MILLER'S

ANTIQUES
Encyclopedia

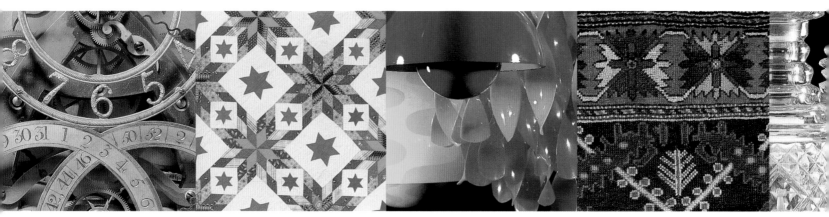

General Editor

JUDITH MILLER

MILLER'S

ANTIQUES
Encyclopedia

MILLER'S ANTIQUES ENCYCLOPEDIA
General Editor **Judith Miller**

First published in Great Britain in 1998
by Miller's, a division of Mitchell Beazley,
imprints of Octopus Publishing Group Ltd,
2–4 Heron Quays, London E14 4JP
Miller's is a registered trademark of Octopus
Publishing Group Ltd
www.millersantiquesguide.com

An Hachette Livre UK company
www.hachettelivre.co.uk

Copyright © Octopus Publishing Group Ltd 1998, 2008
Reprinted 1999, Revised editions printed 2003, 2008

For the original edition
Executive Editor **Alison Starling**
Executive Art Editor **Vivienne Brar**
Senior Editor **Liz Stubbs**
Senior Art Editor **Paul Drayson**
Assistant Editor **Clare Peel**
Designer **Adrian Morris**
Picture Research **Maria Gibbs, Donna Thynne**
Production **Paul Hammond**

For this revised edition
Publishing Manager **Julie Brooke**
Editor **Anna Southgate**
Design **Tim and Ali Scrivens at TJ Graphics**
Production **Lucy Carter**

Specially commissioned photography **Pro Photo,
Tim Ridley, Chris Halton, Ian Booth, Graham Rae**
Illustrations **Amanda Patton**
Maps **Map Creation Limited**
Index **Hilary Bird**

The publishers will be grateful for any information
that will assist them in keeping future editions up to
date. Although all reasonable care has been taken in the
preparation of this book, neither the publishers nor the
compilers can accept any liability for any consequence
arising from the use thereof, or the information
contained therein.

ISBN 978 1 84533 470 3

A CIP catalog record for this book is available from the
Library of Congress

Set in Frutiger and Sabon
Color reproduction by Pica Color Separation
Overseas Pte. Ltd
Produced by Toppan Printing Co., (HK) Ltd.
Printed and bound in China

Distributed in the United States and Canada by Sterling
Publishing Co., Inc., 387 Park Avenue South, New York, NY
10016-8810

Jacket
Back jacket top row: Piero Fornasetti chest, late 19thC French carriage
clock, Regency window seat; bottom row: 18thC Sèvres ecuelle and
cover, American Queen Anne chair; Amphora vase; Regency tea caddy.
Spine: Egyptian Dancer by George Gori. Front top row: vase by Le Verre
Francais; Louis XVI mantel clock; Roseville Della Robbia vase; Italian Art
Nouveau chair; early Worcester beaker vase. Front bottom row: Franz
Bergmann cold painted bronze figure; Louis XV bombé commode.

Contents

Introduction 10

Furniture 16

Ceramics 120

Silver 222

Jewelry 260

Glass 274

Rugs & Carpets 312

Textiles 334

Clocks & Watches 348

Arts and Crafts 368

Art Nouveau 386

Art Deco 412

Mid-century Modern 446

Postmodernism 464

Dolls & Teddy Bears 478

Toys & Games 500

Oriental Works of Art 520

Miscellaneous 530

10 **Introduction**

16 **Furniture**
18 **Furniture: Basics**
18 Construction
20 Styles
22 Woods and patination
24 Decoration
26 Marriages, alterations and fakes, and care
28 **Seat furniture**
28 Stools
29 Early chairs
30 Easy chairs before 1840
33 Country chairs
34 Easy chairs after 1840
36 Dining-chairs before 1840
39 Dining-chairs after 1840
42 Settles and sofas before 1840
44 Settles and sofas after 1840
46 **Tables**
46 Early tables
48 Gateleg and dropleaf tables
50 Dining-tables before 1840
52 Dining-tables after 1840
54 Drum, breakfast, and center tables
56 Pembroke and sofa tables
58 Console, side, and pier tables
60 Sideboards and serving tables
62 Dressing tables
64 Tea tables and tripod tables
66 Occasional tables
68 Games and work tables
70 **Storage furniture**
70 Chests and coffers
72 Early cupboards and meubles en deux corps
73 Cupboards and linen-presses before 1840
76 Wardrobes after 1840
78 Early chests-of-drawers
80 Chests-of-drawers before 1840
83 Chests-of-drawers after 1840
86 Cabinets-on-stands
87 High chests-of-drawers
88 Chests-on-chests
90 Dressers
92 Display cabinets
94 Side cabinets
96 Bookcases and bookshelves
98 **Writing furniture**
98 Bureaux before 1840
100 Bureaux after 1840
102 Escritoires and secrétaires
104 Writing cabinets-on-stands
105 Library and writing tables
106 Davenports
107 Pedestal and kneehole desks
108 **Miscellaneous**
108 Stands and racks
110 Bedside tables and washstands
112 Mirrors
114 Screens
116 Beds
118 Trays, knife-boxes, cutlery-urns, wine coolers, cellarets, and buckets

120 **Ceramics**
122 **Ceramics: Basics**
122 Materials and techniques
124 Decoration
126 Fakes and forgeries
128 Collecting and care
130 **Oriental pottery and porcelain**
130 Map: Pottery and porcelain centers in East Asia
131 China
131 Early ceramics
132 Song
133 Yuan and early Ming
134 Middle and later Ming
136 Later export porcelain
138 Qing before 1800
140 Qing after 1800
141 Korea
142 Japan
142 Arita blue-and-white wares
143 Imari
144 Kakiemon
145 Nabeshima and Hirado
146 Later Japanese ceramics
148 **Pottery**
148 Map: Pottery centers in Europe and the USA
149 Islamic pottery
150 Spain
151 Portugal
152 Italy before 1600
154 Italy after 1600
155 Tiles
156 France
158 Germany
158 Stoneware
159 Faience
160 The Netherlands
162 Britain
162 Delftware
163 Lead-glazed ware
164 Stoneware
165 Creamware and pearlware
166 Wedgwood stoneware
167 Ironstone and transfer-printed wares
168 Staffordshire figures
169 Majolica
170 The United States
172 **Porcelain**
172 Map: Porcelain centers in Europe and the USA
173 Germany before 1800
173 Early Meissen
174 Meissen figures and services
176 Academic and Marcolini
177 Hausmaler
178 Other German factories
181 Germany after 1800
181 Meissen
182 Berlin
184 Dresden and other Meissen imitators
185 Fairings, ribbon plates, and lithophanes
186 The Low Countries, Switzerland, and Scandinavia
188 Austria
190 Italy and Spain
192 France before 1820
192 Early porcelain
193 Vincennes and early Sèvres
194 Later Sèvres
195 Paris
196 France after 1820
196 Sèvres
198 Paris and Limoges
200 Britain before 1790
200 Experimental porcelain
201 Chelsea
202 Bow and Longton Hall
203 Worcester
204 Blue-and-white wares
206 Derby
207 Plymouth, Bristol, and New Hall
208 Britain 1790–1900
208 Worcester
209 Coalport
210 Derby
211 Staffordshire factories
212 Swansea and Nantgarw
213 Rockingham
214 Parian busts and statues
215 Japanesque, aesthetic, and eastern styles
216 Britain after 1900
218 Ireland
219 Russia
220 The United States

222 **Silver**
224 **Silver: Basics**
224 Properties and forming techniques
225 Hallmarking
226 Decoration
228 Fakes, care, and collecting
230 **Candlesticks**
230 Before 1800
232 After 1800
234 Candelabra
236 **Dining silver**
236 Plates and salvers
238 Decorative tableware
240 Entreé dishes and sauceboats
242 Tureens
244 **Flatware**
246 **Drinking vessels**
248 **Serving beverages**
248 Teapots and tea services
250 Tea-caddies, sugar-bowls, and cream-jugs
252 Coffee-pots, chocolate-pots, tea-kettles, and tea-urns
254 **Serving wine and spirits**
254 Claret-jugs, decanters, funnels, coasters, and labels
256 Wine coolers, monteiths, and punch-bowls
258 **Miscellaneous**

260 **Jewelry**
262 **Jewelry: Basics**
264 **Rings**
265 **Pins**
266 **Necklaces, pendants, and lockets**
267 **Earrings and bracelets**
268 **Sentimental jewelry**
270 **Men's jewelry**
271 **Costume jewelry**
272 20th-century costume jewelry

274 **Glass**
276 **Glass: Basics**
276 Materials
277 Forming techniques
278 Decoration
280 Forms and styles
282 **Mold-blown glass**
283 **Pressed glass**
284 **Colored glass**
284 Before 1800
285 After 1800
285 Bohemia
286 Britain, France, and the United States

288 **Enameled glass**
288 Before 1800
290 After 1800
292 **Engraved glass**
292 Low Countries, Bohemia, Germany, and Sweden
294 Britain
296 **Cut glass**
296 Ireland, Britain, and the United States
298 Bohemia, Spain, Belgium, and France
300 **Cameo glass**
302 **Additions to glass**
302 Lampwork
303 Twisted stems
304 Gilding
305 Tassies, sulphides, and jeweling
306 **Lighting**
308 **Paperweights**
310 **Miscellaneous**

312 Rugs & Carpets
314 **Rugs & Carpets: Basics**
316 **Oriental rugs and carpets**
316 Persia before 1800
317 The Ottoman Empire before 1700
318 Persia after 1800
320 The Ottoman Empire after 1700
322 The Caucasus
324 Western Turkestan
326 Flatweaves
327 The Far East
328 **Europe**
328 France
330 Britain and Ireland
331 Spain and Portugal
332 **The United States**

334 Textiles
336 **Needlework**
336 Embroidery
339 Samplers
340 **Quilts**
342 **Costume**
342 Womenswear before 1900
344 Womenswear after 1900
345 Menswear
346 **Accessories**
347 **Lace**

348 Clocks & Watches
350 **Clocks & Watches: Basics**
352 **Wall clocks**
354 **Longcase clocks**
356 **Bracket clocks**
356 Early bracket clocks
357 Later bracket clocks
359 **Carriage clocks**
360 **Precision clocks and chronometers**
361 **Electric clocks**
362 **Novelty clocks**
364 **Barometers**
366 **Watches**
366 Pocket watches
365 Wristwatches

368 Arts and Crafts
370 **Arts and Crafts: Introduction**
371 **Furniture**
372 Britain

374 The United States
376 **Ceramics**
376 Britain
378 The United States
382 **Metalwork**
382 Britain
384 The United States

386 Art Nouveau
388 **Art Nouveau: Introduction**
390 **Furniture**
390 France
392 Belgium, Austria, Spain, and Italy
394 **Ceramics**
394 France
395 The Netherlands
396 Britain, Germany, Austria, and Denmark
398 **Glass**
398 France
400 Austria
401 Britain
402 The United States
404 **Metalwork**
406 **Jewelry**
408 **Sculpture**
410 **Posters**

412 Art Deco
414 **Art Deco: Introduction**
416 **Furniture**
416 The Netherlands, Germany, and Scandinavia
418 France
419 Britain
420 The United States
422 **Ceramics**
422 France, Belgium, and Italy
424 Germany, Austria, and Scandinavia
425 The United States
426 Britain
428 **Glass**
428 France
432 Other European glass
434 The United States
436 **Metalwork**
438 **Jewelry**
440 **Sculpture**
440 France
442 Germany and Austria
444 **Posters**

446 Mid-century Modern
448 **Furniture**
448 The United States
449 Europe
451 New materials
452 **Jewelry**
453 **Lighting**
454 **Domestic wares**
456 **Glass**
458 **Factory-produced ceramics**
460 **Studio ceramics**
460 Europe
462 The United States

464 Postmodernism
466 **Furniture**
468 New technology
470 **Jewelry**
471 **Lighting**
472 **Domestic wares**

474 **Glass**
476 **Studio ceramics**

478 Dolls & Teddy Bears
480 **Dolls & Teddy Bears: Basics**
482 **Wood and papier-mâché dolls**
483 **Poured-wax dolls**
484 **Other wax dolls**
485 **China and parian dolls**
486 **Bisque dolls**
486 France
486 Fashion dolls
488 Bébés
490 Germany
492 **Fabric and rag dolls**
493 **Other later dolls**
494 **Automata**
495 **Soft toys**
496 **Teddy bears**
498 **Dolls' houses**

500 Toys & Games
502 **Wood and paper toys**
504 **Early American toys**
506 **Tinplate**
506 Germany
509 Other European countries
510 **Trains**
510 Germany and Britain
513 Other countries
514 **Lead and plastic figures**
516 **Diecasts**
518 **Other post-war toys**

520 Oriental Works of Art
522 **Metalwork**
524 **Carvings**
526 **Lacquerware**
528 **Jade**
529 **Ivory**

530 Miscellaneous
532 **Scientific and medical instruments**
532 Globes and planetaria
533 Surveying and navigational instruments
534 Telescopes and microscopes
535 Medical instruments
536 **Sporting memorabilia**
538 **Cameras and optical toys**
540 **Metalwork**
542 **Folk art**
544 **Boxes and bottles**
544 Cases and boxes
546 Enamel boxes
547 Tea caddies
548 Perfume bottles
550 **Rock and pop memorabilia**

552 **Where to buy**
554 **Glossary**
565 **Bibliography**
568 **Index**
591 **Picture acknowledgments**

Expert contributors

PAUL ATTERBURY
Arts and Crafts & Art Nouveau & Art Deco
Author of *The Dictionary of Minton*,
Moorcroft Pottery, Poole Pottery, and editor of
Pugin; lecturer and broadcaster

RICHARD BARCLAY
Art Nouveau & Art Deco Posters
Specialist in Vintage Posters,
Christie's South Kensington, London;
special consultant on *Miller's Collecting
Prints & Posters*

VIVIENNE BECKER
Jewelry
Author of *Antique and Twentieth Century
Jewelry, Fabulous Costume Jewelry*, and *Art
Nouveau Jewelry*; curator of Lalique Jewelry
Exhibition, 1987; lecturer and broadcaster

JOHN BENJAMIN
Jewelry
International Director of Jewelry,
Phillips, London; lecturer and broadcaster

BUNNY CAMPIONE
Dolls & Teddy Bears
Senior consultant to the Valuations Department,
Christie's South Kensington, London;
Independent Antiques Advisor;
special consultant on *Miller's Collecting Teddy
Bears & Dolls*; broadcaster

RICHARD CHADWICK
Watches
Specialist in Watches,
Christie's South Kensington, London

STACY MARCUS CHIDEKEL
American Rugs & Carpets
Director of American Indian Art,
Christie's, New York

STEPHEN CLARKE
Silver
Former Director of Silver, Christie's, London;
Independent Fine Art Advisor; Consultant to
Clarke Gammon Auctioneers, Guildford

JAMIE COLLINGRIDGE
Clocks
Associate Director, Clocks Department,
Christie's South Kensington, London

JEREMY COLLINS
Scientific Instruments
Director, Christie's South Kensington,
London

JACQUELINE COULTER
Rugs & Carpets
Director, Sotheby's, London;
broadcaster

NICHOLAS M. DAWES
American and European Decorative Arts
Vice President of Special Projects,
Sotheby's, New York; author of
Lalique Glass and *Majolica*

PHILIP DUCKWORTH
Furniture
Head of Furniture Department,
Christie's South Kensington, London

JOSHUA EVANS
Baseball Memorabilia
Chairman, Leyland's Auctions,
New York City

JOEL KOPP
American Quilts
Owner of *America Hurrah*, New York

SEBASTIAN KUHN
Ceramics
Deputy Director of European Ceramics,
Sotheby's, London

GORDON LANG
Ceramics
Director of Sotheby's Educational Studies;
Honorary Keeper of Burghley House,
Stamford, Lincs.; contributor to many Miller's
publications including *Miller's Antiques
Checklist: Porcelain, Miller's Antiques
Checklist: Pottery & Porcelain Marks*, and
*Miller's Collecting Pottery & Porcelain: The
Facts At Your Fingertips*; broadcaster

MARION LANGHAM
Belleek porcelain
London-based dealer; author of
Belleek: Irish Porcelain

JEFF LOVELL
Miscellaneous
Silver Department, Christie's South Kensington,
London

GRANT MACDOUGALL
Football Memorabilia
Specialist in Sporting Memorabilia,
Christie's, Scotland

MARYBETH McCAFFREY
American Art Nouveau Glass
Associate of J. Alastair Duncan Ltd, New York

LEYLA MANIERA
Soft Toys
Senior Specialist in Teddy Bears & Soft Toys,
Christie's South Kensington, London

HUGO MARSH
Toys & Games
Associate Director, Christie's South Kensington,
London; consultant on *Miller's Antiques
Checklist: Toys & Games*

STEPHEN MAYCOCK
Rock and Pop Memorabilia
Consultant on Rock and Roll & Film
Memorabilia, Sotheby's, London; special
consultant on *Miller's Collecting Prints
and Posters*

EDWARD MONAGLE
Golf Memorabilia
Specialist in Sporting Memorabilia,
Christie's, Scotland

RUPERT NEELANDS
Cricket & Tennis Memorabilia
Specialist in Sporting Memorabilia,
Christie's South Kensington, London

SUSAN PARES
Oriental Works of Art
Editor of *Asian Affairs* and writer on
East Asian subjects

ALEXANDER PAYNE
Post-war Design
Head of Futures: Design, Bonhams,
London

MICHAEL PRITCHARD
Cameras and Optical Toys
Associate Director and Specialist, Cameras and Optical Toys, Christie's South Kensington, London

DAVID RAGO
American Arts and Crafts
Director of Lambertville Antiques and Auction Center, Lambertville, New Jersey; Editor in Chief of *Style: 1900* and *The Modernist Magazine;* broadcaster

NOËL RILEY
Furniture
Author of *The Victorian Design Source Book* and contributor to *Sotheby's Concise Encyclopedia of Furniture*; lecturer

ORLANDO ROCK
Furniture
Vice President, European Furniture Department, Christie's, New York; broadcaster

JOHN SANDON
Ceramics
Director of Ceramics, Phillips, London; author of *The Dictionary of Worcester Porcelain,* contributor to *Miller's Antiques Price Guide,* and special consultant on *Miller's Collecting Pottery & Porcelain: The Facts At Your Fingertips;* lecturer and broadcaster

LITA SOLIS-COHEN
American Advisor
Senior Editor, *Maine Antiques Digest;* contributed to three of the *Miller's The Facts At Your Fingertips* series: *Antiques & Collectibles; Furniture; Pottery & Porcelain*

MARK STEPHEN
Metalwork
Head of Works of Art Department, Sotheby's, Sussex

AUDREY STERNSHINE
Art Nouveau & Art Deco Sculpture
Owner of AS Antique Galleries, Pendleton, Salford, Manchester; a consultant on *Miller's Antiques Price Guide*; contributor to *British Art and Antiques Yearbook*

KERRY TAYLOR
Textiles
Director of Costume and Textiles, Sotheby's, London

EDMUND DE WAAL
Post-war Studio Ceramics
Potter and author of *Bernard Leach*

JONATHAN WADSWORTH
Rugs & Carpets
Deputy Director, Sotheby's, London; broadcaster

MARK WEST
Glass
Glass Dealer in Wimbledon, London; consultant on *Miller's Antiques Checklist: Glass*

THE PUBLISHER WOULD LIKE TO THANK

Keith Baker, Associate Director and Head of the Art Nouveau and Decorative Arts Department, Phillips; **Gail Bardhan**, The Corning Museum of Glass, Corning; **David Battie**, Director, Sotheby's; **Garth Clark** and **Gretchen Adkins**, Garth Clark Gallery, New York; **Philip Collins**, Barometer World Ltd; **Emmanuel Cooper**, *Ceramic Review*; **Roger Dodsworth**, Broadfield House Glass Museum, Kingswinford, West Midlands; **Rachel Evans**, *Hali*; **Marilyn Garrow**, London; **Judith Glass**, Rugs and Carpets Department, Sotheby's; **Jeanette Hayhurst**, Jeanette Hayhurst Fine Glass, London; **Mark James**, Scientific Instruments Department, Christie's South Kensington; **Mayorcas Ltd**, London; **Daniel Morris**, English Furniture Department, Sotheby's; **Nader Rasti**, ociate Director and Head of the Oriental Ceramics and Works of Art Department, Christie's South Kensington; **Michael Turner**, Clocks Department, Sotheby's; **Nicolette White**, Posters Department, Christie's South Kensington; **Robert** and **Josyane Young**, Robert Young Antiques, London; **Sarah Allen**, Bonhams Press Office; **Emma Strouts** and **Camilla Young**, Christie's Images; **Diana Kay**, Phillips Photographic Library; **Sue Daly** and **Joanna Ling**, Sotheby's Picture Library; our writers **Frankie Leibe**, **Suzannah Perry**, **Katherine Sykes**, and **Sarah Yates**; our freelance editors **Tracey Beresford**, **Anna Fischl**, **Laura Hicks**, **Kirsty Seymour-Ure**, and **Arlene Sobel**; our administrative assistants **Joe Burns**, **Giselle Heeger**, **Mary Henderson**, and **Matthew Miller**

The General Editor would like to thank the following for their expert help in the updating of the revised editions:
Matthew Smith of Christies, **Paul Roberts** and **John Mackie** of Lyon and Turnbull, **Mark Hill**, **John Axford** of Woolley & Wallis, **Glenn Butler** of Wallace & Wallace. **Jim Buckley** and **Linda Caine** of Freeman's Philadelphia and **David Rago** of David Rago Auctions, **Jill Bace**, **Nicholas Goodman**, **Steven Moore**, **John Wainwright** and also the in-house team at Mitchell Beazley for all their hard work.

Introduction

For the past 30 years I have been buying, collecting, selling, writing, and publishing books on antiques and collectibles. When I started out they were something of a minority interest. All that has changed. Indeed, since the late 1970s they have enjoyed what can only be described as an explosion of popularity. Various developments have combined to fuel this phenomenon. One has certainly been the tremendous expansion in the types of object either labeled antique, or considered collectible. For example, when I started out, only something that had been made before 1840 was considered an antique. This rigid definition was gradually softened to accommodate pieces over 100 years old. Nowadays, however, the term antique is widely, if not universally, applied to items produced up to and during World War II. In addition, the collecting field has broadened substantially, to encompass previously disregarded items – as diverse as contemporary furniture and rock and pop memorabilia (the antiques of the future).

Equally significant has been the ever-increasing number of prime-time television programs on the subject, some of which regularly achieve viewing figures that stand comparison with the more popular weekly "soaps." Much of their success can be attributed to the manner in which they convey, through expert presenters, the fascinating history, qualities of craftsmanship and design, and often surprisingly high value of the particular artifacts brought in for assessment by members of the general public. Just as influential, however, has been the publication of numerous books on antiques and collectibles, notably Antiques and Collectibles price guides, together with more specialist guides devoted to both mainstream and more peripheral collecting areas. I believe these and other publications have not only done much to explain and demystify antiques, but have also, by providing regularly updated market values, given readers the knowledge and confidence to buy from and sell to (and through) the antiques trade on something approaching level terms. In more recent years, however, the biggest single impact on the world of collecting has been the phenomenally successful internet, with Ebay alone having over 50 million users worldwide. To successfully buy and sell on this, and other sites, it is particularly essential to have authorative information to hand.

Miller's Antiques Encyclopedia was first published in 1998 and took five years in the making. It was driven by a desire to substantially and comprehensively further the dissemination of knowledge about antiques and collectibles to both new and more experienced collectors; in other words, to produce the most authoritative, accessible, and definitive reference work on the market. The fact that this book has been so well received is due to the tireless and painstaking contributions of an international team of distinguished experts and writers. The book works both as an in-depth study of all areas and aspects of collecting, and also as a source of quick reference, in which key facts and features relating to particular subject areas can be assimilated at a glance. During these five years the Encyclopedia has been a great international success (and has been published in seven different languages) but it was felt that, as prices have in many cases changed, it was time to bring out a new edition, with new values again researched by experts in the major fields.

The book begins with a breakdown of styles, which charts the major developments from the Middle Ages to the present day, and pinpoints the

Kraak porcelain jar
This *kraak* jar represents a type of blue-and-white Chinese porcelain made specifically for export to Europe and the Middle East during the late Ming Dynasty. Its heavy, truncated, egg-shaped form and large panels with floral and naturalistic decoration are characteristic features of *kraak* ware.
(c.1620–40; ht 46cm/18in; value I)

Chippendale chair

The work of the English cabinet-maker Thomas Chippendale (1718–79) had a profound influence on furniture-making both in Europe and North America from the mid-18th century, largely through his seminal work *The Gentleman and Cabinet-Maker's Director* (1754–62).

(c.1770; ht 1m/3ft 3in; value Q)

essential characteristics of, and the leading designers and makers associated with, key historical styles, such as Renaissance, Georgian, Victorian, Arts and Crafts, and Art Deco. This, in turn, is followed by the heart of the book, which features comprehensive sections on all the traditional areas of collecting: Furniture; Ceramics; Silver; Jewelry; Glass; Rugs and Carpets; Textiles; Clocks and Watches; Dolls and Teddy Bears; Toys and Games; and Oriental Works of Art. To reflect more recent collecting trends, focusing on particular styles of ornament and decoration, we have also allotted specific sections of the book to the numerous furnishings and artifacts designed and manufactured under the aegis of the Arts and Crafts, the Art Nouveau, and the Art Deco movements. For the same reason, there is also a section dedicated to post-war design. And last but not least, there is a Miscellaneous section, which accommodates other specialized but popular collecting areas, ranging from scientific instruments, sporting memorabilia, cameras, and optical toys, to metalware, boxes and bottles, and rock and pop memorabilia. Finally there is a section on where to buy antiques, which details the comparative advantages (and disadvantages) of purchasing through outlets as diverse as auction houses, specialist and general dealers' shops, antiques fairs, market stalls, and even car-boot (tail gate) sales, junk shops, charity outlets and, of course, the internet.

As you will discover, each section is introduced by an outline of the types of object available, together with an explanation of their particular appeal to collectors. This is followed (where relevant) by detailed information on the basic materials and techniques of manufacture and decoration, and how they have developed over the centuries. There then follows the comprehensive, illustrated, and fully international survey of the subject-matter, with pieces subdivided according to type of object, or country or region of origin, or factory, or individual maker – whichever most closely reflects the manner in which they are traded and collected. Throughout, you will also find sound advice on caring for antiques, an all-important guide to current prices (accompanying each illustration), and numerous feature boxes, each focusing on significant aspects of the subject in hand. Coverage in these boxes includes stylistic peculiarities, influential designers; marks of origin and provenance; and defining features to aid identification of the highly desirable, the simply genuine, and the dishonest fake.

In the world of antiques, it is almost invariably the combination of knowledge and enthusiasm that maximizes the pleasure and the profit of collecting. If *Miller's Antiques Encyclopedia* succeeds in conveying that knowledge and in kindling or inspiring that enthusiasm, then I feel sure you will derive as much enjoyment as I have over the years out of buying, selling, owning, or simply looking at antiques and other collectibles.

Teddy bear by Steiff

This fine Steiff bear is made from mohair and has black shoe-button eyes. The blank button in his ear enables him to be accurately dated; such buttons were used between 1904 and 1906. Steiff teddy bears made before 1930 are the most sought after and can command very high prices.

(1905; ht 36cm/14in; value I)

How to use this book

Miller's Antiques Encyclopedia is designed to work both as a source of quick reference – summarizing key facts at a glance – and as an in-depth study of all aspects of collecting with historical information on many factories, makers, and wares plus known dates for important makers and periods. It is divided into main subject areas, which are subdivided however most appropriate, for example by type or by geographic origin, and then further subdivided by country, center of production, factory, or maker. The text is enhanced by photographs of objects generally found in auctions or at dealers and line drawings, illustrating styles and construction. Key facts boxes, recognizable by their green background tint, summarize important points, give tips on collecting, and show key makers' marks. Some spreads also include feature boxes, highlighting notable aspects of a subject. The book has a glossary and is fully cross-referenced and indexed.

Running headings

Clear running headings assist the reader to find the section of the book that they wish to consult: the running heading on the left-hand page gives the chapter title; the running heading on the right-hand page shows which subsection of the chapter is featured on that page or double-page spread

Page headings

These headings explain exactly what subject is covered on the page or double-page spread for example the type of ware, maker, manufacturer, or area of production

Captions

Each item shown is accompanied by a caption detailing what the piece is, which maker or factory it was made by, and why it is notable; many captions also include tips on collecting

Dates, dimensions, and value codes

This line provides the reader with as accurate a date for the example featured as possible as well as a dimension (**ht** height; **w**. width; **l**. length; **diam**. diameter) and an estimation of its value; the figure for the dimension of the object has been rounded to the nearest half centimeter; the estimated market value of the piece is given in the form of a code (see far right)

Introductions

These brief introductions summarize the main topics raised in a major sub-section and introduce the reader to the key points that will be discussed

Ceramics

Ceramics of one type or anothe made for thousands of years. F earthenware pots through to the m porcelain figures, ceramics have a and diversity of forms and uses. Th can be formed by building or castir

Materials and techni

There are three basic types of ceramic (clay) body: earthenware, stoneware, an porcelain. Earthenware is opaque, porc translucent, and stoneware may be eith understanding the fundamental differen having some knowledge of how a piece been made, it is possible to appreciate c in an object that may not otherwise be a

---

Candlesticks after 1800

By the late 18th century huge numbers of loaded sheet-silver candlesticks were being made using mechanized production in the English industrial centers of Sheffield and Birmingham, primarily to meet demand from the newly prosperous middle classes. The new mechanized techniques of rolling sheet silver, die-stamping, and die-sinking gradually began to replace laborious casting methods (although the best-quality candlesticks were still cast). Candlesticks were also among the earliest items made in Sheffield plate. As the 19th century progressed, elaborate surface ornament, in keeping with Victorian taste, and revivals of 17th- and 18th-century styles characterized the production of candlesticks. They remained popular as decorative items even after the invention of gas and oil lighting and, later, electricity.

LATE NEO-CLASSICAL CANDLESTICKS

At the end of the 18th century candlesticks of all kinds – cast, loaded sheet silver, or Sheffield plate – were made either in the Corinthian column style on a square foot, or in the plain or fluted tapering baluster form on a circular foot: both types are decorated with ornament derived from Classical architecture, such as swags, ram's heads, wreaths, urns, and formal leaves. They are generally 25.5 to 31cm (10–12in) tall. Sheet-silver and Sheffield-plate candlesticks have visible seaming lines where the separate sheet or plate parts have been joined. They may also have small holes in the silver (or patches of visible copper on plate pieces), especially on areas of high relief, caused by overstretching the sheet or plate. Any die-stamped ornament should be sharply defined.

The telescopic adjustable candlestick, a specialty of Sheffield makers, was popular in the late 18th and early 19th centuries. Made in loaded sheet silver and Sheffield plate, it featured a cylindrical stem fitted with telescopic slides rising from the base. Although telescopic candlesticks occasionally appear in auctions today, most do not work properly; their restoration can be costly.

◄ Candlestick by Georg Christoph Neuss
This German candlestick was made in Augsburg. It has the elegant, urn-shaped nozzle and refined form characteristic of the early 19th-century restrained Neo-classical style. However, the faceted stem and nozzle are relatively unusual for the period – most early 19th-century candlesticks have either Corinthian column stems or plain or fluted, tapering baluster stems. The majority of candlesticks made in Germany and Austria during the 19th century are very light and generally not of such good quality as those made in England at the same time. They are consequently also less valuable.
(1819; ht 23cm/9in; value for a pair G)

▲ Candlestick by F.J. Bertrand-Parand
In early 19th-century France, during the Empire and Restoration periods, the austere forms of the Neo-classical style gradually became richly embellished. In this French example, which was made in Paris, the elegant, tapering baluster stem, seen on candlesticks from the late 18th century onward, is surmounted by ornate female busts, and the base is engraved with bands of palms and stylized flowers.
(1819–38; ht 29cm/11¼in; value for a pair I)

THE 19TH-CENTURY REVIVAL STYLES

In the 19th century silver items were produced in an unprecedented range of historical styles, mainly as a result of developments in mechanized production, which meant that manufacturers could reproduce almost any form or type of ornament. The widespread dispersal of aristocratic collections of historic plate also provided inspiration for designers. Motifs such as trefoils and arches derived from Gothic art, while the Rococo – more ornate and bulbous than the original 18th-century version – remained one of the most popular revival styles throughout the century.

► Candlestick by George Fox
This English candlestick, which was made in London, is based on 17th-century French boxwood and fruitwood examples forming part of elaborate toilet services. These imitations are about the same height as the originals; many other 19th-century pieces in revival styles are either larger or smaller than the originals.
(1872; ht 17cm/6¾in; value for a pair I)

REGENCY AND VICTORIAN CANDLESTICKS

In the Regency period (late 18th–early 19th century) candlesticks became more ornate, with richer foliate and scroll decoration on the base, at the top of the stem, and around the socket. From about the 1820s and 1830s candlestick-makers concentrated on imitating 17th- and 18th-century styles, beginning with the Rococo. Candlesticks in the Rococo Revival taste are richly chased all over with scrolls and flowers and have undulating baluster stems, but the curves are heavier, the proportions less balanced, and the sconces more bulbous than on 18th-century originals; most were also made of loaded sheet silver, rather than cast as they would have been in the first half of the 18th century. Since mechanized manufacture resulted in less expensive products, large sets of matching candlesticks were more popular in this period than previously.

Candlesticks in revival styles were produced in both larger and smaller versions of the originals; many were also made as exact copies of originals to replace those that were damaged or lost, although there are a considerable number of fakes. Figural candlesticks were particularly popular during the 19th century, reflecting contemporary taste for novelty pieces. Subjects for figural candlesticks included caryatids, knights in armor, and rustic figures of shepherds and shepherdesses; pairs usually consist of male and female figures.

In the 1890s there was a revival of the fashion for column candlesticks, this time with stepped square bases and with many variations in the patterns of the borders and the capital. These are generally smaller than late 18th-century versions – about 14cm (5½in) high. Many candlesticks in the late 19th and early 20th centuries were wired for electrical lighting as dressing-table or desk lights – in such cases there may be holes in the base for the electrical cord. During the vogue for the Queen Anne style in the early 20th century, some silversmiths produced copies of early 18th-century styles; these can be distinguished from originals by their use of sterling silver instead of the Britannia standard and by their detachable nozzles, which did not appear before c.1740.

With the invention of the self-consuming candle wick in the early 19th century, snuffers became obsolete,

▲ Candlestick by Henry Wilkinson & Co.
The Rococo Revival style was popular during the 1830s. This typical English example is very elaborately chased with swirling acanthus scrolls, rockwork, and flowers, and has an ornate removable nozzle decorated with foliate scroll, rocaille, and flower-head rims. Like most candlesticks made in Sheffield, it is of loaded sheet silver; the areas of relief decoration should be checked for wear, as the silver was usually thin-gauge.
(1834; ht 28.5cm/11in; value for a pair H)

altho tape held cand senti shepl desk taper foun with were
C form quan the la other 19th and with and with inver cham or cy flame 1830 cand a tra shape popu the fc pleat were the o snuff

THE
Cand in the newl With mid-speci enabl unifo 1760 possi manu hamr were meta form with as th and S

◄Car
Classi manul late 19 Sheffie base v carefu metal
(1895;

Feature boxes

These boxes examine a particularly important aspect of a subject such as the history of a style, a notable and definable feature of the subject, or the influence of a celebrated maker; some feature boxes compare and contrast interpretations of a style or technique; others are used to alert the reader to pitfalls of identification

Pictures

More than 1,450 color photographs illustrate objects that are highly representative of items found in auctions or at dealers and fairs

sics

o have been
st utilitarian
d ornamental
lleled variety
material, clay,
by throwing

on a wheel, into flat plates, hollow vessels, and decorative objects in almost unlimited shapes. The wide range of decorative techniques includes piercing or molding the clay itself while it is still wet; coloring with glazes, enamels, or gold either before or after firing; and, relatively recently, using printing processes to transfer a pattern onto the surface.

aste porcelain A typical formula for hard-paste, " porcelain combines 50% kaolin (china clay) with na stone (petuntse) and 25% quartz. Hard-paste vitrifies and becomes translucent during the glaze ecause the body and glaze fuse together at a high ure, it is hard to detect a separate layer of glaze, s Meissen cup and saucer of c.1770. A chip will glass-like conchoidal fracture resembling a chipped flint.
ings: the first (biscuit) to 900–1000°C (1650–) and the second with glaze to 1400°C (2550°F)

FORMING TECHNIQUES

The appropriate process for creating a ceramic vessel is principally determined by the intended shape of the finished object, coupled with the type of body. Earthenware is suited to forming by hand, while sophisticated porcelain clays respond better to mechanical methods of molding. Adjusting the water content determines the plasticity of a body, and this affects the behavior of clay during forming.

Ceramics: Basics 123

Press-molding A modeled relief pattern, as seen on this Italian *jardinière* of c.1760 from Capodimonte or Buen Retiro, or a textured surface is normally produced by pressing clay into a mold. Molds are made of plaster of Paris, which absorbs moisture from the clay, causing shrinkage that prevents the clay from sticking to the mold. A slab, or "bat," of clay is pressed into the various sections of the mold, and this is allowed to dry to a "cheese-hard" or "leather-hard" state. If a vessel is circular in section, press-molding is performed on a wheel; as the mold spins, a machine forces the clay evenly over or within the template mold. For flatware (plates and saucers) this process is called "jiggering," while for hollow-ware, such as cups or jugs, it is called "jollying." The reverse of a press-molded vessel may show the potter's finger marks. The design molded on the outside of a pressed object will not be visible from the inside (not the case with cast shapes).
- Technique involves pressing clay into a mold
- Method used for creating certain relief patterns
- Reverse of an object may show potter's fingerprints
- Design is not visible from inside the object

Casting Also known as "slip-casting," this process uses liquid clay (slip) poured into an absorbent plaster of Paris mold. Clay is first prepared and then mixed with water to form "slip." The molds are assembled from sections held tightly together, and slip is poured into them. The plaster absorbs moisture from the slip, leaving an even skin of clay lining the surface. Excess slip is poured out of the object through a hole – as in the base of this 18th-century English clockcase made by Chelsea – to ensure that the object remains hollow, and the mold is allowed to dry. The formed vessel shrinks slightly, and the sectional mold can then be opened. Complicated objects such as figure groups are assembled from many separately cast pieces.
- Slip-casting is best for making non-round shapes
- The outer pattern appears as a slight impression on the inside
- Thickness varies according to how long the slip is left inside the mold before the excess is poured away

GLAZING

Glaze is a thin covering of glass fused to a ceramic body. Its main functions are to strengthen the body and, in the case of a porous clay, to make it impervious, but glaze also gives pottery a smooth surface beauty that is both pleasing to touch, and practical and hygienic to use. In most cases, crystals of glass are applied as a finely ground powder suspended in liquid, which evenly coats the pottery or porcelain vessel. In a kiln these crystals melt and fuse together to form a permanent and distinctive surface.

Salt glazes At the highest temperature during the firing of stoneware, salt (sodium chloride) is thrown into the kiln, and, as it vaporizes, the sodium reacts with the silica in the stoneware body to form a thin, sometimes pitted glaze, as seen on this 17th-century German jug. The iron impurities present in many stoneware clays cause most salt-glazed stonewares to be brown in color.
- Often a single firing for both hardening and glazing
- Red lead was sometimes added with the salt to make the glaze glassier
- The glaze may have a slightly pitted surface, an effect known as "orange peel"
- Clays need to be rich in silica
- Much salt-glazed stoneware is brown-glazed; a few wares are whitish or light buff in color

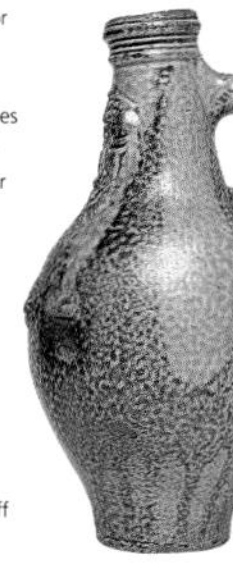

Tin glaze This is used to cover common earthenware bodies to make them resemble porcelain. Tin oxide is insoluble in most glazes and results in an opaque layer of white glass, which covers the body. However, the glaze does not fuse well with the body, and as a result most tin glazes are prone to chipping, as seen on this English porringer.

- Delftware, maiolica, and faience are common tin-glazed wares from different parts of Europe
- Glaze can chip easily
- Color: rich pure white to a bluish glaze

Transparent glazes There are many different kinds of glaze, all producing a smooth, translucent surface on pottery or porcelain. The presence of silica (glass) is vital, but many other minerals are present, especially lead oxide. Lead adds brilliance to the glaze and, above all, reduces the firing temperature needed to fuse the glaze to the body; lead oxide has therefore been widely used in the ceramics industry in glazes fired at less than 1200°C (2200°F). Such colors as green and brown can be introduced to lead glazes. In the 18th century, creamware was sometimes glazed entirely in green, or else with mottled splashes of color, as seen on this Whieldon-type dog of c.1755–60.

- Lead glaze fires at less than 1200°C (2200°F)
- Lead glaze is very glossy, smooth and transparent
- Lead glaze, potentially dangerous to workers and users, was replaced by boric acid in the 19th century; some glazes still contain lead oxide, but within safe limits

Celadon glaze Many Chinese stonewares such as Yue, Longquan (southern China), and Yaozhou (northern China) from the Song Dynasty and earlier were given a high-temperature firing with a semi-opaque, green-tinted glaze, derived from iron. Northern celadon is a gray stoneware covered in a relatively thin, olive-green color, whereas its southern counterpart Longquan has a markedly thicker, cool green glaze over a much whiter, porcellaneous body, as seen on this early Ming barbed-rim dish.
- Yue: similar to northern celadon, perhaps more grayish
- Southern: cool, sometimes bluish green; because of its thickness, it tends to be relatively opaque
- Northern: olive green and semi-translucent
- Celadon wares are sometimes decorated with carved, incised, or molded designs beneath the glaze
- Usually associated with Chinese wares

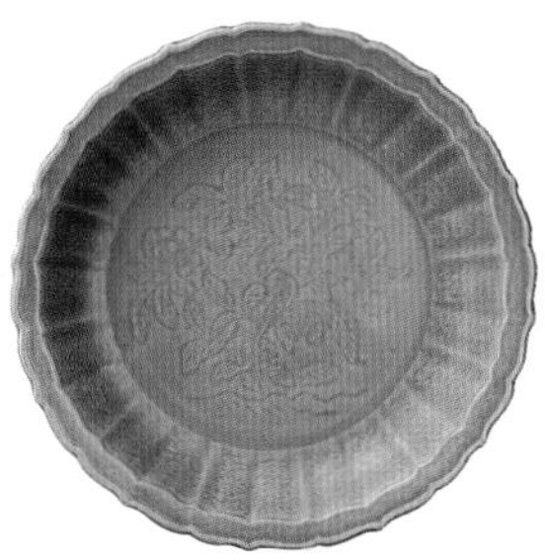

Candlesticks 233

de in revival styles. Similarly, placed by the waxjack (which), but small ornamental s with stems in the form of hildren or shepherds and pular in the 19th century for s. Also produced were "chamber" conical extinguishers like those ndlesticks. They were decorated d foliage around the rims and eld plate as well as in silver. s, among the most utilitarian ere manufactured in vast especially in Sheffield plate from hey usually followed the style of period; in the late 18th and early nple, the socket was urn-shaped and sconce were ornamented sical bands of reeding, beading, examples might also be engraved f arms and marked with an e first half of the 19th century ere often fitted with a bulbous le to guard against unprotected turalistic decoration from the the production of many pan in the form of a leaf, with andle; the sockets were flower-nasturtiums among the more xamples feature figural stems in and dolphins. The octafoil and 8th-century chamber candlesticks duced in the 19th century; unlike ot generally have slots for were rarely used in this period.

AL CENTERS

ng the first items mass-produced Birmingham and Sheffield, using nized methods of manufacture. ndustry in those cities in the lestick manufacture became a olling mill, invented *c.*1740, o be flattened into a sheet of ne fly press, developed in the accurate and repetitive piercing entions reduced labor and nce they replaced laborious iercing. Decorative components ed by die-stamping. The sheet of block with a sunken die in the be reproduced; this was struck relief pattern in the same shape was used for items in both silver a vast range of styles and forms

Bros
-column candlesticks were first century; the style was revived in the of loaded sheet silver manufactured in tick has the characteristic stepped, square oned borders. Pieces like this should be of damage to the corners, where the thin to wear.
for a pair **G**)

was made possible by interchanging the decorative stamped components. As complete sets of dies were highly expensive, they were often used by several manufacturers, resulting in the production of identical patterns by a variety of silversmiths. These new industrialized methods were especially well exploited by the Birmingham makers Matthew Boulton (1728–1809) and John Fothergill (*d.*1782), who pioneered the use of the steam-powered rolling mill in the late 18th century.

▲ **Pair of candlesticks**
Pairs of modern candlesticks such as this are widely available and easier to collect than richly decorated Victorian examples. These pieces have the baluster stems typical of most late 19th- and 20th-century candlesticks but are fairly plain, with bands of die-stamped decoration around the domed bases, shoulders, and molded sockets.
(mid-20th century; ht 18.5cm/7¼in; value **B***)*

KEY FACTS
- DECORATION die-stamped ornament should be well defined; seaming on sheet-silver or Sheffield-plate candlesticks should be visible
- SCALE reproduction or revival-style candlesticks may be smaller than originals
- CONDITION holes or cracks in silver reduce value; loaded and sheet-silver candlesticks may show more wear than cast pieces, as the silver is thinner; Sheffield plate: pinkish tone indicates worn plate, as copper core begins to show under thin silver

Registration marks
From 1842 to 1883 Sheffield plate and electroplated items were sometimes stamped with a lozenge-shaped mark, indicating that the design of the item had been registered with the British Patent Office. In the mark shown (used from 1868 to 1883), the number in the circle at the top indicates the class of the item (Class 1 for plated pieces) and the number beneath this the day. The number of the bundle or parcel of goods is in the left angle, with a letter representing the year (J = 1880) to the right, and a letter representing the month (K = November) at the bottom of the mark.

Key facts boxes
These tinted boxes appear on every page or double-page spread and distil the main points raised in the text; for clarity and ease of reference points may be grouped by type of ware, maker, factory, country, or period

Bullet points
On introductory sections these are used to highlight the main points discussed

Cross references
These refer the reader to related sections within the same chapter and elsewhere in the book

Marks
A selection of important marks and signatures are featured in the key facts boxes: some are illustrated, others are clearly described

VALUE CODES

Throughout this book the value codes used at the end of each caption correspond to the approximate value of the item. These are broad price ranges and should only be seen as a guide to the value of the piece, as prices for antiques vary depending on the condition of the item, geographical location, and market trends.

The codes used are as follows:

A	under $180/£100
B	$180–360/£100–200
C	$360–720/£200–400
D	$720–1,080/£400–600
E	$1,080–1,440/£600–800
F	$1,440–1,800/£800–1,000
G	$1,800–3,600/£1,000–2,000
H	$3,600–7,200/£2,000–4,000
I	$7,200–10,800/£4,000–6,000
J	$10,800–14,400/£6,000–8,000
K	$14,400–18,000/£8,000–10,000
L	$18,000–27,000/£10,000–15,000
M	$27,000–36,000/£15,000–20,000
N	$36,000–54,000/£20,000–30,000
O	$54,000–72,000/£30,000–40,000
P	$72,000–90,000/£40,000–50,000
Q	$90,000+/£50,000+

Conversion rate: $1.80 = £1

Styles

GOTHIC

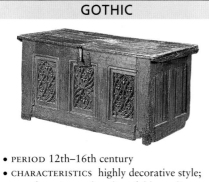

- PERIOD 12th–16th century
- CHARACTERISTICS highly decorative style; use of carving such as linenfold paneling; use of indigenous woods and materials
- MOTIFS tracery, pinnacles, crockets, pointed arches, arcading, trefoils, quatrefoils
- ORIGINS AND DEVELOPMENT Early Gothic style derived from Romanesque architecture and seen in mid-12th century architecture in France; flourished in Italy until *c*.1400; spread by prints from *c*.1500; continued in northern Europe and Iberian peninsula until late 15th/early 16th century; revived as a light, very decorative style in England from the 1740s and known as "Gothick"; more conscientious revivals were seen in Europe (from the 1820s) and in North America (from the 1840s)

RENAISSANCE

- PERIOD 13th–17th century
- CHARACTERISTICS Classical architectural orders; symmetry; influence of Italian artists such as Michelangelo and Raphael
- MOTIFS vases, candelabra, cornucopia, nymphs, mythological and biblical figures, caryatids, masks, putti; northern Europe: strapwork and herms
- ORIGINS AND DEVELOPMENT started and flourished in Italy, where the main center was Florence; introduced to France by Italian craftsmen and spread to the rest of northern Europe by pattern-books, in which it was diluted by Mannerism; in Britain and The Netherlands the influence was felt in the 17th century; revived in Italy (1840s–1890s), North America (1850s–1880s), and Britain from the 1860s

BAROQUE

- PERIOD 17th–early 18th century
- CHARACTERISTICS heavy, grand, and theatrical; sculptural, bulbous forms; elaborate carving and molding; rich gilding; asymmetry
- MOTIFS eagles, cornucopia, trophies, putti, caryatids, pediments, swags, lion's-paw feet
- KEY CREATIVE FIGURES Andreas Brustolon; André-Charles Boulle; Daniel Marot
- IMPORTANT MONARCHS Louis XIV; Charles II; William and Mary
- ORIGINS AND DEVELOPMENT originated in Rome, where the style was representative of the Roman Catholic Church; flourished at the court of Louis XIV at Versailles; spread to The Netherlands and Britain by Huguenot craftsmen after the Revocation of the Edict of Nantes (1685)

PRE 1500   GOTHIC   RENAISSANCE   1600   BAROQUE

REGENCY / EMPIRE

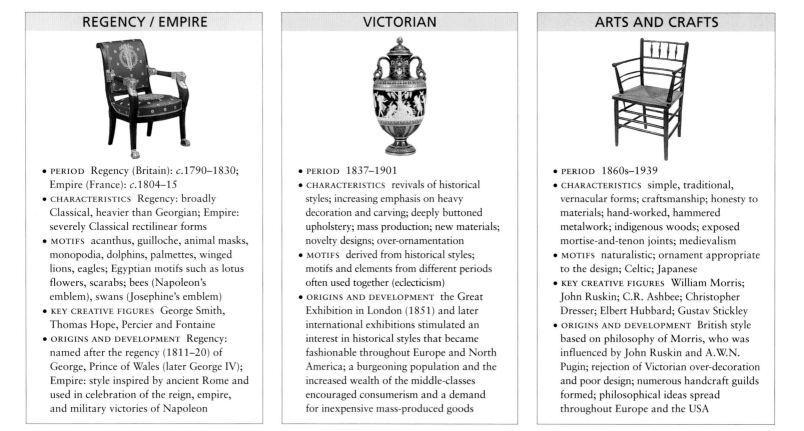

- PERIOD Regency (Britain): *c*.1790–1830; Empire (France): *c*.1804–15
- CHARACTERISTICS Regency: broadly Classical, heavier than Georgian; Empire: severely Classical rectilinear forms
- MOTIFS acanthus, guilloche, animal masks, monopodia, dolphins, palmettes, winged lions, eagles; Egyptian motifs such as lotus flowers, scarabs; bees (Napoleon's emblem), swans (Josephine's emblem)
- KEY CREATIVE FIGURES George Smith, Thomas Hope, Percier and Fontaine
- ORIGINS AND DEVELOPMENT Regency: named after the regency (1811–20) of George, Prince of Wales (later George IV); Empire: style inspired by ancient Rome and used in celebration of the reign, empire, and military victories of Napoleon

VICTORIAN

- PERIOD 1837–1901
- CHARACTERISTICS revivals of historical styles; increasing emphasis on heavy decoration and carving; deeply buttoned upholstery; mass production; new materials; novelty designs; over-ornamentation
- MOTIFS derived from historical styles; motifs and elements from different periods often used together (eclecticism)
- ORIGINS AND DEVELOPMENT the Great Exhibition in London (1851) and later international exhibitions stimulated an interest in historical styles that became fashionable throughout Europe and North America; a burgeoning population and the increased wealth of the middle-classes encouraged consumerism and a demand for inexpensive mass-produced goods

ARTS AND CRAFTS

- PERIOD 1860s–1939
- CHARACTERISTICS simple, traditional, vernacular forms; craftsmanship; honesty to materials; hand-worked, hammered metalwork; indigenous woods; exposed mortise-and-tenon joints; medievalism
- MOTIFS naturalistic; ornament appropriate to the design; Celtic; Japanese
- KEY CREATIVE FIGURES William Morris; John Ruskin; C.R. Ashbee; Christopher Dresser; Elbert Hubbard; Gustav Stickley
- ORIGINS AND DEVELOPMENT British style based on philosophy of Morris, who was influenced by John Ruskin and A.W.N. Pugin; rejection of Victorian over-decoration and poor design; numerous handcraft guilds formed; philosophical ideas spread throughout Europe and the USA

1800   EMPIRE / REGENCY   1850   VICTORIAN   ARTS AND CRAFTS

ROCOCO

- PERIOD early to mid-18th century
- CHARACTERISTICS light, playful, informal; rustic scenes; curved forms; asymmetry; pastel colors; light-colored woods, diaper patterns; light gilding
- MOTIFS flowers, C- and S-scrolls, shells, *rocaille* (rockwork), scrollwork, light grotesques, chinoiseries, singeries
- KEY CREATIVE FIGURES Jean Bérain I, Juste-Aurèle Meissonnier, Nicholas Pineau
- ORIGINS AND DEVELOPMENT developed in France after the Régence period (1715–23) as a reaction to the heavy, ponderous forms of the Baroque; spread to Germany, Austria, Britain, and North America; revived in Europe from the 1820s–1860s, as a reaction to the severe Empire style, and again between 1880 and 1900

NEO-CLASSICISM

- PERIOD mid- to late 18th century
- CHARACTERISTICS Classical antique forms; rationality; symmetry
- MOTIFS vases, urns, guilloche, Greek key, palmettes, husks, fasces, trophies, griffins, anthemion, sphinxes, laurel wreaths, Classical architectural orders
- KEY CREATIVE FIGURES Robert Adam, James "Athenian" Stuart, Karl Friederich Schinkel, Benjamin Henry Latrobe, Samuel McIntyre
- ORIGINS AND DEVELOPMENT reaction to the excesses of Rococo; interest in the styles of ancient Greece and Rome stimulated by the Grand Tour and by excavations of sites such as Herculaneum (1738) and Pompeii (1748); developed into the Louis XVI, Federal (North America), Etruscan, Regency, and Empire styles

GEORGIAN

- PERIOD c.1714–c.1790
- CHARACTERISTICS early Georgian (c.1714–40) architectural in style; mid-Georgian (1740–60) lighter assymmetrical Rococo style; late Georgian (after 1760) strictly Neo-classical style; period from c.1790–1830 usually referred to as Regency
- MOTIFS early: sculpted eagles, herms, swags, masks; mid: chinoiseries, singeries; later: swags, Greek key, paterae, vases
- KEY CREATIVE FIGURES William Kent, Matthias Lock, Thomas Chippendale, George Hepplewhite, Thomas Sheraton
- ORIGINS AND DEVELOPMENT styles reflect the British interpretation of Palladianism (early), the Rococo (mid), and Neo-classicism (late); became the Regency style from c.1790

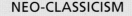

1700 | ROCOCO | 1750 | NEO-CLASSICISM | 1800 EMPIRE / REGENCY
GEORGIAN

ART NOUVEAU

- PERIOD 1890s–c.1910
- CHARACTERISTICS sinuous, organic, asymmetrical forms; stylized naturalism; symbolism; exotic woods; marquetry
- MOTIFS *coup de fouet* (whiplash); plants and flowers; insects – dragonflies, bees, scarabs, butterflies; women with long, flowing tresses and diaphanous gowns
- KEY CREATIVE FIGURES Victor Horta; Emile Gallé; Louis Majorelle; Hector Guimard; René Lalique; Louis Comfort Tiffany
- ORIGINS AND DEVELOPMENT name derived from Samuel Bing's La Maison de l'Art Nouveau in Paris; influenced by the Arts and Crafts movement, Japanese art, and Horta's designs in Belgium; style spread particularly to Britain, Italy, Spain, Germany, Austria, and the USA; revived in the 1960s

ART DECO

- PERIOD c.1918–1940
- CHARACTERISTICS streamlined, stylized, forms based on machines and abstract art; bright, bold colors influenced by Cubism and Futurism; elements from African art, Egyptian art (after the opening of Tutankhamun's tomb in 1922); manmade materials including chromium-plated steel and Bakelite
- MOTIFS fashionable women, chevrons, zigzags, sunbursts, lightning bolts, abstract geometric patterns
- KEY CREATIVE FIGURES Jacques-Emile Ruhlmann, Clarice Cliff, Donald Deskey
- ORIGINS AND DEVELOPMENT originated in France; early decorative and luxurious French style evolved into Modern Movement, which discarded ornament

POST-WAR DESIGN

- PERIOD after c.1945
- CHARACTERISTICS organic, biomorphic, asymmetrical shapes; manmade materials: molded plywood, plastics, fiberglass, PVC, synthetic fabrics; strong, bright colors; mass production
- MOTIFS abstract motifs from the scientific world reflecting atomic and molecular structure; film and cartoon characters
- KEY DESIGNERS Ettore Sottsass; Piero Fornasetti; Charles Eames; Verner Panton; Arne Jacobsen; Eero Saarinen
- ORIGINS AND DEVELOPMENT new technology and materials developed during World War II allowed new forms and construction techniques; mass production encouraged disposable consumer goods and rapid response to changes of style

1900 | ART DECO | 1950 | POST-WAR DESIGN | 2000
ART NOUVEAU

As a domestic necessity in all civilizations, ancient and modern, furniture has been produced in tremendous quantities over the centuries. While the basic categories of furniture are few – seating, tables, storage, and writing – the diversity of pieces that have evolved within these groupings is enormous. Seat furniture, for example, extends from the very simplest wood stools, settles, and chairs to deeply upholstered sofas and settees. Different tables can be used for dining or for making one's toilet, for working or for playing, or simply for decoration. Storage furniture embraces chests-of-drawers, wardrobes, display cabinets, and bookcases. Writing furniture includes bureaux, secrétaires, and desks. Moreover, the diversity of furniture types is echoed in variations in construction, shape, and decoration, which are determined by country or region of origin, maker, and period of manufacture. Much of the collectability of antique furniture lies in these individual differences, but just as important are the aesthetic qualities of the timber from which most pieces are fashioned. Whether hardwood or softwood, solid or veneered, stained and polished wooden furniture, if well cared for, develops a lustrous, mellow patina over time. This visually pleasing, highly prized characteristic plays a significant role in determining both the desirability and the value of an item of antique furniture.

Dressing table (left) This mahogany dressing table with a hinged top, inverted break-front, and a cupboard in the kneehole, is a fine example of mid-Georgian English furniture *(1755)*.

Windsor armchair (above) Made in Philadelphia, Pennsylvania, this comb-back windsor armchair retains its early 19th-century brown-painted finish, over its original white paint *(c.1760)*.

Furniture: Basics

Over the centuries furniture has developed from simple designs cut from one section of the tree, with joints held together by wooden pegs, to skilfully constructed pieces made by using increasingly sophisticated techniques. From the 17th century onward, many items of furniture became smaller and lighter, and seating was upholstered for greater comfort. As wood-turning skills advanced, heavy, plain styles gave way to elegant designs with intricate carving and veneering. In the late 17th century gilding and lacquering were introduced, and exotic timbers began to be imported. Some of these are associated with furniture of particular dates and origins; for example, amboyna veneer was much used in Britain and France in the late 18th century.

Construction

Early furniture was primitively constructed out of the solid, often re-using old pieces of timber. During the 17th and 18th centuries, although the provincial tradition was often slower to change, construction was becoming increasingly sophisticated, with finely executed joints and a carcase that was as well made as the "façade." By the early 19th century the prohibitive expense of craftsmanship, though difficult to improve upon, resulted in the rise of the production of machine-assisted furniture.

PEGGED CONSTRUCTION

Until the early 18th century, what is generally referred to as the "joined" or "pegged" style of construction, using mortise-and-tenon joints held together by wooden dowels or pegs, or occasionally nails, prevailed throughout Europe. Early wooden pegs were of irregular or square-ended tapering form; they acted like wedges and tightened the joints as they were hammered in. Over time, shrinkage "pinched" the pegs and pushed them proud of the surface – this is a good indication that the piece has not been altered at a later date. Pegs from the 19th century are often machine-cut and perfectly round in section, being either flush with the surface or, in some cases, recessed. From the early 18th century, pegged construction was largely abandoned in Britain; after this date it is mainly associated with Continental craftmanship. Pegged furniture in the English style is most likely to be Scottish, Irish, American, or Colonial. Craftsmen from these countries continued to use pegged construction throughout the 18th century.

DRAWER CONSTRUCTION

Early drawers are characterized by their thick (1–2.5cm/⅜–1in) sides or "linings," which were usually channeled so that they could run on bars or "runners" fixed to the sides of the carcase. The angles were usually nailed together, and are sometimes canted (chamfered). During the 17th century, iron-nailed joints were gradually superseded by "dovetailing," whereby two sides are joined together by interlocking, confronting triangular-shaped wedges. Initially large and crude, dovetails became increasingly small and tight during the second half of the 17th century. Such sophisticated thin drawer-linings could no longer be channeled to each side, and from the mid-17th century runners instead were placed beneath the drawers at each side; these ran on further bearers attached to the inside of the carcase. While English carcase furniture was usually made with "dustboards," generally of pine, that divided and sealed each drawer aperture, by contrast, at least until the late 18th century, French and Continental furniture was often left open within the carcase once the drawers were removed.

First introduced in concave form by Thomas Chippendale (1718–79) in the 1760s, quarter-fillets on the inside angles of the drawers were only widely employed in Britain during the 19th century in convex or domed form. In contrast, Swedish and other Scandinavian pieces are often distinguished by the use of wooden pegs, as opposed to nails or glue, to secure the drawer-linings and the backboards. Throughout Europe until the late 18th century, backboards were usually planked. Paneled backs were used exclusively in France from the reign of Louis XIV; these are almost as well constructed and finished as the façades of case furniture.

TABLES

Tables are traditionally constructed with a fixed top, which is supported on a frame with a frieze and legs. They were initially made in the solid, but from the late 17th century veneering was increasingly employed. While the traditional form lent itself well to fashionable ornament and changing tastes, it was not so adaptable to the smaller, lighter tables required for occasional use. The late 17th century saw, therefore, two further variations on the traditional form: the gate-leg and tilt-top tables.

Gateleg tables are characterized by their hinged action, which enables flaps to be supported properly when the gate-leg is rotated through 90 degrees. To provide sufficient strength for the solid drop-leaves, the central section is firmly secured to the table frame by numerous glueblocks and often by tenoned joints. This form was adapted in the mid-18th century for items such as Pembroke tables, where the lighter leaves, made possible by veneering, were instead supported by a "fly bracket" or hinged flap. Tilt-top tables are characterized by hinged tops, which enable them to be stored away when not in use.

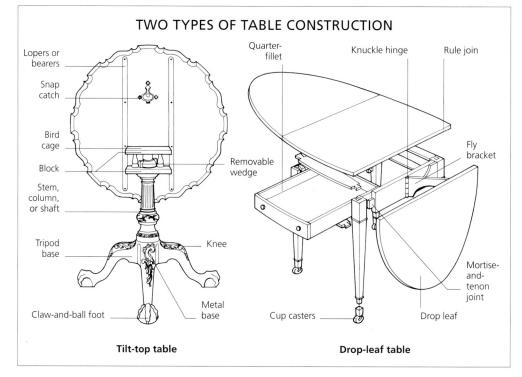

TWO TYPES OF TABLE CONSTRUCTION

Lopers or bearers
Snap catch
Bird cage
Block
Stem, column, or shaft
Tripod base
Claw-and-ball foot
Removable wedge
Knee
Metal base

Quarter-fillet
Knuckle hinge
Rule join
Fly bracket
Cup casters
Mortise-and-tenon joint
Drop leaf

Tilt-top table

Drop-leaf table

Initially introduced for small center or tripod tables during the 17th century, but increasingly used for larger breakfast and dining-tables of the late 18th and the 19th century, tilt-tops are invariably supported on parallel "lopers" or bearers, which are hinged to the top of the pedestal support by wooden or, on later pieces, brass pegs or pins. The tops were designed to be removable, as can be seen particularly well on George II and American "Chippendale" tripod tables. These have a hinged "bird cage" attached to the top, consisting of two parallel platforms joined by columns, through which the top of the shaft or column could be inserted and then fixed by a wedge to the neck. Other 18th-century tripod tables display a turned wooden screw that fixes the shaft to both top and tripod base; the legs are often bound together by a metal brace.

CHAIRS

Until the end of the 17th century, chairs were invariably constructed out of solid timber with pegged tenons. Early walnut chairs from England, America, and The Netherlands tended to have broad, hand-sawn rails with an "adzed" or chipped surface, but as the 18th century progressed the rails became smoother and narrower. Usually designed with drop-in seats that could be supported on the recessed lips of the wide seat frames, early 18th-century English chairs are unique in that their legs are tenoned and glued but not pegged. The back uprights or "stiles" were often made of one piece of timber with the back legs, in order to strengthen the chairs. Splat-backed chairs have stiles that are surmounted by shaped toprails supported by the vertical baluster splat, similarly tenoned to top and bottom and stabilized to the bases by "shoes" or collars.

The large corner blocks of Queen Anne chairs were gradually replaced by diagonal cross-struts that could also support the drop-in seats. This enabled the rails, either constructed in the solid or veneered, to become increasingly thin. Continental chairs of the 18th century are identifiable by their use of pegged construction. Under Louis XIV, chairs and other seating also became increasingly comfortable, and these and other Continental pieces often display not only drop-in seats but also padded backs upholstered *à chassis* (i.e. removable). Owing to their use of pegged construction, rather than animal glue, Continental chairs tend to be made without cross-struts or braces, and only Régence (1715–23) and early 18th-century seating display stretchers. The insides of the seat rails on authentic pieces are rough-hewn and clearly hand-cut with a saw; it was only during the Empire period (1804–15) that *menuisiers* (joiners) finished the seat rails to standards comparable with those of English chair-makers.

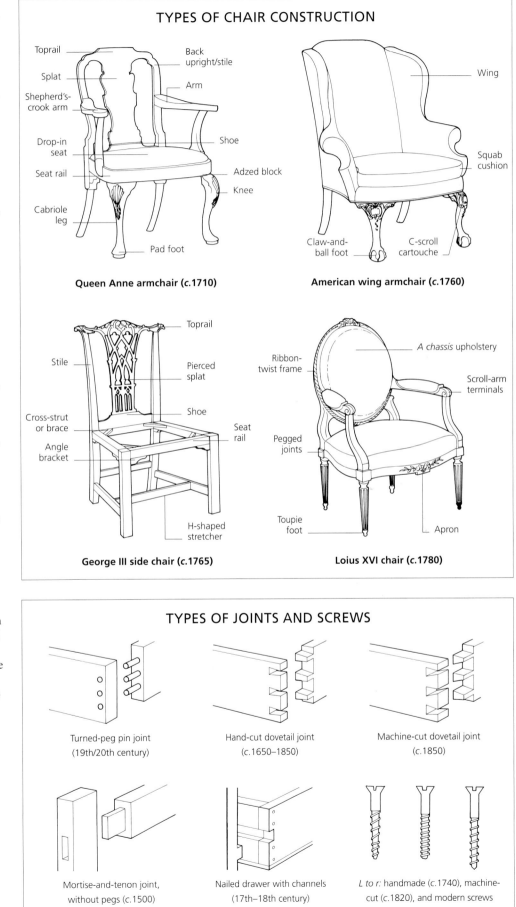

TYPES OF CHAIR CONSTRUCTION

Toprail
Splat
Shepherd's-crook arm
Drop-in seat
Seat rail
Cabriole leg
Pad foot
Back upright/stile
Arm
Shoe
Adzed block
Knee

Queen Anne armchair (*c*.1710)

Wing
Squab cushion
Claw-and-ball foot
C-scroll cartouche

American wing armchair (*c*.1760)

Stile
Cross-strut or brace
Angle bracket
Toprail
Pierced splat
Shoe
Seat rail
H-shaped stretcher

George III side chair (*c*.1765)

Ribbon-twist frame
Pegged joints
Toupie foot
A chassis upholstery
Scroll-arm terminals
Apron

Loius XVI chair (*c*.1780)

TYPES OF JOINTS AND SCREWS

Turned-peg pin joint
(19th/20th century)

Hand-cut dovetail joint
(*c*.1650–1850)

Machine-cut dovetail joint
(*c*.1850)

Mortise-and-tenon joint,
without pegs (*c*.1500)

Nailed drawer with channels
(17th–18th century)

L to r: handmade (*c*.1740), machine-cut (*c*.1820), and modern screws

Styles

Until the mid-17th century, furniture was heavy and architectural in style. Made out of the solid and usually of oak, it was often enriched with simple turned decoration, occasionally embellished with primitive, classically inspired foliage and acanthus carved in relief. During the late 17th century the art of turning became increasingly refined and sophisticated with the introduction of lighter and tighter forms, but these were gradually superseded by the Baroque style. Characterized by its sculptural designs and exuberant wealth of carved ornament, the Baroque to a large extent pre-empted the lighter, freer spirit of the Rococo or *pittoresque* movement, which gained momentum from *c.*1730. During the Rococo period, curves became increasingly exaggerated, and were enriched with foliage and even Gothic and chinoiserie ornament. The excesses of the Rococo were abruptly halted by the Neo-classical movement, which originated in France in the 1750s. Linearity and restraint, inspired by the Classical architecture of ancient Greece and Rome, prevailed until the early 19th century, and was reflected in deliberately Classical ornament featuring urns and paterae, fluting, Greek-key designs, anthemions and acanthus, and even griffins and palmettes. The early 19th century extended the parameters of Neo-classical taste to embrace not only pure Grecian architecture, but also that of ancient Egypt, with motifs such as sphinxes and crocodiles. Inevitably, the 1820s and 1830s saw a reaction to Neo-classicism. This took the form of antiquarianism, which was inspired by 17th-century designs and was fashionable in the 1820s, and also Gothic Revivalism, which reflected contemporary interest in the medieval period. The mid-19th century saw the introduction of exuberant Rococo Revival designs, while late 19th-century, furniture was influenced by yet another revival, with Neo-classical styles once again in fashion.

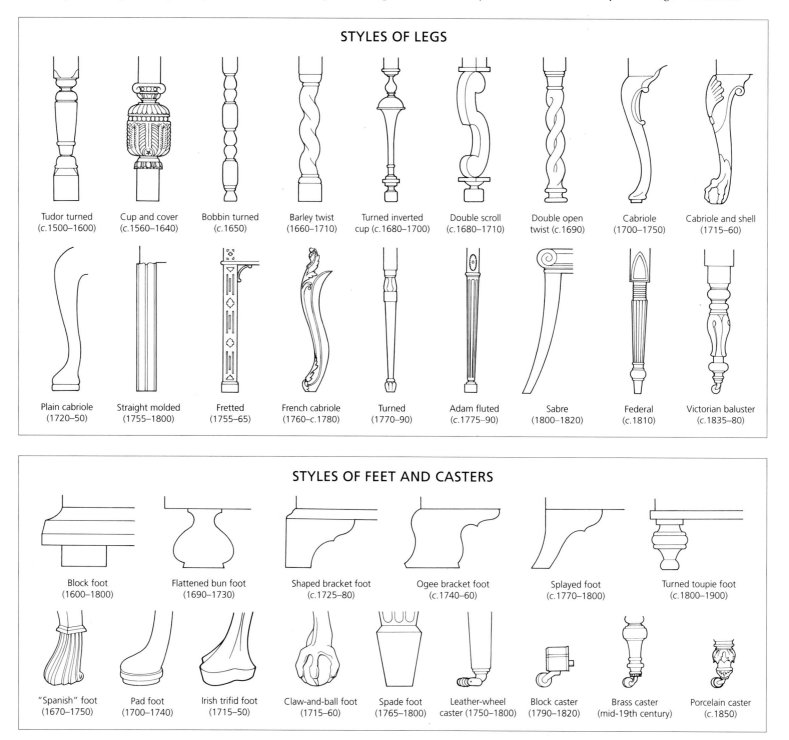

STYLES OF LEGS

Tudor turned (c.1500–1600)

Cup and cover (c.1560–1640)

Bobbin turned (c.1650)

Barley twist (1660–1710)

Turned inverted cup (c.1680–1700)

Double scroll (c.1680–1710)

Double open twist (c.1690)

Cabriole (1700–1750)

Cabriole and shell (1715–60)

Plain cabriole (1720–50)

Straight molded (1755–1800)

Fretted (1755–65)

French cabriole (1760–c.1780)

Turned (1770–90)

Adam fluted (c.1775–90)

Sabre (1800–1820)

Federal (c.1810)

Victorian baluster (c.1835–80)

STYLES OF FEET AND CASTERS

Block foot (1600–1800)

Flattened bun foot (1690–1730)

Shaped bracket foot (c.1725–80)

Ogee bracket foot (c.1740–60)

Splayed foot (c.1770–1800)

Turned toupie foot (c.1800–1900)

"Spanish" foot (1670–1750)

Pad foot (1700–1740)

Irish trifid foot (1715–50)

Claw-and-ball foot (1715–60)

Spade foot (1765–1800)

Leather-wheel caster (1750–1800)

Block caster (1790–1820)

Brass caster (mid-19th century)

Porcelain caster (c.1850)

STYLES OF CHAIR BACKS

Jacobean and Charles I
(1625)

Bobbin turned
(c.1650–70)

Carolean
(1665–85)

William and Mary/
Marot style (c.1695)

Fauteuil à la reine
(c.1730–50)

Splat-back
(1710–40)

Windsor
(c.1750–1850)

Chippendale
(c.1750–65)

Chinoiserie
(c.1755–65)

Louis XVI oval
(1760–85)

George III ladder-back
(1765–1800)

Hepplewhite shield-back
(1780–1800)

Hepplewhite urn splat
(1790–1800)

Provincial ladder-back
(c.1790–1840)

Empire gondola
(c.1800–1835)

Regency Grecian
(1800–1815)

Regency tablet-back
(1805–20)

Federal lyre-back
(1795–1820)

Gothic Revival
(1820–50)

Dished foliate
(1820–50)

Papier-mâché
(c.1830–60)

French buttoned-back
(c.1830–80)

Balloon back
(c.1860)

Victorian buttoned-back
(c.1860–90)

STYLES OF HANDLES

Solid backplate
(1600–1650)

Split tail
(c.1680–1715)

Solid backplate
(c.1710–40)

Chippendale Rococo
(c.1755–65)

Chinoiserie
(1755–80)

American Rococo
(c.1760–80)

Plain drop
(c.1760)

Ring
(c.1770–1800)

American Federal
(c.1790–1810)

Regency lion-mask
(c.1790–1820)

Turned rounded pull
(c.1810–30)

Plain knob
(c.1840–1900)

Woods and patination

The timbers used for constructing and decorating a piece of furniture help to identify the country of origin and the period. Until *c.*1750, indigenous timbers were relatively freely and cheaply available, while the use of more exotic woods is an indication of either colonial access or luxurious extravagance.

Amaranth A dense hardwood with a purplish color and whiteish grain; also known as "purpleheart."
- Imported into Europe from Central America
- Employed in The Netherlands and France from the late 17th century, initially as a veneer on cabinets
- Used for marquetry and parquetry from *c.*1750

Amboyna A hardwood imported from the Moluccas, characterized by its orangey-brown color and tightly curled grain. Widely employed from the late 18th century by French and British cabinet-makers.
- Invariably used as a veneer
- Particularly associated with the work of Adam Weisweiler (1744–1820) and fashionable during the Regency period

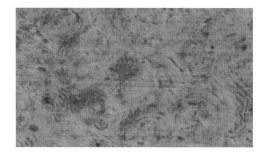

Birch Light-colored wood indigenous throughout northern Europe, particularly Scandinavia and the Baltic.
- First introduced as a veneer in the late 18th century
- Appears in two principal forms: Karelian birch, a tightly figured, gnarled burr, and the lighter satin-birch (widely used in the 19th century); often mistaken for satinwood
- Karelian birch favored by Russian craftsmen from *c.*1800

Bird's-eye maple Closely related in color and texture to satin-birch and satinwood, bird's-eye maple is more richly figured than the standard variety. Maple is indigenous to North America, Canada, and northern Europe.
- Widely employed by 19th-century cabinet-makers both as a veneer and in the solid
- Has distinctive tight, light-brownish spots, caused by branch-bud initials, which resemble birds' eyes when cut
- Fashionable in Britain during the Regency (*c.*1790–1830), and in France during the reign of Charles X (1824–30)

Calamander A dense hardwood, also known as "zebrawood" and distinguished by its strongly streaked yellow bands, alternating with dull-brown to blackish strips.
- So called because it was initially shipped from the Coromandel coast in India; later from West Africa
- Always applied as a veneer in Europe; only Colonial furniture was made in the solid
- Calamander's strong figuring was particularly admired in Britain in the early 19th century

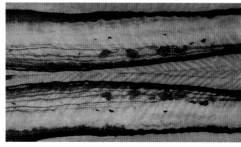

Elm A hardwood distinguished by its wide, jagged, open grain, which often has white speckles. Indigenous to northern Europe.
- Used since the 16th century for construction in the solid
- Particularly favored by provincial cabinet-makers in Britain and The Netherlands
- Richly figured burr-elm is far rarer than the standard variety

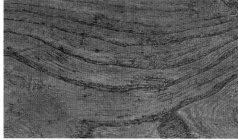

- Burr-elm tends to have a broken surface with tight grains
- Furniture constructed in burr-elm was usually veneered, or in some cases stained to simulate mulberry

Harewood A term used for stained sycamore. Harewood is a light-colored softwood characterized by strong parallel lines on a speckled ground.
- Well suited to staining and frequently seen in marquetry
- Often stained green or brownish-gray

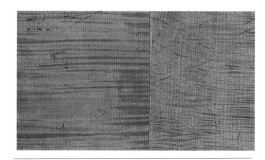

Kingwood A strongly figured, black-grained hardwood from the West Indies; also called palisander.
- Widely employed by French cabinet-makers during the Régence (1715–23) and Louis XV (1723–74) periods
- Seen in parquetry, *bois de bout* marquetry, and crossbanding

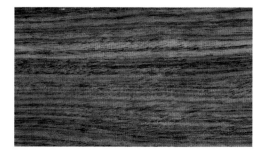

Mahogany A hard, close-grained, wood, impervious to woodworm, it is indigenous to Central America and the West Indies; introduced in Britain from Jamaica *c.*1730.
- Almost exclusively used by British cabinet-makers until the 1760s, when used in France, Germany, and Russia
- Used both as a veneer and in the solid

- Most exotic and richly figured varieties include flame or fiddleback (below) and plum-pudding mahogany

Oak A hard, coarse-grained, dense timber, distinguished by its flecks (rays), which is a light yellowy-brown when cut.
- Provincial oak furniture is often very red in color owing to staining with "dragon's blood"
- Employed in the solid since the Middle Ages, and consistently popular in the provincial tradition
- Increasingly used as a carcase wood on more sophisticated furniture from the 17th century
- Brown or "pollard" oak, a richly figured burr with a broken surface, fashionable as a veneer from the early 19th century

Pine A pale softwood with a wide, straight grain and pronounced knots, indigenous to Europe and North America. Pine was often used for furniture intended to be painted or gilded, but was too soft for elaborate carving; for this reason, much carved giltwood is of lime- or fruitwood.
- Usually employed as a carcase wood, particularly in North America, Italy, and northern Europe
- Scandinavian pine (often has a distinctive purple grain) widely used in Alpine cabinet-making

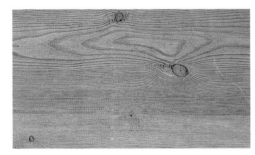

Rosewood A dense hardwood indigenous to India, South America, and the West Indies, and characterized by black streaks on a figured ground. The pronounced figuring often fades with sunlight.
- Widely used for veneering and crossbanding, particularly by British cabinet-makers
- Anglo-Indian pieces often made in the solid

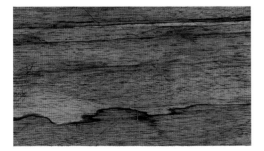

- Darkly streaked Brazilian rosewood used prolifically throughout Europe and America in the early 19th century
- Brazilian rosewood was even carved from the solid

Satinwood An expensive, tight-grained timber from the West Indies, with a curved, smooth grain and light color.
- Introduced into Europe and North America in the late 18th century
- Named after its satin-like figuring

Tulipwood A hard, dense wood with a reddish-pink grain from Brazil and Peru; known in France as *bois de rose*.
- Strongly figured grain and smooth texture well suited to parquetry and marquetry
- Mainly used for crossbanding from the late 18th century

Walnut A fruitwood, the color of which varies from light to very dark, indigenous to Europe and America.
- Used both in the solid or as a veneer
- Largely superseded from the mid-18th century by mahogany and other exotic timbers
- Used in the provincial tradition until the late 19th century

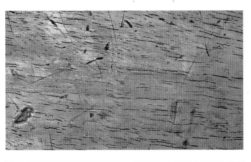

- Burr-walnut (below), is the most admired variety; cut from diseased branches; displays a scrolled, tight grain

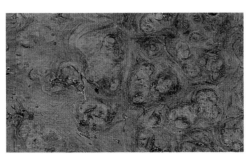

Yew and burr-yew A very hard and slow-growing timber, with a smooth, fruitwood-like surface and pronounced reddish-streaked parallel grain.
- Employed particularly by provincial cabinet-makers in Britain from the late 17th century, and also in Ireland and Russia
- Usually applied as a veneer
- Richly figured "burr" or diseased "root" yew has smooth, tight-scrolled figuring and knots (below)

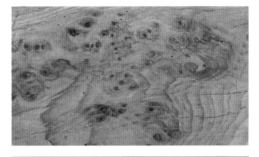

Patination The patina or surface color and texture of a piece of furniture can dramatically affect its value. A rich color and "dry," untouched condition are greeted with real enthusiasm by collectors; to a large extent this is because an old patina is some guarantee that the piece has not undergone extensive restoration or alteration, which might have subsequently been hidden under layers of varnish and stain. English and American furniture – particularly oak, walnut, and mahogany from the 17th and 18th centuries – is the most affected by patina. Unlike their more exuberant Continental counterparts, such pieces are largely unembellished by marquetry, parquetry, or ormolu mounts, and are usually sparsely carved, if at all. They are therefore dependent for their effect on the warmth and depth of color of the timber, and on its finely figured grain. Oak from the 17th century should ideally have a very strong, deep, dark color, built up over time by oxidization, grease, and wax; some pieces feature the dark-reddish tinge of "dragon's blood," a stain characteristic of so many Welsh dressers. Walnut and burr-walnut, and elm and burr-elm, can "sing," or appear flat and bland; this may be due to the application of a thick glossy varnish. On some pieces, the surface may appear to have been "taken back" (i.e. there is too much of one particular color, and the overall color is a little too light). Such flaws may indicate that the piece has had surface problems in the past, and will certainly affect its value. Rich depth of color, and the effects of grease and wax, sunlight and oxidization, as well as the remains of lacquering on the brass and gilt-bronze handles, can all enhance the value of a piece, since they contribute to the original condition, reflecting age and use. Knocks and scratches are not necessarily undesirable, but they should not be either too pronounced or too regular, which may mean that they have been faked. However, fruitwoods such as cherry, burrs such as pollard oak and burr-elm, certain hardwoods such as yew, and exotic timbers such as ebony and padouk all develop a reasonably good color over a short period of time. Different tastes and traditions have inevitably resulted in differing approaches to color and patina. In North America, France, and Germany, the "English" taste for natural-looking pieces is often rejected in favor of varnished and polished surfaces. This is particularly true of French polishing, in which a thick, glossy lacquer or varnish is applied to the surface to imitate the effects of time, sunshine, and color.

Decoration

The decoration of a piece of furniture is often the clearest indication of its period. From the 16th century decoration became more lavish and sophisticated, and, as fashions changed, earlier plainer furniture was frequently embellished in line with contemporary taste. How successfully the decoration works within the overall design is, therefore, often fundamental in determining whether a piece has been altered or embellished at a later date.

CARVING

Although the earliest carved furniture is usually of oak or walnut, specialist 17th-century carvers preferred to use more densely grained timbers, such as lime and boxwood, for very intricate work, and pine and other fruitwoods for carving that was to be over-decorated or gilded. With the invention of mechanical carving in the 19th century, designs became increasingly stylized, and work from this period is often shallow.

- Best examples are freely drawn, of good depth, and with accurately depicted motifs
- Carving was often painted or gilded

VENEERING

Veneering is a technique by which a lamina of expensive timber is applied to a cheaper timber using glue. Exotic timbers were initially employed; finely figured indigenous varieties were later introduced. Veneers from the 17th and 18th centuries are hand-cut and of uneven thickness (under 3mm/⅛in); 19th-century machine-cut veneers are paper thin.

Oyster veneering So-called because the grain resembles an oyster shell, this type of veneering was executed by slicing the veneer transversely across the end grain of smaller branches. These circular "oysters" were veneered one on top of another to resemble a log-pile.

- Technique introduced in the late 17th century
- Usually of walnut, kingwood, laburnum, or olivewood
- Fashionable until the mid-18th century; revived with paper-thin veneering in the early 20th century

Crossbanding and stringing The technique of framing edges on both solid and veneered furniture was widespread from the late 17th century. Matching timber was initially used; later, contrasting and more exotic banding veneers were employed, often laid with the grain at right angles to the principal veneer or timber, a technique known as crossbanding. In stringing and chequerbanding, the banding is framed with metal or wooden "strings" or thin strips.

- Introduced during the Renaissance

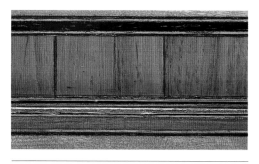

Herringbone veneering A refinement of the technique of crossbanding, herringbone veneering is characterized by the use of two strips of opposing straight-grained veneer cut on a diagonal and laid side by side. The strips are usually cut from the same piece of timber, and present a mirror image.

- Technique particularly employed on the finest early 18th-century walnut furniture
- Often found on bureaux and case furniture
- Used for framing edges

Quarter-veneering A technique in which four sheets of veneer are cut from the same piece of timber and juxtaposed diagonally in pairs, quarter-veneering was much used on the tops of early Georgian walnut chests. It was also widely employed for the sides of commodes on the Continent during the 18th century.

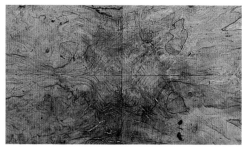

- First introduced on 17th-century cabinets
- Well suited to strong-grained timbers such as laburnum, walnut, burr-walnut, kingwood, tulipwood, and mahogany
- Used for the tops and sides of furniture

Butterfly veneering This technique consists of two opposing end-grain veneers cut successively and diagonally from one branch and applied to "mirror" one another.

- Particularly favored by Régence (1715–23) and Louis XV (1723–74) cabinet-makers
- Usually combined with strongly figured timbers, including tulipwood, kingwood, and olivewood

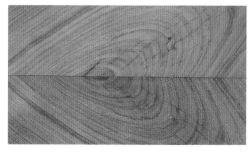

MARQUETRY, PARQUETRY, AND INLAY

The technique of embellishing furniture with marquetry of inlay was first employed during the Italian Renaissance. Rapidly adopted in Germany and the Low Countries, it was introduced to France in the early 17th century but did not reach Britain until after the Restoration (1660).

Marquetry This is a veneer composed of numerous woods, often further enriched by the use of staining, coloring, and engraving, applied to a plain surface to create a pictorial mosaic.

- First recorded in the Italian Renaissance and adopted in the 16th century in Germany and the Low Countries
- Features both symmetrical and asymmetrical designs
- Subject-matter includes flowers, arabesques, birds, architectural *capricci* and chinoiserie designs

Seaweed marquetry This form of marquetry is characterized by symmetrical, spindly, stylized foliate sprigs, often in light woods such as holly and boxwood, inlaid on a darker ground wood, such as walnut.

- Usually employed in circular or oval panels
- Introduced in the Low Countries in the mid-17th century
- Technique popularized by Huguenot craftsmen

Parquetry Veneered parquetry decoration was first used on northern European cabinets in the mid-17th century. It employs geometric designs, as opposed to the figurative or foliate motifs of marquetry. Parquetry was notably adopted by French cabinet-makers during the Régence, but its strong linearity also lent itself to late 18th-century Neo-classicism. The most popular forms of parquetry are the cube, lozenge, trellis (below), and dot trellis.
- Invented during the Italian Renaissance to decorate floors
- Invariably constructed of strongly grained veneers such as tulipwood, kingwood, fruitwood, and satinwood

Inlay While marquetry is always applied as a veneer, inlay is formed from materials cut into a solid groundwood. Employed since the Middle Ages, and widely used in Italy from the Renaissance, inlays were originally of bone or ivory and the technique was called *alla certosina*.
- *Pietre dure* (inlays of hardstones) popular in Italy
- Northern European and German inlays use fruitwoods, exotic colonial timbers, and pewter from the 17th century
- Mannerist-style ivory-and-bone inlay with arabesques, flowers, and festoons very fashionable in the 19th century

Brass inlay This technique involves inlaying brass into a tortoiseshell or exotic hardwood (ebony or amaranth) ground. The inlay was cut from two sheets, one of brass and the other of tortoiseshell or timber, and furniture could be veneered as *première partie* (with the tortoiseshell, as the ground) or *contre partie* (with a brass ground). In pairs of commodes, one inlay usually mirrors the other.
- Synonymous with the work of André-Charles Boulle (1642–1732) and revived in Britain c.1810–40

GILDING

Gilding is the application of gold leaf to a surface prepared with either animal size or a chalky, plaster-like substance known as gesso. The gold leaf binds itself to the prepared, glue-like surface, which has been dampened with oil or water. Oil gilding involves the application of gold leaf to a very thin layer of animal size. This technique requires a high degree of surface finish and is often slightly coarse. By contrast, water gilding is applied to white composition plaster or gesso, which is laid over a smooth bole (often red or yellow), achieving an exceptionally even finish. Oil gilding and *mecca* (a type of gilding that combines gold and silver leaf) were superseded in northern Europe from the late 17th century by gilt gesso. This uses a thick layer of gesso, which is incised with arabesques and armorials on a pounced ground (see below) before the gold leaf is applied. Like ormolu, gilding was increasingly conceived with contrasts between matt (flat) and burnished (highly finished) areas during the 18th century. This contrast was often heightened by the use of differently colored gilding enhanced by the color of the bole.
- Oil gilding suited to richly sculpted and carved furniture
- As a general rule, French and British gilding is applied to a yellowish ground; Swedish, north European, and Italian gilding often has a reddish tinge
- Gilt gesso associated with the work of Moore & Gumley in Britain during the early 18th century
- Regilding widely practiced in the 18th and 19th centuries

GILT BRONZE (ORMOLU)

Only those objects cast in bronze and fired using the mercury gilding process should properly be called ormolu. However, the term is often loosely applied to gilt bronze, which is not fired but dipped in acid and then lacquered. In France decorative ormolu mounts were cast by specialist *bronziers* and gilded by *doreurs*. French mounts executed between 1745 and 1749 should be stamped with the *C Couronne poinçon* (tax mark).

- Ormolu first became fashionable in the late 17th century through the patronage of Louis XIV
- Late-17th- and 18th-century gilding is "soft"; 19th-century gilding is "hard" and gilded to the reverse

LACQUERING AND JAPANNING

The technique of lacquering involves the application of numerous layers of varnish made from the sap of the *Rhus vernicifera* tree onto wood, leather, or fabric. When dry, the layers form a hard crust, which can be carved in relief. Originally imported as boxes, screens, and cabinets during the 18th century, lacquered furniture was often cut up and reused for veneering.
- First used in China in the 4th century BC
- Strong and waterproof
- Most common colors: black, aubergine, red, cream
- Capable of being carved in relief

The high cost and scarcity of lacquer, combined with an ever-expanding demand for so-called "Indian" (i.e. Oriental) designs, led to the development of European "japanning" in imitation of Oriental lacquer. Japanned furniture was made from shellac, seed-lac, or gum-lac, deposited by the insect *Coccus lacca*, which was dissolved in alcohol and then applied in numerous coats and usually decorated with gilt chinoiserie. Unlike lacquer, shellac is both weak and permeable to water; thus it was necessary to imitate the depth of relief possible with lacquer by building up raised areas in sawdust and gum arabic.
- Japanning introduced in the mid-17th century
- Weak and permeable to water

Painting Painted furniture was generally decorated with oil paints on a prepared surface, usually a softwood such as pine. The 18th-century Neo-classical revival, together with the excavations at Pompeii and Herculaneum, led to the increased use of painted arabesques, grotesques, and Etruscan ornament inspired by ancient vases. The fashion for painted furniture reached its peak during the late 18th century due in part to the work of architects such as Robert Adam (1728–92). As a result, satinwood and other exotic timbers began to be enriched with polychrome-painted flowers. This style was widely copied in the late 19th century, when many items of earlier, plain furniture were painted.
- Originally associated with the provincial tradition, especially Alpine and North American furniture
- First became fashionable in Venice and northern Italy from the Rococo period onward

Marriages, alterations and fakes, and care

Most items of furniture are functional, which means that marking and other damage will inevitably occur over time. Honest restoration such as replacement veneer and banding, or handles, locks, and feet, is therefore not only acceptable but also desirable to most collectors as a sign of age. However, all too often pieces have undergone more comprehensive "restoration," and this will certainly have a detrimental effect on their value – but only if the work is declared or detected.

MARRIAGES

A "marriage" is the term used to describe two- or even three-part case furniture that has been "made up" from different pieces, often of a similar date. Most frequently seen on bureau cabinets, and bureau bookcases, but also on larger bookcases and American highboys, marriages are usually betrayed by differences in the color, grain, and quality of the timber, particularly on the sides. Many large items of case furniture have spent some of their lives disassembled, and uneven exposure to sunlight can also cause huge variations in color. As a rule, the backboards on genuine pieces should closely resemble one another, both in the

▲ Sideboard
This Scottish mahogany sideboard was originally fitted with ring-turned legs typical of early 19th-century design. In the early 20th century it was given square tapering legs and spade feet, which belong to the period c.1770 to 1790.
(c.1820–30 and c.1900; ht 1m/3ft 3in; value H)

timber used (usually pine, oak, or ash) and in construction (planked and nailed, paneled and pegged, or with widely chamfered panels). For example, documented furniture often displays paneled tops and planked bases. Similarly, while secondary woods were always employed for backboards hidden behind drawers, or cupboard doors in the base, those of the top of a bookcase or bureau were intended to be seen, and are therefore often made of more exotic timbers, such as mahogany. However, drawers in both sections should display the same constructional characteristics.

Married pieces are often out of proportion, showing a visual imbalance between the joined parts. In addition, they can often be identified by an examination of the junction of the top and base sections, which may not fit tightly. On veneered furniture, a marriage may be apparent when the top section is removed. The veneer should not extend far beyond the point where the base meets the top. Another sign to look for when identifying two sections of different dates is the use of additional molding, intended to widen the top to correspond with the base. All sections of a genuine piece should display stylistic union, and decorative embellishments should be identical in both design and execution.

ALTERATIONS AND FAKES

Reduction in size is undoubtedly the most common alteration made to furniture. Initially, pieces were made smaller for practical purposes, but such alterations were increasingly made for financial gain, as furniture of unusually small proportions has always attracted a premium. Sideboards, bookcases, side tables, and even settees may all be reduced in width and depth, while bookcases may be shortened. Alterations in size are usually betrayed by constructional anomalies. Truncated friezes, redundant tenons

CHECKLIST FOR A BUREAU BOOKCASE: IS IT GENUINE?

Cornice should not have been reduced in width or depth; ornament should conform with that of glazing bars; timber should be the same as that used for the back

Doors should not have been truncated – check for signs of incompatible hinges, and locks

Glazing bars should not have been altered or embellished; they should be tenoned into the sides, not applied to the surface of a continuous sheet of glass

Base should not be veneered under the top and no extra molding should have been added

Grain and figuring of the timber should match, as well as any crossbanding or inlay

Drawer-linings in both the base and, where applicable, top sections should use the same secondary timbers and construction

Feet should be stylistically compatible, and color and distressing should be consistent with age

and re-made drawers are all clearly visible; indeed, reductions in width often necessitate the repositioning of handles and locks. Similarly, reducing the height of a bookcase usually involves shortening the doors, and thus the glazing bars have to be adjusted. It is important to remember that cabinet-makers often re-used and altered existing carcases and even finished furniture according to their clients' wishes, so not all reductions will be of a later period.

Like reductions in size, "improvements" began as innocent alterations motivated by changing tastes. From the mid-18th century handles and ormolu mounts were frequently changed according to the fashion. During the 19th century, simple, early oak was often embellished with florid carving, while plain pieces were often enriched with marquetry, painted decoration, and cross- and chequerbanding. Most common of all such changes are those made to legs and feet, either to disguise damage or to suggest an earlier period. Bun feet, traditionally considered provincial, were replaced from the early 18th century with shaped-bracket feet. More desirable cabriole legs often replaced plainer, club legs on chairs. Legs and feet of a later period than the rest of the piece are usually betrayed by differences in timber, color, and wear.

From the early 20th century, increasingly cynical alterations have been made with the specific intention to deceive. For this reason it has become essential to authenticate items of furniture by examining patina and establishing provenance. Fakes made entirely from new timber are relatively easy to detect, even where traditional methods of construction have been used, but those made up from old material can be very difficult to spot. This is particularly true of pieces built around antique carcases. Careful examination of the carcase, drawer-linings, feet, and surface color will usually serve to arouse suspicion, if it does not provide conclusive evidence. The main signs to look for are the presence of extensive staining; artificial distressing that gives the surface an unnatural

CARE

Color and condition are fundamental to the value of a piece of furniture, making proper care essential. It is important to ensure that furniture is not exposed to direct sunlight, which will lead to fading. Room temperatures and humidity levels should be consistent, as fluctuations cause warping, splitting, and the lifting of brass inlay, marquetry, and banding. Polished timber needs "feeding," ideally with a wax polish and soft dry cloth; silicone-based polishes should be avoided as they can be harmful to antique surfaces. Furniture should also be moved with care – for instance, make sure that chairs are carried by the seat rail, not by the arms or splats. Do not use carrying handles as these are often ornamental. Signs of old woodworm should not cause alarm, unless it has rendered the piece structurally infirm. Checked periodically for live woodworm, which is detectable by deposits of sawdust.

◄ Damaged Italian commode
This commode originally had a marble top. The paper-thin veneer applied at a later date has proved unable to endure the pressure of shrinkage within the carcase and has bubbled and split. One of the sides has also suffered from exposure to direct sunlight.

appearance; pronounced rusting on nails; unevenly oxidized boards; exaggerated adzing to carved areas; and a lack of shrinkage and opening of joints. Frequently, plain oak pieces have been re-veneered in more commercially desirable timbers such as walnut or, especially, pollard oak and burr-elm, which have the advantage of building up a good color rapidly. It is therefore imperative to check that the plugged holes of old handles and locks, and shrinkage splits to the inside of the carcase, correspond with similar scars on the veneer.

Painted furniture is another area in which it is difficult to detect fakes. The commercial viability of this type of furniture, combined with the fact that it has always been refreshed, makes it easy prey to fakers. Detection is further complicated by the fact that in most cases little or no timber is actually exposed. Although painted decoration has always been inspired by engravings, any piece of painted furniture that corresponds to a known design or celebrated model should be treated with caution. The accurate establishment of provenance is vital.

◄ Chest
This apparently genuine mid-17th-century oak chest is, in reality, a plain distressed one that has been heavily restored and embellished. The lid is a replacement, and the front left panel is also of a later date. Made-up furniture is betrayed by such details as the variable quality of the timber and carving, as well as the inconsistent build-up of color and oxidization.
*(mostly mid-17th century; ht 47cm/18½in; value **D**)*

TIPS FOR COLLECTORS

- high-quality restoration that is not intended to deceive should not adversely affect the value of a piece
- marriages are usually betrayed by variations in timber, construction, and style, and by poor proportion; check patina and beware of inconsistencies in color and grain; take particular care when purchasing secretaires, bookcases, highboys, and painted furniture
- look for alterations to cornices, doors, and glazing bars, and also for repositioned handles, re-made drawers, and replacement feet; most likely to be seen on sideboards, bookcases, and side tables
- fakes may be made up from old carcases; pay close attention to feet and drawer-linings; beware of excessive staining and distressing

Seat furniture

Until the 17th century most seating was provided by the stool; box-settles were also common in wealthier households. Side chairs and armchairs were introduced in the 16th century and the settee in the mid-17th century; this evolved over the next 200 years into the fully upholstered sofa. The demand for comfortable seating increased throughout this period, with upholstery gradually eclipsing wood carving and decoration, especially after the introduction of the coiled spring in the 1820s. Over the centuries seating has been profoundly influenced by a succession of styles and forms, from the extravagant Baroque to the austere Neo-classical, all of which have been revived by later generations of craftsmen. The interest in historical design continues to this day.

Stools

The stool has been in use for thousands of years, and was and is common in one form or another to all civilizations. Its often simple construction and its portability have ensured its lasting popularity. Until the 17th century, seat furniture with backs and arms was scarce, and the chair was reserved for the head of the household; most seating was provided by the stool.

17TH-CENTURY JOINED STOOLS

Inventories from the 17th century show that stools existed in large numbers and were reserved for members of the household who had sufficient status to sit at formal occasions. This hierarchy persisted in court circles well into the 18th century. Most stools found today were made from the 17th century onward. As with all types of furniture, examples of stools before 1600 are rare and those that come onto the market can be valuable. The simple, pegged, oak stool with carved decoration is probably the most common type. Called a joined or joint stool, it was made by a joiner, with mortise-and-tenon joints secured by pegs. Although regional variations exist, the design was basically the same throughout Europe. Generally only those pieces that were well made in good-quality wood have survived, and many stools intended for everyday use have long since disappeared.

Joined stools could be extended in length to become benches and were occasionally made with a small drawer underneath the seat. Even at this early date they were often made in sets, a practice that was to become widespread in later centuries. Originally the seat would probably have been softened with a squab cushion but during the 17th century padding became an integral part of the stool as the demand for comfort increased.

LATER STOOLS

Because stools were perennially popular they tended to keep up with fashion trends. In the late 18th century British stools were made after designs in *The Cabinet-Maker and Upholsterer's Guide* (1788–94) by George Hepplewhite (*d.*1786) and French stools after designs by Pierre Fontaine (*c.*1762–1853) and Charles Percier

(1764–1838), as well as those in *Receuil de décorations intérieures* (1801–12). Shapes diversified as the interest in historical styles and forms, whether real or imaginary, took hold. For example, the X-frame form, first made in ancient Egypt and common in Europe during the Renaissance, was revived in Europe and North America during the early 19th century. The 19th century saw an increased use of mechanization, which enabled carving to become extremely elaborate, and stools were made in a variety of bizarre forms with carved and molded decoration. From the third quarter of the 19th century a new type of upholstered seating, the pouffe, was introduced. The upholsterer played an increasingly prominent role in furniture-making as comfort became an ever more important criterion.

◄ **Stool**
From c.1730 mahogany took over from walnut as the preferred wood for fashionable furniture. Cabriole legs were also in vogue until the 1770s. This British mahogany stool has a drop-in seat, introduced in the early 1700s. The "ears" at the top of each leg are vulnerable and are often replaced.
*(c.1740; ht 47cm/18½in; value **G**)*

▼ **Stool after A.M.E. Fournier**
Known as a *tabouret* in France, this French giltwood stool has a deeply padded seat, reflecting the contemporary demand for comfortable seating, and a novel "knotted-rope" frame. Modern copies of this type of stool tend to be stiffer in design and carving than the originals.
*(c.1860; ht 48cm/18¾in; value **H**)*

◄ **Stool**
English-oak joined stools such as this are usually about 59cm (23in) high and always have some form of molding running around the seat edge – this example has a carved frieze. The seat is pegged to the base, and the pegs at the joints of the legs should be visible on the inside of the frame. The seats on such stools may have been replaced and the tips of the legs reduced by wear.
*(mid-17th century; ht 67cm/26½in; value **G**)*

KEY FACTS

- COPIES OF JOINED STOOLS during the 1920s and 1930s many copies were made of the joined stool; signs of a genuine example include wear in the right places, such as the stretchers; irregular pegs that stand proud due to shrinkage and are visible on both the inside and outside of the frame; "dry" wood underneath the seat
- GEORGIAN STOOLS look at the color of the wood under the seat rail (the drop-in seat should lift out) – this should be "dry" and unstained; exercise caution with small stools, which are popular with collectors – fakers may have used the front pair of legs from two damaged chairs and fixed them into a seat rail; check for odd proportions and for tops of legs hidden by the seat rail

Early chairs

Before the 16th century rooms were sparsely furnished, and the range of furniture was limited. Chairs were scarce and, like stools, were viewed as symbols of authority. It was not until the 16th century that more comfortable chairs were made. At this time the major artistic impetus spread northward from Italy, and chairs were made in quantity only in southern Europe. By the 17th century, as lifestyles became more settled, there was a greater demand for comfort in seat furniture.

▲ Turner's or "thrown" chair
Chairs of this type were produced in Britain from the 16th century, and were still made in provincial areas into the 19th century. "Throwing" was an early term for turning. These chairs were often made from ash, which is strong and ideal for turning, although susceptible to woodworm.
(late 17th century; ht 1m/3ft 3in; value H)

SOUTHERN EUROPE

The earliest prototype was the 16th-century Italian X-frame folding chair, usually in walnut, which was adopted in northern Europe from the end of the century. Spanish examples exist that are inlaid with ivory and metals in stellar and geometric designs in the Moorish fashion.

Armchairs of the 16th and 17th centuries were refined versions of the carved *chaise caquetoire* (gossiping chair) which, with its solid, carved back and trapezoidal seat, was not very comfortable. As revealed by the engravings of the Flemish designer Hans Vredeman de Vries (1526–c.1604) in his *Differents Pourtraicts de Menuiserie* (c.1585), the earliest-surviving traditional easy chairs were executed principally in Tuscany, Spain, Portugal, and The Netherlands in the late 16th and early 17th centuries. Known as the *sillón de fraileros* ("monk's chair") in Spain, this type of chair was usually of walnut, with scrolled and acanthus-carved stiles. The upper section was supported by plain legs joined by waved stretchers, and the chair was upholstered with

intricately tooled and embossed leather stretched by ornamental heavy brass nails. Examples from The Netherlands often have lion finials surmounting the stiles.

NORTHERN EUROPE

Turning on a foot-operated lathe (which revolved the legs while the wood was cut to the required shape) became an increasingly popular decorative technique in northern Europe, and by the early 17th century most legs were turned. This form of decoration remained fashionable until the end of the century. Designs became increasingly intricate at this time, culminating in the "barley-sugar" (spiral) twist.

Peculiar to the 17th century is the oak joined chair with arms, often called a wainscot chair in Britain. Similar designs were made in many countries throughout northern Europe, and examples are still found in some numbers. This type of chair commonly has a scroll-carved toprail, sometimes inscribed with initials or a date. Its characteristic feature is a panel back, often symmetrically carved with stylized leaves, lozenges, roundels, and lunettes. The seat is solid, but would originally have had a squab cushion, and the front supports are ring-turned, with the legs joined by stretchers. Chairs of this type were made until the end of the 17th century and represent the final stage of the age of the joiner, as this period is often called. Designs and techniques changed considerably after this time, but in many provincial areas the traditional methods of construction continued to be used.

▼ Sillón de fraileros
This type of walnut armchair was made throughout the 16th and 17th centuries in southern Europe. The leather back and seat, which in Spain were often tooled and held by ornamental nails, were introduced by the Moors. Examples with all the original elements are highly prized.
(17th century; ht 1m/3ft 3in; value D)

▲ Armchair
Iberian walnut armchairs in good original condition are rare. The high arched back, down-curved scroll arms, and pierced front stretcher, mirroring the shape of the toprail, are typical of 17th-century chair design. In northern Europe caning would probably have been used instead of the tooled leather seen here. Such chairs were extensively copied in the 19th century.
(c.1680; ht 1.2m/3ft 11in; value G)

KEY FACTS

- WOODS invariably indigenous – walnut in southern Europe and oak in northern Europe; rosewood was used to a limited extent during the 17th century in Portugal
- DAMAGE examples that pre-date 1600 are extremely rare, and 17th-century examples should be examined closely for repairs; age, wear, and tear will have taken their toll – the legs and the lower part of the back are particularly vulnerable
- DECORATION painted decoration, upholstery, leather, and caning have often been changed; if the originals remain, they increase the value
- COPIES AND FAKES most 17th-century chairs are stylistically of a very simple form, the same designs being produced over a long period, making them difficult to date; turners' chairs are popular with collectors and are often faked – copies are difficult to detect as they may be quite old themselves, and tend to be in the same woods as the originals (ash or oak, not walnut), with good-quality carving; the color of the wood on all unpolished surfaces should be closely examined, as should the overall patina

See also Arts and Crafts: Furniture – Britain, pp.371–73

Easy chairs before 1840

As the Baroque movement swept through Europe during the late 17th century, the design of seat furniture became increasingly luxurious, elaborate, and more importantly comfortable. Caned and leather chairs, which until this time had sufficed, were largely abandoned in favfavor of richly upholstered easy chairs as stiff upright backs were discarded and were replaced by sloped and subsequently shaped backs. The number of types of chairs also increased enormously.

▶ Throne

This giltwood Venetian throne shows the influence of Andreas Brustolon. Its serpentine scrolling arms are richly carved with recumbent putti, and its legs and arm supports with caryatids.
(*c.1700; ht 1.6m/5ft 3in; value Q*)

ITALY AND FRANCE

It was in Italy, particularly in Venice, Florence, and Rome, during the late 17th and early 18th centuries, that the Baroque style found its clearest expression. The most elaborate open armchairs of this period are usually of either boxwood or giltwood. They are carved with scrolling acanthus, *espagnolette* masks, and even mythological figures emblematic of the four seasons. Some Venetian examples feature seahorses in deference to the city's seafaring tradition. Such pieces were usually the work of trained sculptors who had turned their hand to furniture-making; the most celebrated of these was undoubtedly Andreas Brustolon (1662–1732).

In France, under the influence of Cardinal Mazarin, the court of Louis XIV (1643–1715) became increasingly hungry for foreign luxuries and fashions, especially those from Italy. In the mid-17th century French easy chairs became increasingly comfortable and elaborate, owing to their generous proportions, richly turned decoration, and lavish use of velvet upholstery from Genoa or Utrecht.

The Régence period (1715–23) saw significant developments in the design of seat furniture. Although the *menuisiers* (joiners) were slow to abandon the traditional Louis XIV *fauteuil* (armchair) form, they were increasingly lavish in their carving. Chairs were decorated with gadroons, shells, and rosettes, and even richly upholstered in velvet or lavish textiles made at the Savonnerie in Paris (est. 1604 in the Louvre for the production of textiles; from 1627 at the Savonnerie). The stretcher became more sinuous, and was abandoned by the 1720s. Further changes in form and design were

dictated by the fashion for wearing hooped dresses, introduced c.1720, which resulted in the arms of easy chairs being set back by a quarter of the length of the side-rail. The introduction of upholstery *à chassis* allowed the loose covering to be changed according to the season.

Under Louis XV (1715–74) the fashion for placing chairs around the sides of the room was abandoned in favor of a more relaxed arrangement that encouraged intimate conversation and gave birth to the *fauteuil en cabriolet*, with its Rococo form and exuberant carving in the round. Louis XV seat furniture is usually made of either walnut or beech, the latter wood always either gilded or painted; a pegged construction was used, and pieces are very often stamped by the *menuisier* responsible, in accordance with the strict rules of the furniture-makers' guild (Corporation des Menuisiers-Ebénistes). During the 1730s numerous styles of informal easy chair emerged, all of them richly carved. The most luxurious was the *bergère*, which was popular throughout the 18th century and characterized by its deep seat, padded back and sides, and squab cushion. Widely copied throughout Europe, it was to prove inspirational to chair-makers during the Regency period (c.1790–1830) in Britain, and was also much copied in the late 19th and 20th centuries.

BRITAIN AND NORTH AMERICA

The earliest-recorded wing armchairs, known as *bergère en confessionnal* because the identity of the sitter was hidden by the side wings, are French examples from the early 1670s. Invariably of walnut, this form was rapidly adopted in Britain. The wing armchairs made during the late 17th and very early 18th centuries were usually of walnut or, in more provincial examples, of beech stained to simulate walnut. These armchairs are characterized by the exaggerated scroll of the arms, the high, slanted back flanked by high wings, and the stylized carving of scrolls and foliage on the legs and stretchers.

The most celebrated form of wing armchair was made from the early 18th century until c.1750. Examples are usually of walnut, and are supported on cabriole legs, which, unlike their 17th-century prototypes, are rarely joined by stretchers. Wing armchairs made in Britain during the reigns of Queen Anne and George I are often carved with trailed husks and scallop shells on the top of the knees and stand on pad feet, although some later examples have hoof or claw-and-ball feet. The most refined wing armchairs of this period were upholstered in *gros* and *petit point* needlework, often with figures on the back (but never on the seat) within a flower-strewn border.

Wing armchairs continued to be made throughout the 18th century in mahogany, and

▲ Bergère en confessionnal by Pierre Laroque

The low, deeply upholstered form of this late Louis XV French *bergère en confessionnal*, with its high, enveloping back, is designed for an intimate environment. Such chairs are also common in Louis XVI style.
(*c.1766; ht 1m/3ft 3in; value I*)

▼ Wing armchair

Chairs made in New England and New York generally have vertical cone-shaped arms, while those made in Philadelphia, such as this example, generally have double C-scroll arms.
(*1765–80; ht 1.2m/3ft 11in; value Q*)

were widely copied in walnut in the 19th and 20th centuries. North American early 18th-century wing chairs were generally of walnut or maple, with a high arched crest, and block and vase turned legs joined by a stretcher. During the 1720s short cabriole legs with "Spanish" feet, were used and front stretchers were eliminated. From the mid-18th century mahogany was used. Stretchers continued to be used in New England, while easy chairs made in Philadelphia generally did not have them. In 1760 the serpentine crest design was introduced, modifying the verticality, and it was used along with the rounded profile until the 1780s. Between 1780 and 1800 American chair-makers used George Hepplewhite's design for a "Saddle Check Chair," an easy chair with serpentine contored wings, straight legs, and "H" stretchers, a chair design also associated with Thomas Chippendale (1718–79). There are regional differences in construction and upholstery. Maple was often used for the one-piece rear legs and stiles in New England chairs, stained to match the mahogany of the front legs.

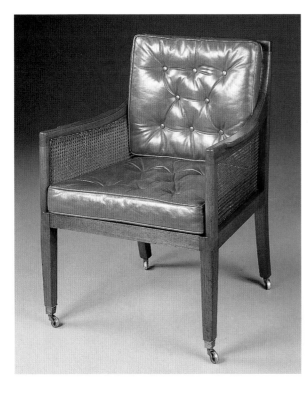

▲ Library *bergère* or "Uxbridge" chair
This British armchair is of a style introduced in the early 18th century for use in the library. It has a cane-filled back and sides, and leather-covered cushions; the best examples have reeded or fluted front legs.
(early 19th century; ht 1.2m/3ft 11in; value I)

Other types of late 18th-century easy chair were based on designs in *The Cabinet-Maker and Upholsterer's Drawing Book* (1791–1802) by Thomas Sheraton (1751–1806) including "conversation" chairs, with deep upholstered seats and padded toprails on which the sitter, facing backward, could rest his or her arms. In Sheraton's *The Cabinet Dictionary* (1803) there is a reference to a "curricle" chair, so-called after a tub-shaped carriage, which was popular in libraries at the time. About 1810 to 1820 *bergère*-type armchairs with deep, upholstered or leather seats and backs, and cane or upholstered sides, were also widely used in libraries.

AMERICAN "CHIPPENDALE"

The carvers of the most elaborate American Rococo furniture were immigrants from England, Scotland, and Ireland, who had served their apprenticeship in London before going to North America. The first of them arrived in the 1740s, but the great wave of craftsmen was in the 1760s. Philadelphia was the city most hospitable to immigrants, and more Rococo furniture was produced there than in other colonies. The major cities in America developed distinctive furniture styles, due to the taste of the gentry, the mix of native born and immigrant craftsmen, and the availability of imported furniture and English pattern-books. It is known that there were copies of Chippendale's *Director* in Philadelphia. The Library Company of Philadelphia acquired a copy between 1764 and 1769, and two cabinet-makers Thomas Affleck (1740–95) and Benjamin Randolph, owned copies. In America furniture was mostly made of solid pieces of primary wood, rather than veneers over a seconday wood carcase as in England.

▶ Side chair from Philadelphia
(c.1755–60; ht 1m/3ft 3in; value Q)

SCANDINAVIA

Trade between England and Scandinavia was well established by the mid-17th century, and some English furniture had been exported to Scandinavia by the end of the century. Craftsmen in these countries produced good copies of English furniture; the joiners (although not the cabinet-makers) were very conservative, with the result that early 18th-century styles continued to be produced until *c.*1800. Around this time, too, mahogany was introduced; before this, walnut was used for expensive pieces. More commonly employed, however, were native light-colored woods such as birch, ash, and pine; these were left bare, stained, or painted in colors.

By the late 1730s French designs had become increasingly popular at the Swedish and Danish courts and also with the upper classes in these countries; the middle classes did not generally adopt the new fashions until the end of the century. French styles were particularly influential in Sweden, and from the Rococo period court architects were trained in Paris. One of the most influential Swedish designers of the period was Jean Eric Rehn (1717–93). Danish court architects learned their trade in Germany, but this situation changed after the reign of Louis XVI, when both countries adopted the French Neo-classical style. In Sweden the cabinet-maker Georg Haupt (1741–84), who had trained in both Paris and London is well known for his work in the Louis XVI style. This style developed into the Neo-classical Gustavian style during the 1770s.

▼ *Fauteuil* by Johan Lindgren
Made during the reign of Gustav III (1771–92), this Swedish armchair shows the influence of French Louis XVI furniture. However, with its parcel gilding and white painted frame, it is a rather heavy example of the style.
(c.1790; ht 1.1m/3ft 7in; value H)

See also Easy chairs after 1840, pp.34–5; Dining-chairs before 1840, pp.36–8

RUSSIA

Throughout the 18th century Russian furniture was inspired by French and to a lesser degree English designs; by *c.*1815 German influence is also apparent. Generally the timbers used for Russian furniture were indigenous; during the early 18th century, when designs were dictated by early Georgian furniture from Britain, they included oak, beech, and walnut. By the 1720s Russian armchairs had tall curved backs with a vase splat and cabriole legs. By the mid-18th century, the taste for Rococo and Chinese ornament had spread to Russia due to the publication of such influential pattern-books as *The Gentleman and Cabinet-Maker's Director* (1754–62) by the English cabinet-maker Thomas Chippendale (1718–79). English-style chairs with pierced splats and sweeping cabriole legs with claw-and-ball feet, usually made in mahogany, were increasingly popular.

However, from the beginning of the 19th century the clearest influence on Russian furniture manufacture was that of France. Particularly favored was the Empire style of the cabinet-maker Georges Jacob (1739–1814), who was based in Paris. About this time, light-colored woods also became popular, anticipating the Biedermeier style in Germany and Scandinavia. From *c.*1815 chairs were executed in indigenous woods such as Karelian birch, maple, and poplar, decorated with restrained stringing.

▲ Fauteuil

This Russian mahogany and parcel-gilt armchair was once owned by a member of the Imperial household. It has a scrolled tablet back with a foliate- and anthemia-enriched triangular pediment, and foliate-carved base. It is inspired by the French Empire style, but embodies the Russian passion for glittering display contrasted with sombre coloring.
*(early 19th century; ht 1.2m/3ft 11in; value **H**)*

THE BIEDERMEIER STYLE

This decorative style was popular in Germany, Austria, and Scandinavia between *c.*1815 and *c.*1848. The name was invented by two German poets who wrote under the pseudonym Gottlieb Biedermeier, formed from a combination of *bieder* (meaning conventional or honest) and Meier, a common German surname. The solid, comfortable appearance of Biedermeier pieces was thought to mirror the unpretentious elegance of the German bourgeoisie. The simple, geometric designs, which eschewed ornate decoration, were inspired by French furniture of the Empire period. Function and comfort were of supreme importance to the Biedermeier craftsmen and to achieve this end they used coil-spring upholstery.

► Bergère

Although this armchair is made from burr-walnut, Biedermeier craftsmen generally preferred to use lightly colored indigenous timber such as elm, ash, Karelian birch, and fruitwoods. The flat surfaces are accented with a simple inlay of ebony. The symmetry and beautiful proportions of this armchair are inspired by the French Etruscan style.
*(1825–40; ht 1m/3ft 3in; value **I**)*

HALL CHAIRS

Hall chairs (and also hall benches) were introduced in Britain from the late 17th century. They may have been inspired by similar chairs known as *sgabelli*, which were popular in the great Italian palaces during the 16th century. Hall chairs were designed to be placed in the entrance hall or passageways used by servants and tradesmen waiting to be called into one of the main rooms. Consequently such chairs were never upholstered, and generally they lacked arms; however, they were increasingly made of mahogany, with solid backs and dished or shaped seats. The designs were bold and simple and were frequently embellished with the painted crest or coat of arms of the family who commissioned them. In some cases they were carved with motifs intended to impress guests and to emphasize the social status of the owner. The importance given to hall chairs is suggested by the fact that there are six designs for such chairs in *The Gentleman and Cabinet-Maker's Director* by Thomas Chippendale, three in *The Cabinet-Maker and Upholsterer's Guide* (1788–94) by George Hepplewhite (*d.*1786), and two in *The Cabinet Dictionary* (1803) by Thomas Sheraton (1751–1806).

► Hall chair

This English hall chair has a shield back painted with a swan. This style of chair back was popular during the Neo-classical and Regency periods. Around 1750 round backs were common for hall chairs, while oval and vase backs were introduced in the 1770s and 1780s.
*(early 19th century; ht 1.1m/3ft 7in; value **D**)*

KEY FACTS

- UPHOLSTERY *gros* and *petit point* are very rare and greatly contribute to the value of a wing armchair
- REGILDING well-executed regilding should not dramatically affect the value of an object; French Louis XV beechwood chairs were usually originally gilded or painted and traces are often found in the crevices
- HALL CHAIRS these are usually found in sets of four or more, although it is possible to find single chairs; they are often decorated on the back with a cartouche featuring the armorial of the family who commissioned them; they are generally very good value for money
- COPIES AND FAKES Brustolon-style chairs were widely copied in the 19th century; Biedermeier chairs have been been widely faked in the 20th century, with many side chairs converted into armchairs – this should be obvious if the proportions seem wrong

Country chairs

Country or, more correctly, vernacular chairs represent an area of furniture-making that holds great fascination for collectors. Such pieces demonstrate the way in which wood-working techniques have changed little from generation to generation. Only occasionally does a hint of a fashionable style, such as the inclusion of cabriole legs, appear in these traditional designs.

▲ Ladder-back chair
This ladder-back (slat-back) chair is much more robust than its design might suggest. Although generally associated with country pieces, the ladder-back design also influenced mainstream mahogany furniture. *(19th century; ht 1.1m/3ft 7in; value for set of four G)*

TYPES OF CHAIR
The best-known country chair in Britain and North America is the "Windsor," which has a solid saddle seat (elm in Britain, and pine or poplar in North America) into which are doweled the bow (ash or yew in Britain, and ash, hickory, or oak in North America) and the turned or roughly rounded spindles and legs (beech in Britain, and birch, maple, ash, or chestnut in North America). There are two basic types of Windsor chair: the comb-back, which has a horizontal toprail (a very popular form in North America); and the hoop-back (also called the bow-back), in which the horizontal bar is steamed and bent into a semi-circle to form the arms and a mid-support for the spindles. Some British hoop-backs have a pierced, decorative splat. High Wycombe, Buckinghamshire, was a major British center of production for this type of chair from the mid-19th century. Other types of country chair include the ladder-back, which has up to six horizontal arched splats, and often a quarter-woven rush or splint seat.

In North America the religious communities formed by the Shakers (so named because of their tendency to shake during their lively prayer meetings) made simple, pared-down furniture, rejecting applied ornament in favor of clean line and color. Their doctrine was "Do not make that which is not useful." During the classic period (1810–60), Shaker furniture-makers simplified existing country designs. Forms were standardized, and hundreds of identical items were produced; chairs with slat-backs and rush or tape seats were manufactured and sold. It is sometimes possible to identify the community in which a chair was made by the design of the finial on the back post. Chairs were light so that they could be moved easily and hung on peg rails.

DECORATION
Some of the appeal of country chairs lies in their distinct lack of, or restrained use of, ornamentation, with furniture-makers often taking advantage of the natural grain and color of the wood. Ash, for example, which was much used by country craftsmen, develops a rich honey-brown patina over time, while cherry acquires a rich red color that is highly sought after today. Painting was the most common form of decoration on provincial chairs, which were often made of pine. Even the Shakers used bright blues, yellows, greens, and occasionally reds, in the 19th century. The Pennsylvania Dutch often stenciled or freebrushed designs of fruit, leaves and flowers on their plank-seat arrow- and balloon-back chairs. However, because these chairs were used every day some of the painted decoration has invariably rubbed off. Early in the 20th century rubbed paint was often deliberately stripped.

◀ Hoop-back Windsor armchair
This is a typical Windsor chair, with component elements made from different native woods. The seat is of elm; the rest of the chair is of ash. *(early 19th century; ht 1.2m/3ft 11in; value E)*

▲ Four-slat Shaker rocker
The vertical proportions of this rocker from the Harvard community in Massachusetts are emphasized by the elongated turned finials on its back stiles. The tops of the slats are arched to give an additional visual lift. Such pieces demonstrate how Shaker craftsmen achieved a purity of form in their desire to create functional furniture. *(c.1840; ht 1.2m/3ft 11in; value O)*

KEY FACTS
- CONDITION many woods used for country chairs are subject to worm (with the exception of oak); elements may have been replaced owing to continual use; rich patination can add considerably to the value of a piece; chairs showing signs of wear are usually preferred
- COPIES many types are still made today, and dating can be difficult; later examples lack authentic patination, and generally have a stiffer appearance
- COLLECTING it is not unusual to find marginal differences in turning and carving within a set; sets of ladder-backs were probably made in the 19th century, and it is rare to find more than six
- MARKS British chairs may be marked with a maker's label, or stamped with the initials, or a name, on the outside edge of the seat; American windsors are sometimes branded under the seat

See also Early chairs, p.29; Arts and Crafts: Furniture – Britain, pp.371–73, The United States, pp.374–75

Easy chairs after 1840

The upholstered chair and the easy chair underwent fundamental changes during the 19th century. The market for such furniture expanded rapidly, with middle-class buyers seeking items that reflected their new-found prosperity. Nowhere was this more apparent than in the desire for increased comfort in seat furniture. With the growth of the railways, easier access to North America, and the international exhibitions, trade increased and designs quickly spread from country to country.

▼ **Gainsborough armchair**
This 20th-century British armchair is copied from one made during the reign of George II (1727–60). Its proportions are stiffer and more pinched than those of an 18th-century example. The backward-swept or "kicked" back leg is a typically British feature.
(c.1910; ht 1m/3ft 3in; value **G***)*

NEW TECHNOLOGY AND MATERIALS
As the layout of 19th-century drawing-rooms (salons) and parlors became ever more informal, so the emphasis on comfort increased. The development of the coiled-wire spring in the late 1820s had a profound effect on seat design. Springs could be incorporated into the chair-frame, which was then upholstered with thick, deep padding to accommodate them, producing a much more comfortable seat than could be afforded by padding alone. The areas enclosing the springs gave a rounded shape to the chair; the form was therefore usually dictated by the need for comfort rather than by aesthetics. In Britain the use of luxuriant upholstery was of paramount importance during the Victorian period (1837–1901), and in the 1840s deeply sunk buttons were introduced in order to emphasize its curves and depth. Deep buttoning that gave a three-dimensional effect came to typify the Victorian easy chair and sofa. The upholstery was secured by tacks and hidden by machine-made cloth beading known as "gimp." Chairs were further embellished with heavy, floor-length fringes, and by tassels and twisted cords in contrasting

colors. The fashion for deep upholstery, which was reflected in heavy drapes and hangings, was at its height in the third quarter of the 19th century. Abundant upholstery had its disadvantages – it harbored dust, moths, and vermin – but to the Victorians, the level of comfort it represented was of greater importance.

Needlework was a popular ladies' pastime during the 19th century. The use of large expanses of upholstery, and the increased number of informal easy chairs, presented an opportunity for displaying different forms of the craft, such as Berlin woolwork, on chair backs and seats. The T-shaped padded back of the *prie-dieu* (kneeling chair), a low seat on short legs, was particularly suited to decoration with needlework. Designs commonly featured large sprays of flowers, and sometimes mirrored the upholstery, drapery, and carpets that surrounded them in the Victorian drawing-room. The most sought-after upholstery covering was that produced at the factory of Aubusson in France, using 18th-century designs appropriate to the style of the chair. These coverings, when found today, add considerably to the value of a piece. The Victorians' desire for comfort and love of innovation spawned a new range of easy chairs and seats, which included the pouffe (cushion seat); the *confidante* (a sofa with angle seats at either end); the *tête-à-tête* or "love seat," often made as two seats facing each other and joined at the sides; and the conversation seat (three seats joined back to back). Chairs for use in the drawing-room were frequently produced in suites, often comprising seven pieces, including a *canapé* (sofa), a *fauteuil* (open armchair), and a *chaise* (chair).

THE INTERNATIONAL EXHIBITIONS
The many new developments in chair design were brought together and displayed publicly and proudly in the international exhibitions that were to become such a feature of the second half of the 19th century in Europe and the USA. The Great Exhibition of 1851 in London set the tone; after it France and Britain, in particular, vied with each other to produce successively larger and better exhibitions. Fashionable fringed upholstery was displayed prominently at the International Exhibition of 1867 in Paris, and the work of the French upholsterers eclipsed even that of the cabinet-makers. Fully illustrated catalogs were produced, disseminating new styles and technological advances. The furniture at these exhibitions was often of the finest quality, but the pieces displayed tended to be virtuoso statements rather than of practical use.

▶ **Armchair**
Copying the popular Louis XVI style, this French giltwood armchair with tapestry back and seat is one of a set of four, which may also once have included a *canapé* or sofa. It is unusual in having blue upholstery – the most popular colors at this time were green and yellow, or pink and red.
(c.1900; ht 1.2m/3ft 11in; value for set of four **I***)*

▲ **Gentleman's armchair**
Items such as this British walnut armchair were often produced as part of a suite and are still found in large numbers today. This example has clearly been influenced by the Louis XV style, with its curves and cabriole legs. It is crisply carved with naturalistic forms. The deep seat suggests that the chair is sprung. Similar armchairs were commonly produced in both rosewood and mahogany.
(c.1850; ht 1m/3 ft 3in; value **F***)*

BELTER'S LAMINATION PROCESS

Between 1847 and 1858 the American manufacturer John Henry Belter (1804–63) developed a way to bend and laminate rosewood, for which he took out a series of patents. Belter's lamination process involved gluing together between four and sixteen sheets of wood with the grain going in different directions. The sheets were steam-molded into shape. Laminated wood is thinner and lighter than solid wood. Its strength allows elaborate piercing and deep carving of leaves, fruit, acorns, vines, and flowers, suited to the Louis XV Revival.

▼ "Rosalie" armchair
This is the most typical Belter design. Unlike much Belter work, it is not pierced, giving the impression of solid rosewood.
*(1845–63; ht 1.1m/3ft 7in; value **Q**)*

middle classes. Relying heavily on the use of C- and S-scrolls, carved flowers, and serpentine forms, easy chairs were either laminated and carved (after the introduction of Belter's lamination process) or carved from the solid, with pierced backs and cabriole legs with casters. The differences between the 18th-century originals and the 19th-century interpretations were often subtle; elements from both these and other periods were often combined, and dark woods or ebonized frames were often used where the originals would have been painted in white and gilded. There was also a heavier interpretation of form, with an increased use of ring-turning, a liberal addition of gilt mounts (so rarely found on 18th-century chairs), and much use of fixed deep-buttoned upholstery rather than the upholstery *à chassis* common on original pieces. Although walnut and mahogany were the most popular woods during the 19th century, much Rococo Revival furniture was made from rosewood, which had a strong grain and rich color. Such firms as Joseph Meeks & Sons (1797–1868) of New York produced fine furniture in the Rococo style during the 1850s and 1860s. The Rococo Revival continued until the 1860s, when it was replaced by other styles.

By the end of the 19th century, the furniture manufacturers' desperate search for novelty designs had resulted in so many revivals and combinations that there was a great confusion of styles. Wealthy Victorian buyers were certainly spoilt for choice in furnishing their homes. The revivals included all of the main European historical styles, as well as Japanese and other east Asian styles, which were widely interpreted during the Aesthetic period from the 1860s.

▲ Armchair
This French armchair with Egyptian-inspired decoration is in the Empire style: the late Neo-classical look influenced by Napoleon's Nile campaigns and revived in France in the late 19th century. It is made of mahogany and gilt-bronze. The quality of the mounts on pieces such as this can vary considerably and should be carefully examined. This type of chair is still being reproduced, but modern examples are often of indifferent craftsmanship.
*(c.1900; ht 80cm/31½in; value **G**)*

◄ Open armchair by Herter Brothers (est. 1860)
The virtuoso carving seen on the winged armrests and on the ribbons and swags on the toprail of this throne-like walnut and burr-walnut chair reflects the exuberant style of the Renaissance Revival in the USA. Herter Brothers of New York was one of the leading exponents.
*(c.1871–3; ht 1.4m/4ft 7in; value **Q**)*

STYLISTIC REVIVALS

The rapid spread of ideas made possible by the international exhibitions led to a range of generic styles in furniture design, with fashions becoming increasingly eclectic as the century progressed. Due to the growing dependence on machines, many national characteristics in design and construction disappeared. It is therefore difficult to determine the country of origin of many pieces made after the 1840s. Most problematic is 19th-century furniture made in the styles of the Louis XV (1715–74) and Louis XVI (1774–93) periods, which were loosely interpreted throughout Europe and North America. The Rococo Revival started in Europe in the 1820s and spread to North America by the 1840s, reflecting the wealth and optimism of the burgeoning

KEY FACTS

- **UPHOLSTERY** original upholstery, especially 19th-century Aubusson covering, is much sought after; it can become threadbare with use, so check for restoration; the quality of upholstery is critical (mending is expensive) since seats in particular have to withstand a lot of pressure, both from body weight and from fitted springs; seats should be taut and well secured to the frame
- **ALTERATIONS** even sprung pieces may be pre-19th century; it is not uncommon for 18th-century chairs, such as wing armchairs, to have been fitted with springs in the 19th century
- **DATING** when fully upholstered, with perhaps only the legs showing, some copies of earlier models can be extremely difficult to date; carefully lift off tacks to look under the seat frame; examine surfaces for variations in color and lack of finish
- **BELTER** laminations are thinner, curves more emphatic, and fruits and flowers richer and more deeply carved on pieces by Belter than on those by his competitors

See also Settles and sofas after 1840, pp.44–5

Dining-chairs before 1840

Chairs without arms were first recorded in Italy, Spain, and The Netherlands in the 16th century, and most examples were made either of walnut or, particularly in The Netherlands, of ebony. Early 17th-century dining-chairs are often supported by baluster-turned legs joined by double stretchers. The seats are generally of brass-nailed leather, particularly those of Spanish chairs, and the backs tend to be elaborately carved with Italian Renaissance-inspired arcades and lion finials.

17TH-CENTURY DINING-CHAIRS

It was not until the late 17th century that side chairs or dining-chairs became fashionable in Europe. English chairs of the Restoration period (1660s) are usually of walnut or beech, with caned seats and central caned back panels. They are often extravagantly carved with dense foliage, arabesques, and putti in the Baroque style; some examples have turned supports, with arched cresting and heavy front stretchers sometimes carved with armorial devices. It is difficult to distinguish

▶ **Side chair**

This yellow-ground floral needlework upholstery seen on this chair is a reproduction; pieces with original needlework are at a premium. Original upholstery can be identified by the use of only one circuit of nail holes attaching the cover to the frame. The legs and feet on chairs such as this will often have been replaced.
(c.1695; ht 1.2m/3ft 11in; value for a pair H)

between Dutch and English chairs of this period, but Continental examples tend to have oval, rather than rectangular, caned-back panels. The turned stretchers on Dutch chairs usually tenon directly into the legs as opposed to square blocks.

Under the influence of the court of Louis XIV, seat furniture from the late 17th century became more comfortable and often more restrained. Frequently of giltwood, the cabriole legs and X-shaped stretchers of Louis XIV side chairs were often channeled rather than carved; the seats were lower and more generous than those of chairs made before this period, and the taller, rectangular backs were padded and upholstered. This type of side chair was swiftly adopted throughout Europe, particularly in The Netherlands and England

after the Revocation of the Edict of Nantes (1685). This forced Parisian-trained Huguenot craftsmen and upholsterers into exile, which led to an almost immediate dissemination of French fashions and taste throughout Europe. Among the most influential Huguenot designers was Daniel Marot (1663–1752). Appointed architect to William II, Prince of Orange, he published numerous designs for dining-chairs in his *Livres d'Appartements* (c.1700). With their characteristic wooden splats depicting masks, interlaced strapwork, shells, armorials, and scrolls, often with a caned seat, Marot's designs were extremely influential in the first decades of the 18th century.

WALNUT AND MARQUETRY DINING-CHAIRS

While side chairs with upholstered backs continued to be produced in the early 18th century, they were considered more appropriate for the furnishing of bedrooms, as 18th-century eating habits required dining-chairs with backs that could be easily cleaned.

Dining-chairs of this period were usually made of walnut or red walnut, although provincial examples in oak and elm were also made. They were characterized by their simple wooden splats (often in the shape of a baluster or vase), deep seat rails with drop-in seats, cabriole legs joined by stretchers, and pad feet. Provincial chair-makers continued in this vein, but from c.1715 to 1720 fashionable walnut side chairs became increasingly sophisticated, with shells and husk-trails carved on the knees. The stretchers were entirely discarded, and the seat rails became much shallower than before. London chair-makers lavished their attention on the splat. While the splats of provincial chairs are usually either made in the solid or veneered onto an oak ground, the most sophisticated examples have splats veneered in figured burr-walnut laid onto a walnut ground. The splat itself is often not only carved with further shell decoration but also curved to fit the arch of the back.

In The Netherlands this form of splat-backed dining-chair was popular throughout the 18th and 19th centuries. Under the influence of cabinet-makers such as Jan van Mekeren (1658–1733), Amsterdam and The Hague became the principal centers for floral marquetry decoration, inspired by Dutch still-life paintings of the 17th century. From the 1730s dining-chairs veneered with floral marquetry were produced. Initially decorated on walnut and, subsequently, on mahogany grounds, Dutch chairs retained the use of stretchers far longer than their English counterparts. During the mid-18th century these floral marquetry chairs were often further enriched with Rococo-influenced, stylized C-scroll and acanthus carving. On the boldest examples the vase-shaped splat is treated asymmetrically. Nineteenth-century dining-chairs are betrayed by their loose quality and stiff floral marquetry.

▶ **Dining-chair**

Although the marquetry decoration on this chair is on a walnut frame, elm and mahogany were also used. The marquetry was usually of stained fruitwoods. The shaped apron and swept stretcher – set back to allow room for the sitter's feet – are typical features of Dutch chairs.
(c.1740; ht 1.2m/3ft 11in; value for a set of six I)

▲ **Dining-chair**

This chair is made of red walnut, a type of mahogany used more frequently for provincial furniture than for furniture made in major centers of production. The provincial origins of this chair are betrayed by the use of a back stretcher. The quality and color of the wood are paramount when determining value.
(c.1730; ht 1m/3ft 3in; value for a set of six K)

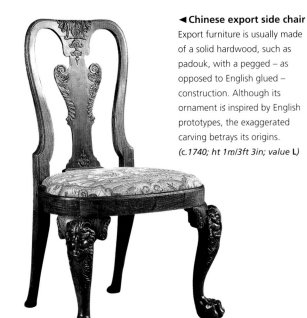

◄ **Chinese export side chair**
Export furniture is usually made
of a solid hardwood, such as
padouk, with a pegged – as
opposed to English glued –
construction. Although its
ornament is inspired by English
prototypes, the exaggerated
carving betrays its origins.
(*c.1740; ht 1m/3ft 3in; value* **L**)

ROCOCO AND NEO-CLASSICAL DINING-CHAIRS

Formal, symmetrical Baroque furniture gave way to the
lighter, freer styles of the Rococo movement, which
reached its maturity in France by the 1730s. Rococo
styles revolutionized English furniture design following
the publication of work by Juste-Aurèle Meissonnier
(1695–1750). The Italian Gaetano Brunetti included
designs for Rococo chairs in his *60 Different Sorts of
Ornament* (1736), but these still have ponderously
Baroque overtones. The upholstered backs of Brunetti's
chairs, formed within a rocaille cartouche carved with
C-scrolls and foliage, are reminiscent of the Rococo
designs favored by Thomas Chippendale (1718–79) in
the 1750s. More influential was the series of pattern-
books (1741–7) by the Frenchman William De La Cour
(*d.*1767), whose chair backs composed of interlaced
bands, often fan shaped, proved inspirational to English
designers and cabinet-makers such as Robert Manwaring
(active 1760–66) and Matthias Darly (active 1750–78).

In the 1750s and 1760s the Neo-classical movement
swept across Europe and in England one of the principal
exponents, Robert Adam (1728–92), encouraged the
adoption of that style. During the 1760s and 1770s,
Chippendale was commissioned to supply Neo-classical
dining-chairs for houses remodeled by Adam. His chairs
for Brocket Hall, Hertfordshire, with their husk-trailed,
square tapering legs, and pierced splats swagged with
laurel and enriched with oval paterae, are sophisticated
examples of the Neo-classical idiom.

HEPPLEWHITE AND SHERATON

The 1780s saw the introduction of the
celebrated shield-back dining-chair. Early
examples were made of mahogany, but
satinwood or polychrome-painted beech
was increasingly used in imitation of
"Etruscan" decoration found at the
excavations of Herculaneum (1738)
and Pompeii (1748). This "antique"
pattern, with its square tapering legs,
may have been conceived by the architect

THOMAS CHIPPENDALE'S *DIRECTOR*

The Gentleman and Cabinet-Maker's Director by Thomas Chippendale (1718–79)
was first published in 1754, and was the first book devoted to furniture design to
appear in England. Containing 160 engraved plates, it illustrated the full range of
contemporary taste, which fell into three principal styles – the French, Chinese,
and Gothick. Among the additional 110 plates included in the third edition of the
Director (1762) was a design for "ribband-back" chairs,
a tour de force of the carver's skill. Very few of these
chairs were ever made, owing to the considerable
expense and expertise required, and fewer still
survive, as, unlike so many of the *Director* designs,
they do not appear to have been copied by
provincial craftsmen. The majority of chairs copied
directly from the *Director* were made during the
Chippendale revivals of the 19th and 20th
centuries. The *Director* is undoubtedly the most
influential Rococo pattern-book, and its fame
has to some extent obscured the fact
that Chippendale was only one of
a number of fashionable London
cabinet-makers working in the
Rococo style in the 1750s and
1760s, which included the firms
of Vile & Cobb (est. 1751) and
Ince & Mayhew (est. 1758).

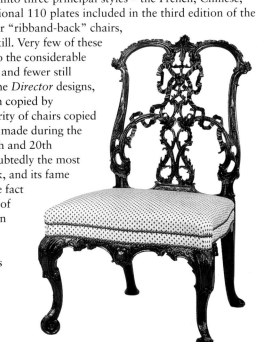

► **Ribband-back side chair by
Thomas Chippendale**
(1755; ht 1m/3ft 3in; value for a pair **Q***)*

▼ **Dining-chair**
This mahogany dining-chair has
a number of features typical of
Hepplewhite's late 18th-century
designs, most notably the
interlaced shield-shaped back.
*(c.1780; ht 1.2m/3 ft 11in;
value for a set of six* **N***)*

James Wyatt (1746–1813) and was certainly made by
the firm of Gillow (est. *c.*1730) of Lancaster, which
published a design for such a chair in 1788. The shield-
back pattern was popularized by George Hepplewhite
(*d.*1786) in *The Cabinet-Maker and Upholsterer's Guide*
(1788–94). The "antique" fluted tapering legs and spade
feet of the 1788 design were discarded by the mid-1790s
in favor of splayed, channeled legs, the precursors of
saber legs. Hepplewhite was certainly influenced by
Adam, and this is perhaps most clearly seen in the backs
of his chairs, where the oval, heart, and shield-shaped
splats are often ornamented with urns and vases, festoons
of husks and drapery, wheat-ears, and rosettes.

The success of Hepplewhite's *Guide* no doubt
inspired the publication of *The Cabinet-Maker and
Upholsterer's Drawing Book* (1791–1802) by Thomas
Sheraton (1751–1806). While several of Sheraton's
designs hark back to Hepplewhite, they also reveal an
awareness of the Louis XVI seat furniture made by such
cabinet-makers as Georges Jacob I (1739–1814). In
particular, the "parlor" or dining-chair patterns almost
all display square backs rather than the more usual oval
or shield shape. Supported by a pierced splat, often in
the form of a slender urn swagged with drapery or a
classical lyre, these linear "antique" splats, together
with the turned tapering legs favored by Sheraton,
were extremely influential during the Regency period
(*c.*1790–1830). Sheraton was also instrumental in
promoting painted seat furniture, producing floral-painted
satinwood chairs in a style associated with George Seddon
& Sons (est. 1785) in London, and ebonized and parcel-
gilt pieces in the "Etruscan" manner practcolord by John
Gee, chair-maker to George III.

"ANTIQUE" DINING-CHAIRS

Early 19th-century dining-chairs bear witness to the contemporary interest in Roman, Greek, and Egyptian ornament. This was inspired by the discovery of such sites as Herculaneum (1738) and Pompeii (1748), and also by Napoleon's campaigns in Egypt (1797–8), which were popularized by Baron Vivant Denon in his *Aventures dans la basse et la haute Egypte* (1802). The patterns often reflect a fusion of Classical ornament with French designs of the 17th and 18th centuries.

▶ Dining-chair

This classic Regency mahognay dining-chair is typical of the work of the firm of Gillow of Lancaster. The design is inspired by the ancient Greek "Klismos" chair and has saber legs and a horizontal paneled tablet. This English example also has a reeded seat rail, and reeded stiles and legs, with a finely carved paper-scrolled top on the tablet back. First introduced in France, this chair pattern revolutionized chair design throughout Europe in the early 19th century.

(1810; ht 1m/3 ft 3in; value for a set of ten K)

The most distinctive Grecian motif employed on early 19th-century dining-chairs was the lyre-back, first introduced in Paris in the 1780s. It was used by such firms as Marsh & Tatham in London, England, and by Duncan Phyfe (1768–1854), the North American cabinet-maker best known for furniture made using the "curule" or Grecian-cross form. The fashion for Egyptian designs was promoted by Charles Percier (1764–1838) and Pierre Fontaine (c.1762–1853) in *Recueil de décorations intérieures* (1801), and was inspirational to Parisian chair-makers. It was adopted in England, where its leading exponents included Thomas Hope (1769–1831), and George Smith (active c.1786–1828), whose pattern-book *A Collection of Designs for Household Furniture and Interior Decoration* (1808) illustrated "Egyptian" dining-chairs and specified that the frames be of bright Spanish mahogany and ebony inlays. The use of ebonized or ebony inlay was a deliberate reference to Etruscan ornament, but the brass inlays also fashionable at this time hark back to the late 17th-century arabesques of Jean Bérain I (1640–1711) and André-Charles Boulle (1642–1732).

▶ Dining-chair

Early 19th-century Viennese dining-chairs are characterized by their use of extremely well-chased ormolu mounts and stylized marquetry. The heavy, thick seat is typical of Germanic and Austrian dining-chairs of this period.

(1800–1820; ht 1m/3ft 3in; value for a set of 18 P)

OTHER DINING-CHAIRS

"Buhl" decoration, so-called after Boulle, who made the technique his own, consists of either brass or marquetry arabesque inlay. The fashion was revived between c.1815 and 1840, and was widely used to enrich dining-chairs. In England, saber-leg dining-chairs with Buhl decoration are asssociated with the firm of Gillow (est. c.1730) of Lancaster, whose chairs are often either stamped or inscribed with the craftsman's name in pencil under the side rail. Gillow dining-chairs were made initially of mahogany, and later of both rosewood and inexpensive beech grained to simulate rosewood. They are of very high quality, and often diplay scrolled stiles joined by paneled or brass-inlaid tablet toprails, spirally turned or baluster bars, caned seats, and saber legs.

Caned seats, introduced in the 1790s, are mostly associated with early 19th-century dining-chairs; perhaps the most common of these is the "Trafalgar" chair, with ropetwist bar, plain channeled seat rail, and saber legs, made to commemorate Nelson's victory at the Battle of Trafalgar (1805). The caned seat was usually designed to support a removable leather squab cushion or seat; the depth of the squab is often revealed by the flared base at the bottom of the stile. Although the more traditional drop-in seat of 18th-century dining-chairs still continued to be used, it was now enclosed within raised channeled side rails, resting only on the front seat rail, and given a pronounced location lug to hold the seat in place.

From the 1820s, although the basic Regency dining-chair pattern still prevailed, inlay and carving became increasingly florid, and examples from the reign of William IV (1830–37) often display pierced, stylized acanthus splats, and rosettes of exaggerated proportions. The refined lines of the saber leg were also discarded from c.1815 in favor of turned legs with Grecian "reeded" or concave-fluted decoration; as the Victorian period progressed, these were gradually simplified into plain, squat baluster legs of heavy proportions.

▲ Side chair by Benjamin Latrobe (1764–1820)

This side chair, with its splayed saber front legs, wide back splat, and painted and gilded decoration, was based on the "Klismos" chair featured on ancient Greek vases and illustrated in *Household Furniture and Interior Decoration* (1807) by Thomas Hope (1769–1831). Benjamin Latrobe, an architect, is also known to have designed a suite of furniture for the White House, which was destroyed by the British in 1814.

(c.1808; ht 88cm/34½in; value Q)

KEY FACTS

- SETS OF DINING-CHAIRS chairs were originally made in large numbers even as many as 36; over the years, such long sets have most often been divided into smaller, more manageable sets; with an uneven number of chairs the "odd" chair has often been "thrown in" and a set of eleven chairs, for example, would probably have the same value as a set of ten; so-called "long" sets are most highly sought after; sets are only really desirable when they comprise over eight chairs
- BEWARE many sets contain armchairs (also known as "carvers," a late 19th-century term) that are often later replaced or even made up from other damaged chairs, either from the same set or from another one
- COLLECTING it is important to examine the full set of chairs before purchasing, as some may have been introduced from other sets to make up an even number (a "harlequin" set); check the consistency of color, decoration, construction, wear, and marks
- MARKS sets of chairs will often be stamped with a Roman numeral under each seat rail; other marks include those of the maker and journeyman

Dining-chairs after 1840

The dining-chair, usually made without arms, reflected the development of fashionable styles more than most items of furniture. The mid-19th century saw a rapid rise in the number of people buying furniture for their homes. A set of dining-chairs was an essential purchase for the new homeowner, whose choice inevitably reflected the current popular style. To cater for the expanding market, furniture was produced on a much larger scale than ever before, and furniture-making changed from a craft to an industry.

◄ Side chair
This mahogany example, which is one of a set of four, was probably made in New York. It imposes a Gothic back on a Neo-classical "Klismos" form. Few Gothic Revival chairs were made in America before 1840.
(c.1835–50; ht 84.5cm/33¼in; value for a set of four **M***)*

REVIVALS OF NATIONAL STYLES

The change in the patronage of furniture-making from upper- to middle-class buyers had a significant impact on the development of designs. The new middle classes showed a preference for styles from earlier periods. At the same time, they lived in smaller houses than their forebears and needed furniture in proportions suited to their surroundings. Above all, they wanted to sit in comfort.

Every country in Europe looked to its own past for inspiration. For example, Elizabethan and Gothic Revival styles were popular in Britain in the 1840s, for both dining-room and hall furniture; different styles could be used for individual rooms in the same house. The Elizabethan Revival, first seen in the 1820s, was linked to a period of former greatness and was encouraged by the publication of novels by Sir Walter Scott. The decision to rebuild the Palace of Westminster, which had burned down in 1834, using Gothic rather than Classical architecture reinforced the new fashions in furniture.

The feel of the Elizabethan period was largely achieved by the use of decoration, with late-16th and 17th-century ornament being applied to existing forms. On new chairs, furniture-makers found strapwork and spiral turnings ideally suited to their labor-saving machinery. As with Elizabethan-style furniture, Gothic chairs feature architectural detail such as crocketed finials and lancet-and-ogee paneling applied to existing

forms. Gothic chairs of the early 1840s still tended to follow the designs of George Smith (active c.1786–1828), whose *A Collection of Designs for Household Furniture and Interior Decoration* (1808) relied for period effect on ornament rather than on purity of shape and form. This situation was radically changed by the work of Augustus Welby Northmore Pugin (1812–52), who was responsible for the architectural vocabulary and interior decor of the Palace of Westminster, reconstructed from 1840 to 1865. Pugin surpassed himself in the invention of Gothic-inspired forms, drawing inspiration from the Tudor period in particular. Through his pursuit of archeological accuracy, the Gothic style became a vehicle of reform, exhibiting a truth to its historical origins that filtered from architecture to furniture, due in large part to the publication of Pugin's book *Gothic Furniture in the Style of the Fifteenth Century* (1835).

Italian furniture-makers also looked to their heritage, which in their case led to a revival of the Renaissance style. In Italy, designs were closely modeled on the originals, but interpretations varied throughout Europe. In Britain, the Renaissance style was considered suitable for the dining-room. The Elizabethan style had merged into that of the Renaissance by the late 1860s, to be superseded by it in the 1870s. Few pieces of British furniture remained true to their Italian originals, which is why the British style is often called "Free Renaissance." It is also known as the "bracket-and-overmantel" style.

The scale of dining-chairs decreased toward the end of the century, along with that of domestic interiors, and proportions also became more attenuated. Dining-chairs were often made as copies of the designs in the reprints of the pattern-books by Thomas Chippendale (1718–79) and Thomas Sheraton (1751–1806), but with more slender legs, thinner seat rails, and taller and more upright backs. However, legs continued to be made in the solid because of the weight they had to bear. These late-Victorian copies of earlier dining-chairs often have a distinctly turn-of-the-century interpretation.

Historical designs were frequently misinterpreted. The term "Elizabethan" was applied to late 17th-century designs as often as to those of the late 16th century, hence the modern term "Jacobethan" for this type of furniture. There was some awareness of the general confusion even at the time, as related in a book called *Beautiful Houses* (1882). Its author, Mrs Haweis, tells how she was shown a Louis XIV mirror described by its owner as "Queen Anne, 'Empire,' you know – genuine Chippendale." The study of furniture was not seriously undertaken until well into the 20th century.

► Dining-chair
This walnut chair could have been made almost anywhere in northern Europe. The enduringly popular style was influenced by the Parisian-born designer Daniel Marot (1663–1752), who spent most of his life in Britain and The Netherlands. The 17th-century-style high back is not a very practical design and can easily be broken at the junction with the seat rail. Originals of this design are rare; most examples are 19th-century copies.
(c.1850; ht 1.2m/3ft 11in; value **H***)*

▲ Dining-chair
With its oval padded back, this German mahogany chair crosses the boundaries between salon and dining-chair. It was made as part of a set with a pair of mahogany *bergères*.
(c.1850; ht 95m/37in; value for set of 4 **G***)*

THE INFLUENCE OF FRANCE

In the 19th century, as in the 18th century, furniture design was profoundly influenced by French styles, especially those of the reign of Louis XV (1715–74). The Rococo Revival style was particularly well suited to the contemporary demand for comfortable seating; adopted in France from the 1830s, it continued to be popular into the next century. In Britain the "Old French" or "Louis XIV" style, as it was loosely called, often featured a combination of Louis XIV (1643–1715) and Louis XV design elements. Originally, British chairs in this style were painted or heightened with gilt, but by the 1840s the fashion was for polished exposed wood. Rococo Revival dining-chairs were reproduced throughout Europe. The style was most fashionable from the 1840s to the 1860s, but it never entirely fell from favor.

◄ **Dining-chair**

The archetypal balloon-back mahogany dining-chair from the middle of Queen Victoria's reign is still found in large numbers, but elbow chairs of the type are rare. Robust examples of similar design were produced in many countries throughout Europe. *(1845; ht 86cm/33¾in; value for a set of six F)*

Although some Rococo Revival pieces have features characteristic of a particular country, it can be difficult to determine the provenance of a Louis XV-style chair, especially if made toward the end of the 19th century.

In the 1850s a naturalistic style, which is now identified exclusively with the 19th century, flourished in Britain. An extension of the "Old French" style, it was characterized by decoration composed of sinuous tendrils entwined with flowers, devised to give an impression of opulence. The wood was handled with great fluidity – seen, for example, in the balloon-back chairs of the period. The wood appears to have been molded as easily as if it were plastic, a feature that is accentuated by the highly polished finish, known as French polishing. The toprails on these chairs were often plain, but on fine examples naturalistic flowers were carved as a cresting.

As well as Louis XIV and Louis XV revivals, the 19th century saw a resurgence throughout Europe of the Louis XVI (1774–93) style. The Empress Eugénie, the consort of Napoleon III, had a great interest in the life of Marie Antoinette, wife of Louis XVI, and was one of the instigators of the revival. The Empress introduced new furniture in the Neo-classical style into her apartments, and her taste had a major influence on fashions from the 1850s to the end of the century.

The 19th-century Classical style in Britain was really a continuation of the Regency designs of c.1790 to 1830. The Neo-classical furniture of the 18th century was reinterpreted, and its purity diminished in favor of flowing forms decorated with richly carved, thickly sprouting ornament (hence the term "Fat-classical," sometimes used to describe this style). The elaborate dining-chairs of the period often had turned legs.

French designs remained a major inspiration for chair-makers throughout the century. Although by 1900 France was no longer the world's leading furniture exporter, the country retained its position as the leading supplier of fine-quality *meubles de luxe*. The term "Made in Paris" continued to command worldwide respect.

Mid-century furniture in France was manufactured in much the same way as it had been a hundred years earlier, although revival pieces tended to be more exaggerated and exuberant than the originals. Nevertheless, these 19th-century interpretations are the recognizable descendants of 18th-century chairs. Toward the end of the century more accurate copies were made, and the choice of styles was less eclectic.

British furniture design took an opposite turn. Although not all British stylistic revivals occurred at the same time, styles became more confused as the century went on, and by 1900 almost any revived style was possible. The designs that developed in the 19th century are now, in their turn, being revived and reproduced.

DEVELOPMENTS IN CONSTRUCTION

The middle years of the 19th century in particular saw a fascination with and respect for ingenuity as an end in itself, rather than as a factor contributing to the success of a design. This ingenuity was seen in the many machines that were proudly displayed at the various international exhibitions, starting with the Great Exhibition of 1851 in London, and was equally apparent in the work of contemporary furniture-makers. Advances in construction went hand in hand with the invention of new machinery.

Seat construction on British and French dining-chairs underwent a major change in the middle of the century. Throughout much of the 18th century, British seat rails had been strengthened on the inside of each angle by a brace, running underneath the seat from one

▲ **Dining-chair**

Made of burr-elm and beechwood, this Dutch chair is one of a matching set and has a shaped back and arched toprail above a solid vase splat. It also has a serpentine drop-in seat, shell-carved cabriole legs, and padded feet. Its style is that of the early 18th century. *(1850; ht 1m/3ft 3in; value for a set of six H)*

► **Dining-chair**

The back of this chair is taken almost directly from a plate in the third edition of *The Gentleman and Cabinet-Maker's Director* (1762) by Thomas Chippendale. The thin, rather pinched and mean lines immediately give it away as a Victorian copy. However, such chairs are often of good quality and highly functional, and are therefore sought after. *(1880; ht 97cm/37½in; value for a set of eight – two elbow and six side chairs – K)*

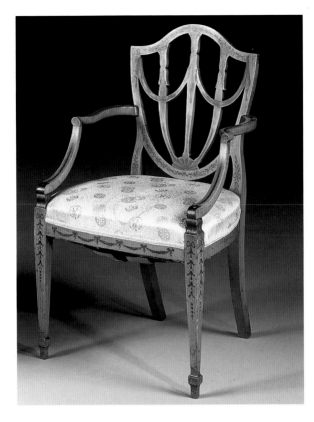

◀ Elbow dining-chair

This Edwardian chair is based on a late 18th-century design by Thomas Sheraton. The style was something of a reaction to the elaborate designs that had been in vogue 20 to 40 years earlier. This type of chair was sometimes made of satinwood, but many examples are made from a secondary, light-colored wood painted to resemble satinwood. Careful examination is required to tell if the painted decoration is original, since the old paint may have rubbed off.
*(c.1900; ht 95cm/37in; value for a set of two **H**)*

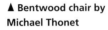

experimenting with ways to economize on labor and materials in his small furniture factory in Boppard on the Rhine. Biedermeier furniture-makers had already discovered how to bend veneers. Thonet developed this practice by gluing together separate parts with their grains running in different directions, allowing curved shapes to be held in tension. He was granted international patents in 1841 and moved to Vienna, where he set up a factory in 1849.

By this time Thonet was concentrating on solid wood. At the Great Exhibition of 1851 in London he showed pieces made of solid, bent rosewood. By the 1860s his factories were turning out vast quantities of bentwood furniture, and by the end of the century they employed thousands of people. Thonet's factories were an example of mass-production through industrialization that was almost unmatched before the 20th century. The bentwood furniture they produced was strong but light in weight, inexpensive, and easy to transport. It was popular throughout Europe, as well as in the USA and in Colonial countries, and also at every level of society. Chairs and other furniture were shipped in pieces and assembled at the country of destination. The snaky, circular nature of Thonet's output was in accord with the Rococo Revival style, with the result that his work made reference to the past while also providing inspiration for the Art Nouveau style.

▲ Bentwood chair by Michael Thonet

Bentwood chairs often had impressed, decorative seats and were produced in vast numbers. Thonet's name is synonymous with bentwood furniture. He was experimenting with laminated and steam-bent wood in Germany at around the same time as Belter in the USA.
*(c.1900; ht 90cm/35½in; value **A**)*

rail to the other. This was now often replaced by three-sided blocks that fitted snugly into each inner angle and were screwed to the two rails they joined; the remaining outside edge was given a serpentine shape. In France, until the mid-19th century, pegs or dowels were used to link the joints on chairs, particularly those on the seat rails. These too disappeared, on all but provincial pieces, in favor of the three-sided block. However, pegs have recently reappeared on chairs in the Louis Revival styles.

In France, as in Britain, beech was widely used as the base wood for painted or gilt chairs and for those with padded seats. Since the carcase was to be covered, there was no point in using an expensive wood. Beech was strong and did not split when nails were knocked into it. However, it could be attacked by woodworm and, for this reason, seat rails on beech chairs often have to be renewed.

THONET AND BENTWOOD CHAIRS

In 19th-century Germany, technology advanced dramatically. The most important development in the production of dining-chairs was the bentwood furniture of Michael Thonet (1796–1871). In 1830 Thonet began

▶ Elbow dining-chair

This yellow-japanned elbow dining-chair was part of a large set that also included a matching extending dining-table. The shape looks back to the end of the 18th century, and the decoration demonstrates the continuing popularity of the Oriental style. The varnish has toned down to a mellow yellow, an unusual color for japanning, increasing the value of the piece. Always check the condition of the japanning on chairs as it is prone to lifting and flaking through wear.
*(c.1850; ht 91cm/35¾in; value for a set of eight **J**)*

KEY FACTS

- SETS OF DINING-CHAIRS elbow-chairs can add to the value of a set and individually are more valuable than a matching chair without arms; some chairs have had arms added to increase value; traditionally made elbow-chairs should be slightly larger and have wider seats than single chairs – check by comparing with a single chair from the same set
- DATING look for pegs in the seat-rail joints in French chairs – these went out of use by the mid-19th century, although modern reproductions using pegs are now being made; in British dining-chairs with padded seats, a corner brace linking and strengthening the corners of the inside angles of the seat rails often indicates a date before 1850; a screwed angle block that fits tightly into the corner indicates a date after 1850
- BEWARE check to see if the legs have been reduced or re-toed; woodworm can be a threat if a chair has been severely attacked, particularly on weight-bearing legs; be especially vigilant with painted chairs made from a wood prone to worm attack, such as beech – an earlier infestation may be hard to detect; seat rails have often been changed on padded-seat chairs, either due to worm damage or to the effect of several generations of upholstery pins; look for strain on high-back chairs at the junction with the seat rail

See also Dining-chairs before 1840, pp.36–8; Dining-tables after 1840, pp.52–3; Art Nouveau: Furniture, pp.390–3

Settles and sofas before 1840

The box-settle was in existence in northern Europe by the 15th century. The earliest examples usually have planked seats and pierced trellis or linen-fold paneled backs, and are often richly carved. A plainer and sturdier form was the oak "monk's table," which had a bench-like seat, often set above an enclosed well used for storage, and a hinged back, which when brought forward served as a table. This basic form was adopted by furniture-makers in Britain (particularly in the provinces), and the Low Countries from the 16th century. Early box-settles were usually of oak, although elm, chestnut, and fruitwood were increasingly used during the 18th century; they continued to be made in the provincial tradition until well into the 19th century.

▶ Box-settle

The box-settle, so called because of the box or well beneath the seat, is among the earliest examples of seat furniture in Europe. This sturdy, George II oak example is characterized by a plain rectangular back, with four fielded panels, and outswept flattened arms on turned supports. The box-seat has a hinged lid, with three fielded panels. The settle rests on stile feet.

(early 18th century; ht 1.9m/6ft 5in; value J)

DOUBLE CHAIR-BACK SETTEES

The double chair-back settee dates from the mid-17th century, and its evolution reflects that of the chair back (splat). Invariably of walnut, this type of furniture is distinguished by caned seats, carved upright splats, and baluster-turned or strapwork legs joined by stretchers. By the late 17th and early 18th centuries the double chair-back settee was characterized by a drop-in, upholstered seat, slightly serpentine toprail with vase or baluster-shaped splats, and cabriole legs with pad feet. Usually made of walnut, it became increasingly bold and elaborate in form and decoration; by the reign of Queen Anne (1702–14) settees were frequently veneered with burr-walnut and enriched with seaweed marquetry on the splats and legs. George I examples (1714–27) were often inspired by the architect William Kent (*c.*1685–1748), and have carved shells, foliage, lion-masks and paws, and eagle's-head arm terminals and claws. Mahogany settees were first made under George II (1727–60); those from the 1750s and 1760s frequently follow chair-patterns in the Chinese, Gothick, and French Rococo styles popularized by Thomas Chippendale (1718–79) in *The Gentleman and Cabinet-Maker's Director* (1754–62). Continental examples were often gilded or painted with flowers and chinoiserie decoration, and are far more Rococo in form than their English counterparts, with exaggerated cabriole legs, serpentine toprails, and asymmetric splats. This latter feature is also characteristic of Dutch double-chair back settees, which parallel English Queen Anne and early

▶ Double chair-back settee

This walnut settee is an extremely desirable example of English early Georgian furniture. The structure is in solid walnut except for the seat rail and splats, which have been veneered in burr-walnut. The carving is of the highest quality, with shell and acanthus crestings, open arms with eagle's-head terminals, and three cabriole legs with shell-carved knees and claw-and-ball feet; the back legs are only rarely carved.

(c.1720; w. 1.5m/4ft 11in; value P)

▼ Canapé

The Rococo style was adopted in northern Italy in furniture-making centers such as Genoa and Venice. The Italian Rococo style was more exuberant than its northern counterpart, as seen in this *canapé*. The carving and gilding on such pieces were of a very high quality, although inexpensive softwoods such as pine and poplar were used.

(c.1760; w. 1.9m/6ft 5in; value L)

Georgian examples, save for the enrichment of floral marquetry. However, Dutch chair-back settees with floral marquetry on a mahogany, as opposed to a walnut, ground are more usually 19th century. English settees of the late 18th and early 19th centuries are usually of carved mahogany or satinwood. Painted designs include peacock feathers and flowers in the manner of George Seddon & Sons (est. 1785), and Etruscan-black decoration, inspired by Classical vases. These painted examples are usually of beech and often display caned or rush seats with squab cushions.

CANAPES AND CHAISES-LONGUES

Canapés with padded backs and seats dating from the reign of Louis XIV (1643–1715) usually have walnut frames with simple channeled decoration to the legs and stretchers, scrolled arms, and cabriole legs. The most sophisticated *canapés* of the Régence period (1715–23) are masterpieces of the carver's art; their giltwood or walnut frames were carved with foliage, shells, and chimerical dragons, and their backs strewn with flowers in the style of Juste-Aurèle Meissonnier (1695–1750).

During the 1730s and 1740s, Rococo *canapés* became even more exaggerated in form and detail. They were usually gilded or of walnut, although Italian craftsmen also employed a mix of silver and gold leaf, a decoration known as *mecca*. Italian *canapés* are often less well constructed than French seat furniture.

The chaise-longue was characterized by its long seat, which enabled the sitter to recline horizontally, and was first recorded in France, Italy, and England in the late 17th century. Louis XIV chaises-longues were usually of carved walnut or beech, with caned seats and squab cushions. During the early 18th century the frames became richer and more florid, often being gilded or japanned in imitation of Oriental lacquer, while the caned seats were rejected in favor of fully stuffed and upholstered seats. Usually carved in lime or beech, and intended to be painted or gilded, mid-18th-century Continental chaises-longues were of a pegged construction. Although rarer, day-beds, usually without side-supports, were also made in England during the mid-Georgian period.

It was under the influence of the Prince of Wales (later George IV) and his circle that the chaise-longue reached its apogee in England. The form was the perfect vehicle for the reproduction of Greek, Roman, and Egyptian ornament. Simpler Regency chaises-longues were also widely manufactured, mainly in mahogany or rosewood, perhaps inlaid with brass in the "Buhl" manner. Painted examples with Etruscan-inspired ebonized and parcel-gilt decoration, or with a grained or stenciled finish, also abound. The earliest Regency chaises-longues are light and elegant, with simple, free-flowing lines, saber legs, and brass caps and casters. Examples from the 1820s and 1830s are increasingly florid and heavy; they are supported on claw feet and are often richly carved with exaggerated, stylized foliage.

▲ Chaise-longue

This Louis XV chaise-longue can be dated to the mid-1730s by the restrained carving of shells and stylized foliage on a hatched ground. The supports, known as "traverses," that cross the width of the chaise-longue are often flat on French examples; those on English chaises-longues are usually dished for comfort. *(c.1735–40; l. 1.9m/6ft 3in; value J)*

DUNCAN PHYFE (1768–1854)

The best-known New York cabinet-maker of the early and mid-19th century, Duncan Phyfe also gave his name to the generic term for American furniture in the Neo-classical style, making use of the forms and ornament of Classical Greece and Rome. The work of Phyfe and his contemporaries incorporates "curule" (Grecian-cross design) legs or saber legs, paw feet, harp and lyre backs, caned toprails, and decoration showing sheaves of wheat, thunderbolts, cornucopia, and swags. Unless documented by a bill or label, New York Federal and Classical furniture should be attributed to the Phyfe school. Phyfe-type furniture was made into the mid-19th century, with a revival in the late 19th and early 20th centuries.

▼ Neo-classical sofa

One of five sofas with winged-paw feet and dolphin arms, this is a very good example of the robust style of American cabinet-makers from c.1815 to 1820. *(c.1815–20; w. 2.3m/7ft 6in; value Q)*

EARLY 19TH-CENTURY SOFAS

The development of the chaise-longue in the 19th century was mirrored by that of the sofa. From c.1805 to 1810 sofas became increasingly bold and luxurious. Frames of plain mahogany were initially fashionable, carved with Grecian ornament as promoted by George Smith (active c.1786–1828) in his book *A Collection of Designs for Household Furniture and Interior Decoration* (1808); these were superseded by more florid examples in rosewood and, later, walnut, upholstered with bolster cushions at each end. This extravagance was continued in the design and decoration of the frames, which often had tightly scrolled arm-terminals and were embellished with gilt-bronze mounts or inlaid in the "Buhl" manner with foliate arabesques, as on sofas by the firm of Gillow (est. c.1730). The sofas were supported by hairy-paw feet. As seen in the designs of Michel Angelo Nicolson (c.1796–1844) in *The Practical Cabinet-Maker, Upholsterer, and Complete Decorator* (1826), the basic Regency form persisted throughout the 19th century. However, sofa designs became heavier as the century progressed, with the introduction of shorter and fatter legs, often reeded, and tapering to brass caps and casters.

KEY FACTS

- BOX-SETTLES the most lavishly decorated settles, particularly those with linen-fold paneled backs, are often examples of 19th-century antiquarianism, in which old paneling has been reused or plain types have been later carved or embellished
- DOUBLE CHAIR-BACK SETTEES the majority of these are 19th-century copies, which may be identified by the quality of the timber and carving, and by the use of carved ornament borrowed from different periods
- CHAISES-LONGUES mid-18th century Continental chaises-longues should be of pegged construction; 18th-century examples were widely copied in the 19th century – these later pieces are usually betrayed by the stiffness of the carving; chaises-longues have very often been regilded (this will not affect the value if the work is of a high quality); examples that were once brightly painted have often faded

See also Easy chairs before 1840, pp.30–32; Settles and sofas after 1840, pp.44–5

Settles and sofas after 1840

The revival of interest in historical styles from the mid-19th century resulted in a multiplicity of designs for all types of furniture, including sofas, which were often made as part of the new salon or parlor suites. A major technical development during this period was use of the coil spring, patented in 1828, which resulted in sturdier, bulkier, and squatter designs that sacrificed form to comfort. These deeply upholstered seats, with their button backs, culminated in the Chesterfield, which was the first fully upholstered sofa.

CHAISES-LONGUES

The design of the chaise-longue allowed the occupant to lie or recline along its length. Introduced in France c.1625, the style came to Britain with the restoration of Charles II (1660). Jacques-Louis David's portrait *Mme Juliette Récamier* (1800) made it fashionable once again; the famous hostess is shown reclining on a chaise-longue, which subsequently was often known as a *récamier* in France. At the beginning of the Victorian period the one-piece chaise-longue, usually of mahogany, walnut, or rosewood, retained the flowing lines of earlier Regency examples and often incorporated a serpentine front. Gradually the curves became more exaggerated, with arched and molded toprails or padded ends joined by pierced and carved scrolling backs. As upholstery techniques developed, the seats were sprung, button backs were used, and the ends were padded and buttoned. Saber or cabriole legs with porcelain casters were gradually replaced by claw feet and, later, by heavier, turned legs. Carving on the legs, armrests, and exposed wooden backrests became increasingly heavy and florid, with stylized foliage.

Gothic Revival chaises-longues were generally of oak, with heavily carved ornament. With the development of sprung upholstery, some chaises-longues were produced with buttoned backs and seats, and with no visible wood. The curves of the Rococo Revival style were

▶ **Settee**
Although of Irish origin, this mahogany "ribband-back" settee is in the style of the British cabinet-maker Thomas Chippendale (1718–79). The original design was featured on chairs in the third edition of Chippendale's highly influential pattern-book *The Gentleman and Cabinet-maker's Director* (1762).
(*c.1850; w. 1.8m/5ft 11in; value* **H**)

◀ *Cassapanca*
The Italian *cassapanca* is a type of settle developed from the *cassone*, with the addition of a back and sometimes of armrests. The *cassapanca* was often decorated in marquetry and ivory, usually depicting 16th-century hunting scenes. The armorial crest on this example suggests that it was intended to stand in the hall of a grand house.
(*c.1880; w. 1.6m/5ft 3in; value* **H**)

▼ **Chaise-longue**
The gentle curve of this rosewood chaise-longue adds to the air of intimacy that made it such a popular form. The occupant reclines in comfort, supported by a padded end and three-quarter back. The curves continue into the simple cabriole legs, which end in porcelain casters. Because of their decorative rather than practical nature, chaises-longues can be found today at reasonable prices.
(*c.1850; l. 1.8m/5ft 11; value* **G**)

ideally suited to the Victorian chaise-longue. From the 1880s this had typically become more rectilinear, with leathercloth upholstery and a solidly constructed rectangular beech or birch frame, often stained to imitate the turned mahogany legs with casters and the turned-spindle gallery along the back.

SALON SUITES

After 1840 in France and Britain the burgeoning middle classes were filling their homes with furniture that they had bought rather than inherited. Rooms were far more densely furnished than in the early 19th century. The salon suite, produced from c.1840, comprised a sofa or settee and a varying number of matching chairs, armchairs, and even foot stools. Settees from this period that survive today may well have originally been part of such suites, which are rarely found complete. Sofas and settees were produced in a great range of historical-revival styles, and "sociable" forms that could seat varying combinations of people were popular; examples include the *confidante*, the *confidante à deux places*, and the *indiscret à trois places*. The triple and double chair-back forms developed into a series of buttoned and upholstered upright backrests, linked by elaborately carved toprails, with padded armrests; many examples also featured circular central upholstered panels and serpentine fronts. In Britain, settees from the early part of this period usually have cabriole legs, while later examples have turned legs. Settees were most commonly constructed from walnut, rosewood, and mahogany, and many were deeply upholstered.

The period *c*.1860 to *c*.1880 was in many ways the golden age of upholstery. Stuffing had been growing steadily thicker from the 1840s, and buttons were introduced to prevent the thread holding the stuffing in place from pulling the covering material. Extra fabric was necessary to create the familiar diamond pattern of buttons or threads characteristic of the deep, luxurious upholstery, with its air of prosperity and comfort, so admired by the Victorian middle classes. The development of the coil spring made increased demands on buttoning. Whereas sofas had previously been stuffed with layers of wadding and horsehair, coiled metal springs were now used. The springs were supported by a layer of hessian webbing, covered with more webbing, which in turn was covered with horsehair stuffing and padding. As a result, Victorian sofas were much more comfortable than early 19th-century examples, but they were also much bulkier; many sofas had button backs to emphasize the new upholstered look. The luxurious

◄ **Settee**

The shield-shaped backs with pierced splats on this double chair-back mahogany settee are derived from the shield back designed by George Hepplewhite (*d*.1786), as are the square, elegant, tapering legs. The ribbon crests are carved with swags and acanthus – both typical Neo-classical motifs – and inlaid with satinwood ovals. This settee was originally part of a salon suite that included two matching armchairs and a set of four single chairs; complete suites are rarely found.

*(c.1890; w. 1.2m/3 ft 11in; value **G**)*

▲ *Canapé*

Canapé usually denotes a sofa with open arms, as seen here. This sofa was produced as part of a salon suite that also included four matching armchairs or *fauteuils*. It is in the Louis XVI Revival style, which was popular in France during the Second Empire (1852–70).

*(late 19th century; w. 1.3m/4ft 3in; value **G**)*

▼ *Confidante*

This carved giltwood French sofa is sometimes known as an *assemblage*. It is formed by combining two one-seater elements with a two-seater settee to form a three-section seating unit. Both elegant and comfortable, this example features Rococo Revival giltwood cresting outlining the padded back and seats, and also has scrolled arms with padded elbow rests. The 19th-century French cabinet-makers' predilection for giltwood and light-colored upholstery gave their Rococo Revival sofas a lightness and playfulness that was in marked contrast to the heavy, often over-extravagant Rococo Revival sofas produced at the same time in Britain and the USA.

*(c.1890; w. 2.9m/9ft 6in; value **I**)*

effect was emphasized by the use of velvet and other elaborate fabrics. Sofas with their original worn upholstery are more collectible today than those with high-quality restoration using an inappropriate fabric.

French sofas were generally lighter in design than British examples, since French craftsmen and manufacturers employed such revival styles as Rococo and Louis XVI, making use of giltwood and lighter upholstery fabrics. In the USA, parlor suites on a grand scale were produced by such leading makers as John Henry Belter (1804–63) of New York, who in the 1850s created laminated and molded rosewood sofas with deep pierced carving. Renaissance Revival suites, with square-backed sofas, were also popular, while the fashion in Europe and the USA for "Turkish" corners gave rise to over-stuffed upholstered sofas with elaborate fringing.

Edwardian sofas of the first two decades of the 20th century borrowed heavily from Neo-classical styles – especially the designs of Thomas Sheraton (1751–1806) – and from Regency styles, but managed to avoid the excesses of Victorian interpretations. Suites of chairs with matching sofas were produced; these were generally made from mahogany, or occasionally from walnut or satinwood. Sofas and chairs often had caned backs and sides, with silk or damask upholstery.

KEY FACTS

- CHAISES-LONGUES these are not particularly commercial as they can be large and not very comfortable to sit on; examples with good shapes are more popular, as are those that are more heavily carved
- GILDING good-quality regilding is quite acceptable if well executed– the highlights should be burnished, and the quality of the carving evident; beware of spray gilding – this will have a flat, matt appearance, with a very even coverage
- RE-UPHOLSTERY the condition of the upholstery should be carefully examined, as seating can be very expensive to re-upholster; furniture with taut webbing is preferable to that with springing, which tends to give an overstuffed look
- COLLECTING many sofas and settees were originally part of parlor or salon suites, which are now rarely found complete; three-seater examples are generally more commercial than two-seater

See also Dining-chairs before 1840, pp.36–8; Settles and sofas before 1840, pp.42–3

Tables

Tables are arguably the most essential item of furniture. Known to have been made in ancient Egypt, they have evolved from the very simplest utilitarian form to items of great splendor and ingenuity. The table is a good record of the changing habits of the societies for which they were made. In the Middle Ages meals were taken in vast halls and suitably large tables were made to accommodate the numerous guests. However, by the 18th century meals were taken in more intimate surroundings, which gave rise to the need for smaller tables that could be set aside when not in use. Of course tables were not just for serving or eating, but also for playing games, working, sewing, reading, or purely for ornamental purposes.

Early tables

During the Middle Ages, banquets were the principal ceremony in any wealthy household and invariably took place in the Great Hall. The high table, usually placed on a raised dais beneath a canopy, was reserved for the master of the house, his family, and guests. Meanwhile, the rest of the household and retainers sat at side tables, drawn into the center of the room and set at right angles to the high table. Flemish, British, and French trestle tables, dating from the 15th and 16th centuries, are usually of massive boards of indigenous woods such as oak or elm, above a central support, and with two or three sturdy trestle supports. Originally functional and plain, the top was draped with a cloth – textiles gave color and decoration to interiors, and the table was another surface to cover. Many tables were later embellished with carving. These earliest trestle tables were often designed to be taken down and removed after meals, the tops themselves being detachable to make way for dancing and festivities in the Hall. Contrastingly, Italian, Spanish, and Portuguese collapsible trestle-tables of the 16th and 17th centuries tend to have planked tops of walnut, rosewood, or chestnut, with X-shaped iron supports or stretchers to stabilize the end-supports.

"JOYNED" AND DRAW-LEAF TABLES

During the 15th and 16th centuries the more stable, although still collapsible, "joyned" tables evolved. The precursors of 16th-century refectory tables, these tables had trestles strengthened by side-rails and stretchers, which were secured through the end-supports by stout, tapering, triangular pegs. Also of oak, elm, or chestnut, these "tables upon a frame" were more permanent fixtures, and were usually supplied with matching stools. When not in use the stools were stored away beneath the table frame, with the seats facing out and resting upon the stretchers. The tables were frequently elaborately carved with Gothic foliage, or even with grotesque beasts.

With their heavy fixed tops, these early trestle tables were not suitable for seating the continually changing numbers of diners, and a more sophisticated design therefore emerged. The innovative "draw-leaf" table was developed in Germany, The Netherlands, and Britain in the mid-16th century; the length of the table could be doubled by pulling out "draw-leaves" at each end, upon which the top rested when closed (hence the appearance of a double thickness top). The basic design of the draw-leaf table was inspirational to Regency cabinet-makers in Britain, as well as to British vernacular furniture-makers of the 19th and 20th centuries.

REFECTORY TABLES

During the 16th century refectory tables – so-called because they originated in monasteries, where the eating room was known as a refectory – became increasingly elaborately decorated. Italian refectory tables were made of walnut and were initially restrained in character, perhaps with turned column legs or carved gadrooned or fluted decoration to the friezes. This style gradually gave way to fabulous tables with boldly sculptural carved end-supports, with figures, foliage, and nymphs or sphinxes on lion supports. The ideas of Italy traveled northward to France, especially the exaggerated and attenuated forms of early Mannerism, as popularized by the painter Giulio Romano (1499–1546) when he left Italy to join the court of Francis I at the chateau of Fontainebleau, outside Paris. Such decorative schemes were swiftly adopted by Flemish and German craftsmen in the later 16th century; it was the latter who developed the fashion for exaggerated vase-shaped legs, often carved with grotesque faces and lion-masks. Through the published designs of northern Mannerist architects such as Hans

▲ Refectory table
This functional form was – and still is – produced throughout much of Europe. On this British oak example, wooden pegs secure the joints as well as the top to the base. The frieze has simple carving, sometimes found on only two or three sides if the table was to stand against a wall. Note the variable wear on the stretchers. The legs all have new tips added to counteract uneven wear, damp, and worm attack to the feet. *(mid-17th century; l. of top 2.9m/9ft 6in; value K)*

◄ Center table
This small walnut table is typically Spanish, because of the shaped iron bars connecting the stretchers, and the fret-carved legs. Although made in the 17th century, this table is designed so that it can easily be dismantled – the form lingered long after the need for the table to be transportable vanished. The long production period of this style makes dating difficult. *(17th century; l. of top 1m/ 3ft 3in; value H)*

Vredeman de Vries (1526–c.1604), as well as the work of immigrant craftsmen, the fashion was transmitted farther through Europe, and spread to Britain. Examples of British 16th- and 17th-century refectory tables are distinguished by their bulbous legs, often carved with foliate arabesques, while friezes are often embellished with naive inlay of interlaced designs incorporating architectural arcades or grotesque beasts.

While walnut was much used in southern Europe and in court pieces elsewhere, oak predominates in central and northern Europe. The carving was bold, individual, and well executed. The carvers worked to a high standard, with good spatial awareness, and there is a robustness about the pieces that diminished toward the end of the 17th century.

The art of wood turning was an important 17th-century development. This was not a new discovery, and had certainly been practiced in ancient Egypt. With the increased use of rigid pieces of furniture, more attention was paid to the way in which the exposed wood was displayed. During the 17th century, table designs became lighter and more refined, with baluster or columnar rather than bulbous legs, finished with ring-turned moldings. Friezes became increasingly restrained, sometimes subtly enriched with parquetry decoration incorporating fine specimen woods or fluting. These later examples are often dated and carved with initials, perhaps to commemorate a marriage. However, beware as these dates can be spurious and applied considerably later, particularly in the 19th century when all things "Jacobethan" enjoyed a revival. Victorian copies of these tables are generally more poorly produced and lack the bold confidence of their 17th-century counterparts.

While trestle and "joyned" refectory tables continued to be made in northern Europe, as well as by provincial furniture-makers in England well into the 19th century, the fashion for eating "in Hall" was gradually abandoned in the late 17th century in favor of smaller dining-rooms. As life became more settled, and merchant classes grew, new types of table developed to suit their needs. Even in aristocratic circles the scale of houses diminished and dining became more intimate.

OTHER SMALLER TABLES

Matching furniture to a specific room was a concept that spread from Spain to the rest of Europe and became a major influence in furniture design. Rooms acquired more furniture, although they were still sparsely furnished by today's standards. As part of this scheme small tables played an important role. Many types, such as the credence table, were designed to perform specific functions, although often those uses have now lapsed. Since the table formed such an integral part of day-to-day life at all levels, its development, style, construction, timber, and name closely reflected progressions and changes within society.

As tables diversified, drawers became common additions. The decorative turnings were more refined; small tables now had slender baluster or

bobbin turnings, which were a significant development from the heavier and more sturdy legs of the previous century. Small, occasional, side tables were produced on a large scale, and fortunately many have survived. Set against walls, they developed into more formalized console tables, which were an important feature in grand interiors from the beginning of the 18th century. The 16th century, with the early 17th, is considered to be the age of the joiner, but as fashions and woodworking skills developed, increasing rapidly throughout the 17th century, his position was taken by the cabinet-maker, who developed and refined the table throughout the 18th century.

◄ Credence table

A credence table was originally a small table or cupboard where food was kept ready to be tasted before being served. Folding tables were made for domestic use from at least the early 17th century, and a credence table now refers specifically to a table with a hinged top; it was either semi-circular or with a three-sided front, as seen on this British oak example.
(c.1680; l. of top 1m/3ft 3in; value L)

▼ Side table

Common features of this style of table are the thin top overhanging the base, and the slender turned legs. They reflect the more attenuated proportions in vogue at the time. Tables such as this British oak example were made throughout Europe from the early 18th century.
(c.1700; l. of top 79cm/31in; value H)

▼ Table

This walnut-and-oak table from Germany is of a type that was for domestic use, and so it is correspondingly plain and functional, displaying none of the exuberance of more lavish German furniture at this time. The top and drawer both slide out, allowing the entire drawer contents to be exposed. The bases of this type were sometimes painted, but the tops were left in the natural state so that they could be used when necessary as worksurfaces for culinary preparation.
(17th century; l. 1.6m/5ft 3in; value G)

KEY FACTS

- **MATERIALS** tables of this period were made in the solid, using indigenous woods; the construction was all pegged mortise and tenon
- **CONDITION** look for areas of wear and damage on stretchers, outer edges of the legs, the top, and at the bottom of each leg – check the height of the table to see if it has been reduced as a result of damage
- **ALTERATIONS** a common fault is that the top will have been "associated" with the base: ensure that all elements concur, and that any marks on the underside of the top relate to the base; although 17th-century refectory tables should have stretchers, it is not uncommon to find them removed to allow room for chair legs

See also Gateleg and dropleaf tables, pp.48–9; Console, side, and pier tables, pp.58–9

Gateleg and dropleaf tables

Tables that can extend are adaptable, and this quality has ensured the continuous survival of the gateleg for at least four centuries. A gateleg table is one with a flap (or flaps) which, when extended, rests on supports swinging out from the the table's underframe. The supports consist of legs, joined by stretchers at the top and bottom to form gate-like structures.

17TH-CENTURY GATELEG TABLES

Small side tables with foldover tops and pivoting gateleg arrangements were already among the luxury furnishings of grand houses in the 16th century. As domestic comfort increased during the 17th century, so such tables proliferated. Early examples tend to be of half-round or half-ellipse shape when folded, with a doubled-over top hinged across the straight edge. When pulled away from the wall and opened out this top forms a circle or an oval, supported firmly underneath by its joined gate-frame, which pivots outward on wooden hinges from the center of the underframe at both top and bottom. Variants of this scheme include square or octagonal tops, and tables with baseboards between the stretchers of the main structure.

As dining habits evolved in the later 17th century, and the large communal hall was replaced by more intimate parlors where meals were taken, the long, rectangular trestle table gave way to rounded gateleg tables, convenient and conducive to conversation. They could be moved away from the center of a room and folded down to a more compact size when space was needed for dancing or music-making.

The later 17th century was the golden period of the gateleg table, with a plethora of variations on the basic structure being made. Foldover tops continued, especially for small tables for gaming and needlework, but they were largely superseded by the type consisting of a fixed central section with a hinged flap and a

▲ Gateleg table
The molded edge to the top, the rule joins between the flaps and the central frame, the baluster legs with faceted cappings, and the elegant scrolled feet all show the very high quality of this British oak round-topped gateleg table. Twentieth-century copies of this table abound.
(late 17th century; w. of top 1.3m/4ft 3in; value I)

gateleg on either side. The supports for the flaps generally swiveled out from one end of the central rectangular structure and folded back parallel with it. Extra large tables, which might seat up to twelve people comfortably, would have two gates on each side to support the flap. Rule joins between the flaps and the fixed central sections of good-quality gateleg tables made after *c.*1690 gave smooth contact between the edges of the central section and the flaps without leaving any gaps.

DESIGN VARIATIONS

In many gateleg tables there was a drawer, or even two, in the frieze of the central section. Small foldover tables of exceptional quality might have three or more small drawers opening in the rounded face of a wide frieze. An unusual type of small table had a single central gate that pivoted in the center of the underframe, to support either a leaf on each side or a vertically tilting solid top, made without flaps. Another rare alternative was a small cupboard at one or both ends of the central section of a two-flap table.

The greatest variation in appearance was given by the decorative treatments of legs and stretchers. Plain bar supports might be grooved or given profile shaping, while baluster, bobbin, or spiral turning resulted in some exuberant underframes, which have developed a rich patina over the years. Carving on friezes and stretchers was common on early tables with foldover tops, but not on larger gateleg tables with fall flaps. The most common late 17th-century gateleg tables were made in oak or elm, while the finest are of walnut, cedar, yew, or some other rare, but usually native, timber. Fruitwoods, such as apple, pear, or cherry, supplemented oak and elm in rural areas.

▲ "Wake" table
Tables of these proportions – long, with large, shallow leaves – are extremely desirable and command high prices. This British example is made in figured mahogany.
*(c.1800; w. of top 1.4m/4ft 7in; value **M**)*

▼ Spider-leg table
This fine spider-leg table, of cocus wood with padouk crossbandings, has a molded edge to the top and baluster-turned feet, set off by the plain legs and gate supports for the rectangular flaps. From the mid-18th century, the spider-leg table was a delicate interpretation of the gateleg principle.
*(c.1770; w. of top 76cm/30in; value **H**)*

DROPLEAF TABLES

Gateleg tables, mainly of oak and elm, were made throughout the 18th century, chiefly for the homes of farmers and the more prosperous country people. Their place at the forefront of fashion was taken from *c.*1720 by the dropleaf table: a type of flap table with a pivoting leg to support the extended leaf but without the under-stretchers of the gate-form underframing. Both types of table reflect the increasingly comfortable and civilized surroundings and activities of the 18th-century middle classes – dining, tea-drinking, card-playing, doing needlework, and conversing in small groups.

As with the design of chairs at this time, the understretcher was relinquished. By the end of Queen Anne's reign (1714), both tables and chairs were usually supported on cabriole legs without understretchers. The underframing of the table was now confined to the underside of the top, and the moving supports. The supports consisted of legs joined at right angles to sturdy rails, pivoted outward on wooden knuckle hinges set into the central underframe. The flaps were generally secured to the central section of the top with brass rule hinges, countersunk into the underside.

Some dropleaf tables were made of oak or walnut, but fashionable mahogany was the choice for most after *c.*1730. The outward curves of the cabriole legs were often embellished with carved acanthus leaves or lion-masks; carved claw-and-ball feet were a similar decorative change from plain pad feet. Less stylish but eminently serviceable were the square and rectangular dropleaf tables, operating on the same principle as round tables and produced for the rest of the century.

The dropleaf table, like the gateleg, continued to be widely made and used, particularly in provincial districts where both types could be considered traditional rather than fashionable pieces of furniture. Plenty of examples still exist and are to be found in such locally available timbers as fruitwood, ash, elm, yew and oak, as well as mahogany. As with most regional furniture of enduring design, it is often very difficult to attribute anything more than a vague date to them.

SPIDER-LEG AND SUTHERLAND TABLES

The gateleg principle was adopted for an exceptionally delicate form of flap-top table, which was popular during the 1760s and 1770s. Appropriately known as a spider-leg table, from the slenderness of its supports, it was a small occasional table for use in the drawing-room, made in fine timbers. Its turned legs and stretchers were usually quite plain, and it had either one or two flaps; some examples have cleverly curved base stretchers to make space for the user's legs.

A new form of flap table was introduced during the mid-19th century. Known as a Sutherland table, it was named after the Duchess of Sutherland, Queen Victoria's Mistress of the Robes, and was a sort of cousin to the

▶ Dropleaf table
This North American dropleaf table was made in Massachusetts, of curly maple, a timber that is rarely found in Europe. The gentle curve of its cabriole legs, the lift to the pad feet, the lively profile of its scalloped apron, the ample extension of its rounded leaves, and its classic proportions all demonstrate the practical simplicity of American Colonial taste. Its appeal is further enhanced by both the warm patina of its top and the old black-green painted surface of its base.
(c.1730–70; ht 66cm/26in; value Q)

▲ Sutherland table
The elaborately fretted trestle ends on this walnut table are typically Victorian in style. So, too, are the rather thin spiral-turned gatelegs and central stretcher of this British Sutherland table on casters. Note how the timber has faded over time, which suggests that it has probably been left stored in direct sunlight near a window. Sutherland tables were hugely popular during the 19th century, and are today too, because they are not only highly decorative but also practical, taking up so little space when not in use.
(c.1860; ht 67cm/26½in; value D)

Pembroke table. It was characterized by an extremely narrow central section supported on a trestle-like, cheval or "horse" base with a relatively deep flap on either side. The base, with its sturdy supports and splayed feet at either end, was often embellished with carving or turning in the full-blown Victorian manner, while the flap supports, which pivoted outward from the center of the underframe just below the top, tended to be comparatively slim. The usefulness of such a table is immediately apparent: its narrowness in the folded position enables it to be tucked away in a small space, while the deep flaps provide a relatively spacious top when opened out. Sutherland tables were made with rectangular as well as rounded flaps. While the best were of figured walnut or some other eye-catching timber, sometimes with inlaid or marquetry decoration as an additional embellishment, more utilitarian versions were produced in oak, elm, or even painted pine. Nearly all of these types have casters attached to the feet for extra mobility.

Other types of space-saver on the dropleaf principle included 18th-century North American butterfly tables, named after the shape of the supports for the leaves, and handkerchief tables, with triangular tops and leaves.

KEY FACTS

- SIZE the standard size of a gateleg or dropleaf table is for four people; the larger examples that can sit up to six people or more (e.g. "Wake" tables) have a considerable premium, which means that they can be popular with fakers
- CONSTRUCTION gateleg tables are more robust in construction than cabriole-legged dropleaf tables, and have therefore survived in greater numbers; the leaves should be the same on both sides; on earlier examples leaves are usually made of two pieces spliced together; sometimes the leaf tip has broken off and been replaced
- COPIES AND FAKES copies from the 1920s and 1930s tend to have barley-twist legs; note that the techniques used should be correct for the period of construction: 17th-century examples should have mortise-and-tenon joints, which have been pegged (the pegs have often lifted slightly and may be uneven, or square), while the copies will only have mortise-and-tenon joints

See also Pembroke and sofa tables, pp.56–7

Dining-tables before 1840

The gateleg table enjoyed enduring popularity in Britain and The Netherlands well into the 18th century, and indeed the provincial tradition carried on virtually unbroken to today. Although gateleg tables were usually oval or circular, rectangular gatelegs, conceived en suite with D-shaped gateleg end-sections, emerged during the reign of George II (1727–60). The earliest recorded extending dining-table was that supplied to Sir Robert Walpole for Houghton Hall, Norfolk, c.1730. Conceived with two single gateleg demi-lune end-sections and two double-gateleg central sections, which could be easily stored away when not in use, it has a molded top and is supported on 32 ring-turned columnar legs with bun feet. However, this design had its failings, as the vast number of legs made it awkward for large numbers of sitters to be seated, and it was only with the introduction of leaves that more guests could be accommodated comfortably.

18TH-CENTURY DINING-TABLES

During the reign of George II, dining-tables with pedestal supports were introduced. Invariably of mahogany, with D-shaped ends and up to as many as five further rectangular tilt-top central sections, the earliest examples made during the 1750s have a separate pedestal to support each section. These pedestals, closely mirroring contemporary tripod tables in design, were initially simple, with a ring-turned columnar or gun-barrel shaft supported on cabriole legs, and pad feet, often with leather casters. During the 1760s the shafts of the pedestals became increasingly rich in both form and carving, perhaps with a vase-shaped baluster and spiral-fluting, or foliate trails to the knees. The tops, joined together by brass U-shaped hooks, were usually covered with linen tablecloths, and were therefore invariably rather plain, as crossbanding was only introduced in the last quarter of the 18th century. Most examples of this period were made of mahogany, with the best timber available being employed to impress. With the advances of Neo-classicism, the pedestals again became increasingly restrained in form and decoration, the vase-shaped shafts of the 1780s and 1790s giving way to ring-turned columns with downswept reeded legs.

▲ Pedestal dining-table
Although the concave-sided platform of this English Regency mahogany quadripartite table allows the sitters to extend their legs, the deep frieze can make it particularly uncomfortable to sit at. A pedestal should never extend beyond the edge of a table, as this suggests that the top has been reshaped or made narrower and as a result the proportions will be wrong.
(c.1820; l. when extended 2.5m/8ft 2in; value **K**)

▼ Dining-table
Such dining-tables as this English mahogany example are generally less commercial than those that do not have a deep frieze, as they can be awkward to sit at. The color and patina of each of the leaves should match, although color variation is to be expected as some leaves will have been more exposed to sunlight than others.
(c.1770; l. when extended 3.2m/10ft 6in; value **I**)

Although, rather surprisingly, designs for dining-tables did not feature in 18th-century pattern-books, Thomas Chippendale (1718–79) certainly supplied several, Sir Edward Knatchbull being charged £5 for "2 Mahogany round ends to Join his Dining-Tables, with 2 pair of strap Hinges, Hooks and Eyes" in 1769. While the tilt-top central sections of pedestal dining-tables could certainly be stored away when not in use, they were still somewhat cumbersome. A sophisticated refinement, therefore, was the Cumberland-action table, which first appeared in the 1770s. Named after Henry Frederick, Duke of Cumberland, brother of George III, these dining-tables have double-gateleg scissor-action central sections and single-gateleg end-sections, which can all support further leaves when opened. They are more stable and easier to enlarge than pedestal dining-tables; their tops are often both molded and thinner, the most accomplished examples being veneered with exceptional richly figured timber, particularly fiddleback (flame) or plum-pudding mahogany, often crossbanded with tulipwood, padouk, or ebony. Provincial versions of this table were also made, usually constructed of solid mahogany. However, rather than having removeable leaves to reduce or enlarge the size, these had instead double-gateleg-action central sections with attached leaves, which hung down when not in use.

During the late 18th century, dining-tables in the Neo-classical taste were made throughout northern Europe and North America. Usually with two semi-circular end-sections, often above a plain paneled frieze, and further leaves, supported on square, tapering or turned and fluted legs, Russian and Louis XVI examples are often enriched with brass collars and flutes. While French and German examples are usually made of mahogany, Swedish, Danish, and Russian dining-tables are often of Karelian birch and cherry.

19TH-CENTURY DINING TABLES

This basic form of dining-table described above could not support more than one leaf between pedestals securely and thus Thomas Sheraton (1751–1806) revealed in *The Cabinet Dictionary* (1803), pedestal dining-tables enjoyed enduring popularity: "The common useful dining-tables are upon pillar and claws, generally four claws to each pillar, with brass castors. A dining-table of this kind may be made to any size, by having a sufficient quantity of pillars and claw parts, for between each of them is a loose flap, fixed by means of iron straps and buttons so that they are easily taken off

and put aside." Such massive "pillar" or pedestal dining-tables, often lavishly decorated with classically inspired motifs, such as claw monopodium and Roman acanthus scrolls, as popularized by George Smith (active *c*.1786–1828), continued to be made throughout the 19th century. In North America, mahogany pedestal dining-tables with columns on platform supports with saber legs were made in the Federal style, and after 1815 in the Regency style, by such cabinet-makers as Duncan Phyfe (1768–1854) in New York. After 1820 this type was largely replaced by Empire pedestal dining-tables, with heavier carved pillar supports resting on platform bases, often with four curved legs and animal-paw feet.

Although telescopic dining-tables (discussed right) were popular during the 19th century, both in Britain and abroad, their form when extended could only ever be rectangular. It was the inventor and cabinet-maker Robert Jupe of New Bond Street who revolutionized the design of oval and circular dining-tables in the reign of William IV (1830–37). In 1835 he was granted a patent – subsequently known as "Jupe's patent" – for the design of a segmental extending dining-table. This mechanism, whereby the segments of the top could be pulled out on their brass-channeled runners and further segments could be placed between them, increased the circumference of the table by up to half as much again, and applied equally well to both circular and oval dining-tables. Jupe dining-tables were invariably made of mahogany and were usually supplied with two sets of leaves, together with a leaf-case, which enabled a typical circular table to be approximately 1.4m (4ft 7in) in circumference when closed, 1.8m (5ft 11in) when partially extended, and 2.1m (6ft 11in) when fully extended. Usually supported on baluster shafts and channeled downswept legs with lion's-paw feet, most Jupe tables are stamped "Johnstone Jupe & Co., New Bond Street" and numbered. Long admired, this pattern was inevitably imitated by Jupe's contemporaries, but those that carry the Johnstone Jupe & Co. stamp command a considerable premium.

▼ **Extending dining-table by Johnstone Jupe & Co.**
Victorian mahogany table such as this are extremely desirable and command a premium, not only because it is labeled but also because it displays an unusually good color and retains all its original leaves.
(1835–70; diam. with smaller leaves 1.8m/5ft 11in; diam. with larger leaves 2m/6ft 7in; value Q)

TELESCOPIC DINING-TABLES

Although the firm of Gillow (est. *c*.1730) of Lancaster is best known for its restrained and often utilitarian mahogany furniture of superb technical craftsmanship, it also manufactured some novel forms. In 1805 Richard Gillow (1734–1811) patented a design for the "Imperial Extending Dining Table," which was "calculated to reduce the number of legs, pillar and claws and to facilitate their enlargement and reduction"; the perennial problem of enlarging a dining-table without having to store numerous tilt-top pedestals was therefore fully addressed. This new device, "whereby the two ends of the table are connected by pieces of wood, so joined together to form what are commonly called lazy tongs," meant that any number of leaves could be added to the "telescopic" frame when it was extended. Distinguished by their finely figured mahogany, reeded edges above a plain paneled frieze, and reeded baluster legs, Gillow's dining-tables are among the most famous and sought after. They were made throughout the 19th century, and their date is usually betrayed by the increasing thickness of the top and the more bulbous, heavier, and often carved legs supported by ceramic rather than brass casters. From *c*.1780 the firm stamped much its furniture with one of several marks including "GILLOWSLANCASTER" and individual craftsmen often signed their work in pencil.

▲ **Dining-table**
American extending dining-tables were based on Gillow's patent of 1805. This mahogany example was made in the Regency style in either New York or Philadelphia. The telescopic action allows the table to extend to receive seven leaves supported by five pedestals, typically with vase and ring-turned columnar supports, and reeded curved legs with brass caps and casters. During the 19th century, tables of this type were much more popular than those with hinged legs and falling leaves; they were also much more expensive.
(c.1805–10; l. when extended 4.7m/15ft 4in; value Q)

KEY FACTS

- ALTERATIONS beware of tables with crossbanded edges in satinwood or exotic woods, as these have often been added at a much later date to "improve" them; as narrower and round forms are more commercial, tables are frequently reshaped or made less wide by shaving off the edges – always check the color of the edge of the table, which should conform with the rest of the table; the underframe of a table may have been replaced because of damage or may be associated
- VENEERING until the late 19th century, dining-tables were almost always made in the solid, never veneered
- COLLECTING color is particularly important with dining-tables; the value of Jupe tables is generally not affected by color, and it is rare to find one with a good color; in today's market circular tables are much more fashionable and therefore commercial than rectangular examples

See also Early tables, pp.46–7

Dining-tables after 1840

The 19th-century middle classes seem to have emphasized their much-vaunted family values with grandiose dining habits. The tendency during the later 18th century to eat in a dining-room furnished with a single large table rather than, more intimately, with several smaller ones, as had been the custom earlier in the 18th century, was developed most spectacularly in the baronial interiors of the Victorian nouveau riche, who recalled picturesque "Merrie England" with long, rectangular dining-tables resplendent with "Tudorbethan" carved legs of massive bulbous form. The various styles of earlier periods were all recorded in the dining-table.

▲ Extending dining-table
The central pillar and grandly scrolled feet of this round burr-walnut table divide to accommodate up to four extra leaves, with two detachable turned legs, forming a long oval when extended. Notice how the extension has a good strong color, whereas the main body is much paler after being consistently exposed to the sunlight.
*(c.1860; l. when extended 3.4m/11ft 2in; value **J**)*

THE LEGACY OF THE EARLIER PERIODS

The fashion for this somewhat pompous dining furniture percolated through to the inhabitants of villas and terraced houses as well as the minor gentry in the country, who now found space for a dedicated dining-room whose central focus was a capacious table suitable for Victorian family meals. Expansion was the order of the day, and while few of these rooms could accommodate the 30- or 40-seater tables that only half filled the awesome spaces of mansion or baronial dining rooms, many were furnished with moderately sized tables that could be made bigger by the addition of leaves or the raising of flaps.

This idea of extending tables was nothing new. Tables with gateleg supported flaps had been in existence for more than two centuries, and "draw-tables," with extending tops that could double the length of a rectangular table, for just as long. Dining-tables with extensions based on the gateleg principle were in use from *c.*1730. The D-end table, which could have extra leaves inserted, proved its worth from the 1750s onward, and the pedestal dining-table, made in sections and most convenient for sitters' knees and feet, was

▲ Extending dining-table
This British walnut table extends by means of a winding mechanism set at the end of the table in the frieze. It has two extra legs, and three extra leaves, each with a hinged frieze.
*(late 19th century; l. when extended 1.5m/4ft 11in; value **H**)*

▼ Extending dining-table
During the early 19th century, George Bullock (c.1777– 1818) championed the use of indigenous woods for furniture-making. This trend was continued by furniture-makers throughout the 19th century.
*(c.1860; l. 3m/9ft 10in; value **H**)*

developed in the late 18th century. Extending tables with the "lazy tongs" telescopic underframing, which had been patented in 1805 by Richard Gillow (1734–1811) of the firm of Gillow (est. *c.*1730) of Lancaster, were a popular introduction during the early 19th century.

All these principles were exploited in the search for adaptability in the dining-rooms of Europe and North America. Some later 19th-century rectangular tables had as many as ten extra leaves to allow expansion from six or eight seats to twenty or thirty, and the round multi-segmented Jupe tables, patented in 1835, were copied with minor variations for the rest of the century.

MATERIALS AND DECORATION

Timbers were as varied as ever; mahogany, walnut or oak were most usual for large extending tables, while busily figured burr woods, amboyna, maple, or birch were favored for the more ostentatious pillar tables, the tops of which might be covered in floral marquetry or intricate Gothic and Renaissance patterns in variously colored woods. Throughout most of the 19th century the majority of dining-tables, of whatever shape or revival style, were fitted with casters, which allowed them to be moved around the room, and also enabled the extensions to run smoothly from the main framework. The architect Augustus Welby Northmore Pugin (1812–52) was probably the first to break this general rule. His reformed Gothic style signaled a departure from the usual revivalist compromises, and his dining and other tables, whether of stark monastic simplicity or great decorative refinement, have their feet set directly and firmly on the floor. Progressive designers of the later 19th and early 20th centuries tended to follow his lead in this respect, but casters continued to be used on most mass-produced tables in the mainstream styles.

The dining-room was traditionally a place for ostentatious display of a distinctly masculine cast, and 19th-century exaggerations of earlier characteristics and styles were often most pronounced in dining-room furniture. The top of the dining-table itself was generally covered with a white damask tablecloth when in use, but

legs offered plenty of opportunity for conspicuous decoration, and even the tops of extending dining-tables, exposed at times, usually had deep molded edges and ornamented friezes.

NEW TYPES OF TABLE

Some of the earlier systems of table extension were refined or slightly altered during the later 19th century, but there was little real innovation. One of the few mechanical developments was the square or rectangular table in two sections with a long metal screw under the top, which could be unwound with a special handle inserted at one end. Once the sections were fully separated, an extra leaf or leaves could be fitted into the middle. This system was adopted widely for the more ordinary dining-tables of the second half of the 19th century, of which examples abound today. The handles are often missing, but these can be easily replaced.

Not all dining-tables were of the extending variety. A popular form, and one which could be embellished in the widest variety of styles, was the round loo table. This table was originally conceived during the early 19th century for the card game of lanterloo, but was probably later used just as often as a dining-table. The top, characteristically supported on a central sturdy pillar, could usually be tipped up when not in use, and was often the vehicle for decoration, with flamboyant inlays or marquetry on the surface, and carving or molding round the edge and on the pillar.

REVIVAL STYLES

Dining-tables were made in 19th-century interpretations of Gothic, Renaissance, Rococo, and Neo-classical styles, and very often in an indiscriminate mixture of several of these at the same time. *The Practical Cabinet Maker and Upholsterer's Treasury of Designs* (1847) of Henry Whitaker (active 1825–50) included illustrations of "Dining-Table Standards [pillars] and Legs" of both "Elizabethan" and "Italian" flavor, liberally carved with scrolls, fluting, and "jeweled" patterns in the Renaissance Revival style, or with fruiting vines. Mid-19th-century attempts to reform taste and purify design were largely unsuccessful, and dining-tables, like other furniture chosen by most of the population, continued to reflect the stylistic confusion and ornamental excess that characterized the period. However, from the 1860s, the efforts of the reformers gradually began to take effect. The firm of Morris, Marshall, Faulkner & Co. (est. 1861) in London, set up by the reformer and designer William Morris (1834–96), produced radical (and sometimes lavishly painted) furniture that became fashionable, at least among an influential élite (alongside furniture in the more commercially successful Chippendale Revival style), and the work of such designers as William Burges (1827–81), Owen Jones (1809–74), and Bruce J. Talbert (1838–81) was conscientiously Gothic in style.

The Japanese taste that swept Europe and North America after the International Exhibition of 1862 in London resulted in a wave of "aesthetic" fervor, turning table legs into spindly supports in real or imitation bamboo or with fretwork. However, on the whole, more solid styles such as "Old English," "Jacobean," or "Gothic" (but of a somewhat simpler and lighter form than before) were preferred for dining-room furniture.

Traditional forms, such as oval tables supported on pillars at either end, or tables with draw-leaf tops, were treated with stylish originality, but there were still plenty of dining-tables in revivalist modes for those who could not wean themselves from the past.

▲ **Extending dining-table**
This French extending table of ebonized wood is made in the flamboyant Parisian manner associated with the period known as the Second Empire (1848–70). This example has gilt-bronze mounts and a central dividing pedestal that gives rise to four massive scrolled legs, each with an upper square pillar. These and two pairs of hinged, turned legs support up to ten extra leaves when the table is fully extended. Such tables were rarer in France than in Britain. The leaves of French extending dining-tables are usually of a poorer quality timber than the rest of the table, as they were never intended to be seen, and the table was covered with a cloth when not in use.
(c.1860; l. when extended 7.4m/24ft 3in; value J)

▼ **Extending dining-table**
This British mahogany dining-table is in the Chippendale Revival style, which was popular in late 19th-century Britain. It has cabriole legs carved with scrolled acanthus leaves, and large claw-and-ball feet.
(late 19th century; l. when extended 3m/9ft 10in; value H)

KEY FACTS

- CASTERS these usually appear on all the legs, as they allow the extension leaves to run easily from the underframe
- CONSTRUCTION the leaves should be of the same timber as the rest of the table (except for French ones, where they are of a cheaper wood); if leaves are missing this will generally reduce the value of the piece; the extending mechanism should be original – the marks made from regular wear should be clearly visible on the underside
- COLOR those leaves that have not been used regularly will usually be of a different color from the rest of the table, which will have been exposed to the light for longer periods and will have been cleaned more frequently; because of the expanse of wood on display, the quality, figuring, and patina will all affect the value
- COLLECTING many examples with legs, or with stretchers, are generally not very popular as they prevent diners from sitting comfortably at the table; the length to which the table can be extended will have a considerable affect on value – some examples can reach up to 16ft (4.9m) long, with up to six separate leaves; make sure that when the table is fully extended it is secure and sound, and that the understructure is strong enough to withstand the weight of a fully laid table; all extending tables are 19th century, as the form did not exist before then

See also Dining-tables before 1840, pp.50–51

Drum, breakfast, and center tables

Drum tables, which were mostly made from the late 18th century, were usually circular, with leather tops, and were used for writing. Breakfast tables, with their hinged flaps, were designed en suite with the furniture in the bedroom, where the first meal of the day was eaten. Center tables, which are multi-purpose but primarily ornamental, were designed to be seen from all sides.

► Breakfast table
Early 19th-century breakfast tables are usually of pillar-and-claw form, and they normally have hinged tilt tops. This British example is of mahogany, with rosewood crossbanding on the border of the rectangular top. It is normal for the base to be darker than the top, as seen here, as the top was more frequently and exposed to the light. On such examples as this, where an expanse of timber is on display, the quality and patina of the wood are very important in determining value.
*(c.1800; ht 71cm/28in; value **G**)*

▲ Drum table
This British mahogany example has a vase-shaped pillar and a tripod base, a leather-covered top surmounting a frieze containing four drawers inlaid with boxwood and tulipwood banding, and brass-capped feet.
*(c.1800; ht 73cm/28½in; value **L**)*

DRUM TABLES
Tables with round, or occasionally polygonal, tops on pillar bases with three or four feet, and with drawers in their friezes, are now known as drum tables, although they were once generally referred to as library tables or writing tables. A leather-covered surface for writing, a slight lip rather than a widely overhanging edge above the frieze, and sometimes a revolving top are also defining characteristics. Such tables were fashionable from c.1790 to 1820. The grandest incorporated bookshelves as well as drawers in the frieze. Others, known as rent tables, had their drawers labeled with the days of the week, or with letters; these provided elegant filing systems for landlords or managers of estates. Some drum tables had wedge-shaped drawers; others had a combination of real and dummy drawers, given decorative coherence with such details as beaded edges, stringing lines, keyholes, and brass knobs or handles. The central pillars were usually turned or faceted; vase shaping, with inward-curving reeded legs, was especially popular c.1800. Later examples, made toward 1820, were usually set on platform bases with carved, and sometimes gilded, feet. Mahogany was most often used for late 18th-century drum tables, but rosewood was also favored for early 19th-century examples. Apart from later reproductions, the type appears to have faded from fashion c.1820.

▼ Center table
The shape of this English table, with its triangular concave base support and ram's-head terminals, is in the French influenced, Neo-classical style of the early 19th century. This exact form appears in *Household Furniture and Interior Decoration Executed from Designs by Thomas Hope* (1807). The large surface area and restrained ornamentation allow the uninterrupted display of the well-figured mahogany.
*(c.1810; ht 77.5cm/30½in; value **H**)*

BREAKFAST TABLES
Small tables, perhaps of the gateleg variety, were used for breakfast and supper, among other purposes, during the 16th and 17th centuries. At this time, and throughout the 18th century, breakfast was generally taken in the privacy of the bedroom or a small parlor.

Examples from this period, which are usually in mahogany, have hinged flaps, supported on fly-brackets, with a drawer in the frieze, and a storage shelf below enclosed by pierced fretwork or brass wire, presumably intended for china and cutlery, or perhaps jams and condiments. To allow room for the user's knees the caged shelf was often concave at the front and back, and if the table's legs had under-stretchers these would be shaped conformingly.

By the 1760s the flaps of breakfast tables were often given a rounded shaping, like butterflies' wings, and the caging around the undershelf was usually dispensed with. Some examples of the 1770s retained a shelf or a decoratively pierced stretcher, but an increasing number were without either, and the type merged imperceptibly into the Pembroke table. Lighter varieties of mahogany, satinwood, and other exotic timbers were used during this period, and they were enhanced with marquetry or painted decoration.

As in earlier centuries, many people would have taken their breakfast from small tripod tables with tip-up tops, known as claw tables. They ranged from plain types, with straight-edged tops, simply turned pillars, and curved legs on pad feet, to those with "piecrust" or scalloped edges round the tops, and delicate carving on the supports.

The most fashionable breakfast tables of the late 18th and early 19th centuries were of the pillar-and-claw (central column with splayed legs) variety. Often seating as many as eight or nine people, they are hardly distinguishable from small dining-tables, save for the absence of extending mechanisms. Early 19th-century breakfast tables of this type were customarily oval, or rectangular with rounded corners. Many had "snap" tops, enabling them to be tipped into a vertical position, as well as casters on their feet, thus continuing the long-established and highly convenient flexibility of the breakfast table.

Mahogany or rosewood were the usual woods used, but the dark striated calamander was reserved for some of the finest tables. Borders were crossbanded or inlaid with stringing lines of darker wood or brass; reeded edges were usual. The central pillar support from which the four claw feet splayed was usually ring- or baluster-turned, with reeding on the legs. Brass cappings, of plain square form or cast into leafy scrolls or lion's paws, generally surmount the casters, which are set at right angles to the feet.

During the mid-19th century the shapes of tops became more varied, with quatrefoil, octagonal, and lobed forms appearing among the circular and oval tables that remained popular. Carved decoration became ever more florid as Classicism gave way to the Rococo Revival and the other historicist styles favored at the time. Walnut and other highly figured woods were used as often as mahogany and oak.

CENTER TABLES

The true center table is one without any specific purpose, designed not only to furnish the space in the middle of a room but also to be the cencenter of attention; while it may host an assortment of activities, its function is largely ornamental. Conventions of room arrangement during the 18th century meant that the most prestigious items of furniture were almost invariably placed against the walls, and the center table as now understood did not come into its own until the early 19th century.

Although most 19th-century center tables are round, oval, octagonal, rectangular, and square ones are not exceptional. Those from early in the century, such as examples designed by Thomas Hope (1769–1831), may be of light mahogany inlaid with classical patterns in dark timbers such as ebony, or with metal and ivory. Inlays of brass, usually in rosewood, were highly fashionable after the revival of the work of André-Charles Boulle (1642–1732) during the early 19th century. The contrast between dark timbers and gilding was also exploited with great effect, during the first three decades of the century.

▲ Center or breakfast table
In the mid-19th century small souvenir wares, including writing slopes and pen boxes, were made in Killarney, Ireland, with marquetry decoration in bog oak, yew, and arbutus. This yew table is a large and unusual example.
*(c.1880; ht 77cm/30¼in; value **K**)*

► Center table
The serpentine oval shape of this table is set with "Buhl" marquetry panels on an ebonized ground with elaborate ormolu mounts. This is a high-quality example of the decadent but influential French taste of the mid- to late 19th century.
*(c.1880; ht 75cm/29½in; value **H**)*

The Victorians produced grand center tables with opulent carving; walnut, mahogany, and oak were the predominant timbers, but burr varieties of native woods, as well as imported exotics such as amboyna, thuya, and maple, were highly regarded. Light timbers were especially valued in eastern Europe and Russia. The tops of the tables were often embellished with floral marquetry, specimen marbles, porcelain plaques or painting decoration, which were favored in most European countries as well as in Britain. The Italians revived their traditional techniques of inlaying, *scagliola* (imitation hardstones) and micro-mosaic, and exported them widely, while the most eye-catching tables were those from Russia, with bright green malachite tops set upon richly gilded bases. However, the French influence was most potent in showy furniture; the Rococo Revival, as interpreted in the rest of Europe, was distinctly French, particularly in the use of gilt-bronze mounts. The French revival of Boullework resulted in ebony and red tortoiseshell tables with brass inlay and sumptous gilded enrichments.

KEY FACTS

- SIZE those tables that were originally intended to be used for eating and are of over 1m (3ft 3in) in length will generally fetch a premium
- BOULLEWORK the brass should be engraved – if it is not it may have been rubbed off through wear; beware of damage as it is extremely expensive and difficult to repair, and this will have a considerable impact on the value; the quality of later designs is usually very varied – the best show a good understanding of the originals and are often quite close copies, while the poorer examples are often only a mass of interlaced foliage
- ALTERATIONS it is common for rosewood or calamander crossbanding and decorative inlay to have been added at a later date, as these boost the table's commercial appeal; round and oval tables tend to be more popular than rectangular tables, and as a result many table tops have been reshaped – look out for poor reshaping, very few signs of real wear to the outside edges, bearers (that provide support and prevent warping) reduced in size, and a top that is too small for its base
- COLLECTING there is a premium on all Irish furniture

► Breakfast table
American forms of this table, which could also be used as a library table, are very rare even though they were popular in the late 1820s and 1830s. This mahogany table made in New York is a precursor of the austere table made later in a style known as "pillar-and-scroll."
*(c.1820–25; ht 74cm/29in; value **Q**)*

See also Pembroke and sofa tables, pp.56–7

Pembroke and sofa tables

The elegant dropleaf table known as the Pembroke table, so called, according to Thomas Sheraton (1751–1806) in his pattern-book *The Cabinet Dictionary* (1803), "from the name of the lady who first gave orders for one of them," was part of the evolution of the breakfast table. The Pembroke table was eventually replaced in the fashionable drawing-room by the sofa table, an extended version of the type, developed in the last years of the 18th and the first decade of the 19th century.

▼ Pembroke table

This English mahogany serpentine Pembroke table is an elegant example of its type. It has square-tapered legs, brass feet, and casters, which are all typical features of Pembroke tables of this period.
(c.1775; ht 73cm/28½in; value I)

PEMBROKE TABLES

Recorded in accounts from the 1750s, Pembroke tables were placed in the drawing-room and the boudoir where they were used for taking meals, playing cards, writing, and needlework. By the 1770s this elegant, useful form was well established, and was often a vehicle for the finest cabinet-making of the Neo-classical period. The basic structure, with its two side flaps supported on hinged brackets, lent itself to almost limitless variations. The opened table may form a rectangle or a square, an oval or an octagon; it can be straight or bow-fronted, with rounded, serpentine, or D-shaped flaps; the wood can be plain or crossbanded, with marquetry, painting, or carved decoration; and the legs may be of cabriole or straight-tapered shape, of round or square section.

A drawer in the frieze is usual, but some examples have sliding sections concealing compartments, while the rare "harlequin" type includes a mechanism to raise and lower compartments of drawers and pigeon holes within the center. Most 18th-century Pembroke tables are supported on their four legs without understretchers, while others have decorated base supports or small platforms. Appropriately for a highly mobile piece of furniture, nearly every example is fitted with casters.

While examples are known in the Gothic and Chinese tastes of the 1760s, those produced between 1770 and 1800 reflect the Neo-classical taste at its most refined.

Veneers are of mahogany, satinwood, or other luxurious woods; lines are simple, proportions carefully considered, and ornament is of the greatest delicacy. The examples illustrated by George Hepplewhite (*d*.1786) in *The Cabinet-Maker and Upholsterer's Guide* (1788–94) are typical of those available to the gentry during the last quarter of the 18th century. Pembroke tables with tapering legs of attenuated cabriole form, ending in the thinnest of scroll feet, were the result of French influence toward the end of the 18th century. Some had finely chiseled gilt-brass mounts.

Decoration took the form of plain stringing or crossbanding, or marquetry borders of anthemion, husks, guilloche, or scrolling acanthus, with such embellishments as shells, medallions, or florets. These could also be painted, although garlands, beribboned swags, or tapering trails were the most usual.

The proportions of late 18th-century Pembroke tables are crucial; the side flaps are usually (but not always) equal to half the width of the central section, and should be one-third of the table height in their fall postion. There should be a frieze drawer at one end with a dummy drawer on the opposite end. An oval table usually also displays bow-fronted end friezes to match the curve of the top. Each flap should have one or two fly-bracket supports, opening sideways on wooden hinges. The legs should be tapered and the tops of the legs should continue upward to form the side frame of the drawer.

Pembroke tables continued to be made in the 19th century, the most advanced design having a central column with splayed legs (called a pillar and claw), which Sheraton illustrated in *The Cabinet-Maker and Upholsterer's Drawing Book* (1791–1802). A slightly later variant was the platform base. Pembroke tables of the 1820s and 1830s are of characteristically squat proportions, with turned tapered legs, and often have two frieze drawers, one above the other.

▲ Pembroke table

The top of this British oval Pembroke table is set with segmented satinwood veneers and decorated with marquetry. The large oval patera medallion in the center of the top is surrounded by a band of sycamore set with scrolling plants and flowerheads, with similar decoration on the outer molded border. Its delicate construction and graceful appearance give it especially feminine associations. As with many tables of this type, this sofa table has a real and an opposing dummy drawer; the legs are decorated with pendent husks typical of late 18th-century Neo-classical ornament.
(c.1780; ht 73cm/28½in; value K)

◄ Pembroke table

In the USA the terms "Pembroke" and "breakfast" table are used interchangeably for small tables with four stationary legs, and falling leaves requiring only short hinged sections of the side rails, known as "flys," for support. The satinwood stringing, which outlines the top of this mahogany example, together with the inlaid ovals on the skirt, and the pendent husks on the tapered legs ending in spade feet, are characteristic of this type of Neo-classical table made in Baltimore, Maryland, at the end of the 18th and beginning of the 19th century.
(c.1790–1800; ht 73cm/28½in; value Q)

SOFA TABLES

The sofa table was as varied as the Pembroke table in the details of its design and decoration and, like its predecessor, it followed a defining form. According to Sheraton in *The Cabinet Dictionary* (1803), the sofa table was specifically for use "before a sofa" where "the Ladies chiefly occupy them to draw, write or read upon."

Sofa tables are usually between 1.52m (5ft) and 1.83m (6ft) long, when fully extended, and 61cm (24in) wide. The flaps, supported on fly brackets, are each about one-quarter of the width of the central section. Some examples have sliding-topped compartments in the middle for games, or rising desks for writing and drawing, but the majority have one long or two short drawers on one side of the frieze, with corresponding dummy drawers on the opposite side.

The edges of sofa-table tops are always straight, and the corners of the flaps rounded, or chamfered to form "octagon corners," but the bases are hugely varied and closely reflect the evolving design styles of the Regency period. The top may be set on end supports, with or without stretchers across the middle, or central supports rising from a platform base. The legs are so designed that the feet can fit a little way under a sofa, allowing the table to be pulled close to the sitter. They are nearly always on casters.

The plainest sofa tables have plank-shaped supports dividing into splayed tapered or saber legs with brass cappings and casters. Alternatively after *c*.1810, rectangular plinths were set at right angles to the uprights, often with scrolls in the angles and with scrolled feet. For more luxurious sofa tables lyre-shaped end supports or patterns of decorative spindles were favored, and while the lion monopodia that were advocated by George Smith (active *c*.1786–1828) in *A Collection of Designs for Household Furniture and Interior Decoration* (1808) were rarely executed, the lion mask often appears on the decorative brass drawer handles. "Hipped" saber or cabriole legs were also popular; they appear often on sofa tables with central supports. All of these shapes could be embellished with reeding, lines of inlaid wood or brass, or strategically placed carved paterae or leaves. Cross-stretchers provided many opportunities for decorative turnings. Inlaid brass decoration on the table top and frieze was sometimes matched on the legs, and/or on the fronts of the fly brackets.

▲ Sofa table

The rarest type of all American dropleaf tables is the long narrow sofa table with leaves at either end made to stand before a sofa. This example, attributed to Duncan Phyfe (1768–1854), is supported by reeded pedestals with outswept reeded legs and brass paw feet on casters. *(1810–20; ht 73cm/28½in; value Q)*

▼ Sofa table

This English rosewood sofa table, crossbanded with satinwood has a central pedestal support with a concave platform, a feature typical of George IV sofa tables. Those examples with brass inlay in the "Buhl" antiquarian taste are commercially desirable, although quite commonplace. *(c.1825; ht 68cm/26¾in; value I)*

The timbers used for sofa tables range from plain mahogany or more fashionable timbers such as rosewood to exotic woods including calamander; lightly colored woods such as satinwood for veneering were now no longer in vogue in the 19th century, except for crossbandings as a foil to the dark woods now in favor; common timbers such as beech could be stained or ebonized to simulate these. By *c*.1815 brass inlays in the manner advocated by George Bullock (*c*.1777–1818) were generally used to create decorative contrasts; the most lavish examples have ormolu mounts as well as inlaid brass. A rare but significant form of surface decoration on sofa tables was black and white penwork, painted by ladies to imitate inlaid ivory decoration.

Because they have been highly desirable for a long time many sofa tables have been "improved" or even fabricated beyond acceptable levels of repair and restoration. As well as "marriages" between tops and associated bases, decoration such as crossbandings or brass inlays may have been added to tops to enhance the commercial value. Bases may have been legitimately repaired, but many sofa tables have been "made up" with the trestle supports from old (and much less expensive) cheval mirrors. These are liable to look somewhat flimsy in proportion to the table tops. Wood grain running the length of a sofa-table top, rather than across it, may indicate a top made up from another larger piece of old furniture.

KEY FACTS

- PEMBROKE TABLES beside the genuine repairs that may be necessary in the course of time, collectors should beware of later restorations and alterations to Pembroke tables: these include substituting an oval top for a (less valuable) square or rectangular one; inserting decorative veneers or crossbandings into a plain surface to increase the value, or later painting, on a previously undecorated table – usually identifiable by the quality
- SOFA TABLES those tables that have low stretchers are generally less popular than those with higher stretchers, which allow more leg room; sometimes lower stretchers have been moved, and the scars that are left should be visible, although often these areas have been re-veneered to hide them; satinwood or rosewood tables are more desirable than mahogany, and end-support tables more sought after than those with central pedestals; the best sofa tables have cedar-lined drawers

Console, side, and pier tables

Tables conceived to stand against walls were first recorded in the 15th century and served as both serving tables and sideboards. It was not until the 17th century that purely ornamental pier tables came into fashion. Invariably executed in giltwood, often by a specialist carver or sculptor, the finest Roman side tables of the 1670s and 1680s are characterized by their thick, marble slabs supported by boldly scrolled foliage, acanthus, and mythological figures. Not to be outdone Louis XIV had pier tables designed for him with caryatid, putto, and scrolled dolphin supports, and side tables, usually gilded, with thick marble tops; legs draped with lambrequins and foliage, are either figurative or of tapered herm form, joined by a waved and scrolled X-shaped stretcher.

◀ **Pier table**
From the 1770s pier tables in the Neo-classical fashion were inlaid with such finely figured specimen woods as burr-yew, harewood, and amaranth. Exponents include the firm of Ince & Mayhew (est. 1758) in London, William Moore (active 1785–1814) in Dublin, and the Seymour family in Boston who worked in the Federal style (1788–1815) and incorporated such motifs as shells, flowers, and eagles into their work.
(1780; ht 83cm/32½in; value L)

THE 18TH CENTURY

The general pattern of the Louis XIV side table was inspirational to cabinet-makers throughout Europe and following the Revocation of the Edict of Nantes (1685), when Huguenot craftsmen settled in England, English side tables became increasingly elaborate and sophisticated, with oyster-veneered parquetry, marquetry, or even inlay in the style of Charles-André Boulle (1642–1732).

Lord Burlington (1694–1753) and the architect William Kent (c.1685–1748) returned from the Grand Tour in 1719. Kent revolutionized the design of English side tables bringing to them a Baroque magnificence. Usually of giltwood or mahogany, his tables are characterized by their architectural design and grandeur, embellished mainly with Vitruvian-scroll, guilloche, or Greek-key fret moldings.

Defined by their bracket construction and designed to be affixed to the wall, console tables are first recorded in the late 17th century. Kent is credited with the design of consoles supported by the splayed wings of Jupiter's eagle, arguably the most celebrated George II pattern. The luxurious tradition of Louis XIV consoles, usually of giltwood, oak, or walnut, survived during the Régence (1715–23). Principally designed as stands to support expensive and exotically figured marble tops, they are usually serpentine-fronted and supported by tapering, double C-scroll front legs, perhaps headed by *espagnolette* masks or dragons, while the X-shaped stretchers are often centered by gadrooned finials or urns. Louis XV consoles are closely related in form to

◀ **Console table**
This English, George II, giltwood console table was almost certainly designed by the architect William Kent. Among the most admired patterns it was adopted by cabinet-makers as far afield as Francis Brodie (1708–82) in Edinburgh, who published such a table on his tradecard of 1793. The eagle, originally a symbol of the Roman Republic, was adopted by the Americans from c.1776 as a symbol of victory during the American War of Independence (1776–83).
(1730; ht 71cm/28in; value O)

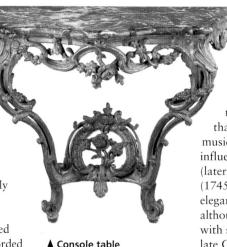

▲ **Console table**
Designers such as Juste-Aurèle Meissonnier (1695–1750) and Nicolas Pineau (1684–1754) were inspirational to mid-18th-century sculptors and carvers, and through their work the console table in the Louis XV Rococo came to fruition. This French giltwood console table is freer and less ponderous than those of the Régence period.
(c.1750; ht 85cm/33½in; value J)

their Régence predecessors, although they are lighter, and often asymmetrically trailed with floral garlands, C-scrolls, and scallop-shells, perhaps even carved with singeries and figures in the style of the designer Jean Pillement (1728–1808). Designed by the architect to be placed within the elaborate *boiseries* (wood paneling schemes) of the room, they were invariably surmounted by mirrors. During the 1750s this style gradually gave way to a taste for the exotic and Oriental, particularly chinoiserie and Turkish motifs, before finally giving in to Neo-classicism in the 1760s.

In England the architects Sir William Chambers (1723–96) and Robert Adam (1728–92) revolutionized the design of English side, pier, and console tables during the late 18th century. Side tables were often gilded or of carved mahogany; pier tables tend to be either rectangular or semi-eliptical, their paneled friezes perhaps fluted or centered by breakfront tablets, and the legs either tapered or turned and fluted, possibly even headed by Neo-classical urns and standing on stepped block feet. From the 1770s the tops of ornamental pier tables were frequently decorated with marquetry. Plainer examples, often in satinwood and inlaid with fans, flutes, husks, and richly figured woods, were also supplied in pairs. During the 1780s there was a fashion for semi-elliptical pier tables that were painted, often on satinwood, with flowers, musical trophies and Classical vignettes. A leading influence in the late 1780s was the Prince of Wales (later George IV) who, with his architect Henry Holland (1745–1806), promoted the fashion for tables in the elegant Louis XVI style. Often of "white and gold," although those of satinwood and mahogany often inlaid with shells or simply crossbanded still found favor, late Georgian tables are light and delicate in form.

The fashion for Neo-classical marquetry side tables was reflected throughout Europe and North America, perhaps nowhere more prolifically than in Italy, where the name of the Milanese cabinet-maker Giuseppe Maggiolini (1738–1814) has since become synonymous with furniture decorated with magnificent arabesque marquetry, sphinxes, and mythological trophies. However, cabinet-makers such as David Roentgen (1743–1807) in Germany, Georg Haupt (1741–84) in Sweden, and Thomas Seymour (1771–1848) in North America were also keen exponents of marquetry in the Neo-classical style.

THE 19TH CENTURY

The console table represents arguably the purest expression of the Empire style. Inspired by the architectural schemes proposed by Napoleon I's architects, Pierre Fontaine (*c*.1762–1853) and Charles Percier (1764–1838), in their *Recueil de décorations intérieures* (1801), as well as by the publication of *Aventures dans la basse et la haute Egypte* (1802) by Baron Vivant Denon (1747–1825), Empire consoles are usually rectangular in form. Their overhanging marble slab tops supported by Egyptian winged herm-caryatids, griffins, and sphinxes, are designed to be reflected by their mirrored backs often mounted with superbly chased and burnished ormolu, the burnished areas often deliberately contrasted with "antique" ungilded bronze elements. Although they are usually executed in the finest figured mahogany, the British blockade of 1806

pushed the prices up prohibitively and forced *ébenistes* (cabinet-makers) to resort to such indigenous woods as maple, ash, elm, and walnut. The Empire style was embraced in Germany by Karl Friedrich Schinkel (1781–1841) of Berlin, and in Britain Thomas Hope (1769–1831) included several designs for console and side tables with winged griffin and sphinx supports in his *Household Furniture and Interior Decoration Executed from Designs by Thomas Hope* (1807). The mounts of Regency mahogany tables were more restrained and sparse, their "Grecian" ornaments – wreaths, palmettes, paterae, sphinxes, and lion-masks – often being carved.

From *c*.1815, side tables and consoles became increasingly elaborate in both form and decoration. The Buhl revival of the 1820s, as well as the fashion under the French King Charles X (1824–30) for furniture *en bois clair* (pale wood), gradually gave way to the Gothic Revival of the 1820s and 1830s, a style in England identified with William Beckford (1760–1844) and subsequently A.W.N. Pugin (1812–52). From *c*.1830, consoles in the Louis XV or Rococo Revival taste again became fashionable; these were gradually superceded by an enthusiasm for all things Italian – particularly of Baroque and, subsequently, Renaissance design including the Milanese ebony side tables inlaid with ivory and copied by the English firm of Gillow (est. *c*.1730) of Lancaster.

▲ Side table by Gustaf Adolph Ditzinger (1760–1800)

Ditzinger was apprenticed to Georg Haupt, cabinet-maker to Gustav III (reigned 1771–92) of Sweden after whom the Neo-classical style in Sweden was named (Gustavian). This side table is decorated with such Neo-classical motifs as acanthus scrolls, husks, urns, and paterae. *(1791; ht 76cm/30in; value **Q**)*

▶ Pier table

This is one of a pair of mahogany pier tables and is typical of a group of Boston tables inspired by similar types illustrated in the *Cabinet–Maker's and Upholsterer's Guide, Drawing Book and Repository* (1826) by the English cabinet-maker George Smith. The two boldly scrolled legs, are taken from a design by Thomas King (active c.1790–c.1839) in *The Modern Style of Cabinet Work Exemplified* (1829–35). The apron drawer is rare on pier tables, but the lower section mirror is frequently found. *(c.1830–35; ht 95cm/37in; value for the pair **Q**)*

▲ Console table

This Italian giltwood table is a curious mix of Baroque and early Rococo styles. The heavily decorated form with its supporting putti has its roots in the Italian Baroque of the late 17th century, particularly in the work of the Venetian sculptor Andreas Brustolon (1662–1732). However, its pierced foliate and shell-encrusted apron and cabriole legs joined by a boldly shaped X-frame stretcher, simultaneously reflect the full-blown Louis XV Rococo style. The fusion of stylistic ornament typifies the fashionable Rococo Revial style, which was popular in Europe from the 1820s and in North America from the 1840s. The Rococo Revival style was eventually superceded by the Louis XVI Revival. *(c.1850–60; ht 91.5cm/36in; value **J**)*

KEY FACTS

- **REGILDING** the fashion for regilding in the 18th and 19th centuries often results in less crisp detailing, as the carved decoration becomes obscured under layers of gesso and gilding; it is not uncommon to find 18th-century furniture with four or five layers of gilding or gold-painted decoration; the commercial value of a piece of giltwood furniture is affected by the quality and condition of the giltwood surface
- **FAKES** many giltwood console tables in the style of Kent have been faked; the provenance of the piece is therefore important
- **COLLECTING** the variety of tables is huge and usually there is something available for every pocket; many console tables were made as vehicles for the expensive marble that topped them, and those examples that retain their original tops will command a premium; pier tables were usually made in pairs, and the value is considerably more for two

See also Sideboards and serving tables, pp.60–61

Sideboards and serving tables

From the Middle Ages, social status was reflected by the lavish display of both the delicacies and the plate that were arranged on the "buffet" or sideboard in the principal Eating Room. Although the dresser, with its tiered superstructure, sufficed during the medieval period, during the 16th century it was superseded in the most sophisticated households by the court cupboard, which was an early type of sideboard.

▼ Serving table
The typical Neo-classical motifs used on this English George III mahogany bow-fronted serving table are the central tablet carved in relief with a Classical urn hung with drapery, oval paterae, heading the fluted legs that terminate in block feet.
(c.1770; ht 59cm/23in; value **L***)*

► Console desserte
Furniture of the French Directoire period (1795–9), named after the government of the time, was inspired by both Greek and Etruscan designs. The first stirrings of this restrained style were felt during the Transitional period (mid-18th century) when the excesses of the Rococo were beginning to be rejected in favor of a more Classical style (Louis XVI), and this *console desserte* typifies the restrained *goût Greque*.
(c.1795–9; ht 88cm/34½in; value **H***)*

18TH-CENTURY SERVING TABLES AND SIDEBOARDS
During the first half of the 18th century serving tables were closely related in form to pier tables, with either wooden or marble tops above plain friezes. The earliest 18th-century examples were usually of walnut, painted or of gilt-gesso, the friezes supported on cabriole legs often joined by stretchers. However, during the 1730s such serving tables became increasingly elaborate under the influence of the William Kent (*c.*1685–1748) and Matthias Lock (*c.*1710–65), with marble tops often being supported by richly carved architectural friezes. This architectural language gave way to a lighter, freer Rococo style, and in *The Gentleman and Cabinet-Maker's Director* (1754–62) by Thomas Chippendale (1718–79) there were several designs for "sideboard" tables of carved mahogany in the Rococo, Gothick, and Chinese fretted styles.

However, these too did not provide for the utilitarian considerations of storage, and although some serving tables from the 1750s were fitted with "pot-cupboards" to the side, it was not until the early 1760s, with the introduction of urns and pedestals conceived en suite with the serving table, that the need for storage was first addressed. This concept was adopted and popularized by the brothers Robert and James Adam in *Works in Architecture* (1773–8), as such suites lent themselves perfectly to the Neo-classical idiom of the

1770s, the pedestals serving as cellarets and plate-warmers to complement the serving table, while the urns often held iced water, or water for the butler to wash the cutlery and plates. Often with break-front tablets to the friezes, these serving tables were usually mahogany. In 1779 the firm of Gillow (est. *c.*1730) of Lancaster, introduced a new type of sideboard, usually with a serpentine or bow-fronted top above a central drawer and kneehole, flanked to one side by a cellaret-drawer, simulated as two drawers and containing bottle-divisions, balanced by a further pair of drawers on the other side. Standing on six tapering legs, perhaps with trailed husks in carved relief or marquetry, and standing on plain or spade feet, such George III sideboards depend primarily on the figuring of the timber for decorative impact – hence the frequent use of flame-figured mahogany. Sideboards were often mounted with brass galleries, upon which fresh linen was hung; Thomas Sheraton (1751–1806) expanded the brass gallery to new extremes in *The Cabinet-Maker and Upholsterer's Drawing Book* (1791–1802), depicting a gallery in the form of a stylized foliate arch incorporating candelabra.

North American sideboards of the Federal period were often based on the published designs of Sheraton, George Hepplewhite (*d.*1786), and Thomas Shearer. Examples usually had square, tapering legs decorated with husks, and such details as quarter fans, and ovals inlaid with shells and the American eagle, motifs often used by cabinet-makers working in Baltimore and Annapolis in Maryland.

▼ Sideboard attributed to Thomas Seymour (1771–1848)
Each prosperous American city produced its own version of the sideboard. The mahogany veneers, light crossbanding, reeded and turned legs, and ivory-urn keyhole escutcheons are typical of Boston sideboards.
(c.1805–15; ht 1m/3ft 3in; value **Q***)*

TABLES A GIBIER AND CONSOLES DESSERTES

In France and northern Europe, the 17th-century marble buffet enjoyed enduring popularity well into the 18th century. However, during the Régence (1715–23) and early Louis XV periods, the *table à gibier*, upon which cooked game was served, became more elaborate, with the marble slab often supported by an oak or a painted base extravagantly carved with acanthus, *espagnolette* masks, and Rococo shells, as well as with Bacchic symbolism appropriate to a room for entertaining.

With Neo-classicism a new linear *console desserte* or sideboard emerged. Often of mahogany or satinwood, it is usually of bow-fronted rectangular form with two tiers of gray-veined white marble above a richly mounted frieze applied with foliate ormolu arabesques, perhaps supported on stop-fluted turned tapering legs, and with a mirrored panel to the reverse. Although the frieze usually encloses a central drawer and, on the most sophisticated examples, spring-loaded drawers to the curved sides, the *console desserte* was principally designed not for storage but for the display of delicacies and plate in the 17th-century tradition. Although examples mounted with Sèvres porcelain plaques were made in the 1780s by such cabinet-makers as Martin Carlin (*d*.1785), they became increasingly restrained in decoration during the Directoire period (1795–9). This form was widely copied in the late 18th century in Russia, Sweden, and Germany, and in the 19th century when the extravagantly mounted examples found favor again.

19TH-CENTURY SERVING TABLES AND SIDEBOARDS

The *Cabinet-Maker and Upholsterer's Drawing Book* (1791–1802) by Thomas Sheraton (1751–1806) also included a design for "a sideboard with knife cases," and this formed the prototype for the early 19th-century pedestal sideboard. Rather than treating the sideboard and flanking pedestals as separate elements, Sheraton's design united them, removing the back legs of the bow-fronted central section and instead supporting it by flanking pedestals. In the first half of the 19th century, pedestal sideboards were manufactured in large quantities, by which time the design had evolved and been considerably simplified. Invariably very well-made, veneered with richly figured flame mahogany, they had bow-fronted central sections which were no longer supported by tapering legs but by the flanking pedestals, which were "battered" or tapered in the manner popularized by Baron Vivant Denon (1747–1825) in

▲ Serving table
This type of monumental George IV mahogany serving table was often made with matching pedestals. The thick top is supported by four paneled legs, which are carved with grapevines and end with panther feet. Importantly these were all conscious references to Bacchus, the god of Wine and Hospitality, whose carriage was drawn by panthers; they were therefore seen as suitable motifs to be used on furniture in a room for entertaining.
*(c.1825; ht 95cm/37in; value **L**)*

▼ Pedestal sideboard
English mahogany pedestal sideboards of this type were were made in large quantities during the early 19th century. Although rather plain and restrained they usually represent excellent value for money both in terms of quality and the lavish timbers employed.
*(c.1820; ht 1.1m/3ft 7in; value **H**)*

his *Aventures dans la basse et la haute Egypte* (1802). Similarly, the linen-hung brass galleries were discarded in favor of solid pedimented splashbacks, often carved with stylized foliage scrolls.

Early 19th-century serving tables, almost always conceived en suite with the dining-chairs and dining-table, were altogether bolder than their 18th-century counterparts and as George Smith (active *c*.1786–1828) stated in *A Collection of Designs for Household Furniture and Interior Decoration* (1808): "These articles of so general use can scarcely be made of any other wood than mahogany." However, indigenous woods such as oak and brown oak also enjoyed renewed popularity in the 1820s. Often with shaped tops and plain, molded friezes, serving tables and sideboards were frequently enriched with Bacchic ornament, of vines, grapes, and satyrs, as promoted by George Smith as being appropriate for the dining-room. They were often fitted with shaped, pedimented, or scrolled backboards to the reverse, which were often removed in the 19th century and replaced with brass galleries.

The sideboards and serving tables of the later 19th century are inevitably inspired by their earlier prototypes. However, they are invariably more lavish and excessive in their decoration. During the 1830s exuberant foliate carved decoration prevailed, but this was in turn superseded by sideboards and serving tables in the "Jacobethan" Revival style, culminating in the late 19th century in Georgian Revival sideboards, with their characteristic Adam-inspired marquetry inlay.

KEY FACTS

- COLLECTING Regency pedestal sideboards can represent great value for money, as they are of a consistently high quality and many were made; they can also be seen as being as rather unfashionable at present, owing to their somewhat heavy form
- ALTERATIONS serving tables and pedestal sideboards have often been altered in both width and depth to make them more commercial: look at the proportions, see if any drawers and veneers have been replaced, or if the back has been altered, or the legs moved; look out for sideboards with later legs: legs should always be constructed of one piece, and although cuts are often hidden behind the decorative molding or crossbanding just below the upper section, differences in color and timber should reveal an alteration

See also Marriages, alterations and fakes, and care, pp.26–7

Dressing tables

The term "dressing table" was used as early as the 17th century to describe a small table designed and fitted for a lady or gentleman's toilet. Such tables became increasingly elaborate and ingenious in design during the 18th century, when they were also known as "toilet tables." Dressing tables were often multipurpose and were also used as desks, with added writing slides, or as small side tables.

BEFORE 1800

In the 17th century, the dressing table was generally small and fitted with two or three drawers, with a shallower drawer in the center to allow for knee room. During the 18th century a free-standing looking or toilet glass, sometimes with uprights fitted into a box base with drawers, would be stood upon the table surface. A looking glass soon became an essential part of the table, either in a fixed easel frame or in increasingly ingenious mechanical designs in which the glass sank or folded into the table when not in use. By the mid-18th century dressing tables with kneeholes or pedestals that could be used both for the toilet and for writing were produced. Elaborate examples in such woods as

◀ **Dressing table**
In this mahogany and ormolu-mounted Empire example, the mirror is on a swing frame, and the concave under-tier allows the user to stand or sit as close to the table as necessary. The marble in the molded top prevented damage from water or other liquids.
(early 19th century; ht 1.3m/4ft 3in; value **G***)*

burr-walnut included a cupboard at the back of the kneehole section, sets of drawers on either side, and a top that lifted to reveal a mirror and fixed compartments for storing toilet accessories; alternatively, mirrors and storage compartments might be concealed in end drawers that swung out, or mirrors simply folded down when not in use. There were equally elaborate designs for dressing tables with mirrors fixed on carved supports on tables with four legs and decorative draperies. By the mid-18th century the dressing table was established as part of leading designers' repertoire. *The Gentleman and Cabinet-Maker's Director* (1754–62) by Thomas Chippendale (1718–79) contains a design for such a "toilet table," and a variation of this design, known as a *toiletta*, was shown in another contemporary book of furniture design, *The Universal System of Household Furniture* (1762) by John Mayhew (1736–1811) and William Ince (*c.*1738–1804). George Hepplewhite (*d.*1786) included dressing-table designs in *The Cabinet-Maker and Upholsterer's Guide* (1788–94), and Thomas Sheraton (1751–1806) designed elegant Neo-classical dressing tables with domed tops, and is credited with the development of the popular kidney-shaped dressing table.

An alternative tradition was the small table that was transformed into a dressing table by the addition of a free-standing mirror. The term lowboy was used for this as such tables were clearly based on the lower part of the tallboy (or chest-on-stand). Early 18th-century lowboys were designed, and known, as dressing tables, and are classic examples of early 18th-century English furniture. They were generally made of walnut veneer (oak and mahogany were used on later Georgian examples), with solid walnut stretcher less cabriole legs with pad feet. The form usually included a center drawer flanked by two side drawers, a shaped and carved apron, and a flat veneered top on which a free-standing toilet mirror could be placed. The fashion for the Queen Anne period lowboy in North America began 20 years later than in England but lasted longer. Walnut was the preferred wood, cherry and maple were used in New England, and mahogany was in use from the 1740s.

AFTER 1800

Before *c.*1820 mahogany dressing tables were produced in the style of contemporary sideboards and may well have doubled up as small side tables. A small gallery along the top of such a table may be the only clue to the dual function. Kneehole dressing tables with foldaway mirrors were also produced, but in the restrained forms typical of the period, often with bow fronts and square tapering legs. In France, dressing tables in the Empire style were characterized by simple lines, minimal carving, and ormolu mounts. They were usually made of mahogany and often incorporated marble tops.

During the Victorian period there was a rapid increase in furniture production, and dressing tables for both men and women were made in large numbers, often as parts of bedroom suites, and in a variety of

---

THE PHILADELPHIA STYLE

The Rococo style was embraced in Philadelphia, the largest and most prosperous city in North America, from the mid-18th century. Although the political climate discouraged the importing of goods from England, London cabinet-makers came to work in the city, one of the most important being Thomas Affleck (1740–95). He arrived in Philadelphia in 1763 with a copy of Chippendale's *The Gentleman and Cabinet-Maker's Director* (1754–62). This design book influenced the development of the style, which is sometimes called "Philadelphia Chippendale." More important than design books were the carvers such as James Reynolds (*c.*1736–94), Hercules Courtenay (*c.*1744–84), and Nicholas Bernard and Martin Jugiez, who were in partnership between 1763 and 1786 and were responsible for some of the best Rococo work. While the Rococo style continued during the early 1780s, it soon gave way to the Federal style of the new Republic.

◀ **Dressing table**
Also called a lowboy in North America, the dressing table and matching high chest-of-drawers (sometimes called a highboy) are the epitome of the Philadelphia style. The knees of the cabriole legs, the claw-and-ball feet, and the apron on this mahogany example provide a place for virtuoso Rococo carving. The lowboy, which went out of fashion in London in the mid-18th century, was made in North America until the early 1780s.
(c.1755–60; ht 78.5cm/30¾in; value **Q***)*

styles and woods. In general the mirror, which came in various shapes and might swing or be fixed, was now centrally placed in a decorated frame on a stand that often formed part of a superstructure with drawers on top of the table itself. Quality varied greatly, from the worst excesses of heavy, over-elaborate pieces in imitations of historical styles to simple, unpretentious, and now sought-after painted pine dressing tables, with porcelain drawer handles and casters and built-in adjustable mirrors that would have been part of modest bedroom suites. The Victorian fashion for papier-mâché furniture extended to the dressing table, and such companies as Jennens & Bettridge (active 1816–64) in Birmingham produced tables with integral adjustable mirrors, cabriole legs, and elaborate japanned decoration on a black background. The multiplicity of designs inspired by the interest in historical styles included Gothic Revival oak dressing tables with lancet-shaped mirrors, frieze rails with carved arcading, and table bases with solid ends pierced by stretchers.

◄ Dressing table attributed to the firm of Gillow (est. c.1730)
Although it closely resembles the design for contemporary desks, with its concave center and central drawer flanked by drawers either side, this piece is identifiable as a dressing table by the three-quarter reeded gallery with a central palmette and glass top. It is also of the same standard type as that for a washstand, which meant that the firm could easily adapt the basic design. The wood is mahogany, and the piece is attributed to the firm of Gillow of Lancaster, an important manufacturer of the period.
(early 19th century; ht 90cm/35½in; value **H***)*

► Dressing table
During the 19th century a dressing table was usually made as part of a bedroom suite; this comprised a wardrobe, a chest-of-drawers, and a pair of night tables. Dressing tables were made in vast quantities during the Victorian and Edwardian periods. Although such an example as this British mahogany chest with satinwood banding is extremely common, the craftsmanship is generally of a consistently good quality.
(c.1900; ht 1.5m/4ft 11in; value **D***)*

◄ Dressing table
The elegant yet playful curves of the French Rococo Revival are used to advantage in this French dressing table. The porcelain plaques are in the style of mid-18th-century ones made by the Sèvres porcelain factory (est. 1756) and are painted with Rococo-style cherubs and flowers. Although the design and decoration are basically 18th century, particularly in the use of such exotic woods as kingwood for the parquetry, and the liberal use of ormolu mounts and porcelain plaques, such an excessive form did not actually exist in mid-18th century France. Mirrors were almost always separate, so this is clearly a 19th-century revival form.
(c.1860; ht 1.4m/4ft 7in; value **H***)*

By the end of the century such London retail outlets as the firms of Liberty & Co. (est. 1875) and Heal & Son (est. 1800) were commissioning and selling simple, plain or stained, well-designed oak and ash dressing tables with adjustable swing mirrors and two drawers that were embellished only by elegant proportions and good craftsmanship. Also modestly priced are the Edwardian mahogany dressing tables, often in Neo-classical style, with shield-shaped (reminiscent of Hepplewhite's shield-back chair) or oval-shaped mirrors over two long drawers supported on square tapering legs. More elaborate pieces with Sheraton-style inlay, mirrors supported by superstructures with drawers, or more complicated forms, such as a kidney-shaped kneehole dressing table, will of course be more highly priced.

KEY FACTS

- **MARKS** furniture by Gillow is signed in pencil under one of the drawers by the craftsman, and is often accompanied by a design number; Gillow kept meticulous records of its designs, and it is possible to check these in the firm's pattern-books
- **COLLECTING** those dressing tables that are of a simple, versatile form, and that can be used for a number of purposes (e.g. a lowboy that can be used as a side table), are generally far more commercial than those that have fixed mirrors; it is common today for bedrooms to have fitted furniture (including cupboards, wardrobes, and dressing tables), which can make older dressing tables redundant; original handles, good-quality veneering, and good color and patina will all add to value

See also Bedside tables and washstands, pp.110–11; Mirrors, pp.112–13

Tea tables and tripod tables

TEA TABLES

Tea was first imported into Europe by the Dutch East India Company in the early 17th century, but it was not until the late 17th century that tables specifically designed for supporting the cups, saucers, and kettles required for drinking tea and coffee were introduced. Very few late 17th-century tea tables survive. Contemporary documents suggest that the earliest examples were either of imported Chinese or Japanese lacquer or japanned in imitation of Oriental decoration.

Although it was initially fashionable to drink tea in the many tea-gardens around London, by the mid-18th century such establishments had become increasingly poorly regarded and it became customary to entertain at home. Inevitably this led to the production of lavishly carved ornamental tea tables in the Rococo taste, and even to the construction of special tea-rooms, often appropriately decorated in the chinoiserie taste.

TRIPOD TABLES

Tripod tables were also made for serving tea, and, although provincial examples were made in indigenous woods, most English 18th-century tripod tables were constructed of solid mahogany. Designed to be folded up and stored away when not in use, they are invariably fitted with either bird-cage supports or tilt-top mechanisms. The former, whereby the top of the shaft is secured by a wedge into the bird cage, which in turn is fixed to the underside of the table by a hinge, allows the top to be removed, and was employed on the most sophisticated English and American tripod tables until the 1760s. Its slightly cumbersome form was replaced by the simpler tilt-top mechanism, whereby the platform at the top of the shaft is joined to the top by two lateral bearers and fixed by a lacquered-brass catch.

During the reigns of George I and George II, tea and coffee were usually served from a silver tray or salver, the tripod table itself being initially conceived as a plain stand. The earliest tripod tables have, therefore, a plain, circular tilt-tops above ring-turned columnar, gun-barrel, baluster or vase-shaped shafts, supported by cabriole legs with pointed pad feet. From the 1750s tripod tables, referred to as "claw tables" by William Ince (*c*.1738–1804) and John Mayhew (1736–1811) in

The Universal System of Household Furniture (1762), became increasingly elaborate, with acanthus and C-scroll carved knees, spirally turned shafts, and claw-and-ball feet. The most expensive examples tend to be the slightly smaller kettle stands of the 1750s, which were conceived to support tea kettles only. Quirky regional types exist, perhaps the most distinctive being the "Manx" tripod, its cabriole legs terminating in shoe-shaped feet, the legs sometimes even carved with breeches.

Although tripod tables are traditionally associated with England and North America they were also executed in Germany, The Netherlands, Scandinavia, and France. From the late 17th century, Dutch painters often decorated the scalloped oval tops of plain-oak tripod tables with mythological scenes and imaginary landscapes, and this tradition survived well into the 19th century. In Brunswick, in Germany, tea tables, invariably with tripod supports, were decorated with "beadwork," whereby polychrome glass beads were strung together to create "mosaic" pictures, often of a walled garden. This concept was later applied to Sevrès porcelain-mounted tables executed for Louis XVI and his court. In the late 18th century the English style became extremely fashionable, and cabinet-makers in Sweden, Denmark, The Netherlands, and France executed furniture in it. The age of satinwood (1780–1800) was particularly admired by cabinet-makers in The Netherlands, and Dutch tripod tables are distinguished by their slender downswept legs, joined halfway up by a circular platform and frequently decorated with elaborate parquetry. Although the thick circular tops appear to be too heavy for the slender bases, these Dutch tripod tables are rendered stable by the construction of the legs, which are veneered onto steel cores.

Although solid mahogany still prevailed, from the 1760s tripod tables were veneered in exotic timbers. No doubt influenced by the French fashion for lighter, more delicate, and refined furniture, they are lighter in design; the heavy mahogany tops and bold proportions of earlier examples were discarded in favor of thin, veneered oval and octagonal tops. Similarly, the richly carved turned shafts were replaced by thinner supports,

◄ **Tripod table**
Although this very simple English George II tripod table is made of good-quality mahogany (typical for the period), provincial examples, were often executed in oak or elm. The signs of fine quality in this table include its rich depth of color (always a determining factor when considering the value of these tables), the fine line of the legs that end in pad feet, and the simple, yet highly sophisticated proportions.
(*c.1750*; *ht 72cm/28½in; value H*)

◄ **Tea table**
The rectangular top of this mahogany tray-top tea table has carved applied molding with notched corners, and candle slides that pull out of the frame. The swelled aprons have rhythmic cyma profiles and integrate with the C-scrolls at the knees, a characteristic of English Georgian furniture used in eastern Massachusetts. The graceful cabriole legs end in platform pad feet. This is a typical example of a group of tea tables, made in Boston where "square" tea tables were preferred to circular pedestal-base tables. In Britain a "square" table with a gallery around the top is known as a silver table.
(*c.1735–70; ht 68cm/26¾in; value Q*)

▲ **Tea table**
Round, tilt-top tea tables with turned pillars and tripod bases were popular in Philadephia in the 1770s. This mahogany example is one of a pair of the largest and most elaborately carved Rococo tables, with a scalloped top made from a single richly grained mahogany board. The fine carving has been attributed to Nicholas Bernard and Martin Jugiez, who were in partnership from the late 1750s to 1783. The bird-cage mechanism, with baluster supports under the top allowing it to turn and tilt, was used more often in Philadelphia than anywhere else.
(*c.1768–75; ht 71.5cm/28¼in; value Q*)

► Tripod table

During the Regency period ebony was used to great effect by furniture-makers, whose work bears witness to the revival of Egyptian, Greek, and Roman ornament and form; for example, ebony or ebonized inlay was used as a deliberate Classical reference to Etruscan ornament. This very simple tripod table is of a type that was made in large numbers, and its bobbin-turned shaft has been ebonized (painted in black), in the antique manner. The bobbin turning is also an antiquarian reference to 17th-century furniture. Although the oval top is common, many other types were also made.

*(1810–20; ht 1m/3ft 3in; value **G**)*

1860) in London. Although Chippendale Revival tripod tables are usually betrayed by their exaggerated ornament, unusual proportions, and the quality of the timber, they are not always so easily distinguished, particularly if they are plain 18th-century examples that have been later carved and embellished.

PIECRUST "SUPPER" TABLES

In the mid-18th century, tripod tables began to be used not only as tea and coffee tables but also as intimate "supper" tables. While tea tables continued to be made with circular or waved rectangular tops, often enriched with balustraded galleries, supper tables with larger "piecrust" or scalloped, dished tops emerged. These piecrust tops, often dished with circular compartments "for holding Each a set of China," as Chippendale stated in *The Gentleman and Cabinet-Maker's Director* (1754–62), are often exceptionally lavishly carved with rocaille decoration, shells, and foliage. Although cabinet-makers such as William Vile (*c*.1700–67) and John Cobb (*c*.1715–78) would certainly have supplied such elaborate piecrust tables, the majority were simpler in form. Others were elaborately decorated with intricate mother-of-pearl or brass inlay.

TEAPOYS

The word "teapoy," from the Sanskrit for "three feet," therefore a tripod, was first used in the Regency period to describe a free-standing vessel for storing tea. Usually in the form of rectangular caskets fitted with lidded tea-caddies and central glass mixing-bowls, they were often supported by central shafts and platforms with four downswept legs with scrolled or claw feet. Frequently the most elaborate examples in lacquer were made for export to Europe. Ivory and sandalwood teapoys were imported via the Anglo-Indian trading links, the finest being made in Vizagapatnam, India. The demand for such items could not be satisfied from abroad alone, and japanned or penwork-decorated examples were made in Europe. Other British teapoys were made of rosewood, perhaps enriched with brass inlay or gadrooned carving to the base of the casket. By the 1820s, teapoys tended to be quite large and relatively plain, with the exception of those of Tunbridgeware.

▼ Teapoy

The majority of teapoys were intended, as with this Regency example with its chinoiserie decoration, as vessels to hold tea. While the most decorative teapoys came from India, Europe provided a secondary, albeit less embellished, source. British-produced teapoys were the plainest of all, with the exception of those of Tunbridgeware, a decorative technique where tiny pieces of timber are cut and intricately applied like mosaic to produce geometric borders and mosaic pictures. It was practiced in Tunbridge Wells, Kent, during the 19th century.

*(c.1810; ht 69cm/27in; value **G**)*

while the cabriole legs gave way to plain, perhaps even slightly arched or downswept legs of square profile. The rare examples from the 1760s that are enriched with carving to the legs are decorated with Neo-classical ornament such as husks and anthemia.

Late 18th-century and Regency tripod tables tend to be far smaller than their earlier counterparts, owing to the fashion for small portable tables. They usually had oval or octagonal tops (although square and rounded rectangular ones were increasingly popular from the 1780s), which were often elaborately inlaid and decorated. While pictorial floral marquetry in the French manner was greatly admired in the 1760s, it was gradually superseded by Neo-classical ornament in the 1770s and 1780s, by geometric parquetry in specimen woods in the 1790s, and by japanned chinoiserie or penwork decoration and brass inlay, in the style of André-Charles Boulle (1642–1732) on a rosewood, ground in the Regency period.

Throughout the 19th century tripod tables were influenced by different revival styles and the eclecticism of the period; during the 1820s and 1830s the influence was medieval and Baroque, with barley-twist supports and ebony and ebonized surfaces, while the Rococo style was revived in the mid-19th century with tripod tables often elaborately carved with C-scrolls, acanthus, and mythical beasts, and usually either of giltwood or at least parcel gilded. The late 19th century also saw a revival of the style of Thomas Chippendale (1718–79) in the work of firms such as Wright & Mansfield (est.

► Tea table

Marquetry and parquetry decoration returned to fashion in the 1840s, and this demand was to some extent satisfied by Italian cabinet-makers in Sorrento, who specialized in the production of elaborately inlaid circular occasional tables, decorated with rustic scenes. The form of the legs harks back to the 17th-century S-scroll form.

*(c.1840; ht 75cm/29½in; value **E**)*

KEY FACTS

- TRIPOD TABLES beware of tables that have been carved at a later date (particularly in the mid-19th century), usually on the knees, legs, and shafts, as a way of making them more expensive; also beware of tripod tables made from the bases of 18th-century polescreens with a later table top: this may be possible to detect by looking at the consistency of color and patination
- ALTERATIONS some flat tops were later shaped with piecrust rims, in which case the table tops will have been "dished"; be careful that the screws of the snap catch do not come through to the top, which would indicate that the wood is very thin and has been scooped out
- TEAPOYS those decorated with chinoiseries were certainly intended as containers for tea; teapoys were fitted with locks to keep the precious contents away from prying hands; some teapoys have been converted into work boxes, in which case their fittings will have been removed, and this will affect the value; penwork and Tunbridgeware teapoys are widely collected

See also Occasional tables, pp.66–7

Occasional tables

In the late 17th and 18th centuries the great palaces and chateaux of Europe were furnished in the Parisian fashion, whereby suites of chairs, tables, and *torchères* (candlestands) were placed against the walls; this left the center of the room open for formal receptions and audiences. Although seat furniture could be drawn into the center for more informal gatherings, inevitably pier tables were less movable and this gave rise to a need for smaller tables that could be brought in for "occasional" use.

EARLY OCCASIONAL TABLES

The earliest occasional tables, recorded in the second half of the 17th century in Paris, Augsburg, and Vienna are of rectangular form, usually with frieze drawers, and were often lavish commissions that are masterpieces of the cabinet-maker's art. Frequently constructed in exotic or expensive materials, such as amber, silver, or ivory, they are extremely rare.

However, at the court of Louis XV, with its increasingly informal social gatherings, the demand for free-standing tables increased. Richly mounted in ormolu and veneered with floral marquetry, architectural *capricci* (fantasies), or illusionistic parquetry, or painted with *vernis Martin*, the French *table ambulante* was emulated throughout Europe. The rapid dissemination of Parisian taste was in part a result of the huge number of foreign cabinet-makers who had either visited or served their apprenticeship under a cabinet-maker in Paris. Under their direction, mid-18th-century occasional tables became not only more elaborate but also more utilitarian. Drawers were fitted with pen-trays and inkwells to create writing tables, while a love of mechanics led not only to the introduction of spring-loaded drawers, on *tables en*

▲ Nest of tables
This type of arrangement of table was made most popular by the firm of Gillow (est. *c.*1730) of Lancaster. This British set of Regency tables is made of bird's-eye maple and rests on twin ring-turned column supports. The crossbanded tops are inlaid with narrow rosewood bandings. This was a particularly popular form of occasional table in the 19th century, and sometimes one of the tables has a chessboard set on it. There are usually four tables in a set.
(c.1810; ht 1m/3ft 3in; value **H***)*

chiffonières, but also to more complicated forms: *tables à transformation*, or metamorphic tables, which could convert into reading tables, library steps, or a *bonheur du jour*; rarer still was the *table rafraîchissoir*, with hinged, fitted compartments devised to conceal the plates, glasses, and provisions for a light supper.

Developed from the late 17th-century *table de cabaret*, a new type of occasional table appeared in the later 18th century as cocoa was imported from the 1750s and the consumption of hot drinks increased. This type of table was required to withstand the heat of coffee and chocolate pots. Although white marble certainly sufficed, in the 1750s the *marchand-mercier* (dealer in luxury goods) Simon-Philippe Poirier (1720–85) conceived a most luxurious refinement. He acquired a decorated porcelain tray, without handles, from Sèvres, and commissioned an elaborate table base to support it; thus the concept of porcelain-mounted furniture was born. This type was greatly admired at the French and Russian courts and was almost exclusively supplied through Poirier and his successor Dominique Daguerre (*d.*1796), who established a shop in London; such furniture became fashionable throughout Europe, even after the Revolution.

PLAINER OCCASIONAL TABLES

Although initially conceived as luxury items, the practical nature of occasional tables inevitably resulted in simpler, more affordable examples for a wider public. In particular, folding or collapsible tables, upon which food or drinks could be served and which could be easily stored away, were particularly desirable for informal entertaining. Of this type, perhaps the most widespread design is the so-called coaching table, first engraved by John Claudius Loudon (1783–1843) in the early 19th century. Closely related in form to the mid-Georgian butler's tray on a stand, and usually of mahogany or oak, these coaching tables were popular throughout Britain and North America from the early 19th century.

COMPARING TWO OCCASIONAL TABLES

The *table en chiffonière* on the left is by Martin Carlin (*d.*1785) Executed in amaranth and tulipwood, with dot-trellis parquetry ormolu, and a Sèvres porcelain plaque (1782), it exemplifies the refined luxury of Louis XVI cabinet-making. During the second quarter of the 19th century, particularly in Britain, there was a renewed enthusiasm for late 17th- and 18th-century French decorative arts. The table on the right, by the firm of Town & Emmanuel (1830–40), which stylized itself as "dealers and manufacturers in antique furniture," is clearly inspired by Carlin's prototype. However, its porcelain plaque is a later French porcelain plate of Sèvres pattern, which is painted with a fake Sèvres mark (interlaced "L"s) on the underside. Similarly, the mounts, although probably cast from 18th-century originals, lack the finesse and quality of Carlin's mounts, with less meticulous chasing. This revival continued in the late 19th century, and numerous faithful copies of Louis XV and Louis XVI furniture abound – they are, however, considerably less valuable than the originals.

► Two occasional tables
(1782 and 1830s; ht 78cm/30¾in; value for original **Q** *and for 19th-century copy* **L***)*

It was multi-purpose tables, particularly nests of quartetto tables, that enjoyed enduring popularity in the 19th century. First recorded in England in *The Cabinet Dictionary* (1803) by Thomas Sheraton (1751–1806), they were often made in the early 19th century in exotic woods such as rosewood, amboyna, ebony, and satinwood. The design of quartetto tables remained remarkably consistent during the first half of the 19th century, the legs becoming gradually heavier in form from the second quarter. Inevitably, Colonial cabinet-makers copied the English design, and although Chinese export examples in padouk, or ivory examples from Vizagapatnam in India, tend to follow English precedents, heavier, more florid examples in ebony from Goa also survive.

Although quartetto tables were often plain, with only crossbanded decoration to each rectangular tier, more elaborate ones were inlaid with a chequerboard to the smallest tier, and occasionally featured a removable, sliding ratchetted, lyre-shaped music stand, which was stored beneath the lowest tier. Although the form altered little, by the 1820s English cabinet-makers began to shy away from exotic hardwoods, reverting instead to indigenous woods such as pollard oak, burr-yew, and burr-elm, but these too were gradually superseded in the 1830s by the Parisian fashion for papier-mâché inlaid with mother-of-pearl.

SPECIMEN MARBLE TABLES
Since the mid-17th century, travellers to Italy on the Grand Tour had acquired panels or table tops of *pietre dure* (hardstones) as souvenirs from Florence. The Florentine workshops became the pre-eminent center for inlay in marbles specializing in panels and table tops with pastoral landscapes, birds, coats of arms, or sprays of flowers. However, for Grand Tourists with shallower purses, table tops decorated with the same motifs could be made of *scagliola* (powdered marble made into to a paste, applied to a gesso ground, and polished), and were a fraction of the cost. This technique enabled an almost painterly freedom in the designs and flourished particularly in the 18th century.

In the early 19th century, under the influence of Napoleon I, who had brought a considerable collection of marbles to Paris as spoils of war, there was a renewed

◄ **Occasional table**
Biedermeier tables are characterized by the use of such richly figured veneers as walnut and Karelian birch, and restrained ebonized or parcel-gilt decoration that is fundamentally Classical in inspiration. Owing much to the designs of Josef Ulrich Danhauser (1780–1829), they are frequently mounted or carved with Egyptian motifs, and stand on lion's-paw feet.
(early 19th century; ht 77cm/30¼in; value **H***)*

▼ **Occasional table**
Such 19th-century specimen marble occasional or *guéridon* tables such as this Italian example became increasingly simple in form and depended on the top for decorative impact.
(c.1850; ht 75cm/29½in; value **G***)*

taste for *guéridon* (candle-stand) tables that supported specimen-marble tops. Exported from Italy, and predominantly circular in form, they were usually inlaid with segments or geometrical patterns of specimen marbles, often on white marble or black slate grounds. Initially these featured Siena (yellow/ red), rosso antico (deep red), and Sicilian Jasper (green-flecked browny/orange) marbles, as well as alabaster and various precious and semi-precious stones such as lapis lazuli and Egyptian porphyry. From 1830 Russian malachite, imported from mines in the Urals, was much used. Such specimen marble *guéridons* became fashionable throughout Europe, and although Italian quarries satisfied much of the demand, northern Europe, especially Russia which had huge mineral reserves, and Britain, produced their own specimen tops. However, the availability of Italian marbles and hardstones was restricted, and they were often prohibitively expensive, so from the mid-19th century, polished slate and granite were used as inexpensive substitutes.

◄ **Coaching table**
This British mahogany coaching table features a hinged divided top on a chamfered X-frame support with turned stretchers. In spite of its name, it is quite possible that such tables were never used for serving refreshments on long coach journeys, and that they are actually a type of butler's tray on a stand. This form of table was produced in vast quantities in Britain and North America during the 19th and 20th centuries.
(early 19th century; ht 72cm/28½in; value **G***)*

KEY FACTS

- NESTS OF TABLES also called quartetto tables; often the height of these tables has been reduced, so look for uninterrupted decoration on the legs; check for reveneering or crossbanding of a later date – patina and consistency of color should be an indication of this; there are usually four tables in a nest, and if one is missing it will affect value; look for consistency of color with each table, and note how the color may change if a table has been protected from the light by the one above
- COACHING TABLES many examples were made in the 19th and 20th centuries
- SPECIMEN MARBLE TABLES many fake examples exist: generally one of the giveaways is that in fake tables resin has been used between the specimens, and when a pin is pushed into this it will make a hole; on the original tables, the specimens would have been set in solid bases of slate or marble, which will remain unmarked by the pin

See also Trays, knife-boxes, cutlery-urns, wine coolers, cellarets, and buckets, pp.118–9

Games and work tables

Small tables for recreational use, such as those for cards, games, and needlework, developed in tandem in Britain and France, each country's designs influencing the other's at different stages and providing a richness that has been imitated the world over. The earliest tables designed specifically for cards were introduced at the end of the 17th century. In the 18th century card-playing and gambling were immensely popular, and furniture-makers catered to an ever-eager market.

▲ Foldover card table

In the 18th century, circular tops on card tables were replaced by square surfaces; dished cylindrical corners held candlesticks and wells for money or counters. The top of this English mahogany table is hinged, with a baize-lined playing surface above a frieze drawer. Many better quality tables have a concertina action underneath.

(c.1735; ht 1m/3ft 3in; value J)

EARLY GAMES TABLES

Tables made c.1700 were often veneered with walnut, with circular folding tops and tapered baluster legs, one or two of which swung out to support the flap, held together by shaped stretchers. The French influence is apparent from about this time. Some of the new card tables were decorated in marquetry, and designed with the finely carved tripod bases that were then popular in France. But where the French made use of tortoiseshell and brass, the British typically employed a variety of indigenous woods including walnut.

Design and construction developed rapidly in Britain in the early 18th century as card-playing became a mania. The fabric, which had traditionally been placed over the surface of the table, now became a fully integrated part of the design, and was commonly made of baize. Simple cabriole legs and pad feet were gradually overtaken by designs of increasing boldness, such as club feet, in turn succeeded by claw-and-ball and lion's-paw.

From c.1730 mahogany became the most common timber used. The construction also developed: the flap supported by a swing leg, which was prevalent c.1700, ran concurrently with a

concertina action on the best-quality tables from c.1720. This was introduced to ensure greater symmetry and stability. Some of the more ingenious tables were designed to incorporate separate leaves for backgammon, chess, writing, and cards; such tables often have unusually deep friezes in order to hide the clumsy arrangement of leaves.

LATER GAMES TABLES

During the mid-18th century British tables became more elaborate. Shaped friezes, lion-masks, feathering, acanthus scrolls, naturalistic moldings, and scrolled feet all made their appearances in turn. Many of the tables were made in softwood and japanned. Tripod tables with triangular tops, for tredrille and other three-handed games, were also made at this time.

In France, tables were made for specific games: square for quadrille, round for brelan, triangular for tri, and marquetry tops for chess. From c.1730 to 1735 the Louis XV style evolved, signaling the triumph of graceful, sinuous lines. Furniture-makers gained complete mastery of their techniques, and design developed rapidly. Free-standing games tables were ideal vehicles for their skill, and were given cabriole legs with double bends, making elongated S-shapes, usually terminating in scrolls or volutes resting on small wooden cubes. Nearly all French games tables were decorated with marquetry in colored woods; Parisian furniture-makers tended to use chiefly imported woods, while provincial makers used regional olive, cherry, pear, and chestnut. Mahogany was unusual in France, and was mainly confined to the Bordeaux region because it entered the port on ships from the West Indies. Its use ceased completely when the British blockaded the French ports in 1806.

By 1770 Britain's enthusiasm for gambling and games had aroused such fervor that George III and Queen Charlotte forbade it at the royal palaces – with little effect. The design and metamorphosis of games tables continued apace. In the last quarter of the century, card

▲ Tric-trac table

Tric-trac was another name for backgammon. This mahogany table, inlaid with ebony and boxwood, may well have been made in a French coastal town, as mahogany was imported into France in such small quantities that it was rarely transported inland. Such tables had reversible tops: this one has a chessboard on one side and a plain top on the reverse. There is also a backgammon board in the recess. Each end, carved with basketwork, stands on cabriole legs with scrolled feet.

(c.1760; ht 74cm/29in; value I)

◄ Card table attributed to Michael Allison (d.1855)

The lyre was a favorite Neo-classical motif in the Federal period in the USA, and was used to support card, work, and sofa tables. This New York table features a pair of lyres with acanthus carving extending to its graceful saber legs, which end in cast brass feet. The lyre strings are brass. The carved drapery panel on its skirt is similar to a panel on a table stamped by Allison. He was one of many cabinet-makers working in the Federal style and was a contemporary of Duncan Phyfe (1768–1854).

(1810–20; ht 79.5cm/31¼in; value Q)

▼ Combined games and work table

This British walnut table has a flap top that opens, revolves around 90 degrees and presents a board inlaid for backgammon and chess. It also has a fitted drawer and a tasseled bag for holding needlework accessories. The carved legs, feet, and stretcher are typical of the Victorian period. *(c.1860; ht 75cm/29½in; value **G**)*

tables were made in a wide variety of shapes, such as oval, circular, square, broken-fronted, or serpentine, with tapered quadrilateral or cylindrical legs, in mahogany or satinwood, and were generally covered with green baize. The dishings for candles or counters were now omitted, and the flaps, when open, were constructed in any one of the earlier styles. In *The Cabinet-Maker and Upholsterer's Guide* (1788–94), George Hepplewhite (*d.*1786) wrote: "The fronts of these tables may be enriched with inlaid or painted ornaments; the tops also admit of great elegance in the same stiles," and he gave four such designs for inlaid or painted surfaces. Marquetry decoration is rare in this period, although in 1781 George, Prince of Wales (later George IV), ordered two circular mahogany card tables inlaid with differently colored woods.

When George III and Queen Charlotte failed to suppress gambling, Parliament intervened with better results. Thus card and games tables became less fashionable during the Regency period, and so fewer were made. In his pattern-book *The Cabinet-Maker and Upholsterer's Drawing Book* (1791–1802), Thomas Sheraton (1751–1806) even went so far as to remark that such tables were "oftener used than to good purpose,"

WORK TABLES

Introduced during the second half of the 18th century, work tables were small tables used for holding needlework accessories. They were originally fitted with either lifting tops or many small drawers, and the accoutrements of needlework, such as reels, needles, shuttles, and bobbins, could be safely stored under the worksurface.

By *c.*1810, work tables were often combined with games tables. Sheraton designed a number of work tables, including some with reversible tops, and increasingly they were constructed with folding demi-lune tops, so that they could be stored out of the way like a side table when not in use. Many games and combination games and work tables were now made using fabric (usually lute string or satin) pouches, or bags, suspended beneath the table for the storage of needlework. On many examples found today these have either been removed completely or are in a tattered state. The pouch design was readily taken up by other designers, who also fitted pouches onto small satinwood Pembroke tables and portable tables with curved wooden handles and small drawers.

19TH-CENTURY TABLES

By the mid-19th century designs had become increasingly convoluted, with the streamlined Regency elegance replaced by the heavier Victorian designs. The Victorians' penchant for resurrecting and "improving" styles of earlier periods gave rise to a number of different types of games and work tables in an eclectic combination of styles. All the basic forms of earlier periods continued to be made: swivel or flap tops, chess and backgammon boards that slid out, reversible tops for different games, D-end sections for holding counters and games pieces, and work pouches underneath where appropriate. The most popular woods were walnut and mahogany, and among the many different types of decoration used were exuberant carving in the Rococo Revival style, or inlaid brasswork on an ebony or hardwood ground in the style of André-Charles Boulle (1642–1732).

◄ Work table

This French work table has a a mirror-paneled lid, lift-out tray, and hinges and lock plates engraved with decoration. The hinged top makes it more impractical than those examples with drawers. *(mid-19th century; ht 70cm/27½in; value **G**)*

▲ Envelope card table

This British satinwood card table is decorated with Neo-classical decoration (foliate scrolls, urns, paterae and husks) in the style associated with the designer Thomas Sheraton (1751–1806). Although this type of table did exist in the 18th century, examples are extremely rare, and any table purporting to be 18th-century should alert suspicion. The leaves of the hinged, baize-lined top open out like an envelope to double the surface area. *(c.1890; ht 76cm/30in; value **H**)*

KEY FACTS

- MATERIALS British tables are mainly in walnut, mahogany, rosewood, and satinwood, while provincial examples are in oak; in France, Parisian makers used imported woods while provincial makers used regional woods such as olivewood, cherry, pear, and chestnut
- COLLECTING both card and work tables are generally quite decorative and can be relatively inexpensive; both types can be used as side tables; good-quality British foldover card tables (1720–70) have a concertina-action underframe, which will carry a premium; sometimes this underframe will have been replaced with a gateleg support – this should be evident by checking underneath where signs of wear should be visible; copies of the concertina-action games table were made in the 1920s and 1930s, but most were not intended to deceive; baize lining on card tables is nearly always replaced – this will not affect value; original pouches on work tables are rarely found

See also Pembroke and sofa tables, pp.56–7

Storage furniture

The earliest movable storage furniture was the hollowed-out log, and these primitive beginnings are still evoked by the name "trunk" for a traveling container. During the medieval period simple chests and coffers were employed as containers for a wide variety of objects ranging from textiles to musical instruments. However, such chests were not the most convenient form of storage, and as furniture-making techniques became more sophisticated during the 17th century, the chest-of-drawers evolved, as did other forms of furniture designed for storing specific objects such as books, linen, or clothing, or, in the very grandest examples, purely for the ostentatious display of wealth.

Chests and coffers

As the main storage furniture of the medieval period, chests were made in large numbers for all kinds of purposes. Chests are containers with flat, hinged lids; they usually have feet but no handles. They were designed for storage inside buildings, their feet keeping the contents clear of damp floors. Coffers are generally traveling trunks without feet that may have carrying handles and a domed lids. From the 13th century chests were produced by the joiner, and coffers by the cofferer, who was primarily a leather worker; coffin-making was another of his tasks.

► Chest
The low-relief carving on the frieze and front panels on this oak-paneled chest is typical of the huge numbers of chests made in various parts of Britain during the 17th and 18th centuries. Many carved patterns have strong regional associations; however, many were added during the 19th century.
(17th century; ht 95cm/37in; value G)

WOODS AND CONSTRUCTION

Oak was mainly used for chests in northern Europe, while walnut was used farther south. Pine was probably used much more than surviving examples would suggest; being subject to woodworm and rot, pre-19th-century pine chests are rare. Aromatic cypress and cedarwood was proof against moths and other insects, and was therefore used in chests intended for clothes and textiles, particularly in northern Italy and the southern alpine regions. Ash and lime were used, notably in southern Germany and Switzerland; chestnut and walnut in southern France. Sometimes more than one type of timber was employed in a single piece.

A simple chest consists of six planks nailed or rudimentarily dovetailed together, with the vertical "slab" ends shaped at the bottom to form feet. Another kind of boarded chest was the hutch, from the French *huche* (chest). In this form the horizontal planks of the front and back are housed at either end in wide vertical members (stiles), which extend downward as the feet. Hutch chests thus have their feet at the front and back,

▲ Cassone
Cassoni were important items of furniture in the Renaissance Italian palace. Many, such as this walnut example, reflect Classical inspiration in their sarcophagus form and decoration. The base was made in the 16th century; the feet, bottom panel, and part of the lid are of a later date.
(late 16th century; ht 70cm/27½in; value I)

EARLY CASSONI

In terms of domestic purposes, the Italian *cassone* has special significance: often, but not always, a marriage piece. Some *cassoni* were embellished with intricate inlay (intarsia) in different woods, while others were finely painted with figurative or mythological subjects or covered in designs in pastiglia, a technique where gesso was laid onto the surface, pressed or modeled into relief patterns, and then painted and gilded. Some of the richest 16th-century *cassoni* were of carved and polished wood, decorated with Mannerist designs. Important marriage *cassoni* were often made in pairs and decorated with heraldic devices and other symbols of the respective families. Farther down the social scale, *cassoni* were used to hold the linen, clothing, and household textiles that constituted a dowry. Some were carved with the initials of the bride and groom and the date, and were handed down.

▼ Coffer
The top of this German oak coffer indicates this type of furniture's origins as a traveling trunk; the domed shape could throw off the rain or sea-spray better than a flat top. Wooden coffers were replaced by smaller, lighter leather-bound traveling trunks. The raised cartouche panel is typical of the type made between the 17th and 19th century. It may have been a marriage piece, and the inscription reads "JOHANN ... MU ... ANNO 1772," which may have been added at a later date.
(c.1772; ht 67cm/26½in; value G)

unlike slab-ended chests with feet at the sides. Some chests of such housed or "clamped-front" construction have framing at the sides, and simple chip-carved decoration on the front. This form survived for high-quality chests in parts of Germany until the 18th century, by which time paneled construction was being used in most of Europe.

Chests of framed and paneled construction were developed during the 15th century, and by the 16th were produced in considerable quantities. Oak chests of the 17th and 18th centuries, and the large numbers of 19th-century reproductions of them, are most often of this type. The front and sides of a paneled chest consist of top and bottom horizontal rails united by vertical bars (muntins), with vertical stiles at each end. In most examples the stiles continue downward to form the feet. The panels, which were of thinner wood and slightly chamfered at the edges, were designed to slide into grooves in this framework, which was fastened together with mortises and tenons secured by wooden dowels. Lids were either paneled, like the front but without carved decoration, or composed of planks jointed together, some with cleated ends. Inside, many of these chests were fitted with a small compartment, or "till," which might be lockable for valuables.

► **Mule chest**

Pieces such as this oak mule chest represent the transition from the basic storage chest to the chest-of-drawers as we know it. First made during the 17th century, it consists of a lidded box compartment with drawers underneath, and is one of furniture's interesting hybrids. Some of the finest examples were decorated with inlay. These chests with drawers continued to be made in some areas until the 19th century. This fine English example is carved with four arched and molded panels above three drawers, quarter columns on the canted corners, and shaped front feet, and was probably made by a provincial craftsman in the mid-18th century.

*(mid-18th century; ht 90cm/35½in; value **G**)*

DECORATION

While carving was prevalent, inlays of contrasting woods, bone, or mother-of-pearl were not unusual. The most elaborate inlays were applied to the so-called "Nonsuch" chests made in Germany and the Low Countries, or by German and Flemish craftsmen working in England in the late 16th and the 17th century. They are distinctive for their patterned architectural inlays filled with vistas of turreted buildings in an intricate mosaic of colored woods. Pine chests were usually painted, particularly in Scandinavia, eastern Europe, Switzerland, and Austria; the mainly floral patterns varied from one region to another. Painted pine became popular in England during the 19th century, but decorative treatments were restrained, and mainly confined to simulations of timber or marble.

The carved decoration imitating pleated fabric, known as linenfold, was used for the panels of many chests. Formalized plants, geometrical patterns, and strapwork and low-relief arcading were other favorite designs for panels and framing. High-relief carving, particularly of figurative subjects, appeared on some northern European chests during the medieval and Renaissance periods.

THE PENNSYLVANIA DUTCH OR GERMAN STYLE

"Dutch" was a general term used in Pennsylvania for all Central European settlers who came to the region in the late 17th century from European villages ravaged by the Thirty Years War (1618–48). Rural settlers continued to use Germanic construction such as wedged dovetails, and also to paint their walnut, pine, or poplar furniture with decoration and the names and dates of their owner. The flat-top blanket chest became the most common piece of furniture in these households, often given to a young girl or boy to store their belongings. Rural communities developed their own styles, and regional differences are based on idiosyncratic construction and painted decoration: in Lancaster County there were three arched panels divided by pilasters; unicorns were painted on chests from Berks County, while stenciled designs were applied to those made around the area of Schwaben Creek in Northumberland County.

▼ **Blanket chest**

This example made in Lebanon County is typical of the painted pine dower chests made between 1770 and 1840. The two long hand-forged hinges visible on the lid terminate in tulip buds.

*(c.1790; ht 66cm/26in; value **O**)*

KEY FACTS

- COLLECTING chests were usually made of oak; after generations of wear and polishing, many examples have developed rich dark patinas; plain plank chests were of the slab-ended type; decoration was minimal, with scratch- or chip-carving; pre-16th-century furniture is usually heavy, and unaltered examples are very rare
- BEWARE decorative panels, sometimes taken from other pieces of furniture (e.g. beds, linen-presses, and wall paneling), were often "recycled" during the 19th century when vast quantities of traditional oak paneled chests were produced using both old and new timbers; many plain old chests were "improved" with chiseled or chip-carved decoration, or were inscribed with spurious dates and initials; such pieces are now antiques in their own right, but should be distinguished from wholly genuine 17th- and 18th-century (or earlier) pieces; feet have been frequently replaced – these were often detached during transportation

See also Marriages, alterations and fakes, and care, pp.26–7; Early chests-of-drawers, pp.78–9

Early cupboards and meubles en deux corps

During the medieval period a cupboard was an open shelf or set of boards for storing cups; what is now understood to be a cupboard – a receptacle fitted with doors intended for storage – was known in England as an aumbry. Later the two terms became interchangeable.

MEUBLES EN DEUX CORPS

The earliest cupboards-on-chests or *meubles en deux corps* – that is, furniture made in two sections and enclosing drawers in both the top and bottom sections – were originally employed for writing or storing papers and valuables. First recorded in Italy during the 16th century, these cupboards, such as *bambocci* made in Tuscany, were almost always made of walnut and are architectural in form; the fall fronts and cornices are supported by putti, armorial cartouches, and Classical arcades, or even carved in relief with biblical or mythological scenes.

Interestingly, it was these Mannerist figurative reliefs, often either biblical or mythological, which were rapidly adopted for the *meubles en deux corps* made for the court of Francis I at the chateau of Fontainebleau, outside Paris, during the mid-16th century. Usually made of walnut, or occasionally ebony, they were sometimes enriched with gilding or polychrome decoration. Conceived both for their decorative and their functional nature, with drawers to the base and either hinged fall fronts (the prototype for 17th-century escritoires or secrétaires) or doors enclosing fitted interiors with further drawers to the top, they are characterized by their exuberant decoration, invariably carved in relief with Mannerist caryatids and arabesques in the style associated with the designers Jacques Androuet DuCerceau (*c.*1515–85), whose engraved publications included *Petites Grotesques* (1550) inspired by the designs of the later Italian Renaissance, and Hugues Sambin

▶ Meuble en deux corps
This French walnut cupboard is a wonderful exhibition of Mannerist ornament, including herms, griffin cartouches, and strapwork. The vigorous carving depicts emblems of the benefits bestowed on good government; the figure panels depict Justice and Virtue on the doors of the upper section, and Peace and Plenty on the lower section. The top is supported by Classical figures, while the lower order is supported by herm pilasters. This example was further embellished during the 19th century.
(partly 16th century; ht 1.8m/5ft 11in; value L)

▼ Cupboard
Made in the southern Netherlands, this oak cupboard shows the influence of Moorish designs in the geometrically molded panel doors and use of inlaid ebony. This type of decoration may well have been introduced in the southern Netherlands by Spanish craftsmen. Note that the cupboard still retains its upper and lower stages.
(17th century; ht 1.5m/4ft 11in; value J)

(*c.*1520–1601), in his *L'Oeuvre de la diversité des termes dont on use en architecture* (1572). These forms and decorative motifs were also inspirational to cabinet-makers in the Low Countries. The 16th-century *meubles en deux corps* were enthusiastically collected throughout the 19th century, and thus numerous copies, as well as others composed of elements of both old and new pieces, survive in some number.

THE LOW COUNTRIES

During the early 17th century cupboards became increasingly important pieces of furniture in the Low Countries; some were carved with Mannerist motifs, while others were painted or decorated with inlay inspired by Italian prototypes. The main timbers used were oak and walnut, with bony inlay. An outstanding type made in the province of Holland in the northern Netherlands was the *Beeldenkast*, the name of which was taken from the term for the carved caryatid figures that decorated the uprights. Like the *meuble en deux corps*, the form was of an upper and lower stage separated by a frieze. In Zeeland in the southern Netherlands, which until 1648 was under Spanish rule, cupboards were carved with geometrical patterns probably introduced into the Netherlands by Spanish craftsmen, who were inspired by Moorish designs. Decorative inlay is particularly associated with workshops in Middelburg.

KEY FACTS

- MEUBLES EN DEUX CORPS these were widely copied during the 1850s through to the 1880s in both England and France while the Renaissance enjoyed a revival; it is extremely rare to find an example that has not had some alterations; 19th-century versions have less crisp carving and generally confuse the motifs used
- ALTERATIONS many pieces that purport to be 17th century were actually made up in the 19th; these can be difficult to identify, although check that the carved elements have not been cut off in mid-flow, and that color and patination are concurrent on all parts, and that distressing and wear are consistent with age

See also Chests-on-chests, pp.88–9

Cupboards and linen-presses before 1840

In the second half of the 17th century, the fashion, and indeed the resulting demand, for domestic furniture became increasingly widespread. Traditionally, walnut *cassoni* and oak coffers, often commissioned to celebrate a marriage, sufficed for the storage of linen and candles. However, their hinged tops prevented ready access to those items stored at the bottom, and so they were seen as impractical and outdated.

NORTHERN LINEN-PRESSES

Although chests and coffers continued to be produced in provincial areas, the princely courts of Burgundy, Frankfurt, Tuscany, and The Netherlands commissioned upright cupboards to fulfil their storage needs. Inspired by early Renaissance precedents, being both strongly architectural in form and linear in design, these presses are characterized by two doors, heavy cornices, molded plinths, and bun feet.

Although designs varied, 17th-century north European presses all display an important refinement from their 16th-century precursors. Unlike Renaissance *cassoni* and chests, which were often made in situ, these presses were executed in a workshop, and could be broken down into sections, which were easily transported and assembled. This was an important development for all carcase furniture and can be most easily seen in the way that the cornice is fixed to the sides – often with long, hand-cut screws or pins.

Usually of walnut or fruitwood, late 17th-century presses from Burgundy are evolved from the mule chest – featuring a storage drawer

► Nasenschrank
This oak storage cupboard is very typical of the style made in Frankfurt during the late 17th century. It has a wonderful sense of rhythm and movement as the light plays on the overhanging molded and canted cornice and on the molded and waved doors. Inside there are four shelves installed at a later date. *(partly late 17th century; ht 2.2m/7ft 3in; value L)*

◄ Armoire
This walnut example from Burgundy, France, is characterized by *à pointes de diamant* decoration, in which the panels are carved with diamond or lozenge-shaped decoration and mounted with cast-iron drop-handles and visible hinges, predicting 18th-century provincial armoires. The doors enclose three later shelves. *(c.1680; ht 2.5m/8ft 2in; value I)*

▼ Armoire
Walnut, as used for this armoire from Lombardy, Italy, was the most popular timber used for provincial furniture during this period. Originally it would have had bun feet, of the type seen on other armoires on this page, which have been replaced at a later date with bracket feet. *(c.1690–c.1710; ht 2.2m/7ft 3in; value H)*

within the plinth. This form was also adopted in the Spanish Netherlands, Amsterdam, and The Hague. Presses from the Spanish Netherlands are usually of ebony (or ebonized wood) and oak, enriched with parquetry decoration and perhaps inlaid with ivory, bone, or slate panels. The earlier, more elaborate examples are enriched with Mannerist decoration and architectural motifs in the manner of Hans Vredeman de Vries (1526–c.1604), including caryatid figures and arabesques. This architectural vocabulary was gradually superseded by more florid decoration, richly carved in relief with flowers and putti, the doors often divided by Solomonic or barley-twist columns.

The *Schrank* and *Nasenschrank* (cupboards) made in Germany during the late 17th and early 18th centuries, represent the purest expression of the northern Baroque style. Usually of walnut or oak, their decoration is restrained in the extreme, often depending entirely on the shaping of mass within the geometrical raised paneling on the doors, or the rich figuring of the veneer, for effect. This architectural purity of design, at first enhanced by the use of geometrical parquetry, was gradually diluted by the use of floral marquetry during the early 18th century. For all their restraint, particularly in the insides, which featured plain pine or oak shelves, these *Schränke* invariably display elaborate iron or, on the most sophisticated examples, steel locking mechanisms of great complexity and ingenuity; these were often engraved with strapwork or foliate arabesques, and occasionally signed and dated.

ITALIAN LINEN-PRESSES

Italian linen-presses were invariably of walnut and architectural in form, the full-length doors no doubt conceived to match the decoration of the room for which they were originally supplied. These presses are characteristically sophisticated on the exterior, while the interiors have a very crude basic construction, typical of all Italian furniture. They are enriched with simple molded paneling on the doors, which in turn are framed as if by pilaster strips. Examples from Lombardy are often distinguished by their ebonized moldings, while Tuscan presses are often lined with marbled paper.

ROCOCO LINEN-PRESSES

As the Rococo movement gained momentum during the second quarter of the 18th century, the linear form of the linen-press (armoire) became both outdated and restrictive. In such principal centers of cabinet-making as The Hague, Dresden, and Mainz, a new Rococo form emerged that, although clearly evolved from the earlier Baroque prototypes, represented a profound reaction to the architectural severity of the 17th century. Of increasingly bombé (swollen) form, Rococo linen-presses clearly reflect the style expounded by such French designers (*ornamentistes*) as Juste-Aurèle Meissonnier (1695–1750).

▲ **Armoire**
This walnut armoire is in a very bold Rococo style, with richly carved decoration. Such Dutch armoires as this typically have waved pediments on which there are two pedestals carved with *rocaille* (rockwork) and flowers, each of which was intended to display a Chinese blue-and-white vase imported by the Dutch East India Company.
*(mid-18th century; ht 2.4m/7ft 10in; value **M**)*

The linearity of the previous period was superseded by more organic forms, which were lighter and more curvaceous. Decoration took the form of asymmetrical cartouches, stylized vases of flowers, C-scrolls, acanthus, and rockwork. Rococo linen presses are distinguished by their waved cornices, above serpentine, molded paneled doors, and deep shaped aprons. These presses were usually made of walnut, tulipwood, or kingwood, and were frequently further enriched with marquetry, and pronounced floral ormolu handles and escutcheons. However, the most important evolution from the 17th-century linen-press was the division of the form into two parts with a high waist; the doors of the upper section were reduced considerably in size to allow for the introduction of a series of long drawers in the base.

This fundamental development, which provided a far more effective means of storage, was subsequently adopted as the basic pattern for linen-presses in England and North America during the 18th and 19th centuries.

PROVINCIAL ARMOIRES

Running parallel to the mainstream tradition were the provincial furniture-makers of Brittany, Normandy, Bordeaux, Frankfurt-am-Main, and the Alps. Unlike cabinet-makers in Paris and London who had access to a range of fine timbers both indigenous and exotic, furniture-makers in the regions were restricted to locally available woods, and thus provincial armoires are usually constructed of fruitwoods such as cherry, chestnut, and walnut, or hardwoods such as elm and oak. However, furniture-makers in such ports as Bordeaux, also had access to cheap tropical hardwoods, particularly mahogany, that arrived as ballast on ships from the West Indies; this distinctive group is known as "Port furniture."

What is most noticeable about provincial armoires of the 18th and early 19th century is that the basic form is essentially that of the 17th century, onto which has been grafted mid-18th century Rococo motifs, years after they were abandoned in Paris. This fusion and continuity of tradition was popular long after the Rococo taste had been discarded in favor of Neo-classicism from the 1760s. Not only were provincial furniture-makers frequently slow to absorb the fashionable decorative language of the day, but they also often slightly misunderstood or diluted these ideas and then showed great reluctance to abandon them. However, this is the mark, and indeed the charm, of provincial furniture.

The provincial tradition also embraced painted furniture, particularly in Britain, Italy, Switzerland, Sweden, Spain, The Netherlands, and Germany. Immigrants from The Netherlands, Switzerland, and Germany took their traditions to North America, which flowered during the 18th and 19th centuries. Decorating onto cheap and locally available softwood carcases, which were usually pine, the artisan painters displayed remarkable imagination, whether in the Rococo or in the later more restrained Neo-classical style. On the plainest armoires, richly figured veneers

▶ **Armoire**
Such painted examples as this Swedish armoire were made in Scandinavia, the Alpine regions, and particularly the Austrian Tyrol. The raised central panels on the doors are painted with brightly colored floral sprays within a marbled frame.
The initials on the upper section suggest that this example was made to celebrate a marriage, although care should be taken as many dates and inscriptions are spurious and of a later date.
*(mid-18th century; ht 2m/6ft 7in; value **K**)*

▲ **Armoire**
The basic form of this French provincial walnut armoire continued unchanged throughout the 19th century. The detailing is of Louis XV inspiration, with the molded foliate cornice and frame carved with ribbon-tied fruiting vines and roses, and the doors carved with foliate scrolls and meandering floral stems. Other provincial armoires were made in fruitwoods, chestnut, and oak.
*(c.1770; ht 2.2m/7ft 3in; value **H**)*

were simulated by exaggerating and enhancing the lines of the grain with paint, a technique known as "graining." On more accomplished pieces of furniture such exotic and expensive materials as tortoiseshell, specimen marbles, and *pietre dure* (hardstones) were convincingly depicted, and on the most elaborate German and north Italian examples, *capricci* (imaginary scenes) and townscapes, or portraits of a patron or ruler were painted on the door panels. On much 18th-century Italian painted furniture, the finest details and pastoral scenes are in fact cut-out prints and engravings, which were applied, in a way similar to a collage to the painted surface and then varnished in imitation of Oriental lacquer. This technique, known as *lacca povera* ("poor-man's lacquer"), was much cheaper than lacquering or even japanning, and enjoyed a considerable revival in the 19th century, particularly in France and Britain as "Decalcomania."

NEO-CLASSICAL ARMOIRES

With the advent of Neo-classicism during the late 1750s, the excesses of the Rococo were cast aside in favor of the Classical ideals of ancient Greece and Rome. Inspired by the excavations of such ancient sites as Herculaneum (1738) and Pompeii (1748), and popularized by the publications of Jean Charles Delafosse (1734–89) and James "Athenian" Stuart (1713–88), to name but two, Neo-classicism embraced the return to sober, architectural linearity of form. Neo-classical presses are, therefore, distinguished by their strongly architectural design and restrained decoration. Usually in finely figured mahogany or, exceptionally, ebonized in the Etruscan taste inspired by ancient vases, the veneer is carefully cut to run through the drawers, and this was to have a profound influence upon furniture-makers during the Empire period throughout Europe, particularly in

Germany and Denmark, and North America. Although often enriched with carved decoration, this is limited purely to Classical architectural vocabulary – dentiled cornices, columns applied to the angles, husks, swagged garlands, and fluted feet inspired by antique fluted columns. The use of ormolu mounts, although lavish on the grandest examples of the Louis XVI period (1774–93), was usually similarly restrained, and often restricted to handles only.

REGENCY LINEN-PRESSES

The uncompromising Neo-classicism of the Parisian *goût Grec* (Greek Revival) of the 1760s gradually gave way to a lighter, although strongly architectural, style that was swiftly adopted in England by the cabinet-maker Thomas Sheraton (1751–1806) in *The Cabinet-Maker and Upholsterer's Drawing Book* (1791–1802) and George Hepplewhite (*d.*1786) in *The Cabinet-Maker and Upholsterer's Guide* (1788–94). Their designs were influential as far as Denmark and Italy, but most particularly on American furniture designs during the early Federal period (1795–1815). These usually enclose three or four oak presses (shelves or trays), from which the name "linen-press" is derived, in the upper section. The most refined linen-presses are lined with cedarwood both for fragrance and to keep moths at bay. Made of kingwood, rosewood, or tulipwood, or inlaid very simply with lines of ebony or boxwood, Regency linen-presses are characterized by their splayed bracket feet, oval or rectangular paneled doors, plain sides, and arched or plain, as opposed to pedimented, cresting. Often of bow-fronted form and with dished aprons, they rely purely on their lines and the finely figured timber for decorative effect. Often linen-presses were adapted at a later date; their shelves were removed and the drawers cut through to allow for a greater hanging space. The simple form of the basic Regency linen-press remained very popular in Britain throughout the the 19th century. Early linen-presses are often only distinguishable from the direct copies that were made during the later Victorian and Edwardian periods by the quality of the timber that was used.

▲ Linen-press

This simple, mahogany bow-fronted linen-press, with dished apron, splayed bracket feet, and two oval panels on the doors, is typical of the type made by the firm of Gillow (est. c.1730) of Lancaster. Those examples with shaped pediments, such as this arched example, are more desirable than those with flat tops. The decoration is kept to an absolute minimum, with only the cornice inlaid with ebonized stringing, lozenges, and star motifs. The doors enclose an interior fitted with sliding trays; these have often been removed. *(c.1790–1800; ht 2.1m/6ft 11in; value H)*

◄ Armoire

The form of this Dutch mahogany armoire is very architectural, with its broken pediment, simple dentil molding, vase-shaped finial, and fluted angle columns. Neo-classical motifs include ribbon-tied flower swags with trophies, and portrait medallions. This type looks back to English Palladian architecture of the 1730s. Dutch armoires are often fitted with handles made in England, in such centers as Brimingham, for export. *(c.1800; ht 2.7m/8ft 10in; value I)*

KEY FACTS

- GERMAN NASENSCHRÄNKE usually of walnut or oak; very plain, with restrained decoration
- PROVINCIAL ARMOIRES because the basic form of the armoire did not change, the style of ornament is the best indication of date; such armoires are usually fitted with hooks or pegs for hanging clothes
- PAINTED ARMOIRES beware, as these often have spurious dates and initials painted on the doors
- REGENCY LINEN-PRESSES often the paneled doors have shrunk or warped, creating gaps at the top and bottom; the quality and use of the timber is of note in such examples; cedarwood is used for the most refined examples
- ALTERATIONS linen-presses are often been converted to make room for a hanging space by removing the shelves or by cutting through the top drawer and introducing a hanging bar

See also Chests and coffers, pp.70–71; Wardrobes after 1840, pp.76–7

Wardrobes after 1840

Wardrobes of the 19th century represent a natural progression from linen-presses and armoires, but the term "wardrobe" did not come into use until the second half of the 18th century, when it was popularized by the designer George Hepplewhite (*d*.1786). Although intended primarily for hanging clothing, rather than simply storing it folded, wardrobes, which were increasingly manufactured, did not completely supersede other storage furniture until the late 1800s. Moreover, in terms of both design and craftsmanship, the wardrobes that were produced are considered to be less interesting than their antecedents.

TYPES OF WARDROBE

Wardrobes produced after *c*.1840 were influenced by the designs set out in the *Encyclopaedia of Cottage, Farm and Villa Architecture and Furniture* (1833) by John Claudius Loudon (1783–1843) and, in North America, *The Architecture of Country Houses* by Andrew Jackson Downing (1815–52), published several times between 1850 and 1866. Designs in the Grecian, or "modern" Italian, Gothic, and Romanesque styles were among those illustrated; each of these wardrobes is tall, and possesses two doors of varied ornamentation, and the inside is evenly divided between hanging and shelf space. One wardrobe of particular interest was described as "a lady's winged wardrobe" and resembled the traditional break-front bookcase in its construction. With a full-length door at either side, the center portion was divided into two halves, the top with doors, the bottom with two short drawers and two long ones; these

are reminiscent of the arrangement of the Georgian linen-press. It was "to be made of any fine wood, French polished, and showing no brasswork in any part of the front. The knobs are of mahogany or ebony, the moldings on the doors are made to project, and the fronts of the drawers are made to recede, and to have a molding raised upon them." Inside the wardrobe great attention was paid to the practicalities: there were pegs provided for hanging dresses, shelves for storing bonnets and shoes, and sometimes even a locker with a fold-down front for dirty linen.

Wardrobes of the mid- to late-Victorian period are characterized by an increase in size and function with a corresponding decrease of ornamental flourishes, consistent with the large, heavy, utilitarian, and somewhat sombre design ethos. Thus by the mid-1880s some wardrobes expanded to tripartite and break-front forms, with a central wardrobe flanked by cupboards and drawer slides, or were "broken up" and lopsided, as in the example of the "Beaconsfield." This was a type of asymmetrical, multi-purpose wardrobe, which had book and display shelves in addition to drawers and cupboards. Sometimes the ends of the wardrobes had open shelves and fret-cut decoration. Fitted wardrobes also gained favor during the mid-1880s, as did corner ones, which were designed to maximize space in small rooms.

Wardrobes also began to be designed en suite with other bedroom furniture. In the "Benedict" bedroom suite, items of furniture were duplicated for the husband and wife; hence the wardrobe had two cupboards and two mirrors and was intended to prevent marital strife. Various other anomalies were also produced, such as papier-mâché suites; first introduced in the late 1830s, these had dark or black grounds that were enriched with mother-of-pearl inlay or brightly colored floral

▲ **Wardrobe by Charles A. Baudouine (1808–95)**
Baudouine, who was based in New York, generally made his Rococo Revival furniture in solid rosewood (as seen here) rather than of laminated construction. (*c.1845–50; ht 2.3m/7ft 6in; value* **M**)

▼ **Wardrobe**
Stamped by the well-known furniture broker T. Willson of London, this mahogany, recessed, break-front wardrobe affords hanging, shelf, and drawer space for the various garments to be stored. Note the plain mahogany handles, which were fashionable at the time. (*c.1850; ht 2.2m/7ft 3in; value* **H**)

MAKERS' MARKS

From 1741, Parisian cabinet-makers were ordered by their guilds to stamp their work, and although the requirement was removed some 50 years later the practice continued. During the 19th century, part of the brasswork was often engraved with a script signature and the date of manufacture. English cabinet-makers were never legally required to identify their furniture, although metal-punched name stamps or brass name tablets were used by some makers during the 18th century. After 1820 attitudes changed, and the practice became more common: so much so that there are plenty of examples of furniture signed not only by its makers, but even by restorers, dealers, or retailers.

The branded mark of Holland & Sons (est. 1803), of London, one of the most famous Victorian furniture makers in Britain.

painting. By the end of the century, some wardrobes had become increasingly ornamented, with marquetry inlaid decoration, molded cornices, and cushion or cavetto friezes. Some Edwardian wardrobes were in painted satinwood, with the doors sporting swags, urns, and scrolling foliage, while others were plainer and more restrained decoratively, featuring only paneled doors.

REVIVAL STYLES

Many styles of wardrobe were revived and popularized in France, particularly the Renaissance and the "Louis" styles, which covered Baroque, Rococo, and Neoclassical. Of these the Rococo Revival was probably the most important as it carried on until the end of the 19th century, when it was combined with Art Nouveau. There was also an interest in Naturalism (with direct allusions to flowers and fruit), Orientalism, and a revived interest in the Middle Ages. The craze for light woods mostly disappeared during the 1840s, and was followed by a taste for the darker woods.

In Germany and Austria, the Biedermeier style, with its geometrical and simplified forms, was still popular in the 1840s, although it ultimately gave way to Germanic interpretations of Gothic and Rococo. German Rococo was generally based on Parisian Louis XV forms, albeit heavier and more exaggerated than its prototype. It was made of carved natural woods, especially walnut and limewood.

The rest of Europe was dominated by various revival styles. Exhibitions, trade catalogs, and pattern-books prompted the dissemination of styles continent-wide, particularly the French "Louis" and the Renaissance styles; the latter was particularly well suited to machine production, and to wardrobes in particular. Each country adapted these styles in its own way, particularly in the second half of the century as each looked to its own cultural roots for inspiration.

◄ **Wardrobe**
Originally this French mahogany wardrobe made in Paris in the Louis XVI Revival style would have been topped with a crest in a similarly grand style. It was made as part of a bedroom suite, which also included a double bed. The tapering legs and classical motifs, seen here in the gilt-bronze mounts, are typical features of the style. The full-length mirror only became a significant feature of wardrobes from the second quarter of the 19th century, when plate glass could be inexpensively produced.
(c.1890; ht 2.4m/7ft 10in; value for a bedroom suite I)

CONSTRUCTION

As the furniture industry of each country was essentially localized, each used different woods for its pieces, especially in the hidden woods of the carcase. The British mainly used mahogany and satinwood for the better pieces, and pine for those less expensive. Mahogany, ebony, oak, and even stained pearwood were the French choice from the 1840s onward. The Dutch used native oak and exotic woods imported from their colonies in the West Indies, whereas the rest of Europe generally imported their exotic woods from the Caribbean. Scandinavian countries used pine, as did rural Alpine regions; it was frequently painted in a variety of colors and designs to hide the poor quality of the wood. Italy also used inexpensive woods in many cases, although walnut and rosewood were still employed for grander pieces, which were frequently enriched with ivory or gilding. Spanish and Portuguese cabinet-makers copied and interpreted the French styles while at the same time continuing their traditional heavily carved 17th-century-style furniture.

The majority of wardrobes were made by cabinet-makers. In Britain they were constructed so that cornices and plinths could be lifted off and drawers and shelving pulled out; French wardrobes were made in many parts, and were often fixed together with long bolts, and a hinge on the door allowed it to be lifted off.

While small free-standing mirrors or those attached to dressing tables were common, full-length mirrored doors on wardrobes were an important 19th-century innovation. Plate glass was used, and no doubt the lowering of the price of producing glass by Pilkington Brothers Ltd (est. 1826), at St Helens, near Liverpool, contributed to its more widespread use. Such mirrors, either sharply beveled (unlike the gently beveled glass of the 18th century), or in a decorative frame, was very thick, and usually placed on the single door in a single door wardrobe or on the center door of a tripartite wardrobe.

▲ **Wardrobe**
This Edwardian satinwood wardrobe was probably originally part of a suite. It is an extremely restrained piece of furniture, with its origins in the Neoclassical style popular at the end of the 18th century. It is the complete antithesis of sombre, heavy Victorian wardrobes, and well suited the desire for simple, uncluttered pieces of furniture that was prevalent at the time. Often such wardrobes are sold individually rather than as part of their original suites.
(c.1905; ht 2.5m/8ft 2in; value E)

KEY FACTS

- WOOD look for good quality and patina
- MIRRORS the effect of damp can cause spotting on the silvering, but the mirrors can be resilvered; old mirrors give a mellow image, while new ones are very bright and give a sharp image
- ALTERATIONS when large break-front wardrobes went out of fashion they were often broken up, and so they can be relatively scarce and very sought after; because of their size they could be reduced in both height and width, and it is usually possible to trace this by the proportions and by looking at the wood – screwholes should not appear on the wrong places; some linen-presses were made into wardrobes in the 19th century
- COLLECTING Victorian mahogany wardrobes are very common; wardrobes in satinwood (a much more expensive wood) are the least common; Edwardian examples are often of the highest craftsmanship and therefore very desirable

See also Dressing tables, pp.62–3; Chests-of-drawers after 1840, pp.83–5

Early chests-of-drawers

The chest-of-drawers as we know it today essentially evolved during the 17th century. During the 1600s it was adapted and modified until the ideal balance and most practical formula were found. The system of graduated drawers, with the most shallow at the top and the deepest at the bottom, was only really reached right at the end of the century. However, it should be remembered that throughout the 17th century chests and coffers were still the principal items of furniture used for storage.

THE EVOLUTION OF THE CHEST-OF-DRAWERS

The 16th and 17th centuries were times of considerable social change in Europe, when a number of new items of furniture were introduced. The chest-of-drawers was one of these new forms, and through its development in the 17th century it is possible to chart the progress of furniture-makers and the emergence of the cabinet-maker. Although new methods of construction (including dovetailing) were developed and refined during the 17th century, the chest-of-drawers was largely made with joints secured by iron nails; only at the end of the century was dovetailing preferred.

From the mid-16th century, the concept of the drawer became widespread in countries that were influenced by the courts of Spain and Italy. In Spain the *vargueño* (writing desk) was one of the most important of the furniture forms that influenced the development of numerous furniture types throughout Europe. The contribution of the Moors, who occupied much of Spain until 1492, is particularly evident in the skilled work of the Spanish craftsmen working in the mid-16th century. The numerous small drawers in the *vargueño* were made using tight dovetails and precisely cut drawer-linings. The *vargueño* could either have a stand in the form of a small table, or a base that was sometimes enclosed by doors, but often had four exposed drawers.

In the province of Zeeland in the southern Netherlands, which was under Spanish rule between 1482 and 1794, a type of square chest, usually measuring 1.5m (4ft 11in) high and 1.7m (5ft 7in) wide, was made. Like the *beeldenkast* (cupboard) made in the northern Netherlands, this type was in two sections, sometimes with a central drawer between the two, enclosed by a pairs of doors.

In Britain, the drawer was not introduced in any significant number until the end of the 16th century, when they were added to coffers and cabinets. They were called "tills" or "drawing-boxes," and the word "drawer" is derived from the latter. From the mid-16th century the term "till" was used to denote a drawer where money was kept, an association it still retains. A coffer or chest could be fitted with drawers, and was then known as a mule chest. An early, hybrid form of the chest-of-drawers and cabinet was made from the mid-17th century; this had a shallow frieze drawer at the top, a deep drawer beneath, and three further drawers enclosed by two doors in the lower section. Graduated drawers were introduced later in the century. These oak chests are still linked to the old form as some had hinged tops, opening to reveal box compartments.

During the later 17th century the chest-of-drawers evolved rapidly. Many were constructed on spiral-turned, double spiral or S-scroll stands (often with a drawer or series of drawers in the stand), stretching to about 1.5m (4ft 11in) in height so that the top drawers were easily accessible. This form is similar to the chest-on-stand. By the end of the 17th century the chest-of-drawers in its familiar form had evolved – the chest was taken down from the stand and rested instead on feet, at first of bun form (introduced c.1690) and later of

▼ Commode

This chest was made in the Italian region of Lombardy. The panels on the drawers have been veneered in burr-walnut inlaid with lines. The other visible parts are all in solid walnut. Italian walnut is generally less well figured than British or other northern European walnut used for veneering. The drawer-linings on much Italian case furniture are of inexpensive woods such as pine. The construction is not usually of the fine and meticulous standard of northern European furniture-makers, as Italians tended to use large, roughly hewn dovetail joints. The chest is robustly carved with Renaissance-style caryatids, fruit, and foliage, although these carvings are reserved for the stiles on either side of the drawers.
*(1680s; ht 96.5cm/38in; value **J**)*

◄ **Secrétaire commode**
As Italy was divided into a number of states, the furniture made there can show strong regional characteristics. Furniture from Bologna, where this walnut example was made, tends to display busy, sometimes fussy, carved decoration. The secrétaire drawer has a drop front, which pulls out to provide a flat writing surface and often encloses a simple interior with a few shelves or pigeon holes. The walnut is carved from the solid, in the southern European style.
*(1680s; ht 1.1m/3ft 7in; value **I**)*

▲ Chest-of-drawers

The construction of this oak chest-of-drawers, like that of many British examples, is of two separate sections, which can be lifted apart for ease of movement. There are usually two tenons rising from either side of the base that fit neatly into two mortises in the top, which should lock it together. The paneled sides and pegged mortise-and-tenon joints should be visible on such chests. The scale has diminished from earlier examples, and the size of the drawers has become more evenly graduated. Sometimes the geometrical panels are inlaid with a more decorative wood, such as fruitwood.

(1675–1700; ht 80cm/31½in; value H)

► Chest-of-drawers

The top of this chest-of-drawers is quarter-veneered in burr-walnut, as was customary for the period, and it is further enhanced with featherbanding. The top and drawer fronts are also veneered, but the sides are in solid and less well-figured walnut. This example is unlike many provincial British chests in that all evidence of the construction has been concealed: the dovetailed joints are hidden beneath the sheets of veneer. Below the drop handles are marks left by the swinging action of the handles; this is often a positive mark of authenticity.

(c.1695; ht 89cm/35in; value K)

► Chest-of-drawers

There are two features of this chest that have been altered over time, either owing to damage or to make it more fashionable. The first is the bracket feet – the originals would have been bun; the second is the handles – the holes where the drop handles were originally secured are clearly visible. Oyster veneering was highly popular c.1700, and the banding not only serves to decorate the chest but also makes the repair of such vulnerable areas easier.

(1700; ht 71.5cm/28¼in; value K)

bracket form (introduced *c.*1725). It is extremely common for feet to have been replaced either owing to damage from wear or woodworm or as a result of changing fashions and the desire to "improve."

CONSTRUCTION AND WOODS

In the Low Countries and Britain during the mid-17th century the chest-of-drawers was made by a joiner. It was constructed of solid oak, often in two parts, with paneled sides and heavy drawers that ran on bearers set into the sides of the carcase. The bearers slid into grooves cut into the drawer-lining (1–2cm/⅜–¾in) along the center of the outside edge. The joined construction was clearly visible from the outside and can now be seen to form part of the decorative appeal.

By the end of the century the cabinet-maker had become increasingly dominant, and joined furniture was therefore relegated to the provincial areas. Chests-of-drawers made in important centers of furniture production now had oak linings, and the carcase and drawers were secured by dovetailed joints. The thick wood that was required for mortise-and-tenon joints disappeared; consequently the thickness of the drawer-linings diminished, and drawers were set to run on their bases or on bearers set underneath the drawers.

In Spain and Italy forms tended to be heavy and thick in construction, still retaining paneled sides, and the drawer-linings were normally made of pine. In central and northern Europe dovetails and drawer-linings became smaller and more delicate; in Italy they remained much less refined, and of much larger form, right through to the 19th century.

Although, throughout most of the 17th century, oak was the preferred wood in England when furniture was made in the solid, walnut was increasingly popular as the veneer for fine furniture because of its figuring and rich color. In Spain and Italy walnut was the most common wood used in the solid. In France timbers imported from the overseas provinces were used from an early stage. Ebony was one such exotic wood and gave rise to the term *ébeniste* (cabinet-maker).

Toward the end of the 17th century, great efforts were made to enrich the visible surfaces of the chest-of-drawers, and considerable expense was lavished on the large surface areas. The most popular forms of decoration were veneering with burr woods, oyster veneering, seaweed marquety, and floral marquetry. This explosion of creativity was a far cry from the heavy, joined chests made just 30 to 40 years earlier. This rapid pace of change – which was much slower in the provinces – continued in construction, decoration, and design well into the next century.

The chest-of-drawers was adopted in all the wealthy circles as a new piece of furniture, and soon gained favor in all the countries of Europe. It took such forms as bachelors' chests, commodes, and chests-on-chests.

KEY FACTS

- SAW MARKS until the end of the 18th century the method of sawing wood for the carcase left straight saw marks; from the end of the 18th century a circular saw was used, which left circular saw marks; these marks should be visible on the inside of the carcase
- FEET it is common to find pieces of this period without their original feet; bun feet have often been replaced by bracket feet; look underneath the chest for old holes into which the bun feet would have fitted
- HANDLES these may have been changed; look for the bruise marks on the woodwork to see where the original handles (usually drop) would have rubbed or swung

See also Chests-on-chests, pp.88–9

Chests-of-drawers before 1840

BACHELORS' CHESTS

Bachelors' chests, so-called because they were originally placed in a "bachelor's bedroom apartments," were conceived as multi-purpose chests for storage, dressing, and writing. Predominantly of walnut, although oak and elm were used for more provincial examples, the earliest bachelors' chests date from the late 17th century. Betrayed by their bun feet and broad, domed moulding framing the deep drawers, early bachelors' chests are usually veneered with straight-grained walnut and simple crossbanding. During the early 18th century the form became increasingly sophisticated, with neat dovetailing and the introduction of a brushing-slide above the top drawer; the heavy bun feet were discarded in favor of shaped bracket feet. Although the form was replaced by the fashionable French commode design in the mid-18th century, provincial furniture-makers continued the tradition throughout the 18th century. However, these later examples are usually betrayed by their larger scale, often with mahogany-lined drawers, and Rococo or Neo-classical handles.

BOMBE COMMODES

The concept of a free-standing chest-of-drawers was first introduced by André-Charles Boulle (1642–1732). Initially known as *tables en bureaux*, and representing perhaps the earliest fusion between the table form and a sarcophagus-shaped coffer, Louis XIV Boulle commodes are characterized not only by their brass inlaid decoration but by their swollen "sarcophagus"

▼ **Bachelor's chest**
Characterized by their small proportions, hinged tops supported by lopers, and graduated drawers, walnut bachelors' chests have long been considered among the finest achievements of early English cabinet-makers. The value of such pieces depends almost entirely on color.
(c.1720; ht 78cm/30¾in; value O)

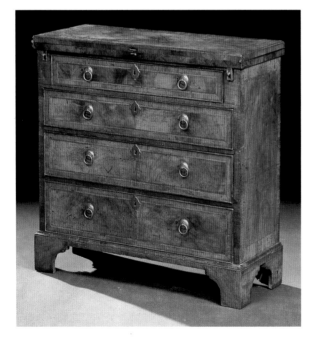

or Roman-tomb form. During the Régence (1715–23), this developed into the *commode en tombeau*, which was widely manufactured by Parisian cabinet-makers. Under Louis XV bombé commodes became increasingly Rococo. Veneered on pine or oak carcases and usually with oak-lined drawers, they are invariably enriched with parquetry or marquetry decoration, usually embracing fruitwoods and numerous exotic woods, particularly tulipwood and amaranth. More elegant and serpentine in shape than their predecessors, these commodes stand higher from the ground on slightly splayed legs with ormolu *sabots* ("shoes"). The geometric parquetry was often subtle, while the ormolu mounts conveyed the full-blown Rococo spirit, perhaps nowhere more so than in the commodes of Charles Cressent (1685–1768).

Inspired by French prototypes, mid-18th-century bombé commodes with parquetry decoration were made throughout Europe, particularly in southern Germany (usually in elm and fruitwood, with long drawers above low aprons), Genoa and Naples (with distinctive dished aprons and starburst kingwood cube parquetry), and Sweden (upright bombé form, pine carcases, and spring-locking drawers, such as those by the cabinet-maker Johann Christian Linning; 1759–1801).

The desire throughout Europe for all things "exotic," particularly lacquer, encouraged such specialist "japanners" as John Stalker and George Parker in England, Gerard Dagly (1657–1715) in Berlin, and the Martin family in Paris to produce their own versions. The name Martin became synonymous with the art of japanning, and indeed the technique is still known as *vernis Martin*. Louis XV commodes mounted with panels in *vernis Martin* painted in imitation of Oriental lacquer, with posies of flowers, and arcadian landscapes, were invariably commissioned by *marchand-merciers* (dealers in luxury goods) such as Simon-Philippe Poirier (1720–85). Regarded as the height of fashion and extremely expensive, they were mounted with luxurious ormolu mounts, and many can be accurately dated to between 1745 and 1749 through a tax mark.

◄ *Commode en tombeau*
Usually of kingwood or rosewood, and often decorated with elaborate parquetry, or inlaid with marquetry, *commodes en tombeau* adhere to a general form with serpentine-fronted marble tops above bombé bases fitted with both long and short walnut-lined drawers. They are usually elaborately mounted with ormolu, as seen in this Louis XV example, with pierced foliate mounts, handles, and escutcheons. On Régence examples the lines of the aprons are often broken by recessed centers with scrolled mounts. The *commode en tombeau* was principally conceived as a vehicle to display rare and costly slabs of marble.
(c.1740; ht 87cm/34¼in; value M)

▲ **Commode**
Although painted furniture was made throughout 18th-century Europe, the best exponents were in Italy, particularly Venice. From c.1750 decoration was distinctly Rococo and included floral posies within an asymmetrical cartouche, or arcadian landscapes within a floral or trellised border. Although the construction of these commodes was often rather crude, the painted decoration, sense of movement, and interplay between the carved and painted areas are extremely sophisticated.
(c.1750; ht 69cm/27in; value J)

▲ Chest-of-drawers
This block-front chest-of-drawers, made in Salem or Boston, Massachusetts, of a brilliantly figured dense mahogany, retains its original patina. It is characterized by an overhanging blocked top with moulded edge above a conforming case with double-beaded dividers, and a green baize-lined dressing-slide with two knobs. There are four graduated, blocked long drawers, each with batwing brasses and escutcheons. Each side of the case is fitted with a brass carrying handle. It has a conforming plinth moulding, a centered, shaped drop pendant, and ogee bracket feet.
*(c.1770; ht 80cm/31½in; value **Q**)*

► Chest-of-drawers
This mahogany chest-of-drawers of the George III period is in the classic Chippendale style; characteristics associated with this style include the chamfered serpentine top, generous canted (chamfered) angles carved with blind Gothic or Chinese fretwork, Rococo handles, and shaped bracket feet. Dressing-commodes have dressing-drawers fitted with mirrors and various compartments for bottles, brushes, and powders. However, beware, as elaborate decoration has frequently been applied at a later date to "improve" the piece.
*(1765–80; ht 1m/3ft 3in; value **M**)*

► Commode
This French, mahogany commode with marble top is typical of those made during the late Louis XVI and the Directoire period (1795–9) when furniture forms were based on straight lines and clean designs, and decoration was kept to an absolute minimum. The plain ring handles and simple escutcheons are now of the very simplest Grecian design, and the fluted tapering legs terminate in neat brass caps.
*(1785–1800; ht 85.5cm/33¾in; value **I**)*

GEORGIAN CHESTS-OF-DRAWERS

The commode reached England through such celebrated pattern-books as *The Universal System of Household Furniture* (1762) by John Mayhew (1736–1811) and William Ince (c.1738–1804) and *The Gentleman and Cabinet-Maker's Director* (1754–62) by Thomas Chippendale (1718–79), who described the form as a "French commode table(s)." However, the majority of George II and George III chests-of-drawers are simple and plain, and the vast majority of those that correspond closely to published patterns are usually Victorian. They are often of mahogany, with canted rectangular or serpentine-fronted moulded tops above graduated drawers and moulded plinths with shaped bracket feet refinements to this basic form include fitted dressing-drawers or brushing-slides; canted angles carved with either trailing foliage, cluster-columns, or Chinese blind-fret; ogee or carved bracket feet; and luxuries such as superb lacquered-brass handles, cedar-lined drawers, and S-pattern keyholes, all of which are characteristic of Chippendale's workshop. However, during the 1760s sumptuous marquetry commodes in the Louis XV manner, introduced by Pierre Langlois (active 1759–81) of Tottenham Court Road, London, became increasingly fashionable. As a result, plain figured mahogany was often discarded in favor of exotic woods, including

sabicu, rosewood, and ebony, and later satinwood, often with parquetry. During the 1770s the marquetry style that had been so swiftly adopted for commodes by cabinet-makers such as John Cobb (c.1715–78) and the firm of Ince & Mayhew (est. 1758) became increasingly linear and Neo-classical in design.

TRANSITIONAL AND NEO-CLASSICAL COMMODES

The explosion of Neo-classicism was slow to filter through, and sometimes during the 1760s there was an unhappy fusion of Neo-classical decoration on Rococo forms. Commodes of this type are known as Transitional, a form particularly identified with the French cabinet-makers Jean-François Oeben (1721–63) and Roger Vandercruse (1728–99).

As the Transitional style became more refined, plain linear commodes, veneered in satinwood or mahogany and virtually denuded of mounts, were made. During the 1770s and 1780s the cabinet-makers Jean-Henri Riesener (1734–1806) and Gilles Joubert (1689–1775) continued to supply the royal household with sumptuous commodes enriched with lavish Neo-classical ormolu mounts and pictorial marquetry panels, while Etienne Levasseur (1721–98) and Adam Weisweiler (1744–1820) promoted a return to the "antique" style of the late 17th century particularly the brass inlay associated with Boulle. On a more modest level the basic commodes remained remarkably unchanged throughout the Louis XVI and Directoire (1795–9) periods. Made in the solid (as opposed to veneered) and usually of mahogany, although more provincial examples are often of fruitwood, they have eared, moulded marble tops above two or three short frieze drawers and long paneled lower drawers, flanked by fluted angle columns, and stand on turned, tapering legs with *toupie* feet in brass caps. Dependent again on the figuring of the timber for impact, although this is often enhanced by brass stringing, they are restrained examples of architectural Neo-classicism. Particularly inspirational to English cabinet-makers through the influence of architects such as Henry Holland (1745–1806), this general form of commode was widely copied throughout Europe. It was through the work of the cabinet-makers David Roentgen (1743–1807), in Germany, and Christian Meyer (active 1787), who worked in Russia but may have trained under Roentgen, that this style reached its apogee.

MAGGIOLINI COMMODES

Neo-classical marquetry commodes were made throughout Europe from the 1770s. The fashion originated in Paris and rapidly spread across Europe. In Italy the Neo-classical style is synonymous with the Giuseppe Maggiolini (1738–1814) in Milan. His work is characterized by superb Neo-classical and arabesque marquetry in walnut, olivewood, and tulipwood, although he also used rosewood in the early 19th century. "Maggiolini" commodes are usually loosely constructed, with a rough-hewn softwood carcase and thickly dovetailed poplar-lined drawers. Owing to the prolific production of commodes from Maggiolini's workshops during the early 19th century, not to mention that of his competitors and imitators, the quality of work inevitably suffered. However, the enormously popular Maggiolini commode continued to be made during the 19th century.

EMPIRE AND RESTAURATION COMMODES

Empire furniture heralded a return to the ornament of Classical antiquity, inspired partly by *Aventures dans la basse et la haute Egypte* (1802) by Baron Vivant Denon (1747–1825). The French Empire style dominated European taste through such influential publications as *Recueil de décorations intérieures* (1801–12) by Charles Percier (1764–1838) and Pierre Fontaine (c.1762–1853). These pattern-books illustrate the finest commodes executed for Napoleon I in the huge workshops of cabinet-makers including François-Honoré-Georges Jacob (1770–1841) and Bernard Molitor (c.1730–1833). However, it is the designs of Pierre de La Mésangère, published as *Collection de Meubles et Objets de goût* (1802–35), that most clearly reveal the type of commode commissioned by less elevated patrons. These were initially veneered with mahogany on oak carcases, but the British blockade of 1806 prevented colonial timbers from getting to France, and the price of mahogany rose so high that cabinet-makers were forced to resort to such

◄ **Commode by Maggiolini**
Commodes from this Milanese workshop can be distinguished, by their lavish Neo-classical marquetry. Most have a quarter-veneered top centered by an oval medallion and stand on square tapering legs that support three long drawers. The top drawer is thinner and treated as a frieze; the deeper drawers are treated *sans traverse* ("without disruption") with a simulated panel centered by a further medallion or Neo-classical inlay.
(c.1790; ht 89cm/35in; value N)

▼ **Commode**
Of modest, squat proportions, and usually made of pitch-pine veneered in, for example, birchwood, Scandinavian Biedermeier commodes are often only enriched with ebonized lines and shield-shaped escutcheons, as on this Swedish example. From c.1825 the plain, square feet were replaced by the splayed or scrolled examples.
(c.1825; ht 91.5cm/35¾in; value I)

◄ **Commode**
This French commode of the Restauration period (1815–25) is typical both in its use of high-quality timber and outstanding craftsmanship. The same piece of mahogany veneer has been cut through so that the figuring goes right through each of the drawers in a waved pattern. The top is set with a simple slab of white-veined grey marble.
(c.1820; ht 91cm/35¾in; value H)

indigenous woods as maple, walnut, elm, ash, and yew. Empire commodes, both those with drawers and those with doors (*à vantaux*), are linear in form, the marble tops often supported above paneled friezes with ormolu mounts, the drawers flanked by columns or Egyptian herm or caryatid figures, and often supported on ebonized hairy-paw feet.

Following the defeat of Napoleon (1815) and the restoration of the Bourbon monarchy, commodes became increasingly restrained and visually heavy relying on flame-figured timber for impact. Often with overhanging frieze drawers and largely denuded of mounts, even handles, they frequently stood on plain plinth bases, although shallow bun feet or plain square legs were also sometimes employed. As this style inspired European cabinet-makers, particularly those in Spain and Germany, it is often difficult the origin of Restauration commodes.

Under Charles X (1824–30) commodes in a lighter, less monumental taste again became fashionable, both in lighter woods, particularly bird's-eye maple, and in the Gothic or *à la troubadour* style. Closely related in form to Restauration commodes, and largely unmounted, commodes in light woods were initially inlaid with stringing in exotic timbers such as amaranth and ebony, but during the 1830s and 1840s this evolved into increasingly lavish Boulle-style marquetry. In contrast, commodes made in the Gothic taste were made in mahogany and oak and were decorated with such carved ornament as crocketed finials and arcades. Although a revival of the Gothic taste had first been proposed by the architect Mansion as early as 1804, it was not until the 1830s and 1840s that it gained more widespread interest.

KEY FACTS

- VENEERING 17th- and 18th-century veneers are hand cut and thick (1–3mm/⅛in); later veneers were machine cut and are paper thin; often the tops of chests-of-drawers have been reveneered because of damage (water, splitting), so it is important to check that the veneers are of the same uneven thickness all over
- ALTERATIONS check that each of the drawers in a chest-of-drawers is of the same construction, as often one of them will have been changed because of damage
- SHRINKAGE this is a common occurrence and is frequently seen in the drawer bases; this is perfectly acceptable, and sometimes the splits have been repaired with canvas; those examples that do not show signs of shrinkage should alert suspicion
- CONSTRUCTION Italian commodes are typically rather loosely constructed and made of cheap timber

Chests-of-drawers after 1840

The practical nature of the chest-of-drawers ensured its continued popularity after 1840. It was considered an essential part of any household and produced in vast numbers throughout Europe. Chests-of-drawers, called commodes if made in France or in the French manner, with serpentine curves and Rococo characteristics, range from the utilitarian to the virtuoso.

▼ Chest-of-drawers
This mahogany chest with two short and three graduated long drawers is of a standard type that was widely produced in Victorian and Edwardian Britain. It is unusual to find small examples of this type. The plain, knob handles would have wooden threads running through to the back and rounded wooden nuts holding them.
(c.1860; ht 1.1m/3ft 7in; value **D**)

WOOD AND CONSTRUCTION
Despite the internationalism of styles, each country in Europe tended to use its native woods especially for the carcases; for example, France and The Netherlands used oak and Scandinavian countries used pine. Typically, Dutch drawer-linings are of oak, nailed together or dovetailed. Satinwood for veneers was imported from the East and West Indies. The satinwood used for furniture of the Edwardian period usually has strong lines, and is more likely to come from the East than the West Indies. Although birch was native to Europe and had been used for a long time on Scandinavian furniture, in Britain it had been confined to cooking utensils and provincial furniture. With the growth of furniture production in the 19th century, satin-birch was used as an alternative to the expensive satinwood; when cut carefully the wood could produce a decorative figure. Birch has subsequently come to be used for plywood and in furniture of modern design. Dovetails throughout central Europe at this time were 10 to 15mm (⅜–⅝in) at their widest point. In southern Europe they were broader and coarser, but all were in marked contrast to those made in Britain. There, the dovetails were consistently much smaller, often finer than a pencilpoint. This is an instantly recognizable feature of British and North American furniture construction.

PLAIN CHESTS-OF-DRAWERS
Many chests-of-drawers made in the 19th century were designed as parts of bedroom suites; the other components would be a bed, a wardrobe, and a pair of night tables. As a result of increased mechanization and the revival of styles, the choice for the Victorian purchaser was huge and designed to suit every pocket. The standard Victorian chest-of-drawers is of the very simplest form with two short and three graduated drawers constructed using traditional methods, with neat dovetailed joints. The proportions were generally rather heavy, and this was accentuated by a heavy plinth base. This type of chest-of-drawers was large and widely manufactured by firms such as Maddox of London (est. 1838) and William Smee & Sons (est. 1817). Pieces found today are likely to be originals and are modestly priced. Their plain, utilitarian design makes these chests long lasting.

The Wellington chest is also a relatively plain form of the chest-of-drawer. Named after the Duke of Wellington, whose succesful campaigns against Napoleon had made him a national hero, it was first introduced in the 1820s and originally intended to contain a collection of coins or other precious artefacts. It is characterized by its tall, narrow form and by the stiles (uprights) fixed to either side of the drawers. One of the stiles is hinged to cover the drawer ends at one side, which allows the chest to be locked. Wellington chests can have up to 12 drawers and occasionally a secrétaire drawer in the middle. They were normally made of mahogany or rosewood, but there are also examples in pollard oak, burr-walnut, burr-elm, and yew.

Another type of plain chest was the two-part campaign chest. These were first made for use in the field during the military campaigns in the Peninsular War (1809–14), although they continued to be made throughout the 19th century. These chests are recognizable by their sunken handles and carrying handles at the sides, and feet that may be unscrewed and stored safely in the drawers while being moved. Of small, neat proportions they are often made in teak.

▲ Chest-of-drawers
This mahogany-and-marquetry chest is Dutch. Such pieces, on oak carcases, are prone to damage and chipping of the veneers. The feet are particularly vulnerable. This example has saber feet, a stepped cornice, a pointed pediment, and an overhanging frieze drawer (which looks back to the Empire style) with five drawers below. The drawers are decorated with ribbon-tied swags, vases of woodland foliage, and fan spandrels between shaped, stylized foliate and urn-decorated stiles. Note that two of the handles are missing.
(c.1850; ht 1.6m/5ft 3in; value **H**)

▶ Chest-of-drawers
Turned, and painted yellow to simulate bamboo, this Victorian chest illustrates the taste for Oriental materials. It is relatively unusual to have a piece still with its original paintwork, and the ageing has mellowed the color. Most of those that are now found have been completely repainted. This example, which is composed of two deep drawers simulated as two short and three long graduated drawers, is decorated with stylized anthemion sprays and ebonized lines.
(c.1850; ht 71.5cm/28¼in; value **G**)

TYPES OF DECORATION

As with other types of furniture, chests-of-drawers made after 1840 were decorated with a wide variety of ornamentation, reviving styles from previous centuries and employing mechanization to speed up production. The fine marquetry decoration that had graced Dutch cabinets-on-stands and other case furniture from the end of the 17th century, by such outstanding craftsmen as Jan van Mekeren (1658–1733), continued to be made throughout the 18th century and was still a popular form of decoration in The Netherlands during the 19th century. The style normally associated with Dutch marquetry is that of flowers with birds and foliate scrolls. However, particularly from the second quarter of the 19th century, more Neo-classical motifs, including ribbon-tied swags, urns, and stiff leaves, were common, usually inlaid on mahogany grounds.

The fascination with Oriental art, dating from the 17th century, had a widespread appeal during the 19th. One of the strongest expressions of this taste can be seen

▼ Commode by François Linke (1855–1946)

This French kingwood and parquetry commode, with fine ormolou mounts is almost an exact copy of a commode of c.1730 in the Wallace Collection, London, by Charles Cressent (1685–1768), one of the finest cabinet-makers working in France during the Louis XV period. Linke was one of the most celebrated cabinet-makers in late 19th-century France, when Paris was the center of luxury, and his work is usually associated with the Louis XVI Revival style.
(c.1880; ht 97cm/38½in; value Q)

▲ Commode

This French commode is made of kingwood with fine marquetry decoration and panels of *vernis Martin*, the best type of japanning, which was developed in Paris by the Martin family during the mid-18th century. The Louis XV style bombé form is painted with a *fête galante* (an idyllic open-air scene) in the style of Rococo paintings. The interior is fitted with two adjustable shelves.
(c.1890; ht 1.2m/3ft 11in; value H)

▼ Wellington chest

Made of burr-walnut, this fine British Wellington chest is one of a pair, which will immediately increase the value considerably. It has a moulded rectangular top above six graduated drawers, flanked by stiles carved with Classical style acanthus leaves and drapery corbels. One side has a hinged locking mechanism, which is one of the characteristics of this type of chest. The whole piece is raised up on a simple moulded plinth.
(1875–1900; ht 1.3m/4ft 3in; value for a pair L)

in the style and furnishings of Brighton Pavilion, designed for the Prince of Wales (later George IV) during the early 19th century. The style of the buildings and its furnishings continued the fashion for chinoiseries already set in the 18th century, using such materials as bamboo, japanning (a European version of lacquering), and caning. While real bamboo was generally used for Regency bamboo furniture, by the 1860s it had largely been replaced by imitation bamboo using such woods such as walnut and beech, and in the USA maple. The wood was turned, carved, and painted to simulate bamboo, in the manner already practiced by the Chinese in the 17th century. The Oriental influence was also strongly felt in the USA, where the production of imitation bamboo furniture was at its height during the 1880s. The forms made were distinctly Western, and the furniture was considered especially suitable for light, summery interiors in country houses, where the hot summer months would be passed, or for use in conservatories and as garden furniture. In Britain the craze for whimsical "bamboo" furniture was given a further boost when Japanese art was shown at the International Exhibition of 1862 in London, which gave rise to the Aesthetic Movement. Between 1869 and 1935 there were over 150 firms registered in Britain manufacturing "bamboo" furniture, including those

with such exotic names as the Aizdu Bamboo Co. (est. 1884) in London and the Mikado Co. (est. 1893) in Birmingham. In the USA, where imitation bamboo was more popular than real bamboo, such firms as C.A. Aimone, the Kilian Bros, and George Hunzinger in New York were notable producers.

Another form of "Oriental" decoration was japanning. During the mid-18th century the Martin family in Paris were well known for their version of japanning, where the carcase was prepared and painted with Oriental designs or *fêtes galantes* (open-air scenes) inspired by the paintings of Antoine Watteau and François Boucher. Numerous coats of amber varnish were then added until a hard coating was achieved. This technique was revived in the 19th century, although the quality achieved was never the same.

Inexpensive timbers could be grained or stained to resemble luxury woods. Thomas Sheraton (1751–1806) had given instructions in *The Cabinet Dictionary* (1803), and Nathaniel Whittock had suggested several ways of imitating timbers such as rosewood in *The Decorative Painters' and Glaziers' Guide* (1827). Whittock also advised on the creation of marbling effects.

Pieces decorated in this way remained popular as occasional and bedroom furniture well into the third quarter of the 19th century, and were revived again in the early years of the 20th. Painted pieces were produced in large quantities, but are now scarce in original condition as the paintwork has rubbed off, or worse, has been stripped off completely. The practice of stripping antiques has now largely stopped, and pieces with original decoration are keenly sought after.

THE REVIVAL STYLES

Throughout the 19th century the revival of styles affected all forms of furniture, and the chest-of-drawers was no exception. Of all styles, the most influential and pervasive throughout Europe were those of the Louis XV and XVI periods. While every country revived furniture styles from periods that had national connotations (Britain "Gothic" and Elizabethan, Italy "Renaissance"), most manufactured furniture in these 18th-century styles. By the end of the 19th century furniture made in different countries was often so similar that it can be difficult to tell where it was actually made. The increasing ease of communication, mechanization, and manufacture continued to dilute national characteristics.

At the International Exhibition of 1867 in Paris, the British firm of Wright & Mansfield (est. 1860) in London, won the supreme award for furniture. It showed a Neo-classical satinwood cabinet in the style of the architect Robert Adam (1728–92), decorated with plaques provided by the firm of Wedgwood. This gave rise in the 1880s to a revival of furniture based on the designs of Thomas Sheraton (1751–1806) and George Hepplewhite (d.1786). Sheraton Revival chests-of-drawers were usually made in light mahogany, satinwood or satin-birch, and decorated with inlaid stringing lines and shells or fan shapes, or painted with flowers and foliate scrolls. A series of books on interior design published in the late 1870s was directed at the middle classes and confirmed the fashion for Adam, Hepplewhite, and Sheraton, and in 1897 Sheraton's

▲ Chest-of-drawers
An interesting feature of this Victorian satin-birch bow-front chest is the way in which the front surface has been conceived as a whole; the veneers are skilfully cut to create the effect of a rippled flame moving upward through the drawers. The cartouche featured on the shaped apron depicts a fruiting oak-leaf. The legs are splayed.
*(1880–90; ht 88cm/34½in; value **G**)*

► Commode
This ormolu-mounted rosewood, parquetry, and marquetry breakfront commode is in the Transitional style (of the type made in France between the Rococo and Neo-classical periods) and was made in Stockholm, Sweden. The break-front section is hinged and opens to reveal an interior fitted with three drawers. Ormolu decoration includes Vitruvian scrolling, a ribbon-tied laurel wreath, acanthus, and paw feet.
*(1916; ht 91cm/35¾in; value **H**)*

◄ Commode
This British commode is in George III style. The ribbon-tied scrolling foliage, anthemia, and floral sprays with urns at the sides are all common motifs for the period. The doors have been quarter-veneered, to focus the eye on the central oval panels and to increase the decorative effect, as the figuring runs in contrasting directions.
*(c.1910; ht 84cm/33in; value **H**)*

The Cabinet-Maker and Upholsterer's Drawing Book (1791–1802) and Hepplewhite's *The Cabinet-Maker and Upholsterer's Guide* (1788–94) were reprinted. Out of these revivals came the Edwardian style, which contained features of all three designers, adapted in shape and proportion, often using mahogany or satin-birch, and with bone inlay or painted ornamentation for decoration. Revivals were subject to misinterpretation, and copies were not always successful. For example, the slenderness of Sheraton forms was often slimmed down even more, and could look too attenuated and rather spindly. After the eclectisism of the earlier 19th century, when various styles from different periods were thrown together, toward the end of the 19th century, there was a move by some firms to reproduce excellent, close copies of the original works. Some of these are indistinguishable from the originals. Firms such as Gillow (est. *c*.1730) of Lancaster, and Edwards & Roberts (est. 1845) of London, developed reputations for these high-quality reproductions. Edwards & Roberts clearly stamped or labeled its chests-of-drawers. However, as it dealt in antiques and modern furniture as well as reproductions, and stamped or labeled everything that that came through its doors, it is often difficult to tell one of its copies from a genuine 18th-century piece. As well as precise copies by top firms, inexpensive imitations were produced elsewhere.

KEY FACTS
- VENEERING check that veneers have not been used to cover poor construction
- DATING most chests look distinctly 19th century, but there were fine copies of 18th-century examples made, which can now be very difficult to distinguish; a 19th-century mark or signature tends to be on mounts or locks rather than on the carcase, as in the 18th century
- SIZE as a general rule of thumb, smaller chests-of-drawers tend to be more commercial – however, beware of fakes and items made from associated pieces
- MARKS some firms marked their furniture with stamps or labels; marks can often be found on hinges

See also Chests-of-drawers before 1840, pp.80–82

Cabinets-on-stands

Created for the storage of papers and valuables, the earliest cabinets, known as "table-cabinets" as they stood on tables rather than stands, came into fashion in the 16th century. During this period they were made in Tuscany with inlaid architectural decoration, and in Augsburg with stylized Mannerist marquetry depicting architectural ruins and mythical beasts in the style of Lorenz Stöer's *Geometrica et Perspectiva* (1567); in Spain cabinets were made with Moorish-inspired *mudéjar* (marquetry), or in ebony with parquetry (these were also produced in the Spanish Netherlands).

MARQUETRY AND LACQUERED CABINETS

The Baroque love of rich, florid decoration led to the fashion for oyster-veneered and marquetry cabinets-on-stands, the production of which was dominated by Huguenot craftsmen trained in Amsterdam and The Hague. In the late 17th century oyster-veneering was gradually superseded by such elaborate decoration as "seaweed" marquetry, which in turn gave way to Boulle marquetry on a tortoiseshell or kingwood ground. Interestingly the illusionistic floral marquetry panels executed by André-Charles Boulle (1642–1732) at the Gobelins workshops in Paris were no doubt inspired by Dutch 17th-century still-life paintings. Floral marquetry cabinets, often enriched with mother-of-pearl or green-stained ivory, were executed throughout Europe from the 1660s, but the most celebrated makers were Jan van Mekeren (1658–1733) in Amsterdam, and Pierre Gole (*c*.1620–84) in Paris. Often decorated with flowers and birds, even exotic parrots, Dutch and English examples of the William and Mary period (1689–1702) are usually of walnut with oak-lined drawers, the stands enclosing two drawers and supported on four, five, or six baluster or barley-twist legs with waved stretchers and bun feet.

◄ **Chinese export cabinet**
It is often difficult to distinguish between Chinese and Japanese cabinets, as each imitated the other; however, Chinese cabinets are often revealed by the character marks painted to the reverse of the drawers. In this example the stand is English.
(late 18th century; ht 1.5m/4ft 11in; value I)

▼ **Cabinet-on-stand**
During the 19th century cabinets exotically decorated with carved ivory plaques were made in Dieppe, while very fine enamel-mounted ebonized examples, such as that shown here, were specialities of cabinet-makers in Vienna.
(c.1890; ht 1.4m/4ft 7in; value O)

Japanese and Chinese lacquer cabinets were first imported by the East India companies in the 17th century. Usually decorated with gilt chinoiseries on aubergine, black, or red lacquer grounds, they were mounted in silver, copper, or brass, with chased hinges and escutcheons. Oriental cabinets were exported without stands, and late 17th-century stands made in The Netherlands, Britain, and Germany tend to be in the florid Baroque taste, with caryatids in the angles and deep, pierced foliate aprons.

In the late 17th century, in response to the demand for and cost of Oriental lacquer, European craftsmen created japanning. This technique was first practiced in Berlin by Gerard Dagly (1657–1715), and in England by John Stalker and George Parker who wrote *A Treatise of Japanning and Varnishing* (1688). Later 18th-century examples are distinguished by the design of their stands, which were usually also japanned, and often enriched with Chinese fret angle-brackets.

In the 19th century the cabinet-on-stand was replaced by the display cabinet. As a result, 19th-century cabinets-on-stands tend to hark back to 17th-century prototypes, in particular those with ebony-and-tortoiseshell veneer, or of a full-blown Baroque character, with Boulle or floral marquetry and *pietre dure* plaques.

◄ **Cabinet-on-stand**
This is a excellent example of the fine marquetry cabinets-on-stands that were first made in the Gobelins workshops in Paris, then in Amsterdam and The Hague, and later in England after the Revocation of the Edict of Nantes (1685), when Huguenot craftsmen sought refuge in Britain from religious persecution in France.
(c.1690; ht 2m/6ft 7in; value O)

KEY FACTS

- MARQUETRY CABINETS a flat stretcher is commonly used on the stand; frequently the legs have been replaced, and this will reduce value; ivory inlay is a sign of good quality; the marquetry on the inside of the cabinet should be of a rich contrast to the outside, as it has not been exposed to sunlight, and should retain its vibrant colors; during the 1770s and again in the 1840s there was an interest in antiquarianism, and 17th-century marquetry door panels were often removed and reused in more fashionable pieces of furniture
- JAPANNING when chipped, it reveals a whitish gesso

See also Early chests-of-drawers, pp.78–9; Display cabinets, pp.92–3

High chests-of-drawers

Chests-on-stands, also known as high chests-of-drawers or highboys, were a development of the chest-of-drawers. The form comprises a series of short drawers at the top, three or four long, graduated drawers beneath, and two or three drawers in the stand. The form was made in England from the end of the 17th century in walnut veneer, with double-twist turned supports, barley-twist or cup-and-cover legs, flat stretchers, and a plain moulded cornice. This piece of furniture became a singularly American form after c.1730.

AMERICAN HIGH CHESTS-OF-DRAWERS

From the 1690s to the 1730s, following the popular London styles, cabinet-makers in New England and Pennsylvania made chests-of-drawers on tall barley-twist, scroll, and trumpet-turned legs, with matching dressing tables (lowboys) for use in the bedchamber. Their arched aprons (skirts) generally accommodated three drawers. Blind frieze drawers are found on some made in New York and New England. The finest are veneered with richly figured burr-walnut, their drawers outlined with herringbone veneer. Others are made of solid maple or cherry, and some are painted. Several from Boston, with four cabriole legs instead of six turned legs, have their original japanned decoration.

By the 1750s high chests with broken-arch pediments had come into vogue. The Philadelphia high chest was lighter and more graceful, with a richly carved middle drawer in the lower section, the upper case, like the lower, flanked by fluted quarter columns, and topped

by a richly carved broken-arch pediment with carved rosettes, a cartouche in the center, and flame finials at the corners. The typanum of the arch, no longer housing a drawer, was filled with Rococo streamers, leaves, and grasses, while carving decorated the apron and knees. *The Gentleman and Cabinet-Maker's Director* (1754–62) by Thomas Chippendale (1718–79) influenced the design of a horizontal cornices, which in the 1760s and 1770s separated the carved scrolled pediments from the unadorned façades of the drawer fronts.

High chests made away from the coastal cities are country versions of those made in urban centers. Those made in Lancaster County inland Pennsylvania, reflect the Philadelphia style, while those from the back country of the Shenandoah Valley are largely influenced by Pennsylvania forms that the settlers of that region were familiar with; eccentric maple chests, stained to simulate mahogany, were made in New Hampshire by the Dunlap family, suggesting their Scottish/Irish origin. In New York and the South they preferred the chest-on-chest form.

◄ High chest-of-drawers
This is a classic example of a walnut high chest-of-drawers with quarter-veneering on the sides and featherbanding decoration. Although the spirally turned legs, shaped flat stretcher, and bun feet have all been replaced. The richly figured timber and color still make it a desirable example of English furniture.
(c.1705–10; ht 1.7m/5ft 7in; value **J**)

◄ High chest-of-drawers
There are specific features about this mahogany high chest-of-drawers from Newport, Rhode Island, that leaves us in no doubt of its origin. These include the closed broken-arch pediment, paneled scroll board, detachable squared cabriole legs ending in pad feet, and ribbed mouldings on the upper, rather than the lower, case. The only carving is the single shell on the gently scrolled apron, unlike the more elaborate Rococo ornament seen on the chest (below right) from Philadelphia. This reliance on the richly figured wood, quiet refinement, and superb proportions are characteristic of the work of the Quaker cabinet-makers in Newport.
(c.1755–79; ht 2.2m/7ft 3in; value **Q**)

▼ High chest-of-drawers
The vertical thrust of this typical Philadelphia high chest is achieved by the spring of its cabriole legs, its fluted corner columns, and the play of solids and voids in its scrolled swan-neck pediment ending in carved rosettes, topped by a Rococo cartouche flanked by flame finials on fluted plinths. It is free of excessive ornament – only scalloping of the apron, the Rococo shell and grasses on the top and bottom drawers, and a cartouche embellish this unique American form, which in London was supplanted by the chest-on-chest by the mid-18th century.
(c.1775–80; ht 2.4m/7ft 10in; value **Q**)

KEY FACTS

- CONSTRUCTION some flat-top high chests were fitted with pedestals for displaying ceramics
- ALTERATIONS high chests were made in two parts, which were sometimes separated; the top was often given feet and sold as a chest-of-drawers, and the bottom given a new top and sold as an over-size dressing table or serving table; even in their altered states, they are considered of value
- COLLECTING in the USA high chests have long been the most highly priced type of furniture; matching high chests and dressing tables will achieve a premium

See also Dressing tables, pp.62–3; Early chests-of-drawers, pp.78–9

Chests-on-chests

Although they were inspired by the 16th-century *meuble en deux corps* that was associated with the period of Henry II in France (1547–59), it was not until the late 17th century that *vargueños* on chests, escritoires, and chests-on-chests (tallboys), without fall fronts or top sections, were recorded in England. Traditionally of oak, although gradually superseded by walnut versions during the reign of William and Mary (1689–1702), the earliest chests-on-chests are rare indeed; they are of a very simple form, with a low "waist," and are supported on plain bun feet.

▲ *Vargueño* on chest
This Spanish *vargueño* and matching chest have characteristic decoration, with geometrical carving with heavy gilding; this is inspired by Hispano-Moresque designs. The shells on the supporting lopers symbolize Santiago.
(17th century; ht 1.5m/4ft 11in; value K)

18TH-CENTURY WALNUT CHESTS-ON-CHESTS

It was under Queen Anne (1702–14) and George I (1714–27) that walnut chests-on-chests became increasingly sophisticated. Usually with plain moulded cornices above two or three small frieze drawers and six or seven long drawers, standing on moulded plinths and bun, or later bracket, feet, these early chests-on-chests are entirely dependent upon the figuring and coloring of the veneer for effect. Burr veneers, and particularly burr-walnut, were therefore highly prized, as this timber displays a far richer figuring than straight-grained walnut. By its very nature, burr-walnut (cut from diseased branches) does not exist in large sections, and so it is a sign of good quality when the veneer has been applied in strips, often mirror-matched, rather than in long sections, as the latter would suggest that the surface has been either reveneered or "grained," whereby straight-grained walnut has been painted to simulate a burr wood. While the plainest, and indeed often the earliest, examples have little or no decoration,

save for a tidy construction of overlapping drawer-mouldings, during the first quarter of the 18th century chests-on-chests became increasingly architectural in form and elaborate in decoration, with dentiled cornices, canted and fluted angles, shaped bracket feet, crossbanding and featherbanding, and even chequerbanded inlay. The most sophisticated examples are inlaid with a "sunburst," usually in ebony and walnut but occasionally in ivory, in the center of the lower drawer, which has a concave front to create a sense of movement. A further development of this period was the secrétaire chest-on-chest, in which the top drawer of the lower section has a fall front that conceals a fitted interior with writing-surface, drawers, and pigeon holes.

As with bachelors' chests, originality, color, and patina are very important when looking at a chest-on-chest from this period. Elaborate crossbanding and inlay, unusually richly figured veneers, and replaced handles and feet are often later "improvements" to enhance the value of the piece. The handles, if original (in which case there is little reason for them all to have ever been taken out), are a very good indicator of quality and craftmanship, and the finest early 18th-century examples are of richly lacquered brass with a pierced, sometimes engraved, backplates.

18TH-CENTURY MAHOGANY CHESTS-ON-CHESTS

Although provincial furniture-makers continued to work with indigenous woods such as oak, elm, and walnut, from the 1730s walnut was increasingly superseded by mahogany. Usually made in the solid, rather than veneered, mahogany chests-on-chests of the George II period (1727–60), built on the architectural legacy of their walnut forebears, reached their Rococo fruition in the 1760s through *The Gentleman and Cabinet-Maker's Director* (1754–62) by Thomas Chippendale (1718–79). Friezes, hitherto always plain, were now carved in relief with mythological deities in the Palladian style, which had been promoted by William Kent (*c.*1685–1748) in the 1730s, with stylized acanthus sprays in the manner of William Hallett (*c.*1707–81) in the 1740s, or with interlaced blind-fretwork in the Chinese manner popularized by William Chambers (1723–96) in the 1750s. Similarly, cornices that had previously been flat became pedimented, swan-necked, and segmental, even centered by splayed eagles or acanthus cartouches, while the restrained bracket feet of the

▲ Chest-on-chest
This English chest-on-chest is an outstanding example of early Georgian cabinet-making. The burr- and figured-walnut (typical of the period) is of the very best color, as are the crossbanding and featherbanding; the half sunburst in the bottom drawer is a feature indicative of the highest-quality furniture.
(1720–25; ht 1.8m/5ft 11in; value Q)

▶ Chest-on-chest
Such features as blind fretwork on the cornice and canted angles, simple drop handles, and ogee-bracket feet make this mahogany tallboy a classic example of George III cabinet-making.
(1770; ht 1.7m/5ft 7in; value J)

STYLES OF PEDIMENTS

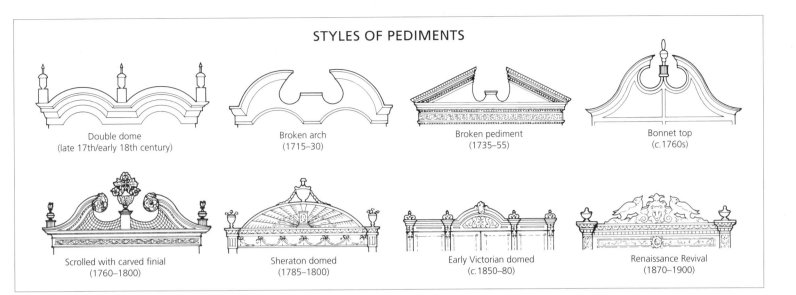

Double dome
(late 17th/early 18th century)

Broken arch
(1715–30)

Broken pediment
(1735–55)

Bonnet top
(c.1760s)

Scrolled with carved finial
(1760–1800)

Sheraton domed
(1785–1800)

Early Victorian domed
(c.1850–80)

Renaissance Revival
(1870–1900)

early 18th century were discarded in favor of Gothic ogee-bracket feet, often with carved and applied decoration. Moreover, this Rococo ornament was echoed in the increasingly elaborate gilt-bronze handles, often manufactured in Birmingham, with a rich lacquered finish, and cast with C-scrolls, flowers, and chinoiserie pagodas.

Perhaps the rarest chests-on-chests are the serpentine-fronted examples executed by Chippendale and his contemporaries during the 1760s. Often still with carrying handles to both upper and lower sections, a surviving trait from the French 17th-century concept of a commode-on-stand, they have cabriole legs and scroll feet.

The Neo-classical style that swept through Europe from the late 1750s and 1760s heralded a return to linearity and architectural purity. This new Classical language, first expounded by architects such as James "Athenian" Stuart (1713–88) and Robert Adam (1728–92) and adopted by cabinet-makers such as Chippendale, John Mayhew (1736–1811), and William Ince (c.1738–1804), was inevitably reflected in chest-on-chest patterns made during the reign of George III (1760–1820). Increasingly plain and usually of mahogany, with plain bracket or, occasionally, square tapering feet and flat-dentiled cornice, the more refined George III chests-on-chests are inlaid with ebony lines in the "Etruscan" manner, or embellished with marquetry decoration including trailed husks to the angles or paterae to the friezes. This Neo-classicism gave way to the lighter "French" style promoted by Thomas Sheraton (1751–1806) and George Hepplewhite (d.1786) in their respective pattern-books, *The Cabinet-Maker and Upholsterer's Drawing Book* (1791–1802) and *The Cabinet-Maker and Upholsterer's Guide* (1788–94). The chests-on-chests of the 1790s, often bow-fronted in form, are characterized by their plain decoration and splayed feet. Although the chest-on-chest was a popular form throughout the 19th century, later ones are usually inspired by 18th-century precedents and patterns.

▲ Chest-on-chest

The blocked lower section and fluted pilasters flanking flat drawers in the upper section are typical of the mahogany chest-on-chest from Massachusetts. Its small size, classic proportions, rich color, and especially the carved and gilded American eagle finial, make this an example of high-style Boston furniture from before the Revolution.
(c.1770–85; ht 2.2m/7ft 3in; value Q)

AMERICAN CHESTS-ON-CHESTS

Mahogany chests-on-chests, also known as "double chests-of-drawers," were to find their true expression in the hands of North American cabinet-makers such as John Cogswell (d.1818) and Stephen Badlam (1751–1815) in Boston, Massachusetts, Thomas Affleck (1740–95) in Philadelphia, Pennsylvania, and Thomas Elfe (1759–1825) in Charleston, South Carolina. Some country examples made by John Dunlap (1746–92) and Samuel Dunlap (1752–1830), and others in New Hampshire, are supported by free-standing frames. In some the top drawers of the lower sections are fitted as secretary drawers. Some examples from Massachusetts have blocked, serpentine, or bombé lower sections; a few made in Boston and Salem are elaborately ornamented with carved figures. Although Philadelphia chests-on-chests were made at the height of the Rococo period (1765–80), evidence of the Rococo is found only in the naturalistic carvings in the pediments and the swirled grain of the mahogany drawer fronts. A horizontal cornice separates the carved pediment with pierced tympanum from the unadorned façade. Chests from Charleston are closely modeled on English prototypes; some have removable broken-scroll pediments, and finely figured mahogany veneer glued of cores of straight-grained mahogany.

KEY FACTS

- **FORM** it is usual for a chest-on-chest to have three short drawers in the top section above three long drawers and three graduated drawers in the bottom section
- **BEWARE** beware of chests of drawers with three short drawers at the top: because of the desire for shorter pieces of furniture that fit in with the scale of houses today, the top sections of many tallboys have been provided with feet and made into chests-of-drawers; it should be clear that the top has later veneering – the top of the tallboy was not veneered, as it was too high to be seen; beware of tallboys inlaid with a sunburst (which is a particularly good feature), as this could be from a later date: on later examples the shaping is clearly more angular and awkward
- **QUALITY OF TIMBER** this is one of the most important considerations when assessing the value of tallboys

See also Early cupboards and meubles en deux corps, p.72

Dressers

The name dresser is derived from the French *dressoir*, a medieval piece of furniture used either as a sideboard for displaying plate and for serving wine, or in the service quarters for preparing and serving food, and for storing dishes and utensils. The ceremonial functions of the *dressoir* were transferred during the 16th and 17th centuries to the buffet or court cupboard. Enclosing the space between the middle and the top shelf with doors established the cupboard as we know it. The later type of court cupboard has an open lower stage and recessed cupboards in the upper section, or is a combination piece with cupboards, drawers, and display shelves – the now familiar dresser.

▲ Low dresser
This oak low dresser has a moulded top above three frieze drawers and a pair of cupboards flanking the central bank of drawers. The geometrical paneled drawers and the inlaid star motif on the arch-paneled doors suggest that it was made in the north-west of England, probably Lancashire or Westmorland.
(late 17th century; ht 92cm/36in; value **K***)*

EARLY DRESSERS

The early dresser consisted simply of a side table with drawers supported on turned legs. Some examples had stretchers, and from the late 17th century this base structure became the framework for a "potboard," or shelf. From the early 17th century these low dressers were also made with cupboards below the drawers and, later, with additional drawers between two cupboards. With the fashion for tin-glazed earthenware after *c*.1650 the "delft rack" – a set of shelves on which to display delftware – was introduced. It was not long before such racks were set up on dresser bases to form an integrated item of furniture – the dresser with a superstructure. The medieval *dressoir*, combining usefulness and display, was thus re-invented *c*.1790 for the homes of the middle classes, particularly in the rural northern and western areas of Britain.

The dresser flourished as an important item of furniture, most particularly in Wales, but also in the north-west and south-west of England, with each type having strong regional characteristics. The dresser was a country type, distinct from fashionable metropolitan furniture, and the object of desire of the well-to-do farmer. Designs were therefore traditional and conservative rather than modish, which makes dating them difficult.

► Low dresser
This oak dresser from the Swansea Valley, with an open base and potboard, is typical of South Wales dressers. The brass handle-plates have been attached upside down to conform with the inlaid holly "line and berry" decoration.
(early 18th century; ht 75cm/29½in; value **L***)*

OPEN DRESSERS

The typical South Wales dresser, with an open rack and an open base below the potboard, is simply a side table with a rack. Similar "open" types evolved in south-west Britain, where the dresser seems to have been established by the mid-18th century. Early 19th-century Cornish examples can be particularly elegant, with bowed cornices in the Regency fashion. Dressers from Devon, whether designed for parlor or dairy, were usually of oak or elm, and plain in style. Those for use in the dairy had open bases. The type with cupboards in the base evolved into the fully enclosed dresser with glazed upper shelves in the early 19th century. Most Somerset dressers were classically simple. One 19th-century type has a boarded back to the upper stage, which generally consists of three shelves, and a pair of drawers surmounting cupboards in the base; elm and/or pine are the usual timbers. Late 18th-century dressers from the Bridgwater area consist of open shelves throughout, with side supports of continuous planks.

▼ Closed dresser
This oak dresser has a moulded cornice and shaped frieze above a "closed" rack. The base has a moulded top and shaped apron, with three drawers crossbanded in yew, and the dresser stands on cabriole legs. Both the crossbanding and the legs suggest Shropshire or Lancashire origins; the superstructure may have been added at a later date.
(mid-18th century; ht 2m/6ft 7in; value **J***)*

Decorative motifs as well as patterns of construction sometimes spread far beyond their areas of origin. The inlaid floral motif, sometimes known as "line and berry," familiar on dressers from around Swansea, appears on dressers from the eastern coastal areas of North America. Oak furniture with inlaid decoration or mahogany crossbanding on drawers suggests a West Yorkshire, Lancashire, or Cheshire origin.

In the 19th century many dressers were decorated with grained paintwork or stains. In Ireland the dresser, which hardly appeared before the 19th century, had a vigorously fretted and often pierced cornice with pilasters flanking the rack, and shaped sides projecting forward to enclose the sides of the working surface. The bases of some are open and may have been curtained, while others have chicken coops in the base. Scottish dressers also typically have upstanding lips at either end of the boards; some have sloping tops to the racks to accommodate the low, angled roofs of crofters' cottages. The so-called hen coop in the center of some Scottish dresser bases was actually a slat-fronted food cupboard.

CLOSED DRESSERS

Dressers from north Wales and northern England (Yorkshire, Lancashire, and Cheshire) are nearly always closed, with boards behind the shelves in the upper part. A distinctive early type from the Caernarvon area in north-west Wales has a pair of spice cupboards set into the rack, and such cupboards also appear in dressers from northern and western England. Small spice drawers placed in varying parts of the upper stages are features of many 18th-century dressers from northern Britain. The "dog-kennel" dresser, with its cupboards flanking a central open space in the base, originated in the Carmarthen area, but was later made in other parts of Wales, and in England.

Some mid-Wales dressers combine the "northern" and "southern" forms, having potboards below and racks boarded at the back. A version of this pattern is the Montgomery dresser, characterized by its broad proportions and pilaster cupboards flanking the shelves in the rack. The Shropshire dresser has cabriole legs, some resting on potboards, while others are free-standing. Either way their broadness is emphasized by square cupboards in the upper section, in contrast to the slender pilaster cupboards of the Montgomery dresser.

TIMBER AND DECORATION

Most dressers were made from oak, but fine examples in elm, ash, fruitwood, yew, chestnut, and walnut exist. Pine dressers were made in Scotland, Ireland, and south-west England, and many of them were painted. While they too can be identified by their regional characteristics, these dressers were primarily utilitarian, in contrast to those made in Wales, the West Midlands, Derbyshire, Yorkshire, and the north-west of England, which were important showpieces, handed down from generation to generation.

▲ **Closed dresser**
This oak dresser on stile feet was made in northern England. It has a moulded cornice above a "closed" superstructure; the paneled base has three frieze drawers above cupboards, and two central dummy drawers. The handles on this example are probably not original, even though they are in the late 18th-century style; there are cuts in the timber in the frieze drawers, which show where earlier handles may have been situated.
(c.1760–90; ht 2.2m/7ft 3in; value L)

▶ **Dish cupboard**
This poplar style of cupboard was made in the Pennsylvania Dutch region, probably in Lancaster County. The cupboard or dresser was designed for practical use in the kitchen. Dressers made of walnut or painted poplar were constructed in the German wood-working tradition, with wedged dovetails on drawers and a backboard held in place by wooden pegs. This example shows traces of the green-blue paint that would once have decorated it.
(c.1750–80; ht 2m/6ft 7in; value P)

KEY FACTS

- MADE-UP DRESSERS during the 19th century dressers were made from recycled timbers, or as reproductions although from new timbers; with over 100 years of patination, many of these look 18th century
- MARRIAGES often bases and racks are put together; some low dressers may have had racks added to them
- ALTERATIONS backboards have often been added to open racks; repairs to the feet are inevitable because of the ravages of wear, damp floors, and woodworm; shaped aprons and carved friezes have often been added to "improve" plain dressers

See also Early cupboards and meubles en deux corps, p.72

Display cabinets

At the end of the 17th century the display cabinet evolved from the cabinet-on-stand tradition, and adopted many of the same features. The principal difference was that the outer doors of the cabinet were not solid, enabling the contents of the shelves – not drawers – inside to be easily viewed.

▼ Display cabinet by Jean-Baptiste Vassou (1739–1807)
The fine techniques used to make this amaranth-and-tulipwood parquetry cabinet are typical of the high standard of 18th-century French cabinet-making. The interior is lined with yellow silk, and the glazing was added in the 19th century.
(c.1765; ht 1.6m/5ft 3in; value J)

▲ Display cabinet
The blind fretwork and pierced-spandrel angle brackets of this mahogany cabinet are typical of Chippendale's "Chinese" style in *The Cabinet-Maker and Upholsterer's Director*, his designs inspired by Chinese lacquer cabinets-on-stands. A similar item was illustrated by Ince & Mayhew in *The Universal System of Household Furniture* (1762); they recommended it for japanning. The glass is heavily beveled and is a 19th-century addition – there may have been no glass originally.
(c.1780; ht 1.2m/3ft 11in; value L)

EARLY CABINETS
Italian cabinets were developed from the cabinet-on-stand tradition, and by the mid-17th century Baroque display cabinets or showcases were also made. These were incredibly grand, opulent, and dramatic, made to display collections of semi-precious stones, minerals, plaques, or other curiosities. In Rome, glass-fronted cabinets were designed by architects, such as Gian Lorenzo Bernini (1598–1680) and Francesco Borromini (1599–1677), and such architectural features as pediments, columns, and sculptural finials prevail. Cabinet-makers in Florence quickly adopted these ideas and combined them with their own tradition of *pietre dure* panels and gilt-bronze mounts.

The fashion for displaying objects arose with the craze for Chinese porcelain and blue-and-white Delftware at the end of the 17th century. Although an elaborate series of shelves was commonly used for their display, fine cabinets attested to the owner's wealth and cultured tastes, and were symbols of great pride,

especially as they were quite rare until the the 18th century. In England the late 17th-century display cabinet had glazed doors with half-round mouldings resembling those found on drawer fronts of the period, and the sides were veneered with walnut, often quarter-veneered. Supported on turned legs and stretchers, it might also have contained two drawers behind the doors, and rested on bun feet. Contemporary cabinets from The Netherlands were influential, partly owing to the Delftware displayed within, and partly because of Dutch craftsmen living and working in England. Marquetry was still used in both English and Dutch designs. In England, after the end of Charles II's reign (1685), colored marquetry became more subtle, and arabesques were more popular than flowers and foliage. Alternatively, colored metal or brass-and-tortoiseshell veneering, in imitation of the latest Parisian fashion inspired by Pierre Gole (*c.*1620–84) and André-Charles Boulle (1642–1732), were also used at this time, although still confined to the wealthiest patrons.

ENGLISH 18TH-CENTURY CABINETS
The earliest 18th-century display cabinets were simple in construction and were almost identical to contemporary bookcases or bureau bookcases and cabinets. The most common features included fine proportions, chamfered corners, gilded mouldings, and rich veneers. Between 1730 and 1750 mahogany gradually replaced walnut as the preferred wood, and also from 1730 the influence of William Kent (*c.*1685–1748) and Palladianism promoted the use of broken pediments and architectural overtones similar to those used in bookcases. Scrolled brackets, eagles' heads, lion-masks, and garlands were typical decoration. The cabinets themselves were variously designed – in three sections with a "break-front," or in two, with stands or on solid bases with doors. Marquetry decoration was replaced with finely carved wood although there were still instances of japanned cabinets and inlay with ivory plaques.

From *c.*1750, cabinets were decorated with Rococo ornament, inspired by France, or with Gothic or Chinese details, largely due to the hugely influential designs of Thomas Chippendale (1718–79) and his pattern-book *The Cabinet-Maker and Upholsterer's Director* (1754–62). Chinese-inspired designs were especially important for display cabinets, as a result of the quantities of Chinese porcelain displayed inside them, and also as a result of the

► Table vitrine
This *vitrine* (fully glazed cabinet) was made in Paris in the Louis XV Revival style. The glass top and sides display the contents while keeping the items dust free, but the top pane is hinged so that objects may be taken out and inspected. The *bijouterie* was a similar display cabinet, also often combined with a tabletop.
(c.1880; ht 79cm/31in; value H)

continuing vogue for Oriental decoration. Pagoda-shaped roofs and mouldings, openwork friezes, latticed galleries, and longitudinal glazing are characteristic of this style. Chippendale favored chinoiserie above all else, although he was not averse to uniting it with distinctive Rococo touches. In *The Universal System of Household Furniture* (1762), John Mayhew (1736–1811) and William Ince (*c*.1738–1804) describe a "china case for Japanning the inside all of looking-glass, in that manner it has been executed, and has a very elegant effect." Japanned cabinets were extremely popular, as were those that featured panels of imported Oriental lacquer. Hanging corner cabinets, made of mahogany and with similar motifs, were also produced, although in smaller numbers than the cabinets.

The design of cabinets was definitively modified by the aspirations of Neo-classicist architects, particularly Robert Adam (1728–92), and cabinet-makers from 1760. Influenced by Classical architecture, the new cabinets were more simple than their predecessors. Doors and cupboards were framed with tapered and fluted columns and pilasters; cornices were surmounted by scrolled and pierced pediments, frequently with urns at the corners and centers; and friezes were delicately carved with anthemia, sheaves of wheat, or honeysuckle motifs. Mahogany was gradually superseded by satinwood or exotic wood veneers, and some cabinets were painted in subtle colors. The construction and look of all these display cabinets were still similar to, but slightly more delicate than, those of contemporary bookcases. The similarity is so close that *The Cabinet-Maker and Upholsterer's Guide* (1788–94) by George Hepplewhite (*d*.1786) does not feature display cabinets as such. The astragals (glazing bars) and cornices illustrated on a separate plate were considered to be equally suitable for both bookcases and cabinets.

REVIVALISM AND THE BELLE EPOQUE

During the 19th century, revivalism dominated fashions in cabinet-making throughout Europe and North America. In Italy the Renaissance Revival (known as Dantesque) was popular, and cabinets made in this style were carved with elements taken from the earlier period. The Florentine cabinet-maker Andrea Baccetti was arguably the greatest exponent of the Italian Renaissance Revival, making richly carved furniture during the 1860s and 1870s. As was usual, the 19th-century revivals were generally loose interpretations of the earlier styles; for example, "Renaissance" cabinets were made of rosewood with parcel gilding, materials unheard of in Europe during the 15th and 16th centuries.

In The Netherlands, the large, traditional 18th-century Dutch display cabinets were reproduced in great numbers during both the 19th and 20th centuries. Usually covered with floral marquetry, these cabinets possessed glazed bureau-style upper halves, with traditional-style bombé drawers below. Sometimes one of the lower drawers was sacrificed in favor of a stand with a stretcher, in the early Baroque manner, but

► **Secrétaire display cabinet**
This double-doored, mahogany-and-marquetry serpentine cabinet, with decoration of foliate scroll tendrils, ribbon-tied drapery swags, flowers, and oval paterae, has been made in the Sheraton style of *c*.1790, in which curved and splayed feet were a typical feature. A drop flap transforms the central lower portion into a writing surface.
(*c*.1905; ht 2.1m/6ft 11in; value **J**)

▼ **Display cabinet made by François Linke**
Like much of Linke's 20th-century work, this piece was designed by the sculptor Léon Messagé of Paris, *c*.1900. This rare display cabinet is veneered in king- and tulipwood. Although the front glazed door is now missing, it still commands a very high price because of the well-known maker.
(*c*.1905; ht 2.3m/7ft 6in; value **P**)

these cabinet-on-stand varieties are less common than their bureau-inspired counterparts.

The cabinet-maker François Linke (1855–1946), working between 1882 and 1935, helped Paris to maintain its position as the world's center of luxury furniture in the sumptuous *Belle Epoque* style. Like that of many distinguished cabinet-makers of the Second Empire (1848–70), Linke's early work is in the Louis XV and XVI styles, many pieces copied directly from 18th-century royal furniture. However, at the International Exhibition of 1900 in Paris he staked his reputation on a lavish display of distinctive furniture in Louis XV style with overtones of Art Nouveau, using the finest mounts applied to simple carcases with quarter-veneered kingwood or tulipwood. His signature motif was the *coquille* (concave scallop-shell), held by acanthus tendrils. Linke kept meticulous records, which demonstrate the staggering number of hours put into each piece of furniture.

KEY FACTS

- **TYPES** the variety is huge, although display cabinets were purpose built only from *c*.1800
- **MATERIALS** watered silk commonly lines French cabinets to offset the gold boxes, trinkets, and curiosities displayed inside; few display cabinets had glass panes until the 19th century; early French pieces often had chickenwire fronting
- **LINKE** the rarity and high quality account for the prices his pieces command; his signature "F. Linke" is usually visible on one of the ormolu mounts in a right-hand corner; much furniture was exported to the USA

See also Cabinets-on-stands, p.86

Side cabinets

Although side cabinets were first made in the 18th century, the golden age was the 19th, when they were produced in a variety of styles that reflected the contemporary fashion for eclecticism. The form may well have been influenced by the French chiffonier – a small shallow cabinet topped by an open shelf or shelves and sometimes a drawer – and the Italian credenza – an early form of sideboard – both of which gave their names to types of side cabinet or *meubles d'appui* as they were known in France.

TYPES OF SIDE CABINETS

Eighteenth-century side cabinets were generally very simple: just shelves and drawers, with few decorative features. A variation introduced in good-quality, late 18th-century side cabinets was the replacement of solid wooden doors with silk-lined ones, sometimes protected by a brass grill. Regency side cabinets retained the simple rectilinear form with enclosed shelves and drawers; decorative inlay (often metal), crossbanding and applied brass mouldings were added. Both features are often found on Regency chiffoniers, many of which also have lyre- or S-shaped supports with brass rails for the exposed shelf sections, which may also be surmounted by brass galleries. Another desirable, but rare, feature is an adjustable shelf.

Credenzas became increasingly popular in the later 19th century. They tended to be larger than chiffoniers and side cabinets, with storage or display shelves fitted at either end. The most desirable pieces have serpentine fronts and glazed side panels; pieces with straight fronts and convex glass sides are generally less desirable. Traditionally the end shelves were lined with velvet. British examples were influenced by Continental models, especially those made in France and Italy. The center-door panels offered good surfaces for decoration and in the best examples will be decorated with good-quality, undamaged *pietre dure*, marquetry, boullework, or panels of ivory or porcelain. Therefore some unexceptional pieces may have exceptional decoration, and vice versa.

► Chiffonier
The shelves on good-quality Regency chiffoniers often had lyre-shaped supports. The superstructure on this rosewood example has turned column supports, with the characteristic pierced brass gallery rail. Another attractive feature is the pleated-silk lining on the paneled doors.
*(1825; ht 1.2m/3ft 11in; value **H**)*

◄ Side cabinet
This Regency mahogany side cabinet, with shelves enclosed by paneled doors, looks back to the simpler forms of late 18th-century examples, but has typical Regency features such as brass rope-twist decoration on the doors, and Egyptian heads and feet on the door pilasters. The hairy-paw feet are original and help to date it. The wooden top seen here was replaced by marble tops on many later Victorian examples.
*(c.1810; ht 84cm/33in; value **H**)*

▼ Credenza
Many desirable features are combined on this French ebonized credenza: the serpentine shape, the velvet-lined cupboards for display, and well-made gilt-bronze mounts; the central panel, frieze, and stiles are decorated with brass-and-tortoiseshell marquetry in the style of André-Charles Boulle (1642–1732).
*(mid-19th century; ht 1.2m/ 3ft 11in; value **H**)*

IMPORTANT MAKERS

After the Great Exhibition of 1851 in London there was a succession of international exhibitions at which British, Continental, and American furniture-makers showed spectacular pieces in the popular revival styles of the time. In France cabinet-makers such as Alexandre-Georges Fourdinois (1799–1871) and his son Henri-Auguste Fourdinois (1830–1907), Guillaume Grohe (1808–85), and Jean-Michel Grohe (b.1804) produced magnificent side cabinets in the Renaissance Revival style, which was popular at the time, for the Paris Exhibition of 1867. Their works were immediately copied by other makers, who made inexpensive versions. Other influential French makers included Louis-Auguste-Alfred Beurdeley (1808–82), principal cabinet-maker to Empress Eugénie, and Henri Dasson (1825–96), who is notable for his superb ormolu mounts. François Linke (1855–1946) is arguably the greatest exponent of the Louis XVI Revival, and his cabinets remain the most

sought after. Pieces by such makers are generally very expensive, but the qualities that made their work so outstanding can be found in more modest forms. They include a well-made carcase (usually associated with French and English makers; Italian carcases are generally less well made, and liable to "move" and split the thin veneers that were used); good-quality ormolu mounts, and inventive decoration that is generous and includes the plinth and sides of the cabinet. In general, British and French examples are the most collectible.

Among the well-known British manufacturers, Wright & Mansfield (est. 1860) in London, was among the prize-winning British companies; its success was largely due to the production of a satinwood side cabinet in the Neo-classical style inspired by the work of the architect Robert Adam (1728–92). Most sought after are those made by such reputable firms as T.H. Filmer of London, which, working in the Renaissance Revival style, combined ebonized wood and *pietre dure* on credenza-style side cabinets with marble tops. The style was also popular in the USA in the 1870s, where it was combined with Louis XVI ormolou decoration by Alexander Roux, a French maker active in New York from *c*.1856. Italian makers were known for their fine ivory inlay, although the pieces were not generally as well constructed as

► Chiffonier

In 1840 G.E. Magnus patented a technique for painting and decorating slate to resemble marble, which was a much more expensive material. The technique was best suited to flat surfaces, such as table tops, and the success of Magnus's pieces at the Great Exhibition inspired more ambitious experiments such as this slate chiffonier, with a shelf and simulated paneled doors decorated with gilt and polychrome flowers. Very few attempts were made to use slate for carcase work, and this somewhat impractical chiffonier may well be unique. However, it is a fascinating example of the Victorian passion for experimenting with new materials.

(c.1850s; ht 1.4m/4ft 7in; value **F***)*

French and British examples. A notable exception was the work of Giovanni Battista Gatti (active 1850–80), prizewinner at the exhibitions in Paris in 1855 and 1878, who produced extremely well-made cabinets set with ivory and *pietre dure* plaques in the Renaissance Revival style.

In France, Rococo Revival side cabinets often had paneled doors with *vernis Martin* (a type of japanning) painted with *fêtes champêtres* (outdoor scenes) scenes after paintings by the 18th-century French artist Antoine Watteau, who specialized in this type of outdoor scene. Others were set with Sèvres porcelain plaques, similarly painted or with flowers and birds. The more formal decorative vocabulary of the Louis XVI Revival included brass inlay and gilt-bronze mounts in Neo-classical motifs. Continental pieces were retailed by such British outlets as W. Williamson & Sons (active *c*.1880–1920) in Guildford, and Maples of London, which imported French furniture during the 1880s.

▲ Credenza

During the period of the Second Empire (1852–70), French makers generally led the field of furniture-making, producing pieces with high-quality carcases and superb decoration. This ebonized credenza has a bowed break-front with a scrolling gilt bronze frieze, and high-quality, crisply cast gilt-bronze mounts. The air of luxury typical of the period is continued in the bold *pietre dure* inlay on the central door. The original bun feet have been removed, which will inevitably reduce the value.

(1852–70; l. 1.8m/5ft 11in; value **G***)*

NEW MATERIALS

In the 19th century British furniture-makers, in particular experimented with some extraordinary materials in an attempt to capture the imagination and the purse-strings of the public. One of the success stories was the papier-mâché furniture made by Jennens & Bettridge (active 1816–64) in Birmingham, who from the 1820s used japanned papier-mâché in conjunction with metal or wood frames to produce a range of furniture, and in 1825 patented a technique for incorporating mother-of-pearl inlay in papier-mâché. In the 1840s and 1850s there were some 30 companies in Derbyshire producing marble furniture, in particular inlaid table tops influenced by the Florentine *pietre dure* models lent by the Duke of Devonshire from his collection at Chatsworth House. As a less expensive alternative, G.E. Magnus patented a technique in 1840 for coloring slate to simulate marble, and at the Great Exhibition he displayed a range of pieces; however, slate cabinet work was very unusual.

KEY FACTS

- TYPES side cabinets were produced in three main styles: the side cabinet with enclosed shelves; chiffoniers (with exposed shelves on top of a cabinet); credenzas (with end shelves)
- DAMAGE the condition of the carcase and decoration is important; *pietre dure* and Boullework is very difficult and expensive to restore
- COLLECTING French and British makers were leaders in the field, with British makers influenced by French and Italian styles; Regency side cabinets and chiffoniers are generally more refined than many Victorian examples that were mass-produced; look for good-quality pieces with brass galleries, pleated-silk door panels, lyre-shaped shelf supports; original decoration, feet, and glass will usually add to value; some pieces of lesser quality may have superior decoration in the form of metal, ivory, or porcelain plaques that were taken from furniture made during an earlier period

See also Display cabinets, pp.92–3

Bookcases and bookshelves

The early history of the bookcase is tied up with the development of monastic and collegiate book collections. Books were a great luxury long after the invention of printing, and even the wealthiest people who knew how to read were unlikely to possess more than a few, which could easily be stored in a chest or cupboard. The bookcase developed both in its own right, as a piece of library furniture, and in conjunction with other pieces such as bureau bookcases. The first bookcases of any significant note date from the early 18th century.

18TH-CENTURY BOOKCASES
Early 18th-century bookcases are extremely rare, and were made in oak veneered in walnut, of simple design and proportions. Examples were flat fronted and of two sections: the upper section was glazed with simple rectangular panes, while the lower section had two doors behind which were drawers. By the mid-1730s the form had become increasingly heavy and architectural, in the manner promoted by William Kent (c.1685–1748). Features include a broken pediment, pilasters, and richly carved Classical decoration.

By the mid-18th century the severely architectural Palladian-style bookcase was displaced by the lighter Rococo style. A familiar bookcase design, comprising a main central break-front section and two side wings retaining its upper glazed section, was developed. The preferred wood for bookcases, as with all furniture of this period, was mahogany. The scrolled pediment above the break-front center was often pierced after 1750. Thomas Chippendale (1718–79) included 14 designs for bookcases in the third edition of *The Gentleman and*

▼ Library break-front bookcase
By 1750 astragals (lightweight wooden mouldings) in patterns were gradually replacing solid glazing bars. The Gothic style, seen in the pointed arches of the side doors of this mahogany example, was popular in the mid-18th century, largely through the influence of Chippendale. *(c.1760; ht 2.7m/8ft 10in; value P)*

► Secrétaire bookcase, attributed to Edmund Johnson (active 1881–1927)
This type is sometimes described as a break-front bookcase because the center section projects forward and the top middle drawer is a fall-front secretary. Sheraton noted that a "gentleman's secretary is intended to stand to write at." Glazed doors, crowned by an undulating cornice, front stiles with bell-flower inlay, drawer-fronts of figured veneer, and six turned legs are typical of this form. It is often called a Salem secretary but was also made in other New England towns. *(1790–1815; ht 2.3m/7ft 6in; value Q)*

Cabinet-Maker's Director (1762). Until *c*.1750, solid glazing-bars were used to retain the rectangular panes of glass in the upper section. After this time they were largely replaced by astragals (glazing-bars with semicircular profiles), which could be arranged in more elaborate and varied patterns, including Gothic and chinoiserie designs. The astragal decoration usually conforms to that on the rest of the bookcase.

From *c*.1770, Neo-classicism became by far the most important influence on the design of fashionable bookcases. The architect Robert Adam (1728–92) specifically designed large bookcases to correlate with the architecture and overall decoration of the rooms for which they were intended; they were usually made to stand in recesses. Some bookcases were made in satinwood while others were made in inexpensive pine and painted in various colors with gilded enrichments. Adam's designs were published and particularly well received in Italy, and his influence may be seen in rare examples of grand, painted, and parcel-gilded Neoclassical Italian bookcases of the late 18th century.

The bookcases detailed in *The Cabinet-Maker and Upholsterer's Guide* (1788–94) by George Hepplewhite (*d*.1786) were even more luxurious; the doors were veneered with waved or curled mahogany, which was sometimes crossbanded and inlaid, and were fitted with simple ring handles. The designs in *The Cabinet-Maker and Upholsterer's Drawing Book* (1791–1802) by Thomas Sheraton (1751–1806) illustrated a new fashion for a lighter, narrower bookcase with a taller lower section. This type of bookcase was typically veneered in satinwood and topped with a lightly scrolled or lunetteshaped pediment, vase finials, and delicate mouldings. Some bookcases contained gathered silk curtains behind

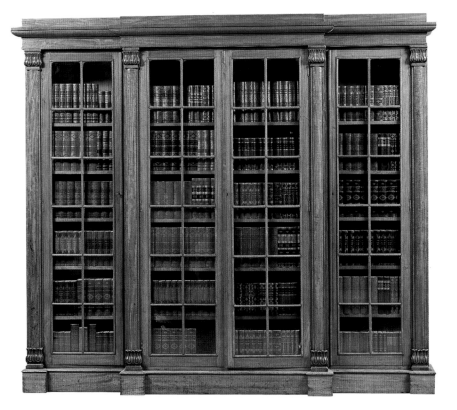

shelves in the center, bordered by panels or doors, "calculated to contain all the books that may be required in a sitting-room without reference to the library." This generally featured applied metal ornaments and gilded columns or terminals. Revolving bookcases were introduced *c.*1810, initially in circular form, although rectangular shapes were also produced; many examples of this space-saving form were made during the Victorian and Edwardian periods.

A great change took place in the early 19th century, initiated by the London publisher William Pickering (1796–1854), who issued books in cloth bindings, thus reducing their price and bringing them within reach of the general public. Machines were introduced for gluing, rather than sewing, the pages together. Together with the expansion of education, book-buying was encouraged. The increasingly literate population therefore created a demand for attractive book-storage space. Gothic Revival bookcases were generally made in oak and were in a style that was interpreted either as a basic functional bookcase, with decorative architectural details grafted onto it, or as a more authentic interpretation with exposed joints. This rather masculine style was considered to be an appropriate one for the Victorian library. One of the most popular types during the 19th century was the secrétaire bookcase.

the glass- or brass-trellis doors, a feature that became increasingly popular in bookcases made during the Regency period (*c.*1790–1830).

French bookcases developed more slowly than their English counterparts. They were generally not so much pieces of furniture in their own right as adapted for books from standard armoire and commode forms. During the 18th century a type of chickenwire was frequently used instead of glazed panels. In many cases, bookshelves were simply incorporated into the interior of an armoire or a desk, so that the books were not actually on display.

19TH-CENTURY BOOKCASES

In *The Cabinet Dictionary* (1803), Sheraton referred to the "bookshelf" or bookstand, which was a set of light, low, open bookshelves with socket casters on the feet, making it easy to move. There was a variety of designs, some of which resembled the open-tiered whatnot or *étagère*. Dwarf bookcases were also in use at this time, and were particularly suitable for delicate Neo-classical decoration. In his book *A Collection of Designs for Household Furniture and Interior Decoration* (1808), George Smith (active *c.*1786–1828) recommended placing a dwarf bookcase at each end of a room, with a library table in between, to produce "a grand and pleasing effect." Also popular was a hybrid version of a low bookcase and a commode, with

▲ Break-front bookcase by P. Moore & Co.

The design of this mahogany bookcase is unusual in that it dispenses with the more traditional solid lower section with doors. In this design all the books are visible down the length of the bookcase. The moulded pilaster stiles with lotus-leaf capitals betray the Classical influence. On such examples the four doors usually open with the stiles.
(*c.*1830; ht 2.3m/7ft 6in; value **L**)

► Hanging shelves

The carcase of these shelves, which are probably British, is made of willow, a wood often used by provincial furniture-makers. The swan-neck cresting and urn-shaped finial decoration have been inspired by contemporary fashions in library bookcases. In addition to the drawers at the front, these shelves feature two secret cedar-lined drawers.
(*c.*1750; ht 1.1m/3ft 7in; value **H**)

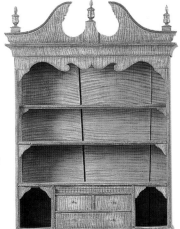

► Revolving bookcase

The patent for the revolving bookcase, a way of storing books and saving wall space, was taken out by Benjamin Crosby in 1808. This type of British rectangular mahogany bookcase was particularly popular in the Edwardian period and continues to be made today.
(*19th century; ht 1.1m/3ft 7in; value* **E***)

KEY FACTS

- ALTERATIONS make sure that the proportions of the bookcase are correct, as some were reduced in height or width in order to fit into the smaller 20th-century room: a large bookcase with up to six sections may well have been reduced to four, which could affect the value of a piece considerably; pediments have often been flattened off, again so that the bookcases can fit into a room with a lower ceiling
- GLAZING the astragals should be rebated into the door frame, and this should be visible on the inside of the door; in later 19th-century versions the glass is usually of one piece, and the mullions are simply laid on top
- PROPORTIONS the glazed section of a late 18th-century bookcase is frequently less deep than the base
- MARRIAGES as in all two- or three-part furniture, it is important to establish that all the parts started life together and that the following features correspond: the quality, color, patina, and figuring of the wood; the methods of construction; the decorative details such as applied moulding

See also Display cabinets, pp.92–3

Writing furniture

Writing furniture can be loosely divided into three distinct categories: first there are those items with sloping fronts to support a book or writing material, into which such forms as the bureau (in all its many and varied styles), bureau bookcase, and bureau cabinet fall. Then there are the flat-fronted, vertical forms, which include such pieces as the escritoire and the sécretaire, both of which developed from the 16th-century Spanish *vargueño*. Finally there are writing tables, and kneehole desks, the latter being first originally conceived as a combination of both dressing table and bureau. Pedestal writing desks and tables were often very grand pieces of furniture designed to occupy a central position in the library of a great house.

Bureaux before 1840

One of the most enduring of furniture types, the bureau has been made since the 17th century. In French the word *bureau* denotes both a study and a type of writing desk; in English it has come to mean a piece of writing furniture with a fall front sloping at about 45 degrees when closed, or a desk with a cylinder front. The bureau should not be confused with the vertical-fronted secrétaire.

ENGLISH BUREAUX

The basic bureau form emerged in France in the second half of the 17th century, having developed from the fall-fronted cabinet (*vargueño*); shortly after, similar desks appeared in England. These had gate-legs to support the fall fronts when open; the insides included drawers and pigeon holes and, in some cases, sliding-top wells for concealing papers. The carcases were generally of oak, or pine, covered with figured veneers, the most common being walnut, sometimes "oyster" veneered, or even with "seaweed" marquetry. By *c.*1700 the gate-leg supports were replaced by sliding lopers at each side. The lower stages were generally separate from the writing sections and were made either as stands on turned or cabriole legs (1710–15), or as chest-of-drawers on bun feet.

▼ Bureau

The usual arrangement of drawers in early Georgian bureaux was two short ones above two graduated long ones. This walnut bureau has both cross- and featherbanding. Color is fundamental to value.
(c.1725; ht 1m/3ft 3in; value **K**)

About 1720 the bureau sections were fused with the chests, and bracket feet gradually superseded bun feet. By this time the classic bureau had evolved. Veneers included walnut, and also burr forms of elm, while provincial craftsmen favored oak and elm in the solid. Decoration generally took the form of herringbone inlay, stringing, or crossbanding. Moldings on the fronts of the dustboards between the drawers were superseded after *c.*1740 by cock-beaded edges to the drawers. This form continued with little change (although mahogany took the place of walnut) throughout the 18th century.

The bureau cabinet, with its superstructure of shelves, drawers, and pigeon holes enclosed by doors, represents a development of the basic bureau. Decoration took the form of fine veneering, marquetry, or even japanning. Early 18th-century examples may have elaborately carved and gilded crestings or simple overhanging straight-molded cornices. After *c.*1715 plain, scrolled, broken, or even closed pediments were usual. Such cabinets were also impressive inside, with architectural features such as columns and pilasters, as well as drawers, cupboards, divisions for documents, and secret compartments. These grand bureaux were made in at least two parts and earlier examples before *c.*1710 in three; the cabinet section was separate from the writing bureau, which in turn was often divided from the chest-of-drawers it surmounted.

The bureau cabinet evolved into the ever more architectural bureau bookcase. The cupboard doors, constructed of chamfered wood panels or, increasingly, featuring molded and glazed geometrical patterns, enclosed shelves instead of the earlier arrangements of storage compartments. The cupboard was set farther forward on the bureau, placing less emphasis on the division between the two parts. Later 18th-century English bureau cabinets were lighter in appearance than early Georgian bureaux; nearly all had glazed upper sections, and some were veneered with either flame mahogany or satinwood. The influence of French cabinet-making is evident in the tambor writing tables and cylinder desks of the late 18th century designed by George Hepplewhite (*d.*1786) and Thomas Sheraton (1751–1806). Some are similar to the contemporary but by this time less fashionable bureaux, with a chests-of-drawers below writing sections fitted with drawers and pigeon holes; others are simply tables with superstructures fitted up for writing, and have no more than two drawers in the friezes.

▲ Bureau cabinet

The richly figured "book-matched" veneers of the bureau section of this bureau cabinet have been carefully arranged to cover the drawer fronts and fall in a continuous pattern. This English mahogany example may well be of provincial origin, as it fuses different stylistic influences from different decades: the pierced pediment is a feature from the 1750s and 1760s, while the ogee feet date from the 1750s, and the astragals in the style of Thomas Chippendale from the 1760s to the 1770s.
(c.1760; ht 2.4m/7ft 10in; value **I**)

▲ Bureau de dame
This French Rococo marquetry bureau, which is set on slender legs ending in gilt-bronze *sabots* ("shoes"), opens to reveal a writing surface with drawers and pigeon holes.
*(c.1760; ht 89cm/35in; value **H**)*

EUROPEAN BUREAUX

Bureau cabinets of this period made in Germany and Italy usually display the full-blown Rococo style. Well before the mid-18th century, German princely courts such as those at Würzburg, Dresden, Ansbach, and Berlin set the pace for Rococo at its most adventurous, and bureau cabinets were among the extreme manifestations of the style. Exaggerated cabriole curves, vigorous serpentine shapes, and concave and bombé forms were inlaid with exotic materials, covered in marquetry and parquetry, and encrusted with gilt-bronze mounts made by virtuoso craftsmen. The Italian Pietro Piffetti (*c.*1700–*c.*1777) took this already exuberant taste even further in the ivory inlaid bureau cabinets he made for the Palazzo Reale in Turin. While bureaux and bureau cabinets from other parts of northern Italy such as Venice and Genoa, were less ostentatious, they were

bold in their curves and often decorated with painting in light colors, or with a type of découpage known as *arte povera*.

By contrast, the wealthy burghers of northern Germany and The Netherlands took a less flamboyant line, favoring bureau cabinets of restrained design, usually made of well-figured walnut. Such pieces increasingly fell under the restraining influence of British design, while conceding to more southern tastes with bombé and serpentine outlines to their bases.

Early 18th-century French writing furniture took an entirely different turn from that of Britain and most of Europe, but some new types related to the bureau were developed around the mid-century. During the Transitional period, when the curvaceous Rococo was being gradually discarded for the restrained and symmetrical Neo-classical style, small desks with cabriole legs, serpentine sides, and fine floral marquetry were especially favored for ladies' apartments. The *bureau de dame* has a sloping top of conventional bureau form. Another type, known as a *bureau à cylindre*, has a horizontally slatted tambor top set into grooves on either side, allowing it to slide over the writing surface within. One of the most accomplished exponents was Jean-François Oeben (1721–63), who is credited with the invention of the roll-top desk with its rigidly curved slide. His successor as one of the leading Parisian cabinet-makers was Jean-Henri Riesener (1734–1806), who continued the tradition of ingenious mechanical pieces and specialized in roll-top desks. Riesener's output ranged from sumptuous pieces decorated with elaborate marquetry and gilt-bronze mounts to plain mahogany desks of no less fine craftsmanship. The German cabinet-maker, David Roentgen (1743–1807), produced bureaux of outstanding quality, in terms of both their marquetry decoration and the ingenious mechanisms with which they were often fitted. In Vienna, which was an important center of furniture-making in the early 19th century, simple cylinder desks were executed in native woods such as walnut, cherry, pear, and maple, mainly for a middle-class clientele.

▲ Bureau à cylindre
This Neo-classical bureau relies for its effect on its superb craftsmanship and the quality of its wood. The brass-mounted and brass-inlaid mahogany clock is flanked by arcaded doors enclosing shelves, while the paneled roll-top hides a fitted interior, with drawers arranged around an arched pigeon hole. The base of the bureau contains three short and two long paneled drawers flanked by fluted quarter columns, set on guilloche inlaid square tapered feet. The clock is related to examples by Peter Kinzing, who is known to have worked with David Roentgen.
*(c.1790; ht 2m/6ft 7in; value **K**)*

◄ Bombé bureau
The sides of the upper section of this fine mahogany serpentine bombé bureau from Boston, Massachusetts, are fitted with brass carrying handles. The upper section also has steep stepped drawers, while the lower section has two graduated drawers set above a molded plinth, on ogee-bracket feet. In North America this type of bureau is known as a serpentine, bombé slant-lid desk.
*(c.1780; ht 1.1m/3ft 7in; value **Q**)*

KEY FACTS

- COLLECTING the color of early bureaux is a crucial factor in determining value – examples showing exceptional color can command very high prices; slope-fronted bureaux are more desirable than secrétaire cabinets or secrétaire bookcases
- BEWARE if the top of a bureau is unusually deep (i.e. over 31cm/12in wide) it may formerly have been the base of a bureau bookcase, in which case the veneering will have been added at a later date
- HANDLES check that all signs of handle holes to the backs of drawer fronts have corresponding scars on the veneered front; if they do not all correspond, the piece has either been reveneered at a later date or the drawer is associated

See also Bureaux after 1840, pp.100–101

Bureaux after 1840

The development of the bureau during the mid-19th century was more a matter of changes in decorative style than of any major technical advance. Desk forms of the 18th century, such as the French *bureau de dame* and *bureau à cylindre*, and the English fall-front bureau, were still current. As an important item of furniture in the middle-class interior, the bureau reflected the prevailing diversity of styles and techniques and was often fashioned with consummate craftsmanship.

▲ Bureau à rognon

This is a fine example of the way the Rococo style was reinterpreted during the 19th century. It features marquetry decoration and gilt-bronze mounts, including a pair of two-light candelabra and a clock surmounted by a figure of Mars.

(c.1860; ht 1.4m/4ft 7in; value J)

MID-19TH-CENTURY BUREAUX

Mahogany and rosewood were still used for a considerable amount of writing furniture, but walnut was most fashionable and provided a greater diversity of figured surfaces, from the relatively plain straight-grained varieties to the variegated dappling of burr veneers. Yellow-toned woods such as satinwood, amboyna, and, especially in eastern Europe, maple, poplar, and birch, were much favored. Locally available fruitwoods, yew, and oak were occasionally used.

The flat-topped writing-desk seems mainly to have been a feature of the male-oriented study, and was often of strikingly plain design, in keeping with the business-like and usually private nature of this room. The bureau, on the other hand, often of small proportions and delicate decoration, appears generally to have been kept in the drawing-room, where it struck a distinctly feminine note. The influence of the French Rococo style is seen in the contored aprons, and tapering cabriole legs with gilt-metal mounts, of bureaux made in England, The

Netherlands, Italy, and eastern Europe, as well as in France, between the 1840s and 1860s. Floral marquetry was the usual surface decoration, and was often more lavish in the 19th century than it had been in the 18th.

There was great variation in the superstructures of these bureaux, which were far from being slavish copies of 18th-century patterns. Some had arrangements of small drawers and pigeon holes around the writing areas; the very best examples might be fitted with gilt-bronze candle sconces or even clocks to match the highly elaborate cast-metal mounts and handles of the main carcases. Others had superstructures of tiered drawers, or combinations of cupboards, drawers and pigeon holes; a central mirror in the upper part suggests a dual purpose bureau-cum-dressing table. More restrained were those bureaux with shelves edged with gilt-metal or brass galleries for books or ornaments. Mechanical features such as rising or sliding sections, and concealed compartments, were sometimes included.

By the mid-19th century writing furniture with brass-and-tortoiseshell marquetry, known as Boullework, was produced both by French cabinet-makers, who enjoyed a lively export trade, and by English firms, some of them employing French craftsmen. Boullework, used in France throughout the 18th century, was revived in England (where it was known as "Buhl" work) by George Bullock (*c.*1777–1818) during the Regency period. The best Boullework-revival pieces are close copies of the originals; the poorest examples have repetitive designs. Elaborate tours de force in ebony, brass, and tortoiseshell were seen in the major exhibitions of London, Paris, and other centers during the 1850s and 1860s. Writing furniture, including some monumental desks and bureaux, was among these extravagant

▲ Bureau de dame

The glass-fronted gallery-topped cupboards of this bureau flank an arched mirror with a drawer below. The fall front encloses a fitted interior and a sliding-topped well. The cabriole legs are embellished with gilt-metal mounts, and the doors, drawer, fall front, and shaped apron are decorated with marquetry in which Rococo and Neo-classical motifs are used indiscriminately. *(1890; ht 1.3m/4ft 3in; value H)*

◀ Tambor-topped *bureau de dame*

The brass gallery on this English satinwood bureau is a very common feature of Victorian and Edwardian bureaux and desks. When pulled out, the tambor shutter will rise by means of a mechanism to reveal an interior of pigeon holes, drawers, and stationery compartments. The marquetry-decorated flap opens out as a leather-lined writing surface, and is supported by the drawer. The undertier is shaped to allow room for the writer's legs. The understated design, and the use of satinwood, suggest that this bureau was made during the revival of the distinctive style of Thomas Sheraton (1751–1806). *(late 19th century; ht 95cm/ 37½in; value I)*

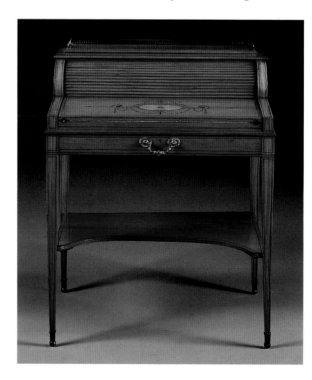

examples of virtuoso craftsmanship. The English firms of Town & Emmanuel (1830–40), Wright & Mansfield (est. 1860), Jackson & Graham (1836–40), Hindley & Wilkinson, and Holland & Sons (est. 1803) were some of the foremost manufacturers of high-quality reproduction Buhl and other French furniture, and the fashion for such pieces continued for the rest of the century. Another cabinet-making firm, Edwards & Roberts, was among the few English companies that regularly marked both the furniture it made and the items it restored. Edwards & Roberts used brass inlays with more restraint and practicality than other cabinet-makers, generally in the form of stringing lines on dark rosewood surfaces. Desks and bureaux in this style provide an elegantly muted contrast to the luxury of full-blown Rococo Revival, lending a note of gravitas to the inevitable abundance of decoration.

LATER 19TH-CENTURY BUREAUX

The Renaissance Revival stimulated ivory-inlaid furniture as well as the heavily carved oak associated with the later 19th century. While carved oak bureaux were produced, the eye-catching qualities of the more unusual ivory-inlaid pieces must have pleased the Victorians. In Italy, where walnut furniture with floral inlays of ivory and bone had a long history, the technique was revived with particular enthusiasm.

While wholly painted surfaces tend to be seen more often on folk and vernacular furniture than on typically middle-class pieces such as bureaux, painted flowers often embellished the delicate ladies' writing furniture of the late Victorian and Edwardian periods, much of it in the Sheraton Revival style. Painted panels were a feature of the Gothic Revival furniture of the 1870s and 1880s, and massive bureaux and roll-top desks in this style are occasionally seen.

Another 19th-century revival was the technique of *arte povera* in Italy, in which Oriental lacquer was (very loosely) imitated by using paper scraps and painted vignettes applied to bright- or light-colored painted grounds and covering the whole surface in varnish. This colorful form of decoration was sometimes applied to bureaux and bureau cabinets of traditional 18th-century design, and even to old items thought to be in need of "improvement."

In The Netherlands, the bureau decorated with floral marquetry remained popular throughout the 19th century. The typical Dutch bureau is based on the English model, with a chest-of-drawers surmounted by a sloping-topped writing section, with or without a cabinet on top; however, its shape, with a bombé swelling low in the base, is of French inspiration. The all-over design of flowers in different woods, usually on a walnut ground, is wholly Dutch. During the 19th century old pieces were often revamped with new marquetry, while new ones were produced with well-executed but rather mechanical flower designs.

From the late 19th century the vast majority of bureaux were made using factory methods, with all the variations of quality and design that a highly competitive industry implies. Most producers followed the prevailing historic Revival, Aesthetic, Arts and Crafts, and progressive trends, tailoring their output to the economics of a growing mass-market. They were rarely innovative. Among the later 19th-century developments was the roll-top desk, a commodious but hardly decorative office cabinet with a kneehole arrangement of drawers beneath a slat-shuttered writing surface fitted with drawers and compartments. These functional desks, in oak, walnut and mahogany, sold in their thousands on both sides of the Atlantic.

Progressive designers of the late 19th century in Britain and on the Continent produced bureaux that met the reformers' dictum of "fitness for purpose" and at the same time reinterpreted historical models in a highly original way, combining vernacular honesty with sophistication. Much of this furniture was sold by Liberty & Co. (est. 1875) in London, while the designers of the Vienna Secession in the early 1900s made a further impact on design philosophy. The effects of the Arts and Crafts Movement have reverberated throughout the 20th century, with individual designer-craftsmen producing bureaux and other furniture of simple, functional design from solid, often locally available timbers.

▶ **Bureau cabinet**
This Italian painted bureau cabinet is of a type still made today. It is decorated with vignettes of Classical ruins and flower sprays in gilt reserves on a blue ground. The design follows 18th-century forms, having a broken-arch pediment above a cabinet of shelves and pigeon holes, a fall front enclosing drawers and compartments, and a serpentine chest-of-drawers in the base.
(late 19th/early 20th century; ht 2.1m/6ft 11in; value J)

◀ **Bureau de dame**
Renaissance and Moorish influences are both apparent in this Italian olivewood bureau with *alla certosina* (bone-and-ivory inlay) decoration. The square-section legs and flattened stretchers are, like the rest of this piece, inlaid with stylized florets and geometrical patterns.
(c.1850–1900; ht 1.4m/4ft 7in; value H)

KEY FACTS

- FORMS most 19th-century bureaux were based on 18th-century designs; roll-top desks were mass-produced in late 19th century
- STRUCTURE cupboards, drawers, and pigeon holes were commonly used; many examples have galleries to hold books and ornaments; examples featuring gilt-metal mounts with matching candle sconces are sought after
- DECORATIVE STYLES marquetry decoration and gilt-metal mounts were fashionable during the Rococo Revival; 19th-century floral marquetry tends to be more elaborate than that of the 18th century; "Buhl" work was widely employed in the mid-19th century by French and English cabinet-makers; inlays of ebony and brass were popular during the 1850s and 1860s; ivory inlays are associated with the Renaissance Revival; painted panels are seen on Gothic Revival furniture of 1870s and 1880s

See also Bureaux before 1840, pp.98–9; Writing cabinets-on-stands, p.104

Escritoires and secrétaires

The essential difference between a bureau and an escritoire or secrétaire is that a bureau has a sloping or curving lid to the writing section, whereas the escritoire and secrétaire are usually flat fronted and vertical. The terms escritoire and scriptor, scriptoire, or scrutoire (the older names for a writing desk) are now usually attached to the fall-front writing box or cabinet made up to c.1720, while secrétaire is generally applied to later types.

EARLY ESCRITOIRES

The direct ancestor of the escritoire was the Spanish *vargueño*, a 16th-century cabinet with a fall front, drawers and compartments, set on a stand or chest. Often highly embellished on the inside, *vargueños* were usually either decorated in the Moorish tradition, with geometrical patterns in wood or ivory, or carved in low relief and painted. The *vargueño* was taken as a model for writing cabinets in other parts of Europe. A cabinet with elaborate intarsia decoration was the specialty of craftsmen in Augsburg and Nuremberg during the 16th and 17th centuries, while Antwerp was famous for cabinets veneered in tortoiseshell and ebony, with ivory embellishments, and sometimes painted inside. In Italy cabinets of architectural form set with colored marbles and hardstones, or decorated with ivory, were produced.

In Britain escritoires were decorated with oyster veneers of walnut or cocus wood and finely wrought silver mounts. The fall fronts were usually supported on

▲ Secrétaire à abattant
This writing desk combines satinwood from the Dutch West Indies, fine marquetry, and Chinese lacquer panels. The fall front encloses drawers and pigeon holes at the back of the baize-lined writing surface; the flower-paneled cupboard doors of the base conceal a shelf.
(c.1780; ht 1.5m/4ft 11in; value **K**)

◄ Escritoire
The architectural cornice, cushion-frieze drawer, walnut veneers, and drop handles make this English escritoire a good representative of its period. The pigeon holes on some examples slide out completely to reveal secret compartments. About 1730 the reading slope was replaced by a sloping-front bureau.
(c.1710; ht 1.6m/5ft 3in; value **L**)

► Secrétaire and bookcase attributed to John Goddard (1732–85)
The height of this imposing North American mahogany cabinet is emphasized by the panel blocking on the bookcase doors, which is carried through onto the desk. The outstanding quality of this piece demonstrates the achievement of the Goddard and Townsend families of master cabinet-makers in Newport, Rhode Island, who are noted for block-front shell-carved furniture.
(c.1760–70; ht 4m/13ft; value **Q**)

cords or chains attached halfway up the sides. Cabinets of this type were placed on stands with spiral or baluster-turned legs. By the 1680s escritoires in two parts and of more architectural proportions were produced. The upper section had an overhanging cornice and sometimes a drawer in the frieze, while the lower part consisted of a chest-of-drawers. The best examples were decorated with floral or "seaweed" marquetry, but oyster veneers remained popular, and burr woods were also used during the early 18th century. From the second half of the 17th century japanning was used for both Dutch and English escritoires. In addition to these fall-front cabinets, a hybrid form of chest, with a secrétaire drawer, was developed. Later 17th- and early 18th-century chests-of-drawers from northern Italy sometimes have shallow drawers fitted for writing; the front of this type of drawer is hinged in such a way that it can be pulled out and let down to form a flat writing surface, often revealing compartments and small drawers for stationery at the back. The most handsome examples of the type are of bombé form in walnut, inlaid with floral patterns in ivory, mother-of-pearl, and pewter.

▲ Mahogany secrétaire bookcase
This superstructure of glazed bookshelves above a writing section with cupboards below follows a pattern established soon after the mid-18th century. However, the Classical cornice with its inlaid shell tablet and urn finials, the circular panels on the doors of the base, and the shaped apron with curved and splayed feet suggest a date of c.1800.
(c.1800; ht 2.5m/8ft 2in; value L)

LATER ESCRITOIRES AND SECRETAIRES

During the early 18th century the most fashionable item of writing furniture in Britain was the bureau, but the chest with a straight-fronted writing drawer continued to be an alternative. On some examples a secrétaire drawer was incorporated into the chest-on-chest. The secrétaire drawer gradually became deeper, and the chest was often surmounted by a superstructure of bookshelves enclosed by glazed or paneled doors. Such pieces were most often made of walnut until *c*.1730, when this was superseded by mahogany. These cabinets were the forerunners of the fine two-part secrétaires, made for parlors or libraries, with glazed upper sections and lower sections with drawers or cupboards, produced in Britain in considerable quantities from the mid-18th century. Designs for a variety of secrétaires were published in *The Cabinet-Maker and Upholsterer's Drawing Book* (1791–1802) by Thomas Sheraton (1751–1806). The usefulness of the secrétaire bookcase or secrétaire cabinet ensured that it continued to be made in the 19th century, with infinite variations of detail in the style of pediments, glazing patterns, and surface decoration.

The French developed the *vargueño*-type desk in a characteristically sophisticated form during the later 18th century. The so-called *secrétaire à abattant* had a fall-front writing cabinet resting on a chest-of-drawers or small cupboard, often constructed as one piece rather than two; this verticality was emphasized by the tall, narrow proportions seen in many examples. Some pieces were produced with substructures of legs with decorative stretchers, giving them a lighter appearance than the standard form. Fine-quality timber was used, sometimes incorporating panels of Oriental lacquer, and the fall front was often the vehicle for elaborate marquetry or, during the 1770s and 1780s, Sèvres porcelain plaques. The lavish use of ormolu mounts added to the richness of the decoration. These models were copied in The Netherlands, where lacquer panels and the finest geometrical marquetry were sometimes combined, and the traditional Dutch floral marquetry rampaged across fall fronts and drawers alike. Similar forms were imitated, usually with more restraint, in Germany, eastern Europe, and Scandinavia. In Britain, marquetry secrétaires of this type are among the finest examples of Neo-classical furniture.

During the French Empire period (1804–15) the *secrétaire à abattant* remained popular, although the outline became more severe and broader, with the fall front above cupboard doors presenting an almost unbroken veneered surface when closed. In Russia and Austria the fall-front secrétaire on a chest, characteristically veneered in such indigenous woods as birch, poplar, maple, or fruitwood, was especially successful in the early 19th century. These pieces were of simple Classical design, relying on the figuring of the veneers for decorative interest. They went on to become staples of the Biedermeier period, which brought a return to grander proportions, with solid but elegant and well-crafted furniture. Some Biedermeier fall-front desks closely resemble English escritoires of the early 18th century.

▲ Secrétaire bookcase
Late 18th-century Neo-classical styles were much copied by Edwardian cabinet-makers. This satinwood secrétaire bookcase, with its elaborate marquetry and crossbanding in sycamore, has the characteristically attenuated form of early 20th-century reproductions.
(c.1910; ht 2m/6ft 7in; value M)

◄ Secrétaire
This French serpentine secrétaire was designed as a *semainier* – a type of chest with a drawer for every day of the week. The fall front encloses a fitted interior for writing, but the drawers are non-functional. The quarter-veneers of tulipwood and rosewood are laid on a serpentine carcase, with gilt-metal mounts and a marble top.
(19th century; ht 1.3m/4ft 3in; value H)

KEY FACTS

- CONSTRUCTION continental *secrétaires à abbatant* often have no visible means of support and are therefore prone to damage, particularly at the bottom where the flap is hinged to the carcase
- CONVERSIONS on some British escritoires the fall front has been converted into two doors, thus making it a cabinet – these are generally more commercial – look for evidence of the old hinge plates or the top central lock
- "IMPROVEMENTS" as many continental examples were very plain, they have often been improved or modified to make them more commercial
- TIMBERS on British examples different woods are often used for the interior (e.g. satinwood) and exterior (mahogany); the interiors should look "fresher" than the exterior as they have not been exposed to light

See also Bureaux before 1840, pp.98–9; Bureaux after 1840, pp.100–101

Writing cabinets-on-stands

Small slope-topped writing boxes were known from medieval times, and during the 16th and early 17th centuries they continued to be associated with the needs of a highly educated elite. With their sloping lids, often lipped at the lower edge, they could double as reading lecterns, and many were decorated with carving, inlay, or painting. Inside they were fitted with compartments and small drawers for papers and writing equipment. Conveniently portable, they could be used on top of a table or chest.

EARLY CABINETS-ON-STANDS

During the second half of the 17th century a new form of writing compendium, with its own base support, was developed. Also known as a scriptor, or, in France, an *escritoire*, the writing cabinet-on-stand was a rectangular structure, based on the Spanish *vargueño* (writing desk) Instead of a sloping lift-up top, it had a fall front concealing drawers and pigeon holes, which opened to form a writing surface supported on cords at either side. The exterior presented an inviting surface for veneering. Fine examples were made with oyster veneers of walnut or cocus wood, or with floral or "seaweed" marquetry; some cabinets were inlaid with ivory and mother-of-pearl, or japanned to imitate Oriental lacquer. The most spectacular, japanned in brilliant colors on white or light-colored grounds, were by Gerard Dagly (1657–1715) of Berlin. The legs of the stand were baluster or spiral turned typical of fashionable furniture of this period. Already, by the close of the 17th century, many of these cabinets had a distinctly feminine flavor, with compartments for toiletries, jewelry, and writing equipment.

Alongside the development of the mainstream bureau and bureau cabinet in the early 18th century was that of the slightly built slope-topped writing desk of bureau form, set upon a cabriole-legged base, with frieze drawers. Some of these desks were surmounted by toilet mirrors, showing their dual function as writing and dressing tables. Typically, they were veneered in walnut or marquetry, but some fine examples are decorated with japanning.

LATER CABINETS-ON-STANDS

In France, luxurious writing-cum-toilet tables for use in ladies' apartments were made in large numbers from the beginning of the Rococo period in the early 18th century. Veneered in fine marquetry of exotic woods, and with cabriole legs, they were embellished with cast- and gilt-bronze mounts. Some of these *bureaux de dames* had sloping lids to the superstructures, while another type, the *secrétaire à capucin*, had a flat writing surface opening out from the table top, and a superstructure of drawers and compartments rising from the back. By the late 1760s the *bonheur du jour* was an established form of ladies' writing table. As its name suggests, it was destined for the feminine "delight of the day," i.e. letter writing. It had a flat writing surface at the front, varying arrangements of shelves, drawers, or small cupboards at the back, and a

drawer below. French examples were lavishly decorated, with gilt-bronze mounts and fine marquetry veneers of unusual woods, and sometimes with porcelain plaques, or panels of Oriental lacquer. By the last quarter of the 18th century the cabriole supports – the last vestiges of the Rococo – were discarded in favor of straight-tapered legs, often with gilded grooves and understretchers.

The English interpretation of the *bonheur du jour* was more restrained, relying for its elegance on finely figured timbers and well-judged proportions; edges were straight and legs square tapered. Mahogany or satinwood was often contrasted with bandings or panels of rosewood, sycamore, tulip, or box. Both French and British styles were adopted by cabinet-makers in other parts of Europe. Porcelain plaques, marquetry, and ormolu mounts all appear on *bonheurs du jour* in Germany, Austria, and Poland, but the structure of such pieces tends to be spare and square rather than voluptuous.

▲ Bonheur du jour
Finely figured timbers, straight lines, and harmonious proportions characterize late 18th-century British *bonheurs du jour*. This example, in satinwood and purpleheart crossbanded with tulipwood, is refined with ivory finials and drawer knobs.
(c.1790; ht 1.1m/3ft 7in; value I)

▼ Bureau-on-stand
This English walnut bureau-on-stand was made when small writing desks were being developed on both sides of the English Channel, specifically for use by women. The sloping fall front encloses drawers, pigeon holes, a well for papers, and a secret drawer.
(c.1720; ht 88cm/34½in; value L)

▲ Bonheur du jtambor
The *bonheur du jour* enjoyed an enthusiastic revival during the mid-19th century. This French example in the curvaceous Rococo Revival style is decorated with walnut and floral marquetry. The elaborate gilt-metal mounts are exaggerated versions of 18th-century prototypes.
(c.1860; w. 1m/3ft 3in; value M)

KEY FACTS

- WRITING CABINETS-ON-STANDS some early very fine examples were decorated with veneered with burr-walnut, oyster veneering or marquetry (floral or "seaweed"), inlaid or japanned; this type of furniture although not always very useful (unlike the bureau in all its forms) is very desirable, so unless the decoration is very badly damaged, they will still generally command high prices
- BONHEURS DU JOUR usually very popular items of decorative furniture; those made in the late 18th-century style of Sheraton are particularly popular

Library and writing tables

The earliest-known tables specifically designed for writing date from 16th-century Italy, when cabinet-makers produced elaborately carved walnut tables with sloping desks fitted into the tops and small drawers below for the storage of writing materials. Similar tables, or bureaux, probably originated in France during the third quarter of the 16th century.

THE 18TH CENTURY

Tables designed specifically for writing were introduced in England after the Restoration (1660). French tables influenced English designs during this period, and both French and English examples were usually made of oak or walnut with a rectangular folding top. The flap was supported by baluster or tapered pillar legs they are often decorated with "seaweed" or floral marquetry and closely parallel the Dutch models. During the early 18th century the Louis XIV concept of a free-standing *bureau plat* (a flat-topped writing table) invented by André-Charles Boulle (1642–1732) was taken up and adapted by English cabinet-makers. Intended to occupy a central position in the library, and to act as a statement of the wealth and power of its owner, such desks reached the zenith of their popularity in England during the mid-18th century, and by the third edition of *The Gentleman and Cabinet-Maker's Director* (1762) by Thomas Chippendale (1718–79), no less than 11 types of carved open pedestal desk were illustrated.

As postal systems developed, and as paper became cheaper and standards of education improved, so the need arose for less stately versions of the writing table, particularly for use by women. Some of these tables appeared in Chippendale's *Director*; while others featured in *The Universal System of Household Furniture* (1762) by John Mayhew (1736–1811) and William Ince (*c.*1738–1804). A great range of new forms came into use at this time, which were notably lighter than their predecessors. Neo-classical tables were made in exotic hardwoods such as satinwood, an expensive and very fashionable wood that was particularly suited to this lighter style of table, and many examples were adorned with fine marquetry.

THE 19TH CENTURY

Several new types of writing table developed during the Regency period (*c.*1790–1830), including the Carlton House desk, named after the London home of the Prince of Wales (later George IV). Another fashionable form featured curved X-shaped supports at either end, with drawers in the frieze, and the flat top enclosed by a three-quarter brass gallery. At the end of the Napoleonic Wars in 1815, furniture designers were given the opportunity to create a wide range of new forms, when the technology required to marry wood to metal – developed for military purposes – was applied to furniture. The furniture of the Regency period was therefore characterized by elegant design combined with ambitious construction techniques. New features included galleries at the top of the table, used either for decorative effect or to hold books safely; numerous small drawers, hinged flaps, and curved ramps, which could be pulled out as required, extending the available surface and facilitating activities such as drawing and painting; and screens that extended beyond the main structure in order to shield the writer's face from the heat of the fire. In addition, revolving circular or polygonal "drum" tables were invented for the library, where they were used for storing and displaying books and paper.

◄ **Writing table**
Based on the sofa table, this Regency writing table would be sought after by collectors today for its fine construction and use of good-quality timbers. The "plum-pudding" mahogany top (a very desirable figured wood) has been crossbanded with olivewood and walnut, and inlaid with ebony stars, which are echoed in the star-shaped brass handles. The two drawers are lined with cedar and mahogany. As with sofa tables, writing tables with high stretchers are more popular than those that are set lower, as this allows for more leg room.
(1810; ht 76cm/30in; value L)

◄ **Writing table**
Although many examples were produced, writing tables with leather tops, such as this English mahogany example, are among the most commercial types on the market today. This style of table has drawers on both sides and often has reeded or fluted legs. The original legs may have been replaced with legs in the style of an earlier period to make the piece more appealing; for example, a Victorian table that originally had heavy legs may have been given lighter, turned, Regency-style legs.
(1780–90; ht 76cm/30in; value L)

▼ **Writing table by Jean-Louis-Benjamin Gros**
This is an example of the revival of the brass-and-tortoiseshell marquetry made famous by André-Charles Boulle (1642–1732) at the end of the 17th century. Although this type of decoration continued to be made throughout the 18th century, it was also revived to great effect in France and Britain. English Boullework made in the 19th century was known as "Buhl" work.
(c.1850–70; ht 89cm/35in; value K)

KEY FACTS

- "BUHL" WORK examples tend to be inferior to those of the 17th and early 18th centuries: the gilding is generally brassier and the tops are inlaid, in contrast to the leather-lined tops of the 17th-century prototypes; the drawer-linings of original examples were usually in oak, while on the copies they are in walnut
- ALTERATIONS leather tops can get ripped and have often been replaced – this should not affect value; heavy legs have often been replaced with lighter legs of an earlier style to make the table more commercial

See also Bureaux before 1840, pp.98–9; Bureaux after 1840, pp.100–101

Davenports

An entry made in the 1790s in the records of the cabinet-makers Gillow (est. *c*.1730) of Lancaster states: "Captain Davenport, a desk." This is thought to be the first recorded example of the small writing cabinets now called by the Captain's name. It is not known whether he ordered the desk for his own use, or as a gift for a lady.

▼ Davenport

Davenports made between *c*.1800 and 1820 are usually narrow and compact, such as this British mahogany example with its sloping desktop. Formerly no more than 46cm (18in) wide and deep, the Davenport broadened from the 1830s to at least 61cm (24¼in) in width. *(c.1820; ht 70cm/27½in; value I)*

For most of the 19th century the Davenport was generally used by women. The basic form, consisting of a small chest-of-drawers with a desk compartment on top, changed very little over the century or so during which most examples were produced. However, there were many minor variations. Most Davenports have four drawers that open at the side of the base sections, with simulated drawer fronts on the opposite sides. Just above the drawers there may be pull-out slides to hold papers or finished letters. Some examples depart from this pattern, with cupboards concealing drawers, but either way the arrangement is symmetrical, with dummy drawers or cupboard doors matching the real ones. Many Davenports are fitted with casters, allowing them to be moved about easily; because of their free-standing nature, they should be well veneered and finished to the same standard on all four sides.

The top section typically comprises a desk with a sloping lid inset with a leather writing surface, and a flat ledge behind it enclosed by a brass or wooden gallery.

One or two small drawers for storing writing implements and ink pull out sideways below. The finest examples have ingeniously concealed hinged drawers.

The first Davenport has a top section that slides forward to accommodate the writer's legs and is anchored by a simple iron rod sliding into holes lined up in the top and bottom. As the Victorian period progressed (from *c*.1847), the desk section was more often fixed in the writing position, and supported on elaborately scrolled or turned supports or brackets, allowing a recessed space for more leg room, and emphasizing the width of the piece. However, the catalog of the firm of William Smee & Sons (est. 1817) of Finsbury Pavement in London, which is undated but was probably produced *c*.1840, shows examples with both sliding- and fixed-desk sections.

While mahogany was the most popular wood for Davenports, some of the finest examples were made in rosewood, particularly during the Regency period. These were often embellished with stringing lines of brass, a contrast carried further by the use of decorative brass drawer-handles, gilt-brass galleries at the back, and brass cappings on the feet.

Most Victorian Davenports had wooden galleries, and these could take the form of simple moldings, turned spindles, or lacy fretwork. Turned wooden drawer knobs also replaced earlier brass handles, but some of the finest mid-19th-century Davenports had brass galleries and gilt-brass candle sconces on rotating arms fixed to the sides of the desks toward the back.

The popularity of the Davenport continued until the end of the 19th century, but few of these late examples, often over-ornamented and of generally clumsy proportions, matched the quality of craftsmanship of those made up to the 1860s.

▲ "Piano-top" Davenport

This Davenport is so called because when the top is closed it resembles a piano. By the mid-19th century, beautifully figured walnut had superseded rosewood for the best furniture, and Davenports with elaborate veneers reflect this development. The secrétaire slide on this example conceals small drawers and fittings, while a stationery compartment rises from the fretworked back. *(c.1860; ht 86.5cm/34in; value H)*

◄ "Harlequin" Davenport

Items of mechanical furniture with concealed drawers or compartments were sometimes known as "harlequin" furniture. This English harlequin Davenport in strongly figured rosewood was operated by pulling a small button on one of the three drawers in the compartment beneath the reading slope; this released the superstructure, which was simply pushed back into the base after use. *(c.1845; ht 86.5cm/34in; value H)*

KEY FACTS

- CONSTRUCTION two main types: the plain Regency box-type, which has a reading slope that slides forward, creating a comfortable knee aperture, and the type introduced *c*.1840, which has a rising superstructure and a recessed knee aperture
- WOODS the most common woods used were rosewood, mahogany, and burr-walnut
- MECHANISM the rise on the mechanical Davenport runs on a leather belt and weights; it is released by a spring lock that opens to reveal pigeon holes and drawers
- COLLECTING the Regency Davenport tends to be more popular than later Victorian examples; although collectible, Davenports are not as usable as bureaux; good-quality examples are well finished on all sides, and also on the inside

See also Pedestal and kneehole desks, p.107

Pedestal and kneehole desks

Conceived as both dressing tables and bureaux, kneehole desks first appeared in France and The Netherlands in the second half of the 17th century. Since the 19th century, at least, they have been known as *bureaux Mazarins* after Louis XIV's First Minister, Cardinal Jules Mazarin (1602–61). Early examples were commissioned by members of the French court as luxury items. Usually mounted with molded brass borders and elaborate escutcheons or ormolu keyhole mounts, *bureaux Mazarins* of the late 17th century are most frequently made of brass-inlaid red tortoiseshell in the style associated with André-Charles Boulle (1642–1732).

▲ Partners' pedestal desk
A pedestal desk fitted with drawers to both sides is known as a partners' desk. The form enabled two people to work at the same desk. This oak example is typical of the rather squat, utilitarian, late Victorian type.
*(late 19th century; ht 78cm/30¾in; value **H**)*

WALNUT KNEEHOLE DESKS

At the end of the 17th century the *bureau Mazarin* kneehole desk was adapted and simplified into the kneehole "burry" or desk. Until *c.*1740 these were usually made of walnut or red walnut, although provincial examples in oak and fruitwood also survive. The most sophisticated examples include those made of burr woods or of stained woods, simulating mulberry, and also "japanned" kneeholes, usually black or red. The most elaborate George I and George II kneeholes (1714–60) have both crossbanded and featherbanded decoration; the tops and sides are often quarter-veneered. The ever-larger kneeholes made under George III (1760–1820) were constructed in mahogany, often in the solid, with mahogany drawer-linings; they are often exotically decorated, and stand on shaped bracket feet, which replaced the earlier bun feet.

▲ Bureau Mazarin
Often constructed with a marquetry top above bow-fronted drawers and with a hinged fall-front compartment over the kneehole, *bureaux Mazarins* are usually supported on legs joined by double X-shaped stretchers to allow for leg room. The carcase was usually oak and pine, with walnut-lined drawers; the underside and the back were often blackened with a wash. The form was widely copied in the 19th century.
*(1700; ht 81cm/31¾in; value **Q**)*

PEDESTAL DESKS

The introduction of pedestal desks – a predominantly British form – reflected the demand for large, freestanding desks, which were more comfortable to sit at than the kneehole desk. First made in walnut *c.*1720 to 1730, they became widespread in mahogany during the reign of George II. Late 18th-century desks usually have three drawers in the friezes; the pedestals are fitted with either drawers or folio cupboards, and stand on molded plinths, often with hidden casters. Pine or oak examples tend to be painted underneath with a reddish wash, and Regency pedestal desks are also blackened. During the early 19th century, exotic timbers, particularly rosewood, calamander, amboyna, and ebony, were used, and firms such as Marsh & Tatham of London enriched Regency pedestal desks with brass inlay. Reacting to this trend, the cabinet-maker George Bullock (*c.*1777–1818) championed the use of indigenous woods, particularly pollard oak and holly. This return to natural woods and utilitarian designs influenced the Victorian cabinet-makers, whose desks are distinguished by their squatter, slightly heavier form and plain wooden knob handles. More elaborate examples were produced in the late 19th century in satinwood and marquetry, or with painted decoration, by firms including Edwards & Roberts.

► Kneehole desk
The original dual-purpose role of the French *bureau Mazarin* was not abandoned in later periods. As seen in this George II burr-and-figured walnut example, sophisticated kneehole desks have brushing-slides and even fitted dressing drawers enabling them to be used as both writing and dressing tables.
*(1715–30; ht 80cm/31½in; value **L**)*

KEY FACTS

- BUREAUX MAZARINS late 19th-century copies often have inset leather tops instead of marquetry ones
- KNEEHOLE DESKS crossbanding and featherbanding to the sides, brushing-slides, or fitted drawers add to their desirability; lacquered-brass handles (often replaced) are a good indication of quality – the finest examples often have either engraved metalwork or elaborately pierced backplates; most examples have thin dovetailed drawer-linings in oak, but provincial kneeholes are often made of pine; early provincial examples have different and cheaper stained timber on the sides

See also Library tables and writing tables, p.105

Miscellaneous

This group of items under the title miscellaneous includes a wide variety of furniture from the utilitarian to the more ornamental. This section includes a discussion of beds, one of the oldest and most important items of furniture, that has always been paid particular attention, to more recent forms such as the canterbury and whatnot, which are indicative of a settled society that required convenient forms of furniture that could be used for a variety of purposes and stored away when not in use. As with all types of furniture the skill and ingenuity of the cabinet-maker is evident from the way in which forms may be disguised as other items of furniture, to the high-quality decoration lavished on such mundane pieces as night tables.

Stands and racks

The term "stand" is used in a wide-ranging sense and implies any kind of support. Although the word can be used for a piece joined to another item of furniture, such as a cabinet stand, this section looks at stands complete in themselves. Such stands were specifically designed to be both highly practical and easily portable. Although they were often embellished with the fashionable decorative qualities of the day, the common feature of these pieces was that function always prevailed over style.

FOLIO AND READING STANDS

The folio stand allowed the reader to store a heavy book temporarily, to browse through at leisure, rather than having to keep taking it down from a library shelf and replacing it. Folio stands were usually adjustable, often with hinged or ratchet actions, to allow for different thicknesses of books or to hold several at once. Before

▼ Folio stand

This figured walnut Victorian folio stand features book shelves as well as the top support. Its pierced center, decorated with strapwork, is still strong enough to take the weight of several books. The bun feet are on casters so that the stand could be moved easily around the room.
(c.1845; ht 1.3m/4ft 3in; value I)

the 20th century it was common practice to read standing up, but books were heavy to hold. A reading stand, designed for resting the book on, provided the solution. Some reading stands were also intended to hold music scores, while others were more robustly constructed to take the greater weight of a book. Like folio stands, reading stands could be adjusted so that the reader was able to place the book at different heights and angles.

CANTERBURIES

Thomas Sheraton (1751–1806) referred to two types of canterbury in *The Cabinet Dictionary* (1803): the music stand and the supper tray. He described the first as "a small music stand," or open-topped rack, with slatted partitions for the storage of loose sheets of music and bound music books. It generally had four short legs on casters, so that it could be moved or kicked away easily, and was short enough to be stored inconspicuously beneath the piano. Commonly used for the storage of magazines today, it was first introduced in Britain in the 1780s. It is thought that the canterbury was named after an Archbishop of Canterbury, for whom the first example was made. Two such stands were illustrated in *A Collection of Designs for Household Furniture and Interior Decoration* (1808) by George Smith (active c.1786–1826). He wrote that "they are intended for holding such music books as are in constant use and may be manufactured in mahogany, rosewood, or bronzed and gilt."

Some stands had sides of wire latticework, and in these examples the slatted partitions were usually omitted. Others, for example some made for the International Exhibition of 1862 in London, were constructed of wood but decorated with mother-of-pearl inlay on papier-mâché, which was then overpainted with gilt and colored varnishes.

The second type of canterbury to which Sheraton referred was "a supper tray, made to stand by a table at supper, with a circular end, and three partitions cross-wise, to hold knives, forks, and plates, at that end, which is made circular on purpose." Much taller than the music-stand type of canterbury, the supper tray resembles a small table. It was used, like the dumb waiter, when service in the dining-room was dispensed with, especially particularly at informal parties. It too stood on casters so that it was easy to move around, and often had splayed legs which provided greater stability.

▲ Canterbury

With four bowed folio sections above a frieze drawer and turned legs, this mahogany canterbury shows the elegance of the Regency period in Britain. It is typical of the "music stand" type described in Sheraton's *The Cabinet Dictionary*.
(c.1800; ht 46cm/18in; value H)

▼ Canterbury

This British walnut example is richly carved with opulent foliate scrolls and leaves in the naturalistic style popular during the early to mid-Victorian period. Note that the handles are inlaid with mother-of-pearl, and that the brass casters support turned, tapered feet.
(c.1850; ht 53cm/21in; value I)

► Dumb waiter

The spiral, fluted balusters and scrolled feet are typical of the British late 18th-century style illustrated in Sheraton's *The Cabinet-Maker and Upholsterer's Drawing Book* (1791–1802). The circular trays are shallow, which indicates that mahogany of the finest quality was used to avoid warping. Rims prevented bottles and glasses from sliding off the trays. *(c.1760; ht 1.2m/3ft 11in; value L)*

DUMB WAITERS

First invented and used in Britain *c*.1725, the dumb waiter consisted of a central shaft with circular trays, which often revolved. The trays increased in size from top to bottom, and terminated in a tripod foot. In *The Cabinet Dictionary*, Sheraton described it as "a useful piece of furniture, to serve in some respects the place of a waiter, whence it is so named." The absence of a human attendant helped confidential dining, and the dumb waiter was generally placed at the corner of the dining-table for diners to help themselves to additional plates, knives and forks, pudding, and cheese. After dinner, bottles of drink and glasses were placed on the trays of the stand.

Toward the end of the 18th century, the use of the dumb waiter had spread to France and Germany in differing forms. At that time in Britain, the dumb waiter was elaborated, and new varieties were introduced. Plain elegance was eschewed in favor of such decoration as Gothic fretwork, leaf molding, and curves. Quadruped supports often supplanted the traditional tripod base. In 1803 Sheraton gave two new designs in his *Dictionary*: the first was "partly from the French taste," and on the top was a thin layer of marble "which not only keeps cleaner and looks neater than mahogany, but also tends to keep the wine cool when a bottle for present use is placed upon it." There were knife trays, shelves for plates, and holes, lined with tin, for bottles and decanters. Sheraton's second design had two levels, not three, although there were drawers underneath the lower for cutlery or dirty plates, and it rested on a quadruped, spider-legged stand.

In the early 19th century in Britain a Classical air, which had no prototype in antiquity, was imparted to many types of furniture, including dumb waiters. Grecian motifs such as lyres provided novelty, and by the Victorian era designs for dumb waiters were as eclectic as those for any other piece of furniture.

WHATNOTS

This type of stand was intended to display a variety of *objets d'art*, ornaments, curiosities, books, and papers. Generally rectangular in shape, with three shelves, and possibly one or two drawers beneath them, they were supported by turned columns at the angles. The first published reference to the whatnot occurred in 1808 in the *Correspondence* of Sarah, Lady Lyttleton, but it is also mentioned in the cost books of the firm of Gillow (est. *c*.1730) of Lancaster eight years earlier. Whatnots were extremely popular throughout the 19th century. They were usually made of mahogany or rosewood, and were sometimes embellished with ormolu mounts. In addition, the shelves of some pieces were edged with pierced brass galleries.

ETAGERES

The French *étagère*, meaning "stand," combined the qualities of the English dumb waiter and the whatnot. A two- or sometimes three-tiered table, it was intended either for displaying objects or for serving food. In some cases the top tier could be removed and used as a tray. Casters and handles on the lower tier enabled the piece to be pulled around a room. French *étagères* were more highly decorated and sinuous than their British counterparts. By the second half of the 19th century there was an enormous variety of designs available, ranging from ones that recalled the Louis XIV and Boulle styles to those featuring ormolu mounts, gilding, naturalistic motifs, and exaggerated Rococo curves and scrolls.

MUSIC STANDS

While the canterbury was for storing music, the music stand was designed for playing a score. Music stands were purely functional before *c*.1770. Professional musicians provided their own, utilitarian, stands and in any case often played sitting down. The development of the music stand as a decorative item marks the fashion in the late 18th century for private recitals, at which works by composers of the chamber form, particularly Haydn, Mozart, and Schubert, were played. Even then, function took precedence over adornment.

◄ Whatnot by Edwards & Roberts

Whatnots were versatile items of furniture, and this mahogany example has an adjustable hinged reading shelf as well as three tiers for display and a drawer at the base for storage. Whatnots were probably a British invention, but similar stands also appeared in continental Europe. *(c.1800; ht 1.7m/5ft 7in; value H)*

▼ Duet music stand

Using a stand with double, adjustable hinged slopes, two people could stand opposite each other and play a musical duet. The lyre-shaped splats of this rosewood stand are an appropriate reference to Apollo, the god of music, who played the lyre and is often depicted with the instrument as an attribute. The decorative potential of music stands was explored only after *c*.1770, and most date from the 19th century. Some stands can have up to four slopes. *(c.1845; ht 1.6m/5ft 3in; value G)*

KEY FACTS

- ALTERATIONS often polescreens have been converted into music stands; ensure that all the platforms on dumb waiters match, and that a three-tier waiter has not been converted into a two-tier one: look carefully at the size of the tier, and the balance and proportions
- COLLECTING canterburies are generally very popular with collectors because of their small size, particularly Regency examples, which because of their delicate form have often had one or more of their divisions replaced; small whatnots with hinged tops are very commercial and are generally made in mahogany; the tiers of some dumb waiters were hinged at either side with two drop flaps so that they could be discreetly stored away; good-quality waiters have galleried tiers

See also Cabinets-on-stands, p.86; High chests-of-drawers, p.87; Writing cabinets-on-stands, p.104

Bedside tables and washstands

Bedside tables and commodes, known as "night tables" in British 18th-century pattern-books, were first made in France during the second quarter of the 18th century. By the latter part of the century they were frequently supplied in pairs, one designed to conceal the chamber-pot, perhaps behind a tambor-fronted slide or simulated drawer, the other to accommodate the basin for shaving and washing. These modest conveniences replaced the early 18th-century commode chairs – so frequently copied in the late 19th century, and betrayed so readily by their exaggeratedly deep friezes.

MID-18TH-CENTURY BEDSIDE TABLES

Known as *tables de chevet*, French mid-18th-century bedside tables were usually veneered in kingwood, tulipwood, and amaranth; provincial examples were made of fruitwood. Often decorated with floral marquetry, sometimes end cut acrosss the grain – a technique particularly associated with Bernard van Risenburgh (*c*.1700–1765) and Pierre Migéon (1701–58) – Louis XV *tables de chevet* are distinguished by their waved galleried tops, pierced carrying handles to the sides, and cabriole legs, often with richly chased ormolu mounts. Extensively copied in Russia, Germany, and northern Italy, particularly in Genoa, they either supported two open tiers with marble tops or, on the most sophisticated examples, had lower tambor-fronted tiers, sometimes with simulated book spines, behind which the chamber-pots were concealed. Although this shaped rectagular form prevailed, Rococo *tables de nuit* of both kidney shape (*à rognon*) and oval form are also recorded, and these were inspirational to Swedish and Russian cabinet-makers in the second half of the 18th century.

▼ *Table de chevet*

This night table decorated with parquetry veneering in rosewood and waved, molded three-quarter galleried top is typical of Louis XV *tables de chevet*. Such examples were copied, particularly by cabinet-makers in Genoa, northern Italy.

(mid-18th century; ht 79cm/31in; value I)

ENGLISH NIGHT TABLES

The French fashion for night tables was adopted in Britain, and the basic form of the British commode had emerged by *c*.1760. Usually of mahogany, with waved or pierced galleried tops, they incorporate carrying handles above pairs of doors and shaped aprons. From the 1770s Neo-classical tables were restrained and firms such as Gillow (est. *c*.1730) of Lancaster, manufactured tambor-fronted night tables with only crossbanding, ebony, and boxwood lines or raised panels to enrich the flamed mahogany veneer. Usually fitted with leather or wooden casters, bedside commodes usually display galleried, plain tray-tops and tambor-fronted slides, above simulated drawers, which pull out to reveal the lidded pots, often set within oak frames. An improvement of the 1780s was the refinement of having "split" front legs, cut diagonally, which, when closed, appeared to be one, the front sections of these pulling out with the pot-cupboard drawer to provide support, as opposed to the more ungainly use of six legs that appears on less sophisticated pot-cupboards.

From the 1770s, as a result of the influence of Louis XVI taste, night tables became increasingly light in both form and color. As a result, bow-fronted commodes, often with slender, turned, tapering legs, veneered in exotic timbers and inlaid with Neo-classical marquetry, emerged. Gradually the rather cumbersome and heavy pattern of the 1760s was also superseded by the growth in popularity of pot-cupboards. Far narrower than their earlier counterparts, late George III pot-cupboards usually have plain three-quarter galleried tops above a single doors or tambor-slides and stand upon elegant turned legs; this form was also widely manufactured in the Victorian and Edwardian periods.

EARLY 19TH-CENTURY POT-CUPBOARDS

The early 19th century saw a renewed and vigorous revival of the designs of Classical antiquity. Napoleon I's succesful campaigns in Egypt, poularized by Baron Vivant Denon (1747–1825) in his *Aventures dans la basse et la haute Egypte* (1802), led to an explosion of Egyptomania, and this was further expressed by Thomas Hope (1769–1831), who simultaneously embraced ancient Greece in his *Household Furniture and Interior Decoration Executed from Designs by Thomas Hope* (1807). Inevitably this renewed Neo-classical fashion was reflected in the design of pot-cupboards in the early 19th century. In France, therefore, firms of cabinet-makers such as Jacob-Desmalter & Cie (est. 1767) in Paris manufactured mahogany pot-cupboards standing on plinths rather than on legs; these were sometimes battered or splayed, and mounted with Egyptian herms and crocodiles in ormolu.

In Germany, Austria, and northern Europe, the Empire style was interpreted in the designs of the Biedermeier movement from *c*.1815, and Biedermeier pot-cupboards are simlarly Classical in inspiration. Usually of mahogany, or indigenous woods, such as birch, Karelian birch, ash, or elm, they are enriched with ebonized and parcel-gilt decoration, perhaps with Egyptian-herm caryatids or lion's-paw feet. Regency

▲ **Commode**

The inlaid oval panel on the front of this English mahogany bow-fronted night table is often indicative of the firm of Gillow (est. *c*.1730) of Lancaster. The lower pot drawer has often been converted into a now more useful drawer.

(c.1790; ht 75cm/29½in; value G)

▲ **Bedside cupboard**

This is the form of a Classical column with an Ionic capital. The hinged top encloses an interior for washing and shaving; the shaft conceals an interior with a pot-shelf. This probably German design was popular in England.

(1820–40; ht 85cm/33½in; value H)

pot-cupboards in England also saw a return to the simple, clean lines and richly figured veneers of early Neo-classicism. They were made of mahogany, often with only subtle, raised panel decoration. Perhaps the most famous design introduced at this time was the multi-purpose bedside steps; made by Gillow, and usually of exceptionally good quality, they concealed the chamber-pot within the sliding first tread of the steps.

VICTORIAN COMMODES

During the 19th century bedside commodes and pot-cupboards became more utilitarian, and the discomfort of the early commodes, with their pull-out bases, was replaced by a comfortable and permanent, but still disguised, seat. These metamorphic chests-of-drawers, first recorded *c.*1830 to 1840, were a huge improvement. Appearing on the outside to be plain chests, usually of walnut or mahogany, and standing on turned tapering feet, these chests of simulated drawers opened to reveal a fitted commode-chair. This design refinement was reflected in the quality of the interior, the commode no longer cheaply set within a carcase wood, such as pine or oak, but within a frame veneered with richly figured timbers such as satin-birch, amboyna, and bird's-eye maple. However, these luxurious Victorian bedside commodes, elaborate as they were, did not last; they were superseded by the widespread introduction of the water closet.

WASHSTANDS

Although basin-stands are recorded in the Middle Ages, it was not until the mid-18th century that washstands became pieces of furniture. Inspired by French prototypes and popularized by Thomas Chippendale (1718–79) in *The Gentleman and Cabinet-Maker's Director* (1754–62), mid-18th-century washstands, often of mahogany, tend to have twin-flap square tops, the flaps opening from the center to reveal a fitted interior with sunken bowl, dressing compartments, and a rising mirror that lifts up from the back. Although the earliest examples are plain, more elaborate examples, carved with Gothic ornament, or pierced fretwork angles in the Chinese manner, were made in the 1750s and 1760s, and these were gradually superseded by Neo-classical

◄ Fiddleback commode
In order to conceal the true nature of this piece of furniture, this Victorian commode has been made to look like a chest-of-drawers. The bottom section is actually a false drawer. This is a much more stable design than the night table seen on the previous page, with its pull-out drawer fitted with a commode. The Victorian commode was gradually superseded by the water closet. This type of commode has most frequently been converted into small chests-of-drawers and this should be evident from the proportions and an inspection of the carcase.
(c.1840; ht 76cm/30in; value **D***)*

▼ Pot-cupboard by Heal & Son (est. 1800)
Late Victorian pot-cupboards, characterized by their three-quarter galleries, paneled doors, and plain plinths, were inspired by those of the French Empire. They were invariably supplied as parts of bedroom suites, their decoration was very restrained until the Sheraton Revival of the 1880s and 1890s. Most have pine or oak carcases and are often veneered in satin-birch, as in this example, or bird's-eye maple, although examples in mahogany, walnut, and burr-walnut also survive, as do others of ebonized wood made from the 1870s.
(c.1870; ht 83cm/32½in; value **C***)*

marquetry in the 1770s. In the 1790s corner-washstands, as featured in *The Cabinet-Maker and Upholsterer's Drawing Book* (1791–1802) by Thomas Sheraton (1751–1806), also appeared, and this pattern enjoyed great popularity in North America. This period also saw the emergence of multi-purpose washstands, such as that designed by Thomas Shearer, which contained a bidet below the dressing-drawer.

In the 19th century, washstands became larger; often they had rectangular tops hinged to the backs and fitted with mirrors on the inside, above central basins and further compartments. From the 1830s they became more practical in design, and are distinguished by wash-boards or splash-backs, which with the basin frame, was often made of white marble. Often conceived as part of a bedroom suite in the late 19th century, the washstand became very elaborate, with cupboards, drawers, and shelves that sometimes framed a toilet-glass. Frequently of satinwood, perhaps painted with flowers and Classical figures, Edwardian and late Victorian washstands were occasionally enriched with Arts and Crafts tiles.

► Washstand designed by William Butterfield (1814–1900)
Although as an architect Butterfield is chiefly renowned for such his work on such Gothic Revival churches as All Saints, Margaret Street, in London, he also designed Milton Ernest Hall, Bedfordshire, which was built between 1854 and 1858. The furniture for the Hall, which Butterfield also designed, is in the late Regency style. This very simple walnut washstand is decorated with elegant sycamore-and-ebony stringing and is fitted with a marble top and splash back.
(c.1855; ht 95cm/37in; value **I***)*

KEY FACTS

- POT-CUPBOARDS mid-18th-century pot-cupboards are extremely rare; pairs of pot-cupboards are among the most commercially desirable objects, and can command a huge premium; however, beware, as they have often been either matched together by later carving or embellished at a later date with elaborate marquetry
- CHAMBER-POTS it is increasingly rare to find the original porcelain or earthenware pot, but this should not affect value
- CONVERSIONS numerous commode sections or commodes have been converted later into drawers or chests-of-drawers; this should be reasonably obvious when examining the carcase and does not dramatically affect the value
- WASHSTANDS many Victorian and Edwardian examples exist; originally washstands were fitted with marble tops with holes cut through for the bowls to sit in – most of these have now been replaced with solid marble tops

See also Chests-of-drawers before 1840, pp.80–82; Chests-of-drawers after 1840, pp.83–5

Mirrors

Although German glassmakers produced convex mirrors from the 15th century, it was not until c.1500 that flat mirror plates were made using the broad-glass technique. This was invented in Venice, and revolutionized mirror production during the 16th and 17th centuries. The technique was later replaced by the plate-glass process first used at the Saint Gobain Glasshouse (est. 1693), in Paris, which allowed the production of larger and more even mirror plates. The Parisian makers enjoyed unchallenged prosperity until the late 18th century when the British Plate Glass Manufactory in London succeeded in manufacturing the large plates, which were so admired.

▲ **Mirror**
The expense of the mirror plate in the late 17th century dictated the luxury of the frame. Flemish frames are of ripple-molded ebony and tortoiseshell, as shown here, while Dutch and later British examples were oyster-veneered with walnut, japanned, or had floral marquetry.
(late 17th century; ht 69cm/27in; value I)

BAROQUE MIRRORS

Late 17th-century southern European mirrors are usually of rectangular form, with the central plates invariably "beveled" or chamfered at the edges and contained within mirrored borders; the plates are often engraved or etched with mythological or pastoral scenes. The carved frames, either giltwood or silvered, usually display a Baroque exuberance, with acanthus, putti, masks, and cornucopiae. Late 17th-century northern European mirrors were often conceived of as dressing mirrors, designed en suite with matching dressing tables and *torchères* (candle stands). Of rectangular form, frequently with convex or cushion-molded frames and usually crowned by shaped crestings, which was often similarly carved, these late 17th-century mirrors display remarkable inventiveness in their use of materials. The production of larger plates led to the introduction of pier glasses, placed between the window piers, the culmination of which are the mirrors in the Galerie des Glaces at the palace of Versailles. Although Paris's lead was followed throughout Europe, particularly in Italy, Britain, and Germany, with mirrored borders often enriched with colored or engraved glass, the plates were almost always divided.

EARLY 18TH-CENTURY MIRRORS

Although French mirror-frames during the Louis XIV (1643–1715) and Régence (1715–23) periods are usually of carved and gilded lime, pine, or oak, enriched with masks, dragons, and serpents, Charles Cressent (1685–1768), the cabinet-maker to the Duc d'Orléans, supplied his patron with vast pier glasses with gilt-bronze frames. These important mirrors, so widely copied in the 19th century, were also produced in Germany and Sweden. However, in the main, German, Swedish, and Danish mirrors made in the first half of the 18th century tended to follow the lead of Paris, although in execution the carving is often slightly flatter.

During the Queen Anne and early Georgian periods a distinctive national style emerged in Britain. Thus, although tall pier glasses with beveled, divided plates, and mirrored borders, enriched the window-piers of the great aristocratic houses, their frames began to be decorated in gilt-gesso, with finely etched and pounced decoration. This gave way between c.1725 and 1750 to the fashion for more architectural mirrors in the Palladian style advocated by Lord Burlington (1694–1753) and William Kent (c.1685–1748). These mirrors often display triangular or scrolled, swan-neck pediments, centered by the mask of a Roman god, an acanthus spray, or an armorial cartouche. Although often gilded or painted cream, these mirrors are most frequently of walnut, with gilding usually reserved for the carved architectural moldings and cresting. In North America mirrors with simple frames topped with arched crests were popular from the 1730s. Carved and gilded openwork shells were often inserted in the crests.

CHIPPENDALE AND ROCOCO MIRRORS

In the 1740s Palladianism gave way to the Rococo style. Inspired by the designs of Nicolas Pineau (1684–1754) in France, Johann Christian Hoppenhaupt (b.1719), in Germany, and Matthias Lock (c.1710–65) in England, the new vocabulary incorporated flowers, acanthus, C-scrolls, and even chinoiserie figures from the 1750s. Even the mirror-plate was decorated, and rare examples survive where the surface was painted in oils with putti and floral garlands. But it was the Chinese who perfected this art with their reverse-painted mirror pictures, which were exported to England from the mid-18th century.

The name of Thomas Chippendale (1718–79) is synonymous with the carved giltwood mirrors of the 1750s and 1760s. His designs were influential throughout Europe, particularly in Portugal, and North America, and indeed served as the inspiration for several 19th-century revivals, most importantly those of the 1830s, 1840s, and c.1900.

► **Convex mirror attributed to John Doggett**
Doggett's Looking Glass and Picture Frame Factory (est. 1802) in Roxbury, Massachusetts, was one of the largest in North America, employing carvers, gilders, and cabinet-makers. This girandole form was popular on both sides of the Atlantic; the mirror was probably imported.
(c.1802–25; ht 1.3m/4ft 3in; value Q)

▲ **Mirror**
In the 1740s the formal architectural style of Palladianism, as advocated by Kent and Burlington, gave way to the Rococo, where the rectangular form was discarded in favor of cartouches, ovals, and scrolled and shaped frames. This English giltwood frame is very close to a drawing of c.1760 by the designer Matthias Lock.
(c.1760; ht 1.8m/5ft 11in; value M)

Rococo "Chippendale" mirrors of the 1750s, as well as those in the early Neo-classical style of the 1760s, are usually of carved and gilded lime or pine, with filigree applied decoration, often of gesso or plaster applied onto wire; papier-mâché examples also survive. This technique, which enables great depth and quality in the detailing but is much more vulnerable, was superseded by gilt-composition, a plaster that is heavier, solid, and cold to the touch, but which could be cast in molds. Early North American Neo-classical mirrors had narrow moldings enclosing rectilinear or oval glass, while later examples became heavier. Often the frame was round, with a convex mirror based on patterns by Thomas Sheraton (1751–1806) and George Smith (active c.1786–1828).

DRESSING AND CHEVAL MIRRORS

It was not until the 17th century that dressing mirrors became free-standing. Initially they were made of silver or silver-gilt with trestle supports to the reverse, and designed en suite with lady's dressing-sets. During the latter half of the 17th century Venetian and Parisian craftsmen supplied exquisitely decorated toilet mirrors of this design to the ladies of the court. By the early 18th century toilet mirrors had become sturdier, often standing on plinth bases, which contained drawers, the most sophisticated being serpentine fronted; numerous examples, particularly from Britain, survive – either of walnut and parcel-gilt or of plain or carved mahogany, and even with painted or japanned decoration. The mirrors were, however, principally rectangular, and it was not until the 1770s that oval dressing mirrors, later popularized by Sheraton, appeared. Regency and American Federal examples tend to be more rectangular, the plates often positioned horizontally, the decoration restrained in the extreme and often found only in the baluster-turning of the upright supports.

Cheval or standing dressing mirrors were first recorded in Paris at the court of Louis XVI, and the design was quickly adopted in Britain. Under Napoleon I cheval mirrors reached a new height of extravagance and luxury, being mounted in gilt-bronze with

▲ Toilet mirror
This type of mirror was made from the early 18th century in walnut or with japanned decoration; this later mahogany example is more commonly found. Of restrained form, this Regency mahogany toilet mirror is typical of examples produced in Britain at the beginning of the 19th century. Of horizontal form, it is made to stand on a chest-of-drawers. The bottom section, fitted with three drawers, sits on bun feet. More luxurious types were sometimes enriched with ivory feet and finials or inlaid with Tunbridgeware decoration.
(c.1820; ht 45cm/17½in; value C)

► Cheval mirror
English cheval mirrors made during the late 18th and early 19th century are usually restrained in form, and are often of mahogany (as seen here) or satinwood. The main benefit of this type was that it was now possible to see a full-length reflection. This good-quality Regency mirror is crossbanded in rosewood and has ormolu urn finials. The most sophisticated examples were adjustable in both angle and height.
(c.1810; ht 1.2m/3ft 11in; value H)

mythological deities, stars, and Classical reliefs, the plates often arched and supported by Classical columns. This style was copied throughout Europe, particularly in Britain, Austria, Germany, and in North America, and it was also revived in the later 19th century under Napoleon III (1852–70).

19TH-CENTURY MIRRORS

In North America mirrors with arched crests in the 18th-century style continued to be made in the early 19th century and had simple ornament, were narrower, and had less top-heavy proportions. The Empire style, which was associated with Napoleon then spread throughout Europe and then to North America. The pier mirrors of the early 19th century are characterized by the use of ebonized and giltwood decoration, often enriched with Classical reliefs and architectural motifs in gilt-composition (gilt-lead in Sweden), or perhaps framing a *verre églomisé* panel. The mirrors of the later 19th century were almost all inspired by precedents of earlier centuries. However, they usually betray their age by a slight misinterpretation or embellishment of earlier ornament. The Rococo Revival was superseded by the "Jacobethan" or 16th- and 17th-century Mannerist designs in the mid-19th century; toward the end of the century both Neo-classical and Rococo styles prevailed and the revival mirrors of this period are frequently directly copied from published designs.

► Mirror
This decorative mirror is an early 20th-century copy of a Baroque 17th-century mirror made on the island of Murano, in Venice. In the original, the border plates would have been divided by repoussé gilt metal and the cresting would have been less stylized. Nevertheless, the mirror still shares the florid yet restrained flavor of the Baroque period.
(c.1900; ht 1.4m/4ft 7in; value D)

KEY FACTS

- MIRROR GLASS 18th-century glass tends to be fairly thin, with the beveling soft and shallow, and the cutting uneven; 19th-century glass is thicker, the beveling cut at an acute angle, and the cutting even; original glass is desirable, and if the glass is cloudy it may be possible to have it re-silvered; replacing glass should generally be avoided
- FRAMES composition frames are vulnerable to damage and are less expensive than giltwood or silvered frames
- COLLECTING "Chippendale" mirrors are notoriously difficult to date, particularly if they have been re-gilded and a discoloring wash has been painted on the reverse of the frame; 19th-century copies do, however, often betray themselves through a misunderstanding of motifs and ornament; Rococo Revival mirrors tend to have over-fussy decoration and heavier carving

See also Dressing tables, pp.62–3

Screens

The earliest known screens were made in China, but they are recorded in Europe from at least the Middle Ages and regularly mentioned in 15th-century inventories. It was not until the coming of electricity that their role in the household changed dramatically, from temperature regulator to decorative art form.

TYPES OF SCREEN

Screens developed from sheer need; until recently, draughts and the excesses of heat from open fires were a way of life in every region where the chills of winter were felt. A number of pieces of furniture were developed to combat these problems – the wing armchair enclosed the sitter and helped him or her to keep warm, and settles, often curved and with solid backs, stopped draughts and contained the heat.

However, the most versatile piece of furniture was the folding screen. It could be large with hinged leaves, sometimes up to 12 in number and occasionally even more. It was practical because, however large, it could easily be folded and stored away. Alternatively, a small screen with an adjustable panel could protect a localized area from the heat of the fire. The screen's place was at the heart of the household, so its quality openly reflected the status of the owner. Screens were therefore made of a variety of materials, from wood to leather and the most expensive and decorative cloths. They could also be made of wicker: one featured in the painting *The Virgin and Child before a Firescreen* (*c*.1440; National Gallery, London) by a follower of the Flemish artist Robert Campin. It shows the Virgin sitting on a low settle, with her head framed halo-like against a circular wicker screen placed before a fireplace.

LACQUERED AND JAPANNED SCREENS

The voyages of discovery opened up the trade routes with the East, and the East India companies were set up to foster this business. By the mid-17th century trade in Oriental curiosities with China and Japan established a taste for the East, which spread and had an enduring impact on furniture ornament and design.

China and Japan had long enjoyed a tradition of sophisticated workmanship. In the West there was a fascination with their blue-and-white porcelain, but furniture was also imported into Europe. The screen was an important feature of the Oriental interior. There the room settings were highly formalized, and in Japan, particularly, solid pieces of furniture were few. Screens were used as room dividers, gave privacy when required, and protected against draughts. They were also designed to be easily movable and, therefore, were ideal for export. The flow to Europe rapidly increased, as Oriental screens translated well to the European interior. More importantly, they gave broad displays

▶ Six-leaf screen
The painting on this Dutch leather screen (in unusually good condition) is less formal and much busier than Oriental designs. The reverse side is generally painted much more plainly than the front.
(*c.1750; ht 2.5m/8ft 2in; value J*)

◀ Polescreen
The needlework panel on this British polescreen is a fragment from something else of a later date than the mahogany frame. Sometimes polescreens were converted into stands for tripod tables; the proportions usually indicate such a change.
(*c.1780; ht 1.5m/4ft 11in; value C*)

of sought-after Oriental lacquer and ornamentation. Chinese lacquer screens were known as "Coromandel" or "bantamwork" screens in the West. However, the demand for lacquer soon outstripped supply; Oriental screens are mentioned in the inventories of every great house between 1700 and 1750. True Oriental lacquer could not be produced in Europe because its main ingredient was the sap of the *Rhus vernicifera* tree, indigenous to China and later introduced to Japan and South-East Asia, but not grown in Europe. Once the sap had been dried, it could be applied in coats, forming a crust so hard that it could be carved in relief. Color, traditionally black, red, and aubergine, could also be added to the sap. In Europe an imitation based on shellac (made from insect secretions) was developed, known as japanning. It is always betrayed by the

▼ "Coromandel" eight-leaf screen
In this form of lacquer decoration many layers are applied and allowed to dry, and are then incised. Unlike that on a European screen, the decoration is not cluttered with figures, even though it is busy. It displays the strongly diagonal features that often characterize Chinese screens. The reverse is decorated with flowering trees and birds, within similar borders.
(*19th century; ht 2.7m/8ft 11in; value L*)

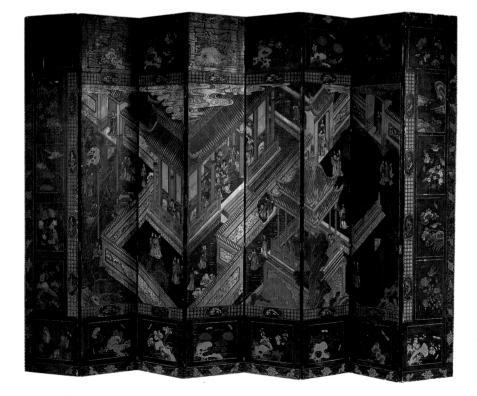

European character of the faces and landscapes. Japanning, in white, blue, and green as well as the Oriental lacquer colors, was applied to many pieces of furniture, remaining an influence through to the present day.

Many imported screens were left as they were, but some were cut up with the idea of making the precious art form go farther. The screen fragments were adapted for pieces of furniture such as mirror-frames, cabinets, tables, and chests, sometimes with no regard for the unity of the designs. Two chests-of-drawers in the State Apartments at Chatsworth House in Derbyshire, England, have been made up in this way, and visibly demonstrate how the scenes have been cut and truncated in order to fit into the appropriate space. The Oriental decoration that illustrated imported screens also influenced European designers. In *The Gentleman and Cabinet-Maker's Director* (1754–62) by Thomas Chippendale (1718–79), designs for screens decorated with Chinese figures, pagoda-like crestings, Chinese railings, and frets abound.

POLESCREENS AND CHEVAL SCREENS

As an essential part of every 18th-century interior, the screen was developed and its form diversified to suit a variety of roles. The large folding screen continued to be produced and, as well as lacquered and japanned screens, examples were made of painted wooden panels, or of a wooden framework covered with leather painted in oils, tapestry, silk, or other textiles. There was also an ever-increasing number of smaller examples for more personal and portable use.

The polescreen was popular as it was small, light, and easily movable. It had a long pole, often capped by an urn finial, with an adjustable panel, which was commonly square, oval, or shield shaped. This was for much more localized use than a free-standing screen, and protected a person's face from the heat of a fire.

The cheval or "horse" screen had a fixed panel typically inset with tapestry or needlework. It was made in the fashionable woods of the day: first in mahogany and later rosewood or satinwood. Cheval screens were sometimes made en suite to the chairs in a room. As the 18th century progressed, more sophisticated examples of cheval screen were made with sliding panels that pulled out from either end or the top. Variations have fixed panels but also enclose hinged flaps, which open to reveal writing surfaces. While writing, sitters could thus have their legs exposed to the warmth of the fire from below while their face was protected from the immediate heat by the panel above.

OTHER 19TH-CENTURY SCREENS

Draughts and open fires continued to remain a way of life during the 19th century. Screens proliferated with the number of homes being built. The panels were often used to display old unwanted textiles or embossed leather panels that, rather than being discarded, were cut up to the required size. A fashion also developed for scrapwork screens. Paper cut-outs of children, animals, houses, and country scenes could be bought in packets

► **Screen by François Linke (1855–1946)**
The central panel of this kingwood, three-fold French screen is inset with a gilt-bronze plaque over an Aubusson tapestry, with jasper roundels and marquetry in the flanking leaves. The woodwork and its gilt-bronze mounts are of the finest quality, as would be expected of Parisian cabinet-maker Linke, who had a long and dazzling career from 1882 to 1935. The screen is in the Louis XVI style, which enjoyed a hugely successful revival after c.1850, as it was the favored style of Empress Eugénie.
*(c.1900; ht 2m/6ft 7in; value **P**)*

▼ **Cheval screen**
This Victorian rosewood screen in the "Elizabethan style" is inset with a needlework panel of a later date. Firescreens were standard features of almost every Victorian drawing-room, and survive in large numbers – although many are neglected and not worth repairing. Rosewood when fashioned in the solid is extremely durable, but pierced fret-carvings, such as the ones featured at the top and bottom of this screen, are vulnerable, and often suffer damage or are lost.
*(c.1845; ht 1.2m/3ft 11in; value **G**)*

and applied to ready-made screens for the nursery or bedroom. The drawing-room was not the only part of the house heated by open fires and so requiring screens. In the dining-room, people often made strenuous efforts to avoid being the ones who sat at table with their backs to the fire. To relieve scorching backs and protect the sitter, a screen of woven cane was introduced, which could be hooked to the back of a chair and extend from the head to the seat. Such small, easily movable screens were also used as splashbacks on washstands to protect the walls.

The increasing introduction of enclosed fires, and particularly of electricity and central heating, has made the screen almost redundant. Some fine-quality examples are works of art in their own right and survive as a result, but vast numbers have been put away and damaged through neglect. Some, for example scrapwork and leather screens, are rarely in complete and undamaged condition. A screen that is in its original state and not in need of repair is a real find.

KEY FACTS

- **CONDITION** leather and scrapwork screens are vulnerable – check that they are complete, as repair is costly; if the panels on a screen display an incomplete picture, the value will be lowered; scrapwork screens in good condition are generally collectible
- **ALTERATIONS** some polescreens have been converted into tripod tables or music stands; check for strange proportions of the top to the stand; check that polescreen insets are contemporary to the frame
- **COLLECTING** fire- and polescreens are the least commercial – other types are more popular, and value is based on scarcity of material, rarity of maker, and quality; when wallpaper and paints replaced 17th-century wall panels of embossed leatherwork, sections of the leather were often made into screens; on 19th-century screens, surrounds of giltwood are more desirable than gilt gesso, and less likely to be damaged

Beds

From the earliest times beds have been endowed with particular importance: as places of rest and privacy, or as symbols of power. The bed was often the most important legacy, as it was regarded as a possession of consequence, representing the continuity of the family.

EARLY BEDS

The earliest European free-standing beds were basic structures comprising roofs, posts, and bases; the fabric hangings that decorated them were of greater value, and when noblemen moved around the country, they took their bedding, curtains, and valances with them, leaving behind the plain wooden construction. An early type of bed was the truckle or trundle bed on wheels, which conveniently slid under a standing bed when not being used by a servant. By the early 16th century most beds in northern Europe were made from oak; the heads were paneled and decorated with coats of arms, lozenges, chevrons, and lettering; squat, carved posts were placed at the corners, and testers (canopies) were added in the middle of the century. This form was replaced during the 17th century with a beech frame, with tester, ornate cornice, and a back covered in the same fabric as the curtains. On grand beds the posts were tall and more slender, with luxurious hangings crowned with finials, covered with the same material as the valance, from which issued ostrich feathers. More ordinary beds were hung with cloth, linen, or moreen.

18TH-CENTURY BEDS

British beds became more subdued at the beginning of the 18th century. Cornices became straight and projecting, and fringes and tassels disappeared in favor of plain trimmings. "Angel," or half-tester, beds, without posts at the foot, imitating the French *lit à la duchesse*, retained the height of their four-poster counterparts.

◄ **Bed**
Originally this important and exquisite Italian giltwood and wrought-iron bed would have been hung with fine cut-velvet hangings from Genoa, or with silk embroideries. Such superb ironwork is typical of the work of Italian and Spanish craftsmen of the 17th century. Iron bedsteads were particularly made on the island of Sicily. The metal is not gilded but instead treated with a lacquer while the square uprights terminate in giltwood finials. The upper rail is hung with lambrequined tassels.
*(late 17th/early 18th century; ht 2.1m/6ft 11in; value **N**)*

▼ **Tester bed**
Although this type of English Tudor bed exists in surprising numbers, many have been composed of parts from other beds. This example is typical, with a canopy surmounting an arcaded backboard with cup and cover posts, and a plinth base with a paneled foot rail. The ornate carving was typical of beds of this kind at the time, but by the end of the century oak bedsteads had become very much less embellished.
*(early 17th century; ht 2.3m/7ft 6in; value **N**)*

The paneled back was reintroduced on mahogany bedsteads of the first half of the century, with cabriole legs ending in lion's-paw feet, and slender posts with vase-shaped plinths replacing silk-covered uprights. By 1775 the cornice had become simple in outline, straight or serpentine, still complemented by vase finials at the four corners; the surface was carved and/or gilded, and cheaper wood frames, such as beech, were painted. On Neo-classical beds the posts were often very elaborately carved with such ornament as fluting, paterae, lion masks, and acanthus. Red damask and moreen were the favored materials for ordinary beds, although in *The Cabinet-Maker and Upholsterer's Guide* (1788–94) George Hepplewhite (*d.*1786) recommended the use of white dimity for "an effect of elegance and neatness." Late 18th-century beds had a much lighter feel, with decoration taking the form of narrow, fluted posts delicately carved with wheat ears or husks or painted with ribbons and garlands of flowers. These clean light lines were echoed in the Federal period beds made in North America by such makers as Samuel McIntire (1757–1811) in Salem, Massachusetts, and Duncan Phyfe (1768–1854) in New York, the posts often decorated with Classical urn-form turnings with delicate reeding. Hangings were based on the designs in *The Cabinet Dictionary* (1803) by Thomas Sheraton (1751–1806) and Hepplewhite's *The Cabinet-Maker and Upholsterer's Guide*.

19TH-CENTURY BEDS

Beds in the French Empire style, particularly *lits en bateau*, are usually richly and exquisitely decorated in a restrained manner; the structure had large unbroken paneled surfaces veneered in both light and dark woods, which were sometimes used in combination, and decorative themes, usually represented in ormolu, included oak, laurel, and olive wreaths, shields, helmets, swans, lions, sphinxes, and vine-leaves. Beds were made in two principal types, both of which were meant to be placed in alcoves and seen from the side; therefore only one of the four faces was properly decorated. The first type was influenced by the beds of the Louis XVI era,

Throughout the later 19th century revivalism dominated fashions. In Italy the Renaissance Revival, known as "Dantesque," was interpreted in heavily carved beds and others decorated with *alla certosina*, a style of ivory and bone inlay, which had been popular in the 16th century. In North America such firms as Berkey & Gay (est. 1859) in Grand Rapids, Michigan, designed suites of bedroom furniture in the Renaissance Revival style, while the firm of Prudent Mallard (1809–79) made high-post beds at his workshop (est. 1838) in New Orleans. In Britain the "Jacobethan" Revival gave rise to the production of heavily carved four-poster beds. Tubular brass was used for bedsteads from the 1820s, and as manufacturing techniques improved during the century, cast-iron beds were made. Iron campaign beds, first made in the early 19th century, were designed to be easily assembled and transported for use on the battlefield.

with straight uprights in columnar or pilaster form, no roof or curtains or excess fabric, but lavishly decorated with bronze mounts. The second type was the *lit en bateau*, as it vaguely resembled a small boat, with two straight ends of equal height, and rolled over, linked by a steeply curved traverse. Both types were sometimes overhung with canopies in the style of earlier fashions. This is a type of bed particularly associated with the Biedermeier period.

The Empire style was the most important influence on English beds of the early 19th century, and numerous examples can be found in *A Collection of Designs for Household Furniture and Interior Decoration* (1808) by George Smith (active *c.*1786–1828), and in the journal *Repository of Arts* (1809–28) by Rudolf Ackermann (1764–1834). The desired goal was to achieve "tasteful simplicity" by having less drapery; mahogany, or rosewood posts decorated with bronzed or gilded "Grecian ornaments"; domed testers, and hangings of red, yellow, or blue silk or calico trimmed with lace or a fringe. By the 1820s the French couch form beneath a canopy was used, although this fashion was short lived.

▲ Lit en bateau

This Empire burr-elm *lit en bateau* has decorations on one side only – the undecorated back was intended to rest against the wall, and the ends were left plain. Possibly intended for an alcove, this bed would have had a canopy of rich fabric attached to the wall above it. Empire-style elements include twin columns at the front, floral paterae and foliate clasps.
(c.1820; ht 1.2m/3ft 11in; value J)

▼ Bed by François Linke (1855–1946)

Linke is arguably the most sought-after cabinet-maker of the late 19th and early 20th century. He started working independently in Paris in 1882, making a wide range of furniture mostly in the Louis XV and XVI styles, many copied directly from 18th-century precedents. This Louis XVI-style mahogany bed is part of a bedroom suite.
(c.1897; ht 1.3m/4ft 3in; value N)

▲ High-post bed

It is rare to find a Federal period bed complete with its original tester frame, as seen in this mahogany example from Salem, Massachusetts. The carving on the end posts is similar in style to that found on beds made in Boston, during the same period.
(c.1800–1815; ht 2.2m/7ft 3in; value O)

KEY FACTS

- ALTERATIONS four-poster beds have often been reduced in height because of changing circumstances; check that the decoration and carving continue up the piece completely; also check to see where any reductions have been made, as the frames may have been cut to make the bed narrower or have added sections of wood to make the bed wider or longer – look along the rails for tell-tale signs in the color and wear of the timber
- MADE-UP BEDS these can be made up of elements from other beds, and usually it is only the front posts that will be original; the most commonly found made-up beds are tester beds from the 16th and 17th centuries

See also Cupboards and linen-presses before 1840, pp.73–5; Wardrobes after 1840, pp.76–7

Trays, knife-boxes, cutlery-urns, wine coolers, cellarets, and buckets

TRAYS
Known as "voyders" in the Middle Ages, and conceived not only for clearing away but also for the presentation of delicacies and sweetmeats, the earliest utilitarian trays were probably made of pewter and wood. During the late 17th century lacquered trays imported by the East India companies and European japanned versions revolutionized tray designs. The fashion for tea in the early 18th century was directly reflected upon all of the component parts of the tea ceremony.

▼ Butler's tray
During the late 18th century rectangular trays on fixed or X-shaped folding stands were usually of mahogany, with occasionally, centrally hinged folding trays. Such trays as this British mahogany example have one long side open for easy access to the glasses.
(early 19th century; ht 89cm/35in; value G)

Modest trays in oak and elm also survive from the early 18th century, and from the 1750s mahogany trays first appeared in pattern-books. Thomas Chippendale (1718–79), in the first edition of *The Gentleman and Cabinet-Maker's Director* (1754), included four designs for trays in the Chinese style with carved fret borders. However, this type is very rare, and Chippendale also supplied designs for plain rectangular trays. From the 1780s trays became increasingly decorative; they were made in mahogany, satinwood, and other exotic timbers, were sometimes richly inlaid with shells, fan-parquetry, and foliate arabesques of stained fruitwood, or were painted. Late 18th- and early 19th-century trays were dominated by the fashion for japanning, particularly in papier-mâché. A process long practiced in Persia (now Iran), it was patented in 1772 by the firm of Henry Clay, in Birmingham, and later by Jennens & Bettridge (active 1816–64) in London. Although papier-mâché trays were often of scalloped form, rectangular trays with similar decoration were also fashionable, particularly those of *tôle peinte* or polychrome-painted metal.

KNIFE-BOXES AND CUTLERY-URNS
Supplied in pairs as ornamental containers for silver and enamel-handled cutlery and designed to stand prominently on the serving table, knife-boxes came into fashion during the reign of George II (1727–60). Although the basic form, with a serpentine front, remained remarkably unchanged until the 1780s, George II knife-boxes were often covered with silk-velvet or shagreen, rather than veneered. From the 1760s knife-boxes in mahogany were made and are characterized by their bow-fronted form, hinged slope with drop-handles, and shaped bracket or claw-and-ball feet; they are unembellished apart from the cockbeaded or chequerbanded edges. The interiors, with slopes pierced with holes to display the cutlery in tiers, were also often silk lined but otherwise restrained. During the 1770s their decoration became increasingly lavish, with crossbanding and featherbanding, ebony-inlaid star parquetry to the slopes, and even stylized green-stained shell inlay – a motif particularly identified with North Country workshops – while the feet were discarded altogether in favor of Classical plinths. With the age of satinwood (1780–1800), elaborate Neo-classical embellishments became commonplace, and these were often complemented by richly engraved Sheffield plate mounts. During the 1780s the vase-form knife-box, published by George Hepplewhite (d.1786) in *The Cabinet-Maker and Upholsterer's Guide* (1788–94), was designed to stand either set at each end of the sideboard or on pedestals. Made of satinwood or other light woods, the most refined examples were painted or inlaid with Neo-classical marquetry, arabesques, and simulated flutes, while the spring-loaded lids opened to reveal a chequerbanded interior with concentric tiers for the display of cutlery. During the early 19th century, knife-boxes and cutlery-urns became increasingly redundant both by sideboards with fitted drawers for storage, and by cutlery-urns being affixed to pedestals.

► Cutlery-urn
This vase form enjoyed enduring popularity, both in carved mahogany, as featured in the *Estimate Sketch Books* (1796) by the firm of Gillow, and in satinwood and marquetry, particularly in the Victorian and Edwardian periods by such firms as Edwards & Roberts.
(late 19th century; ht 45cm/17½in; value I)

◄ Tray by Jennens & Bettridge
The successors to the firm of Henry Clay were Jennens & Bettridge in London. They expanded the business by setting up a branch in New York (1851–2). The firm specialized in polychrome papier-mâché trays, decorated with picturesque landscapes in the manner of the painter George Morland, which from 1825 were inlaid with mother-of-pearl, as seen in this example.
(c.1845; w. 83cm/32½in; value H)

▲ Knife-box
This would have been made as one of a pair, to stand at either end of a sideboard. The interior would have been fitted for cutlery, although, as with most knife-boxes, this example has been converted for stationery.
(c.1760; ht 30cm/11¾in; value for a pair H)

▶ Cellaret by Alexander Norton (active 1822–37)
Distinguished by their solid proportions, restrained Classical ornament, and tapering rectangular form, Regency sarcophagus-shaped cellarets usually stand low to the ground on paw feet. The top of this mahogany example is suitably carved with a grape-and-vine finial.
(c.1825; ht 65cm/25½in; value I)

influence of George Bullock (*c*.1777–1818) increasingly promoted the use of indigenous English woods such as pollard oak and elm, frequently enriched with foliate marquetry arabesques in the "Buhl" style. However, from the 1830s this decoration became increasingly lavish, often combined with carving, and later Victorian cellarets are often betrayed by their squatter, heavier proportions.

PLATE-BUCKETS AND PEAT-BUCKETS
Plate-buckets are distinguished by their one-dished side that enabled servants to remove plates easily, and straight-sided, or even polygonal form. Inspired by the need to ferry plates the long distances from the kitchen to the dining-room, and usually made in pairs, plate-buckets were initially intended to be placed near the fire to keep the plates warm. The plate-bucket lent itself easily to embellishment and carving with pierced Gothick arcades, Chinese blind fretwork, and even marquetry inlay in the Neo-classical style; plain types were also made. The role of the plate-bucket was superseded in the late 18th century by the warmers enclosed within dining-room pedestals, and thus plate-buckets became increasingly plain, purely for use by servants for carrying china to the dining-room. The "peat-bucket" is an Irish term for a container traditionally thought to have been used for carrying peat to the fireplace. However, this is now thought to be unlikely as the bucket and peat together would have been very heavy indeed. It is now thought that they were used for carrying any number of items, including oysters. Although buckets are usually considered an English form, 18th- and 19th-century ones from The Netherlands are among the most common found today, and can be distinguished from their English counterparts by their slightly smaller proportions, ribbed tapering bodies and, most characteristically, by the alternating use of light fruitwood and mahogany to give a streaked effect to the bodies.

▲ Peat-bucket
Wooden peat- and plate-buckets were first recorded in northern Europe in the mid-18th century. Peat had long been used as a fuel in marshland areas, particularly in Ireland, and peat-buckets were needed for carrying peat to the fireplace, although, as discussed, this is contentious. They are usually of tapering circular form, and made of vertical mahogany sections bound together with brass bands, with metal liners and handles. Although peat-buckets tend to be restrained in design, Irish Regency examples are increasingly bold in scale and often elaborately ribbed.
(c.1785; ht 35cm/13¾in; value G)

WINE COOLERS AND CELLARETS
As wine was an expensive luxury, receptacles for cooling and storing wine – whether of open-topped cistern (wine cooler) or lidded cellaret form, fitted with a lock, with divisions for bottles – were often lavishly decorated. Although metal and marble cellarets were first recorded in Britain in the late 17th century, it was not until the mid-18th century that lead-lined mahogany examples carved in the Rococo taste were made. Perhaps the most celebrated wine cooler is the Georgian form with a hexagonal or oval body, made of vertical sections of mahogany held together with two or three brass bands.

Neo-classical wine coolers and cellarets were usually conceived en suite with sideboards and pedestals, and were still predominantly of mahogany, although exotic timbers such as satinwood, padouk, and rosewood were also used. Although wine coolers with serpentine-channeled flutes to the body, which were directly inspired by Roman sarcophagi, and those with elaborate marquetry in a lighter style, continued to be made in the 1780s and 1790s, the most common examples were plainer mahogany hooped with brass, with the lead-lined inside divided with partitions for the bottles. It is from this date that the majority of canted rectangular, circular, dome-lidded, and octagonal examples survive. Increasingly restrained in form and decoration, cellarets were rendered somewhat redundant by the inclusion of cellaret-drawers within designs for dining-room pedestals and sideboards.

During the early 19th century the lidded cellarets of Roman sarcophagus form, which were often of much larger size than its 18th-century predecessors, dominated Regency pattern-books, and generally do not have stands. While firms such as Gillow (est. *c*.1730) of Lancaster, continued to supply cellarets in superbly figured mahogany, from 1810 cabinet-makers under the

◀ Cellaret
This late 18th-century cellaret is typical of the George III style. Made of mahogany with a lead-lined interior and tapering brass-bound body, it has two carrying handles, can be locked, and stands on square, tapering legs with simple brass casters.
(c.1790; ht 64cm/25in; value H)

KEY FACTS
- TRAYS 18th-century mahogany trays are rare; those that exist are often made from the leaves of old dining-tables; papier-mâché trays may suffer from craquelure and flaking; the best papier-mâché examples have mother-of-pearl inlay
- KNIFE-BOXES many have had the insides removed so that they could be converted to other uses – often as writing-cases – in the 19th century; a premium is attached to those that retain their original fitments; examples with shell inlay are usually from the North Country and Scotland; pairs of cutlery urns are very desirable
- WINE COOLERS rare examples are those from the 18th century of carved mahogany or walnut
- PLATE- AND PEAT-BUCKETS these are faked in huge numbers, often from old timber; look out for indications of consistent old damage, shrinkage, and seams to the brass bands, and beware of suspicious stains

See also Sideboards and serving tables, pp.60–61; Occasional tables, pp.66–7

Despite their susceptibility to accidental breakage, ceramics are the most naturally durable of antiques, with some of the earliest surviving examples, of Chinese origin, dated to *c*.6500 BC. They have also proved the most collectible, a status that can be partly attribed to the immense volume of decorative and useful wares that has been produced around the globe, especially since the 16th century. However, the sheer quantity of Oriental, Islamic, European and, more recently, American pottery and porcelain available to collectors has been matched by tremendous variations in the shape, style, and decoration of pieces. Such characteristics are largely determined by the country or region of origin, by individual factories and designers, by advances in technology, and by the aesthetic and cultural preoccupations of different historical periods. These diverse forms and styles of ornamentation have tremendous appeal for collectors, accentuated in many pre-20th-century pieces by intriguingly uncertain provenance, the resolution of which requires the acquisition of considerable knowledge and the skills of a detective. Of equal fascination is the colorful history of ceramics, with its jealously guarded manufacturing secrets, industrial espionage, shipwrecked cargoes, and archeological discoveries.

Detail of a dinner service by Coalport (left) Decorated with delicate floral sprays and foliage and raised floral and gilded borders on a dark blue ground, this is a quintessentially English dinner service *(1820)*.

Teapot (above) This Rococo-style faience teapot, with its organic and vegetal forms and brilliantly painted enameled flowers, was made in Strasbourg, the premier center of faience production in the mid-18th century *(1748–54)*.

Ceramics: Basics

Ceramics of one type or another are known to have been made for thousands of years. From the simplest utilitarian earthenware pots through to the most sophisticated ornamental porcelain figures, ceramics have an almost unparalleled variety and diversity of forms and uses. The pliable basic material, clay, can be formed by building or casting techniques, or by throwing on a wheel, into flat plates, hollow vessels, and decorative objects in almost unlimited shapes. The wide range of decorative techniques includes piercing or molding the clay itself while it is still wet; coloring with glazes, enamels, or gold either before or after firing; and, relatively recently, using printing processes to transfer a pattern onto the surface.

Materials and techniques

There are three basic types of ceramic (fired clay) body: earthenware, stoneware, and porcelain. Earthenware is opaque, porcelain translucent, and stoneware may be either. By understanding the fundamental differences, and having some knowledge of how a piece has been made, it is possible to appreciate qualities in an object that may not otherwise be apparent.

MATERIALS

To make the "body" – the mixture from which a vessel is formed – different kinds of stone are ground into a fine powder and then mixed with water to produce a paste. The object is then fired in a kiln; under intense heat the microscopic crystals in the particles of stone melt and fuse, forming a new, tough material.

Earthenware This includes the basic types of common or coarse pottery, such as this English medieval jug, made from impure clay and fired. Sophisticated tableware and ornaments are composed of refined white clays, which may be mixed with silica and feldspathic minerals. Lightly fired earthenware is often known as "terracotta" (Italian for "cooked earth"). Earthenware is porous, and without a glaze cannot store liquid.

- Firing temperature: 800–1100°C (1500–2000°F)
- Porous and opaque
- Fired body color is usually red-brown or buff

Stoneware Fired to a higher temperature, certain clays will become impervious to liquid, as in this Chinese Yixing teapot, as long as a flux (which lowers the temperature at which the body fuses) is present to assist vitrification. The addition of a glaze makes stoneware hard and durable.

- Firing temperature: 1200–1450°C (2200–2650°F)
- Opaque or slightly translucent, non-porous body
- Can be thinly potted with fine detail
- Can be rough and grainy, through to silky smooth if polished
- Fired body color may be darkish, grayish, red, white, or sand-colored
- Types: various Chinese wares; Wedgwood "jasper"

Hard-paste porcelain A typical formula for hard-paste, or "true," porcelain combines 50% kaolin (china clay) with 25% china stone (petuntse) and 25% quartz. Hard-paste porcelain vitrifies and becomes translucent during the glaze firing. Because the body and glaze fuse together at a high temperature, it is hard to detect a separate layer of glaze, as on this Meissen cup and saucer of c.1770. A chip will show a glass-like conchoidal fracture resembling a chipped piece of flint.

- Two firings: the first (biscuit) to 900–1000°C (1650–1830°F) and the second with glaze to 1400°C (2550°F)
- Components: kaolin, petuntse, and quartz
- Translucent; thin and fine-grained
- White-bodied, with glaze that "fits" very well to the body

Soft-paste porcelain The range of complex formulae for soft-paste, or "artificial," porcelains is vast, but the basic difference from hard paste is the absence of kaolin. Because of its similar firing range, bone china is usually classified as soft paste, even though it comprises 25% kaolin mixed with 25% china stone and 50% animal bone (bone-ash). Soft-paste porcelain and bone china are usually vitrified in the first firing and therefore receive a lower-temperature glaze-firing. This usually results in a clearly discernible layer of glaze sitting on the surface. Soft-paste porcelain is more brittle than hard, and chips appear granular, as seen in this 18th-century Worcester bowl.

- Two firings: biscuit up to 1250°C (2280°F); glaze is lower
- Contains little kaolin or none at all
- Bone china: contains kaolin, china stone, and bone-ash
- Translucent; body ranges from a warm creamy color to a cold grayish white
- Granular chips
- More detectable layer of glaze on the surface
- Glaze: creamy through to grayish or bluish

FORMING TECHNIQUES

The appropriate process for creating a ceramic vessel is principally determined by the intended shape of the finished object, coupled with the type of body. Earthenware is suited to forming by hand, while sophisticated porcelain clays respond better to mechanical methods of molding. Adjusting the water content determines the plasticity of a body, and this affects the behavior of clay during forming.

Slab-building and coiling These are the simplest methods of forming an object from clay. If a vessel has totally flat sides, as in this square bottle by the studio potter Shoji Hamada, it will have been assembled from slabs of clay rolled flat, cut to shape, and joined by pressing the keyed and moistened edges together. Coiling can be used to make vessels with curved sides; long sausage-like clay strips are rolled out, then coiled into the desired shape.

The resultant ridges can be smoothed out, both inside and outside. This method was often used to make pots of large size.

- Most simple and ancient techniques
- Flat-sided objects will have been slab-built
- Objects that were formed by coiling may have visible lines
- Extremely large pots can be made by coiling
- Mainly used by studio potters today

Throwing The potter's wheel is without doubt the most important invention in the history of ceramics production. The potter centers the clay mass on the wheel by throwing it sharply down, and, as the wheel spins, firmly and evenly manipulates the clay, using upward motions. "Throwing rings" – ridges left by the fingers of the potter – encircle thrown vessels, as is seen on this Song stoneware vase. Finally, the completed pot is cut off the wheel using a wire.

- Hand-worked by the potter
- Throwing rings often visible

Press-molding A modeled relief pattern, as seen on this Italian *jardinière* of c.1760 from Capodimonte or Buen Retiro, or a textured surface is normally produced by pressing clay into a mold. Molds are made of plaster of Paris, which absorbs moisture from the clay, causing shrinkage that prevents the clay from sticking to the mold. A slab, or "bat," of clay is pressed into the various sections of the mold, and this is allowed to dry to a "cheese-hard" or "leather-hard" state. If a vessel is circular in section, press-molding is performed on a wheel; as the mold spins, a machine forces the clay evenly over or within the template mold. For flatware (plates and saucers) this process is called "jiggering," while for hollow-ware, such as cups or jugs, it is called "jollying." The reverse of a press-molded vessel may show the potter's finger marks. The design molded on the outside of a pressed object will not be visible from the inside (not the case with cast shapes).

- Technique involves pressing clay into a mold
- Method used for creating certain relief patterns
- Reverse of an object may show potter's fingerprints
- Design is not visible from inside the object

Casting Also known as "slip-casting," this process uses liquid clay (slip) poured into an absorbent plaster of Paris mold. Clay is first prepared and then mixed with water to form "slip." The molds are assembled from sections held tightly together, and slip is poured into them. The plaster absorbs moisture from the slip, leaving an even skin of clay lining the surface. Excess slip is poured out of the object through a hole – as in the base of this 18th-century English clockcase made by Chelsea – to ensure that the object remains hollow, and the mold is allowed to dry. The formed vessel shrinks slightly, and the sectional mold can then be opened. Complicated objects such as figure groups are assembled from many separately cast pieces.

- Slip-casting is best for making non-round shapes
- The outer pattern appears as a slight impression on the inside
- Thickness varies according to how long the slip is left inside the mold before the excess is poured away

GLAZING

Glaze is a thin covering of glass fused to a ceramic body. Its main functions are to strengthen the body and, in the case of a porous clay, to make it impervious, but glaze also gives pottery a smooth surface beauty that is both pleasing to touch, and practical and hygienic to use. In most cases, crystals of glass are applied as a finely ground powder suspended in liquid, which evenly coats the pottery or porcelain vessel. In a kiln these crystals melt and fuse together to form a permanent and distinctive surface.

Salt glazes At the highest temperature during the firing of stoneware, salt (sodium chloride) is thrown into the kiln, and, as it vaporizes, the sodium reacts with the silica in the stoneware body to form a thin, sometimes pitted glaze, as seen on this 17th-century German jug. The iron impurities present in many stoneware clays cause most salt-glazed stonewares to be brown in color.

- Often a single firing for both hardening and glazing
- Red lead was sometimes added with the salt to make the glaze glassier
- The glaze may have a slightly pitted surface, an effect known as "orange peel"
- Clays need to be rich in silica
- Much salt-glazed stoneware is brown-glazed; a few wares are whitish or light buff in color

Tin glaze This is used to cover common earthenware bodies to make them resemble porcelain. Tin oxide is insoluble in most glazes and results in an opaque layer of white glass, which covers the body. However, the glaze does not fuse well with the body, and as a result most tin glazes are prone to chipping, as seen on this English porringer.

- Delftware, maiolica, and faience are common tin-glazed wares from different parts of Europe
- Glaze can chip easily
- Color: rich pure white to a bluish glaze

Transparent glazes There are many different kinds of glaze, all producing a smooth, translucent surface on pottery or porcelain. The presence of silica (glass) is vital, but many other minerals are present, especially lead oxide. Lead adds brilliance to the glaze and, above all, reduces the firing temperature needed to fuse the glaze to the body; lead oxide has therefore been widely used in the ceramics industry in glazes fired at less than 1200°C (2200°F). Such colors as green and brown can be introduced to lead glazes. In the 18th century, creamware was sometimes glazed entirely in green, or else with mottled splashes of color, as seen on this Whieldon-type dog of c.1755–60.

- Lead glaze fires at less than 1200°C (2200°F)
- Lead glaze is very glossy, smooth and transparent
- Lead glaze, potentially dangerous to workers and users, was replaced by boric acid in the 19th centur; some glazes still contain lead oxide, but within safe limits

Celadon glaze Many Chinese stonewares such as Yue, Longquan (southern China), and Yaozhou (northern China) from the Song Dynasty and earlier were given a high-temperature firing with a semi-opaque, green-tinted glaze, derived from iron. Northern celadon is a gray stoneware covered in a relatively thin, olive-green color, whereas its southern counterpart Longquan has a markedly thicker, cool green glaze over a much whiter, porcellaneous body, as seen on this early Ming barbed-rim dish.

- Yue: similar to northern celadon, perhaps more grayish
- Southern: cool, sometimes bluish green; because of its thickness, it tends to be relatively opaque
- Northern: olive green and semi-translucent
- Celadon wares are sometimes decorated with carved, incised, or molded designs beneath the glaze
- Usually associated with Chinese wares

Decoration

The potters, painters, and gilders employed by factories to decorate pottery and porcelain were craftsmen, who learned their trade from their forebears. Their names are rarely known, yet these talented decorators have left us with a legacy of great beauty, ingenuity, and variety. There is a vast range of decorative techniques used on ceramics, and those highlighted below are simply a few of the most common.

APPLIED DECORATION

Widely used on many types of pottery and porcelain, applied decoration is raised up from the ceramic ground in a low relief. Employed in various ways, it can produce designs ranging from the naive and simple to the extremely finely modemodeled and sophisticated.

Slip-trailing The most basic form of ceramic painting is the method of using one color of clay on another, as seen on this English dish of c.1715. Water is added to clay to form slip, which is then trailed onto the body of the ware, and a pointed stick is used to create the desired effect.
• The decoration is flush with the body
• The slip is usually in brown and cream
• Decoration is typically naive but spirited

Tube-lining The process of slip-trailing can be used with careful control to produce a different kind of decoration. Unglazed wares are ornamented with a design drawn in a thick slip, usually by using a quill with a rubber bulb full of slip at the end. This leaves tiny raised lines on the surface, forming enclosed fields, which are filled with underglaze colors. When glazed the colors stay within their shapes, as on this English *jardinière* of 1912 to 1916 by Moorcroft.
• Technique practiced since the 2nd century AD
• Raised lines separate the colors

Sprigging There is a limit to the quality of the relief detail possible with press-molding (see Materials and techniques), and a more finely modeled relief decoration can be achieved by sprigging. Clay is pressed into a mold to form a "sprig," which is then carefully extracted. This molded ornament is attached to the surface of an unfired vessel using water or slip, a process known as "luting." Sprigging is usually carried out by applying clay of one color onto a differently colored ground, as seen on this 19th-century English vase by Wedgwood, but *blanc-de-Chine* porcelain from China and its many European copies used sprigs of the same white porcelain as the ground.
• Very fine detail is possible
• Commonly associated with Wedgwood
• Usually the sprig contrasts in color with the ground

Pâte-sur-pâte In the *pâte-sur-pâte* ("paste-on-paste") technique a design is built up of layer upon layer of painted slip, forming a low relief, which is then carved to resemble a cameo. Once completed and fired, the design is glazed for protection. This English vase of 1911 by Minton & Co. shows the sophisticated effect of translucent drapery that can be achieved. Most examples are in only two colors – usually white on a darker ground – but variations may involve a great many different colors on a single piece. Used in China in the 18th century, the technique was introduced to Europe in the mid-19th century.

• Decoration is in slight relief
• Great depth and translucency are possible
• The effect is intended to resemble a cameo
• Introduced at Sèvres c.1851; its greatest exponent was Marc-Louis Solon, who introduced the technique at Minton

PIERCED DECORATION

Also known as "reticulation," this is a form of decoration carried out when the clay is still wet. After an object has been fully formed, but while the clay is still soft and pliable (a state sometimes referred to as "leather-hard"), it can be cut with a sharp tool so as to create a delicate reticulated pattern. Any kind of clay can be pierced, but usually the technique is restricted to thinly cast porcelain.

• Chinese porcelain was pierced with delicate fretwork during the Ming Dynasty
• In Japan, porcelain makers at Hirado simulated the most delicate pierced ivory
• The greatest exponent of the art of reticulation was George Owen, who worked at Royal Worcester; this saucer by Owen was pierced entirely by hand without any molded guidelines
• On hollow shapes it takes great skill to prevent cut-out pieces from falling inside and spoiling the vessel
• Molded techniques can imitate reticulation, but the result is never as sharp

COLORING

Color may be added to the body either before or after glazing, according to the technique used and the effect required. Many colors are a result of a chemical reaction during firing, and great skill is required to achieve the correct effect.

Underglaze colors These colors are fixed to the body of the ware at the same time as the item is glaze-fired, making this form of decoration much less expensive than other coloring techniques, which require additional firings. Until relatively modern times, blue was the only color that could be applied successfully under the glaze. The process involved mixing finely powdered cobalt oxide with water or oil and applying directly onto the unglazed surface. After a coating of glaze, the black oxide reacts chemically with the glaze, creating a silicate form of cobalt that is blue, as seen on this Lowestoft jug of c.1775.
• Can withstand kiln temperatures of 1200–1300°C (2200–2400°F)
• Blue is the most common underglaze color
• Colors: blue (cobalt), green (copper), purple (manganese), yellow (antimony), and red (iron)

Enameling Colors painted over the glaze are known as "enamels" and require firing at lower temperatures (*petit feu*) to fix them to the body. Enamel colors basically consist of metallic compounds, mostly oxides, that are combined with a flux and ground into a fine powder.

Mixed with oils, enamels are painted onto the surface of the ceramic piece. The colors do not all fuse at the same temperature, so pieces may be subjected to several kiln firings. Many of the colors change totally in the kiln, so painters require considerable skill to ensure that the result is the color they intended. This German sweetmeat dish of c.1745 from Meissen shows a brilliant palette of enamels. Enamel decoration remains on the surface of the porcelain and may be felt with the fingertips.

- Firing temperatures: 900–1100°C (1650–2000°F)
- Most colors are very stable, apart from blue, which can deteriorate
- The range of overglaze colors is greater than that of underglaze colors

Luster Oxides of gold, silver, platinum, or copper are dissolved in acid, and after being mixed with an oily medium are painted onto the glazed ware. Firing produces a metallic or an iridescent surface, as on this English jug of c.1814 from Sunderland. The effect may be used on an entire ground, or to produce or highlight a design.

- Colors: ruby (gold), yellow (silver), silver (platinum), red to pinkish copper (copper)
- Important centers of production: Manises, Malaga, Gubbio, Deruta, Staffordshire, and Sunderland
- First used in the Middle East around the 7th century AD and perfected in Spain in the 15th century

GILDING

Gilding is the process by which gold is used to decorate (mainly) porcelain. Gold is applied as gold-leaf or with a brush, pure or mixed with mercury or (originally) honey, and fired at a low temperature. Mercuric gilding gives a bright metallic gold, honey-gold a dull, rich effect.

Raised gilding Raised gold decoration is intended to simulate the effect of jeweling. To create the pattern – as seen on this English saucer of 1870–80, made by Minton & Co. – the decorator paints the design on the surface using a thick enamel paste. After several layers of enamel have been applied, fine gold is painted over the raised enamel in order to give the appearance of solid gold. The raised enamel is usually yellow, which helps to make it less obtrusive if the gold becomes worn and the enamel underneath shows through.

- Important centers of production: Vienna, Sèvres
- Important craftsmen: Desiré Leroy at Royal Crown Derby; Charley Deakin at Worcester
- Economical use of gold

Burnishing When gold is fired it has a dull, matt surface. Careful polishing by friction, using agate, bloodstone, or metal tools, gives gilded surfaces a brilliant appearance. Spectacular effects, as seen in this cup of 1816 from Sèvres, can be created by tooling designs into a gilded ground; the pattern is left matt when the ground is polished.

- Burnished gold has a rich, soft color
- Brilliant surface effects can be achieved
- Can be tooled into fine and intricate designs
- Popular decorative technique in the early 19th century

PRINTING

Ceramics may be decorated by transfer-printing or lithographic printing, processes that do away with the need for skilled hand-painting. Printed designs were originally in a single color, but as the processes improved polychrome printing became possible.

Transfer-printing This process was introduced in the mid-18th century to replace expensive hand-painted wares. An engraved copper plate is inked and the design transferred onto a sheet of tissue paper or a sheet ("bat") of tacky glue. In bat-printing the design is pressed onto the surface of the object using oil; color is then dusted on with powdered oxides. The design is fixed by firing. Crosshatching caused by the tools on the copper plate is visible in transfer-printed decoration. This English spittoon of c.1820 from Spode shows the problems caused when prints did not fit exactly.

- Transfer-printing was introduced at Worcester by 1754, bat-printing in Staffordshire c.1800
- Often the print does not "fit" and seams are visible
- Blue printing is the most prevalent

Lithographic printing Complicated patterns in full color, which could previously be produced on ceramics only by skilful hand-painters, can be inexpensively mass-produced using lithographic printing. A paper-backed print is laid on the vessel's tacky, varnished surface, and the paper is sponged off, leaving the pattern. The technique is often mistaken for hand-painting, but any area of shading will be composed of tiny dots rather than brushstrokes, as on this 1911 English commemorative mug from Staffordshire.

- Invented in the late 19th century
- Suitable for mass production; most usual printing technique for overglaze decoration
- Colored dots form design
- Same design can be used many times over

Fakes and forgeries

The art of faking porcelain goes back centuries; indeed, most early European porcelain copied valuable Chinese imports to make great profits at the time. These 18th-century "fakes" are today worth far more than the originals that they imitated. More recent fakes are not restricted to copies of items that have a high value, for even inexpensive antique porcelain can be duplicated easily using modern technology. It is, of course, difficult to fake fine porcelain convincingly, and most Victorian fakes would not deceive the ceramics specialists of today. On the other hand, now that some basic pottery and earthenware is highly valuable, and faking is easier, copies can be much harder to detect. Recent court cases have involved alleged fakes of early English pottery worth hundreds of thousands of pounds, and copies of vases by the studio potter Bernard Leach (1887–1979) that were made inside a British jail.

REDECORATION OF WARES

Porcelain can be refired, even after two centuries, and can emerge from the kiln without the look of the original glaze being spoiled. It was common practice in the 1830s and 1840s to add new, lavish, colored grounds to plain white or very simply decorated pieces of 18th-century Sèvres. The porcelain shapes, often bearing the original factory marks, are therefore quite genuine, but now carry painted decoration that is more in the style of the 19th century. Examples of Sèvres wares redecorated in England at Thomas Randall's china works in Madeley, Shropshire, were acquired by many Victorian collectors, who believed them to be original and highly valuable. Rare forms of painted decoration on old Worcester porcelain sold for vast sums at the end of the 19th and in the early 20th centuries, and forgers created many very convincing fakes using 18th-century porcelain with simple, plain patterns, to which colored grounds, lavish gilding, and extravagant painting were added.

These pieces were then sold for huge sums to unsuspecting collectors. Coats of arms and dated inscriptions were added to plain white Delftware, again vastly increasing the value of otherwise ordinary artifacts. More recently, visitors to Russia have been sold apparently old Russian porcelain with valuable pre-Revolution imperial emblems, or portraits of Lenin purporting to date from the 1920s; in fact, the plates were from old but utilitarian Russian dinner sets with the original patterns worn off and fake decoration added. With genuine body and glaze, the deception known as "redecoration" can be the hardest to detect, and great skill is needed to recognize the tell-tale signs of a later kiln firing or inconsistencies in the painting style.

CHINESE COPIES AND FAKES

Chinese porcelain made for the Qing emperors (1644–1911) copied earlier Ming reign marks to show that the skill that produced the centerasured originals still existed. Eighteenth-century imperial fakes of Ming vases are valuable in their own right, especially if they bear the marks of the new emperor's reign rather than spurious 15th-century marks. More recently, vast numbers of clever forgeries of all kinds of Chinese artifacts have regularly fooled collectors in the West. Fine examples of tomb figures from the Tang period (AD 618–907) cannot be sold today without a certificate of a test for thermoluminescence. This measures the amount of radioactive elements present in the clay, from which is determined the likely date the object was fired. About 100 years ago porcelain made during the reign of Emperor Kangxi (1662–1722) was keenly collected in the West, and reproductions were made in China bearing fake early 18th-century marks. These were sold openly as reproductions in such stores as Liberty & Co. (est. 1875), in London, but today these Victorian and Edwardian copies far outnumber genuine marked specimens. This proves that the collector should not rely on the correct identification of the mark alone.

◀▼ **Chinese vase**
The mark on this vase suggests that it was produced during the reign of Emperor Xuande (1426–35); in fact, it was probably made in Taiwan or Korea during the 20th century. Although the design is of the period, it is too blurred to be original. *(20th century; ht 24cm/9½in)*

STAFFORDSHIRE

Because Staffordshire figures have been collected for so long, they have attracted the attention of fakers more than any other kind of collectible ceramics in Britain. Valuable figures by the famous potter Thomas Whieldon (1719–95) were copied during the later 19th century, and an experienced eye is needed to identify the genuine from the copy. Many reproductions of 19th-century Staffordshire figures were made using original molds, the copies often being produced in the same factories. During the 1960s the potter William Kent reproduced the figures which had been made by his family at its pottery in Staffordshire during the 19th century; however, the new figures were of a lesser quality with faked ageing. Kent sold his figures as reproductions, but unscrupulous customers then sold them on as the real thing. Recently, vast quantities of reproduction porcelain Staffordshire figures, made in East Asia, have saturated the antiques markets of Britain, Europe, and North America. Stained to look old, most of these pieces can hope to deceive only inexperienced bargain-hunters, and unfortunately they frequently succeed. These modern ornaments defy the logic that fakers only want to copy antiques that are valuable. The manufacturers sell them as inexpensive reproductions, but traders then enter them into auctions or sell them on to hapless collectors at markets and tabletop sales.

▶ **Redecorated cup and saucer from Sèvres**
The original factory mark with the date letter "M" indicates that these items were made in 1765, too early for this style of jeweling, which was introduced only in the 1780s. When the new decoration was refired in the 19th century, the dirt absorbed through the foot-rim was burned out, causing a mass of black specks. *(1765 and 19th century; ht of cup 6.5cm/2½in; value F)*

▲ "Whieldon" teapot
This teapot was sold in 1989 as being made by Whieldon, but subsequent tests showed that it was actually less than ten years old. A value is therefore not appropriate here.
(c.1979–89; ht 11cm/4¼in)

► *Piper: Scots Guards* made in Staffordshire
The many different models in the old Staffordshire style that have swamped the antiques market since the mid-1990s usually reproduce the original coloring very well. Many such figures, like this one, are unknown in genuine Staffordshire. These reproductions are made in porcelain and do not have earthenware bodies.
*(late 20th century; ht 24cm/9½in; value **B**)*

▼ Two "Wedgwood" plaques showing the triumph of Bacchus
The original blue jasper plaque was modeled for Wedgwood by William Hackwood in 1776. The green jasper copy, which was probably cast from a genuine piece, was not made at the factory and is clearly not as sharply modeled as the original. Wedgwood has regularly attracted the attention of fakers.
(top: 1900s; bottom: 1776; w. 31cm/12in)

▲ Copy of a Meissen dancing group by Samson
Great effort has been made here to reproduce the original coloring used at Meissen during the 1740s. Samson could not be accused of faking, since the Meissen crossed-swords mark was replaced by Samson's own mark of a dissected cross. Unmarked Samson copies are frequently mistaken for the real thing.
*(c.1880; ht 15cm/6in; value **E**)*

EDME SAMSON & CIE
Edmé Samson (1810–91) has achieved notoriety as a faker, yet his Parisian factory survived for more than 150 years openly selling reproductions of the great porcelain of the past. Samson began in the 1830s by making replacements for broken pieces of dinner services. The success of these led him deliberately to copy Meissen, Chelsea, Worcester, and Chinese porcelain, as well as faience, Delft, and English enamel wares. Samson's best pieces are brilliant productions in their own right, and today they can be sought after, mostly because they are highly decorative. The wrong kind of porcelain body is often used for many Samson pieces, and a specialist can usually easily tell a copy from an original.

THE SIGNS OF AUTHENTICITY
If you are concerned about the authenticity of a ceramic piece, it is important to look at the example closely and with an open mind. If it is supposed to be 200 or 300 years old, consider the possibility that the condition is too good. Check for the correct body and glaze, if possible by comparing it closely with a piece you know to be genuine, and question whether or not the colors seem right. Certain colors were not used in the 18th century, and many early makers had trouble with bright-blue enamels, which can appear uneven. Because blue was unstable, figures were never painted

with blue eyes in the 18th century, but these often appear on late Dresden copies. Close examination will reveal clues as to the methods used to make a piece of porcelain, and specialists look for the marks left by molds or kiln supports. Are the tell-tale signs genuine and in the right place? An authentic antique may be dirty or worn, but is not always so. If a piece looks scruffy, is the "dirt" genuine: in other words, is it dirty all over, with grime naturally formed in hard-to-clean parts? Is the rubbing or wear natural, or has it been added by a file or sandpaper? Fakers frequently overdo the signs of ageing by scratching pieces in out-of-the-way places where real objects would never get worn during normal use. Marks are most frequently copied, so check that the maker's mark is correct, of the right size, and in the right place. If a piece of porcelain is fragile – a figure, for example – is it damaged in the places you would expect? Fakes are often too perfect, and consequently may be relatively easy to detect.

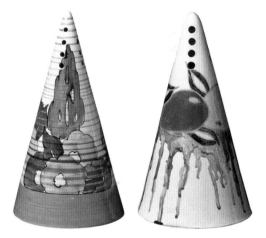

▲ Two "Clarice Cliff" sugar-sifters
The distinctive Art Deco designs of Clarice Cliff (1899–1972) have proved simple to copy, and reproductions are now widespread. Cliff's crisp potting and careful control of the painted colors, seen on the real object (left), have not been reproduced well on the faked example (right). High prices have been paid for some vases and conical sugar-sifters in the belief that they are genuine.
*(c.1930 and late 20th century; ht 13cm/56in; value of original **E**)*

TIPS FOR COLLECTORS
- BODY AND GLAZE these should be correct for the piece
- PALETTE AND DECORATION familiarize yourself with the maker's or factory's output
- CONDITION modern copies are often too perfect for a piece that should be old
- FAKES beware of what may be fake scenterssing; wear and damage should be visible in the expected places
- MARKS these should be in the usual place, but should only be used for authentication once the above elements have been considered

See also Qing before 1800, pp.138–9

Collecting and care

Ceramics are plentiful, and a great deal is available to collect and own. As a result the collector needs to be selective, and to decide what kind of ceramics he or she wants to collect. This has to be determined by a combination of taste, knowledge, and budget. It is right to buy the best that you can afford; but to collect only early Meissen or Renaissance maiolica requires extensive knowledge as well as a bottomless purse. On the other hand, many areas are easy for a beginner, and not expensive. Fine Ming porcelain carries a high price tag, but late Ming porcelain made for the South-East Asian market is reasonably abundant and affordable. The problem with this example is that this less expensive ware lacks quality and may not give you any pleasure, in spite of its Ming name and great age. If funds are limited, it is probably better to acquire good examples of an area of collecting that is currently unfashionable or inexpensive, rather than to settle for poor examples of something that would otherwise be too costly.

THE DISPLAY OF CERAMICS
It goes without saying that you have to like what you collect, but part of the enjoyment of collecting porcelain is that it can be displayed entirely to suit your taste, since it takes little looking after beyond simple common sense. Display cabinets prevent the need for dusting, but it is important to check shelf fixings regularly for scenterngth. Pieces need not be displayed in a cabinet, but always avoid direct heat sources because rapid changes in temperature can cause cracks to appear without warning, even in highly prized and well-made porcelain. Positions to avoid include window-sills in direct sunlight, as on a cold day the sun can heat a piece of china remarkably rapidly, causing terrible cracks and splits. Insurance companies know to their cost that a common cause of breakage to porcelain is a mirror or painting falling off a wall, so if your ornaments are on a mantelpiece, for example, check that any pictures hanging above are firmly secured.

CLEANING AND CARE
It is extraordinary how much porcelain and pottery sent to auctions, or even sold in antique shops, is very dirty; but much of the unsightly appearance can be cleaned up quite simply by the purchaser. A good wash with nothing more than water with a few drops of liquid detergent can transform a piece. A soft cloth should be used, or, for more complicated pieces, a soft toothbrush or a fine paintbrush to get into awkward corners. Under no circumstances should an antique ceramic object be cleaned in a dishwasher. Also, never immerse hollow porcelain ornaments in water, because concealed within them will be tiny blowholes designed to allow the expansion of air during kiln firing. If water seeps inside, figure groups may literally leak water for weeks afterward.

If there is no enameling, gilding, or other decoration applied on top of the glaze, it is safe to use a non-abrasive household cream cleaner to remove dirt from surface scratches. Never use strong cleaning agents on any decoration, or on any piece that is unglazed and so possibly absorbent. As far as possible, try to avoid handling pieces with fine gilding, since the gold used on most porcelain will wear off very easily.

▼ ▶ Cupid
Only half of this European figure of Cupid has been washed. The dirt has not harmed the glazed surface, and a simple clean with a thin brush to access the crevices will reveal the bright colors in their original state.
(late 19th century; ht 35cm/13¾in; value E)

Antique pottery, and some porcelain, may be stained or appear discolored; this is usually the result of years of storage in damp conditions. Professional conservators are generally able to remove severe staining with chemicals, some of which are widely used by dealers and collectors, but no chemical centeratment should be attempted without professional advice, as many valuable ceramics have been ruined by centeratment with ordinary household bleach.

THE MERITS OF DAMAGED CERAMICS
A damaged piece of ceramic – like any other antique – is usually more affordable than a perfect specimen. Most collectors realize that this is perhaps the only way to own a very rare or expensive item. Wares that have been damaged are usually desirable and collectible as long as they are stable and have not been restored with unnecessary overpainting; furthermore, the price should truly reflect the damaged state of the piece.

By its very nature, both hard- and soft-paste porcelain chips and cracks easily; unfortunately even an apparently minor chip will generally greatly reduce the value of the piece. There is nothing wrong with damaged

▲ ▶ Charger with visible metal hanger
The metal hanger on this 19th-century French faience charger has been in place for some years and has chipped through to the body. Such a hanger should only be removed by an expert as the plate may be invisibly cracked and the hanger may be holding it together.
(late 19th century; diam. 50cm/19½in; value E)

▶ Model of a shoe
Although severely chipped, this decorative delftware shoe from London is still very collectible. Restoration of old delft is not generally recommended.
(17th century; l. 16cm/6¼in; value I)

items if you can live with them in your collection, but a collector should be aware that, unless items are very rare, they can prove difficult to resell. A collection that comprises mostly damaged wares is certainly to be avoided. Additionally, if items are of a late date, which includes most 20th-century porcelains, damaged examples will be of little merit and will justify their inclusion in your collection only if they are exceptional, or very inexpensive. Conversely, a damaged specimen of a fine and rare type of porcelain will generally be a better buy than an undamaged but ordinary piece that is offered at the same price.

▼ "Fable" saucer from Chelsea

In perfect condition this saucer, made during Chelsea's Red Anchor period, could have been worth up to ten times the value of this broken example. A "museum-type" repair (conservation) could make the damage less noticeable. Any further spray or overpainting, however, would spoil the unique feel of genuine Chelsea glaze.

*(c.1750–2; diam. 14cm/5½in; value **D**)*

RESTORATION AND CONSERVATION

While most collectors prefer their antiques to be in mint condition, some damage to ceramic bodies seems inevitable. Severe damage (such as chipping, cracking, or rubbing) can be unsightly and can spoil the appearance of a fine object. Restoration of ceramics is today quite widespread, and in many cases a professional repair will do much to enhance a damaged specimen. Nothing looks worse than a broken head on a figure, or a broken spout on a teapot, and paying an expert to put this right is usually money well spent. On the other hand, a lot of repairs that are carried out are completely unjustified from both an aesthetic and a financial point of view.

The practice of repairing broken ceramics dates back to ancient times, and examples are known of Greek terracotta wares and Roman storage jars mended with metal bands or rivets. By the 18th century "china menders" were active in many European and North American cities, joining broken porcelain

▲ Repaired figure of a shepherdess from Bow

The paint used for the repair of the left arm of this 18th-century figure has discolored and turned creamy brown over the years. To detect repair it is necessary to look closely at such danger points as the rim of the hat, the neck, and the fingers, arms, and toes.

*(c.1760; ht 15cm/6in; value **D**)*

together either with special enamel pastes or by riveting with metal "stitches." Riveting was common right up until the 1950s, when strong glues became widely available. If a riveted object is free of rust or corrosion, the repair will remain remarkably strong and last for ever. Complicated riveting can be admired for the great skill involved, but the piece is nevertheless broken and will be valued accordingly. Old rivets can be removed and the breaks disguised, but many collectors today prefer to leave 19th-century repairs showing, as proof that the object was loved and used by the original owner. Riveted wares are an area of increasing interest for collectors, especially in the USA.

Restoration does not make a piece of damaged porcelain perfect again, no matter how skilfully it is carried out. It should not be assumed, therefore, that if restoration is well done the damage will not matter; a restored piece will always be less valuable than an identical piece in pristine condition. A great deal of repair-work is carried out by restorers for dealers who intend to sell the items afterward. Buyers are not always informed of the full extent of the damage, and as this is often invisible it can be impossible for the untrained eye to detect; unfortunately, therefore, buyers are frequently deceived. No collector should be afraid to ask a dealer or auctioneer to explain precisely what repair has been carried out and state this on a written receipt before a purchase is made.

Many collectors and dealers today prefer the "museum-type" repair, in which damage is tidied up and the piece made presentable, with no attempt to camouflage the damage completely. Extensive re-glazing and all-over spraying will hide damage, but this can create a totally synthetic surface that has none of the authentic feel of the original piece. Repair that simply cleans and seals old cracks without spraying, and makes the damaged piece attractive again, should always be encouraged.

▼▲ Dessert dish by Coalport

This dish, which was broken during the 19th century, is part of a fine service in which most of the wares have been riveted. Broken porcelain of that period was repaired by itinerant china merchants, who drilled tiny holes and inserted metal rivets only visible from the back. Once mended, riveted repairs are incredibly strong, and most still hold fast.

*(c.1815; w. 21.5cm/8½in; value **B**)*

TIPS FOR COLLECTORS

- DISPLAY display ware carefully, away from direct sunlight and heat sources, and ensure that surrounding objects are secure
- CARE clean with non-abrasive household cleaners using a soft cloth, a soft toothbrush, or a fine paintbrush; never immerse hollow-wares in water; avoid rubbing gilding; professionals can assist with discoloration using chemicals
- COLLECTING damaged pieces can be difficult to sell, although a rare example that has rectifiable damage should not be discounted; riveted wares still have value, and interest in them is increasing
- RESTORATION a piece with "museum-type" restoration (conservation) is often preferred by dealers and collectors to examples that have been made to appear in perfect condition by means of such aggressive techniques as respraying and glazing, which can strip the piece of its character

Oriental pottery and porcelain

The Chinese Neolithic cultures of the 3rd and 2nd millennia BC are known to have produced pottery wares, and glazes were first used – perhaps accidentally – at the end of the 2nd millennium BC. The development of wares fired at over 1200°C (2220°F) during the Han Dynasty (206 BC–AD 220) signaled an important advance, and, from the 3rd century onward, Chinese ceramics became ever more refined. Fine porcelain was being made by the 14th century, especially under imperial patronage, reaching its apogee in the 15th century in the later Ming period. Ceramics industries grew up in both Japan and Korea, perhaps inevitably influenced to a great extent by Chinese styles; nonetheless, both countries also developed subtly distinct styles of their own.

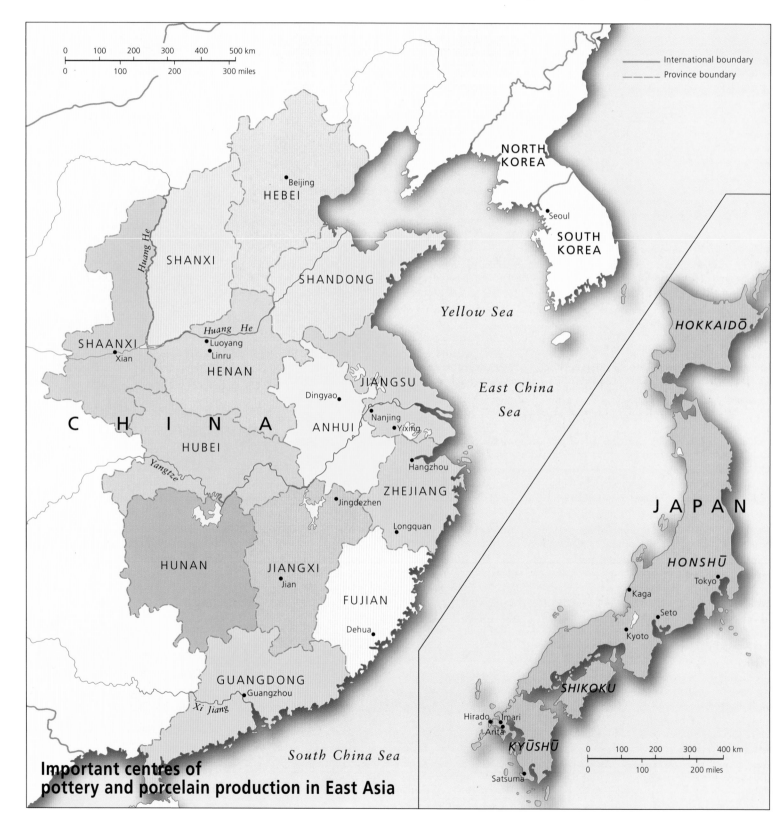

Important centres of pottery and porcelain production in East Asia

China

Early ceramics

By the Shang period (*c*.1600–*c*.1050 BC), when stonewares were first produced in China, there was an advanced ceramic technology, with the separate high-fired and low-fired traditions of Chinese ceramics already apparent. The high-fired Yue stonewares produced from the 3rd century AD were the precursors of the great celadons of the Song period and represent a high level of technical and artistic achievement.

► **Neolithic funeral jar from the Western Yangshao culture**

Burnished earthenware jars such as this have been found in burial sites throughout the province of Gansu in north-west China, which is known for this type of pottery.
(*c.3000 BC; ht 31cm/12in; value I*)

EARLY WARES

The earliest known Chinese ceramics are low-fired earthenwares dating from the Neolithic period. Distinct traditions emerged in the Central (*c*.5000–*c*.2500 BC) and Western (*c*.3300–*c*.1800 BC) Yangshao cultures and in the Dawenkou culture (*c*.5800–*c*.1500 BC) in the north-east. The distinctive bulbous red Yangshao earthenwares were coil-constructed and were sometimes decorated with impressed cord-like patterns or painted with bold black or purple geometric designs, often of spirals and loops enclosing checkered patterns. Dawenkou wares are thin, wheel-thrown pots made of red, gray, or black earthenware, which was burnished.

During the Shang period thick, white, unglazed pots were made of kaolin (china clay), while other fine clays were used to make stonewares, which were then glazed. As ceramics technology developed, wares became increasingly sophisticated; the potter's wheel became more common, and new types of body – such as high-fired stoneware – were introduced. Forms at this time tended to be based on such bronze ritual forms as the *ding* and the *hu*. In the Han period a huge variety of wares was made, including models of houses, farms, ponds, and human figures in lead-glazed earthenware, which were all produced as funerary goods to accompany the deceased into the afterlife.

YUE WARES

Gray-bodied stonewares covered with a green-gray glaze were made in the Yue district in northern Zhejiang Province from the 3rd or 4th century AD until the 10th or 11th century, when they were superseded by the famous Longquan celadons. Yue wares are exceptionally fine and were presented as tribute at the Tang court as well as being exported to South-East Asia and the Near East. Early Yue wares include sophisticated desk ornaments, such as water droppers and brush rests in the shapes of frogs, lions, and other animals, as well as burial urns with applied models of buildings, animals, people, or Buddhist deities. Yue wares also include more functional items, including straight-sided basins. From the second half of the 4th century ewers with characteristic "chicken-head" spouts were produced, and within about 100 years more elegant versions with taller proportions were being made. In general, later Yue wares are more graceful than earlier ones, the glaze becoming progressively less olivey and more jade-like and translucent owing to the use of finer raw materials.

TANG WARES

Some fine white-bodied wares, which led to the production of true porcelain, were made during the Tang period, and included both glazed and unglazed wares. The glaze on Tang wares is particularly distinctive as it has a bright, glassy appearance. In the low-fired range the most characteristic wares of the period are the *sancai* ("three color") wares, namely earthenware vessels and models made as tomb goods, decorated with runny lead-fluxed glazes colored green, chestnut, amber, cream, and, later, blue. Vessels are typically squat and rounded, and include jars, vases, and bowls. Decoration was molded or painted with spotted designs based on contemporary textile patterns. Figures include tomb guardians (whose faces were often left unglazed and painted with colored pigments after firing), camels, and horses. Because these wares have been buried for such long periods they are usually relatively undamaged; nevertheless, they can be very reasonably priced.

▼ **Water dropper made in Yue**

Water droppers were among the desk ornaments designed for the literati during this period. This small one in the shape of a lion has a gray stoneware body and a typical jade-like, green-gray Yue glaze.
(*c.AD 200–300; ht 13cm/5in; value I*)

▼ **Tang-period Fereghan horse**

This magnificent model of a Fereghan horse is a fine example of the *sancai* figures that were made as funerary goods during the Tang period. The body is covered with dappled cream, green, and ocher glazes, which have a tendency to trickle because of the viscous quality of the lead glaze. The horse is splendidly caparisoned, with a finely modeled saddle, extravagantly decorated crupper, and other ornate trappings.
(*AD 618–907; ht 77.5cm/30½in; value I*)

KEY FACTS

Principal Chinese dynasties

Shang (*c*.1600–*c*.1050 BC)	Song (960–1279)
Zhou (*c*.1050–256 BC)	Yuan (1279–1368)
Han (206 BC–AD 220)	Ming (1368–1644)
Tang (618–907)	Qing (1644–1911)

Neolithic wares
- BODY red, gray, or black earthenware
- FORMS funeral jars, cooking utensils, and ewers
- DECORATION cord-like patterns; bold painted designs

Yue wares
- BODY stoneware
- FORMS desk ornaments (water droppers, brush rests, etc); "chicken-head" ewers; bowls and jars
- GLAZE green-gray with an olive tinge in early wares
- DECORATION incised decoration and applied figures and modeling on desk ornaments and burial urns

Tang sancai wares
- BODY earthenware
- GLAZE lead-fluxed green, amber, brown, cream, blue
- DECORATION pots re-create woven textile patterns; horses have superbly modeled tack

See also Oriental Works of Art: Metalwork, pp.522–3

Song

The Song Dynasty (960–1279) is regarded as the classic period of Chinese ceramics, when simple, elegant wares decorated with attractive monochrome glazes were produced. The five "classic wares" – Ding, Jun, Ru, Guan, and Ge – were produced for imperial use, while other wares, notably Cizhou and some of the northern celadons, were made for a much wider market.

▲ Jun bowl
This bowl is liberally splashed with characteristic purple derived from copper oxide on an opaque lavender-blue background.
*(13th century; diam. 18cm/7in; value **K**)*

CELADONS

The most characteristic Song ceramics are the celadons, with their iron-derived, semi-translucent, usually greenish glaze. When the Song court was situated in northern China (960–1126), such centers of production as Yaozhou in Shaanxi Province became important for celadons; the most distinctive northern celadons are those with incised or molded decoration of floral scrolls covered with an olive-green glaze. The later Longquan or southern celadon usually has a pale-gray body that shows the thick, opaque, bluish-green, slightly bubbly glaze to advantage. The best Longquan wares include archaic forms and items for the scholar's desk, bowls, and vases. Jun wares made in Yu xian and Linru in Henan Province are thickly potted stonewares with a lavender-blue glaze often splashed with purple derived from copper oxide and, very rarely, green. Typical forms include chunky globular jars. Ru wares, the rarest and most coveted of all Song ceramics, are simple, elegant stonewares with a crackled blue-green glaze. Guan wares have light buff or dark stoneware bodies with a very thick, pale-grayish glaze that is usually strongly crackled and may be black, brown, or clear. The bodies show dark brown or black on the unglazed rims and feet.

OTHER WARES

Ding wares, made in Ding xian in Hebei Province, are fine porcellaneous stonewares with a warm ivory glaze, made in delicate shapes, including ewers and vases as well as small plates and bowls. Most flatware was fired upside down – the rims were left unglazed, and were bound with gold-colored metal (now patinated). Molded decoration was introduced in the 11th century; in this a reusable stoneware mold was impressed onto the hard clay, creating closely meshed designs; the earlier, more fluid, hand-carved ornament was also used. Qingbai (bluish white) wares from Jingdezhen in Jiangxi Province have a fine white porcelain body and a glassy blue glaze that tends to pool. These items are very delicate and elegant, and include thinly potted conical bowls and beautifully proportioned vases.

Fine black-glazed stonewares were produced during the Song period in Henan Province and at Jian in Jiangxi Province. Blackwares were sometimes decorated with red-brown floral designs. Cizhou wares, named after the kilns in Cizhou in Hebei Province, are sturdy stonewares with robust designs in black-and-white slip; often part of the black slip was scraped away to create a textured pattern (*sgraffito*), while on other wares the designs were sometimes painted on. Common shapes include "pillows" and *meiping* (an inverted-pear-shaped vase).

▼ Longquan celadon vase
This vase, made when the Song Dynasty (1126–1279) was situated in southern China, is in the form of a *cong*, a ritual vessel that was originally made in jade during the Neolithic period. A thick glaze is applied over the light-gray stoneware body to resemble jade. Longquan celadons were exported in great quantities, especially to Western Asia.
*(c.1250; ht 31cm/12in; value **N**)*

▼ Qingbai ewer
Early Qingbai wares (of the 10th and 11th centuries) were made of porcelain stone (petuntse), while from the 12th century kaolin (china clay) was added. The fine white porcelain was covered with a glassy pale-blue glaze, which had a tendency to pool – here, emphasizing the elegant lines of the ewer. Bases were unglazed and reveal a slightly irregular grainy paste with areas of russet. Small intense patches probably indicate where the kiln supports came into contact with the vessel.
*(1127–1279; ht 20cm/8in; value **I**)*

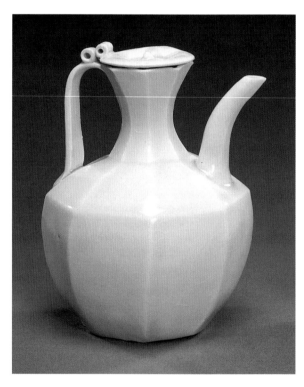

KEY FACTS

- BODY most Song wares are stonewares, although Ding and Qingbai wares are porcellaneous
- STYLE subtle and scholarly, in contrast to the flamboyance of the preceding Tang period and the subsequent Yuan period; from the 12th century there is a strong archaizing tendency, with a fashion for classic jade and bronze shapes
- DECORATION many Song wares are without ornament, relying for effect on the harmony between glaze and form; early Ding and northern celadons are decorated with restrained carved designs – some later wares have busier molded floral and foliate decoration; Cizhou wares show the greatest variety of decorative techniques

Marks
Song wares are generally unmarked, although a few stoneware molds have survived with 12th- or 13th-century dates incised on the surface

See also Yuan and early Ming, p.133; Middle and later Ming, pp.134–5

Yuan and early Ming

During the Mongol occupation and the early reigns of the Ming Dynasty, momentous changes occurred at Jingdezhen in Jiangxi Province. The kilns came under imperial patronage, and fine porcelain with underglaze decoration supplanted the glazed stonewares of the Song period as the most desirable form of ceramic. Exported Longquan celadons remained a vital source of revenue for the government.

◀ Yuan pear-shaped bottle
Both the form of this bottle and the arrangement of the underglaze blue decoration in clear horizontal registers are typical of Yuan-period porcelain. The main motif is floral, contained within bands of classic scroll. The upper neck is decorated with broad plantain leaves, while pendant lotus panels adorn the lower neck and the lower body.
(14th century; ht 28.5cm/11in; value **M***)*

▼ Early Ming dish
Large dishes such as this were prized in Western Asia, and the central motif of grapes with trailing tendrils is a design used exclusively on export wares for the region. The wave pattern around the rim of this piece is found on blue-and-white wares of all kinds from the Yuan period, and also in debased form on later Iznik pottery.
(early 15th century; diam. 38cm/15in; value **Q***)*

PORCELAIN

Although porcellaneous wares had been made from the late 6th century, it was at Jingdezhen that porcelain developed to its full potential. The addition of kaolin (china clay) to the batch made it possible to make much larger pieces than before. *Shu fu* wares, which take their name from the two molded Chinese characters *shu* and *fu* ("Privy Council") found on their interiors, are of thickly potted white porcelain with an opaque, grayish-white glaze; these were made during the Yuan period for the Ministry of Military and Civil Affairs.

UNDERGLAZE BLUE-AND-RED DECORATION

The use of underglaze decoration probably dates from *c*.1330. Cobalt imported from Persia was applied directly onto the unfired body, which was then glazed and fired. Copper oxide, which fires red, was often used in combination with underglaze blue in the earliest painted wares of Jingdezhen, and by the late 14th century it was used on its own. Copper is much more volatile than cobalt and many of these pieces are flawed, the red being grayish and dull.

In 1368, after the Mongols were finally expelled from China, the Ming Emperor Hongwu (1368–98) imposed a strict trade embargo, and foreign cobalt became very rare. The use of copper oxide therefore became more widespread, and copper monochromes were introduced, reaching their peak in the reign of Xuande (1426–35). The Yongle (1403–24) and Xuande reign periods are also regarded as belonging to the classical era of blue and white, when foreign cobalt was once again in plentiful supply. The blue tended to filter through the glaze, creating an effect known as "heaped and piled," much imitated during the Qing period.

▲ Early Ming *meiping*
This high-shouldered, short-necked vase has the conventional horizontal panels of scrolling foliage, with largish petals above and below the central zone, which are characteristic of Ming wares. However, the theme of "windswept scholars" is unusual, since figures were very rarely used as decorative motifs at this time.
(mid-15th century; ht 36cm/14in; value **M***)*

KEY FACTS

Longquan
- FORMS abandonment of archaic forms in favor of large platters and forms dictated by the export market
- GLAZE thinner and more olive than on Song wares
- DECORATION very little space left undecorated

Qingbai
- FORMS large pieces made possible by the addition of kaolin to the paste
- DECORATION increasingly ornate, with little space left undecorated; beading and Buddhist figures common

Shu fu
- BODY thickly potted porcelain
- GLAZE opaque, grayish-white and waxy
- DECORATION may have molded Chinese characters *shu* and *fu* scarcely visible under the glaze; molded floral decoration on the inside and incised decoration on the outside

Blue-and-white wares
- FORMS bottles, bulbous wine jars, and large platters (many with bracketed rims) for the export market
- GLAZE viscous in the Yuan period and inclined to the pitted "orange-peel" effect in the early Ming
- BLUE dark speckled blue, known as "heaped and piled," on some Xuande and Yongle pieces
- DECORATION themes include fish among aquatic plants, flower motifs, grapes, and vine tendrils (specifically for the export market)
- STYLE crowded arrangements in the Yuan, but elegant, harmonious spacing in the Yongle and Xuande periods

See also Fakes and forgeries, pp.126–7; Middle and later Ming, pp.134–5

Middle and later Ming

Ceramic production during the reign of Hongzhi maintained the fine quality associated with wares produced in the Chenghua period. However, during the reign of Zhengde there was a notable decline in both draughtsmanship and potting, which lasted until the end of the Ming Dynasty.

POLYCHROME WARES

From the Chenghua period the use of lead-fluxed, overglaze enamels became increasingly common. Underglaze blue was combined with these colors, which were fired a second time at a much lower temperature. On the finest wares known as *doucai* ("contrasted colors") pieces, the outline of the design was traced in underglaze blue, and then yellow, green, aubergine-purple, and red enamels were painted on before a second firing to create a jewel-like effect. *Doucai* pieces are generally small, fine, and extremely well made; decoration includes figures, plants, and animals, often in briefly painted landscapes. Wares include "chicken cups" – small wine-cups with designs of hens and cockerels with peonies.

The *wucai* ("five colors") style, using the same palette as *doucai*, was introduced in the Jiajing reign period. While underglaze-blue outlines were still used, they were often replaced with overglaze black or red. The decoration developed along different lines, with fish, water-weed, ducks, and figure scenes becoming increasingly popular. Dragons appear in all manner of guises, with wings, and with flowers or jewels in their mouths, arranged around bowls and jars or as circular medallions. *Wucai* decoration was used on large as well as small pieces and is generally not as neat or refined as *doucai*. The color yellow, which had imperial

▲ *Wucai* **dish**
This wide, shallow dish has bold, freely painted designs of fruit and flowers in underglaze blue, while the ground is painted in brilliant, clear yellow enamel over a plain white glaze. The central decoration consists of a flower, probably a gardenia, while around the cavetto there are clusters of grapes, pomegranates, persimmons, and lotus flowers between double line borders.
(1488–1505; diam. 25.5cm/10in; value Q)

connotations, was used together with bold designs of fruits and flowers in underglaze blue from the Xuande to the Jiajing reign period. For example, in the Zhengde period a common design consisted of green dragons on a white background, achieved by marking the design in wax resist then glazing the ground with white, firing, painting the reserved design in green enamel, and finally refiring at a lower temperature.

BLUE-AND-WHITE WARES

Blue-and-white wares made during the Chenghua period are regarded as some of the finest porcelains ever produced. Technically they are superb, with light, thin bodies and a glassy glaze. The blue on early Chenghua pieces is dark – an almost blue-black associated with the use of imported cobalt; the later wares have a much lighter, clearer blue derived from local ore from the Raozhou Prefecture around Jingdezhen. It is applied very evenly, in designs of dragons and phoenixes, landscape scenes, or the very fine flower scrolls that adorn the so-called "Palace" ware. This was made in the imperial kilns at Jingdezhen, the most typical item being a bowl with everted rim, known as a "Palace" bowl.

The reign period of Hongzhi is largely a continuation of the Chenghua style, but it may be viewed as a watershed in the Ming dynasty since after it standards clearly began to decline. Even the best of the later Ming wares never reached the heights of the 15th-century work. As the 16th century advanced, the deterioration manifested itself in the increasing number of flaws in the poorly refined clay, and in the more casual brushwork, although the latter often has great appeal. During the reign of Jiajing the quality of blue improved. A rich, saturated purplish cobalt, termed "Muhammadan" blue, was introduced and was used on many porcelains in this and the later Ming reigns of Longqing and Wanli. Imperial quality wares are dressed in a thickish and smooth glassy glaze with a strong bluish cast. Almost all later

◄ **Dish**
The decoration on this blue-and-white dish consists of a panel of Arabic inscriptions enclosed within a double circle and surrounded by a neat design of stylized lotus blossoms, also enclosed within a double circle. The rim is decorated with a regular geometric pattern. It is extremely rare to find these designs on a bowl, and this example is therefore very valuable indeed.
(1506–21; diam. 38cm/15in; value Q)

▼ **Double-gourd bottle**
This bottle has six bands of decoration. Both bulbs are decorated with landscape scenes that incorporate different symbols of longevity, such as the *lingzhi* fungus, deer, cranes, a peach tree, and the Chinese character *shou*. Note the intense, inky blue (known as "Muhammadan" blue), typical of the Jiajing period when this bottle was made. Both of the bulbs on this vessel have the appearance of being slightly squared off, resulting in a silhouette that is characteristic of many 16th-century bottles and jars.
(1522–66; ht 36cm/14in; value P)

Ming porcelains oxidized during firing, and while this thin reddish veneer may be worn by the passage of time, it is usually still visible at the margin of the glaze on the base or foot-rim.

EXPORT WARES

During the reign of Wanli the export of Chinese porcelain expanded, with large numbers of blue-and-white wares made purely for export. Among these pieces, *kraak* ware, which was produced from the Wanli period, is particularly important. It takes its name from the Dutch rendering of the Portuguese for "carrack," or merchant ship, two of which, carrying Chinese porcelain, were captured by the Dutch in 1602 and 1604. *Kraak* ware of this period has a fairly thin, light body, which is prone to chipping at the edges. The blue, often evenly applied in washes, is inclined to be rather watery and thin.

The use of panels on bowls and dishes increased in the late 16th century; all wares of this type are called *kraak* ware. On *kraak* bowls and dishes the decoration radiates from a central circular panel. After *c.*1570 the most common themes found on *kraak* porcelain are floral, including a highly stylized and barely recognizable form of the peony, lotuses, chrysanthemums, and other flowers issuing from rocks. Other motifs were also popular, such as precious objects or symbols tied with ribbons, and crickets, beetles, and butterflies.

DECORATIVE THEMES

Dragons and phoenixes remained the most important decorative motifs throughout the Ming period, but other designs also became increasingly popular. In the Chenghua period a very fine arrangement of lilies and other flowers in underglaze blue was used to decorate the exteriors of the dishes known as "Palace" bowls. Emperor Chenghua was a devout Buddhist, and this is reflected in the use of Buddhist symbols on some pieces from this period. During the reign of Zhengde, who was tolerant of the Islamic religion in China, a unique style of decoration using Arabic or Persian script was applied to a wide range of blue-and-white wares that were predominantly intended for the scholar's desk. These included pen rests, small lamps, incense burners, and, in a few very rare instances, bowls. The script is enclosed within medallions against a background of scrolls and sometimes stylized lotus designs. These wares always carry the six-character mark of Zhengde, whereas almost all other dishes of this period have a four-character mark.

The decoration of 16th-century Ming wares is less refined, more chaotic in its arrangement, and much more freely drawn than that of the 15th century. The designs show the influence of illustrations from popular literature, which was becoming widely available at this time. On wares of the Jiajing period, children, scholars, animals, and flowers are depicted in gardens, on terraces, or in open landscapes. Daoist subjects, for example the sage Laozi and the Eight Immortals (legendary or historical individuals who are associated with the philosophy of Dao), were increasingly incorporated into the decoration on these wares, as were the associated symbols of long life, such as the *lingzhi* fungus, deer, cranes, peaches, pine trees, the Chinese character *shou* (often elaborated into the form of a peach tree), and herons.

▲ *Kraak* **bottle vase**
Late Ming export porcelains were painted with a series of simple repeated motifs enclosed within linear panels. This bottle is typical of early 17th-century *kraak* porcelain, having crudely executed flowers and pierced rockwork alternating with a *jardinière* of flowers. The top of the neck is decorated with the popular basket-weave known as the "Y" diaper pattern.
(c.1600; ht 27cm/10½in; value **I***)*

▼ **Box and cover**
Boxes, and especially pen boxes, were fairly common both in blue and white and in polychrome (*wucai*) during the late Ming period. The short foot is embellished with the classic scroll motif found throughout this period.
(c.1600; l. 31cm/12in; value **N***)*

KEY FACTS

Ming reign periods

Hongwu (1368–98)	Chenghua (1465–87)
Jianwen (1399–1402)	Hongzhi (1488–1505)
Yongle (1403–24)	Zhengde (1506–21)
Hongxi (1425)	Jiajing (1522–66)
Xuande (1426–35)	Longqing (1567–72)
Zhengtong (1436–49)	Wanli (1573–1619)
Jiangtai (1450–57)	Tianqi (1621–7)
Tianshun (1457–64)	Chongzheng (1628–43)

Doucai wares
- BODY fine white porcelain
- COLORS underglaze-blue outlines with overglaze enamels in red, green, yellow, and aubergine
- SHAPES small, neat pieces: wine-cups, stem cups, bowls, and jars
- DECORATION chickens and peonies; dragons, plants, and floral motifs; neat and jewel-like

Wucai wares
- BODY white porcelain of variable quality
- COLORS overglaze enamels in yellow, red, green, turquoise, and aubergine, with some outlines in red or black and others in underglaze blue
- FORMS small and large pieces, such as huge cisterns
- DECORATION dragons, fish, landscapes, and figures; not as neatly drawn as *doucai* wares

Export wares
- BODY relatively thin and light porcelain of reasonable quality; the glaze has a tendency to break away from the edges in an irregular way – this is often referred to as "moth-eaten" or "tender" edges
- GLAZE high gloss, reasonably thick over the body, tending to be thin on the base
- SHAPES *kendi* (Hindu ritual vessels) and "Persian" flasks, jars, and dishes
- BLUE watery and thin, often applied in washes, sometimes rather silvery gray
- DECORATION division into panels radiating from a central circular field, with animals, birds, plants, landscapes, or baskets of flowers, and often ribbons and medallions between the panels
- FOOT-RIM there is often grit in the glaze

A selection of important reign marks

大德年製宣	大明化年製成	大明靖年製嘉	大明曆年製萬
Xuande	Chenghua	Jiajing	Wanli

See also Later export porcelain, pp.136–7; Blue-and-white wares, pp.204–5

Later export porcelain

The loss of imperial patronage at Jingdezhen in Jiangxi Province in 1608 prior to the death of Emperor Wanli (*d.*1619) encouraged the Chinese potters to seek new markets for their wares. They made dishes to European specifications, introducing new shapes and decorative motifs. They also had an unrivaled artistic freedom, which unleashed a great creativity, while the technical quality of the body and glaze improved noticeably.

◄ **Transitional double-gourd bottle**
The gray-white body, the clear purplish color of the cobalt blue, and the smooth bluish glaze are all typical of the Transitional period, as are the easy naturalism of the brushwork and the subject-matter – a narrative scene of figures in a landscape. These subjects wrap around the vessel (they are rarely if ever found on flatware) in a continuous band.
(1600–40; ht 31cm/12in; value I)

TRANSITIONAL WARES

Blue-and-white porcelains of the Transitional period (1620–83) are characterized by the purplish tone of the blue, and by the easy naturalism of the brushwork. Narrative scenes were common, while landscape painting was given unprecedented importance. Colophons were very rarely added, but when they are found they often give details of where the object was produced, which clearly aids the dating of such items. Enameled Transitional wares are the forerunners of the group of wares known as *famille verte*, and the colors are noticeably bright and clean. The Transitional period also marks the appearance of the first truly European shapes, including table salts, mustard-pots, square flasks, and candlesticks.

EXPORT PORCELAINS FROM JINGDEZHEN

The porcelains produced at Jingdezhen after Emperor Kangxi reorganized the kilns in 1683 are markedly more refined than earlier wares. The potting is economical and neatly trimmed, while the glaze is very thin and glassy. The foot-rims often have a faint amber blush due to oxidization. The blue varies from a silvery hue to an almost purple tone. After *c.*1730 export wares began to decline considerably; this is evident in the poorly trimmed foot-rims and in the presence of sugary kiln grit, as well as in deeper oxidization, and an irregular and bluish glaze.

The range of decorative themes is varied and includes flowers and plants growing among rocks, sometimes enclosed within a fence, especially from the Yongzheng period (1723–35). The landscape designs used during the Kangxi period (1662–1722) have a sense of craggy remoteness, which later gives way to a more comfortable, idealized structure, with pavilioned isles, drifting sampans, and bending trees.

In the early 18th century northern-European clients began to order dinner services decorated with their own coats of arms, although the Spanish and Portuguese had ordered individual pieces with arms more than a century earlier. These armorial services were executed in underglaze blue or in the *famille-verte* palette (green, iron-red, blue, yellow, and a manganese purple). However, the later *famille-rose* armorial services, often embellished with gold, are more numerous; hundreds of thousands of pieces were dispatched each year as wealthy British families ordered vast dinner services.

Europeans commissioned a variety of designs to be copied, sending paper patterns and wooden models to the Chinese. Early during the reign of Qianlong (1736–95), plain, blank porcelains from Jingdezhen were probably sent to be decorated in Guangzhou (later Canton) in Guangdong Province; blue-and-white ware was already fully decorated, as the decoration was underglaze. Their close proximity to the decorators' workshops enabled East India Company employees to complete their private trade orders quickly and effectively. By comparison with general-trade porcelains, these private orders form a much more interesting and collectible group. In addition to the armorial wares, which are by and large formulaic, there are pieces with designs meticulously copied from European engravings.

By the second quarter of the 19th century tailor-made wares were the exception, and production concentrated on heavily enameled decorative wares and dinner services. Pink, green, and gold with touches of yellow and turquoise were the usual palette of these later porcelains, decorated in Canton and known as "Canton" wares. The material and glaze are generally of secondary quality, with deposits of sugary kiln grit.

▲ *Famille-verte* **ewer**
The shape of this ewer is almost certainly derived from a French Baroque silver ewer of *c.*1700 and demonstrates the way in which Europeans commissioned porcelains to suit their tastes. In 1689 and again in 1709 the French aristocracy were forced by sumptuary laws to melt down their silverware in order to finance the wars of Louis XIV. The originals were replaced with faience versions, and it seems logical to assume that porcelain copies were ordered through the East India Company.
(1662–1722; ht 23cm/9in; value H)

◄ **Armorial** *famille-rose* **jar**
It became common practice in the 18th century for wealthy Europeans to commission from Jingdezhen porcelains, especially dinner services, decorated with their coats of arms. Most of these dinner services, like this jar, were executed in *famille-rose* enamels. However, by comparison with armorial tablewares, this jar is of the most extreme rarity. In form and decoration – in particular its smooth and elegant contors and the neat rendition of the birds and flowers – it nearly conforms to Chinese taste.
(c.1723–50; ht 22cm/8½in; value H)

▲ *Famille-rose* "tobacco-leaf" dish
The name of this dish, which is one of a pair, derives from the decorative motif of tobacco leaves. The use of gold highlights is characteristic of *famille-rose* wares intended for export, while the shape and the foliate rim are clearly European in style.
(c.1760; l. 42cm/16½in; value for the pair I)

SWATOW WARES

Named after the port of Shantou (Swatow), Swatow wares are roughly decorated porcelains made around Chaozhou in Guangdong Province from the mid-16th century for export principally to India, South-East Asia, and Japan. Although wares include blue-and-white and slip-painted pieces, it is the polychromes that are best known. The decoration is executed with great flourish in overglaze red, green, and turquoise, with a sparing use of black. Forms include plates and dishes, and *kendi* (ritual vessels), while characteristic motifs include the "split pagoda." Often red character seals are alternated with cartouches around the edges of these wares.

DEHUA PORCELAIN

White porcelain from Dehua in Fujian Province was produced from the Song period. Ming wares from Dehua have a warm ivory tone, while the Qing wares are usually more bluish, or dead white. The most typical forms of Dehua porcelain (known in Europe as *blanc-de-Chine*) are hollow figures of Buddhist deities – most notably of Guanyin, goddess of mercy – although in the Ming period figures of the Madonna and Child were also produced for the Portuguese. Small cups decorated with reliefs of blossoming prunus were also exported. Dehua wares are usually signed with a small seal impressed into the back of the sculpture.

YIXING WARES

Yixing wares are red stonewares, made in Jiangsu Province, which were exported to Europe from the mid-17th century until the end of the 18th century. The most commonly exported wares were small teapots and cups, either left plain or decorated with garden scenes in relief, or with sprigged decoration such as prunus branches. In the 1670s potters in Delft began to produce a low-fired redware in imitation of Yixing, and from the late 17th century potters in Staffordshire produced a similar ware. A number of small Yixing figures were exported to Europe.

SHIPWRECK CARGOES

Among the many ships carrying tea, porcelain, spices, and silk from China to India and Europe, a number inevitably sank before they completed their journeys. In recent years some of these shipwrecks have been salvaged and their precious cargoes auctioned. They include the Dutch ship *Geldermalsen*, carrying the so-called Nanking cargo, which sank in 1752 with 25,000 pieces of porcelain intended for sale in Amsterdam and was found in 1986. The *Diana*, which sank in 1817 in the Strait of Malacca en route to Madras, was salvaged in 1994; just under 24,000 pieces of intact blue-and-white porcelain were recovered from the ship, indicating the popularity of this type of export ware.

► "Fitzhugh"-pattern dish
This plate belongs to a series of graduated oval dishes from a dinner service made for export to Madras in the early 19th century. Salvaged from the *Diana* and intended for sale to wealthy Anglo-Indians, the plate is decorated in underglaze blue with four peony blooms and auspicious objects around a central pomegranate design. The origin of the pattern is unknown, but it is thought to have been named after a family who commissioned a Chinese export service featuring this pattern.
(early 19th century; w. 47cm/18½in; value F)

▼ Jar and cover
Many of the export porcelains of this period were decorated in workshops around Guangzhou (Canton). This piece is covered with very complex, colorful decoration in a variety of themes. The bands around the body and lid have an especially densely meshed pattern reminiscent of *cloisonné* enamels, which were also produced in Canton.
(mid-19th century; ht 51cm/20in; value I)

KEY FACTS

Transitional wares
- BODY grayish-white porcelain
- BLUE rich and purplish, applied in washes
- DECORATION taken from printed sources: narrative scenes and flower studies applied as outlines filled in with a wash, a technique known as "line and wash"
- THEMES narrative scenes taken from literary classics

Kangxi blue-and-white porcelain
- POTTING generally very economical and neatly trimmed around the base
- GLAZE very thin and glassy
- FOOT-RIMS faint amber blush due to oxidization
- BLUE varies from a silvery to an almost purple tone
- THEMES flowers and plants growing among rocks; landscapes

Jingdezhen enameled export porcelain
- SHAPES many European shapes drawn from silverware or European pottery and porcelain prototypes
- DECORATION translucent overglaze enamels with dominant green in densely meshed patterns; gilding

Dehua wares
- BODY white porcelain
- GLAZE warm ivory (Ming); bluish white (Qing)
- SHAPES tall, hollow sculptures of Buddhist deities, figures of the Madonna and Child, and small cups
- DECORATION reliefs of plum blossoms on cups
- MARKS seal signature on the back of sculptures

Yixing wares
- BODY red stoneware
- GLAZE some figures are covered with a pale-gray glaze
- SHAPES small teapots and cups
- DECORATION relief or sprigged decorations
- COPIES made in Europe in the late 17th century by the Elers brothers in Staffordshire and Arij Milde in Delft

See also France before 1820: Early porcelain, p.192

Qing before 1800

Following the overthrow of the Ming Dynasty by the Qing Dynasty in 1644, production at Jingdezhen in Jiangxi Province was severely disrupted until 1677, when one of the classic eras of porcelain production began. This lasted until c.1750.

BLUE-AND-WHITE WARES

Blue and white dominated the export market during this period, but these wares were not prominent among the ceramics made at the imperial kilns at Jingdezhen. Before 1800 Qing imperial blue-and-white wares tended to imitate early Ming versions, particularly from the Yongle (1403–24) and Xuande (1426–35) reign periods, with decoration that was carefully spaced. The designs on these pieces are generally formal, measured arrangements showing stylized lotus flowers among scrolling foliage. The blue was applied in imitation of the "heaped and piled" effect that connoisseurs so admired in the early Ming wares. Often the reign mark used on those wares was used again in deference to the earlier period.

▼ Blue-and-white bowl

The arrangement of the decoration on this bowl deliberately re-creates the style of the Xuande reign period, with the cobalt applied so as to mimic the "heaped and piled" effect. The six-character reign mark on the rim of the bowl is of the Yongzheng period.

(1723–35; diam. 33cm/13in; value N)

ENAMELED WARES

Enameled porcelains came into their own during the Qing period, replacing blue-and-white wares as the focus of technical and artistic innovation. The technical advances signaled by the development of *famille-verte* and *famille-rose* wares greatly enhanced the decorative possibilities of the medium, while the body had now become so refined and delicate as to be the perfect foil for artistic virtuosity. Increasingly, the white porcelain was not so much decorated as painted in the manner of silk-scroll painting.

The *famille-verte* palette was first introduced during the late 17th century as a development of the *wucai* palette. In early *famille verte* the blue is applied under the glaze in the Ming *wucai* style, but distinguished from it by a generally brighter palette. In the mature *famille verte*, which dates from the last years of the 17th century, the blue was applied over the glaze and is transparent. Gold was sometimes applied to *famille-verte* wares of the early 18th century. The designs on these wares tended to be detailed representations of nature, including dramatic rocky landscapes and flowers, or precious objects such as classic vases and items for the scholar's desk.

▲ *Famille-rose* **bottle**

Peaches, the food of the immortals, are often depicted together with five bats, which represent the five blessings – longevity, riches, health, love of virtue, and a good end to life. Note the shading of the colors on the above example, which is possible because of the opaque colors in the *famille-rose* palette. Here the porcelain decorator has adopted the album style of painting, employing the surface merely as an album leaf.

(1736–95; ht 38cm/15in; value Q)

The *famille-rose* palette was created c.1720, at the end of the Kangxi reign period. The palette is named after one of the constituent colors – opaque pink enamel, which was achieved using gold. The palette also includes an opaque white and yellow that made blending and shading of colors possible in a way that could not be achieved with the transparent colors of the *famille-verte* palette. This gave rise to the exquisitely refined decoration seen on porcelain of the Yongzheng period, with ink-and-wash-style landscapes or naturalistic depictions of flowers and fruit rendered in a painterly style against superbly clear white backgrounds. Among the most refined Yongzheng and Qianlong wares are *famille-rose* wares known as *guyuexuan*, which were painted in the imperial workshops. Some of these bear poetic lines or calligraphic designs, and they were copied widely in the 20th century.

MONOCHROMES

In this period monochromes were the ceremonial wares used by the emperor and had to be of the very finest quality. In the early 18th century copper-red glazes, which had been so highly prized in the early Ming period, were reintroduced. However, as a result of a longer firing time, these new colors are not as resonant and fresh as their earlier counterparts, and they can be distinguished from the originals by the extra layer of clear glaze over the copper red. Copper oxide was also used to make the so-called "peachbloom" glaze, which was introduced at this time and applied to a limited range of small wares intended for the scholar's table, including water droppers and brush rests. This glaze is characterized by the combination of a pinkish red and a cloudy greenish bloom, creating a color reminiscent of the blush on a ripening peach.

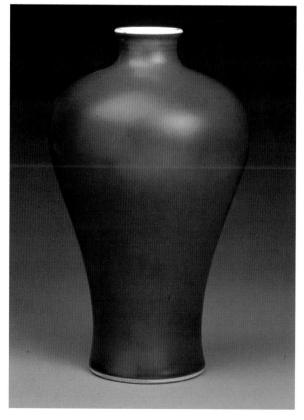

◄ *Meiping* **vase**

This vase typifies some of the aspects of classicism that were so wholeheartedly embraced by the imperial workshops at Jingdezhen. The elegant, high-shouldered form first appeared in the northern Song Dynasty and has remained a favorite of the Chinese ever since. This vase was probably originally used as a wine-jar but, as the name ("blossom vase") suggests, it is perfect for holding a single spray of prunus in blossom. Note the carefully controlled *sang-de-boeuf* glaze, which was used in imitation of Ming wares. To achieve this, pieces were biscuit-fired, then covered with a glaze charged with copper oxide, and a further layer of clear glaze; the result was a very fine, sometimes surface, crackle. The glaze and neat potting are typical of the monochromes of the high Qing period.

(1736–95; ht 23cm/9in; value J)

▲ Bottle
This turquoise-and-blue mottled glaze, known as "robin's-egg" glaze, was developed in the early 18th century at a time when there was a great deal of experimentation with glaze effects. Robin's-egg glaze appears to have been inspired by the Jun wares of the Song period. *(1736–95; ht 24cm/9½in; value H)*

The experimentation with monochrome glazes resulted in many innovative effects, such as the speckled turquoise and dark-blue "robin's-egg" glaze, which is thought to have been inspired by the Jun wares of the Song period. The "teadust" glaze is created when iron oxide is underfired, resulting in a mottled green on a yellowish-brown background. The "iron-rust" glaze is a streaked reddish-brown with a metallic sheen, achieved by cooling the ware very rapidly after firing. The pale-blue *clair-de-lune* glaze was created by incorporating a very small amount of cobalt blue and was applied only to the most delicate wares.

"ARCHAIC" WARES

The Qing emperors, especially Qianlong, were avid collectors of antiquities, and many Qing imperial ceramics closely imitate ancient models. This is particularly evident in the traditional forms that were favored, which include pastiches of early bronzes and jades and also of classic ceramics of the Song and Ming Dynasties; some wares were made using a combination of the two forms. The Qing potters also tried to re-create the glazes applied to the archaistic pieces of the Song period; these included thick, crackled glazes used on Guan wares. The Qing copies are generally smoother and shinier than the originals.

REIGN MARKS

The practice of marking imperial wares with the name of a reign period was introduced during the early 15th century, and continued to the end of the Qing period. Either four or six (or, in very rare cases, eight) characters were inscribed in underglaze blue, and often enclosed within a double circle. In the Yongzheng period, seal-script reign marks became common, and during the succeeding Qianlong period they were the norm. Conventional script became popular again at the end of the 19th century. Reign marks should not be taken at face value when dating a piece, since it was common practice to inscribe wares with the mark of an earlier reign period, particularly those of the much-esteemed Ming period and especially of Emperor Chenghua (1465–87). This was not so much a question of fraud as of admiration for and imitation of antiquity.

 This is the Qianlong reign period mark, shown in seal characters.

▶ *Doucai* bowl
This polychrome bowl clearly shows the mark for the Yongzheng reign period on the base, typically enclosed in a double circle. The mark below shows the reign mark in seal characters. This reign mark was much copied in the 19th and 20th centuries. However, the faker rarely managed to re-create these beautiful characters and formation successfully. *(1723–35; diam. 14cm/5½in; value I)*

▼ *Cong*-shaped vase
Many Qing historicized wares evoke more than one element of past models. Here, while the crackled glaze is based on the classic southern Song and Yuan Guan ware, the form itself is derived from one of the oldest-known forms, the Neolithic jade *cong*, the probable ritual purpose of which remains a mystery. Note the neatness of the potting and the evenness of the glaze in comparison with the Song Longquan prototype featured earlier.
(1736–95; ht 32cm/12½in; value I)

KEY FACTS

Qing reign periods
Shunzhi (1644–61)	Daoguang (1821–50)
Kangxi (1662–1722)	Xianfeng (1851–61)
Yongzheng (1723–35)	Tongzhi (1862–74)
Qianlong (1736–95)	Guangxu (1875–1908)
Jiaqing (1796–1820)	Xuantong (1909–11)

- BODY very fine white porcelain
- POTTING extremely neat with smooth, rounded foot-rims; the bases of bowls and dishes are flat, unlike the slightly convex form of the bases of Ming wares; there are no visible joins on vases and pots
- GLAZES a wide range of innovative glazes appears on monochromes; imitations of crackled Song-period Guan glazes are found on "archaic" pieces
- ENAMELS many colors enhanced with opaque white and yellow in the *famille-rose* palette, permitting shading and more decorative potential
- FORMS small, fine pieces for delicate porcelains as well as imitations of archaic bronze and jade forms
- DECORATION blossoming and fruiting branches rendered in a painterly manner; emblems of good luck, such as the characters *shou* (long life) and *fu* (bat), are often integrated into the designs

Reign marks
Reign marks for Shunzhi and Kangxi are always written in conventional script; for the period of Yongzheng they may be written in the same manner or in seal script; Qianlong, Jiaqing and Daoguang are usually done in seal characters; from the Xianfeng reign onward, marks may be written in either style

大
清
康
熙
年
製

Kangxi

See also Song, p.132; Yuan and early Ming, p.133; Middle and later Ming, pp.134–5

Qing after 1800

During the Qianlong reign period (1736–95) the directorship of the imperial kilns passed from imperial officials to regional supervisors, and from that time there followed a slow decline in the quality of wares from Jingdezhen in Jiangxi Province. While some fine pieces continued to be made, there was a general tendency to over-elaborate in both form and decoration.

BODY AND GLAZE

The changes in the quality of the material were gradual and, when wares are unmarked, it can be very difficult to distinguish between one reign period and another. The dragon and phoenix *wucai* bowls, which were first made during the Kangxi reign period (1622–1722), continued to be made right into the 19th century and are a good example of the problem; their smooth bluish-white glaze and neatly drawn enameling are virtually the same whether they are from the Qianlong or the Jiaqing reign periods (1736–1820). Without reference to the seal marks, most specialists would be hard put to tell the difference.

There was, however, a perceptible decline in quality during the Daoguang reign period (1821–50), and the inferior quality persisted to the end of the dynasty. The cool and lustrous glaze gave way to a grainy off-white, while the enamels were duller or harsher than their brilliant predecessors. The decoration of enameled porcelains was arranged in a crowded or ineffective manner, with over-complicated color combinations.

STYLES, SHAPES, AND DECORATIVE THEMES

The porcelains that had been produced in the 18th century continued to be made in the 19th. They included Ming-style blue-and-white wares such as moon flasks and pear-shaped bottles, as well as large saucer dishes. Likewise, monochromes continued to be produced, notably *sang-de-boeuf* red, "peachbloom," and yellow. There were also artistic innovations, among them the production of "medallion" bowls, which are small

▼ *Famille-rose* "medallion" bowl
This *famille-rose* porcelain bowl belongs to a category of porcelains known as "medallion" bowls, first produced in the 19th century. Each of the four decorative medallions cut out from the ruby-red ground contains lanterns, precious objects, and vases.
*(1821–50; diam. 15cm/6in; value **H**)*

porcelain bowls decorated with roundels containing stylized or figurative subjects reserved on a colored ground. On other bowls the thin walls were pierced with "rice grains" (so-called because the holes resembled grains of rice). There was also a greater use of gilding, while the practice of using the character for long life (*shou*) as a decorative motif became more pronounced, as did the inclusion of other auspicious characters. The dominant wares in both the domestic and the export markets were the heavily enameled porcelains decorated in the style of *cloisonné* enamel. The most typical ground colors were claret and lime green. From the 1870s these wares are found in enormous quantities, often with iron-red seal marks on the base. Many 19th-century decorative porcelains have a thickly applied turquoise wash on the interior, which was sometimes known as "European green."

◄ Vase and cover
During the Qianlong reign period there was a tendency toward the use of highly formalized designs executed in pastel-colored enamels. This type of decoration resembled *cloisonné* enameling. Almost all examples of this group have seal marks in overglaze red as opposed to underglaze blue.
*(1821–50; ht 31cm/12in; value **I**)*

▼ *Fanghu* vase
Throughout the Qing period archaic forms were commonly used. The *fanghu* vase seen here is an imitation of an ancient ritual bronze form. The dramatic flambé glaze, with its vertical curdled streaks of blue, purple, and red set against a copper-red background, adds a note of modernity.
*(1875–1908; ht 30cm/11¾in; value **H**)*

KEY FACTS

- **GLAZE** marked deterioration in quality from the Daoguang period; "European-green" turquoise wash appears on the inside of many vessels
- **DECORATION** tendency to over-elaborate, complicated color schemes and overcrowding; greater use of gilding; introduction of "medallion" bowls and "rice-grain" pierced wares; use of *shou* and other auspicious characters; heavy use of enamels

Reign marks

Reign marks were inscribed on most 19th- and 20th-century domestic, imperial, and export porcelain; the mark shown here is in conventional script for the Guangxu reign period (1875–1908)

大清光
緒年製

See also Qing before 1800, pp.138–9

Korea

Korea's close proximity to China has resulted in a marked Chinese influence in its ceramic production, evident in both the forms and the techniques used by potters. However, Korea has also produced stonewares and porcelains unique to its culture.

THE SILLA AND KORYO PERIODS

During the Silla kingdom (57 BC–AD 935) ceramic production in Korea consisted of gray- or brownish-bodied stonewares of distinctive architectonic form. Tall vessels with hemispherical bowls on an elongated spreading foot were decorated with geometric "windows" and incised bands. Bowls were decorated with punched circlets, small repeated motifs, scratched geometric patterns, and, occasionally, animals or humans. Drawing inspiration from the Yue wares of south-eastern China, Korean potters developed celadon wares during the Koryo period (918–1392). Even if some of the forms are noticeably Chinese, there is almost always a distinctive Korean feel to them. The green glaze is of a subtle tonality akin to the color of the famous Ru wares of the northern Song Dynasty. However, the *sangam* celadons, which are painstakingly inlaid with black-and-white clays, are unique to Korea. A wide range of objects was made, including large blossom vases, ritual water ewers, and tiny covered boxes. Porcelain was also produced, albeit in very limited quantities, during the Koryo period.

CHOSON DYNASTY (1392–1910)

Developed from the *sangam* celadons of the Koryo period are the robust and often crude *punch'ong* wares, a grayish-green celadon-type stoneware made for about the first 200 years of the dynasty. Production ceased at the time of the invasion of Korea by the Japanese leader Toyotomi Hideyoshi (1592–8). The wares are decorated by stamping and washing through with slip. Decoration may feature tiny repeated motifs, flower-heads, or scrolls. Korean wares are generally very heavily potted with a curiously sticky glaze. The grayish-green glaze is thin, translucent, and mostly crackled, and it occasionally flakes. Choson whitewares were made throughout the period; earlier wares were often plain white, although many pieces can be painted in underglaze copper red, iron brown, or blue. Bulbous forms, often with faceted sides, are characteristic of the later Choson period, as are pierced vessels such as brushpots, pipe rests, and waterpots.

◀ *Sangam* **oil bottle**

Tiny and beautifully potted bottles such as this are some of the most successful wares of the Koryo period. The decoration is usually natural, and motifs include the chrysanthemum and the peony. Unique to early Korean ceramics was the use of deep inlay, whereby the decorator cut out a design in soft clay and inlaid pieces of white and black clay. The results, although delicate and appealing, are a little stiff. Nevertheless, they make an interesting counterpoint to the quick and cursory brushwork on painted Korean ceramics. The glaze, as seen here, is typically crackled and filled with bubbles. This *sangam* technique was superseded by a simpler process using shallow stamped designs, which were highlighted by over-washing in a white slip.
(c.1200; ht 8cm/3in; value **G***)*

▼ *Maebyong* **("plum-blossom vase")**

Korean potters are renowned for making some of the most distinctive ceramics in the Far East. This simple vase is very similar in form to the lower section of a Chinese *yen-yen* vase of the Kangxi period (1662–1722). However, the sharply angled return above the recessed foot-rim is entirely Korean. Only a Korean or a Japanese potter could have painted such fluent calligraphic leaves and grasses in underglaze blue and copper red.
(probably 18th or 19th century; ht 25.5cm/10in; value **J***)*

▼ **"Dragon" bottle**

This pear-shaped bottle is typical of Korean production. Most Korean wares are painted in soft grayish underglaze blue with simple flowers or, as here, with a dragon.
(18th or 19th century; ht 25.5cm/10in; value **G***)*

KEY FACTS

Early stoneware
- BODY dull dark gray or brown; potting tends to be very thick, and there is strong tendency for the items to warp
- FORMS "architectural"
- TYPES funerary wares
- DECORATION pierced and incised; often geometric patterns, rarely figures

Celadon
- BODY generally a distinctive grayish blue-green like the classic Ru ware of the northern Song Dynasty
- GLAZE of grayish-olive tone; usually irregular; frequently crackled
- IDENTIFICATION celadon wares were fired on gritty kiln supports, often leaving crude patches on the underside of the foot-rim
- DECORATION the miniaturized inlay technique (*sangam*), using black-and-white clay, is unique to Korea

Porcelain
- BODY heavily potted; sometimes large pieces are warped or cracked; pierced and carved wares of the 18th and 19th centuries are very sophisticated
- GLAZE bluish or greenish irregularly crackled glaze
- DECORATION most common is the dragon; also cranes, tigers, and other animals

Marks
Most ceramics are unmarked before the late 19th century

Japan

Arita blue-and-white wares

Almost all early Japanese porcelain was produced in Arita on Kyūshū, the westernmost of the main Japanese islands and, significantly, the closest to Korea. It is most unlikely that the manufacture of porcelain would have developed in Japan as early as this without the know-how of Korean potters, who were brought to Japan when Toyotomi Hideyoshi returned from his invasion of Korea at the end of the 16th century. Early Arita porcelain is generally, if superficially, classified into three main types: Arita blue and white, Imari, and Kakiemon.

▲ **Ming-style blue-and-white dish**
This large dish is a fairly faithful rendition of late Ming *kraak* porcelain. Emblems used by the Chinese as decorative motifs, including the "Eight Precious Objects" of the scholar (a musical stone, jewels, a coin, a pair of books, an open tied lozenge and a closed tied lozenge, and the artemisia leaf), were often copied by the Japanese. The artemisia leaf can be seen in this dish in the broad panels in the top right corner.
(*c.1660–80; diam. 40cm/16in; value* **H**)

DOMESTIC WARES

The earliest Arita wares were crude-bodied, heavily potted porcelain, casually decorated in blue and white, and were generally not exported. These wares were clearly influenced by both Korean blue-and-white and imported late Ming porcelain. By the mid-17th century the Arita potters were producing a more refined and broader range of objects for the newly established export market, as well as for the domestic market. The type of decoration on these later wares was complex, combining natural themes with geometric patterns; dishes or bowls featured leaf or flower forms and, more rarely, bird or animal shapes. The underglaze blue used ranges from a poor-quality gray or blackish blue through to a bright purplish blue. Wares made for the domestic

market include small dishes and hollow-ware. After *c.1640* Japanese wares include tea whisks and pails. The third type of blue-and-white ware was intended solely for the export market.

EXPORT WARES

In 1647 the civil war in China between the ruling Ming Dynasty and the invading Manchus severely disrupted the well-established trade between China and Europe. The Japanese were persuaded by the Dutch East India Company to supply blue-and-white wares in the style of either the Chinese *kraak* porcelain or the Transitional period, decorated with semi-botanical subjects and narrative themes applied in a mechanical manner. These are not close copies but loose renditions – the Japanese decorators were hampered by the fact that they had to work from wooden models of the Chinese originals supplied by the Dutch.

Wares produced at this time included copies of northern European metal or ceramic forms, for example the *Enghalskrug* (narrow-necked jug) or *Kugelbauchkrug* (bulbous globular tankard), and the *Birnkrug* (pear-shaped tankard). Such specifically Chinese shapes as the *kendi* (a globular drinking vesssel) and the *klapmuts* (a wide-ledged dish) were also made. The trade with Europe continued until the kilns in China were re-established in 1683, after which the Dutch mainly returned to their patronage of Chinese porcelain, which was much less expensive than Japanese wares. However, porcelain made in the kilns at Arita continued to be exported to the West until the mid-18th century.

▼ **Blue-and-white export jar**
Although the general form of this jar is derived from earlier Chinese porcelain, the wedge-shaped neck and ridged foot-rim are Japanese. The landscape is indirectly inspired by late Ming decoration. The collar of chrysanthemum petals is a feature of Arita export ware.
(*c.1680; ht 31cm/12in; value* **H**)

▲ **Blue-and-white export tankard**
Many early Arita export wares copied European forms. The sides of this example are crudely painted with a landscape with pavilions and trees resembling tennis rackets. Surrounding the panels is a band of scrolled foliage called *karakusa*, or "octopus," scrollwork; this was very common in the late 17th century. The hole (not visible) on the handle is for a pewter lid.
(*c.1660–80; ht 20cm/8in; value* **H**)

KEY FACTS

Domestic wares
- CLASSIFICATION early blue and white made before *c.1650* mainly for the domestic market or for South-East Asia; early output influenced by Korea, later blue and white made from the mid-17th century and influenced more by China; later wares not to be confused with the boldly decorated polychrome wares known in the West as "Imari"
- DECORATION invariably sketchy, and generally depicting vegetation or landscapes

Export wares
- DECORATION in the style of Chinese *kraak* porcelain or Transitional blue and white; *karakusa* ("octopus" scrollwork) decoration is very typical of 17th- and 18th-century porcelain; chrysanthemum petals; coin symbols
- GLAZE thick, grayish, and bubbled; blurs the image
- POTTING usually rather heavy
- FORMS copies of European forms, including jugs (the *Enghalskrug* and the *Kugelbauchkrug*) and tankards (the *Birnkrug*)

Marks
Native Japanese dynastic or reign marks were never employed before the 19th century; from *c.1640* potters often borrowed Chinese Ming reign marks – those of Chenghua and Xuande are fairly common; other marks are mainly commendatory or benevolent, e.g. *Fuku* (happiness), as seen in these two examples

See also Middle and later Ming, pp.134–5; Blue-and-white wares, pp.204–5

Imari

Imari is a port on the eastern coast of the island of Kyūshū. The name has become associated with a certain type of porcelain, but it has two different interpretations, one used in Japan and the other in the West. The Japanese terms *Shoki* and *Ko Imari* describe blue-and-white wares made in Arita. However, what is generally known in the West as "Imari" is export porcelain decorated in a palette that usually includes underglaze blue, iron-red, and gilding, but may be extended to include green, brown (manganese), yellow, and (rarely) turquoise. There are also other categories beyond the conventional color scheme; for example, "green family" Imari is dominated by green, with red or other colors being used in a minor role. *Kenjo Imari* (presentation ware) is another sub-group, which uses a similar palette but with a more formal arrangement of paneled zones of color.

Initially developed in the second half of the 17th century, the Imari style matured *c.*1800. The finest examples of the style feature a complex symphony of overlapping geometric or leaf-shaped panels often decorated with conflicting themes, as

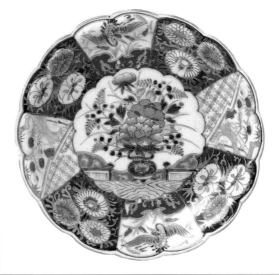

seen in the vase and cover below. Unfortunately the variety of these anti-rational patterns makes it difficult to categorize and present a chronology for this group of wares. Much decoration appears to be based on brocade: a rich silk textile run through with gold or silver thread. The majority of Imari wares are decorative, with pieces intended for display en masse. In the late-17th and 18th centuries the most common objects made were high-shouldered, dome-covered jars, trumpet-shaped beaker vases, and saucer dishes. Tea and coffee wares were also produced, but these are scarce.

▲ Bottle

Imari ware uses not only the basic underglaze blue, red, and gold palette but also several other color combinations, as can be seen on this piece. This unusual color scheme is found mostly on early wares, and includes a dominant red and green, although brown (manganese) and a small amount of yellow are also present. The theme of large blooms connected by straggly branches is taken directly from Chinese Transitional porcelain of c.1640. Based on a contemporary Dutch glass form, this bottle shape was popular in blue-and-white Arita porcelain.
(c.1660; ht 23cm/9in; value **K***)*

◄ Vase and cover

Saturated with decoration, in keeping with the demands of a rich European Baroque interior, this vase epitomizes the Imari style. The design is composed of a mass of restless shapes, each enclosing different motifs, and the overall effect is that of a sumptuous brocade. Indeed, the decoration of early Imari wares may have evolved from that of textiles. The cover of this vase is surmounted by the figure of a woman, but most covers have onion-shaped knops.
(early 18th century;
ht 51cm/20in; value **J***)*

WEAR AND TEAR

Arita porcelain, particularly blue-and-white and Imari, is generally extremely robust and not easily cracked, unlike its more fragile Chinese counterpart. However, although Arita ware is strong, its softish, pale, grayish-blue glaze may be more easily scratched than that of Chinese wares. Some of the Arita export porcelains have crackled glazes, and an intended purchase must be carefully examined to make sure that the body itself is not cracked.

▼ Chrysanthemum dish

Like many other Imari dishes, this piece is shaped like a chrysanthemum, the national flower of Japan. The central design of a *jardinière*, and the paneled border of trellis, birds, and flowers, form a typical early 18th-century arrangement.
(early 18th century; diam. 22cm/8½in; value **F***)*

KEY FACTS

- PALETTE the basic Imari palette comprises underglaze blue, which can be an intense, almost black, color or a pale gray, iron red, and gold; other colors include yellow, manganese brown, green, and turquoise
- POTTING Japanese porcelain is thickly potted and has a tendency to warp during firing, kiln supports were therefore used under the bases of even relatively small wares to prevent them from sagging
- COPIES made in porcelain at Meissen and in tin-glazed earthenware particularly at Delft during the first third of the 18th century
- BEWARE some late-17th- and 18th-century Imari porcelain wares are inscribed with spurious Chinese reign marks

See also Ironstone and transfer-printed wares, p.167

Kakiemon

A type of Arita ware, Kakiemon is a delicate porcelain with a distinctive palette. The name is derived from a family of potters and enamelers working in Arita, who are traditionally believed to have introduced overglaze enameling on porcelain to Japan in the 1640s. The extremely fine, milky-white body (*nigoshide*) was believed to have been exclusive to the Kakiemon kiln, although this is now disputed. Wares include small dishes, bottles, bowls, and vases, many of which are of geometric form.

◄ Tall-necked bottle
Tall-necked bottles, either plain and rounded, or square, hexagonal, or octagonal in form, were made in some numbers at this time. Sensitively and sparingly painted with a vegetal design, this bottle represents the mature stage of the Kakiemon style, in which much of the fine, milky-white surface is left undecorated. The squared form of this elegant vessel was copied at the Meissen porcelain factory, in Böttger stoneware as well as in porcelain, between c.1710 and c.1735.
(late 17th century; ht 23cm/9in; value N)

DECORATION AND FORMS

Although the Kakiemon kilns produced blue-and-white porcelain, they are generally associated with wares expertly painted in a palette of iron-red, cerulean-blue, turquoise-green, yellow, aubergine, and gold. These delicate porcelains form a counterpoint to the heavier Imari wares. Often asymmetrical, the designs enhance the milky-white body of the best Arita porcelain. Kakiemon wares are usually painted with natural themes: birds in branches, flying squirrels, the "quail and millet" design, the "Three Friends of Winter" (pine, prunus, and bamboo), trailing flowers, and banded hedges. Human subjects are rare; some have been given titles such as the "Woman and the Nightingale" and the "Hob in the Well," the latter a design based on the story of a Chinese sage who saved his friend who had fallen into a large fishbowl.

The chrysanthemum, the national flower of Japan, is a very common form for Kakiemon wares, as is the pointed bracket-shape. Many Arita wares, especially the Kakiemon type, are hexagonal or octagonal in form. An iron-brown dressing (*fuchi-beni*) was applied to the edges of many Kakiemon porcelains to embellish them and to protect the rims from being chipped; this was probably introduced around the mid-17th century, following the example set by Chinese potters. Kakiemon porcelain was arguably the most influential Japanese porcelain in Europe; after it was exported to Europe at the end of the 17th century, the forms and decoration were copied by many major factories including Meissen, Saint Cloud, Chantilly, Chelsea, and Bow.

▲ *Koro* and cover
A *koro* is a Japanese incense-burner that was made in either pottery or porcelain. The example shown above has been painted in a combination of both the Kakiemon (main body) and the Imari (base and lid) palettes. This is typical of the way in which the two styles were often combined on much 19th-century Japanese porcelain.
(late 19th century; ht 15cm/6in; value E)

◄ Hexagonal dish
Plain circular forms are rare in Japanese ceramics; the example illustrated possesses a typical faceted shape and asymmetrical ornamentation. The decoration is enameled with the famous *ho-ho* bird (the phoenix) perched among the "Three Friends of Winter." The rim is dressed with an iron-oxide wash (*fuchi-beni*), a feature common to most Kakiemon bowls or flatware. This dish will have small "warts" on the base, left when the kiln supports were snapped off after firing.
(late 17th or early 18th century; diam. 23cm/9in; value N)

KEY FACTS

- BODY a pure milky-white (*nigoshide*)
- GLAZE almost colorless
- PALETTE iron red, cerulean blue, turquoise, brown, yellow, and gold; black is used for detailing; iron-brown edges (*fuchi-beni*) are typical
- FORMS geometric; dishes are hexagonal, octagonal, or decagonal
- DECORATION mainly flower motifs and only rarely figures; asymmetrical and sparse; popular patterns include the "quail and millet," the "Three Friends of Winter" (pine, bamboo, and prunus), banded hedges, flying squirrels, and the *ho-ho* bird (phoenix)
- COPIES made in many European factories from the end of the 18th century, including Meissen, Chantilly, Saint Cloud, Chelsea, and Bow

See also France before 1820: Early porcelain, p.192; Chelsea, p.201; Bow and Longton Hall, p.202

Nabeshima and Hirado

NABESHIMA

The porcelain of Nabeshima (named after the ruling clan) was made at Okawachi, north of Arita, probably from the latter half of the 17th century until c.1870, exclusively for the ruling shogun and feudal lords. As this ware was the preserve of the aristocracy, little of it except "kiln wasters," or seconds, would have reached the West before the late 19th century. A few examples have been sold at auction since World War II (including some of questionable date). Apart from a few pieces of hollow-ware – bottles, vases, boxes, and censers – most surviving items are dishes. In that category the majority are saucer dishes with exceptionally tall foot-rims (over 1.2cm/½in high); the remainder are small pieces of various shapes.

▼ Nabeshima dish

The entire pattern of this typical dish is outlined in a soft and evenly applied underglaze blue. The rich iron red, turquoise, and yellow were added after the glaze-firing (a subtle mushroom/manganese and occasionally black were also available). The majority of Nabeshima designs are natural in theme but tend to be formal and stylized, as here. *(18th century; diam. 19cm/7½in; value **M**)*

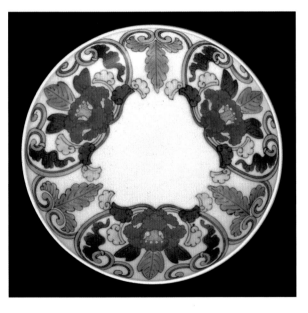

Nabeshima ware is arguably the most refined of all pre-19th-century Japanese porcelain. The decoration is imaginative, timeless, and meticulously executed. The most popular themes are seasonal flowers or wintry trees, sometimes combined with underlying or juxtaposed patterns, which may be derived from waves, Chinese trelliswork, or basketry. This type of decoration could only have been achieved by using a stencil or some kind of transfer-printing technique. For example, the repetitive geometric pattern called "calm-water" (*seigaha*) shows no evidence whatsoever of individual strokes, with their inevitable variations in intensity. Designs are often entirely outlined in underglaze blue with enamel infilling of iron red, turquoise, yellow, pale manganese, and black detailing, in a technique that recalls the *doucai*

▲ Nabeshima dish

Nabeshima is essentially an aristocratic porcelain, and little of the more standard blue-and-white ware was produced. While the saucer-dish form is well known, dishes with flattened or turned-over rims are uncommon. This design seen here is characteristically Japanese in style, climbing all over the surface and also over the lip of the dish.

*(18th century; diam. 18cm/7in; value **M**)*

▼ Hirado inkwell

The fine pure-white Hirado clay allows exceptional definition. Here the contors of the pierced amorphous rockwork are unusually liquid but are counter-balanced by the daintiness of the typical applied flowers. Most Hirado porcelains are either plain white or painted in underglaze blue.

*(c.1850–1900; ht 6cm/2in; value **F**)*

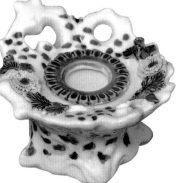

porcelains dating from the early Ming period in China. The glaze is of a soft, pale, grayish-blue tone.

A feature of the characteristic Nabeshima saucer dishes is the underglaze-blue decoration on the tall foot, which is found on most pieces. The decoration consists of a continuous band of elongated "teeth" resembling a comb, known as *kusitakade*. The underside of the rim is usually painted with beribboned coins (known as "cash"), clumps of formal flowers, or undulating foliage. Like much Nabeshima ware, saucer dishes tend to be decorated in colors, as this was more desirable than the standard blue.

HIRADO

Some of the earliest Japanese blue-and-white porcelain was produced at Hirado, near Arita, toward the beginning of the 17th century. Production at the sites of Kihara and Nanko was made possible through the employment of immigrant Korean potters. The later wares, from another site at Mikawachi where production is thought to have begun c.1760, are the most familiar. These wares, either white or blue and white, were made from the very pure clay from the island of Amakusa, allowing the most intricate modeling and refined potting.

Production consisted of censers, brushpots, jars, vases, bottles, teawares, bowls, and dishes. From c.1840 some of the larger pieces were applied with dragons or *shi-shi* (a depiction of the Buddhist lion) as either handles or knops. Other pieces were molded in shallow relief with isolated flower-heads, symbols, or trellis. Blue-and-white wares were sensitively painted in a slightly blurred underglaze blue of varying tone. The most popular themes are children at play or vertiginous landscapes, but birds and large botanical subjects were also used. Border embellishment is invariably small and includes pointed leaves and pendant tassels.

KEY FACTS

Nabeshima
- BODY virtually flawless
- POTTING thin and always very neatly executed
- GLAZE subtly grained; a soft, bluish appearance
- PALETTE usually polychrome – underglaze blue, iron red, yellow, turquoise green, pale manganese/tan, and, very rarely, black
- FORMS mainly flatwares; saucer dishes
- DECORATION natural subjects

Hirado
- BODY pure white with an "icing-sugar" texture
- GLAZE a soft, bluish hue
- PALETTE either white or blue and white

Marks
Nabeshima wares are never marked; Hirado wares are sometimes marked with the place of manufacture, occasionally with the potter's or decorator's name, or, most rarely, with a date

See also Later Japanese ceramics, pp.146–7

Later Japanese ceramics

In 1853 Commodore Matthew Calbraith Perry of the United States Navy entered Japanese territorial waters, forcing the country to accept diplomatic relations and trade with the West after over 200 years of seclusion. One of the effects of this exposure was the introduction of western technology, and this, coupled with the ambitions of the new Meiji Government after 1868, encouraged expansion. The town of Arita, the traditional home of Japanese porcelain, responded not only by making increasing numbers of conventional wares but also with brilliant showpieces suitable for display at international exhibitions and trade fairs, such as those held in London in the 1860s, in Paris (1867), and in Philadelphia (1876). The potters in the most important ceramic centers – Kaga, Satsuma, Kyoto and Seto – also benefited from the liberal policies of the Meiji Government. Vast quantities of pottery and porcelain saturated the markets in Europe and the USA. Such was the craze for all things Japanese that both Impressionism and the Aesthetic Movement were inspired by the imported wares.

The range of Meiji ceramics is vast and includes extraordinarily elaborate and over-decorated earthenwares and the most delicate and flimsy eggshell porcelains. The majority are generally considered to be of variable quality, especially the blue-and-white Arita and Imari porcelains. The mass-produced wares for the export market rarely correspond to the canons of the traditional Japanese aesthetic; the designs are mostly very busy and often lack coherence. They appear either to reflect a western picture-postcard view of Japan or to be re-creations of earlier export porcelains. The emphasis was on space-filling decoration such as *millefiori* (thousand flowers) or overlapping panels of various shapes filled with diverse ornament.

▲ **Imari charger made in Arita**
The complex diaper and floral ground of this charger has been superimposed with "cash" motifs, a flower, and an octagonal panel enclosing Buddhist lions and other motifs. Most late 19th-century Imari dishes have a diameter of about 23cm (9in), but Arita potters also made dishes of about 38cm (15in) or more for the export market.
(c.1900; diam. 46cm/18in; value G)

ARITA

Late Imari porcelain (made in or around the town of Arita) consists mainly of decorative vases, bottles, bowls, and dishes; figures or useful tablewares were rarely if ever made. The majority of the production was of off-white, poorly levigated porcelain covered in a thinnish glaze. Surface pitting, iron flecks, and smudged cobalt indicate the somewhat casual nature of this mass-produced output. Designs are often partly stenciled with outlines in a variable underglaze blue, which were then infilled with an orangey iron-red, green, turquoise, and gilding. The surface decoration featured either a main subject within complicated borders, or an all-over design made up of small panels showing various non-concordant subjects. For such wares the emphasis was on ornamentation – the "more-is-better" school of thought. Output includes enormous Indian club-shaped vases with flared and frilled necks; small shallow saucer dishes; globular bottles with tall narrow cylindrical necks; multi-lobed, high-shouldered jars; and large dishes molded in the form of a chrysanthemum. These wares are generally unmarked, although many have impressed characters. The best Imari wares at this time were made by the Fukugawa family. In 1894 Chuji Fukugawa founded the Fukugawa Manufacturing Co. in Arita, which produced very refined wares with symmetrical, soft, smoky-blue underglaze decoration.

Blue-and-white Arita wares are made of the same material as the Imari type, but the designs are not compartmentalized in the same way, relying instead on ordered floral, bird, or animal subjects. Some of the flatwares, especially the smaller dishes, were decorated entirely using stencils.

KAGA AND SETO

Although Kaga on the island of Honshū was a major center for stoneware, it produced little porcelain of note until the 19th century. The porcelain from the region around Kaga is known as Kutani ware. There are two basic styles of this: the first uses dark washes of green, purple, yellow, and black; the second, which was made specifically for export to the West, is known as "Red Kutani." This export ware has a red ground and grisaille decoration showing people in romantic land- and riverscapes enjoying the delights of the season; decoration may also be heightened with gilding. Another common type of Kutani ware does not use red. Output was dominated by tewares, although decorative bottles and vases were also produced.

By the end of the 19th century there were 434 kilns in Seto in Owari Province, producing mainly export wares. The potters generally appear to have made blue-and-white porcelains, some very close in feeling and design to the Chinese porcelains produced during the reign of Emperor Kangxi (1662–1722). Output consisted of thinly potted ornamental vases and tewares, which were sent to Tokyo for decoration.

▲ **"Old Kutani"-style dish**
Japanese potters have always espoused natural forms such as this irregular leaf-shaped dish. This is an attempt to re-create the so-called "Old Kutani" style of the 17th century. However, this combination of purple, green, and yellow was in fact made exclusively at Arita; only the reproductions were made at Kaga.
(late 19th or early 20th century; w. 16cm/6¼in; value F)

▼ **Vase from the Seikozan studio, Satsuma**
Enameled in the red-dominated palette, this is a conventional example of late 19th-century earthenware. The subjects – elegant women strocolor beside a lake, and bamboo and peony – are typical of the period. On the shoulders of the vase is a favorite subject – a carpet of overlapping chrysanthemums. Such refined wares as this are usually signed on the base.
(c.1890; ht 31cm/12in; value H)

▼ Vase by the Fukugawa Porcelain Manufacturing Co.
Although several other kilns, including Hirado, made pierced ware, the bold, large-scale frieze of irises and the saturated cobalt-blue of this piece are unmistakably by Fukugawa. Openwork was first used on Chinese porcelain of the late Ming period, when it was called "devil's work". Its revival in the 19th century inspired such factories as the Worcester Royal Porcelain Co., where George Owen (1845–1917) made some remarkable examples.
(early 20th century; ht 30cm/11¾in; value H)

► Vase by Makuzu Kozan
The high technical quality that characterizes all this potter's work is evident in the smooth curves and crisp mouth of this vase. The piece is decorated in an underglaze pink on a soft palette of sage-green celadon ground, which is typical of the color combinations used by Kozan. The controlled asymmetry of the scallop-shaped motifs is another notable feature of his work. In addition to the colors seen here, Kozan worked in yellow and blue; he also used overglazed-enamel detailing. Most of Kozan's output bears his idiosyncratic, highly stylized signature in underglaze blue.
(c.1900; ht 26.5cm/10½in; value J)

SATSUMA AND KYOTO
Although Satsuma was an important center of ceramic production from the 16th century, the town is synonymous with the highly decorative export wares made from the mid-19th century. These cream-colored earthenwares with finely crackled glazes and thickly applied enameled and gilded decoration were also produced in the town of Kyoto. Satsuma and Satsuma-type wares were first shown outside Japan at the international exhibitions, resulting in a huge demand for them in the West. While some are of the very highest craftsmanship, many are of rather mediocre or poor quality, intended for sale in department stores.

In Satsuma the Seikozan studio, and in Kyoto such potters as Kinkozan IV (1824–84) and Yabu Meizan (1853–1934), made extremely fine paneled wares decorated with miniature scenes depicting people carrying out everyday activities like fishing, playing, or strolling in parklands or along riversides. Landmarks such as Mount Fujiama were also depicted, together with animals including monkeys, cranes, pheasants, peacocks, and cockerels, and flowers such as chrysanthemums, irises, prunus blossom, and wisteria. Around these panels the ground was embellished with complex patterns or overlapping designs. Wares included *koro* (incense burners), vases, wine or sake ewers, bowls, covered jars, and figures. The most sophisticated wares with the finest-quality decoration appealed to followers of the Aesthetic Movement in Europe and the USA. Most of these wares are clearly signed on the base.

NORITAKE
In 1891 the McKinley Tariff Act passed by the American Congress declared that all Japanese wares imported into the USA should be clearly marked with the word "Nippon" (the Japanese name for Japan). One of the most important factories that produced what were known as "Nippon" wares was the Noritake Co., established in 1904 in Nagoya by Icizaemon Morimura (*b.*1875). The company specialized in the production of

porcelain wares, at first copying debased Rococo-style European wares decorated with flowers, fruit, foliage, and landscapes in pale pastel tones with gold relief highlights. During the 1920s such well-known designers as the American architect Frank Lloyd Wright (1867–1956) were commissioned to supply designs reflecting the current vogue for Art Deco-style tea, coffee and dinner services. After 1921 the American government decided that the Nippon mark was to be changed to "Japan" or "Made in Japan."

▲ Part of a tea or coffee service by Noritake
After World War I the Noritake factory engaged such leading designers as the the American architect Frank Lloyd Wright to revitalize its output. This service was designed for the Imperial Hotel in Tokyo. These Art Deco style porcelains, in a very pure, white, hard-paste porcelain, are very highly sought after today by collectors, especially in the USA.
(c.1925; diam. of plate 12cm/4¾in; value F)

KEY FACTS
Arita
- BODY porcelain
- GLAZE usually fairly thin with surface pitting
- TYPES blue-and-white and Imari-style wares
- DECORATION Imari: busy; blue and white

Kaga and Seto
- BODY porcelain
- DECORATION Kaga: loosely painted with predominant iron red or grisaille; Seto, mainly delicately drawn natural themes in clear, bright underglaze blue

Satsuma and Kyoto
- BODY fine earthenware
- GLAZE Satsuma: warm, creamy, crackled glaze
- PALETTE enameling in bright colors, gilding
- DECORATION landscapes; people carrying out everyday activities; flowers; animals

Marks
Kyoto: seal mark for Yabu Meizan

Noritake
- BODY at first a gray Seto body; from the early 1920s a pure white porcelain similar to that made at the French factory of Limoges
- TYPES good quality utilitarian wares of European/American form intended for export

Marks
Mark used on many Noritake Nippon wares (*c.*1911–1921); "M" is for Morimura

See also Imari, p.143

Pottery

Although pottery production dates from Neolithic times, most surviving examples – and certainly those available to most collectors, rather than in museums – will date from after the early Middle Ages. The brilliant potters of the Islamic world developed a number of innovative techniques, most notably tin-glazing and lustring, which spread across Europe via Spain, and without which European pottery would have looked very different. The maiolica of Italy, the Delftware of the Netherlands, and the faience of France and other countries, are all tin-glazed earthenwares. Europe's potters were also influenced by Chinese blue-and-white wares, and a strong strain of Orientalism is visible in much 17th- and 18th-century pottery.

Important centres of pottery production in Europe and the USA

Islamic pottery

The countries and regions that embraced early Islam were ideally located to absorb the cultural, commercial, and technical cross-currents of the early medieval world. Chinese commodities were one of the major influences in Islamic lands – an area that stretched from India to the Atlantic Ocean. Trade with China was well established by the Tang Dynasty (AD 618–906), since many Arabs were resident in Guangzhou (Canton), and in addition to spices, perfumes, and silks the Chinese sent ceramics to the Middle East.

EARLY WARES

From the 9th century, potters in Mesopotamia (now Iraq) were so inspired by Chinese wares that they strove to imitate them. The first types of ware made were buff or red earthenwares covered with a tin glaze. In an effort to simulate metals potters also developed the luster technique, and during the next 300 years this method of decoration spread through Islamic countries, reaching Spain in the 13th or 14th century. Tin-glazed earthenwares and luster wares were two of the most important types of pottery bequeathed to Europe by the brilliant Islamic ceramic tradition. In eastern Persia (now Iran) the crisply contored 10th- and 11th-century slipwares of Nishapur and Samarkand were subtly decorated with abstract leaf or geometric motifs and Kufic script.

PERSIAN WARES

Unique to the Islamic world is fritware, a glassy composition perhaps developed to copy imported Chinese porcelains produced during the Song Dynasty (960–1279). This grainy, white-bodied ware is often covered in a viscous, deep turquoise-blue glaze. Between c.1215 and 1334 plain and lustered wares were made in the town of Kashan, south of Tehran; the technique was probably introduced to Persia in the 12th century by Egyptian potters.

The sophisticated polychrome *Mina'i* (enamel) wares of late-12th- or 13th-century Persia may often seem crowded and confused, but they are nonetheless outstanding examples of the Islamic decorator's art. *Mina'i* pottery was made in Rayy (now Rhages) near Tehran, and is decorated with figures and painted in a wide range of colors. Many examples of early *Mina'i* ware are painted with large-scale figures in the manner of contemporary lusterware, but later the emphasis was on small-scale, narrative subjects.

Later Persian wares, made during the Safavid (1501–1732) and subsequent periods, include those from Meshed (eastern Persia), Kirman (western Persia), and Kubachi (northern Persia), most of which were painted in the style of late Ming and Transitional Chinese porcelains. The bodies, glazes, and decorations of these Persian wares are very similar and it is difficult to tell them apart.

IZNIK AND KÜTAHYA

In the 16th century, extremely fine copies of blue-and-white Chinese wares were made by the potters in Iznik (east of Istanbul) and Kütahya in central Anatolia. The potters in these towns created superb, crisply painted wares with swirling and scrolling foliage, painted either in blue or in a combination of turquoise, green, and, later, a thick red (Armenian bole). In addition to conventional decorative pottery vessels and dishes, Iznik and Damascus potters produced some of the finest tileworks for mosques and secular buildings. These latter wares were highly influential in late 19th-century Europe, as seen in, for example, the work of the English designer William De Morgan (1839–1917).

▲ Iznik dish
This is an example of the mature Iznik style, in which the decorator has used thickly applied Armenian bole, cobalt blue, and turquoise. Emanating from an axial cypress, carnations and tulips wind about the well of the dish. The flattened rim is typically painted with zones of interrupted whorls, a debased form of the Chinese wave border of the14th century, adopted by Turkish potters in the 16th century. *(mid- to late 16th century; diam. 33cm/13in; value I)*

◄ Mesopotamian dish
This dish is painted in the earliest combination of colors – ruby and gold luster. Designs are complex and all-covering, intended to dazzle the eye.
This quartered arrangement is fairly typical, with geometric segments enclosing dots and lines resembling fish-roe or nets. Other themes include animals or stylized foliage and palms. *(9th century; diam. 20cm/8in; value I)*

▼ Persian bowl
The influence of Chinese porcelain is evident in this fritware bowl. Both Meshed and Kirman produced quantities of similar wares at this time. *(late 16th or early 17th century; diam. 21.5cm/8½in; value H)*

KEY FACTS

Early wares
- BODY buff or red earthenware
- GLAZE tin oxide
- LUSTER ruby, brown, yellow, black, red
- TYPES tin-glazed wares; luster wares
- DECORATION fusion of Chinese and Islamic designs, usually abstract

Persian wares
- BODY *Mina'i*: coarse; Meshed, Kirman, and Kubachi: white frit paste
- GLAZE *Mina'i*: creamy; Meshed, Kirman, and Kubachi: thick and soft
- DECORATION *Mina'i*: underglaze colors and overglaze enamels; Meshed, Kirman, and Kubachi: resemble each other; black design outline may suggest a Meshed piece

Turkish wares
- BODY Iznik: grayish buff, grainy, and absorbent; Kütahya: buff and thinly potted
- GLAZE Iznik: translucent, but slightly bluish tone; Kütahya: irregular, gathers in bluish or greenish pools
- STYLES Iznik: "Golden Horn" (c.1530) decorated with knotted penciled scrolls; "Damascus" (c.1550–70) very sumptuous, with large-scale floral subjects and saw-edged leaf (*saz*); "Rhodian" (c.1555–1700) mainly floral; Chinese-style blue-and-white wares
- PALETTE Iznik: wide range of colors dominated by turquoise and a sealing-wax red (Armenian bole)
- DECORATION Kütahya: crude, floral, and figural

Marks
Islamic pottery is rarely marked, although individual potters' marks do occasionally appear; corruptions of late Ming seal marks are used on Persian pottery

See also Spain, p.150; Tiles, p.155; Rugs & Carpets: Persia before 1800, p.134

Spain

Spain's major contribution to European ceramics history is lusterware. The technique for firing lustered pottery was first developed in the early Islamic world, probably in the 9th century. The Moors conquered Spain in the 8th century, but it was probably not until the mid-13th century that lustered pottery was made there.

LUSTERWARE

The most important centers for lusterware were first at Málaga and later at Manises (near Valencia) in southern Spain. The earliest wares show a strong Islamic influence, with Kufic (Arabic) script, and such motifs as the tree of life, the "Hand of Fatima," and knot patterns. The output consisted mainly of dishes, bowls, pitchers, *albarelli* (drug jars), jars, and tiles. Luster itself varies in coloring; toward the end of the 15th century it became much redder, and later in the 17th century a brash coppery color. During the late 14th and early 15th centuries it is often difficult to distinguish one center of production from another.

Popular 15th-century motifs include bryony, crowns, fern-like leaves, or acacia (the latter is often used alone), parsley flowers, cotton stalks, vines, and ivy leaves. Other tiny geometric patterns were also used as ground

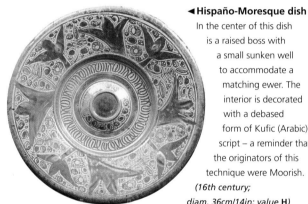

◄ **Hispaño-Moresque dish**
In the center of this dish is a raised boss with a small sunken well to accommodate a matching ewer. The interior is decorated with a debased form of Kufic (Arabic) script – a reminder that the originators of this technique were Moorish.
(16th century; diam. 36cm/14in; value **H***)*

fillers. Coats of arms, not only of the Nasrids (1232–1492), the last ruling Muslim dynasty in Spain, but also later of Spanish royalty, European nobility, and wealthy families, appear on armorial wares.

LATER SPANISH POTTERY

Glazed earthenware appears to have been made in Talavera de la Reina, near Toledo, and at Puente del Arzobispo, from at least the first half of the 16th century. Early wares were decorated mainly in an Italian or a Flemish style, until a regional style emerged in the late 16th century. Dishes, basins, jugs, and other domestic wares were made in increasing quantities to replace silverware, the use of which was severely restricted after 1601 with the introduction of sumptuary laws. Dishes, of which a large number survive, were painted in high-fired colors – brown, a brilliant green, ocher, and blue. The most popular subjects were soldiers, bust portraits, animals, birds, and coats of arms surrounded by a framework of partially hatched foliage. Among the more successful types are scenes with equestrian figures, hunting scenes, and animals careering amid curly foliage. Apart from the

wares already mentioned, the range included *albarelli*, amphoras, and holy-water stoups from *c.*1560 to 1650. Many blue-and-white wares were also painted in the manner of late Ming export porcelain.

In 1727 a factory was established in Alcora, north of Valencia, which soon became the foremost ceramic factory in Spain, making a high-quality faience called *loza fina*. With the help of craftsmen such as Edouard Roux from Moustiers in France, a wide range of beautifully modeled and painted wares was produced. Output included animal-form spice-pots, animal-shaped tureens like those made in Strasbourg, and *trompe l'oeil* dishes decorated with fake comestibles. Decoration was inspired by early Moustiers with blue grotesques or polychrome *lambrequins*, dwarfs, and fantastic creatures. In many cases it is very difficult to distinguish Alcora from Moustiers ware, although the former is composed of a fine reddish clay while the latter is usually of a warm buff clay. The success of Alcora encouraged other Spanish factories to adopt the French style.

In common with other European factories after 1800, Spanish potters continued in the established traditions. Generally the output consisted mainly of more utilitarian objects such as basins, dishes, and jugs intended for the domestic market or for the tourist trade. The themes are mostly simplified renditions of 17th- and 18th-century wares, including animals – the hare, the deer, and the bull – almost all of which are set amid modestly drawn vegetation; armorial ornament; geometrical designs using concentric circles or simple repeated motifs; and foliated decoration. Whatever the type of decoration, the wares are usually painted with bold brushstrokes in the old "hot" colors – green, manganese, yellow, and ocher – and sometimes with a pinkish puce that was virtually unknown before the 19th century. This later production is of variable quality, ranging from crude, gritty ware to the slick, hard-edged appearance of modern mass-produced ware.

▼ **Bowl**
The vigorous brushwork, rampant animals, brisk curly foliage, and palette dominated by emerald green, ocher, and manganese are characteristic of central Spanish faience of this period.
(early 18th century; diam. 25cm/10in; value **H***)*

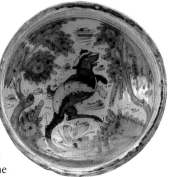

▼ **Ornamental ewer**
Such over-elaborate forms as this are typical of many European historicized wares. While scenes of the hunt were popular in the 17th and 18th centuries, the formal attire of the bullfighter painted on this ewer was not seen until modern times.
(late 19th/early 20th century; ht 38cm/15in; value **F***)*

KEY FACTS

- GLAZE Arzobispo and Talavera: hard and glassy
- WARES tableware, drug jars, basins, ewers, vases, tiles
- PALETTE lusterware: red hue and later a brash coppery color; Arzobispo and Talavera: dominated by rich green, blue, and ocher, with manganese detailing; Alcora: blue and white or polychrome
- DECORATION lusterware: mainly small floral or geometric designs enclosing an armorial bearing and later with large feathery leaves, fish, and other animals; faience: Arzobispo and Talavera wares were vigorously painted with landscapes, figures, or animals; Alcora: *lambrequins* and arabesques similar to Moustiers
- IMPORTANT CENTERS OF PRODUCTION Málaga and Manises (lusterware), Puente del Arzobispo, Talavera de la Reina, Alcora

Marks
Early lusterware is never marked; Talavera: wares were never marked before the 19th century; later they were frequently marked with the full name

Alcora factory wares (1727–*c.*1785) marked in manganese brown

See also Tiles, p.155

Portugal

The beginnings of Portuguese faience are obscure, and prior to the 17th century few pieces can be attributed with any certainty. Although written records indicate that there was production from at least the 13th century, evidence is sparse until the 16th century, when there appears to have been a flowering in this craft. In 1552 there were ten potteries in Lisbon alone. It is most likely that the industry was boosted by migrant potters, perhaps from Italy, France, or The Netherlands. While some European-type wares were made, including Italian-style *albarelli* and late 19th-century wares in the style of the French potter Bernard Palissy (*c*.1510–90), the most characteristic wares were those decorated in the manner of Chinese export porcelain made during the late Ming Dynasty (1368–1644), indicating the importance of the Portuguese trade with China at this time.

Although some of these mainly blue-and-white wares are fairly fine renditions of Chinese porcelain, most have a crowded market-place appeal, with robustly drawn if somewhat garbled motifs in what is known as the "Sino-Portuguese" style. Motifs include the Eight Precious Things (including the artemisia leaf and the musical stone, which often appear in the broad paneled borders of dishes). With time, these designs became simplified or formalized: Chinese-border "sunflowers" evolved into spiky demi-lunes or a radiating scale pattern; the artemisia leaf began to resemble a spider. The compartmentalized borders taken from *kraak* porcelain were retained, although the diverse semi-geometric patterns of the late Ming style were replaced by a simple "cross-stitch" trellis design.

AFTER 1700

During the 18th century Portuguese faience was strongly influenced by French potteries, especially those in Rouen, although the Portuguese wares were never as meticulously drawn as the French. In general Portuguese faience produced in Lisbon, Oporto, Coimbra, and other potteries is very similar in feeling to provincial French faience. Furthermore, there was clearly a reluctance to advance or to experiment with new designs, so wares often seem old-fashioned – the formal Baroque style of early 18th-century Rouen wares is still found in the middle of the century or even later. This time-lag can also be seen on high Rococo faience, the style being maintained until beyond the end of the 18th century. The most important pottery centers were given a great incentive in 1770 when

▶ Jug from Lisbon or Braga

There has been some confusion over these types of jug as they have often been attributed to potteries in Germany, particularly Hamburg. Since there was an extensive trade in ceramics between the two countries during the 17th century, styles of wares were probably copied from one country to the other. This jug almost certainly originates from Lisbon or Braga.
(1635; ht 26cm/10in; value L)

▶ "Goose" tureen made by the Royal factory of Rato

The Italian potter Tomás Brunetto (*d*.1771) was the first director of the Royal factory of Rato (1767–1835) in Lisbon. Wares were usually in the high Rococo style and included tureens in the shape of deer-heads, hens, and geese. The "impressionistic" style of decoration on this tureen is typical of wares made during Brunetto's directorship.
(c.1750–70; ht 38cm/15in; value N)

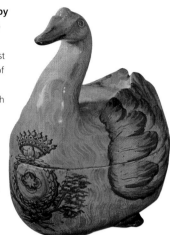

a ban was imposed on all imported porcelain, save that from East Asia, which boosted domestic production.

In the 19th century, in keeping with the European trend, Portuguese potters produced considerable quantities of revival wares, borrowing indiscriminately from the classic wares of Italy, France, and The Netherlands. Among the more frequently encountered types are the lead-glazed wares made in Caldas da Rainha that were based on the wares of Bernard Palissy – dishes or hollow-wares with applied reptiles, covered in dark lead glazes. Nineteenth-century wares were skilfully potted and painted. Much late 19th- and 20th-century pottery is traditional in feel, using an Italianate or a debased Ming export style. In the latter category, deer and rabbits cavort amid formal small-scale vegetation, mostly painted in blue with brown outlines. This refined material may have a silky-smooth glaze of slightly pinkish tone.

▼ Vase from Caldas da Rainha

Portugal's main faience factory was established in Caldas da Rainha in 1885 by Rafael Bordalo Pinheiro and remained in production until 1908. Heavy, treacly lead glazes in sombre, autumnal tones of brown and green were used, which evoke the elaborate and highly complicated 16th-century earthenwares of Palissy. Wares made at the factory include dishes, pots, jars, and vases, such as this example, applied with realistically modeled fish, reptiles, crustacea, and vegetation.
(c.1900; ht 35cm/14in; value E)

KEY FACTS

- **BODY** generally fairly crude; less refined than Spanish wares
- **GLAZE** quite gritty
- **DECORATION** usually very schematic and quickly executed; 17th-century blue-and-white wares: outlined in manganese brown, based on Chinese late Ming and Transitional porcelain; 18th-century faience: inspired by French faience; 19th-century wares: inspired by 16th-century Palissy wares
- **FEATURES** flatware was generally fired on a triangular arrangement of pins visible on the underside of the flange
- **IMPORTANT CENTERS OF PRODUCTION** Lisbon, Oporto, Coimbra, Caldas da Rainha

Marks
Before *c*.1770 Portuguese wares were rarely marked

Lisbon: Royal factory of Rato (1767–1835); mark for wares made under Brunetto (1767–71)

Caldas da Rainha: Mafra factory (est. 1853); mark for wares made under Manuel Gomes (active 1853–7)

See also China: Later export porcelain, pp.136–7

Italy before 1600

Tin-glazed earthenwares were made in Italy from at least the 13th century, and developed from very basic decorated pieces to wares of extremely high artistic quality. "Maiolica" is the term for Italian tin-glazed earthenwares, and is probably derived from the Tuscan name for the island of Majorca through which Hispaño-Moresque wares from Spain were shipped to Italy from the 14th century.

BEFORE c.1400

The earliest period of maiolica production is known as the "Archaic" period and covers wares made until c.1400. The wares are basic in form: simple bowls, dishes, basins, or jugs. Decoration was executed mainly in manganese brown on a copper-green ground, although yellow and blue were also used. The underlying tin-glazed surface is not always white, or even off-white, but a warm biscuity color. Designs were mostly of stylized birds, animals, ribbonwork, hatching, geometric motifs, or occasionally the human figure.

1400–1500

From the early 14th century, maiolica emerged from its humble origins to become a material appropriate for the most elevated patrons. Wares tend to be grouped according to the different types of decoration; the first was the "green" family (c.1425–50), a close descendant of the old Archaic tradition, in which designs were washed in green and outlined in manganese brown. The designs show a greater sensitivity and accomplishment than their predecessors but are still governed by the form of vessel or dish on which they appear. The "blue

▲ Albarello from Faenza
The style of the Gothic label on a ground of undulating scrollwork with parsley-like foliage suggests the attribution of this piece to Faenza. Encircling the neck is a continuous collar of San Bernardino rays.
(c.1480–1500; ht 20cm/8in; value K)

relief" wares (c.1430–60), which were mainly made in Tuscany, were painted in a very thick, rich, cobalt blue, a technique known as "impasto," with detailing in manganese brown and copper green. Wares include *albarelli* (drug jars for use in pharmacies and spice stores) decorated with birds, animals, human figures, coats of arms, or oak leaves. Two-handled jars with oak-leaf decoration are called "oak-leaf" jars.

In the second half of the 15th century Italian potters produced ever more sophisticated work in both form and design. In contrast to the restricted early palette, tiles, *albarelli*, and dishes were painted in a broad range of colors, including blue, green, a translucent turquoise, yellow, and ocher. Designs include a bold Gothic scrolling leaf, the "Persian palmette" (resembling a pine-cone), the "peacock-feather eye," "San Bernardino rays" (wavy radiating lines), tightly scrolled foliage with dotted flower-heads (probably inspired by Hispaño-Moresque ornament), ribbonwork, and geometric motifs.

The development of printing from the mid-15th century onward had a major influence on the maiolica decorators, who used some of the primitive figural images – such as those on tarot cards – to decorate objects. With few exceptions, subjects before c.1500 are allegorical or symbolic, in contrast to the narrative style that developed during the following century. Most of the surviving early figural subjects have been found on wares attributed to Faenza or Florence, the foremost maiolica centers in the 15th century. Other important centers of production included Orvieto, Naples, and Deruta.

◄ Wet-drug jar from Deruta
Deruta was one of the most important centers for the production of maiolica in Italy. It was noted especially for lusterware from c.1500 to c.1550, but more conventional "warmer-colored" pottery was almost certainly made in greater quantities. By comparison with 15th-century wares this wet-drug jar is complicated in form and shows how confident potters had become by the early 16th century. Neat double ribs circle the belly, the "S"-scroll handle is articulated with fancy scrolled terminals, and the vessel is supported on a sophisticated molded foot. The palette has also become hotter to include yellow, ocher, and green. The heavy foliage and the relatively simple minor decorative bands are typical of Deruta at this time.
(1507; ht 26cm/10in; value N)

▼ Vase from Deruta
The form of this vase – a deep hemispherical body surmounted by an inverted trumpet-shaped neck, which is flanked by heavy ear-like handles – appears to be unique to Deruta. Simple repeated patterns were standard decoration and included overlapping scales (as seen here), leaves with curling tendrils, and interlocking zigzag patterns. The ruby luster highlights are an unusual addition to the ocher-gold luster.
(c.1520–30; ht 26cm/10in; value L)

▲ "Cardinal's hat" dish from Urbino

Inspired by engravings, potters translated biblical and Classical themes into colorful pictures. The subject featured on this *istoriato* dish is Jonah being cast overboard. The contors of the vessel or dish were often simply ignored and the whole surface treated as a canvas. With its sunken center and broad ledge, this *tondino* form was dubbed the "cardinal's hat."
*(c.1540–50; diam. 30cm/12in; value **O**)*

1500–1600

About 1480 the ruins of the Domus Aurea (Golden House) of Emperor Nero was discovered in Rome; the walls in the *grotte* (underground rooms) were painted with ornament that included scrolling foliage, fantastic animals, and birds. Known as "grotesques," these designs were translated into engravings and used extensively on Italian maiolica for the next 200 years. Other designs were taken from a variety of printed sources, including the *Metamorphoses* by the Classical Roman poet Ovid, and the engravings of Marcantonio Raimondi – most notable for reproducing work after the High Renaissance artist Raphael, who is considered the single most important influence on Italian *istoriato* (narrative) maiolica. Other artists whose work was incorporated into the painted designs include Albrecht Dürer and Andrea Mantegna. *Istoriato* wares depict biblical, mythological, or historical themes, usually in a brilliant palette that employed the full range of high-fired colors; particularly predominant were a rich orange and a brilliant blue. The most important centers of production for *istoriato* wares were Urbino, Casteldurante, and Gubbio.

Other decorative styles include the "*belle donne*" dishes made particularly around Urbino from *c.*1520, which depicted the heads of beautiful women, and the *a quartieri* style – a patchwork of small, differently colored panels each decorated with scrollwork or grotesques. In the 1520s the *berrettino* (gray-blue) ground was introduced in Faenza, and wares were typically decorated with grotesques and arabesques. The simplified *compendiario* style of decoration was introduced in Faenza during the second half of the 16th century, probably as a reaction to the increasingly busy *istoriato* wares. This simple, rather sketchy style, depicting flowers, figures, or coats of arms, employed a limited palette of blue, yellow, and ocher on a rich white ground known as *bianco di Faenza*. In Montelupo in northern Italy, potters produced very high-quality wares decorated with saints or single figures surrounded by a band of complex decoration. Wares included curious bulbous ewers with dragon-head spouts.

◄ Jar from Venice

Venice was a major maiolica center in the 16th and 17th centuries, producing very distinctive wares. Comfortably rotund, this jar has a general boldness that is emphasized by the broad band of large-scale fruit and foliage, a popular Venetian theme. Typical too are the cross-hatched borders.
*(c.1550–60; ht 25.5cm/10in; value **M**)*

► Dish from Faenza

During the second half of the 16th century, potters in Faenza developed a milky-white ware known as *bianco di Faenza*, which was unlike any other maiolica. This finely reticulated dish is painted with a blue and yellow cherub in a rather impressionistic style called "*stile compendiario*"; the palette was mostly restricted to blue, orange, and yellow.
*(late 16th century; diam. 28.5cm/11in; value **H**)*

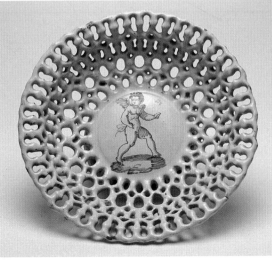

KEY FACTS

Before 1400
- BODY fairly crude brownish or buff color
- GLAZE thin, an off-white color
- PALETTE usually manganese brown and copper green
- FORMS simple bowls, dishes, basins, and jugs
- DECORATION known as "Archaic"; rather crude cross-hatching used as a ground, geometric motifs, stylized birds and animals, occasionally figures
- IMPORTANT CENTERS OF PRODUCTION Florence, Faenza, Deruta, Orvieto, and Naples

1400–1500
- BODY this improved as the century progressed
- GLAZE off-white, sometimes pinky
- PALETTE cobalt blue introduced *c.*1400; ocher and other colors such as turquoise
- DECORATION known as "severe"; groups include the "green" family, "blue relief"; decoration includes oak leaves, birds, animals, figures, coats of arms, Gothic scrolling leaves, "Persian palmettes," "peacock-feather eyes," and "San Bernardino rays"
- IMPORTANT CENTERS OF PRODUCTION Florence, Faenza, Orvieto, Naples, and Deruta

1500–1600
- BODY increasingly refined
- GLAZE whiter, particularly *bianco di Faenza*
- PALETTE high-fired colors, including a deep sky blue and orange; a deep lapis blue in Faenza; metallic lustring in Gubbio and Deruta
- STYLES *istoriato* (narrative); *a quartieri* (quartered); *compendiario* (sketchy); *belle donne* (beautiful women)
- DECORATION grotesques; biblical or mythological scenes taken from printed sources or after famous painters; garlands, arabesques, trophies of arms, portrait medallions
- FORMS *albarelli*, large dishes and bowls, storage jars
- IMPORTANT CENTERS OF PRODUCTION Cafaggiolo, Casteldurante, Castelli, Deruta, Faenza, Gubbio, Montelupo, Pesaro, Rimini, Siena, Urbino, and Venice

Marks
From *c.*1500 the use of initials and/or signatures or inscriptions was introduced by potters; this is a small selection of important makers' marks

Casteldurante: two marks used by Nicola Pellipario

Casteldurante: the mark probably used by Francesco Durantino (active 1543–54)

Gubbio: the mark used by Giorgio Andreoli (*c.*1465–1553)

Urbino: the mark used by Francesco Xanto Avelli of Rovigo (active *c.*1500–1542)

See also Spain, p.150; France, pp.156–7; The Netherlands, pp.160–61

Italy after 1600

Although Italian maiolica reached its apogee in the masterpieces of the 16th century, there is still much to admire in the products of the following 100 years. Potteries in Deruta continued to make colorful *albarelli* (drug jars), although these undoubtedly lack the vigor of their 16th-century predecessors; and, while embossed wall plaques of the Madonna and Child were now virtually mass-produced at Deruta, some still convey a spirit befitting their imagery. The great *istoriato* (narrative) painting of Urbino became debased, and Montelupo dishes are of inferior quality. However, the depiction of soldiers boldly standing with legs apart – the characteristic Montelupo decoration of *arlecchini* – remained a powerful image on dishes and plates.

1650–1800

New varieties of fine maiolica were developed in the second half of the 17th century. At Castelli thin potting was combined with careful painting that employed perspective, quite unlike the Italian maiolica of the previous century. The workshops of the Gentile and Grue families in Castelli produced a large number of high-quality wares, including dishes, vases, and pharmacy jars, the best being made by Francesco Antonio Xaverio Grue (1686–1746) and Carmine Gentile. Most of their wares were essentially functional, but they also included plaques made purely for display. Dishes depicting Classical heroes, spirited hunting scenes, or biblical epics are the successors of 16th-century *istoriato* wares. Production continued at Castelli until the mid-18th century, although there was a gradual decline in quality.

Drug jars continued to be made, although with less spirit than in the past. Instead of bright colors, the influence of Chinese porcelain led to borders of blue-and-white scrollwork or naïve landscapes, which were both pleasing and original. From the late 17th century, dishes produced in Savona represented the *istoriato* tradition in a fresh and lively fashion, combining somewhat sketchy painting with high-quality potting. The standard of maiolica produced by the various Savona workshops varies considerably.

In the 18th century, Italy was no longer the leading force in European pottery. Nevertheless the centers of Le Nove, Bassano, Turin, Milan, and Faenza produced good pottery influenced by silver forms, French faience, and Chinese porcelain. Potters in Milan made dinner services decorated with the Chinese *famille-rose* palette and Japanese Imari patterns. The Ferniani family in Faenza made good-quality dinnerware often decorated with potato flowers or carnations.

▲ **Vase and cover by Francesco Grue**
Made at the Grue family workshop in Castelli, this vase represents the height of quality in Italian maiolica of this period. The continuous landscape exhibiting exceptional perspective is characteristic of Francesco Grue's decoration. The olive green, yellow, and brown are typical of the palette used by the Grue family. The delicate potting adds a dimension of lightness.
(*c.1700; ht 52cm/20½in; value* **L**)

▶ **Ice pail and cover from Milan**
This example illustrates the effects of the competition from porcelain, which led Italian potters to experiment with new shapes for the table. This form is derived from a French porcelain shape and incorporates enameled decoration inspired by the Chinese *famille-rose* palette.
(*c.1775; ht 30cm/11¾in; value* **H**)

AFTER 1800

In the 19th century, Italian pottery was dominated by mostly debased copies of earlier models. Among these, the bold flower painting of G.B. Viero at the faience factory (est. 1728) in Le Nove stands out, as does the work of probably the best-known 19th-century Italian maiolica potter, Ulysse Cantagalli (1839–1901) of Florence. Original 16th-century dishes were already very valuable, and there was an eager market for high-quality reproductions. Cantagalli's famous copies of wares from Urbino and other centers of Italian maiolica production were so good that they fooled many connoisseurs in the 19th century. Many other 19th-century potters also reproduced the glories of the past, maintaining a tradition that continues to the present day.

▶ **Charger by Molaroni**
This large, signed *istoriato* charger by Molaroni of Pesaro is a copy of a 16th-century dish made in Urbino. It depicts a scene from the Old Testament story of Joseph, and is skilfully painted, capturing the spirit of the original.
(*c.1870; diam. 48cm/19in; value* **F**)

KEY FACTS

1650–1800
- BODY new, fine maiolica types, which were thinner than those made in the previous century were developed after *c*.1650
- GLAZE high quality, and generally a grayish cream
- STYLE influenced by silverware, Chinese porcelain, and French porcelain and faience
- FORMS decorative plaques, vases, dinner services
- PALETTE Castelli: naturalistic tones of olive green, brown, and yellow
- DECORATION continuation of *istoriato* (narrative) painting; introduction of perspective in painting of landscapes; allegorical and mythological themes; flowers and figures; Oriental motifs, including Chinese landscapes and blue-and-white scrollwork
- IMPORTANT MAKERS the Grue, Cappelletti, and Gentile families

After 1800
- FORMS a return to classic 16th-century forms; many produced as tourist wares
- DECORATION high-quality reproductions of 16th-century designs (e.g. *istoriato*)

Marks
In the late 19th and early 20th centuries Cantagalli used this distinctive cockerel mark, usually in black; collectors should be wary as unscrupulous dealers have often removed this mark in order to pass pieces off as originals

Savona: this late 17th/early 18th-century representation of the tower or beacon in the harbor of nearby Genoa has been much imitated

See also Italy before 1600, pp.152–3

Tiles

The use of tiles as an architectural element, either as roofing or as decoration for walls, floors, or ceilings, has been a feature of most cultures. In the Middle East, glazed tiles have had a long tradition in creating cool interiors. After the death of Muhammad (AD 632), the culture of Islam expanded rapidly throughout the region, spreading Islamic philosophy and arts. In Iberia, the westernmost outpost of the Islamic world, this influence is particularly evident in such buildings as the Alhambra in Granada.

◄ Dutch tile

The vase was one of the most popular tile subjects in 17th-century Holland. Tiles are often classified by the corner motifs: here the "ox-head" type, named after the symmetrical scrollwork, which resembles the horns and eyes of an ox.

(c.1650; w. 13cm/5in; value **D***)*

▲ English transfer-printed tile decorated in Liverpool

John Sadler supplied a series of copper-plate engravings for use on pottery and porcelain. His designs were varied and included armorial subjects, moralizing scenes, chinoiseries, theatrical themes, and ornamental vases. He and his partner Guy Green were supposedly the first to apply transfer-printing to tiles, thus decorating 1,200 tin-glazed earthenware tiles in 1756.

(c.1757–61; w. 11.5cm/4½in; value **C***)*

◄ Iznik tile

The off-set design on this tile indicates that it is a border tile. Turkish decorators relied almost exclusively on abstract floral and leaf-shaped motifs, and flowing palms. The colors used (turquoise, blue, and red) are typical of Iznik wares.

(c.1550; w. 25.5cm/10in; value **H***)*

EUROPE

In Italy tin-glazed earthenware reached new heights in the late-15th and 16th centuries, and Italian tiles were first used for pavements in churches. Migrating potters transmitted their skills from Italy to France and The Netherlands, and the tin-glazed tiling tradition continued from its epicenter in Antwerp (now in Belgium). In order to escape persecution by their Spanish overlords in the 1560s, many potters fled Antwerp for Rotterdam, Middelburg, Amsterdam, and Delft in the northern Netherlands. By the 1660s and 1670s Dutch potters had adopted a sober blue-and-white palette depicting local interests and activities. In Germany, and many other northern and central European countries, decorative tiles, mostly molded in relief and covered in either a brown or a green monochrome glaze, were used mainly for cladding the exteriors of stoves.

From the 16th century until the latter half of the 18th century, when they went out of fashion, tin-glazed tiles were made in large quantities in Britain. The range and variety of British tiles is great and offers the collector a fertile hunting-ground. From the late 18th century until the latter half of the 19th, decorative tileworks formed little or no part of Western interiors, but after the Great Exhibition of 1851 in London, tiles began to reappear, mainly as fire surrounds but sometimes used either as a tile picture or as a series of repeated patterns creating an exotic interior. Both Minton & Co. (est. 1798) and the designer William De Morgan (1839–1917) embraced the Aesthetic Movement and designed tiles in Japanese, Turkish, and Persian styles. Although a few were hand-painted, the majority were transfer-printed.

NORTH AMERICA

Tiles were manufactured in North America from the second half of the 19th century. By the mid-1870s such firms as the American Encaustic Tiling Co. (est. 1875) in Zanesville, Ohio, and the Star Encaustic Tile Co. (est. 1876) in Pittsburg, Pennsylvania, were making mosaic and inlaid floor-tiles. The Low Art Tile Co. (1877–93) in Chelsea, Massachusetts, produced glazed relief tiles that could compete with the best English tiles. At the Grueby Pottery (est. 1894) in Boston, Massachusetts, a variety of tiles in soft colors with matt glazes was made. Other factories making art tiles included the Trent Tile Co. (est. 1882) in Trenton, New Jersey, and the Rookwood Pottery (est. 1880) in Cincinnati, Ohio.

▲ English transfer-printed tile by E. Smith & Co.

All the largest manufacturers of English tiles, including Copeland and Minton, made earthenware tiles decorated with themes of idealized femininity or knightly gallantry, like this medieval-style depiction of a lady.

(c.1880; w. 20cm/7½in; value **B***)*

▼ Spanish tile

Before the mid-17th century, European tiles were made in a variety of shapes: lozenge, hexagonal, square, or, as here, rectangular. A solitary animal, figure, or bird in a sparsely vegetated landscape is a typical pan-European theme. The palette is a conventional combination of "hot" colors – ocher, yellow, green, and blue.

(early 17th century; w. 28cm/10¾in; value **D***)*

▲ American tile picture by the Grueby Pottery

The tile picture, in which the theme extends over several tiles, first appeared in Europe in the 16th century. It was a rare decorative art form, probably owing to failures in the kiln. With the development of more stable firing techniques during the 19th century, tile pictures became fashionable. These are taken from a larger picture.

(c.1900; w. 13cm/5in; value **F***)*

KEY FACTS

- SIZE early tiles tend to be much thicker than the usual 6mm (¼in) (approx.) of 18th- and 19th-century tiles; sizes became more uniform in the 19th century
- REPRODUCTIONS collectors should beware of reproduction transfer-printed tiles made in the late 1980s and 1990s
- COLLECTING tiles from Victorian fireplaces are available in large numbers; Dutch tiles can be expensive; tile panels and pictures are rare and are usually very expensive; Iznik tiles are among the most expensive tiles available and can measure about 38cm (15in) in width

See also The Netherlands, pp.160–61

France

Tin-glazed earthenware was produced in France from at least the beginning of the 16th century when itinerant potters from Italy first introduced the technique. The ware is called "faience," since much of the early ware resembled maiolica made in Faenza, Italy.

THE 16TH CENTURY

The dominant style for most of the 16th century was Italian; craftsmen from Italy appear to have settled in Lyons (1512), Nevers, Montpellier, and Nîmes, and the output of these centers closely reflects the contemporary Italian polychrome maiolica of Urbino, Faenza, and Savona. The Italian *istoriato* (narrative) style is found on wares made in Lyons and Nevers, while the paneled *a quartieri* style associated with Faenza is seen on the faience of Nîmes and Montpellier. However, in the north of France at Rouen around the middle of the century the work of Masséot Abaquesne (active 1526–59) is more sombre, and the designs show a strong affiliation with the Mannerist work of the Fontainebleau School. Early Rouen was noted for the manufacture of tiles (some still extant in chateaux), *albarelli* (drug jars), saucer dishes, and flat-rimmed dishes.

THE 17TH CENTURY

The first half of the century continued to be dominated by the Italian tradition, but from the mid-17th century a more native French Baroque style developed. Mythological figures after contemporary prints were popular subjects; drawn in a bold, muscular style in which ocher and blue are often dominant, they are somewhat livelier than their Italian *istoriato* predecessors. Dishes, which greatly outnumber hollow-wares (except apothecaries' wares), were typically embellished with heavy foliated borders, usually

▲ Sugar-sifter from Rouen
This sugar-sifter follows a Baroque silver form. The intricate style of embellishment, which is synonymous with the French designer Jean Bérain I (1640–1711), is typical of Rouen wares made at the end of the 17th and the beginning of the 18th centuries. The decoration comprises a *lambrequin* border pattern with pendant tassels and floral swags. This style of decoration remained popular until just before the middle of the 18th century.
(early 18th century; ht 23cm/9in; value I)

interrupted with cartouches enclosing diverse subjects. During the second quarter of the century the influence of imported Chinese porcelain is evident, both in decoration and in form, and consequently the "hot" Italian colors declined in favor of blue and white. Nevers was probably the most important center until the last 20 years of the century and was one of the first French pottery centers to decorate its wares with Chinese motifs. Here the earliest manifestations are garbled versions of the many imported late Ming blue-and-white wares. A large proportion of production was painted in cobalt blue, sometimes outlined in manganese brown with figures in the manner of Chinese Transitional porcelain. Alongside the Italianate and Chinese styles, faience with solid-colored grounds was made, including, most commonly, *bleu persan* (Persian blue), cobalt, and, more rarely, ocher.

Rouen, close to Paris and the French court, developed as a prominent center for faience at the end of the 17th century. The Rouen style of the late 17th and early 18th centuries is formal, utilizing intricate motifs resembling ironwork (*ferronerie*) or lacework (*lambrequin*) but probably owing as much to contemporary Chinese ceramic ornament. The *lambrequin rayonnant* style, so-called because of its radiating "snowflake" complexity, was copied by many other manufacturers in France, including those in Strasbourg and Moustiers. At its height (*c*.1695–1725) Rouen combined this style with vessels based on the shapes of silverwares because the French nobility had been ordered to melt down its silver in order to finance the wars of Louis XIV. Faience therefore became a fashionable substitute for silver.

THE 18TH AND 19TH CENTURIES

Between *c*.1710 and 1720 polychrome wares became fashionable once again. For the next 20 or 30 years bold chinoiseries in high-fired (*grand-feu*) colors eclipsed the blue-and-white wares. From *c*.1750 low-fired (*petit-feu*) enameled decoration became the focus of the leading faience factories of the day, located in Strasbourg, Niderviller, Lunéville, Sceaux, and Marseilles. In an ultimately futile competition with porcelain, these manufacturers decorated their wares with botanical flowers, chinoiseries, and fantastical landscapes in the most delicate brushwork. Forms from the mid-18th century, in keeping with the innate intimacy of the Rococo, were diverse and lively, almost matching porcelain in some instances.

▲ *Bleu persan jardinière* from Nevers
The use of a solid blue ground appears to have been introduced at Nevers in the third quarter of the 17th century. Designs are usually quasi-Oriental, drawn either from Chinese Transitional porcelain or, as here, from Persian/Turkish pottery. Often the design is married to an entirely European Baroque form, as in this example with its square bucket form and rope-twist handles. The dense scrolling foliage and the tulips echo designs on contemporary marquetry furniture.
(late 17th/early 18th century; ht 20cm/8in; value J)

► Teapot and cover from Strasbourg
Possibly the most technically accomplished of all French faience produced in the 1740s and 1750s was that made in Strasbourg. Wares were brilliantly painted in the newly introduced *petit-feu* palette. This teapot epitomizes the eastern-French high Rococo style in the use of natural organic or vegetal forms and neat flower-painting.
(1748–54; w. 25.5cm/10in; value I)

However, in the late 18th century, competition from porcelain and English creamware (cream-colored earthenware) proved too much for faience manufacturers, and many failed around the turn of the century. Some potteries survived the onslaught from English creamware by manufacturing the same material, known as *faience fine*, which although clean and crisp was never as creamy or warm as the English ware. In France, factories such as those in Creil, Pont-aux-Choux, and Montereau, some active before the

mid-18th century, made great quantities of *faience fine*, thus helping to accelerate the decline of faience. Many of these factories decorated their wares with transfer-printing in the style of creamware from the Wedgwood factory (est. 1759) in Burslem, England.

By the mid-19th century Quimper was one of the few surviving faience factories in France, producing wares with simple figural subjects loosely imitative of 18th-century Rouen. Gien, active toward the end of the 19th century, appears to have concentrated on the manufacture of wares in revival styles, using printed designs based on classic Italian maiolica. The output of historicized faience was fairly limited as many factories preferred to produce the fashionable styles current in the dying years of the 19th century. The firm of Samson (est. 1845) in Paris made a wide range of good reproductions of faience. Although this factory applied the original marks, it usually put its own monogram alongside.

▲ Platter made by the factory of Antoine de la Hubaudière, Quimper

Quimper, in northern France, has been a center of faience manufacture since the late 17th century, but is usually known for its popular wares made in the 19th and 20th centuries. Typical painted decoration includes rather stiffly drawn figures of milkmaids and other rustic subjects in simple landscapes enclosed, as here, within a border of scattered flowers. The decoration is in a traditional high-fired palette.
*(c.1885; l. 45cm/17½in; value **D**)*

▲ Dish made by the factory of Robert, Marseilles

The form of this dish is typically associated with Marseilles. The decoration is known as *bouillabaisse* (fish soup).
*(c.1765; diam. 24cm/9½in; value **H**)*

▼ Tureen and cover from St Amand-les-Eaux

Petit-feu enameling was introduced to France from Germany around the mid-18th century. First adopted at Strasbourg, this palette soon spread throughout France. This tureen in the Rococo style is delicately enameled in the manner of Strasbourg, with sprays of flowers and detailed scalloped borders. Although it is well modeled, its contors are slightly awkward.
*(late 18th century; ht 22cm/8½in; value **H**)*

KEY FACTS

- **BODY** Rouen: red; Nevers and Marseilles: buff; Strasbourg: creamy white; Moustiers: grayish
- **GLAZE** Strasbourg: thick and creamy white; Moustiers: creamy gray
- **PALETTE** "hot" colors inspired by Italian maiolica; from *c*.1625 blue and white inspired by imported Chinese porcelain; high-fired colors: cobalt blue, manganese purple, ocher, yellow, green, and iron red; enamels: from the late 1740s a wide range of colors
- **DECORATION** Rouen: *lambrequins* and arabesques; Nevers: narrative style; Strasbourg: botanical studies; Marseilles: naturalistic flowers, *bouillabaisse*; Moustiers: potato flowers, fantastic creatures, Classical figures, and festoons

Marks

These were very randomly applied; marks are usually the initials of the proprietor of the factory; most are in puce, blue, or black; care should be taken since marks of such collectible factories as Strasbourg, Sceaux, Marseilles, Rouen, Lille, and Nevers have been widely copied on 19th- and 20th-century fakes

Strasbourg: Paul Hannong factory (*c*.1740–60)

Marseilles: Veuve Perrin factory (*c*.1740–95)

Moustiers: Olerys factory (1738–*c*.1790)

Quimper: Antoine de la Hubaudière (est. 1782)

Quimper: Fougeray factory (est. 1872): copies of 18th-century originals

See also China, pp.131–40; Italy, pp.152–4

Germany

Stoneware

Stoneware was first made in Europe in the 12th century by potters in the Rhine valley, where there were abundant supplies of wood for fuel. *Steinzeug*, as stoneware is known in Germany, was made mostly in the Rhineland, but also in Saxony. Cologne was the first important center for the production of Renaissance-style Rhenish stoneware in the first half of the 16th century. While there are obvious regional differences, it is not always easy to distinguish the wares of different potteries located close to each other. In terms of production, almost the entire output was of drinking vessels fitted with pewter lids. The few exceptions include flasks (resembling tea-caddies), inkwells, table salts, and small tureens. The complete absence of stoneware dishes or plates indicates a German preference for pewter or wood for use on the table.

SIEGBURG

Siegburg became a center for stoneware production in the 15th century. The most celebrated wares, dating from the second half of the 16th century, are *Schnelle* (tall, tapered tankards), decorated with shallow reliefs molded separately and carefully sealed onto the sides. Subject-matter tends to be either biblical, allegorical, or heraldic. Other wares include *Sturzbecher* ("somersault cups") and *Schnabelkanne* ("beak jugs"). The most important family of potters were the Knütgen, active during the late 16th century. At the beginning of the 17th century the industry declined, owing to increased competition from other Rhenish centers.

RAEREN

Stoneware appears to have been produced in Raeren near Aachen (Aix-la-Chapelle) from the mid-15th century. Early wares are virtually indistinguishable from those of Cologne or other Rhenish areas, and it was not until after the mid-16th century that an individual style developed. This was a gray-bodied stoneware covered in a lustrous brown glaze. The leading makers were members of the Mennicken family, particularly Jan Emens Mennicken. Wares include handsome, bulbous-bodied drinking jugs, the profiles of which reflect the legs on late Elizabethan tables or buffets; these are decorated with a broad central band of relief-molded panels containing arcading, religious subjects, Holy Roman Emperors, or dancing peasants. With their complex, graduated borders of tiny medallions and *Kerbschnitt* (carved, diagonal crosshatching), these vessels have a weighty, architectonic appeal. Raeren continued as a major center through the 19th century, producing 16th- and 17th-century-style wares and beer-mugs.

► *Kugelbauchkrug* **from Westerwald**
This is the most common form of later 17th-century German stoneware. The ground is usually decorated in low relief, with a small oval medallion containing a monogram or armorial device surrounded by repeated masks, geometric panels, or incised scrollwork. The design is highlighted with blue and manganese brown against the grayish "orange-skin" (slightly pitted) salt glaze.
(1575–1600; ht 18cm/7in; value D)

▲ *Schnelle* **from Siegburg**
Schnellen were the principal output of the Siegburg potteries after c.1550. The refined off-white Siegburg body could take remarkably fine detailing, as here. The strapwork and foliation seen on this example have been derived from late Renaissance ornament and are characteristic. Siegburg decoration was often inspired by the printed engravings of such artists as Virgil Solis (1514–62) and Heinrich Aldegrever (b.1502). Early *Schnellen* were extensively copied in the 19th century.
(1582; ht 26cm/10in; value H)

WESTERWALD AND CREUSSEN

The region known as the Westerwald is noted for its manufacture of gray stoneware detailed in cobalt blue and manganese brown. From what survives it is evident that the output was almost wholly of hollow vessels such as the *Enghalskrug* (narrow-necked jug) and the *Kugelbauchkrug* (bulbous globular tankard). Many of these jugs are stamped with a date and the monograms of English monarchs, such as "Anna Regina" and "Georgius Rex," suggesting that they were intended for export to England. Production has continued in the region up to the present day.

Creussen (Kreussen), near Bayreuth, was a center for the production of stoneware from the late 16th century until the 1730s. The product was a light-brownish-gray ware covered in a rich, chocolate-brown salt glaze, and output consisted mainly of tankards and flasks with metal screw-tops. Decoration was applied, molded, or enameled, and included hunting scenes, the 12 Apostles, and figures symbolizing the planets.

► **Tankard by the Mettlach factory**
The tradition of German stoneware has continued uninterrupted to the present day, but for much of the 19th century potters relied on reproductions of earlier wares. The production of the Mettlach factory consisted mainly of dishes and tankards with historical themes, such as the lightly incised and colored image of a troubador depicted on this tankard by the decorator Warth.
(late 19th century; ht 19cm/7½in; value E)

KEY FACTS

- BODY off-white (Siegburg), gray (Frechen, Cologne, Raeren, and Westerwald), or dark brown (Creussen)
- GLAZE salt glaze
- FORMS tankards, narrow-necked and spouted jugs, bellarmines (globular bottles with a bearded mask at the neck, made famous by those produced in Cologne)
- DECORATION applied, enameled, and molded: strapwork and ornamental motifs taken from pattern books; biblical scenes; Holy Roman Emperors; rich figural scenes; coats of arms
- FAKES beware of 19th-century copies of 16th-century *Schnellen*, the bases of which are too finely finished and very flat

Marks

Early wares may bear the initials of the potter or decorator incorporated into the design; marks never appear on the base until the 19th century; factory marks as opposed to individual's initials were unknown before the 19th century

Raeren: mark used for Jan Emens c.1566–94

See also Britain: Stoneware, p.164

Faience

The technique of manufacturing tin-glazed earthenware was spread throughout Europe to France, the Netherlands, Britain, and the German-speaking world in the early 16th century by itinerant potters. German tradition has it that tin-glazed earthenware was first produced by the stove-makers of the south in Bavaria and the Tyrol, and there are a few pieces dated to this time. The majority of German faience, however, dates from the late 17th until the early 19th century.

BEFORE 1700

The arrival of Dutch potters in Frankfurt and Berlin in the later 17th century encouraged the development of German pottery. The first centers of production were Hanau (1661), Frankfurt (1666), and Berlin (1678). Much of the output at this time is in the manner of Dutch Delftware and indeed is frequently wrongly identified as such. Decoration is mainly blue on a white ground, inspired by decoration on Chinese export porcelain, landscapes and figure subjects. Chinese-inspired themes carry on throughout the golden age of German faience in the 18th century, although local themes do sometimes appear. One of the most popular was songbirds among scattered foliage and flowers.

A small proportion of the late 17th- and early 18th-century faience is painted in manganese and yellow as well as blue. Although *petit-feu* (low-fired) enameling was developed here at least as early as the 1680s it is scarce and therefore expensive. As well as plain contored dishes and hollow-wares the potters made lobed wares – both deep dishes, often with 30 or more lobes, and *Enghalskrugen* (narrow-necked jugs).

AFTER 1700

In the 18th century a large number of potteries were established; apart from Hanover (1732) these were principally in the southern and central regions, including Ansbach (1708), Nuremberg (1712), Bayreuth (1719), Brunswick (1719), Fulda (1741), Höchst (1746), and Crailsheim (1749). After 1700 the decorators' repertory included a continuation of their love affair with Chinese ornament – although now in a much-debased form. However, as the century developed, the Chinese designs were gradually replaced by a more native style. Among the most popular themes were birds and foliage, naively painted buildings, figures, landscapes, chinoiserie riverscapes, the double-headed eagle, and coats of arms. Decoration was executed in both the high-fired palette (blue, yellow, and red against a speckled manganese ground) and low-fired enamels.

A considerable portion of the surviving output is the *Walzenkrug* (cylindrical tankard), one of the most characteristic forms of German faience. Also popular were *Enghalskrugen*, dishes, tureens in the form of animals, birds, or vegetables, plates, salts, inkwells, and vases (sometimes in garnitures, or sets). Figures were made by some manufacturers, the majority from the north of the region, such as Brunswick and Münden. Although competition from English creamware (cream-colored earthenware) forced many of the factories to close at the end of the 18th century, some factories continued into the 19th century. The potteries in Kellinghusen established in the 18th century made good-quality peasant-style wares decorated in high-temperature colors with bold flowers; one factory continued until *c*.1860.

▲ *Harvester* from Damm
The Damm pottery (est. 1827) specialized in the manufacture of Höchst-style figures, and its wares bear the same mark as that used on Höchst porcelain.
(c.1850; ht 19.5cm/8in; value E)

▲ **Dish from Nuremberg**
This is a typical example of Nuremberg faience, complex in form and decoration. The finely fluted or ribbed form is washed in pale blue and then painted in grayish cobalt with a highly formalized design – a *jardinière* charged with flowers enclosed within a corona of demi-lune panels and a rim of stylized Oriental flower-heads and floral cartouches. This entire arrangement is a fairly stiff descendant of the Rouen or Delft motifs that were dominant at the turn of the 17th century.
(c.1720–30; diam. 26cm/10in; value G)

▼ *Walzenkrug* from Bayreuth
The high-fired colors and foliated cartouche on a speckled ground were an extremely popular formula for this form. Most such vessels are stamped with the maker's touch-marks on the underside of the lid, but it is always possible that a lid may have been removed from an older piece and may have no relevance to the vessel's date or place of origin.
(c.1750–75; ht 25.5cm/10in; value G)

KEY FACTS

- FORMS multi-lobed dishes and hollow-wares, *Walzenkrugen* and narrow-necked jugs; figures are rare
- DECORATION based on Chinese wares; from *c*.1750 replaced by a more native style
- COPIES in the late 19th and early 20th century, copies of the more exotic *petit-feu* enameled wares were made; 18th-century wares tend to have a pinkish look where the glaze is thin – most evident on the base
- BASES 18th-century wares, particularly from south Germany, have a so-called "thumb print" on the base, created when the item was removed with a string from the wheel; these do not appear on 19th-century wares

Marks

Marked examples are rare before *c*.1700; a considerable number of faience makers used factory marks, but not on every piece.

Bayreuth: this is the mark for Johann Georg Pfeiffer, owner between 1760 and 1767

Hanau: mark used between 1661 and 1806

See also The Netherlands, pp.160–61

The Netherlands

Tin-glazed earthenware has been produced in The Netherlands since the end of the 15th century. Introduced by immigrant Italian craftsmen who settled in Antwerp (c.1500), the techniques and the decorative style gradually spread north during the troubled years of the 1560s and 1570s. While many potteries were established at Haarlem, Rotterdam, and Amsterdam, it was the town of Delft that rose to prominence in the mid-17th century and from which the term "Delftware" is derived.

THE INFLUENCE OF ITALY

During the early to mid-16th century, potters produced what is known as the "Italian-Antwerp" style of wares, which were decorated with pine-cone motifs, scrolling stylized foliage, geometric patterns, and, later in the century, strapwork and half-shaded petal borders (sometimes termed "false gadroons"). Designs are often painted in high-fired colors (copper green, yellow, and ocher) and usually boldly outlined in blackish cobalt blue. Early wares include dishes, plates, *albarelli* (drug jars), and syrup-jugs. Although small household objects such as jugs or double-eared pots were probably made in large numbers, few are extant. *Albarelli* have survived in some quantity and can be recognized by their pronounced flanged bases and crisp mouth-rims. From around the middle of the 16th century the tortuous strapwork and adapted grotesque ornament of the Fontainebleau School in France are seen on more accomplished wares. Northern designers such as Colordeman de Vries of Leeuwarden and Cornelis Bos of Antwerp were also used as sources for this type of decoration.

Time and distance, however, gradually diluted both these influences (although they did not entirely disappear for another century). By the end of the 16th century new, more humble patterns had appeared, employing simple repeated motifs such as dashes, chevrons, or zigzags, and concentric circles enclosing stylized leaves, fruit, or flowers. Tiles were also made in large quantities, first for floors and later for walls.

▲ **Dry-drug jar by The White Star factory in Delft**
Of plain cylindrical form, ultimately derived from the Italian *albarello*, this piece is decorated in underglaze blue in the conventional manner of the Dutch, English, and German apothecaries' ware made at this time. The label is set in a Baroque frame of curling strapwork, a basket of flowers flanked by exotic birds, and a cherub head with attendant swags of flowers. The simple brass cover is almost certainly of a later date.
(early 18th century; ht 18cm/7in; value F)

▶ **Buckelplatte from Delft**
Based on Baroque silver or pewter originals, these lobed dishes were a common form of European flatware. Decorated in the Chinese Transitional style, this dish is painted in the center with figures under a parasol in a mountain retreat, a favorite Chinese setting. Framing this scene, the nine lobes are painted with either a stylized tulip or a solitary figure. Because there is an odd number of panels the decorator has been obliged to repeat the same scene in two panels side by side on the lower edge.
(c.1690; diam. 34cm/13in; value F)

Decoration was usually in blue but also in polychrome, and comprised mainly stylized leaves, flowers, and such fruit as pomegranates, and, later, figures with small corner motifs. The most important centers of production for tiles were Rotterdam, Haarlem, Delft, Gouda, Utrecht, and, later, Harlingen and Makkum.

During the period from 1600 to 1650, the influence of Italian maiolica was still felt. Decorative subjects were extensive and included shadowed foliage, whole and sliced fruit in the manner of Venice or Faenza, scrolling bryony-type flowers, zigzag patterns, and concentric bands of simplified foliage encircling formal flower-heads that resembled "targets." Faenza-style putti and fern-type borders, leaping hounds, equestrian subjects, isolated standing figures, and blue-dash borders were also popular. However, a more local type of decoration that included religious subjects, shipping scenes, and milkmaids was gradually introduced.

THE BLUE-AND-WHITE PERIOD

From the beginning of the 17th century, the Dutch East India Company (V.O.C.) imported blue-and-white Chinese porcelain, known as *kraak* porcelain, into The Netherlands. The name derives from the Portuguese carracks, or merchant ships, that carried large cargoes of Chinese export porcelain, two of which were captured by the Dutch in 1602 and 1604. During the early years of the 17th century, the type of Chinese ornament featured on this porcelain was introduced on Delftware. Within a few decades the high-fired Italian maiolica colors were largely displaced by a palette of blue and white, a switch that demonstrates the growing passion for blue-and-white Chinese porcelain.

As the Dutch brewing industry declined, many of the disused breweries in Delft were turned over to the potters, and from c.1650 Delft became the most important center of production for tin-glazed earthenware. Factories at this time included the Porceleynen Schotel and the Porceleynen Lampetkan.

Probably the single most important impetus for the vast increase in production of tin-glazed earthenwares was the cessation of imports of Chinese porcelain between 1645 and 1650, when the kilns in Jingdezhen were devastated by the invading Manchus. Between c.1650 and c.1680 the number of potteries in Delft rose from eight to nearly thirty. Production of blue-and-white "porcelain," as the Dutch termed their tin-glazed earthenware, focused on reproducing Chinese wares made during the reign of Emperor Wanli (1573–1619) and Transitional porcelain (1620–44), or *kraak* porcelain. Decoration also included Dutch landscapes and biblical subjects. Frederik van Frytom (1632–1702) was the best-known painter of plaques, plates, and dishes decorated with detailed landscapes, with dark-toned foregrounds, lighter-hued middle grounds, and hazy backgrounds. Tiles, drug jars, ewers and other hollow-wares, dishes, and flower-holders, some of great complexity (such as tall tulip vases), were produced. The most important factories included The Metal Pot, whose owner Adriaenus Kocks (d.1701) supplied wares to the court of William and Mary, and The Rose, The Axe, The Three Bells, The White Star, The Greek A, and The Peacock. The still-life paintings of luscious flower displays by Dutch artists such as Jean-Baptiste Monnoyer and Jan van Huysum were very influential on the design of Delftware at this time.

POLYCHROME WARES

From *c.*1683 imports of Chinese porcelain were resumed, affecting the production of Delftware, which was aimed at the same market. From the end of the century, potters in Delft began to experiment with a polychrome palette. Wares follow the colorful *famille-verte* (green, red, yellow, purple, and red) and *famille-rose* (an opaque pink, white, and yellow) export porcelains made in China, which sometimes employed gilding. Another important influence were the Japanese Imari and Kakiemon porcelains, which were imported into The Netherlands in the middle of the 17th century while the Chinese imports were suspended. Dutch polychome wares tended to be restricted to a palette of yellow, blue, purple, green, red, and black. An important producer of polychrome wares in Delft was The Greek A factory (est. 1658), run by the Van Eenhoorn family.

Most of the wares produced during the 18th century are somewhat mundane, decorated with small repeating

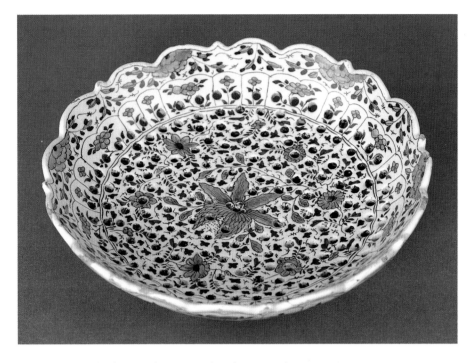

patterns. Biblical subjects, plates painted with images of the months, and whaling and seal-hunting scenes were all popular forms of decoration. Production during the 18th century was extremely diverse and included wall plaques, flower-holders, coffee and tea services, butter-tubs, drug jars, candlesticks, garnitures or vases, punch-bowls, dishes, and small models of shoes. There were more than 30 potteries in Delft in the late-17th and 18th centuries, some specializing in tile production, although it seems that only two of these continued production in the 19th century. The increased popularity of English creamware (cream-colored earthenware) caused the demise of the tin-glazed industry in The Netherlands from the early 19th century.

▲ Drainer from Delft

The ornate shape of this drainer suggests a silver original, but the decoration is pure Chinese, based on early 18th-century imported porcelain. The two outer registers are derived from Kangxi porcelain (1662–1722), and the central zone is a loose rendition of Chinese designs typical of later Delft.
(late 18th century; diam. 20cm/8in; value E*)*

▲ Dish by The Greek A factory

At the beginning of the 18th century the enthusiasm for blue and white waned, and Dutch potters adopted the the colorful palettes of China (*famille verte* and *famille rose*) and Japan (Imari and Kakiemon), often combining them on one piece. This shallow dish molded in the form of a chrysanthemum (a Daoist symbol of longevity, and the national flower of Japan) is painted in the characteristically florid style of the second quarter of the 18th century.
(c.1740; diam. 25.5cm/10in; value E*)*

▼ Cow from Delft

Although difficult to model, a few figures of animals were made. The range included exotic birds, dogs, and horses, but the most popular were farm livestock, most dating from around the mid-18th or the 19th century.
(mid-18th century; ht 15cm/6in; value F*)*

KEY FACTS

- BODY extremely fine, soft, and generally thinly potted
- GLAZE thick, white, and with a "peppered" effect due to air bubbles exploding during firing, seen most clearly on the backs of dishes
- STYLE until *c.*1600: Italianate/Fontainebleau; *c.*1610–20: Chinese *kraak* designs; *c.*1620–50: local styles; from *c.*1650: Chinese-style blue and white; from the early 18th century: an increase in polychrome in the style of Chinese and Japanese wares
- CENTERS OF PRODUCTION Delft, Antwerp, Amsterdam, Haarlem, Middelburg, and Rotterdam
- COLLECTING the choice for the collector is wide since so much was made; the condition will vary, but expect to find chipping on the rims of wares

Marks

These were introduced sporadically from the third quarter of the 17th century; during the 18th century much production was unmarked

Delft: The Golden Flowerpot factory; used from 1654

Delft: The Greek A factory; Adriaenus Kocks and his son Pieter Kocks

Delft: The Porcelain Claw factory (est. 1662); one of various forms used from 1764

See also Britain: Delftware, p.162

Britain

Delftware

The manufacture of British tin-glazed earthenware began in the 16th century, when it was known as "galleyware," possibly named after wares transported by galleys from Spain and Italy. The most important centers of production in Britain were Southwark, Aldgate, and Lambeth in London, Norwich, Brislington, Bristol, Liverpool, Glasgow, and Wincanton.

► "Blue-dash" charger

The term "blue-dash" is given to a series of polychrome dishes on which the rim is emphasized with a band of sloping dashes. The naive decoration of King William III and Queen Mary II on this dish is typical of these wares.
(c.1690–1700; diam. 33cm/13in; value M)

EARLY DELFTWARE

A record of 1567 tells of the arrival in Norwich of such Dutch potters as Jaspar Andries and Jacob Jansen, who had fled Antwerp to escape religious persecution. These potters established potteries locally and later at Aldgate in the east of London. Very few examples of 16th-century British tin-glazed earthenware have survived, apart from some tiles and a number of bulbous-bodied jugs (some with silver mounts). Pottery made during the 17th century is far more common. From the late 1620s virtually until the cessation of tin-glazed production in the late 18th century, there is a considerable body of dated and documentary British delftware, which enables collectors to study the changing shapes and styles of this type of ware over a period of nearly 200 years. From *c.*1600 small quantities of Chinese porcelain began to be imported by the East India Company into Britain, and some British delftware made from *c.*1620 shows the influence of these Chinese blue-and-white imported wares. After *c.*1660 until the end of the 17th century those in the so-called "Transitional" style were copied.

The most notable late 17th-century wares include "blue-dash" chargers, named after the blue dashes around the rim, which were boldly decorated in polychrome with stylized tulips, carnations, oak leaves, biblical subjects, and portraits, particularly of such monarchs as Charles II, William and Mary, and Queen Anne. The majority of this type are covered with a yellowish lead glaze on the back, through which the body is clearly visible – it was considered unnecessary to waste the expensive tin glaze on a side that was rarely seen. These dishes have a thick foot-rim around which a cord could be wound for hanging the object on the wall. Other wares included wine-jugs, drug jars, salts, and wide-brimmed dishes. While a few examples show traces of the old Italian-Dutch style, most embrace the continuing fashion for Chinese blue-and-white wares.

18TH-CENTURY DELFTWARE

From *c.*1720 British delftware became increasingly distinctive, and the decoration less complex and looser in style. Delftware made in the 18th century tends to be more delicate and intimate (with some robust exceptions from Bristol), and a far greater range of wares was made, including punchbowls, plates, flower-bricks, wall pockets, wine-bottles, guglets, fuddling-cups, pear-shaped jugs, puzzle jugs, posset-pots, and, extremely rarely, tea and coffeewares. While many of these wares were painted with contemporary British subjects – figures, buildings, and landscapes – others are decorated in blue with chinoiserie themes – pagodas, pavilions, Chinese figures, birds, and flowers. Production of British delftware virtually ceased at the end of the 18th century because of the competition from creamware (cream-colored earthenware).

▼ Guglet from Lambeth

This form of water-bottle with a bulbous body and tall neck was used with a basin, presumably for minor ablutions. Most examples are painted in cobalt blue with "Chinese" riverscapes or pavilioned gardens. Geese among wispy vegetation are a traditional Chinese theme but rare on British delftware. The use of decorative bands on the neck is borrowed from Chinese porcelain; the trelliswork on the shoulders was a popular form of decoration from c.1740 to 1780.
(c.1760–70; ht 23cm/9in; value H)

▼ Plate from Bristol

River scenes or landscapes with figures in parklands were favorite subjects for Bristol decorators. A feature of this group, in which the painter has ignored the contors of the dish and used the entire surface, is the framing of the scene with sponged trees. The smooth, slightly bluish glaze on much British delftware contrasts with the whiter, "peppered" surface of Dutch Delftware.
(c.1760; diam. 29cm/11½in; value G)

KEY FACTS

- **BODY** British delftware is harder and coarser than the softer, thinner Dutch Delftware
- **STYLE** before 1620 wares are Italian-Dutch in style; after 1620 the influence of Chinese blue and white is clear; 18th-century wares are less formal, and contemporary British figures and landscapes with chinoiserie subjects remained popular
- **GLAZE** generally smoother than Dutch Delftware and chips easily; mainly pinkish or bluish; 18th-century glaze is smooth, as opposed to the whiter and "peppered" surface of Dutch Delftware
- **PALETTE** blue and white dominates; polychrome (iron red, yellow, green, brown, and manganese purple) also used, but rarer and extremely collectible
- **DECORATION** this is cruder than Dutch Delftware: monarchs, bold flowers, oak leaves, chinoiseries
- **FLATWARES** these have knife-like weals under the outer flange or rim since they were fired in the kiln on stilts
- **COLLECTING** flatwares are most available; dates and inscriptions and more unusual forms of decoration can increase the value of a piece substantially

Marks
British delftwares are rarely if ever marked

See also The Netherlands, pp.160–61

Lead-glazed ware

The earliest British lead-glazed pottery was made in the 10th or the 11th century. Recent evacuations of sites at Winchester and Stamford have revealed crude and sometimes partially glazed cooking pots, pitchers, and bottles. In the 17th century a more idiosyncratic type of British pottery developed, including the bold slipwares of Staffordshire and of Wrotham, Kent. A considerable range of different pottery types were covered in lead glaze; red, buff, or white-bodied clays were covered in a clear or colored lead glaze similar to that of the Chinese *sancai* tomb pottery made during the Tang Dynasty (618–907). During the 18th and 19th centuries Staffordshire emerged as one of the most important ceramics regions of the modern age. All the necessary ingredients for high-quality production were found in the area: first-rate clays, local supplies of coal to fuel the kilns, and an extensive waterway system for transporting the finished product.

▲ Slipware dish probably by John Simpson III
Most 17th-century slipware was decorated freehand with robust slip-trailed designs. Here the more intricate design, made up of a number of small elements, has been press-molded, and the low-relief details have been heightened in brown slip by the decorator. The octagonal form was very fashionable from the late 17th until the mid-18th century. (c.1715; diam. 35.5cm/14in; value I)

SLIPWARE

This is a red-bodied ware covered in a brown or white slip (liquid clay), which is then decorated with a contrasting-colored slip in trails and dots, rather like icing a cake. A lead glaze with a small amount of iron is applied to the surface, which when fired turns a distinctive yellow. Other ways of decorating include stamping, *sgraffito* (scratching through the slip to the body below), or press-molding complex designs. The use of molds, probably introduced in the mid-17th century, permitted less skilled draughtsmen to apply simple touches of slip to the raised design. Another type of decoration was marbling, achieved by partly mixing two different-colored slips while they were still in a fairly liquid state. Production included

pitchers, pie plates, salts, tygs (a type of large mug), and dishes. Thickly potted, most wares were boldly decorated with figures, animals, birds, or coats of arms. This latter type remained popular well into the 19th century, especially on oblong oven dishes. Some fine slipwares have the names of such potters as Thomas Toft (*d*.1689), Ralph Simpson (1651–1724), and William Taylor (*b.c*.1630) prominently displayed in the decoration. Because such documentary wares are very expensive, this type has been faked at least since the latter half of the 19th century.

TORTOISESHELL, AGATE, AND JACKFIELD WARE

Thomas Whieldon (1719–95) is usually associated with the production of tortoiseshell ware, although many potteries in north Staffordshire made similar wares from the mid-18th century. They are distinguished by the use of translucent colored glazes, only partially mixed, or mottled, to produce an effect suggested by their title. Combinations of manganese brown, copper green, and cobalt blue were used on domestic wares or figures. Agate ware differs from tortoiseshell in that, instead of differently colored glazes being mixed, it is made by mixing differently colored clays to produce an effect similar to hardstones – hence the name. First made *c*.1740, these salt- or lead-glazed wares were later developed by Josiah Wedgwood (1730–95). The term "Jackfield" has been traditionally given to a reddish-brown ware covered in a very glossy black glaze. This type of ware was probably first made in Jackfield, Shropshire, from *c*.1750, and later produced in many potteries in Staffordshire and elsewhere in the second and third quarters of the 18th century. Production was predominantly of hollow-ware decorated with molding, gilding, or enameling.

▼ Whieldon-type creamer
Milk-jugs modeled as cows were popular for almost 100 years from the mid-18th century, until it was discovered that they might be unhygienic. This is a fine example, covered in a semi-translucent tortoiseshell glaze. (c.1760; ht 14cm/5½in; value I)

▲ Toby jug by Ralph Wood
Toby jugs have been popular since they were first made in the 1760s. The many versions include the "Squire," and the "Thin Man," but this type, the "Toper," or ale drinker, is the most common. The earliest and best examples (such as this) show the feet protruding over the plinth. (c.1770–90; ht 25.5cm/10in; value H)

KEY FACTS

Slipware
- COLORED SLIPS dark brown, tan, and white
- FORMS dishes, tygs, puzzle jugs, and chargers
- DECORATION trailing, combing, marbling; designs: heraldic devices, figures, animals, birds, coats of arms

Tortoiseshell, agate, and Jackfield wares
- GLAZES tortoiseshell: mottled green, yellow, white, manganese, and blue; Jackfield: black and very shiny
- FORMS mainly tewares
- SPUR MARKS two or three left by supporting pins on the base of plates during firing
- DECORATION applied motifs, crabstock handles
- COLLECTING cow creamers are very popular

Toby jugs
- COLLECTING extremely popular area of collecting; Prattware types were made after *c*.1780; the most desirable are those of the so-called "Ralph Wood" type; the most typical and popular figure is the "Toper"

Marks
Slipware is generally unmarked; Toby jugs may have impressed marks such as "Ra WOOD BURSLEM" or paper labels

See also Wedgwood stoneware, p.166

Stoneware

British stoneware was probably first produced in London during the second half of the 17th century. Apart from the fine-bodied Wedgwood-type black basaltes and "jasper"-type wares there are three main types of British stoneware: gray-bodied, brown-glazed wares of Rhenish type; redware in the manner of Chinese Yixing stonewares; and white or off-white salt-glazed wares manufactured in several places including London, Nottingham, Bristol, and Staffordshire.

RHENISH WARE

The earliest datable material, from c.1660, was found at Woolwich, in London. John Dwight (c.1635–1703) was the first documented potter to make brown, salt-glazed Rhenish-style stoneware, and his production of more refined whitewares and red stonewares of the Yixing type began in 1672–3. Production in or near London was centered on Fulham and Mortlake and was generally based on German wares such as those from Cologne (including "bellarmines"), Raeren, and Westerwald. Wares include mugs, jugs, and tankards usually decorated with applied molded motifs or scratched decoration of hunting or drinking scenes. Brown wares continued to be made throughout the 18th and 19th centuries at Mortlake, Fulham, and Lambeth. This group is mostly decorated with applied reliefs under a two-tone brown wash.

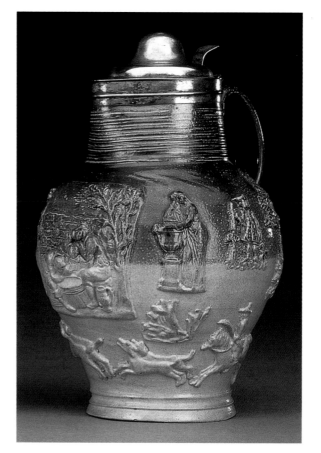

▲ Pecten-shell teapot from Staffordshire

Driven by the competition from porcelain, Staffordshire potters sought to make a more refined white stoneware. This scalloped teapot is a good example of their craft. It was molded by the slip-cast method, which resulted in an extremely thin-walled vessel. Most surviving salt-glazed wares of this type are undecorated, but here the crisp contors are picked out in enamel colors similar to the Chinese *famille-rose* palette.
(c.1750; ht 13cm/5in; value **G***)*

◄ Jug from Mortlake

Both Fulham and Mortlake produced similar types of ware throughout most of the 18th and the early 19th centuries. The two-toned appearance in which the upper register is covered with a dark, iron-brown wash is typical of this series. The jug is actually made of a gray, gritty body, visible only where the salt glaze has been chipped or worn away. Most examples were decorated with applied panels or figures of sporting or wassailing subjects. Many of these vessels are dated and inscribed with individuals' names. The fact that they often have silver lids or metal-sheathed rims suggests that they were treasured and used regularly throughout several generations. The tradition of these stonewares was carried on by Doulton's Lambeth factory, in London, which made bulbous jugs similarly molded in relief with hunting or harvesting scenes.
(c.1800; ht 25.5cm/10in; value **G***)*

REDWARE AND WHITEWARE

Probably introduced to the Staffordshire area by migrant potters, stoneware became more refined during the 18th century, culminating in the sophisticated Neo-classical wares of Josiah Wedgwood (1730–95). Traditionally it is believed that redware was introduced by the brothers John and David Elers from The Netherlands shortly after their arrival in London c.1686. It was strongly influenced by Chinese Yixing stonewares, which were imitated in the Netherlands. Output consisted almost exclusively of tea and coffeewares and other domestic tablewares. Because the body was so hard it could be decorated by engine-turning on a lathe (after c.1765), and by applying delicate sprigs of flowers or scrolled ornament to the smooth, matt body.

Redware was also made in Staffordshire, and is often erroneously described as "Elers ware." Some pieces are impressed with pseudo-Chinese seal marks on the base. This provincial type of redware fell out of favor in the latter half of the 18th century. White stoneware was probably developed in the third quarter of the 17th century. This fine ware could be slip-cast into fairly complicated forms, such as teapots in the form of shells, houses, or animals. Many examples are enameled, and some are transfer-printed. This type of ware was supplanted by Wedgwood's creamware in the late 1760s.

◄ Bear jug from Nottingham

Stoneware was produced in Nottingham for a little more than a hundred years, from the late 17th century until the early 19th. Finely wrought and thinly potted, Nottingham stoneware is usually covered in a smooth, lustrous glaze, or in tiny clay parings simulating fur, as on the bear illustrated. In Georgian Britain, bear-baiting was a popular entertainment.
(c.1750–1800; ht 23cm/9in; value **I***)*

KEY FACTS

- TYPES Rhenish type: gray-bodied; redwares: inspired by Chinese Yixing wares; white/gray wares: bodies became very refined during the 18th century
- GLAZE all wares were salt-glazed; surface has a granular "orange peel" texture
- FORMS mostly jugs, cylindrical tankards, teapots; flatwares were made only after c.1700
- DECORATION sprigging; applied panels of hunting or revelry, or sporting scenes, sometimes taken from printed sources such as Hogarth's *A Modern Midnight Conversation*; engine-turning on redwares; stamping; from the mid-18th century, enameling was used on white wares, mostly copying Chinese *famille-rose* wares; transfer-printing is rare
- MAIN CENTERS OF PRODUCTION London: Fulham, Lambeth, and Mortlake; Staffordshire; Nottingham

Marks

Apart from inscriptions and dates, stonewares are unmarked

See also Germany: Stoneware, p.158

Creamware and pearlware

In the 18th century Staffordshire became the most important area for the manufacture of everyday pottery. Tin-glazed earthenware, for centuries the European staple, was never made there, and very little porcelain was produced before the late 18th century. From the late 17th century north Staffordshire potters gradually refined their wares, until by the middle of the century they were making some of the finest pottery in Europe.

CREAMWARE

Thomas Astbury (1686–1743), Enoch Booth, and Josiah Wedgwood (1730–95) are all associated with the invention and development of creamware (cream-colored earthenware). By the 1760s Wedgwood's creamware was sufficiently developed to excite the interest of Queen Charlotte, who ordered a tea service (1765), and it was subsequently renamed "Queen's ware." For the next 100 years, creamware remained the standard pottery body in Britain and throughout much of continental Europe and North America. The close-grained body was composed of clay from Devon mixed with flint and covered in a very thin but smooth lead glaze. It could be finely molded or cut with great detail. Graymore, it was very receptive to underglaze blue, overglaze enameling, or printing. English creamware includes ornamental wares and sophisticated pierced wares, which were made in Staffordshire and Leeds, and also figures. However, most of the output was of more mundane items such as dinner services, tablewares, and teawares. The versatility of creamware and its acceptance among the higher classes of European society (the 926-piece "Frog" service was made by Wedgwood for Catherine the Great of Russia in 1773–4) ensured its financial success, as well as undermining virtually the entire European tin-glazed pottery tradition.

PEARLWARE AND PRATTWARE

Introduced by Wedgwood *c*.1779 as an improvement on his creamware, pearlware includes more white clay and flint in the body than creamware does. Suggesting an iridescent appearance, "pearlware" is a misleading term; the addition of cobalt oxide to the glaze imparted a bluish-white cast, which is particularly visible where there is pooling. Much pearlware is decorated in underglaze blue by painting or, later, by transfer-printing. Among the most famous printed themes are versions of the "Willow" pattern. In the early 19th century, manufacturers broadened the range of patterns to include Classical designs and English landscapes.

Prattware is associated with the Pratt family from Lane Delph in Staffordshire, although it was also made by a number of other factories. The body is similar to pearlware in weight and color, but the ware is distinguished by a strong, high-temperature palette comprising ocher, brown, green, and blue. Wares include molded teapots, jugs, and figures. From the 1840s the firm of F. & R. Pratt & Co. was famous for multicolored printing, used extensively on pot lids.

◄ Fruit-basket and stand
The pieces shown are very good examples of creamware: the oval dish has been transfer-printed over the glaze with peacocks and other exotic birds in a Chinese-style landscape. The original print for this was produced in Liverpool, where from the 1760s there was a considerable industry for the production of engravings to be used on ceramics. Based on a Rococo silver form, the basket has been skilfully pierced with florets and trellis in the manner of the Chinese "devil's work" popular toward the end of the Ming Dynasty.
(late 18th century; w. of stand 25.5cm/10in; value F)

◄ Jug from Leeds
The scattered sprigs of European flowers on this pearlware jug are the final phase in a long tradition of decoration started at the Meissen porcelain factory *c*.1740. The puce diaper border is derived from contemporary Chinese export porcelain.
(c.1800; ht 20cm/8in; value D)

▲ Figure of a dandy
Late 18th-century pottery figures included biblical and allegorical subjects, actors, and rustics. While the posture is strongly Rococo, the base is decorated with a band of stiff leaves – a favored Neo-classical ornament.
(c.1790; ht 26.5cm/10½in; value F)

KEY FACTS

Creamware
- BODY cream, thin, and lightweight
- GLAZE ivory-tinted lead glaze
- FORMS ornamental Neo-classical wares, tablewares, and more rarely figures
- DECORATION underglaze blue, overglaze enamels, or transfer printing

Pearlware
- BODY white flinty earthenware
- GLAZE bluish glaze to counteract the cream body
- FORMS mainly useful wares: dishes, plates, teapots, coffee-pots, and jugs
- DECORATION usually painted or printed underglaze blue of English landscapes, Grand Tour ruins, etc.

Prattware
- BODY similar to pearlware
- PALETTE high-fired colors: ocher, yellow, brown, green, and blue
- FORMS jugs, teapots, and figures

Marks
The practice of marking pottery became more widespread from *c*.1800; some factories impressed their marks, but the majority are transfer-printed in underglaze blue; in addition the factory might also supply the title of the pattern on the back

Wedgwood: mark used on creamware   WEDGWOOD

Leeds: impressed mark for the firm of Hartley, Greens & Co. (1800–30)   LEEDS.POTTERY

See also Lead-glazed ware, p.163; Wedgwood stoneware, p.166

Wedgwood stoneware

Josiah Wedgwood (1730–95) almost single-handedly transformed British pottery-making into a highly mechanized industry, which supplied fine ceramic wares to a worldwide market. Throughout his life Wedgwood researched and experimented tirelessly with materials and methods of manufacture. The enormous success of his factory was owed not only to his artistic abilities but also to the realization that a wide-based market catering for all levels of society was the key to advancement in such an erratic profession.

From 1754 to 1759 Wedgwood worked in partnership with the potter Thomas Whieldon (1719–95), making experimental and tortoiseshell wares. Because of a leg injury Wedgwood was unable to practice as a potter, and therefore spent much of his time developing pottery bodies and glazes, making very detailed recordings of his discoveries. By 1759 he had set up his own business at the Ivy House Works in Burslem, Staffordshire, where he made redware, Whieldon-type ware with translucent lead glazes, blackware, salt-glazed stoneware, and creamware (cream-colored earthenware). In 1769 he formed a partnership with the Liverpool merchant Thomas Bentley, and opened a bigger factory called "Etruria" (after Etruscan pottery, which inspired some of the factory's production). During the ensuing decade, until Bentley's death in 1780, the company expanded and consolidated its position at the forefront of the market.

▲ Spittoon

The fine-bodied black basalte stoneware perfected by Wedgwood c.1768 was made by staining the stoneware body with cobalt and manganese oxides. Wedgwood was one of the first potters to employ an engine-turned lathe to apply decorative finishes to his work. This simple globular spittoon (also called a "cuspidor") has been cut with shallow vertical channels, and the central band is decorated with a cross-cut pattern. Both these types of embellishment were used by Wedgwood from c.1770.
(early 19th century; ht 12.5cm/5in; value E)

NEO-CLASSICAL STONEWARE

By the 1760s Britain was in the early stages of Neo-classical fever, exemplified in the work of the Adam brothers in architecture, and greatly stimulated by the excavations of the Classical ruins at Herculaneum and Pompeii that had begun in 1738 and 1748 respectively. Seeking to capitalize on the popularity of the Neo-classical style, Wedgwood worked on the refinement of his stonewares throughout the 1760s and 1770s. His first success (c.1768) was black basalte, a fine-grained, unglazed stoneware stained with cobalt and manganese oxides. This type of ware was sometimes decorated with red figures, a style inspired by ancient Greek pottery.

◄ Cachepot

Jasper tricolor ware is relatively scarce, and even small uncomplicated examples such as this cachepot are much sought after by collectors. Tricolor wares were first made during the 1780s. The decoration was often arranged in a grid-like or trellis design (called a "dice pattern"), with the bars and niches applied with delicate jasper quatrefoils and floral scrolls. Here the decorator has used sage green and yellow on a white ground; the range of available stains included a deeper green, dark blue, and lilac. A cachepot is similar to a *jardinière* and serves the same purpose; it is an ornamental container used to conceal a more utilitarian plant pot (the name is derived from the French *cacher*, to hide).
(late 18th/early 19th century; ht 31cm/12in; value G)

Other types of stoneware made include "*rosso antico*," a red-bodied ware largely based on Classical forms, and the yellow-bodied "caneware." However, the most famous type of Wedgwood stoneware is the hard, fine-grained, unglazed "jasper" ware introduced in 1774–5, typically with applied white decoration of Classical figures and motifs. John Flaxman (1755–1826), George Stubbs (1724–1806), and other artists produced designs for ornamental wares, including vases, plaques, cameos, and medallions, based on the illustrations of the excavated Greek and Roman material.

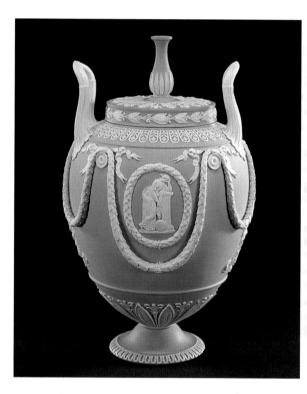

▲ Vase

This type of Neo-classical vase in blue jasper ware was one of the most popular of all Wedgwood's productions. The medallion encloses the Classical figure of Urania, the Muse of astronomy.
(early 19th century; ht 41cm/16in; value H)

KEY FACTS

- **BODY** silky, fine grained, and unglazed
- **FORMS** mostly Neo-classical in style; ornamental vases and urns; portrait plaques; busts; some teawares
- **COLORS** jasper: first colored all the way through the body and later as a surface wash only, in pale blue, sage green, olive green, lilac, lavender, and black; *rosso antico*: a refinement of the existing Staffordshire redware made by the Elers brothers; caneware: yellow wares made by Wedgwood and other Staffordshire potters from the 1770s
- **DECORATION** the stoneware body is capable of taking extremely fine detail; early wares are more detailed than later wares; black basalte is often ornamented with engine-turned ornament; sprigged Neo-classical motifs and mythological figures are typical

Marks

Pre-Etruria wares are rarely marked, but thereafter most wares are impressed with the name; "WEDGWOOD" used after c.1820

wedgwood

Ironstone and transfer-printed wares

In the 19th century, British manufacturers were pre-eminent in the production of functional, durable, and decorative ceramic tableware. Large factories with streamlined production methods made use of transfer-printing, which enabled every piece to be identically decorated to a high standard. Pearlware, widely used from the 1780s, was improved to create a generic type of white earthenware that could be potted evenly and inexpensively.

IRONSTONE AND STONE CHINA

The durable British earthenware services came to supplant the more delicate Chinese porcelain for everyday use both in Britain and abroad. Customers still wanted "Oriental" patterns, and Japanese and Chinese designs were combined in styles called "Indian" or "Japan," with their roots in British wares of the Regency period. In 1813, at Fenton in Staffordshire, Charles James Mason (1791–1856) patented a durable white stoneware body under the name "Mason's Patent Ironstone China." From the 1820s to the 1840s other Staffordshire manufacturers produced similar wares with names such as "Granite China" and "Stone China." The use of the name "china" was blatantly misleading, because these wares were forms of earthenware. To satisfy demand, many Staffordshire factories grew to an enormous size, employing a vast workforce that kept the kilns burning all year round, producing huge quantities of ware for both the home and the export markets.

BLUE-AND-WHITE PRINTED WARES

Ironstone, with its bright colors and occasional gilded decoration, was more expensive than plain blue-and-white wares. Underglaze blue, transfer-printed ware was the staple product of British potteries as far apart as northeastern England, Scotland, the West Country, and South Wales, but it is with the Staffordshire potteries that mass-produced blue-and-white dinner services and other domestic wares are most closely associated. Because the printed patterns were applied beneath the glaze, the design cannot wear off nor the colors fade, with the result that most pieces look as fresh today as when they were made.

▲ Tureen with cover and stand

This tureen is from a large Mason's Patent Ironstone China dinner service comprising dinner plates and various tureens and dishes. The vegetation is in a Chinese *famille-rose* design of c.1755, a popular form of decoration on British Ironstone dinnerwares. The basic design was first transfer-printed and then hand-colored with the low-firing enamel colors. The painting was often carried out by children employed as cheap labor in the Staffordshire factories. This service has impressed and printed factory marks, assisting identification.
(*c.1825; ht 20cm/8in; value of tureen* **E**)

◄ Card-rack

The underglaze blue and the overglaze red and gilded designs of large peonies above zigzag fences on this Mason's Ironstone card-rack were inspired by ornamentation used on brightly colored porcelain exported from the Japanese port of Imari from the middle of the 17th century. Such designs, which often entirely covered the piece, were known during the Regency period as "Japan" patterns. This rare, and therefore highly desirable, unmarked shape can be identified as Mason's Ironstone from the very good quality of the decoration, although it is a little worn in places.
(*c.1820; ht 9.5cm/4in; value* **G**)

The largest producer of blue-and-white printed ware was the Spode factory (est. 1776) in Stoke-on-Trent, where every piece was made to a very high standard. Spode had begun by copying Chinese-style patterns, which were very popular. The demand for English pottery increased when mass imports of Chinese porcelain were suspended c.1800 because the British china dealers had attempted to form a cartel to keep prices artificially low. Gradually new designs were introduced, including views of British stately homes, and American and Indian scenes.

THE "WILLOW" PATTERN

One of the most popular transfer-printed designs, the "Willow" pattern was made by dozens of potteries throughout Britain. The pattern depicts the lovers Koon-see and Chang fleeing their oppressors and being transformed into doves. This "ancient" fable has long delighted owners of Willow services, but in fact it was invented in Britain in order to sell Staffordshire dinner services. Often incorrectly attributed to the Caughley factory (est. c.1772–5), Shropshire, the original pattern was adapted from various Chinese porcelain designs and may have been first used at Spode. Caughley did not make Willow-pattern wares. The design was made in many different versions, and was eventually copied in both China and Japan.

▼ Willow-pattern platter from Staffordshire

This is a standard Willow-pattern platter, with the unusual addition of the name of the original owner.
(*c.1815–20; w. 36cm/14in; value* **C**)

KEY FACTS

- **BODY** a broad range of durable earthenwares and stonewares called by such names as "Ironstone," "Stone China," and "Granite China"
- **DECORATION** mostly transfer-printing; chinoiseries (including the Willow pattern), sporting scenes, Imari- and *famille-rose*-inspired palettes and motifs, and landscapes

Marks

C.J. Mason & Co.: mark used for Mason's Patent Ironstone China

Spode: mark used on blue-and-white and some stone china **SPODE**

See also Creamware and pearlware, p.165

Staffordshire figures

The popularity of porcelain figures in Britain during the 19th century led to a demand for less expensive imitations for the mass market, and the Staffordshire potteries obliged by making exact reproductions of the fine-quality figures made by porcelain factories such as Derby. The rustic charm of Staffordshire figures proved popular at the time, and successive generations have continued to enjoy collecting these generally inexpensive mantelpiece ornaments.

BOCAGE AND SQUARE-BASED FIGURES

The products of John Walton's factory in Burslem (active 1810–30s) were typical of early 19th-century Staffordshire figures. Copying the tradition set by Chelsea and Derby, the factory included flowering trees, a feature known as "*bocage*," behind its figures. Classical deities and allegorical figures (such as the

popular set of three female figures representing "Faith," "Hope," and "Charity"), aimed at more educated customers, were usually mounted on the same style of square base edged with a brown line. Rustic groups of children playing and shepherdesses were mounted on similar bases or on raised green mounds with streams. Biblical characters proved immensely popular, especially "Elijah and the Widow." One distinctive type of group, mounted on "table bases" (scroll-footed platforms), is conventionally referred to as being by Obadiah Sherratt (*d*.1841) after a potter who worked in Burslem from *c*.1815; however, it is now considered unlikely that Sherratt was responsible for the unmarked table-based models usually ascribed to him.

CHARACTERS AND FAMOUS PEOPLE

Victorian Staffordshire figures were intended to be viewed on a mantelpiece from the front only, and consequently the backs were neither modeled nor painted: hence the name "flatbacks" for such pieces. Many figures were simple but highly decorative images of children or lovers. However, from the 1840s there was a demand for portraits of famous people, whose features were copied from journals or the covers of popular printed music. In an age when the public rarely knew what famous people truly looked like, potters sometimes reused discontinued molds to represent more topical individuals. Some figures were even wrongly named, such as a portrait of Benjamin Franklin labeled as George Washington.

Some popular figures were produced for many years and often require a close examination to determine whether they are earlier or later examples; this can greatly affect the value. There are many fake Staffordshire figures on the market, and it is important to learn the correct "feel" of genuine pieces, and to buy only from reputable dealers or auctioneers.

▲ Boy and "zebra"
This "flatback" figure portrays a schoolboy with a horse that has curiously been painted to resemble a zebra. Flatback figures have little or no modeling on the back, a feature that made them easy to mass-produce. It was assumed that flatback pieces would stand on a mantelpiece above a fireplace, and this piece incorporates a spill vase at the back to hold the rolled-paper spills that were used in the 19th century for lighting the fire.
(mid-19th century; ht 24cm/9½in; value C)

▲ The *Eloping Couple*
This elaborately modemodeled Staffordshire group is of the "table-base" type associated – erroneously, it is now believed – with a potter called Obadiah Sherratt, who is said to have specialized in such figures. This charming group depicts a couple being married by a blacksmith in Gretna Green, Dumfriesshire, a Scottish town on the border with England. Between 1753 and 1856, when the English marriage law was tightened, Gretna Green was the scene of many such weddings. Couples eloped from England to marry in Scotland, where they merely needed to declare their wishes before a blacksmith or lock-keeper. The clothes worn by the two figures in this group would have been fashionable in the 1820s.
(c.1830; ht 20cm/8in; value H)

ORIGINAL AND FAKE STAFFORDSHIRE

▼ Two groups of musicians
These two groups look very similar, but the well-modeled and strongly colored example on the left is an original, while that on the right is a reproduction by the firm of William Kent, whose factory (est. c.1870) in Burslem continued potting until 1962 using original Victorian molds. The coloring of the copy is paler and less detailed than that of the original and has been artificially aged with the addition of crazing and scratches.
(c.1820 and c.1920; ht 23cm/9in; values F and B)

KEY FACTS

- FORMS pairs of animals (very popular from the 1840s), portraits of royalty, politicians, military and naval heroes, sportsmen, theatrical celebrities, religious figures, notorious villains
- CENTERS OF PRODUCTION most figures were made in the towns centered around Stoke-on-Trent, although a number were made in north-eastern England and Scotland
- COLLECTING a pair of figures will always be worth more than twice the price of a single piece; later examples are less sharply molded than the originals, with particularly crude painting
- REPRODUCTIONS AND FAKES fake Staffordshire figures are frequently made of pure white porcelain, stained to look old; "crazing" – a network of tiny cracks or veins in the surface glaze – affects most old figures, and fakers sometimes go to such lengths to reproduce it that they over-emphasize; the resulting effect is too regular and pronounced

Marks
Only a few Victorian Staffordshire figures are marked in any way, but research can identify some factories; earlier figures by John Walton and Ralph Salt (both active early 19th century) have their names impressed into a strap of clay at the back of the base

See also Fakes and forgeries, pp.126–7

Majolica

Although the English word "majolica" derives from "maiolica," the term for Italian tin-glazed pottery, the inspiration for this purely Victorian phenomenon in fact came from several quarters: not only Italian Renaissance pottery but also the pottery of the Frenchman Bernard Palissy (c.1510–90), who was famous for dishes with realistically applied reptiles, crustacea, and vegetation. Closer to home, the pottery of the Staffordshire makers Thomas Whieldon (1719–95) and Ralph Wood (1715–72) was also influential. Elements of each of these were combined in the late 1840s into a decorative ceramics material that enjoyed great popularity in mid-Victorian Britain. Majolica was also made in France, Germany, and the USA, where it is popular with collectors.

IMPORTANT PRODUCERS

Majolica was produced by many small manufacturers, but three Staffordshire factories – Minton & Co. (est. 1798), Wedgwood (est. 1759), and George Jones & Sons (est. 1861) – dominated the market and between them account for most of today's collectible pieces. Minton and Wedgwood, the largest makers of ornamental pottery in Staffordshire, made excellent majolica ware, and indeed both claimed to have invented it. Monumental pieces by Minton astounded visitors at such important international exhibitions as the Great Exhibition of 1851 in London. Huge fountains with life-sized human and animal figures formed centerpieces at the major trade shows, surrounded by other furnishings and sometimes by whole tiled rooms that glowed with the colored glazes. Such pieces were too expensive for profitable production and were intended primarily to enhance the companies' prestige at such events. The third important maker is less well known outside this specialist field. George Jones & Sons in Stoke-on-Trent produced some of the finest majolica, but made little else of note and consequently had nothing to fall back on when the fashion for majolica declined at the end of the 19th century. Other British factories that produced majolica, but as a sideline to their mainstream production, include Spode (under the name of Copeland, from the 1840s to the 20th century) in Stoke-on-Trent, and the Worcester Royal Porcelain Co. (est. 1862).

COLOR, GLAZE, AND TYPES

Majolica colors are not enameled but are contained within the substance of the glaze. They are applied either as separate colored glazes or as stains painted onto the body that are picked up by the viscous lead glazes. A sign of good-quality manufacture is that the glazes are well controlled, without blurring or dribbling. The usual majolica palette is blue (including a vivid turquoise), green, yellow, orange, black, and brown.

Majolica wares include *jardinières* of every size and proportion, conservatory seats, vases, dishes, teapots, and tureens. To suit the high Victorian taste, factories vied with each other to cram ornament onto their wares, leading to the creation of extraordinary objects that are both beautiful and bizarre. Such pieces are not to everyone's taste, but after years of neglect majolica is now keenly collected and can be surprisingly highly priced. Nothing exemplifies the frivolity of majolica better than the range of eccentric teapots made by Minton and George Jones in the shape of Chinese people, monkeys, boats, fish, and cats. However, most were too costly for everyday use and survive because they were kept largely for display; some of these pieces fetch very high prices at auction.

▶ *Jardinière* **by Wedgwood**
This *jardinière*, one of a pair designed as containers for ferns or aspidistras in a conservatory, displays molded ornament in the "Japanesque" taste (popular at the end of the 19th century) against checkered grounds. *(1883; ht 21.5cm/8½in; value for a pair I)*

▲ **Vase and cover by Minton & Co.**
This large ornamental vase is decorated in typical high Victorian taste, inspired by the designs of the Renaissance. Well modeled and superbly glazed in a typical, strong, majolica palette, the piece incorporates three seated Bacchic figures (one unseen here), rams' heads, and thick leafy swags, with a cherub on the finial, and such Classical motifs as the Greek key pattern. *(1864; ht 63cm/24¾in; value J)*

◀ **Cheese bell by George Jones & Sons**
Molded daisies, fern-like leaves, and a crabstock handle adorn this very fresh-looking majolica cheese bell. The colored glazes are well controlled, and the underside is typically mottled in brown, giving a tortoiseshell-like effect. This type of decorative tableware was made in large quantities by the important English majolica manufacturers and is very popular among collectors today. *(c.1875; ht 21cm/8¼in; value I)*

KEY FACTS

- GLAZES semi-transparent lead
- PALETTE blue, green, yellow, brown, black, orange
- FORMS domestic wares: teapots, dishes, jugs, vases, dessert baskets, tazzas, centerpieces; umbrella stands; garden ornaments
- DECORATION highly ornamented with an eclectic range
- COLLECTING an exhibition in 1982 organized by the dealers Jeremy Cooper Ltd in London ignited interest in majolica and caused the international collector's market to take off
- FAKES collectors should beware of unmarked pieces by minor makers that have been doctored by the addition of the Minton name etched or engraved through the glaze, in an attempt to pass them off as originals

Marks

Most of the larger producers marked their pieces; marks were usually impressed into the clay under the glaze and can therefore be difficult to see; George Jones & Sons did not always employ a company mark, but did use a distinctive design number, painted in black, usually positioned in the middle of the underside of the pieces; Wedgwood and Minton also impressed date marks into their pieces

George Jones & Sons (est. 1861)

See also Italy, pp.152–4; The United States, pp.170–71

The United States

The manufacture of earthenware by early colonists in North America began as a cottage industry and never grew on a scale consistent with the rapid growth in population and technology in the USA over the last 200 years. The relatively minor impact of domestically produced American pottery may be considered a testament to the extraordinarily high standards of European earthenwares, particularly the products of Staffordshire, which have been exported in enormous quantities since the declaration of American independence (1776). Although a few distinctly American forms and types of decoration emerged during the 19th century, the only pottery that can be considered uniquely American is that made by the Native Americans, the earliest examples of which pre-date European settlement by thousands of years.

▲ Dish attributed to the Smith Pottery
The coloration, cogle-wheel-cut "piecrust" rim, and "pretzel" slip decoration seen on this redware plate are all characteristic of Connecticut slipware. The large size and good condition will affect the value.
(c.1825; diam. 40cm/18in; value G)

EARLY POTTERY

Any domestically produced American pottery made before the mid-18th century is extremely rare. American pottery of this period is limited to simple, thickly potted red or buff earthenware. As the population grew in north-eastern America during the second half of the 18th century, distinctive pottery types were manufactured, all of which were useful. An industry developed for the manufacture of salt-glazed stoneware, which was superior to the porous and brittle common earthenwares. Early American stoneware (pre-1800) was mainly produced by German immigrants in the south-eastern states of Virginia and Georgia.

"Yellow-ware" describes any type of earthenware with an opaque, yellow glaze. This glaze was used in North America throughout the 19th century to make utilitarian wares including mixing bowls or "pans" (deep dishes for cooling milk). Of greater interest is slipware, sometimes erroneously termed "Pennsylvania slipware", which refers to red-bodied (or occasionally buff) earthenware,

made largely in Connecticut, decorated with trailed slip, usually of ocher or chocolate brown. Common forms are deep plates, "pans," and pie dishes, which are often worn through extended use, and so of little value. Common decoration is abstract, but additional inscriptions, dates, figural images, or highly accomplished patterns are particularly sought after.

"Spongeware" and "spatterware" were made throughout the 19th century and describe household mixing bowls, teaware, and platters with random, mottled patterns, typically in pale blues and yellows. Small plates and mugs (often made in Staffordshire) with spattered borders and naïvely painted farm animals or figures are extremely popular. "Mochaware" is of comparable collectibility and interest, especially early 19th-century examples. The term describes glazed earthenware with "tree" forms in the pale glaze, which are caused by the capillary action of the brown slip. Mugs and jugs, most of which were originally made in Staffordshire for the North American market, are typical.

STONEWARE

Most North American stoneware of the 19th century was made in the north-eastern state of Vermont, principally by the Norton family of Bennington. The high standards and successful forms of Norton's stoneware were imitated throughout New England until the beginning of the 20th century, when stoneware became virtually obsolete. Two standard forms of "Bennington crock" were made (one of simple cylinder form with "ear" handles, and one of jug type) for the storage and transport of liquids, including apple cider, ale, and maple syrup. Other forms include covered pots, chamber-pots, spittoons, water coolers, and jugs, some of which were coated in brown glaze.

◄ Crock made by the Norton family
This salt-glazed stoneware crock (water cooler) would originally have been fitted with a spigot. The bold decoration is very typical of the later 19th-century pieces, many of which are signed with the maker's or retailer's name above the ornament, which is typically in underglaze blue. Unusual or particularly fine decoration is the key to the value of crocks.
(c.1880; ht 40cm/18in; value H)

▼ Vase probably from Bennington or East Liverpool
Modeled in the shape of a fireman's trumpet, this Rockingham-glazed vase is uniquely North American, and is a typical example of this form of inexpensive ornamental ware. Rockingham-glazed pieces may be lustrous and streaked, as seen here. Collectors prefer early examples of figural type, such as pairs of dogs or lions. Some pieces bear marks of the United States Pottery of Bennington, active from c.1840.
(c.1890; ht 36cm/14in; value D)

Decoration on American stoneware was rare before *c.*1830 and varied only subtly for the rest of the 19th century. It is typically in underglaze cobalt blue painted in a naïve manner, sometimes over a scratched design. Usual images include flowers (least collectible), insects, ornamental numerals, birds, animals, landscapes, and commemorative designs, the latter being among the most desirable. Some types of decoration are characteristic of a particular potter or date; for example, butterflies are associated with the Norton family in the 1830s.

LATER POTTERY

In the late 19th century American commercial potters were established well beyond New England. New centers included Pittsburgh and other towns in Pennsylvania and neighboring Ohio; Baltimore, Maryland; New York City; and Trenton in New Jersey, which by the 1880s was known as the "Staffordshire of America." The output consisted entirely of utilitarian pieces. Much was in the form of "granite ware," a highly practical, heavy, white earthenware of ironstone type, which was often left undecorated. Typical examples, which are common owing to the robust nature of the ware, include tureens and tableware of all types, comparable to contemporary Staffordshire but larger in scale. Most tableware in daily use took the form of inexpensive transfer-printed wares imported from Staffordshire, the most collectible of which are those decorated with American scenes.

Rockingham-glaze ware – earthenware with a rich, sometimes lustrous, brown glaze – was produced extensively in the USA at this time, notably by the United States Pottery of Bennington, Vermont, founded by Christopher Fenton *c.*1840 and active throughout the century. Most examples are slip-cast, relief-molded hollow-wares, including jugs, figural flasks, spittoons, furniture rests, and statuary. Pairs of "chimney dogs" (based on Staffordshire models but larger in scale) and recumbent lions are characteristic of the Bennington pottery and most desirable.

A uniquely American and fairly rare naïve pottery, consisting of unusual "pinched" forms with applications under green glaze, was made by settlers in the Shenandoah Valley of the Virginias in the mid-19th century. The wares are well-potted, and innovative examples may bear scratched signatures or monograms. Much more common and widely collected is American majolica, which was produced at several factories from the 1860s until the beginning of the 20th century. The best majolica was made by the firm of Griffen, Smith & Hill (1867–1902) in Phoenixville, Pennsylvania.

NATIVE AMERICAN POTTERY

The majority of 19th-century Native American pottery that appears on the market today was made in the states of the south-western USA by nations including the Hopi, the Navajo, and the Acoma. Most wares are unglazed terracotta, and all items are of traditional design and manufacture – either coil-formed or thrown. Decoration is typically painted, with geometric patterns in faded earth tones. Collecting Native American pottery is a rapidly growing area of interest, and examples that can be dated to before the centennial of 1876 are especially sought after. However, dating can be very difficult owing to the continuous production of the traditional forms.

▼ **"Etruscan" majolica butter-pats by Griffen, Smith & Hill**
Tiny butter-pats were a popular 19th-century American majolica product and are very collectible today. The "shell and seaweed" pattern featured on the upper pat is very common. The lower example shows an impressed "GSH" monogram, which appears on some of this factory's ware, sometimes including the trademark "ETRUSCAN" or a design number with prefix "E".
(c.1880; diam. 8cm/3in; value of individual pieces **C**)

▲ **Storage jar made by the Acoma**
Native American pots made before *c.*1920 are thin-walled, light, and brittle, with delicate decoration in earth tones, often painted over a white slip covering a red body.
(c.1890; ht 25.5cm/10in; value **I**)

KEY FACTS

Early pottery
- YELLOW-WARE very collectible, particularly among admirers of folk art, but few pieces have significant value, and many are of European origin
- SLIPWARE well-decorated pieces are most desirable
- SPONGEWARE AND SPATTERWARE reproduction and restoration are quite common
- SIZE American wares are generally larger and more heavily potted than contemporary English wares
- COLLECTING early wares are very rare and are usually so worn that they have relatively little value; examples that bear dates, are well decorated, and are unusual in form or decoration will raise collector interest

Stoneware
- COLLECTING made in large quantities; the most desirable are pieces with unusual decoration

Later pottery
- COLLECTING Rockingham-glazed wares are valuable if the form is unusual and figural; English majolica is more popular than American majolica in the USA

Native American pottery
- COLLECTING wares are difficult to date and are often in fairly poor condition
- MARKS signed examples are usually 20th century

Marks
Bennington: Julius Norton & Co.; impressed mark, *c.*1845

J. NORTON & CO.
BENNINGTON
V.T.

Phoenixville: Griffen, Smith & Hill; impressed mark for majolica and earthenware, *c.*1878–89

Griffen, Smith & Hill; impressed mark for majolica, *c.*1879

ETRUSCAN

See also Lead-glazed ware, p.163; Majolica, p.169

Porcelain

The great secret and success story of the Far East, porcelain was discovered a thousand years before the establishment of the ceramics industry in the West. Its properties were envied and widely imitated, but never matched, and its quality far outstripped that of early Western ceramic production, which was based on stoneware. The first examples of Chinese porcelain arrived in Europe in the early 1500s and caused a near-revolution in the ceramics world, resulting in a thriving export industry from the East that had far-reaching effects on trade. Today, examples of fine-quality porcelain from both the East and the West command the highest prices, and many museums around the world have outstanding collections.

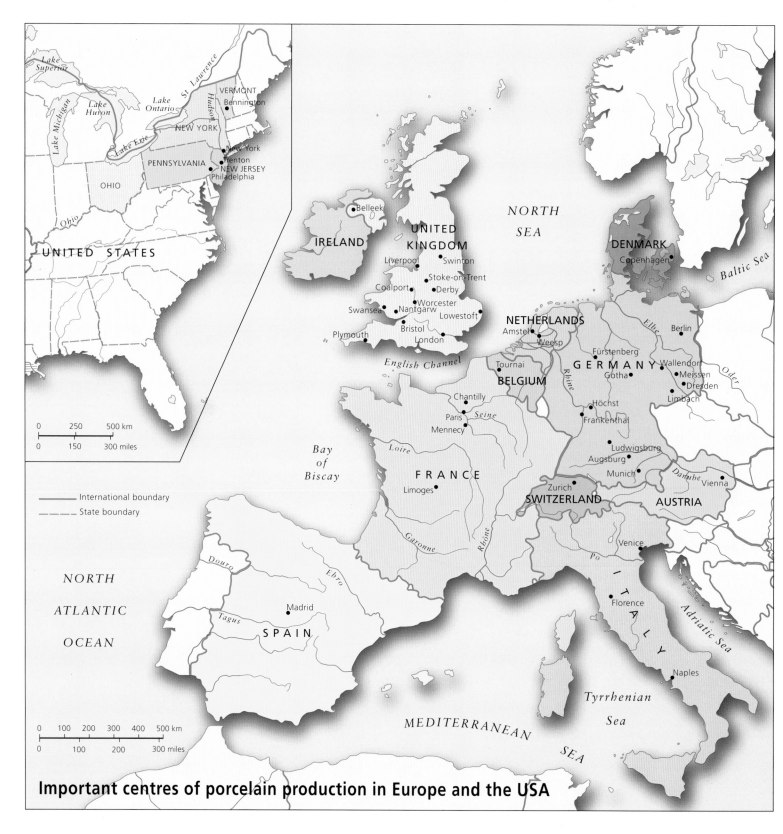

Important centres of porcelain production in Europe and the USA

Germany before 1800

Early Meissen

Imported from the Middle Ages through trade with China, Oriental porcelain was a rare and expensive commodity in Europe. As demand for (and imports of) porcelain became greater, alchemists in the courts of Europe attempted to discover the formula to create "true," or hard-paste, porcelain. The production of the first European hard-paste porcelain was the result of a collaboration between the alchemist Johann Friedrich Böttger (1682–1719) and the scientist Ehrenfried Walther von Tschirnhausen (1651–1708) at the court of Augustus the Strong, Elector of Saxony, in Dresden.

EXPERIMENTAL WARES

Böttger had become famous for his claims that he was on the brink of producing artificial gold. His experiments in this regard failed, but his fame and talents were such that Augustus seized Böttger after he fled from Prussia to Saxony and ordered him to help in von Tschirnhausen's porcelain experiments. The basic formula, which was discovered c.1706–7, produced a fine, brownish-red stoneware. After further experimentation in 1708, Böttger finally produced a white hard paste, and in 1710 Augustus established Europe's first hard-paste porcelain factory in the Albrechtsburg, a palace in Meissen.

Böttger's stoneware was an extremely hard and finely textured material, and is sometimes described as "*Jaspisporzellan*" ("jasper porcelain") because of its resemblance to hardstone. The types of ware produced included and coffee- and teapots, bowls, teacups, and teajars, often imitating Oriental porcelain. One of the first artists to be involved in the modeling of this stoneware was the court goldsmith Johann Jakob Irminger (1635–1724), and many stoneware pieces were based on gold and silver designs. As the material was so hard, typical decoration included polishing or faceting – techniques derived from gem-cutting – although lacquering, enameling, and gilding were also used.

EARLY PORCELAIN

Early Meissen porcelain ("*Böttgerporzellan*"), first produced commercially c.1713, generally followed the stoneware forms, but technical developments at the factory led to a greater range of wares: statuettes of dwarves and saints, copies of Chinese *blanc-de-Chine* wares, and "pagoda" figures. The porcelain was often left white to display the precious material, but some pieces have molded leaf or floral borders, thickly applied and clumsily drawn polychrome enamels, or gilt or silvered scrollwork borders. While all Böttger porcelain is rare, figures and enameled pieces are particularly scarce.

During the 1720s there were rapid technical and artistic advances in the development of porcelain at Meissen, due in part to the arrival in 1720 of the color-chemist and painter Johann Gregorius Höroldt (1696–1775). In the early 1720s, under his leadership, a new source of clay was found from which a slightly creamy white paste was produced. This was used to make a much wider range of wares, including vases, garnitures, bottles copied from Japanese originals, and small vessels with covers, as well as tea and coffeewares.

During the 1720s Höroldt perfected the enameling process, increasing the range of colors. Until the early 1730s the factory owed its success to the skilled painters who copied or adapted Oriental porcelain decoration and eventually developed a distinctive European style of painting. In the early 1720s, underglaze blue decoration was used for copying Chinese originals in the style of wares made during the reign of Emperor Kangxi (1662–1722), and polychrome enamels were employed for making exact copies of Chinese and Japanese wares, including those in the Imari and Kakiemon palettes. Höroldt also produced his own designs for vignettes and chinoiserie scenes. During the mid-1720s the first European-style landscape decoration was introduced; the scenes are typically set within heavy gilt scrollwork cartouches, often embellished with colored enamels. The factory also introduced *Kauffahrtei* ("sea trade") scenes of quaysides, although these became more common in the 1730s.

▲ Beaker and saucer by Johann Gregorius Höroldt
Höroldt's early chinoiserie scenes were painted in a wide range of colors and surrounded by gilt borders embellished in iron red and puce, typical of the Baroque style. The background on early pieces usually took the form of a painted sky; on later pieces it was left white.
(1723–4; ht of beaker 7cm/2¾in; value I)

▼ Coffee-pot and cover
The rectilinear body and the heavy scrolled handle of this coffee-pot are reminiscent of contemporary gold- and silverware. Like pieces of Oriental porcelain, it is also mounted with precious metal around the top rim and foot, while the use of faceting, a technique derived from gem cutting, is clearly evident on the body.
(1715; ht 15cm/6in; value O)

KEY FACTS

Stoneware c.1709–18
- BODY extremely hard, finely textured, mostly brownish red but sometimes almost iron gray or black
- DECORATION polishing, faceting, and other gem-cutting techniques; lacquering, enameling, or gilding (often worn or flaking)

Marks
Generally unmarked, but some pieces have black enamel inventory numbers on the foot

Porcelain c.1710–20
- BODY creamy off-white to smoky white, sometimes with a yellow tinge; small pieces thinly potted, large pieces thick and heavy to prevent cracking during firing
- GLAZE thickly applied glaze often with trapped bubbles, especially in the foot-rim
- DECORATION left white with molded leaf or floral borders; painted gilt or silvered scrollwork borders

Marks
No marks were used at this time

Porcelain c.1720–30
- BODY more consistent, slightly creamy white, with thin, even glaze, which collects slightly in the foot-rims
- DECORATION chinoiseries, copies of Chinese and Japanese wares, and landscapes

Marks
From 1723 crossed swords in underglaze blue, sometimes with "K.P.F.," "K.P.M.," or "M.P.M."; crossed swords in overglaze blue on copies of Chinese and Japanese wares

Mark for c.1730; "AR" (Augustus Rex) monogram for pieces made for the Elector

See also China: Qing before 1800, pp.138–9

Meissen figures and services

From the early 1730s beautifully modeled and painted figures and table services were produced at the Meissen porcelain factory in Germany, establishing its reputation as the pre-eminent porcelain factory in Europe. The extensive range of figures and wares was characterized by an extraordinary virtuosity of modeling, lively expression, and sense of movement, and remains a testimony to the skill of the painters, modelers, and other artisans employed. The factory dominated the mid-18th-century style of porcelain, and Meissen wares and figures were imitated by craftsmen at other porcelain factories throughout Europe.

EARLY FIGURES

Small figures used to decorate the dining-tables of the wealthy were originally modeled in sugar, wax, or gum by cooks and confectioners. Demand for pieces in a more permanent material led to the production of the first porcelain figures at Meissen in 1727, when the modeler Johann Gottlieb Kirchner (1706–after 1738) was appointed the first chief modeler. Kirchner initially produced figures of saints and animals in a strong Baroque style. In the same year Frederick-Augustus I, Elector of Saxony (known as "Augustus the Strong"),

▲ Roller by Kändler
Kändler saw first-hand the unusual birds and animals in the Elector's zoo in Dresden, which enabled him to produce incredibly naturalistic models of these creatures. The vibrant colors and the bases encrusted with flowers, leaves, and insects are typical of Kändler's early style.
*(1740; ht 33.5cm/13½in; value **L**)*

► Harlequin Alarmed by Kändler
The colorful characters of the *commedia dell'arte* provided a rich source of inspiration for Kändler. Here he has conveyed the liveliness of the Italian drama in Harlequin's contorted pose, exaggerated grimace, and boldly painted costume.
*(1738; ht 16.5cm/6½in; value **O**)*

entrusted him with the task of creating 910 monumental figures of animals and birds to decorate his Japanese Palace in Dresden, specially built to accommodate his vast collection of Oriental porcelain. However, the thick body of the porcelain meant that pieces tended to crack or even completely collapse in the kiln. The most famous Meissen modeler, Johann Joachim Kändler (1706–75), joined the factory in 1731 to assist Kirchner, but he too could not solve the technical problems. These difficulties and the high cost of producing such works encouraged Kändler to experiment with the production of small-scale figures.

LATER FIGURES

In 1733 Kändler was appointed chief modeler at Meissen, and during the 1730s and 1740s he was responsible for some of the finest individual figures and groups ever made there. Kändler's early figures have a wonderful sense of liveliness and movement unmatched by his imitators. They are vigorously modeled, dramatic, and sculptural, and make flamboyant or theatrical gestures. Among the extraordinary range of subjects were exotic birds, figures from distant lands, couples in romantic or chivalric poses (known as "crinoline" groups), and humorous depictions of court jesters. Some of the best-known and most popular figures by Kändler are the characters such as Harlequin, Columbine, and Scaramouche from the *commedia dell'arte*, the Italian theater tradition. Kändler also depicted street vendors in two series called the "Cris de Paris" and the "Cris de Londres," some of which were inspired by prints based on the drawings of the French artists Edmé Bouchardon and Christophe Huet. Some of these figures were produced in collaboration with other highly skilled modelers who joined the factory in the mid-18th century: Johann Friedrich Eberlein (1695–1749), Friedrich Elias Meyer (1723–85), and Peter Reinicke (1715–68).

In the mid-18th century the fashion for the Baroque style declined, to be replaced by the delicate, light-hearted Rococo style. Figures of lovers in idyllic pastoral settings, as well as allegorical and mythological figures representing the seasons, the months, and Classical gods and goddesses, were made in keeping with the new, more romantic, frivolous style. From *c*.1750 to 1755 the factory made smaller-scale figures, which were painted with such pastel colors as pale mauve, lemon yellow, and soft green. The simple, flower-encrusted pad or rockwork bases that had been employed during the 1730s and 1740s were abandoned in the 1750s in favor of more elaborately scrolled bases.

▼ Lemon-seller from the "Cris de Paris" series by Kändler and Reinicke
The "Cris de Paris" series featured a range of street traders selling such varied fare as pies, oysters, lottery tickets, rabbits, maps, and trinkets. This figure is clearly of a later date than the *Harlequin* figure shown above, as the colors are softer and it has the gilded scrollwork base typical of the later period.
*(1755; ht 13.5cm/5¼in; value **H**)*

▼ Africa and Asia by Meyer
Allegorical figures and groups representing the seasons and the continents were particularly popular during the Rococo period. In this group, Africa is represented by a black putto wearing an elephant-shaped head-dress and seated on a lion, while Asia is depicted as a white putto wearing a jeweled necklace – two contrasting depictions that are very much a European fantasy of the inhabitants of these two continents. The highly scrolled base and somewhat elongated heads are typical features of Meyer's work and of mid-18th-century Meissen figures. Although Meyer's figures are of very high quality, they are not as collectible as those by Kändler.
*(c.1755; ht 22.5cm/8¾in; value **G**)*

► Armorial dish from the "Swan" service by Kändler
Wares from this famous Meissen service are highly collectible, but they rarely appear on the market. Some pieces made in the 18th century were decorated in the 19th and can be difficult to distinguish from the originals. However, it is sometimes possible to identify later decoration because the gilt borders that were added in the 19th century are often poorly painted and continue to the edge of the rim, whereas on 18th-century pieces the gilding is slightly inset from the edge of the rim.
*(1737–41; diam. 42cm/16½in; value **O**)*

TABLEWARES AND SERVICES

In addition to figures, Kändler and his team of designers and modelers created an extensive range of dinner services, tea and coffee services, centerpieces, candlesticks, ladies' toilet sets, and other useful and decorative wares. By the 1730s Meissen porcelain had become extremely fashionable throughout Europe, and the factory received many commissions.

The commission for Meissen's largest, most famous, and beautifully modeled service, known as the "Swan" service, came in 1736 from the factory's director, Count Heinrich von Brühl, who had recently married. Each plate, painted with the coat of arms of the Count and his new wife, is exquisitely modeled in low relief with a design of swans, herons, pelicans, and rushes, while the tureens are of sumptuous curving forms incorporating an elaborate design of dolphins, mermaids, and other marine creatures. The Count's name, which translates as "swampy meadow" or "marshy ground," may have inspired the theme.

The exquisite and imaginative decoration that the painter and chemist Johann Gregorius Höroldt (1696–1775) had brought to early Meissen wares continued during the 1730s. From 1729 Augustus the Strong commissioned the factory painters to make copies of his collection of Oriental porcelain, and they adapted the decoration on Japanese Kakiemon wares and Chinese *famille-verte* wares to create a new style of decoration known as *indianische Blumen* ("Indian flowers"), so called because much Oriental porcelain was exported into Europe by the East India Companies. In the early 1730s, land- and cityscapes framed with heavy gilt scrollwork or interlaced strapwork borders were a popular alternative to flower decoration, but from *c.*1735 battle scenes and hunting subjects inspired by the French painter Antoine Watteau were favored.

With the development of the Rococo style the popularity of flower decoration increased, and European flowers were used in painted designs. The painter Johann Gottlieb Klinger (active 1731–46) was the best-known exponent of this style. At first petals, leaves, and stems were very

precisely depicted, as the painters followed botanical prints; the design was enlivened with scattered insects and butterflies. The relaxed attitude of the Rococo led to the use of more naturalistic sprays or bouquets in a style known as *deutsche Blumen* ("German flowers"). By the mid-1750s this style had been replaced by looser representations of scattered flowers, described as *Manierblumen* ("mannered flowers").

▲ Teapot and cover
This teapot has a spout in the form of an animal, typical of mid-18th-century Rococo pieces; however, the painted floral decoration is more Baroque in feel. The precise depiction of the sunflowers on this piece is in a style known as *Holzschnittblumen* ("woodcut flowers"), after woodcut botanical studies. The flowers are rendered as though they were casting shadows – a style of illustration that the Meissen painters copied from printmakers.
*(1745; ht 10.5cm/4in; value **I**)*

KEY FACTS

Early figures
- PALETTE dominated by vivid colors – strong red, yellow, and black – applied in broad washes
- BASES simple pad shape with applied flowers and leaves, often turquoise at first but naturalistic green by the 1740s; sculptural pedestals for religious figures
- IMPORTANT MAKERS Kirchner and Kändler

Later figures
- PALETTE pastels – green, mauve, and pale yellow
- BASES unglazed with marks on back or side of figure; Rococo scrolls around the edges, heightened with gilding and enameled colors, and sometimes pierced
- SUBJECTS lovers in pastoral settings; representations of the seasons, the months, Classical gods and goddesses
- IMPORTANT MAKERS Eberlein, Meyer, and Reinicke

Tablewares and services
- BODY off-white, with a thin, glassy glaze giving a bluish tinge, later cold and glassy in appearance
- FORMS early teapots and coffee-pots bulge toward the foot; later shapes tend to be top-heavy
- DECORATION 1730s: "Indian flowers," land- and cityscapes, battle and hunting scenes; 1740s: "German flowers"; mid-1750s: "mannered flowers"

Marks
The initials "AR" (Augustus Rex) appear on pieces made for the court or as gifts from the Elector between 1723 and 1736; the marks "MPM," "KPM," and "KPF" are rare and found only on some wares made *c.*1723–4; the crossed swords from the arms of Saxony are most common after 1724

See also Early Meissen, p.173; Academic and Marcolini, p.176; Other German factories, pp.178–80

Academic and Marcolini

After the end of the Seven Years War (1756–63) there was a period of decline at the Meissen factory, due to the deprivations of the war and the loss of several important painters and modelers. Meissen's share of the burgeoning European porcelain market was further reduced as Austria and Prussia banned Meissen imports, and Britain, France, and Russia placed high tariffs on imported Meissen pieces in order to protect domestic production. Meissen lost its place as the dominant force of innovation, originality, and quality to other factories such as those in Berlin, Vienna, and Sèvres, which it often now attempted to imitate.

▲ Dinner plate
The scattered flowers, mannered style, and lackluster palette seen here characterize the decoration of Meissen wares when the factory, lacking funds and innovative designers, continued to use the outmoded Rococo style. The molded basketwork border with spiraling ribs, known as the "Neue Ozier" pattern, is a distinctive feature of Meissen tableware.
(1763–74; diam. 25cm/9¾in; value B)

THE DOT/ACADEMIC PERIOD

The period 1763 to 1774 is generally known as the "Dot" period, because the mark used at this time consisted of the familiar crossed swords with a dot added between their hilts, or the "Academic" period, because much of the factory's output lacked originality. The factory continued to manufacture figures and wares in the mid-18th-century style but, in a poorer-quality paste, these did not match the standard of earlier pieces. There were few innovations in the design and decoration of tableware in this period, with flowers the most popular painted subject. A debased form of *deutsche Blumen* ("German flowers"), these bouquets can be distinguished from earlier Meissen painting by the often "painterly" style, the pale palette with a predominance of pink tones, and the smaller-scale and often scattered flowers, following the style of Sèvres.

Figures were often reproduced from molds dating from the 1730s but lack the bolder, lively decoration of the originals; the palette is sometimes pale and lackluster, and intricate, fussy patterns often appear.

▲ Coffee-pot
This coffee-pot is decorated with chocolate-colored borders, reserved in white relief with busts and fantastic animals, in an attempt to imitate the forms of ancient Greek and Roman cameos. The Greek key angular handles and oval gilt cartouches also represent the sober Neo-classical influence that evolved as a reaction against the frivolous Rococo style.
(c.1795; ht 20cm/8in; value H)

▼ *Autumn* group
Allegorical figures were popular subjects during both the Rococo and the Neo-classical periods. This group depicts "autumn" through the use of a group of revelers gathered around a barrel of wine. The high, rocky base with guilloche ornament at the bottom, and the small-scale figures, suggest that this group was made at the end of the 18th century.
(c.1800; ht 22cm/8½in; value H)

The Neo-classical style, characterized by simple, geometrical forms and the use of Greek and Roman architectural ornament, was introduced to Meissen by the French sculptor Michel-Victor Acier (1736–99), appointed to work as chief modeler with Kändler. Acier produced small-scale, sentimental figure groups characterized by stiffer modeling in line with the restrained character of the Neo-classical style.

THE MARCOLINI PERIOD

In 1774 Count Camillo Marcolini (1739–1814) was appointed director of Meissen; under his leadership Neo-classicism was more wholeheartedly adopted and the quality greatly improved. Biscuit porcelain was favored for allegorical or Classical figures, because it resembled the marble used for ancient Classical sculpture. In the 1790s the modeler Johann Carl Schönheit (1767–1805) made figures in the Sèvres style after such sculptors as Etienne Falconet.

The Neo-classical taste is also reflected in the forms and decoration of the tableware. Cylindrical coffee-cups with angular handles and covers seem to have been used for display and presentation rather than for drinking. Marcolini also introduced a wider range of very fine decoration that included mythological and pastoral scenes, portraits and landscapes, and, later, portrait medallions, topographical landscapes, and details of paintings. Flower-painting also continued during this period. The bouquets were often large and dense and somewhat stiffly painted, with fewer scattered flowers than in the designs of the 1760s.

KEY FACTS

Dot/Academic period: 1763–74
- BODY poor quality with flecks; off-white in tone
- STYLE continuation of Rococo; development of Neo-classicism
- PALETTE pale, predominantly pink tints for flowers
- DECORATION flowers, especially roses; cupids within garland borders; exotic birds; fable scenes
- FIGURES reproductions of earlier models, stiffly modeled, sentimental or moralizing

Marks
Meissen crossed swords with a dot between the hilts

Marcolini period: 1774–1814
- BODY smooth, slightly off-white; clear, thin, glassy glaze with a bluish tinge
- STYLE severe Neo-classical, with such ornaments as Greek key patterns and laurel wreaths
- FIGURES biscuit figures of allegorical characters, Classical gods, and copies of Sèvres figures
- PALETTE pale colors such as light blues and pinks
- FORMS simple, cylindrical forms for tea and coffeewares, with flat strap or grooved angular handles; saucers with straight, angled sides, imitating Berlin and Vienna wares
- DECORATION cupids, mythological subjects, pastoral scenes, topographical views, portrait medallions, copies of Old Master paintings, flowers
- BASES circular or rectangular with continuous Vitruvian scrollwork or Greek key borders

Marks
Meissen crossed swords with a star between the hilts

Hausmaler

From the 17th century in Germany and Bohemia there was an important industry of freelance artists who decorated faience, to help factories meet the demand for highly decorated pottery. These decorators, known as "*Hausmaler*" ("home painters"), worked in their own studios or workshops. Additionally, hoping to profit from the new porcelain industry, *Hausmaler* in Augsburg and elsewhere bought whitewares from Meissen in bulk and decorated them.

AUGSBURG

Hausmaler from Augsburg were among the first to decorate Meissen porcelain outside the factory, and thus their decoration is usually found on tableware of the 1720s. Gilt decoration is particularly associated with the Augsburg workshops and is the most common form of *Hausmaler* work found today. The best-known and most prolific studio was that of the brothers Abraham and Bartholomäus Seuter (1688–1747 and 1678–1754), who specialized in gilt decoration, particularly chinoiserie scenes in the manner of Johann Gregorius Höroldt (1696–1775) of Meissen, and hunting, genre, and mythological scenes set within ornate gilt scrollwork or foliate borders, or reversed on a solid gilt ground.

The other major *Hausmaler* workshop in Augsburg during the first half of the 18th century was that of the Auffenwerths, who painted chinoiseries in a style that is very similar to the Seuter workshop but which can be distinguished by its more feathery appearance. Sabina Auffenwerth (*b.*1706) is the best known of the family, for her polychrome chinoiserie panels in the style of Meissen, and genre scenes with large figures, sometimes painted in monochrome black, purple, or red, with the faces and arms highlighted in flesh tones.

▲ Meissen bowl decorated by Abraham Seuter
The gilt chinoiserie landscape and elaborate scrollwork ground on this bowl are similar to a design executed by the Meissen painter Höroldt. The use of toothed scrolls at the base is typical of the Seuters' workshop, while the engraved detail animates the rather flat design. The bowl itself may pre-date the decoration by up to ten years.
*(c.1730; ht 8cm/3in; value **H**)*

► Meissen coffee-pot and cover decorated by Ignaz Preissler
This coffee-pot and cover, decorated with *Schwarzlot* (black monochrome), depicts a harbor landscape of galleons and feluccas, castellated towers, bridges, and other buildings; this type of scene was one of the earliest forms of European landscape decoration used at Meissen during the 1720s.
*(c.1720; ht 21cm/8¼in; value **K**)*

◀ **Meissen bowl decorated in the manner of F.J. Ferner**
Ferner's work is particularly well known for his use of gilding and enamels to enhance Meissen porcelain that had already been decorated in underglaze blue. This bowl is finely painted with a central medallion of a castle in the iron-red monochrome typical of *Hausmaler* enamels; in the border, interspersed with flowers, a gallant and a lady are depicted on opposite sides of the bowl. Note how the overglaze decoration seems incompatible with the underglaze blue floral spray in the center.
*(c.1745; diam. 17cm/7in; value **G**)*

OTHER CENTERS OF PRODUCTION

One of the most important *Hausmaler* in Germany was Ignaz Bottengruber (active 1720–30), who worked in Breslau. His work is characterized by detailed designs, high-quality gilding, and varied and subtle tones. He specialized in Bacchic, hunting, and military scenes framed by rich scrollwork, in addition to mythological and allegorical subjects. Ignaz Preissler (1670–1741), the son of a celebrated glass-decorator, Daniel Preissler (1736–1733), also worked in Breslau and later in Bohemia; he painted townscapes, landscapes, chinoiseries, and mythological scenes in black monochrome, known as "*Schwarzlot*" ("black lead"), or even in red monochrome.

The most prolific *Hausmaler* workshop of the later 18th century was that of Franz Ferdinand Meyer (active 1747–94) who worked in Pressnitz, Bohemia. His work is recognizable by a cool palette dominated by light green and iron red, broad gilt scrollwork borders, and bouquets of flowers around the borders. The painter F.J. Ferner (active 1745–50) may have been one of Meyer's assistants, because his style is similar. Ferner added enameled and gilt decoration of flowers, animals, figures, and trees to pieces decorated in underglaze blue at the Meissen factory.

▼ **Meissen tureen painted in the workshop of Franz Ferdinand Meyer**
Hunting scenes and landscapes were Meyer's favorite decorative subjects, and he frequently copied them from German engravings. The predominantly cool palette is one of his distinctive features.
*(c.1750; ht 31cm/12in; value **I**)*

KEY FACTS

- PALETTE monochrome red, purple, or black, and gilding are most typical of *Hausmaler* wares, but polychrome decoration is also found
- SUBJECTS chinoiseries, large figure scenes, landscapes, mythological, and hunting scenes

Marks
Pieces decorated by Meyer and Ferner generally have the Meissen crossed swords mark in underglaze blue; after *c.*1760 Meissen introduced the canceled crossed swords mark on imperfect or blank wares in order to prevent its products from being associated with the work of incompetent decorators

See also Meissen, pp.173–6; Glass: Enameled glass – Before 1800, pp.288–9

Other German factories

The great success of Meissen encouraged other European rulers to set up their own factories in the 1740s and 1750s. By the 1770s there were almost 20 factories in Europe producing hard-paste porcelain, often imitating the wares first produced at Meissen. The most significant are discussed below, although there were also several less important factories in the Saxon province of Thuringia producing high-quality wares on a much smaller basis, including those at Gotha (1756–1834), Kloster-Veilsdorf (est. 1760), Wallendorf (est. 1764), and Limbach (est. 1772).

HÖCHST

In 1746 the Elector of Mainz granted a privilege to Adam Friedrich von Löwenfink (1714–54) to establish a faience factory in Höchst, near Mainz. The factory manufactured porcelain only after the arrival of the arcanist Josef Jakob Ringler (1730–1804) in 1750. Höchst became well known for its porcelain figures modeled by several notable craftsmen, such as Simon Feilner (1726–98), who modeled a dramatic set of *commedia dell'arte* figures and a few elaborate Rococo figures, Johann Friedrich Lück (1727–97), his brother Karl Gottlob Lück (*c.*1730–75), and Johann Peter Melchior (1742–1825), who became master modeler in 1767. Although Melchior's figures often have a stiff or stylized appearance, there is much careful detailing in such features as the folds of clothes. One of the most characteristic elements of Melchior's figures is the mound base, with either grass and earth, or rockwork detailed in green and brown.

The range of wares included *trembleuse* cups and saucers with plain surfaces and small modeled details such as animal or scrollwork spouts and wishbone handles. Wares were painted with landscape vignettes with figures, most frequently peasants or rustic scenes in the style of Dutch paintings, surrounded by small, scattered flowers. Polychrome decoration was common, but a distinctive palette of puce or green monochrome was also used.

The factory's financial situation was always precarious, and it closed in 1796. The molds of the Melchior models were sold to the Damm Pottery (est. 1827) in Aschaffenburg, where the designs were reproduced in faience from *c.*1830, although most existing pieces date from the mid-19th century. These are often very similar to the porcelain originals and are highly collectible in their own right.

◄ **Tureen and cover from Höchst**
This tureen has a bulbous shape, an elaborate finial, and pierced handles molded with "C"-scrolls, all elements that reflect the influence of contemporary Rococo silver forms during the mid-18th century. The dominance of puce and green in the decoration and the use of landscape vignettes are typical features of Höchst tableware.
(1760; ht 33cm/13in; value I)

▼ **Tea-caddy decorated by Jakob Osterspey for Frankenthal**
Osterspey was a noted painter of landscapes and mythological scenes at Frankenthal. Scenes such as this were typically taken from Boucher and painted in the Frankenthal palette of puce, rich green, gray, and brown.
(1765; ht 15cm/6in; value I)

◄ **Pastoral group modeled by Karl Gottlob Lück for Frankenthal**
During the 18th century there was a fashion among European courtiers for dressing up as rustic characters. The most famous practitioner was the French Queen Marie Antoinette, who enjoyed playing at being a milkmaid at her "dairy" at Rambouillet, built for her by her husband Louis XVI and supplied with porcelain from Sèvres. The figures here can be identified as Frankenthal by their doll-like faces and stiff modeling, and also by the applied leaves and moss-like grass on the bases.
(1780; ht 12cm/4¾in; value G)

FRANKENTHAL

From 1752 Paul Antoine Hannong (1700–60) manufactured porcelain at his father's faience factory (est. 1721) in Strasbourg with the help of Ringler, who had previously worked at Höchst. In 1754 Louis XV banned the production of porcelain at Strasbourg in order to protect Vincennes from competition, and Hannong moved the factory to Frankenthal near Mannheim in the German Palatinate; production of hard-paste porcelain started the following year.

Frankenthal is noted for its figures, of which 800 different subjects have been identified. Among the finest are pastoral couples beneath elaborate Rococo arbors characterized by rather stiff modeling. The first modeler, Johann Wilhelm Lanz (active 1755–61), introduced scrolled Rococo bases. In 1762 Karl Theodor, the Elector Palatine, bought the factory and appointed Konrad Linck (1730–93) as chief modeler. Linck modified the style of the figures, enhancing the sculptural qualities of such features as drapery, and adding yellow and green grass or moss to the bases; he also introduced the first elements of Neo-classicism to the factory's style. Johann Peter Melchior joined the factory from Höchst in 1779 and continued to make his distinctive models of children, often in biscuit porcelain.

Frankenthal produced a typical range of tableware, the forms of which were for the most part fairly simple with few sculptural details; plates, dishes, and large tea and coffee vessels often have molded or pierced basketwork rims. Decoration of these wares was in a typical palette of strong, dark colors. The most common subject was naturalistic sprays of large flowers, loosely painted and surrounded by scattered smaller flowers. Jakob Osterspey (*c.*1730–82) specialized in mythological figures and musicians in idealized landscapes, after paintings by Watteau and Boucher. Also popular was *trompe l'oeil* decoration imitating grained wood, while in the 1770s to 1880s crimson and gold flowers over gilt-striped grounds were common.

When the Elector succeeded to the title of Elector of Bavaria in 1777 he moved to Munich, and without his support the factory went into decline. After French troops occupied the Palatinate in 1794 the factory was requisitioned, finally closing in 1799.

▼ *Columbine* **modeled by Franz Anton Bustelli for Nymphenburg**

Some of Bustelli's finest work is in his series of 16 figures from the *commedia dell'arte*. This figure is a fine example of the southern German Rococo style mastered by Bustelli, with its elongated, twisting form and flowing lines emphasized by areas of flat color. The subtle sense of movement is also expressed in the simple, flat, asymmetrical scrolls of the base, which appears integral to the figure as it follows the contors of Columbine's skirt.

(c.1762; ht 19cm/7½in; value **O***)*

NYMPHENBURG

In 1753 the Elector of Bavaria established a porcelain factory in Neudeck, and in 1761 the factory was moved near to the Elector's palace at Nymphenburg. The most outstanding products made at this factory are indisputably the figures by Franz Anton Bustelli (1722–63), one of the greatest exponents of the Rococo style. His forms are stylized and gently twisting, often slightly elongated, with simple, curvaceous forms. Many figures and groups were left unpainted or were painted with broad pastel washes. In 1797 the modeler Johann Peter Melchior joined the factory from Frankenthal and produced Neo-classical biscuit figures. Tablewares include teapots that often have characteristic double-scroll handles and long spouts in the form of a swan's head. The most popular type of decoration during the Rococo period was loose bouquets of flowers. Landscapes were either left unframed, half enclosed by rocaille frames, or framed by gilt cartouches.

LUDWIGSBURG

This factory was established by the Duke of Württemberg in 1758–9. The poor quality of the Ludwigsburg paste compared with some other German factories meant that it was more suitable for figures than for plain or sparsely decorated tablewares. Under the direction of Gottlieb Friedrich Riedel the factory produced a variety of figures that appear rather stiff and very simplified, especially when compared with some of the more sophisticated work of such factories as Nymphenburg. The decoration is restrained, and the painting, most often in pastel colors, is precise. A series of miniatures made in the 1760s is among the most celebrated of the Ludwigsburg figures; representing market traders as well as courtiers, the figures were intended to form a miniature scene of an annual fair in Ludwigsburg. Teapots are generally bullet-shaped, often with fruit knops and bird's-head spouts. Saucers are flared, as opposed to the rounded shape made elsewhere in Germany. Plates, dishes, tureens, and bowls typically feature a band of molded and sectioned basketwork around the rims. Typical painted decoration includes unframed landscapes and scattered flowers. When the court moved to Stuttgart in the 1770s, the factory went into decline, and it finally closed in 1824.

◄ **Dancers modeled by Joseph Nees for Ludwigsburg**

Ballets and masques were popular courtly entertainments in the 18th century, and many modelers who worked in the European porcelain factories took inspiration for their figures from these pastimes. Nees is known to have made more than 60 different figures, many of them dancers. This couple has the stiff pose, particularly evident in the woman's outstretched arms, and the restrained color palette that are typical of Ludwigsburg figures.

(1765; ht 15cm/6in; value **H***)*

KEY FACTS

Höchst (1746–96)
- **BODY** hard-paste porcelain; opaque creamy white; generally flawless
- **DECORATION** landscape vignettes, usually of peasants or rustic scenes in the manner of David Teniers (1610–90) with large figures; chinoiserie figures; naturalistic flower sprays
- **BASES** mound bases with grass and earth, or rockwork detailed in bright green and brown

Marks
Underglaze blue mark used from *c.*1750

Frankenthal (1755–99)
- **BODY** hard-paste porcelain; creamy off-white with a thin glaze but can tend toward grayish off-white, with tiny black specks of ash, or opaque white
- **STYLE** simple forms; plates, dishes, and large tea and coffee vessels, often with molded and sectioned or pierced basketwork rims
- **PALETTE** rich green, gray, carmine, brown, puce
- **DECORATION** naturalistic flower sprays in the style of Strasbourg; chinoiserie scenes with large figures; large birds in wooded landscapes
- **FIGURES** stiff modeling of a variable (often high) quality; pastoral couples; some in biscuit porcelain
- **BASES** elaborate, with undulating and arched Rococo scrollwork, and often tufts of green moss

Marks
Underglaze blue mark used during the period when Elector Karl Theodor owned the factory (1761–93)

Nymphenburg (est. 1753)
- **BODY** hard-paste porcelain; slightly creamy off-white, dense with a wet-looking glaze, with a greenish tone where it collects in hollows and corners
- **STYLE** characteristic double-scroll handle; simple "U"-shape for coffee-cups and sugar-bowls
- **PALETTE** ocher, puce, mushroom-pink, brown, red
- **DECORATION** very skilful naturalistic flower-painting; landscapes with Classical ruins, statues, and small figures; large single figures
- **FIGURES** stylized, slightly elongated and curvaceous forms; later, stiffer Louis XVI-style figures; colored deep pink and orange/tomato red in flat washes
- **BASES** on Bustelli figures these appear integral to the figure – flat, edged with asymmetrical scrollwork; also stepped pedestals

Marks
Impressed on wares made during the "Bustelli" period (1754–65)

Ludwigsburg (1727–1824)
- **BODY** hard-paste porcelain; grayish white and close-grained with distinctive smoky glaze, tends to be green where pooled
- **FORMS** bullet-shaped teapots; saucers with flared rims; spouts in the form of birds or dragons, "C"-shaped scroll handles with shell or feather thumb-pieces
- **PALETTE** russet, puce, dark brown, green, yellow
- **DECORATION** naturalistic flower sprays; realistic figures after Watteau; fruit and flowers in Meissen style; landscapes with two or three tufts of foliage at the base
- **FIGURES** stiff with crisp modeling; colored grayish puce, cobalt, green, yellow
- **BASES** grass and rockwork mounds or slabs, Rococo scrollwork

Marks
Underglaze blue mark used *c.*1770

See also Early Meissen, p.173; Meissen figures and services, pp.174–5; Academic and Marcolini, p.176; Hausmaler, p.177

FÜRSTENBERG

Charles I, Duke of Brunswick, established a factory at Fürstenberg in 1747, but attempts to manufacture porcelain were unsuccessful until the arrival of Johann Kilian Benckgraff (1708–58) from Höchst in 1753. The factory encountered many technical problems, and early wares and figures often have flaws, such as black specks of ash in the body, or are slightly misshapen or cracked.

Many of the figures produced at Fürstenberg imitated those produced at Meissen, Höchst, and Berlin. The most important modeler was Simon Feilner (1726–98) from Höchst, who became chief modeler in 1754; his work included a fine series of miners (1757–8) and, most notably, characters from the *commedia dell'arte* (c.1754). During the Neo-classical period the factory made Classical figures, including a series of biscuit busts of Classical poets and philosophers on pedestals. Copies of figures from 18th-century molds were made in the 19th century, but can be distinguished from the originals by the clumsier decoration and harsher colors.

Early Fürstenberg tablewares are particularly distinctive as they are often decorated with elaborate molded Rococo scrollwork to disguise the flaws in the paste. Early decoration included flower sprays, sometimes in a green monochrome that indicates the influence of the Höchst craftsmen working at Fürstenberg. Landscapes with buildings were generally left unframed and were painted in predominantly dark greens and browns. One of the factory's most easily identifiable decorative themes is finely detailed poultry and other domestic birds perched on fences or branches.

BERLIN

The first porcelain factory at Berlin was founded by Wilhelm Kaspar Wegely in 1752. Some figures were copied directly from Meissen or from prints, and a series of small putti with large heads and limbs, dressed as members of various trades and professions, was also made. Tablewares and vases were painted in the style of Meissen, with naturalistic flowers, landscapes, and figures in the

manner of the French pastoral painter Antoine Watteau. Molded flowers and foliage, and basketwork rims, were specialities of Wegely, and a range of molded baskets was also made. The factory closed in 1757 because of financial problems during the Seven Years War.

In 1761 the merchant Johann Ernst Gotzkowsky set up another factory with craftsmen who had worked at Wegely's factory, but it went bankrupt and was bought in 1763 by Frederick the Great. The new factory, which was known as the Royal Porcelain Factory, produced wares in a distinctive late Rococo style. Tablewares were embellished with trelliswork, pierced rims, and flowers entwined in basketwork patterns. Painted decoration included scale-ground borders and naturalistic flowers, animals, and birds. The modeler Wilhelm Christoph Meyer (1723–85) produced the series "Cries of Berlin" as well as allegorical and Classical figures characterized by elongated forms and small heads. They are set on small, square bases and painted in salmon pink, puce, and black. Neo-classical wares introduced in the 1770s include vases and cylindrical cups. The decoration was sumptuous, with gilded Neo-classical motifs, views of Berlin, and monochrome portrait medallions. During the 1780s figures set on high pedestal or rocky bases imitated Neo-classical sculpture.

◄ **Miner modeled by Simon Feilner at Fürstenberg**
The high quality of Feilner's modeling is evident in the sharply defined face, hands, and clothes, and also in the realistic pose and proportions of this figure. Unusually, it is painted; many similar figures were left white.
(c.1757–8; ht 20cm/8in; value **H**)

▼ **Coffee-pot by Fürstenberg**
The molded wishbone handle and mask spout of this coffee-pot are characteristic Rococo features. However, the curved profile of the body is more Neo-classical.
(c.1775; ht 25.5cm/10in; value **G**)

▼ **Vase and cover by the Royal Porcelain Factory, Berlin**
The cold, bluish-white tone of this porcelain, which suited the refined Neo-classical style, resulted from the use of a new type of kaolin from 1770.
(1775; ht 31cm/12in; value **H**)

KEY FACTS

Fürstenberg (1753–c.1800)
- BODY hard-paste porcelain; generally whitish with a glassy glaze; early paste often had flaws
- STYLE "C"-scroll handles; early pieces sometimes have molded scrollwork or frames
- PALETTE dominated by greens and browns; also monochrome green or purple; figures often left white
- DECORATION unframed landscapes; birds or fowl; portrait medallions
- FIGURES Feilner's miners were both painted and unpainted; Neo-classical biscuit figures are typical; skin is often highly colored
- BASES simple mound or pad

Marks
Underglaze-blue mark used during the early period of production

Berlin: Wegely factory (1752–7)
- BODY creamy white, similar to Meissen but with a thinner glaze lending an opaque look
- GLAZE very glassy, similar to Meissen
- PALETTE white or painted in puce, iron red, or black
- DECORATION molded flowers, trailing foliage, and basket rims; naturalistic flower-painting

Marks
The letter "W" in underglaze blue

Berlin: Royal Porcelain Factory (est. 1763)
- BODY creamy white with thin, even glaze before 1770; white with glassy, blue-tinged glaze after 1770
- FORMS cylindrical coffee-cups with angular handles, Classical or allegorical subjects on high pedestal or rocky bases
- DECORATION molding, scale-ground borders, landscapes, birds and animals, molded basketwork patterns, and pierced rims

Marks
Underglaze-blue mark of a scepter (taken from the arms of Brandenburg) used from c.1763

See also Berlin, pp.182–3

Germany after 1800

Meissen

The attempts by Count Marcolini, director of Meissen from 1774, to improve the quality of Meissen porcelain were not entirely successful, and at the beginning of the 19th century the factory was still in decline. There were several reasons for this: competition from other porcelain factories in Europe, mass production, and the effects of the Napoleonic Wars (1799–1815). When Marcolini retired in 1814, production was at a level just high enough to keep the factory open.

Until the mid-19th century mass production grew steadily, thus reducing costs and meeting demand. From the 1820s the factory kept pace with new developments by using "round" kilns that led to a fourfold increase in production, and introducing new techniques and products. In the late 1820s gloss-gilding was introduced; this inexpensive method of decoration used gold mixed in a solution, which was applied to the porcelain. The time-consuming method of hand-pressing clay into molds to produce plates with molded decoration was replaced by pouring slip into glass molds. One of the new mass-produced items was the lithophane (a thin, translucent plaque with molded decoration that can be viewed by transmitted light), made from 1829, featuring religious or sentimental subjects.

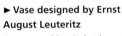

▶ Vase designed by Ernst August Leuteritz
As so many historical styles were popular during the 19th century, a single object of this date can often display a strange mix of influences; the shape of this vase is inspired by Greek and Roman vases, but the curling snake handles and lobed panel ornament on the foot are typically Renaissance ornaments, and the style of the classically inspired decoration is based on Limoges enameling. The rather heavy form is characteristic of 19th-century Meissen.
(1865; ht 28.5cm/11in; value K)

The 19th-century international exhibitions popularized both new and historical styles by displaying artifacts from different cultures and civilizations, and manufacturers copied these objects using new techniques. Taste was now led by the bourgeoisie, and manufacturers' output became more diverse to meet demand. More than one fashion was often popular at any one time, so 19th-century objects often display a bizarre combination of styles. The Biedermeier style was introduced *c.*1830; wares are similar in form to earlier Neo-classical pieces but are heavier, and have less elaborate decoration, often being painted with topographical views.

From the early 1830s the Rococo style was revived, and Meissen enjoyed a renaissance owing to its re-use from the late 1840s of 18th-century figure molds. Rococo Revival figures and wares were greatly in

▶ Cupid Enchained
This mythological figure group of a maiden sitting on a Neo-classical stool, binding Cupid's wings with a ribbon, was produced using a model that had originally been made by Christian Gottlieb Jüchtzer, one of the modelers working at Meissen in the Neo-classical style during the late 18th century. The rather harsh palette, so typical of 19th-century Meissen figures and wares, is especially evident in the red drapery over the attendant's shoulder, which would never have been used on an 18th-century figure.
(1870–80; ht 34.5cm/13½in; value H)

demand and formed the bulk of the factory's production during the second half of the 19th century. Produced under the supervision of the chief modeler, Ernst August Leuteritz (1818–93), these figures are of such typical 18th-century subjects as shepherds and shepherdesses, the aristocracy, and allegorical figures of the Seasons and the Four Continents. They can be distinguished from the originals by their hard, shiny gilding, harsh colors, and overelaborate decoration, such as intricate lacework, made by dipping real lace into the paste. The most notable Meissen products in other revival styles made during the second half of the 19th century include plates and cups and saucers of the 1840s, molded or painted with Gothic arches and tracery patterns, and blue-ground krater vases painted with Classical scenes imitating medieval and Renaissance enamels. From the 1860s large-scale Renaissance Revival vases, often painted with flowers and blue-ground sections and with curling snake handles, became increasingly popular. From the 1870s the factory produced figures in contemporary costume, although these were outweighed by the number of Rococo and Neo-classical reproductions.

▼ Basket
This Rococo Revival basket is in a typical 18th-century form, but the extravagant use of harsh colors suggests that it was made in the late 19th century from an 18th-century mold.
(c.1880; l. 52cm/20½in; value G)

KEY FACTS

- **BODY** pure white hard-paste porcelain with a distinctive hard, glassy glaze
- **STYLES** Empire, Biedermeier, Rococo Revival, Neo-classical, Renaissance and Gothic Revivals
- **PALETTE** harsh versions of 18th-century colors, such as a strong pink and a yellowish green; figures covered completely with paint; hard, shiny gloss-gilding
- **DECORATION** encrusted flowers; topographical views on Biedermeier wares

Marks
This mark was used from 1814 to 1818; thereafter it was sometimes accompanied by a Roman numeral; model numbers consisting of a letter followed by three or four digits are often incised in the base

See also Other German factories, pp.178–80

Berlin

The Royal Porcelain Factory in Berlin (est. 1752) is best known for its superb porcelain made during the late 18th and early 19th centuries, when Neo-classicism was at its height. At this time Prussia was one of the most powerful states in Europe, and it became even stronger after the defeat of Napoleon in 1815. Its prosperity was reflected in the great building schemes undertaken in Berlin and Potsdam, and some of the finest Neo-classical architecture of the age was designed by German architects such as Karl Friedrich Schinkel (1781–1841). Schinkel and the leading sculptor Johann Gottfried Schadow (1764–1850) were among prominent contemporary artists commissioned to design porcelain in the rich Empire style associated with Napoleon, and in the Biedermeier style, a simpler, heavier, Classical style popular with the German middle classes. In contrast to many other European factories, which concentrated on reviving 18th-century styles, the Berlin factory continued to manufacture innovative and stylish wares and figures throughout the century.

BEFORE 1840

In the early 19th century Berlin's particular specialty was wares with finely tooled gilt borders and gilt-ground sections framing sumptuous paintings, creating an opulent effect. In contrast to the vignettes popular in the 18th century, these paintings were highly finished so as to imitate works in oil, and none of the white porcelain was left showing. The most popular painted subjects included profile portraits (sometimes silhouettes) within oval medallions, and Classical themes, but the factory is most renowned for its fine topographical views depicting such celebrated buildings in Berlin as the Royal Palace and the Opera, or the scenery around Potsdam. Topographical views generally feature on cups and saucers, plates, and vases (where they are sometimes titled) intended for display.

◄ Plate
This plate with a fine etched and burnished gilt border of Classical inspiration exemplifies the way in which the Berlin factory treated porcelain as a vehicle for painting during the early 19th century.
(c.1820; diam. 25.5cm/10in; value I)

Frederick the Great, King of Prussia, was an enthusiastic patron of the factory, commissioning and even designing table services for his palaces in Berlin and Potsdam. This tradition continued under Frederick William III; after the defeat of Napoleon, the King ordered elaborate Neo-classical services for both Prussian and foreign generals in celebration of their victory. The most famous of these is the "Prussian" service made between 1817 and 1819 for the Duke of Wellington, which is now displayed at Apsley House in London, his former residence.

One of the most significant developments in Europe during the first half of the 19th century was the increasing power and patronage of the middle classes, a result of the economic boom brought by the Industrial Revolution. Instead of the elaborate table services made for royalty and aristocracy, there was much greater demand for single decorative pieces or small services. The factory adapted to the new market by producing large numbers of "cabinet" cups for display, generally cylindrical and often with covers, and similar to those made in Vienna. From *c.*1815 an elongated, slightly flared version, painted with portrait panels or Classical motifs, was introduced. Also typical of Berlin were octagonal tea services with fine paintings of ancient ruins, birds, or butterflies, surrounded with gilding and elaborate enamels imitating Roman mosaics and *pietre dure* (hardstone) panels.

Vases in a variety of sizes were popular for display and were a major part of the output of Berlin from *c.*1830. Based on antique forms such as urns and kraters, they were usually embellished with topographical paintings or elaborate Classical motifs in panels, surrounded by tooled gilt borders with Neo-classical motifs. The supreme technical and artistic quality of these vases was unmatched.

Like tablewares, figures were inspired by Classical models; they were usually left unpainted or unglazed, in imitation of antique statues, and set on simple cylindrical pedestals molded with regular geometric borders. Although most of the subjects were allegorical or taken from Classical antiquity, the factory also made portraits of the Prussian royal family, and of Prussian generals who had defeated Napoleon. From the 1830s a figure of the Princesses Louise and Frederike was mass-produced with a stepped base or plinth rather than a simple slab.

◄ Vase painted by Johann Eusebius Anton Forst
The urn shape of this vase imitates the form of the krater, or calyx, which was a type of vase for mixing wine and water, made in ancient Greece. Many such pieces were found in archeological excavations made during the 18th and 19th centuries in Europe. The form is characteristic of wares made during the Classical Revival and was used by sculptors and silversmiths as well as by porcelain manufacturers. On this vase, the superbly painted topographical view of Potsdam is surrounded by rich, burnished gilding tooled with such Classical motifs as palmettes and acanthus leaves.
(c.1830; ht 50cm/19½in; value O)

▼ Easter egg and stopper
In 1817 Princess Charlotte of Prussia, daughter of Frederick William III, married Nicholas of Russia. Porcelain eggs provided a good solution to the problem of sending eggs (traditional in Russia) as Easter gifts between the courts of Berlin and Russia. Like this egg, they were typically painted with fine topographical views, reserved on a blue ground with plain gilt borders. Other popular decorative themes included flowers and religious subjects. Examples such as this that have a stopper may have been used as scent bottles.
(1850; ht 9cm/3½in; value H)

Portrait medallions in biscuit porcelain, mostly depicting the royal family, were also made on a large scale. Porcelain Easter eggs were a distinctive product of the Berlin factory from *c*.1820 to the end of the century. They were decorated all over with paintings reserved on colored grounds.

LATER CLASSICAL AND OTHER STYLES

The Berlin factory continued to make high-quality decorated porcelain until the end of the 19th century, even though there was a general decline in European porcelain manufacture because of competition from mass-produced goods. Most mid- and late 19th-century Berlin porcelain displays mainly Classical influences, while other factories such as Meissen concentrated on the revival of 18th-century Rococo models. However, such forms as vases became larger and heavier, and decoration often more ornate: the simple, angular shape for handles, for example, was replaced by animal heads.

Berlin's tradition of treating porcelain primarily as a medium for painting reached its apogee *c*.1840 with the development of porcelain plaques. Like paintings, these were usually rectangular and enclosed in richly modeled gilt frames. They were sold as blanks to outside workshops and painted by independent decorators (*Hausmaler*). The very finely executed subjects were initially copies or details of Old Master works; however, during the last third of the 19th century the themes were less profound: exotic maidens in traditional costume, scantily clad nymphs among flowers, or rather sentimental religious subjects.

From *c*.1850 Rococo Revival elements, such as curling scrollwork, flowers, and shells, appeared in the decoration of tablewares and vases. This decoration, combined with the gilded and colored grounds and topographical views, resulted in an overdecorated effect. This would never have occurred in the 18th century, when restrained decoration was used to create balance. The factory also experimented in mid-century with the Renaissance Revival style by manufacturing copies of Italian Renaissance maiolica and 17th-century German stoneware. These pieces have much heavier forms than the originals. The production of figures at this time was confined mainly to busts and figures of the royal family, ladies in contemporary dress on pedestals, and a limited revival of 18th-century models of such subjects as pastoral figures and tradesmen.

During the 1870s the factory suffered severe financial setbacks, but Hermann Seger, appointed technical director in 1878, revived its fortunes and ensured its future by developing a series of new glazes. The subtle glaze effects on Oriental porcelain were particularly fashionable in the late 19th century, especially after Japanese and Chinese ceramics were displayed at the numerous European international exhibitions. Seger was the first manufacturer in Europe to reproduce rich flambé and *sang-de-boeuf* glazes by developing the "Seger cones," which allowed accurate control of firing temperatures. This type of Oriental-inspired porcelain was known as "*Seger-Porzellan*," and the new technology was taken up in porcelain factories throughout Europe. The Berlin factory continues to produce fine porcelain today.

◄ **Plaque of *Ruth* painted by H. Weigel**

Such biblical subject-matter as this image of Ruth from the Old Testament holding a sheaf of corn was enormously popular in Europe during the later 19th century. As with many plaques, the images depicted were copied from well-known paintings of the time; this example is after a work by the French painter Charles Landelle (1821–1908) who specialized in somewhat sentimental religious paintings during the mid- to late 19th century. Plaques were usually supplied together with frames, and as many were made during the Rococo Revival they would have been scrolled and heavily gilded. On some inexpensive examples it is possible to see the brown outlines of the printed design, which have been overpainted in enamels.
(1880; ht 33cm/13in; value H)

▼ **Cabinet cup, cover, and saucer**

Individual sets of cups and saucers for display were particularly popular among the bourgeoisie, who could not always afford to buy large table services. The scenes depicted include views of the palaces at Koblenz, Godesberg, Bingen, Nonnenwerth, Neuwied, and Winkel-u.-Johanesberg.
(1844–7; diam. of saucer 17cm/6¾in; value F)

KEY FACTS

- BODY high-quality, white, hard-paste porcelain with a glassy glaze and a slightly cold, bluish tinge

Before *c*.1840
- STYLE restrained Neo-classical
- FORMS cabinet cups and saucers; Easter eggs
- DECORATION gilt borders finely tooled with Classical motifs; highly finished topographical paintings imitating oils; colored and gilt grounds

After *c*.1840
- STYLE eclectic, combining both Rococo and Classical elements
- FORMS painted plaques with elaborate gilt frames
- DECORATION very ornate, with applied gilt motifs such as shells and curling scrollwork combined with colored grounds and paintings; paintings of sentimental religious subjects or exotic maidens on plaques

Marks
1832–: this orb mark was printed in blue or red; the KPM stands for the Königliche Porzellan-Manufaktur

KPM

1849–70: this mark was printed in blue; the Prussian eagle holds the orb and the scepter in its claws

Dresden and other Meissen imitators

The success of the Meissen factory in reviving, from the 1840s, its 18th-century figures and wares was reflected in the large number of smaller porcelain factories and decoration workshops that produced less expensive copies and adaptations of 18th-century Meissen in the second half of the 19th century. Most of these enterprises were in and around the Saxon capital of Dresden, but several were also established in the neighboring regions of Thuringia, Silesia, and Bohemia.

▲ **Clockcase from Dresden**
Sentimental and over-ornate, this clockcase is typical of the Rococo Revival style. The manufacture of such elaborate pieces was made possible by advances in slip-casting.
(late 19th century; ht 71cm/28in; value H)

IMPORTANT MANUFACTURERS

In the late 19th and early 20th centuries there were at least 40 porcelain workshops or decorators in and around Dresden, most of them copying the Meissen style. The best pieces may be mistaken for Meissen, but the hard paste used by most workshops is less white and refined than Meissen porcelain. The most common products are individual figures and groups, vases, centerpieces, clockcases, baskets, candelabra, and candlesticks. Figures usually wear 18th-century costume but are larger and far more elaborate than Meissen originals, and groups may include several heavily decorated figures crammed onto one base.

One of the best and most prolific of the Meissen imitators was the factory established by Carl Thieme at Potschappel in 1872, specializing in high-quality items such as candelabra and mirror frames. Other notable manufacturers included the Schlesische porcelain factory in Tiefenfurt, Silesia, the factory of the Voigt brothers in Sitzendorf, Thuringia, and several workshops in Volkstedt, also in Thuringia.

DRESDEN DECORATORS

The most obvious difference between 19th-century pieces and Meissen originals is the quality, and style of decoration. Most 19th-century pieces are in the popular Rococo Revival style. Compared with the delicacy and sparing decoration of original Rococo, they appear over-ornate, with flowers, shells, scrollwork, and figures all together, and are less carefully painted in more garish tones. A distinctive feature is intricate lacework, made by dipping real lace into the liquid paste and firing it.

The workshop of Helena Wolfsohn (est. 1843) in Dresden was one of the most prolific decorating workshops. Wolfsohn specialized in painting vases and tea and coffee wares, often in imitation of Meissen; the decoration was typically divided into quarters decorated with figures in landscapes and flowers, in the style of the French painter Antoine Watteau. Other Dresden workshops included Donath & Co. (est. *c.*1872), Richard Klemm (est. late 1860s), Oswald Lorenz (est. *c.*1880), and Adolph Hammann (est. mid-1860s). These workshops used floral sprays with gilt scroll borders on cups and saucers, and green, blue, or pink scale or "mosaic" borders on ornamental wares.

▼ **Pot-pourri vase by Thieme**
The Thieme factory was one of the best imitators of the 18th-century Meissen Rococo style. Features adapted from the Rococo include painted *fêtes galantes* (alfresco picnics) after Antoine Watteau, garlands of flowers and fruit; and pierced covers and stands.
(c.1880; ht 90cm/35½in; value K)

▲ **Group of festive figures from Dresden**
The crowding of several excessively decorated figures onto one base indicates that this group was made in the 19th century. An 18th-century piece would also be sparingly and carefully painted in paler colors.
(late 19th century; ht 36cm/14in; value G)

KEY FACTS

- BODY hard-paste porcelain, not as white and refined as that of Meissen
- FORMS elaborate figures and groups, ornamental vases, clockcases, baskets, candelabra, mirror frames, tea and coffee services
- PALETTE strong greens, yellows, pinks, reds, and blues, which were never used on originals
- DECORATION painting was not always carefully applied; Rococo Revival style: usually every part of the piece was decorated with painted scenes in the manner of 18th-century French artists such as Watteau and Boucher, or encrusted with heavily modeled or cast flowers, scrolls, and shells; ornamental pieces with richly modeled or cast and painted mythological, allegorical, and pastoral figures, birds, and animals
- COLLECTING wares from such factories as Carl Thieme in Potschappel and the Voigt factory in Sitzendorf are the most collectible

Marks

Some factories used marks similar to the Meissen crossed swords, which are sometimes ground off 19th-century copies to conceal their origins; collectors should beware of an unglazed patch on the back or the base of a piece

Potschappel: factory of Carl Thieme (est. 1875)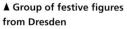

See also Meissen figures and services, pp.174–5

Fairings, ribbon plates, and lithophanes

At the end of the 19th century, industrial investment – coupled with an astute eye on the worldwide market – led German makers to begin the mass production of inexpensive porcelain. In due course, as less costly imported ornaments found eager British buyers, this brought about the demise of the Staffordshire figure industry. By their very nature these German novelties were of somewhat poor quality, but they can still be both decorative and enjoyable.

BISQUE FIGURES AND FAIRINGS

Although there was a tradition in Dresden, stretching back to the 18th century, of producing fine porcelain figures, less expensive figurines by Dresden manufacturers also found a ready market. Unglazed (a state called "biscuit" or "bisque"), such figures were inexpensive to produce and showed the detail of their modeling well. Since they were liable to become chipped and dirty easily, some were put under protective glass domes. Very inexpensive figures would be made in a single two-piece mold, while more elaborate examples, often pleasing and of reasonable quality, were assembled from many pieces. Most figures were issued as pairs and remain inexpensive today. The best makers included the Heubach factory at Lichte near Wallendorf in Thuringia, which was famous for its "Piano Babies" – figures of crawling or seated children designed to sit on a table or piano. Heubach also made bisque dolls' heads.

Another popular range of German items was a series of glazed figure groups aimed mostly at the British market, with English titles on the bases. Originally marketed as "bazaar goods," these pieces are today called "fairings" because they were frequently sold at fairgrounds. The subjects were often risqué or humorous in a "saucy seaside" manner, with jokes about marriage, drink, and lavatories. The principal maker, from c.1880 to 1900, was Conta & Boehme of Pössneck in eastern Germany, which also produced many other inexpensive figures and novelties, including holders for matches.

▲ Bisque figure
This colored German figure in unglazed porcelain is known as a "biscuit" or "bisque" figure. It has a sweet, doll-like face, which is typical of this type of production. These types of figure were made all over Germany and its related areas. They were not made as great works of art, and this example, which is one of a pair, is of better quality than many. The cricketing theme adds considerably to its value.
(c.1890; ht 22cm/8½in; value **C**)

◄ Fairings group
German fairings were popular pieces for displaying on the mantelpiece. The shoeshine boy charging extra for a three-legged Manxman in this figure group would have appealed to the prevailing sense of humor in the late Victorian age.
(c.1880–90; ht 11cm/4¼in; value **C**)

▲ Lithophane
Shown above are two views of the same Berlin porcelain lithophane, lit from the front and from the back. Shining a light through a fine-quality lithophane reveals the hidden picture. This example bears the impressed "KPM" mark of the Royal Berlin Factory.
(mid-19th century; ht 22cm/8½in; value **C**)

RIBBON PLATES AND LITHOPHANES

It is traditionally believed that plates with pierced borders were intended to be hung from ribbons threaded through the holes in the rims – hence the name "ribbon plates." Many were indeed displayed in this way, but many others formed part of fruit sets, and their cut-out borders were purely decorative. A variety of subjects decorated the centers, especially popular German and English tourist towns. Most were inexpensively printed in black or sometimes with color lithographs. Ribbon plates were particularly popular with bargees for their canal boats and also decorated many travelers' caravans. Originally costing very little, the plates remain inexpensive today.

A lithophane is a very thin plaque of unglazed, hard-paste porcelain bearing a lightly molded design that is fully revealed only when light is transmitted through it. A huge variety of subject exists, mostly copies of famous paintings and Rhineland views. Lithophanes enjoyed a long popularity, and were originally mounted into lampshades, firescreens, and window panes. They were also known as '"Berlin transparencies" because that factory was a major manufacturer, as was the Plaue factory at Plaue an der Havel in Thuringia.

KEY FACTS

- **TYPES** ornamental, unglazed single figures or groups, sometimes risqué; pierced plates; decorated plaques
- **DECORATION** ribbon plates were mostly decorated with town views; lithophanes bear Rhineland views and copies of Old Master paintings
- **COLLECTING** bisque figures: usually inexpensive; lithophanes: values vary according to size and subject-matter, and hand-colored examples are very rare; fairings: reasonably priced, the value depending on the rarity of the subject and the quality of the modeling; ribbon plates: generally inexpensive

Marks

Examples made after 1900 were usually stamped "Made in Germany" – but this mark was commonly rubbed off during the world wars

Pössneck: Conta & Boehme (est. 1790); usually impressed, or occasionally printed, with this mark

See also Dolls & Teddy Bears: Bisque Dolls – Germany, pp.490–91

The Low Countries, Switzerland, and Scandinavia

In the 18th century, as the fashion for porcelain reached its peak, many porcelain factories were established outside Germany and France, the main centers of production. Many new factories were founded by arcanists, modelers, and decorators who exploited their knowledge of porcelain manufacture, moving from factory to factory throughout Europe. Unsurprisingly, most of the smaller European operations imitated the styles of Meissen and Sèvres, although their wares sometimes display an interesting mixture of influences.

THE LOW COUNTRIES

In 1750 François-Joseph Peterinck (1719–99) established a factory in Tournai and, with the help of the arcanist Robert Dubois, produced soft-paste porcelain. The influence of Meissen in the tablewares can be seen in the molded basket-weave borders and the spiral patterns around the rims of plates, while the decoration is more English-inspired. The specialities of Tournai were exotic birds and scenes taken from Aesop's fables in underglaze blue, both of which were used at Chelsea and Worcester. Typical of Tournai, too, are landscape vignettes in puce or purple monochrome, surrounded by small sprays of flowers. The factory also made a limited range of *galanterie* – small decorative objects such as snuff-boxes.

◄ *Autumn* by Tournai
Biscuit figures with tree-stump supports on rockwork bases are typical of 18th-century Tournai wares. This figure is vigorously modeled in the round, so that it may be viewed from all sides. It is part of a set of four allegorical figures representing the seasons. This particular example clearly shows the influence of the Sèvres factory.
(*c.1765; ht 12cm/4¾in; value E*)

Tournai produced a large range of figures and groups following contemporary French taste in their subject-matter, in particular pastoral scenes of shepherds and children by artists who had worked at Mennecy. The thickly glazed groups are painted in a pale palette or left in the white, but lack crisp modeling. Also typical of Tournai are figures and groups in biscuit porcelain, especially those on high rockwork bases around a central tree; groups like these were made at Derby.

Peterinck retired in 1796, and ownership of Tournai passed to his daughter Amélie de Bettignies (1757–after 1805). The factory continued making simple household wares, but no more figures, until the mid-19th century. Many 18th-century wares were sold undecorated, and were later painted at a porcelain factory in The Hague set up in 1776 by a German porcelain dealer, Anton Lyncker (1718–81). The Hague factory also made its own hard-paste porcelain wares, decorated in a manner similar to Tournai's. Confusingly, both The Hague factory's own products and the Tournai pieces that it decorated have the same mark; any soft-paste ware bearing an overglaze mark of a stork is likely to be (but by no means definitely is) of Tournai origin.

The first successful Dutch porcelain factory was established in Weesp, near Amsterdam, in 1757 by the Irish arcanist D. MacCarthy, who had been involved in attempts to manufacture porcelain in Copenhagen. This factory has a complex history of ownership. In 1771 it changed hands and moved to Oude Loosdrecht, and in 1782 moved to Amstel, near Amsterdam, where it remained until its closure in 1820. All the Dutch factories used a good-quality white hard paste with a clear glaze. Some small figures of putti holding salts were made at Weesp. At Oude Loosdrecht and Amstel, production was focused entirely on wares – mainly tea, coffee and dinner services. In both form and decoration the wares are similar to Meissen and other German porcelain.

SWITZERLAND

Most porcelain factories in Europe were established by aristocratic patrons who could afford luxury products; in Switzerland, where there was no monarchy, a group of prominent citizens established the first porcelain factory in Zurich in 1763. The factory initially made a soft-paste porcelain but switched to the production of hard paste c.1765.

Reflecting the demands of Switzerland's dominant middle-class market, the bulk of Zurich production was tea, coffee and dinner services. These generally followed German Rococo and Neo-classical styles, but the complex scrolled handles on coffee- and teapots were unique to Zurich. In terms of

◄ Tea-caddy and cover from Weesp
The form and decoration of this tea-caddy, in particular its curved shoulders and chinoiserie design, clearly show the influence of the Meissen factory – many of the craftsmen at Weesp came from German factories. The painting is much more stylized than that which would be found on a similar Meissen piece, and the poses of the figures stiffer.
(*c.1770; ht 12cm/4¾in; value H*)

▼ *Broken Eggs* modeled by Valentin Sonnenschein for Zurich
This charming figure of a maiden weeping over a basket of broken eggs is typical of the sometimes sentimental subject-matter used for porcelain figures during the 18th century. Its rather static pose, the simplified modeling of limbs, and the broad washes of pale green, brown, gray, and pink are all reminiscent of figures made at the German factory of Ludwigsburg, where Sonnenschein had worked.
(*c.1777; ht 14cm/5½in; value I*)

decoration, the Zurich factory is associated with small pastoral landscapes in a palette dominated by blues and greens. Some exquisitely painted landscapes in warmer colors are by Salomon Gessner (1739–79), one of the founders; unfortunately the enamels are often flaky because the paint was applied too thickly. The colorful, naturalistic sprays of flowers familiar on 18th-century Meissen also featured at Zurich, although the flower sprays tend to be looser. Other kinds of decoration included a version of the Oriental banded hedge pattern, usually in purple, and vignettes of birds on branches.

Almost 400 different types of figure and group were made, mostly in the late Rococo style. The famous Meissen series of the street vendors of London and Paris may have inspired the set of 42 street-sellers called the "Cries of Zurich." The finest figures were probably modeled by Valentin Sonnenschein (1749–1828), from Ludwigsburg, and, perhaps because of his influence, many Zurich figures resemble those made there. The factory closed in 1791, owing to financial problems caused by competition from other factories and imports of inexpensive creamware from England.

SCANDINAVIA

In the 1730s several French and German arcanists, including Christoph Conrad Hunger of Meissen and Vienna, produced soft-paste porcelain on a limited scale in Copenhagen. In 1774 the first hard-paste porcelain factory was founded there. Queen Caroline Matilda was the main shareholder of this factory; after her exile it was bought in 1779 by King Christian VII and styled the Royal Danish Porcelain Factory. A fine, white hard paste with a clear glaze was used to make wares mainly in a severe Neo-classical style, much influenced by Berlin, Vienna, and Sèvres.

Cylindrical teapots and coffee-cups with angular handles, and trays with angled sides, are typically embellished with oval and cylindrical medallions enclosing landscapes, topographical views, or portraits in sepia, puce, or pink monochrome, surrounded with swags and colored borders heightened with gilding. Botanical subjects were also popular, the most famous

example being the 1,800-piece "Flora Danica" service (1789–1802) that was probably made for Catherine the Great of Russia.

The factory declined in the early 19th century, but under the direction (1828–57) of Gustav Friedrich Hetsch it produced biscuit figures, notably those based on the work of the Neo-classical sculptor Berthel Thorvaldsen. The factory enjoyed a renaissance when in 1885 the architect and painter Arnold Krug (1856–1931) was appointed artistic director. With new glaze technology, he introduced a revolutionary form of underglaze painting, using simple washes of blues and grays to produce an effect very similar to Japanese pottery.

Johann Ludwig Eberhard Ehrenreich (1722–1803) produced porcelain between 1766 and 1787 at Marieberg, near Stockholm. It initially used a soft paste for Rococo wares, especially spiral-fluted custard cups similar to those made at Mennecy. A hard-paste porcelain was introduced from 1777.

▲ Sauceboat and stand from the "Flora Danica" dinner service from Copenhagen
This service is probably the most celebrated product of the Copenhagen factory. It depicts specimens of Danish flora within bead and foliage borders with gilt dentil rims. On the reverse of each piece, the flower featured is named in Latin.
*(c.1900; ht 17.5cm/7in; value **D**)*

▲ Plate from Zurich
The simple lobed shape, gilt dentil rim, and lack of molding suggest that this plate may have been made in the Neo-classical period, when forms and decoration were restrained. Precisely painted landscape vignettes, as seen on this example, are particularly associated with wares made in Zurich.
*(c.1780; diam. 24cm/9½in; value **H**)*

◄ Teapot from Zurich
Globular teapots seem to have been especially popular at Zurich. This one has the characteristic Rococo animal spout and complex scrolled handle, together with puce highlights. Landscapes were the most common form of decoration; other themes included finely painted birds with very subtle coloring.
*(c.1775; ht 8.5cm/3¼in; value **H**)*

Austria

Vienna

After unsuccessful attempts to make porcelain, Claudius Innocentius Du Paquier (d.1751) bribed the Meissen arcanist Christoph Conrad Hunger (active c.1717–48) to come to Vienna in 1717 to teach him the secret formula. Hunger's expertise proved to be limited, so Du Paquier employed Böttger's kilnmaster Samuel Stölzel (d.1737) in 1719, and the factory made its first successful hard-paste porcelain.

THE DU PAQUIER PERIOD: 1719–44

The shapes of Du Paquier's wares are similar to early Meissen, as they are copied from Baroque silver and are of symmetrical form embellished with scrollwork. The factory also made some original items: tall beakers, sometimes with molded borders and usually on a narrow foot; bottles or flasks applied with masks or modeled with animal-head spouts; and double-handled beakers on large, oval *trembleuse* stands.

Flower decoration was copied from Chinese and Japanese wares with a palette dominated by iron red, green and manganese purple; contemporary Meissen wares are much closer to the originals. Vienna, however, pioneered the use of European flower decoration on porcelain c.1730. At first these were precisely painted in the style of botanical engravings, but from c.1740 to 1745 they are smaller and scattered, with much freer brushwork. Another innovation was the use of black, puce, or iron-red monochrome for battle and hunting scenes and chinoiserie; black monochrome, known as "*Schwarzlot*" ("black lead"), was a common technique among the *Hausmaler* who worked for the factory. These scenes were often enclosed by borders or cartouches of Baroque scrollwork with *Laub- und Bandelwerk* ("leaf- and strapwork") ornament.

▲ *Ecuelle* and cover
The form of this vessel and the mask feet were copied directly from contemporary metalwork. Characteristic of early Vienna wares are its square handles, iron-red trellis ground, and *Schwarzlot* chinoiserie scene.
(1725–30; ht 15cm/6in; value I)

FIRST STATE PERIOD: 1744–1841

Although the early Vienna wares were successful, the factory's finances were always precarious. In 1744 Du Paquier sold the factory to the Austrian state, which had been supporting it for many years. Because its financial troubles might have been due to over-production, the factory did not introduce any new designs until c.1750. From this date, wares and figures were made in the fashionable Rococo style. The paste was improved c.1749 with the use of a much finer clay imported from Hungary.

With the outbreak of the Seven Years War in 1756 there was a new influx to Vienna of Meissen craftsmen who influenced the style of decoration; typical themes were scattered European flowers, unframed monochrome landscapes, and scenes within cartouches and paintings in the manner of Boucher, Watteau, and Teniers.

The greatest innovation of this period was the wide variety of figures, particularly those modeled by Johann Josef Niedermayer (d.1784), chief modeler from 1747. A series of dwarfs copied from engravings by the French printmaker Jacques Callot (1592–1635) is particularly notable. Many were left in the white, while others were painted in very pale colors such as lilac and lemon yellow. The bases are usually a simple pad shape, and are frequently embellished with a wavy gilt border around the bottom edge.

THE SORGENTHAL PERIOD: 1784–c.1830

After several financial problems at the factory Conrad Sörgel von Sorgenthal was appointed director in 1784. Phasing out the Rococo style in favor of refined Neo-classicism, he was responsible for the production of superb wares equaled only by the Berlin factory. Simple, geometric forms were adopted in line with the severe Neo-classical style, and urn and amphora shapes were directly copied from antique pieces excavated at Pompeii and Herculaneum. The factory was particularly famous for its *tête-à-tête* services and solitaires.

The decoration of Vienna wares was among the finest of the period. Colored grounds with sumptuous gilding and rich painting meant that none of the white body of the porcelain was left showing. Vienna is especially associated with raised gilding with tooled architectural ornament. From 1791, following the example of Sèvres, the chemist Josef Leithner developed brilliant ground colors, in particular a claret and a dark blue. The overall effect was enhanced by the fine painting of Classical subjects, topographical views, and botanical subjects in central or reserved panels. The greatest exponent of botanical subjects was Josef Nigg (active 1800–43), whose most celebrated works are minutely painted flower still-lifes on rectangular plaques.

Figures were made on a limited scale at the end of the 18th century. Generally in biscuit porcelain, they were based on Classical sculptures and Pompeian paintings, or were busts of the imperial family and such luminaries as the composer Haydn. The most important modeler was Anton Grassi (1755–1807), who for several months in 1792 visited Rome, where he sketched and noted the recently excavated Classical sculpture.

▲ The *Walper Hollriglin* after a model by Johann Christoph Ludwig Lück
This figure of a dwarf is based on one of the characters depicted by Callot, whose engravings were a popular source of inspiration for porcelain modelers in the 18th century. The very pale washes were much favored by Vienna painters in the Rococo period.
(c.1755; ht 11cm/4¼in; value I)

▲ The Huntsman
Figures such as this were among the most popular of those made by the European porcelain factories during the 18th century. This figure can be identified as a Vienna piece because of the gilt border around the edge of the base, the green and pink pastel coloring, and the slightly stiff pose.
(c.1760; ht 15cm/6in; value F)

After the death of Sorgenthal, Matthias Niedermayer (*d.*1827) became director. The factory was still producing Neo-classical-style wares, but by the 1830s the restrained 18th-century style had been replaced by the heavier, rounded shapes that characterize the Biedermeier taste. Painters continued to embellish plaques, trays, services, and vases with copies of Old Masters, and original botanical, topographical, and Classical compositions; however, the overall decoration is less rich (often with areas of white porcelain showing) and slightly poorer in execution.

◄ **Coffee-pot**

This fine coffee-pot in the Neo-classical style forms part of a *déjeuner* set, or small breakfast service, with each piece decorated with a so-called "named view" of a carefully detailed topographical scene in Italy. Like Berlin pieces of a similar date, the landscape is very finely painted within tooled gilt floral and foliate borders, so as to emulate the effect of an oil painting.
*(c.1801; ht 12cm/4¾in; value **G**)*

AFTER *c.*1830

Although it had encountered various problems from the beginning of the 19th century, from *c.*1830 the Vienna factory entered a serious period of decline, producing inexpensive, rather poor-quality porcelain with transfer-printed decoration to keep up with demand and to try to compete with mass-produced goods, particularly those made in Bohemia. Attempts were made to turn it into an art institute and a model factory, but in 1864 Emperor Francis Joseph ordered its closure.

Subsequently, large quantities of undecorated Vienna porcelain, some dating back to the beginning of the 19th century, were sold off to other factories and decorators. Such wares were decorated in the Classical Revival style of the Sorgenthal period, with heavy gilt borders, Classical motifs, and topographical scenes, often reserved on a claret ground. As the wares were made at the Vienna factory, they bear the underglaze blue shield mark of Vienna and on this basis could be mistaken as original; however, the decoration is much less refined and sometimes verges on extremely coarse. These wares are now described as "Vienna" pieces.

Numerous firms in Bohemia, Silesia, and Germany (particularly Dresden and Thuringia) made their own wares in the Vienna style during the last quarter of the 19th century. The Augarten Factory (est. 1922), in Vienna, continues to reproduce earlier Vienna porcelain, mostly in the Neo-classical and Biedermeier styles; its products are also marked with the underglaze blue shield.

► **Coffee-can and saucer**

A specialty of Vienna during this period was the use of gilt bands on a colored ground, as seen here. At Berlin, in contrast, broad gilt borders were usually employed as framing motifs. A piece such as this would have been displayed rather than actually used.
*(c.1805; ht of cup 5cm/2in; value **G**)*

▲ **Dish in the style of the Vienna factory, made in Austria**

Although many factories attempted to copy the distinctive Neo-classical style of Vienna in the late 19th century, their products do not match the originals. Compared with the refined and sparingly used decoration of fine-quality Vienna wares, this piece is decorated too liberally with gilt scrollwork. The rather erotic representation of a young woman, with its soft brushwork, also suggests a late 19th-century date.
*(1880; diam. 38cm/15in; value **H**)*

KEY FACTS

1719–44

- BODY creamy-white hard paste; smoky, thin glaze with greenish hue
- STYLE heavy Baroque forms and dense, symmetrical decoration
- PALETTE iron red, green, and manganese purple for Oriental flowers; pale, delicate colors for European flowers; black, puce, and iron-red monochrome
- DECORATION Oriental and European flowers, chinoiseries; battle, hunting, and mythological scenes; latticework and *Laub- und Bandelwerk* decoration

1744–84

- BODY grayish hard paste; white and glassy glaze
- DECORATION European flowers, monochrome landscapes, copies of French and Dutch paintings
- FIGURES left white or painted in pale colors
- BASES pad, sometimes with a wavy gilt border

Marks

This mark was made in underglaze blue from *c.*1749; it was sometimes impressed mid-1740s

1784–*c.*1830

- BODY warmer-colored hard paste
- STYLE Neo-classical, rich Empire, and Biedermeier
- DECORATION raised gilding; claret and dark blue grounds; mythological and Classical scenes and topographical views

Marks

As mark above; from 1783 the last two digits of the year were impressed; after 1800 the last three digits of the year were impressed

After *c.*1830

- BODY hard, glassy white paste
- STYLE Neo-classical; heavy gilded borders; less refined; colors stronger than the originals

See also Glass: Enameled glass – Before 1800, pp.288–9

Italy and Spain

Capodimonte, Buen Retiro, and Naples

The first porcelain produced in Europe was made in Florence at the factory started by Francesco I de' Medici, a member of one of the most powerful ruling families in Europe. The duke had a great interest in the applied arts and chemistry, and in the 1570s he initiated experiments in porcelain manufacture that would produce the first successful European soft-paste, or "artificial," porcelain in 1575. The Medici porcelain enterprise was short-lived, however, and it was not until more than 150 years later that soft paste was again produced in Italy.

▲ Coffee-cup and saucer by Capodimonte
The Capodimonte factory used an unusual decorative technique called "stippling," whereby intricate designs were created using dots of color laboriously applied with the point of a brush.
(c.1750; ht of cup 6.5cm/2½in; value H)

CAPODIMONTE AND BUEN RETIRO

The most famous porcelain factory in Italy was founded by Charles IV, King of Naples and Sicily (later Charles III of Spain), in 1743 at the royal palace of Capodimonte. Although wares generally imitated those made at Meissen and Vienna in shape and decoration, a distinctive soft palette and stippled designs were used. Subjects included chinoiseries, landscapes with small figures and fruit and flowers, and battle scenes.

Capodimonte figures by the chief modeler, Giuseppe Gricci (d.1770), rank with those of Franz Anton Bustelli (1722–63) at Nymphenburg and Johann Joachim Kändler (1706–75) at Meissen. Gricci's elegant yet lively modeling is particularly well set off by the fine soft paste, which heightens the effect of the flowing lines.

Many of the figures are undecorated, revealing the beautiful material, while others are painted in muted pastel shades. Gricci gave his figures disproportionately small heads, a feature peculiar to Capodimonte. He is also well known for his fabulous porcelain room in the royal palace at Portici, which is covered entirely with porcelain panels ornamented with chinoiserie figures.

In 1759 Charles succeeded his father as King of Spain, and moved the factory to the palace of Buen Retiro in Madrid. Early Buen Retiro wares are almost indistinguishable from Capodimonte. However, in the 1770s the factory ceased to import materials from Italy, and the quality of the paste deteriorated, becoming grayer and less refined. The Buen Retiro factory concentrated on the production of figures rather than wares; these are generally fairly sculptural in style and include allegorical subjects, peasants, and saints.

NAPLES

After Charles III left for Spain, his son became King of Naples and Sicily as Ferdinand IV. In 1771 he revived the production of porcelain, which continued until 1806 when he was deposed by the French. Biscuit figures and Classical groups were created by the chief modeler, Filippo Tagliolini (1745–1808); the factory also made biscuit copies of antique sculpture from nearby Pompeii and Herculaneum. Most popular with collectors are the figures of peasants and bourgeois in brightly colored contemporary dress. Tea, coffee, and dinner services and vases are typical wares, decorated with views of Naples and its surroundings, including Mount Etna.

▼ Cosmetic pot by Buen Retiro
It is thought that the gilded initials on this cosmetic pot are those of Maria Luisa, wife of Charles IV of Spain (reigned 1788–1808). The number 32, which appears on the front of the pot, may indicate that the piece was one of a series.
(c.1790; ht 8cm/3in; value E).

▲ Figure group from Naples
Figures such as this couple in late 18th-century dress are very popular with collectors today. The broad washes of bold colors, the rocky base, the lack of characterization, and the rather stiff poses are all characterisitc features of Neapolitan figures.
(1790; ht 18.5cm/7¼in; value J)

KEY FACTS

Capodimonte (1743–59) and Buen Retiro (1760–1812)
- BODY pure white and translucent with brilliant glaze, giving a slightly creamy tone; at Buen Retiro grayer and less refined, replaced by hard paste 1803
- DECORATION small figures in landscapes; fruit and flowers; chinoiseries in very pale, soft palette, often in stippled technique; continuous battle scenes
- FIGURES elegant and vigorously modeled; most have small heads; most undecorated or sparingly painted

Marks
Capodimonte: this mark was used from c.1745: impressed, painted in gold or in underglaze blue

Buen Retiro: this underglaze blue mark was used in various forms from c.1760

Naples (1771–1806)
- BODY glassy, white paste, similar to Capodimonte but lacking ivory-toned translucency
- DECORATION views of Naples and surroundings, sometimes very finely painted; also "Etruscan" style in black, white, and terracotta, imitating Greek vases
- FIGURES Classical biscuit groups; miniatures of antique statues; stiffly modeled peasants and bourgeoisie in brightly colored contemporary costume

Marks
This underglaze blue mark was used by the factory in the late 18th century

Vezzi, Cozzi, and Doccia

The production of hard-paste porcelain in Italy began only ten years after the founding of the Meissen factory. The manufacture of hard paste in Italy was in some ways more successful than that of soft paste; whereas the Naples factory closed in the 19th century, the Doccia factory continues today.

VEZZI

The factory was founded in Venice in 1720 by the goldsmith Francesco Vezzi (1651–1740) and Christoph Conrad Hunger, an arcanist who had worked at Meissen and Vienna. The factory was short-lived, and very few pieces of Vezzi porcelain are known today. Production consisted mainly of cups and saucers, coffee- and teapots, and plates. As the material was still experimental, wares were thickly potted so that they did not collapse in the kiln. Vezzi forms were often inspired by contemporary Baroque silver or Oriental porcelain shapes. Among the popular subjects for painting were stylized floral motifs, large *commedia dell'arte* figures, and chinoiseries.

COZZI

The second hard-paste porcelain factory in Venice was established in 1764 by Geminiano Cozzi (1728–97). Its output was larger and more successful than that of Vezzi. Cozzi introduced the lighter Rococo style. Some wares have applied flowers, but most are painted, in a palette dominated by iron red, puce, and an iridescent green. The most common themes are flowers, unframed landscapes, and Classical figures in scrollwork or solid borders. Cozzi figures include Meissen-style pagoda figures, characters from the *commedia dell'arte*, and dwarfs modeled after engravings by the French artist Jacques Callot (1592–1635). They do not often appear on the market today and so are highly prized by collectors.

DOCCIA

The Doccia factory was founded near Florence in 1737 by Carlo Ginori (1702–57). The earliest porcelain was a hybrid hard paste that had a rough, smeared surface and often cracked when fired. The quality improved after 1770, when a glaze that included tin oxide was used to make it whiter and opaque.

The largest part of the factory's output was small and decorative wares, and tea and table services. The factory used some very distinctive types of decoration that make its wares easily recognizable, including designs known as "a galetto rosso" (Chinese-style cockerels painted in iron red and gold), "a tulipano" (iron-red peonies in the Oriental style), and classical figures molded in low relief, with strong flesh tones and gilded details. The style was much imitated in the 19th century, but 18th-century examples are rare. Other techniques included decoration with stenciling ("stampino") in blue and white. The factory also produced figures with well-defined musculature on elaborate scroll bases. Some were left in the white, but others were painted in intense colors or, more rarely, in iron-red monochrome.

In the 19th century the factory continued to produce wares and figures in its 18th-century patterns. In 1896 it was incorporated with the Società Richard of Milan under the name Richard-Ginori.

▲ Sugar-bowl by Vezzi
The compressed, globular, solid form of this sugar-bowl is typical of the Baroque style. Most Vezzi wares were molded in shallow relief, with floral or acanthus leaf borders, festoons, and swags – also features of Baroque silver.
(1725; ht 9cm/3½in; value I)

▲ Dish by Cozzi
Among the most common decorative features of Cozzi wares were molded and scalloped rims, and sprays of flowers in colored enamels, as seen on this example. The dominance of puce and bright green in the decoration of this dish is distinctive of Cozzi. Painted decoration was more common than applied, and flowers were often precisely rendered with careful detailing, especially on early pieces.
(1770; diam. 18cm/7in; value E)

► Figure of a dancing girl by Doccia
Figures produced at the Doccia factory were sometimes decorated in strong iron-red monochrome, as seen here, with the scrollwork bases detailed in puce. The apron on this animated dancing figure has been left unpainted, revealing the glossy, somewhat grayish tone paste, which is so characteristic of Doccia porcelain.
(1770; ht 16.5cm/6½in; value I)

KEY FACTS

Vezzi (1720–27)
- BODY translucent paste varying in color from pure white through creamy white to almost gray with a clear glaze
- PALETTE strong brownish-red or leaf-green enamels; underglaze blue
- DECORATION floral patterns, chinoiserie, large *commedia dell'arte* characters

Marks
This mark was usually in underglaze blue, or gold or red enamel

Cozzi (1764–1812)
- BODY grayish paste with distinctive wet-looking glaze; can vary in quality
- PALETTE dominated by iron red, puce, and an unusual iridescent green
- DECORATION painted flowers, unframed landscapes with buildings, chinoiseries, and Classical figures; applied flowers

Marks
This mark was enameled in red

Doccia (est. 1737)
- BODY gray, somewhat crude paste with distinctive, thin, sticky-looking glaze
- PALETTE dominated by iron red and puce
- DECORATION molded low-relief Classical figures, detailed in bright colors and gilding; Chinese cockerels; red peonies; transfer-printing and stenciling
- FIGURES slip-cast, modeled with stong musculature

Marks
This mark was used from the late 18th century until the first half of the 19th in blue, red, or gold

See also Art Deco: Ceramics, pp.422–7

France before 1820

Early porcelain

The porcelain factories established in France in the early 18th century manufactured soft-paste porcelain, since the kaolin necessary for the production of hard paste was not discovered in France until 1768. Early French porcelain, particularly that of Chantilly, is considered especially attractive by collectors because of its soft ivory or creamy color. The first factory was established in the 1670s in Rouen by the Poterat family, but its output was much less significant than the later factories of Saint-Cloud, Chantilly, and Mennecy.

SAINT-CLOUD

In 1664 Claude Révérend obtained a privilege to experiment with the manufacture of porcelain in and around Paris. In 1674 he employed Pierre Chicaneau (d.1677), who is said to have discovered the recipe for soft-paste porcelain. Through the patronage of the Duke of Orleans, Chicaneau's widow, Barbe Coudray (d.1717), was granted a privilege for the manufacture of faience and porcelain at Saint-Cloud in 1702.

A large range of wares was made at the factory, including ice pails, spice-boxes, snuff-boxes, *bonbonnières*, and cutlery handles. A specialty was pot-pourri vases, usually left unpainted. Early decoration comprised underglaze blue borders of *lambrequins*. From c.1730 wares were left in the white and decorated with molded prunus blossom, imitating *blanc-de-Chine* wares from Dehua in Fujian Province, China. More European designs, such as overlapping leaves and wading birds, were introduced as molded decoration. In the same period, the painters copied Japanese wares in the Kakiemon and Imari patterns.

CHANTILLY

In 1725 Louis-Henri of Bourbon, Prince of Condé, founded a porcelain factory on his estate at Chantilly. The factory is celebrated for its wares decorated in the style of Japanese Kakiemon and Chinese *famille-verte* porcelain. Many items – *jardinières*, teapots, jugs, and plates – were probably copied directly from Oriental originals in the Duke's collection. Figures of Chinese and Japanese characters were also a specialty of the factory before c.1750 and were decorated in the Kakiemon style.

After the mid-18th century, decoration of small scattered sprays of European flowers was introduced. In 1753 Louis XV issued an edict restricting the use of gilding and certain colors by French porcelain factories to protect the commercial interests of Vincennes. Permitted decoration generally consisted of simple floral designs in underglaze blue, or blue or pink enamels. During the 19th century Chantilly porcelain was extensively copied by the factory of Edmé Samson & Cie in Paris.

MENNECY

In 1734 the faience manufacturer François Barbin (1689–1765) opened a factory producing soft-paste porcelain in Paris under the patronage of the Duke of Villeroy. Wares in the style of Vincennes, Saint-Cloud, and Meissen as well as imitations of Japanese Kakiemon porcelain were made. In 1748 the factory moved to Mennecy, near Paris, where custard-cups and covers, molded with spiral or vertical fluting, and bell-shaped ice-cups, influenced by Vincennes and Sèvres, were produced. These were painted with sprays of flowers in a palette dominated by puce and red. Before 1750 the factory produced stiffly modeled Oriental figures, usually decorated in the Kakiemon palette, and after 1750 rustic peasants, children at play, allegorical figures, and, more rarely, *commedia dell'arte* figures.

▲ Pot-pourri by Mennecy
The rockwork base seen here is very similar to those used by the Mennecy factory for its figures. The rim of the cover and pierced openings in the shape of flowers are outlined in puce, because the use of gilding was forbidden to any factory in France except Sèvres (Vincennes).
(c.1760; ht 19.5cm/7¾in; value G)

◄ Strainer cup by Saint-Cloud
The delicate underglaze blue featured here is characteristic of Saint-Cloud. The symmetrical border designs of linear scrolls and scalloping are derived from the designs of Jean Bérain I, the most influential designer of ornamental patterns in the reign of Louis XIV.
(c.1700–25; ht 10cm/4in; value G)

▲ Slop bowl by Chantilly
Slop bowls were an essential part of porcelain tea services from the early 18th century onward. The example shown here is a fine imitation of a Japanese Kakiemon original. As on the original, the design appears rather flat, possibly because the enamels tended to sink into the glaze.
(c.1730; ht 10cm/4in; value H)

KEY FACTS

Saint-Cloud (1664–1766)
- BODY creamy-white or ivory soft paste, with a soft glaze that is greenish where it gathers
- DECORATION *lambrequin* borders in underglaze blue; molded prunus blossom; stiffly painted copies of Japanese Kakiemon and Imari patterns and palettes

Marks
This mark was used after 1722 in underglaze blue or red enamel; the "T" is for Henri Trou, Coudray's second husband

Chantilly (c.1725–1800)
- BODY soft-paste porcelain with a distinctive opaque, creamy tin glaze, which makes it look similar to faience; 19th-century copies are grayish and glassy
- DECORATION before the 1750s Kakiemon and *famille-verte* patterns outlined in black – these wares are the most collectible; from the 1750s European flowers in underglaze blue, or blue or pink monochrome
- FIGURES Oriental figures painted in Kakiemon palette

Marks
This is a common mark, usually in iron red but also found in underglaze blue and other colors

Mennecy (1734–1806)
- BODY similar to Saint-Cloud, with a soft, ivory tone and a slightly green tint to the glaze
- DECORATION Kakiemon style; sprays of European flowers in a pastel palette dominated by puce and red
- FIGURES stiffly modeled figures of Orientals, painted in Kakiemon style; later, figures of peasants, children, putti, and allegorical subjects in line with Rococo taste

Marks
This mark was used from the 1730s and was either incised or painted in blue

See also China: Later export porcelain, pp.136–7; Japan: Kakiemon, p.144

Vincennes and early Sèvres

The Meissen factory went into decline following the Seven Years War (1756–63) and was supplanted in terms of importance by the factory of Vincennes, later moved to Sèvres near Paris. This factory was taken under royal control, and its commercial interests were protected by royal edicts. Employing the finest artists of the day, the factory became the leading producer of porcelain in the Rococo style and, from the 1770s, the more severe Neo-classical style.

VINCENNES

The Vincennes factory was established *c.*1740 at the chateau of Vincennes, with the help of runaway workers from Chantilly. The first director was Claude-Humbert Gérin (1705–50), who discovered the secret of producing a soft paste that was much whiter and finer than that used by earlier French factories.

In 1745 Louis XV granted the factory a 20-year exclusive privilege to produce porcelain. The earliest wares, primarily influenced by Meissen, are heavy in form and painted with small flower sprays, often combined with gilt trellis and scrollwork borders, or landscape and figure scenes. The painting can be distinguished from that of Meissen by its freer brushwork and a softer palette.

Among the more distinctive early products were porcelain flower-heads, which were bought by *marchands-merciers* (dealers in luxury products) and mounted on metal stems. These flower arrangements were placed in vases or used to embellish such items as lamps, clocks, and chandeliers. Figures were made on a limited scale in the 1740s and were usually simply glazed. Popular subjects included birds, animals, nymphs, hunters, and children or putti.

In 1748 the goldsmith Jean Claude Chambellan Duplessis (1690–1774) was hired to create new forms in the Rococo taste. He designed lighter and more elegant shapes that show the influence of contemporary silver. In 1752 the painter Jean-Jacques Bachelier (1724–1806) was hired as artistic director; he introduced light-hearted, designs of children in the style of the Rococo painter François Boucher, and fanciful birds. In 1753 the King granted a new privilege to Vincennes and issued an edict restricting rival factories in their use of subjects, colors, and gilding. In 1751–2 the factory pioneered the fashion for biscuit, or unglazed, porcelain in Europe. Bachelier abandoned the production of small, freely modeled figures in favor of three-dimensional, sculptural pieces designed by such artists as Boucher.

EARLY SEVRES

In 1756 the factory moved to the chateau of Sèvres, near Paris. The quality of the paste and gilding was strictly controlled, and the King issued sumptuary laws banning the use of gilding by any other French porcelain factory in order to protect the commercial interests of Sèvres. In 1768 deposits of kaolin were discovered in the Limoges region, enabling the factory to produce hard-paste porcelain.

▼ **Flared beaker and deep saucer by Vincennes**
This type of ware, known as a *gobelet à la reine*, is decorated with sprays of delicate garden flowers, typical of the Rococo style, and painted with a gilt dentil rim. This beaker was first introduced in 1752 and was made in two sizes.
(c.1745; ht of beaker 10cm/4in; value **G***)*

▼ **Sugar-bowl by Sèvres**
Working with the chemist Jean Hellot, Bachelier developed a number of colored grounds, including a dark blue, known as *bleu lapis*, and a rose-colored pink, known as *rose Pompadour* after the Marquise de Pompadour, mistress of Louis XV, and one of the factory's most important patrons.
(1756; ht 12cm/4¾in; value **G***)*

▲ *Cuvette à fleurs* **by Sèvres**
This basin was intended for holding flowers. It is possible that it was designed by Duplessis, who is credited as being responsible for many of the forms made at Sèvres at this time.
(c.1757; ht 32.5cm/12¾in; value **H***)*

During the late 1750s and the 1760s sculptors, goldsmiths, and designers created larger and more ambitious pieces, such as the purely decorative vases *à tête d'éléphants* (vases modeled with elephant heads supporting candlesticks), and other decorative items, such as pear-shaped ewers with flat covers. In addition to colored grounds, the factory introduced several patterned grounds in the late 1760s: *oeil de perdrix* ("partridge eye"), *caillouté* ("pebbled"), and *vermiculé* ("worm-cast"). The reserve panels are often filled in, with little of the white porcelain left showing, contrasting with the more spare decoration employed at Vincennes. However, large, functional services, tend to have less elaborate painting – typically, small scattered flowers, which are more stylized than those used at Vincennes. Biscuit was the most popular medium for figures and the sculptor Etienne-Maurice Falconet (1716–91), chief modeler between 1757 and 1766, continued the tradition of charming, if sometimes rather sentimental groups of children, lovers, and allegorical subjects.

KEY FACTS

Vincennes
- BODY soft-paste porcelain
- STYLE copies of Meissen; later, Rococo wares
- FIGURES unglazed with tree stump, rockwork, or vase supports in the 1740s; after 1751 three-dimensional, crisply modeled biscuit figures

Early Sèvres
- BODY soft-paste porcelain
- STYLE delicate and elegant Rococo
- DECORATION patterned as well as plain, colored grounds reserved with typically Rococo themes within fine gilt frames
- FIGURES sentimental biscuit figures and groups of lovers and children, inspired by Boucher's paintings

Marks
Vincennes: interlaced "L"s without a date letter were used from *c.*1740 to 1752

Sèvres: the first date letter was introduced in 1753 ("A"); the letter "H" is for 1760

See also Later Sèvres, p.194

Later Sèvres

NEO-CLASSICAL WARES

In the late 1770s the Neo-classical taste became popular in France. At Sèvres, curving, sinuous forms were replaced by strictly geometric shapes or forms based on antique vases and urns. More subdued sepias and grays were used instead of the bright colors of the Rococo, and grisaille (monochrome gray) medallions and white figures on dark grounds based on frescoes uncovered at Pompeii were popular. Decorative Classical motifs include arabesques, palmettes, festoons, garlands, and acanthus leaves. Among the finest examples of this style at Sèvres were the "Arabesque" service (1783–7) and a service for Marie-Antoinette's mock dairy at the chateau of Rambouillet.

Toward the end of century decoration became more varied as the use of hard paste allowed new color effects to be employed, such as various shades of gold. From the early 1780s rich "jeweled" decoration – drops of enamel that simulated beads and pearls – was introduced to embellish the colored grounds. Authentic decoration of this type is rare, but it was widely copied during the late 19th century. Biscuit porcelain was particularly fashionable during the Neo-classical period, as it looked very much like the marble used for antique Classical sculpture. In 1773 the sculptor Louis-Simon Boizot (1743–1809) became head of the modeling workshop, and by c.1780 pastoral subjects had been replaced by mythological and Classical subjects.

AFTER THE REVOLUTION

Following the Revolution, the factory was taken over by the State in 1793. Sèvres concentrated on producing small items in a strictly Neo-classical style. During this period large amounts of undecorated soft-paste porcelain were sold off, and were subsequently decorated in Paris and London in the factory's characteristic Rococo and Neo-classical styles. Some of these imitations can be extremely difficult to distinguish from the originals, but most are unrefined by comparison or are decorated with such subjects as royal portraits, which were never used in the 18th century at Vincennes or Sèvres.

In 1800 Alexander Brongniart (1770–1847) was appointed director of the factory. To make the enterprise financially stable, he continued the sales of old stock, reorganized the operation of the factory, and abandoned the production of difficult and expensive soft paste. The use of hard-paste porcelain enabled potters to make large monumental Neo-classical vases without fear that they would collapse in the kiln. These are typically decorated all over with very high-quality gilding on ground colors, often reserved with panels painted in a similar manner to the Berlin and Vienna factories. The factory also developed more elaborate grounds, imitating tortoiseshell and agate, that could be used only on hard-paste porcelain. In the early 19th century a richer version of the Neo-classical style, known as the "Empire" style, was developed; this is characterized by heavier and more complex forms, and more elaborate Greek and Roman ornament, such as caryatid handles, eagles, swans, and lions. Napoleon's campaigns in Egypt also led to a vogue for Egyptian motifs such as sphinxes and lotus leaves.

▲ **Plate from the "Arabesque" service designed by Louis le Masson**
This service was the first example of Sèvres' Neo-classicism, and one of its finest. The octagonal shape and restrained, compartmentalized decoration contrast strongly with the curving forms and all-over patterns of the Rococo. The delicate border patterns of arabesques and the central medallion of a white figure on a red ground were inspired by paintings discovered during the excavation of Pompeii.
(c.1785; diam. 23.5cm/9in; value **K**)

▲ **Jug from a coffee service**
The lack of any visible white porcelain on this coffee jug is a typical feature of early 19th-century Sèvres. This example illustrates the still restrained yet richer Empire style that followed on from Neo-classicism; the form is still basically geometric – some were based on antique vases or urns – but the broad gilt band of palm and acanthus foliage within arched panels and dotted borders is far more ornate than any 18th- or early 19th-century Neo-classical piece.
(c.1813–17; ht 20cm/8in; value **G**)

◄ **Mercury and Cupid modeled by Le Riche**
In the mid-18th century philosophers such as Jean-Jacques Rousseau expounded the virtues of education and rational behavior. Such ideas influenced the fine and decorative arts, as didactic and moral subjects became popular for sculpture and painting; here, Mercury, the god of skill and eloquence, and the messenger of the gods, is shown teaching the infant Cupid to read from the scroll on his lap.
(c.1770; ht 32.5cm/13in; value **H**)

KEY FACTS

Neo-classical Sèvres
- BODY hard-paste porcelain after 1800
- STYLE restrained and Classically inspired
- DECORATION grisaille medallions, "jeweled" enamel decoration; motifs such as arabesques, palmettes, festoons, and garlands
- FIGURES biscuit mythological and Classical subjects, and scenes from contemporary literature and theater

Post-Revolution and Empire Sèvres
- STYLE strictly Neo-classical; then richer Empire style
- DECORATION more elaborate versions of Neo-classical motifs; grounds imitating hardstones; ground colors with rich gilding reserved with landscapes and other scenes; Egyptian motifs

Marks
This mark, used between 1793 and 1800, replaced the interlinked Ls of the earlier period; the "RF" stands for "République Française"

Paris

Paris became an important center of porcelain production from the 1780s. Several factors led to the vast increase in the number of porcelain factories: the discovery of kaolin in the Limoges area in 1768, which enabled the production of hard paste; sponsorship by members of the French royal and later imperial families; and the relaxation of laws protecting the monopoly of the Sèvres factory. The heyday of the Paris factories was from the 1790s to the 1820s, during which period at least 15 factories and large workshops were operating.

THE DIHL FACTORY
Christophe Dihl (1753–1830) and Antoine Guérhard (d.1793) founded a factory on the rue de Bondi in 1781 under the protection of the Duke of Angoulême. The factory's wares of the 1780s are decorated with cornflowers (known as the "Angoulême sprig"), geometric motifs, and landscapes. The factory's finest period was the early 19th century, when the popularity and quality of its wares rivaled Sèvres. During this period the factory specialized in decoration imitating hardstones. Dihl carried out research into ground colors, producing "jaspered" effects simulating agate and tortoiseshell, usually in combination with fine gilt borders and sometimes reserved scenes. The factory also made biscuit figures of children and allegorical subjects in the Rococo and later Neo-classical tastes; these were sometimes mounted on plinths decorated in matt blue and gilt in imitation of lapis lazuli. Following financial problems during the 1820s, the factory closed in 1828.

THE NAST FACTORY
One of the most successful of all Paris factories, the Nast factory was founded in 1783 by the Austrian Nepomucene-Jean-Hermann Nast (1754–1817). The factory, which operated until 1835, produced a huge variety of items, from luxury tablewares to domestic items such as chamber-pots, jars, and lamps. Its best period was following the Revolution (1789), when it was well known for its development of matt ground colors, in particular a chrome green. Decoration could be very lavish, with high-quality gilding and painted landscapes, Classical subjects, and grotesques; in 1810 Nast developed gilt relief borders imitating bronze, used mainly on cups and saucers. The factory made a range of biscuit figures and busts of Classical and mythological subjects, Napoleon, and other personalities of the Empire period, as well as blue-tinted biscuit wares in imitation of Wedgwood, such as clockcases and candlesticks. It also sold large quantities of undecorated porcelain, which sometimes bears the marks of other Paris factories, such as Darte Frères.

THE DARTE FACTORY
The three Darte brothers – Louis-Joseph, Joseph, and Jean-François – bought a porcelain factory on the rue de Charonne c.1795, which was active until 1804. In 1808 Louis-Joseph and Jean-François founded another factory, trading under the name "Darte Frères," which subsequently gained the protection of the Emperor's mother. Characteristic of this later factory are vases and plates with fine copies of paintings by Raphael. Services are sometimes decorated with fruit or flowers in the

◄ **Ice bucket and cover by Dihl**
The shape of this ice bucket is based on ancient Greek and Roman urns and vases. The blue, green, and gilt cornflowers, here used in a simple, repeating pattern, are a characteristic motif of services made at the Duke of Angoulême's factory.
(c.1790–1800; ht 25cm/9¾in; value F)

▲ **Bust of Empress Josephine by Nast**
The material (hard paste resembling marble) and the style of this imitate antique Roman busts. The plain bust contrasts strongly with the elaborately painted plinth with Classical arabesques and palmettes in bright colors.
(c.1810; ht 50cm/19½in; value I)

trompe l'oeil manner on a blue ground embellished with gilding. Darte fell into financial difficulties in the late 1820s and stopped trading in 1833.

THE DAGOTY AND HONORE FACTORIES
The Dagoty and Honoré factories formed a partnership between 1816 and 1820, after which they operated independently again. The best-known products of the partnership were richly gilded dessert, tea, and coffee services with animal-shaped handles and spouts, and butterfly-shaped knops. Eggcups and inkwells were modeled as snails or mythological figures, and larger cups as swans, shells, and tulips. On some pieces a red ground with gilt chinoiseries, imitating lacquer, was used, which is rare and highly sought after. Colored grounds combined with landscapes, fable subjects, and figures based on Pompeian paintings were popular.

▲ **Teapot**
The cylindrical form of this teapot, the concave shoulders, the decoration of palmettes, and the rich blue ground speckled with gold in imitation of lapis lazuli are all characteristic features of the French Neo-classical style.
(c.1790; ht 12cm/4¾in; value G)

KEY FACTS
- BODY pure white, and even, hard paste with glassy, clear glaze; the dense, slightly sugary appearance of the paste can be seen on the often unglazed foot-rims
- DECORATION simple gilt borders of Classical motifs and scattered flowers; painted scenes with colored and gilt grounds; painted imitations of hardstones and lacquer; rich gilding
- FIGURES biscuit figures of children, allegorical subjects

Marks

Dihl: one of two marks used at the factory between 1780 and 1793

MANUF ʀᴇ de Mᵒʀ le Duc d'Angouleme

Nast: this mark was enameled in red on wares made between 1783 and 1835

Nast

Darte Frères: this mark was enameled in red on wares made between 1788 and 1833

DARTE FRERES A PARIS

See also Sèvres, pp.196–7; Paris and Limoges, pp.198–9

France after 1820

Sèvres

In the 19th century Sèvres remained the pre-eminent porcelain factory in France both in quality and in innovation. Receiving state subsidies and patronage, it employed many eminent chemists, who developed new pastes, glazes, and decorative techniques, which kept the factory in the forefront of fashion. However, during this period there was an increasing divide between domestic or utilitarian wares and the very elaborate ornamental pieces, such as vases and large services, made for the State, for international exhibitions, and as diplomatic gifts.

▲ Plate from the *Service des Pêches* painted by L. Garneray
This plate illustrates how the Sèvres painters continued the late 18th-century tradition of using porcelain primarily as a medium for painting. However, the motifs are no longer strictly Classical as they would have been during the 18th century. Such an elaborate piece as this would have been used only for display in a cabinet.
(1840; diam. 24.5cm/9½in; value J)

THE RESTORATION PERIOD

After France's monarchy was restored in 1815, the country enjoyed a period of relative prosperity and stability until the 1840s. The Sèvres factory continued to produce wares in the Empire style in the 1820s and 1830s, and continued the fashion of treating porcelain as a medium for painting; restrained Neo-classical forms were decorated all over, with little or none of the porcelain left showing. The royal family commissioned large display services, each piece painted with a scene surrounded by gilt borders with motifs such as acanthus, eagles, and trophies. However, portraits of the imperial family, and scenes commemorating the battles and deeds of the Emperor, were replaced by views of France, birds, or scenes of various crafts and trades. The finest examples of this style are the table or breakfast services illustrating industries, agriculture, and history for the palace of Fontainebleau.

The mixture of Classical, Egyptian, and chinoiserie motifs already evident in porcelain decoration before 1830 became more apparent and more complex with the introduction of Gothic and Renaissance Revival shapes

▲ Plate
As well as elaborate vases and plates for display, the Sèvres factory made a wide range of less ornate useful wares. This piece is decorated quite simply with a large spray of garden flowers within a gilt frame and a feather-molded border in a delicate duck-egg blue. Such pieces are relatively inexpensive and appear fairly frequently on the market.
(1846; diam. 22cm/8½in; value D)

▼ Vase
The decoration of this large vase is a typically mid-19th-century mixture of influences from different historical periods: the *campana* shape is Classical in inspiration, being based on the Greek krater, which was used to mix wine and water, while the bearded masks on the sides are typically Renaissance in form. The rich still-lifes of roses in pastel pink and yellow are exaggerated versions of the paintings seen on similar 18th-century pieces.
(1863; ht 63cm/25in; value L)

and motifs, such as grotesques and miniature pinnacles and crockets. Vases were painted in imitation of 16th-century Limoges enamels with grotesques, flower swags, mythological scenes, and scrollwork in gray on blue; this was so successful that a specialist enameling workshop was set up, which operated between 1845 and 1872. Table services made in the 1830s and 1840s for the Duke of Orleans and the Duke of Nemours, based on 18th-century Rococo designs by Jean-Claude Duplessis (1690–1774), marked the revival of Rococo.

From the 1840s the fashion for treating porcelain as a canvas for painting declined. Areas of white porcelain again became visible, particularly on everyday services. For example, the large services made for the royal residences (including those for staff use) tended to be simply ornamented, with a gilt or blue royal monogram in the center and gold-leaf borders around the rims. This decoration was printed rather than painted, since from *c.*1845 the lithographic process was in use at Sèvres, allowing printing in several colors.

THE SECOND REPUBLIC AND SECOND EMPIRE

During the Second Republic (1848–52) Sèvres suffered financial problems because there was little demand for luxury goods. Production increased again during the Second Empire (1852–70), when much of the factory's output was intended either for the residences of Emperor Napoleon III, and as diplomatic gifts, or for display in the many international exhibitions. Plain domestic wares were also made in large quantities.

During the directorship of the chemist Victor Regnauld during the Second Empire there were several important developments in manufacturing and decoration. The production of soft paste was revived, although mainly at an experimental level, and slip-casting was introduced, meaning that very thin or large hollow pieces could be made. In the 1850s the chemist Alphonse-Louis Salvetat created a flambé glaze imitating Chinese porcelain, which was perfected in the 1880s; underglaze brown colors and colored pastes imitating marble and hardstones were also introduced. One of the most popular techniques created during the 1850s was *pâte-sur-pâte*: a process of building up a design in low relief on a tinted ground by applying layer upon layer of white slip and carving the details before firing.

From 1852 the Rococo Revival was the most popular style. The 18th-century forms were reproduced for tablewares and vases, but the gilding and decoration of scrolls, shells, figures, and flowers is more crowded and exaggerated than on original 18th-century pieces. The factory revived landscape panels with figures in the manner of the Rococo artists Watteau and Boucher, as well as colored grounds, particularly turquoise and pink. Factories in Germany and France that had bought the white wares earlier sold off by Sèvres to alleviate its financial problems copied this style in the late 19th century; these copies are usually described by dealers and auctioneers as "Sèvres," too, or as "Sèvres-style."

There was also a revival of the Pompeian and Classical Greek styles between 1845 and 1855, evident in the use of motifs and designs based on engravings of the antiquities of Pompeii. However, the shapes are not always Classical in inspiration, and the colors and decorative techniques, such as painting in matt colors on biscuit porcelain to imitate Classical vases, are different from those used in the 18th-century Neo-classical period. The factory was able to keep up with fashion because it had retained the molds of Neo-classical wares produced in the late 18th century under Louis XVI. This also led to a limited revival of biscuit porcelain figures c.1860.

THE LATE 19TH CENTURY

After the establishment of France's Third Republic in 1871 the factory continued largely to produce ornamental pieces for embassies, ministries, and government buildings, as well as simpler pieces as prizes for lotteries and public competitions.

In 1877 the sculptor Albert-Ernest Carrier-Belleuse (1824–87) was appointed director. He introduced Japanese-inspired designs that contrasted strongly with the overdecorated pieces in a confused mixture of historical styles. The factory also developed a new paste in the 1880s, which was fired at the lower temperature. This made possible an increased range of colors and the perfection of the flambé glazes imitating Oriental porcelain. These wares were particularly fashionable in the 1880s, when there was a vogue for Japanese art.

◄ Vase and cover by Jules Archelais
The delicate decoration of mythological figures on this vase was created in the *pâte-sur-pâte* technique. This type of decoration was first introduced in Europe at Sèvres c.1851, and its enormous popularity spread throughout other European factories. Set against a dark pink ground, the carved white decoration imitates the style of ancient Greek and Roman hardstone or shell cameos.
(c.1870; ht 40cm/16in; value I)

▼ Vase
The slender-shouldered, extremely simple form of this vase shows the influence of Japanese wares, which became fashionable in Europe after the first European exhibitions of Japanese art were held in London in 1854 and 1862. The deep mottled blue glaze sprinkled with gold dust is intended to give the appearance of the hardstone lapis lazuli. A vase of this size could not have been made before the 19th century, when new casting techniques enabled the production of such very large pieces.
(1876–9; ht 1m/3ft 3in; value J)

SEVRES COPIES
Many thousands of imitations of the 18th-century Sèvres style were produced by French and other European manufacturers in the 19th century. After the Revolution huge numbers of blank Sèvres wares were sold off to decorators. Later decorated pieces tend to have poorer-quality decoration and gilding and, if a piece has been refired, there is usually black speckling on the base.

▼ Sèvres-style cabaret set made in Paris or Limoges
Although painted with 18th-century portraits of Louis XV, his wife, and the royal mistresses Madame de Pompadour and Madame du Barry, this type of jeweled decoration was never used at that time.
(c.1880; diam. of tray 20cm/8in; value H)

KEY FACTS
The Restoration period
- BODY fine, white hard paste with a clear, glassy glaze; some items made in soft paste and colored pastes imitating marble and hardstones
- STYLE continuation of Empire style, with introduction of Rococo, Gothic, and Renaissance elements
- FIGURES biscuit portraits and busts in the 18th-century Neo-classical style

Marks
This mark was used from 1834 to 1848; the letters "LP" stand for "Louis-Philippe," who succeeded to the French throne in 1830

The Second Republic and Second Empire
- STYLE Rococo Revival, often combined with Gothic and Renaissance motifs
- DECORATION painting of landscapes in the style of Watteau and Boucher, or large flowers, with gilding, colored grounds, and scrollwork; *pâte-sur-pâte*
- FIGURES small classically inspired biscuit figures revived c.1860

The late 19th century
- STYLE continuation of mid-19th-century styles; Japanesque
- DECORATION plain grounds and glazes in pure colors for Japanese-style wares; Art Nouveau stylized flower motifs in pastel shades

Marks
This mark was introduced in 1900 and used until 1911

See also China: Qing before 1800, pp.138–9; Japan, pp.142–7

Paris and Limoges

The period from 1830 to 1850 may be seen as a transitional phase in French porcelain – during the second quarter of the century there was a noticeable switch in emphasis in its production. For the first quarter of the century, workshop practice had largely followed that of the 18th century, with production in the hands of craftsmen whose first consideration was aesthetic. This highly individual approach could continue in powerful and well-established factories such as Sèvres. For most other factories, however, it proved difficult to survive in an increasingly competitive industry. In an effort to meet the demands of a greatly increased and wealthy bourgeoisie, many factories were forced to streamline production and to simplify decorative techniques in order to remain competitive. Many French porcelains began to use printed decoration and, while there was considerable reliance on conservative "old-fashioned" Rococo or Neo-classical styles, there was also some innovation. The Romantic style, including the Gothic Revival, was much in vogue at the time and influenced porcelain manufacturers.

◄ Scent bottle and stopper by Jacob Petit
During the 1830s and 1840s there was much interest in the Middle Ages in France after the historical novels of Sir Walter Scott were translated into French. Miniature pinnacles and crockets appeared on such ornamental items as this scent bottle. Such motifs were combined with Rococo Revival elements and colored grounds to create the eclectic mixture of styles that characterizes 19th-century taste.
(c.1840; ht 35cm/14in; value G)

JACOB PETIT

Jacob Petit (1796–1868) was the most prominent porcelain manufacturer in Paris from the 1830s. He founded a factory at Belleville in 1830, which he moved to Fontainebleau in 1834 while still maintaining a warehouse in Paris. Using a fine, white, hard-paste porcelain, Petit initially produced simple wares with meticulously modeled or painted flowers, but by the mid-1830s he had mastered the revived historical styles that characterized 19th-century taste.

The factory's products are a typical mixture of mainly Rococo influences combined with elements of the Gothic and Renaissance Revival styles; these include miniature crocketing, pinnacles, and tracery inspired by medieval churches, and brightly colored enamels in the manner of the 16th-century French enamel painter Léonard Limosin who worked in Limoges. The factory also used colored grounds, including garnet and a very bright green, inspired by those used at Sèvres. Few areas were left undecorated, and even fairly direct copies of 18th-century Rococo pieces are mannered and exaggerated by comparison with the originals. Typical wares of the factory include curvaceous tea services and clockcases,

elaborately painted and encrusted with flowers, modeled with exaggerated rockwork and scrolling handles, feet, and spouts, and embellished with lavish gilding. Petit also made a range of novelty items, including elaborate scent bottles in shapes such as cushions, figures, and Gothic or Renaissance buildings; teapots in the shape of maidens; and inkwells in the shape of boats, reclining figures, or fabled animals. Petit was registered as bankrupt in 1848, and the factory was sold in 1862 to an employee.

◄ Clockcase and base by Jacob Petit
Modeled in the complicated and overelaborate Rococo Revival style, comprising endless switch-back scrolls and a liberal encrustation of flowers, this clockcase leaves little space for the painter to show his skill in the cartouche on the base. The rather acid colors, the very hard, glassy nature of the glaze, and the indiscriminate use of somewhat metallic gilding clearly date this piece to the mid-19th century. Although this is a Parisian clock, very similar pieces were made in Limoges during the same period.
(c.1850; ht 42cm/16½in; value G)

▼ Coffee-pot and cream-jug decorated by Victor Boyer
Throughout the 19th century porcelain manufacturers made wares in fashionable styles for display at the many international trade exhibitions such as the Great Exhibition of 1851 in London and the International Exhibition of 1867 in Paris – the latter boasting more than 20,000 exhibitors. These pieces, imitating the 18th-century Sèvres style, were produced for the Paris International Exhibition of 1861. The forms are much heavier and the colors brighter than on 18th-century Sèvres.
(1861; ht of coffee-pot 16cm/6in; value F)

OTHER MANUFACTURERS

The other Parisian manufacturers of the mid- to late 19th century produced a similar range of elaborate items. The manufacturer Gille (*d.*1898), who established a factory on the rue Paradis-Poissonière in 1837, produced monumental tables, mantelpieces, and figures, which were sometimes ornately painted and gilded. Jules-Joseph-Henri Brianchon (*d.*1880) and his brother-in-law Gilet were noted for their wares with iridescent glazes resembling mother-of-pearl; among their specialities were large, realistic pink shells. The firm of Feuillet, later taken over by Victor Boyer, decorated wares in 18th-century Sèvres style.

By the mid-19th century the cost of running or expanding a factory in Paris was so high that many manufacturers sought to establish their factories in the area around Limoges. Labor was cheaper and fuel available, and there were suitable clay deposits. With the completion of the railway between Paris and Limoges in 1857, Limoges was set to become the most important area for porcelain production in late 19th-century France. The Limoges factories kept abreast of fashion and indeed supplied porcelain makers in the capital with blanks virtually identical in form to Paris models.

During the period after 1850 French factories embraced an often eclectic variety of styles; it is not unusual to see simple Classical forms embellished with Rococo handles, or an Etruscan-shaped tazza decorated in the manner of 16th-century Limoges enamels in the new *pâte-sur-pâte* technique. Apart from this historicism and confusion of styles in the period from 1850 to 1880, there was also a return to the Rococo style of the 18th century. Like the Parisian factories, Limoges factories produced thousands of dark-blue, turquoise, and pink-ground decorative wares painted in the manner of early Sèvres porcelain. The tonality of these ornamental wares tends to be much duller than that of the originals, and the painting is decidedly mechanical. French manufacturers, in step with or even slightly ahead of other countries, adopted Japanese designs as part of the fashion for the exotic. The service of more than 1,000 pieces made for President Hayes of the USA by Haviland & Co. in Limoges epitomizes the best in this style with its spare, asymmetrical ornament of bamboo stalks and leaves.

The firm of Edmé Samson & Cie was founded in Saint-Maurice in 1845. Samson began his career as a decorator of white porcelain, but from the 1850s he switched to the direct reproduction of a huge variety of European porcelain, particularly Meissen, Höchst, Ludwigsburg, Nymphenburg, Chelsea, Bow, and Worcester. These were not intended directly to deceive, as most bear Samson's own mark. Samson wares and figures can be distinguished by their lack of sharp modeling and inaccurate palettes, but the most obvious feature is the grayish, glassy hard paste used to copy wares of a creamy soft paste. Very high-quality Samson copies, however, may be difficult to distinguish from the originals, especially when the mark has been ground off.

◄ An 18th-century woman (maker unknown)

This biscuit-porcelain figure is typical of the Rococo Revival style of the 19th century. The very hard, clashing, acid colors (note the blue bows on her scarlet shoes) are much harsher than those used on the original 18th-century biscuit figures. Many figures made at such factories as Sèvres and Tournai did not use tinted washes. This figure is one of a pair, the partner also being in 18th-century costume. They are far more collectible as a pair than as individual figures.

(1860–70; ht 33cm/13in; value **E***)*

▼ Vase and cover painted by E.O. Collot

The attenuated, Classically inspired shape of this vase, and the depiction of Venus and Cupid, represent the revival of the Classical style under the Second Empire (1852–70). The elaborate gilding and modeling are typical of 19th-century porcelain. The painting is signed by Collot, one of the numerous independent decorators who worked in Paris during the mid-19th century.

(1870s; ht 68.5cm/27in; value **G***)*

▲ Cosmetic box and cover from Limoges

The period following the establishment of the Second Republic in 1848 was one of historical revivalism in the decorative arts. This piece is decorated in the manner of Renaissance Limoges enamel, using the laborious technique of *pâte-sur-pâte*, which aimed to reproduce the effect of a 16th-century cameo.

(early 20th century; diam. 13cm/5in; value **C***)*

KEY FACTS

- **BODY** hard-paste porcelain
- **GLAZE** cold and extremely glassy
- **STYLE** an exaggerated Rococo style, sometimes with Gothic and Renaissance influences
- **DECORATION** heavy rockwork and scrollwork; colorful painting of large flowers; lavish matt and burnished gilding; brightly colored grounds; encrusted flowers

Marks

For most of the first half of the 19th century pieces were unmarked, and it is very difficult to attribute work to a specific factory; late 19th-century Limoges was often marked with the initials of the factory's proprietor in dull green

Paris: Dagoty (est. 1785)

Paris: Dihl (1817–29); in red or underglaze blue

Paris: Jacob Petit (1830–62); in underglaze blue

Limoges: A. Lanternier & Cie (est. 1855)

Paris: Samson & Cie (est. 1845); the factory used its own entwined "S" mark as well as imitations of the marks of the factories it copied; here it is the Meissen crossed swords

See also Fakes and forgeries, pp.126–7

Britain before 1790

Experimental porcelain

A great deal remains to be learned about the early years of British porcelain, although much is being revealed through research. The first attempts to produce porcelain in England can be traced back to John Dwight (1635–1703), a potter based in Fulham, London, who succeeded only in producing a fine stoneware. An itinerant chemist, Thomas Briand (*d*.1747), is likely to have made some kind of porcelain in London in the early 1740s, and, although none has been identified, his experimental pieces may have contributed to the success of Chelsea from *c*.1744, since it is believed that it was from him that the formula was acquired.

THE LONDON FACTORIES

During the 17th and 18th centuries Chinese porcelain found a ready market in London, and manufacturers were aware that the production of viable British substitutes would be extremely profitable. The founders of the factory at Bow on the city's eastern outskirts received their first patent *c*.1744, although the works was probably not active until 1747. Joseph Wilson had established a factory at nearby Limehouse by 1746, when blue-and-white Limehouse porcelain was advertised for sale. No examples of Limehouse were identified until 1989, when archeologists discovered the site and dug up shards that had been discarded during manufacture. These matched exactly a type of porcelain previously believed to have been made at the Liverpool factory of William Reid, which is now ascribed to Limehouse. Wares included shell-shaped pickle dishes, sauceboats, and teapots, with blue-and-white chinoiserie decoration. However, Limehouse porcelain clearly proved too difficult to manufacture, and the works closed in 1748.

Charles Gouyn, a jeweler and china retailer, operated a porcelain factory in St James's from *c*.1749 to 1759, but to date no excavations have been possible to confirm the identity of the items produced. However, it is believed that Gouyn made the porcelain figures, scent bottles, and other miniature "toys" (small novelties) referred to as "Girl-in-a-Swing" wares (after the first such figures to be identified), now in the Victoria and Albert Museum, London, and the Museum of Fine Arts, Boston.

About 1752 Nicholas Crisp set up a small factory in Vauxhall on the south bank of the river Thames, making distinctive blue-and-white porcelain, the forms and decoration of which were influenced by Chinese export wares and British and Dutch Delftware. Vauxhall also made rare and very beautiful, brightly painted wares decorated with flowers executed in the style of Meissen. In addition, the factory experimented with polyglaze printing – a form of overglaze printing using several colors at once – but very few of these wares survive. Vauxhall products, like those of Limehouse, were only recently identified, following the discovery of broken porcelain shards on the site of the original factory. The factory closed in 1764.

▲ Tureen from Limehouse
This unique Limehouse porcelain tureen bears curiously European blue-and-white decoration. As with many wares of the period, the shape is derived from a contemporary silver form. This piece would be of even greater value were it not damaged.
*(c.1746–8; ht 24cm/9½in; value **O**)*

▼ Bottle vase from Vauxhall
This is one of the few known examples of polychrome Vauxhall porcelain. It is painted with a chinoiserie design that is distinctly British in style, especially in its bright coloring. The body has sagged slightly during firing.
*(c.1755; ht 18cm/7in; value **L**)*

LUND'S BRISTOL

One of the proprietors of Limehouse moved to Bristol to join Benjamin Lund, and together they produced blue-and-white porcelain from *c*.1749. Lund's Bristol porcelain was not unlike that of Limehouse, but it was more durable owing to its secret ingredient: Cornish soapstone, a substitute for the petuntse (china clay) required to make true porcelain. At Worcester, Dr John Wall and William Davis realized the potential of soapstone and purchased Lund's factory – together with its secret formula for porcelain – in 1752. Worcester became the most successful 18th-century British porcelain factory, and its proprietors went to great pains to protect their secret formula. However, a Worcester employee stole the formula and sold it in 1756 to Richard Chaffers, who made porcelain in Liverpool during the 1750s and 1760s.

▼ Coffee-pot by Lund's Bristol
The shape of this pot is based on a silver form, but the decoration is Chinese in design. This piece was bought inexpensively as a Chinese pot at a country sale, then resold as the real thing for a considerable profit.
*(c.1750–51; ht 13cm/5in; value **N**)*

KEY FACTS

- BODY all the early factories made soft-paste porcelain
- GLAZE Vauxhall: glaze may be "peppered"
- DECORATION Vauxhall: underglaze blue may be inky, wet-looking, and rather smudged; polychrome painting and transfer-printing; designs inspired by Chinese export porcelain and Meissen; Limehouse: wares may resemble Chinese export porcelain unevenly fired
- COLLECTING early porcelain is very rare, and there is a great deal of interest especially in Vauxhall, Limehouse, and the earliest Worcester

Marks

Factory marks were very seldom used by the early porcelain manufacturers, which makes identification a challenge for new collectors; any marks that do appear must be treated with suspicion

See also China: Later export porcelain, pp.136–7; The Netherlands, pp.160–61

Chelsea

The first successful British porcelain factory was founded *c.*1744 at Chelsea, then a village on the outskirts of London, by the Huguenot silversmith Nicholas Sprimont (*c.*1716–71). Unsurprisingly, the shapes of British silverwares were to have a considerable influence on the porcelain made at Chelsea. Production at the factory falls into five periods, four of which are named after marks used at the time.

THE TRIANGLE PERIOD

During the "Triangle" period (*c.*1744–9), Chelsea porcelain was of a beautiful white glassy body, and the shapes were mostly copied directly from British Rococo silver. Early Chelsea porcelain was difficult to control during firing; wares were small-scale and included cream-jugs, beakers, and teapots. The factory was proud of the pure white appearance of its porcelain, and painted decoration was therefore kept to a minimum.

THE RAISED ANCHOR AND THE RED ANCHOR PERIODS

Changes were made to the body and glaze in the second phase (*c.*1749–52), known as the "Raised Anchor" period from the mark of a tiny anchor embossed on a raised pad. The body was now more robust, and tin oxide was added to the glaze to opacify it, which also gave it a silky feel. Popular decoration included copies of 17th-century Japanese Kakiemon porcelain, and landscapes painted in the style of imported European wares from the factories of Meissen in Germany and Vincennes in France. Scenes from Aesop's *Fables*, painted in rich colors, became a Chelsea specialty. A few figures and models of birds were also produced at this time, but these are rare.

During the "Red Anchor" period (1752–6) original forms of decoration were introduced, as well as others copied from Meissen. This period is famous for its dessert table settings, especially covered tureens in the forms of fruit, vegetables, animals, birds, and fish. Painted botanical decoration, a Chelsea invention, was used on "Hans Sloane" wares, named after Sir Hans Sloane, an eminent scientist and patron of the Physic Garden, a botanical garden in Chelsea. Chelsea also made small "toys" – tiny scent bottles and seals in the form of fruit, animals, and people.

Figures became an important part of the factory's production, owing to the skills of the Flemish modeler Josef Willems (*c.*1715–66). When held up to a strong light, Red Anchor porcelain should exhibit the famous Chelsea "moons" – bubbles trapped in the paste, which appear as lighter spots in the body.

GOLD ANCHOR PERIOD

The colored grounds and Rococo shapes of the French factories of Vincennes and Sèvres were the dominant influences in the subsequent "Gold Anchor" period (*c.*1756–69), when the factory's anchor mark was neatly applied in gold rather than red. The use of gilding was significantly increased. Figures, designed for display on mantelpieces or in cabinets and intended to be viewed only from the front, became more elaborate, with masses of *bocage* (small modeled trees and flowers). Although at the end of the 19th century Gold Anchor wares were extremely valuable, their popularity has decreased throughout the 20th century.

Economic problems coupled with the ill health of the founder led to the closure of the Chelsea factory in 1769. John Heath and William Duesbury, the owners of the Derby porcelain factory (est. *c.*1748), bought the works in 1770 and ran the two premises in London and Derby in tandem. This period of production is known as the "Chelsea-Derby" period. The factory finally closed in 1784.

▲ "Sunflower" clockcase
This beautifully modeled clock, from the Gold Anchor period at Chelsea, is a masterpiece of British Rococo design. The elaborately scrolled base is typical of this period and also appears on figures.
(c.1760–61; ht 27cm/10½in; value H)

▲ "Goat-and-bee" jug
The shape of this cream-jug is derived from contemporary English silver, but the effect is somehow more magical in pure white porcelain. The jug bears the incised triangle mark of the earliest Chelsea period.
(1745–8; ht 11cm/4¼in; value H)

◄ "Fable" dish
The silver original of this dish was designed by the founder of the Chelsea works, Nicholas Sprimont. The dish bears the raised anchor mark and is decorated by the celebrated artist Jefferyes Hamett O'Neale (1734–1801) with a scene from one of Aesop's *Fables*.
(1750–52; w. 24cm/9½in; value K)

KEY FACTS

Triangle period (c.1744–9)
• BODY white, glassy, and translucent
• FORMS based on British silverware shapes
• DECORATION often left uncolored
• COLLECTING wares are rare and valuable

Raised Anchor period (c.1749–52)
• BODY milky white and silky; contains impurity specks
• GLAZE tin oxide added to glaze to opacify it; silky feel
• FOOT-RIMS ground flat
• DECORATION based on Japanese porcelain, Vincennes, and Meissen

Red Anchor period (c.1752–6)
• BODY creamy white with dribbling glaze; "moons" appear in paste-firing support marks ("spur marks")
• DECORATION Meissen-style flowers

Gold Anchor period (c.1756–69)
• BODY creamy, prone to staining; bone-ash was added
• GLAZE clear, thickly applied; pools and tends to craze
• STYLE Rococo; influenced by Sèvres
• FAKES beware of 19th-century fakes, usually made in French hard-paste porcelain, the body of which is too white and glassy; they are often marked with gold anchors far bigger than those on genuine pieces

Marks
*c.*1744–*c.*1749: usually incised or painted in underglaze blue

*c.*1749–52: anchor embossed on a raised pad
1752–6: the mark of a very small anchor in red enamel appears on the backs of figures and on the bases of plates and cups
*c.*1756–69: anchor painted in gold

*c.*1769–84: Chelsea–Derby mark

See also Derby, p.206

Bow and Longton Hall

British 18th-century porcelain factories followed their own paths and often aimed their products at very different markets. The proprietors of Bow, to the east of London, responded to the metropolitan demand for Oriental porcelain, which it closely imitated. Longton Hall, in rural Staffordshire, was far removed from the changing fashions of London and produced very individual porcelain with a charm of its own.

▲ The *Fortune Teller* by the "Muses Modeler" for Bow
This early Bow figure group is in the distinctive style of this anonymous craftsman, with wide brows, small heads, receding chins, and long arms. The plain base and the colors are typical of early Bow wares. (c.1752–4; ht 18cm/7in; value **K**)

BOW

The discovery of Bow's porcelain recipe resulted from years of experimentation by the potter Edward Heylyn (1695–c.1758) and the artist Thomas Frye (1710–62). They took out their first patent for a porcelain formula c.1744, but Bow porcelain was probably not on sale before 1748. In 1750 the factory was styled "New Canton," and the influence of China and Japan dominated Bow's useful wares. Bow porcelain was coarser than hard-paste porcelain and less durable than that invented a few years later at Worcester, and the burnt animal bones (bone-ash) used as a principal ingredient at Bow created a body that was liable to stain. Competition from rival makers who used soapstone in their porcelain led Bow to turn its attention to ornamental wares, especially figures. Bow followed the successful example of Chelsea in copying

Meissen figures, although in comparison with the elegance and sophistication of Chelsea figures, those produced by the Staffordshire workmen hired by Bow were clumsy – as typified by the work of the "Muses Modeler," an unknown sculptor, whose work, however, has a distinctive rustic charm. The bright colors on later Bow figures, combined with a strong underglaze blue, resulted in highly decorative ornaments that sold well at the time. The Bow factory remained in production for nearly 30 years but fell victim to an economic recession in the mid-1770s, when figures became unfashionable and the Rococo style that so suited Bow gave way to the Neo-classical taste. The factory closed in 1776.

LONGTON HALL

William Littler (1724–84) founded the Longton Hall factory c.1749 and developed his first porcelain recipe just prior to 1750. This porcelain had a thick, semi-opaque white glaze that has earned the nickname "snowman class" for early Longton Hall figures. By c.1752, however, Littler had perfected his formula to produce porcelain that could be molded quite thinly – ideal for making the forms such as fruit, vegetables, and leaves that dominated Longton Hall's characteristic, brightly painted dishes, jugs, and tureens. The figures, which are not dissimilar from those of Bow and Derby, show the influence of Meissen. The variable quality of Longton Hall porcelain, coupled with heavy kiln losses, led to the factory's bankruptcy and closure in 1760. Littler moved to Scotland, where he later opened a new porcelain works at West Pans, near Musselburgh.

▼ Plate by Bow
This Bow plate exactly reproduces the type of design seen on Chinese plates made during the reign of the Qing Emperor Kangxi (1662–1722). Customers who bought this style of ware would probably have cared little whether their services were made in China or at a London factory.
(c.1757–60; diam. 20cm/8in; value **C**)

▲ Flower-pot by Longton Hall
This small flower-pot is painted with a simple chinoiserie scene, which is typical of British porcelain made during the mid-18th century. The Longton Hall factory was particularly notable for its blue-and-white wares, although, because it was difficult to control the cobalt blue, patterns may often be badly blurred. William Littler invented a distinctive deep underglaze blue, known as "Littler's blue," which had a tendency to blur and run; this blue was also used at his West Pans factory.
(c.1755; ht 6cm/2½in; value **H**)

KEY FACTS

Bow
- **BODY** soft-paste porcelain containing bone-ash; coarser than true porcelain and liable to stain
- **GLAZE** soft and slightly blue with a tendency to pool around the base
- **DECORATION** underglaze, powder-blue ground; *blanc-de-Chine* sprigged prunus blossom; Kakiemon palette; the "quail" pattern (two quails with rocks and foliage), which became Bow's most popular design
- **FIGURES** press-molded rather than slip-cast, and therefore rather heavy; early figures left in the white, later examples decorated in colorful enamels

Marks
Early Bow is generally unmarked, but after c.1765 this "anchor and dagger" mark was painted in red enamel on colorful pieces that were possibly decorated outside the factory

Longton Hall
- **BODY** soft-paste porcelain; sometimes, like Chelsea, the body contains "moons" – tiny air bubbles that appear as pale spots against a strong light
- **STYLE** the factory specialized in colorful jugs, dishes, and tureens in the form of leaves, fruit, and vegetables
- **DECORATION** Meissen-style flowers are attributed to an artist known as the "trembly rose painter," although many artists painted in this manner

Marks
No mark was used; pieces marked with two crossed "L"s in blue, formerly attributed to the factory, are now known to come from Littler's later venture at West Pans

See also China, pp.131–40

Worcester

Worcester was not perhaps the most obvious location for a major British porcelain manufacturer to be established because there were no local deposits of clay or coal; these had to be brought in by river. Nonetheless, it was there in 1751 that Dr John Wall and William Davis invested in a new porcelain factory.

1751–70

The new factory suffered heavy kiln losses, and in 1752 the partners bought up Benjamin Lund's factory in Bristol and with it Lund's secret porcelain formula that included Cornish soapstone. The use of soapstone gave Worcester porcelain increased durability, enabling its teapots to withstand hot liquids – those of most other British makers tended to crack in contact with boiling water. During the 1750s and 1760s Worcester specialized in teawares, sauceboats, pots for pâté, meats and tarts, and pickle-dishes.

Early blue-and-white Worcester shows the influence of the Bristol factory, with shapes derived from British silver. Worcester's colored patterns were in the factory's unique form of chinoiserie that combined elements from China, Japan, Meissen, early Staffordshire, stoneware, and glass. This proved popular in the 1750s and is highly sought after by collectors today. By 1755 Worcester had perfected its blue-and-white wares by eliminating heavy blurring, and was making fine tea services. Worcester can claim the credit for the invention of printing on porcelain, and it used this technique extensively to produce overglaze black enamel and underglaze-blue printed decoration.

1770–83

By 1770 Worcester was England's most successful porcelain factory and even exported blue-and-white wares to the Netherlands. However, the factory had rather neglected the London market and engaged John Toulouse (d.1807), a modeler from Bow, to develop a new range of ornamental shapes – vases, baskets, and figures – aimed at the capital. From c.1767 blank white porcelain was sent to James Giles (1718–80), in Soho, London, for decoration in the latest taste. Giles's designs, copied from Meissen and Sèvres, sold very well in London. The factory perfected a deep, underglaze-blue ground and also invented its famous "scale blue" (in which the underglaze blue ground was painted using a tiny fish-scale pattern) and developed other colored grounds previously made famous by Sèvres and Chelsea. The reserved panels on the colored grounds were decorated with flowers and exotic "fancy birds."

In the 1780s, with competition from Derby and imported French porcelain, and the influx of inexpensive Chinese wares, Worcester lost its premier position. Its recovery was slow, because the success of blue-and-white printed pottery led to the decline of other, more expensive wares. In 1783 Davis, who had managed the firm since 1774, was bought out by Thomas Flight, whose son, John Flight, was to reverse Worcester's ailing fortunes.

▼ Potting pan
Tubs for serving potted meat or pâté – "potting pans" – were an important part of Worcester's output. This example combines a Rococo silver shape with the factory's own brand of chinoiserie decoration.
(c.1754–5; w. 18.5cm/7in; value **L**)

▼ Garniture of vases
The scale-blue ground that decorates this assembled (not originally matching) set of hexagonal vases was invented at Worcester, as was the "fancy-birds" decoration in the reserved panels. Damage to the vases has reduced their value.
(c.1765–72; ht of tallest vase; 41cm/16in; value of set **Q**)

▼ Teabowl, saucer, and coffee-cup
The decoration of brilliant gold scrollwork on a powder-blue ground confirms these examples as the output of the James Giles decorating workshop in London. The figures in the manner of the French painter Watteau reflect the latest styles from Meissen and Sèvres.
(c.1770; ht of cup 6cm/2½in; value **J**)

KEY FACTS

c.1751–60
- BODY soft-paste porcelain with gray-blue cast
- GLAZE fully glazed inside the foot-rims and under the rims of lids
- FORMS teawares, sauceboats, and pickle-dishes
- DECORATION blue-and-white copies of Chinese wares; polychrome chinoiseries; overglaze black transfer-printing and underglaze-blue printing introduced

Marks
Most blue-and-white wares bear a workman's mark, usually a simple sign of uncertain meaning

c.1760–74
- GLAZE evenly controlled with slight yellow-green cast; under-rims of covers unglazed; to avoid glaze running down onto the kiln during firing it was wiped away from the inside of feet c.1758–83 in a technique known as "pegging"
- FORMS teawares, plates, dishes, and vases
- DECORATION blue-and-white printing, much of it for export; Chinese decoration less important; in London Giles decorated many pieces in Meissen or Sèvres style

Marks
Mark used on printed wares (1758–85)

Mark used on blue-ground wares (c.1762–85)

"Pseudo-Meissen" mark used on some colored wares in a European style (c.1760–70)

1774–92
- BODY paste declined in quality; a more straw-colored or yellowish cast; not well controlled
- FORMS traditional styles continued to be made, but were not so well executed
- DECORATION very bright-blue printing, prone to blurring; slow transition from Rococo to Neo-classical decoration; greater French influence

Marks
Crescent mark still used in addition to this cursive "W" printed in blue (c.1770–75)

See also Experimental porcelain, p.200; Blue-and-white wares, pp.204–5; Worcester, p.208

Blue-and-white wares

Trade with China in the 17th and early 18th centuries resulted in a thriving market for blue-and-white porcelain in Europe. In mid-18th century Britain the demand for anything in blue and white appeared almost insatiable. English manufacturers had used delft to copy porcelain since the 17th century, but such copies lacked the magical translucence of the originals. However, because imported Chinese porcelain commanded high prices, there were many early attempts to copy it. Unsurprisingly, such efforts concentrated on the blue-and-white wares that were to be found in so many homes. In the 1740s factories at Bristol and at Limehouse and Chelsea in London produced experimental blue-and-white porcelain, but with little success – although the skills developed during these failed endeavors were put to good use elsewhere. Other factories, such as the ventures at Vauxhall in London and Longton Hall in Staffordshire, enjoyed moderate success, but their products are rare because they ultimately proved unable to compete with the larger china factories at Bow and Worcester.

BOW AND WORCESTER

These two factories succeeded where their rivals failed and between them accounted for a great proportion of the output of English blue and white, far outnumbering all other makers. By 1748 Bow, then just east of London, was producing reasonable copies of Chinese blue-and-white plates, and during the early 1750s it concentrated on direct copies of Chinese and Japanese teaware shapes and patterns. While endeavoring in the main to produce exact – but less expensive – imitations of Oriental porcelain, Bow also made a certain amount of blue-and-white porcelain using English shapes, for which there was a considerable demand, in particular for sauceboats and dishes for serving pickles.

The Worcester factory began production in 1751, also making copies of Chinese plates, but it was unable to compete in terms either of quality or of price with the delicate Chinese teawares that were most in demand. Worcester abandoned its attempts to make exact copies of Chinese porcelain and turned, with great success, to the manufacture of wares with chinoiserie decoration. Shapes derived from English silverware, especially sauceboats and creamboats, were adorned with Chinese-style fishing scenes, and a series of patterns derived from Oriental prototypes, but executed in an English manner, decorated well-made tea services. Worcester's invention of blue-and-white printing in the late 1750s enabled the factory to mass-produce blue-and-white tea and dinnerwares – during the 1760s the output of blue-and-white Worcester reached quite astonishing levels.

◄ **Sauceboat by Bow**
This sauceboat with a high loop handle is painted with a Chinese-inspired rocky landscape, with a pagoda-like house and trees that look like telegraph poles. Inside the rim there is a typically Chinese border of trellis interspersed with a flower design, and in the base there are Buddhist-style motifs. The underglaze blue on early Bow wares is a distinctly royal blue, whereas on later wares it is much more inky.
(c.1750–54; ht 13cm/5in; value E)

▲ **Sauceboat by Longton Hall**
Although this sauceboat is badly misshapen, it is desirable and considerably valuable on account of its rarity.
(c.1756; ht 9.5cm/3¾in; value F)

Although the Bow factory was the larger of the two, far fewer of its blue-and-white wares are extant than those of Worcester, owing to Bow's inferior porcelain body, which was prone to cracking and staining. Worcester's porcelain formula included soapstone, which meant that its wares were as durable as Chinese porcelain. As a result, plenty of examples have survived.

LIVERPOOL AND LOWESTOFT

In the 1750s several factories were established to supply the same markets, many using copies of Worcester's soapstone porcelain recipe. In Liverpool a number of china factories operated in close proximity to one another, a fact that leads to much confusion among collectors today. Richard Chaffers and Philip Christian were the most successful Liverpool porcelain makers. In 1756 Chaffers bought the secret of Worcester's formula and produced durable, thin teawares deriving largely from the blue-and-white patterns of Chinese porcelain. Christian continued the business after Chaffers's death (1765), and it is often difficult to tell this Liverpool porcelain from that of Worcester. Samuel Gilbody made blue-and-white china in Liverpool from 1754 to 1760 but without much success. Three branches of the Pennington family operated their own works in different parts of the city from 1769 to c.1800, and it is only in recent years that it has become possible to distinguish the porcelain of Seth Pennington from that of his brothers John and James. With so many factories working in one city, precise dating plays a vital part in identifying any piece of Liverpool blue-and-white porcelain.

MAKING UNDERGLAZE-BLUE DECORATION

The process used to produce underglaze blue means that the blue coloring is sealed beneath the surface glaze of the porcelain and therefore cannot discolor or wear off. Finely powdered cobalt oxide, a black pigment, is mixed with oil and painted or transfer-printed directly onto unglazed "biscuit" porcelain. To prevent blurring, an initial firing fixes the color onto the surface, which is then covered with a sticky glaze of finely powdered glass. When fired again, the cobalt oxide reacts with the molten glass, becoming the silicate form of cobalt, and turns from black to blue.

▼ **Two saucers by Worcester**
The unfinished saucer (left) is painted in black cobalt oxide on the unglazed "biscuit" porcelain. After glazing, the cobalt would have turned blue, as on the identical finished saucer (right). The unfinished saucer was discarded on the site of the original factory and discovered during excavations.
(c.1770; diam. 13cm/5in; value of finished example A)

◄ Teapot by Chaffers
Painted in well-controlled underglaze blue with a Chinese-inspired scene of a willow tree hanging over a pavilion by a lake, this small teapot is typical of those made during the 1750s when tea was still an expensive commodity in Britain. The slightly grayish look is typical of Liverpool porcelain. Chaffers's ware is usually very translucent, exhibiting an almost white or slightly green color when held up to a strong light.
(c.1758; ht 12cm/4¾in; value **H**)

▼ Milk-jug and cover from Lowestoft
The shape of this large covered milk-jug suggests that it was probably intended for export to Europe. The kickback terminal on the lower joint is typical of the coffee-pots and milk-jugs made at this factory. Although the underglaze blue has sunk into the highly absorbent soft-paste porcelain body, it has remained clear without blurring. From the mid-1760s colored wares were made alongside blue-and-white pieces. However, later blue painting is generally considered to lack the charm of earlier Lowestoft blue-and-white wares.
(c.1780; ht

While the Liverpool factories came and went, one East Anglian factory lasted for more than 40 years from the late 1750s, despite its unlikely location in the fishing port of Lowestoft in Suffolk. The earliest blue-and-white porcelain made there carries some very refreshing, if naive, painted decoration, and shapes tended to follow the forms of salt-glazed stoneware. Later wares from Lowestoft (after c.1765) were largely based on those from Worcester, but were executed in a coarser porcelain body that is somewhat prone to staining. The great joy of any Lowestoft collector is to own one of the many inscribed and dated pieces that were made for the local market, such as mugs inscribed "A Trifle from Lowestoft," or a birth tablet – a disc designed to hang from a baby's crib inscribed with the child's name and birthday. Needless to say, these personalized treats come onto the market very rarely and are highly collectible.

BLUE-AND-WHITE TRANSFER PRINTING
Sometime between 1756 and 1758 the Worcester factory made a discovery that revolutionized the ceramics industry. Josiah Holdship and his brother Richard developed a method whereby ink could be transferred from a design engraved on a sheet of copper to the surface of a piece of unglazed porcelain. This resulted in sets of blue-and-white porcelain bearing an identical printed pattern on every piece, which could be produced at much less cost than by hand-painting. Initially a closely guarded secret, the process of blue printing was taken by Richard Holdship to Bow and then on to Derby, and inferior copies of popular Worcester prints were soon being produced inexpensively at Liverpool and Lowestoft. By the 1770s mass production meant that printed blue and white was being made at all the factories in England, but especially at Worcester and in the village of Caughley near Ironbridge in Shropshire, where Thomas Turner set up a porcelain factory c.1772 in direct competition with his former employers at Worcester. Staffordshire makers applied the same printing process to inexpensive earthenware products (such as pearlware made by the factory of Josiah Spode), which eventually brought about the demise of the English blue-and-white porcelain industry.

KEY FACTS
Body
All wares were made of soft-paste porcelain except Plymouth and Bristol, which are hard-paste porcelain

Quality of underglaze blue
- LIMEHOUSE (1746–8) dark and inky
- BOW (c.1748–75) early very bright, later dark and inky
- VAUXHALL (c.1752–63) bright, so-called "sticky"
- LUND'S BRISTOL (1749–51) bright but blurred
- WORCESTER (1751–90s) well-controlled, dark, and inky, bright after 1780s
- DERBY (c.1760s–80s) bright and dark, very white ground
- LOWESTOFT (c.1757–99) very dark and inky, prone to blurring
- LONGTON HALL (c.1750–60), continued at WEST PANS, Scotland (after 1764) varying tones of blue, prone to extensive blurring
- LIVERPOOL: CHAFFERS (c.1754–65), continued by CHRISTIAN (c.1765–78) light and bright
- LIVERPOOL: GILBODY (c.1754–60) often blurred
- LIVERPOOL: PENNINGTONS (c.1760s–90s) variable
- PLYMOUTH AND BRISTOL (c.1768–81) appears black
- CAUGHLEY (c.1772–99) well-controlled printing, dark inky blue

Quality of glazes
- LIMEHOUSE cloudy
- LUND'S BRISTOL cloudy
- LIVERPOOL: CHAFFERS, continued by CHRISTIAN greeny gray, sometimes blue gray
- LIVERPOOL: GILBODY gray
- LIVERPOOL: PENNINGTONS often of dirty appearance
- PLYMOUTH AND BRISTOL smoky-tinted
- CAUGHLEY light-straw colored

Marks
The following is a small selection of marks used by the factories associated with the production of early blue-and-white porcelain

Worcester: "open" crescent mark for painted wares made between 1758 and 1790

Plymouth: the mark used for the Cookworthy factory (1768–71); this is the alchemical mark for tin, the industry for which Cornwall was well known in the 18th century

Caughley: the "S" mark stands for "Salop," the county in which Caughley was based; the "C" mark was used for painted or printed wares made from c.1775 to 1795

► Tea canister by Caughley
This tea canister has been transfer-printed with the popular "Fisherman" pattern, which was mass-produced at Caughley and other English factories. It is possible to see the crosshatching associated with transfer-printing when the design is viewed close up. With transfer-printed decoration, it is also often possible to see how the design does not quite meet properly where the two ends join.
(c.1785–90; ht 17cm/6¾in; value **D**)

See also China: Yuan and early Ming, p.133; Middle and later Ming, pp.134–5

Derby

Derby already had a long tradition of pottery manufacture by the time that porcelain was made there *c*.1748 by Andrew Planché, a French chemist who had learned the art of making porcelain at factories in continental Europe. Early Derby production was very much aimed at the London market and imitated the white Rococo porcelain made at Chelsea.

EARLY DERBY WARES

The forms of the rare porcelain made during the Planché period are, like Chelsea's, influenced by English silver. Chinoiserie figure groups, unique to Derby, are seen at their best when left undecorated. Derby's slightly creamy, glass-like glaze dribbled freely during the firing. To prevent adhesion to the kiln shelves, the glaze was initially wiped away from around the bases of figures and cream-jugs, giving an appearance known as "dry-edge." During Derby's "transitional" phase (*c*.1755–6) the glaze, over a chalky paste, became whiter, and was lightly decorated in distinctive, rather delicate enamels, which have earned figure groups of this period the title "Pale Family."

In 1756 William Duesbury (1725–86) and his partner John Heath bought the factory. From this time the influence of the German factory of Meissen became more apparent. Wares made under Duesbury's direction are very similar to some made at Longton Hall and were likewise aimed at the London market. Tureens and leaf-shaped dishes were made, alongside some teawares and baskets. Derby developed distinctive styles of bird- and flower-painting that are conventionally associated with artists known respectively as the "moth painter" and "cotton-stalk painter"; in fact such decoration was applied by a number of painters at the factory.

Derby's porcelain body meant that its teawares were prone to cracking during use, and examples are rare.

Instead, Derby became England's foremost figure manufacturer. Influenced by Meissen, Derby figures of the 1750s and 1760s are very Rococo in style, standing on wide, scrolled bases, often backed with intricate *bocage*. To prevent kiln adhesion during firing, the unglazed bases of the figures were supported on raised clay pads that left distinctive "patch marks."

THE CHELSEA-DERBY PERIOD

In 1770 Duesbury bought the ailing Chelsea factory and ran it until 1784 in conjunction with the Derby works. Following Chelsea's adoption of the Derby porcelain formula, production at the factory improved, and new styles of decoration were developed, greatly influenced by the Neo-classical style fashionable in London. Figures continued to form the greater part of Derby's output, but modelers engaged from Europe introduced new subjects and vastly improved the quality. They also developed biscuit figures into a distinctive Derby specialty. The fine detail of the modeling was displayed to full effect on white Derby biscuit figures and groups.

◀ Pickle stand

This is an impressive pickle or sweetmeat stand of the type that was used to grace 18th-century table-settings. On this piece, which is replete with rustic charm, the painting in the scallop shells is associated with a supposed artist known as the "moth painter," as moths have been painted inside the shells. It should be noted that an example such as this is extremely vulnerable to damage, and many such pieces will be chipped or broken.

(c.1762–5; ht 35cm/14in; value J)

▼ "Fountain" vase

Many wares produced during the Chelsea–Derby period, such as this vase, were made in the Neo-classical style. This bright-turquoise ground, a specialty of the period, was inspired by the manufactory at Sèvres, and surrounds a cartouche with cherubs painted in the style of François Boucher.

(c.1775; ht 42cm/16½in; value H)

◀ Chinoiserie group

The figures made at Derby during the early period typically portrayed such popular mid-18th-century subjects as "Chinese" or allegorical figures and pastoral themes. This extremely fine figure group is one of those known as a "dry-edge," where the glutinous glaze was wiped away from the edge of the figure prior to firing to prevent it from sticking to the kiln. Made during the early period of figure production at the factory – evident from the simple base, a style that was later replaced by a scrolled one – this example has clearly been influenced by the figures made by the outstanding Rococo modeler Johann Joachim Kändler (1706–75) at Meissen.

(c.1750; ht 20cm/8in; value L)

KEY FACTS

- **BODY** early Derby paste is chalky white
- **GLAZE** creamy white; *c*.1750–56 Derby porcelain is known as "dry-edge" because the edges of the bases were wiped free of glaze before firing
- **FORMS** tureens, leaf shapes, baskets; teawares are rare
- **DECORATION** birds, flowers; *c*.1756–65 sprays of flowers with very fine stems were painted, formerly attributed to the "cotton-stalk painter"
- **FIGURES** unglazed biscuit was used from 1770s; the styles are Rococo, including scrolled bases and *bocage*; "patch marks" were left by firing supports

Marks

Derby porcelain is unmarked before 1770; from *c*.1770 a model number was often scratched into the base of a figure, greatly assisting identification

Chelsea-Derby period (1770–84); two marks from this: the first is in gold with Chelsea's anchor; the second is usually marked in blue enamel

c.1782 to mid-19th century: mark incised, or painted in purple, black, blue, or (after 1800) red

See also Chelsea, p.201

Plymouth, Bristol, and New Hall

English porcelain belonged to a type known technically as soft-paste, or "artificial," porcelain, which lacked the beautiful hard whiteness of hard-paste porcelain such as that produced in China or at Meissen. However, the chemist William Cookworthy (1705–80) believed that hard paste could be made in Britain and searched for suitable raw materials. Kaolin (china clay), the essential ingredient in true porcelain, had been discovered in Cornwall in 1745, and Cookworthy patented several formulas containing this mineral to make what he believed to be the finest English porcelain.

▲ **Pair of musicians from Plymouth or Bristol**
It is possible that this pair of figures were made either at Plymouth or at Bristol shortly after Cookworthy moved there.
*(c.1770–72; ht 14.5cm/6in; value **H**)*

PLYMOUTH AND BRISTOL

From *c.*1768 Cookworthy produced England's first commercial hard-paste porcelain at his Plymouth works, but it was dogged by serious problems. A pure white glaze was rarely achieved – the creamy surface was frequently covered with black specks that gave it a dirty appearance. Like Meissen and other European makers, Plymouth experienced difficulties with its underglaze blue, which almost turned black, with severe blurring. Painters from Worcester were attracted to Plymouth, and the factory's shapes and Oriental designs closely follow those of Worcester. Few collectors will admit that Plymouth was a failure, but when Cookworthy moved to Bristol in 1770 he had little of any real quality to show new investors.

The porcelain made by Cookworthy at Bristol was probably identical to his Plymouth wares, and it seems likely that much of the porcelain today called "Plymouth" was really made at Bristol. Improvements were made: John Toulouse, a modeler at Bow, came via Worcester and introduced new shapes and figures, mainly direct copies of the latest patterns of Meissen's "Academic" period (1763–74). Bristol sometimes marked its wares with a copy of the Meissen crossed swords, a feature that often confuses present-day collectors – particularly since Bristol porcelain achieved a whiteness similar to that of Meissen after Richard Champion (1743–91) took over Cookworthy's patents

in 1774. Champion made some beautiful porcelain, especially in the Neo-classical style, but never in any great quantity because the works continued to be plagued by firing difficulties, notably "wreathing" – spiral ridges on the surface caused by kiln distortion. Plates and dishes were placed on clay supports during firing to prevent warping. The factory closed in 1781.

NEW HALL

Despite the failure of Bristol, Champion still saw a future for English hard-paste porcelain and visited Staffordshire to try to sell his patent. A consortium of manufacturers showed an interest but realized that Champion's formula had to be adapted for mass production. As the New Hall Co., the consortium opened a factory *c.*1781 at Shelton to exploit an improved version of Champion's porcelain body – the type now known as "hybrid hard paste." The glaze tended to be greenish-gray, but it could be potted very thinly, and wreathing was a less severe problem. The factory was designed to make a profit and aimed its products at a mass market, ignoring more expensive pieces such as ornamental figures and vases. Tea and coffee services in a limited range of patterns comprised the bulk of New Hall's output. Other factories, also concentrating on teawares, were established in competition, and each firm produced its own version of standard shapes – it is therefore important for collectors to learn the differences. New Hall continued into the 1830s, although its later products are not as collectible.

▼ **Vase from Bristol**
An artist from France may have painted this vase as it is distinctly French in style. Many Bristol vases suffered serious distortion in the kiln, but this is a well-fired and successful piece.
*(c.1775–8; ht 44cm/17in; value **K**)*

▲ **Milk- or cream-jug by New Hall**
This early example comes from a tea service painted in the firm's popular "No. 20" pattern, which was an Oriental-style design featuring "bubblehead" Chinese figures. Such standard patterns were inexpensive to produce, and are great fun to collect. The "clip" handle on this example is typical of earlier New Hall output and will add to the value. New Hall was the first manufacturer to assign pattern numbers to porcelain designs, and these are vital clues to the identification and dating of its wares.
*(c.1782–5; ht 9cm/3½in; value **E**)*

KEY FACTS

Plymouth (c.1768–70)
- BODY hard-paste porcelain
- GLAZE a pure white glaze was rarely achieved, because the creamy surface was frequently covered by a smoke of black specks that gave it a dirty appearance
- UNDERGLAZE BLUE almost black, with severe blurring
- DECORATION Oriental patterns following Worcester

Marks
This alchemical sign for tin (which was the main industry in Cornwall) was sometimes used

Bristol (1770–81)
- BODY hard-paste porcelain; very white after 1774
- FEATURES "wreathing" – ridges spiraling around the surface – can often be seen on cups and other hollow shapes owing to firing difficulties
- STYLE Neo-classical, continental
- DECORATION inspired by Meissen "Academic" wares

Marks
Mark in blue enamel, sometimes accompanied by numerals; Meissen crossed-swords mark also copied

New Hall (c.1781–1830s)
- BODY hard-paste porcelain, thinly potted
- GLAZE thick, dull, and greenish gray
- FORMS specialized in tea and coffee services aimed at the mass market; other items are extremely rare

Marks
Pattern numbers were introduced to enable customers to reorder easily, and these help with identification

Britain 1790–1900

Worcester

The best-known Worcester porcelain factory was managed by the Flight family when George III visited Worcester in 1788. However, the term "Worcester" has come to include other factories in the city with which Flight's amalgamated. The King's visit was a turning-point in the fortunes of Worcester porcelain, and he also visited the shop opened by the Chamberlain factory, John Flight's new rival. This royal visit encouraged both factories to realize that their future depended on the production of high-quality wares. Flight opened a new London shop, abandoned the production of inexpensive blue-and-white wares, and used the factory's finest gold on every piece, aiming to revive Worcester's reputation as the producer of the best English porcelain.

FLIGHT'S

After nearly 20 years of decline, the original Worcester factory had begun a revival under the direction of the Flight family. Although John Flight died in 1791, the works underwent a transformation during his short spell in charge. On a visit to France he had seen the exciting new styles of contemporary Paris porcelain; Worcester had relied too heavily on the Rococo style, which had become old-fashioned compared with the Neo-classical styles now in demand. In 1792 the Worcester factory adopted the name "Flight & Barr" when Martin Barr (c.1765–1813) joined the firm, becoming "Barr, Flight & Barr" (1804–13) after Martin Barr junior was brought in. As Barr, Flight & Barr the factory used splendid colored grounds that set it apart from almost all its competitors. Fine hand-painting rivaled that of Derby porcelain, and benefited from the skill of Thomas Baxter (1782–1821), a highly versatile artist, who went on to set up a china-painting school in Worcester c.1814.

The factory also excelled in two other areas. In the 18th century, armorial porcelain came mostly from China; the decline of Chinese imports left this a valuable market for Worcester to exploit. Similarly, the old Japanese Imari patterns were in demand, but trade with Japan had ceased. Worcester decorators developed their own style of "rich Japan" patterns, using the prominent blue and red of the originals but far more lavishly, and making brilliant – and expensive – use of pure gold.

CHAMBERLAIN'S AND GRAINGER'S

Humphrey Chamberlain and his son Robert were in charge of decorating wares at the original Worcester factory during the 1780s, but left c.1786 to set up an independent decorating studio. Within five years the Chamberlains were also making their own porcelain, following the successful French patterns of their former employers and introducing their own versions of Flight's "Japan" patterns and armorial tea and dinner services. However, the body and decoration of Chamberlain's porcelain were rarely as fine as those of its rival. Chamberlain achieved success with its porcelain "souvenirs" – pretty

ornaments and ornately framed plaques, decorated with scenic views of Worcester and nearby Malvern – mainly for sale locally. Such pieces were decorated by new painters, trained under Thomas Baxter. The best artist was Humphrey Chamberlain junior (1791–1824), whose historical and Shakespearean figures were greatly admired.

After half a century of competition, Flight's and Chamberlain's amalgamated in 1840 to form Chamberlain & Co. The new firm still had a rival, in the shape of the factory established c.1806 by Thomas Grainger, a former employee of Robert Chamberlain. Grainger's seldom tried to compete with the best Worcester porcelain, and its output instead had more in common with Staffordshire wares. However, the company did attempt to be fashionable, and its application of printing and specialization to ordinary tea-sets guaranteed Grainger's profitability for almost a century. The factory was bought by the Worcester Royal Porcelain Co. in 1889, but finally closed in 1902.

▲ **Vase probably painted by John Barker for Barr, Flight & Barr**
Panels of shells, as seen on this magnificent vase, were among the most famous subjects to appear on Regency Worcester.
(c.1806–10; ht 33cm/13in; value M)

▼ **Plate by Flight, Barr & Barr**
Taken from the highly elaborate dessert service made for the coronation of King William IV in 1830, this plate displays Worcester's celebrated armorial decoration, gilding, and rich ground-coloring at their most sumptuous.
(1831; diam. 25cm/10in; value I)

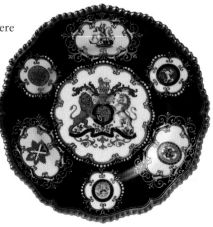

▶ **Souvenir mug by Thomas Grainger & Co.**
The very finely painted monochrome river-view scene of Worcester on this mug by Grainger's includes a careful rendering of the city's famous cathedral. However, the buildings of Barr, Flight, & Barr, Grainger's main rival, have been cleverly omitted from the background.
(c.1812; ht 8cm/3in; value F)

KEY FACTS

Important names and dates of Worcester factories:

Flight's
Flight 1783–92
Flight & Barr 1792–1804
Barr, Flight & Barr 1804–13
Flight, Barr & Barr 1813–40

Chamberlain's
Chamberlain's c.1786–1840
Chamberlain & Co. 1840–51 (joined with Flight's)

Grainger's
Grainger, Wood & Co. c.1806–11
Thomas Grainger & Co. 1811–17 and c.1837–9
Grainger, Lee & Co. 1817–c.1837
George Grainger & Co. from c.1839
Grainger & Co. until 1889

Marks
Barr, Flight & Barr

Flight, Barr & Barr

Kerr & Binns (1852–62)

Worcester Royal Porcelain Co. Ltd (est. 1862)

See also Worcester, p.203; Japanesque, aesthetic, and eastern styles, p.215

Coalport

Today the quiet banks of the River Severn at Coalport, Shropshire, seem an unlikely location for two important porcelain factories: Coalport and Caughley. However, Coalport is close to Ironbridge in an area that once lay at the heart of the 18th-century Industrial Revolution. At the end of the century, the iron furnaces of Coalport were replaced by china works that produced a large amount of good everyday porcelain, especially tea-sets and dinner services. The Coalport factory succeeded by keeping abreast of popular·tastes and fashions, and still exists today (although relocated to Stoke-on-Trent).

▶ Jardinière

This fine Neo-classical *jardinière* was decorated in London at the workshop of Thomas Baxter and bears his signature on the base. Baxter's workshop bought blanks (plain white porcelain) and painted them in a distinctive style – the red and gold striped ground on this piece is typical.
(c.1805–8; ht 15cm/5in; value I)

WHITE COALPORT

John Rose began porcelain production in Coalport c.1796. In 1799 he bought the nearby factory of Caughley, where he continued to make blue-printed teawares. Early Coalport mostly followed New Hall in manufacturing inexpensive enameled copies of Chinese patterns, and such teawares sold well at a time when popular Chinese tea-sets were no longer being imported in any quantity. Instead of trying to compete with the rich porcelain of Worcester or Derby, Rose realized that there were many skilled British china-painters working independently, all of whom required a regular supply of plain white porcelain to decorate. Studios such as those managed by Thomas Baxter in London and George Sparks in Worcester bought white Coalport porcelain and added their own wonderful painting and rich gilding. This accounts for the great variety of decoration found on Coalport porcelain, which causes confusion for collectors. The situation is further complicated by the very similar shapes and designs made by another china factory, located next door to Rose's and owned partly by his brother Thomas Rose. This operated from c.1800 and was bought by Rose in 1814. Rose is also believed to have acquired some molds and designs following the closure of the Nantgarw and Swansea factories in South Wales.

CONTINENTAL INFLUENCES

Coalport's popular Neo-classical and "Japan" patterns gave way c.1815 to the latest French fashion for pretty floral wares using the white porcelain as a ground for delicate gilding. Colorful grounds were introduced during the 1820s, followed in the 1830s by the creation of frivolous Rococo Revival-style wares inspired by the production of the German Meissen factory near Dresden, and therefore known as "English Dresden." This style was epitomized by Coalport's ornamental wares including vases, *jardinières*, baskets, inkstands, and pastille burners, typically encrusted with brightly colored modeled flowers. The term "Coalbrookdale," applied to this type of porcelain (also known as "English Dresden"), originally referred only to Coalport wares, but today is used more loosely to describe encrusted china made by English manufacturers such as Minton & Co. and Samuel Alcock & Co., who based their wares on the same Meissen originals. By the mid-19th century Coalport employed many fine in-house decorators and no longer relied on sending work out to independent artists. The extremely fine work of the bird-painter John Randall (1810–1910), and of William Cook (active 1843–76) who specialized in painting flowers, is unmistakable, and their designs are especially fine when combined with a characteristic turquoise ground.

▲ Vase painted by John Randall

Randall, who specialized in studies of exotic birds, decorated this vase, which is one of a pair. At the Great Exhibition, held in London in 1851, the factory displayed French-style vases by Randall alongside work by the fine flower-painter William Cook.
(c.1850; ht 44cm/17in; value for a pair K)

▶ Vase

This is a typical Coalport piece, almost completely encrusted with porcelain twigs, flowers, greenery, a bird, and a cherub; the style of such wares, similar to those made in Dresden, led to their being known as "English Dresden." They are also called "Coalbrookdale." This type of very overdecorated ware was enormously popular during the Rococo Revival of the 1830s. The strong palette dominated by rather hard, unharmonious colors is different from that which would have been used in the 18th century. Such fragile pieces as this are very prone to damage, as they can be easily chipped, and fine cracks may occur in the body.
(c.1835–40; ht 26cm/10in; value G)

KEY FACTS

- **BODY** hybrid hard-paste porcelain until c.1820, when bone china was introduced
- **FORMS** teawares, dinner services, flower-encrusted ornamental wares
- **DECORATION** Chinese-style enamel patterns; French-style floral designs (c.1815); Rococo Revival wares inspired by Meissen encrusted with floral decoration, known as "Coalbrookdale" or "English Dresden" (c.1830); fine painting and gilding; excellent work by independent decorators including Baxter and Sparks
- **COLLECTING** it is important to examine the shapes of wares as other factories copied Coalport designs

Marks

Most Coalport porcelain is unmarked; however, the factory's distinctive pattern numbers used after c.1820 greatly assist identification

1810–40: mark in underglaze blue — *Coalport*

c.1851–61: mark in gilt or painted —

c.1850–70: mark indicates "C" for "Coalport," "S" for "Swansea," and "N" for "Nantgarw"

Derby

William Duesbury the younger succeeded his father in 1786 and guided the Derby factory through its best and most significant period. Production was aimed only at the wealthiest customers, with every piece finished to the highest standards.

DOMESTIC WARES

The specialty of Derby was cabinet wares, particularly cups or cans and saucers, or cabaret sets – far too expensive to use and intended purely to be admired. Decoration in panels or reserves was executed by such superb artists as Zachariah Boreman (1738–1810) and Thomas "Jockey" Hill (1753–1827) who painted landscapes, Richard Askew (active 1772–95) who was famous for figures, George Complin (active *c*.1755–95) who painted birds and fruit, and William Billingsley (1758–1828),the greatest of all English flower-painters. Derby rediscovered the charm of botanical decoration, and flower prints were accurately copied onto wonderful dessert services. Derby's glaze was creamy white and very soft, accounting for a delightful, smooth, and subtle feeling quite unlike any other English porcelain. In consequence its wares are much in demand today, and the best vases and cabinet cups are hugely expensive.

During the early 19th century Derby excelled at copying colorful patterns inspired by old Japanese wares and really took this form of decoration to heart. Combinations of Chinese and Japanese designs were brought together in a totally English way to suit the

▼ The "Bemrose" garniture designed by Jean-Jacques Spängler (*b*.1752)

Named after William Bemrose, the collector and writer on Derby, this garniture borrows heavily from continental porcelain styles. These vases are also known as "Kedleston" after those in Kedleston Hall, Derbyshire.
(*c.1790–92; ht of vase 38.5cm/15in; value* **L**)

▲ Coffee-can and saucer painted by George Complin

In terms of quality, Derby cups or cans and saucers are so highly regarded that they begin to rival the rich cabinet wares made at the factories of Meissen, Paris, and Vienna.
(*c.1795; ht of can 8cm/3in; value* **K**)

► Pair of figures

Under Robert Bloor's direction (1811–26) Derby figures show the influence of 19th-century Meissen, although the coloring, featuring a deep underglaze blue, is typically Derby. The body is soft and few examples have survived without damage.
(*c.1825–30; ht 14cm/5½in; value* **G**)

Regency taste for Oriental styles. Derby sold its Imari patterns in competition with Coalport and Worcester, and mass-production methods were used to keep costs down. As a result the patterns were painted quickly, giving each piece a spontaneity that can be highly decorative. Some of the Derby Imari designs have names, such as the "Old Witches," the "Tree of Life," or the "Kings" pattern, which was a particular favorite.

FIGURES

Figure-making was always important at Derby, and in the 19th century the factory was still Britain's principal producer; however, there was now serious competition from two other quarters. Staffordshire potters copied every new Derby figure in inexpensive earthenware as

soon as it came on sale, and seriously threatened Derby's monopoly. At the same time Meissen figures were imported in great quantity into Britain and found an appreciative market. Derby countered this new competition by copying other factories' works. During the 1820s and 1830s the reproductions of the latest Meissen models even carried the Meissen crossed swords mark. However, the great period of Derby had ended in 1797 with the death of Duesbury, and the factory went into a steady decline, eventually closing in 1848. Other factories were subsequently established in Derby, the most successful being the Derby Crown Porcelain Co. (est. 1870), which was styled Royal Crown Derby in 1890.

KEY FACTS

- BODY pure white soft-paste porcelain (post-1770)
- GLAZE creamy; frequently stained by surface crazing
- DECORATION gilding is of the very best quality; some gilders are identifiable by a number; fine botanical studies; birds; landscapes; Japanese Imari patterns
- LEADING PAINTERS Boreman and Hill (landscapes), Askew (figures), Complin (birds among fruit), Billingsley (flowers)
- FIGURES style after Meissen; rich coloring, including use of deep blue and gold

Marks

1782–1825: marks carefully painted in blue or purple; after 1800 usually painted in red with less care

c.1820–40: although Robert Bloor suffered from mental illness from 1826, the period through to 1840 is named after him; mark printed in red

See also Japan: Imari, p.143; Derby p.206

Staffordshire factories

The "Five Towns" of Burslem, Stoke-on-Trent, Hanley, Tunstall, and Longton, in Staffordshire, were home to many pottery and porcelain factories during the 19th century, to the extent that the area became known as the "Potteries." Because workers and designers moved from one factory to another, and factories supplied the same china dealers – few factories had their own shops – many shapes and patterns were very similiar. These china shops wanted the continuing patronage of their customers and so discouraged manufacturers from using any kind of factory mark. As a result most English porcelain of this period was sold anonymously and is very difficult to identify accurately.

◄ **Chocolate-cup and saucer by Spode**

This cup and saucer is painted with one of Spode's best and most popular designs, known by its pattern number, 1166. The deep-blue ground was applied first, with reserves left to be filled with colorful flower sprays. The pattern could be adapted to fit a wide range of ornamental and teaware shapes.
(c.1818–25; ht 9.5cm/3¾in; value E)

MASS PRODUCTION

By the 1820s the recipe for bone china was no longer a secret; the ingredients were easy to obtain, and many new factories opened in Staffordshire making fine, affordable wares. Different factories copied each other, making similar pastes and glazes and nearly identical shapes. Pattern numbers painted on certain pieces are sometimes the only clue to the identity of the maker, and the variety of these is huge. Some of the leading factories grew to a great size and made a range of bodies, from very costly porcelain that involved expensive processes and materials to inexpensive earthenware intended for export. Their success lay in the popularity of English bone-china tea and dinner services; these were thinly potted in a pleasing white porcelain, and attractively and fashionably but inexpensively decorated with transfer-printed botanical scenes, birds, topographical views, and "Oriental" patterns and styles, such as "Imari."

▶ **Dish from a dessert service by Ridgway**

Typical of Ridgway wares, this dish is decorated with formal, well-executed flower-painting. The shape of the border was used by several factories, although the precise form of the handles, combined with the pattern number on the base, confirms that it was made at the Ridgway factory.
(c.1830; diam. 19cm/7½in; value B)

IMPORTANT FACTORIES AND LESSER MAKERS

Spode (est. 1776), in Stoke-on-Trent, produced fine painting and Japanese Imari patterns, and a number of services decorated with "bat-printed" designs. An alternative to paper transfers, bat printing involved the application of tiny dots of oil to the surface of the porcelain, using bats of glue; finely powdered color was then dusted onto the oil to form the design. The Davenport factory (*c.*1793–1887), which first produced porcelain *c.*1810, had one of the largest outputs of all the Staffordshire factories. Ridgway (est. 1792) also had a vast production, with a great many different patterns, particularly in the Rococo Revival style with brightly colored grounds; these can be identified by their pattern numbers. Minton & Co. (est. 1793) became the most important porcelain factory in Stoke-on-Trent during the Victorian period; in the 1820s to 1830s it concentrated on quality, with careful gilding and delicate painting.

Many makers of bone china subsidized their richest productions by making inexpensive earthenware, and all had to compete for their share of the market. Other Staffordshire factories included Samuel Alcock & Co. (est. 1826) and H. & R. Daniel (1832–54), both of which carried out very fine work.

▲ **"Shrewsbury" teacup, saucer, and coffee-cup by H. & R. Daniel**

During the second quarter of the 19th century, tea services included a single set of saucers to match both the tea- and the coffee-cups, as these beverages would never have been served at the same time. Teacups were usually wide and shallow, as seen in the example on the left, which has been placed on its side. In 1827 the Earl of Shrewsbury ordered several services from the firm H. & R. Daniel, and the shape of the teacup in this tea service was named "Shrewsbury" to commemorate this. Items are generally marked with a pattern number only.
(c.1828–30; diam. of saucer 13cm/5in; value C)

KEY FACTS

- FORMS wide, shallow teacups in 1830s to 1840s; elaborate shapes with complicated handles
- STYLES Rococo Revival was the most popular
- DECORATION rich and elaborate; colored grounds with reserved panels; use of elaborate gilding
- IMPORTANT FACTORIES Spode (est. 1776); Davenport (*c.*1793–1887); Minton & Co. (est. 1793); Ridgway (1792–1848); H. & R. Daniel (1832–54)

Marks

Few factories marked on a regular basis; pattern numbers vary in style but often appear as fractions on the base of the piece; certain pattern-number sequences are unique and allow the identification of unmarked tableware

Spode: (*c.*1790–1830s) red painted mark   **Spode**

See also Japan: Imari, p.143

Swansea and Nantgarw

The high reputation enjoyed by Welsh porcelain is very much deserved, for the body is truly beautiful and the decoration usually most elegant. Credit for the porcelain and the (albeit short) success of the Welsh factories lies firmly with the painter William Billingsley (1758–1828) who in 1813 brought to Nantgarw, near Cardiff, a new formula he had developed at Barr, Flight & Barr in Worcester. In 1814, with his backer, William Weston Young, Billingsley moved production to the Cambrian Works at Swansea. In 1817 he returned to Nantgarw, and in 1820 left for Coalport.

▲ **Ice pail, cover, and liner from the "Gosford Castle" service from Swansea**
This well-known service is famous for its botanical painting and fine gilding in the style of the best of the French factories.
(c.1815–20; ht 18cm/7in; value **L**)

SWANSEA

Swansea made soft-paste porcelain, closer to the paste produced at Sèvres than to Staffordshire bone china. Swansea paste is a glass-like, highly translucent body; three types were made, known as "glassy," "duck egg," and "trident." However, attempts to perfect the high-quality porcelain led to numerous firing problems; a very large proportion of wares were therefore lost in the kiln, and the factory struggled to make a profit.

Billingsley looked to France for inspiration, and most shapes and forms of decoration were in the French style – the height of fashion in the London market. The delicate white porcelain was an ideal ground for flower-painting, and, in addition to Billingsley himself, many talented flower-painters were engaged at Swansea, including David Evans, Thomas Pardoe (1770–1823), Henry Morris (1799–1880), and William Pollard (1803–54). Thomas Baxter (1782–1821), who later worked at Worcester, painted

atmospheric landscapes, figure subjects, and birds. Simple but elegant formal patterns were painted at Swansea, as well as rich "Japan" patterns; other rich decoration was added in London.

NANTGARW

By 1817 the Swansea venture was failing because of continued firing problems, and Billingsley, striving to succeed on his own, moved back to Nantgarw where he erected new kilns. Nantgarw porcelain was still difficult to control, a problem that resulted most notably in a scarcity of teawares. Instead, plates could be fired with some success, and for a few years Nantgarw plates were made in reasonable quantity, although output was never large. A few wares were decorated in Wales, but most were sent to London to independent decorators, where the finest decoration, in the French style, was added; this included richly colored grounds and ornate painting. Attempts to attribute painting to London artists as opposed to Welsh artists are always controversial, although it is likely that London painting was generally far superior to anything carried out at Nantgarw.

Although Nantgarw made extremely fine, beautiful porcelain, it was unable to make a profit. As a result the venture failed, and in 1820 Billingsley retired to live near Coalport. Many unfinished pieces were left at Nantgarw, and some were decorated up to ten or even twenty years later by local artists such as Pardoe. Auctions held in 1821 and 1822 sold off the last of the wares.

▼ **Plate from Nantgarw**
The border on this plate has been copied from the French factory of Sèvres. Such examples were sent to London as blanks to be painted by decorators in sophisticated and fashionable styles.
(c.1818–20; diam. 25cm/10in; value **H**)

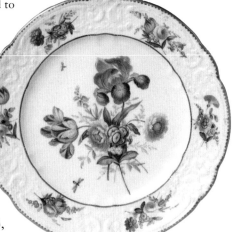

▲ **Plate from the "Duke of Cambridge" dinner service from Nantgarw**
This example is in the flamboyant style that is associated with decorators in London rather than with work produced in Wales. This magnificent service is believed to have been commissioned by the Prince Regent (later George IV) for his brother the Duke of Cambridge.
(c.1820; diam. 24cm/9½in; value **I**)

KEY FACTS

- BODY both soft-paste porcelain; Swansea: types known as "glassy," "duck egg," and "trident"; Nantgarw: extremely fine and translucent
- FORMS teawares, flatwares, cabinet cups, ice pails, tea, dinner, and dessert services
- DECORATION superb flower-painting
- DECORATORS Baxter, Billingsley, Pollard, Pardoe, Morris; study can identify the characteristics of different Swansea flower-painters
- PATRONAGE Nantgarw received important commissions from the aristocracy and local dignitaries
- BEWARE French porcelain was painted in London by the same artists who decorated Swansea and Nantgarw blanks; this can lead to a great deal of confusion
- COLLECTING Swansea shapes are well documented, and specimens must correspond exactly before a Welsh attribution can be claimed; correct identification of body and glaze is important, as Coalport took over some Nantgarw molds and imitations are plentiful; wares are often in good condition

Marks

Swansea: this mark was sometimes painted on by the artists, whose handwriting can help with identification

Swansea

Nantgarw: painted marks are invariably fake – genuine marks are impressed in the clay; "C.W." stands for "China Works"

NANT-GARW
C.W.

Rockingham

During the 1820s an established pottery works at Swinton in South Yorkshire was moved to the Wentworth estate of Earl Fitzwilliam, Marquess of Rockingham, and expanded by the Brameld family to include a porcelain works, with financial support from the Marquess. Bone china was first made there *c*.1825, and the factory, known as "Rockingham," soon developed a very individual style.

THE ROCOCO REVIVAL

The Rockingham factory is synonymous with fancy shapes; indeed, the term "eccentric" is often used for the wares, with some justification. While certain Rockingham designs are plain and elegant, the makers became masters of the Rococo Revival, and specialized in lavish molded decoration. Perhaps the most extravagant examples of this style are the two large "Rhinoceros" vases (*c*.1826) with rhinoceros-shaped finials, one of which is in the Victoria and Albert Museum in London. Tea-sets were made in the shape of plants with overlapping leaves, and handles were often in the form of gnarled branches. Many of the shapes have a rustic quality – even the most celebrated dessert service made for King William IV *c*.1830 included curiously shaped centerpieces. Fine painters, including Thomas Steel (1772–1850), famous for painting fruit, and George Speight, famous for figure subjects, decorated plaques, vases, and dessert services. In competition with similarly styled wares made at the factories of Minton & Co. (est. 1793), in Staffordshire, and Coalport (est. *c*.1796), in Shropshire, Rockingham porcelain encrusted with modeled flowers copied the style of contemporary wares made at the factory of Meissen in Germany.

THE ROCKINGHAM CONFUSION

Rockingham teawares competed with those produced by such factories as Ridgway (1792–1848) and Davenport (*c*.1793–1887), using colored grounds and painted floral reserves. Rockingham figures were often exact copies of Derby, since all the principal English factories supplied the same china shops. The reason that Rockingham achieved greater fame than its contemporaries is that it marked so many of its products. Unfortunately, unmarked tea-sets from factories such as Coalport, Ridgway, and Samuel Alcock & Co. (est. 1826) were mistakenly called "Rockingham" because they represented the same Rococo Revival fashion and looked similar to the marked Rockingham wares. Many Victorian homes owned such tea-sets, and these have been passed on as "Rockingham" china, although very few were actually made by the Yorkshire factory. To identify such sets correctly, it is important to learn the distinctive shapes made at the factory and its pattern numbers. In the same way, Rockingham marks on small animals led to the incorrect attribution of a great range of Staffordshire porcelain ornaments, especially sheep, shaggy poodles, and cottages, which served as pastille burners. Because of such confusion, Rockingham became a household name for inexpensive ornaments.

Rockingham was also renowned for its lavish and ambitious dessert services, such as that commissioned for the coronation of William IV in 1831, which was ready in time for the coronation of Queen Victoria in 1838. Partly because of the costs associated with such services, the factory was forced to close in 1842.

▲ Specimen plate

This is one of a series of sample plates, which were supplied to the English King William IV to allow him to select the design for a dessert service to celebrate his coronation in 1830. In the center of the plate is the royal coat of arms, surrounded by a richly gilded and burnished border. The pattern that was eventually chosen had an even richer border.

(*c*.1830; diam. 24cm/9½in; value **J**)

▶ Group of cat and kittens

Although many English factories produced charming and popular animal groups, this particular example can be ascribed with certainty to Rockingham because of the griffin mark impressed on the base.

(1830s; w. 11cm/4½in; value **G**)

▶ Pot-pourri jar and cover

This type of ware is typical of the production of the Rockingham factory during the 1830s. The twisted handles and extravagant flower encrustation demonstrate how the Rococo Revival style was taken to heart by the factory. This example shows how easily Rockingham output might be confused with the encrusted and decorated wares made at Coalport.

(*c*.1830; ht 25.5cm/10in; value **H**)

KEY FACTS

- **BODY** bone china, ivory toned, prone to crazing and discoloration
- **STYLE** Rococo Revival
- **FORMS** decorative wares, pot-pourri vases, lavish tea and dessert services
- **DECORATION** heavily encrusted with flowers
- **COLLECTING** output was very small; handle shapes on teawares, and the shapes of vases, must match known Rockingham examples

Marks

On tea-sets only the saucers were usually marked; many ornamental shapes were inscribed with a class number, "cl.1" or "cl.2," which help to identify unmarked wares; the mark "Manufacturers to the King" dates from 1830 and is printed in purple; pattern numbers on tea and dessert services and model numbers on figures must match Rockingham sequences

The Fitzwilliam crest used from *c*.1826 was initially printed in red; after Rockingham received royal patronage in 1830, it was changed to purple

See also Coalport, p.209

Parian busts and statues

Parian, or "statuary porcelain," was possibly the most significant ceramics development in Britain during the Victorian period. Named after the Greek island of Paros for its resemblance to the white marble quarried there, parian was a bone china that contained a high degree of feldspar, which meant that it did not need a separate glaze. Decorative wares could therefore be displayed without becoming dirty, unlike earlier biscuit, or unglazed, white porcelain, which was coarse and difficult to clean. First made in the 1840s, parian was capable of being molded without losing any detail, with the result that contemporary sculptors could have their works successfully reproduced for the mass market. Parian was also made in the USA at the United States Pottery in Bennington, Vermont.

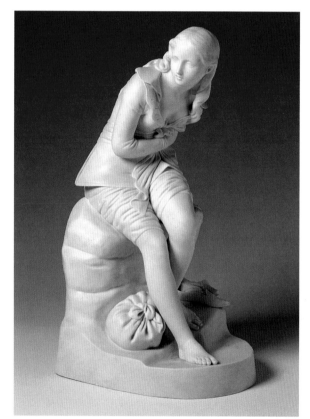

IMPORTANT MAKERS

There remains uncertainty as to which factory invented parian. The firms of Minton & Co. (est. 1793) and Copeland (1833–1933), both in Stoke-on-Trent, claimed to have discovered the secret; both were making parian-like porcelain by the mid-1840s, and at the Great Exhibition of 1851 in London they displayed an extensive range of parian subjects. Other famous makers included Royal Worcester (est. 1862), Coalport (est. *c.*1796), and Wedgwood (est. 1759), all of whom made a range of wares, figures, and busts, while Wedgwood also made impressive, large figure groups. Smaller portrait busts were the specialty of Robinson & Leadbeater (est. early 1860s), in Hanley, and others were made by the firm of Goss (1858–1940), in Stoke-on-Trent. Parian dominated English porcelain production for display objects for about 40 years, and a great deal survives.

BUSTS AND STATUES

Models for parian were provided by eminent Victorian sculptors, whose full-sized statues could be reduced in size and reproduced in quantity for commercial sale without losing quality. The work of contemporary sculptors such as John Bell (1812–95), Raphaelle Monti (1818–81), and Sir Thomas Brock (1847–1922), together with famous Classical statues housed in museums, could be reproduced and sold to a wide public. A device known as "Cheverton's Reducing Machine," patented by Benjamin Cheverton in 1844, was developed to allow subjects to be scaled down and cast in molds for the ceramics factories. Busts were made of various subjects, including royalty, politicians, philanthropists, poets, composers, and characters from antiquity. Figures ranged from meaningful allegories to barely disguised eroticism; for example, *The Greek Slave*, a controversial sculpture by the American sculptor Hiram Powers (1805–73), was displayed at the Great Exhibition of 1851 and copied by Minton & Co. Many parian figures were made either for the Art Union of London or for the Ceramic and Crystal Palace Art Union, which were lotteries set up by philanthropic Victorians to raise funds for the arts; parian works were frequently offered as prizes. The manufacture of artistic parian gradually diminished in favor of the large-scale mass production of portrait busts, and little of any consequence was made after *c.*1880.

▲ **Bust of W.E. Gladstone by Robinson & Leadbeater**
Busts of Gladstone, who served as prime minister four times between 1868 and 1894, and also of his cabinet and political rivals, were made by many ceramics firms. This example was made after a bust by the English sculptor Edgar Papworth the Younger (1809–66).
*(c.1880; ht 20cm/8in; value **D**)*

◄ ***Dorothea* by Minton & Co.**
The character of Dorothea from the novel *Don Quixote* by Cervantes was an especially popular figure with the British public, and the example shown here was based on a sculpture made in 1839 by the English sculptor John Bell.
*(c.1855–60; ht 34.5cm/13½in; value **D**)*

▼ **Bust of Apollo by Copeland**
With the introduction of parian, every Victorian middle-class family was able to adorn its library with Classical-style figures and busts such as this.
*(1870; ht 29cm/11½in; value **D**)*

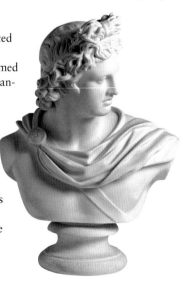

KEY FACTS

- BODY fine, highly vitrified, generally pure white
- FINISH matt, semi-matt, or with a slight surface sheen
- PRODUCTION usually slip-cast, therefore quite light
- FORMS sentimental figures; figures of politicians, royalty, and composers; literary, religious, and allegorical subjects; copies of famous Classical statues housed in museums; works by Victorian sculptors
- IMPORTANT MANUFACTURERS Minton & Co., Copeland, and Robinson & Leadbeater

Marks

Names of important modelers are often inscribed on parian figures, together with the date of the original statue; beware as popular figures remained in production for many years and still bear the original dates; the following is a selection of marks of important factories

Stoke-on-Trent: Copeland (1833–1933); impressed mark

Stoke-on-Trent: Minton & Co.(est. 1793); ermine mark (*c.*1845–65) painted, incised, or printed, often used with other marks; printed globe mark (from mid-1860s), crown added in 1880s

Hanley: Robinson & Leadbeater (est. early 1860s); impressed mark

See also The United States, pp.220–21; Dolls & Teddy Bears: China & Parian dolls, pp.485–91

Japanesque, aesthetic, and eastern styles

After a long period of self-imposed isolation, when it was effectively run by regional shoguns, Japan began a process of modernization in the mid- to late 19th century. Imperial authority was restored in 1867, although trade with the West was already beginning to flourish, the first trade agreement having been signed in 1858. The first big exhibition of Japanese art in London in 1862 caused a sensation, for here was a totally new taste, curious and bizarre to Western eyes, that was of exceptional quality. Leading French and English manufacturers were inspired by this new style of design, and in the 1870s they created a very different style that combined both Chinese and Japanese shapes and designs in a distinctively European way.

MINTON & CO. AND COALPORT

Minton & Co. made porcelain copies of many Japanese and Chinese materials, including *cloisonné* wares, which they imitated using rich turquoise or pink enamel as a background, against which designs were outlined in gold. Some pieces copied Eastern prototypes exactly, while others were rather different thanks to the influential designer Christopher Dresser (1834–1904). Dresser's designs for Minton's *cloisonné* were strangely angular and surprisingly modern, drawing on the dramatic symmetry of the late 19th-century Aesthetic Movement, much associated with the writer Oscar Wilde. At Coalport, jeweled porcelain became a specialty, each piece applied with totally even rows of finely graduated, tiny enamel drops. "Japanese" shapes were also made by smaller producers, including W. Brownfield & Sons (est. 1808), in Cobridge, George Jones & Sons (est. 1861), in Stoke-on-Trent, and Brown-Westhead, Moore & Co. (est. 1862).

ROYAL WORCESTER

The senior modeler at Royal Worcester was James Hadley (*d.*1903), a prolific and highly versatile sculptor. Hadley could turn his hand to any style the public wanted and adapted a great range of Japanese or "Eastern" subjects. Worcester's imitations of Indian carved ivory and Middle Eastern metalwork won universal favor. Many are so clever that it is necessary to handle them in order to realize they are actually made of porcelain. Hadley modeled Royal Worcester's vase shapes, while the brothers James Callowhill (1838– 1913) and Thomas Scott Callowhill (*b.*1843) were responsible for much of the best decoration. Hadley is best known for his figures of Eastern water-carriers and Indian craftsmen, which rivaled at the time the costly painted bronzes of Austria and France. Praise was heaped on Royal Worcester at

◄ **Vase and cover by Coalport**

This very elaborate vase is of Eastern inspiration (Turkish, Indian, and East Asian) and features carefully reticulated honeycomb and scrolling borders. The jeweled decoration on the highly burnished ground is typical of the quality of work carried out at Coalport: each tiny turquoise bead has been individually applied as a thick enamel paste and the piece fired with extreme precision in the intense heat of the kiln.
*(c.1895; ht 26cm/10in; value **I**)*

► **Pair of figures modeled by James Hadley for Royal Worcester**

These fine figures were decorated by the Callowhill brothers. The gold ground imitates Japanese ivory and *Shibayama* lacquer, in which minute pieces of various materials were inlaid into a lacquer ground. This pair is regarded as Hadley's greatest achievement.
*(1870s; ht 40cm/16in; value **K**)*

▼ **Silk-box and cover by George Owen for Royal Worcester**

This reticulated porcelain box and cover has each hole cut out individually with meticulous precision in the manner of Chinese "devil's work." A silk-box was made to contain sewing threads, but this outstanding example would have been far too expensive actually to use and would have been for display only.
*(1917; ht 8cm/3in; value **J**)*

international exhibitions, but, being a factory modeler, Hadley himself achieved little recognition for his work in his own lifetime.

Victorian collectors loved the mystery of Oriental carved ivory. At Royal Worcester the brilliant craftsman George Owen (1845–1917) produced remarkable copies of pierced ivory using thin porcelain, each tiny hole cut out when the clay was still wet. Owen's reticulated porcelain (pierced work in the form of a web or net) is unique, and his vases rank among the masterpieces of Victorian ceramics. Richard William Binns, who became a partner at Royal Worcester in 1852, collected thousands of pieces of Japanese art, which inspired his craftsmen, and he even engaged Po-Hing, a Chinese painter from Canton, to paint designs in a *famille-rose* palette indistinguishable from the porcelain of East Asia.

KEY FACTS

- STYLES Japanese, Indian, Middle Eastern, and the Aesthetic Movement
- PALETTE soft colors; rich gilding
- DECORATION enameling, jeweling, piercing; matt ivory grounds: these include "old ivory," a gentle, even finish, and "blush ivory," which shades from pale cream to deep apricot
- FIGURES these are very popular, particularly examples made by James Hadley
- COLLECTING Owen's reticulated wares are costly; archives are kept at both Minton and Royal Worcester and help to identify the craftsmen and designers

Marks

Minton and Royal Worcester marked virtually all their wares; both factories used elaborate date code systems, which identify the year of manufacture; few pieces carry artists' names as signatures; exceptions include Hadley's molded signature on his figures

Worcester: Worcester Royal Porcelain Co. (est. 1862)

See also Japan, pp.142–7

Britain after 1900

Many beautiful and valuable British porcelain tablewares and a huge variety of decorative ornaments were produced by British factories from the early 20th century. Leading manufacturers subsidized the production of their richly painted porcelains with the mass production of inexpensive, everyday tablewares and popular decorative figures, which were manufactured and sold in large numbers both at home and abroad. The choice for the collector of 20th-century porcelain is wide and extremely varied, and wares regularly come up for sale.

▲ **Cabinet plate by Royal Crown Derby**
Made purely for display in a cabinet, this plate was decorated by the French painter Desiré Leroy. The finely painted bowl of nasturtiums in the center is almost overwhelmed by the extraordinary raised gold border that surrounds the Limoges-style enameled border. All these techniques ensure that this would have been a very expensive plate when it was made.
(1901; diam. 22.5cm/8¾in; value I)

EXPORT AND MASS PRODUCTION

In order to finance very expensive productions, certain English factories such as Minton & Co., Royal Crown Derby, and Coalport started to produce porcelain for the overseas markets, especially the USA and Australia. For these markets, the factories made extremely fine decorative vases and porcelain intended for display in cabinets rather than actually for use. Expensive porcelain was enriched with the very best gilding, and it was this that contributed a sizeable amount to the cost. Raised and tooled gold was used to frame painted panels, which displayed the work of porcelain painters against richly colored grounds. Makers of expensive export porcelain mostly favored traditional designs. Art Deco and modern designs were made by new factories in less expensive ceramics for everyday use.

However, the high cost of fine, hand-painted decoration was prohibitive for much of the world market during the post-war period and the Depression of the 1930s; commercial mass production increased as a result. As photographic methods were improved, litho-printing replaced hand-painting and transfer-printing as a reliable method of reproducing original images at a fraction of the cost. Indeed, many established factories no longer employed painters, as new technology rendered their talents almost obsolete. The many processes and kiln firings needed to produce fine works meant that their manufacture remained extremely expensive. In real terms, many ceramic masterpieces made during the earlier part of the century are actually inexpensive today compared with the original cost of manufacture.

IMPORTANT FACTORIES AND DECORATORS

The "soft" surface of bone china, especially Royal Worcester's glazed parian body, gave English porcelain-painting a freedom that was lacking in the hard-paste porcelain made at Berlin or Meissen. From 1900, English factories encouraged individual hand-painting, and their painters became a new kind of artist, since senior decorators were now allowed to sign their work.

The influential school at Worcester established in 1896 by the modeler and designer James Hadley (*d.*1903) gave rise to a new tradition in flower- and bird-painting on porcelain, using the skills of local painters. Walter Powell and Charles Baldwyn (1859–1943) painted lively birds; Walter Sedgley (active 1889–1929) was famed for his flowers and Italian garden scenes; and Walter Austin (1891–1971) depicted lifelike flowers, the most outstanding of which were his magnificent renditions of delphiniums. The hugely versatile Harry Davis (1885–1970) applied his talents to landscapes, including the Scottish Highlands, garden scenes, views of London, and animal subjects. The name of Stinton has become synonymous with Royal Worcester painting thanks to the prolific talents of John Stinton (1854–1956), his brother James Stinton (1870–1961), and son Harry Stinton (1883–1968). John and Harry Stinton were famed for their Highland cattle in atmospheric landscapes, while James Stinton painted game birds.

At Royal Crown Derby, alongside the reproduction Japanese Imari patterns for which the factory is famous, the craftsmen brought the "Sèvres" style up to date with delicate paintings on richly colored grounds. At the factory, reserved paintings were framed with colored jeweling and the very finest raised gold. Albert Gregory and Cuthbert Gresley painted flowers in the French style, while Desiré Leroy, a French decorator whose work was unrivaled at the time, executed all the different techniques himself and revived the old Sèvres style of reserved flower- and bird-painting framed with incredible tooled goldwork on sumptuous colored grounds.

▲ **Vase and cover by Royal Worcester**
John Stinton, who painted this vase, specialized in Highland cattle. Although he and his son Harry spent their lives painting Highland subjects, neither visited Scotland, and the themes were copied from postcards.
(1910s; ht 43cm/17in; value J)

▼ **Plate from the "London Scenes" tea service painted by Harry Davis for Royal Worcester**
About 1925 Davis visited London to make sketches of famous sites for tea and coffee services. Subjects include Windsor Castle, Tower Bridge, and Big Ben.
(1926; diam. 14cm/5½in; value E)

FIGURES

The origin of the 20th-century British figure lies with James Hadley, whose detailed work for Royal Worcester had been such a success in the 1880s and 1890s. Hadley's figures maintained their popularity after his death. Meanwhile Charles Noke (1858–1941), who had trained under Hadley at Worcester, joined Doulton in 1889 where he produced similarly ambitious figures. Noke also introduced a range of smaller figures at Doulton, although initially these could not compete with inexpensive imported biscuit figures from Germany. During World War I the Board of Trade encouraged British manufacturers to copy goods previously made

in Germany, which resulted in a great expansion in British figure-making. During the 1920s figure designs were streamlined to reduce costs, while at the same time topical and modern styles were introduced to reflect popular fashion. Doulton made "crinoline" figures with bright flame-colored dresses, which the British public preferred to the "lace" figures from Dresden. Noke was responsible for the popular characters from Dickens's novels, as Doulton discovered the commercial advantages of issuing figures in sets that customers could collect. Models were provided by freelance sculptors, who generally designed to a higher standard than factory-trained modelers. Doulton's lead was threatened when Royal Worcester introduced a vast range of new figures in the 1930s, including the naturalistically modeled animal studies by Doris Lindner and the playful children depicted by Freda Doughty (d.1972). Some figures were issued by such factories as Doulton in several different color schemes.

While post-war austerity had affected the home market, ambitious new porcelain sculptures were made for sale in the USA. In 1933 Royal Worcester introduced a series called "American birds," to be followed later by "British birds"; both series were designed by Dorothy Doughty (1892–1962) and are known as "Doughty birds." These realistic studies of birds against a background of flowers and foliage were made until the 1970s. Although Doughty had had no formal training as a

factory modeler, her work took porcelain-figure-making to new heights. Animal and human figures by Lindner and by Ronald van Ruyckevelt (b.1928) and Ruth van Ruyckevelt (b.1931) were made by Royal Worcester from the 1960s as limited editions. Highly prized at the time, limited-edition porcelain has fallen sharply in value, and most pieces could not possibly be made for the low prices they now command. However, the best are surely set to rise. Other collectible, although much cheaper, pottery and porcellanous figures were made by the Staffordshire firms of John Beswick (est. c.1896), in Longton, and Wade Ceramics (est. c.1810), in Burslem.

◄ The *Old Balloon Seller* by Royal Doulton

This figure was originally modeled by Lesley Harradine, and was first introduced into factory production in 1929. Full of character and charm, it became Harradine's best-known work. The figure is actually cast in 21 separate pieces, which are put together by hand by a repairer. Still manufactured today, nearly 70 years after it was first made, it is probably the most common British figure, and examples are now more costly to purchase new than second-hand. *(1929; ht 22cm/8½in; value* **C***)*

▼ *The Evacuees* from the "Wartime" series by Royal Worcester

This sentimental group was modeled by Eva Soper and first issued in 1943. The "Wartime" series, which also included figures called *Take Cover*, *Spitfire*, and *Salvage*, did not sell well in war-torn Britain, and very few were made. This charming group is rare and will command a high value.

(1943; ht 13.5cm/5¼in; value **F***)*

▼ *The Teaparty* from the "Victorian Ladies" series by Royal Worcester

Issued as a limited edition of 500, this group modeled by Ruth van Ruyckevelt rose sharply in value in the early 1970s, reaching a peak in 1973. Unfortunately the value has dropped again; the same group today is worth considerably less. *(1964; ht 20cm/8in; value* **F***)*

KEY FACTS

- **FIGURES** early examples of popular figures are usually better modeled and painted than later versions
- **CONDITION** any damage will affect the price of 20th-century porcelain considerably
- **COLLECTING** figures signed by artists well known for their subjects sell for a premium; any rare variations from the usual color – known as "colorways" – can be surprisingly valuable, but beware of fakes where other colors have been added later in an attempt to increase the desirability of a common figure; choose well-known and established factories over minor or unknown makers; the most collectible items are attractive children and animal studies, and rare figures made in small quantities
- **IMPORTANT MAKERS** Royal Worcester, Royal Doulton, Royal Crown Derby

Marks

Worcester: Royal Worcester; mark for 1892 when the "dot" stystem was introduced; a dot was added for each year until 1916, when an asterisk was added with the dots

Stoke-on-Trent: Royal Doulton; this mark was introduced in 1901; after 1927 it may be accompanied by a year mark

Derby: Royal Crown Derby; this mark was introduced c.1890

Ireland

Belleek

In 1857 a pottery was founded in Belleek, County Fermanagh, by three men: John Caldwell Bloomfield (1823–97), a local landowner who discovered feldspar, kaolin, and other raw materials on his land; David McBirney (1804–82), a wealthy businessman; and William Armstrong (1824–84), an Irish architect who had developed a passion for porcelain and a considerable knowledge of its manufacture while working in various potteries in Staffordshire.

Initially the factory lacked both the expertise and the facilities to produce porcelain and so concentrated on the manufacture of earthenware. Because a local source of coal was lacking, the earthenware was fired with peat. A wide range of articles was made, including floor-tiles and hospital ware. The profits from the earthenware were used to support experiments in porcelain. In 1863 a number of craftsmen were recruited from the Goss factory in Stoke-on-Trent, and porcelain was finally perfected. The influence of Goss is clear in Belleek's early production, and a number of identical pieces, such as a bust of Charles Dickens, were made at both factories.

BASKETS, FIGURES, AND TEAWARES

William Henshall originated the baskets with applied flower-work for which Belleek is justly famous. The first baskets to be introduced were the "Henshall," "Convolvulus," "Twig," "Sydenham," and "Shamrock" designs, but the finest is "Rathmore." Covered baskets were the most difficult to produce, as the base and cover were made at the same time, and if one failed in the firing, both pieces had to be discarded. In addition, the factory turned out a wide variety of highly ornamental and flower-encrusted spills, vases, flower-pots, and centerpieces. Many of the designs had marine connotations and featured shells, seahorses, and dolphins. A range of about 30 figures and busts was also popular at the factory. The rare figure of Erin, symbolizing Ireland and

representing the opening of the pottery, was modeled by William Boyton Kirk. Other figures include *Affection, Meditation, Joy, Sorrow, Prisoner of Love,* and Napoleon's horse *Marengo.*

Teawares were Belleek's most extensive product, and more than 36 patterns have been identified. Most, including the popular "Shamrock" pattern, were introduced in the First Black period (called after the black mark used); others include "Neptune," "Tridacna," and "Limpet," and the less common "Hexagon," "Echinus," and "Grass." The most usual colors, after white, are green or pink; rarely, blue or butterscotch is found. Although most of these services were introduced in the First and Second Black periods, many were continued later. The Shamrock range is the largest, comprising more than 50 pieces.

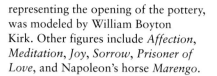

▲ "Neptune" teapot
Green is the most common color variation of this popular tea service, while pink is more rare and is particularly collectible in Japan. The teapot shown here was made in three different sizes. This is the middle size, which is the most common; the smallest size is the most collectible and therefore the most valuable. The nacreous glaze is especially appropriate for this range of wares, whose features, such as the "coral-form" handle and the shell feet, were inspired by the sea. The long spout, which is a distinctive feature of the Belleek teapots, has not been filed down, as is often the case when they have been chipped.
(c.1910; ht 13cm/5in; value E)

▲ "Shamrock" trefoil basket
This shape is the most common of this range of wares. The different flowering buds on each fold of the trefoil make this a collectible piece and suggest an early period; two-strand baskets were first made c.1865, and the three-strand version was introduced soon after. This example has a smooth, rich glaze, which increases the value.
(c.1890; ht 12cm/4¾in; value D)

▼ Earthenware tureen and cover
Both the deep blue and the attenuated form of this tureen are very distinctive of Belleek earthenware. The visible crazing all over the piece is typical of these wares because the kilns were fired with peat rather than coal.
(1863–90; diam. 27cm/10½in; value B)

First Black
1863–90

Third Black
1926–46

Russia

▲ Plate by the Imperial factory, St Petersburg
This plate is decorated with a detailed military painting framed by a delicately tooled gilt border with trophies and eagles, in typical Empire style. Following the Russian victory over Napoleon in 1812, military themes were particularly popular as decoration.
(early 19th century; diam. 24cm/9½in; value L)

The manufacture of porcelain in Russia began as part of a fashion for all things European, and most 18th- and 19th-century porcelain reflects Western European tastes. By 1800 there were at least 20 privately owned factories, and about 70 by 1861, but higher labor costs forced the closure of many factories in the late 19th century. After the Revolution of 1917 the St Petersburg factory was taken over by the State.

THE IMPERIAL FACTORY OF ST PETERSBURG
The first porcelain was made in St Petersburg in 1748 by Dmitri Vinogradov, but production on a larger scale began under the arcanist J.G. Müller. The Imperial factory enjoyed its greatest period under Catherine the Great (1729–96), a collector of French and German porcelain. The factory made Neo-classical wares with blue or violet grounds, elaborate gilding, and Italian-style landscapes. Jean-Dominique Rachette created figures after a series of engravings entitled *Description of All Nations of the Russian Empire*. The factory was reorganized in 1803 by Alexander I (1777–1825), who brought in French craftsmen from Sèvres. During the reign of Alexander II (1855–81) huge vases and services were made for the court, for international exhibitions, and as diplomatic gifts. Easter eggs, decorated with religious subjects or imperial ciphers, were made for the imperial family as presents for the court.

THE GARDNER FACTORY
About 1765 the Englishman Francis Gardner established a factory at Verbilki, near Moscow. It became the most successful private factory in Russia, and the quality of its wares and figures sometimes matches that of the Imperial factory. The most outstanding manufacture was the four services that were made for the imperial orders of St George, St Andrew, St Alexander Nevskii, and

St Vladimir between 1777 and 1785. From the 19th century the factory made brightly colored figures of tradespeople and craftworkers. Other 19th-century wares include tea services painted with roses in white medallions on blue, red, or green grounds, sometimes made for export to Turkey or Central Asia.

REVOLUTIONARY PORCELAIN
After the Revolution the Imperial factory was renamed the State porcelain factory, and in 1925 the Lomonosov porcelain factory. Immediately after the Revolution the Communist government launched a campaign of agitation and propaganda ("agitprop") to reconcile the population to the new regime. Artists and designers in every field played a prominent role in this campaign. The factory decorated its store of blank plates in vibrant colors, with themes and motifs reflecting Revolutionary ideals. In 1922 members of the Suprematist art movement were invited to design pieces for the factory. Suprematist art was typified by arrangements of abstract and geometric forms, intended to represent the "supremacy of pure emotion."

▲ Figure by the Imperial factory, St Petersburg
This fine figure is from a series of Russian craftsmen and regional characters taken from the series of engravings called *Description of All Nations of the Russian Empire*. The high-quality modeling and vivid painting distinguish the Imperial figures from a similar series made at the Gardner factory.
(c.1810–20; ht 20cm/8in; value G)

▼ Dish decorated by Natalya A. Girshfeld for the State porcelain factory
Sergei Chekhonin, director of the State porcelain factory, encouraged the use of porcelain for propaganda. Incribed in Cyrillic "Petrograd 1921," this is one of 23 items created at the factory in aid of the Volga region famine victims of 1921. The plate was made in 1896 and is inscribed on the back with the monogram "IPF" for Nicholas II.
(1896/1921; diam. 37cm/14½in; value H)

KEY FACTS
- BODY hard paste; similar to Paris porcelain
- DECORATION blue or violet grounds, rich gilding with military and topographical paintings; later in the 19th century, scrollwork, shells, flowers; Revolutionary porcelain painted with slogans and worker heroes; in the 1920s and 1930s "agitprop" and Suprematist work
- FIGURES Russian peoples, craftworkers, tradespeople, peasants, and worker heroes
- FAKES owing to the popularity of Suprematist porcelain during the 1980s there has been an influx of copies and fakes, which can be difficult to identify

Marks
Imperial factory: monograms of Catherine II and the later tsars; the mark shown here was used during the reign of Alexander II (1855–81)

Gardner factory: the "G" mark was used during the 18th century in underglaze blue; the Cyrillic mark was impressed and used during the early 19th century

State porcelain factory: this mark of the Soviet period was used from 1917

The United States

The challenge of porcelain manufacture that so intrigued Europeans throughout the 18th century had little impact on North Americans, who preferred to import porcelain from Europe or East Asia. North American porcelain, which is very rarely found outside the USA, has been largely ignored by modern collectors, and even the relatively abundant, post-centennial wares made by large companies are poorly documented, providing one of the few remaining areas of challenge for modern porcelain enthusiasts.

EARLY AMERICAN PORCELAIN

The American China Manufactory was established in Southwark, Philadelphia, by Goussin Bonnin and George Anthony Morris in 1770. The factory failed after about two years of operation, and all products can be considered "experimental." Recorded pieces, of which there are only a few dozen, and archeological evidence suggest that the exclusive product was blue-and-white wares, in painted or (rarely) transfer-printed, soft-paste porcelain. The factory made a complete range of tablewares, including tea and dinner services, cups, and teabowls (some molded with diamond quilting), sauce-boats, "dressing boxes," openwork (chestnut) baskets, pickle-dishes (of shell-and-leaf form), and sweetmeat stands. Typical decoration is crude and boldly painted in inky blue, comparable with some Bow or Liverpool porcelain, with landscapes, chinoiseries, or floral sprays in a naive manner. Molded and applied ornament of shells or sprigs is similarly crude. Unfortunately the increased competition from imported wares proved too much for the factory, and it closed in 1772.

The firm of William Ellis Tucker (1800–1832) operated in Philadelphia from 1826 to 1838. Tucker porcelain, which is also fairly rare, was probably inspired by a combination of contemporary English and French porcelain, both of which were extremely fashionable in the USA. Some of the forms mimicked the later French Empire style. Polychrome decoration tended to be hand-painted floral or landscape designs in the English style, and some teawares are of a form and decoration comparable to contemporary Coalport

▲ Sauceboat by the American China Manufactory

Products of the short-lived Bonnin and Morris enterprise are among the most elusive of all 18th-century porcelain. This Rococo-style sauceboat is characteristic of what is known of the factory's ware. Note the naively painted pagodas and the diaper border in deep blue; the thick paste and relatively crude modeling are typical of Bonnin and Morris wares.
*(c.1770–72; ht 33cm/3in; value **M**)*

► Pitcher by the Tucker factory

Although Tucker's factory was relatively small, it was the largest American porcelain enterprise of the early 19th century. Most fashionable Americans favored British or French porcelain at the time of Tucker's operation, so the firm used elements of both in its products. This example, which is very characteristic, was made in several sizes; the body is comparable to contemporary French wares, but the style of painting is clearly inspired by the factory of Coalport in Staffordshire, England. Ironically, the factory was forced to close because of competition from inexpensive European imports.
*(c.1830; ht 23cm/9in; value **H**)*

porcelain. Simple gilt monograms or sepia and gray painted scenes are common. The standards of potting, decoration, and general finish, including gilding (which wears easily), are inferior. Some painted landscapes are charming in their naivety, and it is not difficult to mistake Tucker in the French style for German or central European Biedermeier porcelain. After Tucker's death the factory was run by his brother Thomas Tucker, until it was forced to close in 1838 owing to the competition from inexpensive European porcelain.

LATER AMERICAN PORCELAIN

Brooklyn, in New York City, was an active potting center in the second half of the 19th century. Porcelain makers included Charles Cartlidge, who, like many members of the American Victorian potting industry, was an immigrant from Staffordshire. The firm of Cartlidge & Co. (1848–56) made wares in white hard-paste porcelain similar to English bone china. Typical products were "fancy" teawares such as slip-cast pitchers molded with corn (maize) stalks, some of which were gilded or painted with American emblems.

The products of the Union Porcelain Works (1861–1922), founded in Brooklyn by Thomas Carll Smith, are of greater interest to collectors. Much of the porcelain, which is of a continental European, hard-paste type, has a distinctly German flavor in palette and use of ornamental modeling, which sometimes borders on the bizarre. Mandarin-head finials, polar-bear handles, and rabbit-form feet are all characteristic of the style of the German sculptor Karl Müller (1820–87), who was art director from the early 1870s. Figural relief panels, partially bisque areas of design, and gilding in the Dresden manner are also typical. Wares include "fancy" tableware and ornamental vases, notably the "Century" vases modeled by Müller for the American Centennial Exhibition in Philadelphia in 1876, which feature a profile medallion of George Washington and

decoration, lustring, and enameling. Many of the wares were sent as blanks to be decorated by outside decorators. American Belleek was made between *c*.1883 and *c*.1930; production fell after the Wall Street Crash (1929), and with the onset of the Depression the demand for luxury goods dropped dramatically. As a result of the short period of production there is less American Belleek than European porcelain of the same period available.

Some American porcelain manufacturers, including Ott & Brewer and a few New York City firms, made good-quality parian porcelain (unglazed, usually white, biscuit porcelain resembling marble), but most American parian ware was made at the United States Pottery (est. *c*.1840), in Bennington, Vermont, founded by Christopher Webber Fenton and active until the end of the 19th century. This factory, which also produced the distinctive brown-glazed "Rockingham ware," used advanced molding techniques to produce extremely ornamental parian wares, as well as figures and busts. Pairs of mantel vases with elaborate applications of berries and flora are typical, sometimes with highlights or backgrounds of pale blue or green. A wide variety of busts and ornamental parian statuary was made at Bennington, but only outstanding examples or rare pieces of American interest have more than decorative value.

▲ **Pitcher by Cartlidge & Co.**
This pitcher, which was made in several sizes, is a distinctive product of the firm of Charles Cartlidge in Brooklyn, New York City. Most examples are plain, or decorated with gilt monograms and painted designs such as this example; such decoration increases the value several times. Some Cartlidge pitchers are signed in script within the painted decoration.
(c.1850; ht 15cm/6in; value I)

buffalo-head handles. Oyster plates were a company specialty. Union porcelain is of innovative design and high quality in manufacture and finish, but is only beginning to be collected in the USA.

The Union Porcelain Co. also made some ivory biscuit porcelain with gilded and painted decoration, in the style of wares made at the Royal Worcester Porcelain Co. in England. American porcelain of this type, which was made at several factories, is generically referred to as "American Belleek," a name that was also used as a trademark by some manufacturers. A number of firms based in Trenton, New Jersey, such as Ott & Brewer (1863–93), Lenox Inc. (est. 1889), the Willets Manufacturing Co. (est. 1879), the American China Works (1891–5), and the Ceramic Art Co. (est. 1889), specialized in the production of American Belleek, while Knowles, Taylor & Knowles Co. (est. 1854), in East Liverpool, Ohio, made fine Belleek from *c*.1883. The term is somewhat misleading, as American Belleek bears little relation to the fine translucent porcelain, with a pearly iridescent glaze, made at the Belleek factory in Ireland. Much American Belleek is very similar in style and quality to the copies of Royal Worcester made at the Royal Bonn factory in Germany. The variety of decoration on American Belleek is wide, and includes hand-painted decoration, jeweling, the use of gold paste to build up

▼ **Oyster plate by the Union Porcelain Works**
Oyster plates, some of which are signed, were a popular product of the Union Porcelain Works and are quite common today. They are often mistaken for French porcelain from Limoges, but tend to be thicker and slightly larger. The most valuable pieces are the ornamental molded and sculptural wares signed by or attributable to Karl Müller, the company's flamboyant art director from the early 1870s.
(c.1876; w. 25.5cm/10in; value C)

▲ **Bottle vase by Ott & Brewer**
The influence of the Royal Worcester factory in England is evident in the decoration on this vase. The design, in the "Japanesque" style, is given depth through the applied gold paste. The factory produced American Belleek only between 1883 and 1893, and consequently the wares are rare; the outstanding quality ensures that they are highly sought after by collectors.
(1880; ht 33cm/13in; value E)

KEY FACTS

- **BODY** Bonnin & Morris: American clays and bone-ash made a "porridgy" paste that is usually thickly potted, with a brownish tint and "moons" visible in transmitted light; Tucker porcelain: hard and glassy, comparable to Paris or German porcelain, often with English-style painted decoration; the glaze is thick, pitted, and bubbly, with a greenish tint in pooling, and unglazed patches appear which may have turned amber; parian: this can be coarse and "chalky" in the manner of continental biscuit porcelain
- **AMERICAN BELLEEK** a generic term describing porcelain made in the ornamental style of Royal Worcester (*c*.1870–1920); it is not comparable to Irish Belleek
- **COLLECTING** the work of Müller made at the Union Porcelain Works is the most collectible of all American Victorian porcelain

Marks
Most American porcelain, of all periods, is unmarked; some examples of Belleek are signed

Bonnin & Morris (1770–72): this is the most typical mark used

P

See also Ireland, p.218; Arts and Crafts: Ceramics – The United States, pp.378–81

Unlike many other antique wares, silver has an intrinsic value that resides in the material from which it is fashioned, although this may be far less than the value of the finished piece. Indeed, since silver was first mined over 4,000 years ago, there have been numerous periods of war and economic uncertainty when silver artifacts were melted down and converted to bullion or coinage. To some degree, investment in objects fashioned from this precious metal and stamped with hallmarks of provenance remains an expression of wealth and status. However, nowadays the collecting of silverware is primarily motivated by aesthetics, notably the reflectivity and luster of the metal, and also by the types of artifact available, the designs and decorative techniques employed, and the craftsmanship displayed in the manufacture of individual items. Many private collections are made up of functionally related objects, such as candlesticks and candelabra; flatware, or cutlery; the many vessels devised for serving, eating, and drinking; toilet accessories; and mirror and picture frames. Usually, such collections consist of pieces that display nuances of shape and decorative embellishments derived from one of the major historical styles of design and ornament.

Detail of a teapot (left) This Victorian silver teapot displays elaborate die-stamped decoration of flowers and foliage. Such teapots were made in huge quantities during the 19th century *(late 19th century)*.
Teapot by Philip Horst (above) Made in Germany, this silver teapot has a fluted pear-shaped form, with a molded spout, a wood handle and a silver-mounted finial *(1736–7)*.

Silver: Basics

Silver has been widely used since ancient times for making an extensive range of domestic, religious, and ceremonial objects. A virtually indestructible material, it was often melted down and refashioned when styles went out of date; this is why little domestic silver dating from before the 15th and 16th centuries survives. Silver can be shaped and decorated by craftsmen, using an extraordinarily diverse range of techniques, from raising and casting to chasing, embossing, engraving, gilding, and piercing. In the mid-18th century the production of silverware was revolutionized by the invention of Sheffield plate, made by fusing silver with copper. The introduction of electroplating in the 1840s led to the rapid decline of the Sheffield-plate industry.

Properties and forming techniques

Valued over the centuries for its rarity, reflectivity, and attractive luster, silver has, like gold, been used for coinage as well as for precious objects expressing wealth and status. For this reason, marking systems were developed for guaranteeing the purity of the metal. Throughout history, silver has been used not only to make objects of religious and symbolic significance, but also to make smaller, practical items, such as spoons, which were owned and valued by all social classes. One of the most important things to remember is that silver has always had an intrinsic value as bullion and was often melted down and converted into coinage during periods of economic and political instability. In the same way, many objects were refashioned into new items when styles went out of date.

PROPERTIES AND STANDARDS

Silver is one of the most versatile metals: it is malleable and ductile and has a relatively low melting point, meaning that it can be cast with basic workshop equipment. It is found mostly in ores combined with lead and other base metals. These ores and the process of extracting silver (known as "cupellation": heating the ore in air on a bed of bone ash to oxidize the lead and other impurities, leaving almost pure silver as a residue) were first discovered in the 3rd millennium BC in Asia Minor and the Near East. Today, most silver is extracted by electrolysis.

In the Middle Ages the most important silver mines were located in Silesia in central Europe, but the Spanish conquest of the Americas led to the exploitation in the 16th century of vast silver deposits in Central and South America. Silver was imported into Europe in enormous quantities, leading to a great increase in production.

Pure silver is too soft for making wrought objects, so it is alloyed with small amounts of other metals, including copper, to harden it. In Britain the established legal standard is the sterling standard (in use in England since 1300), which is 92.5% pure silver. During the period 1697–1720, a shortage of silver led to the raising of the standard to 95.8% – known as the "Britannia" standard – to deter silversmiths from melting coins.

FORMING METHODS

The techniques and tools employed by the silversmith today are in most cases very similar to those in use when the craft first developed, although working processes have been made easier and quicker with the aid of mechanical equipment. The silversmith will often use a combination of the techniques described below to make an object.

▲ Porringer
The simple hollow form of this English porringer was raised from sheet metal, and the handles and foot-rim were made separately and soldered to the bowl.
(1681; ht 8.5cm/3¼in; value H)

"Raising" is the process of making dishes and other hollow-wares from sheet silver. To make the sheet, a silver ingot was cast into flat plates and worked with a hammer; in the mid-18th century the invention of the rolling mill enabled sheet silver of a standard gauge to be produced commercially. The craftsman shapes a disc of sheet metal by working it with a hammer over a rounded metal stake or shaped anvil, folding and flattening the metal until it reaches the required shape. As hammering hardens the metal, it is annealed – heated until red hot, then cooled – to make it easier to work. The process leaves facets on the metal, so it is "planished" with a broad-headed planishing hammer to smooth the surface.

Simple cylindrical shapes, such as beakers and tankards, are made by creating the shape from sheet, soldering the two edges together, and attaching a disc of silver for the base. Complex shapes and components that cannot be raised from sheet, such as handles, feet, and borders, are cast. Cast objects can usually be

► Coffee-pot by Paul Crespin
Early 18th-century English coffee-pots were of a simple, tapering form created from a cylinder of sheet silver soldered together at the two edges. The spout was cast in two halves, soldered together and applied.
(1732; ht 18.5cm/7¼in; value J)

distinguished from raised objects by the thicker metal and heavier weight. In the simplest form of casting, molten silver is poured into a mold conforming to the shape of the finished object, which is removed after cooling.

More complex objects are made by lost-wax casting (*cire perdue*), in which a wax model of the object is made and covered with clay or plaster to form the mold. The whole piece is heated so the wax melts: it is then poured out and replaced with molten silver. After cooling the mold is broken away. Copies are usually made of the wax object, from which further molds can be taken. The raised or cast object is then burnished (worked with a hardstone to bring up "color") and finally polished.

▼ Sauceboat
The scrolling handle and paw-and-ball feet with lion's masks on this English sauceboat were cast separately and applied. On some elaborate pieces with relief decoration, the body may be cast in two halves.
(1820; ht 11.5cm/4½in; value E)

Hallmarking

As silver was easily convertible into coin and vice versa, systems developed for assaying (testing) and marking the purity and consistency of precious-metal alloys. Marks indicating the required amount of pure silver (the standard), the maker, the place of assay, and the official who tested the quality of silver were established in most European countries over the centuries.

The English system is one of the oldest and most consistent. A statute of 1300 decreed that all assayed silver of the legally required sterling standard – 925 parts per thousand pure silver to 75 parts copper – was to be marked with the leopard's head. Makers' marks were made compulsory in 1363, with a third mark introduced in 1478 for identifying the warden or assay master responsible for testing quality. A fourth mark, known as the "date letter," took the form of a letter of the alphabet (using only 20 letters) that changed annually to identify the year the piece was assayed (and probably made).

After the lion passant was introduced for sterling silver in 1544, the leopard's head gradually became recognized as the town mark for London, especially when assay offices, each with a mark, were opened in other cities.

In 1697 the standard was raised to 958 parts to prevent silversmiths from clipping coins to obtain silver, as the demand for silver wares exceeded the availability of bullion. A figure of Britannia and a lion's head erased replaced the lion passant and leopard's head. The sterling standard was restored in 1720. A fifth mark, showing the reigning sovereign's head, should also appear on silver made between 1784 and 1890, indicating that tax was paid.

Marking systems in Scotland, Ireland, and continental Europe are similar, although different standards, such as 800 or 900 parts per thousand pure silver, were often used.

SELECTION OF SILVER AND GOLD HALLMARKS

GREAT BRITAIN

COMPLETE SET

Most British silver carries marks indicating the standard, place of assay, date, and maker. The first and second marks shown here are Britannia and a lion's head erased, used 1697–1720 to indicate that the silver was of the higher Britannia standard. The third mark is the date letter for 1705 and the fourth the maker's mark.

DUTY MARKS

From 1784 to 1890 assayed silver was struck with a mark of the sovereign's head in profile to indicate that duty had been paid. The mark on the left, used 1784–6, shows the head of George III facing to the left (from 1786 to 1837 the head faced to the right), and the mark on the right, used 1837–90, the head of Victoria.

STANDARD MARKS

The mark of the lion passant replaced the leopard's head in 1544 to indicate that silver was of the legally required sterling standard. The form of the lion changed slightly over the centuries: the type on the left was used 1562–1668 and that on the right from 1821.

MAKERS' MARKS

Nathaniel Lock: A number of makers used a symbol as well as their initials for their mark. Here, the key is a reference to the maker's surname.

Thomas Tearle: Between 1697 and 1720, when the Britannia standard was in force, Tearle, like other English silversmiths, was required to use a mark comprising the first two letters of his surname. The other, more usual form, which Tearle registered in 1739, uses his initials.

MARKS FOR IMPORTED PLATE

Silver imported into Britain after 1876 was marked with the letter F (shown left), and from 1904 each assay office was required to use a special office mark for imported items. The symbols shown represent (from left to right) Glasgow, London, and Birmingham.

TOWN ASSAY OFFICES

London: The main center of marking in England. Strictly speaking it has no town mark, but the leopard's head is associated with the London assay office. From 1478 to 1821 the leopard's head was surmounted by a crown.

Birmingham: In the late 18th century Birmingham was an important silversmithing center, particularly for small items such as buckles and vinaigrettes. An assay office was opened there in 1773. The town mark is an anchor.

Edinburgh: Marks were introduced on Scottish silver in the mid-15th century. The town mark of Edinburgh, instituted in 1485, is a castle with three towers.

Chester: Silversmiths were active in Chester from early medieval times, but marking was not regulated there until the late 17th century. The town mark represents a shield with the arms of the city – a sword between three wheatsheaves. The Chester assay office closed in 1962.

Sheffield: Like Birmingham, Sheffield became a major silver-manufacturing center in the late 18th century, and its assay office was established in 1773. Before 1975, the town mark was a crown for silver and a rose for gold.

GOLD MARKS

The same standard marks for gold and silver were used until 1798, when a crown mark was introduced to denote gold of 18-carat standard (22-carat standard from 1844). The marks shown represent a 22-carat standard gold piece assayed in Sheffield (indicated by the town mark of a rose) in 1916 (the date letter A).

FRANCE

After the Revolution of 1789, control of assaying and marking in France passed from the guilds to the State. Two standards were established in 1797: 950 and 800 parts per thousand pure silver, denoted by the mark of a cockerel within a shield with the numerals 1 or 2 to represent the higher and lower standards respectively.

GERMANY

Before the creation of the state of modern Germany in the late 19th century, control of the silver standard in Germany was exercised by guilds in towns and cities such as Augsburg, Nuremberg, and Dresden. In 1888 the mark of a crown and crescent was introduced throughout Germany to denote silver of at least 800 parts per thousand pure silver.

IRELAND

Marking was introduced in Ireland in the 17th century. Because the country was then under British rule, the sterling standard, represented by a crowned harp, was used. Not all Irish silver bears complete marks, as the marking system there was somewhat haphazard.

ITALY

Before Napoleonic rule in 1810, there was no standard system of marking in Italy, and major cities such as Rome and Florence used a variety of marks to denote the place of manufacture and the purity. The crossed keys was the town mark of Rome in the 17th and 18th centuries. A national hallmarking system was adopted in 1874.

SPAIN

Maker's marks, town marks, and a standard of .930 purity were in force in Spain from the 16th century. The letter T was the town mark of Toledo from this period. Standards of .750 and .916 purity were introduced in 1881. The lower standard was shown by the characters "9D" with a crown above.

THE UNITED STATES

Because a comprehensive marking system has never existed in the USA, a great deal of American silver is often struck only with a maker's mark. In contrast to the initials used by English silversmiths, many American makers used their full name or initial and surname as their mark. This is the mark of Paul Revere (1735–1818), the famous American patriot and silversmith.

Decoration

Decoration can be crucial in deciding the period of a piece of silver where there are indistinct marks or no marks at all. It is also useful to be able to identify contemporary decoration, since decoration added later can often reduce the value of silver. Engraved coats of arms were often removed and new ones added, while from the 19th century traditional designs were reproduced by machine.

INTEGRAL DECORATION

The term "integral decoration" refers to decoration forming part of the material or design of the piece of silver. This includes working the surface with gravers, punches, and stamps, turning on a lathe, and removing the metal with saws and chisels to create elaborate openwork designs.

Engraving This describes the decorative patterns cut into a metal surface using a sharp tool known as a "graver" or "burin." It was the most common technique for adding coats of arms and crests, as seen on this English salver of 1752. The style of the engraving is often a good indication of whether the piece was engraved at the time of manufacture. The foliate scrolls and flowers around the rim of this salver are flat-chased.

- Mainly used for crests, coats of arms, and inscriptions
- Removal of engraved arms is often indicated by a thin patch in the metal
- Re-engraved arms are more sharply defined

Bright-cut engraving This technique uses the same basic method as engraving, but the metal is cut with a graver at an angle to create facets that reflect the light. This type of engraving was mainly used for Neo-classical ornament, as seen on this English mustard-pot of 1792.
- Facets are easily worn by over-zealous polishing
- Adds to the value of a piece only if it remains crisp
- Used mainly on late 18th-century silver

Chinoiserie decoration Chinoiserie – decoration depicting Chinese-style motifs such as landscapes, pagodas, and figures – was particularly popular on English and French domestic silver from the late 17th century, following the expansion of trade between Europe and China. Designs were usually flat-chased, as on this English tankard of 1684, but some examples are engraved.
- Exceptionally rare and very collectible
- Used from the late 17th century, mainly on English and French domestic silver

Embossing Embossing, or "repoussé" work, involves creating a relief pattern on the front of a piece of thin silver by hammering from the back with plain or decorative punches or dies. The piece to be worked is placed face down on a block of wood, lead, or pitch; this allows the craftsman to make impressions in the silver, and also offers resistance so that the indentation is not too deep. The front of the relief pattern is usually chased to add definition and detail. The embossed pattern is visible on the reverse of the piece because of the way in which the design is created. Embossed decoration of fruit and flowers, as on this Dutch casket of 1662, is characteristic of European Baroque silver of the mid- and late 17th century.

- Embossing is also called "repoussé" work
- Decoration is usually in quite high relief
- Technique was eventually replaced by die-stamping
- Designs are visible on the reverse of the piece
- Fruit and flowers are the most common motifs
- Often used on 17th-century European Baroque silver

Chasing The craftsman creates a relief design on the front of a metal object, using a chasing hammer and tracing tools to push the metal into a pattern – often to enhance existing relief work. Flat-chasing is chasing applied to a flat surface and leaves an impression of the punched pattern on the reverse. In the 19th century there was such a demand for elaborate decoration that earlier plain silver, such as this English waiter of 1750, was often embellished with all-over chasing. On such pieces the decoration was superimposed over the hallmarks; silver chased at the time of manufacture was hallmarked after it was decorated.
- Does not involve the removal of any metal
- Blurred indentations left by the punches on the reverse
- Lines created on 19th-century chasing are usually broader than those on 18th-century chasing
- Earlier plain silver was often chased with elaborate designs during the 19th century

Hand-piercing This technique involves cutting elements out of a sheet of silver to leave a decorative design. Before the late 18th century most piercing was done by hand, at first using chisels to punch out the patterns and later, from the 1770s, using a fretsaw for cutting out. This was a laborious and extremely time-consuming process, and was later replaced by mechanical piercing. Hand-piercing was particularly popular for use on such 18th-century tablewares as caster covers, dish rings, baskets – as seen on this English cake-basket of 1776 – epergnes, and mustard-pots and salt-cellars with attractively colored glass liners.
- Found mainly on decorative tableware
- Vulnerable to splitting and cracking
- Hand-pierced edges are usually slightly rough
- Used mainly before the late 18th century, when it was replaced by machine-piercing

Machine-piercing The invention of the mechanical fly press in the late 18th century enabled silversmiths to produce pierced designs mechanically in a fraction of the time and at a much lower cost than by the laborious process of hand-piercing. Machine-piercing is generally more precise than hand-piercing. The thin-gauge silver used from the late 18th century is very vulnerable to damage when pierced. The machine-pierced trailing vine

decoration on this English fruit stand of 1912 has been engraved to add further definition.
• Very precise cutting
• Thin-gauge silver used
• Vulnerable to damage

Matting A matt surface can be produced by working silver with small plain or round-headed hammers to create a dense pattern of indentations or dots. This technique is commonly found on utilitarian drinking vessels such as beakers and tankards, as the indented surface aids grip. This German silver-gilt beaker of c.1680 shows how matting was often used to provide an attractive contrast to a highly burnished surface.
• Surface is dull and matt
• Used mainly on utilitarian drinking vessels
• May provide contrast with highly burnished surfaces
• Mainly found on English and German silver
• Particularly popular during the 17th and 19th centuries

Die-stamping This technique involves forcing sheet silver into a die conforming to the finished exterior of the object by means of punches or drop hammers. Developments in machine production, and the creation of strong steel dies from the late 18th century, allowed manufacturers to mass-produce decorative surfaces, such as that seen on this English tea-caddy of 1895, and also entire objects such as spoons and forks. Sheffield plate handles and feet were

often die-stamped in halves, filled with lead, and then applied to an object.
• Fast and inexpensive method of reproducing a design or object
• Metal is stretched: holes may appear, especially in relief decoration
• Used mainly from the 19th century for mass production

Engine-turning Introduced at the end of the 18th century, engine-turning used machine-driven lathes to cut parallel lines (usually curved) into the silver surface to create a regular textured effect. It was mostly used to decorate small objects such as snuff-boxes (as seen on this 19th-century English example), cardcases, and vinaigrettes.
• Textured surface can be covered with transparent enameling, called *guilloché* enameling
• Popular from the end of the 18th century

APPLIED DECORATION
Applied decoration includes all decoration that is not part of the basic form of the object. As well as the techniques described below, it includes precious and semi-precious stones set in mounts, sculptural plaques, inlaid metal, filigree, enameling, and niello. The last is a compound of silver, lead, copper, and sulphur applied to designs cut into the metal and fired to produce a lustrous black surface.

Cut-card decoration This refers to foliate and other patterns cut from thin plates of silver and soldered to an object, particularly around edges, handles, and spouts, and above foot-rims. Although used on some English silver during the reign of Charles II, the technique was perfected by immigrant Huguenot silversmiths who fled to England to escape the persecution of Protestants after the Edict of Nantes was revoked in 1685. Fine cut-card decoration is often engraved or chased with scrolls and foliage, as on this English cup and cover of 1731.
• Can be used to reinforce handle sockets and spouts
• Appears on some English silver made during the reign of Charles II (1660–85); most common on Huguenot silver made during the reign of William III (1695–1702)

Gilding Silver has often been gilded to give it the appearance of the more precious metal gold and also to protect it from tarnishing; the gilding can cover the whole object or can be restricted to specific areas (known as parcel gilding). The earliest form was mercury gilding (fire gilding): gold was combined with mercury to form an amalgam, which was brushed onto the silver and heated until the mercury burned off as vapor, leaving a deposit of pure gold, as seen on this English spoon of 1829. Because mercury vapor is so toxic, this process is now illegal in many countries. Objects made after 1840 were usually gilded using electroplating methods.
• Parcel gilding is a process by which only selected parts of the object are covered in a gold deposit
• Mercury gilding is a highly dangerous method of gilding
• Silver drinking vessels were often gilded on the inside to protect the metal from the acid present in wine and beer

Electrogilding This technique, which replaced mercury gilding in the mid-19th century, involves covering a silver object with a thin film of gold using an electric current. The gold tends to be somewhat hard and brassy in color. This English christening bowl and cover of 1911 would have been evenly electrogilded; over-zealous polishing is probably the reason why the gold has worn away. It is in poor condition compared to the pristine, mercury-gilded, shell-shaped spoon shown above. Electrogilded cutlery, generally intended for use during the dessert course, tends to be in good condition because it was kept for one course only and was usually stored away carefully after the meal.
• Electrogilding tends to have a hard, brassy sheen
• Susceptible to wear, especially with vigorous polishing
• Technique replaced the highly toxic mercury-gilding process after the introduction of electroplating in 1840

Other applied decoration Applied decoration also refers to other types of ornament made separately and added to the body of the silver. Rim wires decorated with beading or reeding were often added to hollow-wares to add strength around the lip, foot, and edge of the silver. Decorative figures, shells, and foliage of elaborate form can be cast using the lost-wax (*cire perdue*) process, whereas simpler forms can be produced by sand casting.
• Rim wires can easily dent or split
• Cast ornament is usually a sign of good quality
• Casting can be used for both simple and more elaborate forms of decoration

Fakes, care, and collecting

Because gold and silver objects are intrinsically valuable, they have been copied and faked over the centuries. The widespread interest in historical silver, particularly from the 19th century onward, meant that not only were large and valuable objects faked, such as 16th-century ewers and salts, but also smaller, increasingly collectible pieces such as apostle spoons. Interest in collecting silver has become even greater in the 20th century. While large pieces such as tureens and cups by well-known silversmiths fetch very high prices at auction, less expensive small silverware, such as wine labels and caddy spoons in a great variety of forms and styles, is also popular.

FAKES

Although the production and quality of silver have in most countries been highly regulated with hallmarking systems, fakes and illegal alterations to silver objects are fairly common. Base metals such as brass were often gilded or silvered and given false hallmarks, while electrotype copies have also been passed off as genuine. In the 19th century reproductions of earlier styles were often produced; many of these were marked with the date of manufacture but some carried false historical marks.

One of the most important features to investigate when determining whether a silver object is a fake is the marks. These may be themselves forged or transposed from an older or more valuable object into one of lesser quality and value. Especially on altered pieces, marks may be positioned incorrectly, distorted, or even missing entirely.

Forged marks can be often be detected by the relatively soft outlines of the marks – the result of using brass punches instead of the hard steel punches employed by assay offices. In many cases, casts or electrotypes were produced from single pieces to give the impression of a pair – candlesticks, for example, were generally produced in pairs or sets, and a single example is often worth considerably less than half the value of a pair. The marks of the original object were therefore reproduced on the copy – a gritty or grainy

▲ **Forged mark**
The soft outlines and lack of clarity seen here are characteristic of forged marks: this is a result of using brass instead of steel punches. The date letter "h" attempts to imitate the real date letter for 1783 – an "h" in Gothic script – but is much less detailed than the genuine mark.

▲ **Transposed mark on a ewer**
Although in the correct place – near the rim to one side of the handle – the marks on this jug have been transposed from an earlier piece. This was done in order to make the Victorian reproduction of an 18th-century jug look older than it actually is. The insertion of the marks has been disguised with elaborate decoration.

▲ **An example of a duty dodger**
Removing the foot of this piece shows how the silversmith inserted an assayed silver disc. Only this part, rather than the whole object, was assayed, so that the silversmith avoided paying duty on the weight of the whole piece.

outline will identify these, as will the identical positioning of the marks on each piece. Genuine pairs or sets were marked separately, so the position of the marks will be slightly different. Some fake marks are now of such a high standard that metallurgical analysis is required.

Transposing marks involves the removal of marks from a small, assayed piece of silver into a larger one or from an older or damaged assayed object into a new reproduction. The insertion can sometimes be disguised with decoration but can usually be detected by breathing on the surface – this will reveal the solder around it. In Britain between 1784 and 1890 there was a widespread practice, known as "duty dodging," of transposing marks to avoid the very high duty, or tax, levied on wrought plate. High-quality or small pieces were sent to be assayed; the marks were then removed and inserted into an unassayed object of lower quality or larger size (since duty was based partly on weight).

Since silver can easily be refashioned, many objects have been altered or converted from redundant pieces into useful ones. In the late 18th century, for example, many tankards were converted into teapots when tea became more popular than beer. These are not necessarily fakes but rather recycled objects. However, some objects are altered specifically to make them more saleable – for example, spoons transformed into early two- or three-pronged forks, which are especially rare and sought after by collectors. In Britain, it is illegal to sell an altered piece of silver if it has not been marked after alteration, even after small repairs such as new handles or finials when originals have been damaged.

When checking to see whether a piece has been altered it is important to look at its proportions, as a faker will often be unaware of such details as different bowl sizes and shapes of spoons. Marks should appear in certain places on certain objects; on early 18th-century English coffee-pots they appear either on the base or on the upper body to one side of the handle. Lids held by a pin and detachable pieces, such as the scrolled or notched rims of monteiths, should also be marked. Erasure of engravings of coats of arms was fairly common when silver changed ownership – there will be a distinct thinness or dip in the metal where the arms should be. The scratchweight (the weight in Troy ounces and pennyweight of the object at the time of its assay, usually lightly engraved on the underside) may also indicate whether a piece has been altered; it may be slightly lighter than its scratchweight owing to removal of metal by polishing, but it should not be heavier.

▼ **Tankard converted into a jug**
Tankards are relatively common in silver, but jugs for beer or wine are rarer and more valuable. A spout was added to this tankard in the 19th century to make it resemble a beer-jug. It was also richly chased with animal and genre scenes to appeal to the Victorian taste for the ornate.

CARE

Silver tarnishes in contact with sulfur, found in the air and in foods such as eggs and peas, because the sulfur combines with the silver to form silver sulfide, discoloring the surface. Regular, careful cleaning will prevent the build-up of tarnish.

When cleaning an object, never use abrasive powder or liquid as these will wear away the surface (especially on Sheffield plate, where removing the thin silver layer will reveal the copper core); abrasive cleaning will also damage the marks. In the 18th century the famous Huguenot silversmith Paul de Lamerie offered advice for cleaning silver that remains useful today: "Clean it now and then with only warm water and soap with a sponge, and then wash it with clean water and dry it very well with a soft linen cloth and keep it in a dry place for the damp will spoil it." If this method is used, the silver will gradually develop a distinctive soft bloom, or "patina." A weak mixture of washing soda and water can be used to clean the stained insides of heavily used teapots and coffee-pots.

Silver objects should be stored in acid-free paper – never in newspaper, because the acid in the print will etch the silver, and never near rubber bands or self-adhesive tape because these also contain acid. Salt is particularly corrosive: salt cellars and any items that have come into contact with salt (such as plates and spoons) should be washed immediately after use. Silver should not be stored anywhere near salt as the salt will permeate the air and deposit itself on objects.

If silver needs to be repaired it should always be taken to a specialist repairer or silversmith; if repairs are not done correctly and hallmarked afterward, if appropriate, the value of the object may be lowered considerably. Items of silver should also be handled carefully – delicate feet on such pieces as cream-jugs can easily be pushed up into the body, while handles and other applied parts are also frequently damaged. Candle stubs should never be removed from silver candlesticks with sharp implements such as knives, because these will leave scratches on the surface.

▲ Collection of christening ware
This is a fairly specialized collection of English and American christening presents dating from c.1870 to c.1920. Mugs, bowls, and cutlery are the most typical christening gifts. Among the items illustrated are a silver bowl and porringer and a silver and niello mug by Tiffany & Co., New York, a hammered bowl and spoon set by Barraclough & Sons of Leeds, and a barrel-shaped mug with Japanese ornament by Gorham & Co., Providence, Rhode Island.

COLLECTING

A great variety of silver objects can be obtained today from different sources, including dealers and auctions, antique shops and markets, and bric-a-brac stalls and fairs. One of the most important things to remember is to buy what appeals to personal taste. It also helps to specialize in a particular area, such as one maker, town, style, or type of object. The last category offers much choice: wine labels, thimbles, and spoons, for example, were made in a great range of styles and forms and are generally much less expensive than larger items such as wine coolers. There are a number of specialist societies that offer information and advice on collecting.

The collector should always try to buy the best quality that he or she can afford, as an object of good quality will always retain its value – consult reputable dealers and auctioneers for advice. Handling objects and researching silver in museum collections also make useful practice for the first-time collector. Condition is the most important factor to take into account when buying – check the color of the metal, and look for holes in relief decoration, splits around handles and feet, and cracks in piercing. Repairs will also lower the value of a piece unless it is extremely rare – it is illegal to sell a piece of silver that has undergone repair and has not been re-assayed and hallmarked afterward. If buying at a sale, always ask for a condition report and read the catalog description carefully. For insurance purposes, it is important to keep accurate descriptions and photographs of objects, as well as catalogs and invoices, and to have silver valued by an expert.

TIPS FOR COLLECTORS

Fakes
- Forged marks often have soft outlines
- Beware of pairs (such as candlesticks) with marks in identical positions – one may have been cast from the other
- Breathing gently on the surface will reveal the solder around transposed marks
- Metal will be thin where armorials have been removed – this will reduce value

Care
- Never store silver in newspaper, or near rubber bands, adhesive tape, or salt
- Never use abrasive cleaners – wash instead in warm, soapy water, rinse, and dry carefully with a soft cloth
- Repairs should always be done by specialists

Collecting
- Always consult and buy from reputable dealers and auctioneers
- Check condition carefully – holes, splits, and cracks around handles, feet, and piercing will reduce value
- Keep up-to-date records for insurance purposes

► Cleaning a silver cream-jug
These illustrations show how a cream-jug has been properly cleaned to remove tarnish. The tarnish was too severe to remove with warm soapy water, so the object has been placed in an electrochemical dip; unlike many proprietary cleaners, this does not remove a thin layer of the silver. The piece must be washed, rinsed, and dried after cleaning.

Candlesticks

Candlesticks are among today's most popular and collectible silver items. The earliest-surviving domestic examples date from the mid-17th century, but most found today were made from the 18th century onward. A great variety of styles is available, from the Classical column shape of the late 18th century to the inventive figural and telescopic forms of the 19th century. Early candlesticks were cast in solid silver, but huge numbers of less expensive examples stamped from rolled silver sheet were being produced in Birmingham and Sheffield by the 1770s – these were among the first-ever items mass-produced by industrial methods. It is important to remember when buying candlesticks and candelabra that most were made as pairs.

Before 1800

Until the age of mass production, silver candlesticks were used mostly by the Church and the wealthy; others tended to be made of less expensive pewter. Examples made before the mid-17th century are rare. Medieval candlesticks, made largely for church altars, featured tripod feet and a pricket (metal spike) to hold the candle: sockets or sconces for the candle were not introduced until the 15th century. Candlesticks were usually made as pairs and are generally sold as such today; single candlesticks may sometimes be worth as little as a quarter of the value of a pair.

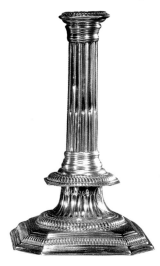

◄ Candlestick by John Barnard
This English candlestick is a late example of the Doric fluted-column style, fashionable in England before the Huguenots introduced the cast-baluster type in the 1690s. The rising base is chased with an oval scroll- and scalework cartouche, engraved with a coat of arms. Like most English candlesticks of this period, it is marked under the base; earlier pieces are often marked at the bottom of the column. *(1703; ht 21.5cm/8½in; value for a pair J)*

BAROQUE AND QUEEN ANNE STYLES

Although many candlesticks are recorded from before the 17th century, few survive; they were often melted down because they were damaged, or for conversion into coin. In particular, there are very few English candlesticks dating from before the 1650s, as much silver was melted down during the Civil War (1642–9).

In the 17th century most silver candlesticks were raised from thin, hammered sheet metal. The earliest candlesticks found on the market today, dating from the 1670s and 1680s, have stems of fluted Classical columns, or clusters of columns, and octagonal or square bases. Some rare examples have scalloped, richly embossed bases – a specialty of Dutch silversmiths. American candlesticks made before c.1760 are rare; the earliest-known pair, made in Boston, dates from 1675.

In the 1690s immigrant Huguenot silversmiths revolutionized the production of English candlesticks by casting them in solid silver rather than raising them from sheet. The base, stem, and sconce were cast separately and soldered together. The earliest pattern of cast

◄ Candlestick by Joannes Andreas Gerardus L'Herminotte
This finely made Dutch candlestick shows the continuing influence of the Rococo style in its domed base with chased spiral fluting; the most fashionable candlesticks of the 1770s and 1780s had plain fluting. Most candlesticks of this date had detachable nozzles, but here the nozzle is missing. This piece is also slightly smaller than most made in the late 18th century. *(1770–80; ht 21.5cm/8½in; value for a pair K)*

candlesticks, generally 15 to 18cm (6–7in) high, had a plain baluster stem with a series of knops (bulbous rings) on a square, round, or angled base. During the 1710s and 1720s octagonal and hexagonal faceted stems and bases, typical of the Queen Anne style, became fashionable. These elegant candlesticks, made in the higher-standard ("Britannia") silver, were plain except for an engraved coat of arms at the bottom of the stem.

ROCOCO AND NEO-CLASSICAL STYLES

The baluster shape remained the most popular design in the early and mid-18th century, but by the early 1730s candlesticks were slightly taller (19–23cm/7½–9in high), with richer ornament of pleated, lobed forms on the base and stem. The influence of the Rococo style is evident in the chased shell motifs and flared, flower-like nozzles of examples from the 1730s to the 1760s. Some exceptionally fine candlesticks of this period have ornately cast and chased stems of figures holding the candle sconce above their heads. In the 1740s detachable nozzles were added to the spool-shaped sconces for saving dripping wax and for easier removal of candle stubs; some candlesticks found today have replacement nozzles because the originals were damaged or lost. Throughout this period some silversmiths specialized in the production of candlesticks; in England, the best known were the Gould and the Cafe families.

In the 1750s and 1760s simpler forms returned under the influence of the Neo-classical style. Candlesticks of this period, averaging 24 to 28.5cm (9½–11in) high, have plain, circular nozzles, square bases, and plain or faceted stems decorated with typically Classical gadrooning around the base, knops, and sconce. By c.1765 Corinthian column candlesticks had become fashionable, and by

▼ Candlestick by Jean-François Balzac (active 1739–81)
French candlesticks of the 18th century are very rare as much French silver was melted down before the Revolution to pay for ambitious military campaigns. This extremely fine example shows the transition between the Rococo and Neo-classical styles: the ovolo borders on the base and sconce are Classically inspired, but the shell motifs on the shoulders of the stem, the cartouches, and the swirling base are Rococo. The original nozzle was damaged or lost and replaced, but this is unlikely to reduce the value of the piece because the replacement nozzle was made only about a decade later than the candlestick. *(1762; ht 26cm/10¼in; value for a pair N)*

◄ **Set of candlesticks by John Parker (active 1758–77) and Edward Wakelin (1716–84)**
The circular nozzles, square bases, heavy gadrooning, and faceted stems of this English set of candlesticks are typical of the mid-18th-century. This pattern, produced by many English silversmiths of the period, was one of the most popular, and remains highly sought after. A set of four good-quality cast-silver candlesticks is considerably more desirable than a pair.
*(1763; ht 28cm/11in; value **N**)*

▼ **Taperstick by Edward Ironside**
This English taperstick follows contemporary candlesticks with an octagonal foot and baluster stem, with fluted borders. A plain spool-shaped socket without detachable nozzle indicates that it was made before the 1740s.
*(1702; ht 10cm/4in; value for a pair **H**)*

the 1770s and 1780s the French style of plain or fluted tapering baluster stem on a circular base, decorated with Neo-classical ornament such as reeding, beading, swags, and ram's heads, was popular. Noted architects such as Robert Adam, James Wyatt, and Sir William Chambers also produced designs for Neo-classical candlesticks as part of their overall schemes for interior decoration.

Simple Neo-classical forms with restrained decoration were particularly suited to new methods of manufacture. Silversmiths in the growing industrial centers of Birmingham and Sheffield used rolled sheet silver, made in flatting mills, to manufacture candlesticks on a large scale. As this silver was often of very thin gauge, the base of the candlestick was weighted, or "loaded," with wood, pitch, or plaster of Paris for stability. Mass production of loaded candlesticks in Birmingham and Sheffield increased after the opening of assay offices in those two cities in 1773; the candlesticks proved so popular that London silversmiths often bought in provincially made pieces and overstamped them with London marks. Loaded candlesticks were significantly less expensive than cast ones because much less silver was used, and they still fetch lower prices today.

TAPERSTICKS, CHAMBERSTICKS, AND SNUFFERS
From the late 17th century silversmiths made tapersticks – smaller versions of candlesticks (10–13cm/4–5in) – for holding a taper, or thin candle, with which to melt sealing wax and light tobacco pipes. Since the designs of tapersticks copy almost exactly those of candlesticks, many such pieces were probably supplied as a set, although tapersticks were usually made singly rather than as a pair. From the mid-18th century the taperstick was replaced by the waxjack, featuring a central rod, around which the taper was coiled, on a circular foot.

Chambersticks were used to light the way at night. Because each member of a household would need one, they were made in large sets, but pairs were common after *c*.1800. They usually have a saucer-like base, decorated with reeding, beading, or gadrooning, with a central socket on a short stem, and detachable nozzles from the mid-18th century. Rare, early 17th-century chambersticks have long, flat handles, but ring- or scroll-shaped handles were introduced from the 1720s, with a thumb-piece and socket for a conical extinguisher. Some chambersticks also have a pierced slot under the sconce

for snuffer scissors, but matching snuffer scissors and chambersticks are rarely found today.

Snuffers (scissor-like implements for trimming and collecting wicks) were an essential accessory for candles before the self-consuming wick was invented *c*.1800. They were produced by specialist makers. The earliest sets, from the late 17th to early 18th century, have vertical stands with faceted baluster stems and bases similar to contemporary candlesticks, sometimes with a conical extinguisher attached. Later sets have oblong or hourglass-shaped stands, like trays, with feet or handles. Snuffer trays are sometimes sold today as pen trays.

▼ **Candlestick by Henri Auguste (1759–1816)**
This French candlestick relates to a large service made in the late 1770s for the Neapolitan Ambassador in England. The tapering, cylindrical stem and ornamentation are typical of the Neo-classical period.
*(1789; ht 30.5cm/12in; value for a pair **N**)*

KEY FACTS

Candlesticks
- NOZZLES detachable nozzles were used from *c*.1740
- COLLECTING usually found in pairs; few survive from before *c*.1670; cast candlesticks fetch higher prices than loaded sheet-metal candlesticks; if loading rattles when candlestick is shaken, it is damaged (costly to repair)

Marks
These appear at the foot of the column or under the base; on pairs marks should be in a different position – if identical it may be that one candlestick has been cast using the other; sconces and nozzles should be marked

Tapersticks
- COLLECTING made in the same patterns as candlesticks but smaller; mostly made and sold singly

Chambersticks
- COLLECTING splitting or cracking and signs of repair around the join of the handle and body, extinguisher hook, and socket reduce value; extinguishers, sconces, or nozzles in Sheffield plate with a silver pan are replacements; often sold in sets or at least pairs

Marks
Most are marked on the inside of the rim or underneath the pan; sconces and detachable extinguishers and nozzles should have the same marks as the main body

Snuffers
- STANDS vertical examples made in the early 18th century are rare and valuable

Marks
If snuffers and accompanying trays are engraved with a crest, this should be identical on both

See also Candlesticks after 1800, pp.232–3

Candlesticks after 1800

By the late 18th century huge numbers of loaded sheet-silver candlesticks were being made using mechanized production in the English industrial centers of Sheffield and Birmingham, primarily to meet demand from the newly prosperous middle classes. The new mechanized techniques of rolling sheet silver, die-stamping, and die-sinking gradually began to replace laborious casting methods (although the best-quality candlesticks were still cast). Candlesticks were also among the earliest items made in Sheffield plate. As the 19th century progressed, elaborate surface ornament, in keeping with Victorian taste, and revivals of 17th- and 18th-century styles characterized the production of candlesticks. They remained popular as decorative items even after the invention of gas and oil lighting and, later, electricity.

LATE NEO-CLASSICAL CANDLESTICKS

At the end of the 18th century candlesticks of all kinds – cast, loaded sheet silver, or Sheffield plate – were made either in the Corinthian column style on a square foot, or in the plain or fluted tapering baluster form on a circular foot: both types are decorated with ornament derived from Classical architecture, such as swags, ram's heads, wreaths, urns, and formal leaves. They are generally 25.5 to 31cm (10–12in) tall. Sheet-silver and Sheffield-plate candlesticks have visible seaming lines where the separate sheet or plate parts have been joined. They may also have small holes in the silver (or patches of visible copper on plate pieces), especially on areas of high relief, caused by overstretching the sheet or plate. Any die-stamped ornament should be sharply defined.

The telescopic adjustable candlestick, a specialty of Sheffield makers, was popular in the late 18th and early 19th centuries. Made in loaded sheet silver and Sheffield plate, it featured a cylindrical stem fitted with telescopic slides rising from the base. Although telescopic candlesticks occasionally appear in auctions today, most do not work properly; their restoration can be costly.

◄ **Candlestick by Georg Christoph Neuss**

This German candlestick was made in Augsburg. It has the elegant, urn-shaped nozzle and refined form characteristic of the early 19th-century restrained Neo-classical style. However, the faceted stem and nozzle are relatively unusual for the period – most early 19th-century candlesticks have either Corinthian column stems or plain or fluted, tapering baluster stems. The majority of candlesticks made in Germany and Austria during the 19th century are very light and generally not of such good quality as those made in England at the same time. They are consequently also less valuable.
(1819; ht 23cm/9in; value for a pair G)

THE 19TH-CENTURY REVIVAL STYLES

In the 19th century silver items were produced in an unprecedented range of historical styles, mainly as a result of developments in mechanized production, which meant that manufacturers could reproduce almost any form or type of ornament. The widespread dispersal of aristocratic collections of historic plate also provided inspiration for designers. Motifs such as trefoils and arches derived from Gothic art, while the Rococo – more ornate and bulbous than the original 18th-century version – remained one of the most popular revival styles throughout the century.

► **Candlestick by George Fox**

This English candlestick, which was made in London, is based on 17th-century French boxwood and fruitwood examples forming part of elaborate toilet services. These imitations are about the same height as the originals; many other 19th-century pieces in revival styles are either larger or smaller than the originals.
(1872; ht 17cm/6¾in; value for a pair I)

▲ **Candlestick by F.J. Bertrand-Parand**

In early 19th-century France, during the Empire and Restoration periods, the austere forms of the Neo-classical style gradually became richly embellished. In this French example, which was made in Paris, the elegant, tapering baluster stem, seen on candlesticks from the late 18th century onward, is surmounted by ornate female busts, and the base is engraved with bands of palms and stylized flowers.
(1819–38; ht 29cm/11¼in; value for a pair I)

REGENCY AND VICTORIAN CANDLESTICKS

In the Regency period (late 18th–early 19th century) candlesticks became more ornate, with richer foliate and scroll decoration on the base, at the top of the stem, and around the socket. From about the 1820s and 1830s candlestick-makers concentrated on imitating 17th- and 18th-century styles, beginning with the Rococo. Candlesticks in the Rococo Revival taste are richly chased all over with scrolls and flowers and have undulating baluster stems, but the curves are heavier, the proportions less balanced, and the sconces more bulbous than on 18th-century originals; most were also made of loaded sheet silver, rather than cast as they would have been in the first half of the 18th century. Since mechanized manufacture resulted in less expensive products, large sets of matching candlesticks were more popular in this period than previously.

Candlesticks in revival styles were produced in both larger and smaller versions of the originals; many were also made as exact copies of originals to replace those that were damaged or lost, although there are a considerable number of fakes. Figural candlesticks were particularly popular during the 19th century, reflecting contemporary taste for novelty pieces. Subjects for figural candlesticks included caryatids, knights in armor, and rustic figures of shepherds and shepherdesses; pairs usually consist of male and female figures.

In the 1890s there was a revival of the fashion for column candlesticks, this time with stepped square bases and with many variations in the patterns of the borders and the capital. These are generally smaller than late 18th-century versions – about 14cm (5½in) high. Many candlesticks in the late 19th and early 20th centuries were wired for electrical lighting as dressing-table or desk lights – in such cases there may be holes in the base for the electrical cord. During the vogue for the Queen Anne style in the early 20th century, some silversmiths produced copies of early 18th-century styles; these can be distinguished from originals by their use of sterling silver instead of the Britannia standard and by their detachable nozzles, which did not appear before *c.*1740.

With the invention of the self-consuming candle wick in the early 19th century, snuffers became obsolete,

**▲ Candlestick by
Henry Wilkinson & Co.**

The Rococo Revival style was
popular during the 1830s. This
typical English example is very
elaborately chased with swirling
acanthus scrolls, rockwork, and
flowers, and has an ornate
removable nozzle decorated with
foliate scroll, rocaille, and flower-
head rims. Like most candlesticks
made in Sheffield, it is of loaded
sheet silver; the areas of relief
decoration should be checked
for wear, as the silver was usually
thin-gauge.

*(1834; ht 28.5cm/11in;
value for a pair H)*

◄ Candlestick by Mappin Bros

Classically inspired Corinthian-column candlesticks were first
manufactured in the late 18th century; the style was revived in the
late 19th century. An example of loaded sheet silver manufactured in
Sheffield, this English candlestick has the characteristic stepped, square
base with die-stamped gadrooned borders. Pieces like this should be
carefully examined for signs of damage to the corners, where the thin
metal is particularly vulnerable to wear.

(1895; ht 29.5cm/11½in; value for a pair G)

although some were made in revival styles. Similarly,
tapersticks had been replaced by the waxjack (which
held a coiled wax taper), but small ornamental
candlesticks, sometimes with stems in the form of
sentimental figures of children or shepherds and
shepherdesses, were popular in the 19th century for
desks and dressing-tables. Also produced were "chamber"
tapersticks, which had conical extinguishers like those
found on chamber candlesticks. They were decorated
with bands of shells and foliage around the rims and
were produced in Sheffield plate as well as in silver.

Chamber candlesticks, among the most utilitarian
forms of candlestick, were manufactured in vast
quantities in silver and especially in Sheffield plate from
the late 18th century. They usually followed the style of
other candlesticks of the period; in the late 18th and early
19th centuries, for example, the socket was urn-shaped
and the rims of the pan and sconce were ornamented
with typically Neo-classical bands of reeding, beading,
and gadrooning. Silver examples might also be engraved
with a crest or a coat of arms and marked with an
inventory number. In the first half of the 19th century
chamber candlesticks were often fitted with a bulbous
or cylindrical glass shade to guard against unprotected
flames. The taste for naturalistic decoration from the
1830s and 1840s led to the production of many
candlesticks featuring a pan in the form of a leaf, with
a trailing stalk for the handle; the sockets were flower-
shaped, with lilies and nasturtiums among the more
popular designs. Rare examples feature figural stems in
the form of snails, fish, and dolphins. The octafoil and
pleated dish shapes of 18th-century chamber candlesticks
were also widely reproduced in the 19th century; unlike
the originals, these do not generally have slots for
snuffers, since the latter were rarely used in this period.

THE NEW INDUSTRIAL CENTERS

Candlesticks were among the first items mass-produced
in the English cities of Birmingham and Sheffield, using
newly developed mechanized methods of manufacture.
With the expansion of industry in those cities in the
mid-19th century, candlestick manufacture became a
specialized trade. The rolling mill, invented *c*.1740,
enabled a silver ingot to be flattened into a sheet of
uniform gauge, while the fly press, developed in the
1760s and 1770s, made accurate and repetitive piercing
possible. Both these inventions reduced labor and
manufacturing costs, since they replaced laborious
hammering and hand-piercing. Decorative components
were also mass-produced by die-stamping. The sheet of
metal was placed on a block with a sunken die in the
form of the pattern to be reproduced; this was struck
with a hammer with a relief pattern in the same shape
as the die. This method was used for items in both silver
and Sheffield plate, and a vast range of styles and forms

was made possible by interchanging the decorative
stamped components. As complete sets of dies were
highly expensive, they were often used by several
manufacturers, resulting in the production of identical
patterns by a variety of silversmiths. These new
industrialized methods were especially well exploited by
the Birmingham makers Matthew Boulton (1728–1809)
and John Fothergill (*d*.1782), who pioneered the use of
the steam-powered rolling mill in the late 18th century.

▲ Pair of candlesticks

Pairs of modern candlesticks such as this are widely available and easier
to collect than richly decorated Victorian examples. These pieces have
the baluster stems typical of most late 19th- and 20th-century
candlesticks but are fairly plain, with bands of die-stamped decoration
around the domed bases, shoulders, and molded sockets.

(mid-20th century; ht 18.5cm/7¼in; value B)

KEY FACTS

- DECORATION die-stamped ornament should be well
  defined; seaming on sheet-silver or Sheffield-plate
  candlesticks should be visible
- SCALE reproduction or revival-style candlesticks may
  be smaller than originals
- CONDITION holes or cracks in silver reduce value;
  loaded and sheet-silver candlesticks may show more
  wear than cast pieces, as the silver is thinner; Sheffield
  plate: pinkish tone indicates worn plate, as copper core
  begins to show under thin silver

Registration marks

From 1842 to 1883 Sheffield plate and electroplated
items were sometimes stamped with a lozenge-shaped
mark, indicating that the design of the item had been
registered with the British Patent Office. In the mark
shown (used from 1868 to 1883), the number in the
circle at the top indicates the class of the
item (Class 1 for plated pieces) and the
number beneath this the day. The number
of the bundle or parcel of goods is in
the left angle, with a letter representing
the year (J = 1880) to the right, and a
letter representing the month (K =
November) at the bottom of the mark.

See also Candlesticks: Before 1800, pp.230–31

Candelabra

Candelabra – table candlesticks with branches for extra lights – began to be made from *c.*1660 and increased in popularity throughout the 18th and 19th centuries. A candelabrum consists of a central shaft with two or more detachable scroll branches supporting candle sockets; sometimes there is also a socket at the top of the shaft. Made in similar styles to candlesticks and by the same makers, candelabra were likewise generally produced in pairs. Most found today are in good condition, because they were better made and much more expensive than candlesticks and therefore were not subjected to the same amount of wear or damage.

▶ Sheffield-plate candelabrum by Matthew Boulton (1728–1809)

This English candelabrum, typical of the plate produced by the famous manufacturer Boulton in Birmingham during the late 18th and early 19th centuries, has the plain stem and branches decorated with reeding and gadrooning common in the Neo-classical period. The central vase-shaped sconce is topped with a flame finial; on other examples the top of the stem has a candle socket.

(c.1815; ht 41cm/16in; value **G***)*

THE EARLY 18TH CENTURY

Although examples are known from the late 17th century, few candelabra dating from before the 1770s survive today. Until the late 18th century most had two branches, but matching branches and stems were not particularly popular or fashionable until *c.*1750. As on candlesticks, detachable nozzles for the sockets appeared *c.*1740. To be of value to collectors, a candelabrum should have all its separate parts – the branches, the nozzle, and the stem – in the same style and bearing the same maker's marks. Before *c.*1750 branches were often considered awkward and so were discarded and the stem used as a candlestick.

French silversmiths created some of the finest Rococo candelabra in the early and mid-18th century. One of the most famous examples is a single three-branched candelabrum designed in 1734–5 by Juste-Aurèle Meissonnier (1695–1750), Royal Goldsmith to King Louis XV of France, and executed by Claude Duvivier (1688–1747) for the English Duke of Kingston. It has an extraordinary, asymmetrical, spiraling stem with three richly sculpted branches ending in flower-shaped sockets, and a cast finial in the form of a cluster of leaves, which can be removed to hold a fourth candle. Such pieces fully exploit the plastic, sculptural qualities of cast silver, and had a particular influence in England, where elaborate Rococo candelabra were made by such leading silversmiths as George Wickes (1698–1761) and Paul de Lamerie (1688–1751) in the 1740s and 1750s. All such pieces are exceptionally rare and valuable today and fetch high prices on the market.

THE LATER 18TH CENTURY

In the early 18th century the hour for dining was generally about 3p.m., but in the latter part of the century it was put back and the main meal of the day was often eaten after dark. For this reason, more light was needed, and so candelabra from the 1770s onward usually have at least three branches. Elegant and light Neo-classical forms, with fluted or plain tapering baluster stems, simple, slender branches, and urn-shaped sockets, all decorated with beading and reeding, were especially popular. Such designs were produced in cast and loaded sheet silver and Sheffield plate; some candelabra have silver stems but Sheffield plate branches, perhaps to reduce the cost. Similarly, candelabra made entirely in Sheffield plate often had a matching set of more expensive silver candlesticks.

THE EARLY 19TH CENTURY

Massive, heavy silver-gilt candelabra are characteristic of the Regency period. Made largely to impress, these often form part of elaborate table centerpieces. Magnificent candelabra were made by the leading English goldsmiths Rundell, Bridge & Rundell (est. 1805) and by Paul Storr (1771–1844) for the Prince of Wales (later King George IV) and his circle. Such pieces – such as one made by Edward Farrell in 1824 – have five or more branches, sometimes with double sockets, and stems in the form of caryatids or mythological figures. Earlier candelabra were often altered to suit new tastes: a pair of candlesticks ordered by the Earl of Carlisle from the firm Parker & Wakelin (est. *c.*1758) in 1770 was supplemented with double branches in 1780 and triple branches in 1826.

▲ Candelabrum by Risler & Carré

In the 18th and 19th centuries the Rococo style was much favored by silversmiths for candelabra because twisting branches and stems fully displayed the plastic qualities of the metal. Unlike the finest 18th-century examples, where the stem is twisted and spiraling, this late 19th-century French three-light candlabrum has a baluster-shaped stem that can be distinguished under the scrolls. As it was probably stamped from sheet, the relief decoration is easily damaged.

(c.1880–90; ht 44cm/17in; value **K***)*

◀ Candelabrum by Robinson, Edkins & Aston for the Soho Plate Co.

Candelabra became slightly smaller in the mid-19th century, after the introduction of gas and oil lighting confined them to a largely decorative role. Naturalistic elements were especially favored by Victorian silversmiths; in this Birmingham example, the base and knops are molded with leaves and the serpentine branches ornamented with foliage. Both the decoration and the hexagonal base show the influence of the Gothic Revival style.

(1843; ht 66cm/26in; value **I***)*

THE LATER 19TH CENTURY

Most candelabra made in the later 19th century are of loaded sheet silver or plate, and many have figures supporting the candle sockets or as decoration on the base. After the introduction of oil lighting, some candelabra were converted to oil lamps. In the second half of the 19th century a huge range of items, including candelabra, was produced using the new method of electroplating. Following the invention of the electric battery in the early 19th century, an English doctor named John Wright experimented with electrolysis to coat the surface of base-metal objects with precious metal. In 1840 the Birmingham firm of Elkington & Co. (est. *c*.1830), in partnership with Wright, took out the first patent for this new process. Known as "electroplating," it involved the immersion into a plating bath of a nickel object attached to a positive anode and a block of pure silver attached to a negative anode. When the electric current was switched on, silver particles passed through the solution and were deposited on the nickel object; the same process could be used both for gilding and for replating worn objects.

The introduction of electroplating led quickly to the decline of the Sheffield-plate industry. The new process was far safer than the old one, but its main advantage was that it enabled objects to be formed entirely by traditional silversmithing methods before being plated, making complex sculptural ornament possible. By comparison,

handles and borders made in Sheffield plate had to be stamped out from sheet silver, filled with lead, and applied.

Elkington & Co. and the many other electroplate manufacturers established in the 1850s and 1860s produced a huge range of electroplated items, from chargers, ewers, and centerpieces richly decorated with ornament in various historical styles to cutlery, cruet frames, and spoon-warmers. Elkington employed the French sculptor Léonard Morel-Ladeuil (1820–88) to design splendid Renaissance-style pieces for display at international exhibitions. The firm also used the process of electrotyping – taking a mold from an object and depositing onto it a thin layer of silver, backed with base metal – to produce facsimile copies of a number of historically important pieces of silverware, in particular a collection of Tudor and Jacobean silver held in the Kremlin Armory in Moscow.

Since such large quantities of electroplate still exist, it is important to buy pieces in the very best condition. Electroplate can usually be distinguished from Sheffield plate by the harsher color of the pure silver (the sterling standard was used in Sheffield plate) and the lack of visible seams and joins, which are hidden by the layer of deposited silver.

◄ Candelabrum by Theodore Starr (active 1900–24)
The curving stem and sinuous candle sockets of this American silver-gilt candelabrum show the influence of the Art Nouveau style, introduced in the late 19th century. The simple lines of this form contrast with the ornate 14-light candelabrum illustrated bottom left, which was made only about 20 years earlier.
(c.1900; ht 25.5cm/10in; value **G***)*

▼ Candelabrum
In the late 19th and early 20th centuries the faceted forms of the early 18th-century Queen Anne style came into vogue in silver. Condition is important with electroplate pieces such as this English three-light candelabrum; so much survives that only good examples are valuable.
(late 19th/early 20th century; ht 41cm/16in; value **D***)*

◄ Candelabrum by Elimeyer
The design of this magnificent, 14-light, silver candelabrum from Dresden, Germany, is based on that of similar pieces produced c.1750 for Augustus III, Elector of Saxony, by the silversmith Christian Heinrich Ingermann. In keeping with the characteristic 19th-century love of elaboration, the number of sockets has been increased from the original four to fourteen. The high standard of casting and chasing in the rocaille, acanthus leaf, and scroll ornament considerably raises the value of this piece.
(c.1880; ht 84cm/33in; value **M***)*

KEY FACTS

- DESIGN early, rare examples have two branches; three were usual by the 1770s; up to five, or sometimes more, were common during the 19th century
- MATERIALS some candelabra with silver stems have Sheffield-plate branches
- CONDITION branches in sheet silver or Sheffield plate are prone to cracking or bending; electroplate is harsher in color and to the touch than Sheffield plate and lacks visible seams and joins; electroplate is also susceptible to wear on relief decoration
- COLLECTING most were made in pairs
- BEWARE it can be hard to tell if candelabra have been converted to oil lamps when well done; if poorly done, joints are badly finished and proportions awkward

Marks
Detachable parts – branches, sconce and nozzles – should have the same marks as the stem and be in the same style

See also Glass: Lighting, pp.306–7

Dining silver

Plates, salvers, tureens, and other items of dining silver first appeared in the late 17th century, when the complete dinner service, with matching dishes and cutlery, was introduced at the French court. From that period, and especially in the 18th century, elaborate dining silver in the latest fashions was often used to display the wealth and status of the host, and finely engraved coats of arms or crests, identifying the owner, are common features of items such as salvers. For collectors today, heavy and elaborately decorated items including tureens and centerpieces are generally more rare and expensive than flatware, utilitarian drinking vessels such as tankards, and casters, cruets, mustard-pots, and salt-cellars, all available in a great variety of styles.

Plates and salvers

Dinner services, comprising individual plates and cutlery as well as serving dishes for specific courses and foods, were first introduced at the French court in the late 17th century. Initially they were the preserve of royalty and the aristocracy, but the fashion for complete services spread in the early 18th century to the minor nobility and gentry, who often acquired different parts of the service over a period of time as their finances allowed. Silver plates, of various sizes, were generally made in sets of 12 (and are normally sold as such today). On both plates and salvers, the main decorative feature is usually the engraved coat of arms or crest of the owner, and sometimes the engraving is of very high quality.

PLATES

The earliest plates found on the market today tend to date from the early 18th century, when the first complete dinner services were made. These plates are seldom larger than 25cm (10in) in diameter and are starkly plain, except for a crest or coat of arms engraved on the broad, flat rim. Marks on these plates are generally found on the underside of the rim and should be clearly visible.

▲ Dinner plate
This German hexafoil plate with reeded rims is engraved with the initials "EC" under a crown and is part of a set made for Elizabeth Christine of Brunswick-Wolfenbüttel, wife of Frederick the Great of Prussia. As well as the maker's mark of Müller, this plate also carries details of its scratchweight (its original weight). Comparing this weight with the actual weight may indicate whether borders have been altered or removed.
*(mid-18th century; diam. 26cm/10¼in; value for a set of 12 **N**)*

Missing or distorted marks usually indicate that the plate has been altered; new borders may have been added and the rim reshaped to accommodate them.

More common than early 18th-century plates are those dating from the 1740s onward. During this time the fashion for complete dinner services, unified by matching ornament, reached its peak, and the custom of dining on a grand scale necessitated services of up to 200 pieces. The standard service included six dozen meat plates, generally 25cm (10in) in diameter (first-course and dessert plates were slightly smaller), and two dozen soup plates. Larger oval dishes for serving roasts were also made en suite.

Eighteenth- and nineteenth-century plates vary little in design except for the borders. During the 1730s the broad, plain, flat rim was replaced by a narrower, wavy rim (giving the plate a five-sided appearance) with gadrooning. With the development of the Rococo style in the 1740s, shell and gadrooned borders became most common; some of the finest plates have separately cast and applied borders, which should be marked. Simpler patterns of reed-and-tie or beading became fashionable in the 1770s and 1780s. The more elaborate gadroon, shell, and foliage border is characteristic of the Regency period. After about 1840 porcelain services were more popular than silver, and most silver plates made were replacements for or additions to earlier services.

▲ Six soup plates by Philip Rollos (d.1721)
These simple plates, decorated only with an engraved coat of arms, are characteristic of English silver c.1680–c.1720. They were made as part of a large service by Philip Rollos, a leading London silversmith who was Subordinate Goldsmith to King William III and Queen Anne. Such sets are particularly rare today and command high prices.
*(1706; diam. 25.5cm/10in; value for a set of six **L**)*

► Dinner plates by Robert Garrard II (1793–1881)
Copies of 18th-century designs were very popular during the Victorian age, and the gadrooned rims with acanthus shell and anthemion ornament featured on these English silver plates imitates Regency patterns. These plates are part of a set of 14 rather than the usual 12. The firm of R. & S. Garrard & Co., of which Garrard was the dominant partner, was appointed to Goldsmith to the Crown in 1830.
*(1842; diam. 26cm/10¼in; value for a set of 14 **M**)*

17TH- TO EARLY 18TH-CENTURY SALVERS

Dating from the mid-17th century, the earliest salvers were of thin-gauge metal with a raised central foot, and were made as stands for porringers or caudle cups. The finest examples were gilded and richly chased and embossed around the border with acanthus leaves, fruit, and flowers in the Dutch Baroque style. From c.1680 to c.1720 heavier-gauge metal was used, and the central foot, sometimes detachable, was often strengthened with applied cut-card work. In the 1720s the central foot was replaced by three or four small cast (usually bracket) feet, especially on the rarer square, octagonal, or octafoil-shaped salvers popular during this period. Salvers before c.1740 often had molded and applied rims of convex and concave curves.

LATER 18TH- AND 19TH-CENTURY SALVERS

Like plates, salvers from c.1740 onward are generally circular or five- or six-sided in shape, with only the borders and engraved armorials changing in style. On salvers, however, the armorials usually appear in the center rather than on the rim. The style of engraving should be contemporary with that of the border and correspond to the date of the marks. In the Baroque period, designs of arms and cartouches were relatively symmetrical, with strapwork and interlacing scrolls; the finest designs on English pieces were by Huguenot engravers such as the Gribelin family.

In the mid-18th century, delicate, asymmetrical designs of flowers, shells, and scrolls reflected Rococo fashions. Salvers were particularly in demand for carrying tea and coffee services. Smaller versions, known as "waiters" (generally less than 20cm/8in in diameter),

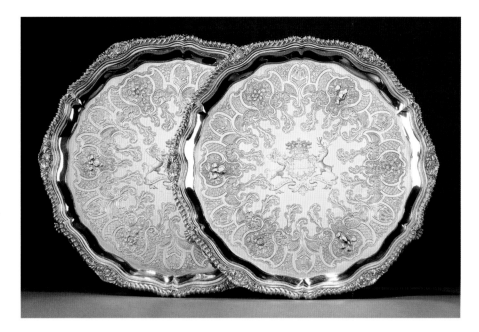

▲ **Pair of salvers by Benjamin Smith**
Regency salvers are distinguished by their great weight, large size, and fine workmanship. This silver-gilt English pair is finely chased, and features ornate lion's-paw, shell, and foliate scroll feet, and gadrooned, shell, and foliate scroll borders.
*(1818; diam. 46cm/18in; value **M**)*

were also made, and sets of two or more salvers became common. The largest, measuring up to 38cm (15in), would usually be engraved with a coat of arms; smaller ones (15–20cm/6–8in) had only a crest. Elaborate Rococo borders appeared, sometimes cast separately, featuring forward and reverse scrolls interspersed with shells, and feet took the form of scrolls or shells. The finest salvers were also flat-chased around the outer edge with designs of scrolls, shells, and foliage.

In the Neo-classical period more restrained borders of gadrooning, reeding, and beading, together with bright-cut engraving of ribbons, husks, and swags, were introduced. However, the taste for more ornate plate in the Regency period led to the appearance of large and heavy, often silver-gilt, salvers with paw feet and richly cast borders of shells, vine leaves, and gadrooning. Throughout the 19th century salvers in 18th-century styles were popular; some earlier salvers were also redecorated with chasing, but the 19th-century style is more elaborate and covers more of the flat surface than on 18th-century examples.

ENGRAVING

Engraved designs were traditionally cut into the metal surface by hand with a sharp steel tool known as a "burin" or "graver"; today, most engraving is done by machine. The technique was particularly popular for reproducing coats of arms, ciphers, and crests. Some of the finest engraving was done in early 18th-century England by such specialists as William Hogarth (1697–1764) and Simon Gribelin (1661–1733). The style of engraving can help to date a piece, but it is not always a reliable method as arms were often re-engraved with a change of ownership.

▼ **Salvers by Thomas Hannam and John Crouch**
This English set of three salvers is engraved with the arms of John Stuart, 1st Marquess of Bute. Sets of salvers became popular in the later 18th century. The plain form, the simple shield of the armorials, and the gadrooned border are characteristic features of the Neo-classical style. The London firm of Hannam & Crouch (active c.1770–1807), concentrated almost entirely on the manufacture of salvers and waiters in the late 18th century.
*(1800; diam. of smallest 20cm/8in; value **K**)*

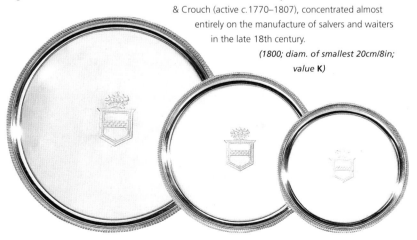

KEY FACTS

Plates
- COLLECTING sets of 12 are most popular – those found today are mostly divided from original larger services; bent or distorted rims may show that borders have been replaced; lack of scratches or knife marks may mean that the plate is over-polished and reduces value

Marks
Marks should be on underside of rim; if a plate does not have a mark, this could indicate replacement borders

Salvers
- DECORATION bright-cut engraving was used in the late 18th century; flat-chased decoration was sometimes added in the 19th century; later engraving or flat-chasing reduces the value
- CONDITION thin silver in center may mean armorials have been removed

Marks
Cast borders and feet should be marked

See also Flatware, pp.244–5

Decorative tableware

In the 18th and 19th centuries the utilitarian plate on dining-tables was complemented by richly decorative pieces such as bread-, fruit- and cake-baskets, epergnes, and centerpieces. Made as much to display wealth as to be practical, these are characterized by high-quality casting, chasing, and, especially on baskets and epergnes, piercing. Such objects are among the most popular with collectors today because they are particularly attractive as display pieces on a table.

EPERGNES

First used at the French court in the 1690s and in England *c.*1715, the epergne was an elaborate centerpiece for the dinner-table or sideboard. The name "epergne" is probably derived from the French word *épargner*, meaning "to save": space could be saved on the table by bringing together several dishes on one stand. By the 1740s the epergne was associated with the dessert course and generally took the form of a central pierced basket surrounded by four to six pierced dishes or baskets for holding fruit or sweetmeats. It was most popular during the mid-18th century, when the light and delicate pierced forms, often ornamented with cast shells and flowers, were particularly suited to the Rococo style. Some epergnes, particularly those by the leading English maker Thomas Pitts (*c.*1723–93), demonstrate the contemporary vogue for chinoiserie, with their pagoda-like canopies with suspended bells.

In the 1760s and 1770s epergnes became wider and heavier with the addition of more baskets, and in the 1780s the influence of the Neo-classical style was evident, with simpler oval or circular baskets, sometimes with blue glass liners, and decorated with Vitruvian scroll borders and swags. The leading specialist maker of epergnes in late 18th-century England was Thomas Pitts's son William Pitts (active 1781–1806). Like other silversmiths, he offered clients a choice between more expensive epergnes, which had cast branches and decoration, and less expensive examples with mechanically produced ornament.

Heavier and more solid than 18th-century examples, Regency epergnes are usually mounted on a heavy square or round foot, with branches ending in large floral sockets supporting cut-glass bowls rather than pierced silver baskets. Very few epergnes were made after this period, as they were generally replaced by the ornamental centerpiece.

CENTERPIECES

Large centerpieces as a decorative focal point for the dining-table or sideboard have always been among the most expensive items of plate and were often displayed as a sign of the wealth and status of the owner. One of the most famous and inventive pieces is the English silver-gilt Poseidon or Neptune centerpiece of 1741, made for Frederick, Prince of Wales. It features an elaborate stand of sculptural cast dolphins and mermen and is decorated with shells and marine creatures. Although this piece bears the maker's mark of Paul Crespin (1694–1770), it may in fact have been designed and made by Nicholas Sprimont (1716–71); both were

▼ Centerpiece probably by Gorham & Co.
This American silver-gilt centerpiece is in the form of a sledge and as such is typical of the novelty silverware that was popular in the late 19th century. The subtly curving form of the sledge and the delicate tendril decoration on the "runners" show the influence of the Art Nouveau style that was fashionable at the time. The company of Gorham, in Providence, Rhode Island, was among the leading North American silver manufacturers of the period. Other novelty items produced by them in silver included an ice pail with handles in the style of reindeer heads and icicle-type decoration.
(c.1890; l. 36cm/14in; value G)

◄ Old Sheffield-plate centerpiece
The form of this English centerpiece is clearly derived from the earlier epergne, which usually had four silver or plate baskets (instead of glass bowls) surrounding a single larger bowl. It is very important to check for chips or cracks in the glass bowls, because any damage reduces value. The copper core of the Sheffield plate may also show through on areas that have been over-polished or subjected to wear, such as the elaborate scrolls on the feet. The flower shape of the glass bowls on this piece is characteristic of 19th-century silver, when naturalism was in vogue in the decorative arts.
(c.1825; ht 50cm/19½in; value H)

leading English Huguenot makers of Rococo silver. The centerpiece was made with many matching salt-cellars and sauceboats, as befitting a grand table service for a royal patron.

Regency and Victorian centerpieces from the 19th century appear more frequently at auctions today (although North American pieces are rare). Made with or without branches for candles, they usually have a central bowl, either solid silver or pierced with a glass liner, for fruit or sweetmeats. Centerpieces with all their original glass liners are rare today. Female caryatid figures supporting a bowl on a stand with heavy scroll or paw feet are characteristic of the Regency period, whereas later 19th-century centerpieces were made in a huge variety of designs – naturalistic, sculptural figures were particularly popular. Many Victorian centerpieces were supplied with a flat, mirrored stand known as a "plateau" to enhance the decorative effect, but very often these became separated from the centerpiece and were sold on their own.

In the 19th century there was also a great demand for presentation plate, and the most important firms, such as Hunt & Roskell (est. 1844), Garrards (est. 1802), and Elkington & Co. (est. *c.*1830) in England, and Odiot in France, employed sculptors to design magnificent silver or electroplate centerpieces for historic or sporting occasions. Such pieces were shown at the 1851 Great Exhibition in London. Centerpieces were also made in Germany and Austria, notably by the firm of Klinkosch, but these are not always of such good quality as English and French pieces because the metal is often thinner. By the second half of the 19th century centerpieces had been scaled down in size and elaborateness, with a single basket on a stand becoming the usual form. This developed into the dessert stand, which had replaced the centerpiece by the end of the century.

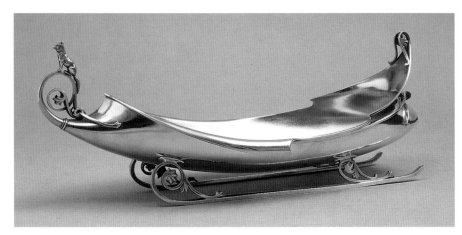

▲ Cake-basket by Philip Freeman
Baskets made in the late 18th century have thinner sheet metal, and are considerably simpler in style and much lighter than those of the early part of the century. It is common for baskets to be engraved with a coat of arms, a crest, or a monogram on the base, but this English example is unusual in that it additionally features a cartouche engraved with the owner's crest on the handle.
(1776; l. 33cm/13in; value G)

BASKETS

Silver baskets designed for holding bread, fruit, cake, or sweetmeats are known from the early 17th century, but most of those surviving today date from *c.*1730 onward. They are oval or circular with pierced sides, a flat base on a raised foot or four cast feet, and a fixed or swinging bail handle. In many cases, the flat base was engraved with a coat of arms. In the late 1730s and 1740s the leading English silversmiths Paul de Lamerie (1688–1751), Paul Crespin (1694–1770), and James Schruder (active 1737–*c.*1752) produced intricate Rococo baskets with delicate pierced designs of scrolls, circles, crescents, and quatrefoils, elaborate engraving and chasing, and asymmetrical handles with cast and applied masks, animals, figures, and birds.

Another feature typical of the Rococo fashion for novelty was the imitation of inexpensive materials in silver; on baskets dating from the first half of the 18th century the sides are often pierced and chased to give the impression of wickerwork strips. Some extremely rare and expensive baskets by the best makers were made in the form of sculptural scallop shells with scroll handles.

By the late 18th century silversmiths used hand-piercing only for the finest baskets, as the majority of pierced parts were mass-produced quickly and accurately using the newly developed fly-punch. The silver sheet was also much thinner than on earlier pieces, so baskets of this date should always be carefully checked to make sure that the piercing is intact. Simple wirework baskets embellished with chased and applied motifs such as flowers, vine leaves, and sheaves of wheat (for bread-baskets) were also popular in the late 18th century.

Regency and early Victorian baskets were produced in a wide variety of styles, but in many cases they can be distinguished from 18th-century examples by an unpierced body that is embossed and chased with heavy scrolls, flowers, and foliage, or radiating lobes. Silversmiths in the 19th century also reproduced the shell-shaped designs and elaborate patterns that were typical of the Rococo period.

Victorian baskets are generally less expensive and more readily available to collectors today than examples from the 18th and 19th centuries. The handles on these baskets are sometimes bent or damaged (or have been removed altogether), as the weight of the unpierced body puts strain on them. Any basket that does not have a handle should be carefully examined to see if the handle has been removed. As on earlier examples, the feet may also have been pushed up into the body of the basket if it has at some stage been overloaded.

▼ Fruit-basket
This Dutch fruit-basket imitates 18th-century styles with its tapering oval form and finely pierced sides engraved with foliage, flowers, beading, and trelliswork, but it does not have a handle – always check that the handle has not been removed. The delicate piercing on this piece should be carefully checked for cracks or splits, since it is particularly vulnerable to damage. This type of basket is more common today than pieces from the 18th century.
(late 19th century; l. 29cm/11¼in; value F)

▼ Bread-basket by Paul Storr (1771–1844)
The design of this English basket, with interwoven reeded hoops and a rope-twist swing handle, is unusual for the Regency period. The deceptively light form belies its weight – approximately 2kg (4½lb). This would be a sought-after piece for collectors as it was made by a leading maker.
(1817; w. 27cm/10½in; value M)

KEY FACTS

Epergnes
- COLLECTING individual baskets may be sold separately; check branches and feet for cracks or repairs

Marks
All detachable parts should be marked; crests or coats of arms on each piece should match

Centerpieces
- COLLECTING mirrored plateaux are now often sold on their own; inscriptions do not add value unless of particular historical interest

Marks
All detachable parts should be marked

Baskets
- DESIGNS solid forms with chased scrolls, flowers, and shells were typical in the early 19th century
- CONDITION piercing is particularly vulnerable to damage and should be checked carefully; ensure that the handle is not bent or damaged due to wear or overloading the basket; feet are prone to pushing up through the body on light, sheet-metal baskets
- COLLECTING early 18th-century baskets in heavy-gauge metal are more valuable than later, lighter ones

Marks
Both the handle and body should feature the same mark; marks are sometimes pierced out

Entrée dishes and sauceboats

Entrée dishes and sauceboats were among the new items of dining silver introduced in France in the late 17th century. French fashion changed European tastes in food: as the new trend developed, the typical plain roast meat served with cold sauces was replaced by soups, stews, and dishes accompanied by hot sauces made from seafood or veal stock, ham and bacon, and herbs and spices. Silver was a particularly useful material for vessels containing these hot foods as it retains heat well. In the 18th century dishes and sauceboats were decorated en suite with plates, tureens and other dining utensils, as the complete dinner service with matching ornaments became the height of fashion.

ENTREE DISHES

Entrée dishes were used for serving the "entrée" – the first course of cooked food that came before the main meat course – for example, small game such as hare, pheasant, or partridge. From about the middle of the 18th century they were also known as "hash" or "curry dishes," from the hot and spicy curries that were introduced to Britain via its extensive trade with India. Today, entrée dishes are more popular for serving vegetables or salads.

Made in various sizes and often in pairs or sets of four, these dishes are shallow with a flat bottom and/or four low feet and usually a domed cover with a handle. As with candlesticks, single entrée dishes are generally less collectible than a pair or set. The handles, which are sometimes wooden on early examples, are generally detachable, so that the cover can be used by itself as a separate dish. The cover should always fit comfortably into the dish, and both should bear the same marks. Some entrée dishes had Sheffield-plate covers, possibly to reduce the cost of the whole piece.

Entrée dishes from the mid- and late 18th century are usually oval in form, with a handle on the cover and very little ornament other than gadrooning or fluting around the edges. The finest entrée dishes have heavy cast handles in the form of a family crest, but simple reeded or plain ring handles, with leaf decoration covering the locking plate, are more common. Most examples are also engraved with a coat of arms, but some pieces have a coat of arms on the cover and a crest on the base. Those made in the late 18th century tend to be much lighter than earlier ones, as the gauge of metal used was considerably thinner. Such pieces should therefore be carefully checked for denting or splitting.

In the early 19th century entrée dishes became larger and heavier, with a more pronounced domed shape to the cover, and with ornate cast handles sometimes in the form of vegetables, reflecting the contemporary taste for naturalistic ornament. Shapes became more varied, being square, oblong, round, and cushion-like as well as oval. The simple gadrooning around the rims was often replaced by more elaborate reeding interspersed with flowers, scrolls, or shells.

To keep the food warm, the dish was generally placed either on a dish cross (incorporating a burner) or, from the early 19th century, on a plated heater base, usually made from Sheffield plate, which contained hot water or a block of heated iron. Only a very few entrée dishes are found today with their original heater base.

Fewer dishes were being made for the entrée course by the mid-19th century, principally because the custom of laying out dishes on the table so that diners could help themselves was replaced by the practice of servants serving food to each of the diners individually as they moved around the table.

▲ **Entrée dish, cover, and heater base by G.R. Elkington & Co.**
This English dish is one of the earliest-surviving examples of electroplate. The pronounced domed shape of the cover, broad fluting, and naturalistic cast vine-and-tendril handles are typical of Victorian dishes. The design, like that of most plated items, follows contemporary fashions.
(1845; w. 36cm/14in; value **E**)

▲ **Entrée dish by G. Falkenberg**
Most entrée dishes had covers to keep hot food warm, but this French dish may have been used for salad since it has no cover. The reed-and-tie border embellished with acanthus scrolls imitates decoration common on 18th-century silver. Unusually this piece is marked on the rim; most entrée dishes were marked underneath or on the sides.
(c.1870; w. 25.5cm/10in; value **F**)

▶ **Vegetable dish and cover by William Adam for Brower & Rusher**
The oblong form of this American dish and the simple decoration of palmettes around the rims are typical of early and mid-19th century entrée dishes. The handle can be removed to allow the cover to be used as a dish; in many cases the cover had decorative rims on the inside so that it matched the base when turned upside down.
(1837–42; l. 32cm/12½in; value **G**)

SAUCEBOATS

First introduced *c*.1715, sauceboats were used for serving gravy or the rich, thick sauces that accompanied meat and fish dishes. They were often made in pairs, and sometimes in sets of four or six for larger services. Like other items commonly made in pair or sets, a single sauceboat is generally less desirable than a pair. The earliest examples of the George I period were double-lipped and stood on a flat oval base with simple scroll handles on either side of the body. The only decorative features were the molded, wavy rim and engraved armorials. However, this form, which was copied by early European porcelain manufacturers, proved impractical for pouring, and by *c*.1725 the familiar bulbous form of sauceboat had appeared, with its single everted (out-turned) lip opposite a handle. It was first made with a central pedestal foot; three or four cast hoof, shell, or scroll feet were introduced in the 1740s, and cast masks or shells applied where the feet joined the body. Some sauceboats were made with a matching circular or oval stand and ladle and sometimes a cover.

The body of the sauceboat was generally raised from a single sheet of silver, so no seaming should be evident. For practical reasons, decoration was restricted to gadrooning or punching to strengthen the wavy rims and the shells or masks where the feet joined the body, although crests were sometimes engraved on either side

of the body or under the lip. Cast double-scroll handles were usual until *c*.1745 and flying-scroll handles (with only one end joined to the body) thereafter, sometimes with leaf decoration.

The sauceboat was a form particularly well exploited in the 1730s and 1740s by the best Rococo silversmiths, often of Huguenot descent – in England, Paul Crespin (1694–1770), Paul de Lamerie (1688–1751), and Nicholas Sprimont (1716–71) – who produced shell-shaped bodies with ornate cast handles in the form of dolphins, caryatids, birds, griffins, and animals, and cast and applied shells and marine creatures. The bodies of Rococo sauceboats are also sometimes decorated with cast and applied scrolls and cartouches. Some of the highest-quality sauceboats are gilded inside. Among the finest examples of this period are the set of naturalistic shell-shaped sauceboats with sculptural figural handles made by Sprimont in 1743–4 for Frederick, Prince of Wales.

The prevalence of sauceboats with shell-and-fish motifs indicates the popularity during this period of rich sauces made with fish. Some rare examples have a body with a double thickness of silver, to be filled with hot water to keep the sauce warm at the table.

In the 1770s the central foot again became fasionable and bowls were deeper, with a tall loop handle replacing the scroll handle. However, sauceboats were generally superseded by sauce tureens in this period, although they returned after the 1820s. In the 19th century, sauceboats were often made in 18th-century styles as part of a ceramic dinner service. Common features of 19th-century sauceboats include a heavy cast foot, applied shell decoration, leaf-capped scroll handles, and three feet. The shell shape was also revived and was produced in Sheffield plate as well as silver; similarly, the early double-lipped sauceboat was popular in the 1820s and 1830s; examples of this date can be distinguished from the early 18th-century versions by their high, inward-curving handles. Sauce-boats of this period were commonly produced in large sets of varying sizes, especially in response to the expansion of the hotel and catering trades after the mid-19th century.

◄ Sauceboat by Joseph Clare

This English sauceboat, with a pouring lip at each end and two side handles, is the earliest form, introduced *c*.1715. Like much silver of this period, it is completely plain. It is more practical to serve sauce with a ladle rather than pour from this boat. The sauceboat with a single lip for pouring replaced this type *c*.1725, although some later 18th-century French and German examples with Rococo decoration survive.
*(1724; ht c.12cm/4¾in; value **I**)*

▼ Sauceboat by James Dixon & Sons

Although sauce tureens were more popular than boats in the last quarter of the 18th century, sauceboats came back into fashion in the 19th century. The bellied shape of this English silver boat, one of a pair, is much deeper, and the floral and scroll feet are more ornate than on 18th-century pieces. Its maker was one of the largest silversmithing firms in Sheffield.
*(1845; l. 19cm/7½in; value **F**)*

▲ Sauceboat and stand by M. Fray

Some sauceboats were made with matching stands and sometimes ladles, but it is unusual to find a sauceboat with its original stand today. Although the decoration around the detachable stand and the rims of this French sauceboat appears to match, it is important to check the marks on each piece to make sure that the boat and stand were originally a set. The elaborate scroll handle is typical of 19th-century silver.
*(1890; l. 27cm/10½in; value **G**)*

KEY FACTS

Entrée dishes
- DESIGN the cover may have gadrooned rims on the inside to match the base when turned over and used as a dish
- CONDITION the cover and handle should both fit properly; lead may show on Sheffield-plate examples – this is caused by bleeding from lead-filled plated and applied handles under heat
- COLLECTING most entrée dishes found today are not in good condition because they have been subjected to considerable use – only the best are collectible; lack of detachable handle (or handle soldered on) reduces value; plated heater bases are often found separately

Marks
The cover and dish should bear the same marks; armorials on the cover should match those on the base

Sauceboats
- CONDITION the handle should be securely attached – seaming under the handle may indicate repairs; pieces in good condition, raised from a single sheet of silver, should have no seaming; rims are thin and often damaged or repaired; feet are vulnerable to damage
- COLLECTING pairs are more valuable than singles

Marks
These are under the body on three-footed pieces and on the edge or inside the foot on pieces with a central foot

Tureens

Tureens were introduced in the early 18th century, reflecting the French fashion for serving stews, soups, and sauces. Legend has it that the tureen was named after the 17th-century Vicomte de Turenne, who reputedly ate his soup from his upturned helmet; in fact, the term derives from the French *terrine*. From the early 18th century, soup usually accompanied boiled meats, fish, and vegetables as part of the first course and was served to the guests by the host or hostess. As such, the tureen became associated with a show of wealth and was often the most richly ornamented and expensive piece in the dinner service. Sauce tureens replaced sauceboats in the second half of the 18th century and were often smaller versions of soup tureens.

◄ Soup tureen, cover, and stand by Nicolas-Richard Masson

The angular lines of this classically inspired oval tureen and matching stand are typically French and contrast with the curved boat shapes popular in England at this time. The detachable cast finial, formed as two putti, is an early example of the solid cast crests and devices found on the best tureens in the 19th century.
(1798–1809; ht 36cm/14in; value L)

▼ George III soup tureen and cover by Thomas Whipham (active 1737–80) and Charles Wright (d.1815)

This tureen shows the influence of the Rococo in its bulbous shape, elaborately cast rose finial, and shell, scroll, and rose bracket handles. Like all early tureens, it is of heavy-gauge silver.
(1763; l. 44cm/17in; value M)

SOUP TUREENS

Soup tureens were introduced *c.*1720, but examples dating from before 1750 are very rare today. Generally circular or oval and of heavy-gauge silver, they were set on four cast scroll, hoof, or ball-and-claw feet with cast scroll, ring, or drop handles at the sides and a domed cover with an ornamental finial; most are engraved with a coat of arms. Tureens designed in the 1730s and 1740s by famous French silversmiths such as Juste-Aurèle Meissonnier (1695–1750) and Thomas Germain are among the most magnificent pieces of Rococo silver. A pair of tureens (1734–40), designed by Meissonnier for the English Duke of Kingston, is cast in the shape of large shells on curving scroll bases, with the covers decorated with cast crustacea, game, and vegetables. These pieces were highly influential: vegetable, fish, and game finials are a feature of European tureens from the 1730s to the 1760s. In the 1750s matching stands and ladles became popular, and many tureens were fitted with detachable liners in thin sheet silver with two end handles; these are often sold separately as baskets. Sheffield-plate liners became more common after the 1770s.

In the Neo-classical period architects such as Robert Adam (1728–92) produced designs for tureens to match the dining-room furnishings. Adam's designs particularly influenced silversmiths, and tureens of this period are generally oval on a single pedestal foot, with high loop handles, a ring handle, or an urn finial on the cover, and reeded, beaded, and gadrooned edges; decoration includes fluting, swags, palmettes, and bands of Vitruvian scrolls. Soup and sauce tureens were often made as sets from the 1770s, but these are now rare. Tureens were also made in Sheffield plate. The handles and feet of such pieces were not cast but stamped in two halves from thin sheet metal, filled with lead, and soldered together; in many cases a silver panel was inserted for engraving the armorials.

Early 19th-century Regency tureens contrast strongly with the elegant forms of the late 18th century: massive and of heavy-gauge silver, they are richly decorated with lion masks and Classical ornament and have four cast shell, scroll, dolphin, or paw feet. The best pieces have solid cast crests and heraldic devices on the cover. Due to the increasing popularity of the ceramic dinner service, fewer silver tureens were made in the first half of the 19th century. However, a distinctive form of the 1830s and 1840s was the melon-shaped tureen with cast vegetable finials, typical of the Rococo Revival style.

▼ Soup tureen and cover by Humbert & Söhne

The applied and chased scrolling roses and bombé form of this German tureen are common features of the Rococo Revival-style silver produced during the 19th century. The form of this tureen will distinguish it from original 18th-century Rococo pieces, which tend to be slightly wider and squatter; 18th-century pieces are also likely to be of much higher-quality craftsmanship. However, the collector will be more likely to find a reasonably priced, 19th-century Rococo Revival piece such as this example on the market today than one of the rarer and more expensive original 18th-century versions.
(1860–68; ht 33cm/13in; value I)

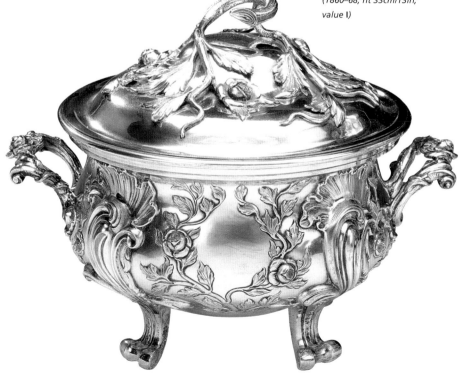

▲ Sauce tureen and cover by William Holmes
This English sauce tureen displays all the typical features of the Neo-classical style: elegant loop handles, gadrooned borders, and finely engraved swags around the body. On more expensive versions, the swags would be cast and applied instead of engraved or chased.
(1784; w. 24cm/9½in; value G)

SAUCE TUREENS

Sauce tureens became popular from the 1770s. Unlike traditional cold accompaniments to meat, such as mustard and redcurrant sauces, the new French sauces were served hot – meaning that tureens with lids were more practical than open sauceboats for keeping them warm. Sauce tureens were usually made in pairs or sometimes as a set of four – one for each corner of the table – and some had matching ladles. Single tureens are generally less collectible than a pair, and sets of four fetch considerably higher prices. Some examples have matching stands, as with sauceboats, to protect the table from the heat of the tureen's contents and to hold the ladle when not in use, although other pieces have covers with a notch inside the tureen where the ladle could be placed.

Like soup tureens of the period, sauce tureens from the late 18th century are characteristically oval or boat-shaped, with elegant upswept loop handles and a single pedestal foot. The cover will often be steeply domed in the center, with the finial at the same height as the top part of the handles. The body of the tureen was raised from a single sheet of silver, while the handles and foot were made separately and soldered onto the body. The majority of early tureens have cast handles, but from about 1790 a number were made from thick silver wire. These delicate handles, which could be very easily damaged by lifting the tureen when full, were sometimes reinforced at the bottom, but it is always important to make sure that the handles have not been pulled away from the body; nor should there be any cracks or tears on the lid where any reinforcing plate that secures the finial has been damaged and/or repaired.

Sauce tureens of this period tended to be sparingly decorated, usually only with reeding, gadrooning, or beading around the rims, covers, and feet; small, urn-shaped finials on the lid were common, but these were generally replaced with a single reeded or plain ring handle from the early 1790s onward. On such plain pieces scratches, dents, and, on versions made from Sheffield plate, inserted

silver disks for engraved coats of arms or crests, are often easily visible. More ornate and expensive examples have cast-and-applied swag ornament, with fruit- or bud-shaped finials; some especially fine pieces made by the renowned Birmingham manufacturer Matthew Boulton (1728–1809) also have radiating fluting on the covers. In addition, some sauce tureens were engraved with a crest or coat of arms on both the cover and the body; any armorials on the cover should match those on the body. In the late 18th century engraved armorials such as these were often enclosed within wreaths or ribbon cartouches.

In the early 19th century silver sauce tureens were made in fewer numbers (sometimes in Sheffield plate), as ceramic examples (particularly those in creamware) became more popular and widely available. However, some heavier versions in both silver and Sheffield plate, with large, cast, drop-ring handles and elaborate mounts, finials, and decorative borders, standing on four feet, survive from this period, while the Neo-classical boat shape was revived at the end of the century.

▼ Sauce tureen and cover by Benjamin Smith II (1793–1850)
The squat, circular form of this English tureen, the bands of flutes, the foliate scroll side handles, and the ring handle decorated with oak leaves are all features of Regency silver. This piece has foliate scroll mantling around an engraved coat of arms on the body – a good indication that the engraving is contemporary with the tureen.
(1824; l. 19cm/7½in; value I)

▼ Sauce tureen and cover by Goldsmiths' and Silversmiths' Co. Ltd
Neo-classical sauce tureens characteristically featured tapering oval forms, fluted loop handles, reeded borders, and domed covers with vase-shaped finials, and were very widely copied from the late 19th century. Such 19th- and 20th-century versions are more commonly found on the market today than the 18th-century originals, and many are reasonably priced. Unlike some earlier pieces, the English example pictured here has not been engraved with a crest or coat of arms.
(1902; l. 27cm/10½in; value F)

KEY FACTS

Soup tureens
- CONDITION seldom good as many pieces suffered from over-use and cleaning; pieces were raised from a single sheet and should therefore not have seams; thinning of metal may indicate removed armorials
- COLLECTING examples were usually made singly but sometimes in pairs; many were produced with stands, liners (often in Sheffield plate), and ladles, but these are typically missing or have been sold separately

Marks
These should appear on both the cover and the base; armorials on the cover should match those on the body

Sauce tureens
- CONDITION with the earliest designs (typically featuring a pedestal foot and loop handles) it is particularly important to check for cracking, splitting, and signs of repair where the foot, finial, and handles, join the body
- COLLECTING examples were made from the 1770s, in pairs or sets of four; from c.1790 reeded or plain ring handles were common on the lid instead of the finial

Marks
The cover and body should feature the same mark; a crest on the cover should match that on the body

Flatware

Flatware, or cutlery, remains among the most popular antique silver today. Spoons, owned and valued by all classes of society, are among the earliest utilitarian silver to survive in any quantity – being small, they had a relatively low value as bullion and were not as readily converted into coin as larger items. Forks were only used for sweetmeats or desserts until the 16th century in continental Europe and the late 17th century in Britain. It was not until the 18th century that matching sets of spoons, forks, and knives were produced, but thereafter they were made on a large scale and in an extensive range of patterns. Complete and original sets of flatware are rare and expensive, since individual pieces were often very heavily used and then replaced.

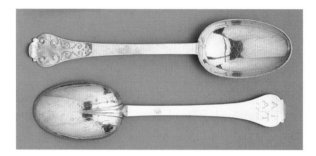

▲ Silver-gilt "trefid" pattern spoons by John Murch
The stems and bowl backs of these spoons are stamped with scrolls and beading, and the terminals pricked with initials and the date. The "rat-tail" strengthens the junction of bowl and stem. Spoons are often the only record of provincial marks.
(c.1700; l. 20cm/8in; value F)

APOSTLE SPOONS

English apostle spoons were made in London and the provinces from the mid-15th to the mid-17th century. They have a fig-shaped bowl and faceted hexagonal stem, and are so called because the cast finials depict the 12 Apostles; originally they were made in sets of 12 or 13 (the thirteenth spoon usually representing Christ), but very few full sets survive today. Spoons were often given as christening presents, the child receiving the spoon representing the saint after whom he was named. Each Apostle can usually be identified by the symbolic object in his right hand – for example keys or a fish for St Peter or a saltire cross for St Andrew. The bowl and stem were created from a single piece of silver, one part being drawn out for the stem and the other hammered into a shaped die for the bowl; the finial was attached with a "V"-joint on pieces made in London; provincial makers used a lap joint. The position of marks on apostle spoons

► Apostle spoon
This is a fairly late example of a London-made apostle spoon, but the fig-shaped bowl, faceted stem, and finial are the same as those on apostle spoons of the 15th century. Typically, the leopard's-head mark for London can be clearly seen in the bowl; the other marks are on the back of the stem.
(1639–42; l. 16.5cm/6½in; value G)

is also distinctive – the town mark is in the bowl; other marks appear on the back of the stem.

Apostle spoons tend to fetch high prices on the market today, as they have been of interest to collectors and antiquarians from as far back as the 18th century. Many fakes were created by cutting off the stem from a similar spoon and adding a reproduction apostle finial. Indistinct features of the apostles are not always a sign that the finial is a fake, because in the 15th and 16th centuries a single mold may have been employed to cast hundreds of finials, so some genuine examples lack sharpness.

SETS OF FLATWARE

French styles of silver were popular in England after the Restoration in 1660, when King Charles II returned from exile in France. Among the new forms introduced was a type of spoon with an egg-shaped bowl and broad, flat stem ending in a simple trefoil, known as a "trefid" spoon. The bowl was joined to the stem by a tapering rib, or "rat-tail," and sometimes the back of the spoon was decorated with scrolls in low relief or engraved with a crest or initials. By c.1690 the trefid pattern had flattened out into the "dognose" – the end of the stem had a central curve with a smaller one on either side. Dining forks, used in France and Italy since the 16th century, were also introduced to England at the Restoration; these followed the styles of trefid and dognose spoons and usually had two or three prongs, or tines. Early forks are rare and much sought after. Some fakes have been converted from spoons, but the proportions are slightly wrong and the tines too thin. Usually, early forks were thick and heavy.

By the early 18th-century forks, knives (with rounded cannon- or pistol-shaped handles), and spoons were made as a set – a trend probably influenced by the fashion for dinner services with matching ornament. The first pattern for matching flatware was the "Hanoverian"; it features a flat, rounded end turned upward and a ridge along the front of the handle. Coats of arms or crests

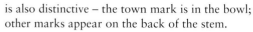
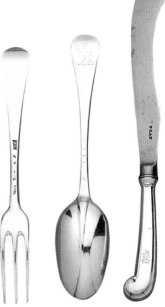

▲ "Hanoverian" pattern fork, spoon, and knife
Although made by different London makers over a 60-year period, this English set of flatware, all of the sought-after "Hanoverian" pattern, is more valuable than a composite service of different patterns. It may have been acquired piecemeal as the original owner's means allowed. The three-prong fork, which bears crests on the back of the stem, dating from 1770, may well have been produced specifically for this service, since by this date many forks featured four prongs.
(1704–70; l. of knife 26cm/10¼in; value for a service J)

► Part of a composite flatware "King's" pattern service
A complete table service would usually include twelve each of tablespoons, table forks, dessert spoons, and dessert forks; nine teaspoons; and a pair of basting spoons. The pieces featured here were all made in 1826. However, like many flatware services, it was augmented during the Victorian period with, among other items, fish knives and forks and dessert knives and forks, so it would not be unusual to find some pieces bearing a later date than the rest of the table service.
(1826 and later; l. of knife 24cm/9½in; value for a service H)

were engraved on the back of the stem, since flatware was laid face down on the table in the French manner.

The Hanoverian pattern evolved by the 1760s into the "Old English" pattern, with a plain, rounded end but turned down instead of up (on spoons), according to the new fashion of placing cutlery face up on the table. In the same period, forks were made with four instead of three tines. With increasingly elaborate dining habits, special silver-gilt services for dessert became popular.

Flatware was made in a huge variety of patterns from the late 18th century, especially with the development of mechanized manufacture in Sheffield, which became the most important center of cutlery production in England. The more popular styles in the late 18th and 19th centuries included the "fiddle" (with the end of the handle in a fiddle shape), and the more ornate "King's" and "Queen's" pattern. Flatware of this date was often supplied with a fitted case.

Today, complete and original sets of flatware, even from the 20th century, are very rare, as pieces were often replaced due to heavy use. When buying flatware, it is important to check for forks that have been trimmed off (this is difficult to detect) and for spoons whose bowls have been reshaped to disguise wear.

CADDY AND MOTE SPOONS

Before the 1770s tea was measured out using the domed caps on tea-caddies; when these were replaced by larger lids a small spoon was kept in the caddy. From the late 18th century thousands of caddy spoons were produced in a diverse range of designs, especially by manufacturers who specialized in "toys" – wine labels, boxes, buckles, and other small items. Like wine labels, caddy spoons are popular with first-time silver collectors.

Among the earliest and most common designs was a spoon with a shell-shaped bowl; other popular novelty forms included a vine leaf with a vine tendril as a handle, a shovel or scoop, and, most coveted by collectors, an eagle's wing and a jockey cap. Most spoons were made by die-stamping, but heavier and more expensive pieces might be cast. Filigree and handles of bone, ivory, or

▲ Part of a flatware service by Tiffany & Co.
This style, with ornate shells, beading, and flowers, is known as the "Richelieu" pattern. Like much American silver, this flatware service is engraved with a monogram instead of a crest.
*(1891–1902; l. of knife 21cm/ 8¼in; value for a service **H**)*

▼ Part of a flatware "trefid" service by Mappin & Webb
This fork and spoon are part of an extensive service decorated in the 17th-century style and supplied with an oak Carolean-style chest. The handles are stamped with foliage and the spoon has a lace-back bowl.
*(1911; l. of fork 19cm/7½in; value for a service **H**)*

mother-of-pearl were also used. In recent years many reproductions of earlier designs have been produced.

Mote spoons, or skimmers, were used to skim tea leaves off tea. Made from the early 18th century, they usually have a pierced bowl, with a pattern of circular holes or crosses and scrolls, and a slender, tapering, pointed stem, for unblocking the spout of the teapot. Mote spoons were often made en suite with teaspoons. Some fake mote spoons have been converted from teaspoons, but teaspoons have larger bowls and no pointed end and are shorter.

LADLES AND FISH SLICES

Ladles for serving soup, sauce, punch, and sugar were produced from the 18th century, sometimes en suite with tureens and punch-bowls. The styles tend to follow flatware, but some soup ladles were made with deep-fluted shell bowls. Punch ladles had circular or oval bowls with a lip and a handle of wood, whalebone, or silver.

Fish slices, produced from the 18th century, have a broad pierced blade and turned wooden or silver handle. Early pieces are pierced with simple patterns, but some Victorian ones depict fishing themes. Fish slices are easily damaged, especially on the piercing and where the blade joins the handle.

▶ Fish slice of "fiddle and thread" pattern
The decorative "fiddle and thread" pattern featured on this English silver fish slice was first introduced c.1820. On a piece with a handle as thin and fragile as this, it is very important to check for splits or cracks where the handle joins the slice.
*(19th century; l. 27cm/10½in; value **C**)*

KEY FACTS

Apostle spoons
- CONSTRUCTION the finial is joined to the stem on London-made spoons with a "V"-joint and on provincial pieces with a lap joint
- COLLECTING very few complete sets survive today; most are provincial pieces

Marks
The town mark is typically found in the bowl; other marks may appear on the back of the stem

Flatware
- COLLECTING it is important to check patterns closely because of small variations in design; complete and original sets are now rare; those with an equal amount of wear on each piece are most collectible; early forks are valuable; knives made before 1800 are abundant but few have survived in good condition

Marks
These were struck near the stem in the early 18th century but near the handle by the 1770s

Caddy spoons
- CONDITION check for badly repaired pieces, with spoons that have snapped where the bowl joins the stem; filigree spoons tend to be very fragile
- COLLECTING designs are extremely varied

See also Dining silver, pp.236–43

Drinking vessels

Like flatware, drinking vessels were made in vast numbers primarily for everyday domestic use. Over the centuries, beakers, tankards, and mugs have changed little in form, and they generally lack the elaborate decoration of more prestigious dining plate such as tureens. Tea and coffee became more popular than beer from the 18th century, after which tankards and mugs were often made as christening presents. Drinking vessels are popular with collectors today, but because so many were heavily used it is important to look for pieces without split rims or cracks around the handle.

◄ Beaker
This is a fairly typical form of mid-17th-century English beaker. It is engraved with a band of strapwork and stylized foliage. Like many beakers, it is also engraved with initials ("AG") instead of a coat of arms or crest, as beakers were often owned by those who did not have family heraldry.
*(1655; ht 9.5cm/3¾in; value **H**)*

BEAKERS AND TUMBLER CUPS
Beakers are among the earliest drinking vessels, with examples surviving from the 15th century onward. The basic form changed very little over the centuries. Sheet metal was curved into a cylinder with a slightly flaring rim, and a base and reeded foot-rim were added; some examples also have a cover. A number of 15th-century German and Flemish examples are set on three cast feet, with covers and elaborate cast decoration of flowers, foliage, and architecturally inspired Gothic ornament such as pinnacles and crockets around the base and center and above the rim.

However, most beakers are plain, apart from a single band of arabesques, stylized flowers, and foliage on 16th- and early 17th-century pieces, or embossed and chased flowers and leaves in the Dutch style on later 17th-century examples; many are also engraved with armorials, monograms, or initials. Elaborately engraved beakers often formed containers for traveling sets of cutlery, spice-boxes, and corkscrews, while some were also made in nesting sets – these are very rare and collectible today.

Tumbler cups are simple, cup-shaped vessels made from the mid-17th century and throughout the 18th, often by provincial silversmiths. They were raised from heavy-gauge silver, with the weight of the metal in the base so that they would return to an upright position when knocked; they were particularly suitable for use at sea or when traveling in a carriage. They are usually very plain except for engraved ciphers, crests, or coats of arms. Some were made in sets or "nests" – these are particularly rare today – and as racing prizes. Most tumbler cups found today range in height from 5cm (2in) to 10cm (4in); early examples are short and squat, while later ones are taller and narrower. Some examples also feature a design on the base.

▼ Beaker and cover
Imitations of medieval silver, like this parcel-gilt silver beaker in the 15th-century style, became popular due to the revival of interest in historical silver in 19th-century Europe. The bands of cast rosettes round the foot, molded bands round the body, lobing around the lip, and orb finial are distinctive elements of the Gothic Revival. This piece is probably German.
*(19th century; ht 17cm/6¾in; value **G**)*

► Lidded tankard
This late 17th-century English tankard, with a stepped lid and scroll handle and thumbpiece, was originally probably very plain. However, like many plain tankards it was redecorated with bands of flutes (and the interior gilded) in the 19th century to make it more acceptable to Victorian taste. The inscription on the underside dated 1866 suggests that it was used as a presentation piece. It is also marked with the maker's mark "TC" with a fish above.
*(1683, with 19th-century decoration; ht 16cm/6¼in; value **G**)*

TANKARDS
In Britain, tankards date from the 16th century, when they were often made of pottery and glass with silver mounts; by the end of the century solid-silver types, flat-chased or engraved with designs of strapwork and fruit, were more common. In Germany, large silver-gilt tankards were chased with biblical and mythological scenes, strapwork, masks, and flowers and sometimes decorated with coins. By the second half of the 17th century the most popular type was drum-shaped on a flat, molded base with a simple, stepped lid. It is important to check that there is a full set of marks on both the body and the lid.

The handles were made from two seamed curved pieces of sheet silver, with a cast thumbpiece in the form of a cusp, openwork lattice, volute, or scroll. There was little decoration on the body, apart from some chased work, and armorials within crossed plumes, scrolling, and foliage. The simple form of tankard on a molded foot was also made in North America from the late 17th century. New York silversmiths specialized in tankards with a corkscrew thumbpiece, a cast mask at the bottom of the handle, and applied leaf ornament above the foot.

After Scandinavian peg tankards were imported into Britain from the late 17th century, many provincial silversmiths, particularly John Plummer of York (active 1648–72), copied the form. The peg tankard has three cast ball or pomegranate feet, and applied leaf scrolls to strengthen the join between feet and body. Some have evenly spaced pegs inside to ensure fair shares in communal drinking. English examples were plain or engraved but rarely chased and embossed all over, as in Scandinavia. From the early 18th century English tankards were still cylindrical in form but with a low domed cover instead of a flat one; by c.1730 the baluster shape was popular, with a more pronounced domed lid, a double-scroll handle, and an applied plain or reeded band around the body. Decoration was limited to engraved armorials or monograms.

Wine, tea, and coffee were more popular drinks than beer in the later 18th century, and tankards became less

◄ Tankard by Michel Olsen
Scandinavian tankards of the late 17th century are particularly distinctive: they have three feet (often in the form of a ball and claw as seen in this example), pegs spaced down the inside serving as markers for drinkers, and all-over embossing and chasing of foliage, flowers, and scrolls. This Norwegian tankard is engraved with names within a cartouche and its cover is inset with a contemporary Dutch marriage medallion, suggesting that it may have been a wedding present. Similar tankards were made in Germany during the same period.
(c.1690; ht 19cm/7½in; value **K***)*

fashionable. One late 18th-century type is the plain, cylindrical tankard with a flat cover, decorated with reeded hoops to imitate a barrel, made in Sheffield plate as well as in thin-gauge seamed silver. Regency tankards are often silver-gilt with cast and applied ornament. In the 19th century older, plain tankards were chased with flowers and scrolls to suit Victorian taste.

MUGS
Mugs, generally following the form of tankards but without covers, date from the mid-17th century. A distinctive late 17th-century type has a flat strap handle and often a central molded rib around the body, with the lower half perhaps decorated with spiral or vertical flutes; applied lobes were used on the Scottish "thistle cup." The most common type in the early 18th century was the baluster form with a cast handle, engraved with armorials or initials; in the later 18th century mugs, like tankards, were made from cylinders of sheet metal with sheet handles. Mugs were given as christening presents, sometimes in a cased set with a knife, fork, and spoon, particularly between 1830 and 1880, and were made in a great range of styles in the 20th century.

GOBLETS
Goblets, or wine cups, were made from the 16th century. Most surviving early examples are beaker-shaped, with a slightly flaring body on a trumpet-shaped foot. An alternative design from the early 17th century, influenced by designs in glass, has a small, tapering bowl, elongated or, later, baluster stem, and spreading, slightly domed foot. The first type is generally plain but sometimes engraved with bands of arabesques, as on beakers; the second type may be chased with vine leaves and flowers. Few goblets were made from the late 17th to the late 18th century, when glass was more popular for wine. The silver goblet was revived with the rise of Neo-classicism and was often made in pairs; like much silver of this period, it was vase-shaped and generally plain except for a gadrooned or beaded rim, armorials or monograms, and/or bright-cut engraving. The vase shape continued throughout the 19th century, often with more elaborate cast and chased decoration.

QUAICHES AND STIRRUP CUPS
The quaich, a shallow bowl with flat handles, or "lugs," that turn down at the ends, was popular in Scotland in the 17th and 18th centuries. Like peg tankards, it was used for communal drinking. Many were made in wood with silver mounts, but there are also solid-silver pieces engraved with vertical staves to imitate wood. Quaiches vary from 8cm (3in) to 20cm (8in) in diameter.

Stirrup cups are silver or silver-gilt drinking vessels in the form of an animal's head, without a handle or base, used by riders before hunting. They were first made in the 1770s, usually in the shape of a fox's head; some from the 1780s onward are in the form of the head of a boar, fox-hound, greyhound, or stag. Some are engraved on the neckband with an inscription relating to the hunt.

▲ Thistle-shaped mug by Robert Brock
The thistle cup is a distinctive type of mug produced in Scotland in the late 17th and early 18th centuries. It has a flaring cup shape, with an applied molded band around the center, and a calyx of applied lobes on the bottom half, imitating a thistle. This piece has a plain scroll handle, but other examples have beaded decoration.
(1694; ht 9cm/3½in; value **H***)*

▲ Stirrup cup by John S. Hunt (d.1865)
Most stirrup cups are in the shape of a fox's head, but this extremely fine and unusual example is in the form of a stag's head. Stirrup cups are most sought after by collectors. The value of this piece is increased by the fact that it was made by Hunt, a partner in Hunt & Roskell, of London, one of the most successful silversmithing firms in 19th-century England.
(1864; l. 18cm/7in; value **I***)*

KEY FACTS
Beakers
- CONDITION well-used pieces may have splits around the rim; look for re-hammering as a sign of repair

Marks
Until the end of the 18th century most were on the underside and thereafter near the rim

Tumbler cups
- WARES most are very plain, utilitarian pieces

Marks
Usually situated underneath or near the rim; often worn

Tankards
- DECORATION minimal – consists mostly of engraved coats of arms or initials
- COLLECTING check for damage around handle sockets
- BEWARE tankards have often been converted into jugs

Marks
These appear on the body on the upper part near the handle; lids should be engraved near the thumbpiece or on the inside with the same mark as the body

Goblets
- DESIGNS 18th-century pieces are mostly vase-shaped
- COLLECTING goblets were often made in pairs; bright-cut engraving should be crisply defined; check for damage where the bowl meets the stem

See also Serving wine and spirits, pp.254–7

Serving beverages

Tea, coffee, and chocolate were introduced into Europe in the late 17th century through trade with China, Arabia, and South America. Initially a great novelty (and a luxury commodity), tea and coffee became extremely popular, and pots, kettles, and urns for making and serving them appeared in a great variety of forms and styles, especially with the advent of mass production in the 19th century. A range of items associated with the preparation of these drinks, such as caddies for storage, spoons, and sugar bowls, was also produced in silver, although matching services became widely popular only in the 19th century. Tea- and coffee-pots were often heavily used, and so should always be carefully checked for signs of damage.

Teapots and tea services

Tea was introduced into Europe from China with the expansion of trade in the 17th century and was a great novelty to people used to drinking only beer, wine, and posset. Although it was extremely expensive – a pound of tea cost £3 10s. in 1660, a year's wages for a maid – it became very popular, particularly as an after-dinner drink, prepared personally by the lady of the house. Those who could afford tea usually also had the means to buy silver, and by the end of the 18th century teawares had became a major part of the silversmith's trade. These practical objects remain among the most popular silver items with collectors today.

THE PEAR SHAPE
The earliest teapots date from the late 17th century, but very few examples survive today. These forms were based on imported Chinese porcelain teapots. Unlike forms such as ewers and jugs, which were also made in pewter, early metal teapots had no established European patterns that the silversmith could follow.

By the early 18th century the dominant style in Britain, the Netherlands, Germany, and North America was a pear shape, with a high-domed, hinged lid; in Britain some teapots were octagonal or hexagonal from c.1710 to c.1725, like much other silver in this period. These pieces are small next to modern examples (11.5–15cm/4½–6in high), reflecting the high price of tea. The handles were of wood (secured with silver sockets and

▲ Teapot by Philip Horst
The pear shape, as in this German example, was particularly common for silver teapots in the first quarter of the 18th century, although the bullet shape was more popular in Britain by the 1730s. The wooden handle and silver-mounted wooden finial were subjected to heavy use, so it is important to check that the wood is not rotten or cracked.
*(1736–7; ht 13cm/5in; value **G**)*

► Teapot by John Main
The bullet-shaped teapot, made during the 1730s and 1740s, was particularly popular in Scotland. The example here, which was made in Edinburgh, features the characteristic decorated spout and bands of chased arabesques around the top of the body and on the lid. Silver handles are a particularly distinctive feature of Scottish teapots.
*(1739; ht 13cm/5in; value **H**)*

pins), so that users would not burn their hands on hot metal. On early pieces the handles were sometimes set at right angles to the spout, but a handle opposite the spout was usual by the 1730s. Foot-rims were made separately and applied to the body, as was the spout, which was cast in two pieces and soldered together, sometimes faceted and with a flap at the end to keep in the heat.

Apart from a finely engraved coat of arms or crest, these early teapots have very little decoration; some may have cut-card work around the spout and handle, which reinforces the weakest points. Some teapots were supplied with a stand and burner, which was replaced by the tea-kettle for refilling the pot with hot water.

THE BULLET AND INVERTED-PEAR SHAPES
From c.1730 a compressed globular, or "bullet," shape was more fashionable than the pear shape. Such teapots are more richly decorated, with bands of engraved or chased scrolls, strapwork, and flowers around the top of the body and the edge of the lid, which is sometimes detachable. An interesting variation on the bullet shape was the fully spherical teapot on a high foot that was a specialty of Scottish silversmiths – these may have silver handles.

An inverted pear shape on a short stem with wide foot-rim, more popular in North America than in Britain, appeared in the 1750s. Its curvaceous shape, curved spout with leaf-wrapped or scroll decoration, double-scroll handle, and embossed and chased scrolls over the top of the body and the lid are typical features of the Rococo style. The finials are also more varied: buds, acorns, and perching birds were popular designs.

▼ Teapot by Abraham Dubois (active 1777–1807)
The very simple urn shape, the concave shoulder and lid, the pedestal base, and the beaded decoration around the body of this teapot from Philadelphia are all typical features of American tea silver of the 1780s and 1790s, when the austere Federal style was in fashion. Most silver in this style was made in the cities of Philadelphia and Boston.
*(c.1785–95; ht 29.5cm/11½in; value **K**)*

◄ Teapot by Paul Storr
The simple drum-and-oval shaped teapots popular in the late 18th century were replaced in the 19th century by the squat, almost boat-shaped form seen in this example. The flutes, flaring gadrooned rim, and ivory handles and finial are also typical of Regency teapots. *(1813; ht 13.5cm/5¼in; value J)*

▼ Teapot
Many tea services were often acquired piecemeal as means allowed. This teapot, from Sheffield, was sold as part of a three-piece service with a milk-jug and sugar-bowl dating from 1895. Victorian teapots were made in a great variety of styles and forms, but the spiral fluting on this piece was one of the more common decorative features. *(1887; ht 10.5cm/4in; value C)*

THE DRUM, OVAL, AND BOAT SHAPES

By the 1770s the availability of rolled sheet silver in thin gauge, produced in flatting mills, enabled silversmiths to produce silver teapots at much reduced prices. Rolled sheet metal was also easy to form into the oval and circular teapot shapes that became popular with the rise of the Neo-classical style. However, such teapots are not as robust as those raised from heavier-gauge metal, and splitting is sometimes evident around the spout, which was made from seamed sheet metal instead of being cast.

Decoration was generally restricted to fluting, beaded or reeded rims, and bright-cut engraving in the form of swags, the key-pattern, laurel wreaths, and other classically inspired ornament. As these pots had flat bases, they were often made with a matching stand with four molded feet to protect furniture from the heat. By *c.*1800 the feet had been transferred to the pot and the pot itself transformed into a larger, curved boat shape, with a swan-necked curving spout and sometimes a broad band of flutes around the bottom half of the body.

VICTORIAN STYLES AND TEA SERVICES

By the end of the 18th century the matching tea service had become popular, although matching tea items had been produced from the early 1700s. The tea service usually consists of a teapot, milk- or cream-jug, and sugar-bowl; a hot-water jug (with a lip instead of a spout to distinguish it from the pot), coffee-pot, and matching tray were sometimes added to the set. Teacups were not generally made in silver because of the heat-conducting property of the metal.

Most teapots made in the 19th century were part of a tea service, produced in an infinite range of styles, from embossed flutes to stamped Rococo, Chinese, and Gothic-inspired motifs. Some teapots were also based on 18th-century porcelain models, such as the teapot in the form of a cabbage, with matching stand, that was made by the leading silversmith Paul Storr (1771–1844) in 1831. Sets have often been broken up and the pieces sold separately, especially those dating from before 1800; a matching set with the same marks on each piece is more valuable today than a composite service. In the 19th century tea services reproducing the plain Queen Anne style were popular; these should never be mistaken for early 18th-century pieces, because only teapots were originally made in this style.

▼ Teapot by Henry Holland (1745–1806)
The vase shape, oval cartouches, elaborate beading, scrolls, and masks featured on this English teapot reflect the revival of the Classical style in the second half of the 19th century. This teapot is part of a four-piece tea service – also including a milk-jug, a sugar-bowl, and a coffee-pot – with matching decoration. A good-quality set such as this is worth considerably more than the sum of the individual pieces. *(1877; ht 23cm/9in; value D)*

KEY FACTS

Pear-shaped teapots, *c.*1680–1720
- CONSTRUCTION most are made of heavy-gauge silver in plain or faceted form; foot-rims were made separately; spouts were cast in two halves and soldered together
- SCALE small size (ht 11.5–15cm/4½–6in), reflecting the high price of tea
- DECORATION minimal – usually an engraved coat of arms, which should be contemporary with date of pot
- CONDITION handles were wooden and therefore susceptible to rotting and cracking; check for damage around handle sockets; also check for splitting, cracking, or soldering on spouts and joins to the body; if the inside of pot is shiny, it may have been restored
- COLLECTING examples in good condition are rare and particularly valuable

Marks
The cover and body should carry the same marks

Bullet- and inverted-pear-shaped teapots, *c.*1730–60
- CONSTRUCTION same as pear-shaped teapots
- DECORATION both shapes often feature bands of decorative engraving or chasing around the top of the body and over the lid; finials tend to be elaborate, e.g. in the form of buds, figures, or birds
- COLLECTING some teapots have detachable lids – these should fit properly; the inverted pear shape is more popular in the USA than in Britain

Drum-, oval-, and boat-shaped teapots, *c.*1770–1820
- CONSTRUCTION most were made in thin rolled and seamed sheet metal in a simple circular or oval shape
- CONDITION examples are sometimes flimsy; check for splits along the seams of the body and spout; bright-cut engraving – popular in the Neo-classical period – is often no longer sharply defined owing to constant use

Victorian teapots and tea services, after *c.*1820
- CONDITION any decoration in high relief – typical of this period – should be checked for wear

Marks
All pieces should preferably have the same marks, although sets are often purchased piecemeal

See also Furniture: Tea tables and tripod tables, pp.64–5

Tea-caddies, sugar-bowls, and cream-jugs

From the late 17th century two types of tea were available to European drinkers: green (or Hyson) unfermented tea or the cheaper, black (or Bohea) fermented variety. As the latter type was generally taken with milk or cream and sugar, milk-jugs and sugar-bowls associated with the preparation of tea were made in silver. Caddies or canisters were also necessary for storing tea, which was imported in large chests and sold loose. By the end of the 18th century milk-jugs, sugar-baskets, and teapots were made with matching forms and decoration as a tea or coffee service.

► Tea-caddy

This is the earliest surviving type of English tea-caddy, with an oval body and rounded cap, which was used for measuring the tea – a form based on Oriental porcelain jars. Caddies of this type, especially those made in Britannia, standard silver as in this case, are rare, but here the value is reduced as the marks are indistinct and the decoration was added about 15 years later.
*(1727; ht 13cm/5in; value **G**)*

TEA-CADDIES

Tea-caddies, very rare before *c*.1700, were initially known as "canisters"; the word "caddy" – derived from the term *kati*, a Malay standard weight of tea – was only used from the 1770s, when tea began to be imported into Europe via Malaya and Java.

Similar to Oriental stoppered porcelain jars, the earliest tea-caddies are small – 8 to 13cm (3–5in) high – and of a plain oblong or oval shape with a flat base and straight sides; there is a sliding base or top for refilling the tea and a rounded cap, which was used as a measure before the caddy spoon was introduced in the 1770s. Caddies were initially made in pairs, and some were marked with the initials "B" and "G" for the two different types of tea, "Black" and "Green."

By the 1720s caddies were generally box-shaped and sometimes fitted with a more practical hinged lid. From the 1730s they were made in sets with a larger canister or bowl for holding the sugar or blending the tea, and kept in a wooden box, often decorated with shagreen, tortoiseshell, leather, or mother-of-pearl, kept locked to prevent pilfering.

A great variety of designs was produced from the late 1740s to the 1770s. For example, vase shapes chased with flowers and scrolls were a specialty of the silversmith Samuel Taylor (active 1744–73), whereas a Rococo-style bombé shape on cast feet or a flat base, with very fine embossed, chased, and cast Rococo flowers, scrolls, and sometimes chinoiserie decoration, was produced by such leading Huguenot silversmiths as Paul de Lamerie (1688–1751).

Some caddies of the 1760s and 1770s were in the form of square boxes engraved with Chinese characters, imitating the bales or chests in which tea was imported.

Caddies were made in thin-gauge sheet silver in the 1770s and 1780s, in drum and oval shapes typical of the Neo-classical style. Simple bands of beading or bright-cut engraving, and fluting or ribbing on the body were common decorative features. Both types were made with cast silver, wood, or ivory finials, possibly detachable. During this period cases for caddies became redundant as the caddies themselves had locks, and sugar was served in separate baskets. From *c*.1800 oval, box-, and drum-shaped caddies continued to be produced, sometimes as part of a tea service, and often had an internal dividing sheet to hold different varieties of tea.

SUGAR-BOWLS AND SUGAR-BASKETS

As the consumption of black tea increased in the early 18th century, containers for sugar became associated with the preparation of tea rather than with other drinks such as punch. The prevalent style was a hemispherical bowl, shaped like a porcelain tea-bowl, usually with a loose, reversible cover surmounted by a ring so that it could be used for holding a teaspoon or as a stand for the bowl. Some examples are engraved with coats of arms. Heavy, octagonal sugar-boxes and covers were also made in this period.

By the mid-18th century a vase shape with a finial instead of a ring had become popular, although in Ireland a squat bowl with no cover, which had three feet and was decorated with flowers, scrolls, and masks, was a

▲ Sugar caster

Sugar casters (or dredgers), used to sprinkle sugar, are similar in form to, but larger than, pepper casters; they were usually produced as part of a cruet set. Unlike a great many European sugar casters, this American example from Massachusetts does not feature an engraved coat of arms.
*(1760; ht 10cm/4in; value **D**)*

▼ Tea-caddy

Tea-caddies of varying quality and styles were produced throughout the 19th century. The box form of this English example, with its die-stamped ornament of Classical figures and gadrooned borders, was quite common during the late 19th century. At this time tea-caddies no longer had locks as tea was much less costly than it had been in the 18th century.
*(1895; ht 8cm/3in; value **D**)*

THE SCARCITY OF 18TH-CENTURY FRENCH SILVER

Most French silver dating from before *c*.1800 is particularly valuable today; because so little of this period survives, any item of good quality appearing on the market will usually be of great interest to collectors. In the late 17th century King Louis XIV commissioned spectacular silver furniture, dining services, and other items to furnish the sumptuous palace of Versailles, but most royal and aristocratic plate was surrendered to the French Mint in 1689 and 1709 to fund the king's incessant military campaigns. Similarly, silver by the leading 18th-century French silversmiths was melted down during the Revolution.

► Sugar-bowl and cover by Jean Clement

This piece is a relatively late example of the heavy but simply decorated Baroque style of the early 18th century. The high-quality engraving and simple fluted rims of the foot and cover are also found on pieces by Huguenot silversmiths of French origin working in England and The Netherlands.
*(1743; ht 13cm/5in; value **L**)*

► **Sugar-basket by Edward Barnard & Sons**

Pierced silver baskets with colored glass liners were a popular form for sugar-baskets in the 19th century, and such items were also used for serving sweetmeats. A piece like this should be carefully examined for splits or cracks in the pierced body and on the handle, which is very fragile. It is difficult to find a replacement for a broken original liner.

(1857; ht 10cm/4in; value E)

► **Cow creamer by John Schuppe**

Vessels for cream in the shape of a cow were made in mid-18th-century England almost exclusively by one silversmith, John Schuppe. This typical example has an applied bee on the cover and a curved tail forming the handle; it has a smooth coat, but some have the texture of hair. Cow creamers were also made in pottery and porcelain and are extremely sought after by collectors today.

(1763; l. 15cm/6in; value J)

distinctive style. Sugar-bowls of this date were often made as part of a set with tea-caddies. By the 1770s the cover was omitted, and the bowl was eventually replaced by a boat-shaped basket with a short stem and a swing handle. These were made of plain sheet silver decorated with bright-cut engraving, or pierced with festoons, stylized leaves, and flowers and with a glass liner. The latter style was dominant throughout the 19th century.

CREAM-JUGS AND COW CREAMERS

The earliest form of cream-jug was plain and pear- or pitcher-shaped or ovoid, with the low foot-rim, the handle, and the lip of the jug made separately and applied. Some jugs were fitted with hinged lids and wooden handles for serving with hot milk, which was popular for taking with tea before c.1720.

The pear shape continued to be produced until the 1770s, but three cast hoof, shell, scroll, or pad feet, a wavy rim, and double-scroll handle were more common. A jug shaped like an inverted helmet, on a spreading foot or cast feet (with lion's mask terminals), sometimes with a molded center rib around the body, is a typically Irish form. Some of the finest versions of both types are chased all over with shells and scrolls.

Other types of vessel for cream produced in the mid-18th century were cream-boats – smaller versions of sauceboats – which sometimes had richly cast and chased Rococo decoration, and cow creamers. The latter were a specialty of John Schuppe (active 1753–73), a silversmith possibly of Dutch origin working in London. Rare and very collectible, these objects have a covered opening on the back of the cow, allowing it to be filled with cream; the curled-back tail acts as a handle, and the cow's mouth as a spout. The feet on cow creamers are particularly vulnerable to damage.

In the Neo-classical period, the dominant style was the tapering urn-and-vase shape with a high loop handle, set on a rounded or shaped pedestal foot, sometimes on a square plinth. Made of thin-gauge silver and heavily used, these types of jug have often been damaged or repaired, even though beaded or reeded wires were frequently applied in order to strengthen the rim. Bright-cut decoration, particularly on pieces made by the Bateman family of silversmiths, adds to the value of a jug, but only if it is sharply defined. From the 1790s most cream-jugs, like teapots and sugar-baskets, were produced as part of a matching tea service in a wide variety of different styles and shapes.

▼ **Cream-jug by James Musgrave**

This piece from Philadelphia, decorated with beaded borders, is typical of the austere forms of American silver in the Federal style made at the end of the 18th century.

(c.1795; ht 14cm/5½in; value I)

► **Cream-jug**

A pear-shape, double-scroll handle, and hoof feet with shells positioned where the feet join the body are common features of mid-18th-century English cream-jugs. The wavy rim and delicate handles and feet are easily damaged, so it is important to check for cracks around the rim and repairs to the handle sockets and around the feet. There should be no seaming evident on the body of the jug, because pieces were usually raised from a single sheet of silver, with the feet and handle being cast separately and applied. On some jugs of this type and period, the rim has been strengthened by punching or applying reeded wire.

(1751; ht 10cm/4in; value C)

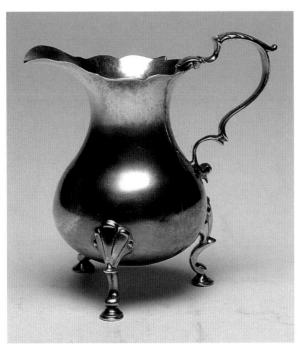

KEY FACTS

Tea-caddies
- DESIGNS locks feature on individual caddies from the 1760s and 1770s
- COLLECTING caddies were usually made in pairs, which are more valuable than singles; they were also made in sets of three in locked cases from the 1730s

Marks
Caddies in pairs or sets should have the same marks

Sugar-bowls and sugar-baskets
- CONDITION pierced baskets should be checked for cracks or splits; handles on baskets are vulnerable
- COLLECTING early 18th-century sugar-bowls are rare and valuable; colored glass liners are hard to replace

Cream-jugs and cow creamers
- CONDITION late 18th-century examples, which were made of thin-gauge silver, are vulnerable to damage: check for splits, cracks, and signs of repair around the handles, feet, and rims
- COLLECTING early 18th-century baluster/pear forms are very sought after; cow creamers made by John Schuppe (active 1753–73) are very rare and valuable today

See also Ceramics: Pottery – The Netherlands, pp.160–61

Coffee-pots, chocolate-pots, tea-kettles, and tea-urns

Coffee first appeared in Europe in the 17th century. Expensive, but less so than tea, it became popular as a breakfast drink. The new coffee-houses that opened from the mid-17th century attracted all classes of society, and became places of such intense political intrigue that in England they were suppressed in 1675. A great variety of coffee-pots is available to the collector today, because they were made in such large quantities. Chocolate, introduced via trading routes to the West Indies, was fashionable as a drink for only a brief period because it required considerable preparation. Tea-kettles and tea-urns were developed to keep water for tea hot.

▲ **Coffee-pot by Thomas Tearle**
The simple, cylindrical form and faceted spout of this piece were typical features of coffee-pots until the 1730s. The marks are placed near the top to one side of the handle. Plain coffee-pots such as this one are generally more collectible than chased pieces of the 1740s.
(1730; ht 20cm/8in; value H)

COFFEE-POTS AND CHOCOLATE-POTS

Coffee- and chocolate-pots are recorded from the 1650s, but there are very few surviving examples from before c.1700. Chocolate-pots follow exactly the same styles and forms as coffee-pots but can be distinguished by their hinged finial designed to allow the insertion of a swizzle-stick to stir the chocolate to prevent it from separating. Some hinged finials, which were easily lost, were attached with a silver chain to the pot. Chocolate-pots were seldom made after 1750, since the drink had mostly gone out of fashion by that date.

Cylindrical or octagonal in shape, early 18th-century coffee- and chocolate-pots were made from a simple sheet of heavy-gauge silver seamed usually down the back of the pot, with a cast-and-applied foot-rim, a straight or curved spout, a rounded wooden handle – on early examples often set at right angles to the spout – and a hinged, domed lid with a finial. Decoration was minimal, generally consisting of engraved armorials or, especially on Huguenot pieces, cut-card work around the spout and handle. North American coffee-pots of the early 18th century were produced in a similar style.

In the 1740s the form of coffee-pots changed slightly, resulting in a flatter lid, tucked-in or incurved foot, beak-shaped spout, and scrolled rather than plain handle. This shape developed into a baluster form on a spreading foot and by the 1760s into a pear shape, which was generally raised from sheet rather than seamed. Both forms were usually decorated with gadrooned rims and sometimes flat-chased bands of shells, flowers, and scrolls around the top and bottom of the body; overall chasing of the body of the pot was common only in the 19th century. The spouts were often cast with shell or wrapping-leaf decoration or fluting to match the more ornate form of the body and handle. The pear shape actually originated in France, where coffee-pots of this type were generally made with three feet, a straight handle, and a small pouring lip – more suitable for the thick Turkish coffee popular in continental Europe. The renowned Huguenot silversmith Paul de Lamerie (1688–1751) produced some elaborate French-style coffee-pots with richly chased and cast Rococo decoration in the 1730s.

The influence of the antique forms popularized by the Neo-classical style is evident in the vase-shaped coffee-pots that replaced the pear shape by the 1770s. Made in both silver and Sheffield plate, these coffee-pots have a tall spool-shaped neck and high loop handles. Typical decoration includes beaded, thread, or reeded borders around the body, neck, and foot and, particularly on fine-quality examples, bright-cut Classical ornament such as swags, medallions, and husks.

From the beginning of the 19th century most coffee-pots were made as part of a matching tea service with a teapot, cream-jug, and sugar-bowl in a vast range of styles and forms. Among the most common designs were coffee-pots with fluted, reeded, and lobed bodies and scroll handles; reproductions of the plain and octagonal shapes of the Queen Anne period were especially popular c.1900.

◄ **Sheffield-plate coffee-jug**
Vase-shaped coffee-pots in silver and Sheffield plate came into fashion with the development of the Neo-classical style in the late 18th century. English coffee-pots always have spouts – this piece is classed as a jug rather than a pot because it has a lip. It is not in prime condition as the copper core of the plate is showing through the engraved decoration and around the bottom of the handle, owing to heavy use or over-polishing. Some coffee-pots and jugs dating from this period have ivory rather than wooden handles, although these crack easily. The high loop handles may have a small "flying" scroll at the top, as an aid to lifting a heavy full pot.
(c.1790; ht 25.5cm/10in; value D)

▲ **Coffee-pot**
Many silver tea- and coffee-pots were made in China during the 18th century for export to Europe. This Chinese export coffee-pot, chased with panels of Chinese landscapes and with a bamboo-form spout, was presumably imported through The Netherlands, as it has a Dutch retailer's mark.
(18th century; ht 15cm/6in; value I)

▲ **Coffee-pot**
This coffee-pot, which is probably Italian, has a baluster-shaped body chased with roses. It is somewhat old fashioned for its date, since by the end of the 18th century most coffee-pots were made in the classically inspired vase shape. This piece has the small pouring lip typical of continental coffee-pots and a pierced foot – this is particularly vulnerable to damage and should always be carefully checked for cracks or splits.
(c.1800; ht 17.5cm/7in; value H)

◄ Chocolate-pot, stand, and lamp by P. & Cie

This French chocolate-pot has the straight handle, small lip, and three feet characteristic of continental European coffee- and chocolate-pots. Chocolate-pots are much more common in continental Europe than in Britain because the drink is a more popular alternative there to tea and coffee. The same ornament – strapwork bands in the Régence style – featured on the stand, pot, and burner indicates that the three pieces form a set; the marks on each should also match, showing that the pieces were produced at the same time.

(c.1900; ht 35cm/13¾in; value **G**)

► Urn by Christofle

The ivory handles, paw feet, eagle's-head spout, masks, and palmette ornament of this French urn imitate the early 19th-century Empire style, which was particularly popular in France. This example may be worth only half the value of an urn that still has its original cover and lamp. The Parisian firm of Christofle – which is still in operation today – was a well-known and large manufacturer of silver and electroplate in the 19th century; the firm was particularly renowned for pieces made in the Louis XV and Louis XVI styles.

(late 19th century; ht 41cm/16in; value **H**)

TEA-KETTLES

Because early 18th-century teapots were so small, large silver tea-kettles developed as a means of keeping water hot for replenishing the pot. Tea-kettles follow the same basic shapes as teapots: early 18th-century versions are plain and pear-shaped, but they have a flat bottom, standing on a plain or pierced ring with a spirit-lamp burner, and a swing handle with a wooden grip. Some of the most elaborate versions were produced in the Rococo style in the 1730s, when the tea-kettle had become bullet-shaped or globular to match the teapot and was often embossed and chased in high relief with flowers, figures, shells, and scrolls. Tea-kettles of this type were large and heavy, and were often supplied with a matching silver stand, generally triangular in shape. In 18th-century paintings tea-kettles are often depicted as standing on the floor away from the tea-table to avoid accidents. Tea-kettles were largely replaced c.1760 by the more practical tea-urn, although they sometimes form part of a 19th-century tea service.

TEA-URNS

Introduced in the 1750s and 1760s, tea-urns tend to be larger than tea-kettles and have a horizontal tap near the base for drawing water – this was much easier and safer than tilting a full tea-kettle. The earliest tea-urns were heated with a charcoal burner, but from the 1770s a heated box-iron was inserted into a socket or tube inside the urn, around which hot water circulated. Most urns are vase-shaped on a stemmed foot, and sometimes the spout of the tap is formed as a cast and chased animal or bird; earlier examples, showing the influence of the Rococo style, are bulbous or gourd-shaped with chased scrolls, flowers, and chinoiserie ornament. Tea-urns are sometimes found as part of a 19th-century tea service; because of the high cost of making such a large item in silver, many were produced in Sheffield plate.

▼ Tea-kettle, burner, and stand by Jean-Valentin Morel (1794–1860)

This elaborate, silver-gilt tea-kettle, with its original burner and stand, has very fine-quality cast, chased, and engraved decoration of flower pendants, strapwork, and masks, imitating the early 18th-century French Régence style. Jean-Valentin Morel (1794–1860), who was based in Paris, was one of the leading French makers of elaborate, luxurious silverware in various historical styles during the mid-19th century.

(c.1845; ht 42cm/16½in; value **I**)

KEY FACTS

Early 18th-century coffee-pots
- CONSTRUCTION typically a simple, cylindrical form made by seaming a sheet of silver, with a seam down the back under the handle; spouts were cast in two halves and joined; handles were mostly wooden and on early examples may be at right angles to the spout
- DECORATION little other than engraved coats of arms or cut-card work
- CONDITION check for cracking, and splitting down the seams and around the handle and spout joints

Mid-18th-century coffee-pots
- FORMS baluster- and pear-shaped examples, often made by raising from sheet, were popular; leaf-wrapped curving spouts and double-scroll handles are typical
- DECORATION little all-over decoration except on Irish pots; some examples feature gadrooned rims and flat-chasing around the top and bottom

Late 18th- and 19th-century coffee-pots
- FORMS the vase shape was most popular
- MATERIALS silver, Sheffield plate, and electroplate; some have ivory handles although wood is more typical
- CONDITION check for splitting or cracking where the body joins the pedestal foot

Chocolate-pots
- DESIGNS made in identical styles to coffee-pots but with a hinged finial for insertion of a swizzle-stick for stirring the chocolate
- COLLECTING rarer and more valuable than coffee-pots – some have been converted from coffee-pots

Tea-kettles
- DESIGNS similar to teapots but with a swing handle, a stand, burner, and sometimes also a tray
- COLLECTING rare, as they were often melted down

Tea-urns
- CONSTRUCTION larger than tea-kettles; typically fitted with a horizontal tap near the base; often made in Sheffield plate; many 19th-century examples were made as part of a tea service
- CONDITION internal fittings should be intact
- COLLECTING not as popular with collectors as tea- and coffee-pots and services, so they can be quite affordable

See also Teapots and tea services, pp.248–9

Serving wine and spirits

Items associated with the preparation and serving of wine and spirits are highly sought after by specialist collectors. In the grandest houses, elaborate silver wine coolers and monteiths stood on the sideboard or table for chilling wine and glasses between servings. In the 19th century punch-bowls were often made as presentation pieces. Silversmiths also made a wide range of gadgets and implements to accompany the often elaborate rituals of wine- and punch-drinking; such items included funnels for decanting wine, coasters for holding bottles or decanters, labels for bottles, and corkscrews (originally described as "steele wormes"), together with nutmeg graters and juice strainers for the preparation of spiced wine and punches.

Claret-jugs, decanters, funnels, coasters, and labels

From the 18th century a large selection of wines was served at dinner to complement the different dishes of each course. It became the custom at the end of the meal for the ladies to withdraw into the drawing-room to take tea or coffee, while in the dining-room the servants were dismissed and the gentlemen passed the port or wine around among themselves. Numerous silver vessels and gadgets associated with wine-drinking were developed; as well as the articles described below, these included nutmeg graters for preparing spiced wine and other drinks, pierced lemon- and orange-juice strainers for punch, and wine tasters for judging the color, clarity, and taste of wine.

▲ **Wine tastevin by Guillaume Baudot**
Wine tasters were shallow circular vessels with a raised center, used by vintners when assessing color, clarity, and taste of wine – silver was considered to be the best material for this purpose. The plain form and single shaped handle of this piece are typically French; English examples have two handles and decorative chasing on the body.
(1740; w. 8cm/3in; value F)

CLARET-JUGS AND DECANTERS
Most covered jugs for wine were made entirely in silver before the 1820s. Decanters – originally made for serving wine at the table after decanting it from the bottle but later more commonly used to serve spirits – are similar in design to wine-jugs but have a stopper and no handle. Early jugs and decanters are generally vase-shaped and decorated with bright-cut engraved bands or beading around the body, neck, and foot. After the 1820s they were usually made of glass with silver mounts forming the neck, the hinged lid, the handle, and sometimes the base. Claret-jugs of the highest quality have cast mounts, but many more, relatively inexpensive versions had mounts of stamped thin silver sheet or electroplate. The glass was also usually frosted, engraved, or etched, sometimes with decoration corresponding to the silver or plate mounts; vine leaves and grapes, relating to the use of the object,

were particularly popular decorative motifs. A plain glass body may be a replacement, as it is particularly difficult to find decorated glass matching the mounts with which to replace broken originals. Handles also have frequently been damaged.

As is typical of 19th-century silver, claret-jugs were made in a broad range of styles and forms. Novelty jugs in the shape of animals such as monkeys or sea-lions were particularly popular; the body was made of glass and the head of silver. In the 1860s and 1870s the well-known Victorian architect and designer William Burges (1827–81) created claret-jugs with colored glass bodies and elaborate mounts inspired by medieval decorative arts. These were set with semi-precious stones, medallions, and enamels, with the silver or silver-gilt handles and spouts in the form of fantastical animals and birds, and the mounts ornamented with stylized flowers and leaves. In contrast, during the same period the English manufacturers Elkington & Co. (est. *c*.1830), Hukin & Heath (est. 1875), and James Dixon & Sons (est. 1835) manufactured jugs in pure geometric forms with minimalist, plain silver or electroplate mounts. Designed specifically for machine production by the progressive British designer Christopher Dresser (1834–1904), these are particularly sought after by collectors today.

◄ **Wine-jug by John Bridge**
This fine English silver vase-shaped jug has a cast vine-tendril scroll handle ornamented with leaves and grapes – a good example of decoration relating to use. The fact that it was made by John Bridge (1755–1834), who was a partner in the prestigious London firm of Rundell, Bridge & Rundell (Goldsmith to George III and George IV from 1802 to 1830), increases its value considerably. This type of all-silver jug is less common on the market today than glass jugs with silver or electroplate mounts, which were made in large quantities throughout the 19th century and also often feature decoration of vine leaves and grapes.
(1832; ht 28.5cm/11in; value H)

▲ **Rye-whiskey silver-mounted glass decanter**
This American red glass whiskey decanter is decorated with naturalistic silver mounts in the form of rye grains and leaves, which was a popular Art Nouveau design during the late 19th and early 20th centuries. Items produced by overlaying colored glass with silver were highly popular in the USA from the 1880s.
(c.1900; ht 33cm/13in; value G)

◀ **Wine funnel**

This Irish wine funnel is typically plain. It has the curved spout introduced in the late 18th century to minimize aeration of the wine when pouring by directing the flow against the side of the bottle, although this has been trimmed to fit in a decanter with a narrow neck. A funnel with a trimmed spout will be less valuable than one in its original condition.

(1808; ht 14cm/5½in; value **D**)

WINE FUNNELS

Silver funnels with a tapering spout were employed for decanting wine from the bottle to serve at table and for removing sediment and pieces of cork. Most surviving examples date from *c.*1770 onward. Light and of thin-gauge silver, funnels were originally made in one piece, but by the late 18th century two sections were standard – either a body with a pierced bottom and a separate funnel, or a body in one piece with a removable pierced inner bowl. Where the body and spout join, there is sometimes a silver ring, originally for securing muslin to catch very fine particles of sediment. Early spouts are straight, but by the end of the 18th century they were curved to allow the wine to flow against the inside of the decanter, thus minimizing aeration. Funnels are usually very plain, apart from simple beaded and gadrooned rims and perhaps an engraved coat of arms or a shell hook on the rim for suspending the funnel on the rim of a punch-bowl. Some funnels, especially Scottish and Irish, have accompanying stands to catch drips.

WINE COASTERS

Wine coasters, made in pairs or sets, were used from *c.*1760 for passing decanters or wine bottles round the table after dinner and have round wooden bases (with baize underneath to avoid scratching furniture) and silver galleried sides. Examples from the 1760s have wavy rims and intricate, fine-quality, hand-pierced designs of delicate leaves, flowers, and arabesques, sometimes incorporating a small medallion for a coat of arms or crest. In the 1770s and 1780s pierced or plain Neo-classical designs of swags, ram's heads, and medallions, sometimes embellished with bright-cut engraving, were popular; a central silver boss on the base now held the crest.

Regency coasters are generally a solid, lobed shape with a gadrooned turned-out rim, often embellished with vine leaves. Cast silver-gilt versions were made *c.*1805–20 by the English firm Rundell, Bridge & Rundell (est. 1805); they featured silver-gilt bases engraved with armorials and openwork patterns of vine leaves, grapes, and putti. In the late 18th and 19th centuries double decanter stands – two galleries on a single wooden base – were popular, as was the "jolly boat" in the form of a rowing boat with four small wheels. A more elaborate version was the decanter wagon, consisting of carriages for the decanters, with wheels and a central shaft with bar and handle.

WINE LABELS

Wine labels (also known as "bottle tickets") for identifying wine were made in silver from *c.*1740, replacing hand-written parchment labels. Usually slightly curved so as to fit closely, they were hung around the neck of the bottle on a chain or, later, a wire hoop, and the name of the wine or spirit was either pierced out or engraved. Approximately 1,500 different names of wines and spirits are recorded. An almost infinite variety of designs, mostly stamped from sheet silver, was made, from the more common oblong, oval, crescent, and escutcheon shapes to anchors, scallop shells, and vine leaves. Heavy, cast, and silver-gilt versions in ornate designs, usually of grapes and vines with putti holding a scroll, were made in the early 19th century. Few wine labels were made after the 1850s, because a Licensing Act of 1860 required wine merchants to label bottles before sale. Decanter labels, intended to hang from the neck of a decanter, are also very collectible. These are mostly slightly larger and even more elaborate than wine labels; decoration of foliage and scrollwork is typical.

▼ **Wine-bottle collars by Reilly & Storer**

Bottle rings or collars to hang around the necks of bottles were a variation on the wine label, or bottle ticket, hung on a chain. Madeira, sherry, port, and claret are among the most common names found on wine labels, and will typically make them much less expensive to collect than those with more obscure names. However, to have a matching set of three or four as seen below is a bonus for the collector. These English examples are very plain, but some wine labels of this period are elaborately decorated with vine leaves, grapes, and scrolls.

(1827; diam. 9cm/3½in; value **E**)

▼ **Coasters**

As seen on these English wood and silver coasters, the simple, circular form with bright-cut engraved bands of leaves was a popular style for wine coasters in the late 18th and early 19th centuries. On the top coaster, the worn patina of the wooden base is clearly visible, showing that the piece has been heavily used – the wood can easily be replaced if desired. A pair will have a higher value than a single piece.

(early 19th century; diam. 13cm/5in; value **G**)

KEY FACTS

Claret-jugs and decanters

- MATERIALS solid silver was common up to the 1820s; after which most examples are of glass with silver or electroplate mounts
- CONDITION glass should be original and unchipped, as it is often impossible or expensive to replace
- COLLECTING decorative glass is more sought after than plain; novelty examples are popular

Wine funnels

- DESIGNS early examples are in one piece; those made after *c.*1770 are in two pieces; before *c.*1750 spouts were straight; curved spouts were popular thereafter; note that a curved spout may have been trimmed to fit the narrower necks of decanters

Marks

These can be very worn; where a funnel is composed of more than one piece, all pieces should be marked

Wine coasters

- CONSTRUCTION many double decanter stands are made from two singles – these can appear crudely joined
- COLLECTING pairs are typically three or four times more valuable than singles

Marks

Typically marked on the plain rim overlapping the base

Wine labels

- COLLECTING rare names or styles are most collectible

Marks

Small examples are often incompletely marked, especially before 1790, after which wine labels were required to carry marks, even though they might weigh less than five pennyweights (originally, the weight of a silver penny)

Wine coolers, monteiths, and punch-bowls

First produced in the late 17th century, wine coolers, punch-bowls, and monteiths were part of a widespread fashion for serving wine and punch. Wine coolers, introduced to Britain from France and made mostly by Huguenot silversmiths in the early 18th century, were placed on the sideboard or table for chilling wine between servings. Punch was introduced to Britain via trade routes with India; most early English punch-bowls and monteiths were made by English-born silversmiths. Wine coolers were used for dining on a grand scale and remained popular throughout the 19th century, while punch-bowls and monteiths were often made as presentation pieces.

WINE COOLERS

Wine coolers developed from the wine cistern, made from the late 17th century. One of the largest and most impressive silver objects associated with serving wine, the cistern was a large oval basin on four feet or a spreading base, with massive drop-ring handles or handles in the form of animal or mythical figures that appeared as part of the owner's coat of arms, such as unicorns and griffins. Used for cooling several bottles of wine in iced water or for washing glasses, these are very heavy objects, some weighing over 1000oz; few have survived as they were often melted down because of their high value as bullion. The cistern was often accompanied by a silver "fountain" for dispensing wine; these are urn-shaped or baluster in form on a spreading foot with a tap and spigot.

In the 18th century cisterns for washing glasses became redundant owing to the production of larger sets of flatware and glasses, while wine cisterns for cooling bottles were replaced by smaller single bottle coolers, set on the table instead of the sideboard. The earliest-surviving examples date from 1698, but early 18th-century examples are rarely seen today. Made mostly by Huguenot makers, these smaller wine coolers are circular or octagonal, with heavy cast and applied ornament such as cut-card work and strapwork. These and later wine coolers were usually made in pairs.

SHEFFIELD PLATE AND ELECTROPLATE

The invention of Sheffield plate in the mid-18th century revolutionized the production of silver objects. In about 1742–3 Thomas Bolsover (1704–88) of Sheffield discovered that copper and silver fused together under heat. Later he found that when the fused metals were rolled under pressure, they expanded at equal rates, producing a large sheet of workable metal. This looked like cast or sheet silver, but, being considerably cheaper, was suitable for inexpensive, mass-produced objects. Among the leading manufacturers of Sheffield plate was the Birmingham silversmith Matthew Boulton (1728–1809). The industry flourished until the mid-19th century, when Sheffield plate was superseded by the introduction of the safer and more efficient process of electroplating (see p.235).

There are a few simple methods of identifying plated objects: worn plate may appear pinkish, as seen on the cooler below; linear decoration, especially coats of arms, are usually flat-chased, because engraving would reveal the copper. In some cases, a pure silver disc was inserted into a plated piece for engraving a coat of arms or crest; this silver may tarnish at a different rate to the plate. Sheffield-plate items are in demand with many collectors today, especially in the USA.

► Electroplated wine cooler

In comparison with the Regency silver-plated wine cooler also illustrated on this page (below), this modern vase-shaped English cooler is in poor condition. The rim is dented and the copper base is showing through, especially on the central engraving and the fluted lower body. A typical hazard with silver plate, this may be due to over-zealous polishing, which has worn away the thin layer of silver over the copper core.
(20th century; ht 23cm/9in; value for a pair D)

► Sheffield plate wine cooler

The antique-inspired vase shape of this fine-quality English wine cooler (one of a pair) was very popular during the Regency period. The cast and applied gadrooned rims, the bands of anthemion motifs, the shells around the body, and the handles formed as reeded foliate branches are typical features on all forms of silver produced during this period. This cooler also retains its original detachable liner and collar, making it more collectible than pieces missing these components. As with other items, a pair is worth more than a single.
(c.1810; ht 24cm/9½in; value H)

Wine coolers went out of fashion from 1730 to 1760, owing to the popularity of claret and port (drunk at room temperature), but were revived in the late 18th century. Throughout the 19th century they were made in a variety of designs. Most have heavy cast and applied decoration, but a popular form from 1780 to 1800 was the lighter bucket type with decoration like staves and with a swing handle or two bracket handles. Massive and silver-gilt forms were made in the Regency period by such leading silversmiths as Paul Storr (1771–1844) and Rundell, Bridge & Rundell (est. 1805) in London and Maison Odiot in Paris; some were based on antique vases, having a single cast foot with decoration of acanthus leaves, vines, lion's heads, and Classical figures round the body. Late 18th- and 19th-century wine coolers were made in three parts – body, liner, and rim (collar); the body should have a full set of marks on the underside, with part marks on the liner and collar.

Many 19th-century wine coolers were made in Sheffield plate, with die-stamped and lead-filled ornament and handles; sets of four were popular, and wine coolers were often made as part of a dinner service.

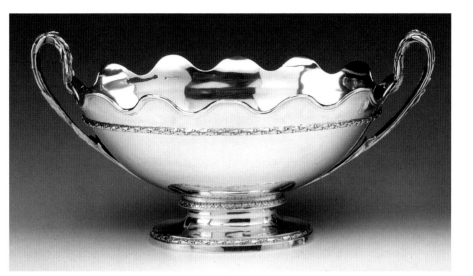

MONTEITHS

The monteith is a large, circular silver bowl with a scalloped or notched rim from which wine glasses are suspended by the foot to be cooled in iced water in the bowl. The name is supposedly derived from a Scot named Monteigh, who was famous for wearing a cloak with a notched edge and is known to have lived in the late 17th century. Monteiths are rare and valuable today, especially the few examples that were made in Ireland and North America.

Made from the 1680s, the earliest type of monteith was decorated with fluted panels on the body beneath the notches and/or flat-chased chinoiserie, with an applied plain or gadrooned foot-rim; nearly all examples are also engraved with armorials. Around 1700, when punch became a fashionable drink, monteiths were made with detachable rims, so that they could also be used as punch-bowls. They also had lion's mask drop-ring handles and more elaborate ornament, such as overall fluting and gadrooning on the body, with shells, masks, scrolls, and cherub's heads on the rims.

Few monteiths were made after c.1730, possibly because from this period glasses were made with smaller feet and so were more difficult to suspend from the rim. They were, however, revived in the late 18th and early 19th centuries in France, and examples in Sheffield plate are also known from c.1780. In the late 19th and early 20th centuries they again returned to fashion as presentation pieces, notably as an alternative to rose bowls for wedding presents.

PUNCH-BOWLS

Punch – made with brandy, claret, sugar, spices, and lemon or orange juice – was introduced from India in the late 17th century and became a popular drink, often mixed by gentlemen at the table after dinner. Punch-bowls are similar to monteiths but lack a detachable rim or handles and have a deeper bowl; some have matching ladles. Many were used as presentation pieces from the 18th century. Rare, early examples are plain except for an engraved coat of arms;

▲ Monteith by Louis-Jean-Baptiste Cheret

This French monteith (*verrière*) is a rare example made during the late 18th century; the value is increased because it is one of a pair. The low, oval form, band of laurel ornament, and loop handles show the influence of the Neo-classical style, and are very different from the circular bowl with drop-ring handles and Baroque decoration used in early 18th-century England.
*(1783; w. 39cm/15¼in; value **N**)*

▼ Monteith by R.F. Mosley & Co.

Reproductions of late 17th- and early 18th-century monteiths were made from the late 19th century. This English piece has a fluted body with a scalloped rim decorated with matted scrolls and shells but the cherub's heads that were common on originals are absent.
*(1915; diam. 25.5cm/10in; value **H**)*

the foot became higher and the bowl larger throughout the 18th century. Chased and embossed flowers and scrolls feature on Rococo punch-bowls and classically inspired motifs on those made in the late 18th century. North American punch-bowls were typically in the form of a plain bowl on a low base. Among the most famous is the "Sons of Liberty" punch-bowl (1768) by the Boston patriot and silversmith Paul Revere (1735–1818); it is inscribed with a dedication to the 92 members of the Massachusetts Bay House of Representatives who refused in 1768 to withdraw a letter hostile to George III on the eve of the American Revolution.

▼ Parcel-gilt punch-bowl and ladle by Gorham & Co.

Like most 19th-century punch-bowls, this extremely handsome American example, with a matching ladle, was made as a presentation piece; the foot of the bowl is engraved with an inscription, and the bowl and ladle with the monogram of the recipient. The scrolling handles are each decorated with a cast-gilt mask of Bacchus with trailing grapevines – decoration relating to the function of the punch-bowl.
*(1871; ht 31cm/12in; value **I**)*

KEY FACTS

Wine coolers
- DECORATION usually heavy cast and applied ornament
- COLLECTING pairs are worth much more than singles

Marks
The body should be fully marked on the underside; the collar and liner should be part marked

Monteiths
- DECORATION most monteiths were engraved with armorials; those without should be carefully examined for signs of removed armorials
- COLLECTING collars have sometimes been removed, but these pieces can still be distinguished from punch-bowls by the plain rim on which the collar sat

Marks
Detachable collars, which were used from c.1700, should be fully marked

Punch-bowls
- DESIGN distinguished from the monteith by fixed, rather than detachable, scalloped rim or handles
- BEWARE plain surfaces are suspect – bowls should feature an engraved crest or a coat of arms

See also Drinking vessels, pp.246–7

Miscellaneous

While large and expensive items such as tureens and wine coolers attract most interest on the market today, a huge variety of smaller items, ranging from dining accessories such as dish rings, cruets, and casters to small boxes and pots, babies' rattles, desk accessories, and scent bottles, is available to the collector with a more limited budget. Such items were produced in vast quantities when mechanized production of silver was introduced in the 19th century.

CRUET FRAMES
Cruets first appeared at the end of the 17th century, when oil and vinegar were introduced as condiments. Early cruet frames had two glass bottles with silver mounts, but by the 1720s they had three silver casters with pierced lids – for sugar, pepper, and mustard – and two glass bottles with silver mounts, set in a frame with a plain base on scroll or shell feet and with a decorative scroll handle. The latter version is known as a "Warwick" cruet frame. By the 1770s a boat-shaped frame was popular, either pierced, or solid with bright-cut swags and festoons; the casters were glass, with silver mounts. In the 19th century the number of bottles increased following the introduction of soy and other exotic sauces, and frames were produced in an infinite range of designs.

▲ Cruet frame
The glass bottles and casters, ornate cast border, and mask handle of this English cruet frame date it to the early 19th century. It has eight glass containers, compared to the five usual on late 18th-century cruets.
(1825; ht 19cm/7½in; value I)

SALT-CELLARS
Rare, early salt-cellars from c.1600 are simply circular or triangular with a central well. These and later salts were usually made in pairs, fours, or sixes. More common are those from the 1730s onward, the most popular type until the 1770s being a "cauldron" form on three or four feet, with cast and applied floral swags and lion's masks; these were supplied with a blue glass liner or gilded to prevent corrosion. Typical of the Neo-classical period are an oval or circular, straight-sided form on ball-and-claw feet, either pierced or of solid bright-cut silver, and also a boat shape with loop handles, similar to contemporary tureens. The pierced circular form remained popular in the 19th century.

◄ Pair of salt-cellars by A. Gelly
These French oval salts on four scroll feet are typical of the elegant salt-cellars made during the mid-18th century. The gilded insides prevent salt from corroding the silver.
(c.1750; ht 8cm/3in; value G)

CASTERS
Silver casters appeared in the late 17th century, when pepper and other spices became popular. Made in sets of three – for black and cayenne pepper and sugar – the earliest were plain and cylindrical with a high, pierced, domed cover. Decoration consisted of ornamental piercing, an engraved coat of arms, gadrooned or rope-twist rims, and a baluster or button-shaped finial. The "lighthouse" form was replaced c.1710 by a plain or octagonal baluster shape, sometimes with a molded rib around the body. This remained fashionable until the late 18th century, when it was superseded by cruets with glass casters.

MUSTARD-POTS
Paste mustard, served in pots, first became popular c.1750. Mustard-pots from the mid-18th century are generally drum-shaped or cylindrical, with a scroll handle and a flat or domed lid with a cast thumbpiece, similar to tankards. More widely used in the 1770s and 1780s were oval, octagonal, and vase shapes with plain, bright-cut, or openwork bodies, usually with a blue glass liner. Novelty mustard-pots such as those in the shape of birds, cats, and pigs are popular with collectors today.

INKSTANDS
Seventeenth-century inkstands are rectangular caskets, containing an inkpot, pounce-pot (for pounce or sand, used to dry ink) and a wafer-pot (containing wax disks for sealing letters). By the 18th century most inkstands consisted of an oblong silver tray on four feet, usually with only an inkpot and pounce-pot, together with a taperstick for melting sealing wax or a small handbell. They are generally plain, except for molded scroll and shell or beaded rims and decorative feet. Glass pots with detachable silver mounts came into fashion from the

▲ Mustard-pot
A small drum shape was a popular form for mustard-pots in the 18th and 19th centuries. This English example, with engraved or flat-chased bands of scrolls and strapwork, has fairly restrained decoration compared to some pieces made in the later 19th century. It is always important to check that on pieces such as this the delicately scrolling handle has not been pulled away from the body and also that the hinge on the lid is in a good state of repair. Pierced examples, especially when used with a blue or red glass liner, were also very popular, although the piercing is prone to damage.
(c.1840; ht 9cm/3½in; value C)

◄ Inkstand by T.J. & N. Creswick
The winged paw feet and elaborately embellished foliage border of this English inkstand are both characteristic early 19th-century decorative elements. The central taperstick, which has a conical snuffer, is original to the stand – some tapersticks (and bells) are now sold separately – and this will add to the value of the piece.
(1826; w. 22cm/8½in; value H)

mid-18th century, along with rectangular trays with pierced galleries to hold the pots. Many inexpensive inkstands were mass-produced in thin-gauge silver and Sheffield plate in the late 18th and 19th centuries.

DRESSING-TABLE SILVER
Dressing-table sets, sometimes fitted in wooden traveling cases, were made throughout the late 19th and early 20th centuries. Most comprised at least a hand mirror and hairbrushes, backed with silver, and often also contained scent bottles or flasks with silver mounts, clothes brushes, combs, and shoehorns. Larger sets could also include eye baths, jewel-caskets, and pomade-jars. Made of silver or gilt-silver, the items were mostly engraved, usually with a monogram or initials, engine-turned, enameled, or embossed.

▲ Hand mirror and brush
This typical English dressing-table set comprises a hand mirror, two hairbrushes, and two clothes brushes, decorated with pink *guilloché* enameling that resembles moiré silk. The enamel decoration should be checked for chipping.
(1931; l. 22.5cm/8¾in; value D)

▲ Picture frame
Silver picture frames, such as this American example, are popular with collectors because they are both practical and decorative. The condition of the mount, backing, and strut should all be carefully checked before buying.
(20th century; ht 15cm/6in; value D)

► Belt buckle
The intricate, sinuous forms of this buckle reflect the influence of the Art Nouveau style of the early 20th century. This English buckle would have ornamented a belt – a standard feature of women's dress in this period. Both parts of the buckle should be marked.
(1907; w. 15cm/6in; value C)

► Silver and tortoiseshell scent bottle by William Comyns
A great variety of scent flasks and bottles was made in the 19th and early 20th centuries. Like this English bottle, examples are usually richly decorated and made of expensive materials. Many have survived in good condition, as they were often given as presents and were protected by a fitted case.
(1906; ht 14cm/5½in; value F)

MIRROR OR PICTURE FRAMES
Most silver frames found today are small and relatively inexpensive, dating from the 1880s onward. Produced in a wide range of forms and styles, they are sometimes ornamented with embossed Classical, naturalistic Art Nouveau, or Art Deco decoration. The silver is very often thin and stamped from sheet and easily damaged; better-quality pieces are cast.

BUCKLES
Buckles became common in England in the 17th century as a replacement for shoelaces. Silver buckles, made of gold, silver, Sheffield plate, or cut steel, were particularly popular during the 18th century for fastening shoes, knee breeches, and women's sashes and neckbands. A wealthy man might possess as many as a dozen pairs of buckles, for different outfits and occasions. In the late 18th century buckles were produced on large scale by manufacturers in the Midlands. In the late 19th and early 20th centuries intricate Art Nouveau-style buckles were made, especially for belts on women's dresses.

▲ Porringer possibly by James Beschefer
The frieze of spiral flutes, scalework, foliate designs, and band of rope-twist molding are typical of 18th-century porringers. Like many porringers, this English example is engraved with initials. Porringers were often given to women after the birth of a child.
(1715; ht 14cm/5½in; value G)

PORRINGERS/CAUDLE CUPS
The porringer, or caudle cup, was a straight-sided or bulbous vessel with two handles, made *c.*1650–*c.*1750 for potage (thick soup) or caudle (fine gruel mixed with wine, spices, and sugar, given to invalids). The earliest types were plain with wirework handles; examples from the 1670s to the 1690s are often embossed and chased with flowers or leaves, and have cast scroll or caryatid handles. In the 18th century decoration of lobes, gadroons, and scalework was popular. In the USA, a "porringer" is a shallow vessel with a flat, pierced handle – called a "bleeding bowl" in Britain.

KEY FACTS
- CONDITION cruet frames: glass bottles should be all the same height and not chipped; salt-cellars: any glass liners should be original and fit properly – check for corrosion; casters: the piercing should be intact and the cover should fit the body closely; mustard pots: beware of hinges and handles that are damaged; mirrors and picture frames: pieces were often stamped from very thin silver and this can easily crack or get worn through over-zealous polishing; avoid mirrors with cracked glass; buckles: look for thin, worn, or cracked silver; porringers/caudle cups: the handles have sometimes been removed and small rough patches may be visible where this has occurred
- COLLECTING cruet frames: the earliest examples had two bottles; by the 1720s "Warwick" cruet frames were produced with three casters and two bottles; salt-cellars: most were made in pairs or sets and are most desirable and collectible as such; inkstands: designs are very varied; individual parts such as tapersticks and bells are often sold separately; dressing-table silver: sets are highly collectible, especially if they are in an original fitted box; complete sets exist in abundance, so any that are worn, broken, or have pieces missing should generally be avoided unless they are very unusual; mirrors and picture frames: many examples still exist of these wares

Marks
These should be visible on the body of the piece, and are often found in a straight line near the rim or on the base; any covers should bear the same marks as the main items; on cruet frames the frame should bear the full set of marks and the handle should feature part marks, although mounts often have the maker's mark only

---

See also Furniture: Mirrors, pp.112–13; Textiles: Costume – pp.342–5, Accessories, p.346; Miscellaneous: Perfume bottles, p.548–9

Jewelry, one of the oldest forms of decorative art, has been worn by men and women since prehistoric times to enhance appearance, to display status, wealth, or grief, and to affirm love, friendship, and loyalty. Jewelry designs are infinitely varied, and are produced using a wide range of techniques and materials, including precious metals, gemstones and hardstones, enamels, wood, glass, ceramics, iron, and even human hair. Jewelry often has symbolic or personal significance, the most obvious examples being mourning jewelry, which dates from the 17th century, and hair jewelry, formed from the intricately woven locks of a loved one's hair. Certain designs are closely associated with particular eras and personalities; for example, snake rings became fashonable in the mid-19th century when Queen Victoria received one as an engagement ring from Prince Albert. *Pietre dure* jewelry, made from hardstones and depicting Classical scenes, was also popular in the 19th century, when many examples were purchased in Italy as tourist souvenirs. To the jewelry collector, the ingenuity of the design, the intrinsic worth of the materials, the quality of manufacture, and the provenence and condition all contribute, in varying degrees, to the desirability of an individual piece. But to the original owner, its true worth often resides simply in its sentimental value.

Selection of cufflinks (left) These examples display a diversity of shapes, sizes, materials, designs, and decorative embellishments *(19th and 20th centuries)*.
Butterfly pin (above) In theme (insects) and composition (red Vauxhall glass) this pin exhibits some of the most characteristic features of Victorian costume jewelry *(c. 1880)*.

Jewelry: Basics

Jewelry is one of the very oldest forms of ornamentation, dating back to antiquity, and embraces a wide range of materials, techniques, and designs. Most surviving examples date from the 18th century or later – very early pieces are rare – and many are in good condition, having been carefully preserved for reasons of sentiment or value.

METALS

There are three main precious metals used for jewelry. Gold, the most popular, is malleable and ductile, and does not tarnish. Its purity is measured in carats, with one carat equalling 200mg of gold. Pure (24ct) gold is so soft that it is usually alloyed with silver or copper. Most quality gold is 18ct or 14ct; 9ct gold is used for less expensive pieces. Silver is malleable but tarnishes, and is usually alloyed with copper for durability: the British standard of purity is the sterling standard, i.e. 925 parts silver to 75 parts copper. Platinum does not tarnish and is rarer, harder, and more valuable than gold.

GEMSTONES

Although some gems can be identified by their color or hardness, many need technical examination to establish authenticity. Among the factors crucial in establishing the value of a stone are its carat weight, color, brilliance, and cut. The color of a gemstone depends on the natural impurities dispersed throughout the stone. Color is the least dependable means of identification, as many types of stone exist in a range of colors, and some stones are heat-treated to improve their color. Most natural gemstones have inclusions, which reduce their brilliance; these will be removed, as far as possible, by a gem-cutter. Synthetic stones and paste and glass imitations may be identified by their lack of inclusions, although paste will sometimes contain bubbles.

Gemstones are cut to enhance their clarity and brilliance, as the different facets of a cut stone alter the amount of refracted light escaping from it. There are many different styles of cut: the brilliant cut, rose cut, old cut, and eight cut are among the most common. Heavily flawed stones are usually cabochon-cut, giving an unfaceted but polished surface.

GOLD TECHNIQUES

In antiquity most gold jewelry was made by punching, hammering, or stamping sheets of gold or by casting molten gold. Wirework and granulation were used from *c.*3000 BC by the Greeks and Etruscans. Such techniques were revived in the 18th century with the discovery of ancient jewelry in archeological sites.

Granulation This is a method of creating relief designs on gold by soldering grains of gold to a metal base.
- The technique was revived in Rome *c.*1826 by the Castellani family – this hinged bangle was made *c.*1880
- Damaged granules may have been resoldered – check for lead solder, which is an inexpensive substitute for gold and silver and will reduce the value of a piece

Cannetille This describes a type of gold or silver filigree design in the form of scrolls or rosettes of tightly coiled wire. The technique, as exemplified in this English amethyst pin of *c.*1830, was particularly popular in Britain, France, and Italy until *c.*1830.
- Fragile and easily damaged
- Some pieces may have missing scrolls, rosettes, or balls – avoid pieces that have been soldered

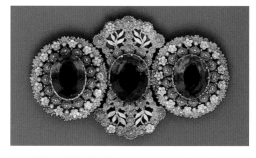

Machine-made New mass production techniques introduced during the 19th century enabled manufacturers to produce inexpensive gold jewelry. One of the most common ways of producing hollow gold jewelry was die-stamping, whereby a flat sheet of metal was enclosed in a die and a pattern produced by applying pressure, thus forcing the metal into the shape of the die.
- Popular for hollow gold pieces with patterns in high relief, as seen on this gold and peridot bracelet of *c.*1835–40
- More vulnerable to damage than solid metalwork – relief patterns wear especially easily
- Dented jewelry should be avoided as dents can be very difficult to repair

CARVING

A wide variety of materials, from wood and ivory to coral, gemstones, and jade, has been carved into decorative shapes for jewelry. Carved coral, such as this pair of earrings of *c.*1850, was produced on a large scale in Naples from the mid-19th century for the growing number of tourists traveling to Italy.

- Good-quality carving should be well defined and smooth, without any jagged or rough edges
- Beads were frequently imported pre-carved, so beads on a necklace or bracelet, for example, may be of slightly differing shapes or sizes
- Fruits and flowers are the most popular designs
- Avoid badly damaged pieces as they are expensive to mend

GEMSTONES

Almandine garnet	Amethyst	Aquamarine
Diamond	Emerald	Lapis lazuli
Opal	Peridot	Ruby
Sapphire	Topaz	Turquojewelry

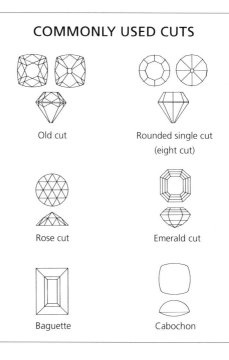

COMMONLY USED CUTS

Old cut	Rounded single cut (eight cut)
Rose cut	Emerald cut
Baguette	Cabochon

MOSAICS

In the 19th century a large number of mosaic plaques or medallions were made as souvenirs for the expanding tourist trade in Italy. Tiny pieces of inlaid glass (Roman mosaic) or hardstones (*pietre dure*) were arranged to depict ancient ruins, landscapes, or figures in national dress. Pins, earrings, and pendants were the most popular forms for mosaic jewelry.

Pietre dure Plaques made with hardstones (*pietre dure*) were a specialty of Florentine craftsmen from the 16th century. This type of mosaic, as in this 19th-century earring, is made of pieces of different-colored hardstones, such as jasper and bloodstone, set into a black slate or white marble background.
- Stones should fit tightly together, with no pieces missing
- Best-quality work uses the stone's natural tones of color to three-dimensional effect

Roman Roman craftsmen employed tiny *tesserae*, or pieces of colored glass, set into a glass background, to create popular designs which included ancient ruins, views of the landscape around Rome, and figures in national costume. Such Egyptian motifs as the pharaoh on this 19th-century locket-back pendant were popular during the first quarter of the 19th century.

- Beware of mosaics with cracked or missing glass, which are difficult to repair
- Good-quality pieces are valuable and collectible
- The mount should be contemporary with the mosaic

CAMEOS

Strictly speaking, a cameo is a hardstone, such as sardonyx or cornelian, with layers of colors, carved to show a relief design and background in contrasting hues. However, the term also refers to relief carvings in lava, coral, and shell, as in the 19th-century example below depicting the goddess Luna. The technique was first used in ancient Greece and Rome but was very popular during the 19th century and widely copied in the 20th century.
- Good examples have crisp, well-defined carving, with no sharp edges, cracks, or chips
- Beware of fakes, made by gluing together bits of stone, shell, or glass
- Mythological subjects were popular in the early 19th century; later, female profiles were more fashionable

ENAMELING

Enameling refers to the process by which colored ground glass is bound into a paste and applied to a gold, silver, or copper base, before being fired in a kiln to revitrify. It can be applied with a brush, like paint, or set into metal depressions, grooves, or compartments. Enamel colors were first employed in Egypt *c.*1600 BC and were extensively used in the Byzantine Empire and during the early Middle Ages. A revival of the techniques during the 19th century led to renewed interest in the art.

Cloisonné **enameling** In *cloisonné* enameling the design is outlined by soldering filigree, wire, or metal strips set edgewise to a metal base to create a series of compartments, known as "cells" or *cloisons*. These cells are then filled with colored enamel and fired to create the final design. The bracelet shown below is a fine example of *c.*1885 by the French maker Lucien Falize (1838–97).
- Popular for jewelry in the Byzantine Revival or Renaissance Revival styles of the 19th century
- Metal *cloisons* can be damaged and the enamel chipped; this will reduce the value of a piece

Geneva enameling From the 17th to the 19th centuries Geneva was an important center of production for painted enamels. The process of enameling involved applying a vitrified coating to a metal base and then firing. Like mosaic jewelry such plaques were produced largely as souvenir pieces for tourists, but some pieces, including this example of *c.*1850 by the firm of Mercier, are of very good quality.

- Designs are often chipped – check for areas restored with modern enamels
- Plaques without their contemporary gold mount are less desirable
- Popular images: figures in Swiss national costume, landscapes, and copies of old master paintings

Guilloché **enameling** This refers to an engraved or engine-turned metal base covered with a layer of translucent enamel that allows the design to show through and creates a shimmering effect, like watered silk. Most designs, as on this French cufflink of *c.*1910, are regular patterns of waves or rosettes. The technique was particularly popular with makers of snuff-boxes and other objects of vertu in 18th-century France.
- Most valuable pieces were made by the jeweler Carl Fabergé (1846–1920) who worked for the Russian imperial family
- Transparent enamel should not be worn or chipped
- Subtle gradations in enamel color are a sign of good quality

SETTINGS

The setting is the mount, usually of metal, in which a gemstone is secured. There are many types of setting, but the most common are the closed- and open-back, claw, pavé, and collet.

Closed- and open-back settings In an open-back setting the back of the stone is exposed, as in this emerald and diamond pin of *c.*1850 (left). In a closed setting the back of the stone is covered with metal, as in this oval pin of *c.*1820 (right). In closed settings stones were often backed with colored foils or painted for extra luster.
- Closed settings were used mainly in late 18th and early 19th centuries; thereafter open settings were typical
- Openwork on open settings can be vulnerable to damage
- Collet setting (see below) is a form of closed- or open-back setting

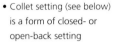

Claw setting In a claw setting the stone is secured by a series of claws, or projecting prongs. It was developed in the 19th century and is mainly used for large cut gemstones as in this gentleman's diamond ring of 1910.

- Only found on 19th-century and early 20th-century pieces
- Beware – if claws are worn, the stone may fall out

Pavé setting A pavé setting refers to a style in which many tiny gemstones, usually diamonds, turquoises (as in this padlock of *c.*1860), or pearls, are set so close together that the metal backing is fully hidden. The stones or pearls are set in holes in the metal base and secured by small raised pieces of metal.

- Typically used on lockets and pins
- Turquoise is typical of the 1860s; Edwardian designs often feature pearls
- Stones must be original

Collet setting In a collet setting the stone is fitted in an open or closed ring or "dish," made from metal tubing or a thin metal band. This setting is commonly used for rings, especially signet rings, and for necklaces, particularly *rivières*.

- Plain collet necklaces such as this garnet necklace of *c.*1840 were popular during the early 19th century
- Check for dents or other metal damage

Rings

The the most popular type of jewelry today, rings have been worn since ancient Egyptian times, not only on the fingers but also on other parts of the body, such as the toes. Various types of ring have specific symbolic significance: signet rings engraved with a personal seal are often associated with power and status, while plain gold wedding rings are tokens of betrothal. Wedding rings have been given or exchanged at the marriage ceremony since Roman times, and from the 16th century it has been the custom to use a plain gold band. Rings have been made not only from such precious metals as gold but also from other materials including jade, amber, opal, turquoise, garnet, and coral.

BEFORE 1800

Rings from this period are fairly rare: before the discovery of large deposits of gold in the USA in the 1840s and diamonds in South Africa in the 1870s, jewelry that was no longer fashionable was often dismantled and the precious metal melted down and refashioned, with the stones being set in new mounts to follow changes in taste. Fashionable 18th-century ring designs include the *giardinetto* ("small garden") ring, so called because it features an openwork design of a bouquet, basket, or vase of flowers set with precious stones of various colors. In the Neo-classical period rings set with small cameos and intaglios were popular. Rings made in Britain after 1738 are easier to date than earlier pieces as an Act of Parliament in that year made it compulsory for jewelers to mark their designs.

► *Giardinetto* ring
These rings were highly popular in the 18th century. As the settings are fragile, surviving examples in good condition are rare. This French silver and gold ring with a pear-shaped emerald at the center and a typical rose-cut diamond bezel in the form of a bouquet of flowers is struck with a control mark, which assists with dating.
(c.1760; value H)

▲ Posy ring
A posy ring is a ring engraved with a posy – an expression of love or sentiment (from "poesy" or "poetry"), usually found on the inside of the ring. Many were used as engagement or wedding rings. This 18ct gold British ring bears the inscription "no recompense but love."
(18th century; value D)

▼ Half-hoop ring
Coral jewelry was particularly fashionable in the first half of the 19th century, although today carved coral necklaces, bracelets, and earrings are more popular than plain coral bead rings. Some imitation coral jewelry has been made with plastic or glass – real coral should feel warm to the touch and will have some natural imperfections.
(c.1840; value B)

◄ Cluster ring
Cluster rings were made in a great variety of shapes and materials, but the combination of cabochon opal or turquoise and diamonds was very popular in the second half of the 19th century. This opal and diamond example, made in Britain, features diamonds held in open claw settings.
(1880; value F)

AFTER 1800

In the early 19th century half-hoop and cluster gem-set rings were introduced, and they remained fashionable throughout the century. Half-hoop rings feature a single or double row of gemstones, while cluster rings generally feature a central gemstone surrounded by smaller gems or pearls. Early in the century gems were always mounted in closed settings and backed with colored foil in order to enhance their color and brilliancy; from the mid-19th century gemstones would typically be set in open collets or claws.

Snakes, symbolizing wisdom and eternity, were a particularly common motif in mid-19th century rings, especially after Prince Albert presented Queen Victoria with an emerald-set snake engagement ring in 1839. Serpent rings consist of one, two, or three bands with single or double serpent heads, often set with diamonds or rubies to represent eyes or simply for adornment. Some bands were engraved and enameenameled to give the effect of scales.

Other types of ring popular in the mid-19th century included mourning rings (a gold band decorated with black enamel) and gold rings in the form of a strap and buckle. Gypsy rings, which were introduced c.1875 and worn by both sexes, consisted of a gold band into which one, two, or three stones were set so deeply (sometimes in a star-shaped recess) that the table of the stone was flush with the surface of the metal.

New patterns introduced in the 1890s reflected the Edwardian revival of interest in 18th-century court styles, and jewelry of this period is characterized by the use of delicate settings. Designs included single and paired hearts set with colored gemstones in a diamond border, characteristically surmounted by crowns and bows; and boat-shaped lozenge or *marquise* rings, which were typically set with graduated rows of gemstones (usually diamonds).

▲ *Marquise* ring
This fine British *marquise* ring, set with high-quality, old, brilliant-cut diamonds, is made of 15ct gold and must therefore date from after 1854, when this standard was introduced.
(1880; value H)

▲ Serpent ring
Rings in the form of entwined snakes are very typical of designs produced during the Victorian period. Like the British example above, which is set with a diamond and a ruby, most serpent rings feature gemstones set in the head or as eyes. The quality of the materials and modeling varies, as many such rings were mass-produced.
(c.1890; value D)

▲ Gypsy ring
Gypsy rings, as shown in the above 18ct gold and sapphire British example, feature stones set deeply into a recess, so that the table of the stone is level with the surface of the metal. Even though the stones are protected by the setting, the gems in gypsy rings are often quite badly scratched.
(c.1890; value D)

KEY FACTS

- **WEDDING RINGS** antique examples are often less expensive than modern versions; most examples found today date from the 19th and 20th centuries and are of 22ct gold; examples are usually plain but may be set with gemstones or engraved with dates or inscriptions
- **ALTERATIONS** some rings, such as half-hoops, cannot be resized because of gemstone settings; most rings are hallmarked – if a ring is resized, marks should not be cut out, as this will reduce the value
- **CONDITION** gem-set rings should have original stones in good condition – replacement stones reduce value; claw settings should also be checked for damage; delicate carving on the sides of a ring may have been damaged if it has been worn next to another ring
- **CARE** rings should be stored in a ring tray with separate compartments to avoid scratching or chipping

See also Sentimental jewelry, pp.268–9; Art Nouveau: Jewelry, pp.406–7; Art Deco: Jewelry, pp.438–9; Mid-century Modern: Jewelry, p.452

Pins

Although now sometimes considered less fashionable than other types of jewelry, pins were among the most popular forms of jewelry in the 19th and early 20th centuries. The fashions of the period were characterized by tight bodices and décolleté necklines for evening dress, with large pins and fancy corsage decoration regarded as highly suitable ornaments for the bodice of a dress.

▲ Butterfly pin
From the late 18th century cut-steel jewelry, using faceted studs of steel to imitate precious stones, was a popular substitute in Britain and France for more expensive diamond jewelry. The technique was developed by the British industrialist and silversmith Matthew Boulton (1728–1809). Butterfly pins such as the above are very collectible.
*(1840; w. 5cm/2in; value **B**)*

BEFORE 1880

In the late 18th and early 19th centuries diamond pins in gold or gold and silver closed settings were popular among the wealthiest members of society. The most fashionable designs were sunbursts, crescents, stars, and, inspired by the Napoleonic wars, trophies of arms. Simple flowerheads and sprays of laurel and bay leaves were also produced and can be distinguished from later Victorian examples by their more formal designs.

Pins with large stones and more ornate settings were introduced in the 1830s and 1840s and thereafter produced in an infinite range of forms and materials. Some Victorian pins were fitted with a loop enabling them also to be worn as a pendant. Pins in the form of leaves and flowers, with the central part of the spray or flower often mounted on springs (*en tremblant*) and hence detachable, were popular, as were animal and bird pins, and insect jewelry, which first appeared in the late 1860s and included insects such as bees, dragonflies, butterflies, and wasps.

► Cameo pin
Hardstone or shell cameos are among the most typical of 19th-century pins. The classically inspired female head in this hardstone piece is typical of mid- and late 19th-century pieces. Early 19th-century cameos usually feature satyrs, mythological beasts, or Roman emperors.
*(c.1870–80; ht 5cm/2in; value **G**)*

► Ribbon pin
Ribbon pins set with diamonds and gems are typical of late 19th- and early 20th-century jewelry. The setting of this piece is gold, but platinum was a popular alternative.
*(c.1880; w. 5cm/2in; value **H**)*

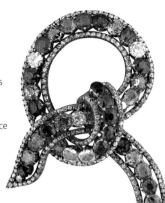

The enthusiasm in the 1840s for the Middle Ages and the Renaissance led to the production of enameled oval plaques imitating Renaissance paintings; particularly notable Greek- and Etruscan-style designs were made in Rome from the 1850s by the Castellani family. Souvenir pins, reflecting the Victorian love of travel, were also popular, and in Italy jewelers produced pins specifically for the tourist market. Designs were usually either in glass micromosaic or in Florentine hardstones (*pietre dure*), depicting Classical scenes; or were cameos carved in lava from Mt Vesuvius, hardstone, or shell. In Scotland "pebble" pins in the form of crosses, shields, or rings were set with such local hardstones as agate and citrine.

Another popular form of pin in the 19th century was the stomacher pin, which was worn on the bodice and usually featured three pear-shaped, often detachable pendants. They were made in a variety of designs, from elaborate foliate scrolls set with diamonds and colored stones to repoussé, or pressed-out, gold settings with amethysts, citrines, turquoises, and garnets.

AFTER 1880

In the 1880s and 1890s there was a revival of interest in 18th-century court jewelry. Star and sunburst pins were usually designed in sets and used to adorn clothing, combs, or tiaras. They are smaller and more delicate than 18th-century originals and are typically set with diamonds, pearls, opals, or moonstones. Ribbon bows and single or paired hearts were also favorite designs.

Introduced in the 1890s, bar pins quickly became popular. They usually consisted of a horizontal gold bar with a gemstone or a decorative motif (flowers, birds, or clovers) at the center. It was fashionable for a name, message, or date to be engraved on a bar pin, and many such souvenirs of Queen Victoria's Diamond Jubilee in 1897 were particularly popular.

▼ "Pebble" pin
Silver pins based on Iron Age originals and set with such Scottish hardstones as agate were typical of the interest in historical jewelry in the 19th century. Such pins are very highly sought after. All stones should be intact, as missing pieces are difficult to replace.
*(19th century; w. 5cm/2in; value **C**)*

▼ *Pietre dure* pin
Pins featuring *pietre dure* (hardstone) designs were mainly produced in Florence in the 19th century as souvenirs for the growing number of tourists. The gold mount of this Italian pin with floral decoration features typically finely detailed bead- and wirework.
*(c.1870; w. 4cm/1½in; value **F**)*

KEY FACTS

- **CONDITION** all fittings, including pendants and pins, should be original; mosaic and hardstone pins should be in good condition, as missing stones are very difficult to replace; any hollow or pressed-out settings will be more susceptible to damage than solid designs
- **COLLECTING** pins are often now considered unfashionable and so may be less expensive than other forms of jewelry; detachable central flowers or sprays mounted *en tremblant* may now be sold separately; novelty animal and insect pins are especially popular with collectors; cameo pins: well-defined detail and depth of carving is a sign of good quality

See also Sentimental jewelry, pp.268–9; Art Nouveau: Jewelry, pp.406–7; Art Deco: Jewelry, pp.438–9; Mid-century Modern: Jewelry, p.452

Necklaces, pendants, and lockets

A huge variety of necklaces was produced in the Victorian period: most are large and ornate, since décolleté necklines for ball and evening gowns were in fashion for most of the 19th century, although less expensive lockets and chains, especially in silver, were also produced in large numbers for the expanding middle-class market from the second half of the 19th century. These are particularly collectible today, as they are easier to wear than heavy, formal necklaces.

▶ *Rivière*

Simple necklaces such as this British *rivière* with a cross pendant are characteristic of jewelry from the 1820s to the 1840s. Garnets were particularly popular for this style of necklace, as were topazes, amethysts, and citrines. Many collectors prefer these necklaces to the more ornate pieces of the later Victorian period.

(*c.1830; l. 46cm/18in; value* **G**)

NECKLACES AND CHAINS

Formal necklaces made in the 18th and early 19th centuries are now rare and very expensive. The most common design for these necklaces was the *rivière*, a string of beads of the same gemstone of graduated size. Such necklaces were often part of a set, or "parure," containing matching earrings and pin. Other fashionable types of necklace in the early 19th century included Neo-classical intaglios and cameos joined with delicate gold chains; aquamarines, topazes, amethysts, garnets, and tourmalines set in cannetille work; and, from the 1840s, snake chains made of interlocking gold links to simulate scales. These snake chains featured a clasp in the form of the head biting the tail and, on the very finest pieces, diamonds, rubies, or turquoises for decoration. From the 1860s Greek- and Etruscan-style necklaces, typically with fringes of urn- or acorn-shaped pendants, were a specialty of top Italian jewelers – including the Castellani and Giuliano families, whose work displays extremely high standards of craftsmanship.

In the 1880s and 1890s the fashionable fringed garland necklace featured collet-set gemstones that were suspended by thin knife-wires from a gold or platinum chain necklet. Light and delicate, this type of necklace could often be mounted as a tiara on a special fitting. The fashion for chokers of several rows of small pearls divided at intervals with gem-set plaques or bars was introduced by Princess Alexandra, later Queen Consort of Edward VII. Chokers were worn with bead or pearl necklaces fastened to the bodice.

Throughout the late 18th, the 19th, and the early 20th centuries gold chains were worn around the neck, shoulders, waist, or corsage, sometimes being used to hang a watch. Most examples from the late 18th and early 19th centuries will be in the form of rounded hollow links or a rope twist in 18ct or 22ct gold or pinchbeck (an alloy of copper and zinc). Clasps are usually barrel- or bobbin-shaped but may also be in the form of gem-set gloved hands. Chains in 9ct gold and silver were produced on a large scale from *c.1850*.

PENDANTS AND LOCKETS

During the first half of the 19th century many pendants were made in the form of a gold cross set with gemstones or carved in hardstone. Latin, Greek, and Maltese crosses were popular as was the "*croix à la Jeannette*" – a Latin cross suspended from a heart, inspired by French peasant jewelry. From the 1860s pendants and lockets – typically worn on gold chains, strings of pearls, or velvet ribbons – were among the most fashionable types of jewelry. Among the most common designs was the "Holbeinesque" pendant, inspired by 16th-century European Renaissance jewelry, in particular the jewelry designs of the Renaissance painter Hans Holbein. Such pendants usually featured a central gemstone and a suspended lozenge-shaped drop. Similar Renaissance-style cross and lozenge-shaped pendants were a specialty of the Neapolitan jeweler Carlo Giuliano (*c.1831–95*), who worked in London from *c.1860*.

Lockets were produced in gem-set enameled gold, chased with monograms, inscriptions, and such motifs as stars and insects, and in less expensive materials such as chased silver, ivory, and tortoiseshell for the growing middle-class clientele. Lockets from the second half of the 19th century are larger than earlier ones because they were designed to hold photographs.

At the end of the century the most popular design for jeweled pendants and lockets was a heart or a cross, surmounted by a ribbon bow. The Edwardian taste for feminine, fragile jewelry is evident in pendants with finely pierced lattice designs and millegrain-set ribbon bows and flower garlands.

◀ "Holbeinesque" pendant

The combination of gold, enamel, and, above all, a large, polished cabochon garnet, as featured on this French pendant, is particularly distinctive of 19th-century pendants imitating 16th-century Renaissance jewelry designs. Pendants such as this were characteristically surrounded by a decorative polychrome enamel foliate and scrollwork border and were sometimes created with a pair of matching earrings.

(*c.1870; l. 5.5cm/2¼in; value* **H**)

▲ Locket and chain

Such decorative silver lockets as this British piece were popular among the Victorians and are as affordable and collectible as they are easy to wear today.

(*1881; w. of locket 2.5cm/1in; value* **A**)

Necklet

This delicate English half-pearl necklet features a combination of gold, pearls, green garnets, and peridots in a scrolling floral design. Green or demantoid garnets, varying in color from dark emerald to light yellow-green, are the rarest and most valuable of all types of garnet.

(*c.1890; l. of chain 60cm/24in; value* **G**)

KEY FACTS

- CONDITION snake necklaces should be in good condition as they are very difficult and expensive to repair; lockets may dent easily, as they are often made of thin-gauge silver; hinges or clasps on pendants and lockets should be original and in good working order; necklaces and chains that have been shortened or altered are less desirable than those with all their original links
- COLLECTING simple necklaces, such as *rivières*, are popular with collectors, as they are easy to wear; lockets with initials are less popular than those with inscriptions; necklaces from the Edwardian period are more abundant than those from earlier periods; complete parures are rare and especially collectible

See also Art Nouveau: Jewelry, pp.406–7; Art Deco: Jewelry, pp.438–9; Postmodernism: Jewelry, p.470

Earrings and bracelets

Most antique earrings found today are of the long, pendent style that would have set off the low necklines of 19th-century ball gowns and evening dresses. Some are so long they reach almost to the shoulders. Since most pendent earrings are relatively lightweight and delicate, so as not to pull the ears, few examples survive in perfect condition. Throughout the 19th century it was highly fashionable for women to wear large numbers of decorative bracelets and bangles on each arm, over the bare wrist during the day and over elegant white evening gloves at night.

During the 1880s and 1890s chain and garland earrings hung from thin wires complemented the dainty fashions of the period. In the 1890s the screw fitting was introduced, allowing those without pierced ears to wear earrings. The loop fittings of many earlier earrings were replaced by screws; such an alteration will lower an item's value.

▲ Mesh bracelet
Pinchbeck was a very popular alternative to gold in the 1830s and 1840s, especially for mesh bracelets, as featured in the example above. However, it was little used after 1854, when lower carat standards of gold (12ct and 15ct) were introduced.
(c.1830; w. 4cm/1½in; value C)

◄ Girandole earrings
This design of girandole earring, set with rose-cut diamonds and amethysts, is very characteristic of 19th-century Spanish and Portuguese pieces. The stones are mounted in closed settings typical of the period, against colored foil to enhance their color. These earrings come with their original fitted retailer's case, which will add to their value.
(c.1780; l. 7cm/2¾in; value H)

BRACELETS AND BANGLES
The main difference between bracelets and bangles is that bracelets are composed of flexible links, while bangles are rigid. In the 1810s and early 1820s both fine bracelets of cameos, intaglios, and gemstones, joined with thin gold chains, and broad, gold mesh bangles with decorative clasps were all the rage. These were superseded in the late 1820s and the 1830s by large, gold, foliate, scroll links; and in the 1840s by snake bracelets of small, gold, articulated links, which curled around the wrist and were sometimes set with gems to represent scales and eyes.

A mid-19th-century novelty was the expanding bracelet, worn on various parts of the arm. The simplest form featured elastic connections, while more complex pieces had hinged, sprung links. Detachable gem-set features could be worn separately as pendants or pins. As with other types of jewelry Greek and Etruscan sources inspired some of the most popular bracelet designs of the 1860s and 1870s, which included pieces decorated with coins, cameos, or wirework. Bangles were very popular in the last two decades of the 19th century, and silver bangles, often with gold overlay in Japanese-style designs, were made in large numbers. More popular *c.*1900 were thin and delicate bracelets, usually with a row of gemstones at the front and expandable platinum or gold links at the back.

▲ Serpent bangle
This Victorian serpent bangle with a scale-like decoration is a fairly unusual piece, since on most serpent bracelets and bangles the snake clasps its tail in its mouth, symbolizing eternity. The use of 15ct gold dates this piece to after 1854.
(mid-19th century; w. 2.5cm/1in; value G)

► Pendent (or drop) earrings
These British earrings feature a fairly common Victorian design of architectural-style gold drops and balusters. Like many earrings from the period, the hollow gold drops would have been pressed out from a thin sheet of gold. Because the metal is thin and fragile, such earrings are easily damaged.
(1870s; l. 9cm/3½in; value G)

EARRINGS
In the late 18th and early 19th centuries the most popular design for formal earrings was the girandole or "chandelier" design, featuring a large, circular gemstone, usually a diamond, from which three matching pear-shaped stones or motifs were suspended. In the 1820s and 1830s the majority of large pendent earrings were still in the form of long, pear-shaped drops hung from a cluster of gems or a single gemstone. In the 1840s earrings went out of fashion as hair was worn parted into two bandeaux, covering the ears; from the 1850s hair was brushed away from the ears, and earrings came back into fashion for day and evening wear.

As is typical of Victorian jewelry, mid- to late 19th-century earrings were produced in a bewildering range of materials and designs, including plain hoops, crosses, stars, naturalistic or novelty designs (insects, flowers, and windmills), and rosettes and *amphorae* inspired by Greek and Etruscan gold jewelry. Favorite materials included coral, jet, ivory, enamel, and tortoiseshell. During the 1870s long, gold, novelty and Etruscan Revival earrings were the height of fashion.

▼ Earrings
Openwork garland designs of flowers and leaves were very popular on Edwardian jewelry. These high-quality British diamond earrings are set in silver and gold. Platinum was sometimes used for mounts in the early 20th century.
(c.1890; l. 5cm/2in; value H)

◄ Bangle
In the 19th century buckles and straps, as on this British example, were popular motifs on silver bangles, bracelets, and rings.
(c.1880; w. 3.5cm/1¼in; value B)

KEY FACTS
- DESIGNS historically, earrings were in either pendent or hoop form – studs are a relatively modern invention; Classically inspired and novelty designs were popular for both earrings and bracelets
- CONDITION loop fittings on earrings should preferably be original but can easily be replaced; alterations will affect value; links and clasps on bracelets and bangles should be original and in good condition
- CARE gold mesh on early 19th-century bracelets is hard to replace; such items should be stored carefully
- COLLECTING earrings and bracelets with signatures of notable makers, such as the Castellani or Giuliano families, are rare and valuable; parures (earrings, necklace, and pin) or demi-parures (earrings and pin) in original fitted cases are particularly desirable, as pieces are generally still in good condition

See also Sentimental jewelry, pp.268–9; Art Nouveau: Jewelry, pp.406–7; Art Deco: Jewelry, pp.438–9; Mid-century Modern: Jewelry, p.452

Sentimental jewelry

Throughout history jewels have been used to express emotions, usually love (and linked to betrothal and marriage), but also friendship, grief, or loyalty to a king or cause. Sentimental jewelry, covering a broad cross-section of periods and styles, has always been a popular area of collecting, not only because of the romantic messages and charming motifs used – often with intriguing secret meanings – but also because so many pieces bear inscriptions, dates, or references, which act as social and historical documentation. Mourning jewelry, which can be much undervalued because of its melancholic associations, was worn from the 17th century, but most abundantly throughout the 19th century, to commemorate the deaths of loved ones. The Victorians immersed themselves in romance, nature, and sentiment, and jewelry that is heavily layered with meaningful motifs dates mostly from the 19th century. Motifs include hearts, cupids, flowers, and messages.

◄ **Mourning pin**
This British pin of Whitby jet is elaborately carved with a central cross, representing faith, and intertwining ivy leaves, symbolizing fidelity. The central boss has a ropework border, a typical feature of carved jet jewels. The pin has a locket compartment at the back, which is intended to hold a lock of hair.
(c.1860–70; l. 4cm/1½in; value B)

MOURNING JEWELRY

The fashion for mourning jewelry developed from the 17th-century custom of bequeathing specially made rings to friends and relatives to be worn in memory of the deceased. In the 17th and early 18th centuries *memento mori* rings were decorated with black enamel, often with such macabre motifs as skulls and bones, hourglasses, and picks and shovels. By the Neo-classical period rings, pins, and pendants were ornamented with allegorical scenes painted in sepia on ivory or enamel, sometimes incorporating hair and seed pearls. Typical scenes featured Classical urns, tombs, crosses, weeping willows, and grieving widows; high-minded mottoes were also often incorporated. Settings were usually of plain gold and of oval, octagonal, or *marquise* shape; they sometimes featured blue, black, and white enamel, or pearls, which signify tears. Black enamel remains one of the most instantly recognizable features of mourning jewelry; white enamel is generally thought to signify the death of a spinster or a child. Dates of birth and death were usually engraved on the reverse of a piece.

The Victorians took mourning etiquette extremely seriously, especially as Queen Victoria spent most of her reign in mourning for Prince Albert (*d.*1861) and her public followed suit. Black jewelry therefore became fashionable. Typical designs, which were all made in such huge quantities and such a variety of styles that many remain available today, included gold or silver-gilt pins with engraved floral frames enameled in black; tortoiseshell jewelry; pieces in jet and "French" jet (a shiny black glass substitute); and brown bog oak jewelry. In Whitby, North Yorkshire, the jet industry flourished from the 1860s to the 1880s: beads, round and smooth or faceted and glittering, were made in profusion, and bracelets, lockets, and pins were elaborately carved with flowers such as lilies, ferns, and forget-me-nots, or fashioned into serpents, love-knots, cameos, or hands holding wreaths. In the USA, where mourning etiquette was also strict, gold jewelry with black enamel, intricate chasing, and gold fringes came into fashion in the 1860s and 1870s.

SYMBOLS AND MOTIFS

The heart is the most obvious and widely used sentimental motif, but an understanding of other symbols adds to the fascination of sentimental jewelry. From the ancient Roman device of clasped hands came the hand of friendship, a popular motif throughout the 19th century, notably for fede rings (from the Italian *fede* meaning "faith"), which featured a clasped pair of hands. These were typically given as tokens of affection or as engagement rings. The love-knot, also derived from an ancient motif, was equally popular for Victorian betrothal rings, as well as for chunky pins in gilt metal, which look surprisingly modern. The love-bird, often formed of intricately chased gold as well as of less expensive silver, was popular during the early Victorian period, and was often depicted with a love letter or a forget-me-not in its beak. The serpent, representing wisdom, is the most ubiquitous of all 19th-century motifs and was frequently depicted with its tail in its mouth to symbolize eternal love. The frog, popular from the 1860s to the end of the 19th century, often in pavé-set turquoises, meant wedded bliss. Other fashionable 19th-century animal and insect motifs include the lizard (the Roman symbol of wedded bliss), the butterfly (the symbol of the soul), the bee (possibly because it was the emblem of the Bonaparte dynasty), and, in men's jewelry, such images of power and agility as the eagle, the horse, and other sporting or hunting beasts. A heart-shaped padlock, sometimes with a tiny key, was a regular feature on much early to mid-19th-century jewelry. Cupid was a popular motif, while an anchor signified hope.

The study of the language of flowers became a fashionable pastime for young ladies. Each flower had a specific meaning: the forget-me-not (usually set with turquoises) meant true love, ivy

◄ **Entwined-heart ring**
This highly decorative and extravagant British example featuring diamonds and a sapphire is likely to have been given as an engagement ring. It incorporates the ever-popular Victorian theme of two entwined hearts, surmounted by a ribbon bow, which symbolizes the tying together of the lovers. Heart rings are still very popular and sought-after as engagement rings, and prices will vary according to the size, age, and quality of the stones.
(l880; value H)

▼ **Gimmel ring**
This is a l9th-century British version of the ancient gimmel ring, revived in medieval times and in the l9th century, in which the gold ring splits into two or more hoops, signifying the uniting of two loves in marriage. Here the clasped hands of faith open to reveal twin hearts, which are brightly enameled in red, the color of love.
(c.l850; value E)

▼ **Forget-me-not earrings**
This subtle, elegant combination of colors and materials – gray cut steel, blue enamel, and white imitation pearl – was particularly fashionable in Britain at the end of the l9th century. Trends in all types of jewelry continued to become increasingly understated into the beginning of the 20th century to suit Edwardian tastes. These earrings feature a circle of eternal love composed of powder blue enamel forget-me-nots – a symbol of true love
(c.l890; l. 3.5cm/1¼in; value C)

signified fidelity, pansies represented thoughtfulness, and the fern, sincerity. The language of stones was also often used in early 19th-century jewelry to convey messages of love. Gemstones or paste gems were arranged in such a way that their initials spelled such words as DEAREST, AMORE, SOUVENIR, or REGARD (perhaps a ruby, an emerald, a garnet, an amethyst, a ruby, and a diamond) in acrostic designs. Occasionally a name could be spelled in this way, but jewelers often had to use old terms or select unusual stones to compose a particular word. The gems were often clustered on small, intricately chased, and finely colored gold charms such as heart padlocks, while forget-me-nots might be surrounded by gem-set petals. In the 1830s and 1840s the combination of turquoises and rubies came to be associated with love.

Inexpensive pins stamped out of silver were produced in Birmingham in huge quantities and with amazing variety during the 1880s and 1890s. They were laden with sentimental motifs, especially symbolic flowers, and often overlaid with rose gold. Inexpensive silver and 9ct gold name pins were made in pierced openwork, along with "mother" or "baby" pins (the latter sometimes also with a pram motif), "good luck" pins, pieces bearing religious mottoes, and jewelry carrying seasonal or festive greetings.

► "Mizpah" pin
MIZPAH was a religious term used on Victorian sentimental pins. MIZPAH (literally translated as "watch-tower") is a modern Hebraic parting salutation meaning "the Lord watch between me and thee, when we are absent one from another." Most such pins were in the form of twin hearts, as in this silver-gilt example. One heart features "MIZPAH" over the biblical text, the other heart bears a cross (faith), an anchor (hope), and a heart (charity).
(c.1880–90; w. 5cm/2in; value **A***)*

◄ "Cupid" pin
Made at the height of the early Victorian craze for romanticism, this highly elaborate British pin features an intricately enameled Cupid, the playful messenger of love, playing a diamond-encrusted lyre, while sitting among diamond- and gem-set clouds. The pin is draped with a gold chain from which hang two freshwater pearls. Other common symbols of love included the heart, the love-knot, the love-bird, the rose, clasped hands, and the forget-me-not.
(c.1830; l. 4cm/1½in; value **K***)*

▲ Anchor pin
In the late 19th century the anchor was used as a symbol of hope and as such was a favorite expression of Victorian piety. Although it was frequently featured as decoration on both love and mourning jewelry, it is relatively unusual to find the jewel itself in the form of an anchor as in the British engraved silver example shown above.
(c.1880; l. 8cm/3in; value **B***)*

HAIR JEWELRY
Human hair was widely used in sentimental jewelry of all kinds, from love to mourning jewelry. In the 17th and early 18th centuries woven hair, along with gold wire initials and seed pearls, was fitted into small gold and crystal buckles or slides, which were then worn on ribbon around the neck or wrist. These are some of the earliest jewelry of sentiment still available. From c.1800 hairwork became enormously popular, with the hair arranged into highly complicated patterns by skilled hairworkers and set into pins or lockets, or even more intricately woven into items of jewelry.

MINIATURES
Miniatures, usually tiny mementos of deceased or loved ones that were carried in specially designed items of jewelry, have been popular since Elizabethan times. Portrait miniatures (and later, photographs) were hidden in lockets, pins, or bracelets – a fashion encouraged by Queen Victoria's passion for sentimental souvenirs. The portrait compartment could be held at the front or, more discreetly, at the back of a piece of jewelry. Mourning miniatures, sometimes holding not only a picture but also a lock of the deceased's hair, were common in the Victorian period. A late 18th-century innovation, popular with collectors, was the painted miniature of an eye, set in an oval or kidney-shaped mount, and recognizable only to a loved one.

KEY FACTS

Mourning jewelry
- COLLECTING mourning jewelry very obviously associated with death is generally unsaleable and inexpensive, but some late 18th and early 19th century pieces can command high prices; very macabre jewelry, e.g. featuring a death's head or a skull and crossbones, is a specialist area of collecting and can be costly

Symbols and motifs
- MAIN DESIGNS hearts, flowers, animals, patriotic emblems, acrostic designs, name pins

Hair jewelry
- DESIGNS hair was used to adorn all types of jewelry from pins and lockets to earrings and miniatures; it was typically intricately woven, plaited, or fanned out to form such shapes as feathers
- COLLECTING most 17th-century pieces are mourning items; 19th-century pieces range from mourning jewelry to gifts exchanged as a mark of affection

Miniatures
- THEMES most feature portraits or pictures; some hold locks of hair; depictions of eyes, often encircled by a serpent border, are an unusual but popular subject
- COLLECTING eye miniatures from the late 18th century are highly collectible, particularly in Britain

► "Regard" pin
Acrostic pins were especially popular in Britain in the 19th century. Early pieces were made of gold set with gemstones; later in the century imitation gold was set with colored pastes to produce less expensive pieces. The example shown is of gilt metal, engraved with twigs to represent the romance of nature, and features paste gems, the initials of which spell REGARD.
(c.1860; w. 6cm/2½in; value **C***)*

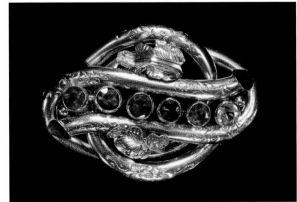

See also Men's jewelry, p.270

Men's jewelry

Men often wore as much jewelry as women until the late 18th century, when leaders of fashion – notably the British dandy Beau Brummell – initiated the trend toward simpler styles of clothing and minimal jewelry. Since the 19th century men's jewelry has been restricted mainly to tiepins, cufflinks, fobs, and signet rings.

TIEPINS

The focal point of fashionable dress was the necktie or cravat, fastened with a tiepin: a long pin with a decorative finial. Late 18th-century tiepins are usually shorter than later examples, with a zigzag pattern in the middle of the pin for security. Designs were fairly simple, and usually made from paste or foil-backed gemstone finials in closed settings.

The Victorian fashion for mourning jewelry resulted in the design of lozenge-shaped tiepin tops, painted with sentimental scenes of weeping willows, urns, or grieving figures. A wide range of designs, ranging from patriotic and political emblems to sporting and hunting motifs, was produced in the 19th century, illustrating the Victorian enthusiasm for novelty. Popular decorative materials included diamonds, carved coral, and turquoises; the very finest examples were highly detailed, with chased gold. Late 19th- and early 20th-century mass-produced tiepins in 9ct gold are mostly simpler in design and setting than those made earlier in the 19th century. Victorian tiepins were typically designed with a spiral ridge near the top of the pin to hold them in place.

CUFFLINKS

Introduced in the early 19th century, cufflinks, now increasingly popular for women as well as for men, are inserted into buttonholes to join the two ends of a cuff around the wrist. They are made in several designs, which generally reflect those of tiepins. The best-quality cufflinks – usually early 19th-century designs – are made in 15ct or 18ct gold and have fine detailing; many late 19th- and early 20th-century pieces were mass-produced and made of only 9ct gold. Most cufflinks were made as identical pairs and, particularly in the late 19th century, were sold in fitted boxes with matching buttons and press studs. Similar to cufflinks, such buttons consist of two separate pieces, which press together to grip the shirt.

RINGS AND FOBS

Among the most common types of ring worn by men are seal or signet rings, originally used for authenticating documents by impressing the seal into wax. Signet rings made before the late 19th century are generally of gold or silver, set with a semi-precious stone, and carved with a coat of arms, crest, or monogram. From the late 19th century signet rings in the form of simple 9ct gold bands engraved with a monogram were produced on a large scale for the expanding middle-class market.

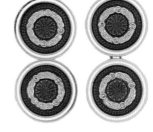

▲ **Selection of tiepins**
The above British tiepins were all typical Victorian designs. They include (from left to right) an inscribed black enamel mourning pin with a hair inset, a Scottish pebble dirk, an archeological revival-style example, and a leaping hare pin.
(all 19th century; l. of longest: 10cm/4in; value for each **A/B**)

◄ **Scarab cufflinks**
These finely detailed, high-quality, 18ct gold scarab beetle cufflinks from Italy show the influence of the Egyptian Revival style, which was popular in jewelry from the 1860s.
(c.1880; value **C**)

▼ **Sporting cufflinks**
These British cufflinks feature polo scenes in the reverse intaglio technique; this involves carving out and then painting a design on the back of a cabochon crystal so the image appears trapped underneath.
(c.1900; value **G**)

Introduced in the early 18th century, fob seals were also used for sealing letters and papers. Worn on watch chains, they were made in many designs, of which the earliest is a simple, domed metal setting with a seal-engraved hardstone on the base. From the 1830s settings were more elaborate, chased with designs of scrollwork, flowers, or animals' heads. Swivel seals – a swiveling, prism-shaped seal mounted horizontally in a stirrup-shaped setting – were also popular from this period.

▼ **Oval-and-baton cufflinks**
These American oval-and-baton cufflinks, typically more ornate than most modern examples, are set with cabochon rubies, emeralds, and diamonds. These are all highly valuable stones, indicating that the cufflinks would probably have been worn with formal evening dress.
(c.1900; value **F**)

▲ **Cufflinks**
The use of blue *guilloché* and white enamel with diamond-set wreaths on these French cufflinks shows the influence of late 18th-century French Neo-classical jewelry.
(c.1910; value **G**)

▼ **Serjeants-at-Law ring**
This ring was made by W. & E. Hopkins, in London. It was the custom for an English barrister to present this type of simple gold ring, often engraved with a Latin legal motto, to the sovereign, judges, officials, and friends on his appointment to the judicial post (abolished in 1875) of Serjeants-at-Law.
(1806; value **D**)

▲ **Intaglio ring**
This British signet ring features a banded agate engraved seal of a bearded man with a chased serpent border around the bezel. Other common materials for hardstone seals include onyx, bloodstone, and amethyst.
(c.1830; value **C**)

KEY FACTS

- CONDITION tiepins should always be in good condition, without damaged or bent pins or replaced tops; signet rings and fobs: seals or engraving should preferably be sharp and well-defined
- COLLECTING tiepins and cufflinks in novelty designs, especially with sporting themes, are highly collectible; cufflinks with original links are more valuable than those with modern replacement links; dress sets of matching cufflinks and studs in original fitted boxes are rare and valuable, especially those with a mark of a well-known maker; gold signet rings are generally more popular than those with large hardstone seals, as they are much more comfortable to wear

See also Textiles: Costume – Menswear, p.345

Costume jewelry

Purely decorative jewelry made of non-precious materials is often more evocative of its age than precious jewels. Worn since antiquity when the Romans excelled at glass imitation gemstones, this "secondary" jewelry exhibits impeccable craftsmanship and clever use of strong period style at relatively low cost. Jewelry on the market dates from the late 18th, 19th, and 20th centuries and is mostly British or European. It is usually either imitative, such as paste, or innovative, such as the Victorian blood-red Bohemian garnets.

PASTE JEWELRY

Jewelry set with cut and polished lead-glass in imitation of gemstones was first created in France in the 1730s by the jeweler Georges-Frédéric Strass (1701–73). Paste (or "strass") was often cut and backed with foil to give color and depth, and set in silver (sometimes gold), in dish-like collet settings. Strass jewels were popular in France and Britain, and in Spain they were worn at court. Late 18th-century *rivière* necklaces, girandole earrings, and stylized clusters gave way in the 19th century to figural designs, love-birds, and crosses. Paste shoe buckles were made in vast numbers; their impracticability has ensured that prices remain low.

▼ *Girandole* pin
This extravagantly decorative Spanish pin in the *girandole* form is set with paste "rubies" in silver. The focus in jewelry in the late 18th century was on the gemstones themselves rather than the settings. This pendant is part of a "parure," still with its original case, and would therefore be very desirable.
*(c.1760; w. 6.5cm/2½in; value **H**)*

◄ Butterfly pin
This British Vauxhall glass pin is highly typical of 19th-century jewelry in its design – insect jewelry was particularly popular during the Victorian period.
*(c.1880; w. 5.5cm/2¼in; value **C**)*

OTHER MATERIALS

Pinchbeck (an alloy of copper and zinc) was invented c.1720 by the English watchmaker Christopher Pinchbeck (1670–1723) as a substitute for gold. The perfect partner for paste, it was intricately chased, engraved, and colored like fashionable goldwork. Popular pinchbeck jewels included wide mesh bracelets, muff chains, hair ornaments, watches, and chatelaines. Other imitations followed in France and Germany, but "genuine" pinchbeck is characterized by its rich burnished color, matt surface, and buttery softness. Later 19th-century gilt metal, often erroneously called pinchbeck, was ideal for less expensive versions of fashionably extravagant jewelry, lockets, bracelets, bangles, and pins.

Cut-steel jewelry made of bluish-gray steel studs, faceted and highly polished to impart a soft sheen, became popular in Britain in the late 18th century. The technique originated in Woodstock, Oxfordshire, and by the mid-19th century had spread to France. From the end of the 18th century, steelworkers produced belt buckles, buttons, chatelaines, hair ornaments, chains, bags, and purses. Until the 1820s jewelry was made with individual multifaceted studs, each separately riveted to a metal backing.

▼ Earrings
In the 18th and early 19th centuries pinchbeck was widely used to create such imitation jewelry as these British pendent earrings. Fashionable techniques used on genuine gold, including intricate filigree work, or cannetille, could also be imitated on pinchbeck. From 1854 when lower, less expensive gold caratage was introduced, pinchbeck proved less popular.
*(c.1820; l. 8cm/3in; value **D**)*

▲ "Berlin ironwork" pin
This romantic floral design is typical of the fashionable iron jewelry known as Berlin ironwork, which was extremely popular both in Germany and France in the early to mid-19th century.
*(19th century; w. 6cm/2½in; value **C**)*

Later jewels were composed of stamped strips of larger, uniform studs with fewer facets. Black ironwork in lacy designs, known as "Berlin ironwork," was first made by Berlin armorers during the Franco-Prussian war (1813–15) in exchange for valuable jewelry offered by women in support of the war effort. Suitable for mourning wear, it lent itself well both to the Neo-classical taste and to the architectural Gothic Revival style.

At the height of 19th-century consumerism, novelty jewelry was made in every conceivable material: ivory, coral, volcanic lava carved as cameos, petrified beetles and birds' heads set in gold or gilt metal, and marcasite, a bright gray mineral that resembles diamonds.

KEY FACTS

Paste jewelry
- PROPERTIES paste: air bubbles in a "gemstone" suggest that it is paste
- CONDITION paste is easily scratched, so condition is important; check that foiling is in good condition
- COLLECTING paste: 18th-century pieces lighter than later examples; Georgian paste (with depth and soft sparkle) is considerably more valuable than mid- to late-19th-century paste, which tends to be imitative of diamonds, and rather lackluster in design; parures are rare and expensive; earrings are desirable but rare

Other materials
- PROPERTIES pinchbeck: has a soft, warm color with a matt finish
- DESIGNS cut steel: early designs are made of studs held in separate facets; later designs feature strips of studs
- CONDITION cut steel rusts easily so ensure that it is protected from damp environments
- COLLECTING pinchbeck: most pieces date from before c.1850, so beware of late-19th-century gilt-metal imitations; later novelty pins: butterflies, keys, arrows, and birds are easier to find than early works; the market for Berlin ironwork is small and specialized; Berlin iron crosses tend to be relatively inexpensive

See also Pins, p.265; 20th-century costume jewelry, pp.272–3

20th-century costume jewelry

The 20th century saw an unprecedented expansion in the market for costume jewelry, triggered in the USA by the 1929 Wall Street Crash. Jewelers working with precious stones struggled to find work and turned to non-precious stones instead. Their inexpensive designs became an affordable luxury for many during the Depression and as prosperity resumed, women bought new costume jewelry regularly, to suit the latest fashions. A similar revolution was happening in France, where

▼ Trifari poinsettia pin

Designed by Alfred Philippe for Trifari, this pin has an elaborate configuration of faux rubies and diamonds. The design incorporates the "invisible setting" technique developed by Philippe for Van Cleef and Arpels – one of various techniques introduced to Trifari by Philippe.

(c.1950s; diam. 7cm/2¾in; value E)

couturier Coco (Gabrielle) Chanel (1883–1971) embellished her simple jersey outfits with multiple gilt chains and faux pearl necklaces and heavy, rigid cuff bracelets. Her rivals Elsa Schiaparelli and Christian Dior were among others to include costume jewelry in their ranges – and so a trend began.

TRIFARI

New York jewelry Trifari (est. *c.*1910) – founded by jewelry Gustavo Trifari, sales manager Leo Krussman, and salesman Carl Fishel – was especially adept at producing jewelry for cocktail parties.

French designer Alfred Philippe imbued Trifari with the idea of using advanced techniques and alternative materials from the 1930s to 1960s. Philippe introduced hand-set rhinestones in necklaces, bracelets, and earrings, which were wrought in a host of different styles. He was also renowned for his high-quality Swarovski crystals, with the company becoming known as the Diamanté Kings. Other popular jewels were the floral, foliate, and fruit pins of the 1930s and 1940s. While metals in retail were prohibited during World War

II, Philippe turned to heavy sterling silver and vermeil (gold-plated) finish, and Lucite, a plastic similar to rock crystal. Among the most notable Trifari pieces was a necklace and earring set, composed of faux pearls, emeralds, and diamonds, for First Lady Mamie Eisenhower in the 1950s.

ELSA SCHIAPARELLI

Italian designer Elsa Schiaparelli (1890–1973) brought bright colors to haute couture in the 1920s at a time when brown, blue, and black were popular. Her pieces were quirky and featured circus imagery and astrological motifs. The arts movements of Futurism, Surrealism, and Neoclassicism influenced Schiaparelli's designs. She was friends with the Surrealist artists Salvador Dali, Jean Cocteau, and Christian Berard, who designed pieces for her. As the new technology of plastic emerged in the 1920s and 1930s, Schiaparelli found another source of inspiration in Bakelite. In the 1950s Schiaparelli moved to New York where abstract, floral, and faunal designs incorporating colorful stones and glass were made under license.

CORO

Reputedly one of the most successful companies in the USA in the 1930s and 1940s, Coro claimed to be the largest costume jewelry manufacturer in the world. The firm started life as an accessories boutique, founded by businessmen Emanuel Cohn and Carl Rosenberger, who outsourced much of the costume jewelry from independent designers, before opening a large factory in Providence, Rhode Island, in 1929. From patriotic motifs, through floral and foliate, to figural, Coro offered a huge number of styles at affordable prices, aimed at the middle and lower sections of the market, while an upmarket brand, Coro Craft, used more expensive materials such as sterling silver and European crystal rhinestones. Design director Adolph Katz created numerous pieces, including the Coro Duette, in 1931, among which the figural Duettes were the most popular. They featured flowers, birds, and other animals, made of vermeil sterling silver and decorated with colorful enameling and crystal rhinestones.

EUGENE JOSEFF

By 1930, the USA – now fully industrialized – offered the technical know-how to produce costume jewelry on a huge scale. Much of the jewelry's popularity lay in Hollywood, where its projection on the big screen triggered a demand for costume copies. American designer Eugene Joseff (1905–1948) supplied the major studios, with Greta Garbo, Grace Kelly, and Clark Gable among the stars wearing his matt finish 'Russian gold' jewelry, developed specifically for the screen.

▲ Demi-parure, designed by Elsa Schiaparelli

This set comprises a necklace, bracelet and earrings. The rhodium-plated links with prong-set blue and green glass stones and aurora borealis rhinestones are typical of Schiaparelli's later costume pieces.

(c.1950s; necklace l. 38cm/15in; bracelet l. 19.5cm/7¾in; earring l. 2.5cm/1 in value G)

▼ Adolph Katz Coro Duette

The Coro Duette, introduced in 1931 allowed two identical or similar clips to be fastened together and worn as one pin, or detached and worn separately. This floral example is set with green crystal baguettes and clear crystal rhinestones.

(c.1940s; ht 6.5cm/2½in; value B)

Joseff, and his company Joseff of Hollywood, created historically accurate jewelry which was loaned, rather than sold, to the studios. In time he built up an archive of three million pieces, many of which were then copied and sold to star-struck fans through department stores. His work can be seen in films as diverse as *The Wizard of Oz*, *Gone with the Wind*, and *Easter Parade*.

MIRIAM HASKELL

The employment of skilled émigré European craftsmen in a booming post-war USA during the 1920s and 1930s benefited designers like Miriam Haskell (1899–1981).

▼ Shell-pendant necklace with a faux pearl, by Joseff

This is a retail version of an original worn by, among others, actresses Virginia Mayo and Pier Angeli. Russian gold plating gave the pendant a matt-gold finish that reduced sparkle under bright studio lights.

(c.1940s; shell l. 2cm1in; value C)

glass, seed pearls, and rose montées. In contrast, her pins and earrings had floral and foliate motifs. To promote her jewelry, Haskell acquired a front-of-store retail outlet in Sak's Fifth Avenue, and had a similar setup with Harvey Nichols, London.

STANLEY HAGLER

Stanley Hagler (1923-1996) worked briefly as a business adviser to Haskell. He similarly produced intricately designed, handcrafted jewelry. His first piece was a gold-plated bangle decorated with hand-wired flowers for the Duchess of Windsor. His faux pearls were handblown glass beads dipped in pearl resin up to 15 times to achieve maximum luminosity. Using fine materials, such as Swarovski crystals and 'Russian gold' filigree, pieces were wired by hand, with stones and crystals prong-set into place. While Hagler won 11 Swarovski awards for "Great Design in Jewelry", the essential feature of his jewelry was that it was often multi-purpose: necklaces can become double bracelets, or the clasp of a necklace a hair ornament or pin.

CHRISTIAN DIOR

French designer Christian Dior's (1905-1957) first haute couture "New Look" collection of 1947 was complemented by well-made and showy costume jewelry and set the tone of women's fashions well in to the 1960s. Dior deployed unusual pastes and stones, such as the iridescent, polychromatic aurora borealis rhinestones, which were honed by a crystal stone supplier. While early Dior pieces were made exclusively for clients such as the Hollywood actresses Marilyn Monroe and Bette Davis, his later pieces were sold through retail outlets under license.

► Christian Dior necklace and earrings

The essence of Dior was the way in which his jewelry was a vital and integral part of his fashion. The use of colorful blue glass and faux pearls in a classic setting, as displayed in this necklace and earring set, is typical of his style.

(c.1960; pendant ht 11cm/4¼in; value F)

▲ Miriam Haskell pin

Alternate bands of small faux baroque pearls and antiqued gilt metal are flanked by large baroque pearls and topped with antiqued gilt metal leaves covered with clear rose montées. The luster of Haskell's faux pearls came from immersion in a secret formula, which Haskell called *essence d'orient*.

(c.1960; l. 7.5cm/3in; value C)

For her innovative and complex jewelry – which enraptured the USA as much as Coco Chanel's did Paris – was handmade to the highest standards, using the best materials, sourced by chief designer Frank Hess. Faux pearls were among the most notable of Haskell's materials, although she also used glass beads from Murano and faceted crystals from Austria. Her necklaces had single or multiple strands of faux pearls, Murano beads, pressed and poured French

► Stanley Hagler camelia pin

Stanley Hagler was renowned for producing handcrafted pieces of the very finest quality. This stylized camelia pin is typical of his intricate designs and uses pearlized metal with pressed red glass, red faux seed pearls, and clear crystal rhinestones.

(c.1960s; diam. 8.25cm/3¼in; value C)

KEY FACTS

- METHODS/STYLES Joseff: Russian gold, set with rhinestones and crystals; Trifari: stones invisible or pavé set, prong and glue set, cold enameling, Jelly Bellies; Schiaparelli: Early pieces inspired by Surrealism, pieces dating from the 1950s usually abstract or floral jewels with colorful stones and glass; Coro: Duettes and Jelly Bellies; Haskell and Hagler: hand-wired beads onto Russian gold filigree backing. Rose montées, fake pearls, Murano glass beads; Dior: High quality, unusual pastes and stones. Diverse inspiration.

Marks
Joseff: "JOSEFF" or "JOSEFF OF HOLLYWOOD"; Trifari: "K.T.F"; "Trifari"; Schiaparelli: "Schiaparelli" in script; Coro: "Coro" or "Corocraft" in script; Miriam Haskell: "MIRIAM HASKELL" in oval cartouche; Steven Hagler: "STANLEY HAGLER N.Y.C"; Christian Dior: "Christian Dior", often with date.

See also Costume jewelry, pp.271

Although much antique glassware remains in domestic use, most pieces are admired today for their aesthetic qualities, with a tremendous diversity of shape, color, and decorative detail found in wares of all periods, from *c.*3000 BC to the late 20th century. However, it is the delicate, almost magical translucency of much glassware that is particularly compelling, and this can be considerably enhanced when pieces are displayed under favorable lighting conditions. The range of glassware available also offers tremendous scope to collectors. Some specialize in certain types of glass, such as soda, potash, or lead crystal, while others acquire according to techniques of manufacture, such as or mold pressing; some collectors focus on shape, or color, or methods of decoration, notably enameling, cutting, gilding, and engraving. Other collectors seek out glassware by provenance, by historical period, or by a particular maker or factory. Many fascinating collections are simply based on one type of object, examples of which range from drinking glasses, bottles, and decanters, to paperweights and dumps (doorstops), candelabra and lusters, and small decorative items, such as bells, rolling pins, balls, walking-sticks, and knife-rests – collectively known as "friggers."

Detail of an armorial service by the Wear Flint Glass Works (left)
This plate and cooler from a British table service have been decorated with fan- and diamond-cutting. The service also includes a rinser (left), decanter, dishes, and carafes (c.*1830*).
Beaker, possibly engraved by Karl Pfohl Produced in Bohemia, this ruby-flashed beaker has a delicate wheel-engraved horse and a boldly cut base (c.*1840–50*).

Glass: Basics

There are three basic types of glass: soda glass (sometimes called soda-lime glass), potash, and lead glass (also known as lead crystal). Each of these types of glass is composed of a different mix of ingredients, which produces the individual characteristics of the glassware, including its weight, resonance, color, and light refraction. Specific handling techniques during the heating and after the cooling processes allows the glass to be worked in different ways; with some of these processes this results in the unique formation of each object and the type and means of decoration that can be done. Decorating techniques range from simple trailing to the very time-consuming and skilled methods of engraving and gilding.

Materials

The mixture or ingredients required to make glass is called a batch, and the components and the different proportions of the ingredients will determine the character of the glass. The basic component is silica (silicon dioxide), an abundant mineral found in sand, quartz, and flint. Coastal sand, although plentiful, is prone to impurities, and glassmakers have tended to use the purer inland sand deposits. Venetian glassmakers used pure white, crushed pebbles from the River Ticino for their supply of sand. Today sand is usually purified mechanically.

Pure silica has an extremely high melting point (1720°C), so a flux, most commonly in the form of soda (sodium carbonate) or potash (potassium carbonate), is added to the batch in order to reduce the temperature and help bind the other components together (vitrification). Broken glass (often fragments of imperfect or fractured pieces), known as cullet, has also been added as a flux since Roman times – an early example of recycling. Lime (calcium carbonate) is added to give the mixture stability. This basic composition is the most typical and comprises 75% silica, 15% soda, and 10% lime.

Soda glass As the name suggests, soda is the alkali used to make soda glass. Silica (60%), soda (25%), and calcium carbonate (chalk or lime; 15%) are heated to 1000°C; the resulting glass is light and, because it remains plastic for longer than other types of glass, is easier to shape and manipulate. This makes it highly suitable for Venetian and Venetian-style (façon de Venise) glass. Generally soda glass has a slightly brown, yellow, or green-grey hue, as seen on the 15th-century German *Maigelein* (small hemispherical bowl) seen above right. The alkali used was ashes of *barilla*, a type of seaweed that was imported from Alicante in Spain. The resulting glass is generally a pale yellow or a slightly grey color. *Cristallo* was a vastly improved type of soda glass that was developed in Venice, possibly by the glassmaker Angelo Barovier (d.1460), during the mid-15th century. Manganese oxide was added to decolorize the glass, and a fine, clear, colorless glass that could resemble rock crystal was produced. In England soda glass was made until lead glass was introduced c.1676 by the glassmaker George Ravenscroft (1632–83).

- Characteristics: soda: generally very light, slightly bubbly and thin walled; *cristallo* is a superior form of soda glass
- Used to make Roman, Egyptian, Venetian, and some Spanish glass

- Has a long working life and therefore is easily manipulated into interesting forms and shapes
- Lacks the resonance associated with lead glass
- Unsuitable for deep cutting or wheel engraving as it is thin and much harder than other types of glass
- Decoration: trailing, enameling, diamond-point engraving, and gilding are the most suitable
- Colors: tinged with yellow, grey, green, or brown; *cristallo* is colorless
- Still used in the 19th century for Venetian-style glass

Potash glass Potash (potassium carbonate) is the other alkali that is used in glassmaking, the alternative to soda, discussed above. In northern Europe, potash (potassium rich ash) was obtained by burning ferns and bracken (in France) or woods such as beech or oak (in Germany and Bohemia). This type of glass was made during from the Middle Ages and is usually referred to as *verre de fougère* ("fern" glass) or *Waldglas* ("forest" glass), as for this 14th-century German beaker seen below. Both types of potash glass have a characteristic green, yellow, or brown hue. Modern potash glass is made commercially with potassium chloride. In Bohemia, chalk is added to the batch to produce a colorless glass that is suitable for engraving. One of the important characteristics of potash glass is that it cannot be worked for long periods (short working life), which means that the forms tend to be simpler than the elaborate Venetian or *façon de Venise* wares made in soda glass. Potash glass is used extensively in the production of modern glassware.

- Characteristics: strong, light, and more brilliant, with a shorter working life than soda glass
- Color: generally has a distinctive green color or is colorless
- Decoration: because potash glass is tough it can be cut and engraved
- Types: *verre de fougère* and *Waldglas* – the names are used interchangeably

Lead or crystal glass This type of glass was discovered c.1676 by the glassmaker George Ravenscroft who, in an attempt to discover a remedy for crizzling (where the glass suffered from a covering of very fine lines in the body of the glass), added red lead (lead oxide) to the batch; not only did he solve the problem of this type of diseased glass, but he also created the brilliant lead glass. This type of glass contains a high percentage (24–30%) of red lead; the proportions have changed over time, but basically remain three parts silica, two parts red lead, and one part potash, with the addition of saltpeter, borax, and arsenic. The glass produced has a heavy, clear, bright, and comparatively soft body. It is easily worked into heavy, simple forms such as this English decanter of c.1800. Because lead glass is very dense, the refractive index is raised, and hence the glass has a characteristic brilliance that from the later 18th century was often enhanced by cutting and polishing. Its strength also made it suitable for engraving.

- Characteristics: heavy and brilliant, with great clarity
- Decoration: can be engraved, cut, and etched
- Can only really be described as full lead glass if it contains 30% red lead
- Uses: fine glassware, chandeliers, and candelabra

Forming techniques

After the ingredients (batch) have been fused together at a very high temperature, the metal is in a liquid or molten state. As it cools the metal becomes viscous and ductile, and can be manipulated into many different shapes and sizes by the use of a wide variety of techniques. The most important are free blowing, mold blowing, and mold pressing and these are discussed in more detail in their own sections below. However, a familiarity with other basic techniques will allow a greater understanding of glassmaking and the terms used, and an appreciation of glass generally. The most basic means of creating a glass object is by pouring the still molten metal into a mold or filling the mold with glass fragments; this technique is known as casting. This enables the creation of solid glass objects, such as beads, or small glass sculptures such as those made in ancient Egypt. Casting was revived in the late 19th century by Art Nouveau and later Art Deco glassmakers who made *pâte de verre* (glass paste) ware. The mosaic bowls made during the Hellenistic period (after the death of Alexander the Great in 323 BC and before the establishment of the Roman Empire *c*.30 BC) and by the Romans were created by laying slices of glass rods side by side on a flat surface and fusing them in the furnace. This fairly solid disc was draped over a ceramic form fashioned in the final desired shape and when placed in the furnace the disc softened and slumped over the ceramic form; hence the technique is called slumping.

Core forming One of the earliest processes for making glass was core forming or core winding, first invented c.2000 BC–c.1500 BC in Egypt and Mesopotamia. It involved building up a core of mud, straw, and clay around a metal rod that was then dipped into a crucible of hot glass. When there was enough glass on the core, it was lifted out and often decorated with a second contrasing color, which was trailed onto the surface and combed in. When the glass had cooled and hardened, the core was dug out, leaving a hollow glass vessel with a rough pitted interior.

- A process of limited use, as it was only really suitable on small and rather crudely shaped vessels such as this Etruscan aryballos (flask) of c.500 BC.
- Objects usually have very thick, roughly shaped bodies

Free blowing The most important breakthrough in the history of glassmaking was the invention of the blowing pipe or blowing iron, a long, hollow, metal pipe, which was probably developed in Syria during the 1st century BC. A gather (parison) of molten glass is collected onto the end of the blowing iron from a crucible in the furnace. The glassmaker rotates the viscous mass on the iron to keep it centered and then inflates it by blowing through the iron at the opposite end to create a hollow shape. A solid pontil

iron is attached to the opposite end of the bubble, which is then separated from the blowing iron. The form is then reheated, and the opening of the object is created. Finally, the shaped glass object is cracked off from the pontil, which leaves the characteristic "pontil mark." Glass blowing is the most difficult glassmaking process and requires great skill and dexterity. The fine mid-17th century flask seen above, which was made in the Low Countries, is a good example of free blowing.

- This technique is extremely difficult and requires great skill from the glassblower
- Thought to have been introduced in Mesopotamia during the 1st century BC
- Suitable for unique one-off pieces, as it is difficult to produce two identical pieces
- Can be left plain or further decorated with trailing

Mold blowing This technique, which was an early development of free blowing, was invented by the Romans in the 1st century AD. In mold blowing a bubble of molten glass is blown into a wooden or metal shaper, or a mold of two or more parts, to create a regular shape and, if desired, pattern, as seen on this English carafe (above right) of c.1850. If a full-size mold is used, then the glass is blown to give the complete shape. With a dip mold, partly blown molten glass is dipped into the mold to produce a pattern or shape, then removed, reheated, and, if necessary, re-blown to achieve the desired size,

while the pattern can be stretched and inflated. Further blowing will reduce the sharpness of the decoration.

- Less skill required than free blowing
- Method used for creating numerous versions of the same form
- Makes interestingly shaped and patterned glassware, including low-relief decoration
- Original molds made of fire-clay; from the 19th century metal molds were used

Mold pressing This technique was used from c.1827 in the USA (from c.1830 in Britain), originally to mass-produce inexpensive copies of elaborate hand-cut glass and then as a technique in its own right. The molten glass is poured into a metal mold of two or more parts that carries a negative of the pattern. A plunger is pressed down into the glass to form a smooth hollow interior and a mold-patterned exterior, as seen on this English "swan" posy bowl by Webb & Hammond of c.1874–5. Alternatively, a flat-ribbed mold was pressed into molten glass, which was then placed over another mold and allowed to "slump" – a process in which gravity forces the molten glass to conform to the shape of the mold on which it rests.

- Method for making many objects of an identical shape
- The glass inside an object is smooth, unlike that of mold-blown glass, which corresponds to the exterior
- Inexpensive method of reproducing copies of cut glass

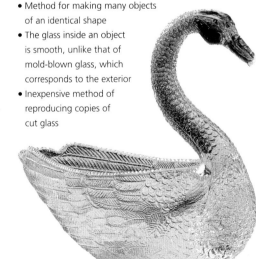

Decoration

Once the basic shape of the object has been completed by one of the forming techniques, it can be decorated in numerous ways. These involve either adding more glass to the object, taking glass away from it by cutting or engraving the surface, or by painting with enamels or gold.

COLORING

There are two main types of colored glass: glass in which the color is produced by impurities in the basic ingredients (for example, green bottle glass derives its color from iron in the silica), and transparent glass that has been colored deliberately by adding metallic oxides to the batch, or by such techniques as staining or flashing, and overlaying. Blue – as seen on this late 17th-century Dutch flask – is one of the easiest colors to produce, while red and orange are notoriously difficult.

- Colors: red (gold, copper, selenium); orange (carbon, sulfur); yellow (iron, cerium, uranium silver); green (iron, copper); blue (cobalt, copper); violet (manganese, nickel); white (arsenic, tin, fluorspar, calcium, phosphate)

ENAMELING

In this technique a mixture of metallic oxides and ground glass is suspended in an oil base; this is painted onto the surface of the glass, which is then fired to harden and fix the pattern. Colors require different firing temperatures, and therefore several firings were required. In cold enameling the decoration is not fired and is therefore very vulnerable to wear, so it was only used on decorative pieces such as this Austrian *Ranftbecher* of c.1850.

- Different colors require different firings, which is risky as the glass may shatter; cold enameling is likely to wear off
- The decoration stands slightly proud of the surface

ENGRAVING

This process involves cutting a design onto the glass using a sharp instrument. First introduced by Roman glassmakers, by the mid-17th century engraving had developed as an art. In wheel engraving the glass is held against a small rotating wheel (usually copper) fed with an abrasive, and the decoration is cut into the surface of the glass. Different sizes of wheel were used to control the precision and detail of the decoration, and the engraved area was either left matt or polished.

Diamond-point engraving One of the earliest forms of engraving was diamond-point engraving, in which a diamond-pointed stylus was used to scratch a surface lightly, and to make free-hand decorations and inscriptions such as on this English "Amen" glass of c.1750; it was suitable for soda glass that was too brittle for wheel engraving or cutting. The best 17th-century decoration was carried out by Dutch craftsmen.

- Technique was possibly used by the Romans but made famous by glass decorators working in the Low Counties during the 17th century on *façon de Venise* glass
- Light surface decoration
- Scratched marks are clearly seen when the glass is observed closely
- Technique superseded by wheel engraving during the 18th century

Stipple engraving In stipple engraving the design is produced by very gently striking a hard steel or diamond point against the glass to produce a series of small shallow dots. The glass decorator builds up areas of light and shade to create a design, as seen on this Dutch portrait glass of c.1780 by David Wolff (1732–98). Glass is an ideal medium for stipple engraving, as the design can be seen from both sides.

- Often only possible to see the design clearly by holding the glass up to the light
- Highlights are provided by the stippled areas, and the shadows by leaving the polished area untouched

Intaglio engraving Also sometimes known as *Tiefschnitt*, this technique involves hollowing out a design using wheel engraving as seen on this 19th-century English wine glass. It was first introduced in the late 16th or early 17th century in Germany and Bohemia, particularly by Caspar Lehman (1570–1622), and is used to create complex patterns. The technique is based on the ancient craft of gem engraving.

- The opposite technique to relief engraving
- Usually used on potash or lead glass, which are much more durable than soda glass
- The surface is usually polished

Relief engraving This technique is also known as *Hochschnitt*. The glass object is deeply cut with wheel engraving, leaving the design standing proud as seen on this early 18th-century Silesian cup and cover decorated by Friedrich Winter (d.c.1712), arguably the most famous exponent, who used a cutting mill driven by water power, which facilitated deep undercutting and carving in the round. The technique is very similar to that used for cutting a cameo. This type of glass decoration was first used in Silesia at the end of the 17th century and was very popular in Bohemia and Germany.

- The most elaborate examples are those in High Baroque style made during the late 17th and very early 18th century
- The opposite technique to *Tiefschnitt* or intaglio engraving
- Suitable for use on potash and lead glass, which because they are durable and thick, will withstand the depth of cutting

Surface engraving This type of wheel-engraving technique only slightly cuts the surface of the object. It is used for sketchy decoration and inscriptions, as seen on this English 19th-century decanter. Different sizes of wheel are used to create precise detail that is enhanced by the contrast of matt and polished glass.

- Used as decoration from the 16th century
- Difficult to feel the decoration on the surface of the glass
- Can be used for both simple and very complicated designs

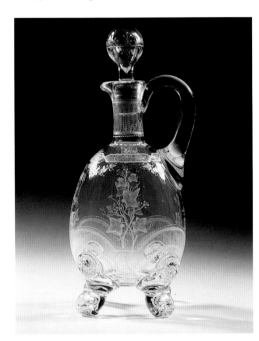

ACID ETCHING

This process uses hydrofluoric acid to cut a design into the surface of the glass. The glass object is covered with an acid-resistant coating (normally paraffin wax) through which the design is cut or scratched. The object is then dipped into hydrofluoric acid, which corrodes or "acid etches" the exposed outline of the design into the glass. The length of exposure to the acid controls the depth of the etching. The technique, as seen on this British tankard of 1873, was introduced for general use in Britain in the mid-19th century.

- An inexpensive, mechanical alternative to the more time-consuming technique of copper-wheel engraving

- Suitable for glass too thin for wheel engraving
- Superseded by sand blasting, a less expensive and less dangerous technique

CUTTING

Cutting glass creates facets that reflect the light and make the object sparkle. The technique was used as early as the 8th century BC, but in the 1st century BC the Romans were using glass-cutting techniques based on those employed by craftsmen working with gemstones. Glass is cut using discs of iron or stone, lubricated with water, against which the glass object is held; the profile of the cutting stone can be changed to give a different pattern, and the main types are: flat edged for facets; "V"-shaped for grooves in straight lines such as the strawberry diamond cuts on this bowl and cover of c.1825; and convex grooved for producing depressions or hollows.

- Steam power, which was introduced c.1830, enabled greater precision and depth of cutting

CAMEO

When an object is composed of two or more layers of glass, the top layer(s) may be cut back in relief to reveal the colors below. The technique was first practiced by the Romans as a way of copying hardstone cameos. The technique was revived during the 19th century, and in Britain one of the leading exponents was George Woodall (1850–1925), who made this vase c.1880.

- Intricately detailed, raised decoration
- An extremely difficult and time-consuming technique

GILDING

In gilding, gold is applied to the surface or the back of a glass object, either using a sticky fixative (e.g. honey) or mixing it into an amalgam with mercury. The gold is then fired in a kiln in order to fix it permanently, as seen on this Austrian scent bottle of c.1880 by Ludwig Moser. In cold gilding (or oil gilding) the gold is applied without firing, and is therefore vulnerable to wear; this technique is generally used to fill cut or engraved decoration so that the gold will be below surface level and therefore more protected. Other gilding processes include sandwiching engraved gold leaf between two layers of glass (*Zwischengoldglas*).

- Gilding was first used by the Romans
- Often used on edges
- Honey gilding has a warm hue, while mercury is thinner and brassier but cheaper and easier to apply

OTHER APPLIED DECORATION

There are many other types of applied decoration, the most popular of which are discussed here. Hot pieces of glass may be applied to a finished or nearly finished item. One of the most common types is prunts – blobs of glass – that can be pulled away from the surface and attached lower down the object or be impressed with a stamp to form "raspberries." Trailing can be a very simple form of applied decoration; molten glass is laid onto the surface of the glass, either as a simple trail, as seen on the English wine glass shown below made c.1870 by the Whitefriars Glassworks (est. 1680; from 1834 known as James Powell & Sons) in London, or spiraled, or as a lattice design as in "nipt-diamond-waies," a type of network decoration in the form of diamonds or lozenges made from glass threads nipped together. A development of trailing was combing, where the trails are marvered (rolled) into the surface and then tooled and combed with a pointed instrument into festoons; this is a distinctive type of decoration used on British Nailsea glass. The stems of drinking glasses can be decorated either by manipulating the air bubbles trapped inside them into extraordinary patterns (air twists), or by introducing glass of another color and creating very fine filigree patterns on the inside of the stem.

- Basic trailed decoration is the easiest and least time-consuming form of decoration.
- The most extraordinary use of trailed decoration is on Venetian and *façon de Venise* glass, made from the 16th century and revived from the mid-19th century during the Venetian Revival
- Decoration that appears on the outside of a glass object is prone to damage

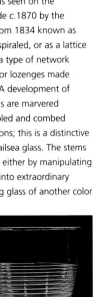

Forms and styles

Decorative patterns in cut glass are made with cutting disks – either flat, grooved, or hollowed, singly or in combination. Flutes, for example, are grooved, using straight or circular lines. Diamond cuts can be raised, flat, or hollow, with areas left cut or uncut. The patterns below have been used on all types of cut table glass.

Decanters and stoppers appear in a wide range of shapes and designs, and can either be uncut or cut; they generally match in decoration. Late 18th-century examples of decanters and stoppers had a plainer shape and pattern, but during the 19th century they became increasingly elaborate. The designs can be dependant upon the type of beverage the decanter holds, for instance spirits or wine.

Drinking glasses can be made of many sections: bowl, knop, stem (sometimes containing a twist), and foot. The shape, size, and design of such vessels are again a result of the type of beverage it is used for, and the decorative embellishments deemed appropriate to the period. Designs of drinking glasses have changed over time, often mirroring the other decorative arts of the period.

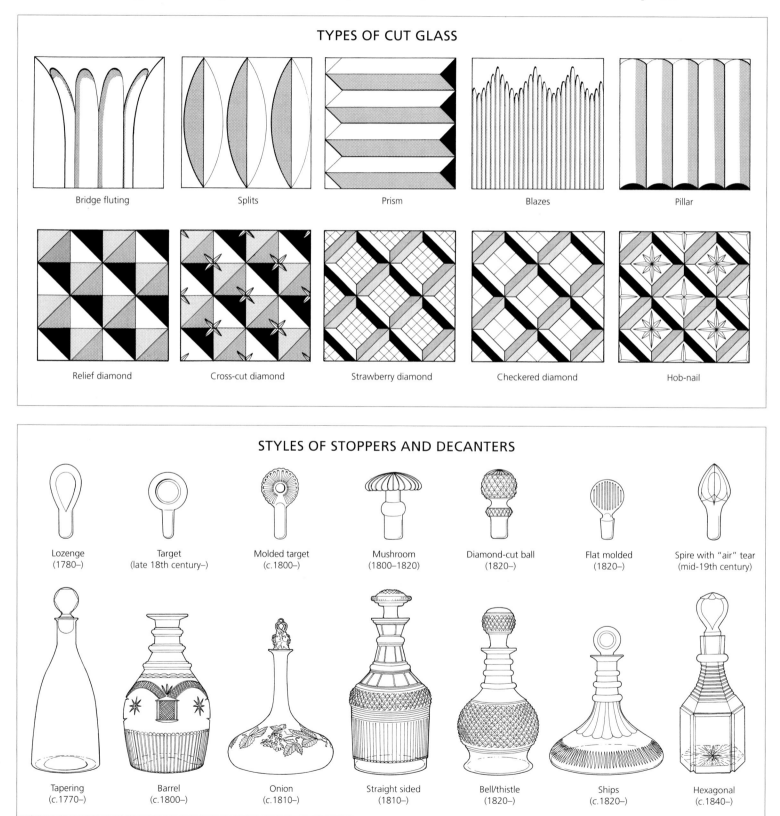

TYPES OF CUT GLASS

Bridge fluting

Splits

Prism

Blazes

Pillar

Relief diamond

Cross-cut diamond

Strawberry diamond

Checkered diamond

Hob-nail

STYLES OF STOPPERS AND DECANTERS

Lozenge (1780–)

Target (late 18th century–)

Molded target (c.1800–)

Mushroom (1800–1820)

Diamond-cut ball (1820–)

Flat molded (1820–)

Spire with "air" tear (mid-19th century)

Tapering (c.1770–)

Barrel (c.1800–)

Onion (c.1810–)

Straight sided (1810–)

Bell/thistle (1820–)

Ships (c.1820–)

Hexagonal (c.1840–)

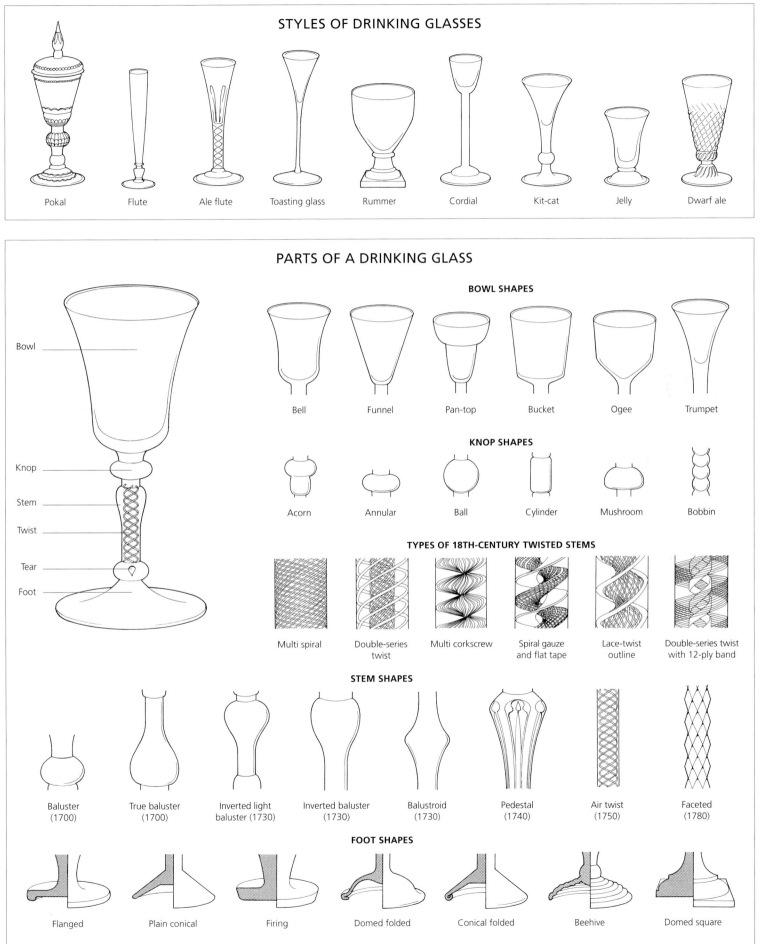

STYLES OF DRINKING GLASSES

Pokal Flute Ale flute Toasting glass Rummer Cordial Kit-cat Jelly Dwarf ale

PARTS OF A DRINKING GLASS

Bowl
Knop
Stem
Twist
Tear
Foot

BOWL SHAPES

Bell Funnel Pan-top Bucket Ogee Trumpet

KNOP SHAPES

Acorn Annular Ball Cylinder Mushroom Bobbin

TYPES OF 18TH-CENTURY TWISTED STEMS

Multi spiral Double-series twist Multi corkscrew Spiral gauze and flat tape Lace-twist outline Double-series twist with 12-ply band

STEM SHAPES

Baluster (1700) True baluster (1700) Inverted light baluster (1730) Inverted baluster (1730) Balustroid (1730) Pedestal (1740) Air twist (1750) Faceted (1780)

FOOT SHAPES

Flanged Plain conical Firing Domed folded Conical folded Beehive Domed square

Mold-blown glass

Mold blowing, a technique that dates back to Roman times, became fashionable when it was used to make Irish and Anglo-Irish glass in the late 18th century. However, its popularity in the USA, where it is known as "blown-three-mold" glass after the three-part mold in which it was produced, declined with the growth of pressed glass in the 1820s.

◄ Unguentarium

Intended to hold aromatic oils, this early Roman jar, known as an unguentarium, would have been blown into a mold, then removed, and the handle added soon after. Small jars such as this were produced in huge quantities, so they are quite common and can be reasonably priced.

(2nd century AD; ht 7.5cm/3in; value D)

EARLY GLASS

Mold blowing was first introduced by the Romans *c.*AD 25 and was one of the most important developments in the production of glass. The simple technique involves blowing a molten, sometimes partly formed, gather of glass (paraison) into a mold. Once shaped by the mold, the piece can be removed and finished, perhaps by reheating and further blowing to enlarge it. The mold, which gives the object both shape and decoration in one operation, was typically made of a non-combustible material such as pearwood, clay, or metal. It was usually made in two or more parts to enable the glass, which does not shrink as it cools, to be removed without damage. Wares made include plain unguentaria, bottles, beakers, and drinking cups, as well as more decorative wares such as inverted bell-shaped "lotus-bud" beakers, hexagonal flasks with decoration showing scenes from the Roman circus, and "mythological" beakers, decorated with events and characters from Roman mythology.

EUROPEAN GLASS

Glassmakers in northern Europe continued to produce mold-blown glass after the Romans left the region. The type of unsophisticated glassware, which included cone and claw beakers, was made of green-tinted soda-lime glass in the forested regions in the Rhineland, France, and Belgium between *c.*AD 400 and *c.*AD 700. The most common wares were simple drinking vessels decorated with trailing.

► Carafe

One of the advantages of making glass by mold blowing was that the shape and the pattern could be produced at the same time, as would have been the case with this French carafe. On early carafes neck rings were applied separately; in later examples they formed part of the mold. The pattern on a piece of mold-blown glass will feel softer than on cut glass; in some pieces the mold seam may be visible down the side.

(c.1860; ht 21cm/8¼in; value B)

In the 18th century mold blowing was popularly used in Ireland to mass-produce wares such as glasses and decanters, with decoration in imitation of cut-glass designs. Most wares were part rather than fully mold blown; this involved blowing a gather of glass into a shallow patterned mold to form the base of the ware – the bowl of a glass or the base of a decanter. The mold enabled the glass-blower to produce a range of wares with a uniform shape and the molded pattern (typically fluted on Irish decanters) helped to hide flaws in the surface of the glass or unsightly sediment from wine settled at the bottom. By the late 18th century Irish glassmakers were also working their factory marks into the base of the mold.

NORTH AMERICAN GLASS

Large quantities and many varieties of blown-three-mold glass, often imitating Anglo-Irish cut glass, were manufactured in Western Pennsylvania, Ohio, West Virginia, and Indiana from *c.*1815. The full-size hinged molds had two, three, or more parts – the name is slightly misleading – and were used to produce pieces with patterns imitating cut glass; wares, which were usually clear, included punch-bowls, decanters, tumblers, and even toy wine glasses decorated with a range of motifs from sunbursts and vertical and horizontal ribs to plumes and scrolls. Very popular at the time were flasks decorated with presidential portraits, the American eagle, or other political symbols, and portraits of celebrities. They were produced from *c.*1815 in a variety of sizes and colors – most common are clear or bottle-green examples, but wares in amethyst, blue, and various shades of green are also known.

Vast quantities of mold-blown glass were manufactured in North America during the 19th century for wine and spirit bottles, patent medicine bottles, and home preserving jars. However, in the 1820s with the development of mold-pressing machinery they were able to mass-produce imitation cut glass.

▼ Celery vase

This American celery vase, intended to hold long stalks of celery, is made of uranium glass. The glass is so called because small quantities of uranium were added to the batch to produce the characteristic yellow color. On this example the mold has been used to create both the basic shape and the vertical bold ribbed pattern, which is very similar to patterns often found on Anglo-Irish cut glass of this period.

(1840; ht 22.5cm/8¾in; value E)

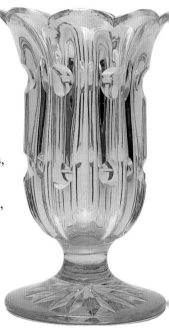

KEY FACTS

General
- DECORATION unlike that on cut or mold-pressed glass, the design may be felt on the inside of the piece; as the glass stretches when blown, patterns are often contorted; mold-seams may be visible down the piece's side

Early glass
- WARES flasks, beakers, cups, bottles, and bowls
- COLLECTING many domestic wares can be commonly found; unusual, colored, or highly decorated items are very collectible and command high prices

European glass
- COLLECTING part-mold-blown Irish decanters (always of clear glass) are particularly sought after

American glass
- TECHNIQUE mold blowing mostly used in North America between *c.*1820 and 1870
- WARES much used for the production of inexpensive bottles, although other wares, including vases, punch-bowls, and drinking glasses, were also produced

See also Pressed glass, p.283; Cut glass, pp.296–7

Pressed glass

The invention and development of mold pressing *c.*1820 revolutionized glass manufacture; previously an exclusive and highly priced commodity, decorative glass became accessible to all. The technique involved pressing a gather of molten glass into a metal mold using a plunger. When the glass cooled, the mold was opened, and any excess glass attached to the seams was removed by hand.

NORTH AMERICA

The most important pressed-glass manufacturer in North America was the Boston & Sandwich Glass Co. (1826–88), founded by Deming Jarves (1790–1869), in Sandwich, Massachusetts. The firm produced inexpensive pressed-glass tableware in "lacy" glass with intricate stippled designs that resembled lace and covered the flaws caused by the pressing process; wares included table services and a range of colored glassware. The earliest pressed patterns of Gothic arches, acanthus leaves, and scrolls were probably copied from cut glass. Another well-known company was the New England Glass Co. (1818–90), originally of East Cambridge, Massachusetts, and also founded by Jarves. Both firms specialized in the production of oil lamps and candlesticks with contrastingly colored glass tops and bases. By the 1850s other pressed glass factories were also established throughout the Midwest.

Many firms produced brightly colored pressed glass with a vivid orange or green iridescent surface, which is known as "Carnival" glass. It was made by spraying pressed glass with metallic powders, and was used to create eye-catching yet inexpensive tumblers, bowls, plates, and vases. Major makers include the Northwood Glass Co. (1888–1925) in Indiana, Pennsylvania, the Imperial Glass Co. (est. 1902) in Bellaire, Ohio, and the Fenton Art Glass Co. (est. 1904) in Williamstown, West Virginia. Between 1925 and 1950 mold pressing was widely used to mass-produce inexpensive glass items, such as trinkets, which were given away as premiums at petrol stations and in boxes of cereal, and also affordable pastel-colored tablewares; these pieces are now known as "Depression" glass. Primary makers include the Jeanette Glass Co. (est. 1898) in Jeanette, Pennsylvania, and the Indiana Glass Co. (est. 1902) in Indiana, Pennsylvania.

BRITAIN

Mold pressing was used in the North of England before 1827, and from the mid-1870s was widely employed by such firms as John Sowerby's Ellison Glassworks (1847–1972) and George Davidson & Co. (est. 1867), both in Gateshead, Henry Greener & Co. (est. 1858) in Sunderland, and John Derbyshire & Co. (1873–6) in Manchester. Commemorative ware was very popular in Britain, and in the 1870s John Derbyshire & Co. introduced patriotic mold-pressed figures to its range, including those of Britannia and Queen Victoria. In the 1860s Henry Greener & Co. produced glass with a ground of small raised dots that was especially well suited to press molding. One of Sowerby's most popular ranges was "Vitro-porcelain" glass, which closely resembled china. Launched in 1877, it was produced in several colors, including cream (registered as "Patent Queen's Ivory Ware"), turquoise, white, green, and a marbled version known as "Malachite." Ranges by George Davidson & Co., introduced in 1889, include opaque "Pearline" glass, which was produced in different shades of turquoise.

► **Bowl by George Davidson & Co.**
Pressed glass with a marbled bluish-purple appearance, as on the English bowl featured here is known as "slag" glass. Produced by skimming waste slag from molten steel and mixing it into the glass batch, it has a characteristic streaky finish. The majority of slag glass was produced in England between *c.*1840 and 1900 by such firms as Davidson & Co. and Henry Greener & Co. *(c.1885; ht 9cm/3½in; value A)*

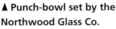

▲ **Punch-bowl set by the Northwood Glass Co.**
This elaborate molded-pressed punch-bowl is made of Carnival glass; it is decorated in the "grape and cable" pattern, with vines and grapes in high relief. The bowl would have been made with a set of eight matching cups, which would also have been decorated with vines and grapes. Amethyst was an especially popular color for this type of ware, but grape-and-cable designs were also made in green, yellow, and blue. Other wares in this design include candlesticks and water jugs. *(c.1910–19; ht 35.5cm/13¾in; value D)*

KEY FACTS

- DECORATION American pressed-glass designs are sharp; pieces with softer patterns are likely to be either copies or European; decoration is often in imitation of cut-glass designs; "lacy" patterns were also popular
- COLLECTING although primarily collected in the USA, pressed glass is now becoming more popular with collectors in Europe; generally, the more ornate the piece, the more desirable it will be
- BEWARE supposedly "rare" examples may be copies

Marks
Most wares feature molded marks, although some Depression glass was marked only with a paper label

USA: Northwood Glass Co.: *c.*1900   **Ⓝ**

USA: Jeanette Glass Co: *c.*1910   **J**

UK: John Sowerby's Ellison Glassworks: molded mark usually found on the base

UK: George Davidson & Co: used in the 1960s

► **Tray by the New England Glass Co.**
American firms produced large quantities of the pressed lacy glass shown here. The detailed surface hid the flaws in the glass that were common in the early days of press molding. Traditionally very popular in the USA, lacy glass is now attracting the interest of collectors in Europe. *(1830–40; l. 30cm/11¾in; value C)*

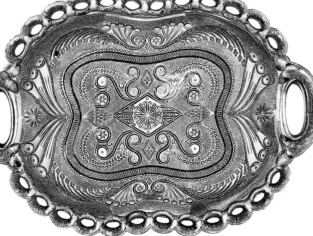

See also Mold-blown glass, p.282; Colored glass, pp.284–7

Colored glass

Colored glass is made by adding metallic oxides to the glass batch. This technique was widely practiced in ancient Egypt and Rome, where brightly colored glass was often favored over clear glass. In the 15th century opaque white glass, slightly translucent glass, and glass in imitation of hardstones were produced in Venice; in Bohemia glass in bold colors of blue and ruby-red was widely produced before 1800. In the 19th century, with advanced technical and mass production methods, production was much more widespread with notable firms operating not only in Italy and Bohemia but also in Britain, France, and the USA. Experimention with new staining and overlay techniques produced a wide array of colored designs.

Before 1800

EARLY GLASS

The Egyptians experimented with colored glass, exploiting their extensive trade routes to acquire the necessary materials. Ancient Egyptian glass comes in a myriad of bright, pure colors. One of the most common was bright turquoise blue, colored by adding copper oxide to the batch. Antimony and tin oxide, imported from Assyria, were used to color glass an opaque white, while pure opaque yellow was trailed over dark blue core-formed objects, with white or pale blue, and combed into festoons or feathery patterns and zigzags. Fine alabastra (bottles or flasks) known as "gold-band" incorporate stripes of real gold.

The Romans continued to experiment with colored glass, producing most famously dark blue glass overlaid with opaque white and cut with cameo decoration. Mosaic glass was made from brilliantly colored canes of glass cut into tiny slices and fused together in a mold. Most colored glass was blue, although purple and amber pieces are also found. Much excavated Roman glass will have an iridescent surface; this is the result of a chemical reaction with the metal oxides in the earth after the glass was buried. Roman wares include bowls, bottles, flasks, and cups.

VENETIAN GLASS

From the mid-15th century the sophisticated know-how of Venetian glassmakers gave rise to many different types and effective combinations of colored glass. In the late 15th century a "milky" opaque-white glass made by adding tin oxide to the batch was developed. This glass (known as *lattimo* in Italy) resembled porcelain, and it became particularly popular in the late 17th and early 18th centuries, when imported Chinese porcelain was in vogue. From the late 15th century a fine marbled glass known as "chalcedony" or "agate" glass was created by mixing together colored opaque metals to resemble hardstones. Opaline glass, which was slightly translucent and less dense than opaque-white glass, was probably first made in Venice in the 17th century by the addition of oxides and the ashes of calcified

◄ Alabastron
This east-Mediterranean alabastron, or small bottle, was made by trailing blue glass around a core of sand, clay, and dung, and rolling (or "marvering") the glass on a smooth surface. The white and yellow decoration would be applied as spiral threads, and the alabastron would be rolled once more. Blue is the most common body color for these wares, although amber-brown, dark green, and, very rarely, red were also used, with turquoise, yellow, and white featured as typical decoration. The interior of the piece is usually rough from the core, which is scraped out once the glass has solidified.
*(c.200 BC–AD 100; ht 28.5cm/11in; value **G**)*

▼ Bowl
Chalcedony glass, known as *calcedonio* in Italy, *jaspe* in France, and *Schmelzglas* in Germany, was intended to resemble hardstones; the fine Venetian bowl featured here has the appearance of agate. This type of glass is extremely rare and is usually only found in museum collections.
*(c.1500; ht 13cm/5in; value **L**)*

bones to the batch; when held to the light it can be distinguished from opaque-white glass by a red or yellow tint, which is known as the "fire."

BOHEMIAN GLASS

In the 16th century a distinctive dark-blue glass was produced in Bohemia by the addition of cobalt oxide. The clear vivid body color was a perfect canvas for the brightly colored naive enameling popular at that time. At the end of the 17th century a deep pink glass was invented by by Johann Kunckel (*c.*1630–1703), a chemist and director at the Potsdam Glasshouse (est. 1679). The color was produced by adding gold chloride to the batch. This "gold-ruby" glass (known as "Kunckel red" or, in German, *Rubinglas* or *Goldrubinglas*) was also produced in Nuremberg and other glasshouses in southern Germany. Gold-ruby glass was decorated with engraving, cutting, or gilding, and was considered a luxury product.

► Beaker and cover
Made in gold-ruby glass, this Bohemian beaker and cover is an extremely fine example of the type of glass perfected by Kunckel at the end of the 17th century. It is made of potash glass, a particularly robust type, developed in the last quarter of the 17th century. Potash glass is thick enough to be able to withstand such cutting as the interlocking thumbnail flutes shown here.
*(c.1700; ht 17.5cm/7in; value **H**)*

KEY FACTS

- **MAIN AREAS OF PRODUCTION** ancient colored glass was made in Egypt and Rome; it was produced from *c.*1450 in Venice and from the 16th century in Bohemia
- **TYPES** blue glass; porcelain-like "milk" glass; colored glass in imitation of hardstones; opaline glass; gold-ruby glass
- **FORMS** densely colored pieces may appear heavy bodied
- **COLORS** ancient glass: many pieces have dark blue bodies sometimes with yellow and white decoration
- **COLLECTING** ancient Egyptian glass is very rare and valuable; generally color will not play an important part in its value; gold-ruby glass is rare and valuable

See also Cameo glass, pp.300–1

After 1800

Bohemia

The 19th century was an age of experimentation in glass technology. Glassmakers, some of whom were also skilled chemists, developed new colors, new ways of applying color, and innovative techniques to produce glass that resembled other materials. The most celebrated types of Bohemian glass from this period are "Lithyalin," "Hyalith," stained, and flashed glass.

◄ Scent bottle
Produced in the workshop of the celebrated Bohemian glassmaker Friedrich Egermann, this scent flask is a fine example of Lithyalin glass. The striations, which are achieved by mixing together glass of different colors, result in a glass that closely resembles a hardstone.
(c.1830–40; ht 9.5cm/3¾in; value **D**)

LITHYALIN AND HYALITH GLASS

Count Georg Franz August Langueval von Buquoy (1781–1851), the owner of a number of glasshouses in southern Bohemia, produced an opaque black glass c.1817, which was inspired by the black basalt wares produced from the end of the 18th century at the Wedgwood factory (est. 1769) in England. In 1819 he produced another dense opaque glass, known as "Hyalith," usually in sealing-wax red or jet-black. Hyalith was usually decorated with gilding.

Von Buquoy's experiments may have inspired Friedrich Egermann (1777–1864), who in 1829 at his factory in Haida, northern Bohemia, patented "Lithyalin" glass, a polished opaque glass that resembled hardstones, which he continued to produce until 1840. The surface of the glass was brushed with metal oxides to resemble veining and marbling. Strong colors are typical, especially red; more unusual are dark-green, blue, and purple. Wares were usually cut and polished and occasionally gilded or enameled. Lithyalin glass was used mainly for purely decorative items, notably vases, beakers, and scent bottles. Lithyalin glass was also produced at the Harrach Glassworks (est. 1714) in Neuwelt (now Novy Svet in the Czech Republic), and by Hautin & Co. in France. Although these copies are difficult to distinguish from pieces by Egermann, they are usually slightly lighter in color.

STAINED, FLASHED, AND OVERLAY GLASS

Egermann also invented an effective and inexpensive method of coloring glass with a thin stain of color, which was called flashing. This involved painting a clear object with a stain and firing it at a low temperature to fix the color. This gave a solid, even, pale color. Egermann is particularly noted for his yellow colored stain, developed in 1818 using silver chloride, and his ruby-red stain, perfected in 1832, using gold

chloride and copper oxide. Wares were often cut through to the thin color to reveal the clear glass beneath.

In casing – a technique reinvented by Egermann – the glass vessel is covered in a differently colored glass and then fired; as the glass cools, the two layers fuse together. Some pieces were "double-cased," i.e. dipped into two differently colored batches of glass to give a multicolored effect. The flashing technique is sometimes confused with casing as the terms were used interchangeably by some glassworks; however, in casing the layers of glass are much thicker. If there is a sharp line between the two colors, this suggests flashing, whereas shading or thinning between two colors suggests overlay. Flashing and staining are characteristic of 19th-century Bohemian glassmakers as they are inexpensive methods of coloring glass and thus well suited to the mass-produced wares made during the 19th century.

OTHER COLORED GLASS

During the 1820s and 1830s a series of industrial exhibitions held in Prague gave rise to the development of other types of colored glass, including violet, pink, green, and blue. Further experimentation with color in the early 19th century sparked the discovery in Bohemia of other ways to color glass. Of particular note is the work of Josef Riedel (active 1830–48), who in the 1830s used uranium to produce a vivid fluorescent greenish-yellow (*Annagrün*) and yellowish-green (*Annagelb*) glass, both named after his wife Anna. However, this glass was mildly radioactive, and the process was later abandoned.

▼ Beaker, possibly engraved by Karl Pfohl
This Bohemian ruby-flashed beaker may have been engraved by Pfohl (1826–94), one of the most distinguished 19th-century Bohemian engravers. The beaker would have been entirely covered in the ruby color and then cut to reveal the clear glass beneath. The delicate wheel-engraved horse contrasts with the heavy, bold cutting at the base.
(c.1840–50; ht 12cm/4¾in; value **G**)

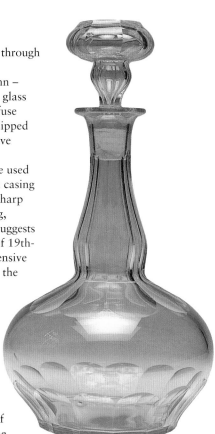

▲ Decanter, probably by the the Harrach Glassworks
The technique of using uranium to color glass yellow was developed by Riedel during the 1830s. Unlike flashed or stained glass, where only the surface is covered with a contrasting color, uranium glass is solid and, when cut, as seen in this Bohemian decanter, does not reveal a contrasting color underneath.
(mid-19th century; ht 30cm/11¾in; value **D**)

KEY FACTS

Lithyalin and Hyalith glass
- CONDITION ceramic restoration techniques are often used, so repairs can be difficult to spot
- COLLECTING display vessels such as vases and bowls are most common; display cups and saucers and pieces with gilt oriental and chinoiserie decoration are rarer; lithyalin overlaid on dark-green hyalith is valuable

Flashed, stained, and overlay glass
- CONDITION check pieces carefully, as damage is often hard to detect on colored glass; good condition is vital
- COLLECTING the condition and depth of the color determine the value; beware when collecting blue-stained glass as it fades easily and can lose value

Other Bohemian colored glass
- TYPES vivid green *Annagrün* and *Annagelb* glass

Marks
Friedrich Egermann: rare mark used c.1830   F. E.

See also Enameled glass after 1800, pp.290–91

Britain, France, and the United States after 1800

Colored glass was widely produced during the 19th century in Britain, France, and the USA. In Britain two important events gave a new impetus to the manufacture of colored glass in the middle of the century. The first was the removal of excise tax on glass in 1845, which encouraged makers to experiment with new techniques and styles, among them colored glass. The second was the Great Exhibition held in London in 1851 at which glassmakers from Europe and the USA were keen to show their new skills and techniques. In France glassmakers at all the major factories manufactured colored glass in a range of styles and forms, and in the USA firms experimented widely with color, producing an extensive range of designs, most characteristically in delicate pastel shades with subtle color graduations.

◄ Decanter

This decanter (one of a pair) is in the typical royal blue of Bristol glass. The bottle has a capacity of one imperial pint, and the gilded decoration on the front identifies the contents, in this case "Hollands" (gin); the other bottle of the pair is for rum. Larger-capacity decanters are rare, and sometimes gilded with wine labels. Also rare are amethyst decanters; most were blue or green. The early gilded decoration is especially associated with the London-based glass decorator James Giles (1718–80) whose work is often found on "Bristol" glass.
(c.1800; ht 20cm/8in; value for a pair **F**)

BRITAIN

All blue, green, and amethyst glass produced in Britain from the end of the 18th to the middle of the 19th century is generically described as "Bristol" glass. The most characteristic color is a brilliant royal blue, produced by adding cobalt oxide to the batch; such glass is frequently embellished with cold gilding. Drinking glasses were generally green, ranging from grass green to a turquoise green. Amethyst glasses are rare, but when found the color is true and clear, with no sign of red, unlike the plum tone found on later Victorian glass.

In the mid-19th century the influence of colored glass manufactured by well-established glass companies in Bohemia became increasingly visible in the products of British factories. Not only did important Bohemian factories such as the Harrach Glassworks (est. 1714) in Neuwelt (now Novy Svet in the Czech Republic) exhibit quantities of colored glass at the Great Exhibition, but Bohemian glassworkers were also employed by British factories where, freed from the constraint of having to produce wares in traditional styles, they were able to manufacture very exciting wares in an outstanding range of new colors.

In the late 1870s a type of opalescent glass, known as "Vaseline" glass due to its greasy, vaseline-like appearance, was developed in Britain and designed to resemble 15th- and 16th-century Venetian glass. The opalescent color was produced by using tiny amounts of uranium together with other metal oxides to create shades of yellow, green, blue, and, more rarely, red. Stevens & Williams Ltd (est. 1847), of Brierley Hill, near Stourbridge, was one of the leading innovators in the field of patent colors and color combinations in the late 19th and early 20th centuries. The company's rare double-cased "Rockingham" ware is particularly sought after, as are the Bohemian-style pieces with alternating panels of engraved color-flashed and clear glass produced by W.H., B. & J. Richardson (est. c.1836), also near Stourbridge. Amber was the most commonly used color for the vases, decanters, and claret jugs in this style, although some pieces were also produced in purple, green, and red.

Gold and uranium oxides combined with sodium nitrate were used to manufacture the "Queen's Burmese" range of glass by Thomas Webb & Sons (est. 1837), near Stourbridge, patented in 1886. Queen's Burmese was inspired by the "Burmese" glassware patented in 1885 by the Mount Washington Glass Co. (est. 1837), in South Boston, Massachusetts, and favored by Queen Victoria who ordered a set – hence the name. It had a body color that shaded from a pale lemon-yellow (sometimes light green) at the bottom through to salmon-pink at the top. Some pieces feature enameled and gilded designs. Although Queen's Burmese ware was made by other British companies – including W.H., B. & J. Richardson – pieces by Webb are the most desirable. Typical wares include vases, posy bowls, and lampshades. Another type of glass introduced by Webb was "Peach" glass, a type of cased glass that shaded from pink through to a deep red.

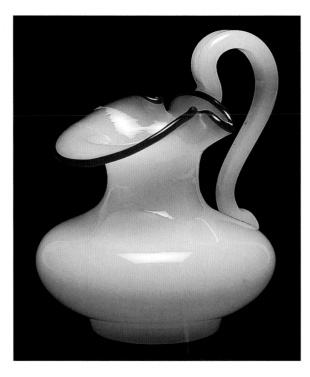

▲ Tazza

The *tazza* is a distinctive Venetian form of serving dish. The revival of 15th- and 16th-century Venetian glass forms and styles of decoration was started in Venice during the mid-19th century and gradually spread throughout Europe. In Britain the Revival was supported by William Morris, who disapproved of the heavily cut glass prevalent at the time. One of the leading British manufacturers of Venetian Revival glass was James Powell & Sons (est. 1834), which produced "Vaseline" glass wares similar to the example shown above, and in delicately tinted glass from the 1870s.
(c.1890; ht 12cm/4¾in; value **D**)

◄ Jug by Baccarat

The curvaceous Neo-classical form of this French opaline jug is typical of the inventive designs by this famous French firm. The white-opaque finish is achieved by adding the ashes of calcined bones to the batch. Opaline glass could also be colored by the addition of metal oxides. Colors include deep blue (as featured on the rim here, and very typical of Baccarat designs), pale green, turquoise, pink, coral, ruby-red, and yellow (rare). Baccarat, which is also renowned for its cut-glass wares and paperweights, is still one of the major French glassworks today. This jug would probably have been produced as a decorative display piece.
(19th century; ht 10cm/4in; value **D**)

FRANCE

In France, the Baccarat Glassworks (est. 1764 as the Sainte-Anne Glassworks) in Baccarat, near Lunéville, Lorraine, produced glass c.1880 in a distinctive, delicate shade of pink known as "tinted-rose." Many wares feature acid-etched Classical decoration. Another fashionable trend was the production of colored opaline glass, a semi-opaque white glass, opacified by the addition of the ash of calcined bones and colored with metallic oxides. The Venetians had been the first to introduce this translucent glass, which was later made in Bohemia and Britain, but the French opaline glass first produced c.1823 at Baccarat was more translucent. The finest French opaline was made at Baccarat, at the Saint-Louis Glassworks (est. 1767) near Bitche, in the Münzthal, Lorraine, and at the Choisy-le-Roi Glassworks (est. 1821) in Paris. Wares were made in delicate pastel shades such

◄ Vase by the Saint-Louis Glassworks

This French vase employs the technique of *latticinio,* a Venetian process that involves working a clear-glass vessel embedded with colored-glass canes. The latter are typically pink, blue, or white. The rim of this piece is in the same color as the rest of the vase, but on many wares of this type the rim is in a contrasting color. Wares with *latticinio* decoration are typical of Saint-Louis but were also made by the Clichy Glassworks (est. 1837), first in Bilancourt and then at Clichy-la-Garenne in the suburbs of Paris.

(mid-19th century; ht 13cm/5in; value F)

as turquoise, pink, and pale green, and include pairs of vases with enameled decoration, and vases, jugs, and dishes of inventive forms, often with colored cane rims. Saint-Louis Glassworks made many pieces in soft pink or blue, with *latticinio* decoration and glass cane rims.

THE UNITED STATES

Throughout the 19th century American glass manufacturers launched and developed a range of innovative colored glass. One of the most popular and now widely collected colors is the transparent "Cranberry" glass, which has a distinctive raspberry pink tint, first produced in the glassmaking region of Stourbridge in England. Huge quantities of useful and ornamental wares were made, most notably at the Boston & Sandwich Glass Co. (1826–88) in Sandwich, Massachusetts.

However, it was only during the 1880s, when there was a move away from cut and pressed glass by the leading glass manufacturers, that they began to experiment in earnest with a more sophisticated range of colored art glass. One of the leading companies at this time was the Mount Washington

Glass Co., which launched the widely copied and enormously popular "Burmese" glass in 1885. Most Burmese glass has a satin finish, although some has a glossy surface, and is characterized by subtle gradations of shading from a light lemon at the bottom of the piece to a delicate pink at the top. In 1883 the firm of Hobbs, Brockunier & Co. (est. 1863) in Wheeling, West Virginia, developed "Peachblow" glass and incorporated it into its range of colored wares. This cased glass is a warm buttery yellow at the base shading through to a purplish-red at the top and is lined in a white opal glass. Peachblow was made at other companies, including the New England Glass Co. (1818–90), originally in East Cambridge, Massachusetts, which called it "Wild Rose." New England was also notable for its "Amberina" range of glass, which it produced as "Pressed Amberina." Both Wild Rose and Pressed Amberina were developed by Joseph Locke (1846–1936), an English glassworker, who emigrated to the USA in 1882. Patented in 1883, Amberina glass contained small amounts of gold, and graduated from pale amber at the base through to a rich fuchsia at the top. It was made until 1900. Hobbs, Brockunier & Co. also made Pressed Amberina under licence from the New England Glass Co.

▼ Champagne pitcher by the New England Glass Co.

This American pitcher, which features elaborate Russian-cut decoration, is made of unshaded Amberina glass, which was patented by Joseph Locke at the New England Glass Co. in 1883. The finest examples shade from deep pink at the top and turn to a rich amber at the base. Typical wares include bowls, candlesticks, epergnes, vases, and decanters.

(c.1884–8; ht 31cm/12in; value E)

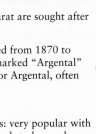

► Trumpet vase by the Mount Washington Glass Co.

This vase features the typical gradations of color of Burmese ware from pale yellow to pink.

(c.1885–95; ht 44cm/17in; value G)

KEY FACTS

Britain
- TYPES Bristol glass, overlay glass, Vaseline glass, decorated opaque and opaline glass
- BEWARE there are many early 20th-century copies of Bristol glass: beware of glasses that are larger than usual (more than c.10cm/4in high) and thin glass

Marks
Thomas Webb & Sons: mark used on Queen's Burmese wares

France
- MAJOR FACTORIES Baccarat, Saint-Louis, Choisy-le-Roi
- TYPES pastel-colored opaline glass and wares with decoration are most notable
- COLLECTING wares by Baccarat are sought after

Marks
Saint-Louis: this mark was used from 1870 to the present day; some pieces marked "Argental" or "Münzthal," the German for Argental, often with a tiny cross of Lorraine

The United States
- COLLECTING Cranberry glass: very popular with collectors; later Cranberry tends to have a less warm hue and a bluey tinge when held to the light

Marks
Mount Washington Glass Co.: mark used on Burmese ware from the 1880s

New England Glass Co.: Amberina ware; mark used from 1880s

See also Miscellaneous: pp.310–11

Enameled glass

The process of enameling has been known since Roman times, and from the end of the 13th century was used to great effect by Islamic glassmakers to decorate mosque lamps. In Europe enameling first appeared in Venice in the 15th century, and spread elsewhere during the 16th century. In Vienna in the early 19th century beakers were decorated with transparent enamels in the Biedermeier style by such artists as Gottlob Samuel Mohn and Anton Kothgasser and in the later part of 19th century copies of earlier styles were made by manufacturers all over Europe, the most outstanding of which were Islamic- and Iznik-style wares, which were made in France, and Historismus wares, which were produced in Germany.

Before 1800

Enameling, which can be used to decorate both colorless and colored glass, was used extensively in Europe from the 16th century. It was employed most notably to decorate armorial wares, but it was also used to create bright and colorful decoration in naturalistic motifs; naive and charming designs of flowers and animals are highly characteristic. On many wares enameled decoration was used in conjunction with gilding.

ITALY

The invention of *cristallo* glass *c.*1450 by Angelo Barovier (*d.*1460) provided a perfectly clear ground that was ideally suited to enameling in brilliant colors. Enameling, a technique that the Venetians probably learned from Islamic glassmakers, was at its peak in Venice from the 15th to the mid-16th centuries. The process involved applying a thick paste of powdered glass and a coloring metallic oxide in an oil medium to the surface of the glass, which was then heated in a furnace, where the enamel and glass fused. Each color required a different firing temperature, and the work could easily burn if overfired. Enameling is a notoriously difficult technique, and most enameling of this period is

◄ Flask from the workshop of Oswaldo Brussa
Although most of the finest Venetian enameling was carried out from the 15th to the mid-16th centuries, good quality enameling was also carried out during the 18th century. The leading exponent was Brussa, who decorated clear-glass pieces with charming birds, flowers, and biblical scenes.
(1740; ht 9cm/3½in; value L)

restricted to the borders, with simple scale and dot patterns. On much more sophisticated wares, such as specially commissioned commemorative *tazze* (ornamental serving dishes), enameling was often combined with gilding, and decoration included portraits, coats of arms, family and guild crests, and mythological figures. Although enameling fell out of favor by the late 16th century, it was revived during the second half of the 18th century by Oswaldo Brussa, who, with his son Angelo, decorated clear-glass beakers, carafes, and bottles with birds, flowers, and biblical scenes in a charming and naive style.

GERMANY AND BOHEMIA

In the 16th century enameling was developed as a popular form of decoration in the regions of Germany and Bohemia. From the mid-16th century German glass decorators, inspired by finely decorated wares from Venice, used brightly colored enamels to decorate large, simple shapes made from coarse, robust soda glass. The technique was especially popular for decorating traditional drinking glasses or goblets, particularly the *Humpen* (simple, cylindrical drinking vessels, the foot rims of which are decorated with white enameled dashes). Variations on the *Humpen* include the *Reichsadlerhumpen* ("Imperial Eagle Beaker"), which was designed to toast and show allegiance to the Holy Roman Emperor, and featured the double-headed Imperial eagle with outstretched wings from which hang shields showing the constituent parts of the Empire; the *Hofkellereiglas* (decorated with armorial decorations), *Wilkommhumpen* ("greeting glass"), usually of large proportions, and *Kurfürstenhumpen* ("Elector's beaker"), decorated with depictions of the Holy Roman Emperor and the Seven Electors of the Empire.

◄ Ochsenkopfhumpen
This type of *Humpen* depicts the Ochsenkopf Mountain in the Fichtelgebirge region between Franconia and Bohemia. The shape of the mountain was supposed to resemble the head of an ox (reinforced here by the actual depiction of an ox's head at the summit). The densely wooded mountain filled with brimming streams and animals was seen as a symbol of fertility. It is not known what the padlocked chain was supposed to symbolize. Such beakers were produced from 1656 until late 18th century, mainly in Upper Franconia, north-east Bavaria.
(1662; ht 17.5cm/7in; value L)

▼ Tankard
The opaque-white glass made in Germany and Bohemia and known as *Milchglas* ("milk glass") was highly suited to brightly colored enameled decoration, as featured on this Bohemian tankard. Vases, flasks, and tankards in traditional shapes were painted in a naive style with folk motifs and scenes of people, animals, and flowers.
(1760; ht 16cm/6¼in; value G)

▲ Bowl, probably decorated by Ignaz Preissler

This Bohemian *Schwarzlot* bowl has several features that make it highly collectible and valuable: it is an unusual shape; the decoration depicts a rare English coat of arms; and the piece was probably worked on by Preissler, who was one of the leading exponents of this type of enameled decoration.

*(c.1736; diam. 25cm/9¾in; value **M**)*

Other German drinking vessels that were enameled include goblets and beakers such as the *Passglas* (a tall cylindrical beaker decorated with horizontal bands, which indicated the amount of beer to be consumed by a drinker before they passed the glass on to the next person) and the *Stangenglas* (a long narrow beaker on a pedestal base). These wares were enameled in very bright colors with decoration such as dated armorial and political motifs, and designs commemorating guilds and trades.

In Bohemia in the 18th century enameling was mostly used to decorate flasks, bottles, and tankards made of opaque-white *Milchglas* ("milk glass"). The white body imitated porcelain, and the decoration featured people, animals, and flowers painted in a naive folk style in bright polychrome enamels.

In the 17th century Johann Schaper (1621–70), a *Hausmaler* ("home painter") based in Nuremberg, developed an enameling techniques which he used to decorate both glass and porcelain. *Schwarzlot* (black-lead) enameling involved decorating glass vessels (mainly tumblers) with black or brown transparent enamel, and was fashionable from *c.*1650 to 1750. Designs were typically inspired by engravings and depicted battle scenes, landscapes, and mythological subjects.

In the 18th century the popularity of *Schwarzlot* decoration spread to Bohemia and Silesia. One of the most celebrated exponents of the technique at this time was Ignaz Preissler (1676–1741), a glass and porcelain painter, who used the technique to decorate glass tumblers and flasks with mythological scenes, townscapes, *Laub- und Bandelwerk* (decoration of interwoven leaves and strapwork), and chinoiserie.

► Decanter made in the Beilby workshop

This enameled, bell-shaped decanter was decorated in the workshop of the Beilby family, probably the best-known British glass enamelers. The decoration is in the characteristic thinly applied white enamel; the additional blue color makes this piece particularly desirable. The decorative motifs of hops and grains underline the function of the piece as a beer decanter.

*(c.1775; ht 28.5cm/11in; value **I**)*

BRITAIN AND SPAIN

Before 1750 enameling was relatively rare in Britain. Among the best-known early British enamelers were the Beilby family. In 1760 William Beilby (1740–1819) and his sister Mary Beilby (1749–97) moved from Bilston, in Staffordshire, to Newcastle-upon-Tyne, in the north-east of England, where they enameled wares between *c.*1762 and 1774. Their most celebrated wares are large pieces, such as the "Royal Beilbys" – goblets featuring the Prince of Wales's feathers and made from 1763 to commemorate the birth of the Prince of Wales (later George IV); their armorial goblets enameled on the bowl and commissioned by local families are also of note. Typical decoration includes simple borders of thinly applied white flowers, fruits, hops, and barley; more ambitious designs include arcadian landscapes, ruins, and even sporting scenes.

Other British decorators who painted with enamels include James Giles (1718–80) and Michael Edkins (1734–1811). Giles decorated glassware for the Falcon Glassworks (est. 1693) in London. Edkins, who worked in Bristol, painted opaque white glass, both with chinoiseries and with charming, naive designs of insects, birds, and other naturalistic motifs.

In Spain enameled glassware was produced most notably at La Granja de San Ildefonso near Segovia. Established in 1728 by the Catalan glassmaker Ventura Sit (*d.*1755), near the palace of La Granja, the factory employed French and German glassmakers, who brought with them a variety of techniques and styles that gave the glass an international character. Typical wares include glasses and tumblers, and although many were embellished with gilded decoration, enameled floral designs, notably tulips and roses, were also popular.

▼ Tumbler by La Granja de San Ildefonso

The factory at La Granja de San Ildefonso, which was established with royal patronage, was the most important glasshouse in Spain. It produced mainly clear glass, and was the only Spanish glasshouse to decorate its wares using enameling or engraving. The simple, clear-glass beaker shown below is boldly painted with opaque enameled flowers. The most common flowers depicted were roses and tulips, suggesting a Dutch influence. La Granja also made beakers with engraved and gilded decoration. *(18th century; ht 10cm/4in; value **C**)*

KEY FACTS

Italy
- GLASS *cristallo* glass is most typical; some wares appear slightly cloudy due to crizzling
- DECORATION many pieces feature naive folk art designs of flowers or biblical scenes; on some examples enameling is used in conjunction with gilding

Germany and Bohemia
- GLASS *Milchglas* should be a slightly off-white color
- COLOR earlier, more collectible glass is often a smoky grayish-green color; most later glass is a strong green
- DECORATION commemorative designs, rustic scenes, and flowers in bright colors are typical
- CONDITION damage to enameling can greatly reduce the value; worn gilding is common but insignificant
- BEWARE be careful with *Schwarzlot* glass that features transfer-printed decoration, as many reproductions were made in the 19th century

Britain and Spain
- GLASS glass is mostly clear, or sometimes blue or white
- DECORATION Britain: some wares by the Beilby family feature armorials; many pieces depict charming, naturalistic designs; Spain: floral designs, especially tulips and roses, are highly characteristic; designs should be neat and well drawn; enameling is often combined with gilded decoration
- COLLECTING Britain: "Royal Beilbys" and armorial goblets with colored decoration are valuable and highly collectible

See also Ceramics: Porcelain – Hausmaler, p.177

Enameled glass after 1800

Styles of enameled glass produced after 1800 are many and varied. In Germanic Europe (a region that included such cities as Prague, Vienna, Copenhagen, and Berlin) the period known as the Biedermeier period (*c*.1815–*c*.1848) was one of middle-class prosperity, and this ensured the continued popularity of such decorative arts as glassmaking. Enameled wares from the early 19th century are typically decorated with topographical scenes, floral designs, and portraits in bright colors. Following the re-establishment of the German Empire in 1871 there was a revival of the production of traditional German styles of glass; this revival is known as "Historismus." Exceptional enameled wares were produced in France in the 19th century, notably elaborate Islamic designs and some delicately decorated opaline wares. In Britain enameled decoration was mainly restricted to monochromatic transfer-printed patterns on opaque white grounds.

GERMANY AND BOHEMIA

During the Biedermeier period Samuel Mohn (1762–1815), a *Hausmaler* ("home painter") in Dresden, pioneered the use of a thin, transparent enamel decoration, which he used to great effect on tumblers and beakers. His son Gottlob Samuel Mohn (1789–1825) learned the technique from his father and in *c*.1811 went

▲ Beaker painted by Samuel Mohn and Augustus Viertel
The technique of painting with thin, transparent enamels was highly popular during the Biedermeier period. It was pioneered by Mohn, who, together with Viertel, decorated the beaker shown here. The topographical scene is typical, as is the gilt border with oak leaves. These beakers, often originally intended as expensive souvenirs, are highly popular and collectible, especially those by Mohn.
(c.1810; ht 10cm/4in; value J)

to Vienna, where he met Anton Kothgasser (1769–1851), a painter at the Royal porcelain factory. Both men used the technique to decorate simple, straight-sided beakers and, from 1814, a type of beaker known as a *Ranftbecher*, with a waisted or tapered body and a thick cogwheel-cut base. Kothgasser's enameled decorations resembled romantic watercolors; his designs included fine landscapes, cityscapes (particularly of Vienna), portraits, and allegorical and Neo-classical subjects. Mohn used silhouettes and allegorical subjects as decoration but is best known for his tumblers decorated with topographical motifs – palaces, cityscapes, and tourist views; his beakers typically have gilded borders. Other distinguished contemporary enamelers include Carl von Scheidt and Andreas Mattoni (1779–1864), who established a school at Karlsbad where Ludwig Moser (1833–1916) was a pupil.

Following the unification of Germany in 1871, there was a fashion for reproducing "historic" styles to create a sense of national identity; this trend (which also appeared in Italy in the mid-19th century) is known as "Historismus." Glassware was just one of the media in which designs were reproduced in the "old German" style, characteristically with decorations of spurious crests, dates, and national insignia. There was a flood of traditional German drinking glasses made, including *Humpen* (simple, cylindrical beakers), *Römer* (drinking glasses with flared feet, wide cylindrical stems, and ovoid bowls), the *Kuttrolf* (a type of pouring flask), and other vessels made in imitation of 16th- and 17th-century originals, with false dates and inscriptions. These copies can usually be recognized by over-elaborate decoration in bright, inappropriately colored enamels, fictitious crests, crests of large towns rather than families, and heavy glass that is free from imperfections (early glass is frequently flawed). Wares, which are often of a very high quality and collectors' items in their own right, may bear enameled signatures identifying the manufacturer. The leading producers included the Rhenish Glasshouse (1886–92) in Ehrenfeld, Köln-Ehrenfeld, situated on the Rhine, near Cologne, and Meyrs Neffe of Bohemia (1841–1922) in Adolfov, known for producing copies of goblets with *Hochschnitt* ("high cut") decoration during the 1890s. *Hausmaler* who worked on "Historismus" wares include Fritz Heckert, a glass enameler who established a glass-decorating works in Petersdorf, Bohemia, in 1866 and a glass factory in 1889. The company was active until *c*.1890 and specialized in the production of *Humpen*, enameled with designs copied from traditional woodcuts and engravings. The strong Bohemian enameling tradition was also continued late into the 19th century by such companies as Ludwig Moser & Sons (est. *c*.1857) in Karlsbad (now Karlovy Vary in the Czech Republic).

◄ *Römer* by the Rhenish Glasshouse
Although produced in 1880, this German *Römer* incoporates the spurious date of 1632 in the enameled and gilded decoration. Traditional styles and forms of wares were made during the Historismus period in Germany, which began in the 1870s. The goblet is a reproduction of an early drinking vessel, complete with applied raspberry prunts (these have a more regular shape than those on authentic pieces) on the stem, an enameled coat of arms, an inscription and a trail-decorated flared foot. It will be marked on the inside of the foot.
(1880; ht 10cm/4in; value B)

▼ Vase
Enameling remained a Bohemian specialty from the mid-16th century to the early 20th century. The form and decoration of this vase were clearly inspired by the glassware produced by the firm of Ludwig Moser & Sons in Karlsbad; the deep green contrasts with the polychrome enameling depicting scrolling plants and flowers on the bowl and foot. Note how the gilding on the foot has almost rubbed off.
(1880; ht 15cm/6in; value B)

FRANCE AND AUSTRIA

In the 19th century French enamelers gained international renown for their fine wares, receiving commissions from all over the world, particularly from Arab states in the Near East. Much French enameling was executed on the finest opaline glass. Some of the best examples are vases decorated with animals, birds, and sprays of wild flowers. Some of the most impressive, although quite rare, French enameled wares were produced by Philippe-Joseph Brocard (d.1896) and I.J. Imberton. Inspired by 13th- and 14th-century Islamic lamps, which were elaborately decorated with arabesques, stylized scrolls, and floral designs in thick, opaque enamel, Brocard experimented with this style from the 1860s. His designs included copies of mosque lamps, vases, ewers, and dishes; these pieces, decorated with thick enameling, jeweling, and gilding, won first prize at the Paris Exhibition of 1878. Imberton also decorated fine Islamic-style wares with stylized motifs. In Austria the style was taken up by the glass company of J. & L. Lobmeyr (est. 1823), in Vienna, which designed a range of Islamic-style glassware for the domestic and export market, and also won prizes for its Islamic-style wares at the Paris Exhibition of 1878.

BRITAIN

In Britain the firm of W.H., B. & J. Richardson (est. c.1836) near Stourbridge, was famous for its high-quality wares and patented designs. It produced glass using many patented techniques. One was known as "vitrified colors," the finest examples of which were shown at the Great Exhibition of 1851 in London. The commercial process involved transfer printing black or colored designs such as a pictorial scene onto the glass body (which was usually opaque), and then firing the design. Sometimes the enamels were hand-painted onto the body, although this is not so common. The firm of Bacchus (est. c.1816; later George Bacchus & Sons) in Birmingham also produced a series of wares in the 19th century, which were decorated with transfer-printed enamels, most of which feature Neo-classical scenes.

► **Lamp base by George Bacchus & Sons**
After c.1845, British producers took advantage of the removal of excise tax on glass to experiment with new decorating techniques. This lamp base has been decorated by transfer printing enamels onto opaque-white glass.
(c.1850; ht 11cm/4¼in; value B)

▲ **Vase**
Art Nouveau was preceded by a period in which French glass enamelers were inspired by Japanese prints and engravings, and this French vase shows this influence. It features delicately painted "Japanesque" decoration of flowers and a butterfly on an opaque-white body. The foot and rim are finely enameled in silver.
(1880; ht 24cm/9½in; value B)

► **Two-handled vase by J. & L. Lobmeyr**
This Austrian ovoid-shaped vase with a flared base and cylindrical neck is a spectacular example of 19th-century "Islamic" glassware. Thick enameling is combined with very richly decorated gilding to create an exotic piece of glass designed for display. The elaborate decoration on this example features tigers attacking deer among a mass of stylized scrolling foliage. The fact that this was made by a distinguished producers and that it is in such superb condition, all add to the value of this piece, which is marked with the Lobmeyr trademark ("JLL") in white enamel.
(c.1880; ht 33cm/13in; value J)

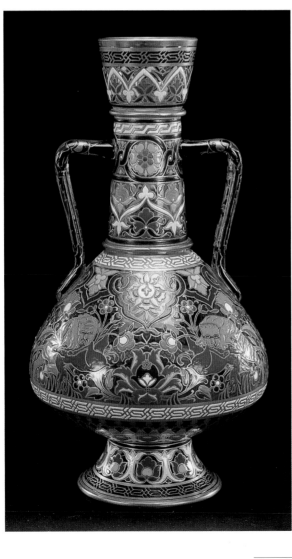

KEY FACTS

Germany and Bohemia
• WARES mainly drinking glasses, beakers, and vases
• STYLES Historismus wares; reproductions of early styles: over-decorated, overly bright enamels, fake crests

Marks
Both Mohn and Kothgasser signed some pieces: Mohn was known to use "G.Mohn f.a.Wien" and Kothgasser used his initials and his full name – often on the base rim

Rhenish Glasshouse: mark etched under the foot; used c.1888

Ludwig Moser & Sons: this mark was usually engraved on the side of a piece

France and Austria
• TYPES enameled opaline glass, Islamic-style wares, some Japanesque wares made in the late 19th century
• COLLECTING Islamic-style wares: in general the more exotic the design, the more collectible the piece; vases were usually made in pairs and a pair will be far more valuable than a single vase

Marks
Philippe-Joseph Brocard: this signature often used in gilt script

Britain
• IMPORTANT FACTORIES W.H., B. & J. Richardson, George Bacchus & Sons
• TYPES transfer-printed enamels on an opaque ground are most typical
• DECORATION George Bacchus & Sons: many feature Neo-classical scenes

Marks
George Bacchus & Sons: this signature was used c.1850

See also Ceramics: Islamic pottery, p.149, Porcelain – Hausmaler, p.177

Engraved glass

Engraving, whereby a decorative pattern is finely cut onto the surface of the glass, dates back to Roman times. The very earliest types of engraving were diamond-point engraving, which involves scratching fine lines into the glass with a sharp instrument (usually a diamond stylus), and wheel engraving, where the design is cut into the glass by means of a rotating wheel. Stipple engraving, a more sophisticated form of diamond-point engraving, where patterns of tiny dots rather than lines are used to create a shaded design, was first used from c.1620; acid etching, which involves burning a design out of the top layer of glass with acid, evolved with the invention of hydrofluoric acid c.1770 and was widely used in Britain.

Low Countries, Bohemia, Germany, and Sweden

Although glass was engraved from Roman times, and examples of fine engraving exist on 15th-century Venetian glass, the widespread use of such techniques as diamond-point and stipple engraving dates mainly from the second half of the 16th century. These techniques were introduced to decorators in the Low Countries by itinerant Venetian glassworkers. Wheel engraving was first used in Germany in the late 16th century.

DIAMOND-POINT AND STIPPLE ENGRAVING

Diamond-point engraving, in which the design or decoration is scratched onto the surface of the glass by a sharp diamond stylus, is particularly suited to thin-walled glass too hard to withstand wheel engraving. It was the only engraving technique suitable to be used on delicate *cristallo* glass. Diamond-point engraving was therefore quite common on 15th-century Venetian and later *façon de Venise* ("in the style of Venice") glass. However, the technique did not reach its apogee until it was taken up in the Low Countries during the 17th century, where it was carried out by both amateur (those who decorated glass as a hobby) and professional glass decorators. Anna Roemers Visscher (1583–1651) was an amateur glass decorator in Amsterdam, where she engraved delicate designs of flowers, fruit, and insects, as well as lines of poetry in calligraphic script, on beakers and *Römer* (a type of drinking glass). Another distinguished amateur glass decorator, Willem Jacobsz van Heemskerk (1613–92), in Leiden, produced most notably free-flowing calligraphic designs on such wares as bulbous serving bottles and jugs. Among the best-known professional engravers was Willem Mooleyser (active 1685–97), from Rotterdam, who used diamond-point engraving on bowls, flasks, goblets, and *Römer*.

In stipple engraving, which is a development of diamond-point engraving, a stylus is very gently tapped on the glass to make a design built up of small dots; these dots create areas of light (dense areas of dots) and shade (sparse areas of dots) to create the delicate design. The detail may be so fine that the design will only be seen clearly when the glass is held to the light. Common designs include portraits and allegorical subjects. Examples of stipple-engraved glass are rare, as the technique is slow, extremely difficult, and requires great skill and patience.

As with diamond-point engraving, the most notable designs were produced by glass decorators from the Low Countries. Visscher introduced the technique to The Netherlands c.1621, but perhaps the best-known exponent was Frans Greenwood (1680–1761), an amateur glass decorator in Dordrecht who employed the technique exclusively from c.1722. He incorporated floral and fruit motifs and also copied designs from contemporary mezzotints and paintings. One of his followers was David Wolff (1732–98), a painter who produced his own designs and portraits. Some of Wolff's pieces are signed and his style inspired other artists toward the end of the century; such pieces are commonly known as "Wolff" glass. Another follower of Greenwood was the painter and engraver Aert Schouman (1710–92). Greenwood, Wolff, and Schouman all mainly worked on glass thought to have been made in the factories around Newcastle-upon-Tyne in northern England, which made a soft glass that was better suited to the stippling technique than the more brittle soda glass.

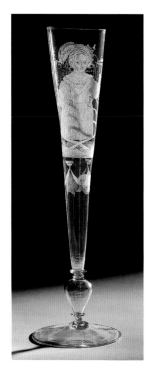

◄ Flute

Cristallo glass, a fine, clear glass originally invented in Venice and generally too brittle and delicate for wheel engraving, was used in the Low Countries for diamond-engraved wares such as this elegant *façon de Venise* flute. It features a portrait of the young Prince William of Orange (later William III of England), holding a baton, and is one of a series of flutes featuring the young Prince. Unusually the slender bowl of this flute is engraved with the date 1657 and the signature "fc M" ("fecit M" or "made by M"); most glassware was signed and dated on the pontil mark. The early date, fine engraving, and extreme rarity of this example mean that it is particularly valuable.

(1657; ht 39.5cm/15½in; value Q)

► Beaker, possibly engraved by Heinrich Schwanhardt

Schwanhardt was a member of a distinguished German family of glass engravers. This fine example of gold-ruby glass is embellished with intaglio wheel-engraved decoration of sunflowers, two coats of arms (unseen), and inscriptions in old German on both sides, a style that was popular in Germany and Silesia from the late 16th to early 17th centuries.

(c.1685–90; ht 10cm/4in; value H)

▲ Goblet and cover, possibly engraved in the workshop of Friedrich Winter

This magnificent Silesian goblet and cover is covered in extremely detailed *Tiefschnitt* (incised or intaglio) decoration that includes putti, small animals, a wild boar, and insects.

(1710–15; ht 29cm/11¼in; value L)

WHEEL ENGRAVING

In wheel engraving a mechanical wheel fed with an abrasive paste (typically a mix of oil and emery) is used to cut a design onto a glass surface. The technique, which has been used since Roman times, is best suited to thick-walled pieces, because the depth of the cut is an essential part of the design. The modern technique was probably developed between c.1590 and 1605, at the court of the Holy Roman Emperor Rudolph II in Prague, by the gem engraver Caspar Lehman (1570–1622), who engraved plaques and beakers with portraits and allegorical subjects.

In Bohemia a new type of glass known as "lime" glass, in which chalk lime carbonate was added to the batch to give a strong, colorless crystal suitable for deep engraving, was developed c.1683. At about the same time water power was introduced to drive the wheels, and this also enabled deeper cutting. Especially notable is the work of Dominik Biemann (1800–1857), whose training at the Prague Academy of Drawing is reflected in his fine engraved portraits on beakers and medallions. Of particular note are the Baroque pokals (lidded goblets) decorated with *Hochschnitt* ("high cut") engraving by the Silesian Friedrich Winter (d.c.1712). One of Lehman's pupils was Georg Schwanhardt the Elder (1601–70), who left Prague for Nuremberg where he established a workshop and founded a dynasty of skilled engravers, including his son Heinrich (1624–93).

The technique was further developed in the 19th century, as Bohemian craftsmen pioneered a process whereby glass was overlaid with a layer of glass in a different color and then wheel engraved to show the design in the color of the first layer. Two layers of glass were standard, but sophisticated pieces were composed of up to four layers. Such pieces demanded great expertise, as each colored layer cooled at a different rate, and with each additional color the risk of cracking increased. Common decoration included forest and hunting scenes, rural views, and castles. However, most sought after are special commissions such as portraits of famous people, battle scenes, and important buildings. Highly skilled Bohemian craftsmen traveled across Europe, so many pieces of this type were produced in various countries.

▲ Goblet
The large surface and cover area of the goblet allowed Bohemian engravers great scope for decoration, as did the use of a second color. In this ruby-flashed Bohemian goblet the engraver has cut through the colored layer, creating an idealized landscape in the clear glass beneath. Goblets that have their covers are more valuable than those without them.
*(c.1800; ht 32cm/12⅛in; value **K**)*

Toward the end of the 19th century some fine wheel-engraved pieces with *Hochschnitt* and *Tiefschnitt* (incised or intaglio) decoration were designed by J. & L. Lobmeyr (est. 1823) in Vienna. The firm produced copies of 18th-century designs and worked in Classical and contemporary styles. Leading engravers who worked for Lobmeyr included Karl Pietsch (1826–83), Peter Eisert (1828–94), and Franz Ullmann (1846–1921).

Engraved glass was also produced in Sweden. In the 20th century some outstanding pieces were made at the Orrefors factory (est. 1898) in Orrefors, in the Småland region. In 1916 Simon Gate (1883–1945) was brought in as a chief designer, and he was joined the following year by Edvard Hald (1883–1980). Gate's designs typically feature elegant Neo-classical figures, while Hald's figures are more caricatured and are mostly shallow engraved. Between 1928 and 1941 Vicke Lindstrand (1904–83) also worked for Orrefors, producing stylish and elegant designs.

▶ Decanter and stopper designed by Simon Gate
Although designed by Gate, the engraving on all four sides of this Swedish decanter was carried out by Gustav Abels. The Neo-classical figures and elegant linear decoration featured are characteristic of the stylish and elegant wares designed by Gate during the 1920s. In the 1930s these refined figures became increasingly robust in style, probably due to the influence of Hald, another chief designer at Orrefors and a former pupil of Henri Matisse. Although Orrefors also produced some elegant, undecorated, free-blown wares, the firm is mostly renowned for its fine engraved designs.
*(1927; ht 27.5cm/10¾in; value **H**)*

◀ Plate made by J. & L. Lobmeyr
This beautifully carved glass plate, attributed to the Austrian decorator Franz Ullmann, is typical of the quality engraved wares made by the distinguished Viennese glasshouse of J. & L. Lobmeyr. The design features a scantily clad, winged young man brandishing a burning torch in one hand and a bow in the other; his quiver of arrows is slung across his back. The border is engraved with cornucopia, amatory trophies, and arabesques in the Renaissance style, characteristic of designs by Lobmeyr.
*(c.1885; diam. 23.5cm/9¼in; value **Q**)*

KEY FACTS

Diamond-point and stipple engraving
- CONDITION diamond-point engraving should be shallow, with ragged, slightly broken lines; minor damage will not greatly affect value of early pieces
- BEWARE copies were decorated by enthusiastic amateurs in the 19th century; when dated there is no confusion, but undated older glasses can be misleading

Marks
Diamond-point pieces may be signed on the foot or in the design

Wheel engraving
- TYPES OF GLASS 19th-century Bohemian colored glass was a popular base; this glass should feel heavy
- DECORATION late 18th-century pieces feature formal designs; heavy, ornate engraving is typical; high-quality pieces have elaborately cut, ornate feet

Marks
A signature may be concealed in an engraved design

See also Cut glass: Bohemia, Spain, Belgium, and France, pp.298–9; Art Deco: Glass, pp.428–435; Mid-century Modern: Glass, pp.456–7

Britain

The earliest engraving on British glass was carried out by the decorator Anthony de Lyse (thought to be of French origin) at the London establishment of the itinerant Italian craftsman Jacopo Verzelini (1522–1605). After a period in Antwerp, Verzelini settled in England, where between 1575 and 1596 he was given permission by Queen Elizabeth I to be the sole manufacturer of glass in the Venetian style; in part this privilege was granted on the condition that Verzelini would pass on traditional Venetian glassmaking skills to English glassworkers. In the 17th century the main method of engraving on British glass was diamond-point; from c.1720 wheel engraving was also popular. However, by the mid-19th century, with the onset of the Industrial Revolution and the demand for inexpensive, rapidly produced decorative wares, acid etching was the most widely used technique.

◀ "Boscobel oak" goblet
The diamond-point engraved decoration of a figure hiding in a tree shown on this British Jacobite drawn-trumpet goblet depicts the story of Charles II, who was forced to hide in an oak tree while escaping from the Battle of Worcester in 1651. Three royal crowns can be seen intertwined among the branches of the oak tree. The combination of intricate engraving and interesting political symbolism make this rare example extremely collectible.
(c.1740; ht 16cm/6¼in; value H)

WHEEL ENGRAVING

Wheel engraving, introduced to Britain from Germany c.1720, was the most common form of engraving in Britain during the 18th and early 19th centuries. This technique was much used for decorating drinking glasses, which were produced in a variety of shapes and sizes. From c.1735 these glasses became lighter in weight, and the decorative wheel engraving on the bowl sometimes reflected the purpose of the glass – a beer or ale glass might feature decoration of hops or barley, while a wine glass might be engraved with a vine motif.

The most famous British wheel-engraved glasses are groups known as "Williamite" and "Jacobite" glasses, decorated with symbols of political allegiance and produced for drinking toasts. Williamite glasses were made from c.1740, to celebrate the 50th anniversary of the Battle of the Boyne in Ireland (1690), when the Protestant King William III of England defeated the Catholic ex-King James II. Williamite glasses are rarer than Jacobite examples and usually feature a portrait of William III on horseback, with the inscription "To the Glorious Memory."

In direct opposition, Jacobite glasses show allegiance to James Edward Stuart, the "Old Pretender," and his son Charles Edward Stuart (known as "Bonnie Prince Charlie" or the "Young Pretender"), both the descendants of James II. Such glasses were made between c.1746 (the date of the Battle of Culloden when Bonnie Prince Charlie and his troops were finally defeated and had to flee to France) and c.1766, the year in which the Old Pretender died and Stuart claims to the throne of England were finally dashed. Decoration usually comprised traditional Jacobite motifs such as the rose (representative of the English Crown), often with one or two buds (the rose for the Old Pretender, one bud for the Young Pretender, and a second, smaller bud for his brother Henry Benedict); the thistle, the lily of the valley, the oak tree and oak leaves (references to King Charles II, a death-bed convert to Catholicism), busts of Bonnie Prince Charlie, and mottos including "*Fiat*" ("May it be so") or "*Redeat*" ("May he return"). Also notable are the "Amen" wine glasses, with diamond-point engraved decoration of a crown, verses from a Jacobite hymn, and the word "Amen"; there are only about 24 genuine Amen glasses known to exist. With Williamite, Jacobite, and Amen glasses reliable provenance is essential as a guarantee of authenticity, as numerous reproductions are known to have been produced throughout the 19th and 20th centuries; these can be identified by an experienced eye.

Following the Great Exhibition in London in 1851, styles and fashions of glassware changed. Engraved glass was manufactured in enormous quantities and varying qualities, and on a great number of subjects. The finer pieces were extremely time-consuming to produce – for example, an exhibition-quality wine jug might take a year. A large number of pieces were produced by skilled craftsmen after designs by master engravers, while others were engraved by less-skilled workers, who decorated wares with designs including ferns, stars, and geometric patterns. These are very common and available to collectors.

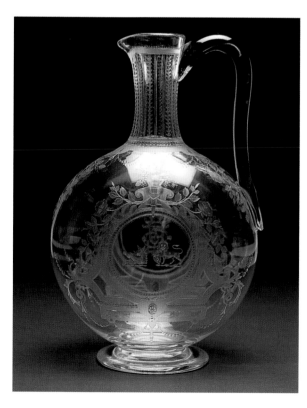

▲ Souvenir goblet
The Great Exhibition held in 1851 in London provided a showcase for new developments in glassware following the abolition of the Excise Tax in 1845. This engraved goblet was made as a souvenir of the Exhibition. The design shows the Crystal Palace, where the Exhibition was held, complete with the inscription "The Crystal Palace; Building for the Grand International Exhibition: 1851." Such memorabilia, in good condition, are very collectible.
(c.1851; ht 23cm/9in; value G)

◀ Presentation jug
The handle on this presentation jug, given as a wedding present, is a clue to its date; it is attached at the top of the neck and then drawn down to the body of the piece, a characteristic of jugs made before c.1870. The flattened "doughnut" shape of the body, which provides a large surface for the finely engraved decoration, is another typical feature of high-quality mid-19th-century English jugs. Much of this type of ware, with armorial devices and naturalistic decoration, is characteristic of wares produced during the mid-19th century.
(c.1860; ht 26.5cm/10½in; value G)

▼ Vase

Acid etching was generally used on clear glass, providing a distinctive matt or frosted finish. The technique was generally not considered successful on colored glass, as designs appeared much less sharply than on colorless glass. This colored, acid-etched vase, with naturalistic decoration on the body and neck and a contrasting angular design around the rim, is therefore unusual. It was produced in Stourbridge, one of the major glassmaking centers in England. *(19th century; ht 15cm/6in; value* **C***)*

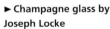

Also sought after are signed pieces engraved by the highly skilled German and Bohemian glass engravers who came to work, and often settled, in Britain. Distinguished names include Joseph Keller, an independent Bohemian glass engraver who worked in the Stourbridge area; William Fritsche (*c*.1853–1924), also from Bohemia, who worked for Thomas Webb & Sons (est. 1856) near Stourbridge; Wilhelm Pohl, who worked in Manchester; J.B. Millar (originally Muller), who worked for Stevens & Williams (est. *c*.1830) of Brierley Hill, near Stourbridge; and Franz Joseph Palme, noted for his engraved animals.

ACID ETCHING

Acid etching, in which corrosive acid (usually hydrofluoric) is used to produce a shiny outline of a design onto the surface of the glass, which was probably first employed in Britain from the 1830s by the firm of Thomas Hawkes in Dudley. Apsley Pellatt (1791–1863) in his book *Curiosities of Glassmaking* (1849) mentions etching by "floric" acid had been introduced but noted that "its 'bite' is not sufficiently rough to be found effective for general purposes." By the 1860s the technique was being used to engrave flatware, wine glasses, bottles, and vases, and by the 1880s it was widely in use as a quick and inexpensive method of decorating mass-produced glassware. Early pieces were often exquisitely decorated, with a combination of acid etching to create the outline and hand engraving to fill in the design; most mass-produced pieces were decorated solely by acid etching, and the designs are therefore usually less finely defined.

Perhaps the most celebrated English exponent of acid etching was John Northwood (1836–1902), who trained at the firm of W.H., B. & J. Richardson (est. *c*.1836) near Stourbridge. The firm was granted a patent for acid etching in 1857. By 1859 Northwood had established his own workshop, in partnership with his brother Joseph Northwood (1839–1915). Northwood

► Champagne glass by Joseph Locke

Although born and trained in England, Locke is best known as one of the major glassworkers in the USA, where he worked for the New England Glass Co. This fine acid-etched champagne glass is signed "Locke Art" at the base of the bowl, and the sophisticated naturalistic design is characteristic of Locke's work. He is especially celebrated for his work on acid-etched, cameo, and colored glass. Although *tazza*-shaped champagne glasses such as this were produced from *c*.1830, narrow, flute-shaped champagne glasses are probably more suitable for preventing the bubbles from escaping. *(c.1890; ht 13.5cm/5¼in; value* **A***)*

▲ Goblet decorated by Laurence Whistler

Whistler (*b*.1912) is one of the artists responsible for the revival of stipple engraving in Britain in the 20th century. This goblet is an example of the inscriptional and emblematic designs of his early period; glass of his middle period is often decorated with landscape scenes; his later work is typically architectural in design. *(1940; ht 27cm/10½in; value* **G***)*

experimented widely with acid etching in continual pursuit of improving the technique; he invented a machine that facilitated template (rather than hand) etching, an etching machine that enabled angular patterns to be reproduced at speed, and "white" acid (introduced 1867), which provided a matt finish and eliminated the need for laborious shading by hand. Another major exponent of acid etching was Joseph Locke (1846–1936), the British engraver who worked for the Richardson firm before emigrating in 1882 to the USA.

KEY FACTS

- **WARES** diamond-point engraving: mostly used for commemorative glasses, particularly those with political affiliations; wheel engraving: typically used to decorate glasses, vases, goblets, and jugs; acid etching: widely used for mass-produced pieces as it is much less expensive and more rapid than the other methods of engraving
- **DESIGNS** the most collectible subjects are battle scenes, landscapes, or portraits; exotic beasts and oriental scenes are also popular
- **COLLECTING** deeply engraved hollow-ware such as jugs, decanters, and glasses are most sought after; Jacobite glasses: copies were made in the 19th century but can generally be identified by their large size (33cm/13in) compared with the smaller originals

Marks

If signed, acid-etched pieces should have an acid-etched mark; many wheel-engraved pieces are marked

Stevens & Williams: one of several marks used

Laurence Whistler: wares engraved with his initials **LW**

Cut glass

Cut-glass decoration has been used since Roman times, but until the 18th century designs were limited to simple, shallow-cut patterns – as most glass was comparatively thin walled, it could not withstand deep cutting and complex decoration. Two major developments brought about change: the invention of lead glass *c.*1676 by the British glassmaker George Ravenscroft, and the development of overlay glass. Lead crystal was an ideal cutting medium, with a soft metal and thick-walled forms that lent themselves to deep and elaborate cutting and prismatic facets; overlay glass – several layers of glass (usually of different colors) fused together – provided thick-walled colored forms that allowed craftsmen to show off their virtuoso cutting skills.

Ireland, Britain, and the United States

Much of the finest 18th- and 19th-century cut glass was made in Ireland, Britain, and the USA. Production in Ireland and Britain was greatly affected by changes in taxation. In Britain an Act of Parliament introducing a tax on glass according to size and weight was passed in 1745. This led to changes in glass design, as makers, keen to minimize the amount of tax payable, concentrated on the production of smaller, lighter wares. In 1777, 1781, and 1788 Excise Acts that further increased taxes were passed; it was not until 1845, when these Acts were repealed, that exuberantly cut glass was able to flourish. The finest Irish glassware was made between 1780 and 1825, when an export tax was introduced on Irish glass.

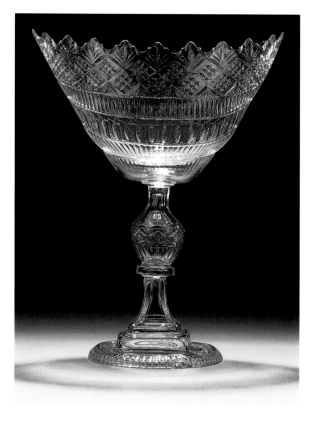

▲ Bowl
This large two-piece bowl is typical of fine, luxury cut-glass wares produced in Ireland between 1780 and 1825. The canoe shape, ornate rim, bands of pattern, and pale grey tone are all characteristic of wares produced in Dublin and Cork. The huge size suggests that this bowl was made as a display piece rather than for serving food.
(1790; ht 50cm/19½in; value O)

IRELAND
The British Excise Acts imposed heavy taxes on glass, and both British and Irish glassmakers took the opportunity to avoid taxes by setting up factories in Ireland. Glassware made in Ireland during this period is known as "Anglo-Irish." Major factories were established in several cities, most notably Richard Williams & Co. (1764–1827) in Dublin; the Waterford Glass House (1783–1851), founded by George and William Penrose, in Waterford; the Cork Glass Co. (1783–1813) and the Waterloo Glass House Co. (1815–35), both in Cork; and the Belfast Glassworks (1803–40) in Belfast. These firms made large bowls, vases, decanters, and jugs in heavy lead crystal. Most 18th-century pieces had simple decoration of geometric patterns cut with shallow, lateral bands. In the early 19th century designs became more ambitious. The charm of many of these large, elaborately cut pieces (often incorporating several patterns) lies in their eccentricities or slight imperfections, such as the foot being set at a slightly wrong angle. Unusual features that add to value include turn-over rims on bowls – these are always found on pieces with "lemon-squeezer" feet.

BRITAIN
Despite the restrictions on glass, by the early 19th century many British glassmakers were producing fine cut-glass tableware known as "Regency" glass. These designs were made largely between 1800 and 1830 and most are very fully cut in only one pattern. In 1845 the Excise Act that had drastically affected British glass production was repealed; most production moved back to the British mainland, and British cut-glass manufacture was able to flourish. Among the major, and now highly collectible, manufacturers were W.H., B. & J. Richardson (est. *c.*1836) and Thomas Webb & Sons (est. 1837), both near Stourbridge, and the F. & C. Osler Glasshouse (est. 1807) in Birmingham. Osler, renowned for its heavily cut high-quality glass, even made glass furniture for export to the Far East. One of the company's most famous creations was the elaborate glass fountain (7m/ 22ft 11in high) that formed the centerpiece of the Great Exhibition of 1851. Ironically, the Exhibition was to prove a turning-point for cut glass: the public were drawn to the lighter, "prettier" glass on show, and heavy-cut crystal, which by this time had become so ornate that designs were described by John Ruskin in his treatise *The Stones of Venice* (1851–3) as "prickly monstrosities," went out of fashion.

▲ Butter dish
Butter dishes are among the most collectible pieces of Irish glass. This example, which is one of a pair, is particularly desirable due to the very ornate cutting, especially around the rim, and the presence of a matching, intricately cut stand.
(1820; diam. 20cm/8in; value C)

▼ Decanter
This lead-crystal decanter combines elaborate hobnail cutting on the body with step cutting on the neck. The latter allows for easier handling as it is not as "prickly" as some cuts. The similarly cut mushroom-shaped stopper is typical of the period.
(late 1830s; ht 26cm/10¼in; value C)

THE UNITED STATES

In the early 19th century Boston, Massachusetts, and Philadelphia, Pennsylvania, were the major American centers of production for elegant glass tableware. However, from c.1818 the focus moved to Pittsburgh, Pennsylvania, where the arrival of a highly talented French glass cutter, Alexis Jardell, signaled the beginning of a period of exceptionally fine glass production, with heavy pieces decorated with cross-hatched diamonds with blaze or strawberry diamonds and fans. One of the leading firms in Pittsburgh was Bakewell's (1808–82; renamed the Pittsburgh Flint Glass Manufactory c.1813), established by Edward Ensell and bought by Benjamin Bakewell in 1808. Cut glass was made from 1810, the technique having been introduced to the firm by William Peter Eichbaum, who had worked for Louis XVI in France.

However, top-quality cut glass was still imported from Europe until the growth of a wealthy middle-class market toward the end of the 19th century resulted in a more developed American glasscutting industry. The firm of J. Hoare & Co. was set up by John Hoare (1822–96), the son of an Irish glasscutter, who arrived in the USA in 1853. After taking over the cutting department at the Brooklyn Flint Glass Co., New York, he moved to Corning, New York, where he founded the Corning Glass Works (1868–1920). Thomas G. Hawkes (1846–1913) came to the USA from Ireland in 1867; he worked for Hoare before setting up the firm of T.G. Hawkes & Co. (1880–1962).

The period 1876 to 1914 is known as the "Brilliant" period of American glassmaking, as much glass was cut with deep cutting, which was highly polished. Glass is typically cut in highly bold, elaborate patterns, which exploit the refractive quality of the glass to the full. Some of Hawkes's top-quality glass was so heavily cut that it was almost too "prickly" to handle. One of the most celebrated of its range of complex, deeply cut patterns was the "Russian" cut, introduced in 1882 and used for a service ordered by the Russian Embassy in Washington, and for another commissioned by the White House in 1885. Fairs were important showcases for glassmakers, and American firms used the Centennial Exhibition of 1876 in Philadelphia and the Columbian World Fair of 1892–3 to show off their work.

◄ **Part of an armorial service, probably by the Wear Flint Glass Works**
This British rinser, plate, and half-pint decanter are part of an armorial service. The crest features an arm brandishing a dagger and is contained within a lozenge-shaped cartouche. The rinser features deeply worked diamond cutting, as does the decanter, although the neck is step cut, making it easier to handle; the plate has an elaborate rim and fan-cut decoration. Each piece has a star-cut base. Also in the service are dishes, carafes, and stands.
*(1820–25; ht of decanter 23cm/9in; value **D**)*

▲ **Pair of *tazze* by T.G. Hawkes & Co.**
This pair of highly decorative American *tazze* combines cutting and engraving, a flamboyant mixture that is rarely, if ever, found on European pieces. These opulent pieces, made from heavy crystal, were produced for the increasingly prosperous middle classes. Most pieces by Hawkes are marked; earlier wares feature the name "Hawkes" and, occasionally, a paper label; later pieces are marked by acid etching.
*(c.1890; ht 20cm/8in; value **G**)*

► **Punch-bowl by J. Hoare & Co.**
This extraordinary American punch-bowl is a good example of the virtuosity, or even excess, of glass cutting in the USA during what is known as the "Brilliant" period (1876–1914). The blown-glass form is completely covered with intricate wheel-cut patterns and features an elaborately cut, scalloped rim and an equally decorative cut foot.
*(c.1890–1910; ht 39.5cm/15½in; value **F**)*

KEY FACTS

Ireland
- FORMS early cut glass is extremely heavy owing to the thickness of glass required for deep cutting; anomalies in shape and construction are common in early pieces but add to their charm; molded feet on large bowls should be square – other shapes indicate later cutting or restoration
- COLOR 18th-century pieces have a greyer tint than the typically brighter pieces of the 19th-century; small white or black flecks (seeds) caused by variations in temperature are common
- DESIGNS lateral bands of decoration should consist of more than one pattern

Marks
Waterford Crystal Ltd: this is a modern mark and will be acid etched

Britain
- PRODUCTION very little between 1745 and 1775 when English glass production was heavily taxed
- DESIGNS these tend to be very heavy and exuberant from 1845 to 1860 when heavy, cut glass fell out of fashion

Marks
Thomas Webb & Sons: used from c.1880

The United States
- METAL most is characterized by a clear, heavy metal
- SURFACE if the surface is very shiny, the piece may have been acid polished; hand polishing is preferable
- CUTTING typically very deep and sharp to the touch
- COLLECTING on a good-quality piece the metal should ring like a bell when struck gently

Marks
T.G. Hawkes & Co.: this mark was usually acid stamped; used between 1895 and 1962

J. Hoare & Co.: used between 1895 and 1920

See also Bohemia, Spain, Belgium, and France, pp.298–9

Bohemia, Spain, Belgium, and France

Cut glass in Bohemia is to some degree eclipsed by the fine 19th-century cut-glass wares produced in Britain and Ireland and the elaborate later designs of the American "Brilliant" cut-glass period. Spain, although more noted for its enameled glass, also produced some delicately cut designs. The influence of "Anglo-Irish" glass was particularly strong in Belgium and France, as many Belgian and French glass factories employed itinerant British and Irish workers. Both Belgium and France produced many elaborate and ornate cut-glass designs, notably some splendid wares designed for the many 19th-century international exhibitions.

BOHEMIA

Early Bohemian cut glass was mostly produced in the region of Silesia , notably at the glassworks at Sklarzska Poreba. Wares typically combined cutting with engraved designs of topographical views, portraits, allegorical subjects, and Rococo motifs. Thereafter glass production in Silesia fell into decline when the area became part of Prussia in 1742.

▼ Beaker engraved by Dominik Biemann

This Bohemian beaker features the heavy cutting on the base and the gold rim typical of the Biedermeier period (c.1815–c.1848). Biemann, one of the top engravers of the time, was noted for his fine portraits.

(c.1830; ht 8.5cm/3¼in; value **H**)

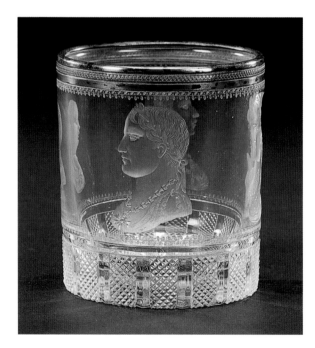

By 1800 the techniques of decorating glass by engraving, enameling, and gilding were more widely used in Bohemia than cut decoration. However, by this time British and Irish wares, made of colorless lead glass and decorated with elaborate, deep-cut designs, were gaining international renown, and Bohemian glassmakers were forced to shift the emphasis of their production in order to compete with the new fashions. The number of colorless, cut-glass wares was increased, although these wares still typically combined cut decoration with engraving, enameling, or gilding in order to retain a characteristic Bohemian style.

As much Bohemian glassware was made of the more brittle soda glass, body shapes of wares with cut decoration were often slightly clumsy with uneven walls, as the glass had to be shaped in thick forms to allow safe cutting. Overlay glass, which was made of several layers of glass and therefore thick walled, was better suited to cutting, and is one of the most common types of Bohemian cut glass.

From c.1830 glasswares were produced using pressing machines molded with cut-glass designs, which enabled the mass production of inexpensive imitation cut glass. Although more accessible and affordable, these wares were mostly of a lesser quality than hand-carved pieces. One major 19th-century Bohemian maker intent on re-establishing a high level of artistic design was Josef Lobmeyr (1792–1855) of J. & L. Lobmeyr (est. 1823) in Vienna. His firm made fine, heavily cut, clear-glass vases, decanters, and beakers; many were carved on blanks bought in from the Harrach Glassworks (est. 1714) in Neuwelt (now Novy Svet in the Czech Republic).

SPAIN

Cut glass was produced in Spain, most notably by the factory of La Granja de San Ildefonso (est. 1728) near Segovia, founded by the glassmaker Ventura Sit (d.1755). The firm made spirit bottles, scent bottles, and small practical wares such as beakers, plates, and bowls with cut-glass decoration from the end of the 18th century, although it is best known for its enameled wares. Designs were decorated in a technique that was more akin to wheel engraving than traditional Irish, British, or American cutting, with cuts that were very shallow, regular in width, and mostly semi-circular.

BELGIUM

In Belgium one of the most innovative manufacturers was the Vonêche Glassworks (est. 1778) near Namur, which employed Irish glassworkers and made British-style lead crystal from 1802 to 1830. Wares were typically elaborate and included vases, dishes, clockcases, and goblets; some of the most ornate were embellished with gilt-bronze mounts. Many fine designs were made by one of its glassworkers, Charpentier (active 1802–16), who decorated wares with cupids and goddesses. In 1802, Charpentier established the firm of Escalier de Cristal, in Paris, which decorated and sold a wide range of glasswares, including glass furniture. Supplied with glass from Vonêche, Escalier de Cristal also decorated wares with intricate diamond cutting and elaborate ormolu mounts. The firm of Cappleman, in Brussels, also received glass from Vonêche, and produced cut-glass wares under the supervision of British cutters.

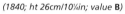

◄ Lily vase

The ornate cutting on this tall vase, designed to support the long stems of lilies, identifies its Bohemian origins. The elegant shape, which closely resembles that of a gently flared drinking glass, is vulnerable, although some stability is provided by the comparatively heavy foot, also decorated with an intricately cut pattern.

(1840; ht 42cm/16in; value **D**)

▼ Decanter

Several features found on original British decanters can be seen on this continental (probably Bohemian) soda-glass version in the Regency style ` of c.1820. Heavy cutting has replaced the gilded and engraved decoration that is more typically on 18th-century decanters, and the piece has a large bulbous body, neck rings and a short neck for ease of handling, and a mushroom stopper – fashionable during the Regency period, and therefore found on Regency-style designs.

(1840; ht 26cm/10¼in; value **B**)

▲ Tureen, cover, and stand by Vonêche

Irish glassworkers were employed by many leading continental glass factories, and this often resulted in interesting hybrid pieces such as this tureen with cover and stand. Manufactured by Irish glassworkers at Vonêche in Belgium, the piece has a continental body shape but is cut in the Irish style, with bands of differently cut patterns.

(1800; ht 28cm/11in; value **H***)*

The Val-Saint-Lambert Glasshouse (est. 1825) in Seraing-sur-Meuse, near Liège, is probably the largest Belgian factory, and is now one of the world's leading makers of cut and engraved glass. During the 19th century it produced very fine cut-glass crystal wares, which were heavily influenced by Irish and British designs as British glassworkers were brought over to direct the cutting department. The most typical wares include elaborate lighting fixtures such as chandeliers and candelabra with faceted lusters, diamond-cut vases, footed bowls, flasks decorated with deep-cut laurel leaves, and tumblers. The spectacular designs of Léon Ledru are especially fine; his "Vase of Nine Provinces" – a massive (2.25m/7½ft high), elaborately cut vase with nine faces, each representing one of the nine Belgian provinces – was designed for the 1894 International Exhibition in Antwerp.

FRANCE

Access to the French market was lost to the Vonêche factory following the annexation of Belgium by the Low Countries in 1815. In 1816 the then owner of the factory, Aimé-Gabriel d'Artigues, bought the French glassworks in Baccarat (est. 1764 as the Sainte-Anne Glassworks) in Baccarat, near Lunéville, Lorraine, which until then had produced soda glass for domestic and industrial markets. The land around Baccarat was heavily wooded, proving an ideal site for a glass factory requiring large quantities of wood for fuel, and d'Artigues's firm was to become one of the leading designers and manufacturers of fine glass, a position it still holds today.

Baccarat is celebrated for its continual quest for better manufacturing techniques, including the invention *c.*1810 of a cutting machine with hydraulically operated (instead of foot-powered) wheels, which speeded up production and made wheel cutting less tiring. The factory's profile

was boosted when the fine cut-glass wares impressed Louis XVIII at the 1823 National Exhibition in Paris. By 1838 artists at Baccarat were also cutting overlay glass. Baccarat produced many monumental pieces such as floor-standing candelabra (including two huge matching candelabra measuring 5.25m/17ft for the Paris Exhibition of 1855), chandeliers, decorative columns, fountains, and vases, some with gilt-bronze mounts in the Victorian taste. Although most pieces were decorated at Baccarat, some were worked on by glasscutters at such independent decorating firms as the Escalier de Cristal. Typical cuts include the simple "flat" cut, used for the "Harcourt" service, the elaborate and intricate "rich" cut used for the "Colbert" service, and the decorative "ornamental" cut used on the "Prestige" service, embellished with elaborate gilt decoration. Notable artists working at Baccarat included François Eugène de Fontenay (1810–84).

Less prolific than Baccarat was the French Saint-Louis Glassworks (est. 1767) near Bitche, in the Münzthal, Lorraine. The factory produced a large quantity of cut glass from the end of the 18th century. Most pieces have heavy bodies made of very good-quality crystal. However, pieces by Saint-Louis can be difficult to identify as they were in the style of many other makers of the period, and were often only marked with vulnerable paper labels.

▼ Lidded jar by Vonêche or Baccarat

The Vonêche Glassworks produced English-style lead crystal between 1802 and 1830. Athough the body shape is continental, it has been cut in the fashionable Irish style and has the characteristic Irish square foot: a result of the many Irish glassworkers who were employed at Vonêche.

(1820; ht 20cm/8in; value **G***)*

▲ Jar and cover by Baccarat

The Irish influence is evident in this lead-crystal jar and cover, decorated with fine swirling cut designs. The square foot and deep cutting may have been the work of the Irish glassworkers employed by the French company. The superb quality and craftsmanship are typical.

(1830; ht 26cm/10in; value **F***)*

KEY FACTS

Bohemia
- DECORATION cutting is often combined with engraved decoration as well as gilding and color
- MATERIAL mostly soda glass with walls of uneven thickness; overlay glass is the most common

Spain
- PRODUCTION mostly small-scale wares
- DECORATION shallow, semi-circular cutting is typical

Belgium and France
- MATERIAL mostly lead glass
- WEIGHT cut glass should feel heavy
- CONDITION the metal should be bright, with a soft feel and no color imperfections
- COLLECTING the finest examples are held in museums

Marks
Monumental pieces occasionally feature a molded mark or a mark on the gilt-bronze mount, but most pieces were marked only with a paper label; an acid-etched or engraved mark indicates a 20th-century piece

Vonêche: pieces decorated at the Escalier de Cristal feature this mark

Baccarat: mark used on cut-glass wares from 1860; this mark is still used today

Val-Saint-Lambert: one of several marks used ✳

See also Lighting, pp.306–7

Cameo glass

Cameo decoration on glass was first used by the Romans in an attempt to imitate small, decorative hardstone or shell cameos. A glass body, which was usually of a deep blue, was covered with one or more layers of glass in a contrasting color, usually white. This layer was then cut back to leave the decoration standing proud in the top color and the background in the base color. Finally, the decoration was lightly engraved to give further definition. The finest example of Roman cameo glass is the "Portland" vase, a cobalt-blue *amphora* with white cameo decoration. Its origins are unknown, but it is dated from the 1st century BC to the 1st century AD. It was brought to Britain by Sir William Hamilton *c.*1783 and bought by the Duchess of Portland (hence the name). Unlike other Roman techniques cameo decoration not revived again until the 19th century, mainly in Britain and Bohemia. The Wedgwood factory (est. 1769) made ceramic versions known as "Jasper" wares.

▼ "Morgan" cup

This small Roman drinking-bowl, thought to be the earliest surviving example of cameo glass, demonstrates the finely developed skills of early gem engravers. The opaque-white, hand-carved frieze that encircles the cup depicts figures involved in a Dionysiac rite and stands in clear relief from the dark blue body.

(c.100 BC–AD 100; ht 6cm/2½ in; value Q)

BRITAIN

The arrival of the Portland vase in England spawned not only copies but also a fashion in the 19th century for cameo glass and decoration featuring Greek and Roman subjects. The most notable area for the manufacture of British cameo glass was Stourbridge in the Midlands, and one of the most important British exponents of the cameo-glass technique was John Northwood (1836–1902), a glassmaker who trained at the firm of W. H., B. & J. Richardson (est. *c.*1836) near Stourbridge. In 1859 Northwood set up his own firm in partnership with his brother Joseph Northwood (1839–1915), and from 1861 it was styled J. & J. Northwood. In 1876, after 20 years of work on the project, John Northwood engraved an exact copy of the Portland vase on a blank made by his cousin, the glassmaker Philip Pargeter (1826–1906) of the Red House Glassworks (est. 1776) in Stourbridge.

▲ Vase by Joseph Locke

This cameo-glass vase was made by covering a cobalt-blue blank in a layer of white glass, acid etching it in order to produce an outline of the design, and then engraving the white glass to give definition. The formal pattern at the neck, rim, and foot, and the use of a cupid with bow and arrows, are in the Neo-classical style. Although Locke worked for leading glass firms in Britain, including Thomas Webb & Sons, in 1882 he moved to the USA, where he went on to produce fine designs for several major glassmaking firms.

(c.1880; ht 19cm/7½in; value H)

► Vase by George Woodall for Thomas Webb & Sons

Woodall is perhaps the most celebrated British exponent of the cameo-glass technique, and the size, detail, and technical brilliance of this large and impressive display piece illustrate his expertise. The formal pattern is intricately executed in pink- and opaque white, and features lion masks and scrolling acanthus leaves. This vase may have been made for the Paris Exhibition in 1889; it was sold by the firm of Tiffany & Co. (est. 1837).

(1889; ht 41cm/16in; value L)

In 1878, together with Pargeter, Northwood produced the "Milton" vase, inspired by Milton's poem *Paradise Lost* and featuring Adam and Eve and the angel Raphael in blue-and-white cameo. In 1882 Northwood completed the "Pegasus" vase for Thomas Webb & Sons (est. 1837) in Stourbridge; this fine piece depicts Amphitrite, the queen of the sea, and Aurora, the personification of the dawn. The finial in the shape of Pegasus, the flying horse, and the sea-horse-shaped handles were carved by Northwood's assistant, Edwin Grice (1839–1913).

Perhaps the most highly renowned 19th-century cameo sculptor was George Woodall (1850–1925), an apprentice of John Northwood, who, together with his brother Thomas Woodall (1849–1926), produced large quantities of cameo glass for Thomas Webb & Sons, mostly in white on a colored background. Typical wares include vases, dishes, scent bottles, and plaques. Woodall also produced some extremely fine display pieces; most feature Classical scenes, some inspired by the sculptures of Antonio Canova and John Flaxman, although some have Chinese-inspired decoration.

Woodall's work exemplifies all the qualities associated with top-quality cameo glass: intricately detailed designs (often with a Classical or slightly erotic quality); sharp, clean edges to the decoration; and superb hand cutting.

Other leading exponents of the cameo technique include the gem engraver Alphonse Eugène Lechevrel (*b.*1850), who worked for Richardson's in 1877. He produced six fine cameo-glass vases decorated with Classical designs, which were shown at the 1878 Exhibition in Paris.

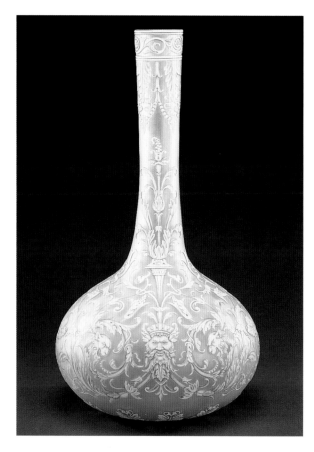

▶ **Scent bottle by Thomas Webb & Sons**

Cameo-glass scent bottles such as this one were very popular in the late 19th century. It is typically decorated with naturalistic designs of flowers and leaves; the silver stopper features matching motifs. Designs incorporating butterflies and small birds were also very characteristic.

(1887; ht 20cm/8in; value **G***)*

As the demand for cameo glass grew, short cuts were introduced to relieve the highly labor-intensive process. The top layer or layers of glass were made thinner and were cut away with an engraving wheel rather than hand tools. From the mid-19th century acid was used to burn through the layers of glass. This resulted in what is known as "commercial" or *faux* ("false") cameo, which although highly collectible is of a different quality from the hand-carved pieces. The definition between the different layers of glass is less marked, the edges of the decoration are softer, and the background is usually matt and slightly rough to the touch. *Faux* cameo vases were produced by many British manufacturers and makers, including Thomas Webb & Sons, Stevens & Williams (est. 1847) of Brierley Hill, near Stourbridge, Northwood's, and Thomas Woodall. All-over naturalistic decoration and the use of such motifs as arabesques became more common than decoration featuring intricately detailed figures.

FRANCE

In the 19th century the fashion for cameo glass soon spread from Britain to France, where such established factories as Baccarat (est. 1764 as the Sainte-Anne Glassworks) in Baccarat, near Lunéville, Lorraine, and the Saint-Louis Glassworks (est. 1767) near Bitche, in the Münzthal, Lorraine, where they began to produce many fine, hand-carved pieces, including vases. However, these factories are best known for their involvement in the development of *faux* cameo, used to produce affordable cameo glass. Wares include mass-produced vases, dishes and bowls, typically decorated with floral motifs and Greek key designs. The cameo technique reached its apogee in France at the end of the 19th century through the distinctive Art Nouveau glass of such outstanding artists as Emile Gallé (1846–1904) in Nancy, and the firm of Daum Frères (est. 1875), also in Nancy.

▶ **Glass by Baccarat**

The French firm of Baccarat made both hand-carved and *faux* cameo. *Faux* cameo was produced using acid to cut away the design, which made production quicker and more cost effective. This hand-carved piece is representative of Baccarat's high-quality designs. The particular example shown has an intricate, symmetrical pattern in pink in relief on a white ground.

(1860; ht 30cm/11¾in; value **E***)*

BOHEMIA

In Bohemia the cameo technique was popular since it was very similar to the traditional Bohemian method of producing overlay glass. The major difference is that the detail and shading on cameo is more intricate than that on overlay glass because the design left in relief is finely engraved after cutting. Wares produced ranged from hand-carved, labor-intensive display and exhibition pieces to mass-produced *faux* cameo items. Decoration is typically Bohemian and includes such themes as forest and hunting scenes, and portraits of German princes and political figures. The Harrach Glassworks (est. 1714) in Neuwelt (now Novy Svet in the Czech Republic) experimented with more avant-garde cameo glass.

THE UNITED STATES

The cameo-glass technique was introduced to the USA by an English glassmaker, Joseph Locke (1846–1936), who had trained under Lechevrel at Richardson's, in Stourbridge. Like John Northwood, Locke gained renown by his production of a copy of the Portland vase, exhibited at the Paris Exhibition of 1878. In 1882 Locke emigrated to the USA, where he worked first for the New England Glass Co. (1818–90) in East Cambridge, Massachusetts, and later at the Libbey Glass Co. (est. 1888) in Toledo, Ohio. He was a highly skilled craftsman and produced fine cameo glass, as well as training American glassworkers and introducing many innovatory types of colored glass. Other American firms working in the cameo-glass technique included Bakewell's (1808–82; renamed the Pittsburgh Flint Glass Manufactory c.1813) in Pittsburgh, Pennsylvania, the Boston & Sandwich Glass Co. (1826–88) in Sandwich, and the Mount Washington Glass Co. (est. 1837) in South Boston, both in Massachusetts.

▼ **Goblet by the Saint-Louis Glassworks**

Acid-etched cameo (*faux* cameo) was a quick and inexpensive alternative to hand carving. This example combines a cameo-glass bowl with a cut-glass stem and foot. The bowl, in shades of pink and white, features a rustic scene of a country boy tending his sheep. The detail is less fine than on hand-carved cameo.

(1870; ht 18cm/7in; value **G***)*

KEY FACTS

Britain
- WARES mainly vases, scent bottles, bowls
- COLORS mostly white decoration in relief on a colored background
- DESIGNS motifs from Classical mythology are the most typical; naturalistic designs were popular on late 19th-century pieces
- COLLECTING early hand-carved wares, especially by a famous maker, will be very highly priced; the finest examples are in museums; 19th-century acid-etched wares are generally quite affordable

Marks
Signatures greatly enhance the value; most appear on the base of the piece or within the decoration itself

Thomas & George Woodall: signature used 1880–1900   *J&G Woodall*

France, Bohemia, and the United States
- TECHNIQUE France: mostly acid-etched cameo glass
- PRODUCTION although France, Bohemia, and the USA produced cameo glass, until the late 19th century none was as prolific or celebrated as Britain

Marks
Saint-Louis Glassworks: this is one of a variety of marks used; some pieces are marked "Argental" or "Münzthal" (German for Argental), often with the cross of Lorraine   *J.Argental*

See also Ceramics: Wedgwood stoneware, p.166; Art Nouveau: Glass – France, pp.398–401

Additions to glass

Methods of working and decorating glass are incredibly varied. In addition to the formulative techniques of blowing, molding, and pressing, decorative glassware can be produced by a technique known as "lampwork." This involves the precise manipulation of tiny rods of glass over a flame and was widely used to produce ornamental, decorative glassware and delicate figures. In addition to coloring, engraving, enameling, and cutting, other methods of decorating glass are the inclusion of twists (clear, opaque, or colored spirals in a variety of combinations), the application of gilding, and decoration with imitation jewels made of colored glass. Others glass additions include medallions with ceramic inlays known as tassies and sulphides.

Lampwork

The technique of lampwork (also known as "lampblown" glass or glass made "at-the-lamp") was used as early as the 5th and 4th centuries BC for the production of jewelry beads. In the 15th century Venetian glassmakers refined the process in order to create small, complex shapes from rods or tubes of glass melted in a localized flame. The glass, which could be clear or colored, was blown or manipulated into intricate shapes over an oil lamp; these shapes were used to produce figures, intricate ornamentation for paperweights, or complex glass motifs used to decorate such wares as drinking glasses, epergnes, goblets, candlesticks, chandeliers, and mirrors.

FACON DE VENISE GLASS

The glass produced throughout Europe in the 16th and 17th centuries in the style of 15th-century Venetian glass is known as *façon de Venise* ("in the style of Venice") glass. Wares are highly decorative, ornate, and delicate. Typical forms include *tazze* (ornamental serving dishes), and winged or serpent-stemmed drinking glasses, which feature elaborate lampwork on the stem. Some of the finest examples of lampwork are the *façon de Venise* drinking glasses with winged stems made in the Low Countries at this time. The stems were tooled into fantastic and ornate shapes, typically incorporating mythical beasts, loops, snake-like patterns, and complex geometrical designs. The term used to describe this type of decoration is "threading," as the decoration is independent of the body of the glass. Most of the glasses are in a combination of colorless and blue glass. Notable producers of this type of ware included the Colinet Glassworks in Beauwelz, in the southern Low Countries, near the French border. In the mid-19th century there was a revival of traditional 15th- and 16th-century Venetian glassware, largely through the efforts of Antonio Salviati (1816–1900). Wares made include *tazze*, goblets with serpent and winged stems, and jugs with elaborate applied decoration.

GLASS FIGURES

The lampwork technique was also used to produce small, highly detailed decorative figures in opaque glass. Production is thought to have originated in France at the Nevers factory (est. 1603) in the Nièvre. The city had passed to the Gonzaga family of Mantua in 1565 through the marriage of Henrietta of Cleves to Ludovico Gonzaga; Gonzaga became Duke of Nevers, and the resulting influx of Italian craftsmen in the town included many glassmakers skilled in lampwork. Similar glass figures were also produced at Nuremberg, in Germany, at Antwerp, in the Low Countries, and in England, but they are now generally referred to as "Nevers" figures.

The technique involved heating rods of opaque-white glass at the lamp and then twisting the softened rods into the shape of a figure. When fired, the opaque-white glass had the appearance of porcelain, and could be decorated with colored enamels. Examples, some of which were built up around a metal armature, are well modeled but unsophisticated, with a characteristic rough surface. Most depict grotesque rustic subjects with stiff, unnatural postures, and exaggerated facial expressions. Some larger pieces depict more elevated subjects, such as saints, characters, or scenes from the Bible, including the Virgin Mary or the Crucifixion, or Classical figures; most smaller pieces are models of animals or miniature groups of pastoral or allegorical figures. Of particular note is a set of four figures, entitled the *Four Seasons*. Each figure holds an item representative of his season: a flowering branch (Spring), a sickle and corn (Summer), two bunches of grapes and a wine cup (Autumn), and a muff (Winter).

▲ Figure from the *Four Seasons*

This figure is Autumn, one of a very rare group of four Nevers figures representing the four seasons. Only two complete sets are known to exist, one of which is in a French museum. *(1775–1800; ht 13.5cm/5¼in; value for a set of four O)*

◄ "Serpent-stemmed" goblet

The skill of the Venetian glassmakers is reflected in the elaborate stem of the aptly named serpent-stemmed goblet. Colored and clear glass was manipulated at the lamp into an extraordinary variety of decorative forms. Such designs were originally produced in Venice in the 15th century and were widely reproduced throughout Europe in the 16th and 17th centuries. *(17th century; ht 28cm/11in; value L)*

KEY FACTS

Façon de Venise glass
- DESIGNS most feature highly elaborate lampwork stems in the form of serpents and dragons; some stems are decorated with interlocking loops
- COLLECTING skilful copies made in the 19th century are much less valuable than originals but are still usually expensive; it is often hard to differentiate between originals and copies

Nevers figures
- SIZE between 2.5 and 15cm (1–6in) tall
- TYPES mostly rustic characters with stiff postures and exaggerated facial expressions
- COLLECTING figures should have a glass base with a slightly rough and dirty surface – a smooth shiny finish suggests a recent piece; sets are very rare and valuable

Twisted stems

When the Excise Tax of 1745 was introduced in Britain, glassmakers had to find a way of manufacturing drinking glasses that were both light in weight and yet still decorative; one of the solutions was the air-twist stemmed glass, which was frequently further decorated with diamond-point or wheel engraving, which did not add to the weight. Opaque- or cotton-twist stems were introduced c.1770 as another way of decorating stems. Twisted-stem glasses were also made in the rest of Europe, although the quality tends to be inferior; glassmakers used soda glass, which cools more slowly than lead glass and is more difficult to control; the result was poorer or irregular twists.

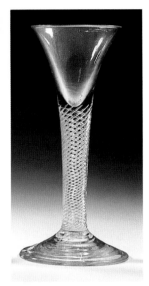

◄ Wine glass with a multiple-spiral, air-twist stem
The multiple-spiral air twist, which may contain up to 12 intertwined filaments, is the simplest form of twisted stem. Multiple spirals are more commonly found on glasses with plain air twists than on those with opaque or colored twists. In this example the twist is combined with a drawn trumpet bowl and a plain conical foot. As this is an early piece the underneath of the foot should feature a pontil mark; these were often ground off on later glasses.
*(c.1770; ht 14.5cm/5¾in; value **D**)*

AIR TWISTS: 1745–1770

In the 18th century glassmakers recognized that air bubbles (or "tears"), which appeared as flaws in the stem, could be pulled and skilfully manipulated into an attractive, decorative pattern. The larger the air bubble, the lower the overall weight of the glass – an important factor after the introduction of the 1745 Excise Act. Air-twist stem patterns were produced in several designs – the simplest type is the multiple-spiral twist, composed of 12 even filaments. Single twists (known as "single-series") feature filaments that are intertwined to create a single spiral; double-series twists are more complex, with one spiral contained within another. Another type of twist is the "mercury" twist, made from two tears, which are pulled into two flattened spirals and then twisted around one another. The flat surface of the spiral reflects the light like quicksilver – hence the name.

OPAQUE TWISTS: 1770–80

Between 1770 and 1780 opaque-white glass, produced by the addition of tin oxide to the batch, was also used to decorate stems. As the 1745 tax only applied to clear crystal, the same financial advantages that applied to air twists also applied to opaque twists. Rods of white glass were placed in the unfinished stem and then pulled and twisted into the desired pattern. Because the pulled white glass has the appearance of thin, white cotton, opaque

twists are also known as "cotton" twists. Single-series opaque twists are rare; more common are double-series opaque twists, where one spiral is contained within another. Triple-series opaque twists, which are composed of three intertwined spirals, are even rarer than single-series opaque ones.

COLORED AND MIXED TWISTS

A further variation on the twisted stem was the use of colored twists, which were produced by inserting a rod of colored glass – typically red and green but sometimes blue or yellow – into the stem of a glass and pulling it into a spiral. The technique is complex, as glass of different colors cools at different rates.

Some stems feature mixed twists. The most common designs are double-series twists composed of an air twist and an opaque twist. Mixed twists made of a combination of an air twist and a colored twist are more rare, mainly due to the complexity of working with colored glass. Mixed twists with an air twist, an opaque twist, and a colored twist were even more difficult to produce and are exceptionally rare.

▼ Wine glass with a double-series, opaque-twist stem
In this glass, a round funnel bowl with a molded base is joined to a double-series, opaque-twist stem. The foot would also have been separately produced. The most commonly found type of opaque twist, the double-series opaque twist is composed of two spirals of opaque-white glass, one contained inside the other. When tapped on the rim of the bowl, fine-quality lead-crystal glasses such as this should produce a sonorous ring. A neat and well-formed twist is also a good indication of quality.
*(1760–65; ht 16.5cm/6½in; value **D**)*

▲ Wine glass with a double-series, mixed-twist stem
This example with a rounded funnel bowl and conical foot combines an opaque and a colored twist. Blue is one of the rarer colors – red and green are more common.
*(1770; ht 17.5cm/7in; value **I**)*

◄ Wine glass with a double-series, mixed-twist stem
An air twist and an opaque-white twist are combined in the stem of this wine glass. The waisted bucket bowl and conical foot would have been made separately and then joined to the stem.
*(c.1760; ht 16cm/6¼in; value **G**)*

KEY FACTS

- MATERIALS British 18th-century drinking glasses are mostly made of lead crystal, which sets slowly and was well suited to the creation of fine twists; most Dutch 18th-century glasses were made of soda glass, which sets more quickly, so twists are less fine
- TYPES air twists, opaque twists, colored twists, mixed twists featuring a combination of twist types
- COLORS on colored twists red and green are most typical; blue and yellow are more rare
- DESIGNS multiple spirals of 12 even filaments, single-, double-, and triple-series twists, "mercury" twists
- CONDITION fine lead crystal should ring when tapped on the rim
- COLLECTING the most collectible glasses are those with the twists that were most difficult to produce such as colored twists and mixed twists; twists on good-quality glasses are usually neat, solid, and well formed
- FAKES twists in faked examples tend to appear more deeply embedded in the glass than in the originals; threads sometimes lack continuity

Gilding

Gilding, the application of gold leaf, gold paint, or gold dust to a glass surface, was a technique primarily used in Continental Europe. On early Venetian drinking glasses and *tazze*, as well as on early Bohemian and German drinking vessels, it was often employed in conjunction with enameling; it was also popular in France and Italy for the decoration of highly ornate wares. Gilding in Britain was used most notably to decorate colored-glass decanters (especially those in "Bristol" glass). There are two main types of gilding: fired gilding and cold gilding. With fired gilding, the gold is applied to the glass surface, which is then fired to fix the gilding; gold decoration of this type has a bright, metallic appearance. With cold gilding, the glass is not fired, and the gilded decoration therefore remains very vulnerable to wear and tear; cold gilding may often have worn away, leaving only residual marks on the object.

◄ Jug
Gilded decoration was often combined with enameled and/or engraved decoration. On this jug, whose gilding is still intact, the intaglio-engraved flowers have been filled with gilding and then fired. Although it was made in Britain, such pieces as this were rarely made by British manufacturers, and are far more typical of French production. However, such rich ornamentation is highly characteristic of the elaborately decorated wares that were popular during the Victorian period in Britain.
(c.1890; ht 15cm/6in; value D)

ZWISCHENGOLDGLAS

The type of glass known as *Zwischengoldglas* ("sandwich gold glass") was developed by Bohemian glassmakers around the beginning of the 18th century; it was particularly popular between c.1730 and 1740. Gold (or very occasionally silver) leaf was applied to the outer surface of a drinking glass, usually a tumbler or a pokal (a lidded goblet), and then engraved with a stylus with such images as hunting scenes, armorial crests, and religious subjects. A slightly larger, protective glass sleeve was then slipped over the engraved decoration, and the glass and sleeve were sealed at the base and top of the vessel in order to protect the decoration.

The technique was revived and developed at the end of the 18th century, mainly through the work of the Austrian Johann Josef Mildner (1763–1808), who perfected the *Medaillonbecher*, a type of beaker inset with a medallion panel depicting portraits or landscapes. During another revival at the end of the 19th century, such firms as Ludwig Moser & Sons (est. c.1857) in Karlsbad (now Karlovy Vary in the Czech Republic), and the Val-Saint-Lambert Glasshouse (est. 1825) in Seraing-sur-Meuse, near Liège, produced a range of *Zwischengoldglas*.

► Goblet and cover
This Bohemian goblet and cover with a double-walled faceted bowl was made during the first fashion for *Zwischengoldglas*. In spite of its age the gilt decoration is particularly well preserved.
(c.1725–50; ht 26.5cm/10½in; value I)

◄ Beaker and saucer
Experiments with colored glass led to the development in Bohemia in 1819 of a dense, opaque glass known as "Hyalith," which could be a sealing-wax red or, as in this example, jet-black. In this set it provides the perfect background for the fired-gilded chinoiserie decoration (pagodas, exotic birds). Made for display rather than use, the decoration does not show signs of wear.
(c.1820; ht 12cm/4¾in; value G)

OTHER TYPES OF GILDED GLASS

In Britain gilding was popularly used to embellish the blue-, green-, and amethyst-colored glass, known as "Bristol" glass, produced from the end of the 18th century to the middle of the 19th. Notable gilders included James Giles (1718–80), a London porcelain decorator who also worked on glass. Decoration is typically calligraphic, although some wares feature chinoiserie designs. Giles was highly influential, and many blue, green, or white Bristol-glass decanters are gilded in his style. Other distinguished names include the gilder Michael Edkins (1734–1811), a freelance decorator who worked in Bristol and gilded opaque-white glass and blue glass. Edkins decorated some wares for the Non-Such Flint Glassworks (est. 1805) in Bristol, run by Isaac Jacobs (active 1790–1835). Wares produced by the firm include decanters, toilet-water and scent bottles, and wine coolers.

In Bohemia large numbers of ornate vases with heavy enameled and gilded decoration were made in the 19th century. In France opaline wares were embellished with delicately gilded flowers and arabesques, and the glassmakers Philippe-Joseph Brocard (d.1896) and I.J. Imberton produced wares in the Islamic style with elaborate enameling combined with gilding and jeweling. Gilded Islamic-styles wares were also made by J. & L. Lobmeyr (est. 1823) in Vienna.

KEY FACTS

- FINISH original gilding should have a smooth, matt finish similar to old gold; regilding will look too bright and slightly grainy; fired gilding has a much brighter finish than cold gilding
- CONDITION cold gilding is vulnerable and rarely survives, but there may be residual marks
- CARE do not use detergent on gilded glass, as this will damage the decoration
- COLLECTING the value of gilded wares is determined to a large degree by the quality of the gilded decoration; early examples of *Zwischengoldglas* are very collectible

Marks

Gilded signatures usually identify the gilder rather than the maker; Isaac Jacobs: some pieces are signed "I. Jacobs Bristol"

See also Colored glass: After 1800 – Britain, France, and the United States, pp.286–7

Tassies, sulphides, and jeweling

Other additions to glass include tassies, sulphides, and jeweling. Tassies are medallions, while sulphides are tiny portraits enclosed within glass surrounds. Jeweling is the name of the technique of applying colored drops of glass to a glass vessel in imitation of precious stones.

TASSIES AND SULPHIDES
Tassies, which were produced in Scotland from 1766 by the stonemason James Tassie (1735–99), are cameo portraits made from a white vilusterous glass paste that was cast in a mold. On early examples the head and bust were mounted on a clear-glass ground, which was placed over colored paper to give the appearance of colored glass. On later examples the portrait and background were cast in one piece. William Tassie (1777–1860), James Tassie's nephew, continued the technique in London in conjunction with John Wilson.

Sulphides are small opaque-white medallions made of china clay or glass paste enclosed in transparent glass. Most feature busts or figures embedded on the side or bottom of clear-glass objects. The technique had been experimented with in Bohemia in the mid-18th century, but was developed by a Frenchman, Barthélemy Desprez (active 1773–1819), in Paris, where he made cameos and portrait medallions of famous people after c.1775. By the early 19th century these medallions were enclosed in transparent glass with a thin layer of air that gave them a characteristic silvery appearance. Some were set in goblets, tumblers, paperweights, and glass plaques. Subjects ranged from portraits of contemporary, historical, and religious figures to military symbols. Notable makers include the Le Creusot Glass Factory (est. 1787), in Mont-Cenis, near Le Creusot, later acquired by the firm of Baccarat (est. 1764 as the Sainte-Anne Glassworks) in Baccarat, near Lunéville, and by the Saint-Louis Glassworks (est. 1767) near Bitche, in the Münzthal, both in Lorraine.

▲ Tassie
Glass-paste portrait medallions, known as tassies, are named after their inventor, James Tassie. Portraits, in this case of the British statesman and politician Edmund Burke, were cast in white paste from molds, which were made from wax portraits modeled in relief. Typical subjects included politicians, members of the aristocracy, and popular contemporary figures.
(1797; ht 11.5cm/4½in; value C)

◄ Sherry glass with sulphide by Apsley Pellatt
This British sherry glass has a characteristically silvery-white sulphide showing the Order of the Garter, the highest order of knighthood in Britain, set in its side. The sulphide was produced by Pellatt, one of the foremost British glassmakers, who introduced the technique to Britain in 1819. Pellatt patented the sulphide technique as the "crystallo-ceramic" process.
(1830; ht 10.5cm/4in; value D)

In Britain the foremost manufacturer of sulphides was Apsley Pellatt (1791–1863), who introduced the technique at the Falcon Glassworks (est. 1693) in London, taking out a patent for what he called "cameo incrustations" or "crystallo ceramie" in 1819. The range of wares made included scent bottles, drinking glasses, and decanters incorporating portrait medallions of British statesmen and monarchs.

In Bohemia sulphides were used in door knobs, glass stoppers, and wine goblets. Paperweights, which were made of a characteristic yellow-brown glass and featured bird or animal subjects, were only produced in the 1920s and 1930s. In the USA fine-quality sulphides were made from c.1814 at Bakewell's (1808–82; renamed the Pittsburgh Flint Glass Manufactory c.1813) in Pittsburgh, Pennsylvania. Other American sulphides were generally of poor quality, although some produced as fairground prizes have a naive charm. Subjects include American military heroes and politicians.

JEWELING
The jeweling technique involves applying colored drops of glass from a heated glass rod to a glass vessel; the "jewels" stand slightly proud of the surface, like tiny cabochon stones. The technique is difficult to master, as different colors cool at different rates, and cracking is a constant hazard. It has been used since ancient times, with early jeweled examples from Egypt, Cyprus, France, and the Rhineland dating from the 4th and 5th centuries AD. The technique was especially popular from the mid-19th century when there was a revival of interest in many historical styles; it was used to fine decorative effect by celebrated firms, including J. & L. Lobmyr (est. 1823) in Vienna, and Baccarat, on glassware displayed at such international exhibitions as the Great Exhibition of 1851 in London. A variation on jeweling is "jewel-and-eye" decoration, where a large drop of colored glass is topped with a small colored drop of glass.

◄ Goblet by J. & L. Lobmeyr
The interest in historical styles from the mid-19th century revived the ancient technique of jeweling, as seen on the foot of this delicately colored Austrian opaline glass.
(1880; ht 14.5cm/5¾in; value F)

KEY FACTS

Tassies
- SIZE most are between 2 and 11cm (¾–4¼in) high and 2 and 9cm (¾–3½in) wide
- SUBJECTS profile portraits of royalty, the aristocracy, and contemporary figures are most typical

Sulphides
- TYPES sulphides were used as portrait medallions and as decoration for scent bottles, glasses, and weights
- COLLECTING American sulphide paperweights are rarely found outside the USA

Marks
Apsley Pellatt: mark used on the firm's sulphide wares

PELLATT & CO. PATENTEES

Jeweling
- WARES mostly used on such ornamental wares as mosque lamps or finely made, decorative glasses
- COLLECTING good early examples are rare

See also Paperweights, pp.308–9

Lighting

The commercial production of glass lighting was sparked by the discovery of lead crystal *c.*1676 by the innovatory British glassmaker George Ravenscroft (1632–83). The highly reflective quality of this type of glass, combined with its suitability for prismatic cutting, was exploited to great effect in Britain throughout the 18th century. The production of single glass candlesticks was followed by the manufacture of multi-branched candlesticks, known as "candelabra"; by the mid-18th century makers were producing magnificent and extremely elaborate chandeliers, designed to hang from ceilings. Other forms of lighting produced in many different styles included lanterns, oil lamps, decorative mosque lamps, and Argand lamps.

CANDLESTICKS

Candlesticks are generally composed of a base, a central column or shaft to hold a nozzle, and a drip-pan to catch any stray molten wax. Most full-size candlesticks were between 20 and 25.5cm (8–10in) tall and were made in pairs. Until the early 18th century, when the first glass candlesticks were produced, the majority of English examples were made of silver. Glass candlesticks were viewed as rare, luxury items – those in silver or brass were far less fragile and therefore less highly priced.

◄ Candlestick

Many early glass candlesticks were based on contemporary wine-glass designs, and this British candlestick – an early example, as very few early glass candlesticks have survived – features a double-series, colored twist in the stem, in the style of 18th-century wine-glass stems. A double-series twist features one twist inside another. The blue color is rare and desirable. The large domed and terraced foot stabilizes the candlestick but makes it heavy – a disadvantage at a time when glass was taxed by weight.
(c.1765; ht 20cm/8in; value M)

In general early glass candlesticks made in Britain followed the styles of contemporary drinking glasses, and were influenced by the forms of brass and silver examples. Most 18th-century candlesticks were produced in clear, colorless glass, but a few were made in colored glass or in clear glass embellished with air-twist or colored-twist shafts. Some were carved with cut decoration to catch and enhance any available light. Facet-stem candlesticks, featuring flat-cut vertical decoration on the shaft, were especially popular, and were widely produced between 1740 and 1820 and were revived at the end of the 19th century.

Toward the end of the 18th century British glass candlesticks were designed with detachable slipover pans, which fitted around the socket of the candlestick and were hung with glass drops, known as "lusters." Lusters were intended to catch and reflect the light,

and were also used on candlesticks made of such materials as gilt-bronze. Other types of candlestick include small taper designs (no taller than 10cm/4in), used to hold the tapers for lighting candles, most of which were produced singly.

In the 18th century fine candlesticks were rarely produced in Europe outside Britain. Examples in blown glass were made in France and the Low Countries, but only a few of them have survived.

In the USA some early glass candlesticks, which were similar in style to English designs, were produced, but in general metal candlesticks were preferred. From the mid-1830s many pressed candlesticks of numerous designs were made in the USA, including one with the shaft in the shape of a dolphin. Other novelty designs that were made in the USA and Europe include candlesticks with the shafts in the form of figures or vase form, and "crucifixion" candlesticks with cross-shaped shafts.

CANDELABRA

Candelabra – a candlestick with at least two arms for candle sockets – only came into common use at the end of the 18th century, although they were produced from the early years of the century. Most had detachable arms, which fitted into a brass plate at the top of the base, and could be lifted out and replaced if damaged. Early examples were usually of clear, colorless glass and quite simple in design, with little ornamentation. With the development of gas lighting *c.*1810, later Victorian examples were often designed to be decorative rather than functional and were typically in colored glass or red or green overlay glass. However, such colored designs did not reflect the light as effectively as clear glass. Decoration also became increasingly elaborate, with larger, more fancily cut pendants characteristic of the Victorian period: glass drops in the form of icicles, triangles, buttons, pears, spears, and lusters were all popular types of ornamentation. The top of the candelabrum was usually decorated with a finial, often in the shape of a spear, a crescent (in imitation of Turkish designs), or a pineapple (a symbol of welcome). Major manufacturers include the F. & C. Osler Glasshouse (est. 1807) in Birmingham, Baccarat (est. 1764 as the Sainte-Anne Glassworks) in Baccarat, near Lunéville, and the Saint-Louis Glassworks (est. 1867) near Bitche, in the Münzthal, both in Lorraine.

▲ Luster

"Luster" is the name for the faceted glass drops hung from the columns of candlesticks to maximize reflected light, but it is also used as a general term to describe this type of candlestick, many of which were made from materials other than glass. In this fine British example, the flat-cut lusters end in round beads, while small beads at the top help the lusters to hang properly.
(19th century; ht 46cm/18in; value for a pair H)

► Candelabrum

This red-glass Bohemian candelabrum has six matching lights, complete with matching lusters; it is supported by an elaborately cut stem with an intricately cut base. Red was one of the most difficult shades of glass to produce but became very popular in the 1830s. However, although visually attractive, the colored-glass and brass fittings did not reflect as much light as clear glass. The arms – all of which are still present – can be lifted out for cleaning.
(mid-19th century; ht 1.3m/4ft 3in; value L)

▲ Chandelier by the F. & C. Osler Glasshouse
This magificent chandelier is so elaborately decorated with chains of glass beads that the basic form is almost obscured. Such a fine piece is typical of Osler, one of the leading Victorian glassmaking firms.
*(mid-19th century; ht 1.3m/4ft 3in; value **Q**)*

CHANDELIERS

Hanging glass chandeliers are basically composed of a central shaft and a variable number of arms or branches, each fitted with a candle-nozzle and a drip-pan. British glass chandeliers were first made in the early 18th century, and were usually designed for the specific interior of a house, a public building, a palace, or a church, as they were usually very large and valuable. Few have survived in their complete original forms as their lusters were often damaged.

Some very fine chandeliers were made in Venice during the 18th century, the most extravagant of which were produced by Giuseppe Briati (1686–1772), whose designs were known as *ciochhe* ("bouquets of flowers") and were decorated with a profusion of fruit, flowers, and leaves. In Britain early 18th-century chandeliers followed the simple lines of brass prototypes: curved arms were usually attached to a central column formed from a series of spheres. In the later 18th century examples were increasingly Rococo in style, with elaborate decorative drops and spirals; they were often fitted with two elaborate layers of arms, which were fixed to a central plate around the middle of the stem.

Irish chandeliers were initially derivative of English designs, but eventually they acquired a separate idiom. Although many were designed by the architect and designer Robert Adam (1728–92), only one can still

be seen in its original setting, at Temple Newsam House, in Leeds, England. Adam's designs were Neo-classical incorporating classic urns and tapered spires and widely influenced other designers and manufacturers. Irish glassmakers were responsible for some superb chandeliers made in the Low Countries in the "Anglo-Irish" style. Many fine chandeliers, characterized by a cascade of hanging droplets, which create a tiered, curtain-like effect around the central shaft, were produced during the Regency period. The French glassworks at Baccarat is celebrated for its grand Empire-style chandeliers. By the late 19th century the firm also produced magnificent floor-standing models, based on the highly successful prototypes shown at the Great Exhibition in London in 1851.

LAMPS

Oil lamps – lamps using oil and a wick – have been used since Roman times. Beautiful mosque lamps with fine enameled and gilded decoration were produced in the 13th and 14th centuries; in the 16th and 17th centuries Venetian-glass oil lamps were made in elaborate forms, including animal-shaped designs. In Britain the earliest glass examples, made from c.1680, were the "floating wick" type, where a wick was floated in a globular reservoir filled with whale oil; these stood on short stems and often had loop handles. In the USA oil lamps with central reservations and two tubes for resting the wicks in were more typical. In 1784 the "Argand" lamp was invented by Aimé Argand in Geneva; it was composed of a reservoir from which the oil was fed down a tube onto a tubular, hollow wick, which allowed access to air; when a chimney was placed over the wick, an updraught caused the oil to burn quickly and brightly.

▼ Whale-oil lamp
Most clear-glass lamps, designed to burn whale oil, were made in the USA in the mid- to late 18th century, before glass candlesticks, which were luxury items, were in common use. However, this item was probably made in Britain. The central vent is used for filling the lamp with oil, while the two peripheral vents are designed to hold wicks.
*(1780; ht 11cm/4¼in; value **D**)*

▲ Argand lamp
This is an extremely good example of an Argand lamp, which was retailed by the firm of Smethurst in New Bond Street, in London. Made of very finely cut lead glass and with a grand ormolu finial in the center, it is an outstanding example of Regency design.
*(1815; ht 1.1m/3ft 7in; value **O**)*

KEY FACTS

Candlesticks
- DESIGNS facet-stem candlesticks are the most common; 18th-century examples have large spreading feet;
- COLLECTING early clear-glass examples and those with air-, opaque-, or color-twist stems are rare and valuable, and a pair will be more valuable than a single candlestick

Candelabra
- COLLECTING candelabra should be complete with all their original arms for maximum value; as with candlesticks, candelabra were usually made in pairs, and a pair will be more valuable than a single example

Chandeliers
- RESTORATION this is acceptable to a degree, but chandeliers with extensive work should be avoided
- CONVERSIONS chandeliers that have been sympathetically changed to gas or electricity are more practical than those that have been untouched; many surviving chandeliers have been adapted to suit different room sizes and fashions
- COLLECTING examples should look well balanced and have an even number of arms and matching elements; the body and arms should appear equally ornate

Lamps
- DESIGNS the most basic design incorporates a central reservoir for oil and a wick
- COLLECTING whale-oil lamps are popular in the USA

See also Silver: Candlesticks, pp.230–35; Cut glass: Ireland, Britain, and the United States, pp.296–7; Miscellaneous: Metalwork, pp.540–41

Paperweights

Paperweights probably originated in Venice, where examples were made from *c*.1843 by the Venetian glassmaker Pietro Bigaglia (1786–1876). The technique, which has changed little over the years, involves placing tiny sliced sections (set-ups) of colored canes or rods on a decorative ground in a mold; this is then covered with a dome of clear glass, which acts as a magnifying lens. The canes may be densely packed together, scattered, or arranged in specific patterns. Some paperweights incorporate lamp-worked decoration in the form of fruit, flowers, or insects. Most weights are circular with a high dome, but faceted weights were also produced. The average size of a weight is 5 to 10cm (2.5–4in) in diameter; the magnum weight is over 10cm (4¼in) in diameter.

Although paperweights were not an immediate success in Venice, the technique was taken by itinerant glassworkers to France, where three companies were to become world famous for their magnificent weights. These were Baccarat (est. 1764 as the Sainte-Anne Glassworks) in Baccarat, near Lunéville, and the Saint-Louis Glassworks (est. 1767) near Bitche, in the Münzthal, both in Lorraine, and the Clichy Glassworks (est. 1837), first in Billancourt, and then at Clichy-la-Garenne, in the suburbs of Paris. After the 1840s many employees from French companies emigrated to the USA, where they founded a highly successful American paperweight industry. British paperweights were produced from 1848.

FRANCE

The firm of Baccarat, arguably the greatest producer of paperweights, manufactured weights between *c*.1845 and *c*.1849, although examples dated 1853 and 1859 are also known. Most weights by Baccarat have less bulging sides than those by other French firms; mushroom weights, where the canes are tightly gathered at the base and encircled with a *torsade* (a spiral ribbon), but flare out in the shape of a mushroom toward the top, were also manufactured, usually in a combination of blue and white. Baccarat produced weights in various sizes ranging from miniatures of 5cm (2.5in) in diameter to magnums. The company specialized in the production of weights with brightly colored "carpet" grounds, made by placing set-ups of tiny canes of glass arranged in a distinctive arrowhead floret design interspersed with those forming the silhouette of a flower, such as a pansy, primrose, or clematis, or an animal, such as a dog, horse, goat, deer, monkey, or elephant. The firm did produce some weights that incorporated fruit, although these were never mixed as they were at Saint-Louis; they include apricots, strawberries, and cherries. Rare Baccarat weights include those featuring a snake, lizard, or butterfly. Baccarat continues to make paperweights in the late 20th century.

▼ Paperweight by Baccarat

This intricate "scattered *millefiori*" paperweight has several features typical of Baccarat's magnificent weights: canes with florets, or animal silhouettes such as the goat and the cockerel featured here, scattered haphazardly on an "upset muslin" ground, where the latticinio rods are organized to resemble twisted muslin.
(19th century; diam. 7.5cm/2¾in; value **G***)*

Saint-Louis produced paperweights from the 1840s. Its weights are made of clear, heavy lead glass and have much higher domes than Baccarat weights. Shapes included mushroom weights and a distinctive crown weight – a hollow globe with walls lined with alternating twisted colored glass ribbons and white filigree twists that meet at a single central *millefiori* motif at the crown. Faceted paperweights were another specialty. Single flowers proliferated and included pansies, fuchsias, dahlias, clematis, and geraniums on a ground of swirling white or pink *latticinio*, or more rarely on a mottled jasper ground. Fruit and vegetable weights incorporating strawberries, cherries, grapes, carrots, and radishes, were produced on a *latticinio* ground. Some examples featuring animal and human silhouettes were also made. In addition, the factory specialized in overlay weights, where the weight was covered in a very thin layer of white glass and then one or two layers of colored glass. Flat "windows" were ground onto the weights (one on the top and three or more around the side). Saint-Louis overlay weights were covered in cases of clear glass.

Clichy Glassworks probably began paperweight production in 1846; it flourished until 1852, after which production was sporadic. Unlike Baccarat and Saint-Louis, which employed lead glass, Clichy used a glass that made the design seem more defined. The clear, light glass weights are almost perfectly globular with flat, very slightly concave bases with narrow rims. The distinctive "Clichy rose" weight includes a set-up of a cane made to resemble an open rose, which is usually in pink. Also distinctive of Clichy are weights with moss-green grounds (although these are uncommon); *millefiori* weights made with concentric patterns of three to eight rings; garland patterns on red, blue, and green grounds; and fine overlay paperweights, some of which won awards at the Great Exhibition of 1851 in London. The colors used by Clichy are generally softer than those used by other French factories and their paperweights weigh a little less. The firm only rarely signed or dated its weights.

▲ Paperweight, probably by Clichy

Glass-paste cameo portraits known as "sulphides" were often incorporated into paperweights. This French example features a portrait of the British Queen Victoria and Prince Albert on a colored ground. Other examples depict major literary, political, or historical figures.
(mid-19th century; diam. 7.5cm/2¾in; value **E***)*

▼ Paperweight by the New England Glass Co.

Most paperweights by this American firm were manufactured between 1854 and 1874. The company drew heavily on French and British techniques, as several of its craftsmen were European immigrants. This design features a delicate white *latticinio* ground topped with a single pink dahlia. The bright green leaves help to identify it as a New England product.
(mid-19th century; diam. 7.5cm/2¾in; value **H***)*

THE UNITED STATES

In the 1850s there was a decline in the fashion for paperweights in France, and the USA became the main center of production. Good-quality weights were made, but they could never rival the products of the three great French firms. François Pierre (1834–72), who had trained and worked at the French firm of Baccarat, joined the New England Glass Co. (1818–90), originally of East Cambridge, Massachusetts, and between 1850 and 1880 the firm produced paperweights in a style and shape that closely resembled French production. The weights have deeply concave bases and incorporate flowers – frequently the camomile flower and the buttercup. Canes used for *millefiori* weights may have been imported from Baccarat.

▼ Paperweight by the Boston & Sandwich Glass Co.

Although flower weights were very popular with American makers, fruit weights, such as this example with berries in clear glass, were also produced. In such weights the accurate positioning of the design is important, as is the perfect condition of the decoration: leaves and fruit should be properly attached and unbroken.

(19th century; diam. 7.5cm/2¾in; value **G***)*

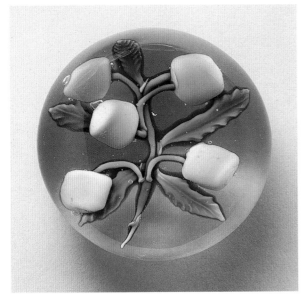

In 1869 another French glassworker, Nicholas Lutz (1835–1906), a former employee of the Saint-Louis factory, joined the Boston & Sandwich Glass Co. (1826–88) in Sandwich, Massachusetts. Although the firm had manufactured paperweights from the 1850s, the majority of its production dates from the 1870s, after Lutz had joined the company. The paperweights come in a wide range of profiles, the most common being low and flat, and they are generally light in weight, with considerable variety in the quality of the glass. The beautiful flower weights are particularly sought after; poinsettias are most common, but wheat-flowers are also quite typical. Some rare examples include upright floral bouquets and baskets of mixed fruit. Other designs feature canes incorporating an animal silhouette, most typically of a bee, an eagle, or a rabbit, at the center of a flower.

BRITAIN

Interest in British paperweights is comparatively recent. In Britain the firm of Bacchus (est. *c.*1816; later George Bacchus & Sons), in Birmingham, briefly produced paperweights from 1848. However, it is estimated that the firm manufactured no more than 400 examples before production declined rapidly in 1850. Most of the weights are large (over 8cm/3in in diameter) and heavy, with a pronounced curve from the widest part of weight to the narrow base; the canes, which are generally less delicate than those on French examples, are set on a high cushion. Concentric *millefiori* weights, usually comprising five circles of florets, at least one of which is made up of large florets, are most typical, as is a thin film of opaque-white glass. Other weights featuring a star, acog, and ruffle canes, as well as a female head in profile, were intended for the tourist market, including sulphide weights – small portrait medallions of china clay or glass paste encased in glass. The firm of John Ford (est. 1810) in Edinburgh, made weights incoporating sulphides of Scottish celebrities such as the poet Robert Burns.

Some of the finest 20th-century paperweights are those made by Paul Ysart (*b.*1904), whose work for the Moncrieff Glassworks (est. *c.*1860) and Caithness Glass Ltd. (est. 1960), both in Perth, include traditional *millefiori* patterns, some incorporating flowers and insects – those showing butterflies and dragonflies are especially highly regarded.

▼ Paperweight by George Bacchus & Sons

Bacchus was one of the leading makers of British paperweights, although it probably produced no more than 400 weights in total. This concentric *millefiori* weight has five circles of canes; the colors appear slightly muted in comparison with French paperweights.

(c.1880; diam. 8cm/3in; value **G***)*

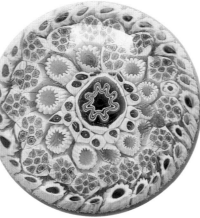

▲ Paperweight by Paul Ysart

Some of the finest contemporary British paperweights are produced in Scotland by Ysart, who was born in Barcelona of Bohemian parents. Many of his designs feature *millefiori* decoration – this example incorporating a green-and-gold speckled snake curled on a red ground is unusual. Snake paperweights were also made by firms in France, including Baccarat and Saint-Louis.

(c.1970; diam. 7.5cm/2¾in; value **E***)*

KEY FACTS

- SIZE weights that are outside the standard size (diam. of 5–10cm/2–4in) are sought after; magnums (diam. of over 10cm/4in) and miniatures (diam. of less than 5cm/2in) are particularly popular
- WEIGHT old paperweights tend to be heavier than reproductions; no two weights are identical
- DECORATION *millefiori* designs are highly typical; other designs include flowers, fruit, vegetables, animals, and silhouettes; sulphide paperweights were made by the firms of Clichy and John Ford
- CONDITION glass should be clear and unclouded with no marked striations; tiny air bubbles are acceptable in rare examples; professional wheel polishing can rectify slightly damaged weights
- COLLECTING French paperweights tend to be more valuable than British or American weights; rare designs such as snake paperweights are especially valuable

Marks

Baccarat: signature canes are often included, which show the letter "B" and the date in blue, green, or red on white canes (1848 is the most common year)

Clichy: examples are rarely marked with the maker or date; some examples feature signature canes as shown

Paul Ysart: his initials are often incorporated within a *millefiori* cane

---

See also Additions to glass: Tassies, sulphides, and jeweling, p.305

Miscellaneous

The Victorian passion for cluttered interiors encouraged the manufacture in the 19th century of a large number of novelty items and decorative "knicknacks," which are best classed as miscellaneous glassware. Other items which do not fit into a specific category include bulb vases and seal-bottles.

FRIGGERS

Friggers are decorative or novelty items made by glassmakers or apprentices at the end of the working day either as showpieces to demonstrate their skills or simply to use up left-over glass. Although friggers were produced in most glassmaking areas, the most notable examples are those produced at the Val-Saint-Lambert Glasshouse (est. 1825), in Seraing-sur-Meuse, near Liège, in Belgium, including glass animal figures, carousels, and wig-stands.

The Nailsea Glasshouse (est. 1788) near Bristol, specialized in inexpensive domestic wares such as jugs and vases. The factory is particularly notable for its wares with looped or combed decoration (the most recognizable being flasks) and spatter glass: wares with a mottled or speckled appearance caused by rolling the item on a surface covered with blobs of usually white glass and marvering (rolling) them into the body. However, the name Nailsea is now a generic term for such items as bells, pipes, walking-sticks, and glass ships made in and around Bristol, the Midlands, and Scotland. Other items were in bright, vivid colors and have the naive charm of folk art. Some items were associated with folk superstitions: "witch" balls or bauble-like spheres, typically of colored glass and often silvered to give a metallic effect, were hung in windows to ward off evil spirits; glass walking-sticks or crops were also hung in windows to draw evil spirits out of the house; when the stick was dusted, the evil spirits were thought to have been banished.

◄ Bell

Bells are the most commonly found items of British Nailsea glass. The majority have colored bodies, usually in red, which may be decorated with white filigree rims, ribbing, and wrythen molding. Handles are usually knopped and joined to the bell with plaster of Paris. Most are of clear glass – colored handles are rare, and some feature air or opaque twists. Bells usually have pear-shaped or, as in this example, made in Stourbridge, marble-like glass clappers. These purely decorative pieces are often made with great skill.
(mid-19th century; ht 30cm/11¾in; value D)

▲ Rolling pin

Decorative glass rolling pins were traditionally given as leaving presents by sailors to their sweethearts. This example is made of dark-blue glass and features the flecks of white or "speckling" typical of Nailsea glass; other rolling pins were decorated with enameled flowers, transfer-printed designs, or looped patterns in red, blue, or pink.
(c.1820; l. 39cm/15¼in; value A)

◄ Crop

This British Nailsea crop is approximately the same length as a real crop but, being made of solid glass, it is purely decorative. It features an internal opaque twist and is a fine example of the virtuoso glassmaking often associated with such wares. Similar items include decorative glass walking-sticks, which were often embellished with twists of colored glass. Decoration in bright colors of blue and red is most characteristic.
(1870; l. 75cm/29½in; value C)

► Bulb vases

These three British hyacinth-bulb vases reflect the different styles used in their manufacture by 19th-century glassmakers. The tall, straight-sided, amethyst-colored vase is a rare early example; the miniature vases such as the piece in the middle are also rare. The blue vase on the left was made in the second half of the 19th century by mold pressing. Although blue, green, and amethyst are most typical, these vases were also made in yellowish-white "Vaseline" glass and pinky red "Cranberry" glass.
(1830–70; amethyst vase (right), ht 18.5cm/7¼in; value A/B)

BULB VASES

Hyacinths were introduced to Europe in the 18th century, and were so popular in the Low Countries that elaborate ceramic vessels were produced in which to grow them. From the end of the 18th century French, Norweigan, and British glassmakers began to produce more modest colored-glass vases in which hyacinths could be grown indoors. The bulb sat in the neck or collar of the vase and the roots grew into the water below. Early vases were made of blown glass in shades of blue, green, or amethyst; most had straight sides and were c.20cm (8in) tall. French makers also produced clear-glass vases, but these were not as popular as colored vases, as they revealed the unsightly root system. When mold-pressing techniques were developed in the mid-19th century, glass manufacturers produced large numbers of short, squat bulb vases in a wide range of colors.

BOTTLES

Seal-bottles, originally made of dark green, almost black glass, were used to store and serve wine. The seal identified the owner when the bottle was refilled by the wine merchant. First produced around the mid-17th century, the free-blown form developed from the "shaft and globe" shape of the earliest bottles to the "onion" shape of early 18th-century examples, with some rare octagonal examples produced in the mid-1800s. By the end of the 18th century bottles were made with the sloping shoulders and straight sides still popular today. Clear, colorless bottles were used from the mid-19th century after the tax on colorless glass was lifted and the

▲ Seal-bottle

Dark green, free-blown seal-bottles, such as this British example, were used for storing wine. The seal set in the side identified the owner when the bottle was refilled by the wine merchant. The sloping shoulders and straight sides are typical of later seal-bottles, and the strong ring at the top of the bottle was used for attaching a stopper. *(c.1780; ht 26.5cm/10½in; value* **C***)*

► Epergne

The epergne – the quintessential Victorian decorative household centerpiece – was very popular from the mid-19th century. It was originally designed with several sections that could hold fruit and desserts; later Victorian examples were used for holding flowers. This British example, made of Cranberry and Vaseline glass, is in fine condition, with all four original sections present. *(1890; ht 41cm/16in; value* **D***)*

Victorians demanded to see the contents of what they were buying. Other mass-produced bottles, which are easy to find and very inexpensive, include the mineral-water bottle introduced by Hiram Codd in 1872, which has a built-in glass stopper, and bottles with embossed advertising labels. Another area of collecting is scent bottles. These include cameo, cut glass, gilded, and faceted bottles, as well as those with double ends, which were made to hold perfume in one end and smelling salts in the other.

OTHER WARES

A quintessential Victorian ornament was the epergne, a decorative table centerpiece composed of several elaborately decorated, trumpet-shaped sections, joined together at the base by a brass collar. Epergnes were often made in shaded and colored glass, with decoration of trailed or pinched designs. The sections were designed to be removed from the brass collar at the base for easy cleaning, and consequently many were lost or broken.

Other popular Victorian ornaments include knife rests, piano rests, and doorstops. Knife rests, designed to hold a carving knife and fork on which to rest cutlery, were made from the 18th century in pairs or in groups of four; they were usually in clear, colorless glass and sometimes embellished with cut decoration. Most were between 10 and 13cm (4–5in) long. Piano rests – chunky, rounded objects with small indentations in the centers – were designed to sit under the four feet of the piano to help conduct the sound. Usually of pressed or molded glass, they are most frequently found in clear

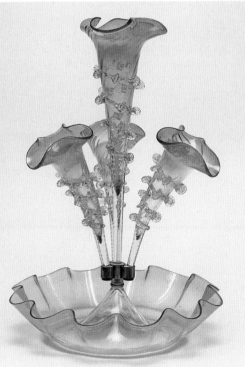

◄ Knife rests by the Val-Saint-Lambert Glasshouse

In Europe it was fashionable in the late 19th century to produce individual knife rests, such as this Belgian set, as the same cutlery was used throughout the meal. The top rest is particularly collectible as it is decorated with a colored twist. *(c.1880; l. 13cm/5in; value* **A***)*

glass but sometimes in green, dark blue, yellow, or amber. It is rare to find a complete set, and individual examples are often confused with ashtrays or paperweights, as they are similar in shape. Doorsteps, known as "dumps," were produced from left-over glass, much of which was bubbled and green tinted. Some glass factories in the center of Britain made doorstops in metal molds; the most common are in the form of sheaves of corn or dogs.

In the USA, red or dark pink glass known as "Cranberry" glass, featuring white or pinky-white enamel decoration of children, is called "Mary Gregory" glass. Designs range from charming to sentimental. Although Mary Gregory has not been identified, it is thought she may have been an employee at the Boston & Sandwich Glass Co. (1826–88) in Sandwich, Massachusetts, between 1886 and 1888. Mary Gregory wares in glass other than Cranberry glass include dark blue, dark green, amethyst, and yellow examples.

▲ Plate

"Mary Gregory" glass is a term used to describe colored glass decorated with white enameling. It is traditionally an American style, but some wares were also produced in Europe. This Mary Gregory plate was made in the USA and has the characteristic decoration of an idealized scene of children at play. Although the background is a greenish-yellow, much Mary Gregory glass was produced on Cranberry glass. *(1900; w. 23cm/9in; value* **C***)*

KEY FACTS

- **WARES** varied novelty glass items known as friggers, bulb vases, bottles, epergnes, knife rests, piano rests, dumps (doorstops)
- **CONDITION** epergnes: check that all sections are present and are undamaged, especially that the frills, or trailed decoration, do not wobble in the brass collar at the base of the trumpets, and match in color and style; knife rests: ensure that the rests are not chipped
- **COLLECTING** bottles: shiny bottles in good condition are most collectible; epergnes: colored examples are more desirable than clear-glass examples; knife rests: cut examples and those with colored inclusions are most collectible; piano rests: full sets are rare; dumps: crown-glass dumps in pristine condition are rare; pairs of dog-shaped dumps are very desirable; Mary Gregory glass: authentic pieces are monochromatic; avoid those in which the figures have colored faces
- **BEWARE** bells copied in the 1950s tend to be coarser and to have thicker glass than 19th-century originals

Marks

The most collectible bulb vases are those marked with the manufacturer's name and the patent date

---

See also Colored glass, pp.284–7; Miscellaneous: Perfume bottles, p.548–9

R eferences to rug- and carpet-weaving in the Old Testament and in Homer's *Iliad* confirm this as among the most ancient of crafts. However, although the majority of handwoven rugs and carpets produced from around the 3rd century BC have had a primarily functional purpose (as table, wall, or floor coverings, as bags, or as animal trappings), the finest examples are viewed as works of art, a status reflected in the substantial prices they can command. Such desirability can be partly attributed to the great skill and ingenuity involved in traditional weaving and knotting techniques, and to the tactile qualities of natural fibers such as silk, wool, and animal hair employed in their manufacture. Equally attractive, in an age of widespread urbanization, are the "romantic" tribal and nomadic origins of many Oriental, North African, and Native American weavings. However, most compelling is the tremendous diversity of vibrant and intricate designs displayed on rugs and carpets, some of the finest examples of which are found in the work of Persian and Turkish court weavers produced between the 15th and 17th centuries. Designs range from the classic religious symbols and patterns associated with Oriental and Native American carpet production, to the secular motifs favored in Western Europe.

Detail of a Karabagh rug (left) The Harshang or "crab" decoration shown here is a classic motif widely found on rugs from the Caucasus and from Azerbaijan *(19th century)*.
Carpet made in Heriz (above) Woven in silk, this wool carpet on a cotton foundation is distinguished by its off-center medallion, ivory field (unusual for Heriz), and vivid colors *(c.1860)*.

Rugs & Carpets: Basics

Historically, in both East and West, rugs and carpets have been made for warmth and comfort, as decorative floor coverings, to adorn walls and furniture, and to be made into functional artifacts such as bags. Whether a domestic object in a nomad's tent or a symbol of opulence of a wealthy patron, rugs and carpets – however simple or complex – are artistic expressions based on long-established and continually evolving traditions.

THE LAYOUT OF A CARPET

There is no hard and fast rule as to when a rug becomes a carpet, or vice versa, but as a general guide, when the size of the piece is more than 2.6m (8ft 6in) long by *c.*1.7m (5ft 6in) wide then the term "carpet" will apply; under this size the object is a rug. The term "runner" applies to a piece *c.*2.6m (8ft 6in) long by 1–1.2m (3–4ft) wide.

Oriental and European carpets have a central field surrounded by a main border, which itself is framed on either side by narrow secondary borders, or guardstripes. A central medallion is often present, or there may be rows of medallions covering the field. Some examples have no medallions at all, but use an all-over repeat design with the impression of an infinite pattern being created by unfinished design elements that end at the borders,

a device called "infinite repeat." Spandrels are usually present when a center medallion is evident. If the two bottom end spandrels are not present, then a directional design is created as the two remaining spandrels form an arch. This is used in the Islamic prayer-rug design, the arch being a representation of the mihrab (prayer niche) set into the wall of the mosque that faces Mecca. The design is sometimes used purely as a decorative device.

FLATWEAVES

Flatweaves consist of only warps and wefts, using no knots and thus having no pile. The designs of flatwoven carpets tend to be simpler than those of piled carpets, often comprising bold, geometric patterns. Flatweaves tend to be less strong and durable than piled carpets.

Kilims Kilims are made by passing a weft thread in and out between the warp threads, after which the fabric is beaten down with a metal comb. They are usually made on narrow, sometimes portable looms, often in two or more separate strips, which are sewn together on completion. The pattern of the kilim is carried by the wefts, and color changes are created in a number of ways. Most common is the slit-tapestry technique, in which the wefts are returned around the last warp of their respective color area – adjacent color areas are therefore marked by a vertical slit, although these may be sewn up later. Slit-tapestry kilims are almost all double-sided as the Turkish kilim shown below exemplifies – the top picture shows the front of the kilim; the bottom picture features the back of the kilim. In this piece, color changes are effected by the single interlocking technique, in which wefts of adjacent color areas are tied around a shared warp. In double interlocking, wefts from adjacent color areas interlock. In dovetailing (a variant of the single interlock method) a group of wefts of one color is applied around a shared warp. These last three techniques are mainly found on Persian kilims; dovetailing is also found in Balkan kilims.
- Technique used in Persia, Turkey, the Balkans, and India
- Kilims are identifiable by slits where the color changes
- Most are reversible, as there are no loose ends of thread

Tapestries The tapestry technique is essentially the same as kilim work but applies to western European flatweaves. Very often carpets made using this technique are not reversible, as the wefts are left floating on the reverse, as can be seen in the Second Empire (1852–70) rug from Aubusson, France, below; the top picture shows the front of the rug; the bottom picture shows the back.
- Technique used widely in Europe, most notably in France
- Tapestries are similar to kilims, but often not reversible

Soumakhs Soumakh technique, or soumakh brocading, is traditionally the term given to flatwoven textiles made by the weft-wrapping technique in the Caucasus and north-western Persia. A ground weft is used to provide the foundation while colored wefts carry the design; these wefts are normally passed over three warps and back over two warps, forming a continuous structure. Soumakhs are one sided, with the back showing loose weft threads. Artifacts such as bags and animal trappings as well as rugs and carpets are made using this technique. A close-up detail of the front of a soumakh is shown below. In Anatolia a supplementary weft-brocading method is used to create a type of flatweave called a çiçim (pronounced "jijim").
- Technique used in the Caucasus and north-western Persia
- Soumakhs, unlike kilims, do not have slits
- Pieces are not reversible: loose threads show at the back

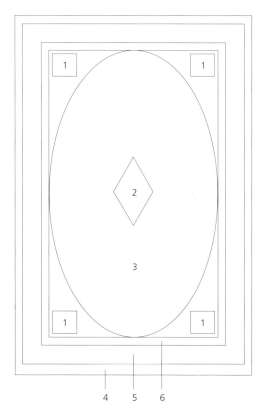

1 Spandrel
2 Medallion
3 Field or ground
4 Outer guardstripe
5 Main border
6 Inner guardstripe

PILE WEAVINGS

Basic techniques in pile weaving have not changed in centuries, with a pair of scissors for cutting the pile being virtually the most sophisticated piece of equipment used. The pile is mostly sheep's wool, although goat hair and camel hair are sometimes used. Cotton is not used extensively for the pile of rugs, but sometimes appears as a highlighter for details in conjunction with wool. Silk also appears as a pile material in technically fine pieces, and may be used in combination with wool for highlighting of details.

A vertical, or upright, loom is used both in town production and for village rugs and is usually a permanent fixture. A horizontal, transportable loom is used by nomadic tribes, who weave on their migrations. In both cases warp threads extend from the top to the bottom of the loom and are the threads to which the knots are applied; the weft runs from side to side and acts as the locking thread for each row of knots – this is achieved by beating down the wefts with a comb device. When the rug is completed several weft shoots are usually run across the warps to lock the whole rug in place. The rug is then cut from the loom and the pile is clipped.

Town weavings: wool Cotton is usually used for the warps and wefts in town weaving, since its fineness allows for a high knot density to be woven onto it; the knots are made with wool. The two pictures below show the front and back of a carpet from Tabriz, and illustrate the detail of the back and the fineness of weave – the pattern is as clear on the back (bottom picture) as on the front of the rug (below, top). Designs are drawn out first on cartoons (scale drawings) by master weavers, or "Ustads"; the weavers then translate this pattern row by row onto the loom. Town weaving is essentially curvilinear in style; the Persian knot is mainly used since it is more suitable for curved forms, although the Turkish knot is sometimes used, or a combination of the two. Workshop town rugs and carpets are generally commercial pieces.

- Wool pile on a cotton foundation is usual, with a high knot density; the Persian knot is typical
- Designs are typically curvilinear and quite detailed

Town weavings: silk Silk is the finest material used in the making of rugs and carpets. Silk warps and wefts are much finer than those in cotton or wool, allowing for a greater knot density to be woven. Silk is usually used to create the pile, and the pattern rendering is extremely detailed. The overall appearance typically exhibits a metallic sheen. Silk town weavings are made in the same way as wool town pieces, although metal thread brocading may be used in pattern detailing; this is found in some fine rugs made in the Kum Kapi workshops of Istanbul in the late 19th century, as seen below – the top picture shows the front of the rug; the bottom picture shows the back.

- Silk is used for the warps, wefts, and the pile
- The knot density is very high so detailed patterns and curvilinear designs are usual; the Persian knot is typical
- The silk pile characteristically has a metallic sheen

Tribal and village weavings Tribal weavings are made on horizontal, transportable looms. Wool is the main material used in the foundation warps and wefts and in the making of the pile. Patterns, which are mostly geometric in style and formed using the Turkish knot, are traditional. Large pieces are rare: the usual output is rugs, bags, and animal trappings. Designs are woven from memory and tend to be more individual than formal town designs. Village rugs are woven on semi-permanent looms. The design principles are the same as for tribal pieces, although cotton may be used in the foundation instead of wool alone, giving a higher knot density and a more detailed design.

Two village rugs are shown below with a reverse detail of each. The two pictures immediately below show a rug woven on cotton (top: front; bottom: back); the pictures below these show a rug woven in wool on wool.

- Detail is finer on a piece woven in wool on a cotton foundation than on a piece woven in wool on wool
- Woven from memory, no two village rugs are identical

- Most village rugs are woven entirely in wool, as below (top: front; bottom: back); the weave is typically coarse
- The rough weave is suited to bold geometric designs

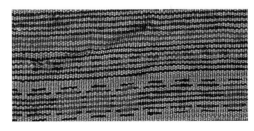

KNOTTING

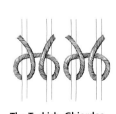 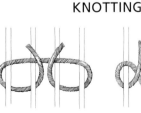  

The Turkish, Ghiordes, or symmetrical knot
Yarn wrapped around two warp strands; used in village and tribal weaving in the Caucasus, west and north-west Persia, Turkey, and Europe; best suited to geometric designs.

The jufti or double Turkish knot
A cheating knot, wrapped around four instead of two strands: coverage is 50 per cent lower than normal, making it twice as fast but resulting in a less durable product.

The Persian, Senneh, or asymmetrical knot
Yarn wrapped around one warp strand; used in town and some tribal work, in central and eastern Persia, Central Asia, and certain Turkish towns; suited to curvilinear patterns.

The jufti or double Persian knot
Like the jufti Turkish knot, this knot covers twice the area of the standard knot (here, two warp strands instead of one); while quick to work, it gives a more fragile product.

Oriental rugs and carpets

The origins of pile weaving are obscure, but that it is an ancient skill is proven by a hand-knotted rug found in Pazyryk, southern Siberia, dating from between the 3rd and 5th centuries BC. Fragments of piled weavings (3rd–6th centuries AD) have been found in Xinjiang (eastern Turkestan); others dating mainly from the 13th century have been uncovered at Fostat in Cairo.

By the 13th century rug-weaving was well established in Anatolia and by at least the 15th century pile carpets were made in Egypt. Persian carpets are mentioned in 10th-century Arab records, by Marco Polo in the 13th century, and by the 14th-century explorer Ibn Batuta. Paintings of the 14th and 15th centuries depict weavings similar to early Turkish carpets.

Persia before 1800

SAFAVID WEAVING

The great trade artery, the Silk Route, ran from Beijing in the east, through eastern and western Turkestan, Persia (Iran), and Turkey, to Europe. Under Timurid rule (1370–1506) Persia established strong links with China, and motifs such as cloudbands, cranes, phoenixes, and dragons were introduced to the Timurid court artists via Chinese textiles and pottery.

The Safavids (1501–1732) conquered Persia in 1501. Tahmasp, the second shah, established royal workshops for weaving carpets and textiles in Kashan, Kirman, Isfahan (now Esfahan), and Tabriz, ushering in the classic age of Persian carpet-weaving. These cities grew into the four great centers of production.

The earliest carpets, from the late 15th to early 16th century, are associated with Tabriz in north-west Persia. They have a large medallion often shaped like a lotus flower with cusped lobes, edged in stylized clouds. Cloudbands and arabesques fill the field. As this design developed, the medallion acquired pendants, and animals in combat appeared in the field. Countless variations on this theme are found in 19th- and 20th-century carpets.

The hunting motifs of a magnificent 16th-century silk carpet from the silk-weaving center Kashan were much borrowed in the 19th and 20th centuries in Tehran, Kirman, Isfahan, and Kashan. The design was popular with mid-20th-century weavers in Qom. Small silk rugs woven in Kashan in the mid-16th century, with a medallion and spandrel design, gave rise to countless modern imitations, many woven in the same city between c.1900 and 1930. In the 17th century, the great Islamic cultural center of Isfahan in central Persia, under Shah Abbas, produced carpets with all-over designs of vine

tendrils supporting huge palmettes, curled "sickle" or *saz* leaves (shaped like a scythe blade with a serrated edge), and bold borders. Such designs are often on a strong red ground.

Certain carpets believed to be from Kirman are known as "vase" carpets. Made from the mid-16th to the late 17th century, some pieces depict Chinese-style vases on a trelliswork of vines, palmettes, and leaves. These carpets have a double layer of cotton warps, and three shoots of weft, the middle one silk. All carpets with this unusual structure are called "vase" carpets, even where the vase pattern does not appear. This trellis, palmette, and leaf pattern was widely copied in the late 19th and 20th centuries.

Many classical Persian carpets were exported to the West, and a great number can now be seen in museums. Wool carpets from Isfahan were popular, as were the silk Polonaise, or Polish, rugs originally thought to come from Poland, but in fact from 17th-century Isfahan. They are woven in bright green, blue, red, and ivory, with brocaded areas in silver or gilt metal (a thin strip of metal was wound around a white or yellow silk thread). Early 20th-century rugs from the Kum Kapi district of Istanbul were inspired by these rugs; modern silk and metal thread rugs from Hereke in Turkey are their distant cousins.

▲ "King Umberto" Polonaise carpet, made in Isfahan
Many Polonaise carpets such as this fine silk and metal piece were presented to European dignitaries by the Persian court. *(mid-17th century; l. 4.1m/13ft 5in; value Q)*

▼ "Rothschild Imperial Silk Hunting" carpet, probably made in Kashan
One of only three surviving large, silk, 16th-century carpets, this piece depicts the synthesis of earthly and heavenly paradise. The cloudbands, winged houris, and hunters relate to motifs from Safavid manuscripts. *(c.1530–40; l. 4.8m/15ft 9in; value Q)*

KEY FACTS

- MAIN CENTERS OF PRODUCTION Kashan, Kirman, Tabriz, and Isfahan.
- SCALE most examples are large carpets, although some small rugs were also produced
- WEAVE most are woven in wool or silk, sometimes with metal thread details; some are woven in silk on a silk and cotton foundation
- DESIGNS early Persian carpets were based on cartoons, many of which were drawn by court artists; the designs of these carpets form the basis of most later Persian weaving patterns
- MOTIFS these include cloudbands, hunting motifs, vegetation (palmettes, vines, lotus-flower-shaped designs, and leaves), cranes, phoenixes, and dragons

See also Persia after 1800, pp.318–19

The Ottoman Empire before 1700

The practice of weaving carpets may have been brought to Anatolia by the Seljuks, a Turkic people from Central Asia who ruled Anatolia from 1077 to 1307. Eight fragmented 13th-century Seljuk carpets were found in the Aladdin Mosque, Konya, in 1905. Some are enormous (6m/nearly 20ft long), several are decorated with geometric floral designs based on Chinese silk brocades, and all have wide borders of stylized Kufic script. These carpets are now in the Turkish and Islamic Museum in Istanbul. Of extraordinary graphic power and grandeur, they reflect a highly developed and sophisticated awareness of weaving as an art form.

THE OTTOMANS

The Ottomans, also originally Turks from Central Asia, established themselves in Turkey in the late 13th century. They took Constantinople (now Istanbul) in 1453 and ruled until 1922. At the height of its power the Ottoman Empire extended from Egypt to Hungary.

Most surviving court weavings date from the 16th and 17th centuries. Early carpets show the geometric *gul* (medallion) patterns that derive from the Central Asian tradition. The "Memling" *gul* (named after the 15th-century German painter Hans Memling, who depicted similar carpets in his work) consists of an octagon enclosing a stepped hooked medallion. Other carpets use the "Holbein" pattern (named after Hans Holbein the Younger), typically comprising rows of octagonal medallions framed by arabesques, interspersed with smaller lozenges. The distinctive "Lotto" design (after Lorenzo Lotto) is a development of the Chinese brocade designs of the Seljuk carpets; it features stylized yellow vines, leaves, and palmettes on a red ground.

Cairo, colonized by the Ottomans in 1517, had under the previous Mamluk rule (1250–1517) created carpets with dense, all-over geometric designs, usually in green, crimson, and white with a little yellow. Weavers from Cairo may have initially been responsible for the group of finely woven mid-16th-century rugs and carpets that show the development of the true Ottoman court style and are very different from the earlier geometric designs. Motifs include the *cintamani* (three balls above a pair of wavy lines), which became one of the most popular devices in Ottoman art (found in tiles, textiles, carpets, and metalwork). Other decoration includes cloudbands and lotus palmettes (from Chinese art), large leaves, and the four favorite Ottoman flowers: carnations, tulips, hyacinths, and roses. Many of these motifs appear stylized in 18th- and 19th-century Turkish village rugs.

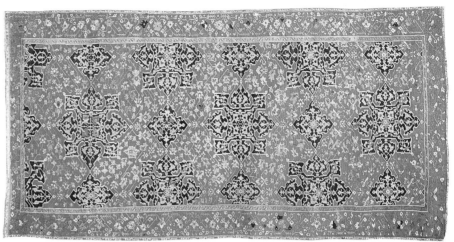

▲ "Star" carpet made in Ushak
The star shape of the main medallion originated in China and is also found in 15th- and 16th-century Persian carpets. The repeat pattern, with its incomplete outer medallions, was intended to suggest infinity. (*c.1550–1600; l. 1.8m/5ft 11in; value* **Q**)

In the late 16th and 17th centuries other designs were developed, including the large "medallion" and "star" carpets of Ushak in western Anatolia. Both these types show an endless repeating design cut by borders. The medallion layout, first used in bindings of the Koran, may have been borrowed from the contemporary Persian carpets of Tabriz (Tabriz artists were employed by the Ottoman court). The ground of the medallion carpets, which is of red vines and palmettes on blue, or vice versa, again recalls Chinese textiles. Other motifs are Persian-influenced, taking the form of sprays of flowers and arabesque scrolls. There are a number of border designs, many used interchangeably on the various carpets, including Kufic, cloudbands, palmettes with flower sprays, and floral cartouches. Turkish carpets were highly prized in the West. Many Tudor (1485–1603) portraits depict their subjects standing proudly on their Turkish carpets. European carpets are knotted with the Turkish, or symmetrical, knot in imitation of these early imports. Most Turkish and many Caucasian rugs of the 18th and 19th centuries have designs developed from the Ottoman production of the 15th–17th centuries.

▼ "Transylvanian" rug made in Ushak
Large quantities of these Turkish rugs were exported to Europe. In Transylvania many were used to decorate Protestant churches in the 17th and 18th centuries – hence their name. This example features stylized mosque lamps. (*1600–1650; l. 1.7m/5ft 7in; value* **P**)

► "Holbein" rug made in Ushak
This type of rug is named after the artist Hans Holbein the Younger, who depicted such rugs in his paintings. The geometric *gul* design was probably brought from Central Asia by the Turkic people. The border is decorated with stylized Kufic script. (*c.1500–1525; l. 1.9m/6ft 3in; value* **Q**)

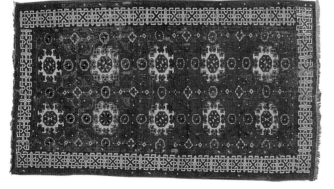

KEY FACTS

- MAIN CENTERS OF PRODUCTION Ushak and Istanbul
- WEAVE most examples are of wool pile on a wool foundation with a symmetrical knot
- COLORS principally terracotta-red, yellow, and blue with small amounts of dark brown, white, and green
- PATTERNS most are geometric; endless-repeat designs are characteristic
- COLLECTING early Ottoman carpets have been prized by western collectors ever since they were first manufactured; examples in good condition will be very highly priced and extremely sought after by collectors

See also The Ottoman Empire after 1700, pp.320–21

Persia after 1800

The quality and quantity of Persian weaving declined greatly in the 18th and early 19th centuries compared to the fine traditions established in the 16th and 17th centuries. However, from the mid-19th century there was a revival of interest, mainly generated by a renewed Western fashion for Eastern products. Demand was accelerated by easier travel and trade links together with a new awareness which was to a large degree generated by British colonialism. Two distinct styles of carpet production emerged in Persia, both firmly based on earlier traditions: the city and town workshop style, and the tribal and village style. Associated with these were the more commercial carpets created to feed the new Western market.

TOWN AND CITY PRODUCTION

Certain towns and cities are synonymous with carpet weaving in Persia. Tabriz in the north-west, Mashad in the north-east, Isfahan (now Esfahan) and Kashan in central Persia, and Kirman in the south-east are of particular importance. Although there are regional variations in the uses of color and in the presentation of the subject-matter, there are several important characteristics in this group that identify the style.

Based on the designs of the earlier classic era (16th- to 17th-century Safavid weavings), the pattern details are essentially curvilinear in form, with particular emphasis on floral design elements. Flower-heads, palmettes (vertically split flowers), and associated vines and foliage are the predominant features, naturalistically drawn to create an image of a colorful garden. Variations on this theme may sometimes include people and real or imaginary animals, emphasizing the link between humans and nature. The designs are generally either all-over repeat patterns or the central medallion style. The prayer-rug design, easily identifiable by the pointed-arch field (mihrab), was originally made for the Muslim to point toward Mecca at the time of prayer, but it was later made for purely decorative purposes to meet Western demand. Essentially, the individual weavers remain anonymous, but in some of the finest town production pieces the signature of the master weaver, or "Ustad", is seen – the Ustad being the designer rather than the weaver of the rug. Other inscriptions on town rugs may read "to the order of…" followed by the name of the person who commissioned the rug; inscriptions may also incorporate lines from Persian verse.

Carpet-producing towns that are situated away from the major city centers are more prone to the influences of tribal or village weaving, and this often results in a notably more angular style in the weaving of designs. The town of Heriz, to the north-east of Tabriz, produces highly desirable and distinctive carpets with patterns based on formal town carpet designs. However, the main distinction is the more angular rendering of the design elements. Both all-over and central medallion designs are woven, the medallions often being characterized by their starlike form. Such open, angular interpretations of the traditional themes vary in quality enormously, depending on the crispness of the drawing and the combination of the colors used.

In western Persia, the town of Senneh (now known as Sanandaj) is renowned for rugs and carpets featuring densely knotted, full-field designs, which incorporate rows of repeated tiny *boteh* (stylized cypress) or *herati* (a diamond flanked by four serrated leaves) motifs. The finely worked design of such pieces stands out especially well owing to the low trimming of the pile. The village of Sarouk in central Persia produced a great variety of carpets, including those of a very distinctive shade of intense salmon pink, which is known as *dughi* pink. These carpets were particularly sought after in the USA, and remain almost as popular today.

▼ "Sayrafiyan" rug made in Isfahan
This rug has a signature cartouche bearing the name of the designer, Sadiq Sayrafiyan. The finely woven, all-over pattern is typical of Isfahan rugs, and the pastel coloring and signature enhance the value.
(c.1950; l. 2.4m/7ft 11in; value K)

▼ Carpet made in Heriz
The shape of the bold central medallion and the angular drawing identify this carpet, made of wool on a cotton foundation. The strong, dark border color contrasts with the pale field palette. White-ground examples are rare and valuable.
(c.1860; l. 3.9m/12ft 10in; value K)

◄ Carpet made in Tabriz
The design is based on earlier, classic Persian "vase" carpets. Made from wool on a cotton foundation, this piece is finely woven with an all-over tile pattern using the infinite-repeat device (in which incomplete medallions are cut by the borders). With its multicolored yet harmonious color scheme, this style is popular with decorators in today's market.
(c.1900; l. 4.7m/15ft 5in; value L)

▲ Prayer-rug made in Kashan

This fine-quality rug has a silk pile on silk foundation (with a cotton weft) and features crisp, naturalistic drawing depicting the "tree of life." It is very rare, bearing the signature "Mohtashem" (the name of the designer); most pieces of this type are unsigned. White- or yellow-ground examples like this one are particularly popular.
(c.1890; 1.3m/4ft 3in; value **K**)

TRIBAL AND VILLAGE PRODUCTION

Tribal rugs are woven by the various nomadic groups during migrations with their flocks, and have been subject to few outside influences. The tribal tradition of rug-weaving is quite different from that of town manufacture: designs are woven from memory, with patterns passed down from generation to generation, or adapted from other products seen by the weavers on their travels; designs are therefore often highly original. The designs of tribal rugs are always geometric, and represent stylized versions of the more naturalistic drawing seen in town rugs. The geometric patterns are mainly determined by the use of the Turkish knot, which is suited to creating angular lines. Tribal products are woven with a wool pile on wool foundation; being a thick material, wool does not allow for such intricate detail as is possible on the cotton or silk foundations of products made in the towns.

Floral motifs abound and are often highly stylized. Animals, birds, and humans are also often depicted, although they are sometimes barely recognizable. Persian tribal rugs tend to be more densely decorated than their northerly Caucasian neighbors, whose designs are bolder and even more rigidly rectilinear.

The best-known Persian tribal groups are the Kashgai, the Khamseh, and the Afshar, all of which use wonderful, jewel-like colors – blues, reds, yellows, greens, and ivory – in all tones. Their work includes all-over designs and medallion formats, and they occasionally produce prayer-rugs. It is sometimes difficult to distinguish between the products of these three tribes, since they often borrow each other's ideas.

Technical quality in tribal work can vary enormously, from extremely coarse to extremely fine depending on the experience or competence of the weaver. It is important to note that the value of a piece is not necessarily based on technical fineness, but may also depend on its visual appeal or its individuality. As well as rugs, artifacts such as bags and animal trappings are woven. Carpets are rarely seen, although in some villages around the main marketing towns settled tribespeople weave large-scale pieces.

WESTERN INFLUENCE

In 1882 Ziegler & Co., a British/Swiss firm exporting Persian goods to the West, set up carpet workshops in Sultanabad (now Arak) in north-west Persia. Traditional designs were adapted for the Western market, incorporating bold floral motifs linked by lattice vines and framed within wide borders. Such carpets are highly popular and valuable, although central-medallion carpets of this type are less sought after. A particular Western-led innovation was the employment of the human figure as the main, pictorial element of a design.

▼ Carpet made by Ziegler & Co.

The spacious all-over design, the delicate pastel color scheme, and the size of this carpet represent the best attributes of Ziegler & Co. style. Although relatively coarsely woven, such carpets are popular. This piece is wool on a cotton foundation.
(c.1890; l. 4.3m/14ft 1in; value **N**)

▼ Rug made by the Kashgai

This rug is a typical, fine example of nomadic work, made by the Kashgai tribal group from south-west Persia. It exhibits an essentially formal design arrangement, with the three large medallions, the field, and the spandrels all in geometric interpretation. The crablike ornament in the medallions is very distinctive to the Kashgai. The piece is, like most tribal work, woven of wool on a wool foundation.
(c.1880; l. 2m/6ft 7in; value **H**)

KEY FACTS

- MAIN CENTERS OF PRODUCTION Tabriz, Mashad, Isfahan, Kashan, Kirman, Heriz, and Senneh
- MAIN TRIBES the Kashgai, the Khamseh, and the Afshar
- TYPES town and city production: mostly rugs and carpets; tribal and village production: smaller wares – rugs and artifacts such as bags and animal trappings are typical; carpets are rare
- WEAVES town and city rugs and carpets are generally finely woven with either wool on a cotton foundation or, sometimes, silk pile on a silk foundation; tribal and village designs are mostly woven in wool on wool
- COLORS these vary enormously from the broad range of pastels and bright colors used in towns and cities to the bold, jewel-like colors typical of tribal production
- DESIGNS town and city pieces are based on cartoons; curvilinear designs, typically featuring floral motifs, are common; tribal and village rugs and carpets are woven from memory, so no two examples are exactly alike; design and coloring have often been governed by the export market – the use of the human figure as the principal design was mainly inspired by Western tastes
- COLLECTING avoid pieces in shades of orange and garish shades of red; tribal rugs made before 1900 are prized by collectors; modern 20th-century examples are likely to be well made and attractive but lack the individuality in color and design of older 19th-century pieces; fine tribal weaves can be very valuable

See also Persia before 1800, p.316

The Ottoman Empire after 1700

The Ottoman tradition of weaving established between the 15th and 17th centuries formed the inspiration for rug production in Turkey in the 19th century. What emerged was the creation of far more commercial rugs and carpets to appeal to a wider, Western audience – products that were still traditional in approach, but more accessible. This commercialization affected both village rug production and town and city workshop production, with designs evolving or being adapted from the earlier classic traditions.

VILLAGE AND NOMADIC PRODUCTION

Rugs woven in villages throughout Turkey share similar design formats, construction, and traditional influences with their Persian and Caucasian neighbors to the East and North, and with those from Central Asia farther East. Village products incorporate essentially geometric design elements, woven on woollen warps and wefts, and made with the Turkish knot. Inspiration is drawn from earlier classic renditions; the *guls* (medallions) used are frequently similar to *guls* seen in Turkoman carpets from Central Asia, while the influence of the early "Holbein" rugs is often evident in the shape of the medallions. Designs that were popular in the 18th and 19th centuries are reproduced today in similar formats and contemporary shades, although as is typical throughout the industry, products made after *c.*1900 lack the individuality and vibrancy of the earlier pieces.

▼ Rug made in Bergama

This village rug from western Anatolia displays a design popular among local weavers. The four octagonal medallions are adapted from the "Holbein" rug design of the early 16th century. The size and color scheme are typical of later commercial productions.

(*c.1900; l. 2m/6ft 8in; value* **H**)

Very little of the Turkish rug production is actually nomadic; most is cooperative and village-based. The Yuruk and the Kurds are two nomadic peoples who weave on their migrations. Rugs from these two groups share similarities with Caucasian Kazak and Karabagh rugs, with their bold, geometric patterns and strong palette. The pile is usually even deeper than in the Caucasian carpets. One of the major differences between the Caucasian and the Turkish village and nomad rugs is the lack of zoomorphic and human forms in the Turkish pieces: the design elements are almost exclusively floral-based.

TOWN PRODUCTION

Like Persian town production, Turkish town rugs and carpets have formal curvilinear designs, and in some centers are woven from cartoons (scale drawings); most production is on cotton or sometimes silk foundations, although town rugs and carpets in Turkey are also woven on woollen foundations. In western Turkey the town of Ghiordes (the name used to describe the Turkish, or symmetrical, knot) was a main weaving center from the 17th to the early 20th century. Although on a wool foundation, the pile of Turkish town rugs and carpets is finely woven on red- or pink-dyed warps, and a cotton weft is used. Rugs from Ghiordes are often of prayer-rug form; others recall earlier design traditions. Zigzags, hexagonal medallions, and stylized floral motifs are typical. This type of rug design was popular in the 19th century.

Prayer-rugs are widespread in Turkish rug production. Ladik in central Anatolia is famous for those made in the 18th and early 19th centuries, depicting a plain mihrab (prayer niche) supported by a detailed border, presenting a striking image. These rugs also demonstrate the use of design elements adapted from older rugs. The town of Konya, close to Ladik, is also a center for the production of prayer-rugs. Alternative prayer-rug formats included the use of a double mihrab – again a feature associated with similar rug production from the classic era. Konya produces bold geometric-design rugs very similar in character and color to Kazak rugs from the Caucasus. Both Ladik and Konya rugs are highly sought after by collectors, due to their powerful and distinctive images.

◄ *Kiz* rug made in Ghiordes

Kiz means "girl" (particularly of marriageable age), and weavings of this type were made as part of a girl's dowry, by the bride herself, to be given to the groom on her wedding day. Each area had its own traditional designs, but typical of most is the hexagonal medallion, as in this example, which was based on the earlier "Transylvanian" rugs from Ushak in western Anatolia. The white field is also typical, and was often piled in cotton. Like the Transylvanian rugs, this finely woven piece has a zigzag effect created in the borders. It is made of wool on a cotton foundation.

(*c.1820; l. 1.5m/4ft 11in; value* **G**)

▲ Prayer-rug made in Ladik

The central Anatolian town of Ladik is prolific in its production of prayer-rugs. The piece featured here, made of wool on a wool foundation, represents a typical example, with its bright-red mihrab and blue spandrels. The floral panel above the mihrab – incorporating three stylized tulips or poppies on long, straight stems – is a characteristic feature of Ladik rugs, as is the border of stylized floral motifs. The stylized tulip or poppy is a motif often found in Anatolian weavings and Ottoman art.

(*c.1850; 1.6m/5ft 3in; value* **H**)

▲ Prayer-rug made in Konya

Konya, an ancient city of religious learning, produces many prayer-rugs, with strong, vivid coloring and a generally simple, open design format. This example features a double mihrab, or prayer niche. The broad border with bold flower-heads is a basic version of a typical Anatolian theme. This rug is coarsely woven of wool on a wool foundation.

(c.1810; l. 1.6m/5ft 3in; value H)

▼ Carpet made in Ushak

Produced on a large scale toward the end of the 19th century, these pale-colored rugs with all-over designs based on Persian models are popular and highly decorative, although they tend to be somewhat coarsely woven. The stronger-colored examples and those with central medallions are considerably less desirable and valuable.

(c.1890; l. 3.5m/11ft 6in; value K)

MASTERPIECES OF TURKISH WEAVING

The town of Hereke, east of Istanbul, is famous for its extremely fine silk rugs with refined, elegant decoration. The finest silk rugs in the world are made there today. At the same time that Hereke started its production (late 19th century), workshops were established in Kum Kapi, the Armenian quarter of Istanbul. Exceptional, finely woven silk rugs were made there by Turkish Armenians who came from the weaving centers of Kayseri and Sivas; technically advanced in the art of rug-weaving, they produced rugs of a quality that had not been seen since the 17th century. They drew their inspiration from the Ottoman court style and the classic 16th-century Persian rugs of the Safavid period (1501–1732). Many of the products from these workshops are signed by the master weavers, with names that are now legendary: Zareh Penyamian, Hagop Kapoudjian, and the Tossounian family. These exquisite masterpieces are highly regarded and command high prices.

WESTERN INFLUENCE

In the late 19th century Western demand for decorative large-scale carpets increased, affecting both Persia and Turkey. Turkish carpet production during the 1890s responded to the new market, and Ushak in western Anatolia produced large, coarsely woven, decorative carpets for the European and American markets. These were often made to order by stores such as Liberty & Co. (est. 1875) in London, and carpets may still be found bearing their labels. Loosely woven on woollen foundations, many of these carpets were of indifferent quality and unattractive, the design most frequently produced being bright red with all-over bold green-and-blue lozenges and palmettes: these are often referred to as "Turkey" carpets. However, some attractive products were made, generally based on Persian models of the same period.

▼ "Sultan's Head" prayer-rug made in Kum Kapi

This silk rug, made in the Kum Kapi workshops of Istanbul, incorporates metal-thread brocading, in conjunction with flat-woven colored silks, in the arabesques. Seven different colored silks are used in this way. As is characteristic of Kum Kapi production, this rug exhibits an extremely high degree of technical excellence, with 121 knots to the square centimeter. The intricate, complex, curvilinear design is made possible by the high knot count and the use of silk yarn.

(c.1905; l. 1.7m/5ft 7in; value O)

KEY FACTS

- MAIN AREAS OF PRODUCTION Ghiordes, Ladik, Konya, Hereke, Kum Kapi (Istanbul)
- WEAVE most town pieces are either cotton or silk on a wool foundation; less fine examples are woven in wool
- DESIGNS many patterns take their inspiration from classic prototypes and Persian models; nomadic and semi-nomadic rugs usually feature geometric designs
- COLORS these vary enormously from bright, vibrant jewel colors to washed-out pastel shades – the latter especially typical of town production pieces; poor examples feature harsh bright colors; modern nomadic and semi-nomadic pieces are characterized by the use of soft pastel shades
- COLLECTING look out for harmonious color combinations and well-balanced designs; fine silk rugs from Hereke and Kum Kapi are rare, exquisitely made, and usually extremely valuable; it is advisable to buy rare antique rugs only from reputable dealers – the most beautiful examples would have been made for export purposes so it is not usually advisable to travel to the country of production to find the best pieces

See also The Ottoman Empire before 1700, p.317

The Caucasus

The mountainous region between the Black and Caspian seas is inhabited by many ethnic groups, whose weaving traditions go back centuries. However, very little is known of the type of carpet produced here prior to the mid-17th century, although what emerges from this time is a clearly identifiable group of carpets based on a nomadic and semi-nomadic style of production. The designs incorporate both bold and finely drawn geometric motifs in bright, vivid, contrasting colors, and characteristically depict stylized animal and floral forms. These strong, geometric, individual renderings are highly prized by collectors, particularly examples that date from before c.1900. Later examples lack spontaneity, and are inclined to appear dull and stereotyped by comparison.

▲ "Dragon" carpet made in Shirvan
On this early piece from the eastern Caucasus, four white stylized dragons adorn the field, with moustache-like, jagged leaves forming a lattice. Unfinished pattern details running into the borders suggest a design running into infinity – a device used frequently in classic and later carpets. The floral and animal forms are intensely stylized. This rug is woven with a wool pile on a cotton foundation.
(c.1650; l. 4m/13ft 2in; value **M***)*

▲ Long rug made in Seichur
This rug is highly distinctive and easily recognizable as being from Seichur, with the "St Andrew's cross" motif on the field. Collectors prefer white field examples, as this allows the jewel-like colors to shine out. The stylized bird's-head outer border is also very characteristic.
(c.1880; l. 3.1m/10ft 4in; value **H***)*

EARLY CAUCASIAN WEAVINGS

The oldest identifiable group of Caucasian carpets is the so-called "Kuba dragon" carpets, which appear to date from about the mid-17th century. The name "Kuba" is likely to be spurious, as it is now generally thought that these carpets were woven in the Karabagh district of the southern Caucasus and the Shirvan district of the eastern Caucasus. The dragon rugs represent a bold and powerful provincial rendering of Persian animal and vase carpet designs from the towns of Tabriz, Kashan, and Kirman during the Safavid period (1501–1732). They incorporate stylized dragons and other motifs such as cloudbands, cranes, and phoenixes, which are associated with Chinese art and which also appear, naturalistically drawn, in Persian Safavid town production.

The overall design format with an endless repeat of animal and floral forms without a lattice arrangement also stems from the established format adopted by the Safavid court style. The degree of stylization of the drawing varies from carpet to carpet, with some carpets displaying motifs whose origins are barely identifiable. The production of large carpets, taking a characteristically long, narrow form and decorated with designs derived from classic production, virtually ceases by the mid-18th century.

LATER NORTH- AND EAST-CAUCASIAN WEAVINGS

Most Caucasian rugs date from the 19th century and were made in village workshops by weavers who combined a nomadic tradition, often based on an earlier Anatolian work, with formal designs based on the earlier dragon carpets or directly on Persian town influences. Northern and eastern Caucasian rugs are mostly on a cotton foundation or a combination of wool and cotton. The design repertory is endless, but there are certain consistent features in the group. The pile is in most cases tightly woven and closely wrapped, which allows for greater crispness and definition of design. The colors are jewel-like and vibrant. Kuba, Shirvan, and Dagestan are the three main districts where

▼ "Akstafa" long rug made in Shirvan
This design is called "Akstafa," after the town in the eastern Caucasus to which the pattern is attributed. This rug, made of wool pile on wool warps and a cotton weft, is easily identifiable as belonging to the genre, which is characterized by fantailed birds supporting or flanking a column of usually star-shaped medallions. Fine, crisp definition of the pattern drawing, as here, is typical. The supporting cast is made up of brilliant multicolored stylized flowers, animals, and birds.
(c.1890; l. 3.2m/10ft 6in; value **H***)*

technically fine Caucasian rugs are produced. Within each district, particular towns are associated with carpet production: Perebedil, Chi Chi, and Seichur in Kuba, and Marasali and Akstafa in Shirvan are the best known. Dagestan rugs are named after the district.

Rugs from the village of Seichur are particularly distinctive; mainly in runner format, they usually feature a repeating "St Andrew's cross" medallion in a typically formal arrangement, as seen in such earlier classic pieces as the "Holbein" rugs. The remaining field is often crammed with stylized flowering branches. White is rare as a background color, with shades of blue and red being much more usual. Dark blue is particularly common in northern and eastern Caucasian rugs; small details are frequently picked out in brighter colors, and contrast strongly against the dark background. Visually appealing examples will, additionally, incorporate a background border color that contrasts with the field

color. Prayer-rugs are typically woven with the mihrab, or prayer niche, consistently geometric in shape and very easily identifiable.

The north-easterly region of Dagestan is renowned for its well-made prayer-rugs with white or ivory grounds. The light ground is filled in with diagonal rows of multicolored, stylized plants in a serrated lattice. Borders are typically in a contrasting color to the ground.

LATER SOUTH- AND WEST-CAUCASIAN WEAVINGS

Bold and open designs epitomize rugs from the Karabagh and Kazak districts in the southern and western Caucasus, respectively. In contrast to that of rugs from the North and East, the wool pile is long and usually much more loosely woven, resulting in bolder, less detailed motifs. Designs are based upon earlier classic forms, both Persian and Anatolian. Good examples exhibit a fine balance between scale and color contrast in the pattern details. Carpets are seldom produced, mainly owing to the predominantly village-oriented nature of production, but also because the bold designs lend themselves to a smaller, rug-sized scale, as well as to runner formats. Bold prayer-rug designs are also found.

In establishing the quality of rugs from this area, it is important to look for bright, vibrant colors that are not brash or conflicting. Also look for lustrous wool in the pile and a good balance of design. Fineness of weave is not usually a factor in determining the quality of rugs from this region. Pieces made after 1880 may display harsh chemical dyes, with bright shades of orange and purple very noticeable. These were the first chemical dyes produced, c.1870, and do not harmonize with more traditional, natural colors. Shades of brown and charcoal are often used – these are prone to natural corrosion or oxidation due to the iron in the dyestuff. With rugs using these shades, the pile in the colored areas sometimes appears worn, but if the supporting pile is good, and only natural oxidation has occurred, this is not considered to be a flaw.

▲ **Rug made in Karabagh**
This rug features what is often referred to as the "eagle" or "sunburst" design, named after the medallions in the field. The design comes from Chelaberd, a village in the Karabagh district, and is one of the most celebrated in the southern Caucasus. An adaptation and simplification of the classic Ushak "star" medallion, it has a vibrant color scheme typical of Chelaberd rugs, with a characteristic red field and narrow ivory border. Armenian dates and inscriptions are not uncommon on these rugs. This example is loosely woven in wool on a wool foundation.
(c.1880; l. 2.5m/8ft 2in; value I)

▲ **Prayer-rug made in Dagestan**
Once seen, never forgotten, this striking design is typical of the rugs produced in the north-eastern Caucasian region of Dagestan (although the area does produce some designs that are not in prayer-rug format). The finely woven design comprises a white ground under the toothed arch of the mihrab, with an all-over pattern of stylized plants in diagonal rows forming a serrated lattice. Animal forms are often incorporated to break down the rigidity of this design. This example has the Islamic date 1327, equivalent to AD 1909.
(1909; l. 1.7m/5ft 7in; value H)

▼ **Rug made in Kazak**
The column of bold polychrome medallions in the field of this rug is a designed developed from the octagonal, latchhook medallions of classic Ottoman "Holbein" rugs. The simplified border is taken from Turkish "Transylvanian" rugs. This rug, from the western Caucasus, is made of wool on a wool foundation.
(c.1890; l. 2.4m/7ft 11in; value H)

KEY FACTS

- MAIN AREAS OF PRODUCTION the Kuba, Shirvan, Dagestan, Karabagh, and Kazak districts
- WEAVE mostly wool on a wool foundation although some finer pieces are produced on a cotton foundation
- SCALE most pieces are of rug size although runners and practical artifacts were also produced
- COLORS jewel-like colors are characteristic for the field, especially red, blue, white, and sometimes yellow; avoid pieces in shades of orange as well as any examples with color run; particularly beware of red bleeding into white
- DESIGNS these are almost always geometric; prayer-rugs are typical of the area
- MOTIFS floral and animal motifs are typical
- COLLECTING pieces are usually identifiable by district or by village; rugs produced before 1900 are highly sought after by collectors; later examples tend to feature poor color combinations and usually lack the individuality of earlier pieces; examples are copied in Turkey but colors are likely to be pastel-based

Western Turkestan

Western Turkestan is a loosely defined area bordered by Iran and the Caspian Sea to the West, Afghanistan to the South, and China to the East. The region is inhabited by the Turkomans (Turkic peoples), whose tribal structure has historically always been complex and shifting. Many of the tribal groups under this heading changed over the years as alliances were formed, broken, and re-formed. The main tribal subdivisions within this group are the Tekke, the Yomut, the Salor, the Ersari, the Beshir, the Saryk, and the Belouch. Their weaving tradition dates back centuries, but most examples found today can be confidently dated only to the 18th century or later. Western Turkestan came under the control of the Russian empire in the late 19th century, and later of the Soviet Union. Russian domination gradually eroded the tribal structures and consequently tribal weavings became more stereotyped and commercialized, and less highly collectible.

TURKOMAN WEAVINGS

Turkoman weavings, as a group, are easy to recognize, but to identify the exact tribal subdivision can prove difficult. Based on nomadic traditions, their woven products included rugs and functional artifacts of daily life such as *torba* (long, narrow bags), *juval* (deeper bags), and trappings. Large carpets (more than 3.5m/ 12ft long) are seldom seen. Most pieces have a limited color scheme – usually Turkoman weavings have the same ground and border color. The background color is usually red in all its shades, ranging from a very bright terracotta through burgundy to brown or aubergine. The designs, in dark brown, white, and blue, with occasional yellow, crimson, and green, are abstract and geometric in form, following the typical nomadic custom, and are woven from memory with patterns passed down through the generations. Wool is used for foundation and pile.

Prior to any commercialization the Turkomans used their weavings to decorate their circular tents, known as *öy*; the motifs they wove identified the tribe. As in certain Ottoman designs, the primary motif is the *gul*,

◄ **Carpet made by the Saryk**
This rug, from southern Turkestan, is a very typical, and impressive, example of Saryk work, although the upper border is missing. The design of the *gul*, the reddish-brown field, and the checkered borders are characteristic of this tribe. Another distinctive feature is the occasional use of cotton or silk pile to pick out details in the patterns of carpets and artifacts. Unusually for a Turkoman tribe, the Saryk used a Turkish, or symmetrical, knot. Like most Saryk weavings, this rug is of wool on a wool foundation.
(*c.1860; l. 2.8m/9ft 2in; value* **K**)

▼ *Juval* **made by the Salor**
This *juval* (bag) from southwestern Turkestan, identifiable by the large, rounded, turreted *guls* on a crimson-red ground, illustrates true Salor work in every sense. Only one, horizontal row of *guls* is present, with purple-pink silk highlights. The Salor *gul* was later taken up by the Tekke and the Saryk, but their version is flatter and they use six (in two rows) rather than three on a *juval*. Salor pieces are rare, and highly prized by collectors. This is of wool on a wool foundation, and is Persian-knotted.
(*c.1820; l. 1.1m/3ft 7in; value* **H**)

▼ *Juval* **made by the Tekke**
Formal rows of *guls* with a skirt at one end identify this piece as a *juval* (bag). The rich terracotta coloring and the full, finely woven design, are true Tekke attributes. Tekke rugs often have a grid of black lines (not present here) joining the *guls*. This piece, from central Turkestan, is of wool on a wool foundation; it is Persian-knotted.
(*c.1870; l. 1.2m/3ft 11in; value* **E**)

a geometric, highly stylized floral motif, and its shape is (or was originally) the distinctive signature of the tribe – its symbol or emblem. The *gul* is used in repeated parallel rows in the main field design, which is framed by a complementary border. Difficulties of exact tribal attribution can arise, as *gul* motifs were copied from neighboring tribes, or, during times of conflict, motifs were stolen and adapted by the victorious group.

By the end of the 19th century, commercialization along with increasing demand from Western markets led to the emergence of a more stereotyped style. The Tekke *gul* proved especially popular, and as a result other tribal groups abandoned their own *gul* to use that of the Tekke instead. By the end of the 19th century, although commercial production was a success, the individual weaving traditions of the tribes had virtually died out.

THE TRIBES

The Tekke were the most powerful tribe in western Turkestan during the 19th century until they were defeated in 1881 by the Russian army. They were prolific weavers, their products ranging from main carpets to functional pieces. Their carpets are among the most copied in Pakistan and Afghanistan today. Tekke carpets are often incorrectly called "Bokhara" carpets, while the famous Tekke *gul* is sometimes incorrectly described as the "elephant's foot" *gul* after its shape. Tekke carpets often display a characteristic grid of black horizontal and vertical lines joining the *guls*. Weavings made prior to the end of the 19th century are extremely collectible and of high quality.

The Yomut were also prolific weavers. It is sometimes difficult to identify a Yomut piece, since the tribe used a great variety of designs, but various shades of brown and aubergine for the grounds, and bright reds, yellows, blue, and ivory for pattern details are typical. Yomut *guls* often have hooked edges and may be arranged in diagonals. Like the Tekke, the Yomut are famous for certain artifacts, such as *asmalyk* (camel trappings).

The Salor, a notorious warring tribe, were heavily defeated by the Persians in 1831, and later by the Tekke in a land struggle in 1859. The tribe then effectively disintegrated and members were swallowed into larger groups such as the Ersari. Their large, rounded *gul* containing a trefoil motif (known as a *gülli*, or "flower," *gul*) was subsequently adopted by the Tekke and the Saryk, but was used by these tribes in greater density, giving the pattern an overcrowded appearance.

In contrast to the finely woven work of the neighboring Tekke and Yomut, the weaving of the Ersari is crude and loose. The Ersari are closely associated with the Beshir, and both were prolific weaving groups until the late 19th century. A typical Ersari design uses the *gülli gul* repeated in tightly packed rows. Borders of stepped medallions are also common. Ersari carpets are often labeled as Afghan, mainly because the Turkoman plains of northern Afghanistan formed part of the tribe's territory. Their designs, particularly the large *gul* format, were also imitated by later Afghan mass production.

The Saryk were one of the least prolific weaving groups in Turkestan: pieces identifiable to them are rare, and sought after by collectors. Unusually for Turkoman work, Saryk carpets use the Turkish (symmetrical) knot. They also use several different *guls*, similar to those of the Tekke and the Salor. Most typical is a large octagonal *gul* with 24 facets, often containing cross-shaped motifs; large and small *guls* may alternate in rows.

The Belouch (now the Baluchi) inhabit an isolated region straddling the Afghan-Iranian border. Their work is distinctive and original, making use of wonderfully soft natural camel wool. Prayer-rugs are one of their most highly regarded formats, while the tree – often a stylized tree of life – is one of their most typical motifs.

▲ Prayer-rug made by the Belouch

Rugs produced by the nomadic Belouch tribe, whose territory extends across the Afghan-Iranian border, are characterized by somber coloring. This piece – a prayer-rug, which features a geometricized mihrab – is an example of one of the best and most sought-after designs. The natural camel wool ground with the stylized tree of life crisply drawn in darker shades is very appealing. This prayer-rug is woven in wool on a wool foundation.

*(c.1870; l. 1.4m/4ft 7in; value **G**)*

▲ *Asmalyk* made by the Yomut

Easily identifiable with its pentagonal shape, the *asmalyk* was used to decorate the bridal camel. This serrated *gul* and vine lattice is the most common design. Tassels would originally have run the full length of the bottom end. This piece is of wool on a wool foundation.

*(c.1870; l. 1.2m/3ft 11in; value **F**)*

► Carpet made by the Ersari

Large *guls* on a terracotta-brown field, together with the use of broad kilim ends, identify this example as Ersari. The delicate use of yellow and white is also characteristically Ersari. The design is often seen in later Afghan carpets in strong red shades. This carpet is made of coarse but lustrous wool on a wool foundation.

*(c.1865; l. 3.8m/12ft 6in; value **H**)*

KEY FACTS

- **MAIN TRIBES** the Tekke, the Yomut, the Salor, the Ersari, the Beshir, the Saryk, and the Belouch
- **TYPES** rugs, carpets, and artifacts such as bags and animal trappings
- **WEAVE** wool pile on a wool foundation is typical
- **COLORS** the field is usually characterized by extremely distinctive shades of red and brown; Turkoman weavings typically have the same color ground and border; decorative motifs are typically in dark blue or ivory
- **DESIGNS** these are almost exclusively geometric in form and are based upon motifs of flora and fauna; repeat designs of the *gul* or flower-head are usually featured in the field
- **COLLECTING** examples are subdivided into tribal groups and are usually identified by the shape and style of the primary *gul* motif; pieces made before 1900 are sought after by collectors; later pieces lack the individuality and subtlety of color of early pieces and tend to be more coarsely woven
- **BEWARE** pieces from western Turkestan are often erroneously classified as "Bokhara" weavings after the exporting town in the region; however, no rugs were ever made in Bokhara; collectors should beware that designs are often copied in Pakistan using considerably inferior colors and materials to the originals

Flatweaves

Traditionally, flatweaves in the Middle East were made for domestic use rather than for sale. It is really only since the 1960s that collectors have taken an interest, and historical details are sparse. Geometric designs predominate, since they are the simplest to execute. In addition to large floor coverings, bags, saddlebags, horse covers, and cradles are made using the flatweaving technique.

KILIMS

The word commonly used to describe Middle Eastern flatweaves is "kilim," from the Persian *gelim*. They are usually tribal or village products, normally in wool, sometimes also including cotton (used to give a very bright white) and occasionally silk and metal thread.

A small number of 16th- to 18th-century Turkish Ottoman court kilims with curvilinear designs based on textiles survive, but the majority are geometric. As with piled weavings, colors and designs are regionally different, and a wide variety of distinctive types exists. Kilims from Balikesir and Bergama in north-western Anatolia, for example, are mainly dark red and blue with horizontally emphasized designs of hooked bars. Those of Konya in central-southern Anatolia often have a white ground. Reyhanli kilims from near the border with Syria typically have three panels with floral trelliswork enclosing rectangles with geometric *guls* (medallions).

Commercially, Caucasian kilims are usually described as being from either Kuba or Shirvan, although they were almost certainly made elsewhere as well. Kuba kilims usually have red or blue fields with offset rows of interlocking hooked and stepped medallions. Shirvan kilims are often horizontally banded with rows of stepped *guls* and narrow stripes of geometric motifs in strong, bright colors. Karabagh produced a distinctive European-style kilim with *gul ferangi* ("foreign flowers") – usually cabbage roses – in imitation of 19th-century French carpets, often on a brown ground. Later examples have brash chemical dyes in orange and pink.

About 40 Safavid Persian kilims from the 16th and 17th centuries survive. Executed in silk and metal thread with designs similar to those of piled carpets, they are unlike any 19th- or 20th-century production. Fewer kilims were made in Persia than in Anatolia. Among the most distinctive groups are those made by the Kashgai of south-western Persia, in bright colors with "eye-dazzler" (concentric multicolored blocks), diamond, and panel patterns. White cotton may be used, and they often have dark-blue and white diamond borders. Finely woven kilims from Senneh (now Sanandaj), the capital of Persian Kurdistan, are also easily identified, having small *boteh* (stylized cypress) or *herati* (a diamond flanked by four serrated leaves) designs, occasionally in prayer-niche format. The finest have silk warps or silk details. Later kilims from Bidjar, north-east of Senneh, copy Senneh designs but are rarely of such good quality.

Kilims were also made in the Balkans, Thrace (now part of Turkey, Greece, and Bulgaria), and Bessarabia. These kilims often have European designs, with sprigs or pots of flowers, ribbons, and birds. Curvilinear designs are also produced using supplementary wefts. Pieces from the 18th century and earlier are rare; 19th-century examples with vegetable dyes are popular and relatively inexpensive.

▲ Kilim made in Bessarabia

Kilims such as this are woven with supplementary wefts – additional rows of weft inserted so as to create curves. A design of all-over flower sprays, here with ribbon bows, is very typical of Bessarabian kilims, which take inspiration from European rather than Oriental textiles.
(late 19th century; l. 3m/9ft 10in; value H)

► Soumakh horse cover made in the Caucasus

The main part of this weaving lay over the animal's back and the two projections were tied under its neck. It is heavily embroidered with two-headed animals and stylized peacocks. Animal forms are probably intended to bring the user prosperity (measured by the size of his herds). Elaborate examples such as this are keenly sought by collectors.
(late 19th century; l. 1.8m/5ft 11in; value I)

SOUMAKH, PALLAS, AND CICIM

The "soumakh" technique gives a harder-wearing fabric than the kilim, and is used for floor coverings, bags, and horse covers. It may be combined with pile-weaving, notably for bags. Soumakh carpets usually come from the Caucasus. The usual design is a row of three long blue medallions on a red ground. "Pallas" is the term used to refer to the flatweaves of Afghanistan and Baluchistan. *Çiçim* (pronounced "jijim") are heavy, plain-woven Turkish fabrics with surface embroidery.

► Kilim made in Konya

Most large Anatolian kilims were woven in two strips, the weaver being limited by the width of her loom. Often, as here, the joins do not match perfectly. The desirable white ground and open design are typical of this area (central-southern Anatolia).
(c.1850–80; l. 2.8m/ 9ft 2in; value G)

KEY FACTS

- TYPES domestic artifacts and floor coverings
- MATERIAL wool is most typical
- DESIGNS patterns are characteristically geometric
- CONDITION flatweaves are less hard-wearing than pile carpets; they have a tendency to split at the joins and on areas of color change
- COLLECTING look for natural dyes and strong colors; avoid pre-faded pieces (colors often appear "chalky") or those with any color run, indicating late chemical dyes; pieces are best hung on the wall or over furniture

See also France, pp.328–9

The Far East

Eastern Turkestan, Mongolia, China, Tibet, and Nepal are all areas of carpet production. They are known for their heavy weavings, using a large, Persian (asymmetrical) knot, generally on a cotton foundation.

CHINA

China is not known to have made rugs before the 17th century, although silk textiles have been made there for thousands of years. The technique of knotting reached China via trade with Turkestan, and early Chinese weavings (17th to mid-19th century) are especially associated with Ningxia in north-west China, a stop on the Silk Route between Beijing and eastern Turkestan.

Chinese culture has for centuries been dominated by several major religions, including Buddhism and Daoism, and these have inevitably influenced the arts. Unlike Middle Eastern rugs, Chinese rugs feature symbols with specific meanings: the dragon is the symbol of the emperor; bats mean luck; cranes represent immortality; the peony stands for nobility and wealth, and the lotus for purity; the Lions of Fo, the guardians of Buddhist temples, protect against evil. Chinese weavings use a mixture of geometric and curvilinear designs, often in the same rug, and designs are elegant and harmonious. Colors tend to be less strong than those of the Middle Eastern palette, with yellows and blues dominating. Partly for warmth, the pile is usually left quite long.

Carpet-making flourished principally in the northern and western provinces (Xinjiang, Ningxia, Gansu, Inner Mongolia); designs are broadly similar, with a few regional differences. For example, Baotou, in Inner Mongolia, is known for its pictorial rugs. From the mid-19th century, carpets were produced commercially, and imperial factories such as those in Beijing gradually replaced the small workshops. Carpets from the 1920s and 1930s, often called "Nichols Chinese" after the company they were made for, are in non-traditional colors such as purple, green, and maroon, with floral decoration imitating 19th-century French Aubusson and Savonnerie styles. In the 20th century China has used cheap labor to make carpets for the Western market.

The Chinese also made "pillar" rugs to decorate the columns of Buddhist temples. These depict dragons and symbolic motifs which, when the rug is wrapped around a pillar, form a continuous design. Woven covers for ceremonial seats and chair backs were also made.

▲ "Peony and dragon" rug made in Ningxia
The coloring of ivory, yellow, apricot, dark blue, and light blue is very characteristic of early Chinese carpets. Note the dragons with cranes' wings in the corners. The narrow, dark-brown outer border is common on 17th- and 18th-century Ningxia weaves.
(1723–35; l. 2.8m/9ft 2in; value **P***)*

◄ "Lotus blossom" carpet made in western China
This example has the typical soft, long pile and monochromatic color scheme of 19th-century Chinese carpets. The medallions are stylized lotus flowers. Also characteristic is the two-tone blue fretwork inner border. Many pieces of this type were exported to the West in the late 19th and early 20th centuries, and were particularly popular in the USA.
(second half 19th century; l. 3.6m/11ft 10in; value **H***)*

EASTERN TURKESTAN (XINJIANG)

This region includes the production centers of Khotan, Yarkand, and Kashgar. Often called "Samarkands," carpets typically include designs of one or three large circular medallions with fretwork spandrels, or stylized pomegranate trees in vases. Colors are usually bright reds and blues; some were woven in yellow and a purple dye called "fuchsine," which fades to a pale lavender.

TIBET AND MONGOLIA

Tibetan weavings include rugs, pillar carpets, and saddle and seat covers, typically with a long pile. Unusual checkerboard designs are found, often in blue and ivory, as well as pelt rugs that imitate tiger skin. Lotus flowers, chrysanthemums, and peonies were popular motifs. Vegetable dyes were used until the early 20th century, after which bright synthetic pinks, oranges, and reds were used. Recent Tibetan rugs, made by refugees in Nepal, come in a variety of patterns, often in pastels.

Mongolian weavings tend to be coarse, and are mainly in red, brown, and white. Their production is limited: warm felts are used for rugs, cloaks, and coverings.

◄ Saddle cover made in Tibet
Coarsely woven, with a heavy pile, this saddle cover has Chinese-influenced decoration. The binding of thick red woollen fabric is frequently found on Tibetan weavings.
(mid-19th century; l. 90cm/35½in; value **B***)*

KEY FACTS

- MAIN AREAS OF PRODUCTION Xinjiang; Ningxia; Gansu; Inner Mongolia; Khotan; Yarkand; Kashgar; Nepal
- WEAVE mostly wool on a cotton foundation using an asymmetrical knot; examples tend to be weighty
- DESIGNS these reflect the local religion and culture: dragons, bats, cranes, peonies, and lotus blossoms are all highly characteristic of Chinese carpets
- CONDITION the glossy wool pile of examples with a plain field is difficult to repair, so avoid stained or damaged examples
- COLLECTING many Chinese carpets were produced in response to Western demand, so a great number of examples exist; modern copies have little resale value

See also France, pp. 328–9

Europe

Spain is the only European country that can be said to have an indigenous hand-knotted carpet industry, owing to the influence of Moorish culture. Spanish carpets of the Moorish period (up to the 15th century) were similar to early Anatolian patterns. Carpet-weaving was established in France in the 17th century. The French workshops produced magnificent carpets in the first distinctively European style, with extravagant, naturalistic floral patterns. English carpet-weaving centers were established in the 18th century to compete with those in France, and their designs mainly imitated fashionable French production. The decline that set in with industrialization was briefly halted by the efforts of individuals such as William Morris.

France

The most highly prized European carpets are those from the great French factory known as the Savonnerie. This name is often used to describe not only true Savonnerie production but also the piled weavings of other French factories, including Aubusson, and even carpets from Spain, Belgium, Germany, and Austria.

THE SAVONNERIE

A workshop for the weaving of furnishing fabrics was established by Pierre Dupont in the Louvre Palace in 1604, and in 1627 its production, with the royal permission of Louis XIII (reigned 1610–43), expanded to rugs and carpets. The enterprise moved to the Savonnerie, an orphanage and former soap factory at Chaillot, near Paris. Many of the orphans were the factory's first apprentices, forming a convenient source of cheap labor. The early production of the factory, under Louis XIII, is characterized by dark blackish-brown grounds strewn with naturalistically drawn flowers. This style, known as "Louis XIII," remained popular into the second half of the 17th century.

The Savonnerie enjoyed its greatest success under Louis XIV (reigned 1643–1715), the "Sun King," whose rule saw the high point of French power in Europe and a great flourishing of French culture. These were the years in which 13 carpets for the Apollo Gallery in the Louvre and 92 (of 93 commissioned) carpets for the Great Gallery (connecting the Louvre to the Tuileries Palace) were woven. These carpets are distinguished by their size; the Great Gallery measures 442m (1,450ft) long, and each carpet was approximately 8 to 9m (26–30ft) in length and 5m (16ft 6in) wide. Special looms and new workshops were built to accommodate their dimensions.

◄ **Carpet designed by Perrot, made at the Savonnerie**
This model was woven at least 16 times between c.1744 and c.1756 for several of the royal residences. The dark ground echoes Louis XIV production, but the less formal hand of the 18th century is epitomized by the garlands of summer flowers. The pleated and *rose moresque* medallion, shells, mosaic, and corner jewel clasps are typical features of Perrot's designs. *(mid-18th century; l. 3.6m/11ft 10in; value Q)*

▼ **Carpet made at the Savonnerie**
This is one of 93 planned for the Great Gallery of the Louvre. The background featuring polychrome *rinceaux* (scrolling foliage), the architectonic borders echoing the ceiling decoration, and the royal emblems – here orbs with fleurs-de-lis surmounted by crowns and entwined "L"s (for Louis XIV) – are all characteristic. *(c.1668–1680s; l. 9m/29ft 6in; value Q)*

The carpets were woven as pairs, and those depicting landscape vignettes were alternated with examples depicting allegorical figures such as "Peace and Abundance," and "Victory and Strength."

Louis XIV eventually lost interest in the Great Gallery, as the focus of his attention shifted to his palace at Versailles. The carpets, used only rarely, survived the 18th century, but many were cut down or sold to raise money during the period of the Directory (1795–9). Most are now in museums. Louis ordered new works for Versailles, as well as for other royal residences, including those of Fontainebleau and Choisy-le-Roi.

The influence of the designer Pierre-Josse Perrot (active 1725–50) is evident in the bold designs and exuberant colors of Rococo production. Many of the popular designs were rewoven over a period of 30 or 40 years, so it can be difficult to judge the age of individual pieces. Other articles woven at the Savonnerie include bench covers, screen panels, and, occasionally, panels imitating paintings.

Savonnerie weavings have strongly depressed warps, making the back heavily ribbed. They use a Turkish-style (symmetrical) knot, and the dense pile is neatly clipped, giving great clarity to the designs. Patterns – designed by artists – were deliberately non-Oriental, reflecting instead contemporary French tastes in architecture and design. After the self-conscious grandeur of the Baroque era, 18th-century examples were less ostentatious and formal, while never losing the extravagance of their design. Bright colors are typical. Even as styles evolved, floral decoration with twining arabesques and foliage, often with a central medallion, remained a basic theme.

▲ Carpet made in Tournai by Piat Lefebvre
Carpets were woven in Tournai to supplement Savonnerie production. After a design by the artist Louis de la Hamayde de Sainte Ange, this carpet includes swans and floral cornucopia, typical First Empire motifs.
(c.1809; l. 6.9m/22ft 8in; value Q)

AUBUSSON

By the mid-18th century demand for Savonnerie carpets had outstripped the capabilities of the factory. In 1740 Aubusson in central-southern France, already famous for its tapestries, began production of piled carpets in the Savonnerie style. Aubusson was not a specific factory: the workers were spread throughout the city in independent workshops, working either on their own account or producing piecework. The quality of their weaving and dyeing had historically been rather mediocre, but the greatest difficulty lay in obtaining suitable cartoons (the design for a tapestry or carpet). For this reason, until *c*.1750 Aubusson carpets were usually copies of Oriental carpets, such as Ushaks. Old cartoons from the Savonnerie were used from *c*.1760. Although production is in the Savonnerie style, the workmanship is less skilled and the weaves are looser, making the designs of the carpets less crisp and regular. Aubusson pile carpets have single-layered warps, and the pile is therefore less dense than that of the Savonnerie.

In 1771, in order to create more employment for the tapestry weavers, Aubusson began to weave *tapis-ras* (flatwoven carpets made using the tapestry technique), and this is the type for which it became famous. Late 18th-century production uses a coarsely spun "dry" wool and has a "hairy" surface. Designs are typical of the period, often copying Savonnerie.

THE 19TH CENTURY

During the French Revolution, production effectively ceased at the Savonnerie and in Aubusson. Napoleon Bonaparte became emperor in 1804 and was obliged to redecorate the royal palaces, since much of the furniture and carpets had been dispersed. His designers, Charles Percier (1764–1838) and Pierre Fontaine (*c*.1762–1853), were primarily responsible for the stylistic revolution of the First Empire period

(1804–15). Popular motifs included bees (Napoleon's personal emblem), military trophies, and elements from classical antiquity. New carpets were required by the new, fashion-conscious bourgeoisie, and the industry was revived. The imperial household commissioned carpets from the Savonnerie, Aubusson, and other smaller factories such as Tournai (now in Belgium).

Under the Bourbon Restoration of Louis XVIII (1814–24) and Charles X (1824–30) the Empire style remained popular. Aubusson produced large numbers of *tapis-ras*, to supply the growing middle classes. Under Louis Philippe (1830–48) the typically refined, elegant, and intricate patterns became denser and more elaborate, and stronger colors such as chocolate brown, dark red, olive green, and gold were used. Drawing is extremely realistic on these pieces. During and after the Second Empire period (1852–70), colors softened. Late production is very pale pink and beige with floral bouquets and, often, a dark-red surround. This type is most frequently seen in today's market. First Empire *tapis-ras* are similar in texture to late 18th-century weaving, while carpets made during the reign of Louis Philippe and later have more tightly spun wool and a smoother surface. The better-quality carpets may include silk or metal thread.

▼ Flatwoven carpet made in Aubusson
This part-silk carpet was possibly woven by the principal Aubusson firm of Charles Sallandrouze de la Mornaix, renowned for their Rococo Revival carpets. Its eclectic and unusual design includes a Chinese-style trellis and a central medallion showing fishing tackle and a picnic.
(c.1840–50; l. 2m/6ft 7in; value K)

▲ Flatwoven *entre-fenêtre* made in Aubusson
This panel would have hung on the wall between two windows. Aubusson also produced *cantonnières* (window pelmets) often with *trompe l'oeil* fringing and tassels, and *portières* (coverings for doorways).
(1852–70; l. 3.6m/12ft; value I)

◄ Flatwoven carpet made in Aubusson
This example is highly typical of late 19th-century production in the Louis XVI style. Imitations of Louis XIV and XV carpets were also produced, including pile examples, usually in pale colors.
(late 19th century; l. 4.1m/13ft 5in; value L)

KEY FACTS

- MATERIALS Savonnerie: wool pile with a symmetrical knot; Aubusson: some piled production but most examples are flatwoven *tapis-ras*
- SCALE Savonnerie: most are very large carpets
- DESIGNS pieces closely reflect fashionable taste
- COLLECTING carpets produced by the Savonnerie are much rarer than those made in Aubusson; if in good condition, Savonnerie carpets are among the most valuable weavings on the market; Aubusson carpets were produced on a relatively large scale and are therefore quite easy to find; however, as flatweaves are very prone to wear, examples in good condition will carry a premium
- BEWARE always buy from a reputable dealer, as there are many reproductions directly copied from 19th-century pieces on the market; most are made in China and can be distinguished by their pastel coloring

Britain and Ireland

P ile carpets were little known in Britain before the early 16th century; floors were usually covered with straw or rushes. Portraits of Henry VIII (1491–1547) show him standing on Turkish "Holbein" and "Lotto" carpets and "star" Ushak carpets.

BEFORE 1800
From the late 16th century, Persian and Turkish carpets were imported to Britain and became increasingly popular. Carpets were generically known as "Turkey" carpets; pile was called "Turkey-work." Early British designs, typically on a hemp foundation, take their inspiration from Oriental models, but traditional Far-Eastern motifs are often replaced with motifs more familiar to the British market such as strawberry leaves and roses. Armorials are also characteristic.

During the mid-18th century, organized production in England began on a commercial basis in an attempt to rival the fashionable French carpets. Early ventures were dogged by financial difficulties, and factories were short-lived, so these carpets are rare. One of the earliest manufacturers was the Frenchman Pierre Parisot, who, with two weavers from the Savonnerie in Paris, set up a workshop in Fulham, London. He produced carpets in imitation of those from the Savonnerie between 1751 and 1755; the business was taken over by the Swiss maker Claude Passavant (d.1776) and transferred to Exeter, but went bankrupt in 1761.

Thomas Moore (1700–1788) had a workshop at Moorfields in London (est. by 1757) and produced carpets for the Scottish architects Robert Adam (1728–92) and James Adam (1730–94), who pioneered the Neo-classical movement in Britain. The carpets commissioned by the Adams were designed to echo the architecture (usually the ceilings) of the buildings for which they were intended, such as Syon House and Osterley House, both in Middlesex. Production ceased in 1795.

Thomas Whitty of Axminster in Devon was the most successful 18th-century English maker. The Axminster factory (1755–1835) produced carpets mainly in the French style, which were renowned for their quality.

◄ Carpet made in Exeter
This example features a woven inscription, "EXON. 1758," identifying it as the work of Claude Passavant. The design is clearly indebted to contemporary French carpets from the Savonnerie, with its mosaic ground, jeweled corner clasps, masks, and architectural frame. Exeter carpets are particularly rare. This piece is composed of a wool pile and wool warps and wefts.
*(1758; l. 4.2m/13ft 9in; value **Q**)*

► Carpet made in Wilton
This floral design is typical of the popular English taste of the mid-19th century. Naturalistically drawn flowers are designed to appear three-dimensional against a damask pattern ground. The bright-blue field is often seen in English carpets of this period, although not in French equivalents.
*(c.1850; l. 5m/16ft 5in; value **M**)*

▼ Carpet made in Axminster
Although similar to contemporary French examples, this piled carpet has several very English features, including strawberry plants at each end of the medallion and Tudor-style roses in the border. The dark-brown ground is typical of Axminster production of this period. Axminster carpets from the 18th century are extremely desirable and valuable.
*(c.1765–70; l. 5.3m/17ft 5in; value **Q**)*

AFTER 1800
In the early 19th century the Axminster factory was the main center of weaving in Britain; carpets were woven in all the fashionable styles, including Savonnerie, Neo-classical, Oriental, and Regency. After 1835 carpet production moved to the nearby town of Wilton, where Wilton carpets (with a tufted rather than a knotted pile), ingrain carpets (in a thick, double-faced fabric), and jacquard carpets (named after the inventor of the jacquard loom, which was particularly suited to the production of repeat-pattern carpets) were all made by machine. Hand-knotted carpets were also made until 1957. Most Wilton carpets were luxury commissions for the wealthy aristocracy, and feature a rich velvety pile.

In the late 19th century William Morris (1834–96) and his partner John Henry Deale wove hand-knotted carpets inspired by 17th-century Persian designs. Other smaller factories included Alexander Morton and Co. in Killybegs in Donegal, Ireland, which wove carpets from designs by such artists as C.F.A. Voysey (1857–1941).

KEY FACTS
- WEAVE all British carpets are woven with the symmetrical (Turkish) knot
- SCALE most are large pieces, designed to impress
- MOTIFS strawberry plants, roses, armorials
- INSCRIPTIONS Moorfields carpets are sometimes inscribed with the name "Moorfields"
- COLORS these reflect the fashions of the day
- PRODUCTION many British carpets were produced to rival imports from France and the Middle East
- COLLECTING examples in good condition are now very highly priced and are rarely found outside of museums and large country houses; Axminster carpets and any examples by important craftsmen are rare and valuable

See also The Ottoman Empire before 1700, p.315, France, pp.328–9

Spain and Portugal

The Iberian peninsula was partially ruled by the Moors from the 8th to the late 15th century and Moorish artisans had introduced carpet-weaving to Spain by at least the 12th century. A distinguishing feature of Spanish carpets is their knot, which is tied around alternate single warps in offset rows. Weaving centers were concentrated in the south-west of Spain, in areas dominated by the Moors; these include Murcia, Alcaraz, Chinchilla, and Cuenca.

A Spanish fragment found at Fostat in Cairo dates to the 12th or 13th century, but the oldest virtually complete Spanish carpet is of the 14th century. Decorated with stylized trees and with a Kufic border, it was found in 1880 in a church in the Austrian Tyrol. Also notable are the c.30 surviving carpets and fragments that are related to the celebrated 15th-century "Admiral" heraldic carpet; these combine Anatolian geometric motifs and Kufic script with the armorials of Spanish noble families. Spanish weavers also imitated 15th- and 16th-century Turkish carpets – several examples exist with "Holbein" designs (repeated polygonal medallions), showing the Anatolian influence. In the 16th century, this pattern became more European in character, developing into a wreath of oak leaves with acorns. Other designs were based on contemporary textiles. In the 17th century Cuenca produced carpets with designs based on Turkish "Lotto" carpets, which featured a grid of arabesques. A combination of yellows, blues, and ivory is particularly typical of Cuenca and Alcaraz carpet production of the 16th and 17th centuries.

In 1721 the Madrid royal tapestry factory was founded by Jacobo van der Goten from Antwerp, at the behest of Philip V of Spain. The factory initially wove tapestries, but in 1786 was given permission to weave carpets. It was destroyed during the Peninsular War (1808–14) but reopened in 1819, and by the late 19th and early 20th centuries, its output was considerable. Copies of earlier Cuenca and Alcaraz carpets were produced in shades of pale blue, pink, green, and yellow; these copies have a "dry," flat look in comparison with the originals. Other carpets were woven at Cuenca and Alcaraz in the 18th-century European style.

▼ "Admiral" heraldic carpet made in Alcaraz

Woven for Don Fadrique Enriquez, 26th Admiral of Castille, and bearing his armorial three times, this carpet has many charming details such as a border of birds, bears, and swans.
*(mid-15th century; l. 5.8m/19ft; value **Q**)*

▼ Ogival-lattice carpet made in Cuenca or Alcaraz

This pattern, featuring palmettes enclosed within a trellis of vines clasped by crowns and leaves, is derived from late 16th-century Turkish and Italian textiles.
*(late 16th century; l. 3.3m/10ft 10in; value **L**)*

▲ Savonnerie-style carpet, probably made in Madrid

From the 18th century, Spanish weavers produced carpets imitating the fashionable output of the Savonnerie and Aubusson, in France, to supply their domestic market. This carpet is in the style of the late 18th century, but has been produced in the very pale colors that were particularly popular in the late 19th and early 20th centuries.
*(20th century; l. 7m/23ft; value **L**)*

PORTUGAL

There is no tradition of knotted-pile carpets in Portugal. Instead, the Portuguese made embroidered carpets, called *arraiolos*, after the principal place of manufacture: Arrailos, in the Alentejo. The earliest, rare, examples are 17th century. Production declined in the 19th century but was revived in the 20th century and still continues. Carpets usually have a mixture of floral and folkloric motifs such as birds and animals. Modern production is in a wide variety of styles, dictated by contemporary fashions.

KEY FACTS

- **WEAVE** Spain: carpets are produced using a version of the symmetrical knot, woven around one warp only
- **MATERIAL** Spain: most are wool pile on a wool or cotton foundation; Portugal: embroidered carpets in wool (sometimes in silk) on linen are most typical; early 18th-century pieces are usually on jute canvas
- **DESIGN** Spain: many pieces show a French or Turkish influence; Portugal: mostly folk-art and floral motifs
- **COLOR** Spain: 18th- and 19th-century carpets are predominantly in shades of shocking pink, electric blue, vibrant yellow, and emerald green
- **COLLECTING** Spain: early carpets are rare and valuable; those inspired by French designs are more affordable

See also The Ottoman Empire before 1700, p.317

The United States

Beautiful textiles have been woven by Indian tribes in the south-west of the USA for centuries. The earliest evidence of weaving in the region dates back to the Anasazi culture (from c.1000), who twined and braided clothing from human and animal hair and vegetable fibers. From c.1600 the Pueblo Indians of the Rio Grande area (now New Mexico) developed a rich tradition of weaving with cotton on a loom. When the Navajo Indians migrated to the Rio Grande between the 11th and 16th centuries, they adopted Pueblo weaving techniques and developed them to create a unique weaving tradition that has since produced some of the most stunning textiles in the world.

MATERIALS AND TECHNIQUES

The wool and dyes used by the Navajo are central to the production of the bold designs that characterize their work. In general, the Navajo do not ply their yarn while spinning; instead they create a continuous thread whose thickness is often subtly varied. Wool is from two breeds of sheep, Churro and Merino. The wool of the Churro sheep is coarse and usually gray or brown; that of the Merino is softer and a creamy-white color. Natural wools were used exclusively until c.1870, when the Navajo were detained at Bosque Redondo by the North American government and forced to weave with commercially produced yarns, most notably those from Germantown, Pennsylvania, sometimes known as "Germantown" yarns.

Whereas earlier Navajo weavings were characterized by their natural colors – browns and shades of gray, blue, red, and yellow from natural dyes – those made using commercial yarns were colored with new, mass-produced, synthetic (or aniline) dyes, which were available in a wide array of colors. However, at the beginning of the 20th century the Navajo returned to the

use of natural dyes. Blankets woven solely with synthetic yarns have a stiff feel due to the very tightly woven ply, and are prone to fading, since aniline dyes are less durable and resistent than natural dyes.

Most Navajo weavings are made using the tapestry technique. They are worked in sections with a diagonal edge, which are then sewn together with wool; the joins appear as faint diagonal lines ("lazy lines"), which are incorporated into the pattern.

CLASSIC WEAVINGS

Weavings produced between c.1825 and c.1875 are referred to as "classic." The two most notable types of blanket produced during this period are the chiefs' wearing blankets and serapes, both of which were prestigious robes.

Chiefs' wearing blankets are among the earliest Navajo textiles. They are similar in shape to Pueblo capes in that they are wider than they are long; they were mostly woven in handspun wool, often in natural white and brown with accents of indigo and red. Variations are divided into three categories, according to the style of the striped pattern. The first-phase pattern is composed of simple broad stripes in contrasting colors – the stripe or band being the basic design element in all Navajo weavings. Second-phase examples are divided into zones: the top, center, and bottom bands are each

▲ Classic chief's wearing blanket made by the Navajo
The simple horizontal bands of alternating brown, cream and blue indicate that this is a first-phase Navajo blanket. It is made entirely of handspun wool. The brown-and-white areas are woven from natural, undyed wool, while indigo has been used to dye the blue areas. This particular design, with its broad center band, was very popular among the Ute tribe.
(early to mid-19th century; l. 1.8m/5ft 11in; value Q)

◄ Late classic serape made by the Navajo
A longer, narrower, and more highly decorated version of the chief's wearing blanket, the serape traditionally conferred honor on the wearer. This particularly fine example features bold horizontal bands, which lead the eye from the narrow stripes to the broad triangle motifs in the foreground. It has been woven using a combination of plied Saxony yarns, which gives it a very soft feel that is extremely sought after by collectors. The blue areas have been dyed with indigo.
(mid-19th century; l. 1.9m/ 6ft 3in; value N)

▼ Late classic serape made by the Navajo
This textile features a typical serape design, with triangle motifs at the top and bottom and a center band of diamonds. The narrow stripes help to maintain the traditional horizontal zones characteristic of classic Navajo serapes and chiefs' wearing blankets. This is an exceptionally fine piece with an unusual color combination.
(mid-19th century; l. 1.8m/5ft 11in; value O)

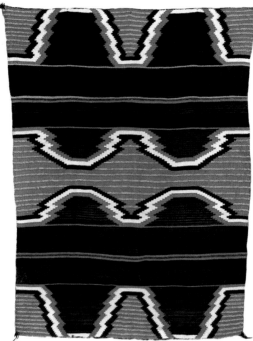

broken up by rectangular blocks on each side and in the center. Third-phase patterns are divided into the same zones, but the rectangles are replaced with diamond-shaped blocks. Within each phase there are early and later examples: in general, narrower stripes are typical of early examples; later examples feature wider bands.

In contrast to the chief's blanket, the serape is long and narrow and typically has a much more elaborate geometric pattern. Early examples feature bands of serrated lines and diamond-shaped designs on a striped ground. On later serapes, the striped ground is less prominent, and the geometric design stands out more from the ground.

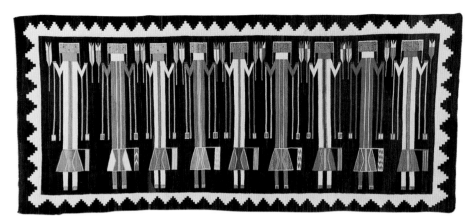

▲ Yei rug made by the Navajo

Yei figures are an important aspect of Navajo ceremonial and religious life, but are considered secular when used in textiles. They are typically arranged face on, and depicted in an elongated fashion. This geometric design is well suited to representation in weaving. The images are most often framed within the center field. The example shown here is exceptionally large and finely woven.

(late 19th century; l. 3.6m/11ft 10in; value K)

▼ Pictorial rug made by the Navajo

Pictorial weavings represent only a small percentage of Navajo work. They were often produced as status symbols, and many examples show trains or other modes of transport. This weaving depicts a wedding scene.

(late 20th century; l. 1.8m/5ft 11in; value G)

◄ Regional rug made by the Navajo

Regional weavings share few of the designs of classic Navajo textiles, deriving inspiration from sources as varied as Oriental textiles and Spanish weavings. The edges of the weaving are often braided and the elements in the central field are framed by a band motif or a more elaborate pattern.

(early 20th century; l. 1.9m/6ft 2in; value G)

COMMERICIAL WEAVINGS

At the end of the 19th century, after losing much of their land during their detention at Bosque Redondo, the Navajo had to find new ways of rebuilding their villages, and it became common for them to weave textiles for commercial purposes. Better communications due to the railroad and the growing tourist trade also encouraged commercial production. In an effort to make the Navajo textiles more broadly marketable, regional styles developed around trading posts such as Two Gray Hills, in the Chuska Mountains in what is now New Mexico, and Teec Nos Poc and Ganado, in what is now Arizona. Weavers were encouraged to respond to trends in fashion, for example by incorporating popular Oriental motifs into their designs. Woven in irregularly handspun wool as rugs rather then blankets, these commercial textiles are often much coarser in texture than earlier pieces; they are typically in tones of brown with red and other subtle color accents, in line with the Navajo's return at this time to the use of natural colors.

With the commercialization of Navajo textile production, images that were once prohibited on religious grounds slowly gained acceptance. Figurative images were reproduced, such as those derived from religious sand paintings (ephemeral designs drawn using minerals on sand or, for longer-lasting work, on buckskin), as well as images of the American flag, animals, birds, trains, and, later, cars. Rugs depicting Navajo deities are also typical. These rugs are known as "Yei" rugs and feature brightly colored, finely woven deities either alone or in groups. "Yeibichai" rugs are similar but feature Navajo Indians impersonating Yei deities.

KEY FACTS

- TYPES chiefs' wearing blankets, serapes, pictorial rugs
- MATERIALS most are woven in unplied, handspun wool, the quality of which is not consistent, since Navajo herds were not always prevented from interbreeding; from *c*.1870 commercial wools (mainly Germantown and Saxony yarns) were also used
- DESIGNS chiefs' wearing blankets and serapes are distinguished by their bold, geometric designs; the range of motifs used on pictorial pieces is very wide
- CONDITION pieces should be in good condition with no fraying or damage at the edges; examine both sides as one may be significantly more faded than the other
- COLLECTING early classic chiefs' wearing blankets and early serapes are the most highly sought-after Native American weavings; fine pictorial textiles are becoming increasingly popular among collectors

See also Ceramics: Pottery – The United States, pp.170–71

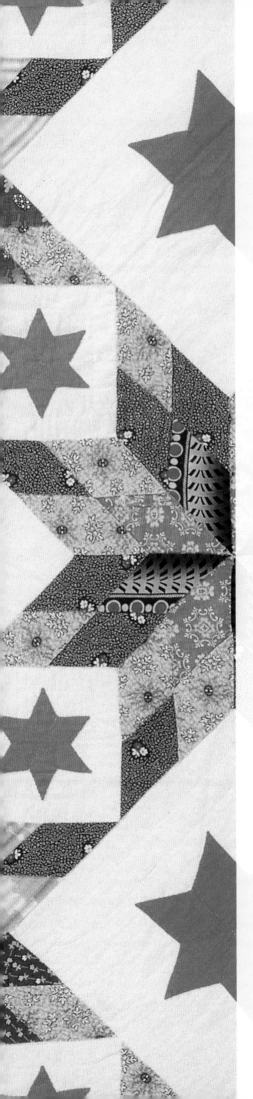

The vast majority of textiles can be categorized as either soft furnishings or costume (and accessories), although a few, such as needlepoint and bobbin lace, have been utilized for both of these purposes. Among the soft furnishings regularly found on today's antiques market are bed- and wall-hangings, picture panels and mirror frames, chair and cushion covers, firescreens, and patchwork and appliqué quilts. Such items clearly had an important domestic use, but they are chiefly appreciated today for the specialist needlework and embroidery skills employed in their manufacture, and for the diverse abstract and figurative motifs and patterns (derived from a multi-national vocabulary of ornament) that they display. Beyond this, they also provide a tangible record of the social and cultural practices of previous centuries, notably the domestic craft skills acquired by young girls and women. Period costume, and accessories such as purses, bags, fans, and parasols, show a similar use of sophisticated manufacturing skills, combined with an ingenuity of design. Much of their collectibility lies in the way in which they have stylistically reflected changing social and economic aspirations running much deeper than the vagaries of fashion.

Detail of a quilt (left) The pattern on this North American quilt from New England is known as "Prairie Stars"; the quilt is made in a range of multi-colored cottons (c. 1845–55).
Parasol (above) Designed to match an Edwardian lady's dress, this pretty parasol features a silk canopy decorated with machine-made blonde lace and a wooden handle and ferrule (c. 1905).

Needlework

Needlework is an area in which women of all classes over the centuries have displayed their skills and creativity. In 17th-century Britain stumpwork, crewelwork, canvaswork, and samplers flourished, and an equally strong tradition developed among the settlers in the New World; such skills continued to thrive in the 18th century on both sides of the Atlantic. However, in the 19th century skilled embroidery lost ground to amateur "fancy work" – where charted designs were worked with brightly colored, chemically dyed wools – and the new embroidery machines. The efforts of such design reformers as William Morris, and the establishment of art needlework schools, partly helped to redress the balance in the late 19th and early 20th centuries.

Embroidery

CREWELWORK

Crewel is a type of loosely twisted, fine, two-ply wool yarn used for embroidery. Crewelwork, which may describe any embroidery using crewel, is particularly associated with the bed-hangings and curtains made in Britain from the late 17th to the early 18th century and subsequently copied in North America. Wool was an inexpensive thread and therefore suitable for large-scale designs. From *c.*1650 twill-woven linen and cotton bed furnishings and curtains were embroidered at home, often in crewel stitch, satin stitch, or long and short stitch. The freehand designs were influenced by the printed fabrics imported from India. Popular motifs

▶ **Stumpwork picture**
Stumpwork, or raised work, was popular throughout the 17th century. This British portrait of Charles I would have represented the culmination of a girl's education in embroidery and taken several years to complete. The raised details were composed of hundreds of tiny buttonhole stitches; the hands and faces of the figures were formed from carved wood, padded, then covered in satin.
(1640; w. 34cm/13¼in; value L)

included exotic birds and animals among flowers and in the branches of gnarled, twisted trees on hummocks; early examples were worked in well-blended vegetable dye shades of green, blue, and brown. These so-called "Jacobean" designs were taken to the American Colonies by the Pilgrims, and had an important influence on early needlework there. However, the latest fashions were slow to cross the Atlantic, and styles generally remained popular in North America long after they had disappeared in Europe. Many surviving examples have unfortunately been remounted, with the crewelwork motifs removed from their original ground and transferred to new, sturdier fabric.

STUMPWORK

Raised work (known as stumpwork from the 19th century) was the apogee of a girl's needlework education in mid-17th-century Britain. Young embroiderers created three-dimensional, pictorial panels of needlework, which were mounted as pictures, used for mirror frames, or made up into boxes or caskets by a cabinet-maker. The more elaborate and valuable caskets, which could take several years to complete, sometimes featured double doors, shallow drawers, and silver locks and handles.

Designs were drawn or traced onto a white satin ground, and flat details were worked in silk, chenille, or metal threads in a variety of different stitches. Raised elements were built up from hundreds of tiny buttonhole stitches. Figures were made separately and then appliquéd to the ground. Heads, hands, and legs were often carved from wood, with the heads and hands covered in white satin with embroidered or painted features. Hair and wool were also used to create a three-dimensional effect, and beads, seed pearls, and metal wire were often added to enrich details. Panels usually depict scenes from the Old Testament or mythological stories or are derived from Dutch or Flemish engravings.

BRITISH AND AMERICAN CREWELWORK

Although the design of this American piece (left) is based on early 17th-century English Jacobean designs, it is typically much less ornate and covers less ground fabric than the more densely worked design on the British piece (right). British crewelwork is characteristically even more densely worked than this example, which is loosely based on late 17th-century designs, but lacks the vitality and the vigor of such early pieces.

American crewelwork curtain
(c.1740–60; l. 1.9m/6ft 3in; value L)

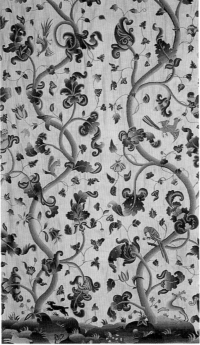

British crewelwork curtain
(c.1900; l. 2m/6ft 7in; value E)

▲ Canvas-work picture
As patterned dress fabrics became fashionable in the mid-18th century, embroiderers turned their skills to the production of needlework pictures. This British example, depicting a typical idealized rural setting, is worked in silk using tent stitch.
(mid-18th century; ht 55cm/21½in; value **H***)*

CANVAS WORK

Canvas work is a broad term that covers a range of embroidery worked with counted stitches on an open-weave canvas. The canvas, ranging from a fine silk net to a coarse jute, is completely covered with wool or silk. (Colored wool was common until the 1780s, after which silk was also popular.) In the mid-16th century wall-hangings, table carpets, and bed furnishings were worked in wools and silks in tent stitch, often by professional embroiderers, to depict scenes from Classical mythology, the Bible, and contemporary life.

In the early 17th century fine canvas-work pictures were introduced as an alternative to expensive tapestries, and, as wood paneling in houses increased, small framed pictures replaced large tent-stitched panels. Book covers, bags, purses, and cushion covers were made, often by amateur needleworkers. Designs became less extravagant and began to feature animals. By the late 17th century designs became more exotic, due to the increased trade with East Asia; also popular were the bolder, shaded designs in wool with silk highlights, based on the floral paintings by Dutch artists. In the 18th century the fashion for embroidering seats and backs of upholstered chairs was at its height.

As with crewelwork, the Pilgrims took British canvas-work designs with them to the New World, where styles lingered long after they had gone out of fashion in Europe. American designs generally were less sophisticated and made more economical use of thread. Utility was a priority, and the tight, flat surface of canvaswork was densely worked in flame stitch (also called "bargello" or "Florentine" stitch), tent stitch, and cross stitch to form a robust and hard-wearing surface.

BERLIN WOOLWORK

The vogue for charted designs worked in brightly colored wools reached its zenith in the mid-19th century. The first "Berlin woolwork" patterns – in which the number, the color, and the position of the stitches and threads were clearly marked – were produced in Berlin, Germany, *c.*1804 by a printmaker named Philipson. The early colored silks were replaced in the 1820s by thick, felt-like merino wool, enabling the basic stitch to be enlarged so that patterns could be completed more quickly. By 1831 patterns were being imported into Britain by Wilks's Warehouse of Regent Street, London, and by 1840 they had also become fashionable in North America.

Berlin woolwork was extremely popular, and was used to produce numerous Victorian knicknacks, including firescreens, book and cushion covers, picture frames, lamp mats, and tobacco pouches. Pictures of famous people, royalty, animals, religious and literary scenes, and works of famous painters were popular. Earlier pieces were more restrained and subtle. Designs were often floral, with life-size plants on light backgrounds worked in muted-colored silks on fine canvas. By the 1850s the use of aniline dyes (based on benzene, a derivative of coal tar) produced stronger, brighter but cruder colors, and impressive roses, peonies, and lilies replaced more modest flowers. The canvas background became coarser and the stitches larger, and glass beadwork and sheared pile were added. In the mid-1850s the bold, brightly colored embroidery popularized by the Great Exhibition in London in 1851 was the height of fashion.

▼ Flame-stitch wallet
This brightly colored American wallet is produced in flame stitch (or "bargello" or "Florentine" stitch), which consists of a pattern of coarse upright stitches designed to create the effect of flames. The technique was used across Europe and North America and was particularly popular during the 18th century.
(18th century; w. 15cm/6in; value **E***)*

▼ Berlin-woolwork picture
By 1840, when Berlin-woolwork designs were first exported to North America, an impressive 14,000 designs were available. Religious scenes, such as on the example featured below, were just one type. In general these designs are less valuable than some of the more exuberant examples that included beadwork, plushwork, and the bold, vivid colors associated with the new aniline dyes.
(19th century; ht 40cm/ 15¾in; value **C***)*

KEY FACTS

- MATERIALS the most popular fabrics (silk, wool, linen, cotton, canvas) and threads (silk, wool, metal, cotton) vary according to fashion, but all have a collecting niche depending on style and price
- DESIGNS stumpwork: in earlier examples the use of relief and the range of stitches are limited; stitching on later pieces is more varied; canvas work: simple square or rectangular formats preferred to elongated shapes
- CONDITION good condition is usually essential: faded, worn, or damaged fabric will reduce value; fading is a major problem, especially with aniline dyes used post-1850; acid from wood mounts may make the satin ground in stumpwork brittle and cause cracking
- COLLECTING early pieces in good condition are rare and expensive; crewelwork: pieces with re-applied motifs are far less expensive than original pieces; large 17th-century pieces are most expensive; smaller, later items such as firescreens and pocket books (the latter are popular in the USA) are more accessible; stumpwork: later, more elaborate pieces are most desirable; caskets are highly sought after but very expensive; pictures and mirror frames are more commonly found; canvas work: few 16th-century examples survive outside museums; 17th-century examples are sought after; smaller pieces (pictures, firescreens, and cushions) are more widely available; Berlin woolwork: elaborate examples incorporating beadwork and plushwork are very sought after – peak production was between 1850 and 1860

See also Furniture: Screens, pp.114–15

PICTURES

In the early 18th century, as printed dress fabrics achieved popularity, embroiderers turned their skills to needlework pictures. Those worked in the first half of the century are typically executed in wools on a linen canvas ground in tent stitch. They often depict idealized pastoral scenes involving love-lorn shepherds or shepherdesses frequently with a mansion and/or a huntsman in the background; the landscapes have hummocky, grassy mounds, often spotted with improbable combinations of animals. Chinoiserie and Indian-inspired designs also became popular as trade via the Dutch East India Company brought oriental treasures to Europe. The latter part of the 18th century saw a fashion for embroidered needle paintings. These are usually worked in satin stitch in silk and chenille threads. The more difficult or laborious areas, such as facial features or the sky, are often of painted silk. Pastoral themes were popular, and Neo-classical figures abound.

In North America the death of George Washington, the first President, in 1799 sparked a fashion for memorial or mourning pictures. Typically these featured stylized austere gardens with weeping willows and cypresses, and a figure, usually a woman in Classical dress, by a tomb. More personal mourning pictures were sometimes embroidered using hair from the deceased, often for inscriptions, which gives a characteristically fine, silky line. In the 18th century American schoolgirls based needlework pictures on engravings of famous paintings they had seen in books. These memorial pictures are interesting if the maker, school, and date are included, or if there are contemporary topographical pictures such as views of New York or Mount Vernon (Washington's birthplace).

▲ **Appliqué picture of**
***The Goosewoman* by George Smart**
This commercially produced British picture is composed of small scraps of wool, velvet, and cotton chintz. The vista behind the brightly colored figure of the goosewoman shows a typically soft and gentle Kentish landscape; the town that is featured in the background has been identified as Tunbridge Wells, Kent. As in this example, complex or intricate background details were usually painted rather than worked in appliqué.
*(late 1830s; ht 23.5cm/9¼in; value **H**)*

◄ **Mourning picture**
The death of the American statesman George Washington launched a vogue for mourning pictures. Many, such as this American example, combined silk embroidery with watercolor painting. Personal mourning pictures (commonly listing the demise of numerous children) are highly collectible, because most are family heirlooms and do not often come onto the market. The fact that the dense embroidery is worked onto fine silk means that such pieces are prone to splitting and fading; examples in good condition are therefore rare. Similar European works, perhaps featuring the death of Nelson, are worth a fraction of the value of their American counterparts.
*(c.1805; l. 48cm/19in; value **K**)*

WHITEWORK

Whitework is embroidery in white thread on a white ground. Late 16th- and early 17th-century pieces were usually of white linen worked with white linen thread and were heavier in style than the elegant whitework fashionable throughout much of Europe during the early and mid-19th century. Whitework was particularly popular in Scotland, especially in the county of Ayrshire (now part of the Strathclyde region). In the 1820s a flourishing hand-embroidery industry was established by a Mrs Jamieson of Ayr. Outworkers produced babies' robes and caps, and women's collars, caps, and other accessories, in a fine soft muslin embroidered in white cotton thread and satin. Whitework reached its peak *c.*1850, and subsequently became increasingly coarse. The embargo on cotton imports to Europe during the American Civil War (1861–5) and the introduction of embroidery machines contributed to its decline.

▼ **Whitework christening gown**
Produced in Ayrshire, Scotland's most renowned whitework area, this whitework gown has a delicate embroidery of leaves and flowers. Many babies' robes were carefully stored and kept for sentimental reasons, so collectors should ensure examples are in good condition.
*(c.1900; l. 60.5cm/24in; value **A**)*

KEY FACTS

- MATERIALS pictures: 17th century – satin or linen; first half of 18th century – usually linen canvas; latter part of 18th century – fine silk was common; 19th century – commercially produced canvas, or linen, wool, or jute grounds for samplers; whitework: most is made of linen, muslin, and cotton
- CONDITION all textiles are prone to damage from light; silks and watercolor details are liable to fade
- COLLECTING mourning pictures: these are a collecting niche, with personal examples the most popular but rare; American school project pictures with personal details are especially popular; whitework: earlier pieces are highly desirable; pieces made after the 1850s are less desirable; on babies' gowns look for a characteristic triangle of embroidery with the base at the hem and the apex at the bodice

Samplers

The earliest samplers were exactly what their name suggests: samples or examples (Latin *exemplum*) of a wide range of stitches and patterns. They were referred to by amateur and professional needleworkers, then rolled up and put away when not in use. In Britain an early example is dated 1598, and examples from the 17th century are common in Europe. In the 18th century developments in public education meant that most girls were taught needlework as a vital skill for employment or accomplishment. The sampler was both an instruction tool and a chance for them to practice their skills before working on more valuable pieces. Most sought after are pictorial samplers that show something of the child's personality. From c.1850 wool largely replaced silk, the fabric ground became coarser, and the range of stitches became increasingly restricted.

EARLY SAMPLERS

Early samplers were usually narrow strips of unbleached linen, long and rectangular in shape, and sometimes finished with needlepoint lace. They were practical working tools rather than decorative items, with horizontal bands of a wide variety of stitches or random designs, such as spot motifs – flowers, animals, insects – for use on embroidered items. They were densely worked in colored silk, sometimes combined with silver metal threads. The more complex pieces feature stumpwork details and even figures worked in needlepoint lace. Many southern German and Dutch samplers feature large Christian motifs or small motifs of women engaged in domestic tasks.

18TH-CENTURY SAMPLERS

During the 18th century, although the sampler was still used to test a girl's dexterity with a needle, it became less functional and more pictorial. The shape of the sampler changed from the long rectangle to a square. Girls used cheap, coarse, loosely woven linen for their first attempts at simple alphabets. Once they had proved their skill they were given finely woven pieces of linen or wool. From the 1720s a fine tabby-woven wool ground was used in addition to unbleached linen. Decoration became less dense and more pictorial – houses, plants, and figures all appeared; names and dates were often included, together with the alphabet, numbers, and short, edifying verses. The sampler also became an educational tool and was used to give moral guidance; some of the verses can be quite dour. Geography was taught through the "map" sampler, popular in the 1790s; however, since they tell us nothing of the embroiderer, these are less popular with collectors.

▲ Sampler
The form of this British sampler dates it to the 17th century. At that time samplers were used as a reference compendium of stitches and designs rather than as decorative items; when not in use, they were rolled up and stored. Typically, the ground is linen, and stitches and designs are worked in colored silks. Such early examples, in good condition, are very valuable.
(1660; ht 67.5cm/26½in; value I)

◄ Sampler by Catherine Low
The popularity of Berlin woolwork in the mid-19th century resulted in wool threads replacing silk, and woollen and canvas grounds replacing linen ones. This Scottish sampler has some Berlin woolwork and shows the typical mid-century combination of pictures, alphabets, and numbers; most desirably it includes details such as the maker's name and date.
(1847; ht 51cm/20in; value G)

19TH-CENTURY SAMPLERS

During the 19th century the more pictorial form of sampler remained the most common sort made in both North America and Britain; other types included those with religious and "improving" texts, alphabets, and personal details. However, in The Netherlands darning samplers became popular during the 19th century, while in Germany, France, Belgium, and Spain, panels worked with numerous, seemingly randomly placed, cross-stitched motifs prevailed.

The growth in formal education meant that in the USA and Britain certain "types" began to emerge, stemming from, for example, the schoolmistress in a particular area teaching needlework skills using favored designs, themes, or materials. One of the factors that makes samplers so desirable is the possibility of tracking down the location of these particular schools and styles. The research into the provenance of a sampler is as much a joy to many collectors as the quality of the needlework itself. In the USA, enormous research into samplers produced in different styles and regions has been carried out; however, in Europe there still remains great scope for investigation.

▲ Sampler by Mary Butz from Kutztown, Pennsylvania
Several desirable features contribute to the high value of this American sampler. First, it is a piece of American history, recording the Franklin Academy (still standing) and the old St John's Church (replaced in 1876) in Kutztown, Pennsylvania; the linen ground is in good conditon, and the colors of the wool and silk needlework remain fresh and vibrant; and it is signed and dated, and has an exceptionally luxuriant border.
(1842; ht 44cm/17in; value O)

KEY FACTS

- CARE professional cleaning and restoration are advisable for all samplers; keep samplers out of direct sunlight and protect them from direct sources of heat
- CONDITION this is critical to value: check for moth or mold damage, for colors that have faded through exposure to direct sunlight, and for run-stained grounds
- COLLECTING early, fine-quality samplers in good condition are the most desirable to collectors; bold, colorful, humorous, original, and pictorial designs are highly sought after; personal details such as dates and the names of makers, teachers, and schools are also desirable; American collectors prefer American samplers and early examples are especially sought after; original frames and backboards add to the appeal and value of a sampler

Quilts

Quilting is a method of securing padding between two layers of fabric, using stitching in decorative patterns. The technique has been used from ancient times to make warm garments and furnishings. In the Middle Ages quilted jackets were worn beneath armor, and bed-quilts were first recorded in the 14th century. Quilting techniques were taken to the American Colonies by European settlers in the 17th century, and by the 18th century the ability to make warm quilts was an essential skill for women in the new settlements. The "quilting bee" – when a group of women gathered to produce a quilt in a day – became a social ritual. Most European and American quilts found today date from the 19th and early 20th centuries, when patchwork was the most popular method of producing decorative covers.

EUROPEAN QUILTS

Quilts were made by rich and poor alike: the more affluent the maker, the more expensive the fabrics used. Finely made 17th-century silk quilts, made in India for Portuguese merchants, still survive. Decoration includes a mixture of European figures, hunt scenes, naked women, and exotic beasts. Quilted silk cradle covers, petticoats, and maternity wear were common in the 18th century. However, most plain quilts available today date from the late 19th to the early 20th century. Patterns of stitching ranged from roses, leaves, hearts, spirals, and waves on Welsh quilts to lovers' knots and feathers on quilts from the north of England. Northern makers, especially in 19th-century Co. Durham, specialized in "strip" quilts, where alternating strips of fabric were sewn together and quilted with border patterns.

Another popular technique in Europe was cord quilting, where cords or twisted threads were inserted between two layers of fabric, held together with narrow, parallel lines of stitching. The cord quilts produced in 18th-century Marseilles are especially renowned. Plain quilting was used in the 17th and 18th centuries to make dresses and petticoats, but during the 19th century cheap printed cotton became widely available, and patchwork became more popular than traditional stitched quilting.

BRITISH PATCHWORK AND APPLIQUE

The earliest known examples of British patchwork are a bed-quilt and hangings made *c*.1708 from pieces of Indian printed cotton for Levens Hall in Westmorland. The fashion for piecing together (patchwork) or cutting out pictorial motifs and applying them onto grounds (appliqué) lasted throughout the 18th century. British patchwork tended to be of a mosaic pattern, the patches being joined one by one, unlike the American coverlets that were formed from well-thought-out patterned blocks. They often had central designs, such as an eight-pointed star or a printed chintz medallion. Repeated motifs such as baskets, hearts, stars, and feathers were common on early 19th-century British patchwork and appliqué quilts. "Crazy" patchwork quilts, made from scraps of fabric arranged randomly, were popular from the 1870s to the early 20th century.

▲ Military quilt

In striking design and color, this unusual quilt was made by a British soldier in India using scraps of red, black, green, and ivory wool fabric from uniforms. *(c.1866; l. 2.2m/7ft 3in; value* **G***)*

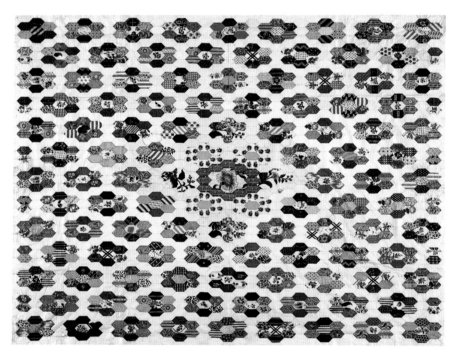

AMERICAN ONE-PIECE QUILTS

Although patchwork and appliqué quilts are the most familiar types of American quilt, the earliest examples from the 17th and early 18th centuries were similar to one-piece European quilts. The top was made from a single piece of cloth (or from strips of fabric joined together), stitched with flowers, fruits, and leaves for decoration. Fabrics included wool, linen, a mixture of the two known as "linsey-woolsey," and calamanco, a fine, sometimes glazed worsted. In the late 18th century fashionable imported chintzes were used for quilt tops. Printed cottons became popular with the development of the cotton-printing industry in the early 19th century.

▲ Chintz mosaic quilt

This arrangement of clustered colored hexagons interspersed with rows of white hexagons is known as "grandmother's flower garden" and was very popular throughout the 19th century. Although hexagon patterns were also used in the USA, they were commonly associated with British quilts. *(c.1825–30; l. 1.2m/7ft 3in; value* **G***)*

▼ Strip quilt made by Isabella Calvert of Co. Durham

Striped quilts were popular in northern England and, like this example, were often quilted with long border patterns or rows of rosettes and shells. This sateen quilt was probably made as a wedding present. *(c.1900; l. 2.3m/7ft 6in; value* **D***)*

AMERICAN PATCHWORK QUILTS

In the late 18th and throughout the 19th century, patchwork quilting was both common and popular in rural American communities, where economical use of scraps of materials was important. Patchworks made entirely from men's suiting fabrics, early denim jeans, or even flour sacks appear occasionally. Patchwork for quilts usually involved making one block of a design at a time, then sewing together several blocks, perhaps alternating them with squares of solid-colored fabric. Blocks could be arranged in infinite patterns, and this method proved so widespread that from c.1830 women's magazines published a huge variety of patterns for quilt blocks. It is this strong design aspect that sets American quilts apart and makes them dramatic and visually exciting.

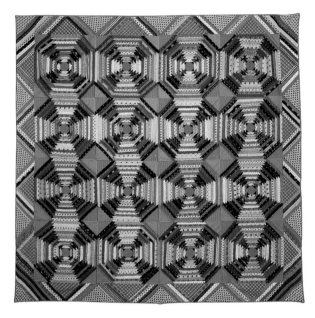

The simplest patchwork quilts were designed in geometric patterns of triangles, squares, rectangles, hexagons, and octagons. More elaborate patterns developed in the second half of the 19th century, notably the "tumbling blocks" design, made of diamond shapes to give a three-dimensional effect, and the "log cabin" pattern, built from interlocking strips of fabric set around a central square (representing the chimney of the cabin). Other motifs were inspired by Colonial life or the American landscape and wildlife, such as "Rocky Road to Kansas," "Pine Trees," and "Bear's Paw." Crazy patchwork, using scraps of fabric arranged randomly, was fashionable from c.1870 until c.1900.

European settlers brought designs from their homelands to the New World, an influence that is highly evident in the quilts made by Dutch- and German-speaking communities such as the Amish, the Pennsylvania Germans, and the Mennonites. Amish quilts are striking in their use of dark, plain fabrics in simple abstract or geometric patterns. Those of the Pennsylvania Germans typically feature bold primary colors and motifs such as star compasses and tulips.

◄ "Album" quilt

This elaborate album quilt, which was made in Baltimore, Maryland, features motifs typical of this type of quilt, including flowers and foliage, perhaps found in the area in which the quilt was made, patriotic emblems (eagles and flags), and scenes of daily rural life. The intricate pattern is characteristic of quilts made in Baltimore in the 1840s and 1850s by a group of women belonging to the Methodist Church. Such an elaborate and sophisticated example as this would be highly sought after by collectors.
(c.1850; l. 2.6m/8ft 6in; value P)

◄ Patchwork quilt made in Pennsylvania

The octagon-shaped "windmill" pattern featured on this wool challis quilt is an elaborate version of the more rectangular "log cabin" design. Both the central pattern and the "sawtooth" border are indicative of the great variety of printed fabrics available in North America in the mid-19th century.
(c.1865–70; l. 2.2m/7ft 3in; value J)

▼ Quilt made by the Amish

Amish quilts are characterized by dark, plain fabrics and simple, strongly geometric patterns. The woollen cloth used for this "diamond in the square" quilt from Lancaster County, Pennsylvania, would also have been used for clothing. The contrasting squares in the corners are distinctive of the work of the Pennsylvania Amish.
(1920; l. 1.9m/6ft 3in; value L)

AMERICAN APPLIQUE QUILTS

Appliqué work is similar to patchwork but involves stitching pieces of fabric onto a flat textile as opposed to joining pieces together. Appliqué was often more elaborate than patchwork because the technique allowed greater freedom in creating images. From the late 18th century a popular technique was *brodérie perse*, which involved sewing cut-out floral and bird motifs in printed cottons and chintzes onto a plain ground. Patterns popular in the 19th century include oak leaves (a symbol of long life), pineapples (hospitality), and, on wedding quilts, hearts. American flags, patriotic mottoes, and eagles feature on quilts made c.1876, the Centennial year. Among the most sought-after and elaborate appliqué quilts are "album" quilts, composed of squares of different motifs. They were usually a group effort, with individual squares signed by their makers.

KEY FACTS

European quilts

- DESIGNS plain quilts: many feature fine stitching in intricate patterns; brightly colored chain stich and motifs of birds, trees, and flowers were popular; patchwork and appliqué: motifs include stars, baskets, hearts, and feathers; designs are more random than on American quilts
- MATERIALS 17th–18th centuries; brocaded silk patchworks; late 18th–19th centuries: cottons, wools, and linens; late 19th century: velvets combined with satins and silks
- COLLECTING European quilts are commonly available; plain quilted or Co. Durham-type quilts are inexpensive; patchworks (except Regency) are moderately priced

American quilts

- DESIGNS block-to-block quilts were made from the 1830s; crazy patchwork and the "log cabin" designs were used after 1865; pastel textiles are typical of the early 20th century
- MATERIALS one-piece quilts: wool, linen, or linsey-woolsey; chintz from the late 18th century, printed cottons from the 19th; patchwork: printed cottons, silk, and wool; appliqué: cotton, chintz
- CARE consult an expert before washing antique quilts
- COLLECTING generally more expensive than European quilts; early pieces are sought after; pieces bearing the name of the quilter are considered to be folk art

Costume

Much antique clothing has unfortunately been lost because of recycling. In the 18th and 19th centuries women's gowns were often altered to keep up with rapidly changing fashions, a practice that allowed valuable fabrics to be re-used, but which means that many original styles have not survived. Garments that have survived in quality and in their original state are usually those with sentimental value, notably christening and wedding gowns, which were packed away and handed down as family heirlooms. Fashions in the early 20th century were led by haute couture designers; later in the century the growing range of less expensive, artificial fabrics used for mass-produced clothing increased the variety of styles and materials on the market.

Womenswear before 1900

Throughout most of the 18th century women's fashions in Europe and North America were dictated by the Rococo and Neo-classical tastes of the French courts of Louis XV and Louis XVI. Nineteenth-century fashions were influenced by such prominent figures as Queen Victoria and Empress Eugénie, wife of Napoleon III; overall, the 19th century was notable for its cumbersome, uncomfortable, restrictive, and often highly impractical fashions for women.

◄ Lady's robe

Like so many fine early gowns, this magnificent silk *sacque* has been altered to accommodate changing fashions. In this case the sleeves have been shortened, the ruffles re-applied, and a section of the rear petticoat removed. Alterations do affect value, but 18th-century alterations are preferable to later ones. The beauty of the fabric and the generally "fresh" appearance of the gown make this a desirable piece despite its minor alterations. It is probably Spanish, and the formal style and high-quality fabric suggest that it was worn at court.

(1765–70; value L)

18TH-CENTURY DRESSES

Throughout the 18th century the open robe was the most commonly adopted form of gown. This consisted of a skirt, or "petticoat" as it was called, together with a bodice with long, flowing skirts worn on top. If the drapes at the back fell in long, flowing box pleats the gown was known as a *sacque* or *robe à la française*. If the back was fitted and curved into the waist it was known as a *fourreaux* or *robe à l'anglaise*. The gown was unboned and loose, and was worn over a heavily boned corset. The front of the bodice was usually open, and a decorative stomacher was pinned in place. In the 1770s Queen Marie Antoinette liked to dress up as a shepherdess in flowing muslin gowns. Empress Josephine continued to wear diaphanous muslins but in Neo-classical styles. Inexpensive imported Indian muslins made the fashion more widely accessible.

19TH-CENTURY DRESSES

The minimalist Neo-classical shifts popular in the opening decade of the 19th century were not suited to the British climate, although devoted followers of fashion were known to wet their Classically inspired muslin gowns to make them cling to their naked forms beneath. By 1815, frills, appliqué flowers, and padded bands were added to the basic gowns, and by 1820 the waistline was lowered. By 1823–4 the waistline had crept up to the bottom of the ribcage, and wider skirts were supported by horsehair petticoats. The leg o' mutton sleeve, first seen in 1827, had become as wide as the skirt by 1835, with a sloping shoulder line on designs from the 1830s, as the width in the sleeve gradually shifted from shoulder to elbow.

Queen Victoria's marriage in 1840 made the image of the wife and mother the fashionable ideal; the waistline returned to its natural place, hems fell to conceal the feet, and sleeves became smaller. Tartan silks were popular, inspired by Victoria's love of Balmoral Castle in Scotland. By the mid-1850s the Victorian fondness for decoration and clutter was reflected in the elaborate trimmings that were applied to day dresses, and by 1855 the cage – a sprung steel frame that increased the size of skirts – was introduced. Extremely tight, constricting corsets were worn under formal dresses to pull in the waist and structure the upper body.

From *c.*1860 women's fashions were dictated to a large degree by the British designer Charles Frederick Worth (1825–95), who founded the Maison Worth in Paris in 1858. He was appointed dressmaker to Empress Eugénie in 1859 and established the French tradition of haute couture (made-to-measure garments bearing the designer's own label). In Britain and the USA a reaction against the constraints and extravagance of haute couture was led by the Pre-Raphaelite Brotherhood, who designed relaxed medieval-inspired wrap-over garments. The firm of Liberty & Co. (est. 1875) in London sold Arts and Crafts-style gowns, but these were nonetheless still worn with corsets, which the majority of the female population continued to don, together with bustles, and other similarly constrictive devices. Throughout the 19th century the silhouettes may have changed, with bustles replacing crinolines, but the discomfort levels remained essentially the same.

▼ Wedding dress

Owing to their sentimental value, many wedding dresses have survived unaltered and in good condition, and so they are usually inexpensive. However, this ivory moiré silk example made in Britain is more desirable because of its early date. It features a matching lace-edged tippet and the leg o' mutton sleeves and frilled skirt bottom that were typical of the period. In the early decades of the 19th century wedding dresses were not of any special color, although Queen Victoria's ivory bridal gown influenced fashion, working-class women still tended to marry in their best frocks regardless of the color.

(c.1835; value E)

KASHMIR AND PAISLEY SHAWLS

On Kashmir shawls hand-weaving is evident in the slight irregularities in the pattern on the front and in the short, tied-in threads on the reverse, as the individual shuttles carrying the threads only traveled the width of the pattern. While the size, shape, and pattern of Paisley shawls closely resemble the Kashmir originals, they were, in fact, mass produced, and if examined on the reverse they have flat, even surfaces with threads that carry across the width of the shawl.

▼ Kashmir shawl (left) and Paisley shawl (right)
(1860; ht 3m/10ft; value **G***; 1855–60; ht 3.2m/10ft 6in; value* **E***)*

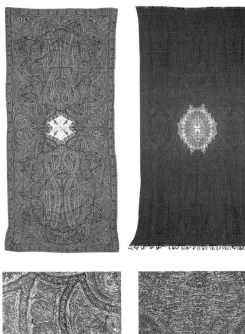

GLOVES, HATS, SHOES, AND SHAWLS

In the 17th century gloves were an essential part of an outfit, especially since the main means of transport was on horseback, and finely embroidered kid-leather gauntlets were often commissioned to be given as very special gifts. During the 18th century gloves became more functional looking and less intricately adorned. By the 19th century the wearing of gloves was socially *de rigueur* for women, because the contact of a lady's naked hand with a gentleman's was thought highly improper. Many of these gloves, which are tiny as hands were much smaller then, are unwearable by women today, and hence are usually very affordable.

Hats were also essential items, and until the 1950s it was considered unacceptable to be seen in public without one. During the 18th century high-domed, silk taffeta bonnets were typical outdoor wear, while embroidered caps – now rare and usually very highly priced – were worn indoors. Nineteenth-century hats have survived in reasonable numbers. Most common are

small straw bonnets designed to fit over a bun, dating from the 1880s and 1890s, and the caps worn indoors by married women.

Leather was not commonly used for fine shoes until the end of the 18th century; most examples of 18th-century fine ladies' shoes are of brocaded silk or velvet – these are delicate items, which would have been typically protected by wooden clogs. The fashion in footwear early in the 19th century was for flimsy, low-cut, satin shoes that were often tied with ribbons. Designed primarily to show off the wearer's tiny feet, and sometimes incorporating embroidered decoration, such shoes were principally decorative rather than functional. More robust fabric and leather button boots and elasticated ankle boots became standard practical wear from the 1850s. By the end of the century women's increasing desire for social and physical emancipation was reflected in the range of leather lace-up and court shoes that were both fashionable and practical.

Shawls became a necessity with the advent of the late 18th-century Neo-classical shifts. Such dresses were only wearable in northern Europe if accompanied by a warm shawl. Hand-made shawls were first produced in India's Kashmir region from the 15th century and were warm, soft, and light. By the early 1800s, mass-produced copies were made in Paisley, Scotland, Norwich, England, and in Paris and Lyons, France. These used a pine-cone-shaped version of the Kashmir *boteh* motif, and the pattern became known as "Paisley."

▼ Paisley day dress
The sloping shoulder line of this British woollen day dress, the fitted lower waist, and the more modest width of the sleeves are typical of dresses of the time, as is the lack of frills at the bottom of the skirt.
(c.1850; value **D***)*

▲ Camisole top
Loose cotton undergarments, including waist-length petticoats and camisole tops such as the one above, are among the few items of 19th-century women's clothing large enough for contemporary wearers. Desirability is usually dictated by the amount of lace and ribbonwork. More modest cotton examples are hand-embroidered and pinned and tucked. The more extreme examples of Victorian laced corsets are becoming a cult collecting area.
(c.1890; value **A***)*

KEY FACTS

- DECORATION items with unusual decoration are particularly desirable
- CONDITION good condition is critical, since damaged fabric with detract from value; alterations will also reduce the value, especially more recent ones; quality of color and decoration is critical; rarity, luxurious fabric, and brilliant color will increase value
- DRESSES AND UNDERGARMENTS dresses: brightly colored dresses are more collectible than sober grays and browns; although 18th-century black dresses are very collectible, 19th-century black mourning wear and white bridal wear are very common and not particularly sought after; later alterations on 18th-century dresses can reduce the value of a dress; look in the waistband of 19th-century dresses for a label – those bearing the name "Worth" will command a high price in good condition; look for examples with an interesting provenance; Victorian gowns made from the mid-19th century are very affordable, even those in perfect condition; undergarments: Victorian corsets are becoming popular with collectors; examples in unusual colors and fabrics are the most desirable; late 19th-century camisole tops and petticoats are abundant; fine embroidery or lace will increase the value of these items
- GLOVES, HATS, SHOES, AND SHAWLS gloves: highly adorned, early examples are much sought after; plain, 19th-century kid gloves are very reasonably priced; hats: 18th-century examples are rare and expensive, while 19th-century examples are common and still inexpensive; an original box adds value; shoes: these are very collectible – particularly some 18th-century examples; shawls: Kashmir shawls are expensive and very collectible; Paisley shawls were produced in vast quantities and are usually found for reasonable prices

See also Womenswear after 1900, p.344

Womenswear after 1900

In the early 20th century, fashion was still dictated by French haute couture. The move toward comfort began in 1911 with high-waisted gowns by the French designer Paul Poiret (1870–1914). The onset of World War I meant that ease of movement was a necessity, and rigid boning and tight corsets were banished. The clothes of the 1920s, 1930s, and 1940s are unboned and more loosely flowing; wasp waistlines and tight corsets appeared again in the 1950s, while the clothes of the late 20th century were typically informal.

BEFORE WORLD WAR II

The Italian artist and designer Mariano Fortuny (1871–1949) produced unstructured, flowing gowns that were set apart from the main trends and favored by rich, artistic types. During the 1920s social emancipation and a growing interest in sport led to a fashion for shorter skirts and a straight, tubular silhouette. Fashion was still led by Paris, with some of the most famous names being Poiret, Edward Molyneux (1891–1974), Mme Joseph Paquin (d.1930), Jean Patou (b.1880), Gabrielle "Coco" Chanel (1883–1971), Madeleine Vionnet (1876–1975), Jacques Doucet, and Elsa Schiaparelli (1890–1973). The "flapper" tunic dress of the 1920s was often decorated with beadwork in Art-Deco-inspired patterns. By the 1930s Vionnet was producing glamorous, bias-cut dresses in sculptural silks and satins, while Chanel made famous the "little black dress."

Long kid gloves, sequinned or feather fans, and embroidered purses were essential evening accessories. Glamor was a major factor in the design of evening shoes; made in stunning fabrics and colors, they were held securely in place by a bar strap, allowing women to enjoy energetic dances such as the Charleston.

POST-WAR FASHION

After the privations of wartime rationing, the "New Look" that Christian Dior (1905–57) launched in 1947 caused a sensation. Designs such as the "Bar" suit combined a close-fitting, waisted jacket with a full skirt to give a curving, hourglass shape, and the boned bodices, tiny waistlines, and explosion of fabric from the skirt was genuinely shocking. Other major 1950s and 1960s designers include Pierre Balmain (1914–82), Christóbal Balenciaga (1895–1972), Yves Saint Laurent (b.1936), Hubert de Givenchy (b.1927), and Paco Rabanne (b.1934).

The 1950s have become a popular area with collectors interested in mass-produced clothes typical of the era rather than in exclusive haute couture. There are many collectible, inexpensive examples of brightly colored, printed cotton day dresses in patterns of fruit, vegetables, and flowers. Other

▲ "Flapper" dress
This French black georgette dress was mass produced and has machine-stitched beadwork. It is far less valuable than a one-off couture model that is made by one of the couture houses and has hand-stitched beadwork and oversewn seams.
(c.1928; value **C***)*

▶ Suit by Christóbal Balenciaga
The slim skirt and box-shaped, waistless jacket with three-quarter-length sleeves are typical of Spanish designer Balenciaga's elegant designs. Weights are sewn into the lining to maintain an even line.
(late 1950s; value **C***)*

popular and moderately priced 1950s designs include ready-to-wear evening gowns, especially puffball styles.

In the 1960s Pop art and popular culture gave rise to clothes intended to be ephemeral and fun. New fabrics, including vinyl and PVC, were used for often unisex clothing. Young British designers took the lead over Paris couture, and street fashion dictated the style. Hemlines soared under the influence of such designers as Mary Quant (b.1934). The austere lines of Jean Muir (1928–95) inspired an almost cult following, as did the chiffon and silk designs of Ossie Clark (1942–97).

Recent successful auctions of London street fashion have aroused interest in the boutique ranges of the 1960s and 1970s and the punk styles of the 1970s and 1980s. By 1969 the original tiny Biba boutique, opened in 1964 by Barbara Hulanicki (b.1936), had expanded to occupy an Art-Deco emporium in London's High Scenteret Kensington, and clothes produced by designers for the Biba label are now collectors' items. Also desirable are punk clothes, such as tartan bondage trousers, produced by Vivienne Westwood (b.1941) and Malcom McLaren under the Seditionaries Personal Collection label, and the Conceptual Chic collection launched in 1977 by Zandra Rhodes (b.1940).

Increasing informality has meant that hats and gloves are no longer essential dress. Most hats that come up for sale are haute-couture items, although 1940s designs, including close-fitting bandeau hats, are also popular with collectors. Popular footwear includes 1950s stilettos, 1960s thigh-high leather boots, 1970s platform shoes, and Westwood's now infamous platform soles.

▶ Shoes by Vivienne Westwood
Once the *enfant terrible* of British fashion, Westwood is now a fashion icon whose sexy designs have endured the test of time. The platform soles of these "prostitute stiletto" shoes are one of her hallmarks.
(1996–7; value **C***)*

KEY FACTS

- IMPORTANT DESIGNERS Poiret, Fortuny, Chanel, Schiaparelli, Dior, Balenciaga, Yves Saint Laurent, Paco Rabanne, Mary Quant, Muir, Clark, Westwood
- CONDITION this is important, since damaged fabric or alterations will affect the value
- CARE beaded "flapper" dresses: store flat to protect delicate fabric and heavy beadwork
- LABELS always look at the side seams and waist seams to check for labels; haute-couture labels have hand-written or stamped client numbers behind the main label – such labels can sometimes increase a piece's value tenfold, depending on the design and the period; Dior: ready-to-wear collections are labeled "Christian Dior London" rather than "Paris"
- COLLECTING fine quality unlabeled or ready-to-wear gowns are often cheaper than inexpensive modern boutique gowns; haute-couture pieces need to be in good condition, labeled and made by designers at the peak of their inventiveness (e.g. Chanel in the 1920s or 1930s, Balenciaga in the early 1960s); collectible fun boutique labels include Biba, Westwood and McLaren's Seditionaries, and Ossie Clark

Menswear

In the 18th century men's clothes were as colorful as women's. Suits in luscious velvets or floral brocades were the norm; not until the late 18th century, probably as a reaction to the French Revolution, did menswear become more muted, with tailcoats in dark colors, pale breeches or trousers, and colorful embroidered waistcoats. The three-piece suit as we have come to know it was a mid-19th-century invention which men have adopted ever since.

► Waistcoat

Waistcoats are one of the few items of early menswear to have survived in any quantity. The English example shown here has the characteristic ivory silk front, but is adorned with applied borders and pocket-tops of olive green satin with chenille work and cut-steel hearts. The more elaborate the decoration, the more valuable the waistcoat.
(c.1780; value E)

THE 18TH CENTURY

Fabulously colorful 18th-century suits are extremely desirable and do still survive, although they are found in smaller quantities than the female equivalents. It is important to find the tailcoat, waistcoat, and matching breeches together. Everyday wear is incredibly rare, since it was generally only expensive, highly decorative outfits that were deemed worth saving rather than discarding. Eighteenth-century waistcoats are found in sufficient quantity and range to mean that they are reasonably priced and highly popular with collectors. In the early part of the century the waistcoat was usually a contrasting color to the suit and was elaborately decorated with embroidery, metal lace, and bullion fringe. As the century progressed, menswear became more lightweight and elegant, relying for effect on fine tailoring rather than elaborate fabric. By c.1765 waistcoats had become shorter and were made of light silks, with delicate embroidery or trimmed with gold and silver lace. By the 1790s the fashionable light-colored, close-fitting breeches (intended to give the impression of Neo-classical nudity) were accompanied by waistcoats that reached only to the waist and were often plain, and the fashionable frock coat.

Collectible headwear from the 18th century includes embroidered caps which, although commonly known as "night caps," were popular informal wear at home. Surviving examples are of linen, silk, velvet, or wool, and are often densely embroidered.

THE 19TH CENTURY

At the beginning of the 19th century George "Beau" Brummell (1778–1840) employed impeccable tailoring to transform the fashionable simplicity of British country wear into the elegant black evening suit. By 1810 the length of trousers had dropped from calf- to shoe-length, while a strap under the foot maintained the desired line. Overcoats were in sober colors such as black and brown – black worn in town, and gray and brown more typically in the country. Early 19th-century full-dress waistcoats were decorated with embroidery, as were the "fancy" waistcoats of the 1830s to 1870s and the intricately patterned wedding waistcoats. Also popular with collectors are waistcoats in brocaded silk or brightly embroidered Berlin woolwork. The growing aristocratic predilection for sportswear was led by the Prince of Wales, later King Edward VII, who loved bright tweeds and checks.

Hats were an important part of a man's standard costume, and styles were immensely varied, ranging from silk top hats and exotically decorated smoking caps to bowlers, trilbies, panamas, and boaters.

THE 20TH CENTURY

In the 1950s the New Edwardian clothes that were the uniform of the Teddy Boys were popular, particularly suits with long, draped jackets and velvet lapels. Designs of the 1950s became increasingly colorful, and denim was introduced as a uniform for the young and rebellious. In the 1960s the "mod" style was in vogue, followed by the relaxed dress of the hippy in the 1970s, and by the aggressive punk look in the late 1970s and early 1980s. Notable 1990s designs include the unisex underwear of Calvin Klein (*b*.1942) and the outrageous skirts of Jean Paul Gaultier (*b*.1952). As with women's costume, men's clothing has become less formal since World War II, and hats and gloves are no longer considered an essential part of standard dress.

▼ Top hat

Top hats were worn throughout the 19th century and as formal wear in the early 20th. Earlier top hats were of beaver felt, later ones of silk hatter's plush. Shape helps with dating: early examples have broad crowns and brims, the "Cumberland" of the 1830s was taller, and the high-crowned, narrow-brimmed "stove pipe" of the 1850s was the extreme. This British hat has the elegant proportions typical from the 1890s onward.
(c.1910; value B)

▲ Jacket and plus-fours

Usually made of tweed or checked wool, plus-fours were long, wide knickerbockers that were popular casual wear in the 1920s and 1930s. Popularized by the Prince of Wales, they were worn when playing golf, game-shooting, or simply relaxing. Plus-fours gained their name because the overhang at the knee necessitated an additional 10cm (4in) of material.
(1930s; value A)

KEY FACTS

The 18th century
- CONDITION this is vital: stained, torn, or faded fabric will detract from the value; the suit needs to be complete, with coat, breeches, and matching waistcoat
- COLLECTING early menswear is rare; only waistcoats have survived in large numbers – their value will depend on the condition and the quality of the embroidery

The 19th century
- CONDITION good condition is crucial, since damaged and worn fabric will affect the value; the quality of color and any decoration is critical
- COLLECTING 19th-century menswear is rare, because the coats and trousers tended to be comparatively drab and were usually destroyed rather than stored away; waistcoats abound, and their value depends on their decorative appeal and size; hats: top hats are plentiful and inexpensive; an original box adds value; hats and gloves generally are modestly priced

The 20th century
- DESIGNS styles are varied and exist in a wide range of new materials and colors
- COLLECTING popular culture-inspired fashions such as punk are particularly collectible; the more outrageous the style, the more the potential value; boutique labels – Granny Takes a Trip or Westwood and McLaren's Seditionaries – are also desirable

See also Jewelery: Men's jewelery, p.270; Miscellaneous: Sporting memorabilia, pp.536–7

Accessories

Accessories provide the perfect alternative for collectors with neither the budget nor the space for costume. Many are miniature works of art, and, not having been subject to the alterations so common with clothing, provide an insight into the fashions and craftsmanship of their day.

PURSES AND BAGS

Drawstring purses date back to medieval times, when they were used to carry sweet-smelling herbs, sweetmeats, and money. In the 16th century women kept long drawstring pouches under their skirts; by the early 17th century purses were increasingly decorative, with canvas examples embroidered and lined with silk. Surviving 18th-century purses are decorated with silk, metal threads, and *sablé* work (a type of very fine beadwork). Such early examples are rarely found and highly priced. More common are the many types of purse and bag produced from the 19th century onward, with French evening bags of the 1920s and 1930s particularly common. Less expensive models have gilt or imitation ivory frames, often combined with beaded or embroidered velvet. Exclusive 1930s bags often feature jeweled frames.

With the development of plastics in the 20th century, PVC fabrics such as Lizadex, Crocadex, and even Emudex replaced expensive animal skins; from the 1950s, plastic purses were made in large quantities, particularly in the USA. There is still a market for exclusive designs, notably the quilted, scallop-shell purse of the 1980s and 1990s and purses by such designers as Chanel (1883–1971).

FANS AND PARASOLS

Although fans are no longer an essential part of the fashionable wardrobe, they remain popular with collectors. Fixed fans are rigid fans, usually with a central stick. Folding fans fall into three main categories: the *brisé* fan, with the leaf formed entirely from overlapping sticks in one material, such as ivory; the standard folding fan, where the sticks have a pleated leaf that allows the fan to open and close; and the cockade fan, which forms a circle when fully open. Leaves were made from silk, "chicken skin" (a fine papery vellum), paper, lace, or feathers. Fan sticks were of horn, mother-of-pearl, sandalwood, tortoiseshell, or ivory, and painted, carved, inlaid, or decorated with gold and silver *piqué* work. Some of the most desirable fans are those produced by George Villeroy in Paris and shown at the Great Exhibition in London in 1851. Also popular are the late 18th- and early 19th-century Italian fans made for travelers on the Grand Tour, featuring Classical images or copies of

◀ **Parasol**
From the 1830s the parasol was an essential part of a woman's fashionable wardrobe. Square-form parasols are rarer than round examples. This European parasol is typical of the period; it has a long, wooden handle and ferrule, with a silk canopy applied with flounces of machine-made blonde lace, and it would probably have been bought to match dresses in an Edwardian day wardrobe. Examples with carved grips in expensive materials and canopies in silk with hand-made lace covers are more valuable than those intended for everyday use.
(c.1905; l. 80.5cm/31¾in; value **B**)

◀ **Purse**
The decorative metal mount and chain handle of this elegant purse may well have been made in Germany, the production center of metal frames at the end of the 19th century. Typically the fabric bag is decorated with embroidery, in this case an attractive and unusual example of elaborate Turkish Maresh work.
(1900–1910; l. 26cm/10¼in; value **A**)

▼ **Fan**
This French fan is painted with a scene from Classical mythology, depicting Neptune, the Roman god of the sea, and his consort Amphitrite arising from the ocean. The fan has pierced and gilded sticks of mother-of-pearl, which are finely carved with shepherds and shepherdesses, another Neo-classical theme.
(c.1840; w. 29.5cm/11½in; value **I**)

famous Italian paintings. A niche collecting area is the advertising fans that were produced in the 1920s and 1930s to advertise perfumes, restaurants, and nightclubs.

From the 1830s to the 1920s parasols were an essential fashion accessory. The ribs were initially made of whalebone, with copper and steel becoming more common later. In the late 1830s parasols were delicate and elegant, while in the late 1860s they were frequently made of fabrics to match the dress and edged in deep fringes. By 1900 parasols were long (usually walking-stick length), with heavily knopped or tapering grips; the canopies were often very frilly or lacy. Many surviving examples have folding ivory or bone handles, which made alighting from a carriage easier. Some of the ivory grips are superbly carved, and this increases desirability.

KEY FACTS

General
• COLLECTING early accessories are rare and highly priced; later examples are more abundant, can be both fun and usable, and are still inexpensive; early Hermès and Gucci bags are very collectible

Purses and bags
• CARE 17th to 19th century examples require special care; beaded bags from the 1920s deteriorate if over-used

Fans and parasols
• CONDITION parasols: beware of spending too much on a parasol with a perished canopy, as they are expensive to restore; even if the canopy is badly perished it may still be worth pursuing if the parasol has an interesting novelty grip, or if the grip is of finely carved ivory, or enameled, or of precious metals
• COLLECTING parasols: check to see what the canopy struts are made of – if they are of baleen or whalebone, the parasol is an early example and as such highly collectible; fans: 18th-century hand-painted fans are very desirable; examples made by such Parisian firms as Maison Duvelleroy (est. 1827) are good quality and still affordable

Lace

In the 16th, 17th, and 18th centuries fortunes were spent on lace, whose beauty and highly skilled execution were recognized by those rich enough to commission it. Lace was a status symbol, not merely a trimming, and both men and women took great care in its selection and use. There are many forms of it, the most common being needlepoint lace and bobbin lace.

NEEDLEPOINT LACE

Needlepoint lace is sewn with a needle and built up from layers of buttonhole stitches on threads laid down on a parchment pattern. Loosely worked, the stitches form a mesh ground; or the ground may consist of linking bars (brides), and may have added decoration in the form of tiny projections (picots). The solid part of the pattern is built up from rows of simple looped stitches; a three-dimensional effect is achieved by working over a thread padding, as in *gros point de Venise*. The simple yet laborious needlepoint technique was used to make a wide range of patterns associated with various centers of production. In the 17th century Italy produced superb, finely worked examples, and France made *point de France*, *point d'Argentan*, and *point d'Alençon*, some of the most complex and desirable laces; in the 19th century Ireland produced a fine lace at the Parchment Convent in Youghal, and Brussels produced *point de gaze*.

BOBBIN (PILLOW) LACE

Bobbin lace is woven rather than sewn. Threads wound onto weighted bobbins are twisted, plaited, or woven together around pins marking out the pattern on parchment attached to a pillow. There are two types of bobbin lace: straight lace, a continuous piece of fabric in which the ground and pattern are worked together; and part lace, where the motifs are made separately and the ground is worked around them afterward. From the 18th century each major center of production had a distinctive style. Bobbin lace was produced in Caen and Valenciennes in France, Bruges in Belgium, and Genoa and Milan in Italy. In the 19th century Chantilly in France, Brussels in Belgium, and Honiton in Devon became famous for the lace used to trim taffeta gowns and accessories.

THE BASIC TYPES OF LACE

NEEDLEPOINT LACE

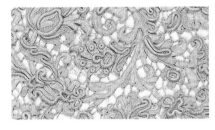

Gros point de Venise The characteristic three-dimensional effect is built up by thread padding *(late 17th century)*

Point de gaze Brussels lace made of layers of buttonhole stitches, usually in the form of roses *(c.1880–90)*

BOBBIN LACE

Flemish bobbin lace Open-mesh ground, dense pattern *(1750–60)*

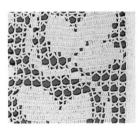

Honiton bobbin lace Plaited brides among bobbin blooms *(c.1890)*

Brussels lace Hexagonal mesh with flowing designs *(c.1860–80)*

OTHER TYPES OF LACE

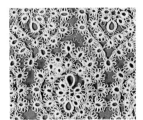

Crocheted lace Popular from c.1900 to c.1930 *(1910–20)*

Tatting Lace formed using a shuttle *(early 20th century)*

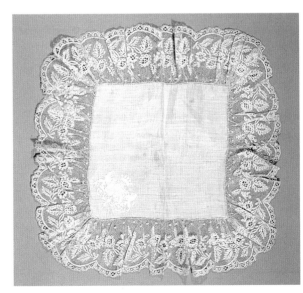

Machine lace Usually identified by its regularity *(20th century)*

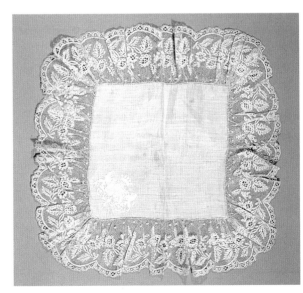

◄ **Bobbin-lace handkerchief**
A distinctive type of bobbin lace was produced in Valenciennes, France, in the early 18th century. It was worked in one piece – ground and pattern together – with a characteristic solid, strong, diamond-mesh ground and solid motifs. In the mid-19th century there was a revival of the handmade lace industry after a vogue for embroidered machine-made net. Valenciennes developed a bobbin lace with a new and lighter diamond mesh ground, as seen in the trimming on this handkerchief.
*(mid-19th century; w. 27cm/10½in; value **A**)*

KEY FACTS

- IMPORTANT CENTERS OF PRODUCTION Belgium: Antwerp, Bruges, Brussels, Louvain, Mechlin (Malines); France: Chantilly, Valenciennes; Britain: Honiton, Nottingham; Italy: Genoa, Venice; Ireland: Youghal
- MAIN TYPES needlepoint lace: *gros point de Venise*, *point de France*, *point d'Argentan*, *point d'Alençon*, *point de gaze*; bobbin lace: Valenciennes, Chantilly, Brussels, Honiton
- CARE cleaning should be undertaken by an expert; lace can usually be repaired very successfully
- COLLECTING fine museum-quality 17th- and 18th-century pieces command high prices, as do large dress flounces of 19th-century *point de gaze*; however, lace is still very undervalued generally, especially when compared with modern mass-produced trimmings; bobbin lace: still quite inexpensive because it can be hard to display unless it is in the form of a cap-back, collar, or similar accessory small enough to be framed

Mechanical clocks, invented in the late 13th century, and watches, first made at the end of the 16th century, are among the most fascinating of antiques. This is in no small part due to the numerous innovations and improvements introduced to their mechanisms for keeping accurate time, particularly since the 17th century. Their attraction, like that of related instruments such as barometers (for recording atmospheric pressure), thus resides to a large extent in our enduring appreciation of technological ingenuity, although on a more fundamental level it also stems from the near-universal preoccupation with the passing and recording of time. However, clocks and watches also have tremendous decorative appeal; for example, many pocket watches and wristwatches are sought after as much as for the qualities of their design as for the accuracy of their time-keeping. Similarly, most types of clock – including wall, longcase, bracket, and carriage, to name a few – display the skills not only of the clockmaker, but also of the cabinet-maker, polisher, engraver, brass caster, and dial painter. Such timepieces can therefore be appreciated in much the same way as a piece of furniture, or even a painting. Indeed, some of the more elaborate examples have been described as mechanical pictures.

Detail of a skeleton timepiece by John Pace (left) Three dials, showing time, date, and 52-week power reserve, are shown on this rare British timepiece *(c.1850)*.

Mantle clock (above) This mass-produced French clock is faced in black slate and displays a Neo-classical influence in its details *(late 19th century)*.

Clocks & Watches: Basics

Until the 19th century the clock was one of the most sophisticated machines in the world, and over the centuries clockmakers have created increasingly accurate mechanisms in a variety of case designs. Knowledge of mechanisms, dials, and cases will help in determining a clock's age and authenticity.

THE EVOLUTION OF THE CLOCK
In ancient Egypt, Greece, and Rome, time was measured by sundials or by waterclocks, but the history of the clock until the Middle Ages is obscure because the same Latin word – *horologium* – was used to describe any means of recording time.

The first mechanical weight-driven clocks, which were used in monasteries and churches, appeared in Europe sometime after 1280. These large clocks were scaled down to smaller domestic versions by the late 14th century; the application of the coiled spring in the early 15th century led to the development of portable clocks and eventually to watches.

THE MOVEMENT
A clock is composed of a movement, or mechanism; a dial, showing the time; and a case, housing the dial and movement. The movement comprises a system (train) of wheels and pinions (gears), set between flat brass or wooden plates, which are held together by pillars. The wheels were initially made of iron or steel, but brass was used from the late 16th century. The movement is powered through the constant pull of weights, attached to a line wound around a barrel ("weight-driven"), or by the release of energy in a coiled spring contained in a barrel ("spring-driven").

THE ESCAPEMENT
The escapement is a device that regulates the transfer of power from the weights (or spring) to the movement. It is so called because it allows one tooth of a wheel to escape at a time. The most basic escapement is an arm with two pallets, or "flags," which engage the teeth of the wheel. The earliest form was the verge escapement, consisting of a "crown," or toothed wheel; a verge, or shaft, with two pallets; and a large horizontal bar ("foliot") or a wheel ("balance"). The foliot or the balance releases the two pallets in turn, which engage the toothed wheel, resulting in an alternating backward and forward motion. The foliot verge escapement was never very reliable, losing or gaining up to fifteen minutes a day.

In the 1670s the invention of the anchor escapement, used with the pendulum, provided a more accurate means of regulation. The arm, with a pallet at each end, is in the shape of an anchor. As a tooth of the escape wheel escapes from the pallet at one end, another engages the pallet at the other end. In locking, the pallets tend to push the teeth slightly backward; this is known as "recoil." The anchor escapement was first used in longcase clocks but became standard in most clocks by *c*.1800; some were converted from the verge to the anchor to improve their timekeeping. Another type of escapement is the platform lever escapement, used mainly in carriage clocks as it does not have a pendulum: instead, an oscillating balance wheel, regulated by a coiled spring, is mounted above the movement. A carriage clock may thus keep time while being moved.

THE FUSEE
On spring-driven clocks the spring loses force when it unwinds, so in the mid-15th century the fusee was invented to equalize this force. Used particularly by British makers, it is a spirally grooved, truncated cone that takes up a wire or gut line wound around the spring barrel. When the spring is fully coiled and its force greatest, the wire unwinds from the small end of the fusee; when the energy of the spring is nearly spent (usually after eight days), the wire unwinds from the large end, compensating for the weakness of the spring. Many continental European clocks have a going barrel instead of a fusee, transmitting force directly from the spring to the train.

PARTS OF A SIMPLE CLOCK

1	Hands	11	Back plate
2	Dial wheels	12	Main wheel
3	Winding arbor	13	Pinions
4	Dial plate	14	Center arbor
5	Dial feet	15	Center wheel
6	Front plate	16	Third wheel
7	Barrel	17	Anchor
8	Seatboard		escapement
9	Weight	18	Pillars
10	Pendulum	19	Backboard

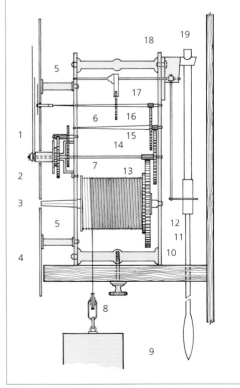

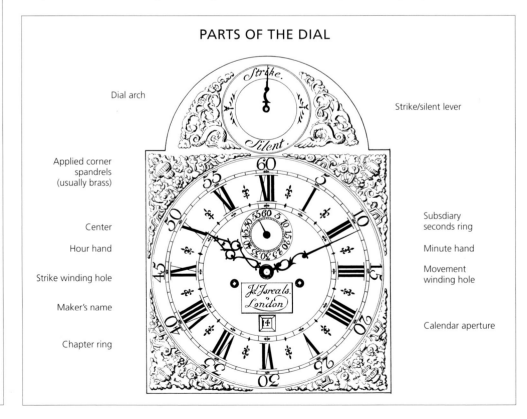

PARTS OF THE DIAL

Dial arch

Strike/silent lever

Applied corner spandrels (usually brass)

Center

Hour hand

Strike winding hole

Maker's name

Chapter ring

Subsidiary seconds ring

Minute hand

Movement winding hole

Calendar aperture

THE MECHANICS OF A CLOCK

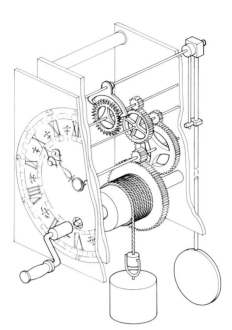

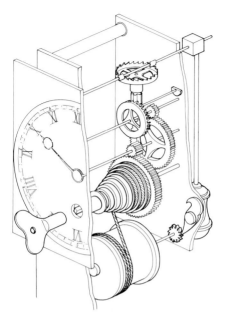

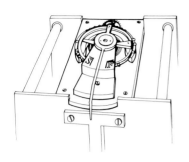

▲ Platform escapement
Carriage clocks commonly have a lever escapement mounted on a platform on the top of the movement rather than the backplate. This type of escapement does not have a pendulum and so is especially suitable for traveling clocks.

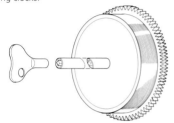

▲ Anchor escapement
Developed from c.1665, this escapement is so called because it resembles a ship's anchor. First employed in longcase clocks with a seconds-beating long pendulum, it was used from c.1800 in bracket clocks with a half-second-beating shorter pendulum. The pendulum used in conjunction with an anchor escapement swings in a narrower arc than that fitted with a verge escapement; it also has a disc-shaped rather than a bulbous bob.

▲ Verge or crown wheel escapement with fusee
The earliest clocks were regulated by a verge or crown wheel escapement, so called because the teeth were cut to give the appearance of a crown. It was widely used until c.1800 with a short bob pendulum and as such was most often fitted in portable bracket clocks. British spring-driven bracket clocks were generally fitted with a fusee, attached by a wire or chain to the spring barrel, to equalize the force of the spring as it ran down.

▲ Going barrel
The going barrel is a cylindrical brass barrel containing the spring; it has teeth around its edge that transmit power directly to the wheels of the train. A clock with a going barrel may be less accurate than one with a fusee as it winds down.

THE PENDULUM

The pendulum, regulating timekeeping, was first applied to clocks by the Dutch scientist Christiaan Huygens (1629–95) in the 1650s. As the pendulum is isochronous – it swings in a regular arc – accuracy improved so much that the clock kept time within a minute or two every day. Attached to the arbor on which the escape wheel turns, the pendulum is usually a brass or steel rod with a metal disc (bob) at the end; by altering the height of the bob, the pendulum swings faster or slower, altering the speed of the clock.

Although more accurate than the verge, the pendulum and anchor escapement still had disadvantages: the pendulum lengthened or shortened as it expanded and contracted with temperature changes. This altered its swing rate and the accuracy of the clock. The recoil of the anchor escapement had a similar effect.

A desire for greater accuracy led to the design of various precision timekeeping devices, notably the deadbeat anchor escapement c.1715, purportedly by the British clockmaker George Graham (c.1673–1751); this featured an arm with two curved pallets rather than one curved and one flat pallet. When a tooth on the escape wheel was released it fell into a locking face without causing recoil.

Another device designed to improve the clock's accuracy was the temperature-compensating pendulum, of which two main types were invented. The mercurial pendulum, designed by Graham in 1726, was composed of a steel rod with a glass jar of mercury as its bob: the expansion of the mercury with heat countered that of the steel. John Harrison (1693–1776) another British clockmaker, invented the gridiron pendulum, with up to nine alternating steel and brass rods. As steel and brass expand at different rates, the length of the pendulum remained constant. A simpler temperature-compensating pendulum featured a wooden rod, as wood is little affected by heat or cold.

THE STRIKING MECHANISM

A clock with a simple striking mechanism for the hours has two trains: one for the clock and one for striking. More complex clocks that strike the quarter hours have a third train; some have a cord or button that causes the striking mechanism to sound. Early clocks used a countwheel or locking plate for striking, but in 1676 Edward Barlow invented a more accurate device, the "rack and snail," which linked striking with hand movement. Until the second quarter of the 19th century a bell was used, with a gong becoming popular thereafter.

THE DIAL AND CASE

The dial consists of a square, round, or arched metal or wooden plate (the "dial plate"), fixed to the frontplate of the movement. The earliest dials were of brass; painted wood and metal or enameled metal were popular in the 19th century. Early clocks have only an hour hand – the minute hand was introduced in the mid- to late 17th century after the invention of the pendulum improved accuracy. Most dial plates have two or three winding holes for winding the movement; some also feature subsidiary dials showing the seconds, a calendar aperture or dial showing the date, or a strike/silent lever to turn the striking mechanism on or off.

Cases are so varied that is impossible to generalize about designs and materials. They were usually made by a specialist casemaker, and designs, especially for bracket and longcase clocks, mostly follow furniture styles of the day. British and American makers favored wooden cases: walnut and ebony were used for bracket and longcase clocks in the late 17th and early 18th centuries, while mahogany was common in the 18th century. Continental, particularly French, makers specialized in elaborate gilded metal cases. Some of the best clocks feature marquetry, lacquer, brass, silver or gilt-bronze mounts, and tortoiseshell veneer.

Wall clocks

A wall clock is simply a clock that can be fixed to a wall. Lantern clocks of the late 16th and 17th centuries were the first domestic wall clocks, but from the early 18th century large wall-hung clocks were made for taverns, inns, and other public buildings. Wall clocks of the 18th and 19th centuries range from elaborate, gilded French cartel clocks to the mass-produced, wooden-cased clocks of the USA.

LANTERN CLOCKS

A lantern clock is a weight-driven wall clock that strikes the hour on a bell. It is especially associated with Britain, where it was first made *c.*1620, but versions were also produced in continental Europe and Japan. Made almost entirely from brass – "lantern" may be derived from the old English word "latten," meaning brass – the clock resembles a domestic lantern: the square brass case has four small ball or urn feet, an engraved dial plate, three pierced frets, and a bell, covered by four straps and

▼ **Lantern clock by William Bowyer of London**
The detailed engraving of tulips in the dial center, decorative dolphins on the frets, and elaborate hand tip of this British brass clock, are all typical features of late 17th-century lantern clocks.
(c.1670; ht 31cm/12in; value J)

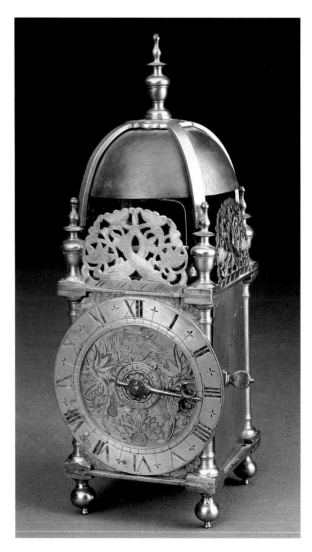

topped with a finial. The chapter ring, showing hours and quarter hours, was very narrow on the earliest examples and extended over the sides of the clock. In the dial's center are the maker's signature and engraved designs – typically foliate scrolls and flower-heads – and often an alarm setting disc. The single hand is usually of iron but may be of brass or blued steel. Hands were "blued" by heating – this process not only strengthened them but also altered their color to a dark blue-gray that was clearly visible against the dial.

Early lantern clocks were regulated by a balance wheel escapement, but after the pendulum was invented in the mid-17th century, most clocks were converted to or made with the more precise pendulum-controlled verge or anchor escapements. The verge escapement was especially popular throughout the 18th century with provincial makers. Lantern clocks went out of fashion in the early 18th century, but in the 19th century reproductions were made (and old clocks fitted) with spring-driven movements. Some clocks were refitted with balance wheel escapements as lantern clocks have become increasingly valuable in recent times.

TAVERN AND DIAL CLOCKS

Wall clocks for taverns, inns, assembly rooms, and public buildings were first produced in the 1720s. The first such clocks are known as "tavern" clocks and sometimes erroneously as "Act of Parliament" clocks: in 1797 a tax on clocks and watches was instituted by the British Parliament (although repealed one year later), and this led to the popular misconception that these clocks were placed in taverns for customers who could not afford clocks in their homes. However, most tavern clocks predate this act by several decades. Measuring up to 76cm (30in) in diameter, and with a long trunk for the weight and pendulum, tavern clocks were designed to be seen clearly from a distance, and are usually only timepieces. The earliest examples from the 1720s have virtually square dials with arched tops; these developed into shield-shaped wooden dials. The numerals and chapter ring are usually gilt, and gilt designs of flowers and scrolls feature in the corners of the dial, often with chinoiserie designs on the trunk.

▲ **Wall clock by Bushman of London**
This is a rare example of an early British wall clock, probably intended for use in a domestic setting rather than a public place. It has a curved wooden trunk, and – unlike later tavern clocks – a brass dial with an applied silvered chapter ring. It also has a date aperture.
(c.1700; ht 1.5m/4ft 11in; value H)

▶ **Dial clock by Joseph Jump**
The simple but functional design of a large white dial with clear black numerals was characteristic of the many inexpensive public clocks produced in the 19th century. This British clock has no five-minute ring on the dial, as this feature (a second ring of minutes in Arabic numerals on the outside of the ring of Roman numerals) disappeared from clock design at the end of the 18th century.
(second half of 19th century; ht 38cm/15in; value C)

Gilt finials sometimes ornamented the top of the case, but on some clocks these have broken off. Round dials were introduced in the mid-18th century: the dial itself was initially black with gold numerals, but from the 1770s a white dial with numerals and chapter ring in black was popular. As neither shield nor round dials had glass covers, the numerals and chapter ring are often worn away or repainted. Many round-dial tavern clocks also had black lacquered cases with chinoiserie decoration. From the 1790s lacquered tavern clocks declined and gave way to mahogany cases.

Dial clocks, made from the 1750s, became possibly the most popular style of clock ever produced. Simple in design, they consist of a round dial of engraved, silvered brass (18th century), painted wood (from *c*.1805), or painted iron (from *c*.1830), covered with glass and a brass bezel, and housed in a wooden case. The first dial clocks appeared with mahogany cases, but oak, walnut, and rosewood were also used in the 19th century, when these clocks were made by many British, German, and American firms to meet the demand for inexpensive timekeepers in offices, shops, and railway stations.

CARTEL CLOCKS
Cartel clocks are decorative, spring-driven wall clocks that were made in France, and to a lesser extent Britain, Austria, and Sweden, in the 18th and 19th centuries. "Cartel" is probably derived from the Italian word *cartella*, meaning "bracket." The clock, with a verge or anchor escapement, typically featured a white-enameled dial and a finely cast and gilded bronze or brass case. Elaborate, asymmetrical scrollwork, flowers, fruit, and shells are typical of mid-18th century Rococo cases; more symmetrical Neo-classical designs of sunburst rays,

masks, and urns were popular from the 1780s. Cartel clocks were produced in Britain on a limited scale from the 1730s to the 1770s; many are copies of French designs but are less exuberant than the Rococo originals.

AMERICAN WALL CLOCKS
Clockmaking began in New England *c*.1750 and was initially a very small industry, with parts such as dials imported from Europe. In the early 19th century such clockmakers as Eli Terry (1772–1852) in Connecticut used streamlined methods of production and standard parts to mass-produce inexpensive clocks. As brass was expensive in the USA, movements as well as cases were often of wood. Most wall clocks from before *c*.1870 are weight-driven, with an anchor escapement.

Although many early American clocks were based on European designs, some distinctive new types were created in the 19th century. In 1802 Simon Willard (1753–1848) of Massachusetts invented the "banjo" clock, which featured simple but well-made brass movements and a white-painted metal dial. The long trunk, holding the weights and pendulum, was flanked by curved brass frets, with a box at the bottom decorated with *verre églomisé* (reverse-painted glass) panels. Only about 4,000 such clocks were produced and these are very collectible today.

Simon's brother Aaron Willard (1757–1844) introduced a variant of the "banjo" clock, known as the "lyre" clock, which had a curving trunk of carved wood and a pendant-shaped bracket at the bottom of the case. In the mid-19th century the clockmaker Chauncey Jerome (1793–1868) of Bristol, Connecticut, designed an inexpensive, 30-hour duration shelf or wall clock known as the "OG" (ogee) clock, which took its name from the shape of the molding around the dial and door. These mass-produced clocks had cheap brass movements, ogee-molded veneered softwood cases, white-painted zinc dials, and *verre églomisé* panels. Early, rare American wall clocks are highly sought after in the USA.

▲ **Half-pillar and splat shelf clock by Solomon Stowe of Connecticut**
This type of clock is so called because its case is decorated with architectural-style pillars at the sides and a splat at the top. This clock has a number of features that are highly characteristic of American wall clocks, including a veneered softwood case inset with a decorative *verre églomisé* panel – which, in this typical example, depicts an American folk art scene – a weight-driven, bell-striking, wooden movement, and an original maker's label.
(c.1830; ht 72cm/28½in; value **H***)*

◄ **Cartel clock**
In the 19th century there was a revival of interest in 18th-century French Rococo art, and decorative cartel clocks in the Rococo style became extremely popular. This elaborate, gilt-bronze example, made in France, is richly decorated with scrolls and flowers, and is a fine imitation of earlier pieces. Cartel clocks were also manufactured in Britain, but French examples are typically much more ornate than their British counterparts – even the pierced, brass hands on this clock are more elaborate than those found on British examples. French cartel clocks were predominantly made of gilded bronze or brass whereas the British versions were usually made of less expensive gilded wood.
(c.1880; ht 58.5cm/23in; value **H***)*

KEY FACTS
Lantern clocks
- MOVEMENT a spring-driven mechanism indicates a clock made or altered in the 19th century
- CONDITION any shiny or artificially distressed parts are likely to be replacements; these should be good quality in order not to reduce the value

Tavern and dial clocks
- DESIGNS shield-shaped dials are typical of tavern clocks made between the 1720s and 1750s; later versions have round dials
- MOVEMENT dial clocks made before 1800 had verge escapements; anchor escapements were usual thereafter
- CONDITION some repainting of the numerals, chapter ring, and signature is common; clocks with extensive repainting should be avoided

Cartel clocks
- DESIGNS a gilt-bronze or brass case usually indicates a French make; most British versions are of carved, gilded wood

American wall clocks
- DESIGNS *verre églomisé* panels are typical
- LABELING few are signed on the dial: instead they often have a label at the back of the inside case

See also Precision clocks and chronometers, p.360

Longcase clocks

The weight-driven longcase clock, regulated by a pendulum, was introduced *c*.1660. The long case may have developed as protection for the pendulum and weights – they hung below the movement, which was held with the dial in a hood. Cases were mostly made by cabinet-makers and so reflect the style of contemporary furniture. Longcases are especially linked with Britain, but fine versions were also made in continental Europe and in the USA, where they are known as "tallcases."

EARLY BRITISH LONGCASES

The earliest British longcases, made from the 1660s mainly in London, had cases of ebony-veneered oak with architectural pediment tops, but walnut-veneered clocks, typically with flat or crested tops and Baroque twist columns on the hood, were fashionable toward the end of the 17th century. The square brass dial had a narrow, applied and silvered chapter ring, applied spandrels of cherubs' heads, scrolls, or foliage, a roughened or matted brass center, and heat-treated, durable, blued-steel hands; most examples also had a seconds dial. Perhaps the leading clockmaker of this period was Thomas Tompion (1639–1713).

Marquetry decoration was very popular on the best longcases from the 1680s to *c*.1710. Before the 1690s this usually consisted of panels of birds and flowers, or geometric patterns, or parquetry, on the trunk and base. Later examples are decorated all over with elaborate designs of arabesques, scrolls, flowers, birds, and figures. Another common feature of late 17th-century longcases is the lenticle: a small, oval, glass window in the trunk door, revealing the pendulum. With the fashion for larger rooms in the early 18th century, very tall longcases – up to 2.5m (8ft 2in) in height – were popular. Classical hood columns that were influenced by contemporary architecture replaced Baroque twists. Dials increasingly became larger and *c*.1715 the arched or break-arch dial was introduced.

Japanned decoration reflected the European interest in Chinese and Japanese art from *c*.1700 to the 1770s. Japanning was a European version of the costly, time-consuming process of lacquering. Japanning – usually black and green but occasionally red, yellow, blue, or cream – was painted all over the case on a layer of gesso; gilt chinoiserie designs were then added to the ground.

DUTCH LONGCASES

Longcase clocks were produced in the Netherlands from *c*.1670 to the end of the 18th century. Although in many ways they resemble contemporary British clocks, some features are distinctively Dutch. These include the bombé base, sometimes with projecting scrolls; C and S scrolls at the top and bottom of the trunk door; a cast-metal lenticle surround; large paw or ball feet; and gilded figural finials. Cases were typically veneered in walnut, with ebony or light-colored wood stringing or marquetry decoration. Musical work and automata in the dial arch were common features.

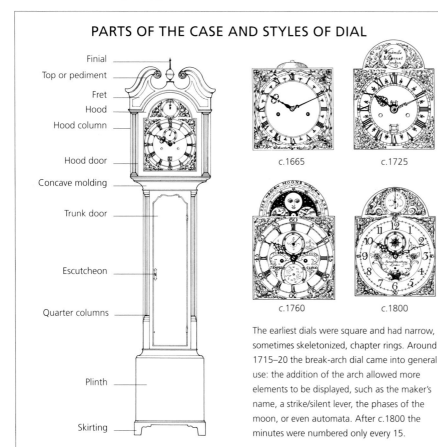

PARTS OF THE CASE AND STYLES OF DIAL

Finial
Top or pediment
Fret
Hood
Hood column
Hood door
Concave molding
Trunk door
Escutcheon
Quarter columns
Plinth
Skirting

c.1665

c.1725

c.1760

c.1800

The earliest dials were square and had narrow, sometimes skeletonized, chapter rings. Around 1715–20 the break-arch dial came into general use: the addition of the arch allowed more elements to be displayed, such as the maker's name, a strike/silent lever, the phases of the moon, or even automata. After *c*.1800 the minutes were numbered only every 15.

▲ Longcase by Vermeulen
The rich, all-over marquetry on this Dutch walnut clock indicates that it was made in the very late 17th or the early 18th century – on earlier pieces the marquetry is confined to panels on the trunk and base. The plinth has awkward proportions, indicating it has been changed or rebuilt. *(very late 17th or early 18th century; ht 2.4m/7ft 10in; value I)*

◄ Longcase by Conyers Dunlop of London
Such fine mahogany longcases as this elegantly proportioned George III example were produced by London makers from the middle to the end of the 18th century. The paneled base, shaped plinth, and brass, stop-fluted, reeded columns are typical features of London mahogany longcases. *(c.1760; ht 2.2m/7ft 3in; value J)*

LATER BRITISH AND AMERICAN LONGCASES

In the 18th century high-quality longcase clocks were produced in English cities outside London and in Scotland, especially in Bristol, Oxford, Liverpool, and Edinburgh. From *c*.1750 the majority of fashionable London makers used mahogany for cases, while oak was popular elsewhere in Britain; makers in the USA, where the industry was well established on the eastern seaboard, preferred indigenous woods such as maple and cherry, although mahogany was also used. London cases of this period typically feature an elaborate pagoda top, two or three brass ball-and-spire finials, and sometimes quarter columns at the corners of the trunk and base, with decorative brass stop-fluting.

◄ **Tallcase clock**

American tallcase clocks, such as this example made in Philadelphia, can often be identified by the combination of veneers. Here, tiger maple, a local wood, is inlaid with contrasting panels of mahogany. Most American makers also used iron for the dial as an alternative to brass, which was expensive in the USA: the dial of this clock features colorful shell spandrels and a disc showing the phases of the moon.

(c.1810; ht 2.4m/7ft 10in; value K)

► **Longcase by Robert Milne of Aberdeen**

Painted dials were used in many British provincial longcase clocks in the 19th century because they were much less expensive than brass dials. Allegorical figures are typical – such as the maidens representing England, Scotland, Wales, and Ireland in the four corners of the dial plate of this early Victorian clock. White dials first made their appearance in Britain *c*.1770. The wood that is used in this Scottish longcase is mahogany.

(c.1840; ht 2.2m/7ft 3in; value N)

The arched brass dial with applied chapter ring and spandrels remained popular and some dials from the 1770s also featured a subsidiary calendar dial, instead of an aperture. Engraved one-piece brass or silvered-brass dials appeared between 1750 and 1770. Iron dials, painted with floral motifs, portraits, or mythological and allegorical figures, were introduced in the 1770s and used extensively on British provincial longcases and in the USA, where supplies of brass were limited.

In the Victorian period longcases suffered a decline in quality: painted dials, broad, flimsily constructed cases, and mass-produced movements were common. Novelty and bracket clocks were more popular than longcases, although longcase regulators remained in fashion.

FRENCH LONGCASES

Weight-driven longcases were never made on a large scale in France. More popular at the beginning of the 18th century was the *pendule sur socle*, a spring-driven bracket clock on a matching tall pedestal or plinth. Cases were made by such leading French cabinet-makers as André-Charles Boulle (1642–1732). Examples by Boulle are typically surmounted by a gilt-bronze figure. In the mid-18th century the best French makers produced a type of longcase which, although not a true regulator or precision clock, was known as a *regulateur*. With its outward-curving, bombé trunk, it was very different in style from British longcase clocks. Cases were finely veneered in walnut or rosewood, with rich ormolu mounts and details in mahogany, sycamore, tulipwood, and olivewood.

Production of the *pendule sur socle* and the *regulateur* was confined mainly to Paris, but other major centers of clockmaking in the 18th and 19th centuries included the Jura region and the Franche-Comté, the latter renowned for its *Comtoise* longcases. Most late *Comtoise* clocks featured an elaborate pressed-brass pendulum, visible through a teardrop-shaped, glazed trunk section where the case was at its most bulbous; these pendulums were matched by elaborate pressed-brass dial frames.

► **Chiming longcase**

Longcases with chimes were popular in the Victorian and Edwardian periods. This British piece has a solid door but glass was also used so that the gong could be seen. The massive, extravagant base, ornate carving, and Art Nouveau-style Arabic numerals of this mahogany clock are typically Edwardian.

(c.1910; ht 2.9m/9ft 6in; value I)

KEY FACTS

- **WOODS** Britain: ebony-veneered oak was used in 1660s, walnut and olivewood veneers in 1670; walnut-veneered cases were used *c*.1715; mahogany first appeared in 1720s and by *c*.1750 had largely supplanted walnut; oak remained popular in the provinces in the 18th century; USA: indigenous woods such as cherry and maple gave a distinctive style; some mahogany was also used
- **DIALS** square dials were typical until *c*.1715; thereafter the break-arch dial, often featuring a rolling moon or the maker's name, was popular; silvered dials appeared *c*.1760, white dials *c*.1770, circular dials *c*.1800; painted metal dials are typical on American pieces
- **CASES** earliest British cases are in simple architectural style; after 1670s marquetry decoration was used, also on Dutch clocks; lacquer was used in the Netherlands mid- to late 17th century and was popular in Britain *c*.1720–70s; chinoiserie designs were very popular
- **MARRIAGES** dials and movements were often removed from one case and placed in another: look for a pendulum that appears too large for its case, a dial that does not fit the hood, or any parts that are not original
- **CUT-DOWNS** longcases that have been shortened are known as "cut-downs"; peg holes will be visible if feet have been removed; outline of removed cresting or finials may be visible; proportions may look awkward

See also Precision clocks and chronometers, p.360

Bracket clocks

Early bracket clocks

The invention of the pendulum in the mid-17th century made possible the production of spring-driven clocks with a short pendulum, designed to stand on furniture, shelves, or wall brackets. These clocks, often portable, are usually known in Britain as "bracket" clocks, although few were actually made with matching brackets; they are also known as "mantel" or "table" clocks. The cases and dials of early 17th- and 18th-century examples largely follow those of contemporary longcases.

◄ Bracket clock by Henry Jones

This early British clock with an ebony case, elaborate brass handle, pierced ("basket") brass top, applied brass spandrels, and skeletonized chapter ring is of exceptional quality and very rare. The blued-steel hour hand is pierced and scrolled, in the typical style of many 17th-century lantern clocks.

*(c.1680; ht 28cm/10¾in; value **B**)*

THE 17TH CENTURY

The earliest bracket clocks, made from the 1660s mostly in England, have cases veneered with ebony, walnut, or olivewood, a pediment-shaped or domed top, a brass carrying handle, bun or block feet, and pierced wooden panels or frets at the sides and/or the front, which were backed with fabric so that the striking mechanism could be heard. Damaged delicate wooden frets were often later replaced by glass panes. Some examples have gilded or silver feet, pierced (known as "basket") brass tops and frets, and tortoiseshell veneer. The square brass dials often feature an applied, silvered chapter ring, spandrels in the form of winged cherubs, and blued-steel hands. Most 17th-century (and 18th-century) bracket clocks are of eight-day duration, strike the hours, and have a verge escapement; some were converted to the more accurate anchor escapement in the 19th century. Backplates were often engraved with Dutch-inspired tulips and leaves.

French 17th-century bracket clocks are usually more ornate than their English counterparts. One of the earliest forms was the *pendule religieuse* or Louis XIII clock, with tortoiseshell inlaid with silver and brass, gilt finials, and often gilt acanthus leaf swags or scroll mounts. From the 1690s French examples featured white enamel plaques for each numeral on the dial, on a velvet ground. Dutch clocks also featured velvet-covered dial plates, but their cases – typically in ebony – are plainer.

THE 18TH CENTURY

Bracket cases were usually veneered with walnut or ebonized until *c*.1730, and veneered with mahogany thereafter. Arched brass dials were introduced *c*.1715, with calendar work or strike/silent dials in the arch, and an applied, silvered chapter ring. Some 18th-century examples have quarter-hour as well as hour striking and often a repeat mechanism, operated by a cord.

The backplate continued to be engraved, usually with such fashionable motifs as foliate scrolls and flowering urns.

In France curvaceous, asymmetrical forms were popular from the 1690s, typified by the waisted bracket clock with its inward-curving case and matching wall bracket. Extravagant inlay with exotic materials was typical until *c*.1750, as were tortoiseshell veneer and gilt mounts; ormolu, lacquer, and porcelain were all popular, with ornate asymmetrical scrolls, shells, and flowers. From *c*.1750 to *c*.1800 more restrained lines and rustic, sentimental, and Classical motifs prevailed. Dials on most early 18th-century examples have an enameled center, with enamel plaques for numerals – this is called a 13-piece dial; from the mid-18th century clockmakers used a one-piece, white, enameled dial.

▲ Bracket clock by Samuel Denton

Finely figured mahogany was the most popular type of veneer for high-quality bracket and long-case clocks in the 18th century. This British clock is in the "bell top" case style used from *c*.1770, having convex molding at the top and concave molding below. "Inverted bell" tops, also typical of the 18th century, have concave moldings above and convex moldings below. This example lacks its brass finials to the corners of the top.

*(c.1770; ht 52cm/20½in; value **H**)*

▲ Bracket clock

The use of exotic veneers, known as "Boulle marquetry" after the cabinet-maker André-Charles Boulle (1642–1732), were characteristic of many French clocks made from the late 17th century. This Louis XV clock is veneered in tortoiseshell with brass inlay and features ornate gilt scrolls and figural mounts, which were very typical of the highly extravagant Rococo style of the mid-18th century. This clock also has individual white enamel plaques (cartouches) for each hour numeral – a style that was especially popular in France.

*(c.1740; ht 81cm/32in; value **I**)*

KEY FACTS

- CASE designs are similar to contemporary furniture and longcase clocks; British clocks tend to have wooden cases; French cases use a variety of materials
- MOVEMENT early bracket clocks have verge escapements: these were sometimes converted to anchor escapements and if so the apron over the pendulum rod may be missing or the pendulum bob will be disc-shaped instead of conical; some clocks were reconverted back to verge, often with a new apron in a style different from the rest of the clock
- ALTERATIONS finials and feet are often missing or replaced in a different style; delicate wooden frets may have been replaced by glass
- COLLECTING clocks with a matching bracket are fairly rare and so especially collectible; original escapements are desirable; early clocks are highly sought after

Later bracket clocks

Although the longcase clock went into decline in the early 19th century, the bracket clock remained popular. The majority of 19th-century European bracket clocks are typified by elaborate case design in a variety of styles. The clock industry expanded in the USA, and from the 1840s mass-produced, inexpensive American bracket clocks, or "shelf" clocks, were imported into Europe, contributing to increased competition but ultimately to a decline in the European industry, especially in Britain.

REGENCY BRACKET CLOCKS

From the 1790s to the 1820s British bracket clocks were produced in diverse styles, from the satinwood-veneered "balloon" case, similar to the French waisted style, to the chamfer-top case. The chamfer-top style has a flattened pediment top, influenced by the contemporary Greek Revival style in architecture, and is crowned by a cast and gilt finial. Cases were usually veneered in mahogany or rosewood or ebonized, often with brass strip inlay in delicate scrolling designs. From the end of the 18th century bracket clocks were usually kept in one position rather than transported around: for this reason they often no longer had carrying handles at the top, although most chamfer-top clocks have ornamental brass ring handles on the sides, often held by lion masks.

The large, round, convex dials are among the easiest of faces to read: made of silvered brass, painted iron, or white-enameled copper, they are usually very plain except for the maker's signature. The simple brass or blued-steel hands are typically pierced or feature ornamental spade or heart tips. The movement is spring-driven with an anchor escapement.

VICTORIAN BRACKET CLOCKS

By the mid-19th century novelty of case design was all-important. The numerous revival styles, especially the Gothic Revival, were particularly influential. Gothic Revival clocks, popular between the 1830s and 1850s, have the same basic form as Regency clocks, but the dial plate is in the shape of a pointed arch, the fretted side panels imitate Gothic tracery, and cluster columns, copied from medieval architecture, ornament the corners. In contrast to the simpler Regency forms Victorian clocks tended to be elaborately decorated with heavy carving and mounts. Some featured complex striking mechanisms, with chimes on bells, and gongs on the quarter hour. Substantial three-train chiming "director's" or "boardroom" clocks are typical of the high Victorian period.

Dials were made in a wide range of materials, including plain or silvered brass and painted iron; the use of Arabic numerals was common from c.1870. As with most 19th-century European clocks, the name on the dial is frequently that

of the retailer, although the best makers also sold their own clocks. The British clockmaking industry gradually declined from the 1840s owing to growing imports of mass-produced American and German clocks, but fine bracket clocks were made in Britain until World War I.

AMERICAN SHELF CLOCKS

Large-scale production of clocks first began in the early 19th century. Although many were exported to Europe, most surviving examples are found in the USA, where they are popular with collectors. Connecticut-based Eli Terry (1772–1852) was the first to produce inexpensive movements, mostly of wood, using slick production methods and standard parts. In the 1830s Chauncey Jerome (1793–1868) invented 30-hour duration movements from rolled brass, which were both easier to make and more reliable than wood.

Although less expensive materials were used for American cases than European ones, designs were just as varied. Most carcasses were softwood veneered with mahogany, with a maker's label on the interior, and thin, sheet-metal or wooden dials painted white. Clocks were simply designed to meet functional domestic demands, and used little brass so as to keep costs down. Notable designs were the "pillar and scroll" clock (until c.1830), with elegant side pillars, a scrolled pediment with finials, and simple, scalloped feet and skirt; the "three deck" design, with the case divided into three and decorated with half columns at the sides; the "acorn" style, with a wide, curving trunk; and the "steeple" clock, with a pointed gable and pinnacled side pillars. Most clocks are embellished on the front door with *verre églomisé* (reverse-painted glass) panels. At the end of the 19th century many American makers copied French marble mantel clocks, using imitation marble of enameled iron or painted wood; some cases were of papier-mâché inset with mother-of-pearl and painted with floral designs.

▲ **"Steeple" shelf clock by Birge and Fuller, Bristol, Connecticut**
This design of clock, with a pointed gable and pinnacled pillars, was probably influenced by Gothic Revival clocks made in Britain between the 1830s and 1850s. Its movement is signed by the maker, and, as with the majority of 19th-century American shelf clocks, there is an original maker's label inside the case. The *verre églomisé* panels are replacements. (c.1845; ht 66cm/26in; value **G**)

▶ **Bracket clock by Grant of London**
It is unusual to find a Regency bracket clock with its original matching bracket. Many chamfer-top clocks of this type were made in mahogany or rosewood, but this example has an ebonized wood case. Brass strip inlay, bun feet, pineapple finials, and large, round, white-painted dials are typical of early 19th-century British bracket clocks. (c.1820; ht excluding bracket 48cm/19in; value **H**)

KEY FACTS

Regency bracket clocks
- HANDLES many examples have brass side handles, commonly with lion mask or cornucopia mounts
- CASES a variety of styles was produced but most were made of mahogany or rosewood with ball or bracket feet; the best examples have brass strip inlay in scrolling or floral designs
- DIALS most are round and convex, and of silvered brass, white-painted iron, or enameled copper; hands, plain or pierced, are of simple, elegant design

Victorian bracket clocks
- CASES designs are varied, since originality of case was sometimes considered more important than the movement or any mechanical refinements; cases for chiming clocks were elaborate and heavily carved
- DIALS Arabic numerals were popular from c.1870; any name is often that of the retailer rather than the maker

American shelf clocks
- CASES most are softwood, veneered with mahogany; styles are varied but the majority of cases are decorated on the front with *verre églomisé* panels
- DIALS these are usually of wood or metal, painted white; dials were not usually signed – instead a label with the maker's name was usually pasted to the case
- MOVEMENTS early clocks have wooden movements with steel pivots; thin rolled brass was used from 1830s

**▲ Mantel clock by Cailland
of Paris**

The extensive use of gilt bronze,
or ormolu, on this French
example is highly characteristic
of 19th-century French clocks.
Elaborate cases – particularly
with figures in Classical dress in
miniature interior settings – were
often far more significant than
any mechanical refinements.
White enamel dials of this period
typically feature ormolu bezels.
Cases often represented Classical
or allegorical themes such as
"Love" or "Wisdom." The
combination of the female
figure and a globe on this
example indicates that the
figure represents Urania, the
Muse of astronomy.
*(early 19th century;
ht 45cm/17½in; value* **H***)*

FRENCH BRACKET AND MANTEL CLOCKS

The late 18th to early 19th century was a great period
for French clockmaking, and a tremendous range of
clocks was produced, some of them highly sophisticated.
The work of the casemaker was as important as – and
sometimes more important than – the complexity of the
movement: cases are typically made of marble or bronze,
embellished with rich gilt-bronze (ormolu) mounts, and
generally more ornate than those on British examples.
Most such clocks were made in Paris and reflect the
influence of the Neo-classical style; ornamental motifs
include Classical urns, vases, palmettes, festoons, and
swags. One notable design – intended to illustrate the
technical sophistication of the clock – is the lyre clock,
which features a central gridiron pendulum with metal
rods like the strings of a lyre. The multiple rods that
form the gridiron pendulum expand and contract at
different rates and in varying directions with changes in
temperature, ensuring that the length of the pendulum
remains constant and the clock highly accurate.

Most late 18th-century French mantel clocks feature
round, convex dials, usually enameled in white with
black numerals. A few rare and highly collectible clocks
produced in the 1790s have Revolutionary dials: in 1793
the Revolutionary government decreed that clocks and
watches should show decimal time, with ten hours in a
day and one hundred minutes for each hour. This system
was, however, very short-lived.

Classical influences continued into the Empire
period, but case designs became ever more ornamental
and elaborate. Some were miniature replicas of the
furnishings of the period, with figures in Grecian
dress seated at tables or with musical instruments.
As industrial production was encouraged by the French
government, mechanisms were increasingly standardized
– most were fitted with an anchor escapement.

A huge variety of clocks was made in the mid- to late
19th century. A distinctive French design of the second
half of the 19th century was the mass-produced, black
marble mantel clock, assembled from pre-shaped marble
or marble-faced cement. Polished black slate was often
used for facings to reduce costs. Only the better-quality
pieces, embellished with bronze relief decoration or such
mechanical refinements as a perpetual calendar or moon
phase dials, are of interest to collectors today. Other
designs included the four-glass clock (from *c*.1850),
featuring four panes of glass, and 18th-century revival
styles, most of which were produced in gilt metal in the
later 19th century. Most 19th-century examples are of
eight-day duration. After *c*.1870 many cheaper versions
of ormolu clocks were made of inferior gilt spelter.

◀ Mantel clock

Many 18th-century styles were
revived in the 19th century, but
objects made during this period
are generally more ornate than
the originals. The figures on this
French clock are copied from
late 18th-century Neo-classical
designs, but the use of gilt scrolls
is typical of the Rococo Revival.
Porcelain panels were also
popular in the mid-19th century.
(c.1860; ht 51cm/20in; value **H***)*

▲ "Marble" mantel clock

In the late 19th century French
clockmakers turned to mass
production to compete with the
inexpensive wood-cased clocks
from the USA. This "marble"
clock, faced with black slate,
would have been assembled
from several parts. The scrolled
pediment, gadrooning, and
mask-head handles show the
influence of Neo-classicism.
(c.1880; ht 46cm/18in; value **B***)*

KEY FACTS

- CASES most have ornate cases made of bronze or
marble, decorated with rich ormolu mounts; mass-
produced marble- or black-slate-faced mantel clocks
were common from the late 19th century and are
generally inexpensive
- DIALS most are round and convex, with ormolu
surrounds; gilt-metal hands were used *c*.1800;
later examples have blued-steel hands
- COLLECTING some clocks were produced with
matching pairs of candelabra or vases, designed to
stand either side of the clock on the mantelpiece;
a complete set is desirable and enhances value

Carriage clocks

Carriage clocks – small, portable, spring-driven clocks with carrying handles – are among the most popular clocks with collectors today. Abraham-Louis Breguet (1747–1823), one of the leading French clockmakers of the late 18th and early 19th centuries, developed this type of traveling clock, called in France a *pendule de voyage*, at the turn of the 19th century. Carriage clocks were made throughout the 19th and early 20th centuries mainly in France, although the largest market for them was in Britain and the USA.

FRANCE

The manufacture of carriage clocks was well established in France by the mid-19th century. Movements were usually made in the Franche-Comté region, Lyons, or Normandy, with the escapements produced by specialist artisans along the French–Swiss border. These escapements were placed on a horizontal platform at the top of the clock, visible through a glazed aperture and thus are called platform escapements. Similar to those used in watches, and are not affected by movement. Makers in Paris assembled the workings of the clock and the case and stamped their marks on the movement.

The cases of carriage clocks are usually rectangular: the earliest versions have a brass frame, cast in one piece, with beveled glass panels on the front, sides, back,

and top, revealing the movement. After *c.*1845 makers assembled cases from several parts, allowing greater variation in design. Cases were made in various patterns and sizes – *mignonnette* (below 11cm/4¼in high); full size (between 14cm/5½in and 23cm/9in high); and giant (over 23cm/9in high). The finest cases were gilded and entirely engraved (including the rear door) with foliate or floral patterns. In the last quarter of the 19th century a relatively small number of carriage clocks with decorative enamel or porcelain panels were produced, which are now highly collectible. Most clocks were sold with close-fitting, leather-covered, wooden carrying cases, but few are still intact.

Dials are generally white enameled copper, with blued-steel hands. As most French clocks were sold in Britain, the signature or name on the dial is often that of a British retailer. A serial number and maker's stamp may also appear on the movement. All French carriage clocks are of eight-day duration with a going barrel; some are timepieces (i.e. without a striking mechanism), while others have complex striking such as *grande sonnerie* (striking both the hour and the quarter hours). Many striking clocks also feature a repeat mechanism: when a button on top of the case is pressed, the last hour or quarter will strike again.

BRITAIN

In Britain carriage clocks were produced in smaller numbers than in France but they are generally of far higher quality, as they were made only by the best makers, often to order. They can be distinguished from French examples by their plainer and heavier cases. Movements feature a fusee instead of a going barrel.

The signature on the dial (and the backplate) is usually that of the maker; the firms of Frodsham, McCabe, and Dent were among the well-known British makers, and also retailed French clocks.

◄ **Carriage clock**
Carriage clocks set with decorative panels of enamel or porcelain were produced in fairly modest numbers during the last quarter of the 19th century. Many of the enameled panels, as seen on this example, depicted idyllic 18th-century pastoral scenes. Here, the panels have been silvered and engraved before being set with enamel plaques; others featured all-over enameling. *Cloisonné* decoration (where enamel was fired into separate compartments divided by wires or pieces of metal) was also popular.
(c.1880; ht 14cm/5½in; value **H***)*

▲ **Carriage clock**
Carriage clocks featuring a simple brass frame, plain white enamel dial, and glass panels were produced well into the 20th century. The case of this French example is of brass, in the *corniche* ("cornice") pattern – the most common case style for mass-produced carriage clocks. This clock is a timepiece so does not chime. It features simple, elegant "moon" pattern hands.
(c.1900; ht 13cm/5in; value **A***)*

◄ **Carriage clock by Charles Frodsham (1810–71)**
Charles Frodsham was the most eminent of the renowned family of British clockmakers. Most British carriage clocks are relatively plain, but this early 20th-century example is particularly fine: it features an engraved dial mask, a white enamel dial, a subsidiary up-and-down dial (indicating power reserve), and a well-proportioned gilt-brass case with simple, but decorative carrying handle.
(c.1905; ht 23cm/9in; value **M***)*

KEY FACTS
- CASE the finest French cases have engraved gilt-brass frames with enameled or porcelain panels
- DIAL French dials often feature the name of a British retailer; British dials more often give the maker's name
- COLLECTING examples with original traveling case and winding key are sought after; more complex clocks are more collectible; British clocks, usually higher quality, are more valuable; replaced escapements reduce value

Precision clocks and chronometers

Clockmakers were continually searching for new ways of making their clocks more accurate. In 1715 George Graham (c.1673–1751) invented the deadbeat anchor escapement, which eliminated all elements of recoil when the pallets engaged the escape wheel, and in 1726 he created a pendulum with a glass, mercury-filled bob that compensated for temperature changes. Such mechanisms were used in precision clocks that in turn were used to regulate other timekeepers and became known as regulators. John Harrison (1693–1776) invented the marine chronometer, which enabled mariners to establish exact longitude at sea.

BRITISH, FRENCH, AND AMERICAN REGULATORS

Regulators were made in Britain and France in the 18th and 19th centuries and in the USA from the end of the 18th century. British longcase and wall regulators had plain mahogany cases and silvered-brass dials. Minutes were indicated on the chapter ring, hours and seconds on subsidiary dials. Early longcase regulators had solid trunk doors and pediment tops; from c.1750 glazed doors and rounded tops were usual. French regulators were elaborate, with ornate finials, a square top, and ormolu mounts. Dials were usually in enamel with a brass bezel. Most regulators were timepieces, so the vibrations of a striking mechanism did not affect accuracy; many had a system of springs for maintaining power to ensure that time was not lost during winding. Graham's mercurial pendulum was used in some regulators; others had gridiron or wood-rod pendulums.

VIENNA REGULATORS

Vienna regulators of exceptional quality were produced during the first quarter of the 19th century. These weight-driven clocks, usually wall-hung, are of two main types: the *Laterndluhr* ("lantern clock") and the more common *Dachluhr* ("rooftop clock"). A few longcase designs were also produced. Cases were relatively plain but well made, with a pediment top. Dials were enameled or of silvered brass, with hours around the chapter ring. Some cases also have a beat scale – a small plaque with equal divisions – to indicate whether the pendulum is swinging equally. From the 1840s cases were more ornate, often with decorative carving. Imitations of varying quality were made in the late 19th and the early 20th century in Silesia and the Black Forest (and also in the USA), with striking mechanisms and enamel dials. The movements of later examples are often of poorer quality.

CHRONOMETERS

Mariners relied on accurate, spring-driven chronometers to calculate longitude so as to work out their position at sea. Chronometers were made from the late 18th century, but most common today are 19th-century examples. The best were made in Britain and France. Most feature a spring detent escapement – more accurate than an ordinary regulator's escapement. Most chronometers were mounted in brass gimbals (pivoted rings) to offset motion at sea, and held in a glazed wooden box with a lid. The case was often mahogany with brass side handles. Most examples are of one-, two-, or eight-day duration, with an engraved, silvered dial. A subsidiary up/down dial shows how long the clock has left to run before rewinding. Dials were usually signed by the maker or retailer and have a serial number.

▲ **Marine chronometer by John Roger Arnold**
Unlike many chronometers, this British example has its original wooden lid – navigators often removed the lids so that they could see the time more quickly; the chronometer was protected by the glazed middle section. The lock and the ivory plaque with the maker's or retailer's name are clearly evident: some original ivories are replaced with plastic ones.
(c.1820; w. 17cm/6¾in; value J)

◄ **Longcase regulator by Depree of Exeter**
This 19th-century British clock features a pediment top, solid trunk door, and finely figured mahogany case. It also has a distinctive British-style regulator dial with the minutes marked around the chapter ring and separate dials to indicate hours and seconds. The restrained design of the (nonetheless expensive) case is typical – its simplicity is intended not to detract from the clock's main purpose: accurate timekeeping.
(c.1850; ht 2.1m/6ft 11in; value H)

► **Vienna regulator**
This fine Austrian regulator is of the *Dachluhr* type, which usually featured a hood and a one-piece trunk with glazed panels. This example has a cherrywood case, six glazed panels, and a steel pendulum rod with a brass-faced, dish-shaped bob; gridiron pendulums of brass and steel rods were also typical.
(c.1825–50; ht 83cm/32½in; value I)

KEY FACTS

British, French, and American regulators
- CASES most British cases are of mahogany and very plain; French cases are more ornate, typically with ormolu mounts
- DIALS British dials have minutes around the chapter ring, with subsidiary dials for seconds and hours
- MOVEMENTS most have a precision deadbeat escapement, often with jeweled anchor pallets to reduce friction; wooden rod, mercurial, or gridiron pendulums were used to balance temperature changes

Vienna regulators
- CASES these are usually in a very fine Classical style, with a pediment top and six or nine glazed sections
- DIALS most are of enamel or silvered brass, with hours around the chapter ring
- MOVEMENTS these are very similar to those on other European regulators and extremely finely made

Chronometers
- CASES most are mahogany, but those made for private yachts may have more expensive veneers such as rosewood; lids are often missing or replaced
- DIALS subsidiary up/down dials showing time left before rewinding were typical; Arabic numerals were common on American 1940s chronometers
- MOVEMENTS escapements are sophisticated and need regular overhauling to keep accurate time

See also Longcase clocks, pp.354–5

Electric clocks

Electricity and magnetism were phenomena known in the ancient world, but the first experiments into magnetic fields produced by electric currents did not take place until the early 19th century. Among the first to experiment with the use of electrically induced magnets to drive clock mechanisms was the Scotsman Alexander Bain (1810–77), who patented an electric clock in the early 1840s. In the 19th century most electric clocks were used as precise master timekeepers, but from the early 20th century electric clocks for domestic use were also produced.

MASTER ELECTRIC CLOCKS

Bain's first electric clock of the 1840s was powered by an earth battery, which supplied an electric current alternately to two coils on either side of a magnetized bar on the pendulum bob. These regular electric impulses maintained the swing of the pendulum. Sliding contacts on the pendulum rod delivered the current alternately to coils in the movement, and the hands of the clock moved forward at each double swing of the pendulum. The movement was usually set in a simple wooden case, either wall-mounted or floor-standing. Most surviving examples of Bain's clock are museum-pieces. In Switzerland Matthäus Hipp (1813–93) developed the Hipp toggle c.1834, although it was not applied to clocks until 1842. This mechanism, featuring a toggle attached to the pendulum, gave an electric impulse only when the swing of the pendulum fell below a given arc. The inventions of Bain and Hipp facilitated the production of master timekeepers, which were much more accurate than purely mechanical clocks.

Further designs for electric master clocks followed in the early 20th century. In 1910 Percival A. Bentley of Leicester patented his "Earth Driven" clock, produced in a variety of case designs: his longcases typically had well-made mahogany cases with beveled glass trunk doors. One of the most precise electric master clocks, the "Shortt Free Pendulum" clock, was developed by William Hamilton Shortt (1882–1971) and Frank Hope-Jones (1867–1950) between 1921 and 1924. This clock was extremely accurate – losing or gaining only one or two-thousandths of a second every day – and was used as a standard timepiece for observatories until the development of the caesium atomic clock in the 1950s.

◀ **Electric wall regulator by L'Heure Electrique**
A clock such as this would have been used to regulate other timekeepers. Like mechanical regulators, this French example has a very plain mahogany case because it was primarily a functional piece.
(late 19th century; ht 1.6m/5ft 3in; value J)

▶ **Electric clock by the Eureka Clock Co.**
The large, vertically mounted and electrically impulsed balance wheel is visible beneath the dial of this British Eureka clock. It has a brass case and would originally have been protected by a glass dome; other case styles include "balloon" cases imitating early 19th-century bracket clocks. On this example the serial and patent numbers feature on the front plate; on other clocks these numbers are marked on the back of the movement.
(c.1910; ht 34cm/13¼in; value E)

▼ **Electric clock by Bulle**
Many clocks by Bulle had skeletonized movements on a mahogany base, but this early piece, made in France, has a serpentine-molded, four-glass, brass case, with the battery in the base. Bulle clocks from the 1930s often have Bakelite plastic cases and nickel-plated, not brass, parts.
(c.1920; ht 34cm/14¼in value D)

DOMESTIC ELECTRIC CLOCKS

Probably the most successful early domestic electric clock was that manufactured between 1909 and 1914 by the Eureka Clock Co. in Clerkenwell, London. Patented in 1906, it used the same principle as Bain's electric clock, but instead of the pendulum the balance wheel was impulsed. Eureka clocks were very well made with a variety of case designs: the most desirable are those in which the movement is visible. This type, like the skeleton clock, was covered by a glass dome.

One of the most common electric clocks found today is the Bulle clock, invented by Monsieur Favre-Bulle. This clock was patented in 1922 in Britain, but most examples were manufactured in France; production ceased at the beginning of World War II. The earliest Bulle clocks have circular mahogany bases, with the battery housed in a vertical brass pillar and the movement covered by a glass dome; in later examples the battery is housed in the base. In the 1930s some electric shelf clocks with plastic cases operating from mains electricity were produced: these are becoming increasingly collectible with the growing popularity of 1930s Art Deco pieces and the interest in such early plastics as Bakelite.

KEY FACTS

- CARE glass domes supplied with skeletonized Eureka and Bulle clocks may be missing and are difficult to replace; reversing the battery connections of a non-working Bulle clock may be sufficient to restart it; if a Bulle clock requires a battery, this should be no more powerful than 1½ volts
- COLLECTING 19th-century electric master clocks are rare; the most collectible Eureka clocks are those with a visible oscillating balance wheel; visible movements are generally more desirable than concealed ones

See also Novelty clocks, pp.362–3

Novelty clocks

Clocks have always exerted fascination because of their complex mechanisms. Since the 17th century clockmakers have created unique timekeepers that incorporate musical work, mechanical figures, elaborate cases and dials, and complicated striking mechanisms. Most novelty clocks available today were produced during the 19th century (particularly in France), when in the face of mass production there was a great demand for unusual clocks. These novelty clocks were fashioned in numerous designs and with a great variety of intricate and complicated mechanisms.

AUTOMATON CLOCKS

One of the most popular types of novelty clock was the automaton clock, featuring automata or mechanical figures. The earliest automaton clocks were made in the late 16th century, especially in Germany and central Europe, and include such devices as griffins that flapped their wings and opened and closed their beaks at the striking of each hour. In the 18th and 19th centuries rocking ships, phases of the moon (on a revolving dial), and figures of musicians playing were common. These features were often fitted in the dial arch of longcase and bracket clocks. Some of the most elaborate 19th-century examples from France and Switzerland have very ornate cases with figures appearing through doors, windmills with turning sails, and rocking ships.

Most automaton clocks available today are of eight-day duration and are spring-driven, with a third winding hole for winding the concealed automaton mechanism, musical work, and/or a quarter-hour striking mechanism. Many automata have minor damage, and prospective buyers should always make sure that the automata work before purchasing.

▶ Automaton clock
The chased gilt-bronze case of this fine French automaton clock is in the form of a rocky cave and encloses a rocking ship against a painted background. This piece has musical work, playing three tunes either in sequence or individually.
*(1840; ht 47cm/18½in; value **H**)*

▶ Cuckoo clock
This fine Black Forest cuckoo clock is spring-driven (most were weight-driven) and intended to stand on a shelf or table rather than to hang from a wall. It has an ornately carved walnut case; the cuckoo emerges from an aperture above the dial. This clock has a high-quality British-style fusee movement, whereas most table cuckoo clocks had barrel movements. Carved bone hands and numerals were common on these clocks.
*(mid-19th century; ht 65cm/ 25½in; value **H**)*

◀ Picture clock
The fashion for novelty clocks sparked a variety of inventive designs, including the picture clock, where a movement was housed behind a painted canvas. The dial appeared through a hole in the canvas, often, as in this French example, as the clock on a church tower in a rustic landscape. Many also had a musical movement concealed behind the canvas, operated by pulling a trip to one side.
*(c.1840; ht 70cm/27½in; value **G**)*

BLACK FOREST CLOCKS

Clocks have been made in Germany's Black Forest region since the late 17th century, but most pieces on the market today are from the 18th and 19th centuries. In the 18th century a cottage clockmaking industry grew up, making wall-hung, weight-driven, 30-hour clocks with anchor escapements and long pendulums. With the great local tradition of woodcarving, and the high cost of brass, clockmakers used wood for almost all features of the clock: the shield-shaped, painted wooden dial, often decorated with floral motifs, was fixed onto a wooden frame housing the movement – also mostly of wood. In the 19th century the clockmaking industry turned to mass production in the face of competition from mass-produced, wooden-cased clocks from the USA. Painted shield clocks were still popular, but most 19th-century examples have steel or brass rather than wooden movements. One of the most famous types of Black Forest clock is the cuckoo clock, supposedly first made by Franz Anton Ketterer c.1730; table cuckoo clocks were made from the 1850s. Cuckoo clocks have elaborate, carved wood cases, often in the form of a hunting lodge or chalet. Some have a matching carved pendulum bob and weights modeled as pine-cones. The wooden cuckoo usually pops out of an aperture on the hour and the half hour; the finest clocks also feature musical work, with birdsong emitted by two small pipes with miniature bellows inside the case. The more unusual trumpeter clocks, from c.1857, are similar, but have trumpeters rather than a cuckoo.

SKELETON CLOCKS

The skeleton clock evolved in France in the mid-18th century, probably out of the desire of the great French clockmakers of the time to show off their skill. The pierced or fretted brass frame revealed the mechanism, which typically featured cut and pierced brass plates secured by blued-steel screws. The base was usually of marble or wood, decorated with elaborate gilt-bronze mounts, and the clock was covered with a glass dome to protect the movement from dust. Most dials were of white enamel, with the center often cut out to reveal the movement behind. Usually made to commission for wealthy patrons, French clocks were of extremely high quality, featuring sophisticated mechanical refinements, calendarwork, and often fine gridiron pendulums.

The skeleton clock was not introduced in Britain until c.1820; production tailed off by 1890 and stopped in 1910. British skeletons usually have a fusee movement, an anchor escapement, an engraved and silvered or white-painted brass dial, and blued-steel hands. Dials were often pierced or fretted, with the dial center cut out. Because the movements were on display, they were usually very finely finished, and the frame was lacquered or gilded. Like French skeletons, British pieces usually sat on marble or wooden bases, often with a velvet-covered center; the base had a step or groove to hold the glass dome cover.

Before the mid-19th century fine skeleton clocks were made in Britain by a few individual makers; after that time (following the Great Exhibition of 1851) they were produced in large numbers by specialized manufacturers. Skeleton clocks became virtuoso pieces of design, with elaborate, scalloped, pierced, and fretted frames, often modeled on famous buildings – on some pieces the hands are hardly visible against the profusion of miniature spires and arches. Early skeleton clocks are timepieces, whereas these complex clocks strike the hour and sometimes the half hour on a gong, visible behind the clock. Some of the most elaborate skeleton clocks strike on two or more bells or have musical chimes.

MYSTERY CLOCKS

The earliest mystery clocks date from the 17th century, but the principal period of mystery clock production was the 19th century in France. They are so called because there is no apparent connection between the pendulum and the movement; or no apparent connection between the movement and the hands. These perplexing clocks were usually spring-driven, and the visible pendulum, which mysteriously appears to swing unaided, was therefore a mainly decorative feature added for intrigue. The pendulum was often held by a bronze or spelter (an alloy of zinc) figure, and the movement in the marble base: each impulse of the escapement caused the figure to rotate virtually imperceptibly to the right and left, and this rotating movement in turn enabled the pendulum to swing. Another design was that of a glass dial supported by a column: the dial kept the time without any visible connection to the movement. The quality of the figure determines the price of the clock – those with bronze statues are the most highly sought after.

▲ Mystery clock
The movement of this French clock is housed in the globe held by the figure: the large, three-pronged pendulum appears to be powered on its own but in fact it only moves because it is attached to the rocking globe. A small pendulum inside the globe is the true regulator.
(c.1890; ht 1.1m/3ft 7in; value **H**)

▲ "Rolling ball" clock
In the early 19th century Sir William Congreve (1772–1828) invented an ingenious variation on the skeleton clock, which was known as the "rolling ball" clock and featured an escapement impulsed by a rolling ball moving across a tilted plane. Few were made in the early 19th century, but many reproductions have been produced commercially in the 20th century.
(c.1970; ht 29cm/11in; value **F**)

◄ Skeleton clock
The movement is clearly visible behind the white-painted, cut-out dial of this fairly simple, brass-framed, British piece. This skeleton is a simple timepiece, and not as desirable as those with more complex movements.
(c.1870; ht 41cm/16in; value **D**)

KEY FACTS

Automaton clocks
- DESIGNS automata were often combined with complex musical workings
- CONDITION automata should always be original and in good working order as they are difficult to fix

Black Forest clocks
- CONDITION wooden cases, dials, and movements may suffer from woodworm or be cracked or split; wooden carvings should be intact
- COLLECTING the finest examples also play music

Skeleton clocks
- DESIGNS the best pieces have ornate pierced and fretted frames (perhaps modeled as a cathedral), an original glass dome, complex striking, and sometimes chimes
- CARE cleaning should be carried out by specialists; broken or missing glass domes are difficult to replace
- COLLECTING the more complicated the design and mechanism, the more collectible the clock; original domes are important

Mystery clocks
- COLLECTING figures should be original; bronze is more desirable than spelter; bad repairs reduce value

Barometers

The barometer – an instrument for measuring atmospheric pressure – was invented by the Italian philosopher and mathematician Evangelista Torricelli in 1643–4. Torricelli discovered that the height of mercury in a glass tube immersed upside down in a cistern of mercury is dependent on atmospheric pressure. The British scientist Robert Boyle was the first to relate changes in the height of the mercury to variations in the weather, and the first domestic barometers were made from the 1670s. Barometers were often fitted with a thermometer, calibrated with the Royal Society scale from 0 to 90 degrees until *c.*1725 and the Fahrenheit scale thereafter.

STICK BAROMETERS

The stick barometer, the earliest and simplest type, consists of a long, straight, glass tube of mercury immersed in a glass cistern full of mercury. Late 17th-century British examples are mounted on a wooden walnut-veneered frame, decorated with Baroque-style twist pillars and fretted scrolls, and have a solid walnut cistern cover and a silvered-brass graduated scale (the "register plates") at the top with a recording pointer. Made by clockmakers, most follow the form of contemporary clocks.

The closed-cistern stick barometer is usually attributed to Daniel Quare (1649–1724) in 1695: being sealed, it was more easily transportable. Most early 18th-century barometers found today are of this type. Made mainly in London, they are similar to late 17th-century models but tend to have shorter hoods, gilt finials, and plainer cases. Mahogany veneer was used from *c.*1740.

While earlier barometers followed clock styles, later 18th-century examples were influenced more by furniture. After the mid-18th century cases became plainer, the engraving on the register plates less ornate, and trunks narrower; the influence of long-case clocks disappeared. From *c.*1750 the Vernier scale, accurate to one-hundredth of an inch, was used for mercury readings, and the principal weather indications of "fair," "changeable," and "rain" were standardized. Hinged glass doors to protect the register plates appeared at the end of the 18th century.

In the early 19th century finely crafted barometers featured stringing in dark ebony or lighter woods. From *c.*1840 rosewood as well as mahogany was used for cases, and ivory or paper for the register plates. The "Admiral Fitzroy" barometer, a popular design by the British meteorologist Admiral Robert Fitzroy (1805–65), featured a glazed, rectangular oak case, paper register plates, a thermometer, and a storm glass – a bottle of crystals in a camphor solution that supposedly forecast weather changes. Two recording pointers allowed atmospheric pressure to be recorded on successive days.

The stick barometer went out of fashion in favor of the aneroid barometer in the early 20th century, but earlier designs were reproduced on a limited scale.

► Angle barometer by Howorth

The angle barometer was never as popular as the stick or wheel barometers because of its awkward design. This type, featuring two tubes, was invented in the second quarter of the 18th century, reputedly by Charles Orme (1688–1747), to reduce the length of the unwieldy horizontal arm without reducing the barometer's scale. *(c.1820; ht 1m/3ft 3in; value* **H***)*

◄ Stick barometer by J. Ramsden

Bow-fronted stick barometers were particularly popular between 1815 and 1830. In this British example the bow shape emphasizes the fine figuring of the mahogany veneer. Many barometers of this type have an ebony or ebonized cistern in an urn shape, showing the influence of the fashionable Neo-classical style. *(c.1820; ht 1m/3ft 3in; value* **H***)*

ANGLE BAROMETERS

The angle or "signpost" barometer uses the same principle as the stick barometer, but the upper part of the tube is bent. Invented in the 1670s and made until *c.*1880, this design was intended to give a more accurate reading, as the mercury moved over a greater length in the upper part of the tube. However, it was less accurate than hoped and never widely popular because of its expense and its unwieldy shape. Rarer than other types, angle barometers are particularly collectible today.

Barometer-makers invented new designs to obscure the awkward form: in the early 18th century the maker John Patrick mounted the angle barometer on a square or rectangular wooden frame with a large mirror in the center and a thermometer on the other side to balance the design. To reduce the horizontal part of the arm without reducing the scale, some makers used two or three tubes, set side by side and angled at different heights, so that the tubes would cover the full scale.

WHEEL BAROMETERS

The wheel barometer, invented in 1663 by Robert Hooke (1635–1703), featured a U-shaped tube with long and short arms. A float resting on the mercury in the short arm is attached to a lighter counterweight by a thread over a pulley wheel, which in turn is connected to a pointer on a dial. The movement of the mercury in the tube raises or lowers the float, rotating the pointer. The wheel barometer was not made in large numbers in Britain until *c.*1770, when the "banjo" design was introduced by Italian glassblowers and

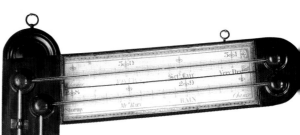

▼ Wheel barometer by Belloni

This British "banjo" wheel barometer is of the "five dial," scrolled-pediment type and is fitted with a hygrometer, a thermometer, a clock, and a spirit level as well as a dial. More usually, the five dial barometer is seen with a convex mirror in the center. The squared case features directly above and below the dial were introduced *c.*1830. *(c.1835; ht 1.3m/4ft 3in; value* **G***)*

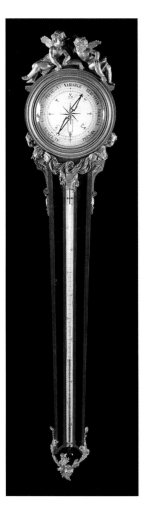

◄ Barometer

Barometers were produced in France from the late 17th century and tended to be highly decorative. Like French clocks, this barometer has an elaborate gilded wood case with ormolu mounts. Other examples were made in tortoiseshell and *vernis Martin*, in contrast to the more restrained lines of British barometers. As in Britain, however, makers usually followed the styles of contemporary furniture.
(late 19th century; ht 1.1m/ 3ft 7in; value H)

► "Admiral Fitzroy" barometer

Admiral Robert Fitzroy, first Superintendent of the British Meteorological Department, produced a detailed system for forecasting the weather and designed a highly sophisticated barometer, which was named after him. Its two recording pointers – one for "Yesterday," the other for "Today" – enabled atmospheric pressure to be recorded on successive days.
(c.1875; 1.3m/4ft 3in; value D)

ANEROID BAROMETERS

Invented by the French engineer Lucien Vidie in 1843, the aneroid ("liquid-free") barometer completely transformed barometer making. Instead of mercury, it featured a small, vacuumed, metal chamber that rose and fell with atmospheric pressure change. Very accurate and easily portable, by *c.*1900 it was the most successful type of barometer. Aneroid barometers were initially used by scientists, surveyors, and engineers, but from *c.*1860 models were made for the home in a wide variety of case designs, from round brass cases to marble mantel ornaments; some were fitted into mantel or carriage clocks. Imitation "banjo" wheel barometers were also popular. Domestic versions featured silvered-brass or less expensive cardboard dials; marine barometers had enamel or porcelain dials, less likely to corrode in sea air. Pocket aneroid barometers, used by travelers and climbers, were produced *c.*1860 by the firm of Negretti & Zambra. Most were fitted in leather-covered wooden cases; some also had a scale on the dial for measuring altitude, a curved mercury thermometer, or a compass.

► Wall aneroid barometer

This British aneroid barometer has an elaborately carved oak case, characteristic of late 19th- and early 20th-century examples. It also imitates the "banjo"-style case used for wheel barometers. Fewer barometers were made with open dials revealing the mechanism, so examples such as this piece are generally more valuable than those with ordinary dials.
(1930s; ht 81cm/32in; value C)

instrument-makers. The "banjo" wheel barometer, the most popular type of wheel barometer in the 19th century, consists of a dial and thermometer in a banjo-shaped wooden case. The silvered-brass dial has a blued-steel indicating hand and a brass fixed hand for recording readings. The scale, measured in inches, ranged from 71 to 79cm (28–31in), the average atmospheric pressure in northern Europe, and was divided into tenths or twentieths of an inch. Later examples are usually equipped with more detailed scales graduated to hundreths of an inch.

Many wheel barometers were also fitted with a spirit level at the bottom for checking that the barometer was hung vertically – if it was not level, the float would jam. Another useful device was the hygrometer, indicating humidity (which, like temperature, affected the height of the mercury): a beard of oats, which curled and uncurled with changes in air moisture, was set on a dial with the indications "moist" ("damp" from *c.*1800) and "dry."

Before *c.*1825 most wheel barometer cases were veneered in mahogany, with the best examples made in satinwood, maple, or pearwood. From *c.*1815 to *c.*1825 "Sheraton shell" inlay, copied from Regency furniture, was especially fashionable as a form of decoration. The mid-19th century saw the appearance of the "onion" or "tulip" top case, and the finest examples were veneered in mahogany or rosewood, inlaid with mother-of-pearl, tortoiseshell, and brass. Later 19th-century cases, influenced by the 1851 Great Exhibition, tended to use solid wood (often oak) cases, with increasingly elaborate carving. The wheel barometer was superseded by the aneroid barometer in the late 19th century.

KEY FACTS

Stick barometers
- DESIGNS the Vernier scale was used from *c.*1750; register plates were usually made of silvered brass until 1840, bone and ivory thereafter
- COLLECTING barometers made in the late 17th to early 18th century are very rare and valuable today

Angle barometers
- DESIGNS some were mounted on a wooden frame with a mirror and thermometer
- COLLECTING few were made after *c.*1880, and fewer were made than other types, so they highly sought after

Wheel barometers
- DESIGNS the "banjo" shape was the most popular design from the late 18th century; scroll pediments were fairly standard after 1825; "Sheraton shell" inlay was used *c.*1815–25; convex glass mirrors were put in the center from *c.*1840; best later Victorian examples are inlaid with brass, mother-of-pearl, and tortoiseshell
- COLLECTING most British barometers are signed by Italians, who dominated the industry

Aneroid barometers
- DESIGNS case shapes were varied, but the "banjo" style was especially popular; wheel barometer types were made from the 1860s; pocket examples were produced from *c.*1860

Watches

Pocket watches

The first pocket watches, made during the second half of the 16th century, were powered by a three-wheel train, a fusee, and a verge escapement. By the beginning of the 17th century the familiar four-wheel train was introduced when it was realized that a higher wheel count effected a smoother transmission of power. Distinctively, watches of this early date have only one hand – this was typical until the late 17th century. Reflecting the puritanical climate of the period, British mid-17th-century watches are usually either very plain or decorated only with simple engraving. Continental watchmakers created watches with highly colored and beautifully painted enamel cases. Watches pre-dating 1700 are scarce.

► Verge watch by Daniel Quare
Quare was an important British watchmaker based in London, whose work is collectible today. This gold verge pocket watch, which is signed and numbered "2112" on the back plate features a fine champlevé dial.
(c.1700; diam. 5cm/2in; value **H**)

BEFORE 1800

By the end of the 17th century Britain was producing the finest and most innovative watches. A particular feature of watches before c.1720 is the *champlevé* dial, made of metal inlaid with black wax; after c.1720 enameled dials were more popular. A watch with a *champlevé* dial, verge fusee movement, and pair cases (inner and outer cases) can be dated to the late 17th or early 18th century. Minute hands were introduced during this period and provided more accurate time readings. Watches at this time were mostly the preserve of members of the court and wealthy merchants.

During the second half of the 18th century, watches became more generally accessible, as the methods of production became more advanced. The pair-cased verge watch was the most common. Component parts were largely unchanged from the late 17th century; although usually made of silver, they were also made of gold.

AFTER 1800

The general construction of the watch did not change until the very beginning of the 19th century when watchmakers in continental Europe started to produce slimmer watches, often still using the traditional verge escapement. High-quality, decorative, enameled cases are often a feature of watches of c.1800; some were produced with novelty cases in the shape of violins, beetles, pistols, and snuff-boxes.

During the mid-19th century the keyless watch with winding as an inbuilt mechanism was introduced, and by the 1870s most pocket watches were keyless. Watches became slimmer in design and several different

types were introduced, the most common being open-faced (glazed front, hinged back cover), half-hunting-cased (hinged front cover with small glazed aperture, chapter ring, and hinged back cover), and hunting-cased (hinged covers at both the front and back). During the 19th century the two dominant types of escapement were the cylinder and the lever. The cylinder, although widely used, was eventually superseded by the more efficient lever.

While complicated and precision watches have been produced throughout watchmaking history, these were often one-off pieces or regarded as scientific instruments rather than practical, everyday watches. Toward the end of the 19th century, however, a great variety of special features was added to more standard pocket watches, including repeating mechanisms that sounded the hours, quarter hours, and sometimes also the minutes, calendarwork, chronograph (stopwatch) mechanisms, and moonphases. Such watches typify the high-quality Swiss work produced at the end of the 19th century and are highly collectible.

▲ Hunting-cased watch
Watches such as this Swiss gold piece, which features not only a repeating mechanism and calendarwork but also a moonphase and a chronograph, are very highly sought after. A piece with this many additional features may be fairly valuable.
(c.1900; diam. 6cm/2½in; value **G**)

▼ Verge watch
This French heart-shaped gold watch is intricately set with pearls and embellished with an enameled picture. The unusual form combined with high-quality decoration is therefore highly collectible. The dainty size of this piece, as well as the feminine design and decoration, make it an ideal lady's watch. Enameled watches are very sought after: value will depend on the quality, subject-matter, make, and condition. Any restoration will considerably reduce the value of the piece.
(c.1820; diam. 4.5cm/1¾in; value **I**)

KEY FACTS

Before 1800
- CASES in the 16th and early 17th centuries, most cases were single and either plain, engraved, or enameled – when decoration is present it is usually of a religious nature; later cases were typically pairs and of silver, gold, or gilt metal
- DIALS engraved metal was popular until the mid-17th century; champlevé dials were typical in the late 17th and early 18th centuries
- HANDS most clocks featured a single hand until the late 17th century; two hands were typical thereafter, usually in the "beetle and poker" design
- MOVEMENT most watches from the 18th century were fitted with a verge escapement
- COLLECTING even 19th-century copies of early watches are reasonably valuable

After 1800
- DESIGNS watches were slimmer after c.1800 especially in continental Europe; by the 1870s the majority of pocket watches were keyless
- CASES most are decorative and of painted enamel; novelty shapes popular in the early 19th century; from the mid-19th century cases were of three principal types: open-faced, half-hunting-cased, or hunting-cased
- DIALS enameled dials are typical; many watches also feature several subsidiary dials
- MOVEMENTS various escapements were used, including verge, cylinder, and lever mechanisms
- COLLECTING watches with chronographs, repeating mechanisms, moonphases, and calendars are especially collectible

Important makers
British: Thomas Tompion (1638–1713); Daniel Quare (1648–1724); George Graham (1674–1751); E.J. Dent: 1790–1853; Charles Frodsham (1810–71); French: Abraham-Louis Breguet (1747–1823); Vacheron & Constantin (est. 1755)

Wristwatches

The watch was first worn on the wrist in the early years of the 20th century. Early wristwatches were in the form of small pocket watches that had been converted to wristwatches either by the addition of wire strap lugs soldered on to the case or by the use of a leather pocket, designed to hold the watch and fix onto the wrist with a strap. Such watches are easily identifiable as they are usually profusely chased and engraved on the reverse and the dial is not positioned in the usual wristwatch manner. These early wristwatch conversions are historically interesting but generally of low value. The first true wristwatch was produced by the Parisian firm of Cartier *c.*1904 for the aviator Alberto Santos Dumont; this design became known as the "Santos" and is still in production today. The Swiss firm of Rolex, at the forefront of watch production, began to manufacture wristwatches as early as 1911. With the outbreak of World War I, wristwatches were issued to servicemen, and many interesting variations of these watches can be found. The "Trench" watch is one of these and is readily identifiable by its pierced grille, intended to protect the glass and dial. Until the 1920s watches were generally of plain circular form with either silvered or enamel dials, Swiss movements, and either chrome, silver, or gold cases.

AFTER 1920

During the 1920s the range of wristwatch styles broadened to include rectangular, square, oval, and octagonal shapes. Most designs featured simple clean lines and bold numerals. During the 1930s case and dial designs became more abstract, numerals were more exaggerated and elongated, and two-color cases and bold Odeonesque features were introduced. Watches from the 1920s and 1930s are among the most sought after by collectors: a classic style coupled with a maker renowned for high standards such as Patek Philippe, Rolex, Cartier, Jaeger le Coultre, Audemars Piguet, and Vacheron & Constantin would be especially desirable.

In the 1940s watch styles resembled jewelry designs of the period with styles such as the "cocktail" watch being typical. After the outbreak of World War II standard wristwatches were issued to members of the armed forces. These watches can be identified by their robust steel construction and their characteristic black dials and luminous numerals. The British Government property mark in the form of an arrow on the back of the case can also help to confirm

▲ **Lady's wristwatch**
This decorative Swiss watch featuring diamonds and synthetic rubies is unsigned. Its angular form is highly typical of the Art Deco period.
(c.1930; l. of face including setting 5cm/2in; value G)

▲ **Wristwatch by Rolex**
During the 1920s this classic silver cushion-form wristwatch was the height of fashion and it is still extremely popular and collectible today. This example, which was made in Switzerland, features 15 jewels and a Glasgow import mark for 1927 on its case.
(1927; diam. 3cm/1in; value E)

▲ **Military wristwatch by Longines**
Most eminent firms designed military wristwatches, and they are becoming an increasingly popular area of collecting. This Swiss example is made of steel and is water resistant. It is slightly unusual in that it features a white dial – most World War II wristwatches had black dials.
(1940s; diam. 3.5cm/1¼in; value D)

the identification of British watches. Since military wristwatches were made by most eminent makers, including Longines, I.W.C., and Omega, collectors are taking an increased interest in these watches.

From the late 1940s into the early 1950s wristwatch design captured the futuristic look that was popular at the time: hands and baton numerals were severely pointed and streamlined and lugs were typically in exaggerated teardrop shapes. The inclusion of such features as calendars, moonphases, and chronographs was also highly characteristic of the period.

The following decade, the 1960s, produced many abstract and interesting watch designs, which are instantly recognizable as products of their age. While these characteristically bright-colored watches in new synthetic materials are currently of little interest to the serious watch collector, they are avidly sought after by followers of modern design. Most wristwatch collectors today seek the classic designs from the 1930s, 1940s, and 1950s. When assessing value, the style, maker, model, and complexity of a watch are vital considerations, as are condition and any replacement parts. Wristwatches of recent manufacture are also sought after when made by one of the exclusive designers.

► **Triple calendar and moonphase wristwatch by Universal**
In general, the more complex a good-quality watch is, the more highly sought after it will be – such a complicated and sophisticated example as this Swiss gold watch, featuring a triple calendar and moonphase, will therefore be very collectible. Its classic design also adds to its desirability.
(1950s; diam. 3.5cm/1¼in; value G)

KEY FACTS

Before 1920
- DESIGNS these were usually of plain circular form with wire strap lugs and enamel dials; the "Trench" watch, distributed to soldiers in World War I, featured a protective grille over the glass dial-cover
- DIALS these were often unsigned – check the movement for the maker's signature

After 1920
- DESIGNS unusual case shapes were typical; most military wristwatches from World War II are slightly larger than average, with black dials
- COLLECTING calendars, chronographs, moonphases, and repeating features can add value; automatic wristwatches are more sought after than manual-wind watches; British military watches are usually inscribed on the reverse with a Government issue arrow

Collectible makers
Patek Philippe, Rolex, Cartier, Vacheron & Constantin, Audemars Piguet, Jaeger le Coultre

high in the wood · high oft
aloft i rise · when low

Pioneers of the Arts and Crafts Movement, which emerged in the 1860s and endured until the late 1930s, were united in their rejection of the stylistic eclecticism and historicism that dominated mass-produced Victorian furnishings and artifacts. They criticized such items for their over-ornamentation and general poor quality. Underpinning this reaction was the belief that the decoration of household objects should be an integral part of their design, rather than a superfluous addition. To Arts and Crafts designers this meant, in practice, a revival of medieval standards of craftsmanship and the adoption of unpretentious patterns and motifs, usually derived from the medieval English and secularized Gothic styles. Thus, on many of the fine examples of Arts and Crafts that survive, decoration, when employed, is in the form of floral and faunal imagery. The movement was particularly successful in Britain and the United States, where some designers and craftsmen produced works of exceptional quality utilizing traditional hand-crafting methods. However, while some designers and craftsmen may have rejected techniques of mass-production, there were many who recognized their potential, and who were able to embrace them without losing sight of the Arts and Crafts principles.

Detail of tapestry by William Morris, "Greenery" (left) This tapestry, designed for Morris by John Henry Dearle, harks back to the Middle Ages, both in style and content, and depicts a medieval woodland scene. (c.1892).
Table lamp by Grueby (above) The base of this lamp – hand thrown with a thick green glaze and hand-carved design – is characteristic of the work of this American potter of the New England School (c.1905).

Arts and Crafts: Introduction

The Arts and Crafts Movement, which aimed to revive quality craftsmanship in the face of industrial mass production – and as such was as much a social as an artistic movement – was born in Britain during the 1860s, and spanned the period from the early years of Queen Victoria's reign (1837–1901) to the beginning of World War II. The popularity of the style grew in opposition to trends for the extravagant revival styles that were admired by most Victorians but ardently rejected by Arts and Crafts enthusiasts, who favored artistic, individually crafted wares.

INFLUENCES
One of the champions of the movement was the art and social critic John Ruskin (1819–1900), who railed against industrialization in his treatise *The Stones of Venice* (1851–3). The Gothic Revivalist architect Augustus Welby Northmore Pugin (1812–52) was also highly influential, promoting the Gothic architecture of the Middle Ages as representing a better, pre-industrial era.

The historicism of earlier decades continued but with a preference for simpler styles which reflected the skills of the individual rather than the power of the machine. Also influential were Japanese art and design following the reopening of Japan's borders to the West in 1853. First shown at the 1862 London International Exhibition, the arts of Japan (ceramics, ivory, prints, and textiles) influenced those in Europe and the USA. Leading designers working in this style include Christopher Dresser (1834–1904) and E.W. Godwin (1833–86), whose use of ornament and stark geometrical designs contributed to the foundations of 20th-century Modernism.

▲ Vitrine by George Walton
The simple, elegant form and slim, tapering, legs of this mahogany vitrine are typical of the furniture of the Scottish designer Walton (1867–1933).
(c.1900; ht 1.5m/5ft; value H)

◄ "Morris" chair by Philip Webb (1831–1915) for Morris, Marshall, Faulkner & Co.
This reclining chair of ebonized wood features the original tapestry upholstery in a design typical of Arts and Crafts.
(c.1870; ht 99cm/39in; value I)

BRITAIN
The major pioneer in the emphasis on using traditional skills to create beautifully crafted objects was William Morris (1834–96). From the mid-1860s his London-based design company, Morris, Marshall, Faulkner & Co. (later Morris & Co.), promoted a broadly coordinated style based on medieval sources, using local and natural materials and traditional handicraft techniques. Decoration was inspired by natural or medieval themes, with narrative designs from myths and legends being especially characteristic.

The influence of Morris's philosophies led to the foundation of a great many enterprises, including art potteries, furniture and metal workshops, textile studios, and medieval-inspired guilds, all reflecting an individual approach to design and manufacture, and drawing on the talents of graduates, both male and female, from the national government-run schools of art and design. Apart from Morris, leading exponents of the movement in Britain include the industrial studio potteries run by Minton & Co. (est. 1793) and Doulton & Co. (est. 1815) and such notable designers as

William De Morgan (1839–1917), the Martin brothers, Charles Robert Ashbee (1863–1942), Mackay Hugh Baillie Scott (1865–1945), and Charles Rennie Mackintosh (1868–1928). The popularity of the movement was underlined by the establishment in 1884 of the Art Workers' Guild in London and in 1906 of the Arts and Crafts Exhibition Society, where members' work was exhibited annually.

THE UNITED STATES
Arts and Crafts design in the USA dates mainly from the 1870s and is largely confined to architecture, domestic furniture, pottery (including tiles), and metalwork (including lighting). The same principles of craftsmanship and simplicity of design that were hailed by followers of the movement in Britain were supported by their American counterparts, with Ruskin and Morris highly influential figures, particularly on the East Coast. As in Britain, Arts and Crafts wares were shown at exhibition: the first exhibition dedicated solely to the movement was held at Copley Hall in Boston in 1897. The pre-eminent American Arts and Crafts designer was Gustav Stickley (1858–1942); other important furniture designers include Frank Lloyd Wright (1867–1959) and the Greene brothers.

Arts and Crafts pottery divides roughly into two main types: hand-painted wares, examples of which were made at the Rookwood Pottery, in Cincinnati, Ohio, c.1880 to 1941, and at other Ohio-based potteries such as Roseville from 1898; and hand-carved or modeled wares, by such potters as William Grueby (1867–1925) and George E. Ohr (1857–1918). Designs feature organic decoration and experimental glazes. Notable American Arts and Crafts metalwork includes the hand-hammered designs of the Dutch-born metalsmith Dirk Van Erp (1860–1953) and the Roycroft shops as well as the more refined silver wares of Robert Jarvie (1865–1941).

◄ Vase by William Grueby
The form and the moss-green color of this earthenware piece are both characteristic of the work of the American potter Grueby. The thick glaze, which gives the surface of the vase a textured effect similar to that of a watermelon skin, is also typical. Examples by Grueby featuring such details as petals tend to be more valuable than plain pieces; a design in more than one color will also be more sought after.
(c.1900; ht 40cm/15¾in; value H)

Furniture

Although Arts and Crafts furniture cannot be identified by a single style, its designers and makers, who were based mainly in Britain and the USA, shared the same priorities of simplicity in design, modest use of ornament, honesty in construction, and emphasis on the importance of the role of the individual artisan. In practice these ideals were translated into extremely well-made, functional furniture, characteristically based on traditional designs, in which the construction itself was the most important decorative feature. Thus, Arts and Crafts furniture typically incorporated many highly traditional elements, such as exposed mortise-and-tenon joints, dovetailing, faceting and chamfering, and metalwork strap hinges.

Britain

William Morris

Architect, designer, painter, printer, socialist, and poet, Morris was strongly influenced by the ideas of both Ruskin, the art and social critic, and Pugin, the architect who spearheaded the Gothic Revival movement. In 1861 Morris and a group of like-minded friends, including Ford Madox Brown (1821–93) and the painter Dante Gabriel Rossetti (1828–82), set up the firm of Morris, Marshall, Faulkner & Co. in London. Early furniture designs by Philip Webb (1831–1915), an architect and close friend of Morris's, were Neo-Gothic in style and clearly influenced by the furniture designs of Pugin and other Gothic-Revival architects including William Burges (1827–81) and Charles Locke Eastlake (1836–1906). Their expensive, collectible pieces were made by the London-based companies of J.G. Crace and Howard & Sons, and the Lancaster firm of Gillow (est. c.1730). From the 1850s to the 1870s these companies also made their own ranges of plain, simply constructed oak furniture.

In 1875 Morris took sole control of Morris, Marshall, Faulkner & Co. (subsequently known as Morris & Co. or the "Firm") and produced solid, heavy pieces of traditional furniture, usually in mahogany with satinwood inlay. The company also produced a wide range of stained glass, wallpaper, ceramics, and fabrics, mostly at Morris's printworks, the Merton Abbey Workshops (est. 1881), in Surrey. One of its most successful furniture designs of the 1880s was the "Sussex" chair. The original design by Webb – an ash frame with a handwoven rush seat and decoration restricted to turned vertical spindles on the back – was based on a traditional country chair. The design was produced as a single chair, an armchair, a corner chair, a round-seat piano stool, and a settee; round-seated versions were designed by Brown and Rossetti. Another notable design is the "Morris" chair – a large, box-like, adjustable armchair, typically with upholstery also by Morris in medieval-inspired designs.

Under the influence of George Jack (1855–1932) furniture designs of the 1890s made by Morris & Co. were more elaborate than earlier designs and showed the influence of the newly popular Queen Anne Revival style, favored by Webb and the architect Richard Norman Shaw (1831–1912). Typical examples include large mahogany buffets and dressers featuring glazed doors and pierced carving.

▲ **Chair probably designed by Ford Madox Brown**
Made of stained ash with a rush seat, this chair is based on the highly popular "Sussex" chair produced by Morris & Co. The traditional design harks back to simple country styles.
(c.1864–5; ht 86cm/33¾in; value H)

▼ **Cabinet-on-stand by Morris, Marshall, Faulkner & Co.**
The form and decoration of this mahogany, oak, and pine piece reflect the medieval influences that inspired the early practitioners of the Arts and Crafts. Designed by Webb, with panels depicting the legend of St George painted by Morris, it was made for the London International Exhibition of 1862. Such fine pieces are rarely found outside museums. *(1861–2; ht 96cm/37½in; value Q)*

KEY FACTS

- MATERIALS early designs were typically in ebonized wood; later designs are mostly in woods traditionally associated with country furniture such as oak and ash, although some were also made in mahogany; rush seating is common on dining-chairs
- DESIGNS these are handcrafted and based largely on traditional country designs; most pieces are very sturdily made
- DECORATION joints and hinges used in construction play an important part in the decoration of a piece; many armchairs feature fabrics inspired by medieval designs, also by Morris
- COLLECTING all furniture made by Morris & Co. will be valuable and highly collectible; the finest pieces are found only in museums

Marks
Although many copies of the "Sussex" chair have been produced, any originals will be clearly marked – usually with a "Morris & Co." stamp

See also Furniture: Chairs – Country chairs, p.33

Other British makers

Inspired by Morris, a succession of major designers embraced the Arts and Crafts style in Britain. Their interpretations, although varied, all focused on the same fundamental principles of craftsmanship and quality. An early influential figure was Edward William Godwin (1833–86), whose elegant, striking furniture sparked a trend for Japanese design that was to continue into the 1930s. Also notable were the host of medieval-style guilds based mostly in the Cotswolds, and the angular, architectural work of the Scottish designer Charles Rennie Mackintosh (1868–1928). The production of furniture by commercial firms also helped to increase the accessibility of work in the Arts and Crafts style.

▼ Desk probably designed by Edward Godwin

Although Godwin was identified with the Aesthetic Movement, his emphasis on materials and superb construction, as in this Japanese-style desk, echoes principles central to the Arts and Crafts Movement. *(c.1875; ht 75cm/29½in; value M)*

THE AESTHETIC MOVEMENT

The Aesthetic Movement, influenced by stark, unadorned Japanese designs in dark woods and elegant, minimally decorated forms, overlapped with Arts and Crafts both in the ebonized furniture produced by Morris & Co. and in the simple, elegant, Japanese-influenced furniture designed by Godwin. The latter, an architect and designer, was an early pioneer of the Arts and Crafts total design ethic, in which the building, interior decoration, and fittings would all reflect a single ideal. From 1865 he designed furniture for his own architectural practice but after 1870 he was far more successful as a designer of furniture than of buildings. Simplicity, elegance, and refined proportions are the hallmarks of Godwin's exclusive, ebonized wood furniture. Decoration is minimal: molding and carving are virtually eliminated and are replaced with inset panels of embossed Japanese paper, or sometimes with painted or stenciled symmetrical decoration of stylized geometric designs. Godwin's designs were produced by such notable London cabinet-makers as William Wyatt, John Gregory Crace (1809–89), and the firm of Collinson & Lock (est. 1870).

GUILDS AND WORKSHOPS

In the 1880s a large number of Arts and Crafts organizations sprang up in London, with the aims of breaking down the hierarchy between fine and applied art and fostering the ideal of the artist/craftsman. The Century Guild (est. 1882), headed by Arthur Heygate Mackmurdo (1851–1942), the Art Workers' Guild (est. 1884), the Arts and Crafts Exhibition Society (est. 1888), and the Guild of Handicraft (est. 1888), set up in London's East End by Charles Robert Ashbee (1863–1942), brought together the growing number of talented Arts and Crafts furniture designers.

Ernest Gimson (1864–1919), William Lethaby (1857–1931), and Sidney Barnsley (1865–1926) were among the founders of the short-lived Kenton & Co. (1890–92), a London-based furniture company that used professional cabinet-makers to make mahogany and oak furniture. After the demise of Kenton & Co. in 1892, Gimson and Barnsley, along with Barnsley's brother Ernest Barnsley (1863–1926), set up a new workshop in the Cotswolds, south-west England. Gimson's designs, featuring exposed pins and joints, and exploiting the natural color and markings of the wood, were finely executed by carefully trained craftsmen in such local woods as ash, oak, elm, and fruitwoods. Gimson's pieces include rush-seated ladder-back chairs and plain oak furniture, as well as more elaborate cabinets featuring fruitwood, holly, mother-of-pearl, shell, and ivory inlay. After Gimson's death, his foreman Peter Waals still worked to Gimson's designs and in 1920 set up his own workshop in Chalford.

The Guild of Handicraft moved to the Cotswolds in 1902, producing furniture to designs by Charles Francis Annesley Voysey (1857–1941) and Mackay Hugh Baillie Scott (1865–1945). The last in the line of the Cotswold School was Gordon Russell (1892–1980), whose work bridged the gap between the one-off, handmade pieces of Gimson and Barnsley and the need for functional, well-designed, affordable furniture for a mass market.

The Omega Workshops (1913–19), in Bloomsbury, London, established by Roger Fry (1866–1934), was the last of the Arts and Crafts groups. Superficially the group closely resembled the original Morris company, but it celebrated amateur craft skills and was more interested in aesthetics than social reform. Omega furniture to designs by Fry, Duncan Grant (1885–1978), and Vanessa Bell (1879–1961) was made by local cabinet-makers and then painted by Bell, Grant, and many others.

IMPORTANT DESIGNERS

Voysey, one of the most innovative Arts and Crafts furniture designers, never established his own workshop; his designs were produced not only by craftsmen such as William Hall, who had worked for Kenton & Co., but also by commercial cabinet-makers and such piano-makers as Bechstein. From *c.*1895 Voysey produced designs that were simple, elegant, abstract, and stylized, relying heavily on the innate beauty of the wood. Stained oak, large metal strap hinges, and exaggerated, often tapering vertical supports were features popular with Voysey, among other designers, although they had originally been used by Mackmurdo. Other common features (by no means exclusive to Voysey) are heart-shaped decorative motifs and rush chair-seats.

▲ Chair designed by Ernest Gimson

Such superbly constructed individual pieces as this walnut chair with a drop-in upholstered seat were usually made from locally grown wood and crafted by highly skilled, specially trained, local cabinet-makers. *(c.1905; ht 91.5cm/36in; value I)*

▼ Chair designed by Voysey

The plain oak, the tapering, vertical uprights, the traditional rush seating, and the minimal pierced decoration are all typical of Voysey's work. Such an elegantly proportioned chair as this is highly collectible. *(c.1900; ht 1m/3ft 3in; value H)*

► Cabinet designed by Mackay Hugh Baillie Scott

The restrained and symmetrical decoration on this inlaid cabinet (a leading member of the second generation of Arts and Crafts practitioners), is typical of Arts and Crafts furniture. Baillie Scott's work is especially popular in Germany, where he is noted for his furniture designs, commissioned in 1898, for the artist's colony in Darmstadt.
(c.1904; ht 1.2m/3ft 11in; value M)

The same stylish simplicity can be found in the furniture of Baillie Scott, who was strongly influenced by Voysey. His simple, box-like furniture was mass-produced by the firm of J.P White, Bedford, while his other, more complex designs were produced by Ashbee's Guild of Handicraft. Most of Baillie Scott's furniture is in oak or inlaid mahogany, with the color and grain of the wood providing the main decoration.

The two most famous Scottish interpreters of Arts and Crafts furniture were George Walton (1867–1933) and Charles Rennie Mackintosh (1868–1928), both based in Glasgow. Walton set up a design and decorating business in 1888, and in 1896 was commissioned for the overall interior design of the Glasgow Buchanan Street Tea Room, for which Mackintosh provided some of the interior decoration. Walton's highly collectible chairs for Buchanan Street were based on a traditional Scottish design, with a narrow back featuring a pierced heart-shaped motif, curving arms, and a rush seat. Other chair designs by Walton are more elegant and typically have narrow, tapering, outwardly curving legs. Mackintosh designed distinctive high-backed chairs with elliptical panels for the Dutch Kitchen extension that was added to the Argyle Street Tea Rooms (also in Glasgow) in 1906; for the Willow Street Tea Rooms he produced a side-chair in ebonized oak with a rush seat (1903).

COMMERCIAL FIRMS

Far less expensive than the exclusive pieces by the major Arts and Crafts designers was the furniture produced by commercial companies. Liberty & Co., which opened in Regent Street, London, in May 1875, was a staunch supporter of the Aesthetic Movement and also produced and sold a wide range of Arts and Crafts furniture. Ambrose Heal (1872–1959) exhibited regularly at the Arts and Crafts exhibitions in London, and from 1897 his London-based firm of Heal & Son (est. 1800) sold furniture made to his designs, which were strongly influenced by the Cotswold School. Other well-known commercial manufacturers include Timms & Webb and Wylie & Lochhead, both in Glasgow, the firm of John Sollie Henry in London, and the Dryad Works (est. 1907) in Leicester, which specialized in the manufacture of cane and wicker furniture.

▼ Chair designed by Charles Rennie Mackintosh

This chair was designed for the Glasgow Argyle Street Tea Rooms owned by Miss Catherine Cranston. Made of stained oak, with an exaggerated high back and elliptical decoration, it is one of the best known of Mackintosh's designs. His work is characterized by accentuated, tapering verticals, which often intersect with horizontals, and a sophisticated idiosyncratic style. Pieces by Mackintosh rarely come up for sale and always achieve exceptionally high prices.
(1896–7; ht 1.4m/4ft 7in; value P)

► Sideboard produced by Liberty & Co.

One of the leading retail outlets for Arts and Crafts furniture was Liberty & Co., founded by Sir Arthur Lasenby Liberty (1843–1917). Well known for its interest in and support of new artistic ventures, the company sold an extremely successful range of Arts and Crafts furniture, including some pieces by such notable designers as Walton. This sideboard has many features characteristic of Arts and Crafts design, including plain oak construction, symmetrical design, and very restrained decoration.
(c.1910; ht 2.4m/7ft 10in; value H)

KEY FACTS

The Aesthetic Movement
- MATERIALS most pieces are in dark, ebonized woods
- DESIGNS elegant, simple forms with a strong Japanese influence are typical; many of Godwin's designs feature a central cruciform block with radiating stretchers
- COLLECTING all pieces by Godwin are rare and highly sought after; the value of pieces in ebonized wood will depend on the condition, as ebonized furniture is difficult to restore; an original finish in good condition is critical for maximum value

Marks
Godwin's pieces are never marked; attribution is usually based on the style of his few surviving design sketches

Guilds and workshops
- MATERIALS oak is the most typical but other local woods such as elm, ash, and fruitwoods were also used
- DESIGNS most pieces are plain in design; decoration is mainly limited to the effect of the wood's natural grain and color and the construction of joints
- COLLECTING the superb quality and workmanship of pieces by either Gimson or Barnsley will be matched by correspondingly high prices

Important designers
- MATERIALS Voysey: oak is typical of his work
- DESIGNS Voysey: furniture is characteristically of traditional design, often with heart-shaped decoration, long tapering verticals, and rush seating; Baillie Scott: most of his pieces have simple, unadorned, boxy forms; Mackintosh: tall, geometric forms, reflecting his training as an architect, are characteristic
- COLLECTING pieces by well-known makers will be sought after by collectors; all of Mackintosh's work is extremely highly priced and valuable

Commercial firms
- MATERIALS pieces by Liberty & Co. were usually in oak; most pieces by Heal & Son were in oak, with versions also available in mahogany and chestnut
- COLLECTING commercially produced furniture will be more affordable than pieces by leading designers

Marks
Liberty pieces are marked simply "Liberty & Co."

See also Arts and Crafts: Furniture – The United States, pp.374–5

The United States

The majority of American Arts and Crafts furniture produced between the 1890s and the 1920s is of oak and made by or in the style of one of several members of the Stickley family. Such furniture is commonly referred to as "Mission oak," although this term, which suggests a stylistic influence of the early mission churches of the American Southwest, is misleading.

THE STICKLEY FAMILY

Gustav Stickley (1857–1942) was the eldest of six brothers, most of whom worked in the furniture trade. He trained as an architect and designer and in 1898 established the Gustav Stickley Co. in Eastwood, New York State. In 1900 he introduced his "Craftsman" furniture range, the majority of which is of heavy, solid construction in American white oak. Production of Craftsman furniture continued until 1915. From 1901 Stickley produced a magazine called *The Craftsman*, in which examples of his work were shown. Although many Stickley forms, including high-backed settles, stools, and trestle tables, show the influence of 17th-century colonial furniture in their style and use of traditional joinery, the most valuable examples of his work are those that are innovative and more modern in design. Typical forms include both horizontal and vertical slat-back chairs (including rocking-chairs and "Morris" chairs, which were based on the upholstered reclining chair by the British Arts and Crafts designer William Morris), benches, dining-, writing-, and library-tables, fall-front desks, sideboards, bookcases, magazine and umbrella stands, and mirrors. Spindle-sided and spindle-backed chairs in Modernist taste were produced from 1905, perhaps inspired by the furniture designed by Frank Lloyd Wright (1867–1956) in 1904 for Darwin House, near Buffalo, New York State; this style of Stickley furniture is keenly sought after by collectors.

The oak that Stickley used for his furniture was fumed for preservation, a process that imparted a warm patination, which he described as a "friendly" finish. The subtlety and originality of color and patina of his wood is important when assessing value, as is rarity of design. Upholstery is typically in green or brown leather and although original upholstery is preferable, pieces that have been well re-upholstered are still popular with collectors. Most Stickley furniture is in very good condition owing to its sturdy construction and strong, well-reinforced joints.

Albert Stickley and John George Stickley (1871–1921), operating as the Stickley Brothers Co. from c.1890 in Grand Rapids, Michigan, produced furniture in a style similar to that of their brother. Some of their work is marked "Quaint Furniture" but it is not greatly

▲ "Craftsman" bookcase #716 by G. Stickley
This popular design was made in four widths, ranging from approximately 1m to 1.5m (3ft 3in–4ft 11in); the height, however, remained standard at 1.4 meters (4ft 6in). The richly colored oak, exposed jointing, and "arrowhead" drop handles are typical features of Gustav's mature work after 1904.
(c.1905; ht 1.4m/4ft 6in; value K)

▼ Chair by L. & J.G. Stickley
Progressive designs – as typified by this strongly horizontal, oak "Prairie" chair – show the influence of Frank Lloyd Wright, the Glasgow School, and the Vienna Secession. This was one of the firm's most successful designs and is popular with both collectors of modern design and Arts and Crafts enthusiasts.
(c.1905; ht 71cm/28in; value M)

appreciated by collectors. In 1900 Leopold Stickley (1869–1957) left Gustav's Eastwood workshop to establish with John George the firm of L. & J.G. Stickley (known from c.1904 as the Onondaga Shops and from 1906 as Handcraft) in Fayetteville, New York State. Designs include settles, spindle chairs, serving-tables, and bookcases, and are typically produced in carefully finished oak. Upholstery is usually in leather, sometimes fastened with round-headed tacks. Hand-hammered copper hardware is characteristic on furniture in the "Handcraft" range. Better furniture by the brothers compares in quality to the less startling Craftsman pieces by Gustav and, being more widely available than these sought-after designs, has a strong following.

▼ Settle for the Onondaga Shops
Large or unique pieces by L. & J.G. Stickley & Co. such as this mahogany settle, with back and side slats carved with stylized leaves, command prices comparable to those for original Craftsman furniture by Gustav Stickley. The original coarse fabric upholstery of this example renders it particularly desirable.
(c.1905–10; ht 94cm/37in; value L)

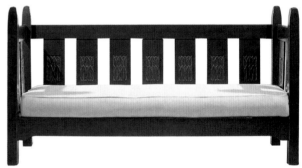

CHARLES ROHLFS, GREENE AND GREENE, AND THE ROYCROFT FURNITURE SHOP

Charles Rohlfs (1853–1936), a successful cabinet-maker in Buffalo, New York State, from c.1890 until the mid-1920s, employed a team of eight craftsmen to execute his furniture designs. Rohlfs participated in the 1902 International Exhibition of Modern Decorative Art in Turin, Italy, and the influence of Art Nouveau is evident in his use of carved or cut-out tendrils. Forms include desks, chairs, small tables, and storage pieces, some with carved Gothic lettering and a signature. The oak used for Rohlfs's pieces is relatively pale compared to the wood used for most American Arts and Crafts furniture. Rohlfs's work is less pure in design than that of Gustav Stickley, but its rarity and high standards of craftsmanship make it extremely popular with collectors.

The brothers Charles Sumner Greene (1868–1957) and Henry Mather Greene (1870–1954) operated to commission in Pasadena, California, in the early 20th century, and their furniture combined high-quality Arts and Crafts workmanship with simple, Chinese-inspired designs in mother-of-pearl or metal inlay. Hardwoods, including teak and ebony, often subtly carved with Oriental motifs, are characteristic. Joinery is usually by squared, ebony pegs. Some of the brothers' work was produced by the furniture-maker John Hall; these pieces are very rare and considered the most finely executed of all American Arts and Crafts work.

▲ Armchair by Greene and Greene

The attention to detail seen in the silver, abalone shell, copper, and pewter inlay on the back of this mahogany chair is typical of the high-quality craftsmanship of the Greene brothers. The combination of mahogany and exposed ebony pegging is a common feature of their work. (*c.*1905; ht 1m/3ft 3in; value **O**)

▼ China cabinet by the Roycroft Furniture Shop

The simple construction and the hammered metal hardware such as the square-faceted door-pulls on this oak cabinet are typical of designs by the Roycrofters. The prominent position of the orb-and-cross mark on the bottom rail is also characteristic. (*c.*1915; ht 1.5m/4ft 11in; value **J**)

The Roycrofters were an idealistic Arts and Crafts community founded in 1895 in East Aurora, New York State, by Elbert Hubbard (1856–1915). Hubbard, who has been called the "American William Morris," produced furniture from *c.*1901 in the Roycroft Furniture Shop. Roycroft pieces are always in oak, of solid, heavy construction, and normally have a warm, nut-brown patina. Forms are extremely plain and simple and sometimes incorporate hammered copper hardware.

OTHER ARTS AND CRAFTS FURNITURE

It is widely agreed that the best work of the architect Frank Lloyd Wright was that produced during the first decade of the 20th century, when he worked principally as a residential architect in the Midwest. His furniture was produced mostly in oak in a style that blended American Arts and Crafts designs and ideals with European progressive Modernism. Most of Wright's pieces were produced for architectural commissions and rarely come up for sale; prices are still among the highest of all American furniture from this period.

The architectural design firm of Purcell, Feick & Elmslie, near Chicago, produced furniture to commission in pale oak, mahogany, brass, and copper between *c.*1906 and 1922. After the work of Wright, the designs of George Grant Elmslie (1871–1952) and William Gray Purcell (1880–1965) are considered the most progressive of all American Arts and Crafts pieces. Tall, architectural forms with spindling, inlay, and carved details are typical and reflect the strong influence of the Glasgow School and the Vienna Secession. Purcell, Feick & Elmslie furniture is rare, particularly outside the Midwestern states, where it is most keenly collected.

The Furniture Shop was founded in San Francisco in 1906 by Arthur Mathews (1860–1945) and his wife Lucia Mathews (1867–1956). Unlike most American Arts and Crafts furniture, their work was painted in polychrome and gilded, or mounted with polychromed, embossed leather. Carved oak or mahogany is typical in forms evocative of medieval France and Germany. Images include troubadors or medieval saints, together with romantic Californian landscapes painted by Lucia. Output from the Furniture Shop was modest, but small items sometimes appear on the market. The style is referred to as "California Decorative" and objects are of lesser appeal to most collectors than the purely designed work of the East Coast craftsmen.

Charles P. Limbert (1902–44) produced oak furniture in New Holland, near Grand Rapids, Michigan, in the early 20th century. Forms can be compared to those of Gustav Stickley, but many show the direct influence of the Scottish designer Charles Rennie Mackintosh (1868–1928) and the Glasgow School. Pieces are commonly of pale oak and crafted to a high standard and most are marked with a large brand featuring a craftsman at work. Prices are comparable to those commanded by Roycroft designs.

▼ Drinks cabinet by C.P. Limbert

This elegant, well-proportioned oak drinks cabinet, with neat hardware including square-faceted drawer-pulls – which often appear on Gustav Stickley's furniture – is a fine example of Limbert's craftsmanship. (*c.*1912; ht 61cm/24in; value **I**)

KEY FACTS

The Stickley Family

- FORMS designs are simple, geometric, and very solid; typically larger and bulkier than European counterparts
- WOOD white American oak, often quarter sawn, is typical, as is a reddish or gray tone achieved by fuming the wood in ammonia; some pieces may appear faded
- HARDWARE most features a hand-hammered surface
- COLLECTING Gustav's work is rare outside the USA; all forms are recorded in *The Craftsman* magazine; the work of L. & J.G. Stickley is most common

Marks

Gustav Stickley: pieces are usually inscribed "Als ik kan" (Flemish, "As I can"), after the Antwerp art society of that name, in a joiner's compass, and signed beneath

Charles Rohlfs

- DECORATION carved or cut-out whiplashes are usual
- COLLECTING his fine-quality work is very sought after

Greene and Greene

- DECORATION Oriental designs in metal and mother-of-pearl inlay are characteristic; visible dark pegs – often in ebony – may feature as decoration
- COLLECTING their work is extremely rare and very desirable; designs are unsigned but well documented

The Roycroft Furniture Shop

- FORMS most are rectilinear designs with strong proportions; many feature a distinctive tapered leg terminating in a bulbous foot
- DECORATION this is limited to hand-wrought iron or copper hardware

Frank Lloyd Wright

- FORMS most are rectilinear, with a vertical emphasis
- CONSTRUCTION complex and innovative; spindling is common on seat furniture and tables

The Furniture Shop

- DECORATION embellishment is mainly restricted to polychrome paintwork and embossed leather
- COLLECTING the output was relatively small; pieces are less desirable than the work of the East Coast designers

Charles P. Limbert

- COLLECTING interest in his high-quality work is growing following an exhibition in New York in 1995

See also Arts and Crafts: Furniture – Britain, pp.370–73

Ceramics

In a reaction against the mass-produced, overly embellished ceramic designs of the Victorian period, from *c.*1866 a small but influential band of potters created designs that were typified by the elegant Japanese-style decoration promoted by the Aesthetic Movement, the high-quality designs of William Morris, new types of glazes, and highly inventive forms. Inspired by the individuality and quality of these designs, several major ceramics manufacturers invested in art potteries, which also produced wares in the Arts and Crafts style. In the USA ceramics were perceived for the first time as a decorative rather than a purely functional medium, and potters experimented with forms, glazes, and naturalistic decoration.

Britain

From *c.*1866 major individual makers designed ceramics inspired by the wave of interest in all things Japanese and the organic motifs lauded by devotees of the Arts and Crafts Movement. Commercial firms took advantage of the talents of graduates from major art schools, funding them to produce individualistic, high-quality designs that could then be mass-produced in their newly founded art potteries. However, as the Arts and Crafts potters became technically more experienced, their independence grew: they made their own tiles, supervised the throwing of forms, and even worked as true artist/craftsmen in traditional craft potteries.

IMPORTANT MAKERS

One of the most influential and prolific potters was William De Morgan (1839–1917), who from 1873 decorated factory-made tiles with animals, birds, and grotesques, and finished them with luster glazes. After *c.*1875, inspired by 15th- and 16th-century Iznik pottery, he specialized in "Persian" wares in purples, blues, and greens. In 1882, after moving to Morris's Merton Abbey Workshops in Surrey, he made his own tiles and developed a range of pots with bluish-gray, gold, and ruby-red luster glazes after Hispaño-Moresque wares, or Persian decoration. In 1888 he set up a pottery at Sands End, London, developing his "Moonlight" and "Sunlight" series with double and triple luster effects.

▲ **Vase designed by Walter Crane for Maw & Co.**
This vase, depicting Nordic figures, is the result of a fruitful collaboration at the end of the 19th century between an Arts and Crafts designer and a major commercial manufacturer. The ruby luster glaze highlights Crane's flat, symmetrical design. *(c.1889; ht 23cm/9in; value H)*

◄ **Charger by William De Morgan**
Not only was De Morgan highly influential in ceramic design, he was also extremely prolific. Most typical of his 300 designs are those featuring flowers, fish, eagles, peacocks, and mythical creatures. *(late 19th century; diam. 44cm/17in; value I)*

► **Tobacco jar by Robert Martin**
This head of this eccentric, salt-glazed bird, which is typical of Robert Martin's work, lifts off to reveal a tobacco jar. Martin also produced a range of jugs decorated with grotesque faces – these quirky designs are highly popular with collectors. *(c.1907; ht 21cm/8¼in; value L)*

The designer and illustrator Walter Crane (1845–1915) joined the Artworkers' Guild when it was formed in 1884. He produced decorative designs for reputable ceramics firms including Maw & Co. (1850–1967), in Broseley, and Pilkington's Tile & Pottery Co. Ltd (est. 1897), in Clifton Junction, near Manchester. The flat areas of color and simple, asymmetrical forms typical of his dishes, vases, and tiles show the influence of Japanese prints.

The Martin brothers – Robert (1843–1923), Charles (1846–1910), Walter (1857–1912), and Edwin (1860–1915) – set up a pottery in Fulham, in London, in 1873, but by 1877 they had moved to Southall, Middlesex, where they produced an individualistic range of salt-glazed stoneware. Although Robert Martin designed some wares for Doulton & Co. (est. 1815), in Stoke-on-Trent, of premium interest to collectors is his range of birds and grotesques. Also desirable are vases in browns, greens, and blues, with organic *sgraffito* decoration.

The distinctive, organic designs of Christopher Dresser (1838–1904) were influenced both by his training as a botanist and by a visit to Japan. During the 1870s he began work for Minton & Co. (est. 1793), in Stoke-on-Trent. In 1879 he became Art Director of the newly formed Linthorpe Pottery (1879–89), near Middlesbrough, which was under the management of Henry Tooth. Dresser's range of vases, jugs, and other vessels for the Linthorpe Pottery have inventive forms, typically inspired by pre-Columbian and Japanese ceramics; these include gourd-shaped vases with multiple handles, and "camel-backed" jugs with poured or dripped glazes in dark brown with green, or blue with green or yellow. From 1892 to 1895 Dresser produced designs for the Ault Pottery (est. 1887), in Swadlincote, Derbyshire; jugs, vases, pedestals, and *jardinières* were all made in earthenware, some with a shimmering aventurine glaze.

Sir Edmund Elton (1846–1920), who set up a pottery on his estate in Clevedon, launched Elton Ware in 1882, and from 1883 it received acclaim at international exhibitions. Handmade vases, jugs, cups, and covers in inventive forms, often with multiple handles or strange spouts, were glazed in more than one color, frequently swirled to create a marbled effect, with incised and heavily enameled decoration. After 1902 Elton developed a range of crackled luster glazes; pieces in gold or silver are especially collectible.

▶ **Vase designed by Christopher Dresser for the Linthorpe Pottery**

The eccentric form of this vase, which imitates a Peruvian pouring jug, is typical of Dresser's imaginative designs. The subtle combination of brown, green, and blue glazes is also characteristic of Dresser's work, which is among the most highly sought after of all Arts and Crafts ceramics.
*(late 19th century; ht 21.5cm/8½in; value **H**)*

COMMERCIAL COMPANIES

Such commercial giants as Doulton & Co. (est. 1815), Minton & Co. (est. 1793), and Wedgwood (est. 1759), in Stoke-on-Trent, all took advantage of the opportunities offered by collaboration with Arts and Crafts designers. Doulton in particular played an important role through the links set up by Henry Doulton (1820–97) with the Lambeth School of Art. The profits from its contract to provide salt-glazed stoneware pipes for the new sewage schemes were used to establish an art pottery, where from *c.*1870 hand-thrown, salt-glazed stoneware vessels were produced. The typically buff or gray bodies were adorned with incised, carved, and modeled decoration in subdued brown, gray, blue, and green glazes by students from the Lambeth School of Art. Some of the most successful students include George Tinworth (1843–1913), and members of the Barlow family – Hannah Barlow (1859–1913), Florence Barlow (*d.*1909), and their brother Arthur Barlow (*d.*1909).

The short-lived Minton Art Pottery Studios was set up in 1871 under the direction of William Stephen Coleman in Kensington Gore, London, in order to establish links with students from the nearby National Training School, and until 1875 (when it burned down) it provided facilities for both amateur and professional painters to decorate tiles, plaques, and other wares supplied by the factory, with flowers, animals, genre scenes, and figures in medieval costume. Competitions set up by Minton were continued after 1875 by Howell & James, a London-based pottery retailer, and some successful entrants went on to work on Doulton's painted "faience" ware. Most commonly found are pieces decorated with indigenous British flowers, but pieces with figural decoration, in particular children, are the most sought after by collectors.

Burmantofts Faience (1858–1904), established by Wilcox & Co., near Leeds, Yorkshire, only began to produce art pottery from 1880. Wares, which include tiles, vases, pedestals, *jardinières*, bottles, jars, and pilgrim-bottles, were all made from local clay and decorated with monochrome or streaked glazes in orange, lime green, yellow, and *sang-de-boeuf*. More sought after by collectors is the range of vases that are intricately decorated with Iznik-style patterns – stylized flowers or arabesques decorated with brilliant green, blue, and turquoise glazes – inspired by 15th- and 16th-century Turkish ceramics and the work of De Morgan who was producing work in a similar vein.

ART POTTERIES

More in strict keeping with Arts and Crafts ideals than the commercial art studios were the art potteries. Wall tiles were one of the first products of Morris, Marshall, Faulkner & Co. (est. 1861). Plain white tiles were hand painted with designs by, among others, Dante Gabriel Rossetti, Ford Madox Brown, and Morris himself. Some were commissioned for large decorative schemes for interiors, others were produced as individual designs to be sold in the firm's shop. The Della Robbia Pottery (1894–1906) set up in Birkenhead by the painter Harold Rathbone, a former pupil of Ford Madox Brown, made a large range of hand-thrown pots, decorated with flowers or figures in lead glazes. Low-relief panels and plaques were also handmade and painted. Other notable art potteries include the Bretby Art Pottery (1883–1920), in Derbyshire, set up by Henry Tooth and William Ault, and the Ruskin Pottery (est. 1898) set up by W. Howson Taylor.

▶ **Vase designed by Liz Wilkins for the Della Robbia Pottery**
Art pottery by Della Robbia is popular among collectors, especially if, as in this case, a piece is by one of their most distinguished designers.
*(1903; ht 38cm/15in; value **F**)*

▼ **Vase decorated by Florence Barlow for Doulton & Co.**
Barlow was one of the many students from the Lambeth Art School employed by Doulton & Co. at their nearby works during the Arts and Crafts period. The muted palette, the depiction of small British birds, and the use of *sgraffito* decoration over a colored slip are typical of her designs, as is the elaborately decorated border on this hand-thrown stone vase.
*(1903; ht 38cm/15in; value **G**)*

KEY FACTS

Important makers
- DESIGNS De Morgan: naturalistic decoration in luster glazes; Crane: asymmetrical forms influenced by Japanese designs, also in luster glazes; Martin brothers: salt-glazed grotesques in autumnal colors are typical; Dresser: most of his highly original designs show the influence of Japan in their exotic luster glazes and stylized decoration; brown, green, and blue are typical
- COLLECTING De Morgan: all pieces will sell at a premium; tiles with ruby luster glaze are more sought after than those with Persian motifs and colors; Martin brothers: Robert's birds and grotesques are popular and highly priced; items by Edwin can be affordable; Dresser: his work is among the most highly sought after of all Arts and Crafts pottery; early Linthorpe pottery is noted for Tooth's dripped glazes

Marks
De Morgan: the most typical mark is shown here

Martin brothers: all wares are marked on the underside with hand-incised details of the maker, address, and date; the most collectible pieces are those made before 1873 and marked "Fulham"

Dresser: pieces feature an incised facsimile of Dresser's name in addition to Tooth's monogram

Commercial companies
- DESIGNS Doulton: stoneware in a palette of subdued colors; Minton: decoration of flowers is most typical; Wedgwood: mostly themed designs in luster glazes

Marks
Burmantofts Faience: the most typical mark

Art potteries
- DESIGNS Morris: most feature medieval-inspired or organic decoration; Della Robbia: typically organic forms and all-over *sgraffito* decoration on a rough surface; muted autumnal palette

Marks
Della Robbia Pottery: the most typical mark

See also Ceramics: Islamic pottery, p.149, Spain, p.150, Tiles, p.155

The United States

Philadelphia's Centennial Exhibition, held in 1876, had an unexpected and dramatic effect on the nation's ceramics industry. Designed to showcase the country's newly emerging industrial power, it was the first major "World Fair" to be held in the USA. Among the exhibits were major displays of European "art" ceramics, which inspired American producers to manufacture such wares in the USA.

Until now, the American ceramics industry had mainly focused on the production of domestic wares necessary for the settling of a new continent – roof tiles and butter churns. The late 1870s were a period of burgeoning confidence in America, however, and this was reflected in the establishment of a number of new

► Rookwood Pottery scenic "Vellum vase"
The Rookwood Pottery is considered the pre-eminent American Art Pottery whose hand-painted wares define the high end of the Ohio Valley style. This vase with closed-in rim, depicts a wintry woodland scene and was decorated by Kataro Shirayamadani. The vase is finished with the matt Vellum glaze, patented in 1904, which is particularly suited to floral and faunal scenes.
(c.1908; h 23cm/9¼in; value H)

ceramic manufacturers concentrating primarily on "art wares." The timing was perfect: the nation was ripe for change, seeking to decorate its new homes and enjoy its rising affluence.

Most American art pottery from c.1880–1920 falls into two categories: "true" art pottery, where a vase was used as a canvas or was hand-carved or modeled; and more commercial wares that relied less on manual techniques and more on molded or glazed decoration.

THE OHIO VALLEY SCHOOL

Rich clay deposits in the Ohio Valley, together with easy access to major water routes, enabled the cities of Cincinnati and Zanesville to embrace decorative ceramics on a large scale. The two largest producers, the Rookwood Pottery in Cincinnati, and the Roseville Pottery in Zanesville, were competitors for nearly 70 years, each satisfying their own sector of a nationally based market.

Rookwood was by far the most important of these enterprises, established by Maria Longworth Nichols in 1880. A society lady, she had been inspired by the 1876 Philadelphia Centennial Exhibition to decorate blank china as a hobby. Under the tutelage of Benn Pitman of the Cincinnati School of Design, she felt confident enough to make her hobby a business in 1880. The Rookwood Pottery

▲ Rookwood "Standard Glaze" vase, by Grace Young
This is one of a series of portraits of Native Americans on Rookwood pieces and depicts Wanstall Arapahoe. Particularly rare, such portraits are sought after by collectors. The pottery's glazes are imbued with the natural color of the Ohio clay.
(1900; h 34cm/13½in; value K)

▼ "Della Robbia" vase by Roseville
Roseville's "Della Robbia" range is now among the most collectible of its wares, and is typified by the precise design and production quality of the pieces that were made. This example is decorated with daisies and spade-shaped leaves on a forest- green ground and is finished with a Rozane seal.
(c.1905; h 26.5cm/10½in; value K)

was established in a former schoolhouse bought for the purpose by Nichols' father, the name deriving from the family's country estate. From the outset, Nichols saw Rookwood as an artistic enterprise rather than a commercial one and had strict quality controls. Hired artists were often accomplished easel painters or sculptors rather than commercial potters. Any item that failed the quality controls was marked with an "X."

Among the first employees was Henry Farny, at Rookwood from 1881, known for his native American subjects. He was soon followed by Albert Robert Valentien who later went on to form his own pottery in San Diego. Artus Van Briggle joined the firm in 1887. He was inspired by Ming dynasty wares, whose matt glazes he recreated. The next important appointment was that of William Watts Taylor who, as manager, attracted many important artists as well as the chemists who developed Rookwood's unique glazes.

Rookwood's designs are typified by a precise, naturalistic under-glaze slip decoration of indigenous flora and fauna, landscapes, oriental flowers, dragons, as well as Native American portraits, under crisp, limpid glazes. Rookwood wares featuring delicately applied brown, yellow, and ocher slips on dark grounds, and a clear glossy glaze, are known as "Standard Glaze" and are strongly associated with the factory.

Facing competition from more commercially run factories, such as Roseville, Rookwood introduced a commercial line from c.1900, based on glaze effects rather than hand-painting. Although it met with some success, this was not the work for which the firm is most remembered. In 1904, the factory patented a matt glaze called "Vellum," which works particularly well with stylized flora such as wisteria, or landscapes, and is marked by a "V" on the base of the vessel.

The Roseville Pottery, while producing lesser-quality wares, was the best of the second-tier Ohio Valley companies working in the Arts and Crafts style. It was established in 1892 in Roseville, producing art wares from 1898. Much of its work comprised less expensive copies of the lines made famous by Rookwood. The "Rozane" range was based on Rookwood's "Standard" glazed pieces, for example. However, these "imitations" lacked the care and spontaneity of the originals. Occasionally, as with their "Della Robbia" line, designed by the celebrated British potter Frederick Hurten Rhead (1880–1942) and introduced in 1906, Roseville produced pieces of comparable design and quality to Rookwood.

Zanesville's established place in the American pottery industry attracted Sam Weller to found his pottery there in 1889. Having worked at Fultonham since 1872, Weller began his career producing utilitarian wares, but under the influence of his new neighbors, introduced "art wares" with great success. Inspired by a visit in 1893 to Chicago's "World's Columbian Exposition," his work moved toward a more naturalistic style, heavily influenced by Rookwood. Cleverly combining hand-decoration and mass-production techniques, Weller's pieces straddled the space between the expensive and arty Rookwood wares, but held higher artistic pretensions to most of those made by Roseville.

▲ Rare Grueby vase, by Ruth Erickson

William Grueby was among the first art pottery manufacturers to use matt glazes in a range of colors on his wares, and it is for the distinctive green glaze of this vase that his company became particularly well known. A stunning example of Arts and Crafts pottery, the crisply tooled design of this vase alternates stylized, full-height leaves with delicate amber buds.

(c.1905; w 18.5cm/7¼in; value L)

▲ Table-lamp by the Fulper Pottery Co.

From *c*.1910, the Fulper Pottery Co. in New Jersey began to produce art ware in the Arts and Crafts style alongside the more utilitarian products for which it was better known. The company enjoyed tremendous success with its "Vasecraft" range of vases and table-lamps, which typically had organic forms. Table-lamps like this one became extremely popular and were sold in prestigious department stores across the USA.

(c.1905; h 53cm/21in; value K)

THE NEW ENGLAND SCHOOL

While the Ohio potters chose to paint their vases, decorators and designers in New England tended to sculpt or model organic designs into their wares. Where the work in Ohio established a clear delineation between the vessel and the decoration, the New England School blended the two in search of an organic, unified aesthetic, believing that a unique work of art captured a moment in time, and that a hand-thrown piece would always be more successful at accomplishing this than the finest molded pot.

William Grueby (1867–1925) was greatly influenced by the French potter Auguste Delaherche (1857–1940), whose work he saw at the Chicago "Worlds Columbian Exposition" in 1893. Grueby pioneered the use of matt glazes, such as yellow, aqua, and pink, but it was his distinctive green that would make his name. This prized glaze, produced at his studio in Boston, Massachusetts, from 1894 to 1907, won a gold medal at the Paris Exhibition in 1900 and inspired many imitators, including Rookwood.

Grueby worked closely with firms such as Tiffany of New York, and manufactured lamp bases for the firm. A close association was also formed with Gustav Stickley, taking joint stands at exhibitions, where Grueby's wares were shown off to great effect on Stickley's furnishings.

Another New England art pottery that shared Grueby's Arts and Crafts sensibilities was the Saturday Evening Girls' Club in Boston, whose work is typified by freely inscribed designs of flowers, farmyard animals, and stylized landscapes under soft, porous glazes. Early pieces use a simple palette of mostly yellow, blue, and green, with white and brown. Shapes are hand thrown or molded, with very early examples hand formed.

Established by Edith Brown and Edith Guerrier, with the support of benefactor Helen Storrow, the pottery emerged out of the women's movement and the numerous library clubs. Known as the "Ediths," Brown and Guerrier met Helen Storrow while she volunteered at the Boston Public Library, where Guerrier worked and ran a number of popular girls' clubs, each named after the day of the week upon which they met. Helen Storrow, in a spirit of generosity and support for the library clubs, erected a 14-bedroom house to act as a summer camp for the various girls' clubs.

► Four-sided vase by the Saturday Evening Girls' Club

This vase is typical Saturday Evening Girls, later known as the Paul Revere Pottery. Decorated using the cuerda seca technique, some light tooling and a soft palette, the vase depicts stylized trees in a landscape on an indigo ground. The colors epitomize the work of this pottery.

(1920; h. 9.5cm/3¾in; value E)

After a trip to Europe in 1906, the "Ediths" conceived the idea of establishing a small pottery to produce work for sale. Initially just a kick wheel and a kiln in the basement of the "Ediths" shared home, Helen Storrow bought a house in Hull Street, Boston, to act as workshop and store to sell the pottery. Being in close proximity to Old North Church where Paul Revere hung his signal lamps, the pottery was named in his honor.

The Hull Street premises were sold in 1915 and, through the continued patronage of Helen Storrow, a purpose-built pottery was established at Nottinhill Road, Brighton, Massachusetts, which continued until its closure in 1942.

NEW JERSEY

The Fulper Pottery Co. of Flemington, New Jersey (est. 1814), became renowned for its Arts and Crafts pottery under the direction of William H. Fulper II, at the turn of the 20th century. He saw potential in producing "artware," and the company enjoyed some success with a range of new glazes, which sought to recreate those from ancient China. It was for "Vasekraft" lamps that the firm became best known. Designed by ceramics engineer Martin Stangl employed by Fulper in 1910, the lamps were of organic form, with ceramic shades that frequently featured slag glass inserts.

KEY FACTS

The Ohio Valley School
- DECORATION Rookwood: many wares are embellished with a hand-painted slip or raised, painted decoration
- COLOR Rookwood: brown grounds; "Sea Green," "Ariel Blue," and "Iris" introduced after 1894
- GLAZES Rookwood: early wares are mostly glossy; the soft "Vellum" glaze was not introduced until 1896
- FAKES collectors should beware of modern copies of Rookwood wares made from old molds

Marks

Rookwood: mark from 1887; most wares were impressed with the factory name, a date, and the artist's monogram; from 1886 this "RP" monogram was used, with a "flame" (as seen above) being added for each year from 1887 to 1900; from 1901 the Roman numeral I was added below and changed accordingly each year.

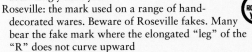

Roseville: the mark used on a range of hand-decorated wares. Beware of Roseville fakes. Many bear the fake mark where the elongated "leg" of the "R" does not curve upward

Weller pieces bear Weller name or the various range names such as "Aurelian," "Eocean," "Louelsa"

The New England School
- FORMS Grueby: pieces are organic and highly stylized
- DECORATION most pieces feature carved or modeled designs; Grueby: mostly leaves or flowers; Paul Revere: stylized flora and fauna are typical
- GLAZES Grueby: these are typically extremely thick, opaque, and pitted; most give a matt effect, resembling the skin of a watermelon, and are usually moss green

Marks

Grueby: pieces are marked with the name "Grueby" accompanied by this vegetal motif
Saturday Evening Girls' pieces marked "SEG" or "PRP" usually with a date and initials

See also Arts and Crafts: Ceramics – Britain, pp.376–7; Other American makers, pp.380–1

Other American makers

THE SOUTHERN SCHOOL

The South, ravaged by the American Civil War (1861–5), began production of art pottery in a vastly different way from the Ohio Valley and New England schools. The decimation of the male population resulted in women taking on more dominant roles at work, and ceramic decoration was a popular choice.

Newcomb College Pottery, an adjunct of Tulane University in New Orleans, Louisiana, operated from

▼ **Newcomb College Pottery vase**

Carved by A.F. Simpson, this vase is one of a number of Newcomb pieces depicting a moonlit bayou landscape. The rich matt finish is usual for glazes used on Newcomb College Pottery wares made after 1910.

(1923; ht 17cm/6¾in; value **F***)*

1894 to 1945 and sought to bring women into the workforce by teaching them these applied skills. Here, the pots were first thrown by master potters and then decorated by the students. Newcomb was primarily a studio and its wares reflect its careful approach, each piece being an individual creation bearing the proud label "Newcomb Pottery. Designs are not duplicated."

Three people were responsible for the pottery's establishment, which was part of the college's art department. Ellsworth Woodward devised the vocational courses and he brought in Mary Given Sheerer, from Cincinnati, to teach pottery design and decoration. Joseph Mayer was responsible for throwing the wares, usually to Sheerer's designs. Paul Cox joined the team in 1910 to improve the glaze and body and it was Cox that developed Newcomb's signature semi-matt, almost waxy glaze.

Early Newcomb pieces are simply marked with the college's name, but from 1897 the famous mark of an "N" within a "C" was employed.

Newcomb's products can be divided into three fairly distinct groups. The earliest pieces are finished with a

clear glossy glaze that, from 1909 to about 1914, becomes a waxy matt glaze. Following this period, the better-known rich matt finish is introduced.

As Newcomb was a training college the quality of work varies. Generally, the best work is by the tutors and not the students, although several of the latter graduated and stayed on to teach, including the renowned Sadie Irvine, who graduated in 1906, and taught at the college until her retirement in 1952.

The studio is known for its blue and green palette and decoration that sought inspiration from nature. Popular decoration included incised moonlit bayou scenes, native flora such as cotton plants, tobacco plants, and jonquils, and such indigenous creatures such as lizards and waterfowl. Other colors were used, particularly during the early phase, and again during the late 1930s and up to the studio's closure in 1945. Between 1901 and 1942, a unique dating system was used at the studio. Each piece bears a letter or letter combination, plus a number from 1 to 100. Thus "A1" was the first piece produced in 1901.

Another famous southern pottery was the Biloxi Pottery, founded in Biloxi, Mississippi, and worked solely by its owner, George E. Ohr (1857–1918), from 1880 to c.1907. Ohr's eccentric appearance and way of life earned him the nickname "the mad potter of Biloxi," and it is difficult to classify him as anything but an anomaly, since he pursued an extremely focused, iconoclastic vision.

Perhaps he was the truest of the Arts and Crafts potters, because his work, above that of all others, captured the spirit of "one moment, one creation." Each vessel is distinctly different. Ohr is reported to have claimed: "God made no two souls alike and I'll make no two pots alike." In general, his work is characterized by thin walls, a severely manipulated and pinched asymmetrical form with deep, spiraling ridges and daring and improbable glazing, usually in shades of brown, green, and red.

Ohr's later and most mature work is characterized by extreme manipulation and a lack of glazing; he is quoted as stating: "God put no color on souls and I'll put no color on my pots." Although Ohr produced some 10,000 pieces during his career, including both practical and ornamental wares – such as vases, jugs, inkwells, and bowls – he sold hardly a single item. He stopped potting extremely abruptly, leaving behind a legacy of pieces that had been produced well before their time. His collection was left to his family and eventually came on to the market in 1972; only now is the Biloxi Pottery attracting the attention it deserves.

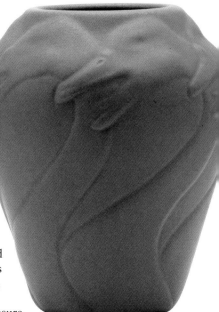

▲ **Van Briggle vase**

Working in his own studio in Colorado from 1899, Van Briggle continued to use the matt glazes he had perfected at Rookwood. While employed by Maria Longworth Nichols at Rookwood, Van Briggle had spent three years studying in Paris, and the embossed design of this vase, with its stylized goose pattern, betrays the influence of the European Arts and Crafts Movement.

(1903; ht 16cm/6¼in; value **I***)*

▶ **George Ohr vase**

The deep twisting and crimping of this vase is typical of Ohr's style. Almost always hand-thrown, his pieces are extremely thin, with early glazes lustrous and mottled in brown, black, orange, and bronze.

(1890s; ht 9cm/3½in; value **L***)*

▼ Rhead "Santa Barbara" vase

This iconic Arts and Crafts landscape-etched vase is a fusion of American decorative trends with Rhead's European tastes. *(1915; ht 28.5m/11¼in; value Q)*

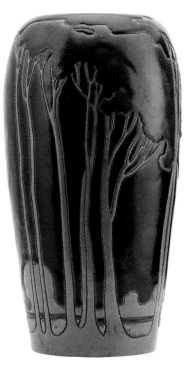

In Colorado, Artus Van Briggle (1869-1904) began to produce wares of his own. Until 1899, he had worked for Rookwood as a senior decorator, but had been forced to leave on grounds of ill health. With his wife Anna he relocated to Colorado Springs, Colorado in 1899 in the hopes of easing his tuberculosis. There, he founded Van Briggle Pottery, favoring organic-shaped ceramic vessels decorated with sumptuous matt glazes.

Artus had long been experimenting with matt glazes in the hope of discovering the secret of the lost 'dead' glazes of the Chinese Ming Dynasty. In 1900, he finally succeeded. Under his direction the company won medals in the 1903 Paris Salon (where 24 designs were shown) and the 1904 Lousiana Purchase Exposition. Most of the finest Van Briggle ware was produced before Artus' death in 1904. However, with Anna in control, the company continued to produce high quality art wares in a variety of distinctive hues. She sold the factory in 1912 but it remains in operation today, making it unique among the major potteries of the Arts and Crafts period.

THE CALIFORNIAN SCHOOL

California was the last American state to be settled by the pioneers and its pottery industry was consequently several years behind that of the rest of the country. However, this delay was not wholly to California's disadvantage, as extremely rich clay deposits and beautiful, inspirational vistas attracted some of the best potters to the West Coast.

The British potter Frederick Hurten Rhead (1880-1942), who worked at Roseville, Jervis, University City, Vance/Avon Faience Company and Weller, established several potteries in California, including the Rhead Pottery in Santa Barbara. The most famous of his California ventures was the Arequipa Pottery, in Fairfax (1911–18), set up to provide occupational therapy for working women with tuberculosis at the Arequipa Sanatorium. The high turnover of patients as well as the working methods make Arequipa's wares harder to categorize than other studios. Rhead was the first master potter to work Arequipa. He was followed by fellow Englishmen Albert Solon and Fred Wilde. The experimental nature of both the directors and the patients gave Arequipa's pieces a unique "naturalness" and spontaneity.

Linking the Ohio Valley and Californian schools is the short-lived pottery established by Albert R. Valentien (1847–1913) and his wife Anna Marie Valentien (1862–1947), who created art wares at their Valentien Pottery (1911– *c.*1913) in San Diego.

The Valentiens were essentially artists, who, after leaving employment at Rookwood in 1905, pursued painting as a career and traveled to California in order to paint the many wild flowers there. Employing many of the glazes and decorative techniques used at Rookwood, the Valentiens' pieces are either painted or decorated in low relief. Typical themes are peacock feathers, swirling plant forms, dragonflies, and fish. Anna Valentien is known to have modeled pieces with human subjects in low relief. Although the quality is not always as good as that made by other firms, Valentien pieces have an individuality that ensures an enduring popularity.

▼ Valentien vase

Wares produced by the Valentien pottery were typically embossed and painted with floral designs in soft matt colors on a soft matt ground. This green example is embossed with maple leaves. A number of Valentien pieces, including this one, are Art Nouveau in design, although the glazes, based on those that Albert and Anna Marie Valentien encountered when working at Rookwood, are more clearly associated with the American Arts and Crafts movement. *(1911-14; ht 17cm/6¾in; value H)*

◄ Arequipa vessel

Both the squat, bulbous shape of this vase and the embossed decoration are indicative of Arequipa wares. Here, the embossed wreath of stylized flowers is finished with a matt ivory-to-pink glaze. Frederick Hurten Rhead left the Arequipa pottery in 1913, to set up his own pottery at Santa Barbara, California. *(c.1910; w. 16.5cm/6½in; value G)*

KEY FACTS

The Southern School

- DECORATION Newcomb: incised decoration of stylized flora and fauna, moonlit bayou scenes
- GLAZES Newcomb: early wares clear high glaze, after 1910 soft matt glazes; Ohr: most early pieces lustrous and mottled; later works bisque-fired with no glazing

Marks

Newcomb: wares are impressed with an "N" encircled by a "C," a number, and the artist's monogram

The California School

- DECORATION Arequipa: slip-trailed decoration typical, matt after 1910; Valentien: embossed and painted floral designs; Van Briggle: molded organic shapes

Marks

Arequipa Pottery: mark used 1911 to 1918 Valentien: "V," "P" either side of a stylized Californian poppy

See also Arts and Crafts: Ceramics – Britain, pp.376–7; The United States, pp.378–379

Metalwork

In the late 19th century a number of designers and artists in Europe reacted against the poor quality of mass-produced metal objects and attempted to revive traditional methods of manufacture. Pieces typically boasted "hand-crafted" origins and celebrated nature in their design. A feature was made of hammered surfaces and organic ornament as well as Celtic-style decoration, cabochons, and enameling. The best examples today are those that were made by craftspeople as opposed to those produced on a more commercial basis.

In Britain several designers founded guilds at which apprentices could gain experience of metalwork, and which were often run on idealist – almost socialist – principles. While they sought to give opportunities to working people, however, they often produced goods that were only affordable to the rich.

LIBERTY & CO.

Liberty & Co. of Regent Street, London, was founded in 1875 by Arthur Lasenby Liberty (1843–1917) and operates on the same site today. Metalwork joined the famous fabric lines in the mid-1890s, and by 1902 the firm was selling its distinctive silver and pewter ranges:

▲ **"Tudric" pewter and enameled vase**
Made of pewter, many pieces in Liberty's "Tudric" line were similar or identical to those of the silver "Cymric" line and included designs for vases, boxes, candlesticks, and chalices. This piece was designed for Liberty by Archibald Knox.
*(c.1905; ht 29cm/11½in; value **G**)*

"Cymric" (silver) and "Tudric" (pewter). The "Cymric" range was made until the 1930s and is not especially rare today. Most examples are of neo-Celtic design, featuring entrelacs and stylized leaves or flower-heads, and are often decorated with vitreous enamel in vivid bluish-green. Boxes, picture frames, inkwells, jewelry, candlesticks, and spoons are typical. "Tudric" pewter includes such designs as decorative chalices, clocks, and vases.Examples that can be attributed to Archibald Knox (1864–1933), Liberty's foremost metalwork designer, are most desirable. The company also worked with Jessie M. King, Oliver Baker and Rex Silver.

◄ **"Tudric" pewter vase designed by David Veazey for Liberty & Co.**
This rare Arts and Crafts pewter vase is from Liberty's sought after "Tudric" range. The vase is of compressed form with a cylindrical neck. The piece has elegant applied handles and honesty roundels.
*(c.1900; ht 34cm/13¼in; value **G**)*

▼ **C.R. Ashbee silver vase**
Under Ashbee's direction, the Guild of Handicraft created works with a high Arts and Crafts aesthetic. This piece, designed by Ashbee, is set with garnets; tiny hammered depressions, made using a rounded planishing hammer, create the matt surface.
*(1900; ht 18cm/7in; value **H**)*

ASHBEE AND THE GUILD OF HANDICRAFT

Founded by Charles Robert Ashbee in 1888, in the true spirit of Ruskin and Morris, the Guild of Handicraft was a major exponent of the British Arts and Crafts Movement. Combining an understanding of medieval forms, techniques, and materials the guild produced works of outstanding quality. Based at Essex House on the Mile End Road (from 1890) in London's East End, it was set up on the lines of a working guild in the medieval tradition of masters teaching journeymen and apprentices. Ashbee's innovation was that apprentices learnt a craft as they made objects, as opposed to watching articles being made.

Although members learnt metalwork, woodwork and leatherwork, the guild is principally known for its small silver objects and jewelry, usually made to Ashbee's designs. Covered cups with sinuous handles are typical, often decorated in part with vitreous enamel in shades of green or brown and cabochon hardstones. Items using archaeological finds are known, as well as pieces incorporating specially commissioned Whitefriars glass. Some examples show the influence of Celtic metalwork in design and materials.

The best vessels are meticulously hammered on the surface and are of a very thin gauge. This is an important feature. Whereas hammered metalwork was a major feature of much contemporary metalwork, the best guild pieces are hammered in such a way that the tiny hammer marks texture the surface, rather than dominate it, giving it an almost matt look.

The guild prospered and opened a gallery just off London's Bond Street in 1890 and, by 1902, moved to the Cotswold village of Chipping Campden. Although the move was initially a success, the impracticality of transporting goods to London proved too much, and by 1907 the guild was wound up.

BENSON, RAMSDEN, AND FISHER

William Arthur Smith Benson (1854–1924) produced some of the most innovative British Arts and Crafts metalwork at his factory in Hammersmith, London, from 1883 to 1923. His commercial metalwork included practical wares in brass, copper, electroplate, and other base metals; items such as kettles may have ebonized wood handles. Influenced by the Aesthetic Movement, Benson's

▼ **Ramsden & Carr silver and enameled bowl**
The trefoil was much used in Arts and Crafts design – here in the shape of this silver bowl. Each "lobe" has a twin-branched wirework handle, with a red-enameled plaque.
*(1902; ht 12cm/4¾in; value **H**)*

style combined elements of Japanese simplicity with traditional European techniques.

Born in Sheffield, Omar Ramsden (1873–1939), was an important maker of silverware. Joining forces with Alwyn Carr in 1898, he established a studio in Chelsea, producing silverware of a very high standard, often set with hardstones or enamel, or made from turned and polished wood mounted in silver.

London-based painter and silversmith Alexander Fisher (1864–1936) specialized in innovative, pictorial enamel and foil plaques on silver; caskets are typical. His work resembles the best Liberty "Cymric" wares but is rare and more collectible.

KESWICK AND NEWLYN

Linked by their use of copper, the Keswick and Newlyn Schools produced distinctive craft pieces reflecting the artistic movements of the period.

Set up as a night school in 1884, and held in the parish rooms of Crossthwaite church, the Keswick School of Industrial Arts was established by Cannon Hardwicke Rawnsley, a friend of John Ruskin and founder of the National Trust. Early success saw a move to purpose-built premises in 1894. Producing a range of both copper and silver items, early products took inspiration from the Celtic and Norse heritage of the English Lake District, but by the early 20th century the work fits into a more traditional Arts and Crafts style.

Of a similar date and style are the pieces made at the Newlyn Industrial Class. Begun in 1890 teaching metalwork, enamel, and embroidery to fishermen, it was established by artist John Mackenzie. John Pearson joined in 1892, having previously been a member of the Guild of Handicrafts. Pearson was a major influence on Newlyn's style, which makes a strong feature of plant forms, but especially marine subjects. Pearson's style is heavily influenced by the pottery of William de Morgan, with whom he was associated.

Although Newlyn wares are marked, and occasionally signed by the maker or artist, almost as many were unmarked. Genuine pieces are very well made, often of patinated copper, although brass and pewter were worked too. Attention to detail is a feature, as is the decorative treatment of seams and hinges, which were often shaped into curves.

CHRISTOPHER DRESSER

Born in Glasgow, Dr Christopher Dresser (1834–1904) was a highly influential designer working across many media, and his work was often visionary.

Unlike many of his contemporaries, Dresser was a keen proponent of manufacturing, believing that industrialized processes brought good design to the many. Always a strong advocate of Japanese design, he visited the country officially in 1876, bringing back examples of Japanese goods to be exhibited by the New York firm Tiffany and Co.

Working mainly in electroplate as well as copper and japanned tin, Dresser's most productive and influential period was the late 1870s, when he acted as a designer for several smaller companies. James Dixon & Co. of Sheffield and Hukin and Heath of Birmingham are among the firms that manufactured electroplated pieces to Dresser's ground-breaking designs.

▲ **W.A.S. Benson dished copper tray**
Benson used traditional European techniques and materials. This copper tray has both repoussé decoration and embossing.
(c.1900; ht 48cm/19¼in; value **D**)

▲ **Newlyn school copper repoussé tea caddy**
Marine subjects often feature – a reminder of Newlyn's origins as a school for fishermen.
(c.1905; ht 15.5cm/6in; value **E**)

▼ **Glasgow School mirror**
The sinuous lines of this copper mirror are reminiscent of the Art Nouveau style taking root in Europe at the same time.
(c.1910; ht 59cm/22¼in; value **L**)

THE GLASGOW SCHOOL

Although termed a "school," events in Glasgow at this time resulted in more of a movement. A group known as "The Four" (sisters Margaret and Francis McDonald, Herbert McNair, and Charles Rennie Macintosh) collaborated on a number of projects including metal wares. "Glasgow School" pieces tend to be more Art Nouveau than Arts and Crafts, having a much more European-inspired aesthetic. Plant forms, flower heads, and almost abstract human forms are typical of this distinctive style.

KEY FACTS

Ashbee and the Guild of Handicraft
- DECORATION hammered surfaces, green or brown enamel, and cabochon hardstones are typical
- CONDITION pieces with damaged or restored enamel outnumber perfect examples, since enamel splinters easily if the silver ground is bent
- COLLECTING jewelry and large, complex pieces are most sought after, especially ecclesiastical ware

Marks
Most designs are impressed "CRA" and often also "G. of H. Ltd" for "Guild of Handicraft"

Liberty & Co.
- MATERIALS silver, pewter, brass, and copper were all used, characteristically combined with vitreous enamel plaques or details, cabochon hardstones, and turquoise
- CONDITION poor condition or restoration of enamel is common and reduces value of a piece
- COLLECTING most Tudric pewter and other base-metal pieces are fairly common; pieces by Knox and/or with original presentation boxes are more valuable
- FAKES recent forgeries of picture frames can be spotted by a metallic glint to the enamel and the newness of the blue velvet back

Marks
Most pieces are impressed "CYMRIC" or "TUDRIC," with the name or initial; many Tudric pieces may be unmarked; modern fakes bear fake English hallmarks

Benson, Ramsden, and Fisher
- COLLECTING light fixtures and table-lamps by Benson are particularly sought after – they are seldom found outside Britain; work by Fisher is rare and collectible

Marks
Pieces by Ramsden are stamped or incised

Keswick and Newlyn
- MATERIALS Keswick: copper and silver steel; Newlyn: copper, brass, pewter
- DECORATION Newlyn: marine subjects – ships, fish, octopus, and crabs feature often

Marks
Keswick: "K S I A" for "Keswick School of Industrial Arts"
Newlyn: either stamped "NEWLYN" or unmarked

Christopher Dresser
- MATERIALS Often ground-breaking designs in electroplate, copper, and tin

Marks
Pieces usually carry a facsimile of Dresser's signature

See also Arts and Crafts: Metalwork – The United States, pp.382–3

The United States

The Arts and Crafts movement that engaged craftsmen through much of Europe toward the end of the 19th century also found favor in the USA, where a number of artist and immigrant metalworkers established workshops of their own.

The most valuable examples of American metalwork from this period are the "weed holders," or slender, sheet-copper vases designed by Frank Lloyd Wright (1867–1959) and made c.1893–1902 by the firm of

▶ **Hammered copper inkwell by Gustav Stickley**

The inkwell has an applied owl figurine and a dark patina. It also bears the Stickley "Als ik kan" stamp on the base. Although not all Stickley ironwork is signed, it can be easily attributed as all designs are well documented.

(c.1910; w. 14cm/5½in; value C)

James A. Miller of Chicago. Fewer than ten examples are known to exist, but copies and fakes of the design are common. A large, bulbous sheet-copper jardinière made by Miller after a Wright design in 1903 is equally rare and valuable.

GUSTAV STICKLEY

Gustav Stickley (1858–1942), famed for his simple "Mission Oak" furniture, produced an important range of highly collectible metalwork. The metalworking studio at his Craftsman Workshops in Eastwood, New York, made strap hinges, key escutcheons and handles for his furniture as well as simple, of heavy gauge copper pieces, often of a dark patina, and uniformly finely made. Inkwells, bookends, and desk sets are typical. Wrought iron was also used, particularly for firedogs and companion sets. Firedogs are typically large and heavy with hammered surfaces with a dark, silvery patina, often unified by a connecting chain. Designs in copper and brass were also produced, including furniture hardware in the manner of pieces by Roycroft. Some, but not all, Stickley pieces are signed, with the joiners' compass logo.

Gustav's brothers, Leopold and John George, set up the Onondaga Workshops in Fayetteville, New York, in 1902. They produced furniture similar to Gustav's, and a variety of hammered copper wares. The company became L. and J.G. Stickley in 1907.

▶ **Coal bucket by the Onondaga Metal Shops**

A coal bucket with dark patina and exposed rivets, both characteristic of Onondaga Metal Shops Arts and Crafts style. Embossed with a stylized floral design, the coal bucket is stamped OMS.

(c.1904; ht 42cm/16½in; value H)

THE ROYCROFTERS

Founded in 1895 in East Aurora, New York State, by the writer and craftsman Elbert Hubbard (1856–1915), the Roycrofters were an idealistic Arts and Crafts rural community. Hubbard was a colorful and visionary character who was greatly influenced by a visit to William Morris's Merton Abbey Workshops, in Surrey, England, in 1894.

The Roycroft Shops grew in a totally organic way, beginning with the publishing shop, established by Hubbard after he was unable to find a publisher for his writing. A blacksmith's shop was added in 1899, making fireplace equipment and some architectural pieces, such as hinges, door plates, and furniture hardware for domestic use; these were influenced by medieval European art. A copper shop followed in 1902. Such was Hubbard's fame that a hotel was erected to house the many visitors. As the hotel needed to be furnished, a furniture shop was established.

The commercial sale of copper wares was introduced in 1906. Roycroft copper is typified by simple shapes, with a handmade look and a heavily hammered appearance. Cut-out overlays in copper or silvered metal is typical. Early Roycroft pieces are also heavily influenced by European styles, particularly that of the Vienna Secession.

Roycroft pieces are patinated and the condition of this patination is paramount for collectors. Three main patinas are used: "Aurora Brown," a rich brown tone popular with collectors, "Old Brass" and "Modern Sheffield," a silver patination. The later Italian Polychrome range (a rich caramel brown with green-painted highlighting) was introduced in 1911. This is a rare and desirable range.

Pieces by Karl Kipp or Walter Jennings (who left in 1912 to form their own "Tookay" shop, before returning to Roycroft in 1915) are particularly sought by collectors.

DIRK VAN ERP

Dirk Van Erp (1860–1953) was a Dutch immigrant who settled in Oakland, California, in 1886. The son of a metalworker, he began his career at the Union iron works where, in his spare time, he reworked old shell cases into vases, which he sold to gift shops and galleries in San Francisco.

Setting up his own business in 1908, Van Erp's early metalwork is superbly executed with meticulously hand-hammered surfaces, often with exposed riveting, and strapwork decoration. Van Erp pieces with an original, reddish patina are sought after by collectors today,

▲ **Roycroft andirons**

A large orb-and-cross is incorporated into the design of this extremely rare pair of Roycroft andirons. The curled elements and twisted rings are finished with black enamel. The overall design betrays medieval inspiration.

(c.1901; h. 78.5cm/31in; value I)

▲ **Dirk Van Erp hammered copper and mica table-lamp.**

This lamp is typical of those made in collaboration with Ellen D'Arcy Gaw and bear's the stamp of both names. D'Arcy Gaw was a particularly skilled designer as is evident in the pleasing proportions of her pieces. The four-panel shade with spade-shaped riveted straps is characteristic of these lamps.

(c.1910; h 42cm/16½in; value I)

particularly as he considered this to be his most successful work.

In 1910, he formed a short-lived partnership with the prominent American craftswoman Ellen D'Arcy Gaw, who is credited with the introduction of the well-known range of lamps. Items bearing both D'Arcy Gaw's and Van Erp's names are highly prized. These tablelamps (and some hanging fixtures), have characteristic conical shades and hollow, vase-shaped bases. Most were produced between 1910 and 1915. The shades are made of thin sheets of mottled amber mica.

TIFFANY STUDIOS

Tiffany Studios, part of Tiffany & Co. (est. 1837) founded by Charles Lewis Tiffany (1812–1902), produced a variety of Arts and Crafts metalwork in the 1890s under the direction of the founder's son Louis Comfort Tiffany (1848–1933). Together with bases and

▲ Tiffany bronze eight-light candelabrum
Among the pieces produced by Tiffany were a number of desk items made from bronze, of pulled naturalistic form.
(c.1900; h 38cm/14in; value I)

fittings for lamps, the firm produced a wide range of bronze desk items and small, enameled copper inkwells and objets de vertu. Some of its best pieces were made in "mixed" metal, reflecting the company's interest in new and experimental metalworking techniques.

JARVIE

Recently, interest in the work of Robert Jarvie (1865–1940), who operated the Jarvie Shop in Chicago from 1904, and specialized in candlesticks, has increased among collectors. Most of his designs are in cast brass or turned copper, simple and elegant in form, and are

marked with the name "Jarvie" in script. Silver objects by Jarvie are even less common.

KALO

Formed in 1900 by Clara P. Barck, the Kalo Shop initially produced pokerwork items and leather work. Copper wares soon followed. Barck married George Welles, a coal merchant and amateur silversmith, in 1905, after which silver holloware and silver and gold jewelry were also made.

The best examples, most of which are stamped, are comparable in style and quality to the work of Jarvie. Candlesticks and small items for the desk or dressing-table are most typical. Although the Kalo Shops continued in operation until 1970, its Arts and Crafts pieces are among the most collectible.

THE ARTS CRAFT SHOP, BUFFALO NY

Established in 1902 by Bernard Carpenter and Otto Heintz, the Arts Craft Shop began by making enameled, handcrafted copper wares. In 1906 the company name was changed to the Heintz Art Metal Shop and a switch to machine-formed bronze vessels, overlaid with silver took place. Typically, Heintz pieces are patinated and overlaid with cut silver in floral or landscape themes.

GORHAM MANUFACTURING COMPANY

Particularly recognized for its silverware, typically cutlery, combs, and jewelry, the Gorham Manufacturing Company was established in 1831, in Providence, Rhode Island, by master craftsman Jabez Gorham (1792–1869). His son, John (1820–1898), took over in 1847. Impressed by events in Europe, John Gorham employed a number of skilled European craftsmen to train his own silversmtihs.

▼ Gorham Manufacturing Company tray
Although better known for their silverwares, Gorham also produced items made from mixed metal. Applied silver crabs decorate this copper and sterling silver tray.
(c.1881; w. 25.5cm/10in; value G)

◄ Jarvie Alpha candlesticks
A pair of Robert Jarvie candlesticks, in spun brass with their original bobeches. Jarvie's candlestick designs were frequently based on abstractions of plant forms. They were particularly praised for their simplicity and elegance and are sought after by today's Arts and Crafts collectors .
(c.1910; ht 29cm/11½in; value D)

▼ Heintz bronze vase
This small vase has a flared neck and a jonquil design overlay. Silver overlays were a regular feature of Heintz bronze ware, which was also typically highy polished. The method of silver application was patented by the company.
(c.1920; ht 16.5cm/6½in; value B)

KEY FACTS

The Roycroft Shop and Gustav Stickley
• MATERIALS beaten sheet copper is most characteristic
• FORMS typically plain and simple
• COLLECTING small Roycroft pieces are inexpensive; all of Stickley's work is valuable and highly sought after

Marks
Roycroft: designs are normally stamped with the firm's name; Stickley pieces are usually inscribed "Als ik kan"

Kalo Shops
• MATERIALS copper, silver

Marks
Various, but usually mention "Kalo" or "Kalo Shops"

Van Erp and other American Metalwork
• COLLECTING original designs of Van Erp, Wright, and Tiffany are rare; collectors should beware of forgeries

Marks
Van Erp: most lamps are marked with a stamped name below a windmill; early pieces are marked with a closed box; Tiffany: pieces made after 1900 may be impressed with "TIFFANY STUDIOS"

See also Arts and Crafts: Metalwork p.382–3

Art Nouveau style appeared in embryonic form during the 1880s and, prior to falling out of fashion by the outbreak of World War I, had blossomed during the 1890s and the first decade of the 20th century. Like the Arts and Crafts Movement that had emerged before it, Art Nouveau was in-part fueled by a rejection of the stylistic eclecticism of most mass-produced mid-19th-century furnishings. At its heart, however, was a particularly enthusiastic re-appreciation of the forms of Nature. In part this had been prompted by a return to "naturalism" in the Gothic Revival style, but it also had some parallels in contemporary Symbolist art and poetry. Most Art Nouveau designers and graphic artists represented the forms of Nature – primarily plant forms, but also female figures – in a highly distinctive style that drew for inspiration on the serpentine lines of 18th-century Rococo decoration, the sinuous interlacings of ancient Celtic ornament, and the asymmetry of traditional Japanese design – a stylistic fusion that, ironically, often proved well-suited to techniques of commercial mass-production. Although by 1914 Art Nouveau had been superseded by a more angular and less embelished "modern" aesthetic, it did enjoy a notable revival in the 1960s, following a series of retrospective exhibitons.

Stained glass and painted lead glass panel, entitled "La Plume," by Alphonse Mucha The work of Alphonse Mucha represents many characteristics of the Art Nouveau style, not least the frequent use of beautiful young "maidens" and stylized plant forms. *(1899)*.
Van Briggle "Mermaid" center bowl Asymmetrical forms were a feature of Art Nouveau design and, in this respect, were reminiscent of pieces from the Rococo period of the early 18th century *(c.1905)*.

Art Nouveau

Art Nouveau took its name from "La Maison de l'Art Nouveau," the shop opened in Paris by Samuel Bing, in 1895, to display the wares made in this new style. A number of trends emerged and were classed by different names in their countries of origin. In Germany it was termed Jugendstil, while in Spain it was known as Arte Joven or Modernismo. In Italy it was called Stile Floreale, or Stile Liberty – the latter in recognition of the British store. In Britain it was sometimes referred to as the Glasgow Style, after the work of various Scottish craftsmen, while in the USA it was often described as Tiffany Style. In Austria, the term Secessionist embraced not only Jugendstil and other Art Nouveau styles, but also the ensuing Modern Movement.

European origins

Although with hindsight, French designers and craftsmen such as Emile Gallé were producing Art Nouveau style artefacts, most notably glassware, in the 1880s, the Art Nouveau style really emerged in coherent form in the early 1890s, in Belgium, in the work of architects Victor Horta (1862–1947) and Henri van de Velde (1863–1957). Horta's Hotel Tassel, built 1893–94, is considered by many to be the first true Art Nouveau building. Here, Horta developed a new aesthetic that took its cue from natural plant forms and embraced the entire building – from decorative schemes, stained glass and furniture, to door handles and hinges. Here Art Nouveau became a "total art" that fused architecture and interior decoration as one whole; at the Tassel, Horta also developed the "whiplash" motif that was to become such a feature of both the style and the era.

Trained as a painter, Henri van de Velde turned his hand to architecture and interior decoration in 1892. In 1894 he published his important pamphlet *Le Déblaiement d'Art*, in which he set out his agenda for the "new art." He is principally remembered today as the designer of the gallery in Paris from which this movement derives its name.

Opened in Paris in December 1895, "La Maison Bing," a shop owned by the art dealer Siegfried Bing (1838–1905), was soon renamed "La Maison de l'Art Nouveau" and became the launch pad of the new style in France. Bing had been sent to the United States by the French government to write a report on American art, which was published in 1896. Inspired by the "newness" and freedom of the continent, unconstrained by old ideas, Bing resolved to capitalize on this spirit.

◄ **Art Nouveau necklace**
Much Art Nouveau jewelry is characterized by its use of relatively inexpensive materials. This piece, possibly by Sydney & Co. uses 9-carat gold and moonstones in its elegant tapering scroll design with rope-twist borders and wirework surrounds.
(c.1900; l. 63cm/24¾in; value G)

▶ **An Italian Art Nouveau side chair**
Although unmarked, this is an exceptional carved chair from the Art Nouveau period, sharing a number of characteristics with much contemporary furniture, particularly pieces emerging from Belgium, France, and Italy. The asymmetrical, sinuous nature of the design, the whiplash curls, the maidens' heads, and the use of motifs from nature (among them a frog and floral details), are among the many features that sum up the style.
(c.1900; ht 99cm/29in; value G)

The building, with rooms created by Henri van de Velde and façade by Victor Horta, was not only a showcase but also a store selling the very best of the "new" from Europe and America. It combined glass and iron with stone to create a gallery space within a department store, where even the filament light bulbs were left uncovered and proudly "new." Entered through a huge "arch" of terracotta sunflowers designed by Louis Bonnier, Bing sought to create an avant-garde world celebrating the new spirit, but importantly proclaiming good design, be it rare and hand-made or mass produced.

The opening show proved a controversial one and was much criticized. High-brow Parisian critics were shocked at the newness and described it as either too English, too Belgian, too Jewish, or all three. Bing (who was Jewish himself) was not distracted. Paintings by Van de Velde and Georges Lemmen were shown alongside stained glass designed by Edouard Vuillard, Paul Ranson, Pierre Bonnard, Henri-Gabriel Ibels, Felix Vallotton, and Henri de Toulouse-Lautrec. Bing also sold more "traditional" fabrics and wallpapers by William Morris, as well as silks from Liberty and metalwork by W.A.S. Benson, and was also the principle agent for Rookwood Pottery in France.

ART NOUVEAU EXHIBITIONS

As in America, exhibitions in Europe played an important role in showcasing emerging styles. Although pioneered by Bing, Art Nouveau was launched onto the world stage by the Paris International Exhibition of 1900. Here the new

◄ **Tiffany "poinsettia" table-lamp**
The Art Nouveau style in the USA is synonymous with the work of Louis Comfort Tiffany, best-known for his exquisite glass designs, often used in the making of his unique, handmade lamps. One of several lamps to use a floral design, this 1950s reproduction has a band of delicate, pink-red poinsettia heads within a background of mottled green leaves and stems. Tiffany's style, including his designs have been much copied over the last hundred years.
(1950; ht 73cm/28½in; value D)

▲ "Amphora" vase
Produced by the porcelain manufacturer Reissner, Stellmacher & Kessel, the "Amphora range" became the most desirable line of Bohemian ceramics from this period and remains collectible today. This example is painted with a long-haired maiden and bears the familiar R.S.K. stamp.
(c.1905; ht 42cm/9¾in; value **H***)*

▼ W.M.F. pewter card tray
The focus of this pewter card, the work of the German Württembergische Metallwaren Fabrik, is a graceful maiden with flowing hair and robes. She seems to emerge out of the piece in a fluid and organic way.
(1906; ht 29cm/11½in; value **G***)*

style was greeted with universal acclaim and seen as a true expression of something genuinely different. Bing's presence, with his "Pavilion Art Nouveau Bing," underscored his innovation. It included furniture by Georges de Feure (1868–1928) and Eugène Gaillard (1862–1933) of the Paris School, naturalistic designs by the German potter Max Läuger (1864–1952), and enamel jewelry by Eugène Feuillâtre (1870–1916).

In the "Palais des Arts Décoratifs" the work of the "botanist decorators" (known from 1901 as the Nancy School) included furniture in organic forms by Emile Gallé (1846–1904) and Louis Majorelle (1859–1926).

In Turin at the "International Exhibition of Modern Decorative Arts" in 1902, the exotic, elaborately inlaid, Moorish- and North African-inspired work of the Italian designer Carlo Bugatti (1856–1940) attracted great attention. Also shown in Turin were the distinctive, geometric furniture designs of the Scottish architect and designer Charles Rennie Mackintosh (1868–1928), which helped to inspire the angular designs of the Austrian Josef Hoffmann (1870–1956) and other members of the Wiener Werkstätte. Ironically, the style seen as "new" in Paris in 1900 was greeted ominously by some as not looking quite so new any more. Bing closed his ground-breaking gallery in 1904 and, by 1914, the style was being superseded by newer forms of expression.

MOTIFS AND MATERIALS
The basic inspiration for Art Nouveau motifs was the natural world: either directly observed, in the form of flowers, animals, birds, insects, and exotic plants, as in the designs of the Nancy School; or translated into the stylized and symbolic forms of the Paris School and the "coup de fouet" (whiplash) motif associated with the Belgian designer Victor Horta (1861–1947); or, from c.1904, the more geometric, angular lines of the Wiener Werkstätte. The other principal motif was the female figure, inspired by the stage acts of the American dancers Loïe Fuller and Isadora Duncan, and the actress Sarah Bernhardt, and idealized as an ethereal maiden with luxuriant, flowing hair and diaphanous, floating gowns. In contrast, in Scotland the core motif was an almost geometric and totally stripped-down rendering of the rose. Materials used by furniture makers were typically exotic, with strongly grained woods such as amaranth, purpleheart, and teak. Veneers were characteristically in banana, coconut palm, locustwood, and bougainvillea, with elaborate inlays in brass and mother-of-pearl.

Members of the Nancy School introduced marquetry panels, often in fruitwoods, depicting local and idealized landscapes, animals, insects, flowers, and plants.

The supremely plastic nature of glass, clay, and metal rendered them especially suited to the curving Art Nouveau forms. Leading glassmakers such as Gallé and René Lalique (1860–1945) experimented extensively with, respectively, cameo and iridescent glass, while jewelers often abandoned ostentatious mediums in favor of mixing materials such as mother-of-pearl, moonstone, opal, horn, tortoiseshell, glass, and plique-à-jour enameling with precious metals. Many of these, particularly horn, tortoiseshell, and moonstone, were chosen for the way in which light affected their appearance and emphasized the "naturalness" of the design. The Württembergishe Metallwaren Fabrik, known simply as W.M.F., was renowned for its art metal works, creating exquisite Jugendstil designs for domestic wares from its own art studio.

▲ Scottish Art Nouveau embroidered panel with a pair of birds perched on a flowering tree
Typical of the Scottish Art Nouveau style, this silk-work embroidered panel has a geometric element to its design, more in keeping with the later work of the Wiener Werkstätte than the fluid lines of the French and Belgian Art Nouveau. The stylized flowering tree and floral motifs are also characteristic of the Scottish School.
(c.1900; ht 71cm/28in; value **D***)*

Furniture

National and regional differences in the Art Nouveau style – that is, differences in both form and decoration – were particularly evident in furniture design. Although Nature was the recurring source of inspiration, the way in which it was represented often varied significantly. For example, many of Frenchman Emile Gallé's extravagant pieces recall Louis XV forms and display extravagant and exotic marquetry, whereas the German Michael Thonet's "bentwood" chairs, although incorporating "roco-coesque" curves, are more "machine-like" and relatively unadorned. Even more idiosyncratic are the Moorish-, Egyptian- and Japanese-influenced designs of Carlo Bugatti in Italy, and the unique sculptural forms of Antonio Gaudí in Spain.

France

The two main centers of Art Nouveau furniture production in France were Nancy, in northeastern France, and Paris. The Nancy School drew heavily on nature for inspiration – a theme that was central to all Art Nouveau design. Furniture typically features superb, intricate marquetry panels, used to decorate organic-, naturalistic-, even zoomorphic-shaped supports and moldings. The furniture made by the Paris School also took inspiration from nature but in a much more stylized and restrained manner.

◄ **Desk by Hector Guimard**
The stylized, sculptural style of the Paris School is exemplified in this pearwood desk, in which decoration is restricted to fine, carved whiplash motifs and two gilt-bronze handles. Such a large, one-off piece – possibly a commission – is very rare and valuable.
(c.1903; ht 86cm/34in; value P)

THE NANCY SCHOOL

The Nancy School began as an informal grouping of artists and makers who had personal and business links, often inspiring one another. This "Provincial Alliance of Art Industries" was formed around 1890 and, under Emile Gallé, became the Nancy School in 1901.

Gallé studied extensively in Paris, London, and Weimar; not only art, but botany and chemistry. Having set up his own glass studio in 1873, he took over his family firm of glass and faïence makers in 1874. In 1885, a cabinetmaking and marquetry workshop was added to Gallé's glassworks in Nancy: tea-tables, nests of tables, and "guéridons" are typical products, most often inlayed or carved with zoomorphic details.

He often ignored the conventions of traditional furniture design and created sinuous, curving forms such as tables supported by huge dragonflies' wings, bronze mounts in the form of insects, and handles in the shape of snails, grapes, corn, and barley. Much of his furniture is embellished with fine marquetry decoration. In the truest sprit of the movement, Gallé's workshops produced two lines of work: a luxury one of exhibition standards, and a more affordable line.

A younger contemporary of Gallé's, and his deputy at the school, was Louis Majorelle (1859–1926). The son of a cabinetmaker, Majorelle studied art in Paris, before returning to Nancy to run the family firm on his father's death in 1879. La Maison Majorelle had specialized in making reproductions of 18th-century French furniture of the highest quality. From 1890, however, Louis introduced new styles influenced by Gallé, but less bound by his tradition and methods of construction.

An accomplished cabinetmaker with a sound knowledge of veneers, Majorelle adhered to the established limits of furniture design, applying superb floral decoration to carcasses inspired by conventional forms, but he treated wood in an almost plastic way. Such was his desire for fluidity of design, he sculpted many pieces in clay before making them in wood.

▼ **Cabinet by Louis Majorelle**
The detail on this piece, together with superb exotic wood marquetry, intricate carving, and pleated silk back panels, is based on natural motifs. Majorelle's marquetry signature confirms its authentic provenance.
(c.1903; ht 1.8m/5ft 11in; value N)

Majorelle combined dark, exotic, strongly grained hardwoods with mother-of-pearl and metal inlays. Although he worked mainly to commission, he also produced catalogs featuring more affordable pieces. Distinctive characteristics such as superb marquetry, often incorporating a chicory-leaf motif, pleated silk back panels, inlaid decoration, and symmetrical forms are found on his individual, elegant pieces. His finest pieces were produced between c.1898 and 1906 and were decorated with beautiful ormolu mounts of waterlilies and orchids. From 1906 to 1908, Majorelle's workshop was industrialized and produced a wider range of lightly sculptured furniture, which was aimed at a more general market than his earlier, one-off pieces. Bronze and ormolu were produced in the workshop, which also made mounts for Daum Frères' glass lamps In turn, they made glass for inclusion in Majorelle's

KEY FACTS

The Nancy School
- STYLE most designs are highly imaginative in form, typically inspired by nature, and extremely decorative
- DECORATION designers used exotic-wood veneers, mother-of-pearl and metal inlay, ormolu mounts, and superb marquetry, often combined with chicory-leaf or whiplash motifs
- COLLECTING all pieces are rare and valuable

Marks
Gallé: designs are marked in elaborate inlay

Majorelle: pieces are typically signed in marquetry

L. Majorelle

The Paris School
- STYLE this is more stylized than that of the Nancy School, with nature often used symbolically
- DECORATION whiplash motifs are typical
- MATERIALS fruitwoods are most characteristic

▲ Silver-plated wall mirror by Georges De Feure
Among the exhibits at the 1900 Paris Exposition was this wall mirror. It depicts a relief-molded scene of a woman in a stylized landscape setting and is mounted within a molded oak frame. Simplicity is a key characteristic of De Feure's furniture design.
(c.1900; w. 45cm/17¾in; value L)

furniture. This symbiosis is typical of the Nancy school.

Other Nancy designers included Eugène Vallin (1856–1922) and Emile André (1871–1933). Cabinetmaker, turned designer, turned architect, Vallin designed whole interiors in the Nancy style. His early pieces were floral in nature, inspired by Gallé, but his work moved toward a more curvilinear form, often featuring unobtrusive mounts and handles. Emile André became one of Nancy's most prominent architects, responsible (with Vallin) for the redesign of the main area of the city, the Grand Magasins, in 1901. André, like his contemporaries, also produced interiors and furniture, often of a more restrained – almost Parisian – style. His chairs have a distinct triangular back, a motif he incorporated into many pieces, and much-copied by other makers.

THE PARIS SCHOOL

If the Nancy school focused on flowers and elaborate inlay, the look of the Paris school was more simplified. Curves were still in evidence, but the form of Parisian furniture was more restrained and sculptural than that of the Nancy School, although decoration was still influenced by nature.

Siegfried Bing's gallery, "l'Art Nouveau – La Maison Bing," provided a focus for the Paris School. His ground-breaking and controversial exhibition of 1895 launched the style on unsuspecting critics – who hated it – and on a curious public, who flocked to see this shocking "new" style. Bing was a great patron of new arts and made protégés of its designers. Among these were Georges de Feure (1868–1928), Edouard Colonna (1862–1948), and Eugène Gaillard (1862–1933). Gaillard's work was closer to Majorelle's than others in Paris, while de Feure and Colonna took a more simple, organic approach.

If Art Nouveau had not been an instant hit in 1895, by 1900 it was a definitely a success. The Paris exhibition became its launch pad and Bing – as ever – was the "eminence grise." His "Pavilion de L'Art Nouveau" was a massive success with the critics and featured work by all of his designers. For example, de Feure designed a dressing room and boudoir, Gaillard designed the vestibule, the dinning room, and a bedroom, and Colonna designed the drawing room. Also connected to Bing was Hector Guimard (1867–1942). Heavily influenced by Victor Horta, whom he met in Brussels in 1895, Guimard is best known for the wrought-iron entrances he designed for the Paris Métro, which are the epitome of Parisian Art Nouveau. His finely made furniture, crafted mostly from fruitwoods, was equally stylized and sculptural.

▲ Emile Gallé mahogany display cabinet
Gallé saw flat surfaces as blank canvas and richly decorated them with exotic wood inlays. This cabinet has a clematis motif. Sometimes Gallé also inlaid text or phrases in his furniture – a type known in French as "meubles parlants" or furniture that talks.
(c.1900; ht 80cm/31½in; value I)

◄ Double bed for the house of Solvay in Brussels
An early Art Nouveau piece by Victor Horta, this double bed shares a number of features with the French furniture that was so clearly influenced by the Belgian's designs. Among the classic Art Nouveau characteristics are the light-brown stained mahogany, the fluid, serpentine lines of the paneled head- and foot boards, and the ornamental bronze handles.
(1894; l. 200cm/80in; value O)

See also Art Nouveau: Glass – France, pp.398–9

Belgium, Austria, Spain, and Italy

In Belgium Art Nouveau first took a clearly defined form in Brussels with the building of the Hotel Tassel, designed in 1892–3 by Victor Horta (1861–1947), but the style was short-lived and was quickly moderated after the International Exhibition of 1905 in Liège. However, Horta's influence was longer-lasting, with his ideas and motifs – in particular his whiplash design – reinterpreted by many European designers. Elsewhere in Europe, although nature's curves were a source of inspiration for all designers, interpretations of Art Nouveau were varied. Austrian designers preferred rectilinear, often severe forms, and Spanish and Italian designers created highly idiosyncratic furniture.

▲ "Silex" sideboard designed by Gustave Serrurier-Bovy
Desiring to make good design accessible to all, the Belgian designer Serrurier-Bovy created the Silex range of self-assembly furniture. The oak frames were attached with black metal grips, and hinges worked with linear and geometrical motifs applied with small screws.
(c.1904; ht 2m/6ft 7in; value I)

BELGIUM

The main exponents of the Art Nouveau style in Belgium were Horta, Gustave Serrurier-Bovy (1858–1910), and Henri van de Velde (1863–1957). Serrurier-Bovy's early furniture, typified by curving forms in mahogany and brass fittings, was strongly influenced by the British Arts and Crafts Movement; his later pieces owe much to German and Viennese design and are more restrained. In 1904 he launched the "Silex" range of affordable but high-quality oak furniture for self-assembly, which was intended to make good design accessible to all.

The painter, architect, and graphic designer Van de Velde gained renown after he created three rooms for La Maison de l'Art Nouveau, the Parisian gallery owned by Samuel Bing (1838–1905) that acted as a center of artistic inspiration for the Paris School. Van de Velde's designs – similar to those of the Paris School – are characterized by an overall restrained sculptural form with little applied decoration. Chairs typically have slender splats, out-curving legs, and upholstery held in place by studwork. Van de Velde designed whole interiors, including that of his own house, Bloemenwerf, at Uccle, near Brussels, which he completed in 1896. He produced furniture mainly to commission, so his designs are rare, and correspondingly keenly sought after.

AUSTRIA

One of the major factors in the development of Art Nouveau furniture in Austria was the pioneering of the bentwood technique by the innovative furniture designer Michael Thonet (1796–1871). The process involved steaming solid or laminated wood so that it could be bent into shape, allowing angular corner joints to be replaced by gentle curves. The sinuous curves associated with Art Nouveau featured heavily in the first catalog of bentwood furniture, produced by the Viennese firm of Gebrüder Thonet (est. 1819) in 1859; the first bentwood rocker was created the following year.

One of Thonet's major designers was the architect Josef Hoffmann (1870–1956), a leading member of the Vienna Secession, an independent group of architects and designers who aspired to introduce a purer, more abstract style of design. Hoffmann was one of the founders of the Wiener Werkstätte (1903–32), an association formed with the aim of producing

▼ Recliner by Gebrüder Thonet
The elegant, curving shapes typical of bentwood furniture were a precursor of the Art Nouveau style and have remained popular. Larger examples, such as bentwood rocking-chairs, are highly sought after and valuable. This Austrian bentwood and cane recliner (no. 7500), with an adjustable back hinged in the center, is a rare and collectible model.
(c.1880; l. 1.5m/4ft 11 in; value I)

▲ Side-chair designed by Henri van de Velde
This elegant Belgian walnut side-chair was made for the dining-room of Van de Velde's home, Bloemenwerf, near Brussels; he also designed silver, cutlery, and decorative fixtures for the house. The spartan, unadorned design is highly characteristic of Van de Velde's work. Although in general chairs are among the most commonly found and reasonably priced items of Art Nouveau furniture, the rarity and desirability of Van de Velde's elegant, finely crafted work explain the high price of this particular piece.
(1894–5; ht 93.5cm/37in; value K)

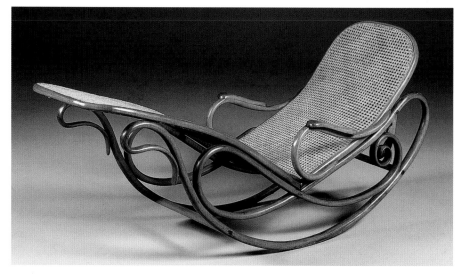

aesthetically pleasing objects, including furniture, for everyday use. Hoffman's furniture designs for the Wiener Werkstätte were strongly influenced by the work of the Scottish architect and designer Charles Rennie Mackintosh (1868–1928), and included tables and chairs made from beechwood, mahogany, limed oak, and other ebonized woods. The forms were characteristically linear and geometric, although his bentwood designs have gently rounded corners. Decoration consists largely of open-centered rectangles or squares, with a ball motif at intersections. From 1903 these rectangular and rectilinear shapes replaced the more French-influenced floral and curving style of the earlier Austrian Art Nouveau style.

SPAIN

In Spain the Art Nouveau style was dominated by a small group of Catalan architects, most notably Antoní Gaudí (1852–1926). Gaudí's highly idiosyncratic furniture was generally designed for the interiors of his extraordinary, sculptural buildings: for example, he designed a kidney-shaped chaise-longue and dressing-table for the Güell Palace (1885–9) in Barcelona, the home of the textile-manufacturer Count Eusebi Güell, who was one of Gaudí's major patrons. Especially striking in the designer's work is his bold rejection of symmetry and his use of twisting, strangely contorted forms. The employment of the central Art Nouveau theme of nature is evident in Gaudí's preference for extremely sculptural, curving, organic structures over straight lines, and his frequent use of floral decoration. In common with other Spanish Art Nouveau furniture, Gaudí's pieces often serve multiple roles: sofas sometimes incorporate small tables, while display-cabinets house mirrors and cupboards. Gaudí's preferred wood was oak, but other Spanish designers used pale woods including ash, birch, and sycamore, which were characteristically combined with burnished metal and fine marquetry decoration.

ITALY

The major designer of Italian *Stile Liberty* (Art Nouveau) furniture was Carlo Bugatti (1855–1940), who, like Gaudí, designed furniture for specific locations, notably the Moorish interior he created for the Italian Pavilion at the Turin International Exhibition of Modern Decorative Arts in 1902. The influence of North Africa is evident in his use of subdued colors (largely browns and blacks), circular seat-backs, strips of beaten and pierced metal, tassels, and vellum upholstery. Bugatti's lavish use of ivory, brass, and pewter inlay is also a predominant feature, but such intricate decoration is very vulnerable and often slightly damaged. However, the rarity and desirability of Bugatti's work means that even less than perfect examples are still highly collectible. His range of designs included larger pieces

such as sectional bench seats, elements of which were produced as cabinets, tables, and chairs. As with Gaudí, Bugatti's designs were highly inventive and often involved a combination of different elements – seats had integral lamps, and tables sometimes included cabinets. Another Italian designer of this period was Carlo Zen (1851–1918), whose furniture is typified by inlaid mother-of-pearl, silver, and brass and restrained forms similar to those of the Paris School.

▶ Table designed by Carlo Bugatti

This table is typical of this Italian designer's North African-inspired furniture. The circular top and square lower shelf are covered in vellum, the piece is inlaid with beaten metal strips, the legs have angular blocks at the terminals, and the frieze is intended to mirror the outline of a mosque.
(c.1900; ht 72cm/ 28¼in; value **L**)

▲ Dressing table designed by Antoní Gaudí

The keynote to this dressing-table, designed for the Güell Palace in Barcelona, is asymmetry. The piece rests on five inlaid and carved legs, each of which is a different shape, with a curved iron stretcher. The mirror is placed at an angle, and the cylindrical cupboards at the sides are placed at different levels. Such a rejection of traditional forms is absolutely typical of Gaudí – both in his fantastic architectural work and in his furniture design.
(c.1887–8; ht 1.8m/6ft; value **Q**)

KEY FACTS

Belgium
- STYLE Serrurier-Bovy: designs are more restrained than French pieces; Van de Velde: pieces have a restrained, sculptural form with no applied decoration; most chairs have slender splats and out-curving legs, with upholstery (often leather) held in place by studs
- COLLECTING commissioned furniture is rare and sought after; Serrurier-Bovy: Silex furniture is more accessibly priced; fakes are virtually unknown

Marks
Serrurier-Bovy: the Silex range is all clearly stamped "SILEX"; Van de Velde: work is rarely marked; pieces can often be identified from contemporary photographs

Austria
- STYLE Thonet; bentwood furniture is strongly characterized by sinuous curves; Wiener Werkstätte: their work is typified by geometric, angular designs
- COLLECTING Thonet: bentwood chairs with cane seats were mass-produced in various designs and in large quantities so are readily available; more desirable are the rarer large rocking-chairs and recliners

Marks
Wiener Werkstätte: pieces are rarely signed but the quantities of original designs and contemporary photographs that survive make identification easier

Thonet: designs are marked as shown   **THONET 2**

Spain
- DESIGNS Gaudí: exotic, amorphous shapes are common, often in the form of multi-purpose furniture
- COLLECTING Gaudí's work is extremely rare

Italy
- DECORATION Bugatti: exotic inlay is typical
- CONDITION minor damage to decoration will not affect the desirability of larger pieces
- COLLECTING large commissioned pieces are rare and highly priced; smaller, functional pieces, especially chairs, are more accessible; fakes are virtually unknown – copies are more common

Marks
Bugatti: some of his furniture designs feature a painted signature, usually within the vellum panels   *Bugatti*

See also Art Deco: Furniture – The Netherlands, Germany, and Scandanavia, pp.416–7

Ceramics

Ceramics were an ideal medium for the Art Nouveau style as form and decoration alike adapted very easily to the new curving shapes and trailing, naturalistic motifs, which were typically applied by transfer-printing, slip-trailing, or hand-painting. Artists, notably artist-potters in France, were keen to break with the constraints of tradition, and experimented with glazes, developing a range of stunning lustrous, iridescent effects. Surface decoration on wares made by commercial firms in France, The Netherlands, and Britain was firmly rooted in the characteristic Art Nouveau theme of the organic, and while the work of makers in Germany and Austria is typically stylized and restrained, it still features much naturalistic decoration.

France

In France, Art Nouveau ceramics inspired by Japanese styles and distinguished by new luster and iridescent glazes were successfully developed both by individual artist-potters and by larger, commercial manufacturers.

ARTIST-POTTERS

French artist-potters led the field in developing the new glazes that were a feature of Art Nouveau ceramics. Joseph-Théodore Deck (1823–91) created his *bleu de Deck* glaze in 1861 and was a pioneer of *Japonisme* in the 1870s, experimenting with flambé and copper glazes.

▲ **Plaque by Clement Massier**
Massier's major contribution to Art Nouveau pottery was his iridescent or luster decoration. This plaque, with a molded, low-relief model of the American dancer Loïe Fuller, is typical of his work.
(c.1900; diam. 49cm/19¼in; value I)

Clement Massier (1845–1917) focused on developing iridescent glazes and in 1883 produced a range of earthenware pieces intended as a canvas for subtle iridescent or luster glazes. Experimental glazes were also the province of Auguste Delaherche (1857–1940), who won a gold medal at the Paris International Exhibition in 1889 for pieces with engraved or raised decoration and unusual glazes. A notable success was his use of the flambé glaze. In 1894 he moved to the village of Armentières, where he decorated simple forms with deep monochrome glazes. After 1904 he made mostly one-off white porcelain vases featuring pierced decoration of stylized flowers.

▼ **Vase by Sèvres**
Sèvres vases are among the finest examples of French Art Nouveau commercial ceramics. This example has the typical slip-cast, fine white porcelain body with equally typical hand-painted floral decoration in muted colors with gilded highlights.
(late 19th century; ht 46cm/18in; value G)

◄ **Vase by Auguste Delaherche**
The elegant, understated form of this gourd-shaped stoneware vase is set off by the reduced copper flambé glaze – a characteristic deep crimson streaked with turquoise blue. A well-known maker and an unusual glaze make this piece highly collectible.
(c.1889–90; ht 66.5cm/26in; value K)

THE SEVRES PORCELAIN FACTORY

The established commercial ceramics manufacturers in Europe were swift to adapt their production to include Art Nouveau wares. There were two major trends: one based on the organic, naturalistic style and the other a more stylized, formal response. The Sèvres porcelain factory (est. 1756), the most notable French commerical producer of Art Nouveau ceramics, largely followed the first trend. Its porcelain vases were very successful at the Paris International Exhibition in 1900 and are among the best of all French Art Nouveau pieces. Slip-cast in white porcelain, the vases often had a sculptural form that showed a Chinese influence. The decoration was hand-painted in underglaze colors – subdued soft greens, yellows, and mauves – with gilded highlights; gilt-bronze mounts or plinths in naturalistic designs were also typical. They have only recently become sought after and are thus a good area for collectors. A more radical response to the Art Nouveau style was the vases designed for Sèvres by Taxile Doat (1851–1938), whose organic-shaped vases featured gourd-flower stoppers.

KEY FACTS

Artist-potters
- GLAZES experimental flambé and iridescent glazes are highly typical of the period
- DECORATION Art Nouveau motifs, including organic designs and women, feature heavily
- COLLECTING pieces are very desirable and valuable

Marks
Deck: pieces were impressed with these initials

Delaherche: pieces were impressed with this mark

The Sèvres porcelain factory
- FORMS Chinese-influenced vases are typical
- BODY most pieces are of high quality and made of slip-cast, pure white porcelain
- DECORATION mostly hand-painted, floral designs; many pieces feature top-quality gilding
- COLORS soft, subdued colors are a major feature of pieces by Sèvres
- COLLECTING the name of a well-known decorator will add to the appeal of a piece; Art Nouveau Sèvres vases are a relatively new area of collecting

See also Ceramics: Porcelain – Sèvres, pp.196–7

The Netherlands

The art pottery that developed in The Netherlands from the 1880s fell into two broad styles: that of The Hague, which corresponded approximately to the French Nancy School, where forms had sinuous curves and both symmetrical and asymmetrical floral decoration; and that of Amsterdam, which featured simpler shapes and formalized, even geometrical decoration, more akin to the stylized line of the Paris School. Some of the most notable examples of the Amsterdam School were the earthenwares made at the Amstelhoek Factory, which had brick-red or ochre grounds inlaid with symmetrical designs in colored clay. However, the dividing line between the two styles was as fluid as the Art Nouveau curves, and many designers and companies worked in both styles.

◄ Vase by the Rozenburg factory
Rozenburg's "eggshell" porcelain wares were the major Dutch contribution to Art Nouveau ceramics. The curving, elongated, exotic form of this vase is characteristic of the work of Schellink, one of the company's chief designers and decorators. The delicate decoration of sunflowers and spider's webs are typical of the "eggshell" wares. This vase has a hairline crack, which will reduce the value of an otherwise highly desirable pot.
(1900; ht 32.5cm/13in; value K)

THE HAGUE SCHOOL

The Rozenburg factory (1883–1916) was founded in The Hague by Wilhelm Wolff von Gudenberg with the intention of producing art wares. In the late 1880s and early 1890s, under the artistic directorship of Theodoor C.A. Colenbrander (1841–1930), it produced innovative earthenwares with bold abstract decoration influenced by both Art Nouveau and Japanese art. However, the company's major contribution to Art Nouveau ceramics was their range of what was called "eggshell" porcelain, which was developed in 1899 by J. Jurriaan Kok (1861–1919). These wares, which were extremely well received at the Paris International Exhibition in 1900, were slip-cast into elegant and inventive forms, which were characteristically razor-thin, often elongated in design, and slightly concave apart from the rim. No two pieces were ever exactly alike as the decoration, typically depicting such naturalistic motifs as wildflowers, birds, and insects, was hand-painted. Two of the most inventive and sought-after designers and decorators at the Rozenburg factory were W.P. Hartgring and Sam Schellink; the latter's pieces

are usually marked with his monogram as well as the factory mark. Wares such as vases, ewers, and teawares in exotic shapes are now very sought after by collectors, and the high quality of these vulnerable pieces means that they are equally highly priced.

Weduwe N.S.A. Brantjes & Co. (1893–1920), based in Purmerend, produced wares in the style of those made at Rozenburg. During the factory's short period of operation, a distinctive and highly collectible range of decorative earthenwares in strong, symmetrical forms was produced, characterized by brightly colored glazes and bold, all-over floral decoration.

THE AMSTERDAM SCHOOL

The Amstelhoek factory (1894–1910), in Amsterdam, was established by the jeweler W. Hoeker and is noted for its range of earthenwares, which were made from red- or yellow-fired clays, partly inlaid with white-fired clay. Pieces were designed in 1900–1901 by the sculptor Lambertus Zijl and thereafter by Christiaan J. Van der Hoef. Decoration consists mainly of stylized, Japanese-inspired designs of plants and animals.

Another well-known manufacturer of Art Nouveau ceramics was the Distel factory, also in Amsterdam, founded in 1895 by J.M. Lob. The major designer associated with the company was Bert Nienhuis (1873–1960), who from 1902 was the head of the decorating department, and whose early pieces include tiles decorated with animal and flower motifs. Most sought after, however, are his pieces in white porcelain, in symmetrical forms; these are typified by matt glazes and restrained decoration in soft pastel colors and symmetrical designs.

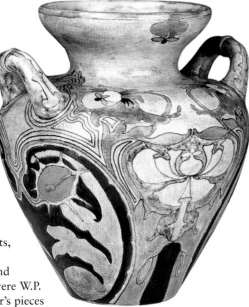

▼ Vase by Weduwe N.S.A. Brantjes & Co.
This two-handled earthenware vase has several of the characteristics of the pieces manufactured by the short-lived Weduwe N.S.A. Brantjes & Co. These include a strong, robust symmetrical form, a bright glaze, and boldly colored, all-over, naturalistic decoration, highly typical of the Art Nouveau period.
(c.1896–1904; ht 36cm/14in; value G)

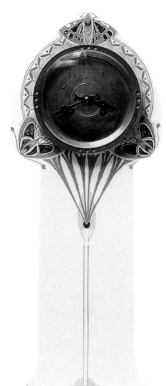

▲ Clock designed by Bert Nienhuis for the Distel factory
Nienhuis joined Distel in 1895, and this clock is typical of his porcelain designs: it has a symmetrical form, emphasized by the restrained pastel-colored decoration, and a matt white glaze. The delicacy of such pieces is in marked contrast to the robust, brightly colored earthenware pieces that were also manufactured during the firm's short period of production.
(c.1895; ht 28.5cm/11in; value I)

KEY FACTS

The Hague School
- DECORATION typically naturalistic; most earthenwares feature boldly colored abstract designs; Rozenburg "eggshell" pieces feature delicate designs
- COLLECTING Rozenburg: pieces are very delicate: check for cracks or fine crazing; no fakes or copies are known

Marks
Rozenburg: this is the mark used on early wares; after 1900 a crown or painted monogram and a year symbol were used

Weduwe N.S.A. Brantjes & Co.: wares are stamped as shown

The Amsterdam School
- DECORATION Amstelhoek: stylized organic designs; Distel: early earthenwares are in the Rozenburg style; later porcelain wares are in soft pastel colors and more stylized in design

Britain, Germany, Austria, and Denmark

Although British art potteries of this period are especially celebrated for their Arts and Crafts wares, ceramics in the Art Nouveau style were well suited to mass production by the larger ceramics firms. Major Staffordshire companies opened art pottery studios, where designers could experiment with flowing, organic forms, new methods of glazing and decorating, and naturalistic surface designs. In Germany the response to the style was more restrained but the use of nature as the overriding source of inspiration nevertheless dominated. Designs that were used to adorn the fine wares made at Meissen (est. 1710) are typically restrained and stylized, paving the way for the geometric designs of the Vienna Secession and, later, for the bold, stylized work of the Modernist movement. Designers in Denmark, who were influenced by the newly popular Japanese styles, experimented with luster and iridescent glazes and made use in their designs of the human figure, which was another central Art Nouveau motif.

◀ **"Iris" pedestal vase by William Moorcroft for Macintyre & Co.**

Decorated all over with the distinctive tube-lining technique favored by this British potter, the example shown is from Moorcroft's successful Florian range of wares. Designs were typically in blues, yellows, and white, with decoration of flora used to complement the form of the piece. Decoration of animals is rare, although some "butterfly" vases are known to exist; peacock feathers were also used.
(1900; ht 25.5cm/10in; value H)

BRITAIN

From 1898 William Moorcroft (1872–1945) led the art pottery department at Macintyre & Co. (est. 1847), in Burslem, Staffordshire. His early designs, known as "Aurelian" wares, were generally printed in underglaze blue with overglaze red and gilding. His later work for Macintyre retailed as "Florian" ware and was possibly the foremost contribution to British Art Nouveau ceramics. At Macintyre, Moorcroft produced designs for both utilitarian wares and the now more collectible art pottery including vases, jugs, loving-cups, biscuit barrels, and *jardinières*. His inventive forms were applied with symmetrical floral designs in blues, yellows, and white. He took tube-lined decoration – fine lines of slip applied to the surface of the object – to new heights, using it to decorate an entire surface.

At the firm of Minton & Co. (est. 1793), also in Staffordshire, a range of Art Nouveau earthenwares decorated with tube-lining was produced under the direction of the influential Léon Solon (1872–1957), who was Art Director of the company from 1900 to 1909. This range was influenced by the designs of the Vienna Secession, whose members also experimented greatly with tube-lined decoration.

▲ **Vase by Minton & Co.**
The glazes on this strikingly colorful tube-lined vase by the British firm of Minton are typically blurred, having been unevenly fired. The red decoration in particular has run beyond its bounds and up toward the neck of the piece. The vertical decoration reflects the influence of Viennese Art Nouveau designers, who made extensive use of such geometric patterns and stylized flowing plant forms. The slightly avant-garde shape of this vase also shows a Viennese influence.
(c.1900–1909; ht 28.5cm/11in; value D)

GERMANY

The early response (before 1910) to the Art Nouveau style at the Meissen firm, near Dresden, was more conservative than that in France and the Netherlands. The superb-quality porcelain remained the major feature; earlier forms were largely retained; and the new style was mainly confined to contemporary underglaze decoration with matt, semi-matt, or crystalline glazes. Among the most successful pieces (now much sought after) were the vases designed by Julius Konrad Hentschel (1872–1907); these were mainly ornamental, with symmetrical decoration of trailing flowers, often in *pâte-sur-pâte* (a technique in which layers of paste are used to build up relief decoration). Hentschel and his brother Johannes Rudolf Hentschel (1869–1951) made good use of the superb Meissen body in their collectible range of services, vases, candlesticks, and sculptures. Less successful were the table services that were commissioned from the Belgian painter, architect, and designer Henri van de Velde (1863–1957) and the German designer Richard Riemerschmid (1868–1957). Although sought after today, these table services were not popular at the time and were produced in relatively small numbers. The more formal, geometric Secessionist forms and decoration worked better on the larger vases with covers that were made from 1910, in which the quality of the porcelain was the predominant feature.

Although Meissen encountered mixed fortunes, with the popularity of its earlier French-inspired vases being offset by the relative lack of success of the table services commissioned from some of the leading Secessionist designers, the Berlin porcelain factory (est. 1763) produced a range of tablewares featuring Art Nouveau decoration. Designed by Theodor Hermann Schmuz-Baudiss (1859–1942), these tablewares were extremely successful at the time of production, and they are now highly collectible.

Max Läuger (1864–1952) was one of the few German potters to be influenced by the French style. Originally an architect, engineer, and sculptor, in 1895 he established a pottery at Tonwerke Kandern at Kandern, near Baden. The forms of his robust pots (mainly vases) were influenced by the rural pottery made in the Black Forest area and have a characteristic slightly irregular glaze. The slip-trailed organic or floral decoration – often long-stemmed flowers and grasses – was in the French style. Läuger's pieces are usually marked with the Kandern mark and his own monogram.

◀**Plate designed by Henri van de Velde**

Van de Velde, who played a major part in the evolution of the Belgian style of Art Nouveau, has adapted the stylized, geometric whiplash design of another influential Belgian Art Nouveau designer, Victor Horta (1861–1947), for this piece's underglaze blue decoration. His work is always sought after, and his ceramic pieces may include his monogram alongside the factory mark.
(1903–4; diam. 27cm/10½in; value F)

AUSTRIA

In 1905 Michael Powolny (1871–1954), an Austrian ceramics decorator, and Bertold Loffler (1874–1960) co-founded the Vienna ceramics factory (merged from 1913 to become United Vienna and Gmund ceramics factory). One of the most collectible ranges produced by the company is the popular series of small, figural earthenware sculptures made by Powolny. The figures are usually small, cherubic boys (although some pieces featuring young women were also produced), typically holding flowers, and are of white earthenware with detail in black. The figure usually stands on a restrained base, which is decorated with black chevron-style designs. Powolny figures are rare and seldom signed, but their distinctive style makes them readily recognizable.

Desirable Art Nouveau sculpture was also produced by the Austrian ceramics factory of Riessner, Stellmacher & Kessel (est. 1892; known as R.S.K.), in Turn-Teplitz, Bohemia. Most sought after is the company's mass-produced earthenware "Amphora" range of vases, which typically took fantastic, exotic forms with molded organic decoration of berries, leaves, and stems on thick enameling.

▲ Vase and cover designed by Julius Konrad Hentschel

German-born Hentschel was one of the most successful designers of Meissen's earlier French-influenced Art Nouveau pieces. This decorative porcelain piece has the typical toned ground and organic floral decoration that were associated with the Nancy School; especially characteristic of Meissen is the symmetry of the decorative clematis flowers and buds and the *pâte-sur-pâte* technique that was used to produce them. *(1905; ht 23cm/9in; value I)*

► "Amphora" vase by Riessner, Stellmacher & Kessel

This earthenware vase is based on a design by Riessner, one of the founders of the company that produced these highly popular vases. This fine example features rich decoration, including a pierced and gilded neck, and the naked maiden and stylized flowers with brightly colored ceramic centers so characteristic of Art Nouveau. The lavish use of gold coupled with deep red is also typical of R.S.K.'s designs. Handles were often whiplash- or branch-shaped, culminating in decorative tendrils. R.S.K. capitalized on the Amphora label, using it also for a rare range of small wall-hung masks. *(c.1900; ht 45.5cm/18in; value H)*

DENMARK

In 1883 Bing & Grondahl (est. 1853) and the Royal porcelain factory (est. 1775) merged to become Royal Copenhagen. Under the inspired direction of Arnold Krog (1856–1931), who was influenced by Japanese ceramics, the company produced a successful Art Nouveau range, distinguished particularly by innovative glazing and decorating techniques – notably the use of underglaze grays and blues to produce naturalistic, misty paintings of landscapes, and (c.1904) crystalline liquid and crackled glazes. Designs included such mildly erotic sculptural pieces as the now-famous *The Rock and the Wave*, as well as more demure figures of children in a pastoral setting. All such pieces were mass-produced in slip-cast porcelain, with characteristically subdued coloring of pale blue-gray and flesh tones. In 1895 Royal Copenhagen began production of a series of Christmas plaques, distinguished each year by a different design; this series is still produced today, and early examples are highly collectible.

► The *Rock and the Wave* designed by Theodor Lundberg for Royal Copenhagen

Both the symbolic and stylistic elements of Art Nouveau are combined in this celebrated slip-cast porcelain Danish figure. Designed by Lundberg in 1899, it is still produced by Royal Copenhagen today, although early examples are most highly sought after by collectors. Royal Copenhagen marks provide useful clues as to the date of such pieces, because different styles of mark have been used by the company over the years. *(1899; ht 46cm/18in; value J)*

Glass

The supreme plasticity of glass made it the medium best suited to expressing the concepts of the Art Nouveau style. Glass artists moved away from the industrial methods that had produced the heavily decorated cut glass of the 19th century, experimenting instead with new techniques and exploring the sculptural possibilities of glass to create daring forms in fine technicolor.

Eager to reach the mass market, factories used such industrial techniques as acid-etching, while continuing to produce limited edition and studio pieces. In France Emile Gallé took inspiration from flora and fauna, while in the USA Louis Comfort Tiffany produced a range of beautiful iridescent and mosaic glass, which was widely imitated by glassmakers throughout Europe.

France

Art Nouveau glass in France was dominated by the work of makers in Nancy, especially Emile Gallé, the Daum and Müller brothers. Also typical of Nancy was the use of *pâte-de-verre* ("glass paste"), which was used to create small, sculptural glasswares.

EMILE GALLE

The name of Emile Gallé (1846–1904) is synonymous with the Art Nouveau movement. His wonderfully organic forms inspired by the beauty of nature assured his position as the most influential glass artist of the early 20th century. Gallé studied botany in Weimar and trained as a glassmaker at Meissenthal, Germany, and at his father's glass and faience factory in Saint-Clément, France. In 1874 he took over the family business and moved the factory to Nancy. His early work was in clear, amber, or green glass enameled with heraldic devices and designs inspired by historical and Islamic art. While he quickly established himself as an outstanding designer, he also became known as a highly accomplished glass technician, whose experiments produced exciting effects.

Perhaps Gallé's most important development was that of cameo glass in the 1880s – a technique first perfected by the Romans. Two or more layers of colored glass were fused together and a design engraved with a wheel through to the glass beneath. This type of glass was hugely popular, and in order to speed up production Gallé introduced the use of acid-etching, where layered glass was covered in a design in an acid resist and then plunged into a bath of hydrofluoric acid, which slowly ate away the unprotected glass. Items that have been mass-produced using this technique are known as "standard" Gallé and include floriform, baluster-shaped, and squat, pinched vases, table-lamps with mushroom-shaped or conical shades, and floriform boxes, stoppered bottles, and lampshades for metal bases. They lack the depth of the hand-finished pieces and consequently do not command such high prices.

Although Gallé supervised all the designs for the factory, his constant experimentation only allowed him to work on a few one-off or limited-edition pieces. Greater interest is focused on "artistic" Gallé than on his standard wares, particularly on vases in the *marqueterie sur verre* ("glass marquetry") technique (c.1897) and *verreries parlantes* ("talking glassware"). *Marqueterie sur verre* involved pressing shapes of hot glass onto the surface of a glass object, and then merging them with the body by rolling it on a slab; *verreries parlantes* are pieces that are engraved or decorated in cameo with verses from French poetry.

◄ Vase by Emile Gallé
Cameo vases and lamps decorated using the "blowout" technique, with portions of the design mold blown in naturalistic relief, are valued according to the depth of color, as well as the rarity of the piece and its general condition. "Blowout" vases such as this one were produced in large numbers and in a wide variety of colors and thus are commonly found today. Prominent, organic-inspired decoration as featured here is typical of all of Gallé's work – both his glass and his exquisite furniture.
*(c.1910; ht 38cm/15in; value **L**)*

▼ Table-lamp by Daum Frères
The technique used here to depict a winter landscape is acid-etching and enameling – wares decorated in this way are mostly not as valuable as cameo glass, although pieces featuring a rain-streaked effect are collectible. Landscapes depicting autumnal and winter scenes are typical on lamps, vases, and bowls; the effect of the design disappearing over the edge of the shade is also characteristic.
*(c.1900; ht 63cm/24¾in; value **L**)*

OTHER NANCY SCHOOL MAKERS

The firm (est. 1875) of Auguste Daum (1853–1909) and his brother Antonin Daum (1864–1930), also based in Nancy, produced cameo and other art glass in the manner of Gallé from the 1890s. Fascinated by the endless possibilities offered by color, the brothers experimented widely with complex internal polychrome effects and mottled coloration; they also experimented with texture, for example with the *martelé* ("hammered") technique, where the surface of the glass was held against an abrasive wheel and faceted so that the background of the design resembled beaten metal.

One of the most highly distinctive hallmarks of the firm of Daum Frères glass is their use of frosted grounds, which are achieved by rolling a gather of hot glass in powdered glass; when reheated the glass vitrified with the main body providing an opaque, matt background. Another effective (although highly complicated) technique, which was used not only to create an impression of perspective but also to depict such meteorological effects as rain or snow, was known as *intercalaire*. This involved fusing layers of glass together, carving them with a design, covering them in another "skin" of glass, and carving them again. The firm of Daum Frères is still in production today but does not make reproductions of its early pieces.

Another principal Nancy School maker of cameo glass was the firm of Müller Frères, founded in Lunéville by Henri and Desiré Müller and active from 1895 until c.1933. Most of their wares are in cameo glass or enameled in the style of Gallé and Daum Frères, but are of inferior quality and less valuable. Dark brown and yellow are characteristic colors. Lamps and artistic pieces using innovative techniques or featuring Japanese-inspired decoration are the most highly sought after.

PATE-DE-VERRE

Pâte-de-verre ("glass paste") is a glassmaking technique that was first practiced in ancient Egypt and successfully revived by French glass artists in the late 19th century. The technique involved grinding glass into a powder, adding a flux (a substance that facilitates the melting of the powder), and then adding color. The mixture was then melted and applied in layers or poured into a mold and refired. The main pioneer of the technique was the sculptor Henri Cros (1840–1907), who used it mainly in the production of small, solid items – the instability of glass made in this way makes it most suited to small-scale, solid objects such as paperweights. Wares have a characteristic "sugary" surface texture and are commonly in matt, mottled coloration.

Examples of work by Cros are rare and often appear "experimental." Most common are plaques and some lightweight bowls, which are thickly cast or molded with Neo-classical figural decoration in pale, matt colors. Cros's work is fragile and often in poor condition and is considered mainly of academic interest by collectors. More generally sought after is the work of Albert Dammouse (1848–1926), a follower of Cros who worked chiefly in ceramics at the Sèvres porcelain factory (est. 1756). Dammouse perfected the medium to produce a range of porcelain-like pieces that are decorated with figural and floral imagery. These pieces are now rare.

Other notable *pâte-de-verre* artists include Gabriel Argy-Rousseau (1885–1953), Alméric Walter (1859–1942), and François-Emile Décorchement (1880–1971). Argy-Rousseau, who produced wares in the medium between c.1900 and 1925 in Nancy, was extremely prolific. His repertoire included vases, pendants, statuettes, ashtrays, paperweights, lamps, illuminated plaques, and perfume burners. Most pieces were produced in series from molds, and popular models were produced in large numbers over several years. Among the rarest, most collectible items are table-lamps, later examples of which have glass shades and bases; most are of *veilleuse* type with wrought-iron or bronze foliate bases. Walter, who worked at the firm of Daum Frères between c.1906 and 1914, produced a wide variety of *pâte-de-verre* wares, which were comparable in style and standard to the work of Argy-Rousseau, although more vibrant in color. He specialized in delicately made *vide poches*, paperweights, and ashtrays, which are typically molded with animals or floral sprays.

▲ Vase by Müller Frères
Both the form and the coloration of this double overlay cameo vase are typical of Müller Frères' etched cameo glass, which is gaining respect among cameo glass collectors.
(c.1905; ht 45cm/17½in; value J)

◀ *Pomme de pin* pendant by Gabriel Argy-Rousseau
Argy-Rousseau specialized in *pâte-de-verre*, producing a range of small-scale wares such as this decorative pendant. His pieces are usually richly colored and distinctively opaque. Pins, perfume burners, and bowls are also typical.
(c.1921; w. of pendant 5.5cm/2¼in: value F)

▼ *Vide poche* by Alméric Walter
This piece exploits the varyingly opaque and translucent qualities of *pâte-de-verre*, a material favored by Walter; it has a waxy surface and a solid, heavy finish.
(c.1900; w. 11.5cm/4½in; value G)

KEY FACTS

General points
- TABLE-LAMPS pieces in overlay glass by the Nancy School are typically more valuable than vases or coupés
- ALTERATIONS shades and bases are often married; old shades on modern bases are common; tall vases are often skilfully reduced at the neck
- CONDITION damage to rims and bases, including drilling vases for lamp conversion, may be hidden by authentic-looking metal mounts
- COLLECTING desirability is determined by the scale and the complexity of technique; pieces in the high Art Nouveau style are most valuable

Gallé
- DESIGNS naturalistic motifs in warm, muted colors are typical; some designs feature applied or *marquetrie de verre* decoration; many vases and lamps feature an opaque white ground
- COLLECTING unique, "artistic" pieces by Gallé can be extremely valuable; *verreries parlantes* are popular with collectors; most late, commercial ware are of modest value only; the majority of Gallé glass on the market bearing the Gallé name was made after his death or is a modern forgery
- BEWARE fakes are widespread and often convincing; most copy later, commercial overlay vases and lamps with floral or landscape designs

Marks
This starred mark was used from Gallé's death in 1904 until 1914

Other Nancy School makers
- DESIGNS mottled or "frosted" grounds are typical; some pieces feature applied decoration of dragonflies or snails; many wares have innovative, organic forms
- COLLECTING Müller Frères: cameo or enameled work is of inferior quality to pieces by Gallé or Daum
- BEWARE collectors should beware of authentic Daum pieces with spurious applied decoration

Marks
Daum Frères: signature is usually enameled or in intaglio on the side of a piece or gilded or engraved on the underside of the foot. The cross is the regional emblem of Lorraine

Müller Frères: most are signed in cameo or in red; "Lunéville" was added after 1910

Pâte-de-verre
- DESIGNS Cros: most pieces are thickly cast and appear "experimental"; Walter: his work includes salamanders and chameleons, some modeled by the sculptor Bergé
- CONDITION *pâte-de-verre* is often cracked owing to its fragile state; dark-colored pieces can be repaired but restoration is easily spotted with transmitted light
- COLLECTING the value of a piece is determined by the condition, the pattern, and the intensity of color; deep, rich tones are the most sought after
- BEWARE copies tend to be brighter, more contrasting in color, and less finely modeled than original pieces; fake pendants and figural bowls may be very convincing; Argy-Rousseau: some signed pendants and figural paperweights have been reproduced in recent years and are often misrepresented as original

Marks
Argy-Rousseau: most pieces are incised with a signature

Walter: some sculptural works also feature a stylized "B" for "Bergé"

See also Art Nouveau: Furniture – France, p.390–1

Austria

Austrian art glass is commonly in the *Jugendstil* taste, a formal, sometimes architecturally inspired form of modern design contemporary to Art Nouveau but without the naturalism of the French style. The best examples, showing influence of the Wiener Werkstätte (1903–32), are among the most admired of all European art glass. The influence of the American Louis Comfort Tiffany (1848–1933) is strongly evident, notably in the iridescent vases by the firm of Loetz.

LOETZ AND PALLME-KÖNIG & HABEL

The most widely available and collectible Austrian glass was made at the factory of Johann Loetz-Witwe, in Klostermühle, near Vienna, from *c.*1890 until the 1920s, mostly under the direction of Max Ritter von Spaun. Loetz glass is typically of iridescent bluish-green color, sometimes streaked with red or golden yellow. Surfaces may be spotted with patches of silvery iridescence, intended to appear like the wings of a butterfly but known as "oil spots." Vases, ranging from squat and symmetrical to tall, asymmetrical shapes, are most collectible, especially those featuring applied decoration in the form of vertical lappets, handles, or feet in silvery or gold iridescence. Some Loetz vases and lamps may be attributable to such designers as Gustav Gurschner (*b.*1873) and Maria Kirschner (1852–1931); designs by such notable artists as Josef Hoffman (1870–1956) or Koloman Moser (1868–1918), who both designed for Loetz while working for the Wiener Werkstätte, are extremely collectible. Other renowned Wiener Werkstätte designers whose pieces for Loetz can be identified include Dagobert Pèche (1887–1923), Otto Prutscher (1880–1949), and Michael Powolny (1871–1954).

The firm of Pallme-König & Habel, in Kosten, near Teplitz, manufactured iridescent glasswares in the style of Loetz from *c.*1887. Designs are varied, ranging from small, squat vases with ruffled rims to brass-bound inkwells and vases with applied floral motifs. Many wares are of a purplish or pea-green color with trailed decoration. Pallme-König & Habel glass tends to be thicker and of a lesser quality than wares by Loetz; iridescence is also typically less controlled.

J. &. L. LOBMEYR AND KARL KÖPPING

The Viennese firm of J. & L. Lobmeyr (est. 1823) was a prolific manufacturer of Art Nouveau table glass and also produced some of Austria's most innovative art glass, mostly under the direction of Ludwig Lobmeyr (1829–1917). The firm specialized in cut and polished vessels and elegant drinking ware with extremely thin walls. Lobmeyr commissioned designs from such leading Wiener Werkstätte designers as Hoffmann and Prutscher; their pieces include tall-stemmed wineglasses flashed with a color and cut with geometric designs, goblets with painted decoration in polychrome enamel or grisaille, and flaring, geometric bowls in dark colors including amethyst.

The work of Karl Köpping (1848–1914), produced in his Berlin studio, is some of the rarest and most valuable *Jugendstil* glass. From *c.*1896 Köpping specialized in the design of tall-stemmed, extremely fragile drinking glasses made "at-the-lamp," where rods and tubes of glass were manipulated under the heat of a lamp rather than at the furnace. Köpping's virtuoso pieces typically feature extremely delicate, applied tendrils of glass, floriform shapes, and foliage motifs.

► Goblet attributed to Otto Prutscher
Glasses of this type were made at several Austrian glassworks after designs by Wiener Werkstätte designers. The technique of cutting through the flashed surface color is traditional to Bohemia and much used for conventional designs.
*(c.1905–8; ht 21cm/8¼in; value **G**)*

▲ Vase by Loetz
This rich blue iridescent coloration, particularly when decorated with silvery threading, is generally preferred by collectors to a predominant green. The pinched form is typical of Loetz designs.
*(c.1898; ht 21.5cm/8½in; value **I**)*

▼ Vase by Pallme-König & Habel
This iridescent vase with red and green trailed decoration is typical of wares made by the firm. Vessels of this type may be identified as being of a lesser quality than pieces by Loetz by a lack of pontil mark, a molded surface, and thick walls.
*(c.1900; ht 13cm/5in; value **C**)*

KEY FACTS

Loetz
- COLOR pieces are almost always in an iridescent greenish-blue, sometimes with red or yellow streaking; vivid colors or unusual ground colors, notably red, yellow, and purple, are the most sought after and typically denote a higher-quality piece
- BASES vases normally feature a ground pontil mark
- QUALITY fine edges and thin walls are typical
- COLLECTING Loetz glass has gained greatly in popularity in recent years; pieces in the high Art Nouveau style or those attributable to designers – especially members of the Wiener Werkstätte – are the most valuable; vases are particularly sought after

Marks
This engraved mark was in use from 1898

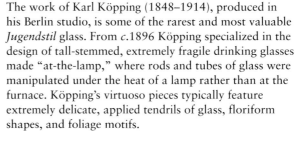

Pallme-König & Habel
- COLOR purple and bright pea-green are typical
- BASES there is generally no ground pontil mark
- DECORATION trailed colors are very common
- QUALITY pieces are often misrepresented as Loetz but are inferior, lacking the high design standards, delicacy, and quality of finish of Loetz wares

Marks
Pieces were never signed; some are spuriously engraved with a Loetz signature

J. &. L. Lobmeyr and Köpping
- COLLECTING Lobmeyr: stemware has limited value despite high style and fine quality; pieces by Wiener Werkstätte designers for Lobmeyr, especially those by by Hoffman and Prutscher, are rare and collectible

Marks
Wiener Werkstätte: pieces are typically engraved or acid-etched as shown with two interlocking initials

Lobmeyr: an engraved monogram is characteristic of his pieces

Köpping: most pieces feature a tiny engraved signature

See also Art Nouveau: Glass – The United States, pp.402–3

Britain

Although Art Nouveau glassmaking is principally associated with continental Europe and the United States, several British glassmakers worked in distinctive styles and to high technical and artistic standards.

JAMES COUPER & SONS

The Glasgow glasshouse of James Couper & Sons (est. 1880) produced some of the best British Art Nouveau glass from 1880 until the early 20th century. The firm specialized in iridescent, streaked, bubbly glass, free-blown into unique, asymmetrical forms. Shapes are often similar to the work of Loetz in Austria or Tiffany Studios in the United States. Many vessels were enhanced by the inclusion of mica or metal foil specks, a technique rarely practiced outside Britain. Couper named this line "Clutha" and employed several designers specifically to work on the range, notably Christopher Dresser (1834–1904). Clutha glass is fairly common: the most collectible examples are Dresser's large designs, in particular the slender "goose-neck" or trumpet vases and vessels of unusual form.

STOURBRIDGE GLASS

The most widely collected and distinctive British Art Nouveau glass is cameo glass produced in the Stourbridge area of the West Midlands from c.1875 by such factories as W.H., B. & J. Richardson & Sons (est. c.1836), Thomas Webb & Sons (est. 1837), and Stevens & Williams (est. 1847). The glass is almost exclusively white, cut back over a deep red, blue, or – less preferable – vibrant yellow ground. Typical wares include small vases, plaques, plates, boxes, perfume bottles, and vials with silver-gilt tops; small "boudoir" lamps with cameo-glass shades and bases are especially rare.

Particularly notable by Thomas Webb & Sons are the large, documented cameo-glass pieces by George Woodall (1850–1925) or his brother Thomas Woodall (1849–1926). Stevens & Williams is most celebrated for its wares by the glass sculptor John Northwood (1836–1902), best known for reproducing the famous Roman cameo "Portland" vase in 1876. In 1882 Northwood became art director at Stevens & Williams, which produced a wide variety of art glass. Distinctive lines include "Silveria," introduced c.1900 by his son – also John Northwood (b.1870) – comprising oviform vases of opaque, richly colored, and metallic speckled glass coated in applied, trailed, thin glass "threads."

OTHER MANUFACTURERS

Between c.1885 and 1920 the Whitefriars Glassworks (est. c.1680), in London, produced a range of iridescent Art Nouveau vessels under the direction of Harry J. Powell (1853–1922). The finest and most collectible pieces are of pale, yellowish color with thin, opalescent streaking, free-blown into floriform or stemmed vases with ruffled rims. Glassware with

twisted or curled stems is distinctive but is fairly rare, partly owing to the brittle nature of the soda glass from which it is made. Other British Art Nouveau glassworks include the Moncrieff Glassworks (est. c.1864), in Perth, Scotland, best known as makers of "Monart" ware, a heavy, bubbly, pale-colored glass used for a variety of vases from c.1918 to c.1950. Monart glass was developed and made by Salvador Ysart (1887–1956) and his son Paul Ysart (b.1904).

▲ "Clutha" vase designed by Christopher Dresser for James Couper & Sons
Typically of amorphous form, Clutha glass is bubbly, and may have foil inclusions. The word "Clutha" is said to mean "cloudy" in Old Scottish and is also supposed to be the Gaelic name for the river Clyde, which runs through Glasgow.
(c.1885; ht 27cm/10½in; value **G***)*

► "Monart" vase by the Moncrieff Glassworks
This is a typical example of Monart glass, produced by Moncrieff in the 1920s. Monart glass was sold through such important department stores as Liberty & Co. (est. 1875), in London, until after World War II. Forms are generally heavy and the glass is characteristically bubbled.
(c.1920; ht 16cm/6¼in; value **C***)*

KEY FACTS

James Couper & Sons
- DESIGNS Clutha wares are distinguished by bubbles and heavy streaking
- COLLECTING Clutha pieces of asymmetrical form by Dresser from 1890s are highly collectible

Marks
Clutha wares are marked as shown

Stourbridge glass
- FORMS Webb: designs include plates, plaques, boxes, perfume bottles, and lamps in formal Victorian style
- COLORS Webb: red, blue, and yellow are typical
- COLLECTING Webb: their work is very popular in the USA, Canada, and Australia; designs by Woodall, and signed pieces, are most collectible

Marks
Webb: most of their wares bear an etched or printed mark as shown; some cameo glass was etched in full with "THOMAS WEBB & SONS"

Stevens & Williams: this mark was etched or printed onto some pieces; other marks feature the firm's full name; individual designers did not sign their wares

Other manufacturers
- DESIGNS Whitefriars: delicate floriform pieces decorated with streaked color and twisted stems; Moncrieff: Monart glass is typically heavyweight, bubbled, and usually pale in color
- COLLECTING Whitefriars: the finest pieces are thin, blown floriform pieces or vases of pale yellow featuring opalescent streaks; Monart glass: currently few pieces have significant value; there is no market outside Britain

Marks
Moncrieff: this circular mark featuring the Monart trademark and the factory name is the most typical stamp that is used on Monart wares

◄ Tazza designed by Harry Powell for the Whitefriars Glassworks
Whitefriars glass can be identified by its consistently high quality, lightness, and a typically delicate and elegant form. Most popular with collectors are the iridescent, floriform vases in the style of Tiffany; these often feature opalescent streaks within pale, gold glass.
(1902; ht 21cm/ 8¼in; value **H***)*

See also Glass: Cameo glass, pp.300–1

The United States

The exponents of the Art Nouveau style in glass in the USA, in-part inspired by developments in Europe, introduced a new grammar of ornament to the medium. A distinction was made between glass as a medium of artistic expression and glass as a household item, leaving designers free to experiment with innovative new glassmaking and decorating techniques in their attempts to produce beautiful wares.

ART GLASS

The most influential figure in American Art Nouveau glass was Louis Comfort Tiffany (1848–1933). From 1885 he operated under various names, including the Tiffany Glass & Decorating Co. (est. 1892), in Corona, Queens, New York, and the Tiffany Studios (est. 1900), in New York City. After the death of his father, Charles Lewis Tiffany, he was appointed Artistic Director of Tiffany & Co. (est. 1837) from 1902 until 1918, during which time he continued to run his own firm, Tiffany Studios, which focused on his own artistic identity. He experimented widely with new techniques and produced many types of new glass, notably the extraordinary range of iridescent glassware sold under the tradename "Favrile." Other hallmark techniques include "mottled," "drapery," and "fractured." Many of Tiffany's technical innovations in glassmaking simulated different elements of nature.

▲ Vase by the Steuben Glassworks
This glass vase of flattened bottle form with applied raised handles is part of the "Aurene" series, which was introduced by the firm in its early years of production. The range included a number of colors, of which red is the most desirable, on account of difficulties encountered when producing art glass in this color, particularly at the firing stage.
(c.1914; ht 33cm/13in; value **G**)

◄ Quezal lily lamp
This eight-light lily lamp with iridescent shades is a fine example of the range of art glass manufactured by Quezal. Such pieces can easily be mistaken for Tiffany wares, as the two firms used almost identical decorating techniques and colors. Collector's may be further confused by the fact that Quezal did not always mark their pieces.
(c.1920; ht 45.5cm/18in; value **G**)

Especially notable are "Lava" glass, characterized by a rough, pitted surface and iridescent stripes or patterning, intended to appear as molten lava; "Cypriote" glass with a pitted, opaque surface to give an antique finish; iridescent, multicolored "Paperweight" glass, typically with floral decoration; light-green "Aquamarine" glass, embedded with decoration of marine plants and animals; and "Agate" glass, intended to resemble the stone.

The Steuben Glassworks (est. 1903; known as Steuben Glass, Inc. from 1933), in Corning, New York, was another important contributor to the creation of modern art glass. The British glassmaker Frederick Carder (1863–1963) was lured away from the firm of Stevens & Williams (est. 1847), near Stourbridge, to become the firm's founding director. Under Carder, Steuben introduced a variety of glass types, notably gold and blue "Aurene" tablewares, which take their name from the Latin *aurum* meaning "gold" and the Middle English word for "sheen"; as well as the "Intarsia" series (1916), characterized by a boldly colored design encased within two layers of clear glass. Other types include the slightly bubbly "Cintra" glass (c.1917), and "Cluthra" glass, which is typified by larger bubbles (but is thought not to be related to the Clutha glass made by the British firm of James Couper & Sons). Notable glass in the style of Tiffany was made by the Quezal Art Glass & Decorating Co. (1902–24) in Queens, New York, set up by Martin Bach and Thomas Johnson, both formerly of Tiffany.

LAMP MANUFACTURERS

Thomas Edison's invention of the incandescent filament bulb in 1885 revolutionized domestic lighting. Tiffany Studios was the first to capitalize on the invention, and produced a wide range of lamp designs – including table-lamps, chandeliers, wall-sconces, and floor-lamps – from the late 1890s until its closure in 1932. Popular models were those with floral themes, such as peony, wisteria, poppy, daffodil, and laburnum, typically produced in brilliant shades of red, purple, blue, orange, and yellow. Geometric designs were produced in neutral palettes of greens, blues, and golds. With a few exceptions, the bronze bases, which were manufactured in numerous styles and sizes, are interchangeable with the leaded shades. Tiffany Studios was not the only firm to recognize the exciting possibilities offered by the new technology

▲ Tiffany "Favrile" glass
The floriform vases of Tiffany's delightful "Favrile" range were never intended as receptacles for flowers, but for purely decorative and ornamental purposes. Typically, each one captures an entire plant form within a single fluid shape. The gold bowl of this example reflects a lavender iridescence onto the domed circular foot. Tiffany's floriform vases are sought after by today's collectors who consider them to be highly representational of the Art Nouveau period.
(c.1905; ht 27cm/10¾in; value **??**)

◄ "Windswept Tulip" table-lamp by Tiffany Studios
Tiffany's floral lamps are particularly popular with enthusiasts of Art Nouveau.
(c.1900; ht 65cm/21½in; value **P**)

of electricity: soon a number of other American glasshouses, inspired by Tiffany's artistic and commercial success, branched out to manufacture ranges of electric table- and floor-lamps alongside their more traditional glasswares.

The Glass Handel Co. (1885–1936; known as the Handel Co. from 1903), in Meriden, Connecticut, was founded by Philip Julius Handel (d.1914) and produced leaded shades as well as a distinctive range of mold-blown and lightly etched lampshades, which were intricately decorated on the interior with hand-painted landscapes, birds, and flowers, and which, when illuminated, gave a three-dimensional appearance. The firm concentrated solely on decorating glasswares and relied on commercial glasshouses for the production of its glass. Table-lamp designs were particularly popular, as was a line of smaller-scale cylindrical desk- and piano-lamps.

The Pairpoint Corporation (est. 1900), in New Bedford, Massachusetts, manufactured a series of blown shades known as "Puffies," which were molded in high relief with flower sprays hand-painted on the inside of the glass. Common floral themes included roses, dogwoods, pansies, and apple blossoms, in tones that were generally softer than those by Tiffany, with golds, oranges, pinks, and browns predominating. Smaller models were known as "boudoir puffies." These shades were beautifully proportioned and provided a different aesthetic to the standard leaded-glass shade popularized by Tiffany Studios. The Pairpoint Corporation also manufactured several other types of shade, most notably those of ribbed and scenic styles. Several other, smaller firms, including Duffner & Kimberly in New York City, produced leaded-glass

▲ "Puffy" lamp by the Pairpoint Corporation

"Puffy" lamps were produced in a wide variety of designs, of which this hummingbird and chrysanthemum version is just one. The molded, high-relief surface of the "Puffy" shade is characteristic of the ground-breaking designs produced during the Art Nouveau period. A number of designs were produced in a range of sizes and on a selection of interchangeable bases, intended to complement a variety of domestic interiors.
(c.1905; h 54cm/21¼in; value **G**)

◄ Table-lamp produced by the Handel Co.

A table-lamp with hemispherical acid-etched shade reverse-painted with pink roses and yellow butterflies. The colorations of Handel's lamps was chosen to coincide with the time of year in which they were painted. In general, paler colors were used in the spring and summer months, while lamps painted during the fall and winter months used much warmer colors, with golden or brown tones. The mellow, glowing colors of this example, suggest that it was made in the fall or winter.
(c.1905; ht 59cm/23¼in; value **J**)

shades in a variety of designs and sizes similar to those of Tiffany Studios. However, Duffner & Kimberly was only in operation from 1906 until 1911, and its overall production was therefore relatively small. The range of items that they manufactured included leaded-glass table- and floor-lamps, chandeliers, and blown shades. Unfortunately, however, the firm did not always sign its work, which can make identification sometimes rather difficult. Also worthy of mention are the Art Nouveau designs of the glass manufacturers Miller Co. and Jefferson Co.

KEY FACTS

Louis Comfort Tiffany
- DECORATION this tends to be integral to the object; new iridescent finishes were popular
- BEWARE fakes and copies are common; items are well documented – numbers can be checked; Quezal vases are often misidentified as Tiffany

Marks
Art glass is commonly inscribed "Louis C. Tiffany – Favrile," "L.C. Tiffany – Favrile," or "LCT," all with accompanying numbers

Steuben Glassworks
- DECORATION iridescence is characteristically brighter than that of Tiffany's Favrile glass
- TEXTURED EFFECTS "Cintra" glass has a powdered interior; "Cluthra" glass has a bubbled interior

Marks
Many pieces (1903–32) feature an inscribed or a stenciled signature to the pontil

Quezal Art Glass & Decorating Co.
- FORMS these are typically asymmetrical and organic
- DECORATION the surface is always iridescent and satiny; colors are brilliant; frequent use is made of the "pulled feather" device; naturalistic floral motifs
- COLLECTING pieces tends to be more heavily walled than designs by Tiffany

Marks
This mark was used from 1902 to 1924

Lamp designs
- SHADES Tiffany: geometric and leaded shades in green, orange, and gold; Handel: usually domed or conical, with a reverse-painted image and a hand-painted shade; frosted "chipped" or sand-finished effect; Pairpoint: shades were frosted before decoration
- BASES Tiffany: always bronze with a green-brown, brown, or gilt-bronze patina; Handel: white metal and pewter; Pairpoint: bronze, silver plate, copper, glass

Marks
Tiffany: many shades bear a stamped metal tag with "TIFFANY STUDIOS NEW YORK" and a model number; most bases are impressed with the same mark on the underside and a model number

Handel: lamps often have a molded signature in capitals; many shades bear a painted signature, a design number, and sometimes the artist's name or initials

Pairpoint: shades are signed on the inside or outer edge; bases are often signed on the underside with "THE PAIRPOINT CORPORATION" and the firm's logo, which is the letter "P" in a diamond

See also Art Nouveau: Jewelry, pp.406–7; Art Deco: Glass – The United States, p.434–5

Metalwork

As in the other decorative arts, avant-garde silversmiths and metalworkers at the turn of the century rejected the historical styles of the 19th century and attempted to create a new style, based on the formal, almost abstract representation of the natural world. The success of the Art Nouveau style in silver and metalwork encouraged commercial manufacturers, especially in Germany, to produce affordable items in the modern style for a wider market.

FRANCE

The leading Art Nouveau metalworkers and jewelers were René Lalique (1860–1945), Eugène Feuillâtre (1870–1916), Lucien Falize (1839–97), and Lucien Gaillard (b.1861). Lalique made silver openwork cups featuring naturalistic designs of stalks and pine-cones, as well as silver scent bottles. Feuillâtre specialized in decorative items such as vases with rich *plique-à-jour* enameling, where enamel is held in an unbacked metal framework. Falize and Gaillard were both influenced by Japanese art, which during the 1890s was promoted in France by such dealers as Samuel Bing (1838–1905). In 1878 Gaillard became an apprentice in his family's jewelry firm and in the early 1880s began a detailed study of Japanese methods of coloring, inlaying, and patinating silver and other metals. In such items as vases, he combined precious and non-precious metals.

Among commercial manufacturers, the Parisian firm of Cardeilhac produced good-quality repoussé copper and silver vases, which feature naturalistic motifs, but in a much more restrained style. The firm of Boucheron (est. 1858), also in Paris, produced high-quality tablewares inspired by late 18th- and early 19th-century silver. Although the firm used a combination of hand and mechanized methods of production, the quality of craftsmanship in its work is exceptional. Bing and other leading dealers such as Julius Meier-Graefe also sold a range of mass-produced domestic silver and metalwork by leading designers, including Paul Follot (1877–1941) and Georges de Feure (1868–1943).

► **Table-lamp cast after a model by Leleu**
During the Art Nouveau period, when electric light was a recent invention, many sculptors turned to the design of elaborate table-lamps. This French example has typical Art Nouveau organic decoration of spiky dandelion leaves on the shade and flared base, with the flowerheads represented by claw-set, cabochon, opalescent glass – a popular material at this time. Cast-bronze lamps such as this should have a natural patination and not be over-polished.
(c.1900; ht 40cm/15¾in; value J)

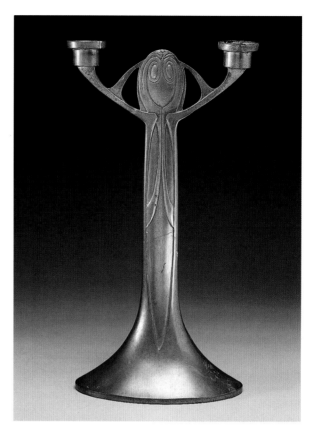

GERMANY AND AUSTRIA

At the turn of the century the Art Nouveau style became widely popular in Germany, where it was known as *Jugendstil*. The most important centers for design in the new style were Munich and Darmstadt. In Munich, Fritz von Miller (1840–1921) opened a workshop in 1876; he began by making silver centerpieces in historical styles but from the mid-1890s used formalized floral and animal motifs in his designs. Miller's assistant, Ernst Riegel (1871–1939), established his own business in 1900, making decorative silver wares using traditional techniques such as piercing and chasing. His designs are also distinctive for his use of stylized birds set among dense foliage – motifs strongly inspired by Persian art. In 1907 Riegel joined the avant-garde artists' colony at Darmstadt, established under the patronage of Grand Duke Ernst Ludwig von Hesse. Other members of the colony included the architects Peter Behrens (1868–1940) and Josef Maria Olbrich (1867–1908). Their designs for silver and metalwork, like those of their Belgian contemporary Henri van de Velde (1863–1957), who also worked in Berlin and Weimar, are distinctly different from the flowing French style: for example, jugs and vases are elongated and subtly curved, with angular contors, twisted handles and finials, and ornament confined to small areas.

Commercial manufacturers were encouraged by the government to employ progressive designers to strengthen the ties between culture and industry. For example, the metalwork manufacturer Peter Bruckmann of Bruckmann & Söhne helped in 1907 to found the Deutscher Werkbund, a coalition of designers and industrialists. Bruckmann commissioned silver designs

◄ **Candelabrum designed by Josef Maria Olbrich for Eduard Hueck**
The Austrian architect Olbrich was a member of both the Wiener Werkstätte and the Darmstadt artists' colony in Germany in the early 20th century. He produced many designs for furniture, jewelry, and posters, as well as silver and pewter. This elegant candelabrum, which is made of pewter, features the elongated, curving forms and stylized naturalistic motifs that are highly typical of German Art Nouveau metalwork.
(1901; ht 36cm/14in; value H)

▲ **Jug designed by Albin Müller**
The simple, linear decoration and slender, tapering form of this pewter jug are typical of the fine metalwork designed by avant-garde artists and architects, for German commercial factories. The restrained use of low-relief decoration makes the form well suited to machine production. This piece is stamped with the number "1866," which is most probably the reference number of the design in the company's archives.
(1902; ht 39.5cm/15½in; value F)

for machine production from both Behrens and Olbrich. M.H. Wilkens & Söhne of Bremen also made metalwork and silver designed by Behrens, and the Eduard Hueck metalwork factory of Ludenscheid produced pewter, characterized by elongated forms with decorative interlacing, from designs by Behrens, Olbrich, and the architect Albin Müller (1871–1941).

The most successful makers of commercial Art Nouveau pewter were the Württemberg Metalwork Factory (known as WMF; est. 1880), in Göppingen, and Kayser & Söhne (1885–c.1904), near Düsseldorf. The style of wares made by these factories was flamboyant and closer to the French Art Nouveau style than to the restrained, angular forms of the German avant-garde designers. WMF specialized in such decorative wares as vases, trophies, and picture frames in Continental pewter (an electroplated metal alloy), typically embellished with sinuous foliage and figures of women. Kayser produced practical pewter items such as ashtrays, vases, and dishes in flowing, organic forms, sold from 1896 under the trademark "Kayserzinn."

In Austria the Wiener Werkstätte (1903–32) produced a large range of silver and metalwork, distinctive for its use of pure lines and geometric forms. The workshops employed professional silversmiths, who worked in close collaboration with such designers as Josef Hoffmann (1870–1956) and Koloman Moser (1868–1918) and used mainly mechanized processes, although some pieces were handmade to order. Hoffmann's designs are of two types: from the early 1900s he designed starkly geometric, pierced fretwork desk-stands, vases, and candlesticks in silver or painted metal, but from c.1910 his silver or brass bowls and dishes were more organic in inspiration, with lobed and fluted or ribbed sides and planished surfaces. Like Hoffmann, Moser was influenced by the geometric style of the Scottish designer Charles Rennie Mackintosh (1868–1928). Moser designed small, decorative items such as vases in simple shapes, often cylinders and spheres, decorated only with planished surfaces and hardstones.

◀ **Vase designed by Josef Hoffmann for the Wiener Werkstätte**
Hoffmann's early silver and metalwork designs, produced between 1903 and c.1910, for the Wiener Werkstätte are among the most distinctive of this period because of their pure, geometric forms and striking pierced fretwork decoration. The silver-colored trumpet form of this vase has a smooth surface, whereas later pieces designed by Hoffmann are characterized by a faceted, planished surface. Pieces by such a notable designer as Hoffmann are especially collectible today. Designs include vases, baskets, candlesticks, and desk-stands.
*(c.1905–7; ht 32cm/12½in; value **K**)*

DENMARK AND ITALY

The leading silversmith of the period in Scandinavia was Georg Jensen (1866–1935), who worked as a sculptor and potter before opening his own silversmithing workshop in Copenhagen in 1904. Jensen's style was a distinctive adaptation of Art Nouveau, featuring simple, rounded forms with smooth rather than planished surfaces, and detailed and sculptural naturalistic decoration of fruit, roses, pod, and tendril forms for handles, feet, and finials. Items such as tureens were made by a combination of hand and machine methods, and few pieces were specially commissioned. Many of Jensen's designs, as well as those designed for the firm by the architect Anton Rosen (1858–1928) and the painter Johan Rohde (1856–1935), are still manufactured by the Jensen firm today.

In Italy the painter, sculptor, and designer Carlo Bugatti (1856–1940) was best known for his designs for Art Nouveau furniture and interiors, but he also designed silver, featuring the typical Art Nouveau motifs of naturalistic plants, animals, and insects, especially after he moved from Milan to Paris in 1904. His designs were executed by silversmiths employed at the Parisian bronze foundry A.A. Hébrard.

▲ **Vase and cover designed by Georg Jensen**
The simple, rounded forms of Jensen's Danish silver wares are reminiscent of 18th-century silver. The cover of this vase features typical Jensen ornament of finely sculpted flower-bud forms, with cabochon amethysts – some of his pieces have ivory handles, which act as heat insulators as well as adding decorative contrast. Jensen's work was very popular in both Scandinavia and the USA, to where large quantities were imported.
*(c.1910; ht 21cm/8¼in; value **H**)*

▼ **Cigar bowl designed by Carlo Bugatti for A.A. Hébrard**
Insects were one of the most popular motifs among Art Nouveau designers. In this silver cigar bowl by Bugatti, the cigar rests are formed by the outspread wings of three naturalistically detailed cicadas.
*(c.1900; ht 10cm/4in; value **G**)*

KEY FACTS

France
- STYLE asymmetrical, fluid ornament of flowers, plants, and birds, influenced by Japanese art, is typical
- MATERIALS the French made lavish use of enamel, ivory, rock crystal, glass, and hardstones

Marks
Feuillâtre: most pieces feature an engraved signature
Boucheron: most pieces are stamped with the firm's name or "B" in script

Germany
- STYLE forms are more elongated, angular, and stylized than French forms, except for commercial pewter
- REPRODUCTIONS copies of WMF pewter have a bright rather than patinated surface; modern backstands on picture frames are most likely covered in velor
- COLLECTING it is important that any glass liner, especially for Kayser pewter, should be original

Marks
Albin Müller: impressed monogram

WMF: this mark was used after 1914

Austria
- FORMS pierced or solid geometric forms by Hoffmann in silver or painted metal are very characteristic
- COLLECTING all pieces by the Wiener Werkstätte are highly sought after by collectors

Marks
Wiener Werkstätte: pieces are stamped "WW" and often with the designer's monogram; mark for Josef Hoffmann

Denmark
- STYLE most pieces have simple, rounded forms
- DECORATION finely sculpted, often repoussé flowers are common, as are pod and tendril motifs for handles, feet, and finials

Marks
Georg Jensen: stamped as shown or "GJ"

Jewelry

In the late 19th century there was a reaction in artistic circles to the low quality of mass-produced jewelry and the ostentatious use of expensive materials such as diamonds. Artists throughout Europe and the USA attempted to re-establish the traditions of fine craftsmanship, often – as in Britain with the Arts and Crafts Movement – as part of the push for social reform. Jewelry became an art in its own right and not just an accessory for the display of wealth, and pieces were valued for their design and workmanship rather than for the cost of the precious stones and metals. Art Nouveau jewelry is distinctive for its use of comparatively inexpensive materials including opals, moonstones, turquoises, silver, rich enameling, ivory, horn, bone, and frosted glass. There is also particular emphasis among collectors on the work of individual designers, and pieces signed by the best makers or still in their original boxes are especially valuable.

▶ **"Butterfly" pin by Charles Robert Ashbee**
Typically of both Arts and Crafts and Art Nouveau designs, this British pendant incorporates such precious materials as gold and a pearl with less valuable silver and enamel. The visible marks of hand craftsmanship, especially in the hammered silver wings, are a distinctive feature of Arts and Crafts jewelry.
*(1900s; l. 6cm/2½in; value **H**)*

BRITAIN

British jewelry made from the end of the 19th century differs from French and American Art Nouveau jewelry in its use of simple floral and figural patterns and decorative interlacing motifs inspired by Celtic art. This was largely the result of the influential social and aesthetic philosophy of the late 19th-century Arts and Crafts Movement. Craftsmen's guilds, organized on socialist principles, encouraged craftsmen to design and make objects, including jewelry, from start to finish. Arts and Crafts designers deliberately used inexpensive materials so as to make their jewelry affordable to working people. Cabochon stones such as garnets, turquoise matrix, mother-of-pearl, and baroque pearls, as well as dull, hammered metal are among the most distinctive features of Arts and Crafts jewelry. Plain collet settings were preferred to claw settings, and necklaces in the form of loops or festoons of chains, pendants decorated with wirework, enamel, and baroque pearls, and clasps and buckles were favorite forms.

The jewelry of the architect and designer Charles Robert Ashbee (1863–1942), who established the Guild of Handicraft in the East End of London in 1888, is especially characterized by the use of turquoise enamel and a distinctive four-leaf design of billowing petals. The architect Henry Wilson (1864–1934) turned to metalworking in 1890 and made jewelry inspired by medieval and Renaissance forms.

Large commercial firms were quick to imitate the avant-garde Arts and Crafts designs, and their pieces were often machine-made with hand-finishing. These pieces were more popular than the handmade pieces of the guilds, particularly as they were less expensive. The most important firm was Liberty & Co. of London, established in 1875 by Arthur Lasenby Liberty (1843–1917). By the 1890s Liberty employed leading British Arts and Crafts designers, such as Archibald Knox (1864–1933), Jessie M. King (1876–1949), and Oliver Baker to design jewelry, silver, and pewter for factory production. Liberty insisted on anonymity for his designers, so pieces lack designers' signatures. However, Knox's style in particular is very distinctive, characterized by the use of Celtic interlacing, whiplash motifs, and complex knots in silver, and decorated with turquoises, mother-of-pearl, and blue and green enamels. King was known for her range of belt buckles in curled and interlacing hammered silver, set with cabochon hardstones.

Murrle, Bennett & Co. (1884–1914), founded by the German Ernst Mürrle and an Englishman named Mr Bennett (about whom very little is known), was another important retailer of Arts and Crafts and Art Nouveau jewelry. The firm specialized in inexpensive silver and gold pieces, some of which came from the factory in Pforzheim, Germany, owned by Theodor Fahrner (1868–1928), since Mürrle had connections with German and Austrian designers and makers. Much of Murrle, Bennett & Co.'s jewelry is in the plain, bold, geometric styles distinctive of the German *Jugendstil*. Pieces such as necklets and pendants are set with turquoises, misshapen pearls, and opal matrix, with gold and silver wires and pierced geometric forms.

▼ **Waist clasp designed by Jessie M. King**
King was one of the leading figures in the British Arts and Crafts Movement, designing jewelry for Liberty & Co. The trelliswork and stylized enamel roses of this clasp are influenced by the work of Charles Rennie Mackintosh, one of the most important figures in the Glasgow School, where King trained.
*(c.1900; w. 4.5cm/1¾in; value **H**)*

▲ **Bracelet by Murrle, Bennett & Co.**
Jewelry produced and sold by the British firm of Murrle, Bennett & Co. shows the influence of the more abstract jewelry designs made in Germany and Austria, as the company had strong links with avant-garde designers in those countries. Turquoise matrix – turquoise embedded in its parent rock – was a particularly popular stone, much used in jewelry at this time.
*(c.1900; l. 18.5cm/7¼in; value **G**)*

▲ **Pendant in the style of Charles Horner**
Horner, who worked in Halifax, England, specialized in relatively inexpensive mass-produced jewelry such as hatpins and pendants in simple geometric designs, similar to styles made by Liberty & Co. Mass-produced pendants such as this are much more abundant and affordable than one-off pieces by well-known craftsmen.
*(1910; w. 4cm/1½in; value **B**)*

THE UNITED STATES

The Art Nouveau style was particularly influential in the USA, where the leading maker of jewelry in this style was Tiffany & Co. (est. 1837) of New York. Its director, Louis Comfort Tiffany (1848–1933), the son of the firm's founder, is mainly associated with stained glass, but he also opened an art jewelry department in 1902, for which he produced designs for necklaces, pins, and other pieces of fine jewelry. These usually combined hardstones or precious stones with glass and enameled metal.

The firm of Unger Bros (1881–1910) of Newark, New Jersey, manufactured commercial stamped and cast jewelry in silver and low-carat gold, which was intended for the less expensive end of the market. Buckles, pendants, and pins are especially typical forms, and these were mostly decorated with floral and other naturalistic motifs and the archetypal Art Nouveau female with long, flowing hair.

CONTINENTAL EUROPE

Some of the finest and most stylish Art Nouveau jewelry was produced in France: dramatic and impressive, jewelry in this style is characterized by the use of asymmetrical and flowing lines. Necklaces, pendants, and hair-combs were among the favorite types of jewelry. The most innovative and influential designer was René Lalique (1860–1945), who achieved international renown for his shockingly beautiful works of art, particularly after they were shown at the Paris International Exhibition in 1900. Lalique pioneered the use of inexpensive materials such as horn and revived the delicate technique of *plique-à-jour* enameling (in which the enamel is held in an unbacked metal framework) for features such as the wings of "dragonfly" pins and pendants. He also introduced such subjects as female nudes, girl's faces with windswept hair, and overripe fruit. Lalique's jewelry has been widely copied, but few imitations achieve the exceptionally high standard of his poetic design and fine craftsmanship.

Other French Art Nouveau jewelers include Paul Vever (1851–1915) and his brother Henri Vever (1854–1942) of the Maison Vever (est. 1821), who used such inexpensive materials as silver and horn in a more angular manner than Lalique. The silversmith Lucien Gaillard (*b*.1861) took over the firm of his father, the furniture designer Eugène Gaillard (1862–1933), in 1892 and produced Japanese-inspired jewelry in mixed and patinated metals and horn carved into simple organic shapes. Another leading jeweler, Georges Fouquet (1862–1957) commissioned Alphonse Mucha (1860–1939) to design jewelry in the Art Nouveau style for the actress Sarah Bernhardt. Also notable is the work of Eugène Feuillâtre (1870–1916).

Jewelry by the Austrian designers Josef Hoffmann (1870–1956) and Koloman Moser (1868–1918) of the Wiener Werkstätte (1903–32) is unusual in its use of geometric forms and textured metalwork. In Germany the firm of Theodor Fahrner in Pforzheim employed such artists as Josef Maria Olbrich (1867–1908) and Patriz Huber (1878–1902) to create designs for mass production. Although machine-made, their pieces are of the finest quality and typified by architectural lines.

◄ Pendant and chain by Tiffany & Co.

The firm of Tiffany was the leading American manufacturer of high-quality Art Nouveau jewelry at the end of the 19th century. Like French pieces, the firm's jewelry frequently features stylized vegetal forms, as in this necklace and pendant, which is finely decorated with *plique-à-jour* enameling and opals. The blue, yellow, and green color scheme is characteristic of Art Nouveau jewelry, whereas the use of gold rather than silver is specific to Tiffany for this type of jewelry.

(*c*.1902; w. of pendant 5cm/2in; value **L**)

▼ Ring by René Lalique

Lalique was the foremost French designer of the Art Nouveau period; his copious range of jewelry includes hatpins, pins, pendants, bracelets, chokers, stomachers (which were worn as bodice decoration), hair-combs, and rings. Combinations of materials such as opal and enamel, as in the *marquise* ring shown here, are typical, although the use of gold suggests that the ring was made for a wealthy client – silver is more prevalent in the jewelry of this period.

(*c*.1890–1900; value **L**)

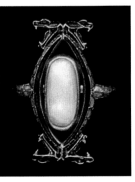

▲ Pin by Gaston Lafite

Graceful female figures with flowing drapery and delicate butterfly-style wings are among the most distinctive features of Art Nouveau jewelry. This figure's wings are made in fragile *plique-à-jour* enamel — popular among the best Art Nouveau jewelers. This piece would have been made for a wealthy client (with avant-garde tastes), as the figure is made of gold and the wings set with diamonds and rubies.

(1900s; l. 5.5cm/2¼in; value **K**)

KEY FACTS

- DECORATION cabochon stones, baroque pearls, and *plique-à-jour* enameling are predominant
- ALTERATIONS belt buckles have sometimes been converted to pins – this reduces the value
- CONDITION enamel should be in good condition as it is difficult and expensive to repair; hollow metal used in mass-produced pieces is vulnerable to dents
- COLLECTING Arts and Crafts: jewelry in this style is a rather academic collecting area, appealing only to specialized taste; jewelry was often made by students of guilds and is therefore rarely signed; Art Nouveau: designers' or makers' signatures add to the interest and value of a piece, even though it is not always possible to identify minor jewelers – signed jewelry by Lalique is particularly sought after; Art Nouveau earrings are less common than other forms of jewelry such as necklaces and pendants; hair-combs are less popular with collectors than other types of jewelry as they are not very wearable today

Marks

Jessie M. King: some pieces bear a signature

Murrle, Bennett & Co.: designs are stamped with "MB & CO" or as shown

René Lalique: marks vary – some feature a cross and initials as shown, others bear a signature

Georges Fouquet: pieces should be marked as shown

See also Jewelry, pp.260–73; Art Deco: Jewelry, pp.438–9; Mid-century Modern: Jewelry, p.452; Postmodernism: Jewelry, p.470

Sculpture

During the 19th century Paris was considered the home of sculpture and attracted sculptors from all over Europe and the USA. They studied at the Ecole des Beaux Arts and submitted their work to the salons for exhibition. Only selected work would be displayed at one of the prestigious annual salon exhibitions, attended by important government and institutional purchasers. Artists and sculptors relied heavily on the commissioning powers of these people for their economic survival. Thus the salons exercised considerable control over the artistic output of the 19th century. They upheld strong Classical traditions, demanding sculptors continue to interpret the work of their masters in a Classical idiom. By the 1890s sculptors had become more daring. Many sought to pursue more romantic ideas and were charmed by the concept of sculpture as pure decoration.

The break with the artistic restrictions was aided by a number of founders, who increasingly used a machine called a pantograph, invented in 1830. This was a type of tracing machine that enabled founders to produce scaled down models of monumental pieces. Thus huge Classical statues could be reduced to domestic proportions and be produced as limited editions. This fueled a new desire for sculpture in the home. Founders encouraged a growing body of young sculptors, providing them with a new vehicle for their work and introducing them to a wider audience. The royalties earned from the serial production released artists from the need to earn commissions from one-off pieces. Some founders negotiated copyright with major sculptors to reproduce (edit) their work in metal, but often they commissioned artists to make models in wax, clay, or plaster, which were then cast in metal and made in serialized editions.

▲ *Butterfly Girl* by Francis Renaud (*b*.1877)
This charming French bronze is typical of the period, combining the image of a young woman with long flowing hair and a butterfly. Cicadas, stag beetles, and butterflies were motifs that were characteristic of the Art Nouveau period.
(*c.1901; ht 25.5cm/10in; value* J)

► *Girl with Monkey* by Youngman
This piece, which portrays an Edwardian woman holding a monkey, displays the more restrained, conservative style of the British artists, who tended to be less flamboyant than their continental peers.
(*c.1900; ht 40cm/15¾in; value* H)

MATERIALS

Most works of sculpture in the late 19th century were cast in bronze, although there was also a resurgence in the popularity of ivory. Casting in bronze involved labor-intensive and highly skilled processes. Consequently leading sculptors would often work closely with the most prestigious founders. Such celebrated French names as Louis Ernest Barrias (1841–1905), George Henry Lemaire, Louis Florentin Chauvet (1878–1958), and Franz Hoosemann experimented with bronze in combination with other materials, usually marble or ivory. Exotic minerals such as hardstones were also used, either carved to form an integral part of the model or applied as gems to give decorative detail to an elaborate head-dress or bodice. In the late 1880s, while studying in Paris, the British sculptor George Frampton (1860–1928) developed an interest in combining materials. He presented his polychrome plaster relief panel *Mysteriach* at the Royal Academy in 1893, and in 1895 produced the work *Mother and Child*, fashioned from silvered bronze against a copper plaque with a white enameled disc at the center.

Many sculptors modeled works that were executed in a variety of materials. The French factory of Sèvres (est. 1756) commissioned a series of dancers from Agathon Léonard (*b*.1841), which were issued in white biscuit porcelain. The same series of dancers by Léonard was cast in bronze by the Susse Frères founder in Paris. The firm of Goldscheider (1885–1954) in Vienna produced models in a variety of materials, and arguably some of their most striking late 19th-century pieces of Art Nouveau sculpture were figures and busts of sultry women in painted terracotta.

THE FEMALE IMAGE

The portrayal of the female preoccupied Art Nouveau sculptors to an extraordinary degree. The slightly innocent but teasingly erotic depiction of the semi-clad female form was probably the most repeated image of the era. The "new woman" was liberated from the constraints of a 19th-century literary tradition that portrayed her as stiflingly respectable. Most typically she was modeled in full relief with long flowing hair to form the fluid asymmetrical shapes that define the Art Nouveau style; she was also cast clinging to the sides of organic-shaped vases, her head and torso cast in high relief; or as a mermaid, languishing amid seaweed and waves on bronze or pewter vases, bowls, or platters. These maidens had their antecedents in the Symbolist movement that pervaded the world of art and literature in the 1880s. Works such as *The Secret* and *Ophelia* by Maurice Bouval (*d*.1920), *Eve* by Thomas Brock, and the *Spirit of Contemplation* by Albert Tofts all display a typically Symbolist air of mystery, tinged sometimes with a hint of melancholy or a suggestion of the sinister.

▼ *Circe* by Bertrand Mackennal (1863–1931)
Mackennal was an Australian sculptor who worked in Britain. When this figure of the Greek enchantress Circe was first exhibited at the Royal Academy in London in 1894, the naked figures around the base caused an outrage, and the piece was covered up to avoid corrupting the viewing public.
(*1893; ht lifesize; value* Q)

Many sculptors were inspired to create models of contemporary female celebrities, most notably dancers and actresses. The American dancer Loïe Fuller arrived in Paris in 1892 and performed at the Folies Bergère, where she devised and performed illuminated dances featuring billowing scarves. Fuller captivated her audiences and inspired many artists, including the celebrated sculptor Raoul Larche (1860–1912), whose exquisite gilt-bronze models of her are considered to be among his finest works.

ELECTRIC LIGHTING

The electric light bulb (invented in 1885) was a great novelty to Art Nouveau sculptors who thoroughly explored and experimented with its properties and effects. The French sculptor Léo Laporte-Blairsy (1865–1923) was particularly inventive. His figure *The Milky Way* depicts a pensive female holding and gazing into a blue and opal glass globe, etched with stars and illuminated from within. In another of his works, *Fairies with Casket*, the subject carries a large, openwork bronze casket in front of her; the casket's sides and top feature stained-glass panels, which glow to full dramatic effect when lit. The Austrian artist Gustav Gurschner (*b*.1873) modeled lamps with finely cast stylized female forms, incorporating a nautilus shell; when lit the natural translucence of the shell gave a soft, warm luminescence. Sometimes the shell replaced a shade made from a more conventional material, but often it was cleverly incorporated into the modeling, and formed part of the figure's anatomy. In other forms light bulbs were subtly concealed in the floral boughs that were held aloft by female dancers, or used to replace the stamen in the flower heads of a myriad of lamps that combined flora and the female form.

Some of the finest sculptors and glassmakers collaborated in the design and execution of single pieces. Tiffany & Co. (est. 1837) in New York made the glass panels for at least one of Gurschner's lamps; the French firm of Daum Frères (est. 1875), in Nancy, designed the blue glass globe that is held by the figure in Léo Laporte-Blairsy's *The Milky Way*. Daum also produced tiny glass shades for a lamp featuring a kneeling female figure, which was modeled by the German sculptor Guerbe.

◄ *Daphne* **by Ernst Whallis**
This Austrian sculptor, whose work is always of notably fine quality, produced many models of Art Nouveau females in a variety of materials including glazed ceramic and (as here) terracotta. This example depicts Daphne, the Greek nymph loved by Apollo; her diaphanous clothes and floral head-dress are typical of the period.
(1900; ht 76cm/30in; value **I***)*

▼ **Lamp by Gustav Gurschner**
This exquisite lamp is one of several by Gurschner that incorporates the nautilus shell. The twirling, stylized plant-form base together with a sinuous maiden with long flowing hair and outstretched arms epitomize the Art Nouveau style. Such pieces are highly prized.
(c.1900; ht 53cm/21in; value **M***)*

► **Lamp by Agathon Léonard**
This French gilt-bronze lamp is one of the figures in the series of dancers modeled by Agathon Léonard and produced by Sèvres in white biscuit porcelain.
(c.1898;. ht 60cm/23¾in; value **L***)*

KEY FACTS

- IMPORTANT SCULPTORS Raoul Larche, Léo Laporte-Blairsy, Gustav Gurschner, Maurice Bouval
- MATERIALS most figures are made of bronze, but many sculptors also worked in marble, ivory, porcelain, and terracotta or a combination of various materials; shell was popularly used in lamp designs
- TECHNIQUES bronze figures are either sand-cast in sections and then patinated, or cast using the lost-wax (*cire perdue*) technique
- MOTIFS the female figure, typically swathed in floating gowns with long hair, is highly characteristic; some more daring pieces feature the naked or near naked body; imagery from the natural world often applied as motifs to sculptural forms are also characteristic, especially stag beetles, cicadas, and butterflies
- SIZE size is not always an indication of price when purchasing sculpture; small exquisite examples of the work of leading Art Nouveau sculptors can be more valuable than large mediocre pieces
- LAMPS figures in the form of lamps have a dual appeal and this ensures that they are very popular with collectors
- CONDITION bronzes that have retained their original patina are more valuable than those that have not; wear to the patina will affect the value of a piece adversely
- COLLECTING the finest examples of Art Nouveau bronze sculpture are keenly sought by collectors and command high prices; good examples that include elements of ivory are relatively rare and so command a premium; incorrect anatomical detail and clumsy modeling will be reflected in the value of a piece; small editions of bronzes were sometimes numbered and this has a strong appeal to some collectors; female figures are generally more sought after than male

Marks
Many pieces are signed by the artist and some bear a stamped or impressed mark of the founder in the bronze, for example "SUSSE FRERES EDITEURS PARIS"; the following are a selection of marks:

Agathon Léonard: most commonly used mark

Gustav Gurschner: one of several variations

Francis Renaud: most commonly used mark

See also Art Deco: Sculpture, pp.440–1

Posters

Although letterpress posters have existed for several centuries, posters as we now know them were first developed in the 1860s when the French artist Jules Chéret (1836–1932) – generally considered the father of the modern poster – adapted the printing process of lithography to commercial poster production. This development enabled bright, color reproductions to be produced at speed. The instant commercial success of this new form of advertising meant that within two years the walls of Paris were covered in posters and the demand for them was such that examples were stripped overnight from public billboards by keen collectors.

▼ Poster designed by Henri Toulouse-Lautrec

This sought-after French poster of the café-concert *Divan Japonais* depicts a typically Parisian *fin-de-siècle* artistic scene. The spectators who form the focal point of the poster are the cabaret artist Jane Avril and the literary, art and music critic Edouard Du Jardin.
(1893; ht 81cm/32in; value **M***)*

THEATER AND CONCERT POSTERS

Chéret was very prolific, producing more than 1,000 poster designs as a commercial artist. The most collectible of his works include advertisements for the Moulin Rouge (1892), the Folies Bergère (1893–97), and the Palais de Glace (1893–96), in Paris. In contrast to Chéret's extensive output, the best known of all Art Nouveau artists, Henri de Toulouse-Lautrec (1864–1901), designed only 31 posters from 1891 to 1901. Toulouse-Lautrec immersed himself in the theaters, cabarets, music-halls, circuses, bars, and brothels that were central to Parisian life of the 1890s, and the colorful characters he encountered feature frequently in his posters. His most sought-after posters depict such café-bars as the Chat Noir, theaters such as Moulin de la Gallette, and

▶ Poster designed by Alphonse Mucha

This French poster for Alfred de Musset's play *Lorenzaccio*, depicting Bernhardt as the eponymous male protagonist, is one of Mucha's most celebrated designs. His richly decorated posters typically feature beautiful women and elaborate imagery.
(1896; ht 99cm/39in; value I*)*

celebrated stage personalities of the era including Yvette Guilbert, Aristide Bruant, Jane Avril, May Milton, and May Belfort. Toulouse-Lautrec's reputation as an artist was one of the most crucial contributing factors in the establishment of the ephemeral, commercial poster as a recognized major art form, and his posters are now among the most sought-after works on the market.

The theater was also a common subject for Alphonse Mucha (1860–1939), a Czech-born designer working in Paris, whose style is synonymous with Art Nouveau. The focal point of the majority of Mucha's posters is a curvaceous, flowing-haired, often richly adorned woman, usually featured on a circular background. Mucha's first and most famous poster design was for Victorien Sardou's *Gismonda*, starring Sarah Bernhardt, at the Théâtre de la Renaissance. So impressed was Bernhardt by Mucha's work that she enlisted him to design posters for all of her stage performances for the next six years.

DOMESTIC ADVERTISING

As the influence of the poster became increasingly apparent, designs appeared for such varied items as biscuits, chocolates, cigarettes, and beverages. Posters promoting newspapers became common and include designs for *Le Monde*, *Le Courrier Français*, and, by Chéret, for *L'Echo de Paris* and *Le Petit Bleu*.

Although France was at the forefront of poster production, most other European countries quickly followed suit, with T. Privat-Livemont (1861–1936) producing influencial designs in Belgium. His best-known poster was for Absinthe Robette, a green liqueur flavored with wormwood, which was later found to affect the nervous system and universally prohibited. Privat-Livemont also produced posters for the Belgian chocolate firm Cacao Van Houten, as well as for perfume companies including J.C. Boldoot. In his designs, the commodity promoted always takes second place to the Art Nouveau female.

In Italy the German-born Adolpho Hohenstein (1854–1928), a prominent name in Italian *Stile Liberty*, produced his first poster in 1895 for Puccini's opera *La Bohème*. Many early Italian posters promoted opera, as it was such an important national institution. By c.1898 artists including Hohenstein and Leopoldo Metlicovitz (1868–1944) also produced posters for such diverse products as Monowatt Bulbs, Bitter Campari, and the Milan evening newspaper *Corriere della Sera*, and for companies as varied as Mele's, in Milan and Naples, and the jewelers A. Calderoni, in Milan. Other Italian posters of the period, which are becoming increasingly scarce, feature figures from Classical mythology.

▼ Poster designed by T. Privat-Livemont

As in all of the Belgian designer Privat-Livemont's posters, this example features an Art Nouveau maiden with an elaborate head-dress and flowing locks, seen in profile.
(1900; ht 79cm/31in; value **H***)*

Spanish artists of the period were greatly influenced by the evolution of the poster in the rest of Europe. Alexandra de Riquer (1856–1920) was Spain's most successful exponent of Art Nouveau, producing posters for everyday goods as well as for such specialist groups as Mosaics Hidráulicos, a Barcelona mosaics firm. Spanish posters from this period are rare because, unlike in France, collectors did not exist at the time of production, and many copies were therefore destroyed.

TRANSPORT

Travel posters, covering bicycles, automobiles, aviation, and shipping, are a major field of collecting. The bicycle gained popularity during the 1880s and 1890s, and such firms as Stella, Hurtu, and Wonder in France, Raleigh in Britain, and Victor, Columbia, and Crawford in the USA made extensive use of posters in publicity campaigns.

The development of the car in France followed the cycling boom and firms were soon promoting both modes of transport in the same poster. Cars were rarely the sole subject of paintings during the period so posters featuring cars on their own are collectible. The artist René Vincent (1879–1936), a car fanatic who held one of the first driving licenses in France, designed posters that are notable for their close attention to the contemporary setting; early Grand Prix posters show the same careful attention to detail.

Posters promoting early aviation meets, particularly those depicting hot-air balloons and precarious flying machines, are also highly sought after by collectors. Notable aviation posters include those for the French Pastilles au Miel, produced c.1900 by the artist known as "Lovis," those for Aéroplanes Blériot, and designs for the 1912 Premier Grand Prix.

Sea travel became an increasingly popular subject for promotion, being the principal commercial method of intercontinental travel. A desire for luxury was reflected in the transatlantic travel posters advertising such British liners as the ill-fated *Titanic*, *Lusitania*, and the *Mauritania*. The immigrant shipping lines, which trawled their way to Australia, New Zealand, Africa, and other European colonies, were also popular subjects. Important artists include Herbert K. Rooke, who designed posters for the P. & O. shipping company, and the French artists Henri Cassiers (1858–1944) and Louis Lessieux, designers for the Compagnie Générale Transatlantique.

▲ Poster designed by Alexandra de Riquer

This poster uses a typically Art Nouveau motif with its exploitation of a flowing-haired maiden to promote a mundane agricultural product – the chicken grain *Granja Avicola*. Its designer, De Riquer, is the most notable of Spain's poster artists of the period.
*(1896; ht 64cm/25in; value **G**)*

◄ Poster designed by Josef R. Witzel (1867–1924)

This boldly colored poster designed for the German car manufacturer Audi illustrates how cars were first promoted as a new mode of transportation for the wealthy. The woman, elegantly dressed in stylish, fashionable clothes of the period, is seen to favor the car over the horse, the more traditional mode of transport.
*(1912; ht 1.3m/4ft 3in; value **I**)*

► Transport poster

This poster is a good example of the many joint promotions undertaken by the London & South-Western Railway Co. in England and the Chemins de Fer de l'Ouest in France. By incorporating both St Paul's Cathedral in London and the Arc de Triomphe in Paris into the design, the artist aims to entice passengers to travel economically and comfortably between the two cities by rail and sea. Such a poster as this would be of interest to shipping enthusiasts as it depicts the type of vessel in use at the beginning of the 19th century.
*(c.1900; ht 1m/3ft 3in; value **F**)*

KEY FACTS

General
- DESIGNS AND COLORS extensive use of the female form, intricate decoration, mosaics, and circular designs are typical; pastels and gold were popular
- CARE restoration and cleaning should be done by a professional; backing: some posters are left unbacked, others are backed on linen or japan paper using acid-free glue – the preferred method differs from country to country; mounting: posters should never be dry-mounted; framing: UV plexiglass is preferable to glass
- CONDITION as posters are multiples, condition is important, although a rare poster in poorer condition will still be collectible; creases, folds, and staining will lower the value and posters with large losses should be avoided; any trimmed margins will greatly affect value
- FAKES these do exist; check for ageing of the paper and the printing; a list of fakes is available from the International Vintage Posters Dealers Association

Theater and concert posters
- MAJOR DESIGNERS Chéret, Toulouse-Lautrec, and Mucha predominate
- SUBJECTS Parisian theaters, cabarets, cafés, bars, and contemporary actors and actresses were most popular

Domestic advertising
- MAJOR DESIGNERS Privat-Livemont, Hohenstein, Metlicovitz, and De Riquer are the biggest names
- SUBJECTS designs were produced for tobacco, biscuits, chocolates, beverages, newspapers, and major stores

Transport
- MAJOR DESIGNERS Vincent, Rooke, and Cassiers
- SUBJECTS posters were designed to promote travel by bicycle, car, train, airplane, and luxury sea-liner

See also Art Deco: Posters, pp.444–5

D erived from the Exposition Internationale des Arts Décoratifs et Industriels Modernes, held in Paris in 1925, the term Art Deco encompasses the distinctive decorative styles that emerged prior to World War I as Art Nouveau waned in popularity. Up until the late 1930s Art Deco furniture- and glassmakers, ceramicists, silversmiths, and sculptors – among others – continued to develop new works characterized by the use of bright colors and stylized designs and decorative motifs. They drew for inspiration on such diverse sources as Léon Bakst's designs for the Ballets Russes, the Western art movements of Expressionism, Cubism, Futurism, and Modernism and, following the excavation of Tutankhamun's tomb and the discovery of Aztec temples in the early 1920s, ancient Egyptian and native Central American art. The gradual assimilation of these influences resulted in significant stylistic changes: prior to the late 1920s, Art Deco designs featured rounded, oval, and spiral shapes with romantic motifs such as formalized rosebuds and garlands and baskets of flowers; thereafter, the designs and motifs became increasingly geometrical, abstract, and vigorously streamlined – a development the influential French designer Paul Iribe described as sacrificing "the flower on the altar of the machine."

Detail of a screen by Paul Fehér (left) A wonderful example of Art Deco design, this American screen was made in the Rose Irons Works, Cleveland, under the personal direction of Martin Rose. It is constructed from silver-plated iron, gold-plated brass, and the then "new aluminum" *(1930)*.
Jug by Clarice Cliff (above) Bright colors, hand-painted, abstract renderings of natural scenes, and innovative tableware shapes characterize the style of this British ceramicist *(c.1932)*.

Art Deco: Introduction

The Art Deco style of the 1920s and 1930s, which derived its name from the 1925 Paris Exhibition – the Exposition des Arts Décoratifs et Industriels Modernes – was the first truly modern style of the 20th century. In their subject-matter, style, and bright colors, Art Deco furniture, jewelry, ceramics, posters, sculpture, and other decorative arts reflected the general atmosphere of optimism that prevailed after the devastation of World War I. The increased liberation of women, the rise of jazz music and Hollywood film-making, the preoccupation with speed, travel, and leisure pursuits, and the growth of commercial competition and advertising all had a strong influence on Art Deco designers. Until the late 1970s Art Deco pieces attracted little interest among dealers and collectors, but since that time, with numerous exhibitions and publications on the subject, the popularity of collecting Art Deco has increased enormously.

THE 1925 PARIS EXHIBITION

The Art Deco style, although mainly associated with the 1920s and 1930s, did not suddenly emerge fully formed in this period. Rich ornament, exotic materials, and emphasis on comfort – all features of the style – were already evident in the decorative arts, especially in French furniture, before and during World War I. However, the development of the Art Deco style is mainly associated with the 1925 exhibition in Paris, which lasted from April to October. This exhibition was originally planned for 1915, as a continuation of the French government-sponsored international exhibitions that were held in Paris from the 19th century, but was postponed because of the war.

Like the Paris Exhibition of 1900 – which had been the showcase for the Art Nouveau style – the 1925 Exhibition aimed to promote France as the pre-eminent center for the production of luxury goods. Most European countries, except for Germany, were involved; the USA declined to take part, deciding that it could not meet the entry requirements for examples of work of "new and original inspiration" stipulated by the organizers. The exhibition was therefore dominated by pavilions displaying the work of leading French designers, such as the furniture designer Jacques-Emile Ruhlmann (1879–1933) and the glassmaker René Lalique (1860–1945). The design studios of the major Parisian department stores, such as Primavera at Printemps, La Maîtrise at Galéries Lafayette, and Pomone at Au Bon Marché, displayed complete interiors, with examples of furniture, household wares, textiles, and carpets in matching styles.

Most of the exhibits reflected the "official taste" of the exhibition; forms were adapted from historical or traditional styles, but with lavish ornament of stylized flowers, figures, and animals, and geometric patterns such as zigzags and chevrons. This was particularly evident in Ruhlmann's Pavillon d'un Collectionneur, with its chairs influenced by 18th-century design, boldly patterned wall coverings, and elaborate chandeliers, and also in the design by André Groult for an ambassadorial boudoir with shagreen-covered furniture.

This style contrasted strongly with the few displays by Modernist designers. The Pavillon de l'Esprit Nouveau was designed by the avant-garde Swiss-born architect Le Corbusier (1887–1965) and exemplified his vision of a new, minimalist architecture and lifestyle. His small two-storey house, with its doors, windows, and other structural elements based on a modular system of standard-sized units, contained mass-produced furniture and was decorated with abstract paintings. Although this style made a strong impact, its influence did not become widespread until the 1930s, when it was represented at the 1937 Universal Exhibition in Paris and also at the 1939 World's Fair in New York.

▲ **Vase by François-Emile Décorchement (1880–1971)**
The rich turquoise-and-black mottled colors of this *pâte-de-verre* vase were much favored by French Art Deco luxury glassmakers. The technique was used to create complex patterns in colors imitating those of semi-precious stones, and involved the use of colored ground-glass paste, which was fired in a mold. The horizontal bands of berries are a typical Art Deco motif.
(c.1926; ht 23cm/9in; value K)

MOTIFS, INFLUENCES, AND NEW MATERIALS

The standard motifs of the Art Deco style included such traditional decorative elements as bouquets of flowers, animals, and figures of young maidens. However, these were always stylized and angular rather than naturalistic and were often combined with purely geometric motifs, including chevrons, zigzags, sunbursts, and lightning bolts. This emphasis on stylization and abstract and repeated forms was influenced by the growing impact of the machine, especially automobiles, trains, and airplanes, and by such abstract art movements of the early 20th century as Cubism and Futurism. The taste for bright colors was also inspired by the vibrant Fauvist

▼ **Coffee-pot by Shelley (1872–1966)**
Practicality is combined with innovative design in this piece from the British pottery's "Eve" range. The clean lines, simple decoration, and red-and-black trim are typical of the period.
(c.1932; ht 25.5cm/10in; value B)

◄ **Poster by Joseph Binder (1898–1972)**
This poster promoting a music and theater festival in Vienna is a typical example of the development of the Art Deco style in Austria. The combination of the stylized faces, clothes, and musical instruments of the performers with the bright, flat colors creates a stunning visual impact.
(1924; ht 1.3m/4ft 3in; value F)

paintings of Henri Matisse, André Derain and Maurice Vlaminck, which used contrasting tones and non-naturalistic colors.

Such movements were in turn influenced by the stylized, abstract forms of African masks and sculpture, which were widely collected and imported into Europe in large quantities at this time. Certain elements of Art Deco decorative arts, such as ceramic wall masks, show the inspiration of African art, while African figures featured as decoration on the ceramics of such potters as René Buthaud (1886–1987). Also around this time, black American culture in the form of jazz music was introduced into Europe from the USA; the jazz-inspired Revue Nègre in Paris, featuring the black dancer and actress Josephine Baker, influenced the work of Buthaud and other Art Deco designers.

The taste for Oriental art was encouraged between 1911 and 1920 by the exotic stage and costume designs of Léon Bakst (1866–1924) for the Ballets Russes. These had a significant influence on the Art Deco style, and sparked a fashion for Oriental black-and-red color combinations as well as lacquered furniture, metalwork, and *objets d'art*. One of the best exponents of the style was the Swiss designer Jean Dunand (1877–1942). Leading sculptors in France, such as Dimitri Chiparus (1880–1950), also produced figures of dancers in exotic costumes. Egyptian motifs such as

◄ **Cigarette case attributed to Jean Dunand**

This case uses the Oriental-style combination of red-and-black lacquer, with eggshell (*coquille d'oeuf*) added for contrast.
(*c.1925; l. 13cm/5in; value* **G**)

▲ *Dancer* **by Dimitri Chiparus**

The French sculptor Chiparus was one of the leading Art Deco exponents of chryselephantine (the combination of bronze and ivory) sculptures of exotic dancers, and his pieces are particularly collectible today. This figure wears a tight-fitting cloche hat – fashionable at the time, and a distinctive feature of many of Chiparus's sculptures – and has finely carved limbs and detailed costume. The green onyx base is also typical of the artist's work.
(*early 20th century; ht 38cm/15in; value* **K**)

THE MODERN MOVEMENT

An alternative to the luxury Art Deco style developed mainly outside France, especially in Germany, during and after World War I. Progressive artists, architects, and designers argued that the new era demanded good-quality, functional design for all; that new technology and machine production should be exploited fully; and that form must be derived from function, without unnecessary ornament.

This movement began in 1907 with the Deutscher Werkbund, an alliance of designers and industrialists. In 1919 the Bauhaus was founded in Weimar by the German architect and designer Walter Gropius (1883–1969); in 1925 the school moved to Dessau, and it was closed by the Nazis in 1933. Bauhaus members designed high-quality furniture, lighting, metalwork, and textiles for industrial production, using new materials, including plywood and tubular steel. Many designs, such as the tubular steel furniture by Marcel Breuer (1902–81) and the glass and metal lamps by Marianne Brandt (1893–1983), are still widely produced. Other Modernist designers of the period included Le Corbusier in France, Alvar Aalto (1898–1976) in Finland, and Gerrit Rietveld (1888–1964) in the Netherlands.

Both the decorative and the Modern strands of Art Deco had a strong influence in the USA, where the style's vibrant colors and rhythmic patterns expressed the optimism of a young country that was also the world leader in the mass production of consumer goods. Designers including Paul T. Frankl (1886–1958) and Donald Deskey (1894–1989) used materials also favored by European Modernists, such as chrome-plated tubular steel. In the 1930s designers such as Norman Bel Geddes (1893–1958) and Walter Dorwin Teague (1883–1960) began to develop their own distinctive version of Art Deco, known as "streamlining."

sphinxes and hieroglyphs, and materials such as turquoise, proved highly popular in the decorative arts after Howard Carter discovered the tomb of Tutankhamun in 1922.

Art Deco designers used an extremely wide range of materials. Luxury manufacturers, including Jacques-Emile Ruhlmann, Paul Follot (1877–1941), and the cabinet-makers Louis Süe (1875–1968) and André Mare (1887–1932), specialized in fine-quality pieces veneered in exotic woods such as amboyna and Macassar ebony, combined with ivory, shagreen, enamel, gold and silver leaf, and lacquer. Modernist and industrial designers, especially in the USA, showed greater interest in new materials such as aluminum, chromium, and tubular steel. Lavish cinema interiors were created relatively inexpensively from combinations of chromium, colored glass, and painted concrete. Bakelite, a type of cheap, easily molded plastic patented in 1907, was widely employed as a substitute for wood in such mass-produced items as radios.

► **Table by Donald Deskey**

Deskey was one of a number of American furniture designers who employed new materials and technology to produce both unique pieces and prototypes for mass production. Like most of his furniture, this chromium-plated steel and Vitriolite table with X-shaped stretchers makes use of simple, geometric forms and straight lines. Although this example is plain, Deskey also used contrasting stripes of bold primary colors on some of his furniture.
(*c.1928; ht 38cm/15in; value* **K**)

Furniture

After World War I, furniture designers combined luxury and practicality in their products, and created both traditional types of furniture and innovative forms. In France, traditional Art Deco furniture was typified by elegant styles looking back to the 18th or 19th centuries, using inlay and exotic woods. After 1925 French makers started to incorporate the "new" materials that were part of the Modernist aesthetic, such as chromium, aluminum, and tubular steel – as advocated by the innovative German Bauhaus, whose industrial designers created functional furniture for mass production. In the USA, designers were influenced by both traditional and Modern European Art Deco, using materials such as laminated wood and chromed metal.

The Netherlands, Germany, and Scandinavia

In the early 20th century, Dutch, German, and Scandinavian furniture designers were at the forefront of the Modern movement. Designing specifically for machine production, they rejected ornament and experimented with the new materials of tubular steel, aluminum, chromium, and preformed plywood, aiming to create standardized, functional furniture accessible to all markets.

THE NETHERLANDS

Among the earliest furniture designs inspired by the new machine aesthetic were those of Gerrit Rietveld (1888–1964). From c.1918 Rietveld was associated with the Dutch magazine *De Stijl* (*Style*), whose contributors, a group of avant-garde architects, painters, designers, and theorists, aimed to create a new "universal" art based on lines, geometric shapes, primary colors, and black and white. Rietveld's "Red-Blue" chair, designed in 1918, is one of the best-known expressions of *De Stijl* ideas. Its straightforward construction meant that it was highly suitable for mass production. Versions made before 1923 are stained, varnished, or limed, reflecting Rietveld's traditional training in carpentry. Only after this date was the chair painted in red, blue, black, and yellow. From c.1918 Rietveld's furniture designs were constructed from linear wooden elements; from the mid-1920s they featured flat wooden planes. Rietveld produced his own furniture until 1924, when he sold his business to his assistant Gerard van der Groenekan. Rights to the designs were sold in 1971 to the Italian furniture company Cassina, which still reproduces them today.

GERMANY

Most of the well-known furniture designers in Germany in the inter-war period were associated with the Bauhaus. Founded in 1919 in Weimar by the architect Walter Gropius (1883–1969), the Bauhaus was one of the first schools to train artists and craftsmen to design high-quality goods specifically for industrial production. It is particularly renowned for the functional, geometric style of its products and its experimentation with new materials such as tubular steel and plywood.

The best-known furniture designs associated with the Bauhaus were those produced by the Hungarian-born architect Marcel Breuer (1902–81), head of the school's carpentry workshop from 1925 to 1928. His earliest designs feature linear wooden components, similar in style to Rietveld's furniture. However, by c.1925, Breuer was designing chairs with tubular steel frames, and his "Wassily" chair (1925) was one of the first tubular steel pieces to be produced on a large scale. Designs including the "Wassily" chair and the tubular steel-framed, cantilevered "B32" chair (1926) were manufactured by such firms as Standard-Möbel Lengyel & Co. in Berlin and Thonet in Vienna. In 1932 Breuer began to design aluminum furniture for the Wohnbedarf furnishings stores in Switzerland; since aluminum is weaker than steel, these designs are more complex in construction than his tubular steel pieces. In 1935 Breuer emigrated to Britain, where he met Jack Pritchard (b.1899), owner of Isokon (1932–9), which produced furniture in the Modern style and promoted the use of plywood. For Isokon, Breuer designed the "Long Chair," a sculptural plywood reclining chair that molded to the position of the body, and lightweight tables and chairs created from single sheets of cut and molded plywood.

The avant-garde architect Ludwig Mies van der Rohe (1886–1969), artistic director of the Bauhaus from 1930 to 1933, designed cantilevered tubular steel furniture for mass production by the firm of Berliner Metallgewerbe from 1927 to 1931. Many of his other designs, although functional in appearance, were in fact handmade for the luxury market. A notable example is his padded leather and chrome "Barcelona" chair and stool, designed for the German pavilion at the 1929 International Exhibition in Barcelona. With a curved X-frame inspired by Classical furniture, the chair was designed as a "throne" for King Alfonso XIII of Spain for the opening

▲ **"Red-Blue" chair by Gerrit Rietveld**
Rietveld's earliest (1918) and best-known furniture design, this striking piece is constructed from thirteen standard squared wooden units screwed together and supporting flat arm rests, an angled wood seat, and back-rest. This relatively late example was made by Rietveld's former assistant van der Groenekan. (c.1955–60; ht 88cm/34½in; value J)

▶ **"Wassily" club chair "B3" by Marcel Breuer**
Named after the abstract painter Wassily Kandinsky, this chair was among the first pieces of furniture constructed from chrome-plated tubular steel. Such an example as this will command a premium as it was manufactured at Standard-Möbel Lengyel & Co. in Berlin shortly after it was first designed. It is unusual in that it has a black canvas rather than a hide seat. (1927–8; ht 76cm/30in; value N)

ceremony of the exhibition. Original Berliner Metallgewerbe models are exceptionally rare and valuable today, but since 1947–8 the chair has been mass-produced by the American firm of Knoll, and these reproductions are more accessible to collectors.

SCANDINAVIA

In the 1920s and 1930s, Scandinavia was less industrialized than the rest of Europe or the USA, and its craft tradition was still highly evident in furniture and interior design. This tradition continued even with the advent of Modernism, Scandinavian designers preferring curving forms and wood to the angular shapes and tubular steel favored by their German peers. This is well illustrated by the furniture designed by the Finnish architect Alvar Aalto (1898–1976), who from 1929 experimented with plywood for such items as chairs and trolleys, and in 1933 patented a method of bending wood to make stacking stools. Like other Modernist furniture of the period, Aalto's designs are simple in construction, with no surface decoration, although they may be painted in bright primary colors. His furniture was produced from 1930 to 1933 by the firm of Otto Korhonen in Turku and from 1935 by his own manufacturing company, Artek, in Helsinki. Aalto's versatile furniture, especially his stacking stools, proved particularly popular in Britain, where it was imported and distributed by Finmar Ltd (est. 1934–5).

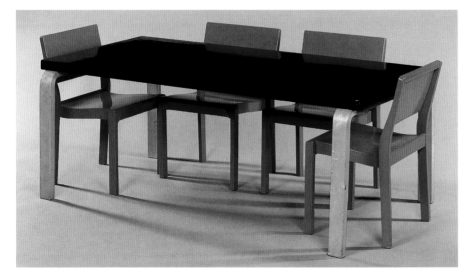

◄ "Barcelona" chair by Mies van der Rohe, manufactured by the Bamberger Metallwerkstätte

Although it is now mass-produced by the American firm of Knoll and has become one of the most popular chair designs of the 20th century, the "Barcelona" chair was in fact one of the few Modernist chairs not originally designed for machine production. This early example, in padded leather and chrome, was manufactured only a couple of years after the design was first produced in 1929, and is exceptionally rare and valuable.

(c.1931; ht 76cm/30in; value **M***)*

▼ Table and chairs by Alvar Aalto

The Finnish architect Alvar Aalto's simple and practical furniture designs tended to be more widely popular in the 1920s and 1930s than German furniture designs. Their gently curved lines and wooden construction gave a warm and humanizing effect, in contrast to the somewhat clinical feel imparted by angular lines and industrial tubular steel. The pieces shown here were produced separately but match; all the pieces in Aalto's furniture range were designed to complement one another. Imported into Britain by Finmar Ltd, they bear metal labels with model numbers.

(chairs 1929, table 1933–5; ht of table 71cm/28in, ht of chairs 79cm/31in; value **K***)*

▼ Tea trolley by Alvar Aalto

This example, model number 98, was designed *c.*1935–6 and retailed in Finland by Artek and in Britain by Finmar Ltd. Although straightforward in design, it is made of a combination of woods: bent laminated and solid birch, plywood, and lacquered wood. Versions without the lacquered-wood wheels were also produced.

(after 1936; ht 56cm/22in; value **I***)*

KEY FACTS

General points
- COLLECTING original 1920s and 1930s pieces are rarer and more valuable than recent versions; many designs were sold to large furniture companies from the 1940s and have been in continuous production since

Gerrit Rietveld
- CONSTRUCTION linear elements were typical before the early 1920s; planar designs thereafter
- COLORS primary colors, plus black and white; early versions of "Red-Blue" chair are unpainted

Marcel Breuer
- MATERIALS tubular steel, aluminum, or bent and laminated plywood; leather and cane for seats
- CONSTRUCTION simple contors, cantilevered construction; chairs and tables made after 1925 have runners rather than feet; Isokon side-chairs and tables are made from single sheets of cut plywood

Marks
May have a label if made or distributed by a company such as Isokon or Finmar Ltd

Ludwig Mies van der Rohe
- MATERIALS tubular steel combined with padded leather upholstery, raffia, or glass
- CONSTRUCTION some chairs are cantilevered; the "Barcelona" chair and stool have a distinctive X-frame; careful hand-finishing is typical
- COLLECTING on early, handmade "Barcelona" chairs the top rail is in bent chromed steel with lap joints and chrome-headed bolts; on later, mass-produced pieces (after 1947–8) the top rail is of cut and welded stainless steel

Alvar Aalto
- MATERIALS woods, especially plywood, bent laminated (which may flake), and solid birch

Marks
Some Finnish furniture is marked "Aalto Mobler, Svensk Kvalitet Sprodurt"; most pieces have an applied metal label bearing a model number

See also Art Deco: Furniture – Britain, p.419

France

Some of the finest Art Deco furniture was produced in France, where designers reacted against the Art Nouveau style. Many were inspired instead by the lines of 18th- and early 19th-century French furniture. Cabinet-makers such as Jacques-Emile Ruhlmann (1879–1933) created one-off pieces in exotic woods; others were influenced by African and Oriental art, while from 1925 the machine aesthetic of Modernism gained prominence, with such materials as tubular steel.

▶ **Occasional table by Jacques-Emile Ruhlmann**
The elegant, restrained design of this fine-quality table is typical of Ruhlmann's furniture of the 1920s. Like most of his pieces, its only form of decoration is the exotic-figured, burr-amboyna veneer, simply inlaid with ivory. The cabriole legs with scrolled feet are a modern adaptation of 18th-century French furniture.
(c.1922; ht 64cm/25in; value **K***)*

TRADITIONALIST DESIGNS

The leading French furniture designer from c.1918 to the mid-1920s was Jacques-Emile Ruhlmann, whose exceptionally fine handmade furniture is an elegantly pared-down version of the Neo-classical and Empire styles, with typical 18th-century features such as tapering, fluted legs. Decorative effect is provided by exotic wood veneers, sometimes with inlaid ivory, mother-of-pearl, and tortoiseshell. After 1925 Ruhlmann used Modernist materials, such as tubular steel, but continued to work in a traditional style.

Other designers inspired by historical furniture were Louis Süe (1875–1968) and André Mare (1887–1932), who in 1919 formed the Compagnie des Arts Français to produce a range of pieces including chairs, commodes, and desks, typified by massive forms and veneered in exotic woods with carved or inlaid stylized flowers, fruits, and plants. Their designs are heavier in style than Ruhlmann's, as they favored adaptations of the Louis-Philippe furniture of the 1830s and 1840s.

Many leading Paris department stores had separate studios that provided a complete interior-design service. From 1921 Maurice Dufrène (1876–1955) directed La Maîtrise, the design studio of Galéries Lafayette, and from 1923 Paul Follot (1877–1941) was artistic director at Pomone for Au Bon Marché. Follot designed a wide range of furnishings; his furniture,

▶ **Chair by Paul Follot**
Follot rarely designed single pieces – this black lacquer and giltwood chair made for Pomone is part of a set. The frames with slender, fluted uprights and scalloped aprons are typical, as is the use of patterned upholstery.
(c.1925; ht 82cm/32in; value **H***)*

like Ruhlmann's, is based on 18th-century forms, but is distinguished by giltwood frames and richly colored, patterned upholstery. Although his designs became more geometric after 1925, Follot continued to prefer wood, gilding, lacquer, and inlay to tubular steel, plastic, or glass.

EXOTIC AND MODERN DESIGNS

The geometric motifs typical of this period were derived from Cubist painting, which itself was influenced by the stylized forms of African masks and sculpture. The furniture designer Pierre Legrain (1887–1929) took inspiration from African art, fashioning African-inspired designs in Western materials.

The Art Deco taste for Oriental art is evident in the popularity of lacquered furniture, the leading exponents of which were the Swiss-born Jean Dunand (1877–1942) and the Irish-born Eileen Gray (1879–1976), both active in Paris. Dunand's early lacquered furniture featured floral designs; his work from the 1920s depicted geometric forms in red-and-black lacquer and sometimes panels of crushed eggshell (*coquille d'oeuf*). Gray studied lacquering in Paris with the Japanese master Sougawara, and in 1920 she designed a furnished apartment for the milliner Suzanne Talbot, featuring a collection of African-inspired pieces. From c.1925, influenced by Modernism, she produced furniture of tubular steel, glass, and aluminum.

The leading designer of Modernist furniture was the architect Le Corbusier (1887–1965). At the 1925 Paris Exhibition he designed the Pavillon de l'Esprit Nouveau, a stark, geometric space sparsely furnished with mass-produced items such as bentwood furniture by Thonet. From 1926, with Charlotte Perriand (1903-1999) and his cousin Pierre Jeanneret, Le Corbusier designed his own functionalist furniture using tubular steel and other "new" materials. These and other Modernist designs have been reproduced since the 1960s by the Italian furniture company Cassina.

▲ **Armchair by Le Corbusier**
Le Corbusier was one of the progressive Modernist designers who created furniture for industrial production, but this rare and unusual piece was hand-built for a specific client and is therefore highly collectible, especially since it has its original fabric seat cushions. The frame, with adjustable back panel, is made of tubular steel, a material much favored by the Modernists because of its suitability for mass production. The clean, even stark lines and simple, functional form are typical of Le Corbusier's work and reflect the minimalist ethic.
(1932; ht 1m/3ft 3in; value **M***)*

KEY FACTS

Jacques-Emile Ruhlmann
- FORMS simple, elegant forms based on 18th-century designs, with a very high standard of workmanship
- MATERIALS exotic wood veneers, such as Macassar ebony, amboyna, palisander, and amaranth; ivory inlay
- COLLECTING all work collectible, and highly priced

Marks
Ruhlmann's work carries this signature

Compagnie des Arts Français
- MATERIALS marble tops, velvet upholstery

Legrain, Dunand, and Le Corbusier
- FORMS Legrain: African-inspired with angular, stepped features; Dunand: naturalistic floral designs, geometric designs; Le Corbusier: stark, Modernist designs
- TECHNIQUES AND MATERIALS Dunand: lacquering, crushed eggshell; Le Corbusier: tubular steel frames
- COLLECTING Le Corbusier: modern reproductions mass-produced by Cassina are more accessible

Britain

Many major British designers used elements of the Art Deco style in their furniture, while remaining true to their Arts and Crafts roots and making little use of lavish ornament or exotic woods. Art Deco furniture was more typically produced by minor makers, whose work included copies of popular pieces shown at the 1928 Exhibition of Modern Art in Decoration and Furnishing. Held in London, the exhibition introduced decorative, continental Art Deco furniture into Britain. The Modernist influence of the 1930s is seen in the mass-produced furniture by Isokon (1932–9).

TRADITIONALISTS

The designers of the Cotswold School concentrated on the Arts and Crafts tenets of truth to materials, form derived from function, and traditional construction techniques. Native woods such as oak and walnut were favored, and decoration was minimal. Luxury furniture was made by, among others, Sidney Barnsley (1865–1926), Peter Waals (1870-1937), and Robert Thompson (1876-1955), the "Mouseman," who used a carved mouse as his signature. Gordon Russell (1892–1980) made the most successful transition to both traditionalist and Modernist styles of Art Deco. While using traditional construction techniques, he incorporated such exotic materials as Macassar ebony and ivory into some pieces, together with Art Deco motifs like sunbursts and chevrons. His belief in the need for good-quality, mass-produced furniture led him to develop a range of furniture that used tubular steel and other synthetic materials, with machine-made parts.

Heal & Son (est. 1800), in London, maintained its role as a manufacturer and retailer. Oak, especially limed oak, was used for a range of Arts and Crafts designs with some Art Deco features. Decoration was minimal, and while contemporary construction techniques such as screw-fixing were used, pieces were hand-finished.

▶ "Letchworth" tallboy chest by Heal & Son

A piece of fine proportions with an asymmetrical design, this Heal's oak chest bridges the gap between the exclusive, luxury furniture created by such well-known designers as J.F. Johnson and the mass-produced Art Deco furniture made by minor manufacturers. Heal's produced a successful and collectible range of oak furniture, much of which was limed. In many ways the designs of these pieces looked back to the firm's range of Arts and Crafts furniture, produced at the beginning of the 20th century.

*(c.1930; ht 149cm/30in; value **G**)*

▼ Secretaire chest by Edward Barnsley

Although this walnut secretaire chest by Sidney Barnsley's son Edward (1900-1987) does not display the elaborate and exotic elements often associated with Art Deco, the molded top, richly figured veneer, and inlaid ebony diamonds mark this as a luxury item that appealed to the "less-is-more" philosophy of the Modernist-minimalist strand of Art Deco and which remained popular after the war.

*(1969; w. 109cm/43in; value **L**)*

MODERNISTS

In 1934–5 Finmar Ltd was set up in Britain to distribute Alvar Aalto's molded plywood furniture. The plain, simple pieces had clean contors, decorated with blocks of color; solid wood was often combined with laminates. The firm of Isokon (Isometric Unit Construction), founded in London by the architect Jack Pritchard (1899-1992), produced a range of simple furniture, generally more adventurous than that distributed by Finmar. Designers associated with the company include Marcel Breuer (1902–81). Typical of the period are its lightweight stacking "cutout" tables and chairs made from a single sheet of cut and molded plywood.

More exclusive Modernist Art Deco furniture was designed by Betty Joel (1896–1984), who used curving shapes, minimal decoration – wood grain or contrasting veneers – and native woods such as sycamore; from the 1930s she also used chromed steel and plywood laminates. One of the few truly innovative British Art Deco designers was Gerald Summers (1899–1967). In the 1930s he designed side-chairs and open armchairs, cut and shaped with curved backs and seats, in laminated birchwood. The Birmingham firm of PEL (Practical Equipment Ltd, est. 1931) commissioned collectible steel-frame furniture from designers such as Oliver Bernard (1881–1939) and Wells Coates (1895–1958).

KEY FACTS

- **MATERIALS** light woods were popular – sycamore, limed oak, walnut, and burr-walnut
- **CONDITION** plywood furniture must be in good condition: check laminated pieces for chips or flaking
- **COLLECTING** one-off, commissioned pieces by well-known makers are very expensive; minor furniture is collectible if well designed and in good condition; pieces by members of Cotswold School most desirable; forms associated with Jazz Age most sought after

Marks

Heal & Son: work is stamped with this mark, inset in a circular ivory plaque on the insides of doors or inside drawers

Isokon: most work carries this mark

See also Arts and Crafts: Furniture – Britain, pp.371–3

The United States

The late 1920s saw the emergence of a "Modern movement" of innovative American furniture designers. Inspired by European immigrants, including several key members of the Bauhaus, they explored new materials such as tubular metal. American Modernism was relatively small-scale, but it set the stage for a generation of industrial designers who from the mid-1930s reshaped interiors with enormous flair.

American Art Deco furniture falls into three broad categories: commercial copies of formal French pieces in exotic wood veneers and inlay; innovative and avant-garde work, which was never produced in large quantities and is scarce today; and industrially produced, mostly metallic and laminated wood furniture, based loosely on Bauhaus concepts. Produced from the 1930s until after World War II, this third category is much collected today.

PAUL T. FRANKL

Frankl (1886–1958), an Austrian architect and engineer, emigrated to the USA at the outbreak of World War I. He began designing and manufacturing furniture in New York City c.1920, working in a traditional European formal style. By the mid-1920s he was designing economical, compact, practical, modular furniture, inspired in part by the architect–designers Walter Gropius (1883–1969) and Le Corbusier (1887–1965). The best Frankl furniture (1925–c.1930), produced under the tradename "Skyscraper," was inspired by the evolving New York skyline. Bookcases and tall cabinetry of stepped, rectilinear form are typical, often with a black, red, or pale-green lacquer finish with silver-leaf edging. Natural woods, including California redwood and oak, were also used, with a red, black, or silver trim.

▲ **Pair of "Skyscraper" bookcases by Paul T. Frankl**
The most sought-after Frankl pieces, like these lacquered wood and metal bookcases, evoke the art of Mondrian. Original condition is closely related to value, and a black trim is generally preferred.
(c.1930; ht 1.9m/6ft 3in; value **K**)

Dressing tables, desks, and mirrors are also found, often with mirrored-glass tops or shelving and Bakelite drawer-pulls, which suggest a slightly later date. Bookcase cabinets usually have simple wooden pulls. Skyscraper furniture was designed to be economical, and standards of cabinetry are basic.

During the inter-war years Oriental interiors were extremely fashionable in the USA, and Frankl produced lacquered furniture such as dining-chairs, cocktail bars, dressing-tables, and small tables, usually in black, pale green, or red with gold- or silver-leaf details, sometimes with brass fittings. This furniture is less popular than the Skyscraper range, because collectors prefer pure, Modernist lines, particularly if they evoke the works of the Dutch painter Piet Mondrian, who was also inspired by mid-1920s New York architecture.

DONALD DESKEY

The designer Donald Deskey (1894–1989) collaborated with Frankl during the late 1920s, designing screens and large cabinetry in lacquered and metallic-leaf finish with vivid, jazzy decoration featuring zigzags. He also produced more mainstream designs for numerous other American manufacturers, working mostly in hardwood veneers. He is best known as the principal interior designer for New York's Radio City Music Hall, which preserves many of his pieces *in situ*. Pieces with Radio City provenance occasionally appear on the market and are eagerly sought.

Between 1927 and 1931 Deskey worked in partnership with Phillip Vollmer, designing furniture in Bauhaus taste, made of metal and glass, sometimes together with Bakelite and cork. Most of Deskey's work is unsigned, but his designs are well recorded in contemporary catalogs, and many specialist dealers in the USA recognize them.

FRANK LLOYD WRIGHT

Frank Lloyd Wright (1867–1959) is one of the best-known and most influential American architects and designers. Any designs attributed to him command a premium, particularly the Modernist oak creations from the first decade of the 20th century. However, his later post-war commercial furniture, mostly oak and maple tables and low, horizontal seating, is currently of little more than decorative value.

Most of Wright's work cannot be considered Art Deco, but some of his furniture of the inter-war years appeals to Art Deco enthusiasts. The best examples were designed for Wright's residential buildings, and are therefore extremely scarce. Pieces for commercial interiors were made in larger numbers and are more common today. Enameled metal furniture, such as that made for Wright's S.C. Johnson Administration Building (Wisconsin) in 1937, and several types of wooden chair are relatively common on the market.

▼ **Folding screen by Donald Deskey**
This three-panel lacquered screen with its bold, abstract, geometric pattern and zigzag lines was designed for the Paul T. Frankl Gallery and is typical of Deskey's jazzy style.
(c.1927–31; ht 2m/6ft 7in; value **M**)

▼ **Office chair by Frank Lloyd Wright**
The innovative form and industrial style of this enameled tubular steel chair for the S.C. Johnson Administration Building are typical of Wright's 1930s office furniture, which is found on the market fairly often.
(c.1937; ht 79cm/31in; value **K**)

THE CRANBROOK ACADEMY OF ART

In 1925 the Finnish architect Eliel Saarinen (1873–1950) began work on the Cranbrook Academy of Art in Bloomfield Hills, near Detroit, Michigan. In 1932 he became president and art director of the academy, serving there until his death. The building retains many of the original furnishings that he designed.

In most of Saarinen's designs a formal, Scandinavian influence is evident in the elegant lines and relatively small scale, although some are comparable to the more organic style of the Wiener Werkstätte designer Dagobert Pêche (1887–1923). Saarinen preferred rich wood veneers and natural materials, which he sometimes used in combination with steel or polished metal.

The Cranbrook Academy, like the German Bauhaus school, is best known for its influential alumni. The most celebrated Cranbrook graduates from the 1930s are Florence Knoll (*b*.1917), whose name appears on much American Modernist furniture made under her direction; Charles Eames (1907–78), who designed laminated wood, leather, and fiberglass furniture for the Herman Miller Co. and others from the late 1930s; and Eero Saarinen (1910–61), Eliel Saarinen's son, who collaborated with Eames as well as pursuing an independent career as both an architect and a furniture designer. Popular designs were produced over several decades (some are still made); earlier pieces can be identified by tags and generally higher-quality craftsmanship, as well as by wear and tear. Followers of Eames whose work is of interest to collectors include Gilbert Rohde (1894–1944), who designed Bauhaus-influenced tubular steel furniture produced by the Herman Miller Co., and George Nelson (1907–86).

OTHER AMERICAN ART DECO FURNITURE

During the 1930s, American Modernism took root throughout the USA, partly because so economical a style of design was appropriate to a country in the grip of the Depression. Leading designers include Russel Wright (1904–76), Walter Dorwin Teague (1883–1960), and Raymond Loewy (1893–1986), who all specialized in industrial-style commercial products and lighting, using new materials such as aluminum, chrome, and plastic. Karl Emmanuel Martin ("Kem") Weber (1889–1963) studied under Bruno Paul in Berlin before moving to California in 1914. He designed both individually commissioned and mass-produced furniture, typically in laminated wood, chromed metal, and sprung steel. The architect Eugene Schoen (1880–1957) designed elegant furniture in Modernist materials including glass and nickel. Examples of tubular steel furniture influenced by the Bauhaus include pieces designed by Wolfgang Hoffman (1900–69), son of the famous Austrian designer Josef Hoffman (1870–1956), during the 1930s. Prestigious firms included John Widdicomb, Johnson Furniture, and Barker Brothers Furniture Co., all in Los Angeles, and S. Karpen of Chicago, all of which employed leading designers.

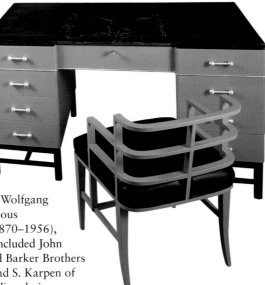

► Cabinet by Eliel Saarinen

Saarinen's original designs are rare, although his son Eero designed pieces that were commercially produced on a large scale, sometimes in collaboration with Charles Eames, a fellow graduate of the Cranbrook Academy. This marquetry cabinet designed by the elder Saarinen was made for the Saarinen House at Cranbrook. The style is typically very plain, with a simple pattern provided by panels of contrasting woods. Furniture by Eliel Saarinen is extremely rare and is usually custom made. This example was constructed by Tor Berglund, using African walnut, green hart, rosewood, and maple veneers.
(1930; ht 1.5m/4ft 11in; value **P***)*

▼ Desk and chair by Kem Weber

Weber was one of only a handful of Modernists working on the West Coast of the USA, where, among other things, he produced designs for Hollywood film sets. He also designed a few pieces to commission for Mr and Mrs John Bissinger of San Francisco, including this bird's-eye maple, lacquer, and silver-leaf desk and chair. Weber's designs were typically sleek and functional, showing the influence of the Bauhaus, and most were commercially produced. They may bear a Lloyd Manufacturing Co. tag.
(1928–9; ht 80cm/31½in; value **J***)*

KEY FACTS

Paul T. Frankl
- COLLECTING rarely found outside New York City; Oriental style is less popular than Skyscraper; collectors prefer signed pieces in unrestored condition; surface restoration is common as decoration is easily worn

Marks
Authentic Skyscraper pieces are stamped "SKYSCRAPER FURNITURE, Frankl Galleries, 4 East 48th Street, New York"

Donald Deskey
- VALUE interesting provenance, such as Radio City Music Hall, adds greatly to value
- COLLECTING Deskey-Vollmer signed pieces are more desirable than Deskey's later, traditional designs; vivid, jazzy designs are very collectible – beware of fakes

Marks
Some pieces of Deskey-Vollmer have a metal tag

Frank Lloyd Wright
- COLLECTING Art Deco style is less valuable than pieces from *c*.1900 to 1910, but more valuable than post-1945 pieces; original condition is all-important; provenance from notable interior schemes adds greatly to value

Marks
Wright furniture is rarely marked, but is well documented and easily identifiable through style

Saarinen and The Cranbrook Academy of Art
- COLLECTING Saarinen: designs are scarce but well documented; Eames: very collectible, particularly early work

Other designers
- COLLECTING identifiable pieces by lesser-known American designers are rare but still not greatly sought after; provenance is important in determining value; commercial furniture is less valuable than domestic

Marks
Pieces are rarely signed by the designer but may bear a maker's or retailer's mark; Weber pieces may bear a tag from Lloyd Manufacturing Co.

See also The Netherlands, Germany, and Scandinavia, pp.416–17

Ceramics

In the 1920s and 1930s the Art Deco style filtered through into the designs of commercial ceramics manufacturers throughout Europe. Factories such as Sèvres in France employed top designers to create fashionable pieces with such typical Art Deco motifs as stylized flowers, plants, female nudes, and exotic animals in bold colors. Commercially produced pieces survive in larger numbers than those of artist-potters and are becoming increasingly popular with collectors. Geometric shapes and clean, functional forms were a legacy of the Bauhaus in Germany, being eminently suitable for mass production. British ceramics remained essentially traditional, but bold, bright Art Deco designs were produced by Clarice Cliff.

France, Belgium, and Italy

FRENCH ART POTTERY

Immediately prior to and following World War I, many potters continued to work in the tradition of the reform movements of the 19th century, in which the artisan was responsible for all phases of the production of his or her work. Most of these artist-potters were based in France and explored a wide variety of techniques, including painting, *sgraffito* and crackle glazing. Many of them employed the typical Art Deco motifs of stylized female figures and animals, often representing episodes from Classical myths, or geometric forms.

▶ Vase by René Buthaud

This painted earthenware vase depicts the Greek myth of Europa, in which Europa is carried off by Zeus in the form of a bull. The female figure and the bull are set against a stylized landscape with a Classical temple. The buff crackle-glaze ground, the palette of blue, green, brown and black, and the stylized wavy hair of Europa are characteristic of Buthaud's ceramic designs.
(c.1925; ht 41cm/16in; value I)

An influential forerunner of the artist-potters was André Metthey (1871–1921), who produced richly colored faience and stoneware vases with decoration designed by such well-known avant-garde artists as Henri Matisse, André Dérain, and Edouard Vuillard. After World War I Metthey turned to painting his wares with pure geometric motifs of his own design, as well as stylized flowers, plants, and Classical figures in bright colors, usually in friezes or set in medallions.

In the early 20th century many French potters were strongly influenced by Oriental ceramics. Among these was Raoul Lachenal (1855–c.1930), who produced simple, symmetrical stonewares inspired by Oriental forms and painted with stylized floral or geometric patterns in strong, plain colors. Henri Simmen (1880–1969) was greatly interested in French peasant pottery, and worked with salt and flambé glazes before World War I. After the war he produced handmade stonewares, using natural products to create rich glazes. Simmen's wares were sometimes incised with symmetrically placed geometric motifs; ivory, precious wood, or horn lids, finials, and stands were carved by his Japanese wife, O'Kin Simmen. The early designs of Emile Décoeur (1876–1953) were in the Art Nouveau style, but in the 1920s and 1930s he rejected elaborate surface decoration in favor of pure, symmetrical, Oriental-style forms with a single, brilliantly colored glaze.

One of the best-known figures in Art Deco French ceramics was René Buthaud (1886–1987), whose work is rare and highly collectible. In the mid-1920s he produced simple, bulbous vases and bowls with painted, crackle-glazed, or incised decoration, generally in brown tones. His designs of linear, stylized female figures were influenced by the paintings of Jean Dupas and by African art. Buthaud was among the artists who designed wares for Primavera, the design studio of the Printemps department store in Paris. The Longwy factory also produced wares for Primavera, including pieces with crackle-glazed grounds, which were used as a base for painted decoration.

The painter Jean Mayodon (1893–1967) turned to working in ceramics in 1912 but did not exhibit his pieces until after the war. His vases, bowls, and plates are painted in rich colors and decorated with Classical figures. As well as small decorative pieces, Mayodon produced panels and tiles, some of which were used for the French ocean liners of the 1930s. The French painter Raoul Dufy (1877–1953) collaborated with the Catalan potter Josep Llorens Artigas (1892–1980) on ceramic vases, fountains, and planters decorated with Dufy's trademark motifs of dancers, flowers, and nymphs.

COMMERCIAL WARES

Some of the highest-quality Art Deco ceramics were produced at Sèvres from 1920, when the factory came under the direction of George Lechevallier-Chévignard. At the 1925 Paris Exhibition, Sèvres displayed vases and tablewares with decorations designed by a number of eminent contemporary artists, including Suzanne Lalique (b.1899), daughter of the jeweler and glassmaker René

▲ Charger by Longwy for Primavera

In the 1920s and 1930s the firm of Longwy produced many distinctive wares for Primavera, which, like this charger, were typically painted in brown, black, and reddish colors against ivory-and-gray crackled grounds. Stylized female figures such as those seen here feature in many Primavera wares. The scroll border is inspired by Classical motifs.
(c.1928; diam. 38cm/15in; value F)

▶ Vase by Mlle de Mezence for Sèvres

Decoration such as stylized leaves enhanced with gilding, as here, is typical of Sèvres wares of the Art Deco period. Most of the factory's vases of this time are based on Neo-classical shapes; the cylindrical form and elongated neck of this porcelain piece are slightly unusual.
(c.1925; ht 33cm/13in; value G)

Lalique (1860–1945), Jacques-Emile Ruhlmann (1879–1933), and the painter Jean Dupas (1882–1964). These wares were traditional in form but were elaborately embellished with Art Deco motifs. The restrained use of gilding to highlight or outline motifs is also a familiar feature of Sèvres wares.

The Limoges firm of Théodore Haviland & Cie (est. 1797) also employed Suzanne Lalique and Dufy and consequently produced pieces similar to those of Sèvres. Lalique designed plates depicting grapes and vines in a palette of black, silver, and green, while Dufy's wares featured foliage and floral motifs in bright colors. Tableware for Haviland by the glass designer Jean Luce (1895–1964) is characterized by gold-and-platinum stylized clouds, angular sunbursts, and zigzags.

In the 1920s and 1930s the design studios of Parisian department stores produced a wide variety of Art Deco wares for the mass market. La Maîtrise, the studio of Galéries Lafayette, produced a range of household wares manufactured in Belgium. The Compagnie des Arts Français (est. 1919) produced a variety of utilitarian and decorative wares in an architectonic style, as well as tablewares such as tureens and vegetable dishes with heavy scrolls and floral motifs.

The most important manufacturer of Belgian Art Deco ceramics was the firm of Keramis, owned by Boch Frères, in La Louvrière. Its artistic director from 1907 was Charles Catteau (1880–1966), who designed simple, ovoid-shaped vases, with thickly applied glazes on an often ivory, crackle-glazed background. Like Lachenal, Catteau sometimes used patterns imitating *cloisonné* enamel, although in the 1920s and 1930s his favored forms of decoration included such animals as leaping gazelles and stylized pendant flowers and plants.

In Italy the architect Gio Ponti (1891–1979) created a range of wares between 1923 and 1930 for the porcelain manufacturers Richard-Ginori (est. 1896) in Doccia. His range included tableware, vases, and urns, which were painted with strongly stylized geometric patterns, architectural forms, figures, or drapery.

▶ Vase by Charles Catteau for Keramis

Animals in natural settings were among Catteau's favorite motifs for his Art Deco vases for Keramis. The thickly applied enamels, creating a relief pattern, and the ovoid shape of the vase are common features of his designs. Like many Keramis wares, this vase is painted on the underside with the designer's name.
(c.1925; ht 49cm/19¼in; value E)

FIGURES

Most French figurative ceramics reflect the general trend for stylized forms. Among the earliest Art Deco examples are the porcelain tea- and coffee-sets (1916–17) designed by the Swiss sculptor Edouard Marcel Sandoz (1881–1971) for Haviland. The teapots, creamers, and other items are modeled as formalized, angular animals and birds. The Parisian firm of Robj produced useful wares in the form of brightly colored, almost toylike figures in national dress or representing different professions.

From 1928 the Italian firm of Lenci (est. 1919) in Turin produced earthenware and porcelain figures, mainly of women, either nude or in contemporary dress. These figures are more naturalistic than most French examples and are distinguished by elongated limbs, bright-yellow hair, and a combination of matt and glossy glazes. Most Lenci designers are anonymous.

▶ Figure by Lenci

This girl perched on a bookcase is typical of the Art Deco figures made by Lenci, with its bold pose and use of bright colors and stylish, modern dress. Many female figures by Lenci wear fashionable small hats and feature intricately worked details – here, the scarf.
(1937; ht 38.5cm/15in; value I)

◀ Bowl by Gio Ponti for Richard-Ginori

Typical of the highly stylized wares designed by Ponti for the Doccia-based firm, this large porcelain bowl is decorated with an imaginary landscape with a church set on a rounded hill, a leaping traveler, and shooting stars flying through a clouded sky. It is marked "Richard Ginori Pittoria di Doccia."
(1927; ht 21cm/8¼in; value D)

KEY FACTS

French art pottery
- DECORATION *sgraffito*, painting, and crackle glazing
- INSPIRATION Classical and Oriental wares

Marks
Buthaud: painted "R. Buthaud," or painted or incised monogram "RB"

Primavera: Dufy/Artigas: each piece should be individually numbered (1–110)

Sèvres
- STYLE conventional forms based on 18th-century designs are typically decorated with stylized leaves and flowers, and geometric patterns; gilding is common
- COLLECTING pieces are high quality so are relatively expensive even though mass-produced

Keramis/Boch Frères
- FORMS simple, ovoid shapes
- DECORATION patterns imitating *cloisonné* enamel; stylized flowers, plants, or animals; colors: turquoise, also blue, black, green, and brown

Marks
Several marks used, including this overglaze mark after 1914

France
- FORMS useful wares such as tea- and coffee-services and decanters, as well as decorative pieces, made in the form of stylized animals, birds, or human figures

Lenci
- FORMS figures of women, nude or in stylish modern dress, often wearing hats; mostly single subjects
- GLAZES matt often combined with shiny finish
- COLLECTING sophisticated pieces most sought after

Marks
The name may read backward on some pieces as the stamp was set in positive rather than in reverse in the mold

See also Mid-century Modern: Studio ceramics – Europe, p.460

Germany, Austria, and Scandinavia

COMMERCIAL WARES

In Germany, the Bauhaus (est. 1919) opened a ceramics workshop at Dornburg near Weimar, but ceramics were abandoned when the school moved to Dessau in 1925. However, the pure, functional forms used by Bauhaus designers did have some influence on mass-produced ceramics. In 1930, at the State Porcelain Factory in Berlin, Marguerite Friedlander-Wildenhaim (1896–1985), a former Bauhaus student, created the simple, geometric designs of the "Halle" service. Geometric shapes, with soft, rounded contors, were also used by Dr Hermann Gretsch for his designs for the "Arzberg 1382" service of 1931, which was manufactured by the Carl Schumann factory in Arzberg.

▲ Tea service by Marguerite Friedlander-Wildenhaim for the State Porcelain Factory, Berlin
The aesthetic appeal of this tea service lies in its very simple banding and elegant proportions. Designed by a former Bauhaus student, it shows how good design can be compatible with mass production.
*(1930; ht of teapot 11.5cm/4½in; value **F**)*

Among the most distinctive Art Deco ceramics are those designed by Wilhelm Kåge (1889–1950), artistic director of the Gustavsberg porcelain works in Sweden. His "Argenta" range of hand-thrown or molded green-glazed vases, bowls, plates, and boxes (1929–52) is inset with chased silver in typically Art Deco motifs of mermaids, nude female figures, and flowers. Such wares are becoming more popular with collectors but are still relatively inexpensive.

FIGURES

Along with tableware, figures are among the most widely collected Art Deco ceramics today. While some factories continued to produce figures of traditional subjects, such as characters from the Italian *commedia dell'arte*, many Art Deco figures represent women, either nude or in contemporary dress. Some are accompanied by elegant greyhounds or borzois. Stylized human, animal, or bird figures and wall masks, influenced by contemporary Cubist abstract sculpture, were also popular during this period.

During the 1920s and 1930s the Vienna firm of Goldscheider (1885–1954) was one of the few Austrian producers of earthenware and porcelain in the Modern style. Figures made by Goldscheider include dancing couples in contemporary dress, ballerinas, and Pierrettes from the *commedia dell'arte*. Colors are typically rich and contrasting, and costumes are exotic. Goldscheider

also produced polychrome cast plaster and ceramic copies of bronze and ivory sculptures by Joseph Lorenzl and Bruno Zach. Among the factory's most collectible products today are its terracotta wall masks. These elongated, highly stylized female faces are hand-painted in bold colors, typically red, yellow, green, and black, and usually have brightly colored hair in ringlets. The firm also had a subsidiary in Paris, which at the 1925 exhibition displayed Cubist-inspired, angular statuettes with simplified features. In the late 1930s the British firm of Myott, Son & Co. Ltd produced Goldscheider figures. These pieces, clearly marked with their origin, are less collectible than Goldscheider figures made in Austria.

In Germany, fine-quality, detailed, naturalistic porcelain figures of dancers in colorful costumes, women in modern dress, and animals were produced by the firm of Rosenthal (est. 1879) in Selb. However, some of its most distinctive figures of the late 1920s and 1930s are very different in style; modeled by the artist Gerhard Schliepstein (*b*.1886) they depict svelte, elongated, and stylized women and greyhounds in pure-white porcelain. The Art Deco taste for the exotic was reflected in the figures of snake-charmers, Spanish dancers, and belly-dancers made by the Dux porcelain factory in Bohemia in the 1920s and 1930s.

▼ Wall mask by Goldscheider
Ceramic wall masks were particularly popular during the Art Deco period and were made by a number of European factories, but those by the Austrian firm of Goldscheider are among the most sought after today. A series of six or more designs was produced in terracotta. Hand-painted, usually in bold colors, the stylized faces have serene expressions.
*(c.1930; ht 31cm/12in; value **E**)*

▲ Bust by Gerhard Schliepstein for Rosenthal
The pieces designed by Schliepstein for Rosenthal are among the most distinctive Art Deco figural ceramics. Like this porcelain bust, they are highly stylized and sculptural and, unlike many ceramics of the period, are left white. The elongated limbs are also typical of Schliepstein's designs.
*(1929; ht 46cm/18in; value **H**)*

KEY FACTS

German commercial wares
- STYLE usually influenced by the Bauhaus designs; simple, geometric shapes are typical, often with soft, round contors

Gustavsberg porcelain works
- STYLE Argenta tablewares, vases, and boxes with green-glazed grounds, inset with chased silver motifs; some with diaper-patterned or floral borders
- COLLECTING Argenta wares are increasingly collectible; hand-thrown pieces are more heavily molded

Marks
Printed in black or gold (1910–40)

Goldscheider
- FORMS figures of couples in modern dress, dancers, and stylized wall masks
- COLORS wall masks are painted in bright tones of red, yellow, green, and black
- CONDITION masks are prone to chipping as they are made of earthenware; paint may also be worn

Marks
Mark used 1918–46; versions by Myott, Son & Co. Ltd marked "Goldscheider made in England"

Rosenthal
- FORMS naturalistic dancers, women in modern dress; Schliepstein: stylized figures of women and animals
- STYLE naturalistic figures are colorful. Schliepstein: highly glazed and left undecorated

Marks
Incised with designer's name on underside or side of base; printed mark

See also Sculpture: Germany and Austria, pp.442–3

The United States

American Art Deco ceramics were mainly inspired by European design, and today many collectors in the USA actually prefer French Art Deco porcelain or pottery to American-made pieces.

COMMERCIAL CERAMICS

Cleveland, Ohio, was the center for progressive American ceramics during the inter-war years, owing to the influence of Julius Mihalik, a Viennese professor at the Cleveland Institute of Arts and follower of the Wiener Werkstätte. Several students and independent designers worked for the Cowan Pottery, founded outside Cleveland in 1913 by Reginald Guy Cowan (d.1930). Cowan designed most of the pottery's early pieces himself; these consist mainly of inexpensive, slip-cast earthenware figures and figural "flower frogs" with matt monochrome glazes. The work of independent designers, generally made after 1927 for the Cowan Pottery Studio, was often issued in limited editions, and is most collectible. Some pieces show a distinctly Austrian influence, while others, particularly the work of Paul

▲ "Jazz" punchbowl by Victor Schreckengost for the Cowan Pottery Studio
This well-known design depicts scenes of New York City on New Year's Eve and is glazed in "Egyptian Blue." Each piece in the rare limited edition of 50 is slightly different. A commercial, mass-produced edition also exists.
(1931; ht 20cm/8in; value of limited-edition bowl K)

Manship (1885–1966), are sculptural. The designs of Waylande Gregory (1905–71), who worked at Cowan from 1928 and later at the Cranbrook Academy of Art in Bloomfield Hills, near Detroit, Michigan, are often Neo-classical in inspiration. A famous allegorical image, "Radio," personifies the medium as a woman depicted in the Classical style, holding a lightning bolt.

The Rookwood Pottery (est. 1880) of Cincinnati, Ohio, produced an extensive range of Art Deco ceramics, mostly figures, bookends, and paperweights, in monochrome glazes. The Art Deco wares of the Roseville Pottery, in Zanesville, Ohio, are generally considered inferior to those of Rookwood, but such lines as "Futura," introduced in 1928, are lively and attractive, which

makes them of greater interest to collectors. Most common in this line are well-marked vases featuring angular handles or "skyscraper" stepping.

In 1936 Frederick Hurten Rhead (1880–1942) introduced the "Fiesta" line for the Homer Laughlin China Co. (est. 1877) in East Liverpool, Ohio. This was a popular kitchenware in vibrant colors. Collectors are widespread, and Fiesta is sold at special auctions throughout North America. Comparable to Fiesta ware are the monochrome teapots and dinnerware in streamlined style made at the Hall China Co. (est. 1903) in East Liverpool; like the Fiesta range, these have been authentically reproduced.

STUDIO POTTERY

Studio potters active in the inter-war years in the USA include Susi Singer (1895–1949) and Vally Wieselthier (1895–1945), who were both potters at the Wiener Werkstätte before emigrating in 1932. Typical of their work are hand-modeled earthenware figures, most of which are clearly signed. Wieselthier produced designs for General Ceramics in New York. From 1923 to the early 1930s the designer Wilhelm Hunt Diederich (1884–1953) made a limited amount of pottery, rare and now highly sought after, at his studios in Woodstock, New York. Other potters of note include Henry Varnum Poor (1888–1971), Carl Walters, and Maija Grotell.

▼ Vase by the Rookwood Pottery

Decorated by Wilhemine Rehm, this vase is somewhat unusual for Rookwood, whose Art Deco work is typically plain, with matt, monochrome glaze, and of limited interest to collectors. This colorful vase, which features an abstract pattern, is undoubtedly more collectible. Some Rookwood pieces, especially the small, geometric wares, bear impressed marks on the base.
(1930; ht 16.5cm/6½in; value F)

▲ "Futura" vase by the Roseville Pottery
This vase from the Futura range illustrates the typical, stepped "skyscraper" form and is decorated with vividly colored glazes. Although not regarded as high-quality ware, Futura is among the most valuable and collectible American Art Deco pottery, owing to its interesting design and lively colors.
(c.1935; ht 20cm/8in; value C)

KEY FACTS

Cowan Pottery
- COLLECTING Cowan Pottery Studio is the most collectible commercial ware; pieces by independent designers after 1927 (especially limited-edition "Jazz" bowls) are more collectible than early pieces

Marks
Most pieces are impressed or printed with marks showing artist's name or monogram

Other commercial ceramics
- ROOKWOOD Art Deco pieces are less collectible and valuable than pre-1914 pieces, although colorful, abstract-patterned vases are popular with collectors
- ROSEVILLE more collectible than Rookwood; "Futura" is most popular; beware of modern forgeries, which are difficult to distinguish from originals
- FIESTA made until 1972 and reintroduced in 1986; widely collected in USA; early pieces include red (most desirable), blue, yellow, green, and ivory (least popular); most new colors are pastel; modern versions are widely available

Marks
Homer Laughlin China Co.: mark used from 1936 on "Fiesta" wares

Roseville Pottery: impressed mark used from 1930

Studio pottery
- TYPES various pieces, including polychrome, hand-modeled earthenware figures, and platters hand-painted with stylized figures and animals
- VALUE pieces by independent studio potters are higher in value than mass-produced ceramics
- COLLECTING wares are generally signed by the artist; work by Hunt Diederich is rare and very collectible

See also Arts and Crafts: Ceramics – The United States, pp.378–81; Mid-century Modern: Studio ceramics – The United States, p.462–3

Britain

Art Deco had little immediate impact on the forms of commercial British ceramics; most firms simply added the newly fashionable, brightly colored, geometric, and abstract designs to existing shapes. By the late 1920s the success of such innovative designers as Clarice Cliff (1899–1972) encouraged others to develop original shapes alongside traditional ranges, and by the 1930s the influence of Modernism was evident in the increasingly functional and geometric forms of tableware, minimally decorated in neutral matt glazes. A whimsical trend in ceramics continued in the range of popular ornaments, from Wedgwood's sculptural animal designs to porcelain figures embellishing such items as dressing-table wares.

▲ **"Lotus" jug by Clarice Cliff**
This earthenware jug is one of Cliff's early "Bizarre" wares and is covered in the characteristic warm honey glaze. It is hand-painted with the design known as the "House and Bridge" pattern.
*(c.1932; ht 30cm/12in; value **E**)*

CLARICE CLIFF
British Art Deco ceramics are virtually synonymous with Cliff. In 1916 she joined the firm of A.J. Wilkinson Ltd (est. 1896), near Burslem, Staffordshire. In 1920 the firm acquired the nearby Newport Pottery and its range of old-fashioned white wares, and, recognizing Cliff's talent, set her up in a studio there. Cliff and her team of decorators hand-painted biscuit-fired tablewares with brightly colored enamels over a distinctive ivory-colored glaze, known as "honey" glaze. In January 1928 the "Bizarre" range of inexpensive and cheerful pottery for everyday use was launched; by October of the same year the range had become hugely successful. Cliff went on to design more than 500 shapes, including the "Conical," "Bonjour," and "Stamford" ranges, and 2,000 patterns, including "Inspiration" (now rare and desirable), "Appliqué," "Tennis," "Sunray," "Solitude," and "Mountain." As well as traditional shapes, she designed many futuristic or otherwise innovative forms, such as

beehive-shaped honey-pots, cone-shaped sugar-sifters, and highly stylized, geometric versions of conventional items. The majority of her output was tablewares, but she also produced a range of novelty wares, among the most collectible being figures and the newly fashionable wall masks, which usually depicted the subject face-on and featured a floral head-dress. Cliff also commissioned designs from other artists, among them Laura Knight (1877–1970), who produced the now highly collectible "Circus" series.

SUSIE COOPER
Although somewhat overshadowed by Cliff's bright, flamboyant designs, Susie Cooper (1902–95) designed an equally distinctive and now sought-after range of shapes (including "Kestrel," "Curlew," "Wren," "Jay," "Falcon," and "Spiral") and patterns (including "Dresden Spray," "Tadpoles," "Scarlet runner beans," "Nosegay," "Polka dots," and "Cromer"). In 1922 she undertook a work placement with A.E. Gray & Co. Ltd (1912–61) in Hanley, Staffordshire, and her success in designing surface patterns in luster pigments and enamel colors for bought-in white wares was such that she was given her own mark. By 1929 she had established a ceramic decoration company at George Street Pottery, Tunstall, and by 1932 was designing her own shapes; these were produced at Wood & Sons, in Burslem, Staffordshire, where Cooper had her own production unit, Crown Works. Most sought after are her tablewares in traditional, rounded shapes such as "Kestrel," "Curlew," and "Wren." Other early and desirable ranges include the more brightly colored, abstract, geometric designs such as the banded patterns, polka dots, and exclamation marks produced for the large retail outlets of the John Lewis Partnership in the early 1930s. Her hand-painted designs were carefully adapted for transfer-printing, and the two methods of decoration are virtually indistinguishable and equally collectible. After World War II Cooper produced light, translucent, bone-china teawares made in Longton and sent to Burslem for decoration; these are less collectible.

WEDGWOOD AND DOULTON
The commercial giants Wedgwood (est. 1759), in Burslem, Staffordshire, and Doulton & Co. (est. 1815), in London, both produced ranges of functional tablewares and purely decorative Art Deco pieces. For Wedgwood the Modernist architect Keith Murray (1892–1981) designed a range of simple, geometric forms, including vases and bowls, with lathe-turned decoration and semi-matt glazes, often in soft gray, green, and ivory white. In complete contrast to Murray's plain, functional designs were Wedgwood's more conventional, intricately decorated lusterwares, the most popular and expensive of which was the "Fairyland" series.

▼ **"Kestrel" teapot by Susie Cooper**
The most collectible Cooper teawares are those made before 1939. The form of this teapot is transfer-printed with "Dresden Spray," one of the most popular patterns. Typically, her patterns are understated and executed with great attention to detail, making them equally successful whether hand-painted, transfer-printed, or lithographed.
*(c.1935; ht 15cm/ 6in; value **C**)*

▼ **Vase by Keith Murray for Wedgwood**
The simple, geometric, ribbed form with lathe-turned bands and matt-green glaze identifies this Wedgwood earthenware vase as one of Murray's designs. Originally trained as an architect, Murray produced a range of highly collectible Modernist ceramics, from vases and commemorative wares to tablewares, and used distinctive, often matt, glazes.
*(c.1935; ht 20cm/8in; value **D**)*

▲ *The Bather* by Lesley Harradine for Doulton

This figure is one of the most famous of the decorative, hand-painted figures produced by Doulton in the 1930s. The casual pose reflects the increasing freedom enjoyed by women at this time. Unlike the more modest, clothed brunette shown here, most versions of *The Bather* are in the form of a blonde nude.

*(1935–8; ht 35cm/13¾in; value **D**)*

Although the imagery on the "Fairyland" pieces bears no resemblance to that usually associated with Art Deco, the original shapes and bright colors are typical of the period, and the success of Wedgwood's lusterwares inspired other manufacturers to produce more strictly Art Deco luster ranges. From 1926 the modeler and sculptor John Skeaping (1901–80) designed a range of 14 stylized Art Deco earthenware animals and birds for Wedgwood in black basalt, cream, celadon, and tan glazes; these pieces proved popular and were produced well into the 1950s.

Doulton produced a range of Art Deco tableware – such as the "Dubarry" dinner service – but it is the company's decorative bone-china figures of the 1920s and 1930s, many designed by Lesley Harradine (1887–1965), that are particularly collectible today. These figures, most of which are full length, usually depict young, fair-skinned women in informal poses, and as such are celebrations of women's increasing freedom and independence.

OTHER FACTORIES

The Art Deco wares produced by the Shelley Pottery Ltd (1872–1966; originally Wileman & Co.; trading as Foley 1892–1925, and as Shelley from 1925) owe their continuing popularity at least in part to the talented designers employed by the company in the 1920s and 1930s. These include the illustrator Mabel Lucie Attwell (1879–1964), who in 1926 introduced a range of charming nursery wares. In 1930 Eric Slater (*b.*1902) introduced two new, Modernist forms – "Vogue" and "Mode" – in clean, streamlined, architectural shapes that were perfectly suited to Shelley's fine bone china. However, more successful was the "Eve" range of tablewares, introduced *c.*1932, combining practicality with stylish, geometric design; it featured cup rims narrowed to prevent heat loss, and triangular handles pierced, rather than solid, for easier handling.

The Poole Pottery in Dorset (est. 1873 as Carter & Co.; trading as Carter, Stabler & Adams from 1921, and from 1963 as Poole Pottery, the name now also used to describe early wares) produced collectible Art Deco tablewares during the 1930s. Designs include "Studland," which has elaborate angular handles combined with a plain body of mottled green or blue, or the fashionable leaf and floral pattern; "Picotee" and "Everest" in plain colors with solid diamond-shaped handles, and rounded and ribbed shapes respectively; and "Streamline," which as the name suggests was influenced by the American streamlined style.

The Carlton Works at Stoke-on-Trent (est. 1890; from 1958 Carltonware Ltd) produced a distinctive range of ceramics during this period. Rare and highly sought after are their geometric-shaped vases, hand-painted in bright contrasting colors. The success of Wedgwood's lusterwares inspired Carlton to produce a range of richly colored pieces, featuring enameled decoration on a dark glaze and a pearlized effect on the interior. Most of the company's production took the form of molded tableware, with leaf-molded dishes being especially common.

▲ Vase by Truda Carter for Poole Pottery

Hand-thrown, ornamental earthenware vases were one of the main Poole products during the 1920s and early 1930s. This example has the characteristic stylized floral motifs in the typical Poole palette of deep, subtle colors in which blue often dominates. Irregular ribbing on the inside confirms that it was hand-thrown.

*(c.1932; ht 18cm/7in; value **E**)*

KEY FACTS

Clarice Cliff

- **DESIGNS** strong geometric forms in bold, bright colors; some traditional shapes
- **BEWARE** fakes proliferate: check for washed-out color, poor-quality painting, and an uneven or murky glaze
- **COLLECTING** increasingly rare and expensive; pieces are collected by pattern or type; desirability is determined by pattern, shape, and condition; wall masks and "Age of Jazz" figures are highly sought after

Marks

Most pieces marked, with the pattern name alongside the signature, and a stamped factory mark

Susie Cooper

- **DESIGNS** traditional, rounded forms; tea-sets usually in autumnal colors
- **COLLECTING** pre-1939 wares are most collectible; archive catalogs help to distinguish between pre- and post-war issues of the same designs; hand-painted, transfer-printed, or lithographed designs are all equally collectible

Marks

Printed in brown on earthenwares from *c.*1932

Major manufacturers

- **DESIGNS** Murray for Wedgwood: geometric, often ribbed pieces; Doulton figures: young women, typically bathing or dancing; Shelley: architectural forms with conical bodies and solid, triangular handles; Poole: streamlined shapes produced in combinations of subdued, two-color glazes
- **DECORATION** Carlton: flowers, butterflies, chinoiserie, and silver-luster lightning motifs are typical
- **COLLECTING** a wide range of tablewares is available; porcelain figures command premium prices; Wedgwood: designs by Murray and Skeaping are highly sought after, particularly Murray's lathe-turned wares, "Annular" teawares, and the "Bournvita" drinking set; Shelley: designs by Slater are highly desirable; Carlton: leaf-molded forms are abundant but not popular with collectors

Marks

Poole Pottery: almost all pieces are impressed with this mark or the entwined initials "CSA" and will include the decorator's monogram; few pieces are dated

◄ Ginger jar by the Carlton Works

Carlton's lusterwares were inspired by Wedgwood's highly successful range. The surface of this jar has a rich, jewel-like appearance, produced by the use of a glossy, pearlized, iridescent glaze. The cobalt-blue ground is characteristic of Carlton's lusterwares. The enamel and gilt chinoiserie decoration was applied by hand after glazing, giving a slightly raised effect.

*(c.1930; ht 25.5cm/10in; value **E**)*

Glass

After a decline at the end of the Art Nouveau period, art glass became popular once again during the inter-war years. France was the leader in design and innovation, with the prolific René Lalique being the foremost glassmaker in the Art Deco style. Functional pieces were very often turned to purely decorative purposes, and Lalique's molded, opalescent, or frosted glass, ranging from vases to architectural panels, spawned a great many imitators. In the USA the Steuben Glass Works produced fine engraved stemware. Molded glass was usually mass-produced and sometimes hand-finished; makers also used such techniques as enameling and engraving to embellish glass with the fashionable stylized motifs of the era.

France

Lalique, Daum, and Marinot

European industrial decorative-glass manufacturers of the Art Deco period, most of which operated in France or Bohemia, were primarily influenced by the work of René Lalique (1860–1945). Many chose to copy his style and techniques, making clear or opalescent glass vessels and statuary with a frosted finish. The wealth of output provides a wide range of choice for collectors, and many focus on only one category, or even on one color or motif. The present-day market is similarly led by Lalique prices, and most glass by other manufacturers, found throughout Europe, North America, and beyond, rarely rises above decorative value.

◄ "Tourbillons" vase by Lalique
Lalique vases are either mold-blown, or, like this model, power-pressed. Vases made in this way may be very heavy, which makes them susceptible to chipping and "bruising." This model is more valuable in clear glass with black enamel details.
(c.1926; ht 20cm/8in; value **K**)

RENE LALIQUE

Lalique began glassmaking in 1910, having already established a successful career as the leading jeweler of the Art Nouveau period, and in 1921 he took over a large glassworks at Wingen-sur-Moder in Alsace to produce his designs. He was a prolific designer, and made an enormous variety of items, ranging from perfume bottles, vases, and tablewares to clocks, lighting, and architectural panels. Most of his work was machine-made to a high standard. Lalique relied on metal molds for casting or mold-blowing glass, and many items, particularly panels and larger vessels, show evidence of "chill marks," or ripples, on the surface. Mold seams were often left, or only partially polished off. Certain objects, including vases, were made by Lalique himself (rather than by the workshop) using the *cire perdue* (lost-wax) technique. Since the mold has to be broken in order to retrieve the glass, each *cire perdue* cast is unique, and such items are highly collectible.

The majority of Lalique wares, and virtually all architectural panels, lighting, and table glass, are clear with a frosted or partially frosted surface. Opalescent glass was also used. Some vases were produced in colors,

including amber, electric blue, and black, and these command premium prices. Lalique created various forms of lighting, often in inventive shapes or containing geometric or figural decoration. Clear or opalescent light bowls are generally more desirable than those of a yellow color. Lalique designed several hundred perfume bottles, the rarest and best of which are as valuable as some colored vases. Other categories of collectible interest include the range of 27 automobile-hood ornaments (car mascots), made from 1925 to 1932, boxes, inkwells, ashtrays, and letter seals.

THE INFLUENCE OF LALIQUE

Marius-Ernest Sabino (1878–1961) produced a wide range of vases, statuary, and lighting from c.1923 until the closure of his glassworks in 1939. Much of his work clearly displays the influence of Lalique; however, few examples are as finely executed as Lalique wares, nor were Sabino's designs as imaginative. The best examples are in deep, opalescent glass of milky blue. Most popular are the highly stylized figures of women, while colored vases, mostly black or smoky topaz, have a limited following. Sabino also produced car mascots, often copies of designs by Lalique. Reproductions of Sabino's wares using the original molds have been made since the 1960s.

Edmond Etling & Cie (active 1920s–1930s) commissioned molded opalescent glass, comparable in standards of design and manufacture to Sabino. Figures of draped female nudes produced during the mid-1920s, often in a pale-bluish tint, are especially collectible, with values rivaling Sabino and lesser Lalique. Other typical subjects were animals and ships, and some vases were also produced.

Other French glassmakers in Lalique style include the firm of Verlys, which operated in France and the USA; André Hunebelle, who specialized in lighting and frosted vases of geometric design; and the firm of Genet & Michon, makers of innovative lighting, frosted architectural panels, and vases. A large variety of frosted glass, geometric-patterned lampshades, and hanging lights is reproduced today and can be found at reasonable cost.

◄ Car mascot by Marius-Ernest Sabino
Glass car mascots were originally conceived by Lalique (who produced two dragonfly models) in 1925, and were copied by several manufacturers. This piece is similar to those of Lalique but less well executed. This is one of many of Sabino's models that the factory has reproduced since the 1960s.
(c.1930; ht 15.5cm/6in; value **E**)

▼ Figure by Edmond Etling & Cie
This opalescent figure on a chromed-metal stand is the best-known and most successful of Etling's Art Deco figures. The draped female and bluish-tinted glass are typical of work commissioned by Etling.
(c.1925; ht 20cm/8in; value **I**)

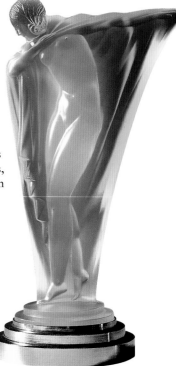

DAUM

The factory operated by the Daum family in Nancy from 1875 to the present day produced some of the best and most distinctive French Art Deco glass of the late 1920s and early 1930s. Daum specialized in artistic Art Nouveau overlay and etched glass until the 1920s, but introduced new lines in the Art Deco style before 1930, mostly under the direction of Paul Daum. The two most characteristic types of Art Deco Daum glass are the mottled and the acid-etched lines.

Mottled glass was usually of amber color, often with golden metallic inclusions, and was used for vases and some lamps (which are far more desirable than vessels), blown into heavy metal armatures. The typical wrought-iron metalwork may be signed "Edgar Brandt" or attributable to the firm of Louis Majorelle (1859–1926) in Nancy. Daum glass of this type is relatively low in value as pieces tend to be cumbersome and a little somber.

Vases, bowls, and table-lamps in heavy, thick-walled, vividly colored glass with deeply acid-etched decoration are the most collectible Art Deco Daum. Colors include green, amethyst, amber, turquoise, and gray; monumental vases in "electric" colors, particularly bright blue and vibrant yellow, are highly sought after. Matt and polished surfaces were sometimes combined. Value is directly in proportion to the depth and complexity of the etched decoration; vessels with shallow, sparse decoration tend to be of later origin and are relatively inexpensive. Pale colors and a smoky gray are also indicative of late origin (possibly post-World War II). Table-lamps are usually in thick, clear glass with a frosted or grainy surface texture and vertically etched grooves forming a geometric, abstract pattern. Lampshades are bullet-shaped (the more popular) or mushroom-shaped. Any authentic Daum etched table-lamp is of considerable value, particularly if it is of large scale. A few hanging shades of similar style were also made, but are generally less popular than lamps.

MAURICE MARINOT

Maurice Marinot (1882–1960) was a painter and glass artist who worked largely independently from c.1911. This glass was not mass-produced and is rarely found on the market; however, it is easily identifiable and widely collected, particularly in Europe. Marinot created mostly functional pieces such as vases, jugs, and bowls, often of abstract, sculptural form, and experimented with decorative techniques such as trapping bubbles or metal foil within thick, heavy walls of glass. Between c.1915 and 1918 Marinot made enameled glass, which is somewhat less collectible than his later work and consists mainly of pale-colored or bubbly vases and decanters painted with Art Deco-style flora, fauna, or figures in bright polychrome enamel. Later, internally decorated pieces are often in the form of stoppered bottles (the stopper may be a glass sphere), free-blown in thick, clear glass decorated with bubbling, inclusions, and streaks of color, and sometimes deeply etched with geometric or figural patterns.

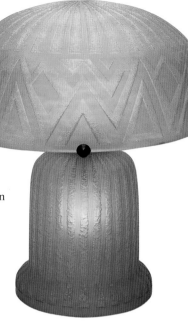

▲ Table-lamp by Daum

Daum table-lamps are among the most valuable French Art Deco glass items. This example is acid-etched in pale-amber glass with the characteristic frosted or granular surface texture. Most Daum lamps are of clear glass, which is preferred by collectors. Depth of etching is a factor in determining value, shallow work being less valuable.

(c.1930; ht 47cm/18½in; value K)

▼ Perfume bottle by Maurice Marinot

This internally decorated, clear glass bottle with facet-cut surface is engraved "Marinot 1755." The heavy form and small scale are typical of the work of Marinot, who produced unique pieces that rarely appear on the market today. All are signed and many are numbered.

(c.1925; ht 6cm/2⅜in; value H)

 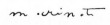

Other French makers

ARGY-ROUSSEAU, DÉCORCHEMONT, WALTER

The style of the *pâte-de-verre* (glass paste) specialists Gabriel Argy-Rousseau (1885–1953), Francois-Émile Décorchemont (1880–1971), and Amalric Walter (1870–1959) evolved from the Art Nouveau to the Art Deco style during the 1920s. Argy-Rousseau is best known for his modern, richly-colored purple and mauve hand-finished vases, patterned in relief with geometric or stylized flower and bird designs or dramatically posed ancient Egyptian, Greek, and mythological figures. His innovative and fanciful wares also included plaques, ashtrays, bowls, sensuous female figurines, translucent vessels in *pâte de-cristal* and table-lamps – the most highly prized of all Art Deco *pâte-de-verre*.

Trained as a painter and ceramicist, Décorchemont established a glass studio in the village of Conches in 1902. There he experimented with the technique of *pâte-*

◄ **"Aux Musiciens Grecs" vase by Gabriel Argy-Rousseau**
Vases such as this *pâte-de-verre* model are among the most collectible of Argy-Rousseau wares. Collectors (mostly American and Japanese) prefer heavy walls, deep, vibrant colors, and well-defined detail. The opaque glass and slightly mottled effect are typical features of the *pâte-de-verre* technique. Ancient Greek and Egyptian figures were often used by Argy-Rousseau.
(c.1928; ht 25.5cm/10in; value **K***)*

de-verre, at first producing thin-walled vessels in the Art Nouveau style that eventually gave way to solid, eye-catching bowls and vases decorated with relief masks and simple floral and animal motifs. By the 1920s his *pâte-de-verre* and *pâte-de-cristal* vessels had grown even larger and heavier, boasting both classical and contemporary decoration in rich jewel-like or marbled colors – deep blue, green, tortoiseshell brown, or amethyst – and often featuring inner bubbles and streaks. Although his work is less collectible than that of Argy-Rousseau, Décorchemont also adapted to contemporary styles and he embraced the sharp abstract forms and motifs favored by Art Deco fashion, with small vessels in Neoclassical shapes typically decorated with delicate geometric engraving.

One of the most prolific artists to work in *pâte-de-verre* was Amalric Walter. Having worked in the Art Nouveau tradition at the Daum Frères factory since 1903, Walter set up his own workshops in Nancy after World War II. Here, in addition to animal and figure subjects he produced vases, pots with covers, bowls, trays, plaques for jewelry, bookends, and paperweights decorated with abstract patterns in the Art Deco style. The glass was opaque and colors were typically dense, ranging from greens and blue-greens to luscious shades of amber and ocher.

▼ **Vase by Marcel Goupy**
The scale, decoration, and palette of this vessel are characteristic of Marcel Goupy's works, as are the simple form and the monochrome ground; the colors are bright but not loud or garish. The applied decoration has been hand-enameled, although probably not by Goupy himself. From around this date, Goupy's work, like that of many Art Deco designers, became increasingly geometric in style, showing the growing influence of the Modern Movement.
(c.1925; ht 26cm/10¼in; value **E***)*

GOUPY, LEGRAS

From his Paris workshop between 1918 and *c.*1936, Marcel Goupy (1886–1954) designed glass and ceramics sold mainly through the gallery of Georges Rouard in the avenue de L'Opera. As artistic director of the firm, Goupy created thin-walled vases, carafes, bottles, and goblets in clear or pale monochrome glass that were painted on both the inner and outer surfaces with stylized flora, fauna, or figural decoration using semi-matt polychrome enamels. Goupy also produced a variety of one-off vases and bowls, many in faded, dusky hues embellished with classical figures such as archers or nymphs, deer, floral garlands, and fashionable 1920s ladies.

Auguste-Claude Heiligenstein (1891–1976) worked at Rouard from 1919 until 1926, where, as Goupy's assistant, he executed many of the director's designs. He also produced ceramics and glass for several commercial firms and for private clients. Specializing in figural decoration, Heiligenstein's distinctive vases, bowls, decanters, pendants, and boxes were enameled with translucent, naturalistic colors and

◄ **Vase by Charles Schneider**
Large-scale pieces with bright colors and interesting forms, such as this vase modeled as a Japanese lantern, with etched overlay decoration, are the most collectible of Schneider's wares marketed under the name "Le Verre Français."
(c.1925; ht 45cm/17½in; value **H***)*

KEY FACTS

Argy-Rousseau, Décorchement, and Walter
- WARES after *c.*1920, symmetrical items, including vases
- RESTORATION may be visible on heavy, opaque pieces through transmitted light, and reduces value
- COLLECTING rich, deep colors and well-defined decoration are most desirable; heavier vases are popular

Marks
Argy-Rousseau: molded or engraved signature on most pieces; Décorchement: most pieces marked; two digits for the year a piece was made; Walter: "A Walter Nancy," often with monogram or name of sculptor

Goupy, Heiligenstein, and Legras
- DECORATION polychrome enameling
- COLLECTING Goupy: large-scale works and figural work are his most collectible pieces

Marks
Goupy: enamel or gilt script in the design or on underside of foot; Heiligenstein: enamel or gilt signature, dates, and title of decoration; Legras: variety of marks – "Legras," "Mont Joye & Cie," "Pantin," and "De Vez"

Lesser known makers
- COLLECTING Luce: desk items are popular; Schneider: large pieces, geometric forms, lamps, and pieces with applied elements are the more valuable Schneider wares

Marks
Schneider: work is engraved with a signature or "Le Verre Français" engraved or in overlay

Val St Lambert
- WARES geometric cut glass; free-blown artistic pieces; engraved vessels
- COLLECTING free-blown glass made at Jemeppe-sur-Meuse; and engraved work by Charles Graffart

▲ Amalric Walter pâte de verre bowl
Amalric Walter played a key role in the revival of the ancient pâte-de-verre technique. This yellow bowl bears the modeler's mark, M Corrett.
*(c.1920-1930; ht 10cm/4in; value **H**)*

often feature mythological scenes centered within medallions or frames; these were sometimes gilded with floral, geometric, wave, or other opulent patterns. In the 1930s, Heiligenstein created for the Legras Pantin glassworks thick-walled vessels that were elaborately decorated to reflect the revival of classical themes, so popular with many Art Deco designers.

Other French Art Deco glass artists who practiced enamel decoration include André Delatte, who worked near Nancy in the 1920s and made cameo glassware and vases in opaque, bright colors. In his finest art glass pieces the decoration combines etched overlay in two or three hues with polychrome enamel painting. Muller Frères in Lunéville (est. 1895) developed their own decorative technique called "fluogravure," which used

▼ Legras "Egyptianesque" glass vase
Like a number of the glass wares produced by Legras, this vase of globular form has an opaque white body, overlaid in a transparent color – in this case, red. Legras pieces were also further decorated in a number of ways, including enameling, acid-etching, and, as here, gilding. The "Egyptian" design is reminiscent of the Empire style, favored by Napoleon in the early 19th century and revived by several Art Deco designers.
*(c.1920; ht 10cm/4in; value **B**)*

hydrofluoric acid to etch both the body of the vessel and the areas of applied geometric decoration, producing an effect of rich, luminous color. Muller Frères also made speckled glass comparable to Daum *c.*1930, which may be fixed with metal armatures. The most valuable glass of this type was used for a series of animal-form lamps.

The glassworks founded by Auguste JF Legras in the Paris suburb of Saint-Denis earned a formidable reputation for its distinctive cameo glass carved to imitate carnelian stone and embellished in vivid enamels with floral, landscape, or fruit-inspired decorative patterns. Legras also produced pieces in opaque glass, made with layered shades of rich colors ranging from golden beige to rosy pink, which were then acid-cut to create sumptuous designs featuring flower bouquets, bunches of fruit, or seaweed. The glass was then colored in red or brown with leaves highlighted in rich shades of green.

LESSER-KNOWN MAKERS
French Art Deco glass by small or lesser-known makers is widely available and varies greatly in quality. The unique, deeply acid-etched sculptural work of Aristide Colotte (1885–1959) in clear crystal, ranks among the highest achievements in Art Deco decorative glass, but is not widely collected. Jean Luce (1895–1964), who exhibited ceramics at the 1925 Paris Exposition Universelle, created glass vessels boasting motifs echoing the Cubist movement. After 1925 he abandoned enameled surfaces in favor of bold geometric or simple horizontally lined patterns, etched and engraved on monumental vases or occasionally contrasting rough sandblasted sections on a vessel with segments of smooth mirrored glass.

At his glassworks in Epinay-sur-Seine, Charles Schneider (1881–1953) created a popular range of useful glass wares from *c.*1918 until the early 1930s. His mottled, bubbly glass, which was mold-blown into thick-walled vases, bowls and lamps – many with applied feet or handles in a contrasting color – are relatively common. Schneider and his brother Ernest also produced cameo, carved, and acid-etched, internally-decorated art glass, as well as a range of large vases and table lamps called "Le Verre Francais," typically made in overlay glass and etched with Art Deco decoration.

VAL-SAINT-LAMBERT
Established in 1825 near Liège in Belgium, the Val-Saint-Lambert glassworks first employed English craftsmen to produce English-style crystal glassware. By the late 1890s, the company had come under the influence of the Art Nouveau movement and later, under the guidance of Belgian architect-designer Henry van de Velde (1863-1957), it made a specialty of high-quality, cased-glass vessels with deep-cut, abstract decoration that appealed to the prevalent taste for Art Deco.

▲ Val-Saint-Lambert vase
In cased red glass and cut with vertical bands and horizontal step cutting, this vase is typical of the Art Deco pieces produced by the Belgian gassmakers Val-Saint-Lambert under the direction of van de Velde. Val-Saint-Lambert contributed a major display at the Paris 1925 Exposition Internationale, for which the factory created a novel series of vases using decorative themes and techniques in the Art Deco idiom. The wares were widely celebrated and recognized for their exceptional quality.
*(1930s; ht 25.5cm/10in; value **G**)*

See also Art Deco: Glass – France, pp.428–9

Other European Glass

ITALY

Italian glassmaking had always been focused on the island of Murano. From the first decade of the 20th century until the late 1930s, Muranese studios and glass factories produced a wide variety of wares including new forms and decoration, while also using traditional techniques. The result was a style of bold Italian Modernism that would cement Italy's international reputation for high-quality glass of distinctive design.

Leading this renaissance of Venetian glassmaking were Paolo Venini (1895–1959) and Ercole Barovier (1889–1974). Both came from families with long histories of glass production, and they continued the

tradition of employing talented and innovative designers in their factories. Venini & C. (est. 1921 with partner Giacomo Cappellin) produced Art Deco shapes that were at once striking and practical, playing with surface textures and internal color effects. Barovier explored the potential of achieving different textures. Typical of his work are his *vetro gemmato* glass with a randomly dimpled surface, introduced in 1936, and his *vetro rugiada* in 1940, where the glass had a surface texture resembling a delicate covering of dew-drops. Classical subjects in the Art Deco style were the forte of Guido Balsamo-Stella, who ranks as the most celebrated Italian designer of fine-quality engraved decorations for glass.

AUSTRIA, GERMANY, AND CZECHOSLOVAKIA

The path forged by Josef Hoffmann in concert with avant-garde artists and designers at the turn of the 20th century, saw their crisp, functional approach become a perfect match for the clean, bold shapes of the Art Deco style. The glass-decorating workshops of the Wiener Werkstätte produced wares by a number of talented artists, including Michael Powolny, Kolomon Moser, Dagobert Peche, and Otto Prutscher. The Bohemian firms of Lobmeyr, Meyr's Neffe, and especially the Loetz family glassworks, also manufactured vases and tableware after the precise, geometrical designs of the Wiener Werkstätte artists. These included a range of

▲ Barovier glass vase
Barovier conducted innovative experiments in texture and color, which he generally applied to plain, fluid shapes. In this example, a red vase is cased with clear bubbles and side decoration.
(1930s; ht 28cm/11in; value H)

◄ Round glass vase by Venini & C.
Designed by Napoleone Martinuzzi, this vase has a round shape with thick horizontal ribbing in cased opaque-white and opaque turquoise-blue glass. Venini evolved from producing reinterpretations of traditional Venetian forms to simple yet bold Art Deco shapes influenced by functionalism and Modernism. Among Venini's chief designers, Napoleone Martinuzzi was celebrated for his exuberant sculptural pieces including trees and giant cacti.
(1930; ht 29cm/11¾in; value D)

► Loetz-Witwe coupe
Designed for the Loetz-Witwe glassworks by Maria Likarz, this coupe is an Art Deco interpretation of a Classical form. The iridescent, mottled, oil-spot decoration is characteristic of the factory's output during this era. Perhaps better known for her textile designs, Maria Likarz was one of the leading female designers of the Wiener Werkstätte.
(1920s; w 25.5cm/10in; value G)

robust forms in white or orange glass decorated with black bands and stripes designed by Michael Powolny. In Germany, the celebrated Württembergische Metallwarenfabrik (WMF), made the greatest contribution to the nation's interpretation of Art Deco glass. Alongside functional clear glass pieces by Bauhaus designer Wilhelm Wagenfeld (1900-1990) they created ranges of ornate, highly original art glass. Wiedman's "Ikora-Kristall" glass vessels, which boasted internal decoration of air-bubbles and color was followed by "Myra-Kristall," simple shapes with sumptuous iridescent surfaces in the manner of Tiffany and Loetz glass. External whorled motifs and crystalline detailing characterizes the range of opaque "Lavaluna" glass that was introduced by Wiedman in the mid-1930s.

SCANDINAVIA

During the 1920s and 1930s Scandinavian, and particularly Swedish, glass designers developed what had been a minor commercial enterprise into an influential international industry. By applying functionalist, Modernist theories to industry and manufacture, the Swedes and their Scandinavian neighbors successfully set a dynamic new standard for all areas of the applied arts – including glass production – by bringing quality design to mass-produced wares.

At the heart of this new burst of creativity was the glassworks at Orrefors. Originally an iron foundry, the factory had manufactured simple domestic glassware since 1898. After buying the company in 1913, Johan Ekman turned Orrefors into a highly productive and innovative firm specializing in decorative art glass. He hired two creative artists, painters Simon Gate (1883–1945) in 1916 and Edvard Hald (1883–1980) in 1917, whose prodigious talent brought energy and inspiration to Orrefors. Neither had any previous experience working with glass, but both designers understood the potential of the medium. They developed an admirable repertoire of glassmaking techniques in collaboration with a team of highly-skilled craftsmen, directed by master glass-blower Knut Bergqvist.

Orrefors became celebrated for two types of finely-crafted glass wares: "Graal" and "Ariel." "Graal," a type of glass with internal decoration cased in clear

glass, came in various colors and designs with subtle and muted decoration. "Ariel," developed in the mid-1930s by designer Vicke Linstrand, saw pieces sandblasted with intagio patterns that were then cased, trapping air in channels and pockets and enhanced with inlays of color. The fine, delicately, engraved pieces of the 1920s gave way after 1930 to simple, eye-catching and dynamic designs including stylized nudes and a series of swimming figures, featuring deeper engraving on a base of heavier glass.

GREAT BRITAIN

New Zealand-born architect Keith Day Murray (1892–1981) pioneered a dramatic change in the staunchly traditional and conservative British glass industry in the 1930s. Impressed by what he had seen at the 1925 Paris Exposition and the Swedish Exhibition in London in 1931, Murray created a variety of handsome, functional, clear, and colored glass vessels and undecorated tableware during his seven-year tenure at Stevens & Williams near Stourbridge. A typical Murray design comprised of parallel horizontal fluting was used for vases, decanters and other tableware as well as for a limited quantity of mid-1930s flaçons and powder boxes with ivory stoppers and lids. His celebrated rectangular crystal decanter wheel-carved with a cactus, is boldly Modernist with echoes of the Viennese and Scandinavian glass he had seen at the 1925 Paris Exposition.

Several other companies followed Murray's lead in challenging tradition to create glass with a new, decidedly modern spirit. Founded in the 17th century in London, the Whitefriars Glassworks, which was acquired in 1834 by James Powell (1774–1840), forged a reputation as a forerunner of English glass in the Art Nouveau style, and ventured into the production of Art Deco designs for hand-blown vases, bowls, decanters, and other tableware during the 1920s and 1930s.

▲ WMF vase

The Württembergische Metallwarenfabrik explored a wide range of glassmaking techniques during the Art Deco period, including layering different colors, sometimes with metal inclusions, and the use of innovative shapes. This molded, clear-glass vase has green marbled and gray oxide inclusions, overlaid in red. Glassmaking reached a peak at the WMF during this time.

(c.1935; ht 33cm/13¼in; value **B***)*

▶ Relief-decorated vase by Orrefors

A dark green, pressed-glass vase, with bold, geometric relief decoration, designed for the Orrefors glassworks by Simon Gate. The Swedish company became one of the leading glass makers of the interwar years. Both the Classical shape of the vase and its strong geometric patterning are typical of designs emerging during the Art Deco period, not only in glassware, but also in the ceramics and textile industries.

(c.1930; ht 16cm/6¼in; value **C***)*

▲ Whitefriars glass bowl

All of the glass wares produced at Whitefriars were hand-blown. This amber footed glass bowl has the applied swirling hand-applied "ribbon trail" decoration characteristic of many Whitefriars pieces from this period, seen in bowls and vases in a variety of colors.

(c.1930s; diam. 26.5cm/10½in; value **A***)*

▶ Whitefriars vase by William Wilson

Wheel-engraving became a popular technique during the 1930s, enabling glassmakers to achieve the geometric patterns that appear in so many domestic wares of this period. William Wilson, Barnaby Powell, and Albert Tubby were among the Whitefriars designers who championed the technique.

(c.1936; ht 31cm/12in; value **C***)*

KEY FACTS

Italy

- WARES Venini: functional glassware in bold Modernist shapes, some with colorful internal patterns and a variety of innovative surface effects, as well as Martinuzzi's sculptural pieces featuring trees and cacti; Barovier: *Vetro gemmato* – glass with a haphazard dimpled surface – and *vetro rugiada* – glass with a dew-drop surface texture

Austria, Germany, and Czechoslovakia

- WARES Austria: faceted monochromatic designs by Josef Hoffmann led the trend toward chunky forms; Bohemia: glass with dramatic shapes and strong colors are preferred over wares with intricate ornate decoration

Scandinavia

- WARES Orrefors: colorful "Graal" glass with internal decoration cased in clear glass with muted decoration and "Ariel" glass sandblasted with intaglio patterns

Great Britain

- WARES Keith Murray: architectural vases in clear or colored glass with flat-cut or engraved decoration are highly collectible; Whitefriars Glassworks: produced hand-blown glass vases, bowls, and tableware in the Art Deco style

See also Mid-century Modern: Glass, pp.456–7

The United States

Most American glass made during the inter-war years was press-molded in the traditional styles, although relatively inexpensive interpretations of French glass, especially that of René Lalique (1860–1945), were popular during the early 1930s. American glass of this period is rarely found outside the USA, as little was exported; while a thriving network of American-glass collectors exists, it is only relatively recently there has been interest in this type of Art Deco glass elsewhere in the world.

STEUBEN GLASS
Founded in Corning, New York, in 1903 by Englishman Frederick Carder (1864–1963), Steuben Glassworks earned an impressive reputation as a maker of ornamental glass of exceptional quality. This prestigious American glassmaker owes much to its elegant and distinctive work in the Art Deco style.

Before 1933, Carder designed much of Steuben's ware himself, creating new types of glass in many shapes and colors, and exploring different surface effects. After that date most Steuben Art Deco glass was designed by architect John Monteith Gates (1905-2004) or sculptor Sidney B. Waugh (1904–1963), who worked almost exclusively in high-quality clear crystal glass, developing blown vessels in simple, robust shapes that were enhanced with fine engraving. In the midst of the Depression, it was a bold move to abandon the colored and luster wares that had been the mainstay of production since the Art Nouveau era, but Steuben succeeded against the odds. After the 1937 Paris Exposition, the company commissioned 27 internationally renowned painters and sculptors, including Salvador Dali, Aristide Maillol, Georgia O'Keefe, Henri Matisse, Eric Gill and Jean Cocteau to design motifs – and in some cases forms – for limited-edition engraved Steuben crystal.

Neither Modernist nor avant-garde, ornamental pieces of imaginative design with highly accomplished engraved decoration – comparable to that of contemporary glass made by the Swedish firm Orrefors (est. 1898) – became Steuben's strength and cemented its stature as the première glassmaker in the USA. Vase shapes are typically sleek and restrained, often of Neoclassical or Chinese inspiration, and much of the engraving is figural, featuring slender forms with subtle, geometric stylization. During the late 1930s and 1940s Steuben also produced a range of heavy, cast, clear animals, some in geometric Art Deco designs, for use as bookends and paperweights; these remain highly collectible today. Decanters, often with air-trapped stoppers, are also typical.

Stylish stemware, bar items, and vases created for Steuben in the early 1930s by the leading industrial designer Walter Dorwin Teague (1883–1960) are considered among the most innovative examples of

American Art Deco glass. Teague's slender, elegant Art Deco cocktail and wine glasses are comparable in value to the finest Lalique pieces.

VERLYS AND LALIQUE-STYLE GLASS
The trademark "Verlys" derives from "Verrerie d'Andelys," a French glassworks (est. 1920) in Les Andelys, Normandy, founded by the American Holophane Glass Company. However, from c.1933 until 1955 most decorative Verlys wares were made in the USA, where pieces have grown in popularity in recent years along with an emerging market in Europe. Typical of the factory's output are press-molded vases and bowls in deep-bluish opalescent glass, mostly with symmetrical patterns evocative of Lalique. Smoky-gray, blue, and pink are rare but generally less popular, and even the finest designs share values with the most commonplace vessels produced by Lalique.

From 1926, under the direction of Reuben Haley, the Consolidated Lamp & Glass Company of Coraopolis, Pennsylvania produced an inexpensive range of conventional mold-blown vases and bowls and some

▲ **"Ruba Rhombic" vase by the Consolidated Lamp & Glass Co.**
Most Ruba Rhombic is in this color, called "Smokey Topaz." All pieces are rare, but collectors prefer vibrant colors and unusual forms such as candlesticks or monumental pieces.
(1931; ht 19cm/7½in; value G)

◄ **Vase by Walter Dorwin Teague for the Steuben Glassworks**
Teague's work for Steuben is limited to a small number of commissioned designs, mostly functional, elegant stemware. Vases of this form were also produced without decoration or with conventional cutting – such pieces are less valuable.
(1932; ht 29.5cm/11½in; value E)

▼ **"Thistle" vase by Verlys**
This opalescent vase has been made using the press-molding technique. The opalescent coloring emulates the style of fashionable French Lalique ware. Most Verlys vases and bowls found in the USA were made there after 1933.
(c.1935; ht 25.5cm/10in; value C)

KEY FACTS

Steuben Glassworks
- FORMS Neo-classical or Chinese-style vases, clear crystal animals, decanters with air-trapped stoppers; Art Deco stemware, vases, and barware by Teague
- ORNAMENT engraved, stylized figures or fauna
- COLLECTING elegant Art Deco vases, cocktail and wineglasses are most valuable

Marks
Most pieces are engraved or acid-etched with "Steuben" or a small "S"; fleur-de-lis used before 1932   *Steuben*

Verlys
- FORMS press-molded vases and bowls, with Lalique-style symmetrical patterns
- COLLECTING becoming increasingly popular; opalescent colors are more desirable than smoky gray, blue, or pink

Marks
Molded or engraved, sometimes also with "France"   *Verlys*

Phoenix Glassworks
- STYLE some copies of, or attempts to emulate, Lalique are found, but they can be distinguished by their light weight, poor definition, poorly finished rims, sugary frosted texture, and use of matt, pastel staining, sometimes in two colors
- COLLECTING a developping collecting market

Ruba Rhombic glass
- FORMS angular, heavily molded vases and tableware, mostly in pale monochrome
- COLLECTING angular "Ruba Rhombic" pieces in vibrant or rare colors such as green, yellow, lavender, and black are most desirable

Carnival glass
- FORMS molded vases, bowls, and platters decorated with Oriental motifs, fruits, and flowers; iridescent colors include orange-gold, blue, green, and purple; red is rare and pastels are not favored.

▲ Ruby peacock feather vase by the Vineland Flint Glassworks

This peacock feather pattern became one of the Vineland Flint Glassworks' best-known designs and was produced in various colors, including blue, green, ruby, and, although very rare, yellow. With origins in ancient Egypt, the pulled feather technique inspired a number of Tiffany's Art Nouveau pieces. *(c.1924–1931; ht 16cm/6¼in; value* **C***)*

figural plates inspired by the style of Lalique. With Reuben's son Kenneth Haley in charge, production of glassware that brazenly copied Lalique designs continued on the same site under the name Phoenix Glassworks until into the 1940s.

"RUBA RHOMBIC," DEPRESSION, AND CARNIVAL GLASS

During the late 1920s and 1930s the most popular type of glass in the USA was mass-produced, molded "Depression" glass, a recently coined term applied to a huge variety of useful and fancy, traditional, and Modernist wares that were inexpensive, widely appealing, and commercial. Although clear and opaque varieties were also available, Depression glass was typically translucent and colored. Makers of Depression glass included, among others, Anchor Hocking, Federal, Indian, and Hazel Atlas.

Between 1923 and 1933 the Consolidated Lamp and Glass Company produced a stylish line of vases and table glass called "Ruba Rhombic." This was considered the finest of the so-called Depression glass that was manufactured by scores of regional firms. Pale monochrome, heavily molded kitchen or tableware in the Art Deco style, "Ruba Rhombic" Depression glass is collectible in the USA and still relatively affordable. Among the most common pieces are liqueur sets and small vases in a smoky gray color. Vessels in vibrant and rare colors such as green, yellow, amber lavender and black are highly prized. It is estimated that fewer than 1,500 of these pieces exist today.

For many collectors, "Carnival" glass is synonymous with Depression glass, but in fact the former is more accurately applied to those inexpensively pressed, iridescent vases, bowls, and platters that were offered in the USA as prizes at country fairs. Also referred to as "poor man's Tiffany," much of this Carnival glass was produced by Imperial Glass in Ohio and Fenton Glass in West Virginia, and looked back to Victorian

styles for inspiration. Favorite patterns included Oriental motifs, fruits, and flowers. The most popular iridescent colors were marigold, blue, green, and purple, which were sprayed on and heated to fix.

OTHER US GLASSMAKERS

Other glassmakers active in the USA during the heyday of Art Deco include French immigrant, Victor Durand Jnr (d.1931), who set up the Vineland Flint Glass Works, in Vineland, New Jersey, in 1897, and produced art glass from 1924, under the direction of Martin Bach, who had worked for Tiffany. Among the employees were a number of glassworkers from the recently closed Quezal Art Glass Company and, initially, most Vineland pieces were reminiscent of the Quezal style. Glass makers were encouraged to develop designs of their own, however, and soon a very wide range of domestic wares, including glasses, plates, candlesticks, and perfume bottles were produced in many colors and styles. The firm became particularly known for the frequent use of its yellow "oil glass," or "ambergris."

In West Virginia, Fostoria Glass employed talented outside designers to create new products in the popular modern taste. During the 1920s New York interior designer George Sakier was celebrated for his elegant, cylindrical fluted vases in sumptuous hues including amber, ebony, topaz, and wisteria along with other affordable wares in what he termed the "classic modern" mode.

One of the most innovative American glassmakers in the 1920s and 1930s was the pioneering studio-glass artist Maurice Heaton (1900-1989), who shared the Bauhaus philosophy that useful, everyday objects could be both well designed and pleasing to look at. He created sheets of bubbled glass decorated with geometric patterns of white and colored spirals, circles and triangles in enamel glaze, as well as innovative designs for multiple objects including lighting fixtures.

► "Moderntone" glass trio set by the Hazel Atlas Glass Co.

"Depression" glass became the generic name for the vast quantites of glass products that were made in the wake of the Depression in order to statisfy the growing demand for stylish, yet affordable domestic wares. This colbalt blue "Moderntone" set from the Hazel Atlas Glass Company is typical in its modern, ridged design and the use of translucent, colored glass as opposed to opaque glass. The set comprises a plate and a coffee cup and saucer. *(c.1934–42; Plate diam. 15cm/6in; value* **A***)*

► Phoenix Glass Company freesia vase

The Phoenix Glass Company is best known for its copies of pieces by the French designer, René Lalique. Here, a blue pressed-glass vase is decorated with relief-molded freesias very much in the style of Lalique, although its value is less than that of a similar piece designed by the Frenchman. *(1930s; ht 21cm/8¼in; value* **B***)*

See also Art Nouveau: Glass – The United States, pp.402–3; Art Deco: Glass – France, pp.428–31; Postmodernism: Glass, pp.474–5

Metalwork

A rt Deco metalwork followed the same trends as other decorative arts, with geometric and angular shapes favored by Modernist designers, and stylized floral and plant motifs and adaptations of historical styles preferred by more traditional artists. The use of wrought iron, copper, and brass was revived for decorative and utilitarian objects; silversmiths combined precious metals with ivory, ebony, and precious stones, while industrial designers experimented with chromium, aluminum, copper, and industrial sheet metal, particularly in the USA during the Depression.

FRANCE

The most important French Art Deco silversmith was Jean Puiforcat (1897–1945), who established his workshop in Paris in 1922. He produced a wide range of high-quality silver, based on geometric forms such as spheres and cylinders. Puiforcat rejected traditional, applied decoration, exploiting instead the interplay of light, reflection, and shadow created by smooth surfaces. The major Parisian firm of Christofle (est. 1827) mass-produced wares throughout the period, including much of the plate for the ocean liner *SS Normandie*. Many of Christofle's pieces are typified by geometric forms, and the firm also commissioned a series of distinctive wares from such notable designers as Louis Süe (1875–1968).

Decorative ironwork was revived during this period and proved particularly popular in France, where it was used for such features as grilles, window guards, doors, screens, console tables, and light fixtures. Leading ironworkers include Edgar Brandt (1880–1960) and Raymond Subes (1893–1970), artistic director of the construction company Borderel & Robert. Subes created decorative grilles and panels for buildings throughout France, and also designed wrought-iron, brass, and copper furnishings. His pieces of the 1920s are characterized by scrolls and curls, his work of the 1930s by such architectonic motifs as stepped plinths and fluted columns.

Several artists and designers also specialized in *dinanderie* – decorative work in non-precious metals. Jean Dunand (1877–1942), a Swiss furniture designer, metalworker, and lacquerer based in Paris, created high-quality, Oriental-influenced vases decorated with red-and-black lacquer in abstract and geometric designs. His apprentice Claudius Linossier (1893–1955) made richly textured, handmade vases, plates, and bowls in patinated copper inlaid with brass, silver, and alloys.

▲ Tea and coffee service by Jean Puiforcat
This service shows the way in which Puiforcat skilfully exploited the angles, planes, and reflective surfaces of silver to animate his plain forms. The ebony handles, typical of his otherwise unadorned wares, and the gilding inside each piece indicate high quality. The tray, although by Ravinet d'Enfert, is in keeping with the style of the service. Incomplete sets are considerably less valuable than sets with all their pieces.
(1928–30; ht of coffee-pot 19cm/7½in; value L)

▼ Vase by Claudius Linossier
This piece has the hammer-textured surface characteristic of Linossier's handmade vases. The combination of black, silver, and copper-red colors and the use of decorative bands of lozenges are distinctive of his designs and reflect the influence of Dunand. *Dinanderie* pieces are usually made from a single sheet of metal, often copper, on which silver or other metals are inlaid.
(1927; ht 17cm/6¾in; value E)

AUSTRIA, GERMANY, AND DENMARK

By the 1920s many of the designers of the Austrian Wiener Werkstätte (1903–32) were creating wares in a highly ornate style. Foremost among them was Dagobert Pêche (1887–1923), whose elaborate designs feature organic motifs such as repoussé berried plants, leaves, and flowers. Other Wiener Werkstätte designers, including Josef Hoffmann (1870–1956), created elegant silver vessels with fluted bodies and hammered surfaces.

By contrast, the students at the Bauhaus (est. 1919) in Weimar, and later in Dessau, designed attractive and functional objects, devoid of decoration, for industrial production. Bauhaus designs were severely geometric in form and manufactured in such "new" materials as chromium and nickel, considered more suitable for mass production than silver. One of the leading designers was Marianne Brandt (1893–1983), director of the metalwork studio in 1928–1929.

The Danish silversmith Georg Jensen (1866–1935) was one of the most successful of the period, producing high-quality handmade and mass-produced silver. His style is distinctive: highly polished, smooth bodies are left plain, but handles, stems, and feet are in the form of detailed, naturalistic berries, pods, tendrils, and flowers.

▲ Teapot designed by Hans Przyrembel for the Bauhaus
Some of the most influential designs in silver and base metals of the 1920s and 1930s were produced by the Bauhaus. The solid-brass teapot featured above is of typically austere and geometric form, with a simple, ebonized wood handle and knop.
(c.1926–7; ht 10cm/4in; value H)

THE UNITED STATES

Wilhelm Hunt Diederich (1884–1953) and Oscar Bach (1884–1957) were the USA's foremost studio metalsmiths of the inter-war years, active mainly in the early 1920s. Diederich worked largely in sheet iron, creating skeletal and elegant Art Deco weather-vanes, firescreens, floor-lamps, and other lighting. Images of horses in the form of silhouettes are particularly common. Sheet metal is thin and usually painted, patinated, or oxidized black, while mesh screens are used as backing.

Bach favored wrought and delicately cast iron, sometimes partially gilded or of patinated gun-metal color. Some examples, including floor-lamps, smoking stands, and lighting, feature Renaissance-style elements blended with Art Deco and are of lesser interest to collectors. Bach's large studio worked on projects of more ambitious scale than Diederich's, including architectural fixtures and mirrors, some inspired by the work of the French designer Edgar Brandt.

"Streamlining" as a design trend evolved during the late 1920s and was applied to virtually all decorative arts and industrial design within a decade. Objects were smooth, slender, and often elongated or aerodynamic in form. All American Modernists designed some streamlined metalwork, and several designers specialized in it. Collectors today are able to find streamlined chrome and other metal housewares, including lighting, throughout the USA at flea markets, antiques centers, and a few specialist dealers.

The largest chrome manufacturer was the Chase Brass and Copper Co. (1876–1976) in Waterbury, Connecticut; it concentrated on producing inexpensive household chrome from 1930 to 1941. Chase's vast range of products is well documented in a reprinted trade catalog, and most items are stamped on the base. Collectors focus on large or rare models, items with particularly striking design, or pieces by commissioned designers, notably Rockwell Kent, Walter von Nessen (1889–1943), and Russel Wright (1904–76). Original boxes, interesting or colorful Bakelite or blue-glass fittings, and complete sets add value. Wright also designed aluminum dinnerware for West Bend Aluminum, which is becoming collectible but is still relatively inexpensive.

The best Art Deco chrome is probably by Norman Bel Geddes (1893–1958), a leading exponent of the streamlined style. He designed metalware for several manufacturers, including 17 pieces for the Revere Copper and Brass Co. in the late 1930s. Many of the designs are barware – especially popular after the repeal of Prohibition in 1933. They include the "Skyscraper" cocktail set, the "Normandie" water pitcher, and the "Manhattan" drinks tray. Cocktail shakers in innovative forms are popular with collectors, although many prefer European to American examples. Other designers of

streamlined metalware include Donald Deskey (1894–1989), who made mostly light fittings; Henry Dreyfuss (1904–72), who designed office equipment and kitchen appliances; Walter Dorwin Teague (1883–1960); and "Kem" Weber (1889–1963).

American silver of the inter-war years is typically in historic revival or formal taste and rarely innovative. Some pieces in the geometric style, inspired by the work of the French silversmith Jean Emile Puiforcat, were produced by Gorham & Co. (est. 1831) in Providence, Rhode Island, and Tiffany & Co. (est. 1837) in New York and also in Mexico, but they have limited interest for collectors, who prefer American Arts and Crafts silver.

▲ **"Soda King" soda siphon by Norman Bel Geddes for the Walter Kidde Sales Co.**
This soda syphon in the streamlined style is made in chrome-plated and enameled metal with rubber fittings. An extremely successful design, it was produced until the post-war years in several colors by the Walter Kidde Sales Co. in Bloomfield, New Jersey. Barware of this type is still widely available in the USA and generally very affordable.
(c.1935; ht 25.5cm/10in; value **C***)*

◄ **"Zephyr" digital clock by Kem Weber for Lawson Time Inc.**
Weber produced Modernist and Art Deco designs for interiors, furniture, and Hollywood film sets, as well as household items such as this copper and plastic clock. Trained in Germany, Weber typically made sleek, functional pieces that often show the influence of the German Bauhaus.
(1934; ht 9.5cm/3¾in; value **F***)*

▶ **"Franconia" bowl and dish by Gorham & Co.**
This beautifully decorated silver bowl and dish show the influence of contemporary French Art Deco silver by such designers as Jean Puiforcat. The Odeonesque handles, the stepped interior, and the sunburst design on the rim are all typical Art Deco motifs.
(c.1930; diam. 36cm/14in; value **J***)*

KEY FACTS

Jean Puiforcat and Christofle
- FORMS simple and geometric, with plain surfaces
- DECORATION hardstones, ivory, or hardwood knobs and handles

Marks
Puiforcat: all pieces are stamped   JEAN PUIFORCAT PARIS

Christofle: usually stamped with the name on the base

Edgar Brandt and Raymond Subes
- MATERIALS Brandt/Subes: wrought iron, (silvered) bronze, brass, copper; Subes: aluminum, steel in 1930s
- DECORATION richly textured, hammered surfaces, with stylized scrolls, flowers, and animals; work by Subes has minimal decoration after late 1920s

Marks
Brandt: work is stamped with this mark   E BRANDT

Jean Dunand and Claudius Linossier
- MATERIALS copper inlaid with brass and silver
- COLORS rich tones of brown, red, silver, and black
- DECORATION bands of diamonds and lozenges; textured, metal-encrusted surfaces

The Wiener Werkstätte and the Bauhaus
- STYLE Werkstätte: generally organic, often fluted forms, with planished surfaces; Bauhaus: geometric
- COLLECTING highly collectible

Marks
Werkstätte: work is stamped with this mark; many pieces also carry the artist's monogram

Wilhelm Hunt Diederich and Oscar Bach
- STYLE Diederich: thin, painted, or patinated sheet iron; Bach: larger-scale wrought or delicately cast iron
- COLLECTING Bach is more common and less collectible than Diederich

Streamlined style
- TYPES household wares, barware, and lighting
- DESIGNERS streamlined and Art Deco chrome is of higher value if by Bel Geddes or Kent
- COLLECTING abundant on the American market and often available at reasonable prices; unusual items and lighting are more collectible than barware and tableware; commercially made metalwork is less popular with collectors than studio pieces; Chase: chrome in good condition and blue glass or colorful Bakelite fittings are most collectible

Marks
Chase Brass and Copper Co.: chrome wares carry this mark

See also Silver, pp.222–59; Art Deco: Jewelry, pp.438–9

Jewelry

Art Deco designs are among the most sought after by jewelry collectors today. Characterized by bold colors and abstract or stylized forms, both fine and fashion jewelry of the 1920s and 1930s reflects the general design trends of the period, when "style" was all important. As with Art Nouveau jewelry, color and design were valued as much as the intrinsic worth of materials. There are two distinct stages in Art Deco jewelry design: before 1925 pieces were opulent, with extensive use of precious materials such as diamonds and platinum, in stylized figurative designs; after this date more abstract and geometric forms appeared, inspired by machine production and by Cubist and African art.

▶ Pendant by Emile David

In the 1910s and 1920s, African art had a strong influence on avant-garde art in Europe, and African-inspired designs also eventually appeared as jewelry. The elongated and stylized face of this French silver and enamel pendant is taken from African masks. This type of work is rarer than Art Deco pieces in geometric designs, although the use of semi-precious metal and colored enamel is typical of Art Deco jewelry.

(c.1925; l. 6.5cm/2½in; value J)

FORMS AND FASHIONS

The radical new women's fashions of the 1920s, especially the long, slim silhouette, demanded distinctive types of jewelry: long neckchains of beads in amber, ivory, carnelian, coral, and pearls, or plain chains with pendants, complemented the long line of the body and the dropped waistlines. *Sautoirs* – long necklaces of jewels or pearls with a tassel at the end – were popular, as were bandeaux worn around the head. With the increasing fashion for sleeveless dresses, elaborate bangles worn around the upper arm became a common feature. The new short-cropped hairstyles led to the revival of long, pendant earrings, often in the form of jeweled tassels with flexible settings so that the earrings could move. Designs of linked circles, oblongs, or triangles were especially popular for all forms of jewelry. Large and chunky "cocktail" rings of geometrical form were widely worn.

Pins, for outdoor wear (especially on coat collars) as well as for evening dresses, became extremely popular, and one of the most typical forms of Art Deco jewelry is the double-clip pin. Clips with two parallel pins without fasteners were usually made in pairs so that they could be worn on either side of a neckline or lapel or joined together as a single pin. Clips were made in a very wide variety of designs, including geometric, floral, and figural, and in many different materials, from precious gems and hardstones to paste and plastic – catering to all tastes and price ranges.

MATERIALS AND MOTIFS

The extravagance of the post-war period led to a demand for ostentatious jewelry set with large precious stones and hardstones. Luxury jewelers such as the Paris firms of Cartier (est. 1847) and Boucheron (est. 1858) created exquisitely crafted pieces in costly materials, notably the "all-white jewelry" combining platinum with diamonds. The combination of rubies, sapphires, and emeralds reflected the vogue for bright and bold designs. Less expensive pieces, made particularly after the mid-1930s, featured colorful and large hardstones such as aquamarine, topaz, and citrine. New cuts of stones, including the step and the emerald cuts, were developed to create fashionable geometric shapes and to accentuate the color of the stones. Many stones were also calibré-cut to fit a particular design. Synthetic diamonds, rubies, and sapphires were invented in the 1930s and 1940s, when the export of gems from India and Burma (now Myanmar) was halted by World War II. A fashion for strong color contrasts resulted in the extensive use of the combination of crystal and black onyx to create "black-and-white" jewelry in geometric designs. Chinese-influenced designs became fashionable in the 1920s, which made jade a popular material. Jade carvings, often dating from the 19th century, were imported into Europe and the USA in large quantities and set in precious-stone mounts. Beads and stones, including rubies, sapphires, and emeralds, carved in the shapes of fruits and berries were imported from India and used to make colorful pendants and pins, known as "tutti-frutti" jewelry. Costume jewelry in marcasite, plastic, paste, and bright enamels on metal was a popular fashion accessory, and is often more avant-garde in design; being inexpensive, it could easily be discarded and replaced with the latest fashion.

Geometric and abstract designs are particularly associated with Art Deco jewelry, but there were many other influences on jewelry design, especially in the 1920s. Carved jade pendants, earrings, and pins and Japanese-garden scenes in lacquer illustrate the widespread interest in Oriental art; Oriental motifs such as prunus blossom, bonsai, and dragons were especially popular. The discovery of the tomb of Tutankhamun in 1922 inspired jewelers to create elaborate enameled gold jewelry with ancient-Egyptian motifs such as sphinxes and pyramids, together with materials such as turquoise and lapis lazuli that were used in authentic Egyptian jewelry. Pins and pendants featuring stylized and angular flowers, garlands, and leaves, particularly those set with precious stones, show the lingering influence of 18th-century jewelry design.

▼ Clip pin

Geometric forms and the combination of jade, coral, and enamel with diamonds are characteristic of clip pins made in the 1920s and 1930s. Black, white, and red were often used to contrasting effect. Art Deco jewelry has become extremely popular in recent years, and a well-made piece such as this will be especially sought after by collectors. Some clip pins have been converted into ear-clips, more suited to the fashions of today – the back of the setting will show the original pins if this is so.

(c.1925; w. 5cm/2in; value K)

▼ "Tutti-frutti" bracelet by Cartier

One of the most famous jewel houses, Cartier has branches in Paris, New York, and London, and is renowned for its opulent jewelry. Cartier Art Deco work often shows an Oriental or Indian influence. The firm made a specialty of "tutti-frutti" jewelry, set with imported Indian rubies, sapphires, emeralds, and other precious stones carved into the shape of fruit and berries. Such pieces may originally have been commissioned by the wealthy Indian maharajas who figured among the company's impressive list of clients. These luxurious pieces are among the most expensive items of Art Deco jewelry today.

Pins in particular feature a very wide range of motifs reflecting modern life and the obsession with speed and movement. Designs of miniature airplanes, cars, ocean liners, and simple arrows were made in both gold and precious stones and also in inexpensive plastics, chrome, and enamels. Figures of women in 1920s dress with sleek greyhounds were also simply stamped or cut out of sheet metal. Palm trees – the symbol of the Hollywood film industry – featured palm leaves carved in hardstone, with the trunk in gold or platinum.

The trend toward streamlined geometry and abstraction really began in the mid-1920s, with circles, arcs, squares, and triangles used for all types of jewelry and in every type of material. Larger and heavier bows, scrolls, buckles, and fans, with an emphasis on the metal settings rather than the gems, are distinctive of the "cocktail" jewelry made from the late 1930s.

FAMOUS DESIGNERS

In the Art Deco period, as in the Art Nouveau, Paris was the center of jewelry design. Elaborate luxury pieces were made by long-established firms such as Boucheron and, especially, Cartier. Under the direction of Louis Cartier the firm produced colorful and exotic pieces featuring unusual combinations of precious stones such as diamonds, sapphires, and emeralds with coral, onyx, carved jade, platinum, and gold. The firm was particularly famous for its jeweled clips – widely imitated in less expensive materials such as paste and base metals – and wristwatches and pendant watches set with precious gems. Other leading firms making luxury Art Deco jewelry included Mauboussin – noted for its use of black enamel – and Lacloche Frères (est. 1897), both based in Paris, and the American firms of Tiffany & Co. (est. 1837) and Van Cleef & Arpels (est. 1906), both in New York.

Similarly, most of the leading avant-garde designers of Modernist jewelry were based in Paris. Jean Dunand (1877–1942), Jean Fouquet (1899–1984), Jean Desprès

◄ **Bangle**
The stylized lotus leaves and combination of gold with blue, orange-red, and turquoise enamel on this bangle, which is probably French, reflect the vogue for Egyptian-style jewelry that was sparked by the discovery of Tutankhamun's tomb in 1922. Complete with pendants on chains, this bangle was probably designed to be worn on the upper arm – a popular fashion in the Art Deco period, when dresses were frequently sleeveless.
(1920s; diam. 7cm/2¾in; value D)

(1889–1980), Gerard Sandoz (b.1902), and Raymond Templier (1891–1968) introduced purely geometric designs in the 1920s and 1930s. Dunand is known for his designs for earrings, pinses, and bracelets, composed both of interwoven lines and zigzags and of openwork squares and triangles in silver with red-and-black lacquer. Fouquet produced geometric pendants combining hardstones and semi-precious stones. Desprès, an industrial designer, made strongly mechanistic and abstract designs in black lacquer and hammered silver, with silver balls representing ball-bearings. Templier favored platinum and silver combined with black onyx and other colored hardstones.

Most Art Deco jewelry produced elsewhere in Europe, for example at the factory of Theodor Fahrner (1868–1928) at Pforzheim in Germany, imitated the fashionable French designs. British designers such as Sybil Dunlop (1889–1968), H.G. Murphy (1884–1939), and Harold Stabler (1872–1945) continued to produce Arts and Crafts-inspired pieces in silver with cabochon stones, moonstones, chrysoprases, and chalcedonies.

▼ **Ring by Theodor Fahrner**
Fahrner was well known for his Art Nouveau jewelry, but he also made other fashionable styles in the 1920s. Fahrner's jewelry, which is much sought after today, often incorporates such materials as silver, marcasite, and semi-precious stones, including lapis lazuli and chalcedony, as in this typically chunky ring.
(c.1925; value H)

◄ **"Philadelphia-style" bracelets**
During the 1920s and 1930s, when it was fashionable to wear obviously fake jewelry, newly developed plastics – originally a substitute for more precious natural materials such as ivory, amber, jet, and coral – became acceptable for jewelry in their own right. Plastic was also seen as an exciting modern material, appropriate to avant-garde jewelry designs. This very collectible pair of American plastic bracelets, brightly colored and geometric in design, shows how the most innovative jewelry styles could be easily manufactured using the new materials. Costume jewelry was mass-produced in large quantities, and often discarded when it went out of fashion.
(1920s; w. 7cm/2¾in; value D)

KEY FACTS

- MATERIALS semi-precious stones and hardstones, often in the same piece; jade; Indian carved beads; costume jewelry: plastic, paste, marcasites, and bright enamels
- STYLES large, ostentatious stones; geometric and abstract designs; African, Oriental, Egyptian, and Indian motifs; images of "modern" life
- QUALITY French Art Deco jewelry is usually very well made, although most pieces are unsigned
- REPRODUCTIONS many exist – stones should be of correct cut and shape; metalwork should have a good-quality finish without visible machine marks
- CONVERSIONS earrings often converted from pins or bracelets: check settings for breaks and attachments
- CARE large stones are prone to chips and abrasions; calibré-cut stones are expensive and difficult to replace
- COLLECTING signed jewelry by well-known makers, especially Cartier, is sought after; avant-garde plastic pieces are affordable and collectible; synthetic stones may be hard to identify – consult a gemmologist

Marks

Cartier: most Cartier jewelry is stamped with this signature   *Cartier*

Boucheron: stamped with "B" or "Boucheron"   ℬ

See also Jewelry, pp.260–73; Art Nouveau: Jewelry, pp.406–7; Mid-century Modern: Jewelry, p.452; Postmodernism: Jewelry, p.470

Sculpture

The sculptors who emerged during the Art Deco period eschewed the romantic forms of Art Nouveau, producing work that directly reflected the fast-changing world around them. Women were a major subject for these artists; portrayed as bold, stylish, and self-assured, they were shown engaging in contemporary pastimes or sports. They were also depicted as muscular Amazons, erotic fantasies, exotic characters from distant lands, or figures from Classical mythology. Other popular subjects included children and exotic animals. Working mainly in Paris, Berlin, and Vienna, Art Deco sculptors experimented with materials and finishes, producing among other statues chryselephantine figures in bronze and ivory.

France

During the 1920s enormous quantities of ivory tusks were shipped from the Congo to be sold in Antwerp, Belgium. Eventually supply outstripped demand, and a glut occurred. Artists were encouraged to carve the excess ivory, and in some instances were offered free tusks. Partly because of the high costs involved in working in bronze, many sculptors took up the offer. Nonetheless, bronze remained the favored material for sculpture, since new methods of serial production had enabled founders to produce and market affordable bronzes. Some figures were modeled in bronze with carved ivory elements (often the head and hands). The term chryselephantine was used to describe this combination in Art Deco sculpture.

PIERRE LE FAGUAYS AND MARCEL-ANDRE BOURAINE

Pierre le Faguays (b.1892) exhibited at the salon of the Société des Artistes in the early 1920s. Like many of his contemporaries he concentrated on the female form; his women were modeled predominantly in bronze and portrayed as strong, athletic warrior types, naked or semi-clad, bearing swords and waving shields. Work by le Faguays often has a highly dramatic flavor; pieces include dancers, sometimes playing pipes or cymbals, and stylized allegorical figures. Le Faguays modeled in wood and stone as well as in bronze and ivory; notable examples in this medium include *The Marionettes*, and *Harem Dancer*. Le Faguays produced much of his work for the firm of Goldscheider (1892–1948) in Paris.

Like le Faguays, Marcel-André Bouraine exhibited at the salon of the Société des Artistes Français in the early 1920s; indeed, it is possible that

◄ *Messenger of Love* by
Pierre le Faguays
An archetypal simplicity of form, with a hint of the influence of Egypt, is displayed in this highly stylized silvered-bronze figure.
(c.1930; ht 75cm/30in; value K)

the two artists worked together, since Bouraine also cast some of his women as noble warriors. His kneeling *Amazon* and Le Faguays's *Female Warrior* bear a strong resemblance to one another. Clowns, pierrots, and harlequins were other favorite subjects, often displaying a strong Cubist influence. Bouraine's pieces were generally cast in bronze, and often have enameled or silvered surfaces. Many of his figures are in exaggerated poses – clowns may balance ivory balls on their outstretched limbs, dancers may balance on one leg – or carry an object such as a fan, spear, or bow. Much of his work was produced by the firm of Etling in Paris.

DIMITRI CHIPARUS

Dimitri Chiparus (1880–1950) was born in Romania, and, like many other contemporary sculptors, studied in France. He exhibited at the salon of the Société des Artistes Français in Paris in 1914, receiving an Honorable Mention. The most prolific artist of his era, Chiparus worked largely in bronze and ivory. The Etling foundry was responsible for editing most of his models, and many bear its foundry seal and the artist's signature. A number of models were executed for Goldscheider and the foundry of Les Neveux de J. Lehmann.

Many of Chiparus's models are of theatrical subjects – the inspirations derived from a vast array of sources, not least the Ballets Russes. Sergei Diaghilev brought to Paris this troupe of Russian dancers who, because of World War I and the Russian Revolution, were stranded there in 1917. The Ballets Russes had an extraordinary impact, and fired the imagination of artists and designers with their dramatic choreography and their exotic costumes and sets designed by Léon Bakst (1866–1924). Chiparus's *Russian Dancers* is thought to be a portrayal of Vaslav Nijinsky and Ida Rubenstein in their roles in *Scheherazade*. Chiparus created many fanciful images of women clad in jewel-encrusted costumes and head-

◄ *Amazon* by
Marcel-André Bouraine
The Amazonian figure with windswept hair was a recurring subject in Bouraine's work. As well as the artist's signature, this silvered-bronze figure – a model produced in several sizes – bears a seal of the Etling foundry, which produced many of Bouraine's designs.
(c.1930; l. 24cm/9½in; value H)

▲ *Little Sad One* by
Dimitri Chiparus
This gilt-bronze and ivory figure departs from the more usual dramatic, exaggerated style that denotes Chiparus's work. The quality of the naturalistic modeling of this figure indicates why Chiparus is one of the most highly esteemed Deco sculptors.
(c.1930; ht 30cm/12in; value K)

dresses, which he cast in bronze. The heads and torsos of the figures were usually carved from ivory, although a small number were cast totally in bronze.

Another source of inspiration for Chiparus, as for many Art Deco artists, was the opening of the tomb of Tutankhamun in 1922. Chiparus modeled Egyptian dancers such as *Nubian Dancer* both in bronze and in bronze and ivory, embellishing the bronze of their costumes with scarab motifs and beaded and jeweled decorative detail, which was then highlighted using the cold-painting process. He exploited the visually exciting and exaggerated, stylized movements, recognizable as the "Dance of the Pharaohs." Although Chiparus created images for maximum dramatic and exotic effect, he also created naturalistically modeled figures, such as *Little Sad One* and *Innocence*, and models of small children, some of which are charming but others rather sentimental.

CLAIRE-JEANNE-ROBERTE COLINET

Claire-Jeanne-Roberte Colinet was one of a very small number of successful female sculptors. Born and educated in Brussels, she studied sculpture with Jef Lambeaux and then moved to Paris. Colinet was elected to the Société des Artistes Français in 1929. She is renowned for her series of dancers of different nationalities, often wildly exotic and usually clad in rich gold-patinated costumes bedecked with jewels. Her women are naturalistically modeled, provocatively revealing fleshy ivory midriffs and fulsome calves and thighs. Perhaps the most sensational of Colinet's works is *Ankaran Dancer*, which portrays an exotic dancer poised on one foot: the other knee is raised to meet the bowed head, while a green patinated-bronze snake rises from the marble base on which the dancer stands and winds itself around her leg.

OTHER SCULPTORS

There was a great number of other French sculptors who produced fine work alongside those mentioned above. Joé Descomps (1869–1950) was a regular exhibitor at the salons of the Société des Artistes Français. A number of his chryselephantine figures are eclectic or derivative, paying tribute at times to both Chiparus and Colinet. However, *Beauty of Paris*, *Regal*, and *Enchanted* illustrate his own creative originality. His small female nudes in carved ivory are particularly charming and well executed.

Sculptors such as Affortunato Gory, A. Godard, A. Gilbert, Amedeo Gennerelli, and Pierre Laurel modeled figures that were stylistically similar to the work of the artists already discussed above. Others, such as Alexandre Kéléty, were distinguished by their unique stylization. Kéléty's figure *The Archer* is among the most visually striking of all Art Deco bronze figures. Rarely found but totally engaging are his small chryselephantine figures of children modeled in a semi-abstract style, with chubby knees and round faces reminiscent of the drawings by the British illustrator Mabel Lucie Attwell.

▲ *Hindu Dancer* **by Claire-Jeanne-Roberte Colinet**

Colinet modeled a series of flamboyant females in a similar manner to this gilt-bronze and ivory figure. The finely cast bronze bases embellished with Egyptian or other exotic motifs were often seen supporting the finer examples of her work. Other figures in the series include *Roman Dancer*, *Mexican Dancer*, and *Theban Dancer*. They frequently carry a symbol of their country, and, as in the example shown here, the bronze base is often carved with motifs of the country. Several versions were made of each figure, generally in bronze and ivory with a cold-painted or (as here) gilt surface, but sometimes in patinated bronze. New dancers in the series are occasionally still identified.
(c.1920; ht 35cm/14in; value **M***)*

◀ *Beauty of Paris* **by Joé Descomps**

This model is one of Descomps's most successful and celebrated figures, exemplifying a style that was far less derivative than much of the rest of his work. The intricate detailing on the bronze surface of this chryselephantine figure points to the fine work of the chaser whose task it was to recreate a true representation of the original model supplied to the foundry by the artist.
(c.1930; ht 38cm/15in; value **J***)*

Mention should also be made of Maurice Guiraud Rivière, who modeled a number of seated female nudes with pensive expressions, some attended by playful goats or other small animals. More notably, he was captivated by movement and speed. His futuristically stylized figure *The Comet* depicts a flying female with ankle-length hair cascading backward as she moves through the air. Rivière modeled several versions of racehorses and jockeys. His racing motorist is a truly evocative piece of work: a driver, in helmet and goggles, sits at the wheel of an open-topped car; little of the car exists in the modeling, yet the simple detail of the driver's scarf blowing straight out behind him conveys an impression of speed.

KEY FACTS

- MATERIALS bronze (often gilded, silvered, or cold-painted), ivory, spelter (an alloy of copper and zinc)
- CHRYSELEPHANTINE a term originally used to describe Classical statuary made of gold and ivory, and in the 1920s extended to include objects of ivory in combination with another material, usually bronze
- EDITORS they commissioned models from artists that would then be produced in series by the foundries; some French editors owned their own foundries
- BASES the most popular were made in black slate, striated marble, and green onyx, and are usually stepped or of an architectural form; the most impressive were designed by Chiparus, who often carved them or set them with low-relief bronze plaques
- BEWARE sometimes spelter, which presents as a white metal (bronze is yellow) under a patinated surface, may be passed off as bronze; it was used for inexpensive, mass-produced figures: these have less defined modeling, as they were not hand finished, and are generally lighter in weight (bronze is usually quite heavy), and the metal is warm to the touch (bronze is cold); fake chryselephantine figures exist in spelter with hands and faces in molded ivorine, an inexpensive, synthetic material with properties akin to plastic, which is aged to look like the real thing
- CONDITION ivory: although fine lines may be tolerable, where possible ivory should not have too many deep cracks – these are particularly distracting on facial features and can substantially affect the value of the piece; bronze: cold-painted surfaces should have as much of the original color detail as possible; silver-plated surfaces should not be so worn that the bronze is highly visible
- CARE ivory: do not let the material dry out, and keep out of direct sunlight; bronze: do not attempt to repolish bronze or alter the patina as this will reduce the value of a piece – dusting is adequate care

Marks

Signed work is always desirable, but the quality of the work is more important; the value of poor-quality work is not increased by a signature; signatures may appear on the base or be cast in the bronze

Dimitri Chiparus: the signature appears in the bronze or on the base	D.H.Chiparus
Claire-Jeanne-Roberte Colinet	CJ&Colinet
Joé Descomps	Joé Descomps
Pierre le Faguays	P.leFaguays
Foundry marks: this is the mark of Les Neveux de J. Lehmann, Paris	LN PARIS JL

See also Germany and Austria, pp.442–3

Germany and Austria

With some notable exceptions, much of the work of the German and Austrian sculptors of the Art Deco era was concerned with the naturalistic portrayal of beautiful, healthy people pursuing wholesome, everyday activities. There were far fewer editors and founders than in France, although their commissioning powers certainly influenced the ultimate output.

FERDINAND PREISS

Ferdinand Preiss (1882–1943) was born in Erbach, Germany. The town had a strong tradition of ivory carving, and Preiss's maternal relatives had been employed in the trade. At the age of 15 Preiss was apprenticed for two years to the ivory carver Philip Wilmann, and he continued to work for Wilmann after completing his apprenticeship. However, Preiss was ambitious and still eager to learn, and after a few years he left Erbach to travel and work in Germany and Italy. In 1905 he joined the firm of Carl Haebler in Baden-Baden, where he met Arthur Kassler, and the following year they set up the firm of Preiss-Kassler in Berlin, the name being shortened to "PK" in 1910. In these early years Preiss was employing about six designers, but

► *The Bather* by
Ferdinand Preiss

The superbly carved detail and the translucent quality of the cold-painting seen on this ivory model are hallmarks of Preiss's work. The figure is a typical portrayal of a contemporary woman in a fashionable bathing suit engaged in a leisure pursuit that was particularly popular during the period with the opening of public lidos.
(c.1930; ht 33cm/13in; value **L**)

with the advent of World War I the firm closed, and it did not re-open until 1919. By 1925 Preiss had a team of ten ivory-carvers, including Ludwig Walter, Louis Kuchler, Dorothea Charol, and Philip Lenz.

Preiss had an extraordinary talent for carving life into ivory, and the quality of the work that issued from the PK firm was consistently excellent. Almost all of the figures produced were naturalistically modeled, usually in ivory or bronze and ivory but occasionally in bronze alone. In common with his peers he attempted to evoke the world around him, depicting most of his figures engaged in "modern" activities such as smoking, bathing, or dancing. A typical example is the cold-painted chryselephantine figure *Airwoman*, said to be based on the English aviator Amy Johnson, reflects the changing role of women. The music hall was also a source of inspiration; Preiss's figure *Lighter Than Air* was based on the actress and singer Ada May, who appeared in the 1930 C.B. Cochran Revue in Paris. He is known to have produced the figure specifically for the English market, where he had a loyal following.

Preiss executed a number of themed series, one of the most notable depicting sporting figures, often based on real sportsmen and women and inspired by the Olympic Games held in Paris in 1924. Skaters, javelin-throwers, golfers, tennis-players, bathers, and archers are caught frozen in action and naturalistically rendered. Other successful models depict dancers, *Con Brio*, *Autumn Dancer*, *Flame Leaper*, and *Cabaret Girl* being some of the most stylish and sought-after examples. Preiss also carved a number of small Classical female nudes in ivory, and a series of young children. Preiss's figures are usually mounted on green or black onyx bases.

OTTO POERTZEL AND PAUL PHILIPPE

Otto Poertzel (1876–1963) was the son of a porcelain designer and spent some time studying porcelain before setting up as a sculptor in 1900. He received many commissions to model portrait busts and figures of the reigning ducal family of Saxe-Coburg; he also modeled music-hall performers and famous names from the world of theater and ballet. Some of Poertzel's chryselephantine sculptures are indistinguishable from those made by Preiss, and it is thought that he may have worked alongside Preiss. However, certain works, such as his exuberant *Snake Dancer*, exhibit an original, dramatic style.

Paul Philippe was a talented and prolific sculptor. He was born in Berlin but spent about 15 years studying and working in Paris, from the beginning of the century until the outbreak of World War I, when he returned to Germany. His earlier work consists of figures such as *Russian Dancer* and *Rhada*, which are similar to those by the Paris-based Belgian sculptor Claire-Jeanne-Roberte Colinet. Philippe worked in marble and wood as well as bronze and ivory. Some of his most successful models, such as *Awakening*, were of nude women with curvaceous bodies and full hair, executed in an assortment of materials and a variety of sizes. After the war Philippe lived in Berlin and designed for the founder Rosenthal and Maeder (RuM; taken over by Preiss-Kassler in 1929). At this time the style of his work

▲ *Snake Dancer* by
Otto Poertzel

This rare and highly dramatic chryselephantine sculpture was also produced in a smaller size. A version cast entirely in bronze exists, but this only very rarely comes onto the market. The skin-tight costume in simulated snakeskin is embellished with black enamel detail.
(c.1930; ht 52cm/20½in; value **L**)

◄ *Three Dancers* by
Paul Philippe

Most Art Deco sculptures were modeled as individual figures – groups such as this are relatively rare. This chryselephantine group of women in chic and elegant evening dress is particularly desirable because of its fine and slightly unusual composition. The sculptor succeeds in conveying a sense of movement in the dancers' contrasting poses, while at the same time certain elements, such as the flowing dresses, are more angular and stylized. The delicately carved ivory heads and hands and cold-painted bronze bodies are typical of Philippe's later models.
(c.1930; ht 46cm/18in; value **L**)

► *Exotic Dancer* by Gerdago
It is rare to find examples of Gerdago's work in really fine original condition. The vulnerable intricate enameled detail has usually suffered some degree of wear. The exotic costume worn by the dancer shown here is typical of Gerdago's style, as are the use of colored enamel to pick out parts of the dress, and the exaggerated pose.
(c.1930; ht 31cm/12in; value L)

changed completely, and throughout the 1920s and 1930s he produced highly stylized models. His new figures were mannequins, pierrots, and dancers with subtly tinted ivory heads and hands, and cold-painted cast-bronze costumes, of a similar style to work by Preiss. Philippe's female figures were characteristically long and lean with fashionably bobbed hair.

GERDAGO AND GUSTAV SCHMIDTCASSEL

The work of Gerdago and that of Gustav Schmidtcassel show great similarities. Both artists modeled futuristic-looking, exotic dancers in bronze and ivory, inspired by contemporary costume designs for ballet and theater. At this time a number of ceramic artists in Germany and Austria were producing polychrome porcelain models based on the same designs. Gerdago and Schmidtcassel picked out and enameled the fine details of the dancers' costumes in strong, bright colors and applied black enamel to the carved-ivory hair, which was sometimes visible beneath an elaborate head-dress. No two figures are decorated identically.

BRUNO ZACH

Unlike his contemporaries, who portrayed wholesome, healthy athletes and beautiful, flawless Aryan women, Zach depicted the "after-dark" side of Berlin life in his sculptures. His models were finely cast, mostly in bronze but sometimes in bronze and ivory. They conjure up images of the actress Marlene Dietrich in the film *The Blue Angel* (1930), smoke-filled rooms, and late-night cabarets. The women are tall, haughty seducers, lightly fingering long cigarette holders. Some rather racy figures are modeled in their underwear sporting riding crops, while others are clad in fur coats half-opened to reveal their near-naked forms. One figure group depicts women dancing a riotous "cancan" in short frothy dresses and high heels. Zach is notable for his accurate depiction of the somewhat masculine women's clothes of the period. Groups of figures are relatively rare, although pairs are more commonly found, typically either dancers or lovers. Zach's erotic subjects are highly sought after; he also modeled a number of other figures, including sporting characters, but these tend to be less popular.

► *Cigarette Girl* by Bruno Zach
As with so many Zach figures, this young woman, modeled in cold-painted bronze, adopts a confident, self-assured stance and has a seductive, provocative air.
(c.1930; ht 71cm/28in; value L)

JOSEPH LORENZL

Joseph Lorenzl was born and worked in Vienna. He was an extremely prolific sculptor and his models have been a great commercial success. His bronze, and bronze and ivory, figures, mostly of female dancers, are highly stylized and instantly recognizable, with their elongated limbs, small breasts, and slim, boyish figures. They are usually nude or semi-clad, caught in acrobatic or athletic poses; they may hold or wave tamborines, scarves, cymbals, or fans – props employed to enhance the dramatic shape of the sculpture. The surface of the bronze is usually silvered or cold-painted. Occasionally the costumes are decorated with enameled floral detail, and figures of this type may bear the signature "Crejo," the artist-craftsman who carried out the enameling for Lorenzl. Most of Lorenzl's work was edited by the firm of Goldscheider (1885–1954) in Vienna, for which he also designed a number of ceramic figures; these were equally successful and are avidly collected today. Lorenzl's bases are often faceted and of plain green onyx; some figures have bases inset with black-slate sections.

► *Dancer* by Joseph Lorenzl
Most figures modeled by Lorenzl were between 24 and 38cm (9½–15in) tall. However, some examples, usually cast totally in bronze, were as large as 70cm (27½in). This example, with its slender, stylized limbs and acrobatic pose, is very typical of the artist's style.
(c.1930; ht 68cm/26¾in; value J)

KEY FACTS

- MATERIALS bronze and ivory
- IMPORTANT SCULPTORS Preiss, Poertzel, Philippe, Gerdago, Schmidtcassel, Zach, and Lorenzl
- FOUNDERS Preiss-Kassler (Berlin), Rosenthal and Maeder (Berlin), Goldscheider (Vienna)
- TYPES OF FIGURES mostly healthy young women engaged in everyday contemporary activities such as dancing, playing sports, and smoking
- ATTRIBUTION occasionally sculptors would use the same photographic reference, resulting in near-identical versions of the same model – for example, the figures *Aristocrats* and *Butterfly Dancers* are very similar and likely to bear the signature of either Preiss or Poertzel
- SIZES these vary: most figures were produced at between 25 and 45cm (10–17½in) high; some were produced in more than one size; many bronzes by Lorenzl were issued in a variety of sizes up to 70cm (27½in) high, although larger sizes are not so common; his large figures tend to be cast totally in bronze
- COLLECTING the most desirable figures are stylized, usually depicting females captured in motion, examples typical of an artist's work, and in good condition

Marks

Ferdinand Preiss: cast in the bronze plinth above the base or engraved on the base

F. PREISS

Bruno Zach: this mark is usually cast

B.Zach

The foundry seals of PK and RuM are occasionally found on a single piece of sculpture; this suggests that the model was produced by the RuM foundry but was unsold at the time the firm was taken over by PK in 1929

See also France, pp.440–1

Posters

In the 1920s posters were used as an advertising medium, promoting such varied commodities and activities as household products, leisure pursuits, transport, and centers of artistic or cultural activity. In the USA the poster was even used as a method of advocating the work ethic. Posters of the period were designed with simple lines and bold, strong colors, and the typography was styled to catch the viewer's attention. Substantial amounts of money were spent by advertisers on poster campaigns, since a successful publicity poster was considered the most effective of all promotional vehicles.

LEISURE POSTERS

Striking poster designs were used to promote a host of new brands that came onto the market following the end of World War I, including cigarettes, perfumes, champagne, chocolate, household products, and clothing. In France some of the most popular artists of the period working in this field were Jean Carlu (*b*.1900), Daniel DeLosques (1880–1915), and Charles Gesmar (1900–28). Paris's reputation as a fashionable center of entertainment, established at the end of the 19th century, continued during the Art Deco period, and many posters were commissioned by musicians and cabaret performers such as Mistinguett and Alice Soulie. Posters by Paul Colin (1892–1985) depicting the celebrated jazz performer Josephine Baker are particularly sought after.

No less significant were poster designs from Austria and Germany, particularly the work of such artists as Joseph Binder (1898–1972), Walter Schnackenberg (1880–1961), and Ludwig Hohlwein (1874–1949). Hohlwein, the most prolific artist in Germany, produced designs characterized by a strong use of color, flat pattern, and simplified lines. He designed many posters for both new and established products, including Casanova cigarettes, Marco Polo tea, and Toblerone chocolate, as well as for popular Munich social haunts such as the Café Odéon and the Odéon Casino.

Winter holidays became increasingly common at this time, with ski resorts proving particularly fashionable destinations. The Paris-Lyon-Méditerranée (P.L.M.) railway network used posters to entice tourists to resorts in the Alps, the Pyrenees, and the Jura, with designs often incorporating textual instructions explaining how to reach the resort by train. The most sought-after skiing posters include those advertising skiing techniques, equipment, and the newly founded ski-schools. The P.L.M. also worked hard at promoting the French coastal resorts. Roger Broders (1883–1953) worked extensively for them, producing a celebrated series of travel posters that covered all of the glamorous Riviera resorts. Broders's posters often feature stylized, fashionable women set against

► Poster by Roger Broders for the P.L.M. railway

Broders's posters are typically Art Deco in their use of simple, effective lines, areas of bold, bright color, and striking shapes. This example illustrates the designer's characteristic and skilful use of perspective to set the glamorous, stylized model in the appropriate context. The poster also features a typically bold new Art Deco typeface. Fashionable seaside resorts such as the one promoted here were often depicted on posters advertising railway companies, as a means of encouraging people to travel by railway.
(1928; ht 1m/3ft 3in; value J)

▼ Poster by R. Michaud

The development of skiing as a leisure activity in the 1920s and 1930s resulted in the production of a great variety of Art Deco skiing posters, often advertising resorts in France and Switzerland. This poster promoting cable-car access to the ski slopes of Mégève makes use of bold lettering and characteristic Art Deco lines. A dramatic and eye-catching advertising tool, it is notable for its strong, simple, and stylized central image.
(1933; ht 96.5cm/38in; value I)

a vibrant background, and his use of perspective enables a scene to be viewed in a realistic context. His posters, with their bold colors and simple lines, are typical of the period. Posters advertising the Belgian coast were also widely produced and feature resorts such as Coxyde-Plage, Saint Idesbald Plage, Heyst, and Duingerben.

TRANSPORT AND TRAVEL

The 1920s saw a huge growth in travel for pleasure, and shipping companies and railways advertised widely to gain a share of the burgeoning market. Emphasis was given to the speed, magnificence, and comfort of the new methods of transport, especially in the case of the transatlantic liners. The most acclaimed poster designer of the period was the French artist Adolphe Mouron Cassandre (1901–68), whose striking travel advertisements now command some of the highest prices of all Art Deco posters. Cassandre created many works of this type for the French national railway as well as for the great ocean liners. His architectural style, characterized by simple design, clean lines, and bold color, influenced designers worldwide. His most dynamic posters include those for the liners *Statendam*, *L'Atlantique*, and *SS Normandie* and for the *Nord Express* railway service. Another notable designer working for shipping companies was the Dutch artist Willem Frederik ten Broek (*b*.1905), who produced many posters for Dutch shipping routes, including the Holland–North America line.

The car was also a popular subject for posters in the 1920s, and manufacturers such as Renault, Favor, and

◄ Poster by Alberto Bianchi (1882–1969) for Fiat

Fiat made extensive use of posters to promote its cars, and this poster for the Ardita car evokes the stylish and sophisticated Italian designs of the period. Using simple lines and bold colors, the poster conveys an impression of speed and excitement. Although Italian posters were produced on large print-runs, they are now scarce. *(c.1933; ht 2m/6ft 7in; value I)*

Peugeot in France, AC in Britain, and Buick in Germany used posters to advertise their new collections. These typically featured the car itself as the central focus, with careful attention paid to typography. Advertisements showing models posing with the latest make of car appeared in glossy publications such as *Vogue*. Posters promoting automobile races and Grands Prix, especially the Monaco Grand Prix, are highly sought after.

The travel posters of the 1920s and 1930s, displayed in railway stations and on billboards, marked the heyday of poster design in Britain. Leading designers were employed by the four regional rail networks to depict attractive countryside and sunny beaches in an attempt to entice passengers to travel by rail. These posters act as an interesting record of the towns that were the most popular destinations of the time. Landscapes were often featured, as illustrated by the series by Edward McKnight Kauffer (1890–1954) for the Great Western Railway, which portrays six scenes in Devon and Cornwall. The most sought-after British travel posters are those depicting stylish figures, bathing-suit-clad beachgoers, locomotives, and sporting images. Golfing posters for Gleneagles, St Andrews, and Cruden Bay are particularly popular.

London Underground established itself as a major advertising patron during the Art Deco period, using a wide range of European and American artists to design promotional posters for such destinations as London Zoo and the Natural History Museum. Actual tube trains rarely feature in these posters, as the designer was instructed to portray the destination of the train rather than the train itself. Kauffer produced many highly sought-after posters for the London Underground during the 1920s and 1930s, most notably his 1924 poster advertising the winter sales and his 1930 design for the West End theaters. Other artists include Fred Taylor (1875–1963), Frank Newbould (1887–1950), Austin Cooper (1890–1964), the French designer Jean Dupas (1882–1964) and the Swiss-born artist Frederick Schneider Manner (1889–1961). Posters advertising major sporting events, such as the Wimbledon Tennis Championships, are also extremely collectible. These posters were produced in small panel sizes because they were displayed inside the cars of the trains.

AMERCIAN WORK-INCENTIVE POSTERS

American work-incentive posters, invented by Charles Mather in Chicago, are an unusual example of the medium, intended not to sell a product but to motivate workers. Mather aimed to sell his posters to manufacturers, claiming that they would save time and money and improve morale. Production began in 1923, but Mather's most sought-after series of 75 posters was produced in 1929. These follow the same format as earlier designs, each having a bold headline, a short message and a punchy caption. The visual impact was crucial, since many immigrant factoryworkers in the USA spoke limited English. Mather devised the captions himself and commissioned the Chicago-based artists Willard Frederick Elmes, Frank Beatty, Robert Beebe, and Henry Lee to create the designs.

▼ Poster by Frederick Schneider Manner for the London Underground

The weather was a popular theme on London Underground posters during this period. This stylized umbrella poster makes use of the idea that the underground-railway system functioned as London's "umbrella" against the unpredictable English weather. This is the only poster recorded as having been designed for London Underground by the little-known artist Manner. It is typical of Art Deco Underground posters in having a bold and stylized subject – here, almost abstract. The typography reflects London Underground's own specially designed typeface. *(1929; ht 1m/3ft 3in; value H)*

▼ Poster by Willard Frederick Elmes

This example was part of the series of work-incentive posters produced by Mather and his company in Chicago in 1929. The format was simple and effective: an attention-grabbing headline followed by an educational message, rounded off with a punchy slogan or caption. The image is clear, helping to get the message across to the workers who spoke little English. *(1929; ht 1.1m/3ft 7in; value F)*

KEY FACTS

- STYLES AND DESIGNS clean lines, bold colors, striking typography, highly stylized images
- NOTABLE DESIGNERS Carlu, DeLosques, Binder, Schnackenberg, Hohlwein, Cassandre, Elmes, Beatty
- SUBJECTS new household brands, musicians, holiday and cultural destinations, ocean liners, cars, sports; American work-incentive posters: timekeeping, motivation of the workforce, teamwork
- CARE cleaning and restoration should be undertaken by a professional restorer; backing: some posters are left unbacked, others are backed on linen or japan paper using a water-soluble glue; preferred method of backing differs from country to country; mounting: never dry-mount posters; framing: use UV Plexiglass rather than glass
- FAKES some exist, so check the printing and ageing of the paper; the International Vintage Posters Dealers Association will supply a list of known fakes
- CONDITION AND COLLECTING although rare posters in poorer condition will be very collectible, condition is important, and creases and staining will affect value; posters with large losses should be avoided; any trimmed margins will also greatly reduce value

See also Art Nouveau: Posters, pp.410–11

The years immediately following World War II saw the emergence of the "New Look," a term coined by Christian Dior to describe his extravagant, witty, and romantic haute couture collection of 1947. This reaction to the austerity of the war years and the functionalism of Modernism revolutionized contemporary design and profoundly influenced the other applied arts, so that designers of furniture, ceramics, glass, lighting, and jewelry developed new and exciting forms. The designs of the 1950s – particularly those from the USA and Italy – were imbued with a new optimism and became altogether more curvaceous, sculptural, and organic in both outline and decoration. Furthermore, the ghost of wartime sobriety was fully laid to rest by the brightly colored, often outlandish designs of the 1960s, a decade in which the distinction between fine art and design was often blurred. Behind many of these post-war developments was the introduction of new, malleable materials, especially plastics and alloys, that were not only well suited to mass-production, but to the designs themselves, which increasingly sought to challenge convention. And it is the resulting quality of design and craftsmanship, rather than the intrinsic value of the materials used, that often characterizes the most exciting work of this period.

Wall lights by Verner Panton for Louis Poulsen, Denmark (left) The emergence of new plastics in the 1960s and 1970s enabled designers to introduce bold color to their work. *(1969/70).*
Cone chair by Verner Panton for Fritz Hansen, Denmark (above) So radical was Panton's design for his parents' restaurant, the "Komigen Inn" at Langeso, Denmark, that New York police were forced to remove the chair from a shop window, when huge crowds gathered to look at it. *(c. 1960).*

Mid-century Modern

Furniture

In the immediate post-war era, wood made a return as the material of choice for many furniture designers, although it was soon superseded by metal, or metal with wood, fiberglass, and, later, new plastics. Advanced molding techniques such as wood lamination, the invention of malleable plastics, and the growing popularity of metal, afforded designers greater flexibility in their work, enabling them to produce stunning furniture with the human form in mind. Most designers were now commissioned by large firms, where their work was mass-produced at an affordable price, and many such designs are still in production today. All these factors make the post-war period one of the most interesting for enthusiasts of furniture design.

The United States

Developments in technology during World War II, such as the introduction of new techniques in molding and wood lamination, combined with shortages of raw materials, forced designers to seek new forms. Mass-production methods used during the war made it possible – for the first time – for designers to produce well-made items that were truly egalitarian.

Among the designers leading the way in post-war America was Charles Eames (1907–78). Having initially studied architecture, he was asked to leave his studies, as his ideas were considered "too modern." Establishing his own practice he returned to studies following an offer of a fellowship from Eliel Saarinen (1873-1950) at the highly regarded, hotbed of modern thinking, the

◄ Lounge chair designed by Charles and Ray Eames
This molded plywood chair, designed in 1945, was first produced c.1946 by the Molded Plywood Co. at Evans Products Co. in the USA. From 1949 until 1957 it was made by Herman Miller, also in the USA, in several versions. The rubber shock mounts to the seat back and frame were intended to provide flexibility and comfort. Examples must be in good condition for maximum value.
(1946; ht 62cm/24¼in; value F)

Cranbrook Academy of Art in 1938. Eames later taught there and became head of industrial design. During his time there, Eames formed two very important relationships, the first with his future wife Ray Kaiser (1912–1988) and the second with collaborator Eero Saarinen (1910–1961), the son of Eliel. In 1940, Charles Eames and Eero Saarinen won a prize for a molded plywood shell armchair at the Organic Design in Home Furnishings exhibition, held at the Museum of Modern Art (MOMA), New York, in 1940. This competition was judged by Alvar Aalto and Marcel Breuer.

In 1941, Eames divorced his then wife and married Ray, moving to Los Angeles to establish a studio. They remained there, collaborating closely, for the rest of their lives. Many of their plans were delayed by the war, but from 1945 they introduced ground-breaking designs to the world. Some of the first were the DCW and DCM chair series made from plywood (DCW) or metal and plywood (DCM).

Typical of Eames' work, these came in dining or lounge heights, as well as an office version, and had complimentary multipurpose tables, including a coffee table, child's table, card table, and dining table. The inclusion of a table for children emphasizes the family-friendly nature of the couple's designs.

By 1948, their attentions had turned to the use of fiberglass. However they made a triumphant return to wood with their iconic lounge chair of 1956 with its matching ottoman. Inspired by an earlier collaboration with Eero Saarinen, it is indicative of one aspect of their working methods, the revival of previously used themes. In later life Eames said that the lounge chair had "a certain ugliness to it" but conceded that it "had given a lot of pleasure to people." Its makers Herman Miller has sold over $100 million dollars worth of the chairs to date.

Although the Eameses were the leading designers in post-war America, other important figures were producing important work. The Herman Miller furniture company played an important role in developing the taste for Modernism. Its design director, George Nelson, produced his own work and commissioned other leading makers like Harry Bertoia (1915–1978) and Isamu Noguchi (1904–1988).

Other notable designers are George Nakashima (1905–1990) and Vladimir Kagan (b.1927). Like most of the American Modern school, Nakashima had studied as an architect. Among his pieces are a number of organic, free-form tables with tops made from a single piece of wood, often walnut, where the natural shape of the wood has been retained. Vladimir Kagan was among a number of designers not backed by a large company, and so produced work on a much smaller scale. His designs are organic with splayed, angular legs.

▲ "Wishbone" chair designed by Hans Wegner
The gentle curves of the steam-bent back and arm rail of this chair, and the solid frame made either of ash, beech, or oak (sometimes painted) are complemented by the natural woven cord seat to produce a harmonious, organic design, highly typical of this designer's work. This chair was produced by Fritz Hansen and is marked with the company's label. With his simple, elegant pieces, Hans Wegner was one of the most prominent Danish furniture designers of the 1950s.
(1950; ht 73cm/28½in; value D)

◄ "Hilleplan" sideboard designed by Robin Day
This very minimalist sideboard, which features a teak body, black vitriolite doors, and gray tubular steel legs, was manufactured by Hille Co. Ltd and is marked on the inside of one of the two sliding drawers with a circular badge, reading "Hille of London."
(c.1953; w. 1.4m/4ft 7in; value D)

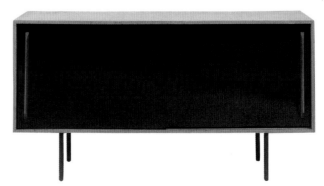

▲ **"Thin Edge" rosewood chest by George Nelson**
An important designer of the Modern school in America, George Nelson is perhaps better known for his appointment as design director of the Herman Miller Furniture Company. It was through Nelson that many prominent American designers of the era had their first pieces produced on a large scale. This piece is one of a number designed for the "Thin Edge" range, which included tables, chests of drawers, and nightstands. Typical features include the use of richly figured veneers with no additional surface decoration, porcelain drawer pulls, and metal legs.
*(1956; w. 85.5cm/33¾in; value **G**)*

Europe

BRITAIN

In Britain the first taste of the stark post-war Modern style was introduced by Sir Gordon Russell (1892–1980). In 1942, he was commissioned by the government to design a range of "Utility" furniture to refurnish bombed-out houses and help young families to set up home. Russell saw it as a chance to wean the British public away from imitation period furniture and to introduce clean, modern lines free of carving and extraneous detail. From 1943, "Utility" designs were produced in a variety of materials, with hardboard being the most common. Only 20 designs were released, with no sofas or three-piece suites, and many are now collectible.

Post-war, the lack of raw material forced a new generation of British designers to look to newer ways of furniture making and post-war longings for something new allowed Modernist designs into many people's homes for the first time. Two principal figures were involved in this movement: Ernest Race (1913–64) and Robin Day (b. 1915)

Race set up Ernest Race Ltd (with JW Noel Jordan) in 1945 and sought to produce pieces that crossed English traditions with Swedish Modernism. His light, practical designs, which often minimized the amounts of materials used, found a natural audience at the 1951 Festival of Britain – a celebration of the work of British architects and designers – and where his wood and steel "Antelope" chair became extremely popular.

Like his near contemporary Charles Eames, Robin Day found fame by winning a design competition at New York's MOMA, this time in 1948. This brought him to the attention of Hille Co. Ltd (est. 1906), a traditional furniture maker that wished to produce a Modernist range. Comissioned in 1949 to design for Hille, by 1950 he was appointed design director where he produced a range of good-quality, affordable, and now collectible contemporary furniture. This included molded plywood armchairs with steel under-frames and the "Hillestak" stacking chair, which combined beech legs with a plywood seat and curved plywood back.

ITALY

In Italy a wide variety of designers produced an equally wide range of furniture. One of the most important post-war designers was Carlo Mollino (1905–73), whose furniture was inspired by a combination of surrealism and erotic curves. His "Arabesque" table (1950), one of the most curvaceous and popular of his designs, consists of two asymmetrical pieces of glass supported by a whiplash-shaped wooden support; the support is pierced with decorative asymmetrical holes.

In complete contrast is the "Superleggera" ("Superlight") chair, which was designed by Gio Ponti (1891–1979) and produced by the firm of Cassina (est. 1927), in Milan, from 1952. This chair, which features a solid ash frame and traditional woven rush seat, was mass-produced in a wide range of colors. Incredibly light yet very strong, it was inspired by a traditional design from Chiavari, in northern Italy, traditionally closely associated with woven cane and rush work.

▲ **Walnut cabinet by Gio Ponti for Singer and Sons**
Ponti's cabinet shares a number of features with the prevailing designs of the 1950s, not least the unembellished wood veneers, and the clean, Modernist lines. Several pieces for Singer and Sons had brass feet.
*(1950; w 177.5cm/70in; value **L**)*

KEY FACTS

- COLOR good color will add to value: avoid bleached, faded, or inappropriate colored paint
- CONDITION this is important: check for signs of damage, repair, woodworm, or any inappropriate restoration, including re-upholstery in a non-contemporary fabric
- COLLECTING look for designs that strongly echo the period, such as atomic motifs from the 1950s; many designs are still in production; some have been reissued; early or original pieces remain the most collectible

Marks

Makers' marks, stamps, and labels are usually found on the back or the base of a piece, or inside the drawers

▲ **Vladimir Kagan sofa**
This piece is one of several designed by Vladimir Kagan, and is characteristic of his organic, sometimes biomorphic style. The floating seat and back are typical, as are the sculptural, angular walnut legs, which feature in a number of his pieces .
*(1950s; w. 203cm/80in; value **L**)*

See also Art Deco: Furniture – The Netherlands, Germany, and Scandinavia, pp.406–7

SCANDINAVIA

The clean lines of Scandinavian design were very influential, establishing a trend for stylish, Modernist furniture, which is still the height of fashion. Much of what is seen after 1945 has its origins in the prewar era. Although plywood had been used earlier, it was Finnish designer Alvar Aalto (1898–1976) who was arguably the earliest and best known Scandinavian designer to use the material. Like many of the best furniture makers of the Modern period, Aalto trained as an architect. His major foray into furniture occurred in 1931–32 when he designed the Paimio Sanatorium in southern Finland.

For this project Aalto designed the seminal "armchair 41" and the cantilevered "chair 31." Both eschewed the current trend for metal and leather, choosing wood, a material that Aalto felt was on a more human level. Not only was this chair designed for maximum comfort, but also the angle of the back was raked to assist patients at the sanatorium in easy breathing. Aalto and his wife and collaborator, Aino (1894-1949), established the firm Artek in 1935 to manufacture their furniture designs, many of which were exported worldwide.

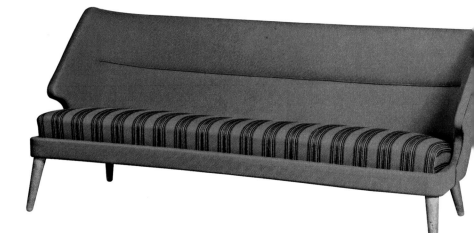

▲ **Finn Juhl red sofa**

Although plastic and synthetic materials were very fashionable from the late 1950s, designers in Scandinavia continued to use wood such as ash and birch as an integral design element. The best designers sought new ways of working with wood – be it in construction or decoration – such as the use of wood for armrests and table or chair legs. This sofa has a number of features that are characterstic of post-war Scandinavian design. Essentially, they relate to the paring back of its main elements to the absolute minimum – the wrap-around back, the single seat cushion, the tapering wooden legs, and the use of a single bold color over a large area. The piece is also typical of Finn Juhl's work, embracing curved forms to achieve an elegant, sculptural piece of furniture. Juhl is particularly known for his work with teak.

(1950s; w 191cm/75in; value H)

Denmark was also a powerhouse of design, owing to three influential designers: Arne Jacobsen (1902–71), Hans Wegner (1914-2007), and Finn Juhl (1912–89).

Jacobsen designed one of the most popular mass-produced chairs of the 1950s, the three-legged "Ant" chair, which was made from molded plywood in a waisted shape and produced by the company Fritz Hansen. Although wood and natural materials remained central to Jacobsen's designs, he made two notable exceptions. The iconic "Egg" and "Swan" chairs from 1956, were conceived as part of his entire scheme for the SAS Royal Hotel in Copenhagen. Jacobsen designed every part of the hotel. Here, he conceived an upholstered form on a crossed metal base. The "Egg," featured a womb like "egg" form that fits the body, while the "Swan" has two "wings" that form armrests.

Wegner trained as a cabinet-maker, and his chairs, designed to be made by hand, combine traditional materials, attention to detail, and elegant, ergonomic design. His classic chair design – known simply as "The Chair" (1949) – combines a solid wooden frame of oak or mahogany with a woven cane seat. Made by the firm of Johannes Hansen (est. 1915), it is the epitome of Scandinavian excellence in furniture design in the 1950s.

Juhl, who had also trained as a cabinet-maker, produced exaggeratedly curved designs, which were far more sculptural than Jacobsen's pared-down designs or Wegner's subtle and elegant furniture in natural materials. His designs were handmade by another Danish cabinetmaker, Niels Vodder, as well as manufactured by Bovirke and France & Sons.

▲ **"Swan" chair designed by Arne Jacobsen**

An Arne Jacobsen "Swan" chair, manufactured by Fritz Hansen, Denmark. The continuous curvilinear seat is supported on a four-prong aluminum swivel base and bears the manufacturer's label and control mark. This example has been reupholstered in a contemporary color, which affects its desirability to collectors.

(1956; ht 76cm/30in; value E)

▶ **Alvar Aalto "Tank" chair**

This chair has a birchwood frame and red wool upholstery. Aalto championed wood over all other materials and pioneered the use of bent plywood, which he used for so many of his furniture designs. Each arm of this chair is made from a single strip of plywood, bent to create its sculptural, organic cantilevered form.

(1936; w. 77.5cm/30½in; value F)

KEY FACTS

- ATTRIBUTION few pieces bear designers' names, so attribution can only be formed on a stylistic basis. Some pieces bear makers' marks, which can be helpful, particularly in knowing if the piece is from an original issue or a later example
- COLLECTING as many of these designs have never been out of production, early examples are keenly sought, as are pieces with a provenance. e.g. a Jacobsen chair from the original commission at the SAS Royal Hotel in Copenhagen would always be worth more than a later example
- CONDITION originality is desirable too; look out for original coverings or finishes on pieces and be wary of painted wood finishes, as they may have been overpainted more recently

New materials

In line with the general trend in the immediate post-war years for bold, bright designs, makers working with plastics exploited vivid citrus colors, while metal was popular for creating architectural pieces with a distinctly minimalist feel. This new attitude to furniture design is typical of Harry Bertoia (1915–78). A student of the Cranbrook Academy, Bertoia was offered, in 1950, free reign to design whatever he wanted – be it sculpture or furniture – by fellow student, Florence Knoll (b.1917).

Bertoia had always considered himself to be an artist first and designer second. It is no surprise that the pieces he produced for Knoll were highly sculptural. In describing his "Diamond" chairs, Bertoia said; "they are mainly made of air, like sculpture. Space passes right through them."

Having worked with Eames on wooded pieces, Eero Saarinen moved away from wood toward fiberglass and aluminum. At the same time as designing his wood structured "Grasshopper" chair from 1946, he also showed his "Womb" chair. The design was produced from 1948 by Knoll Associates. Featuring steel legs and an upholstered fiberglass body, it began a move away from traditional shapes that would see his "Tulip" series realized in 1955. Consisting of high and low tables, and matching chairs with aluminum bases and fiberglass reinforced plastic seats, the clean lines betray Saarinen's early desire to be a sculptor.

The Dane, Verner Panton (1926–1998), was one of the leading post-war designers. His K1 cone chair, was a totally new form: from a crossed metal base an upholstered cone rose to form both seat and back rest. This was followed up 1959 by the wire cone chair, a stripped version with a wire frame and upholstered seat.

From these early ventures into new forms, Panton moved more and more toward Pop Art and more conceptual pieces. This interest in concept is summed up by his prototype "Pneumatic Cushion" introduced in 1960 and the world's first "inflatable" item of furniture, although a commercial way of making this design could not be found. Indeed, it was not until 1967, with the "Blow" chair that Panton's concept of inflatable furniture became a reality.

Exploration of materials, often pushing them beyond the limits of current technology, led to the design and production of Panton's most iconic piece, the so-called

► "Djinn" chair designed by Olivier Mourgue

This French chair is named after an Islamic mythological spirit that could take animal or human form. The steel frame is upholstered with stretch-jersey-covered polyurethane foam to create gentle curves with a futuristic feel. The "Djinn" series also included a sofa, a stool, and a chaise-longue.
(1963; ht 68cm/26¾in; value E)

► "Stacking" chair by Verner Panton

The revolutionary, single-piece, cantilevered design of this Danish chair is the first example of its type in plastic. The original prototype was of fiberglass-reinforced plastic; early models were made of molded PU-hardfoam; and from 1970 injection-molded thermoplastic was used. The latter can be identified by fins under the curve where the seat and foot meet.
(1968; ht 89cm/35in; value D)

◄ The "Blow" chair

Taking inspiration from Verner Panton, this inflatable chair was designed by Gionatan De Pas, Donato D'Urbino, and Paolo Lomazzi. It is made of PVC, which has been radio frequency welded, and was produced by Zanotta, Milan.
(1968; ht 89cm/35in; value D)

◄ "Diamond" chair designed by Harry Bertoia

This American chair, made of welded steel, was made by Knoll Associates from 1952; it came with either a detachable vinyl seat pad or a full padded cover. The chair has a light, airy quality that makes it as much a piece of sculpture as an item of furniture.
(1952; ht 70cm/27½in; value D)

"Panton Chair." His initial concept of a one-piece chair that could be mass-produced took decades to develop. Launched in 1967, Panton was constantly revising the design until it could be made, in 1971, as a fully mass-produced, injection-molded design.

In France, two notable designers were producing pieces in a similar vein to Panton. Pierre Paulin (b. 1927) and Olivier Mourgue (b. 1939). Both made full use of new materials, particularly Pirelli foam, which when wrapped around forms of wood or

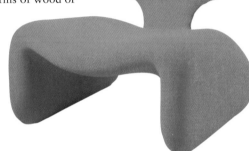

metal, could produce new shapes. Typical of Paulin's style are the pieces he made in association with Dutch manufacturer Artifort from 1956 onward. Here he found the support to transform his vision into reality, producing such examples as the No.582 "Ribbon" chair in 1966 and the "Tongue" chair in 1967. Both pieces were formed from a single piece of metal, covered in foam and upholstery.

Using similar materials to Paulin, Olivier Mourgue designed, in 1963, the "Djinn" series, manufactured in France from 1963 to 1976 by Airbourne International. The series had a futuristic, curving shape that made it an ideal choice for inclusion in Stanley Kubrick's science-fiction film '2001: A Space Odyssey' (1968).

KEY FACTS

- CONDITION good condition is vital: plastic is very hard to restore, so avoid pieces with deep scratches or cracks or that have faded in the sun
- COLLECTING most designs are extremely popular; the Panton "Stacking" chair was made in different types of plastic: most sought after are the earlier versions, which have thicker bodies

Marks
Italian plastic furniture has molded marks

See also Art Deco: Furniture – The Netherlands, Germany, and Scandinavia, pp.416–17; Mid-century modern: Furniture, pp.448–9

Jewelry

In the post-war years, new materials and technologies in jewelry-making developed alongside the more traditional forms. In the 1940s and 1950s wartime shortages of luxury materials led to the use of non-precious metals and plastics in imitation of precious jewelry. However, at the end of war-time privations, the launch of Christian Dior's "New Look" in 1947, and the fascination with modernity and the space race brought about a new style of jewelry, introducing a new

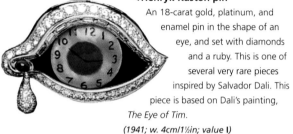

◀ **Henryk Kaston pin**
An 18-carat gold, platinum, and enamel pin in the shape of an eye, and set with diamonds and a ruby. This is one of several very rare pieces inspired by Salvador Dali. This piece is based on Dali's painting, *The Eye of Tim*.
(1941; w. 4cm/1½in; value I)

breed of artist-jewelers who designed jewelry for those who saw it more as wearable art.

THE 1940S AND 1950S

In Denmark, the company established in 1904 by Georg Jensen (1866–1935) was especially noted for its range of minimalist, sculptural jewelry; these designs, often produced in polished silver, reflected the "New Look" in their rounded, abstract sculptural forms.

One of the best known and most collectible of Jensen's designers was the sculptor Henning Koppel (1918–81), whose minimally decorated pieces in strong abstract shapes set a trend that developed well into the 1960s. Inspired by Alexander Calder, Jean Arp, and Constantin Brancusi among others, his sensuous, organic shapes have a sculptural quality. His first pieces, a series of bracelets and necklaces that resemble whale vertebrae and microscopic organisms, are asymmetric and organic in shape and were launched in 1948.

Many ground-breaking designs for post-war pieces were created by artist-designers who worked across a range of disciplines, Pablo Picasso, Nikki de Saint Phalle, and Harry Bertoia among them. Polish-born Henryk Kaston (b.1910) started his career as a violinist, but also trained as a jeweler. Much of his jewelry is on a musical theme and, impressed with the refinement of these pieces, Salvador Dali invited Kaston to create a series of surrealist designs.

Surrealism heavily influenced the work of Sam Kramer (1913-64) – the New York jeweler said by many to be the most important post-war Modernist jeweler. A surrealist who worked in Greenwich Village, Kramer worked in the biomorphic style also seen in the work of

▶ **Fire opal and onyx brooxh by Sam Kramer**
Surrealist Sam Kramer's work is often biomorphic in form, emphasizing not only the hand of the artist but also the natural potential for the fluidity of the metal.
(1950; l. 10cm/4in; value I)

Henning Koppel. He made his first jewelry in 1936 and went on to advertise his work as "Fantastic Jewelry for People Who are slightly Mad." Kramer studied gemology and developed a fondness for precious stones as well as exotic materials, from Burmese rubies to glass eyes. Among the first to blur the line between fine and decorative art, some of his designs include non-precious materials such as seashells and glass, while others use multiple layers of different patterns to create an overall abstract design.

This new type of jewelry was celebrated in 1946 when the Museum of Modern Art held an exhibition of "Modern Handmade Jewelry." The pieces on show, by established artists such as Alexander Calder and Lacque Lipchitz, as well as studio jewelers such as Kramer and Margaret de Patta (1903–64), aimed to show the "jeweler as artist" and the "artist as jeweler."

THE 1960S

The rise of popular culture and street fashion brought the role of jewelry and its place in society into question; non-precious metals and plastics were used as materials in their own right rather than as substitutes for more elite materials, and the value of a piece therefore lay more in its design and craftsmanship than in the basic value of its materials. In 1961 the International Exhibition of Modern Jewelry 1890–1961, the first of its kind, was held at the Goldsmiths' Hall in London.

One of the exhibitors was Italian-born Andrew Grima (1921–2007), whose rough-textured, asymmetrical pieces were influenced by natural forms and the newly fashionable Abstract Expressionist painters; and Austrian-born Gerda Flockinger (b.1927), a pioneer of studio jewelry in Britain, whose work is distinguished by its organic, textured surfaces, often set with precious stones. In Germany, another group of distinguished and highly collectible makers, among them Hermann Jünger (1928–2005) and Reinhold Reiling (1922–83), created new styles in precious metals.

Jünger, a skilled and talented goldsmith, developed a style that celebrated imperfections rather than rejecting them, and resulting in jewelry that appeared to be "unfinished." Reinhold Reiling was among the first avant-garde jewelry designers in Germany.

▲ **Bracelet designed by Henning Koppel for Georg Jensen**
This silver "star-form" bracelet features a number of abstract star shapes. Strong organic forms and minimal surface decoration are common in Koppel's work .
(1960s; l. 19.5cm/7¾in; value G)

KEY FACTS

- MATERIALS gold, silver, aluminum, brass, copper, plastics, ceramics, glass, quartz, enamel.
- COLLECTING value is based on design and the quality of craftsmanship rather than expensive materials; pieces by Jensen are a good starting-point for collectors as they combine good design and reasonable affordability

Marks

Sam Kramer: circle with mouse ears on top and a mushroom inside; Henning Koppel: HK within an oval cartouche

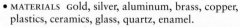

See also Jewelry, pp.260–72; Art Nouveau: Jewelry, pp.406–7; Art Deco: Jewelry, pp.438–9; Postmodernism: Jewelry, p.470

Lighting

Lighting design in the post-war years became increasingly sculptural, bold, and innovative, with designers exploiting the growing range of new materials available to them. Lighting was no longer viewed by the general public as a merely functional concern, but as an art form that could be produced to very high levels of design and used to create a wide variety of visual effects.

◄ **Arredoluce "Eye" lamp**
The design of this lamp is attributed to Italian designer, Angelo Lelli. The central fixture is mounted on the polished chrome shaft using a magnet and is, therefore, adjustable. This example bears the "Arredoluce Moza" paper label.
*(1964; ht 62cm/24⅛in; value **G**)*

THE 1940S AND 1950S

In the post-war years lighting design was dominated by Scandinavia and Italy. In Denmark Poul Henningsen (1894–1967) designed a range of architectural and domestic lighting for the leading lighting manufacturer Louis Poulsen (est. 1892). Being an architect, Henningsen viewed lighting as a fundamental component of an interior rather than as a decorative accessory. He designed for both public and domestic interiors, and it was while seeking a large-scale and striking design for the Langelinie Pavilion in Copenhagen that his "Artichoke" lamp came into being. Having taken its name and cone shape from the globe artichoke, its "leaves" were made of copper sprayed clear on the upper surface and pink on the underside. The leaves served to diffuse the strong light at the center and to protect the eyes from glare. Another successful design by Henningsen was the "PH5" lamp (1957), with a shade that was mass-produced from sheet metal. Lampshades were a specialty of the Danish firm of Le Klint (est. *c.*1944), which produced a range of acclaimed lampshades in paper and plastic-coated paper.

In the USA the designer, architect, and writer George Nelson (1908–86) launched the "Bubble" shade in 1952. The concept – a steel-wire frame cocooned with semi-translucent plastic – was simple and lent itself to the newly popular organic shapes and light, bright domestic interiors. These shades were mass-produced by the Howard Miller Clock Co. and influenced a generation of young designers, including John and Sylvia Reid. These British architects designed a range of molded plastic lampshades for Rotaflex which were inexpensive, light, strong, and washable.

THE 1960S

The bold new directions in lighting design taken by Italian companies such as Arteluce (est. 1939) were often

▲ **"Artichoke" lamp by Poul Henningsen**
Originally designed as a piece of large-scale architectural lighting, this lamp, produced by the firm of Louis Poulsen, is now available in three sizes. It is a fine example of organic Scandinavian design.
*(c.1958; diam. 72.5cm/28½in; value **F**)*

▼ **1960s American chromed metal satellite table-lamp**
An exploration of new materials and innovative design each of the six arms of this table-lamp terminates in a chrome-plated spherical shade that rotates on the baluster-form lamp base.
*(c.1960s; h 68cm/26¾in; value **E**)*

the result of collaboration with architects. For example, in 1967 Flos (est. 1959) launched the "Snoopy" lamp designed by the architect-designer Achille Castiglioni (1918-2002) and his brother Pier Giacomo Castiglioni (1894–1967). Based, as the name suggests, on the highly popular American strip-cartoon character, the collectible lamp is a combination of elegant styling, meticulous attention to design detail, and high-quality materials. Designed by Castiglioni, Flos' "Viscontia" and "Gatto" lamps were very similar to Howard Miller's "Bubble" lamp range. Flos' rivals employed versatile new plastics to create sculptural 'Pop' designs.

In the 1960s, a new generation of artists took Pop culture more seriously, producing outrageous and informal commodities that were in tune with the outlook of a newly empowered youth movement. Artemide's designer, Vico Magistretti, produced a range of Pop lighting that featured bright colors and geometric shapes. However, some of the most iconic work of this period sits between functional lighting and artistic sculpture. Once again, Pop was evoked by the "Pillola" lamps by Cesare Casati and Emanuele Ponzio for Ponteur, which were funky, fun, and fresh. In the mid-1960s the Italian Joe Colombo (1930–71) designed a number of highly successful and collectible lamps for O-Luce (est. 1946), including the "Coupé" wall lamp (1964) and the "Spider" lamp (1965). In a table-lamp for Kartell in the 1960s, Colombo explored the applications of plastic, a material in which he was particularly interested.

► **A 1960s Vistosi chandelier,**
Venetian glass factory Vistosi was renowned for its innovative glass creations. From the 1960s, the company collaborated with a number of architects and designers to produce a wide range of domestic wares, with lighting among them. Designers included Gae Aulenti and Vico Magistretti.
*(c.1960s; h 55cm/22in; value **G**)*

KEY FACTS

- DESIGNS lampshades are less expensive to collect than hanging lights but they must be in perfect condition
- CONDITION pieces must be in good working order and complete with appropriate bulbs, i.e. the type used in the original design
- COLLECTING original packaging, in good condition, adds to value; check for manufacturer's labels, which enable the collector to trace pieces back through catalogs to establish dates and designers; 1950s molded plastic lamps by John and Sylvia Reid are becoming increasingly popular; early versions of the "Artichoke" lamp are highly sought after

See also Glass: Lighting, pp.306–7; Postmodernism: Lighting, p.471

Domestic wares

In the wake of World War II, demands from an increasingly fashion-conscious consumer public led to the application of affordable design to a wide range of household goods. New materials and manufacturing processes were utilized to bring new ideas to the home. With the growing importance of corporate identity, branded goods became the height of fashion. Advances in technology made sophisticated electronic goods available to domestic consumers, opening up a whole new world to designers.

THE 1940S AND 1950S

In the early post-war years, the emphasis on rebuilding homes provided an eager market for domestic wares in new styles, bright colors, and modern, easy-care materials. The clean lines of Scandinavian design were well suited to the more informal domestic interiors of post-war houses, and such firms as Dansk International Design (est. 1954) made cast-iron wares in bright colors that won medals at the Milan Triennale of 1954 for designer Jens Harald Quistgaard (1922-2008).

Quistgaard founded Dansk Designs with American Ted Nierenberg in 1954, and became the company's

▲ **Casserole designed by Jens H. Quistgaard for Dansk International Design**
This enameled cast-iron casserole is a good example of the new shapes and light, pastel colors that were highly popular in the early post-war years. When collecting avoid any pieces that have been chipped or rusted as good condition is essential for maximum value. This example is marked "Dansk, Made in Denmark"; and also features the initials of the designer – "I.H.Q."
(1950s; ht 11cm/4½in; value **B***)*

principal designer for 30 years. He worked in many media and is especially known for his wooden and stainless-steel pieces as well as furniture and ceramics.

In the USA, George Nelson (1908–86) produced a wide range of revolutionary pieces, including the now collectible "Atomic" clock. American manufacturers were quick to realize that successful styling equaled increased sales, and through a new streamlined design, the industrial designer Raymond Loewy (1893–1986) transformed both the look and the market profitability of the "Coldspot" refrigerator, made from 1935 by Sears & Roebuck Co. Loewy worked design in a new way. Not only was style paramount but he took on considerations of cost as well as brand promotion. Typical of this approach is his redesign of the Lucky Strike cigarette packet. Challenged in 1940 by the head of British American Tobacco that he could not improve the look of the iconic packet, Loewy removed the green background and added logos to the sides. Sales took off and Lowey won the $50,000 wager!

Multinational companies such as Coca-Cola used corporate furnishings and graphics to sell their products worldwide, producing a vast range of bright, colorful merchandise – examples from the 1950s that also reflect the American way of life are especially sought after.

THE 1960S

The growing economic prosperity of the 1960s and the coming of age of the baby boomers resulted in the rise of a youth market. In came Pop – bright colors, synthetic materials, and inexpensive, disposable, mass-produced objects that could respond quickly to rapid changes in

▲ **Coca-Cola tray**
This tin tray is an example of the advertising merchandise produced by the American multinational giant Coca-Cola in the 1950s. The presence of American Allied occupation troops all over the world helped to encourage a taste for the American way of life, and large American companies were swift to capitalize on this. Coca-Cola was one of the first examples of a branded food product being strongly identified with a particular culture and way of life, achieving enormous worldwide sales. Coca-Cola memorabilia has become a cult collecting niche, but examples must be in mint condition to be of interest.
(1950s; w. 76cm/30in; value **A***)*

▲ **"Multiwind" fan designed by Reinhold Weiss for Braun AG**
Designed in 1961, this plastic fan is typical of this German company's production: modern, clean, monochromatic, and with functional elegance. Such pieces, which are marked and therefore easy to identify, are always popular, as Braun products have a cult following.
(1966; ht 14cm/5½in; value **B***)*

◄ **"Compact" dinnerware designed by Massimo and Lella Vignelli**
This practical, space-saving, stacking dinnerware, which features molded handles, was designed in Italy in 1964 and produced from 1969 in a wide range of bold, bright colors by Heller Designs.
(1960s; ht of large container 14cm/5½in; value **C***)*

style. In the hands of Italian designers plastic, previously seen as a cheap material, became chic, colorful, and stylish. Notable designers include Gino Colombini (b.1915), who produced a range of brightly colored, quality kitchen implements for Kartell. Founded in 1949, Kartell specialized in making plastic objects and appointed Colombini its design director in 1953. After leaving the firm in 1960, he continued to produce designs for it, including his well-known umbrella stand from 1965.

Other notable Italian designers include Massimo Vignelli (b.1931) and Lella Vignelli, who designed neatly stacking molded-plastic dinnerware; and Ettore

▼ National Panasonic "Toot-a-Loop" radios

Designed to be worn on the wrist (if your wrists were reasonably small!) "Toot-a-Loop"' radios were produced in a range of bright colors, including white, red, blue, and yellow. Today, collectors seek out the rare orange (made for the Australian market) and the even rarer green (made for South Africa)

*(1970; h 15cm/6in; value **A** each)*

◄ "Atomic" wall clock by George Nelson

Nelson's atom-ball clock, manufactured by the Howard Miller Clock Co., incorporates the new scientific imagery of rods and spheres, that was popularized by a number of designers of this era. Here, each of the brass rods making the clock face terminates in a black-laquered wooden sphere.

*(1947; diam. 33cm/13in; value **E**)*

▼ J.V.C. Videosphere

Made in the USA from 1969 to the mid-1970s, the design of this futuristic-looking television is clearly based on a spaceman's helmet and was influenced by the American lunar landing of 1969. These televisions were made in white and orange for the UK market and red, black, and gray for the US. There is a later version with a radio and alarm clock in the base, which is more valuable.

*(c.1970; h 33m/13in; value **C**)*

companies as Sanyo, J.V.C., Panasonic, and Sony produced a wide portfolio of futuristic designs for both hi-fi and multimedia equipment, which were strongly influenced by the continuing space race and visions of the new technological future.

Mass production and miniaturization meant that electronic items could become fashion accessories. This new feeling is typified by Panasonics innovative "Toot a Loop" radios launched in 1972. A novelty radio design to be worn as a bangle it "splits" to reveal a tuner and a speaker.

In Britain Clive Sinclair (b.1940) harnessed micro-electronic technology in his ground-breaking design of the first pocket calculator, the "Executive." Made in 1972 by his company Sinclair Radionics (est. 1962), it has since become a collectible design classic.

Sottsass (1917-2007), who transformed the typewriter into a chic domestic accessory, with his bright-red plastic "Valentine" model for Olivetti.

By contrast, from 1954 the German firm Braun AG (est. 1921), in Frankfurt, developed a team committed to the Bauhaus principles of pure and elegant design. All Braun products of the 1960s, recognizable by their functional design and monochromatic colors, are now identified with high quality and excellence. Collectors have a wide range of pieces to choose from, but of particular note is the radio and record player designed by Hans Gugelot (1920–65) and Dieter Rams (b.1932) and produced from 1956: known as "Snow White's Coffin," it has a perspex cover and a white-painted metal body.

In Britain, radio and television manufacturer Bush (est. 1931) brought in streamlined designs with their "TR82" radio. The development of batteries and transistors meant that portable electronics emerged for the first time.

THE 1970S

By the very late 1960s or early 1970s Japanese expertise in mass production and miniaturization had brought a whole range of affordable electronic goods on to the world market. Such multinational

▼ Bush "TR82" radio, designed by David Ogle

Originally designed in 1959, manufacture of the Bush "TR82" radio continued until the mid-1970s. Models were available in a range of two-tone color schemes, including the tan and cream version shown here. Reproductions are available today, still produced by Bush.

*(1959; w. 33cm/13in; value **A**)*

KEY FACTS

- MATERIALS plastic wares were highly popular in the immediate post-war years
- DESIGN these are extremely varied and range from kitchen wares such as plastic dishes and trays to a wide variety of complex electronic machines, including calculators, televisions, radios, and hi-fi systems, and electrical pieces such as razors, hair-driers, and alarm clocks; in the 1950s designs with an "atomic" influence were especially fashionable
- BRAND NAMES Dansk International Design; Coca-Cola; Olivetti; Braun AG; Philips; Panasonic; Sinclair Radionics are all important
- CONDITION scratched or faded plastic should be avoided; electrical pieces do not necessarily have to be in working order to be collectible
- COLLECTING domestic wares are a good area to start collecting, because pieces are often small and reasonably priced; designs from the 1950s are becoming especially sought after by collectors; other highly popular pieces include small kitchen appliances by Braun and radios and televisions by Philips; the presence of the original packaging will always add to the value of a piece

Marks

Objects are usually marked on the base, typically with the maker's name, the place of manufacture, and the individual model number

See also Postmodernism: Domestic wares, pp.472–3

Glass

Since the 1940s, glass has increasingly been used as a medium for bold artistic expression. Designers – aided by technology and the growing expertise of glassblowers able to achieve sophisticated forms – have capitalized on its fluid and malleable properties to create ever more sculptural forms. Bold experimentation with color is also characteristic of the post-war years, particularly in the work of Italian glassmakers.

THE 1940S AND 1950S

In the early post-war years Scandinavian designers were at the forefront of glass design, producing pieces typified by clean, organic-inspired lines. The glassware designed in the 1930s by the Finnish architect–designers Alvar Aalto (1898–1976) and his wife Aino Aalto (1894–1949) had already demonstrated the suitability of such a flexible material as glass to the creation of these newly popular organic shapes. Other Finnish designers, most notably Tapio Wirkkala (1915–85), continued the trend for glass forms inspired by nature. Particularly collectible are Wirkkala's delicate and sculptural blown-glass "Kantarelli" series of vases (1946–57), based on the chanterelle mushroom, his angular mold-blown "Iceblock" and textured "Lichen" vases (1950), and his later 'Pinus' range (1972) inspired by tree bark, all of which were manufactured by the leading Finnish glassworks Iittala (est. 1888). The designer Timo Sarpaneva (1926-2005) also worked for Iittala, producing a large number of collectible pieces; these range from highly sculptural glass designs such as the dart-shaped "Kayak" (1954) to the domestic "i-glass" series (1956) of tableware in which he experimented with subtle colors and forms. The smooth, curving lines of Sarpaneva's "Orchid" sculpture are highly characteristic of the organic designs that were so popular in all areas of design in the 1950s.

The Swedish designer Nils Landberg (1907-91) used another popular and fashionable shape of the 1950s – the tulip – as the inspiration for his "Tulpenglas" ("Tulip glass"); this fragile design demanded enormous technical expertise and was produced from 1957 by Orrefors (est. 1898), one of the most celebrated Swedish glassworks. Two other well-known designers who worked for Orrefors were Sven Palmqvist (1906–84), who developed the innovative "Kraka" (1941) and "Ravenna" (1948) effects, and Ingeborg Lundin (1921-92), who is best known for her "Apple" design (1955) and her "Ariel" vases using a complex technique developed in the 1930s by Edvin Öhrström (1906-94) and Vicke Lindstrand (1904–83). Lindstrand also produced a wide range of designs for the other leading Swedish glassworks, Kosta (est. 1742). Many comprised abstract or figural motifs engraved onto simple, curving forms. The technical expertise of the Scandinavian glassworks allowed the talented freelance designers a virtually free hand.

▼ Orrefors "Fiskegraal" vase

This vase was designed by the celebrated Swedish artist, Edward Hald, employed by Orrefors since 1917. He exploited the fluid potential of glass in his designs, as demonstrated by the "movement" created in this underwater scene, the result of using extremely thick glass walls.

(1942; h 14.5cm/6in; value E)

In Denmark, the designer Per Lütken (1916-98) produced an enormously varied range of experimental designs for the Holmegaard Glassworks (est. 1898) from 1942. His most notable designs are probably his organic, asymmetrical vases in dusky grays and cool blues, such as the "Beak" vase of 1951. By the mid- to late 1950s his designs were aimed more at the rapidly expanding middle-class market and consisted of affordable, mass-produced, domestic glassware. These elegant and restrained mass-produced pieces are less expensive than Lütken's more experimental pieces and are a good starting-point for collectors.

Glass companies in other parts of Europe shared with Scandinavia the competitive spirit of the post-war years. Among the most innovative and avant-garde glass designs were those produced in the Netherlands by Andreas Copier (1901–91) for the Leerdam Glassworks. In addition to his distinctive "Unica" series begun in the early 1920s, Copier invented several highly original techniques, including enameled decoration – usually of fish and seaweed – between layers of colored glass and the vacuum technique where air is sucked out of a vessel to create dents, depressions, and irregular shapes. He was one of the first to experiment with non-functional free-blown pieces, which in the 1960s inspired the nascent Studio Glass movement in the USA. Under his directorship other talent also blossomed, notably that of Floris Meydam (b.1919) who started out designing "Unica" pieces and, from the early 1950s, made free-blown abstract vessels in clear crystal that was then cut using techniques typically applied to optical glass.

In Czechoslovakia, the glass industry was nationalized in 1948 and high quality production continued. Designers received a thorough education in glass, which began at a specialized glass school. Training usually culminated at the Academy of Applied Arts in Prague under the influential professors Karel Stipl, Josef Kaplicky (1899-1962) or Stanislav Libensky (1921-2002). As the Communist government did not deem glass to be an art form that was ideologically threatening, designers could work largely free from official control. This resulted in the creation of highly innovative, modern designs that updated traditional methods of glassmaking. The country participated in the World Exposition in Brussels in 1958, and the Milan Triennale exhibitions in 1957 and 1960. Designers won

▲ Vase from the "Carnaby" range by Kastrup and Holmegaard

This vase was designed by Per Lütken and is an iconic example of 1960s mold-blown glass. Designers explored more elaborate shapes, as seen in this double-waisted, red and white cased form. There were several forms in this range, which also mimics plastics of the Pop era in its coloring.

(c.1969; h 30cm/12in; value D)

▼ "Finlandia" vase designed by Timo Sarpaneva

This is one of many glass products designed by Timo Sarpaneva for the Finnish glassworks, Iittala. Employed by the company for almost 30 years, he also designed its distinctive logo. This molded, smoke-gray vase is cylindrical in shape and has an flared rim. The surface has etched marks in places and has raised bubbles in others, typical of the Finn's work.

(1964; h 20cm/8in; value C)

prestigious awards for their glass designs, and were also able to witness developing styles from outside the Iron Curtain.

Many designers worked across different techniques, some with architectural glass, and important names include Stanislav Libensky, René Roubíček (b.1922) and his wife Miluse Roubícková (b.1922), Jiri Harcuba (b.1928), and Pavel Hlava (1924-2003). Important factories include Skrdlovice (est. 1940), and the Borské Sklo and Podebrady groups.

In the UK, cut glass saw a revival in a modern style, led by designers such as Irene Stevens (b.1917) at Webb Corbett, John Luxton (b.1920) at Stuart & Sons, and David Hammond (b.1931) at Webb & Sons. Laurence Whistler (1912-2000) and John Hutton (1907-78)

▶ "Pezzato" vase, designed by Fulvio Bianconi

Designed by Bianconi for Venini & C. of Murano, this "pezzato," or patchwork, vase demonstrates an iconic technique of the 1950s and 1960s, in which patches of colored glass were fused together. The colors here, red, green, blue, and clear are collectively recognized as the "Paris" decorative design, and is highly sought after by today's collectors of 20th century glass.
(c.1951; h. 21cm/8¼in; value H)

revived diamond point engraving on vases and architectural features. RCA graduate Geoffrey Baxter (1922-95) joined Whitefriars in 1954 and, along with William Wilson (1914-72), designed thick walled vases and bowls in curving, organic forms.

THE 1960S

Venetian glass of this decade is especially known (and collected) for its variety, technical expertise, and bold, bright colors. One of the major Italian glassworks was the company established in 1921 by Paolo Venini (1895–1959), on the island of Murano. Venini used early Venetian glassmaking techniques to produce a range of colorful, delicate, textured pieces, which are highly sought after and often copied. One of the best-known designers working with Venini was Fulvio Bianconi (1915-96), who helped design the range of asymmetrical "Handkerchief" vases in c.1949. Bianconi also worked in an alternative style, using clear-cased glass and simple forms with dense, contrasting colors.

The firm of Vistosi, although better known for its contribution to lighting design, also produced pieces that typified bright, bold Italian glass design. Fine examples are the playful pieces designed by Alessandro Pianon (1931-84), who worked for Vistosi from 1956. Another celebrated Murano glassworks was Barovier & Toso (est. 1942), which was well known for applying colored decoration to molten glass. Ercole Barovier was one of its leading designers and produced some fine pieces incorporating fused mosaic, and "Intarsio" glass comprised of geometric patterns in colored glass.

In the USA, developments in small furnace

▶ "Efeso" vase designed by Ercole Barovier

A glass vase of oval form, designed by Ercole Barovier for the Murano glassworks, Barovier & Toso. This piece is typical of their output, and a good example of their work during the 1960s, in which they sought to create different effects by applying a different colored decoration to molten glass. Here the light blue vase has had dark gray bubbles of varying sizes blown into the surface.
(1964; h 40.5cm/16in; value H)

technology meant that designers could work from their own studios rather than having to be based at a factory, and this led to the introduction of the term "studio glass." Developed by Harvey K. Littleton (b.1922) and Dominick Labino (1910–87) in 1962, a glass program was subsequently founded at the University of Wisconsin which totally transformed glassmaking. One early student, Dale Chihuly (b.1941), went on to develop an exuberant and influential style, with inspirations including nature and tribal artefacts. He and his contemporaries have become responsible for teaching new generations of studio glass artists.

In England, glassmakers had begun to rival those in Scandinavia. From 1967, Geoffrey Baxter's colorful mold blown textured designs for Whitefriars, and those produced by Frank Thrower (1932-87) for Dartington, proved highly popular. Studio glass techniques were brought to the UK in 1967 by Littleton's student Samuel Herman (b.1936) who taught at London's Royal College of Art.

▼ Aureliano Toso "Oriente" vase by Dino Martens

The "Oriente" range was introduced at the Venice Biennale in 1952. This early carafe is overlaid with a dark violet and white star murrine, and multicolored panels of opaque enamels. At the neck is an applied, colorless, foliate band with gold foil inclusions.
(c.1952; h 33cm/14in; value I)

▶ Glass bird, by Alessandro Pianon

Working for the Italian glassmakers, Vistosi, Alessandro Pianon is well-known for his characterful glass birds, which he produced in a range of shapes and colors. This cobalt blue example is typically of his work – hand blown, with internal murrines and raised on wire legs, in this case, copper.
(c.1960s; h 29cm/11½in; value G)

KEY FACTS

- **IMPORTANT FIRMS AND MAKERS** Iittala; Orrefors; Kosta; Holmegaard; Lütken; Venini; Bianconi; Vistosi; Chihuly; Herman; The Glasshouse; Peiser; Andreas Copier, Leerdam Glassworks; Meydam; Libensky; Roubícek; Brychtova; Hlava; Baxter
- **CONDITION** post-war studio and factory glass must in perfect condition; generally damage is unacceptable; the work of influential makers is more desirable
- **COLLECTING** one-off designer pieces will often be high in price; serial-production or mass-produced pieces by the same designer will generally be much more affordable; although studio glass is usually signed, much factory glass is unmarked and is best identified from the color and shape

Marks

Scandinavian glassworks usually marked their pieces with details of the factory, the designer's initials, and a code number; Venini glass has an acid-etched mark on the base, but Italian glass may be unmarked

See also Glass: pp.274–311

Factory-produced ceramics

The mass-produced domestic ceramics of the post-war years reflected the new, informal style of living and entertaining. The accessible designs were to a large degree inspired by the vibrant, imaginatively decorated work shown at the influential Organic Design in Home Furnishings exhibition held at the Museum of Modern Art (MOMA), New York, in 1940.

THE UNITED STATES

In the early post-war years American ceramicists played a major part in translating the "New Look" into affordable domestic wares. In 1937 Russel Wright (1904–76) designed the colorful "American Modern" tableware that was made from 1939 to 1959 by Steubenville Pottery Co. (est. 1879) and intended to "mix and match"; the series had a soft, organic form and an innovative streamlined shape. Also influential was the work of Eva Zeisel (b.1906), a Hungarian-born ceramicist, whose work appeared in MOMA's Organic Design exhibition. A commission from MOMA for a "Museum" tableware service followed, and in 1942 Zeisel produced curving, free-form designs that were made in porcelain by Castleton China in 1946. The new desire for color contributed to the success of the vibrant "Fiesta" tableware range designed by Frederick Hurten Rhead (1880–1942).

▼ "Fiesta" ware designed by Frederick Hurten Rhead

"Fiesta" tableware was first produced in the USA in 1936 by the Homer Laughlin China Co. (est. 1877) in East Liverpool, Ohio. It remained successful throughout the 1950s and its style is particularly associated with that era. The name reflects the bright, vibrant range of colors available, including red, blue, yellow, and green.

*(both c.1950s; ht of jug 25cm/9¾in; value for each **B**)*

BRITAIN

During the 1950s the firm of Wedgwood (est. 1759), in Staffordshire, launched a range of tableware decorated by Eric Ravilious (1903–42). The designs had been commissioned in 1938 but were not put into production until after World War II. The typical "Englishness" of Ravilious's designs, in which there is no hint of the otherwise highly fashionable "New Look," perfectly complements the traditional Wedgwood forms. Although not very popular in the 1950s, all designs by Ravilious, ranging from Coronation mugs to the "Queensware Travel" series of dinnerware, are now highly sought after by collectors.

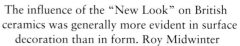

▲ "Homemaker" plate designed by Enid Seeney

The design of the "Homemaker" series is typical of the abstract patterns popular in Britain during the 1950s. The series was made by Ridgway (est. 1792) from 1955 and the objects shown, such as the reclining armchair by Robin Day (b.1915), reflect contemporary designs. The "Homemaker" series was seen as the perfect starter range for newly married couples.

*(c.1950s; diam. 11cm/4¼in; value **B**)*

► Coronation mug designed by Eric Ravilious

The design for this British mug, made in the 1950s by Wedgwood, was originally commissioned from Ravilious in 1936 for the coronation of Edward VIII. The original design in blue was adapted to green for the coronation of George VI and then pink for Elizabeth II. The design features fireworks, a favorite theme of this designer.

*(c.1951; ht 10cm/4in; value **B**)*

The influence of the "New Look" on British ceramics was generally more evident in surface decoration than in form. Roy Midwinter (1923–90), sales director of the family firm of W.R. Midwinter (est. 1910), was inspired by the work of Wright and Zeisel to introduce organic shapes in such innovative ranges as "Stylecraft" and "Fashion," but he is probably better known for his imaginative commissions for decoration from young designers such as Jessie Tait (b.1928) and Terence Conran (b.1931). The latter was responsible for the "Plantlife" tableware range, which imaginatively combined bright colors and plant forms. Ridgway produced a highly successful "Homemaker" series, in which the designer Enid Seeney (b.1932) combined line drawings of many of the new and contemporary fashions of the 1950s to form an abstract design. The mass-produced series sold through the high-street chain Woolworth's, so pieces must be in fine condition to be collectible. The firm of Troika (est. 1963), in St Ives and later in Newlyn, produced a range of domestic wares inspired by the local Cornish landscape and the St Ives group of abstract artists, which included Ben Nicholson (1894–1982) and Barbara Hepworth (1903–75). The rare white Troika range draws particularly heavily on Nicholson's white reliefs.

◄ "Plantlife" tureen designed by Terence Conran

This tureen, made by the British firm of Midwinter, is a very fine example of the firm's innovative policy of commissioning ceramic designs from young, up-and-coming artists and designers. Conran's decoration shows a departure from traditional floral ornamentation.

*(c.1957; w. 30cm/11¾in; value **A**)*

SCANDINAVIA

The production of ceramics in Scandinavia was dominated by a few major companies and the designers associated with them. In Sweden the Gustavberg Pottery (est. 1825) owed much of its success in the early post-war years to two outstanding designers: Wilhelm Kåge (1889–1960) and his pupil and successor Stig Lindberg (1916–82), whose designs and decoration often anticipated trends by some ten years. In the 1950s Lindberg used bright, colorful, playful decoration on tin-glazed earthenware; other designs from the early 1950s included leaf-shaped bowls decorated with leaf designs. By the late 1950s he anticipated the Op art movement with the "Domino" series of precise, angular shapes with black and white geometric designs. In Finland ceramics production in the 1950s was dominated by Arabia (est. 1873), for which Kaj Franck (b.1911) designed the "Kilta" tableware service made from 1953 to 1974. Produced in five colorways – black, blue, green, white, and yellow – it worked on the "mix and match" principle.

ITALY

Unlike Scandinavia, where the small number of factories and designers led to a consistent and recognizable Scandinavian style, the range of ceramics produced in Italy was as diverse as the numerous workshops and designers that produced them. One of the principal manufacturers in the 1950s was Richard-Ginori in 1896 in Doccia. The principal designer was Giovanni

▼ Dish designed by Stig Lindberg

During the 1950s the name of the Gustavberg Pottery in Sweden was almost synonymous with that of their chief designer, Stig Lindberg. This plate is a fine example of the playful, colorful, hand-painted decoration that Lindberg employed on tin-glazed earthenware made at the factory; other wares have smaller, abstract, linear patterns. All work by Lindberg will be highly collectible.

(c.1950s; l. 26cm/10¼in; value C)

▲ Vinaigrette by Arabia

The Finnish firm of Arabia (est. 1932) was well known for its tableware designs. Here scratched decoration over an "anthracite" glaze suggests the coat and hands, and the head is made from the stopper topped with a pilgrim hat. All pieces made by Arabia are stamped and marked.

(early 1950s; ht 20cm/8in; value A)

► Plate from the "12 Mesi/12 Soli" series designed by Piero Fornasetti

The concept behind this series of Italian plates is the calendar (*mesi* means "months" in Italian). This example is the only design of the 12 to feature monochrome decoration – the others are all decorated in color. Fornasetti, who also designed the celebrated "Themes and Variations" series, was such a prolific designer that it is often difficult to date his pieces accurately. However, all are clearly marked – usually with both the designer's signature and details of the manufacturer.

(late 1950s; diam. 26cm/10¼in; value B)

Gariboldi (1908–71), who produced tableware and tiles with linear, abstract printed patterns. In contrast, Piero Fornasetti (1913–88) produced a range of designs that were generally transfer-printed onto blanks. Among the best known are the "Themes and Variations" and "12 Mesi/12 Soli" series of plates. Fornasetti was a very prolific designer and drew his inspiration from an eclectic range of sources, including both Renaissance and Surrealist art. All of his pieces are clearly marked, although the marks will vary and are often stylized to reflect the theme of the design.

GERMANY

In 1955 the firm of Rosenthal (est. 1880) introduced a "New Look"-inspired range designed by Beate Kuhn (b.1927); this consisted of extravagantly shaped vases, decorated in many cases with patterns inspired by the paintings of Joan Miró. Rosenthal also commissioned designs from many non-German designers, including the "Service 2000" range, designed in 1954 by the celebrated American industrial designers Raymond Loewy (1893–1986) and Richard Latham (b.1920), and distinguished by its highly fashionable, curving, hourglass forms.

KEY FACTS

- DESIGNS 1950s: curving, free-form shapes inspired by the "New Look" were popular, as were abstract linear decoration and bright colors; "mix and match" tableware was also especially fashionable; 1960s: favorite designs featured bold abstract decoration or psychedelic color combinations
- IMPORTANT DESIGNERS well-known makers include: Wright; Zeisel; Hurten Rhead; Ravilious; Tait; Conran; Kåge; Lindberg; Franck; Gariboldi; Fornasetti; Loewy
- COLLECTING only collect pieces that are in perfect condition; look for examples that complement contemporary furniture, especially those in soft, streamlined shapes and light, pastel colors; pieces such as the "Homemaker" plate featuring illustrations of contemporary designs are also highly collectible

See also Arts and Crafts: Ceramics – The United States, pp.378–9

Studio ceramics

The 20th-century revival of interest in handmade and hand-decorated pottery is known as the studio ceramics movement. Although potters pursued individual aims and styles varied widely, they shared a common interest in the qualities found in handmade pots. The movement flourished as a reaction against the standardization of industrially manufactured ceramics. Its main tenet was that the manufacture of a pot should involve as little interference from machines as possible, resulting in more natural and spontaneous pottery. Oriental ceramics were inspirational, and there was great interest in declining folk-pottery traditions: many of the pioneers of the studio ceramics movement learned from surviving folk-potters.

EUROPE

BRITAIN

Studio ceramics in Britain have been strongly influenced by the pottery of the Far East. Following the first significant exhibition of Chinese ceramics from the Tang Dynasty (618–907) and Song Dynasty (960–1279), held in London in 1910 at the Burlington Fine Arts Club, much of the effort of the early pioneer potters was spent attempting to emulate their glazes and forms. Typical Chinese and Japanese glazes, such as the blue-green celadon and the rust-black tenmoku, are common.

Bernard Leach (1887–1979) was the dominant figure not only for the Anglo-Oriental school of ceramics but also for all studio ceramicists. He studied art in London and ceramics in Japan, returning to start a studio in St Ives, Cornwall, in 1920. He was accompanied by Shoji Hamada (1894–1979), a young Japanese potter who remained in Britain until 1923. The significant characteristics of their ceramics were the contrasting areas of glazed and unglazed surfaces, and an austere approach to the tones of their glazes. Pots were fired in a traditional Japanese-type, wood-fired kiln. Their early pots, often technically deficient, are prized for their vigorous decorative character.

Leach's first apprentice, Michael Cardew (1901–83), also became a pivotal figure in the studio ceramics movement. He was the first studio potter to revive the technique of slipware, which he employed on his pitchers and chargers. Cardew's pots have a fluidity of decoration that indicates the speed and facility of his approach. Both Leach and Cardew had many pupils; their influence has been substantial, particularly as they held strong views on the need for functional handmade pottery as the basis for all studio ceramics.

ABSTRACTION IN POTTERY

Whereas Leach saw beauty in craft and domestic objects, William Staite Murray (1881–1962) regarded pottery as the equal of sculpture and painting, and exhibited his work alongside the leading abstract artists of the 1920s and 1930s. His pots were given expressive titles such as "Vortex," "Cadence," or "Purple Night" and were shown once a year at a special exhibition in Bond Street. Staite Murray was notable at the time for charging high prices for his wares. His forms, thrown on the wheel, were often large (up to 1m/3ft 3in in height) and of a free-flowing, undulating character. The decoration seemed equally spontaneous.

Prominent among Staite Murray's pupils was Thomas "Sam" Haile (1909–48), an abstract artist of considerable talent. Although his shapes were much influenced by Murray, his surrealist decoration, sets him apart from his contemporaries. Few pieces come on to the market and those that do are highly collectible.

MODERNISM FROM EUROPE

The dominant Orientalist influence of Leach within studio ceramics was challenged in the late 1930s by the arrival in Britain of two potters. Lucie Rie (1902–95) was born in Vienna where she studied with Josef Hoffmann (1870–1956). She came to Britain in 1938 and established a London studio. Her early domestic wares made in the 1950s, in particular her coffee-sets, are highly collectible; austere with finely inscribed parallel lines and delicately inlaid colors, they are exact rather than spontaneous, and controlled rather than exploratory. Her pots betray a deep knowledge of glazes.

Hans Coper (1920–81) was born in Germany and settled in Britain in 1939. From 1946 he shared a studio with Rie and worked with her on her domestic wares; some of these are marked with both their seals. Coper developed his own repertory of distinctive forms. These have a deep tonal range of ochres and metallic black that derive from his use of oxides applied to the unglazed,

▲ "Leaping Salmon" vase by Bernard Leach
Leach repeated this notable design over 30 times and considered it one of his most successful decorative motifs. The slender tapering form and light glaze reveal the Oriental influence; both come from Korean ceramics.
(c.1960; ht 30cm/11¾ in; value H)

◄ Vase by Shoji Hamada
This stoneware bottle vase displays Hamada's strong use of different decorative glazing techniques. The juxtaposition of his depiction of a spray of foliage with the deep-rust glaze is characteristic. The pot was made to his design, using slabs of clay luted together and fired in a wood kiln. Hamada did not sign his pots after leaving Britain in 1923, preferring the Japanese custom of signing the box in which they were wrapped.
(c.1963; ht 24cm/9½in; value I)

► Vase by William Staite Murray
This is a characteristic form of Staite Murray: a broadly based "Oriental" type of vase. He was capable of producing pots that were either wholly representational, as in this case, or wholly abstract in their decoration. The boldness and confidence of line that this vase shows reveal Staite Murray's interest in brush painting.
(c.1939; ht 31cm/12¼in; value G)

► Large stoneware bowl by Dame Lucie Rie

This bowl is typical of Lucie Rie's later work. She frequently used banded glazes on top of each other – a technique that gave a piece of pottery the effect of great depth. This example has a mottled pale turqoise ground within a broad bronze colored band and an additional band of "dribbled" brown decoration. This piece bears an impressed "LR" seal. Rie's pottery, when compared to that of Bernard Leach, is considered less rural and recognized for its use of brighter colors. There is also less obvious influence from the Far East. Known particularly for her bowls and bottles, Rie employed no figurative or patterning brushwork but invariably used color.

(c.1975; diam. 25.5cm/64¾in; value I)

▼ Ceramic vase by Georges Jouve

This vase is characteristic of Georges Jouve's work, with its simple, traditional form and applied high-relief sun decoration. Jouve peferred to work with his hands rather than on a wheel and much of his work was produced this way – from vases to lampstands and mirror frames. Much of his work is organic and sculptural in appearance, in keeping with post-war trends in other disciplines such as glass making.

(c.1948; ht 30.5cm/12in; value N)

textured surface. Unlike Rie's, Coper's pots can best be described as a process of formal exploration: Coper used to create his ceramics by the meticulous joining together of elements thrown on the wheel. They betray his training as an engineer in their construction. These different multiple forms are known as "Thistle," "Poppy," or "Spade" forms.

GERMANY AND FRANCE

German potter Otto Meier (1903-96) is indebted to both the disappearing folk traditions of functional pottery and with the Chinese sources, although his ceramics also have a softer and more organic feel to them. His use of fluxed running glazes is also important. In France, Georges Jouve (1910–64) took inspiration from ancient forms, while developing vivid glazes with his use of selenium leading. Studio ceramics of these kinds can be seen to have had a positive impact on the design of contemporary industrial ceramics, particularly in Germany, France, the Netherlands, and Scandanavia.

SCANDINAVIA

Unlike Britain, where most studio potters had their own workshops, the practice in Scandinavia was for established potteries to take on artists to form studios. They produced both designs for general production as well as artist-made studio pieces. Such was the high quality of production pieces that the distinction between them and "studio work" is not always clear.

In Sweden the two main factories, Gustavsberg and Rorstrand both ran important studios. The former was run by Willem Kage (1889–1960) who was succeeded in 1949 by Stig Lindberg (1916–1982). Rorstrand's studio was run by Gunnar Nylund from 1930, who had established Saxbo, his own studio with Nathalie Krebbs in 1929. Saxbo is regarded as the most important independent studio in Denmark, producing pottery of simple shapes often with oriental style glazes.

ARTISTS AND POTTERS

Many of the most famous 20th-century painters have experimented with decorating blanks. From the late 1950s the painter Jean Cocteau (1889–1963) combined the decorative skills of a painter with a novel approach to form, playing with the different viewpoints of a pot. One of his favorite forms was the plate, which he often decorated with linear designs of faces, shown in profile in a limited range of colors. The ceramics of Pablo Picasso (1881--1973) are the best known of any artist's ceramics and the most truly collaborative. They fall into two types; first there is his ceramic sculpture, where each piece is unique, and then there are his ceramics, where the work has been reproduced in limited editions such as 40, 100, or 300.

▼ Ceramic charger by Jean Cocteau

Like many artists of his generation, Jean Cocteau explored different media, including ceramics. Generally, pieces were similar to his graphic work; spare and unadorned and decorated freely, Cocteau called it "tattooing the clay." Painted in bright yellow and red glazes, this charger depicts a man chasing a woman with a snake.

(1958; ht 30.5cm/12in; value F)

► Pablo Picasso Madoura white clay vessel

A Pablo Picasso/Madoura White clay figural vessel of a peasant woman with a face painted and incised on her apron. The subject matter painted on Picasso's ceramics was similar to that of his graphic work and included such diverse motifs as birds, fish, goats, bulls and bull-fighting scenes, faces, and mythological creatures such as centaurs. Picasso's most common wares were round and square plates, platters, jugs, and vases. Picasso did not throw the pieces himself, but was closely involved in the design of the forms.

(1950s; ht 35cm/13¾in; value H)

KEY FACTS

Marks

Bernard Leach: Personal seal or a mark for Leach Studio
William Staite Murray: impressed "M" in pentagram
Lucie Rie: all works impressed with her seal
Hans Coper: from 1947 marked his works with an incised or painted personal sealmark
Kahler: "HAK" monogramme or name and "Nestved"
Rorstrand and Gustavsberg: factory marks with individual artist monogrammes
Saxbo: early pieces marked "Krebbs" and "Nylund"
Otto Meier: incised or impressed monogram
Jean Cocteau: painted signature on base
Pablo Picasso: "Picasso" stamped or incised on base

See also Arts and Crafts: Ceramics, pp.376–81; Mid-century Modern: Studio ceramics – The United States, pp.462–3

The United States

ORIGINS AND PIONEERS

The studio ceramics movement in the USA developed much later than the comparative movement in Europe, and in a somewhat different way. Despite this, however, a number of European immigrants had a significant impact on its development.

Unlike Europe, where studio pottery most often emerged out of a craft tradition, in the USA, the movement found favor in art schools, which made the link to art a much stronger one. One major, prewar, school existed: The New York State School of Clay Working and Ceramics (now the State College of Ceramics), at Alfred University, New York. Established in 1900, it was directed by Charles Fergus Binns (1857–1934), the English-born son of a director of the

▲ Natzler small flaring bowl
With forms worked on the wheel by Gertrud and glazed by her husband Otto, the Natzlers' studio pottery was made using local Californian clay. Early forms were primarily bowls, but Gertrud later produced gourds and bottles as well. This elegant flaring bowl is reminiscent of Lucie Rie's work and is finished with a porous uranium volcanic glaze. The bowl is signed "Natzler."
(c.1960s; diam. 15cm/53⁄4in; value **H***)*

Royal Worcester Porcelain Company. Binns is credited as having introduced studio ceramics to America.

Binns brought with him an important working method, not yet seen in America. Previously it was customary to have one person produce a pot and another person decorate it. Binns introduced the arts-and-crafts inspired practice of the same maker both producing and decorating a piece, thereby uniting the art of making and decorating.

Emigrating from Finland in 1927 (where she had studied under Alfred Finch), Maija Grotell (1899–1973) encountered Binns. Trained as a painter and sculptor in Finland, ceramics were Grotell's first love. She had been unable to pursue this in her homeland, and so had emigrated to the USA in 1927. Following her studies, Maija pursued a teaching career, notably at The Cranbrook Academy of Art, Michigan, from 1938–1966. She is remembered particularly for her glazing techniques and the number of students she taught who went on to find fame themselves, such as Toshiko Takaezu, Susanne Stephenson, and John Glick.

Arriving later than Maija Grotell, Otto (1908–2007) and Gertrud Natzler (1908-71) had similar influence. Fleeing the Nazi annexation of their native Austria in 1938, they settled in Los Angeles,

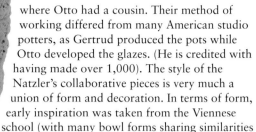

▲ Vase by Beatrice Wood
This flaring vase is typical of the pieces produced by Beatrice Wood during this period. The rough, pitted surface is characteristic of the "volcanic" glazes she developed using either earth tones or bright colors including the Persian Blue seen here. With an emphasis on the sculptural quality of a piece, it was not unusual for vessels to have small apertures.
(c.1960s; ht 13.5cm/5¼in; value **G***)*

▼ Scheier charger
Depicting Adam and Eve, this charger is typical of much work produced by Edwin and Mary Scheier. It embodies their interest in the human form and life experience and captures their fascination for folk-art traditions. Pieces were oftern formed by Mary and decorated by Edwin, as here, in simple outlines reminiscent of tribal art.
(1945; diam 38cm/15in; value **H***)*

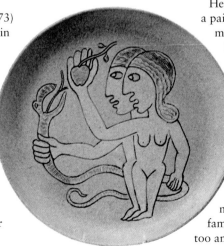

where Otto had a cousin. Their method of working differed from many American studio potters, as Gertrud produced the pots while Otto developed the glazes. (He is credited with having made over 1,000). The style of the Natzler's collaborative pieces is very much a union of form and decoration. In terms of form, early inspiration was taken from the Viennese school (with many bowl forms sharing similarities to Lucie Rie's work). The couple later developed their own forms. After Gertrud's death, Otto initially refused to glaze some two hundred pieces that she had left behind, but eventually glazed them one by one, as well as producing his own wares. His later, slab-formed pieces are equally collected.

The Natzler's took on students, including Beatrice Wood (1893–1998). The daughter of wealthy San Francisco socialites, Wood had an extraordinary life. She knew such figures as Marcel Duchamp, Francis Picabia, and Man Ray and was an early American adherent of the Dada movement. Encountering ceramics by accident, she is remembered for her bowl and vase forms and her later "sophisticated primitives," a series of figurative studies. Luster glazes were a life-long love, which she developed throughout her career. Although she possessed a great skill in glazing, she lacked the technical brilliance of her teacher Otto Natzler. Instead, she was content to explore errors and happenstance. This was a method of working that she also employed in her forms; Wood took inspiration from many sources, but with a natural skill and Dadaist sense of humor, she somehow managed to make them her own.

Equally individualist were Edwin Scheier (b. 1910) and his wife Mary (1909–2007). Initially producing individual works, with Mary specializing in thrown pieces and Edwin sculpture, they increasingly began to work together from their marriage in 1937; Edwin decorated Mary's work in a distinctive style. The Scheiers worked using a number of techniques, but the human form and themes of the human journey from birth through life is one that recurs often. Figures formed inside animal forms, or human figures within human forms, are seen throughout their long careers. Much of this work was inspired by their early trips to Mexico, where they had lived together for ten years.

Henry Varnum Poor (1887–1970) was principally a painter, having been encouraged by his artistic mother to pursue a career in the arts. A farm boy from Chapman, Kansas, he studied art at Stamford University, The Slade School in London, and the Académie Julian, Paris. Having moved to Rockland County in New York in 1920, he focused his attention more and more on ceramics.

A self-taught potter, Poor began to explore ceramics after his paintings were poorly received at an exhibition at the Kervorkian Galleries in New York. Whereas ceramics began as a need, Poor soon mastered them and began making a name for his work. On the back of his fame as a potter, his paintings began to be recognized too and he produced works in both media.

LATER AWAKENING

These early pioneers paved the way and created a structure for the success of later artists, such as Toshiko Takaezu (b.1922) and Peter Voulkos (1924–2002), who both rose to prominence during the 1950s. Although of a similar generation, Voulkos and Takaezu explored clay in different directions, and yet both produced mainly sculptural studio pieces.

Voulkos (born Panagiotis Harry Voulkopoulos) produced work that is more akin to sculpture than traditional studio potting. His earliest pieces explore form, but he soon moved toward an abstract and highly sculptural aesthetic. His uncompromising style has often being aligned to the abstract Expressionist movement. Tearing, gouging, and ripping clay, he sought to produce freely formed works, often on a monumental scale. Much of his later work comprises his so called "stack pots," where disparate forms were forced together to make one complete work. Voulkos employed this technique to produce works cast in bronze, further endorsing his sculptural ambitions.

While Voulkos sought to express sculptural forms through the force of his vision, Toshiko Takaezu's early work owes much to her Japanese heritage. Born in Hawaii to Japanese parents, she was a pupil of Maija Grotell at The Cranbrook Academy from 1951 to 1954, studying in Japan the following year. Her work embraces both glaze and form as well as decoration in the Japanese tradition, but explores other cultures too. She is a consummate technician, greatly admired for her use of hand forming and hand-poured and hand-painted glazes and decoration. Takaezu's hand-formed, "closed" vessels are synonymous with her work, and are often of a monumental scale. From 1966 to 1992 she taught at Princeton, establishing her own studio after her retirement where she continues to work (2008).

THE 1960S

The "Funk" ceramics movement, where commonly found objects and images were expressed in new and often humorous or disturbing ways, was also specifically American. The work of Robert Arneson (b.1930) dominated the 1960s, with its refusal to be tasteful and its positive embrace of garish modernity.

Funk pre-figured the return to an exploration of the vessel form, and historical ceramics were used as source material for witty and irreverent re-workings; for example, Adrian Saxe (b.1943) combined the forms of 18th-century Sèvres vases with cartoon imagery as a commentary on current extravagant taste. Betty Woodman (b.1930) also appropriates from historical sources, often making pieces that include their own plinths in an ironic statement on museum displays.

▼ Toshiko Takaezu ceramic vessel
Takaezu is perhaps best known for her large-scale, "closed" vessels, which were typically hand formed. This example has modeled buttresses and a flattened top, and is finished in brown glazes. It is signed "TT."
(c.1960s; ht 30cm/12in; value I)

KEY FACTS

- CONDITION good condition is generally a prerequisite for the value of a piece; look for signs of restoration
- COLLECTING early pieces by major ceramicists, though rare, are not necessarily more valuable than the artists' later work; if collecting a single piece by an artist, select one that is representative of his or her mature style; an unusual piece can add greatly to a collection of work by a specific artist; proof of provenance is crucial for important studio wares; many pieces are signed and look on and around the base for impressed seal marks or monograms; contemporary works that have been illustrated in key publications and magazines are also especially collectible; biggest is not necessarily best – some artists are more successful on an intimate level

Marks
Charles F. Binns: pieces marked with a conjoined "CFB" within a circle

Maija Grotell: pieces signed "MG" or fully signed

Natzlers: pieces fully marked, or with an "N"

Beatrice Woods: pieces fully signed with her mark; "Beato"

Peter Voulkos and Betty Woodman: both sign their work

Toshiko Takaezu's: pieces bear her "TT" emblem

Henry Varnum Poor: ceramics usually signed with "HVP" followed by last two digits of the year

▲ Faience charger by Henry Varnum Poor
This charger is characteristic of the vast majority of Varnum Poor's work; primarily he produced vases and chargers, which he hand-painted. His training as an artist is evident in the decoration of his pieces, which he achieves using *sgrafitto* technique. Here, the charger is incised with a coffee pot and fruit bowl still life. It has a crackled polychrome glaze and is signed "HVP 57."
(c.1957; ht 32cm/12½in; value F)

► Hand-thrown porcelain bowl by Maija Grotell
This fine bowl is typical of Maija Grotell's work, particularly in terms of size and color. Grotell was recognized for her ability to work large pieces on the wheel, with considerable precision and control. She is also well known for her glazing techniques, among which were a range of bright blues, made from using copper oxide. This example has a banded wave pattern in coral on a teal and cobalt matt glaze, and is incised "MG." From 1938–66, Grotell held a teaching post at The Cranbrook Academy of Art, producing some of her finest work and inspiring, among others, architects Eliel and Eero Saarinen in their use of glazed bricks.
(c.1950s; w. 28cm/11in; value I)

See also Arts and Crafts: Ceramics pp.376–81; Postmodernism: Studio ceramics, pp.476–7

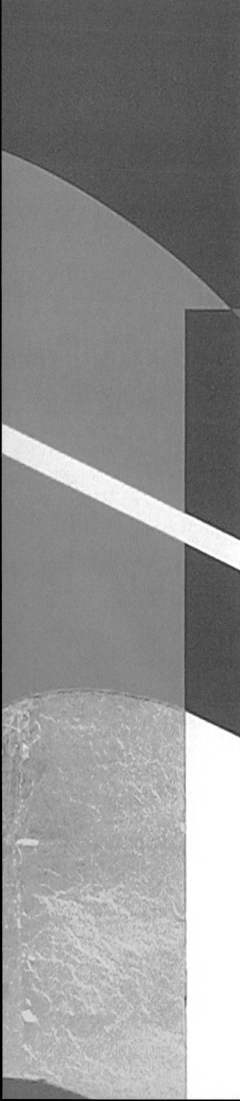

Epitomized by the outlandish designs of the 1980s, Postmodernism was, essentially, a rejection of the design style that had prevailed for the last forty years. Designers across all disciplines began to express a deep cynicism of the Modern Movement. Not only did they reject the Modernist mantra "form follows function," but they actively sought ways in which to undermine it. Italian design groups Alchimia and Memphis led the way, encouraging furniture designers, glassmakers, potters, and product designers to plunder the past in a bid to create witty, ironic, and irreverent pieces of a wholly disparate nature. The result was a wealth of innovative designs that were rich in color, where discordant materials or motifs sat boldly beside one another, and whose forms adopted shapes that defied not only convention but also, in some cases, gravity! A new breed of "celebrity" designer emerged and, aided by better technology, low-cost materials, and cheaper manufacturing methods, produced numerous novel and emphemeral domestic wares and accessories at affordable prices. Toward the end of the century, the Crafts Revival Movement saw a number of designers return to an emphasis on craftsmanship, fine materials, and the one-off or limited production of very beautiful, exclusive furniture designed to last.

The top of an Alchimia "Atropo" table by Alessandro Mendini (left) features a graphic handpainted design with gold foil highlights that is typical of Alchimia's design aesthetic (1984).

Post Design "Sgaboo" stool by Markus Benesch (above) Twenty years after Memphis disbanded (1988), Alberto Albrichi's Post Design firm continues to produce pieces in the Memphis spirit, such as this multi-colored solid foam rubber and plastic stool (2005).

Furniture

Postmodernism is a difficult subject to grasp properly. By its very nature – a desire to move on and be more "modern" than the "modern" movement – it can be hard to define. Its often uncompromising style can make it hard to access and its bold use of color and material can seem to be more at home in a gallery or museum than in a domestic setting. It is generally applied to pieces that were produced by designers working after the Modern movement (making them "postmodern") and therein lies the problem; when does the Modern movement end and where does Postmodernism begin? The answer isn't obvious, as the postmodern movement is a generalized style of pieces made by a disparate group of designers.

Postmodernism brought an abrupt halt to the idea that a style emerges organically, as had been the case in the past. Instead designers deliberately sought something totally new, perhaps intentionally shocking, and avant-garde. Above all, they pioneered the idea of art over functionality. Integral to the idea of shock and invention, postmodern designers (often out of irony) heavily referenced historical forms or decorations, but used these references in quirky or wholly new ways.

POSTMODERN ORIGINS

Amongst the first proponents of Postmodernism was the American architect, Robert Venturi (b.1925), who advocated as early as 1966 an approach to design in which various hybrid elements combined to produce designs that were somehow "distorted" or "ambigious" – challenging the accepted norm.

In post-war Italy a sense of renewal was apparent in all parts of society, along with a desire for change.

▲ Steel cocktail table by Paul Evans
The base of this table is made from steel, which has been sculpted and painted. Paul Evans experimented frequently with color in his work, typically painting metal surfaces. This was a technique he had employed during his partnership with Phillip Lloyd Powell in the 1950s and early 1960s. In this example, the metal base supports a plate glass top.
(1973; ht 91.5cm/36in; value L)

► Wendell Castle three-legged corner vanity
Typical of the furniture designed by Wendell Castle during the late 1980s and 1990s, this corner vanity is made from expensive materials, including exotic hardwoods and bird's-eye maple veneer, and is of exaggerated angular form.
(c.1992; h 137cm/54in; value !)

Architects and designers like Gio Ponti (1891–1979) stepped into the void to bring new forms in built and interior architecture. Furniture that Ponti made in collaboration with Piero Fornasetti (1913–1988) is an early manifestation of the ideas behind postmodernism, as is his "Billia" lamp of 1931. Formed as a globe atop a cone, if colored differently, this could have been a 1980s Memphis design. The collaboration with Fornasetti was an important one and many of the their pieces make statements that are often seen in later, more radical ideas.

EUROPE

Although these early pieces are often classed as "pre" Postmodern, the movement itself began later with the establishment of Studio Alchimia in Milan, in 1976, founded by Alessandro Guerriero (b. 1943). Seeking to "produce a new emotional and sensual relationship between the user and the object," concerns with utility and or mass production were ignored. These were pieces made for a few or nobody! Typical of this approach, the Alchimia group took everyday objects and turned them into "golden" objects of design. In doing so they often rendered them useless, but this was not always the point.

Classic design pieces by the great leaders of the modern moment were transformed in the same way. In 1981, Studio Alchimia launched its collection entitled: "I mobili infiniti" (unfinished furniture). Over 30 artists, architects, and designers collaborated on individual parts such as handles, legs, and so on, which could be applied using magnets to create an intentionally discordant look.

The previous year, an important figure, Ettore Sottsass (1917–2007), left the Alchimia studio and

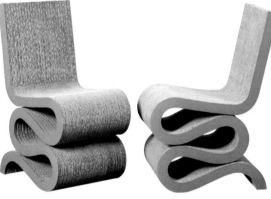

▲ "Wiggle" chairs by Frank Gehry
These chairs were designed by American architect Frank Gehry, in response to the greater awareness of environmental issues that arose in the 1970s. Made from multiple layers of bonded corrugated cardboard, and finished at the edges with brown hardboard, the "Wiggle" chairs are one of several furniture designs in the "Easy Edges" series, which also comprised a table and armchair. Originally intended to be affordable to a large number of people, the range was priced at $35–100 when introduced.
(c.1972; ht 85cm/33⅓in; value F)

◄ "Queen Anne" chair by Robert Venturi
This is one of nine postmodern designs for Knoll International. Typical Queen Anne features have been simplified and literally "flattened" in this molded plywood interpretation of the historial style. Other designs include a Sheraton chair and Chippendale chair.
(c.1984; h 61/24in; value N)

▲ **"Biedermeier" sofa by Ettore Sottsass**
Founding member of the Memphis Group, Ettore Sottsass was at the leading edge of the Postmodern movement. In name, as well as in execution, this sofa is an archetypal example of Sottsass' design. The overall styling is reminiscent of the Biedermeier furniture of the early 19th century, and there are other borrowed historical elements, including the raised "plinth" and the "marbled" columns that recall ancient Classical architecture. Many postmodern designers also used plastic laminates to great effect, using patterned examples as well as those in bright, often clashing, colors.
(1983; ht 137cm/54in; value **K***)*

established the Memphis Group. Sottsass had a long association with design, but Memphis was something of a revolution, perhaps more like a revolt.

The Memphis group designed furniture and objects using bright colors that concealed cheap materials such as MDF or plastic. Objects were designed to look like toys or skyscrapers. Considered by the group themselves to be a fashion, there was always something of the "emperors new clothes" about Memphis and, by 1988, the fad was over. Pieces look very dated today but the group had great influence on many designers, such as Philippe Starck and Jasper Morrison. Several members of the Memphis group, such as Sottsass and Michele de Lucchi (b. 1951), established their own studios.

In Britain and America, revived interest in the 19th century brought about the Crafts Revival Movement. Such furniture designers as John Makepeace (b.1939) returned to an emphasis on craftsmanship, fine materials, and the one-off or limited production of beautiful, exclusive furniture designed to last. He established his first workshop in 1961, where he produced his own work as well as designing pieces for retailers such as Liberty and Heal's.

THE UNITED STATES

Postmodern furniture emerged differently in the USA, where there were no large groups like Memphis or Alchima. Instead many individual designers worked in a style that can be termed "postmodern." Sometimes this look is called "Art Furniture" in the USA. This is an important distinction. Many designers working after World War II sought to make exclusive pieces that fused, traditional "art" techniques, such as sculpture, with ones more normally associated with furniture.

Paul Evans (1931–1987) is typical of this American synthesis of furniture and art. Trained as a silversmith at The Cranbrook Academy, Michigan, Evans opened a shop in 1951 with his then partner Phillip Lloyd Powell (1919–2008) in New Hope, Pennsylvania, an established artistic colony. Evans and Powell produced unique pieces, often fusing disparate materials like stone, wood, glass, and metal together. The inclusion of silver or gold into pieces is not unusual. Doors are formed as sculptures or with found objects, such as paintings. Color is frequently employed: a piece may be painted bright red inside or the metal work is colored. From the mid-sixties the partnership was over, and Evans went on to work for furniture company Directional, for whom he designed one-of-a-kind pieces as well as production lines.

Inspired by both John Makepeace and the Memphis Group, Wendell Castle is best known for his work from the mid-1980s to the 1990s. Borrowing richly from the past, his designs focus on color and form over function. Pieces often have a sculptural quality and can be loaded with symbolism.

▲ **"First" stools by Michele de Lucchi**
Michele de Lucchi first designed these in 1983, while working with the Memphis design group. They epitomize the group's desire for the aesthetic appeal of its furntiure, at the expense of functionality. The spherical armrests intentionally make the stool uncomfortable to sit on, as do the small back and flat seat. The stools are more a work of art – sculpture – than a piece of furniture.
(1992; ht 62cm/24½in; value **D***)*

▶ **"Palladian" demi-lune chest by Piero Fornasetti**
Borrowing motifs from classical Italy, Piero Fornasetti's three-drawer demi-lune chest is typical of his work. He is well known for decorating pieces of furniture by applying his own printed designs. Here he uses a black and white print of a typically Palladian building to embellish the front of this classical form. The piece is in keeping with a number of items that Fornasetti collaborated on with Gio Ponti. Typically, the two designers explored new ways of presenting traditional furniture forms, as here, primarily by applying engravings or trompe l'oeil designs that confused the perspective of a piece.
(1950s; ht 101.5cm/40in; value **I***)*

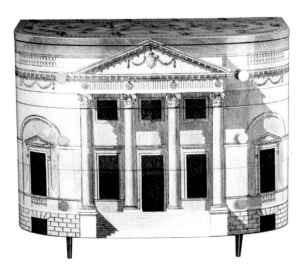

KEY FACTS

- MATERIALS preference for cheap materials, plastics and laminates; found objects; laminated wood; painted metal
- DESIGN witty, often ironic inclusion of elements from historical styles; focus on aesthetic appeal over function

Marks
Fornasetti: pieces are marked with a label; Studio Alchima and Memphis: usually well labeled and bear reference to the collection/exhibition; Memphis: pieces bear label and designer names; Paul Evans: usually signed pieces, often on metal parts; Wendell Castle: pieces usually signed.

See also Mid-century Modern: Furniture, pp.448–451; Postmodernism: Furniture – New technology, pp. 468–9

New technology

It may seem surprising that so many designers seeking a new and Postmodern aesthetic chose to use "old" materials like wood so often. Apart from any considerations of style, wood was often the only choice, as technology had not yet caught up with designers' visions. This began to change in the 1970s and by the 1980s plastics had come to the fore.

The new possibilities created by plastics, foams, and other modern materials were explored by Turin-based

◀ **Gufram "cactus" hallstand**

Guido Drocco and Franco Meilo designed this outlandish coatstand for Gufram, made from green polyurethane. Gufram were at the forefront of innovation when it came to using the exciting plastics that became available from the early 1970s onward.

(*c.1972; ht 166.5cm/66½in; value* **G**)

firm Gufram (est. 1952). Its "Multiples" series was launched in 1967 as a series of objects designed by a number of artists. Using new molding techniques and polyurethane foam they produced extraordinary creations that shared the uncompromising spirit of Postmodernism, before the name was applied to furniture. A series of "seats" formed as "stones" designed by Piero Gilardi launched the range which was produced in limited editions. "Pratone" was perhaps the most daring design. A seating unit formed as blades of grass, it was introduced in 1971, the same year as "Bocca," a sofa formed as a pair of red lips, inspired by Salvador Dali's portrait of Mae West.

Foremost among the later designers choosing plastic was the French designer, Philippe Starck (b.1949). After studying design, he established his own company, in 1968, that produced inflatable furniture. In 1969 he became design director of Pierre Cardin, followed by a spell in the USA. Returning to France, he set up "Stark Product" in 1979. He soon became renowned for his furniture designs, following a commission for President Mitterand's private apartment in the Elysée Palace, 1982.

Starck is strongly associated with a "total design" look, often taking on projects in which he has complete control, such as hotels and restaurants. These projects often result in many pieces of furniture made for sale. Unlike others working at this period, Starck saw nothing wrong with mass production or mass appeal.

This is one of the reasons that he made extensive use of plastic in designs ranging from toothbrushes to furniture. His "Louis Ghost" chair (2002) has become a classic of the 21st century. Also notable are his "Super Glob" and "Louis 20" chairs, which are practical – they

are portable and stackable, can be used both inside and outside, and come with or without arms, as well as environmentally friendly – the aluminum rear legs unscrew from the polypropylene body so that the parts can be recycled.

METALS

The 1980 oil crisis and economic recession had sparked a trend in furniture made from recycled metal objects. In Britain the Israeli-born Ron Arad (b.1951) used recycled salvage to make such limited-production pieces as the "Rover" seat and the "Big Easy Volume 2" chair, in his London design workshop One Off Ltd (est. 1981). Arad moved onto more exclusive furniture, producing pieces in heavily polished metal, that if touched or even sat in, would be changed.

Equally exclusive is the one-off and limited-edition furniture designed by André Dubreuil (b.1951) – also based in London – notably his "Spine" chair (1988), which was made of bent and welded mild steel.

Marc Newson (born 1963) came to prominence with his iconic "Lockheed Lounge" chair of 1986. Made from aluminum panels over a fiberglass shell, it owed some inspiration to both Starck (the three legs) and Arad (use of metal). Following this early success, Newson spent the next few years eking out an existence and designing prototypes until 1989 when he moved to Tokyo to work for Teruo Kurosaki. Newson established his own studio in Paris in 1992, settling in London in 1997.

Another notable London designer is the self-taught Tom Dixon (b.1959). An art school drop out, Dixon fell into design after a motorcycle accident. Teaching himself welding he designed pieces often made from found scrap metals. His growing reputation brought him to the attention of Italian furniture makers Cappellini in 1989, for whom he produced his celebrated "S" chair; it featured a welded steel frame topped with either wicker, raffia, latex rubber, or fabric upholstery, and his "Pylon" chair of 1992. From 1994 Dixon turned his attention to plastics, looking at new methods of molding, and set up his own company "Eurolounge" to produce his own designs. One of the first products was his "Jack" light, a large "sitting, stacking lighting thing" designed as a furnishing feature light.

The American-born designer Danny Lane (b.1955) combines glass and metal in his designs, which are made at his studio (est. 1983) in London. Trained as a painter, Lane mixes a range of materials to produce pieces that blur the distinction between art and design. A more classic combination of metal and glass is the "Nomos" table that was designed by the architect Norman Foster (b.1935) in 1986 as part of a complete office furniture system. Pared-down, modernist metal design was also popular in Japan in the 1980s; the designer Shiro Kuramata

▶ **"W-W" stool by Philippe Starck**

Designed for a fantasy office environment for the German film director, Wim Wenders, Starck's sculptural, sand-blasted and lacquered aluminum stool champions the aesthetic value of a piece over its function. The design is such, that it can be used for sitting on, but also as a support when standing.

(*c.1990; ht 98cm/38½in; value* **H**)

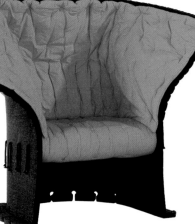

▲ **"I Feltri" armchair**

Designed by Gaetano Pesce for Cassina, this sculptural chair is made entirely of a thick, resin-infused wool felt over a plastic frame, and tied with string laces. Described by Pesce as an "object of uncertain form" the chair has a metamorphic quality, and molds to the body of the sitter. The back of the chair can be raised to full height, as shown, or folded down to provide armrests, depending on the preference of the user. Principally an architect, Pesce is highly regarded as one of the most innovative and unconventional designers of the period.

(*c.1987; ht 122cm/48in; value* **G**)

▲ **Laminated-wood folding screen by Piero Fornasetti**
Fornasetti's delightful folding screen is printed to depict the
open trumeau of a sporting gentleman.
(1950s; ht 200cm/78¾in; value Q)

(1934–91) used nickel-plated wire mesh to create "How
High the Moon," a glittering, airy chair designed for the
Vitra Edition collection and made as a limited edition
from 1986 by the Swiss firm of Vitra GmbH (est. 1934).

ARCHITECT DESIGNERS
Keeping the tradition of architects producing mold-
breaking furniture is Iranian born, London-based Zaha
Hadid (b.1950). Her uncompromising, curvilinear
architectural style was realized in a furniture collection
launched in 2006. Her painted polyester-resin pieces look

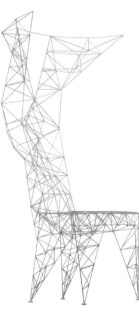

◄ **"Pylon" chair by
Tom Dixon**
As the name suggests,
the design of this chair
was inspired by electricity
pylons. In keeping with
Dixon's early work, each
chair is made by hand,
each joint welded in
turn, resulting in a
unique piece each time.
*(1992; ht 128cm/50¼in;
value H)*

▶ **Chair sculpture by Pedro Friedeberg**
This is one of a number of "Butterfly" chairs created by Pedro
Friedeberg, and is perhaps more a piece of sculpture than a
furniture form. Ornately decorated, carved-wood pieces are
typical of Friedeberg's work, as are the use of human forms
and partial application of gold leaf.
(c.1960s; ht 85cm/33.5in; value L)

more "alien" and sculptural. Produced in small limited
number of between six and twelve these expensive items
may well become modern classics of the 21st century.

Also emerging from architecture, Michael Graves
(born 1934) is one of America's most influential
designers. Post graduation, Graves worked initially for
the veritable firm of George Nelson Associates, but left
in 1960 to study in Rome for two years. Returning to
the USA, he established his own architecture studio
and began to move away from the Modernist style.

From 1979 –81 Graves designed furniture for
Sunnar Hauserman Inc. and from 1981 he was
associated with the Memphis Group. He
produced a number of important designs for
Italian firm Alessi (founded 1921).

WOOD
Postmodern designers sought new ways to
use wood, among them Pedro Friedeberg.
Born in 1937 to German Jewish parents,
his family fled to Mexico in 1940. A painter
and architect his early influences were from
the Dada movement as well as the Mexican group "Los
Hartos" (the fed up) of which he was a member. He
began to make furniture in 1961, which does not fit
easily into any European or American styles.

His first chair is typical of his uncompromising style.
An oversized, upturned open hand, carved from Mexican
mahogany, is raised on a conical base. At first – and this
is intentional – it is not apparently a chair, it could be
seen as a pure sculpture, the gilded surface adding to the
inferred misconception. Friedeberg further developed this
model, raising it on a human foot and soon produced
tables, whose glass tops were raised on hands or legs or
hands with legs, the fingers often grasping and holding
the glass in place. Continuing to play with form and
function, he designed, slightly later, the "Butterfly" chair,
of which he made several. The "seat" was formed from
one solid piece of carved wood in two planes, which,
when painted by Friedeberg appears to be formed as two
butterflies. The chair is raised on "human" legs and has
"arms" for antennae. The bright colors and gilding are
inspired by Mexican folk art.

▲ **"Plaza" dressing table, by
Michael Graves**
Graves designed this dressing
table while part of the Memphis
group in the early 1980s. The
piece borrows a number of
architectural elements, and
include a pediment, which
appeared on a good many
Postmodern buildings during this
era. True to the Memphis code,
Graves' dressing table is finished
colorfully and "cheaply" in
plastic-laminated wood.
(1981; ht 226cm/89in; value O)

KEY FACTS
- CONDITION; good, original condition is vital: plastic
  and laminates are often very hard to restore, so avoid
  pieces with deep scratches or cracks, or missing
  sections, or those that have faded in the sun
- COLLECTING; one-off pieces or prototypes by major
  designers are typically the most valuable, but some
  designers produced designs for more affordable, often
  limited edition, production ranges such as Gaetano
  Pesce's "Fish Design" range of homewares

Marks
Most pieces tend to bear a combination of marks, often a
designer, maker or model number, or name; with all or
some of this information it is almost always possible to
identify pieces
Pedro Freidberg signed his pieces, either with a painted
signature or "branded" into the wood. Decorative
miniature versions of certain pieces were also made
and are more affordable

See also Mid-century Modern: Furniture, pp.448–451; Postmodernism: Furniture, pp.466–7

Jewelry

From the 1960s, jewelry was no longer identified predominantly with wealth and status – and a new breed of young designer-craftworkers experimented with inexpensive synthetic materials, such as plastic, to create extreme, sculpture-like designs that questioned the traditional role of jewelry.

THE 1970S

Many young, art-school-trained jewelers now explored new combinations of materials and forms. In Britain Susanna Heron (b.1949) combined silver and acrylic to produce jewelry in figurative and abstract designs. By 1976, she was producing acrylic and Perspex bangles. Wendy Ramshaw (b.1939) and David Watkins (b.1940) experimented with a range of paper jewelry, sold flat-packed for self-assembly. Ramshaw also designed her now highly celebrated ring sets, in which rings of precious metal, set with polished stones on upright spikes, could either be worn in different combinations or displayed as sculptures on stands.

Dutch jeweler and product designer Gijs Bakker (b. 1942) began his career in the 1960s, aiming to make jewelry equal to other disciplines in the fine arts so that it was seen as something more than simply decorative. He went on to use industrial materials in his jewelry in an aim to undermine the traditional concept that jewelry is an ornament or precious object.

THE 1980S AND 1990S

By the 1980s, the whole concept of jewelry had been pushed to its limits. Broadhead and Heron had moved into "wearables," which blurred the distinction between textiles, sculpture, and jewelry. Pierre Degen (b.1947), who trained in Switzerland but works in London, also looked at jewelry as something that could transform a whole body, and as a means of commenting on society. He used non-precious materials to make jewelry and sculptural forms. Another Swiss-trained craftsman who

▼ **Sun Wheel necklace by Bernhard Schobinger**
Schobinger often juxtaposes found objects with materials associated with traditional jewelry-making, as in this stone and gold piece.
*(1987; diam. 23cm/9in; value **M**)*

► **"Pebble" necklace by Paul Derrez**
This necklace comprises twenty smooth oval pebbles fashioned from cork – identical in size and shape – and secured with thin red yarn. Derrez' jewelry involves a range of media; he works primarily with silver but has also used other metals, such as aluminum and steel, and plastics.
*(1985; w. 4cm/1½in; value **??**)*

saw his work in this light is Bernhard Schobinger (b.1946). He used cast offs, including bottlenecks, saw blades, and nails to create works inspired by youth movements such as punk. These may be combined with gold and precious stones to create memorable pieces.

Traditional metals such as gold and silver were still used by such distinguished jewelers as the Japanese designer Yasuki Hiramatsu (b.1926), but in new abstract forms. Hiramatsu's work is characterized by textured, matt surfaces and is highly sculptural and minimalist. Similarly German Otto Künzli (b. 1948) made minimal pieces from precious metals which are noted for their meticulous craftsmanship and consideration of the materials' potential as well as making challenging and provocative comments on contemporary culture.

Many of these new jewelers saw their work promoted through new specialist galleries, often started by fellow craftsmen. One such jeweler-turned-gallery owner is Paul Derrez (b.1950) who trained as a goldsmith. While he mostly works in silver, he has also used aluminum, steel, and plastics.

In contrast, jewelry makers such as American Jan Yager (b.1951) have been inspired by, and have used, found or recycled objects to make jewelry that is more political statement than adornment. Yager's "City Flora"/"City Flotsam" series used discarded items from the streets near her studio (eg; pen tops or used syringes) or plants growing in an abandoned lot nearby (clover, grasses, and chicory).

▼ **A 24-carat gold, epoxy resin and gold leaf bangle by Professor Yasuki Hiramatsu**
Hiramatsu's work is characterized by an interest in reinterpreting traditional metalworking techniques. His simple, often minimalist, forms are an exploration of shape and texture
*(c.2000; diam. 6.5cm/2½in; value **I**)*

KEY FACTS

- **MATERIALS** new materials used in jewelry design include acrylic, non-precious metals, and textiles
- **CONDITION** very good condition is important
- **COLLECTING** value is based on design and the quality of craftsmanship rather than expensive materials; 1960s and 1970s jewelry is increasingly sought after; Look for examples from iconic ranges which sum up their time or the work of their maker.

Marks
Most designer jewelry is marked or signed.

See also Jewelry, pp.260–72; Art Nouveau: Jewelry, pp.406–7; Art Deco: Jewelry, pp.438–9; Mid-century Modern: Jewelry, p.452

Lighting

The revolution inspired by the Pop Art movement continued into the 1970s, as everyday objects were scrutinized and then enlarged to over-sized proportions. Gaetano Pesce's 1970 "Moloch" floor lamp was a giant version of the best-selling "Luxo" or "Anglepoise" desk lamp, but the room-filling design would never fit on a desk. Similarly, "Pillola" by Cesare Casati and Emanuele Ponzio was a run of gigantic, brightly-colored pill

▼ "Pillola" floor lamp set

Designed by Cesare Casati and Emanuele Ponzio, and produced by Ponteur, this set of five huge "pill capsules" embraces the malleabilty of the new plastics that became popular during the Pop era. Each lamp is a different color, with its own bulb, and can be moved independently. *(1968; h 55.5cm/21½in; value I)*

capsules. Equally distinctive is the lighting designed by the Italian architect-designer Ettore Sottsass (1917-2007). He used the wood substitute MDF together with laminates to create the "Svincola" lamp, produced by Alchimia (est. 1976). Expensive and exclusive, the lamp is 2.5m (8ft 2in) tall and is lit by pink and blue fluorescent bulbs, each 0.7m (2ft 3½in) long. Although sought after as a superb example of Alchimia's witty, anarchic designs, size and the scarcity of replacement bulbs make this a piece for committed collectors only.

THE 1970S

While the lighting designers of the 1960s found plastic to be a malleable material to work with, the oil crisis of the early 1970s pushed the price of plastic up to prohibitive levels. Designers returned to a more rational style of design – known as High-Tech – as a new, more staid approach emerged. Italian designer Gino Sarfatti (b.1912), who set up his own company Arteluce (est. 1939), ensured that his lighting fixtures attracted attention in the same way as an unusual sculpture. His "NR 607 Halogen Lamp" of 1971 was the

► "Dalu" table-lamps by Vico Magistretti

Originally designed for Artemide in the 1960s, these lamps are still in production today. Like Verner Panton's stacking chair, these lamps were revolutionary for their time, as they were one of the earliest continuous forms to be made from plastic. *(1970s; ht 26.5cm/10½in; value B)*

► "Treetops" lamp, designed by Ettore Sottsass for Memphis

Many of Sottsass' designs were synonymous with the postmodern era, and so have become sought after by collectors. Typical features include the bold colors, the use of geometric forms, and the whimsical nature of the design. The handle on the side featured in several Sottsass pieces. *(1981; ht 31.5cm/71½in; value F)*

▼ Table-lamp by Garry Knox Bennet

Knox Bennett's work embodies the 1990's rebellion against the consumerism that had defined the 1980s. This table lamp, composed of what appear to be "found objects" has a burl wood base, gold-painted metal arm and, painted parchment shade. *(1995; ht 43cm/17in; value E)*

first to use halogen bulbs and was typical of the High-Tech movement. In the late 1970s a new, more abrasive generation of designers, including Gaetano Pesce, Alessandro Mendini, and Michele De Lucchi produced lights that defied convention. Lamps looked more like artists' sketches as these designers used a motley collection of materials and loud, discordant colors.

THE 1980S AND 1990S

In the 1980s, lighting became more playful as consumer confidence returned, though in contrast to the fun-loving products of the 1960s, pieces were now more cerebral in design. Lights – often made of recycled materials – resembled sculptures that just happened to have a bulb or two attached. The "A Nite On Lindquist Ridge Table Lamp" by Gary Knox Bennett of California, was constructed with stovepipe housing with five flexible black-and-white shaft fixtures and characterized the salvage look. German designer Ingo Maurer works with both cutting edge and primitive materials. Having set up Studio M in 1966, Maurer has created many innovative designs.

In Britain the rebirth of the designer-craftworker resulted in a return to handmade pieces. Tom Dixon (b.1959) works in metal from his own London studio, and produces one-off and limited-production ranges of highly individualistic lights. Dixon's designs make highly effective use of the light emitted by the bulb, and also the reflections.

As research in the 1990s showed that lighting could affect people's mood, productivity and eyesight, design became a more serious subject. While Droog, the Dutch design collective, produced inventive and amusing lighting, the fantastical designs of the 1970s and 1980s were becoming things of the past. However, the "85 Lamp Chandelier" (1993), designed by Rody Graumans for the Dutch The Product Matters Company, cleverly combined simple individual light bulbs on wires to give a dramatic and opulent effect . The "Italian wireless WL01C table lamp," designed by Andrea Branzi and distributed by Design Gallery Milan, was battery powered; the main body of the lamp could be opened to reveal a rice-paper shade.

KEY FACTS

- DESIGNS collectors tend to collect designs by a known designer or company. Pieces made in the style of, but not by, the big names can represent value for money if they are well made.
- CONDITION: if replacement bulbs for a lamp are hard to come by this may affect price – and the chances of using the lamp.
- COLLECTING look for pieces typical of the era. Popular designs by well-known designers are usually more common than rarer pieces by big names. However, while some rare pieces are valuable, designs that are less typical of any given style will generally be less desirable.

See also Glass: Lighting, pp.306–7; Mid-century Modern: Lighting, p.453

Domestic wares

In the 19th century, William Morris advocated good design for all, but in effect much of what he and his followers produced was too expensive for anyone but the rich. During the 20th century, manufacturing began to change that. In the 1950s and 1960s, particularly in the USA, rising prosperity and the rise in consumerism meant that good design was beginning to be available to all.

Another difference is that manufacturers began to realize that well-designed and targeted products sold, so many designers turned their attention to smaller objects in everyday use. The rise of electronic goods created a whole new field to be "made over."

▲ "Bubble sculpture"
Indicative of this era was the emergence of easily affordable designs whose purpose was purely decorative. Pieces like this fun sculpture could be produced cheaply and in large numbers.
(c.1970s; diam. 46cm/18in; value A)

CELEBRITY DESIGNERS

Low-cost materials, such as plastics, together with new techniques and cheaper labor in the Far East meant that, for the first time, product designers could create ephemeral, fashionable pieces. Also new was the idea of marketing that created desire and boosted brands in order to make them global names. Whereas once product designers were anonymous, from the 1980s onward they were heavily marketed and "designer collections" were launched. Individual designers like Philippe Starck and Ettore Sottsass became celebrities.

Typical of this new breed of designers, and strongly associated with product design is Ettore Sottsass (1917–2008), who joined Italian company, Olivetti, in 1959 as a designer in its new electronics section. Unique to his job, however, was that he also fronted a "cultural relations" department, liasing with the management and media, which involved design in all aspects of the company. As well as his "Valentine" typewriter, Sottsass designed the highly successful "Synthesis" range from 1969–73. A range of household and office pieces set out

to bridge the link between work and play – a theme that Sottsass would later explore in his Memphis days – "Synthesis" included everything from coat racks to chairs and ashtrays to desk tidies.

Alessi (founded 1921) was another design-conscious Italian company. Originally makers of handmade home and kitchen goods, machine making was introduced during the era of post-war reconstruction. From 1955, Alessi began to use external designers including Carlo Mazzeri, Luigi Massoni and Anselmo Vitale.

Under Alberto Alessi (b. 1946), during the 1980s, Alessi became the pre-eminent maker of designer domestic wares. Alessi sought to make beautiful pieces that could be used every day, ranging from lavatory brushes to bottle openers to musical kettles. The designs are colorful and often playful.

Stefano Giovannoni (b. 1954) began to work for Alessi in 1989. His "Merdolino" lavatory brush (designed 1993) is typical. Designed as a green "cactus" emerging form a "terracotta" pot (both made of plastic), its cartoon-like design, as well as its humor, were intentional. Even its name (politely "pooh pusher") is part of a whole design ethos.

Many Alessi products of the era became objects of desire to numerous households. By buying one you were making a statement – you had good taste and understood design. Among the "must haves" were the "bird whistle kettle" by Michael Graves, Philippe Stark's "Juicy Salif" lemon squeezer and Alessandro Mendini's (b. 1931) "Anna G" corkscrew from 1994. Graves's kettle has a small bird that whistles when the water boils. Designed in 1985, its still a strong seller. Fusing steel and plastic elements, part Art Deco, part pre-Columbian, part Pop Art, Graves makes an obvious homage to his Memphis Group connections, but in a wholly accessible way.

Stark's "Juicy Salif" of 1990 became a phenomenon and no smart 1990s' home with any design pretensions was without one. The "reamer" is raised on three legs (a typical Stark feature) and looks more like an alien spider from a 1950s' sci-fi than a practical object. Made in aluminum, it looked great, but was somewhat impractical. Despite this, it sold massively and Alessi produced a gold-plated, numbered edition of 10,000 pieces to mark its tenth anniversary. A gray and black version was also made and both of these are highly collectible.

The playfulness of Alessi's products is seen in the work of American designer Peter Shire (b.1947), who has worked across many different media. He is known for his

▲ Olivetti "Synthesis" coat and umbrella stand
This metal and lacquered ABS plastic coat and umbrella stand was designed for Olivetti by Ettore Sottsass. It was one of a range of pieces in the "Synthesis" range that sought to soften the office environment, making it a calm and harmonious place in which to work. The effect was, to some extent achieved by Sottsass's use of warm, soft colors and by the basic shapes of his designs.
(1973; diam. 151cm/59½in; value E)

▶ "Sol" glass fruit bowl, designed by Ettore Sottsass for Memphis
There is no mistaking the work of Ettore Sottsass in this fruit bowl. A typical feature of postmodern design is his whimsical reference to a historic form – in this case the ancient Roman tazza – emphasized by the fact that the piece is made from glass and not stone, as would be the case for an ancient example, so challenging the viewer's preconceived ideas.
(1982; h 26cm/10⅛in; value F)

▲ Swid Powell "Medici" bowl, designed by Ettore Sottsass
A transfer-printed soup bowl, in which three design elements are juxtaposed, each influenced by a different historical style or theme.
(1984; diam. 23.5cm/9¼in; value A)

ceramic teapots, which he began to make in the 1970s. Unlike Alessi's mass-produced pieces, Shires' work, is individual and exclusive. The intersection of shape and form interested Shire, as did color, and his work influenced Ettore Sottsass, who invited him to work for Memphis in the 1980s.

Inspired by Memphis, two American furniture designers Nan Swid and Addie Powell, established New York based "Swid Powell" in 1982. Both had a background in contemporary furniture but saw a need for high-quality, "designer" home wares. The company commissioned pieces in silver, glass and ceramics from leading designers such as Ettore Sottsass, Robert Venturi, Zaha Hadid and Michael Graves. The playfulness of Postmodern design, combined with a more commercial sensibility is typical of Swid Powell's pieces. Among these is Graves's "Little Dripper" ceramic tea and coffee service (1986). Its Art Deco inspiration is typical of Graves, as is his use of color. The cruciform base is colored red to suggest heat and the blue wavy lines hint at the liquid contained within the vessels.

FASHION AND TECHNOLOGY
Fashion began to play a more important element in design, and the most successful companies combined good design with marketing. The first Swatch watches were

launched in 1983 and were a typical designed-led "fashion" item.

Created to recapture the market lost by Swiss manufacturers to the Japanese, as well as to re-popularize the analog watch in an increasingly digital world, "Swatches" were defined by their bold styling and colors as well as heavy marketing, and soon became "must-have" items. Even the name itself – a contraction of "second watch" suggests their ephemeral quality.

The Swatch gained instant worldwide popularity and early models are highly sought by collectors. They suited the faddishness of the 1980s well and fashions such as wearing two Swatches or using one to tie a ponytail became commonplace. Under the direction of their design consultant, Alessandro Mendini, appointed in the mid 1980s, Swatch devised a number of limited editions and other innovations such as the "Pop" Swatch, which could be attached to clothing. They also released artist collections, collaborating with artists such as Keith Haring (1958–1990), which ironically gave heightened status to a once-cheap article.

The fusion of technology and design is most apparent in the products of Apple Inc. (est. 1976) the California-based computer manufacturer. Noted for individuality, their iMac (1998), iPod (2001), and iPhone (2007) were all designed by British-born designer Jonathan Ive (b.1967). Melding Loewian streamlining with the playfulness and color of Sottsass, the iMac computer was revolutionary. Initially produced in white and "Bondi blue," other bright colors were introduced in 1999. The iPod and iPhone took the minimalism further and have become instant design classics.

▼ Alessi "Vaso Viso" ceramic vase, Alessandro Mendini
This huge vase stands at almost a meter (3 feet) tall. Released as a limited edition of just 2,000 pieces, it is very rare.
(2001; h 91cm/35¾in; value H)

◄ Swatch "Cosmesis" wristwatch
Alessandro Mendini designed a number of wristwatches for the company, including "Metroscape" (1990) "Lots of Dots" (1992). All Swatch wristwatches were (and still are) released as one-off limited editions, for that season only.
(c.1990; l. 3.5cm/1½in; value A)

▲ Peter Shire teapot
Possibly best-known for his teapots, Peter Shire produced pieces for both Alessi and Memphis. Not all of his teapots are functional, Shire being interested in challenging traditions in teapot design. The spout on this teapot, for example, is straight-sided, as opposed to the more curved spout associated with easy pouring. The handle, also, defies convention, being a perfect circle and not the usual "D" shape. The teapot is hand-painted in a style vaguely reminiscent of designs from the Art Deco era.
(c.1996; w. 23cm/9in; value D)

KEY FACTS
- **WARES** wide range of household utensils and fashion accessories – kitchenalia, vases, ornaments, picture/mirror frames
- **DESIGN** typically bold and colorful, challenging the function of a piece, defying convention; motifs borrowed from a range of historical styles, including Classical, and Art Deco
- **CONDITION** this is always an important consideration, as many pieces were originally intended for use. Some plastic items can suffer from sun exposure
- **PACKAGING** look out for original packaging on wares like Swatch watches or Alessi pieces; this will increase the value of a piece
- **LIMITED EDITIONS** always collectible and, as many designs were made over a long period, (or are still in production) it is these pieces that will become more collectible
- **DESIGNERS** "Celebrity" branding important: designers associated with numberous pieces, particularly those produced by Alessi and Swatch; with pieces commissioned by Swid Powell, the designer is key to value – the more significant the designer, the greater value a piece will have

Marks
Sottsass' pieces for Oilvetti Synthesis are not signed but marked "Olivetti Synthesis"

See also Mid-century Modern: Domestic wares, pp.454–5

Glass

Much of the glass produced toward the end of the 20th century was influenced by the studio glass movement, championed in the USA by Harvey Littleton (b. 1922), whose father was a leading glass scientist at the Corning Glassworks in New York. In collaboration with Dominick Labino, Littleton organized two glass workshop seminars in 1962, suggesting that "glass should be a medium for the individual artist." Together, they introduced the idea that glass could be melted, worked, and blown by the artist in a studio, rather than demanding the elaborate and costly equipment and disciplined production process that was standard in the glass industry. Their ideas were taken up enthusiastically by a number of artists in the USA, and then in Europe.

THE UNITED STATES

Working in the studio glass tradition, Dale Chihuly (b.1941) is probably the best-known glass artist working today. He spent time at the Venini Glassworks in Murano in 1968 and, in the 1970s, experimented with folded forms and loops. Chihuly shares Littleton's desire to promote the purely formal aesthetic potential of glass objects and he is also interested in interrelated shapes. He makes groups of basket-like objects, which, although separate, depend on one another for a corporate existence. He has also worked on a series of cylindrical shapes in translucent colored glass with brilliantly colored inlaid woven patterns. These reflect his background as a weaver and are inspired by Navajo textile design. Chihuly's sculptures rely on intense colors and look for inspiration to the natural world, including ocean creatures, trees, and flowers. From the 1990s he has created dramatic large-scale architectural glass installations including three-dimensional chandeliers and wall sconces.

Also working in the United States is Dan Dailey, whose confident and colorful glass compositions combine humor and stellar craftsmanship. He often uses many different glass-making techniques – plate glass, blown glass, engraving, and sandblasting, as well as mixed metal media including aluminum, bronze, or nickel-plated brass, in a single piece – to create highly-polished postmodern pieces. Dailey worked on the refurbishment of the Rainbow Rooms in New York's Rockefeller Center, and has forged a distinguished career as an artist. He is in great demand for commissions.

► **"Face" vase by Eva Englund**
Eva Englund joined Orrefors in the early 1970s and stayed there until 1990, after which she set up her own studio. During her time at Orrefors, Englund created a number of "Face" pieces, including limited-edition vases and plates with her dream-like images captured between the layers of glass.
(1990; h 32cm/13in; value H)

Other American glass-artists on the contemporary scene whose imaginative and highly original works deserve mention include Marvin Lipofsky (b.1938), Joel Philip Myers (b.1934), Tom Patti (b.1943), Mark Peiser (b.1938), and John Kuhn (b.1949).

GERMANY

Germany is perhaps the most important European country recognizing and supporting the art-glass industry. Since the 1960s, Erwin Eisch (b.1927) has been the dominant influence among German glass-artists: more than any other single European glass-artist, Eisch was responsible for pioneering the Studio Glass Movement in Europe. Bursting with both wit and cynicism, his glass vessels tend to be free-blown and embellished with enameled and gilded decoration. He also relies for inspiration on "Pop" culture with a strong leaning toward "Funk."

Another brilliant German glass-artist and technical perfectionist was Klaus Moje (b. 1936), who worked most of his life in Germany until moving to Australia. He was a master of many traditional methods including cutting, polishing, and the firing of painted decoration, and he used these techniques to bring about a variety of aesthetic innovations in glass. His intricately-worked bowls and plates in brilliant or opaque glass have an unrivaled elegance, and with his wife Isgard Moje-Wohlgemuth, he developed a process where the blown glass shape is ground and then painted with metallic oxides fired at high temperatures.

ITALY

On the island of Murano many independent glass artists continuously create works of striking innovation.

Alongside a younger generation of talent stands Toni Zuccheri (b.1937), for whom the animal and vegetable world of nature has for decades been a source of inspiration – in particular his poetic blown glass constructions embellished with bronze, copper, iron, and brass.

Dividing his time between the USA and Murano, Italian-born Lino Tagliapietra (b.1934) continues to be celebrated as one of the most sensitive contemporary interpreters of the expressive potential of blown and wheel-ground glass. His design-driven artistic pieces continue to dazzle and testify to his consummate ability to create complex and imaginative patterns.

▲ **Vase by Toni Zuccheri**
Designed for Murano glass-makers, Barovier & Toso, this vase by Toni Zuccheri takes the form of a stylized flower. In keeping with the postmodern tradition, the form challenges conventions, and has a vertical "cut" from the top edge, the glass peeling away like a petal. Known as the "Spacchi" vase – derived from the Italian verb *spaccare* (to split) – this was a form that Zuccheri experimented with on several occasions. Here, he has used colorless glass with white and dark-violet bands.
(1989; h 32cm/12½in; value G)

▼ **"Hopi" blown glass in blue, by Lino Tagliapietra**
A number of pieces were created by Tagliapietra for his "Hopi" blown-glass series, many in rich, vibrant colors. The artist claims to have taken inspiration from the indigenous art of southwestern America. Prominent features of such pieces are the broad shoulders, and the incredibly fine surface patterning, both reminiscent of Native American textiles, basketry, and ceramics.
(2003; h 38cm/15in; value N)

◄ **"Messager de L'Espace" sculpture by Yan Zoritchak.** Zoritchak is probably best known for the large, sculptural pieces in this series, which translates as "Messenger from Space." Typical features include detailed interior decoration – often conveying scenes of nature – within smooth-surfaced, crystal-clear glass walls. The artist was interested in the potential of the glass to distort what lay within. *(2003; h 46cm/18in; value J)*

Founded in 1859 by Antonio Salviati, the glassworks that bear his name changed the face of Murano as the production center of lavish and expensive glass pieces since the Middle Ages to one that mass-produced high-quality glass for export. Today the company continues to make a wide variety of ornamental glassware and tableware – from cased, colored, and mosaic glassware to enameled and gilded wares.

SCANDINAVIA

At a number of the more sizable glass manufactories in Scandinavia, designers were encouraged to create pieces of art glass that were subsequently issued in small editions. One such example of this practice was Eva Englund at Orrefors during the 1970s, who brought a new concept to art glass by incorporating her dreams into the images captured in the glass forms. Her expressive, eloquent "face vases" brought about a renaissance in the "Graal" technique, whereby multiple-layered cameo glass was encased in clear crystal to produce the effect of paintings within glass.

BRITAIN

The late 1960s witnessed the start of the studio glass movement in Britain, pioneered by American-born Sam Herman (b.1936), who established The Glasshouse, a cooperative with a combined workshop and gallery in London. In an effort to combat the high cost of the equipment needed to set up a glass studio, small workshops were set up with a handful of Herman's

talented students from the Royal College of Art. This venture formed the nucleus of British glass artists throughout the following decade and included now well-established and collectible makers as Annette Meech (b.1948), Pauline Solven (b.1943) and the American-born Steven Newell (b.1948).

CZECH REPUBLIC

René Roubícek (b.1922) and Miluse Roubícková (b.1922) continued to be influential during this period, particularly with their hot-worked forms which were made with similar working practices to studio glassmakers in Europe and the USA. Pavel Hlava (1924-2003) and Jiri Suhájek (b.1943) are also notable in this area. After the "Velvet Revolution" in 1989, many artists increasingly worked both for factories and independently. Jiri Harcuba (b.1928) has remained important for his expressive cut and engraved portraits on vessels and plaques. The use of cut and polished optical glass to produce typically geometric, sculptural forms also grew. Important artists include Václav Cigler (b.1929), Frantisek Vízner (b.1936), and the Slovakian Yan Zoritchak (b. 1944).

► **Periwinkle glass vase by Clare Falkenstein for Salviati glassworks** An organic blue vase form with three opalscent supports. Salviati have worked with a number of the world's leading designers – including Ingo Maurer, Francesco Lucchese, and Tom Dixon – in creating their impressive range of contemporary glass forms. *(1972; h 41cm/16¼in; value G)*

◄ **"Sparklers" by Dan Dailey** This is a two-part blown vase in honey yellow with a sky blue wrap, and with cobalt rim and balls. Characterstic of several Dailey pieces, this vase uses a range of media, including fabricated, patinated nickel, gold-plated bronze, and pâte de verre. *(2003; h 76cm/30in; value P)*

KEY FACTS

- **FORMS** Chihuly: organic, freeform pieces in clear glass or bold colors; large-scale multi-piece forms; Dan Dailey: witty Postmodern pieces; the influence of Pop Art designs for glass continues to attract collectors
- **DECORATION** Dan Dailey: use of other media, including various metals (copper, bronze, aluminum); Eisch: enameling, gilding; Englund: revival of "Graal" technique at Orrefors
- **CONDITION** all one-off studio pieces and limited editions should be in perfect condition if they are to return to, or increase, their value
- **IMPORTANT FIRMS AND MAKERS** studio glass by American glass artists Dale Chihuly, Tom Patti, and Mark Peiser continues to be highly collectible; in Britain The Glasshouse artists; in Europe: Toni Zuccheri and Paolo Martinuzzi (Venice), Frantisek Vízner, Václav Cigler and René Roubicek (Czech Republic), Eva Englund (Sweden) and Oiva Toikka (Finland), and Klaus Moje and Erwin Eisch (Germany)

Marks

Pieces produced at The Glasshouse in Britain by artists including Annette Meech or Pauline Solven should be marked on the base with the maker's name, the number of the piece and "The Glasshouse" and the date. Most other works are signed, but signatures can be hard to read and monograms hard to decipher.

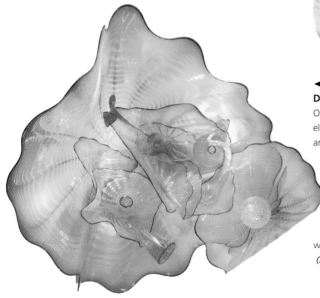

◄ **Orange "Persian" set by Dale Chihuly** Often comprising a number of elements, Chihuly's Persian series arose from his desire to explore new forms. Many of the shapes are of Eastern influence, as is suggested by the name, and make use of the threaded glass techniques Chihuly discovered while working for Venini. *(2001; w. 70cm/27½in; value O)*

See also Mid-century Modern: Glass, pp.456–7

Studio ceramics

For many years the tradition of ceramics in America was essentially a European one – inspired by European styles and forms or produced by European immigrants. This began to change in the late 1930s as a number of studio potters began to develop specifically American styles. Part of the problem was the few colleges and universities that offered ceramics as part of

▲ "Chief Fat Lazy Bullfrog" by David Gilhooly
This two-piece earthenware sculpture, is one of several made by David Gilhooly in the "Frog World" series, which became something of a signature. In fact, Gilhooly "commemorated" the UCD Bicentennial celebrations, in 1975, with a number of large frog busts.
(1976; h 55cm/21½in; value G)

the syllabus. After World War II, however, this began to change, and during the 1950s and 1960s a number of important American studio potters began to emerge, challenging the "craft" status of ceramics.

PETER VOULKOS AND THE "CLAY REVOLUTION"
Some of the first steps in creating a truly American clay aesthetic were taken by Peter Voulkos (1924–2002), who headed the ceramics school of The Los Angeles County Art Institute from 1954. Here, he began to redefine ceramics from craft to high art/sculpture. He was joined by his first student, Paul Soldner (b.1921), who was soon followed by John Mason (b.1921) and Mac McCain (b.1923).

As the new department had few pieces of equipment, Voulkos and his students sought out equipment themselves and soon began to produce work on a "guild" system of collaboration. The early period at the Institute is typified by experimentation. Voulkos and his students explored form and decoration while producing more conventional pieces, such as his "Face" vases, which he would exhibit at the yearly "Californian Design" shows.

At the same time Voulkos challenged convention with

his radical "Rocking Pot" of 1954, in which he broke the "rules" by adding "rockers" made from discarded slabs of clay to a regular vase.

During 1957–58 he began a series of works with which he is strongly associated; his so-called "Stack Pots." Here, he began with a form thrown on a wheel, but this is where any convention stops. Each form was beaten, torn, cut, or ripped and then "forced" together with others to form massive sculptures. Individual pieces were "stacked" together, often dictating themselves how pieces would come out. One such work, the five foot high, "Black Bulerlas," won the Rodin Prize at the first Paris Biennale in 1959.

Despite this growing reputation, Voulkos and his students, free thinking and radical, caused a clash with the administration at the Institute, and Voulkos was dismissed in 1959. Soon after, he was offered a teaching job at Berkeley, where he stayed for almost 30 years.

KEN PRICE
Born in 1935, a generation later than Voulkos, Kenneth Price explored similar themes of form, but in a very different way to his elder peer.

Whereas Voulkos and his students (of which Price was one) looked to redesign pieces by disruption, Price sought to produce more organic, flowing forms, which he calls "Gloops." To achieve the almost unreal finish he desired, Price fired his ceramics, but rather than glazing them, finished them in acrylic paints. These layers of paint are sanded down and layered to create different surface patterns, none of which are achievable with normal glazing techniques. After a number of years spent at Taos, Mexico, he was influenced by Mexican native pottery and, more recently, paints graphic acrylic scenes of American life on simple thrown forms.

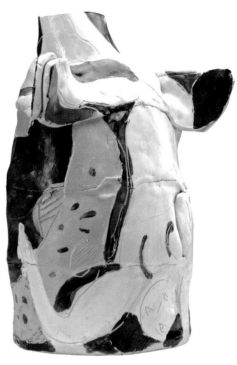

▲ Rudy Autio torso-like sculpture
A porcelain-slab sculpture of a torso, incised and painted with figural decoration, and signed "AUTIO/HKI/81." Autio's torso-like vessels are among the best-known pieces produced by Autio This particular example was made at the Arabia Factory in Helsinki, Finland, where Autio spent some time in 1980/1981, and is accompanied by an original letter from the artist discussing the piece and his great satisfaction with it.
(1981; w. 33.5cm/13¼in; value I)

◄ Peter Voulkos stoneware charger
A Peter Voulkos large stoneware charger, with a gouged and incised surface under a buff glaze. Voulkos and his students sought to explore the nature of clay, and its potential for use. Above all, they regarded clay as a medium that should be used, not simply as a substance for making an object whose clay origins end up being disguised, but for pieces in which the natural qualities of the clay are evident.
(c.1970s; diam. 199cm/78½in; value K)

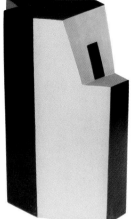

◀ **Ken Price ceramic vessel**
Ken Price is known for his abstract shapes – here in geometric form – but also, later, more organic, free-flowing forms. This ceramic vessel has a small rectangular opening and has been painted, using acrylic paints, in black, light blue, and red. The sculptural quality of the piece is characteristic of numerous ceramics being produced in the USA during the Postmodern era.
*(1980s century; w. 37cm/14½in; value **G**)*

RUDY AUTIO

Born Arne Rudolf Autio to Finnish immigrants, Rudy Autio (1926–2007) spent most of his life in his native Montana. He met his contemporary and life-long friend Peter Voulkos at Montana State, Bozeman, and later established the ceramics faculty at the University of Montana at Missoula, where he taught for over 28 years. He is known for his torso-like vessels painted in a linear style, or in ways that challenge the form and decoration. He had a connection with Finland's Arabia pottery where he worked in 1980/81. His experiences at Arabia, introduced more color into his work.

THE "FUNK" CERAMICS MOVEMENT

The emergent nature of ceramics teaching at colleges and universities is typified by the set-up at the University of California at Davis (UCD). Established as an agricultural college, its art faculty was very much in the background. Spread across a number of temporary buildings, ceramics were taught by Robert Arneson (1930–1992) who came to UCD in 1962.

Influenced by abstract expressionism, Arneson's early work at UCD, like that of Peter Voulkos, attempted to move away from traditional vase forms; after a pot was thrown on the wheel, it would be rolled on the floor, pushed, beaten, changed in some way. This style of working led to his "stoneware trophies," which were his first "Funk" pieces made at UCD. Stoneware required a high temperature firing, which ruled out color. This frustrated Arneson greatly as his wished to use color more. Through experimentation a new white ware body was developed that fired at a low temperature (allowing greater use of color) and dried evenly, which allowed large sculptural pieces to be built in stages.

This new clay mix, developed by Arneson and his student Peter Vandenberge (b.1935), freed Arneson's vision and marked the beginning of "Funk ceramics." Against the tyranny of the vase form, "Funk" potters took pieces from everyday life and recreated them in clay. Cars were a specialty of Margaret Dodd, (b.1941) scenes from everyday American life were recreated by Chris Unterseher (b.1943).

David Gilhooly is another important figure in the "Funk" movement and was, at one time, Robert Arneson's assistant. Exploring the new possibilities allowed by the white clay mix, Gilhooly began to make his well-known "cookie jar" forms from around 1966, as well as his animal forms, both of which were influenced by the Tarzan films of his youth. He is perhaps best known for his important "Frog World" series. Still working on a large scale he produced pieces that were given titles like "Black Doris Day Vegetable Fertility Goddess," a frog-like bust with vegetables emerging from the head and breast.

In 1971 Gilhooly moved to Ontario, teaching part time, and began making vegetable forms, soon adding donuts and pizza, which he would sell from a stall at art shows. He also continued developing his Frog World series, which became ever more playful.

▼ **Rudy Autio sculptural vessel**
Autio is probably best-known for his figurative and sculptural vessels. This example, a table-sized piece in muted colors has a number of features: the two, central flat masks are surrounded by four candles and a bird's head between a flaring bowl rim and foot. The beige clay has a deep iron-red finish and is covered in white, beige, and black matt glazes. The piece is , signed "Autio."
*(c.1970s; h 52cm/20½in; value **K**)*

▼ **Betty Woodman "French Garden" jardinière**
Betty Woodman is known for creating pieces inspired by historical styles. This example is Woodman's interpretation of a jardinière, slab-built and embellished with applied decoration.
*(c.1970s; h 16.5cm/6½in; value **F**)*

KEY FACTS

- **WARES** Peter Voulkos: radical designs, challenging conventional form, large-scale "stacked" pieces; Ken Price: organic flowing forms – "gloops" – often finished in acrylic paint; Rudy Autio: "torso"- shaped vessels, good use of color
- **CONDITION** this is always important, a number of pieces may be more susceptible to damage, particularly those of artists like Ken Price, who used acrylic varnishes, which chip/flake easily
- **COLLECTING** certain artists are associated with a specific style of work, which is often more valuable than atypical work – thus Voulkos's Montana pieces and his less radical work for the California design shows are often underrated compared to his better-known style; pieces from David Gilhooly's Frog World series are particularly sought after
- **PROVENANCE** Voulkos occasionally glued pieces together, with these items the provenance is important

Marks
"Funk" movement: Members of the "Funk" movement usually signed their work. However, many works are not dated and can only be dated to a general period from their style.
Robert Arneson: Some early, pre-UCD, pieces are signed "ARNE."

See also Mid-century modern: Studio ceramics – The United States, pp.462–3

Dolls are among the oldest and most universally popular of toys, being common to civilizations both primitive and modern. To children, they have served as playmates and as preparation for adulthood, through their use in role-playing games and activities such as making clothes. Since the early 20th century, when they were first made, teddy bears and other soft toys have performed a similar function. To adults, the primary appeal of dolls and teddy bears is nostalgic, derived from their link with childhood. However, dolls also provide a record of changing fashions, concepts of beauty and, via dolls' houses, styles of architecture and furnishings. Equally fascinating is the diversity found in the types of doll produced. Notable examples include the early "penny woodens," *Parisiennes* (fashion dolls), "bébés" (idealized young girls), "caricature" dolls (inspired by illustrations from children's books), and "character" dolls based on film stars and cartoon characters (also the source of inspiration for many soft toys). The materials used in toy construction range from carved wood to celluloid and vinyl. These, together with a pronounced degree of articulation, may make a doll or bear attractive to a collector, as may special features, such as the ability to blink, laugh, cry, or speak, or to play a musical instrument.

Selection of dolls, teddy bears, soft toys, and an automaton (left) Among the toys shown here are a bébé, a character dog (Bonzo), a character doll, teddy bears, and an Oriental tea pourer *(late 19th to mid-20th century)*.
Teddy bear by Steiff (above) This teddy is notable for its rounded ears, small, close-set eyes, long arms and feet, and spoon-shaped paws. Steiff bears are very collectible today *(1910)*.

Dolls & Teddy Bears: Basics

Dolls made from a variety of materials have been favorite playthings since ancient times – so popular indeed that makers also designed miniature accessories, wardrobes, and houses for them. In the 16th and 17th centuries wooden dolls carved in the forested areas of Germany and Austria were sold throughout Europe. In the 18th century quality wooden dolls, skilfully carved in detail, then painted and dressed in the latest fashions, were made in Britain. By the late 18th century quality had declined, and British dolls were superseded by German imports and dolls made of wax, papier-mâché (a mix of glue, shredded paper, ashes, and flour), china, parian (a fine, porcelain-like marble), and bisque (a versatile, unglazed, tinted porcelain). German makers led the market until *c*.1860, when the French introduced exquisite bisque fashion dolls and bébé dolls. In the 20th century makers in the USA developed character dolls based on the entertainment industries; mass-marketing and new materials (such as plastic and vinyl) gave rise to popular teenage fashion dolls. It was also in the 20th century that teddy bears, now hugely popular with collectors, were first commercially produced. Soft toy animals stated slightly earlier (*c*.1880) but these are still a relatively new collecting area.

DOLLS: HEADS

Dolls are usually classified according to the material from which the head is made and its construction. There are three main types of head: shoulder heads, swivel heads, and socket heads. On shoulder-headed dolls, the head, neck, and shoulders are molded in one piece and then sewn or glued to a cloth body. Shoulder heads were first used on papier-mâché dolls and were then extended to bisque dolls. The swivel head is a modification of the shoulder head in which the head and shoulders are separate, allowing the head to turn or swivel. The head fits into a small cup, often kid-lined, in the shoulder plate. The socket

► Swivel-headed fashion doll by François Gaultier (active 1860–99)

On swivel heads such as this French example, the head and shoulder plate are made of the same material but are separate. The shoulder plate houses a cup, sometimes lined with kid, into which the head fits, thus allowing it to swivel.

*(1870; ht 41cm/16in; value **G**)*

▼ Socket-headed doll by Kämmer & Reinhardt (1886–c.1940)

This common head is found on most French and German bébés. The base of the neck is rounded so that it fits into a cup shape at the top of the body. This German example features an open crown onto which a pate (or circle) of cork or cardboard is glued; a wig is then attached to the pate.

*(1912; ht 60.5cm/24in; value **F**)*

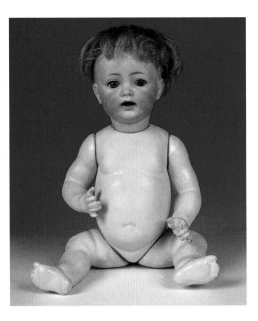

head is a common head type in which the rounded base of the neck fits into a cup shape at the top of the body. The head turns, but there is no separate shoulder plate as in the swivel head. On a reverse-socket head, the neck extends up from the body and fits into a hollow at the base of the head. Bisque-headed dolls usually have an open head in which the open crown is covered with a separate pate (or circle) of cork or cardboard onto which the wig is attached. Some have a solid-domed head onto which the wig is glued or, more rarely, held by string through special holes. Some dolls with soft bodies have flange-neck heads, where the base of the neck flares outward and is pierced on either side, allowing the head to be sewn onto the body.

DOLLS: BODIES

The body, which may not necessarily have been produced by the same manufacturer as the head, is also often of a different material or may be made from a combination of materials. The heads and torsos of early wooden dolls – those produced before *c*.1780 – were usually carved in one piece, with a tapered waist. Upper arms were typically made of cloth, while lower arms were often made of wood and ended in forked hands. Legs were of jointed wood. After *c*.1780 skittle-shaped

torsos were very popular with makers, and these typically featured sloping shoulders, a high bust, and no waist.

The bodies of fashion dolls were shaped to show off stylish costumes to advantage. Their bodies were mostly of gusseted kid with wide shoulders, tapering to a tiny waist before flaring out again into wide hips. Forearms were made of bisque, with wooden tenon joints at the shoulders, elbows, and knees. Although china was used for some early examples, most fashion dolls had bisque shoulder heads, either swiveling or rigid. Early French bébés (child dolls) had shorter, plumper bodies with chubby limbs and slightly protruding stomachs. They had jointed bodies, usually of composition (an inexpensive base material made of a combination of plaster of Paris, cloth, size, wood, glue, and sawdust), and their limbs were connected by means of a ball, which was fixed onto one of the limbs. Ball-jointed bodies – generally associated with bisque-headed dolls – usually have six ball joints, which are sometimes known as "floating-ball" joints. The limbs slide over an independent ball joint that "floats" between them connected only by elastic.

Baby and character dolls made between 1910 and 1939 often had five-piece bent-limb bodies made of composition. This type of body is also found on later plastic dolls. German "toddler" dolls had jointed composition or wood bodies with plump stomachs and accentuated side hip joints. The "Ne Plus Ultra" body, which featured jointed knees and elbows, was patented by the dollmaker Sarah Robinson in 1883 in the USA; unusually the thighs formed an integral part of the doll's torso. This design was superseded by the "Universal" joint, patented in the USA by Charles Fausel in 1895. Used on kid and fabric bodies, this was a three-part joint that allowed dolls' joints to move sideways as well as backward and forward.

◄ Reverse-socket head by British National Dolls

On a reverse-socket doll, as in the British example shown here, the neck forms part of the body and fits into a hole at the bottom of the head. The advantage of this type of head is that the neck join is not obviously visible when the doll is looked at face-on. Reverse-socket heads are a variation on socket heads.

*(c.1950; ht 36cm/14in; value **B**)*

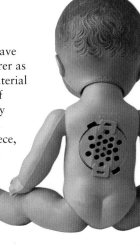

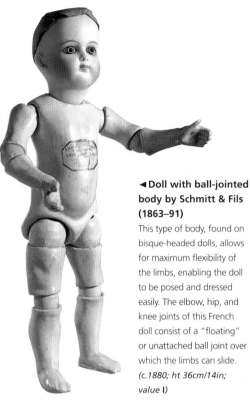

◄ Doll with ball-jointed body by Schmitt & Fils (1863–91)
This type of body, found on bisque-headed dolls, allows for maximum flexibility of the limbs, enabling the doll to be posed and dressed easily. The elbow, hip, and knee joints of this French doll consist of a "floating" or unattached ball joint over which the limbs can slide. *(c.1880; ht 36cm/14in; value I)*

DOLLS: FEATURES

Eyes play a large part in determining the attractiveness of the doll's expression. Painted eyes were used on virtually all types of doll. Intaglio painted eyes are hollowed out of the head and the interior highlighted with white paint. Glass eyes come in several types: fixed glass eyes are found on wooden, wax, china, bisque, and papier-mâché dolls; "paperweight" blown glass eyes – sometimes fashioned as "sleeping" eyes that open and close – are mainly found on French bisque dolls and are so-called because they feature fine white threads of glass running through the iris to create an illusion of extra depth; "flirty" eyes are "sleeping" eyes that also move from side to side. Exaggerated, sideways-glancing "googly" eyes are painted or of glass and are found on 20th-century character dolls.

The mouth is another distinctive feature that adds greatly to a doll's appeal. Most were painted closed until the introduction of the "open–closed" mouths of early bisque dolls, in which the molded mouths appears to be open but in fact has uncut plaster between the lips.

► Doll with shoulder head and "Ne Plus Ultra" body by Kämmer & Reinhardt
This German doll has a kid "Ne Plus Ultra" body, in which the thighs form part of the torso; it also features "Universal" knee joints. The shoulder head has the characteristic glossy sheen associated with celluloid and a wig of real hair. *(1920; ht 46cm/18in; value D)*

Open mouths with teeth – either one or two rows of molded teeth or inserted teeth – were used from c.1890. "Kewpie" and "Googly" dolls had characteristic "watermelon" closed smiling mouths.

Other important features include ears and hair: ears may be carved – as on wooden dolls – molded, or applied separately, and are often pierced. Hair may be painted, molded and painted, applied as a real-hair or mohair wig, inserted and sewn, or, with later 20th-century dolls, synthetic and rooted.

TEDDY BEARS

Teddy bears come in a great variety of shapes, sizes, and colors. The most collectible are those by well-known makers, which can be identified by marks; however, as many bears were unmarked, a knowledge of the distinct characteristics of notable makers is helpful. The shape of the bears and proportions of the limbs are important. Stuffing may be of excelsior (made from fine wood shavings and used in early German bears) or kapok (a soft fiber made from seed pods), which gives a softer, cuddlier bear, or sometimes a mixture of the two. After World War II washable synthetic stuffing was used for many bears. Many pre-1945 bears are made of silk mohair plush in a variety of colors and lengths; after 1945 synthetics in a variety of colors were used. Synthetic stuffing and fabric are less popular with collectors.

Paws are often covered with different material from the rest of the body; their size and shape often help identify the maker. Early bears usually have beige, brown, or cream felt-covered paw pads, and these are typically reinforced with cardboard or fabric. Leather was also used, as were cotton, velveteen, and Wrexine, a type of oilcloth, popular between 1930 and 1950. After c.1950 many bears had synthetic plush paws.

The shape of the head and the size, shape, and position of the ears are also important clues to age and maker. Early bears have hand-stitched noses; the shape and the type of stitching varies. From c.1930 celluloid or sealing-wax noses were typical; after 1950 rubber noses were introduced. Early bears have large, wide-set ears; early (pre-1930) bears by Steiff (est. 1877) have rounded, wide-set ears; early bears by the Ideal Novelty & Toy Co. (est. c.1906) have ears on the side of the head.

Eyes also reflect the age and maker. Early German bears have boot-button eyes made from black plaster or wood, which were attached by wire or stitched; glass (usually amber and black) eyes with wire shanks were also used. From 1955 safer, plastic eyes were common.

▼ Teddy bear by the Ideal Novelty & Toy Co.
Although rarely marked, early American teddy bears by Ideal can be identified by certain distinctive characteristics including the large, rounded ears set wide apart on a triangular face, shorn muzzle, and slightly pointed feet that are shown here. Another clue to this bear's identity is its excelsior-stuffed body, which has disc joints at the neck, hips, and shoulders. The early date and well-known and desirable manufacturer make this bear very collectible. *(1910; ht 60.5cm/24in; value G)*

TIPS FOR COLLECTORS

Dolls
• Dolls should be examined as a whole and undressed, to ensure a correct match between head and body – damaged heads and limbs may have been inappropriately replaced
• Check for original limbs: replacement limbs should be reflected in the price
• Clothes and hairstyles should reflect contemporary fashions at the time of production

Marks
Dolls may be marked with the maker's name, the country of origin, and the mold number; wood, papier-mâché, china, and parian dolls are rarely marked; bisque dolls are usually marked on the back of the head or on the neck; fashion dolls may be branded under the kid on the shoulder or on the back rim of the shoulder plate; cloth dolls will be marked either on the foot or with a textile label

Teddy bears
• Value depends mostly on the age and maker
• Fakes are common: beware of unworn or unrestored "old" bears, with uneven, thickly stitched seams, unworn noses, or old labels on new paw-covering
• Missing fur or ears cannot be replaced; new paw pads are acceptable if properly replaced

Marks
These can be problematic as many marked buttons were removed by safety-conscious parents; embroidered or printed fabric labels may be sewn onto feet or into side seams

Wood and papier-mâché dolls

In Europe during the 16th and 17th centuries crude wooden dolls, known as "babies," were produced on lathes, often by chairmakers, and sold as toys at fairs. Many finely carved wooden dolls were made in Britain in the early 18th century, but quality declined toward the end of the century due to competition from less expensive wooden and papier-mâché German imports. By the 19th century Germany and Austria were the main centers of wooden and papier-mâché doll production.

► Wooden doll

This doll has many of the typical features of early British wooden dolls, including a head and torso carved from a single piece of wood, a tapering waist, and wooden lower arms with forked hands. Also characteristic are its round face, which has been covered in gesso and then painted with pink cheeks, its dark, elongated, enameled glass eyes with no pupils, and its thin eyebrows. Even though one of its arms is missing, such an early doll as this, still in its original clothing and unrestored, is extremely rare and therefore very highly sought after.

(c.1740; ht 36cm/14in; value H)

EARLY WOODEN DOLLS

Those dolls made before *c*.1780 had a very distinctive body shape, and this helps with identification. The head and torso were made in one piece, peg-jointed legs and arms were attached separately, and forked hands were large and carefully carved. The face was round and the neck long and thin. The head was typically covered in gesso and then painted with pink spotlike cheeks, a thin mouth with a rosebud center, and herringbone eyebrows. The eyes had no pupils and were usually of black glass. Hair was real, attached to a cap, and nailed onto the head. Very early dolls (before 1702) may sport fashionable beauty spots and have painted eyes.

LATER WOODEN DOLLS

Dolls produced after *c*.1780 were generally less well made than early dolls and were crudely shaped and carved. Although the head and torso were still carved as one piece, the torso was skittle-shaped, with a high bust, very small waist, and sloping shoulders. Facial features became increasingly crudely carved, with the nose often little more than a small wooden triangle. Eyes were usually close set and sometimes blue with black pupils – unlike the exclusively dark eyes found in early dolls. Cheeks were usually bright red rather than pink, and the hair was sparser and generally attached to the doll in the form of a fringe or a white wig.

▲ "Penny wooden" doll

This crudely carved and painted doll from Grödnertal is just one of the many thousands sold at market stalls and fairs in Europe. Known as "penny woodens" or "Dutch" dolls, they have simple features, black painted hair, and jointed limbs. Paint was applied directly to the wood, but only to visible areas that were not covered by a costume.

(late 19th century; ht 31cm/12in; value A)

▼ Papier-mâché dolls

Although unmarked, these German dolls are easy to identify as they have several features typical of early papier-mâché dolls. An early date, original clothes, and good condition make them desirable.

(both 1840; left: ht 25cm/9¾in; value E; right: ht 46cm/18in; value F)

GRÖDNERTAL DOLLS

Grödnertal dolls – named after the region of Austria where they were first made – were produced in the 18th and 19th centuries as a response to the British demand for more affordable dolls. They came in a variety of sizes, from 2.5cm to 61cm (1in–24in), and were originally inexpensive. The least costly versions had simple wooden peg joints; more sophisticated dolls had ball joints and swivel waists. All Grödnertal dolls featured "spade" hands and narrow, well-defined waists; their faces were gessoed and varnished, which with age gives them a characteristically yellow tinge. Most sought after are the better-quality dolls made before the 1830s, typically with shiny grey- or black-painted hair in elaborate curls with a comb or coronet. Simpler versions were also known as "Dutch" (possibly a corruption of *Deutsch* meaning "German") dolls or "penny woodens," which reflects their cost when they were sold at fairs at the end of the 19th century.

PAPIER-MACHE

Although papier-mâché dolls had been produced by hand in France from the mid-16th century, they became popular as an inexpensive alternative to wood only when mass-produced by the German dollmaker Friedrich Müller in the early 19th century. Müller used molds to mass-produce papier-mâché dolls' heads and was the founder of the Sonneberg doll industry, which exported German papier-mâché heads to Britain, France, and the USA. Most popular with collectors are the so-called "Biedermeier" dolls, made from *c*.1815 to *c*.1848, whose elaborate hairstyles were successfully molded in papier-mâché. Their features were similar to those of wooden dolls, with painted eyes and eyebrows and black molded hair. The papier-mâché shoulder head was glued to a kid body with limbs (usually unjointed) of wood or kid. Hands were typically spoon-shaped with a separate thumb. Papier-mâché dolls can be dated by hairstyle, clothes, and facial features as well as by more easily identifiable details such as flat, painted shoes, which were used on dolls made before 1860, and glass eyes, which were used only after *c*.1870.

KEY FACTS

Wooden dolls
- CONSTRUCTION body shape will help with dating (eg early 17th century, tapered waist; late 17th century, no waist); doll with jointed elbows, hips, and knees and carved fingers and toes is probably of very high quality
- CONDITION excellent condition suggests restoration (visible with an ultraviolet lamp); this may reduce value
- COLLECTING check the provenance: a doll with a known history and/or from an important collection will be more valuable than an undocumented doll; original clothes will greatly add to the value; larger dolls are generally more valuable than small dolls; British wooden dolls made before *c*.1702 are rare and valuable

Papier-mâché dolls
- CONSTRUCTION arms are usually unjointed; bendy wire arms suggest a later date or an addition
- CONDITION a cracked head (common) will reduce value

Poured-wax dolls

Wax dolls probably evolved from the funeral effigies and religious figures made in the Middle Ages. Wax – generally bleached beeswax mixed with red pigment and other additives such as animal fat to resemble human skin – was a costly material, making these dolls expensive and exclusive. Pressed-wax dolls with molded or carved solid wax heads were produced until 1840, when British dollmakers – many of Italian descent – began making poured-wax dolls. This less expensive technique involved pouring molten wax into a mold, allowing the outer crust to harden, and then pouring off the excess and repeating the process until the desired thickness was achieved. The dolls had hollow, wax heads with inserted glass eyes and real hair (also for eyelashes and eyebrows), a cloth body with hollow, wax limbs, and well-defined wax hands and feet. British makers remained at the forefront of production until c.1890, when bisque dolls became more popular.

IMPORTANT MAKERS

The Pierotti family company (c.1780–1930), based in London, made high-quality dolls with characteristically gentle, well-modeled expressions and slightly turned heads with folds and creases in the neck. Henry Pierotti (1809–71) invented the first baby dolls, basing them on the numerous children of Queen Victoria; these dolls were known as "Royal Model Babies." All Pierotti dolls are highly collectible, and although wax dolls are rarely marked, Pierotti dolls sometimes feature the company name scratched on the back of the head.

One of Pierotti's greatest rivals was the London-based company founded in 1849 by another dollmaker of Italian descent, Augusta Montanari (1818–64), who was joined by her son Richard Montanari in 1855. Rarely signed, Montanari dolls can often be identified by their heavy shoulders, chubby limbs, and somewhat petulant expression. They were dressed in highly elaborate costumes, the condition of which plays an important part in their value. A Montanari doll in its original box will now be very valuable. Like Pierotti, Montanari produced a popular range based on Queen Victoria's children, known as "Royal Wax Baby Dolls."

◄ Doll by Montanari
Augusta Montanari ranks alongside the Pierotti family as one of the best-known makers of British poured-wax dolls. The example shown here features the distinctive, petulant Montanari expression, inserted blue glass eyes, and inserted hair. The handmade clothes feature embroidery and conceal the doll's characteristically chubby limbs and slightly heavy shoulders. Few dolls by Montanari are signed.
(1860; ht 51cm/20in; value F)

OTHER MAKERS

Other distinguished and collectible British makers include John Edwards (1831–1907), W.H. Cremer & Son (c.1860–73), Charles A. Marsh (1865–1914), Herbert John Meech (1865–1917), and Lucy Peck (1891–1930), all of whom were based in London. Edwards established a factory c.1868 and produced a huge range of dolls from inexpensive models to royal commissions. As is the case with most poured-wax dolls, those by Edwards are usually unmarked – only one marked example, with the initial "E" on its shoe, is known – but their pale skin tones and detailed modeling may help to distinguish them.

The firm of W.H. Cremer & Son sold imported German dolls from a Bond Street toyshop and acted as agent for such distinguished makers as Pierotti. Cremer also bought wax limbs and heads from which he assembled his own dolls. Cremer dolls usually have the company name stamped on the chest and may also bear the maker's name. Other retailers who stamped their dolls include Hamleys and Aldis. Meech produced fine-quality dolls, including some for the royal family.

▼ Crying doll by John Edwards
This unusual British doll is one of the many poured-wax dolls made in London by Edwards. Its well-molded, expressive face has the detailed modeling and pale skin tones generally associated with this maker, whose dolls are rarely marked. The hair has been inserted with a knife or needle rather than added as a wig. Its rarity, good condition, and original costume contribute significantly to its value.
(c.1880; ht 46cm/18in; value I)

◄ Baby doll by Pierotti
Pierotti is one of the most sought-after British dollmakers, and this poured-wax baby is typical of the firm's high-quality production. The hollow shoulder head is made of several layers of peach-colored wax and is attached to a stuffed cloth body with poured-wax limbs. This doll has the typical Pierotti sweet expression and closed mouth. Other characteristic features are inserted blonde human hair and blue glass eyes. The surface crack on the doll's shoulders can be easily repaired and will not detract much from its value.
(c.1860; ht 51cm/20in; value G)

KEY FACTS

- DESIGNS few dolls are marked (some may have a maker's name stamp on the chest and/or shop or distributor details) so an informed knowledge of famous makers' characteristics is important; most Pierotti dolls have sweet faces with blue eyes, inserted hair, and chubby necks; Montanari dolls typically have plump limbs, heavy shoulders, and a despairing expression; dolls by Edwards can be recognized by their characteristically pale complexions and finely modeled faces
- CONDITION good condition is important as wax is a vulnerable material: check for pale color caused by exposure to light, and malformed limbs damaged as a result of exposure to direct sun or heat; cracks in wax dolls are easy to restore and will not greatly affect price
- COLLECTING the presence and quality of original clothing is crucial in determining value: check for fashions and fabrics contemporaneous with production

Other wax dolls

Dolls made of wax over composition or wax over papier-mâché were mass-produced in Britain, France, and Germany from 1830 to 1890. They were developed as an inexpensive alternative to poured-wax dolls and their variety and affordability make them popular with collectors. The technique consisted of covering a molded core of composition (a mix of cloth, wood, wood pulp, plaster of Paris, glue, and sawdust) or papier-mâché with layers of wax. Heads were more crudely modeled than those made of poured wax, but they were stronger and could support "sleeping" eyes; the main disadvantage of this technique was that it often produced a network of fine lines, or crazing, due to the different rates at which the wax and the composition or papier-mâché expanded and contracted. These dolls divide into three main types: "slit heads," "pumpkin heads," and "wax overs."

SLIT-HEAD DOLLS

Dolls known as slit heads or "Crazy Alices" were made in Britain from 1830 and named after the slit in the crown of the papier-mâché head into which human hair was inserted. The body was made of fabric with kid forearms; the face was crudely modeled with pupil-less glass eyes and a closed mouth. Crazing will not detract from the value of a slit head, as these dolls are early and therefore highly collectible.

PUMPKIN-HEAD DOLLS

Slit heads were gradually replaced by pumpkin-head dolls, which were made in Britain and Germany from c.1860. Their large, hollow, molded, pumpkin-shaped, papier-mâché heads were dipped in wax and then painted; hair was usually molded and painted blond. Pumpkin heads with molded bonnets were known as "bonnet heads" and are especially collectible. These dolls usually have brown eyes, and limbs of turned wood attached to cloth or papier-mâché bodies.

▲ "Slit-head" doll
This British doll has a shoulder head, made of wax over papier-mâché, and a fabric body. Although its features are rather crudely modeled, their wax covering makes them appear softer and more appealing. The crazing on its face and shoulders will not detract from its value; this is based mainly on the fact that it is an early doll, has not been restored, and has an abundant head of hair and original garments.
(1845; ht 46cm/18in; value L)

◀ "Pumpkin-head" and "bonnet-head" dolls
This group of dolls includes a large German pumpkin head at the rear and a German bonnet head directly in front of it. Both have typical molded blond hair, pupil-less brown eyes, and closed mouths. Dolls with blue eyes and open mouths are rare and therefore highly sought after. Only dolls with heads in perfect condition are worth collecting; examples with an elaborate original costume in pristine condition will be considerably more valuable than dolls that are in shabby or restored costumes.
(both c.1860; pumpkin head: ht 66cm/26in; value L; bonnet head: ht 31cm/12in; value L)

WAX-OVER DOLLS

Known as wax overs, wax-over-composition dolls were produced in France and Germany during the 1870s and are more realistically modeled than slit- and pumpkin-head dolls. Wax overs often appear very similar to china and parian dolls of the same period. Most have closed mouths, fixed or sleeping glass eyes, and elaborate, blond, mohair wigs. The shoulder heads were attached to fabric bodies through eyelet holes; the lower limbs were often made of wax over composition. French dolls typically have "paperweight" eyes, whereas German dolls generally have flatter, spun-glass eyes. Some French examples were produced with elaborately molded boots and these are particularly sought after. A charming addition to the range of wax overs was fairies produced as inexpensive decorations for the Christmas trees introduced to Britain by Prince Albert. Many are in good condition because they were brought out only once a year and were then carefully wrapped and stored. They usually have blond mohair wigs and blue glass eyes; later example can distinguished by their deep pink color.

► "Wax-over" doll
This French doll is typical of the more realistically modeled wax-over-composition dolls produced in the late 19th century. It is a particularly fine example and has detailed features, which are more characteristic of those found on china or parian dolls than on wax overs. The blue paperweight eyes are usually found only on valuable bisque dolls. Unusual features are the dark hair – blond was more popular – and the open mouth. The doll's stylish original costume reflects its French origins, as do its (hidden) molded boots.
(c.1870s; ht 36cm/14in; value M)

KEY FACTS

- HEADS slit heads: remaining hair should still be reasonably abundant; crazing will not be detrimental to the value; pumpkin heads: the more elaborate the molded hairstyle and bonnet, the higher the value of the doll; wax overs : good condition of the head is paramount; crazing on the face will detract from value
- CLOTHING colorful and elaborate original clothes in good condition will add to desirability; wax overs: original clothes are essential for maximum value
- CONDITION on all examples, good condition is a must; crazing will detract less from the value of slit heads than of later dolls, especially wax overs
- COLLECTING pumpkin heads: examples with molded bonnets are highly desirable; wax over fairies are especially popular with collectors and are usually preserved in good condition as they were only used at Christmas and then carefully packed away

China and parian dolls

China dolls were first produced by porcelain factories in Thuringia, Germany, and were particularly popular between c.1840 and 1880, when they were superseded by bisque dolls. Although the best-known and most prolific makers were German, the French companies of Maison Huret, Rohmer, and Barrois were also noted for their refined and elegant dolls. Parian dolls were made mostly in Germany between 1870 and 1900 and are characterized by an unglazed matt finish. Both china and parian dolls are extremely fragile and are consequently rare and sought after by collectors. As they were rarely marked, clothes and hairstyles reflecting contemporary fashions will help with dating.

▶ "Highbrow" china doll

This superb-quality German china doll was modeled on, and named after, Empress Eugénie, the wife of Napoleon III. Its finely painted black hair is elaborately styled and decorated with a gold-painted snood and tassels. Its wide, high forehead makes it a highbrow; it also has the finely modeled, delicately painted features associated with top-quality dolls, and an original silk dress. Its value reflects its status as one of the finest of the German china dolls.
(c.1850; ht 38cm/15in; value G)

GERMAN CHINA DOLLS

Early china dolls, known as highbrows, were delicately modeled and featured dark brown or black molded and painted hair set back on the forehead. The shoulder heads were made from glazed, hard-paste porcelain and attached to the fabric or leather body by glue or nails, or stitched through four or, later, two holes. Facial features – rouged cheeks, blue eyes, and a red, rosebud-shaped mouth – were painted on to the doll and fired to prevent chipping. Limbs were also sometimes made from china and legs painted with dainty black boots and fancy garters. Most sought after are the so-called "Biedermeier" china dolls, produced between 1845 and 1860, which have bald heads with a black dot covered with a curled plait of real hair, fine features, and delicately painted faces. Dolls produced by the Berlin porcelain factory (est. 1761) are marked with the company initials and can be dated accurately; most have dark-brown molded hair. Early dolls are highly collectible and typically have flat shoes and a red line above the eye. Dolls made after c.1860 tend to have rounder faces, shorter necks, and short black curly hair with a center parting. Dolls made after c.1880 and known as "lowbrows" because of their low-set short curly hair are less popular.

FRENCH CHINA DOLLS

Although French makers were far less prolific than their German counterparts, the china dolls they produced were generally more refined. Special features included swivel heads, glass or painted eyes, closed, smiling mouths, and exquisite handmade costumes. French china dolls often had real hair wigs, and the painting on the faces was subtle and refined. Well-known and collectible makers include the Paris-based companies of Maison Huret (1850–1920), Madame Marie Antoinette Rohmer (active c.1857–80), and Madame Barrois (active 1844–77).

PARIAN DOLLS

"Parian" was originally a trade name used by the British firm of Copeland (1833–1933), but became the generic name for a fine half-vitreous porcelain, which superficially resembled marble from the Greek island of Paros. Parian dolls were manufactured predominantly in Germany between 1870 and 1900, and have a white, matt, marble-like skin tone. The characteristic shoulder head had molded blond hair, often in an elaborate style, painted blue eyes (brown or glass eyes are rare), and a closed mouth. Molded and painted jewelry, highlighted with luster, was a common feature, and many parian dolls had pierced ears. Hair was sometimes also decorated with luster. The stuffed fabric or kid body may have kid or bisque lower limbs; some examples also have molded boots. Parian dolls are generally unmarked, so clothes and hairstyles will provide the collector with essential dating clues.

◀ Parian doll

This German doll has a delicate, marble-like skin tone typical of parian dolls. Also typical are the closed mouth, blond hair, and elegant, molded, gold-luster boots; the glass eyes, however, are unusual and add to the value. This doll is in perfect, unrestored condition and is wearing its original costume, including the hat (often missing).
(1890; ht 31cm/12in; value F)

▲ China doll by Rohmer

The Paris-based company owned by Madame Rohmer is reputed for its rare, high-quality, china fashion dolls. This fine example features a gusseted kid body with lower forearms made of bisque, a swivel head, and the rounded face with delicate detailing highly characteristic of Rohmer dolls. Its stylish and elaborate original French costume is still in very good condition and this will add considerably to its value.
(c.1860; ht 41cm/16in; value I)

KEY FACTS

- UNUSUAL FEATURES china dolls: desirable features include dark-brown hair in an elaborate style, and glass eyes, especially in brown or grey; rare swivel heads are also highly collectible; parian dolls: dolls with brown glass eyes are rare; look out for dolls with molded ruffled shirts, dress tops, jewelry, and feathers
- CONDITION original clothes will enhance value
- COLLECTING china and parian dolls are rarely marked; clothes, footwear, hairstyles, and jewelry will all help with dating; dolls made before 1880 are more collectible than later dolls; highbrow and Biedermeier china dolls are especially popular, as are parian lady or adult dolls

See also Fashion dolls, pp.486–7

Bisque dolls

In the 1850s German makers produced heads made from bisque, which sold well throughout Europe. Between *c*.1860 and 1890 French makers were pre-eminent, introducing two popular new doll types: fashion dolls and bébés. These elegant, high-quality, exquisitely dressed dolls were intended for the luxury market and were priced accordingly. By the 1890s competition from inexpensive German dolls led a number of French dollmakers to form the Société Française de Fabrication de Bébés et Jouets in 1899, with the aim of competing together against German imports. However, the S.F.B.J. led to a deterioration in quality, and from *c*.1900 to *c*.1930 German makers were again market-leaders, notably with their individualistic bisque character dolls.

France

Fashion dolls

Fashion dolls (or "*Parisiennes*") were produced between *c*.1860 and 1890 in Paris – then the fashion capital of the world. Bisque heads were attached to flexible, elaborately jointed and gusseted, wood or kid bodies, which were designed to show off elaborate costumes to full advantage. The clothes and accessories of these collectible dolls are fundamental to their value: whereas original costumes of early dolls were handmade copies of contemporary couture outfits, after *c*.1880 clothes were factory-made, reflecting a deterioration in quality. Attribution generally has to be based on a good knowledge of the characteristics of different makers, as many dolls were unmarked and heads and bodies were often from different sources. Fashion dolls can be distinguished from bébés by their slender waists.

ROHMER

Among the most sought-after dolls are those made by Madame Marie Antoinette Rohmer, who produced dolls between *c*.1857 and 1880. Her exquisite, high-quality dolls are scarce and usually unmarked; however, they can be identified by their characteristically soulful, expressive, painted (rather than glass) eyes and rounded faces with delicate detail. Heads may be of fixed or swivel design; bodies are usually made of leather, either gusseted at the elbows, hips, and knees, or gusseted at the hips and knees and accompanied by bisque forearms and wood tenon joints at the shoulders. The most valuable Rohmer dolls are those accompanied by their own trunk containing an original handmade wardrobe; this will typically include night attire, slippers, and a grooming kit as well as such luxurious fashion accessories as fur muffs, scarves, gloves, jewelry, parasols, and fans.

► **Doll by Rohmer**
Rohmer fashion dolls are scarce and rarely marked, and the great variety of body types and heads makes identification difficult. Most, however, have a distinctive, characteristically round face, with delicate coloring and detail, and soulful eyes, as typified by this example. Its swivel bisque head and painted eyes add to its value, as does the charming, original, brown-checked costume.
(*c.1865; ht 41cm/16in; value* **H**)

JUMEAU

The firm of Jumeau (1842–99), was founded at Montreuil-sur-Bois by Pierre François Jumeau, whose dolls, like Rohmer's, are noted for their soulful eyes; most Jumeau dolls, however, have large, blue, fixed eyes made of "paperweight" glass, whereas Rohmer dolls have painted eyes. Early Jumeau dolls are marked only with a number; those made after 1875, when Emile Jumeau, the founder's son, took over the company, may feature a red tick mark on the head. Other characteristics that help with identification include swivel heads, applied pierced ears, and a closed mouth. Bodies were typically made of gusseted kid and usually had separate fingers and toes. Jumeau dolls are particularly reputed for their elegant, fashionable costumes, and a surviving doll with an intact, original wardrobe will be extremely collectible.

MAISON HURET

Maison Huret (1850–1920) is most highly famed for the inventiveness of one of its founders, Mademoiselle Calixte Huret, who applied for patents for molded articulated body types in 1850 and a swivel head in 1861. The latter was an immensely popular design with other French fashion dollmakers as it enabled them to produce heads that moved easily and realistically from side to side; in general dolls that have swivel heads are much more valuable and collectible than dolls with rigid heads. Huret dolls often bear a blue company stamp, but they may also be identified by typical body types. Popular combinations include composition with ball-jointed hips and jointed knees, or leather over gutta-percha (a fibrous material typically used to make doll's bodies), wood, or kid. Arms and hands were made of bisque, composition, china, or metal, which is especially rare and highly collectible.

▲ **Doll by Maison Huret**
Madame Huret patented the swivel head in 1861, and this fashion doll, which features an unusual, wooden, spring-jointed body with a swivel waist, is a very early example of its use. The doll's early date is confirmed by its painted eyes, lashes, and brows and its closed, smiling mouth. Its blond mohair wig is attached to the cork pate on the crown of the head used on most early French dolls, and it has pierced ears. Its metal hands are rare – hands made of bisque, composition, or china are more typical – and therefore make this doll particularly valuable.
(*c.1860; ht 46cm/18in; value* **L**)

▶ Doll by François Gaultier

This elegantly clothed doll has a bisque swivel head, kid feet (hidden), and kid hands with separately stitched fingers. Its closed, slightly smiling mouth with a well-defined top lip and its large, piercing eyes are typical features of all Gaultier's dolls (fashion dolls and bébés). It is important that the head and body of a doll should match, as they do in this example, which still has the original, now somewhat faded, pink and green costume. Complete fashion dolls by Gaultier such as this one are usually marked, which should help with identification.
(c.1865; ht 46cm/18in; value I)

GAULTIER

François Gaultier (active 1860–99), who produced dolls for other makers as well as for his own firm (est. 1860 as Gauthier; known as Gaultier, 1875–99), specialized in the manufacture of bisque fashion dolls and bébés. Most of his fashion dolls feature shoulder heads with cork pates, and these were produced with both rigid and swivel heads – the latter inspired by Mademoiselle Huret's innovation of 1861. Gaultier's dolls are characterized by large, piercing eyes, and a closed, slightly smiling mouth with a well-defined upper lip. Body types were varied and included gusseted kid, gutta-percha, and articulated wood or metal padded with kapok and then covered with stockinette. Hands and feet are usually of either bisque or kid – those made in kid are more desirable if the hands have separately stitched fingers and toes than if they have "mitten" hands. Costumes were usually highly decorative and elaborate, in line with contemporary fashions; most dresses featured bustles, which helps to date them to the late 19th century.

Because Gaultier was such a prolific maker, identification of his dolls can be slightly difficult, although it is aided by marks. These are most typically found on the shoulder and/or on the back of the crown on fashion dolls made entirely by Gaultier's own firm. The bisque heads, which he also manufactured for other companies, are generally unmarked except, possibly, for a size identification number.

The Geslend Co. (1860–1915) is often linked with Gaultier as they used many of his mass-produced bisque heads to assemble their own designs; they also used parts produced by Gaultier to repair damaged dolls. One of their most successful lines was dolls with Gaultier heads, who were clothed in French regional dress. These dolls were especially popular as souvenirs for late 19th-century travelers on the Grand Tour.

BRU JEUNE & CIE

Bru Jeune & Cie (1866–83), founded in the Rue St Denis, Paris, by Léon Casimir Bru, and known as Bru Jeune from 1877, was another major manufacturer of French fashion dolls. They introduced several notable novelties into their range of bisque-headed dolls including a crying and laughing/crying doll with a revolving head, designed in 1867, and a smiling doll with a swivel head on a bisque shoulder plate, which was registered in 1873. Bru Jeune dolls are usually smiling, and characteristically have a closed mouth and fixed "paperweight" eyes. Body types include all kid with a square-cut torso and all wood with a swivel waist and joints at wrists, elbows, knees, and hips. Early dolls were sometimes marked "Déposé" and/or "Bru Jne & Cie"; lady dolls or "smilers" may be inscribed with a letter (A–M), which relates to the doll's size.

▼ Doll by Gaultier

The shape of the body can be an invaluable aid in identifying and dating French fashion dolls, especially as many examples are unmarked. This doll was made by Gaultier, one of the leading Parisian manufacturers, who also produced heads for other makers. The exaggeratedly wide shoulders, narrow waist, and generous hips are designed to support the doll's original dress, which was bustled. The combination of gusseted kid body with a swivel bisque head is also highly typical of Gaultier and may help with identification.
(late 19th century; ht 41cm/16in; value H)

▼ Doll by Bru Jeune & Cie

This smiling bridal fashion doll has a swivel head on a bisque shoulder plate. Registered by Bru Jeune in 1873, this type of doll is thought to have been modeled on Empress Eugénie, wife of Napoleon III. Several different body types were used – all were jointed to allow the elaborate costume to be displayed to best advantage. This doll has a gusseted kid body with bisque forearms. It is marked "K" on the shoulder plate and "Déposé K" high on the forehead.
(c.1875; ht 64cm/25in; value K)

KEY FACTS

- COSTUME original, handmade, couture clothes and accessories are essential for maximum value; factory-made clothes of the 1880s are less valuable than earlier, hand-produced clothes
- IDENTIFICATION this can be tricky as many dolls are unmarked; heads and bodies were often produced by different firms, which can also confuse; collectors must build up knowledge of different makers' characteristics
- CONDITION firing defects may reduce value: check for firing lines, raised pink or black spots, and speckling caused by dust in the kiln
- COLLECTING French fashion dolls are valuable and much sought after; rarity will determine value

See also Bébés, pp.448–9

Bébés

Bébés (child dolls) are probably the type of doll most sought after by collectors and early examples in good condition are very valuable. The first bébé doll, made in 1855 by Pierre François Jumeau, was an idealized version of a young girl, with chubby limbs and a rounded stomach, rather than a model of a slim-waisted adult woman like previous dolls. From c.1860 to the 1890s – the golden age of French bébé production – many top-quality, expensive dolls in handmade, fashionable clothes were produced for the luxury market. Early bébés, usually with closed mouths, fixed wrists, and, on the finest examples, pale, flawless, bisque heads, are highly sought after. Later bébés had highly colored bisque heads, open mouths, and articulated wrists. Quality declined after 1899 when the competition from less expensive German dolls led to the formation of the Société Française de Fabrication de Bébés et Jouets (S.F.B.J.).

JUMEAU

Having created the bébé in 1855, the French firm of Jumeau (1842–99) went on to introduce portrait bébés, the "Jumeau Triste" ("sad" or "long-faced" Jumeau), and "two-faced" dolls. Portrait bébés, dating from 1870, were allegedly based on real-life models and typically feature lightly painted eyebrows as well as blue eyes with a black outline and long lashes. Most have eight-jointed bodies made of composition with wooden ball joints and fixed wrists, and were typically sold with elaborate clothes and accessories. The Jumeau Triste dates back to c.1880 and surviving examples are extremely collectible. As the name implies, they are characterized by a melancholy expression; most have

◄▲ "Two-faced" doll by Jumeau

One of the many novel types of bébé introduced by Jumeau was the two-faced doll shown here. The crying face could be turned round to reveal the smiling face by means of a knob situated in the top of the hair. Although the pink coloring of the bisque and the expressions on these dolls are less appealing than those on more conventional bébés, their rarity and novelty value make them sought after.
(c.1890; ht 66cm/26in; value K)

▼ Bébé by Bru Jeune & Cie

This unusual boy bébé has a bisque swivel head, pierced ears, a dark wig, and a typical jointed wood and composition body with fixed wrists. Notably, the gender of the doll is conveyed by the choice of clothing rather than great variation in the facial features. Its splendid original matador costume makes it of particular interest to collectors.
(1880; ht 47cm/18½in; value K)

fixed blue "paperweight" eyes and a closed mouth. Bodies are usually stamped "Medaille d'Or Paris" in blue – Jumeau was awarded this prize in 1878 so examples produced between then and 1885, when the stamp was changed to "Diplôme d'Honneur," are easy to date; heads are typically branded with a number. Two-faced Jumeau dolls, most notably laughing and crying, are also rare and collectible. These dolls were operated by means of a knob on the top of the head, which twisted the face around to produce, alternately, a cheerful and an unhappy doll. From 1899, after the foundation of the S.F.B.J., the quality of Jumeau dolls deteriorated as the company used less expensive, imported German heads to reduce costs.

BRU JEUNE & CIE

Bru Jeune & Cie (1866–83) produced a number of unusual bébés, including the now rare "Bru Brevété," with a kid body and a bisque swivel head and hands. This doll was patented in 1879 and produced until c.1883. Other innovations included the "Bru Teteur" (1879), which could suck from a bottle, and the "Bébé Gourmand," which could be fed through its open mouth, via a tube leading to a hole in the foot. The Bébé Gourmand was less popular than the Bru Teteur and fewer examples were produced, meaning that they are now rare and highly collectible. In 1883 the company was bought by Chevrot, which produced luxury and innovative, award-winning dolls, including a swimming doll. After 1883 dolls were produced with a new body type, featuring a small shoulder plate, a large head, and wooden lower limbs with clearly defined toes; these dolls are marked "Bru Jne." A range of now rare and collectible ethnic dolls was also introduced. In 1899 the firm of Girard took over the company but their dolls were less refined than earlier designs.

▲ Bébé by Jumeau

Jumeau was the first company to produce the bébé and this early example, manufactured during the golden age of French dollmaking, highlights many characteristic qualities associated with these perennially popular and collectible dolls. It has a pale-colored bisque shoulder head with large, blue, almond-shaped, fixed glass "paperweight" eyes outlined in black (a feature of early Jumeau bébés) and lightly painted eyebrows. The head is likely to be incised "Déposé Jumeau."
(1870; ht 28cm/11in; value G)

▲ Bébé by Jules Steiner
Although Steiner was well known for his mechanical dolls, he is most famous for his bébés, in particular those produced during the 1880s. This slightly later example, wearing a lace-trimmed dress and bonnet (not the original clothing), has a jointed papier-mâché body, which is also characteristic of this maker. On some dolls the purple wash used on the body is visible beneath the paint.
(c.1892; ht 47cm/18½in; value **H**)

GAULTIER AND STEINER

François Gaultier, a family firm (1860–99), produced bébés that were especially noted for the size and quality of their fixed glass paperweight eyes. Other typical features include chubby cheeks, pointed chins, and pierced ears. Early bébés, produced before 1885, had lightly arched eyebrows, an open mouth with two rows of teeth, and papier-mâché bodies. Later dolls had dark, glossy eyebrows, and, if open-mouthed, upper teeth only.

Jules Nicholas Steiner (1855–1910), originally a clockmaker, produced walking, talking dolls at his factory in Paris. Exact dating of Steiner dolls is difficult as faces were painted by different artists; however, heads have cardboard pates, the mouth is always close to the nose, and many have "wire eyes," which opened and closed by means of a wire lever at the side of the head. Bodies are usually papier-mâché and jointed, and often purple beneath the flesh tones; most Steiner dolls have stubby fingers.

OTHER MAKERS

Many other French dollmaking firms flourished in the late 19th century, notably that of A. Thuillier (1875–93), which produced fine-quality dolls with French, jointed bodies, paperweight eyes, and real or mohair wigs. Some of Thuillier's designs used bodies by Steiner; others incorporated heads made by Gaultier. The firms of Rabery & Delphieu (1856–1930), Danel & Cie (1889–95), and Schmitt & Fils (1863–91) also manufactured dolls, although their designs were not as sophisticated and of as high quality as those by Thuillier. Dolls by Schmitt & Fils include the "Bébé Schmitt," which was advertised as being indestructible. The production of bébés was also undertaken by several factories in Limoges, a city already famous for its porcelain, and these factories created a wide range of designs of varying quality between *c*.1897 and *c*.1925.

THE SOCIETE FRANCAISE DE FABRICATION DE BEBES ET JOUETS

The S.F.B.J. (1899–*c*.1950) was an association of leading French doll-manufacturers formed to challenge the threat from German competition at the end of the 19th century. Although its members included such leading names as Bru Jeune & Cie and Jumeau – the S.F.B.J. was based at the Jumeau factory – the quality of the dolls it produced was compromised owing to the need to maintain low costs. Bébés by the S.F.B.J. were slim with high-cut legs, wood and composition bodies, and bisque heads. Ironically, some were made from imported German parts. More successful were the character dolls produced from *c*.1911; these were of better quality and were produced in a wide range of body types.

◄ Bébé by Gaultier
This doll with finely made, large, fixed, brown glass eyes, chubby cheeks, and small, pointed chin is typical of Gaultier's bébés. Its one unusual feature, for an early bébé, is its thick, dark, glossy eyebrows, which are usually found on dolls produced after *c*.1885. Identification of dolls made entirely by François Gaultier is quite straightforward as most examples were marked with the maker's initials.
(c.1880; ht 61cm/24in; value **I**)

▲ Bébé from Limoges
Many Limoges porcelain factories branched out to manufacture both dolls' heads and whole dolls between 1897 and 1925. The quality was generally fairly low and the coloring was often exaggerated. The example shown above displays the rather crude, over-pink coloring and molded teeth typical of Limoges dolls. However, it also features "sleeping" eyes and pierced ears, which are more characteristically found on better-quality dolls. Although its attractive face, original costume, and good condition help to compensate for this doll's undistinguished origins, its price remains reasonable.
(c.1910; ht 46cm/18in; value **E**)

KEY FACTS

- COSTUME original, fashionable clothes in luxurious fabrics will increase the value of a doll; French clothes and shoes may be sold separately
- CONDITION look out for hairline cracks, which will reduce value; restored dolls are less desirable: check for repainting, and replacement pates (originals will be cork) and wigs (originals will be hair or mohair)
- COLLECTING bébés are in general the most sought-after type of doll and therefore can be very valuable; earlier dolls are especially desirable and can be identified by pale, flawless, bisque heads; later dolls are often made from high-colored bisque (quality declined after 1899); dolls by famous makers are very collectible

See also Fashion dolls, pp.486–7

Germany

As early as the 1850s German manufacturers in Thuringia were producing bisque dolls' heads and exporting them throughout Europe. Although French makers reigned supreme from the 1860s to the 1890s, German makers started to make bébés (child dolls) in 1870. Their larger, cheaper workforce made German dolls more affordable than French examples, and French makers were forced to compromise on quality to match prices. From the late 1890s until the early 20th century German makers produced character bébés – lifelike bisque-headed character dolls – which were more realistic and less idealized than the French versions. There were many different makers manufacturing dolls in a range of styles and prices. Among the most popular were "Googly" dolls (from c.1911) and "Kewpie" dolls (from c.1913), which were made in vast quantities for export to the USA.

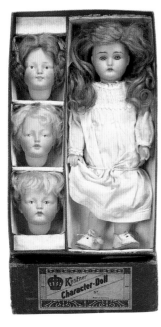

◄ Character doll by Kestner & Co.

This rare doll, with a ball-jointed, wood and composition body, has three extra, interchangeable bisque heads. The head with blue glass eyes, brown mohair wig, and an open mouth with upper teeth can be substituted by a head with painted brown eyes, brown hair, and an open or closed mouth, a head with painted blue eyes, blond hair, and an open or closed mouth, or one with painted brown eyes, blond hair, and a pouty mouth The presence of the original instructions and box makes up for the small firing crack on the original head and the detached lower right leg.

(c.1910; ht 28cm/10¾in; value J)

SIMON & HALBIG

One of the most prolific manufacturers of china and bisque shoulder heads was the firm of Simon & Halbig (c.1869–c.1930), which supplied bisque heads to such other well-known makers as Kämmer & Reinhardt, and the French firm of Jumeau (1842–99), from their factory in Thuringia. Their early child dolls had solid, domed heads with fixed glass eyes, flat, painted brows and lashes, and a closed mouth. Later dolls had socket heads with an open crown and cardboard pate and an open mouth. Their main specialty was ethnic dolls. The heads can be identified by marks and, in particular, mold numbers.

KESTNER & CO.

The firm of Kestner & Co. (1816–1930) was founded in Walterhausen, Thuringia, by Johannes Daniel Kestner, whose grandson Adolphe made bisque-headed child dolls from the 1880s and character dolls from 1910. The company merged with Kämmer & Reinhardt in 1930. Their dolls were very popular in the USA, where they were distributed by the major New York-based importer George Borgfeldt (1881–c.1930). Their child dolls had high-quality bisque heads with mohair wigs on

◄ Character doll by Kestner & Co.

This doll is a superb example of the popular exotic character dolls created by German makers in the early 20th century. This example is a rare doll, made from mold 243, and features weighted brown glass eyes and a black wig of real hair; the open mouth reveals two tiny upper teeth. The bent, five-limbed body, which is typical of character dolls, is made of composition. This doll is one of the collectible "200" series, which was produced from c.1910, and for which Kestner manufactured both the heads and the bodies. The presence of an original silk jacket adds still further to the value of the piece.

(c.1914; ht 33cm/13in; value H)

a plaster pate and blown-glass "sleeping" eyes of blue or brown – grey is rare and more collectible. Dolls with shoulder heads had kid or muslin bodies; those with socket heads typically had composition bodies. Much sought after are character dolls in the Kestner "200" series, produced from c.1910, for which they made both the heads and the bodies. The latter have plump tummies, chubby arms, and well-defined feet and toes. The comparatively rare, and therefore more valuable, toddler bodies have higher-cut legs and are able to stand. They are marked only on the head.

KÄMMER & REINHARDT

Kämmer & Reinhardt (1886–c.1940) was founded in Walterhausen by the designer and model-maker Ernst Kämmer and the entrepreneur Franz Reinhardt, and was the first company to produce character dolls. Kämmer designed the heads until his death in 1901, when Simon & Halbig took over production, using Kämmer's designs. The company's golden era was from 1909 – when the first character doll was introduced – to 1914. One of the best known of the Kämmer & Reinhardt character dolls is the "Kaiser" baby, the first example in the "100" series. The rarest and most sought-after numbers in the series are: 102, 103, 104, 105, 106, 107, 109, and 112. More appealing and collectible are the firm's character children; these were often recorded with names and were available in boy or girl versions. Notable features include painted eyes, painted, closed mouths, and mohair wigs. Character children came with either bent-limbed or jointed bodies, but the latter type was more popular as it enabled the dolls to stand.

▼ "Mein Liebling" doll by Kämmer & Reinhardt

Mein Liebling ("My Darling") was one of the most popular character dolls produced by the major German manufacturer Kämmer & Reinhardt. This example was produced from mold 117 and has the characteristic sweet expression that made these child dolls such favorites both when they were first produced and with collectors today. It has a closed mouth, sleeping glass eyes, and a brown mohair wig, and is still wearing its original costume. Its popular mold number and good condition make it very desirable. Dolls made from mold 117/A are similar to this example but they have an even sweeter expression and are slightly more collectible.

(c.1911; ht 71cm/28in; value H)

GEBRÜDER HEUBACH

The Thuringia area of Germany was traditionally associated with porcelain production and so adapted easily to bisque doll manufacture. Gebrüder Heubach (active 1840–c.1945), near Wallendorf, set up by the brothers Christoph and Philipp Heubach, expanded from the manufacture of figures and dolls' heads to the production of whole dolls from 1905. Most notable is their wide range of bisque-headed character dolls. Bodies were of composition or cloth and were quite crudely modeled. Greater emphasis was given to the design of the heads, which featured rosy cheeks and exaggerated, characterful expressions. The painted eyes were realistic and intaglio-molded with an indented pupil; the iris was often highlighted with a white dot. One of the most popular ranges by this firm was the "Piano" babies – bisque figures designed to sit on the household piano.

ARMAND MARSEILLE

Russian-born Armand Marseille (active 1885–1930) took over a porcelain factory in Thuringia, and by 1890 he and his son, also called Armand, were producing bisque dolls' heads. Their production was prolific and from 1900 to 1930 they also supplied other makers. The most commonly found Marseille doll is the "390" series, made from c.1900. It varies in quality, however, and the bottom end of the range is marred by over-simplified features and line eyebrows. The most popular range was the "Dream Babies," which was registered in 1926.

Armand Marseille the younger married the daughter of another major dollmaker – Ernst Heubach (1887–1930) of Koppelsdorf; in 1919 the two companies merged to form the Koppelsdorf porcelain factory. Their bisque character and baby dolls were less costly and of slightly poorer quality than their earlier designs; the decline in quality is reflected in the over-red cheeks. The company also made black dolls in ethnic costume.

◄ "Dream Babies" by Armand Marseille

Dream Babies, made from 1926, were the most popular dolls made by the Marseille firm. They were produced in large quantities and a variety of sizes and colors (including black). Some, like the larger doll here, have flange heads with soft bodies; others, like the smaller, have five-limbed composition bodies. Most popular are small Dream Babies with closed mouths and a composition body. *(both: c.1925; left: ht 56cm/22in; value **C**; right: ht 25cm/10in; value **C**)*

▼ "Googly" dolls by Kämmer & Reinhardt

Inspired by the drawings of an American illustrator, Googly dolls were named after their large, round, bug-like, sideways-glancing eyes, and were made by various German makers from 1911. This particular pair (from the 131 mold) combines the high quality associated with the German maker Kämmer & Reinhardt with such typical Googly features as tiny snub noses, closed, "watermelon" mouths, and high-set, short, slanting eyebrows. Their high value reflects their distinguished maker and the good condition of their charming, immaculate, and highly detailed costumes. *(both: 1914; ht 36cm/14¼in; each doll: value **H**)*

GOOGLIES AND KEWPIES

Googlies were popular caricature dolls inspired by the drawings of the American illustrator Grace Debbie Drayton. They were produced from c.1911 to c.1931 by various German makers, including Gebrüder Heubach, Armand Marseille, Kämmer & Reinhardt, and Kestner & Co. All Googlies have bisque heads, large, round, sideways-glancing eyes, short, slanting eyebrows, tiny snub noses, and closed, "watermelon" mouths. Bodies are of jointed composition or wood "toddler" type.

Kewpie dolls were inspired by another American illustrator, Rose O'Neill. The first cupid-like (hence "Kewpie") figure was designed in 1912 by O'Neill and made c.1913 by Kestner & Co., with other makers soon following suit. Authorized Kewpies were produced in huge quantities for export; almost equally large numbers of unauthorized versions were produced in Japan and Europe. Kewpies are instantly recognizable by their bald heads with a blond tuft in the center, pedestal legs, outstretched arms, and tiny blue wings below the ears. The usually painted eyes are sideways-glancing beneath short line eyebrows, the nose is snub, and the "watermelon" mouth is smiling. Kewpie bodies may be of celluloid, rubber, composition, or – most desirable and valuable – bisque. All authorized Kewpies are marked "Rose O'Neill."

► "Kewpie" doll by Kestner & Co.

Kestner was the first German manufacturer to produce the popular Kewpie dolls. This example, with a bisque head and composition body, is very collectible because it has glass rather than painted eyes and is unusually large. It carries the maker's mark "J.D.K. 10" on the neck and is stamped with an authorized signature on the bottom of the foot. Although its costume is very appealing, clothes do not play a large part in the value of a Kewpie doll. *(1913; ht 27cm/10½in; value **H**)*

KEY FACTS

- COSTUMES these range from highly traditional regional outfits to exotic, Oriental costumes
- DESIGNS these are also wide-ranging, from realistic Dream Babies to 20th-century caricature dolls (Googlies and Kewpies); exotic dolls were popular
- MARRIAGES check for a correct match between the head and body: repair and restoration may lead to inappropriate combinations
- CONDITION repainting to disguise cracks will reduce value; original clothing in good condition is important
- COLLECTING dolls by well-known makers are the most sought after; pale bisque, detailed painting, and a rare mold number all add to a doll's value

Fabric and rag dolls

Safe, soft, and affordable, fabric and rag have been used in dollmaking from earliest times. However, because cloth dolls were inexpensive and vulnerable, they were often thrown away and replaced; as a result the first significant examples date only from the second half of the 19th century. There was a strong domestic rag doll tradition in the USA, where the first rag doll patent was taken out in 1873. In Europe high-quality dolls were produced from the mid-19th century. Mass production of printed cut-out fabric dolls began after fabric color printing developed c.1830.

▶ Cloth doll

This doll, made in the USA, is based on a "Mammy" from the deep South. It is wearing its original decorative bead necklaces, bracelets, rings, and a turban. Its body is well formed, with full thighs and shapely legs, and its features are stitched – it even has embroidered red nipples. The fingernails are made from porcupine quills.
(c.1880; ht 31cm/12in; value D)

THE UNITED STATES

Famous early makers, whose dolls are now rare, include Izannah Walker and Martha Chase (active 1880s–1925), both of Rhode Island. Walker patented a cloth doll in 1873 and produced designs with oil-painted features and stitched hands with separate thumbs. Chase applied for a patent in 1890 and produced mask-faced stockinette dolls, also with oil-painted features. More often found are "Raggedy Ann" and "Raggedy Andy" dolls, which were based on a story by the artist John Gruelle and made in a range of styles. Gruelle's family initially made 200 Raggedy Ann dolls with hand-painted faces, eyes with six lower lashes, and wooden hearts; from 1918 Volland & Co., Gruelle's publisher, produced more copies in response to demand. Raggedy Andy was created in 1920. Variations were made by several firms, notably the Georgene Averill (or Madam Hendrer) Manufacturing Co. (1876–1963), in New York.

GERMANY

The two major German manufacturers associated with cloth dolls are the firms of Margarete Steiff (est. 1877), in Giengen, and Käthe Kruse (est. 1910). Steiff, although better known for her teddy bears, produced felt dolls from 1889 and character dolls in plush and velvet from c.1903. She designed a large range of characters such as policemen, soldiers, firemen, film stars, and musicians; most are marked with paper labels or metal buttons and have blue or black button eyes, a hand-painted face with a vertical seam, and large feet. Käthe Kruse's first dolls,

intended to be safe and washable, were made by Kämmer & Reinhardt (est. 1886). In 1912 production shifted to her own workshop in Bad Kosen, and from World War II to a factory at Donauworth. Her range was small: she made just one type of doll from 1911 to 1920, expanding to five by 1956. Early dolls are sought after and can be recognized by the three hand-stitched pate seams on the calico heads, which had oil-painted hair and features, and by the separately stitched thumbs. They had wide hips and realistic legs with five seams.

BRITAIN

From the early 1920s Chad Valley (registered as Chad Valley 1897) produced dolls made of stockinette, felt, and velvet, most notably models based on the young princesses Elizabeth and Margaret. In 1926 Norah Wellings, a former Chad Valley designer, set up her own company (1926–60), in Wellington, Shropshire, with her brother, Leonard, and produced a wide variety of character dolls, including sailors, South Sea islanders, and pixies in an equally vast range of sizes and prices. Her creations typically have very well-modeled velvet or felt heads with zigzag-stitched seams on the back of the head and the body. Wellings's prolific output means that her dolls are readily found, but good condition and original clothing are essential (cloth is hard to restore).

ITALY

The Italian firm of Lenci was founded in Turin in 1918 by Enrico di Scavini. Lenci is an acronym of "Ludus Est Nobis Constanter Industria" ("play is work for us") and is also supposed to have been Di Scavini's pet name for his wife. The sophisticated dolls produced by the firm were primarily intended for adults, and between c.1920 and 1940 a vast range of dolls in elaborate costumes was produced. The pressed-felt faces, with painted eyes (usually brown) and painted eyebrows, are unusually expressive; costumes are brightly colored and must be in good condition to retain value. Marks vary: in the 1920s and 1930s dolls were branded with a black or purple stamp on the foot, in the 1930s labels were marked with model numbers, and after c.1938 these changed to cardboard tags. From 1925 to 1950 ribbons with the company name were sewn into the costume.

▲ Felt soldier doll by Lenci

The golden age of Italian Lenci dolls was between c.1920 and 1940, when this doll was made. It has several characteristics very typical of Lenci dolls: an expressive pressed-felt face with a slightly sulky expression, painted eyes and eyebrows, a mouth with a paler lower lip, and hands with two joined middle fingers and separately stitched outer fingers. As Lenci dolls were designed primarily for adults rather than children and intended to be displayed, the condition of the costume will significantly affect a doll's value.
(1930; ht 38cm/15in; value G)

◀ Cloth doll by Käthe Kruse

This doll is a fine and highly collectible example of the early dolls made in Germany by Käthe Kruse. Like most early dolls by this designer, it has a number on its left foot and the maker's signature.
(c.1920; ht 38cm/15in; value G)

KEY FACTS

- CARE storage and display arrangements must protect delicate fabrics against fading by sunlight and damage caused by insects, especially moths
- CONDITION cloth dolls should be in good condition and clean as they are difficult to restore; many cannot be washed
- COLLECTING the large range of types and prices offers a wide choice for collectors; early American and German dolls are especially highly sought after

See also Soft toys, p.495

Other later dolls

Composition was used by doll manufacturers as an inexpensive alternative to bisque and china in the 19th and early 20th centuries. German makers led the field until World War I, after which American firms launched a highly successful range of innovative designs. Celluloid, patented in the USA in 1869 by the brothers James Wesley Hyatt and Isaiah Smith Hyatt, was developed as an alternative to bisque and composition. It was used by German makers from 1873, mainly for hands and heads, but also to produce inexpensive copies of bisque dolls. Hard plastic was used in dollmaking from the end of World War II until the 1950s, when it was superseded by vinyl, which was softer to the touch. Millions of dolls have been made out of vinyl, notably the phenomenally successful teenage fashion dolls "Barbie" and "Sindy."

COMPOSITION

Composition is made from wood or paper pulp, which is reinforced with other ingredients: in Europe, rags, bones, and eggs; in the USA, wood and plastic. European dollmakers used it to make baby dolls, bodies, and limbs, but makers in the USA were more adventurous, and developed a collectible range of composition dolls that included film stars such as Deanna Durbin and Shirley Temple, cartoon characters such as "Betty Boop," and advertising characters. Good condition is important but rare; composition is vulnerable to flaking and crazing, and hard to clean as it is damaged by water.

CELLULOID

Although celluloid was patented in the USA, it was used mostly by French and German dollmakers. From 1873 the Rhineland Rubber & Celluloid Co. (1873–c.1930), in Bavaria, produced celluloid dolls modeled as babies and children; other German makers such as Kestner & Co. (1816–1930) and Kämmer & Reinhardt (1886–c.1940) followed suit, as did the French company Jumeau (1842–99). Large numbers of celluloid dolls were made, often from bisque molds. The main advantage of celluloid was that it did not flake or peel; disadvantages included high flammability, a tendency to crack, dent, or fade, and a resistance to restoration. Nevertheless celluloid dolls in good condition remain popular with collectors owing to their affordability and wide range of types. Celluloid dolls have a characteristic glossy sheen and may give off a smell of camphor if rubbed briskly with a cloth.

◄ **Plastic crying doll by British National Dolls**
Huge quantities of plastic dolls were made in Britain in the 1950s. This typical example, with molded hair, "sleeping" eyes with eyelashes, and crudely shaped fingers and toes, is lacking its original clothes. It cries "Mama" when tilted. *(early 1950s; ht 30cm/11¾in; value A)*

PLASTIC AND VINYL

Inexpensive and durable, hard plastic was used to make dolls from 1945 until the 1950s, when it was replaced by vinyl. Collectible hard plastic dolls were made by such American companies as the New York-based Alexander Doll Co. (est. 1923), which produced a huge range of named dolls, including the popular "Little Women" series. In Britain, Rosebud (est. 1947; merged with Mattel 1967), Pedigree (the trademark of Lines Bros; est. 1942), and British National Dolls Ltd (est. c.1930), all in London, made hard plastic dolls.

The advent of vinyl heralded the mass production of probably the most successful doll ever – Barbie. Launched in 1959 by Mattel, Barbie has been mass-manufactured ever since. Most sought after are early (pre-1961) Barbies with ponytails, pale complexions, and pierced feet for a stand, rare brunette and red-headed Barbies, and unusual outfits. Barbie's British rival was Sindy, a vinyl doll made by Pedigree from 1962 and promoted on television as "the doll you love to dress." Most desirable are black Sindys, only 250 of which were produced. "Sasha," another collectible vinyl doll, was created in Britain c.1970 by the Swiss designer Sasha Morgenthaler. Sasha dolls apppealed to children for their notable realism rather than as fashion icons.

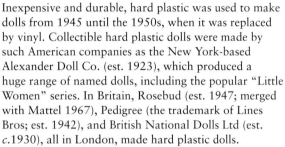

▲ **"Barbie" by Mattel**
Barbie is probably the most successful doll ever produced, with sales of several million since it was first launched by the American company Mattel. This doll, with rooted hair based on Jackie Kennedy's style, reflects the height of 1960s glamor. *(1966; ht 25cm/9¾in; value A)*

◄ **Celluloid doll**
This French doll has a swivel head, molded and painted hair, and glass eyes. Although well made and desirable because of its eyes and original clothes, its price reflects its later date. Most celluloid dolls are marked; this one is marked on the back and neck with the initials "SNF" (Société Nobel Française). *(1930; ht 46cm/18in; value C)*

KEY FACTS

Composition
- CONDITION this will determine value as composition dolls are difficult to clean
- COLLECTING American dolls are more collectible than British ones; unusual features, such as sleeping eyes, will add to value; a lively facial expression and original clothes are also very desirable

Celluloid
- CONDITION this is crucial as celluloid is easily damaged and hard to restore: check for dents, cracks, and fading
- COLLECTING better-quality dolls have glass eyes; original clothes add to value; Kestner character dolls are especially sought after

Plactic and vinyl
- CONDITION mint boxed condition is essential for maximum value, especially with recent dolls
- COLLECTING Barbie: brunette or red-headed dolls are more collectible than blond dolls; "fake" Barbies are generally poor quality and unmarked; check for pristine, recently drilled holes in feet to "age" the doll; Sindy: black versions are rare and collectible

Automata

The precursors of automata were the novelty clocks animated by moving figures that were produced by German clockmakers in the 16th century. In the 18th century, exclusive and highly complex mechanical figures with musical accompaniment were made to commission by the Jacquet-Droz family in Geneva. The more commercial production of automata with simple mechanisms began in France in the early 19th century. The golden age of automata lasted from c.1880 to 1920, when increasingly elaborate and sophisticated automata were produced for the luxury market. In Germany and the USA, such firms as Althof Bergmann (est. 1856) in New York, concentrated on simpler, less expensive automata, often with hand-operated mechanisms, designed primarily for children.

FAMOUS FRENCH MAKERS

The finest, most collectible automata are those produced by manufacturers in and around Paris in the late 19th century. From the 1870s they were made from a combination of mass-produced Swiss musical movements, figures with French and German dolls' heads, and exquisite, highly detailed French costumes and accessories. Among the leading makers was the firm of Roullet & Decamps (1832–1972), founded by Jean Roullet (d.1907), who was joined by his son-in-law Ernest Decamps (d.1909), who in turn was followed by his son Gaston until 1972. They designed complex, high-quality drawing-room automata as well as simpler models aimed at children. Another notable Parisian firm was founded by Blaise Bontems (c.1840–1905), and was renowned for its automata featuring singing birds. Like Roullet & Decamps, Bontems produced two ranges, and their simpler, less valuable singing birds are a good starting-point for new collectors.

Other early firms of note include Théroude (c.1845–72), founded by Alexandre Nicolas Théroude, whose products were intended for children and included animal automata and simple dolls mounted on wheeled platforms. Circus clowns, pierrots, and the "Man in the Moon" were favorite subjects for automata made by the firm of Vichy (1862–1905), founded by the Vichy brothers Antoine Michel, Henri, and Gustave Pierre. The brothers took out a patent for a mechanical doll in 1862 and their figures are noted for their very expressive faces; the fine-quality heads were individually designed. Another maker, Leopold Lambert, who had trained with the Vichy brothers, went on to establish his own company (c.1888–c.1923), which specialized in mechanical figures that performed simple actions. Lambert's high-quality dolls had bisque heads (some supplied by the distinguished dollmaking firm of Jumeau) and elaborate costumes; they covered a range of characters from the well-known "crying" dolls to figures that smoked cigars and blew bubbles.

Some of the most complex and luxurious automata were made by the Paris-based company Phalibois (c.1850–c.1910), founded by Jean Marie Phalibois. Designs were complex and featured large-scale groups of mechanical figures assembled under glass domes; these were supported on finely decorated bases, which incorporated brass, mother-of-pearl, and ivory inlay. Many automata by Phalibois also featured monkeys dressed as humans. These exclusive drawing-room automata were luxury objects in their day and this is reflected in their current market value.

◄ **"Monkey Violinist" automaton by Phalibois**
The Paris-based company of Phalibois was noted for its exclusive and sophisticated drawing-room automata, of which satin-dressed monkeys were a favorite subject. This example shows a monkey with a papier-mâché head and articulated upper lip and eyes. It nods, turns its head, moves its eyes, and lifts its upper lip as it plays two different tunes. This example would normally be covered by a large, protective glass dome, which would add to its value.
(c.1880; ht 67cm/26½in; value **F**)

▼ **"Tricyclist" automaton by Bergmann**
Although not as complex as most French contemporary automata, this American tricyclist with a papier-mâché head does possess a certain naive charm. The simple clockwork movement rocks the young rider backward and forward as he pedals along.
(c.1870; l. 25.5cm/10in; value **F**)

◄ **"Le Cuisinier" automaton by Vichy**
The example shown here, which features a chef with an expressive papier-mâché head and articulated eyes, is highly typical of the fine automata produced by the leading Parisian firm of Vichy. The chef nods, turns his head, and takes a swig from the bottle, while the little cat pops its head out of the saucepan and cheekily sticks out its tongue.
(c.1885; ht 74cm/29in; value **K**)

KEY FACTS

- MOVEMENT the complexity and originality of the movement will determine the value of a piece
- CONDITION the quality of the head, original costume, and movements are crucial: appropriate replacements are acceptable but will be reflected in the price
- COLLECTING French automata are highly sought after; German, British, and American pieces are less refined and less expensive; designs produced for children are mostly less valuable but more abundant and accessible than those aimed at adults; restoration and repair work is highly skilled and correspondingly priced
- BEWARE automata are a difficult area for collectors, so novices should buy from specialists only

See also Clocks & Watches: Novelty clocks, pp.362–3

Soft toys

Although toy animals have been made in stone and wood since ancient times, animals in cloth, velvet, plush, felt, or leather became popular only in the late 19th century, when Margarete Steiff created a range that was to launch the soft toy industry. She inspired other European firms to design soft toys, many based on characters from children's books. From the 1950s firms in the USA capitalized on the popularity of animals from Walt Disney films and cartoons. By 1970 Japanese firms were making huge quantities of soft toys, and other Far Eastern countries have since followed suit.

▲ Pig by Steiff
The German firm of Steiff produced a wide range of soft toy animals, but pigs, traditionally very popular with children, are among the most desirable. This example is still in fine condition and highly collectible.
*(c.1910; l. 33cm/13in; value **E**)*

BEFORE 1950

From *c.*1880 in Giengen, southern Germany, the firm of Margarete Steiff (est. 1877) produced elephant-shaped felt pincushions, which were developed into a range of small, jointed animals including elephants, monkeys, pigs, dogs, and possums. The most common materials were mohair, velvet, and felt, with stuffing made from excelsior (a soft mixture of long, thin woodshavings), and black boot-button or glass eyes. Steiff animals can be identified by their superb quality, beautiful modeling, and attention to detail. Other notable German makers producing novelty soft toys included Schuco (the trademark of Schreyer & Co.; 1912–78) and Gebrüder Bing (1879–1933), both in Nuremburg.

In Britain manufacturers such as the London-based J.K. Farnell (*c.*1840–1968), Chad Valley (registered as Chad Valley 1897), and Dean's Rag Book Co. (est. 1903), as well as Chiltern Toys (est. 1920), in Chesham, Bucks, and Merrythought Ltd (est. 1930), near Ironbridge, Shropshire, produced successful ranges of soft toys. There was great rivalry over acquiring licenses to produce contemporary animal characters. In 1927 Chad Valley acquired the license to produce "Bonzo," a bull terrier based on a cartoon in the *Daily Sketch*, and his girlfriend "Oolo"; the latter, made in the 1930s, is particularly rare. Dean's acquired the license to produce toy versions of Mickey Mouse

and friends; other successful Dean's characters include "Peter Rabbit," "Bambi," and a dalmatian dog, initially issued as "Dismal Desmond" and joined in 1933 by "Cheerful Desmond." Farnell were granted the license to produce "Jemima Puddleduck" from Beatrix Potter's *Peter Rabbit* books.

AFTER 1950

Shortages after World War II forced producers to use synthetic materials and many soft toys were designed fully clothed to cut down on the scarce natural materials required to make their bodies. Major pre-war German and British makers were joined by new firms such as the British company Clifton and manufacturers in the USA, keen to exploit the market for spin-offs from films, television, and books. In the 1960s Eden Toy Inc. in America made versions of "Peter Rabbit" and "Paddington Bear"; Sears, Roebuck & Co. issued the Disney version of "Winnie-the-Pooh"; and both Merrythought and Chad Valley designed characters from the *Winnie-the-Pooh* books.

In Germany Steiff continued to dominate the market, introducing a range of large, unjointed animals. They expanded their range of smaller, jointed animals, and marked each toy with a name-tag around the neck. In the 1980s Steiff launched a range of limited-edition replicas of early designs, made in the traditional way; these can be identified by a black-and-white label. The many glove puppets produced by most of the major makers are a good area for collectors, and, as always, Steiff animals are at a premium. The company produced a wide variety of glove puppets following the success of "Sooty," the puppet bear on children's television in the 1950s, and a Steiff puppet will command a higher price than one by Dean's or Chad Valley.

▼ Hedgehog by Steiff
In addition to the Steiff ear button and label, this hedgehog has a swing neck label that identifies it as one of the Joggi series of hedgehogs made by the company in the 1950s.
*(1950s; l. 15cm/6in; value **C**)*

▲ Duck by Clifton
The appeal of this felt duck lies in its unfaded, bright colors, which would have been a welcome relief after the austerity of the war years. Good condition is vital for such mass-produced toys – damage from moths or owners will considerably reduce value. A bonus is the original label identifying its British maker.
*(1950s; ht 25.5cm/10in; value **B**)*

◄ "Peter Rabbit" by Eden Toy Inc.
The great popularity of Beatrix Potter's stories of Peter Rabbit led to the production of various different soft toy versions clad in the unmistakable blue coat, as this example, still with its original blue coat and slippers, illustrates. Eden Toy Inc. was noted for its character soft toys and as well as its designs based on Beatrix Potter's books, also produced versions of "Paddington Bear."
*(1960s; ht 23cm/9in; value **B**)*

KEY FACTS

- **POPULAR SUBJECTS** famous animal characters from children's literature, films, and television
- **IDENTIFICATION** any original labels, marks, and swing tags will add to the value of a toy, although unmarked toys are still collectible if well made and of unusual design; Steiff: their toys can generally be recognized by a button in the left ear, the markings on which will vary (some feature an elephant); animals wearing slippers, such as Peter Rabbit, will feature an elephant trademark on the sole of the foot
- **CONDITION** good condition is critical: value will be reduced by moth-eaten fur, wear (especially to the face), faded colors in felt animals, and inappropriate restoration; Steiff replicas: fur sometimes deliberately "distressed" and "aged" in order to appear original
- **COLLECTING** pre-1914 toys are rare; a famous make will determine price: Steiff is the most sought after; an original box will add to the value
- **BEWARE** Steiff fakes are known: be suspicious of crudely made, inaccurately modeled animals

See also Teddy Bears, pp.496–7

Teddy bears

Although a comparatively late arrival on the toy scene, teddy bears have become very popular with collectors and now reach record prices at auction. There are several rival claims as to which company produced the first teddy bear. The German company of Margarete Steiff (est. 1877), in Giengen, produced jointed bears from 1902–3, and in 1904 a Steiff bear won a medal at the World's Fair in St Louis. The New York-based Ideal Novelty & Toy Co. (est. c.1906), founded by Morris Michtom, produced a jointed mohair bear that became known as "Teddy's bear," supposedly after a cartoon showing the American president Theodore Roosevelt sparing a bear cub on a hunting trip. Such was the popularity of the new toys that manufacturers in Germany, Britain, and the USA all diversified into teddy bear production. During and after World War I British companies expanded to fill the gap left by banned German imports, while French manufacturers developed their own home market. All European bear manufacture was severely disrupted by World War II, following which there was an increased use of less desirable synthetic plush. Children's books spawned models based on such famous literary bears as Winnie-the-Pooh, and with the growth of cartoons, films, and television, new teddy bears based on media characters developed alongside the more traditional styles.

GERMANY
The name Steiff is virtually synonymous with collectible teddy bears. Margarete Steiff was already well known for her production of soft toys when, in 1902, she made her first jointed teddy bears, designed by her nephew Richard Steiff (active 1902–c.1934), who modeled them on living bears. They were an immediate success and in 1903 the company sold more than 12,000 bears. By 1904 the string joints of the early design had been replaced by metal rods; these bears with metal rod joints are very rare and correspondingly valuable. Also in 1904 Steiff registered the elephant trademark that appears on the ear button of Steiff bears; from 1904 a blank button was used, replaced by a button with the company name

► **Early bear by Steiff**
This blond mohair plush bear has many features common to early German bears by Steiff. Most distinctive are its long, curved arms and legs, its spoon-shaped front paws with stitched claws, and its large, oval feet. It also has typically close-set eyes and wide-set, rounded ears.
(1910; ht 71cm/28in; value K)

in 1905–6. The early (pre-1930) Steiff bears are very sought after. They have distinctively long, curved arms, slim ankles, large oval feet, and a pronounced hump at the top of the back. Black shoe-button eyes were standard until World War I, after which glass eyes were used; these were set close together, near the muzzle. Steiff bears were produced in a variety of colors: those in white, blond, or silver plush had brown stitched noses; bears in brown or gold plush had black noses; black bears were also produced but are extremely rare – they were too frightening for most young children – and are consequently highly sought after by collectors; cinnamon-colored bears are also popular, although they are rarely found in perfect condition because they age more rapidly owing to the dye used.

Although Steiff is by far the most prominent German bear manufacturer, the firm of Gebrüder Bing (1879–1933), in Nuremberg, best known for their metal toys, also made highly collectible bears, in particular mechanical bears that could walk and play football. Their designs were typically dressed in bright, colorful outfits of silk or felt. Other well-known makers include Schuco (1912–78), in Nuremberg, who were famous for their innovative miniature mechanical bears.

THE UNITED STATES
Morris Michtom, founder of the Ideal Novelty & Toy Co. (est. c.1906), launched the first American teddy bear. His jointed mohair "Teddy's bear" was very popular when first designed and remains so with collectors today. Early Ideal bears were unmarked, however, and fakes proliferate. Fake bears look suspiciously pristine and unhandled: their noses are unworn, and their seams may be thick and uneven. All Ideal bears have jointed hips, necks, and shoulders. Early examples have a characteristic "American football" shape and are mostly made of short, gold or beige mohair plush with matching felt paws, and distinctive, sharply pointed foot pads. They have shoe-button or glass eyes, and the fur around the muzzle may be shorn. Later bears were made in a large variety of colors and types – for example, pandas – and had longer fur.

Other collectible bears include those manufactured by the Knickerbocker Toy Co. (active 1924–5), in New York, whose bears are clearly marked with a label in the front seam. Similar to many early American bears, Knickerbocker bears usually have long bodies, small feet, and short, straight arms and legs. Their later bears can be recognized by their large inverted ears and big noses. Also collectible are bears produced by Gund Manufacturing Co. (est. 1898), now in New York, and such novelty designs as "Hershey's bears," which were designed to promote Hershey's chocolate bars.

▲ **Novelty bears by Schuco**
These two bears are fine examples of the brightly colored novelty miniature bears produced by the German company Schuco. They were constructed in metal and covered in plush; unusual colors, such as the pink and green shown here, are particularly sought after. The body of the pink bear conceals a scent bottle; the green bear is a powder compact.
(c.1920; ht 9cm/3½in; value for each M)

▲ **Bear by the Ideal Novelty & Toy Co.**
The short gold plush fur and matching gold felt paws of this American bear are highly typical of early Ideal bears. Other characteristics include the pointed long snout, long legs and slightly pointed toes, an accentuated back hump, and rounded, wide-apart ears.
(1910; ht 60.5cm/24in; value G)

BRITAIN

One of the best-known British teddy bear makers was Chad Valley (registered as Chad Valley 1897), a major toy manufacturer, which produced bears from the 1920s. Production continued throughout World War II and in 1967 the company acquired Chiltern Toy Works (est. 1920). In 1978 Chad Valley was bought by Palitoy and records and catalogs were destroyed, so dating their bears can be very difficult.

◄ Bear by Chad Valley
Luxuriant orange mohair plush, a chubby body and limbs, and a wide head with a heavily stitched, bulbous nose all help to identify this British bear as an early Chad Valley. Confirmation is provided by the company label on the comparatively small feet, and the original metal ear button. Good condition, an early date, and a distinguished maker will all influence the value.
(1930s; ht 31cm/12in; value E)

As is the case generally, early Chad Valley bears are more desirable than later bears. Most have large, golden mohair plush bodies stuffed with kapok and excelsior; their short, fat limbs are stuffed solely with kapok and so feel softer. Their wide heads have long, blunt snouts with horizontally stitched noses and amber and black glass eyes. Other identifying features are large, flat ears and relatively small feet. From 1920 Chad Valley bears were marked and are therefore easy to identify.

Bears made by Chiltern before the takeover by Chad Valley are also collectible, especially early bears, which were made from high-quality, long, soft mohair and had long, curving arms and wide feet with cardboard-reinforced velvet pads. Other distinctive features are wide ears, a shaved muzzle, and upward stitches at the end of the stitched nose. Most have a label on the foot.

Other distinguished makers include Dean's Rag Book Co. Ltd (1903–72), in London, noted for their unusually colored bears and such novelty designs as bears on wheels, and Merrythought Ltd (est. 1930), near Ironbridge, Shropshire. Both firms employed ex-Chad Valley staff, and this makes it difficult to distinguish between early bears made by the two companies. Traditional early Merrythought bears are highly sought after and are usually marked with a celluloid button in the ear; this button was later moved to the back, and a fabric foot label was added. Modern limited-edition Merrythought bears are increasingly popular long-term investments.

J.K. Farnell & Co. (1897–1968), a famous London-based toy manufacturer, also claimed to have invented the teddy bear. A more likely claim to fame is that it was almost certainly a Farnell bear that inspired the books written by A.A. Milne, featuring the archetypal British teddy bear Winnie-the-Pooh. Other British celebrity bears, made by various international companies, include "Rupert the Bear," "Paddington," and "Sooty."

◄ "Bertie" bear by Dean's Rag Book Co.
Bertie bears were mass-produced in Britain by Dean's Rag Book Co. and were relatively inexpensive because the firm's founder, Samuel Dean, believed that every child had the right to own one. This example, which is still in good condition, has typically thick, shaggy yellow fur, is stuffed with kapok, and is jointed. The maker's label can be seen on its foot.
(1938; ht 30cm/12in; value C)

◄ Bear by Merrythought Ltd
Merrythought bears are often confused with those by Chad Valley as the same chief designer worked for both firms. This British bear has the bulbous, black and amber glass eyes, large, flat, wide-set ears, and clipped, pointed muzzle common to both companies. Unique to Merrythought is the distinctive stitching on the felt paw pads and the fabric company label on the foot.
(1930s; ht 41cm/16in; value H)

▼ Bear by J.K. Farnell & Co.
This teddy bear was made by Farnell, one of the most sought-after of British teddy bear manufacturers. It was probably a Farnell bear that inspired A.A. Milne's literary bear Winnie-the-Pooh. Early Farnell bears, such as this example, were made from high-quality mohair plush and had slightly heavy-looking bodies, with long, curved arms and vertically stitched noses.
(1920; ht 51cm/20in; value I)

KEY FACTS

- **STUFFING** British bears, stuffed solely with kapok, are softer than German, excelsior-stuffed bears
- **CONDITION** this is important: missing ears or fur cannot be restored but new paw pads are acceptable
- **COLLECTING** maker, condition, and age will determine value: Steiff and Ideal bears are very popular; rarity (Steiff metal rod bears) and an unusual color (Chad Valley "Rainbow" bears) will also influence value
- **BEWARE** fakes proliferate: check for signs of wear or restoration (fakes will be suspiciously pristine), uneven seams, thickly stitched, unworn noses, and old labels on new paws

See also Soft toys, p.495

Dolls' houses

Early dolls' houses were the preserve of the wealthy (the first known example was commissioned in 1558 by Albrecht V, Duke of Bavaria, for his daughter) and were primarily designed as cabinets to display collections of valuable miniatures rather than as children's playthings. From its origins in Germany and the Low Countries in the mid-16th century, the fashion for dolls' houses (or "baby houses") reached Britain in the early 18th century, when Queen Anne gave her goddaughter a fine example made c.1700; the first American dolls' houses were made in the late 18th century. By the mid-1800s, during the reign of Queen Victoria – herself a dolls' house enthusiast – middle-class interest was aroused, and from 1860, with the development of chromolithography, dolls' houses were mass-produced in Germany, Britain, and the USA. Dolls' houses from the 1950s were smaller than earlier designs and were made of printed paper, cardboard, and plastic; from the 1960s dolls' houses were made for the first time as television and merchandising tie-ins.

▲ **Dolls' house by Hacker**
German manufacturers were at the forefront of dolls' house production between c.1860 and 1914, and this example is typical of the French-style houses produced by one of the most notable German makers of that period, Hacker. This piece would have been less expensive than many of Hacker's earlier houses as the bricks are not painted on but applied as brick-printed paper. Typically the house has a mansard roof decorated with simulated blue slate; it also has a working doorbell.
(c.1895–1900; ht 71cm/28in; value **G**)

GERMANY

In the 19th century miniature room settings were as popular in Germany as dolls' houses. German toymaking expertise led to a virtual world monopoly, and most 19th-century dolls' houses, regardless of country of production, were furnished with German-made dolls' furniture. Among the best-known and most collectible makers are Gebrüder Schneegass of Waltershausen, and Rock & Graner (c.1830–1905). From c.1860 until World War I Germany also monopolized the international doll's house market, producing houses in different styles to suit the tastes of all their export markets. Two of the best-known post World War I firms are those of Christian Hacker (1870–c.1930), in Nuremberg, and Moritz Göttschalk. Hacker specialized in French-style houses with mansard roofs covered in the diamond roof tiles typical of northern France. His houses, usually marked with the intertwined initials "CH" topped by a small crown, remained popular until the 1930s. Göttschalk, who also specialized in French-style houses, is known for his "blue roof" houses, in which blue printed paper was used to simulate slate tiles. Göttschalk was adventurous in his designs and was one of the few makers to produce a Modernist dolls' house (c.1930); some of his ultra-modern houses are even equipped with lifts.

BRITAIN

Most British houses were individually crafted until mass production and chromolithography transformed the market c.1860. Thereafter London-based wholesalers such as Silber & Fleming (est. c.1890) distributed houses made in Germany and Britain. These tended to be mainly simple wooden designs with box backs and no embellishments; the façade, usually an imitation of a terraced London house of the 1820s, opened to reveal four plain, empty rooms, which the owners could furnish as they pleased. Notable British manufacturers of dolls' house furniture include J. Bubb of London and

▲ **Dolls' house by Göttschalk**
Moritz Göttschalk was one of the best-known German makers of dolls' houses in the 19th century. The porch and veranda of this wooden house are both typical of his designs, as is the blue roof. Such houses were inexpensive, as the detail was chromolithographed.
(c.1890; ht 69cm/27in; value **G**)

▼ **"Stockbroker Tudor" dolls' house by Triang**
Stockbroker Tudor dolls' houses were produced in a wide range of sizes and models. This British example is one of the largest made and, like the real houses on which it is based, is furnished predominantly with reproduction furniture. It does, however, have contemporary kitchen equipment and a desirable radiogram.
(1930s; ht 75cm/29½in; value **C**)

Evans & Cartwright (1802–50) of Wolverhampton. From c.1895 G. & J. Lines in London included dolls' houses in their toy range. Their wooden houses with brick-printed paper and imitation stucco surrounds came in a variety of styles and prices, with some examples being extremely expensive. Lines Brothers (the company established by Joseph Lines's sons in 1919) continued the dolls' house tradition, and from the mid-1920s produced a range of houses in modern styles under the trade name Triang, which are now eagerly sought by collectors. Particular favorites include the "Stockbroker Tudor" houses, which represented the dream home of aspirational urban British families of the time, and copies of Y Bwthyn Bach, the playhouse made in 1932 by the Principality of Wales for Princess Elizabeth (later Queen Elizabeth II).

From c.1930 Dinky Toys launched the "Dolly Varden" range for girls, which included hollow metal dolls' houses and a range of small-scale furniture. More vulnerable were the flat-packed cardboard houses made by the English Toy Co. (est. 1889), in London. Other well-known dolls' house manufacturers include Tudor Toys, who produced imitation Tudor houses, and Chad Valley (registered as Chad Valley 1897), in Birmingham, who manufactured tinplate houses. From the 1950s dolls' houses were smaller than earlier versions but were filled with all the furniture, domestic appliances, and consumer durables that real householders could only dream about. These highly desirable accessories were produced by such major manufacturers as Tiny Toy, Dol-Toi, Pit-a-Pat, Elgin, and Britains (est. c.1893), in London, and Meccano (c.1901–64), in Liverpool.

◄ **New York brownstone dolls' house**

Carpenter-built from wood, this fine American dolls' house has been painted to imitate the iron-rich brownstone used in New York terraces in the mid-19th century. The three-storey flat front, with real glass windows and imposing double mahogany doors, opens to reveal the true glory of this house – five extremely grand rooms furnished in sumptuous style.

(c.1850; ht 1.4m/4ft 7in; value **G**)

THE UNITED STATES

The earliest surviving American dolls' house is dated 1744; known as the "Van Cortlandt Mansion," it was a special commission and became a family heirloom. Carpenter-made houses were usually based on contemporary styles, and from the mid-19th century were furnished with German-made furniture and dolls, adapted to American styles. Well-known American dolls' furniture makers include Rufus Bliss (est. 1832) of Pawtucket, Rhode Island, who produced painted tin furniture and highly popular and collectible "cottage furniture" – wooden bedroom furniture decorated with lithographed paper. Notable cast-iron dolls' house furniture was produced by J. & E. Stevens (c.1870–1930), in Cromwell, Connecticut. Some of the finer dolls' houses, especially those in the style of grand New York town houses, were extremely sumptuously furnished.

In 1889 Bliss introduced the now celebrated papered wooden houses known as "Bliss" houses, which were made of lithographed paper glued to a wooden frame, and came in a range of styles; most had the characteristic porches, balconies, cupolas, and balustrades associated with American houses. Bliss houses are all carefully marked, although the signature may be printed on doors, under gables, or hidden on floors. Another regular feature on Bliss houses is turned wooden balusters. In 1894 the McLoughlin Brothers of New York launched a "New Folding Dolls' House" – a cardboard house that could be assembled from flat board printed with wallpaper and floor coverings; flat cardboard furniture was also supplied. Dolls' houses made by Bliss or McLoughlin are very rare and are consequently valuable.

A more accessible area for new collectors is the wide range of television-marketed, plastic houses, which have been mass-manufactured since the mid-20th century. These include the Mattel "Barbie" house, a pure Hollywood, shocking-pink and blue plastic edifice that was designed to be furnished with a wide range of shocking-pink matching furniture and accessories. Less overwhelmingly feminine is the mass-marketed house based on the set of the American television series *Sesame Street*, by Fisher Price. This small-scale version of "Hooper's Store" was first produced c.1980 and features signs in English and Spanish.

▲ **"Bliss" dolls' house**

The above example is an inexpensive wooden house covered in chromolithographed paper by the prominent American maker Bliss.

(1895; ht 36cm/14in; value **D**)

▼ **Dolls' house accessories**

Accessories that complement dolls' houses are collectible items in their own right. This furniture is by the American firm Tynietoy; the figure is German.

(figure: 1920s; ht 13cm/5in; value **A**; furniture: 1930s; ht 5cm/2in; value **A**)

KEY FACTS

- IMPORTANT MAKERS Germany: Gebrüder Schneegass; Rock & Graner; Britain: J. Bubb; Triang; Chad Valley; USA: Bliss; McLoughlin Brothers
- FURNITURE this need not be original but should be appropriate; fine-quality furniture, especially in rare styles or by famous makers, is a collecting area in its own right
- CONDITION check for damage from worms or moths
- RESTORATION this should always be carried out by professionals: over-restoration or amateur restoration can reduce the value of a piece enormously
- COLLECTING early, carpenter-made houses are rare and valuable; mass-produced post-war houses are a good area for novice collectors

SPEISEWAGEN

19420

RIC   Gew.d.W. 47800 kg

In terms of their type, styling, and construction, toys and games have usually reflected the underlying social and technical developments of the era in which they were first popular. Thus, 18th-century jigsaws were produced as dissected maps to serve as teaching aids when the colonization of new territories and the expansion of trade placed increasing importance on geographical knowledge. Toy theaters and circuses proved fashionable until the cinema and television provided more "sophisticated" and readily accessible forms of entertainment. As their life-size equivalents became the most up-to-date means of travel, toy trains, automobiles, airplanes, and spaceships gradually superseded one another in the imaginations of children and in the output of manufacturers. Similarly, since the mid-19th century, mass-produced toys have supplanted handmade, while wood, paper, and lead have been generally replaced by, in turn, tinplate, steel, and plastic. To adults, the appeal of antique toys and games lies in a nostalgia for earlier technologies and lifestyles, and for childhood itself. However, the premium on "mint-and-boxed" (unused) toys and games reveals them as anything but children's playthings to the serious collector.

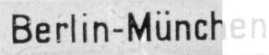

Dining car and engine shed (left) Produced by Märklin, the painted tinplate dining car is an accurate representation of a train of the period. The lithographed tinplate engine shed is by Hornby *(c.1937 and 1939)*.

"Goofy the Walking Gardener" (above) This clockwork toy depicting a popular Disney character, produced under license by the American firm of Louis Marx, is made from lithographed tinplate *(c.1955)*.

Wood and paper toys

Wood was the most common material used for making toys until the mid-19th century, when it was largely superseded by tinplate. By the 18th century the central European tradition of carving and painting toys had grown into a cottage industry, notably in Germany. The development in Germany of lithography (from 1797) and chromolithography (in 1870) enabled toymakers to combine wood and paper. Lithograph decoration was printed in black and then hand-colored; chromolithography produced detailed decoration in subtler and more diverse colors. From 1870, American manufacturers went into mass production, using jigsaws and chromolithography to replace hand-carving and hand-painting. Many British manufacturers used the outstanding Bavarian printers until World War I, when Germany's domination of the European wooden toy market ended. Although wooden toys were produced in huge quantities, few have survived in good condition.

◄ **Swing toy**
This wood and composition swing toy is typical of the many moving toys produced in Altdorf, near Nuremberg, from the late 18th century. The brightly colored hand-painted couple swing to and fro when a lever is moved at the side. Very few of these fragile toys have survived.
(c.1840; ht 20cm/8in; value **H***)*

SMALL WOODEN TOYS

Germany was the leading producer of carved wooden toys from the early 18th century to the 19th century. In some villages of the Erzgebirge, in Saxony, everyone worked from home producing small wooden figures. Erzgebirge Noah's Arks were exported worldwide; by 1911 the R. Bliss Manufacturing Co. (est. 1832; toy production c.1871–1914) of Pawtucket, Rhode Island, was importing Erzgebirge animals for its own arks.

The European tradition is evident in the work of Albert Schoenhut (1850–1934), who set up his own company (c.1872) in Philadelphia and went on to become one of the major American producers of wooden figures. His "Humpty Dumpty Circus" sets, produced from 1903 to 1935, were extremely popular; each set comprised more than 20 figures and animals. The most sought-after Schoenhut models are animals with glass eyes, and figures with glass eyes and bisque heads. One of the most popular toys ever made was the wooden Tinkertoy Construction Set, devised by Charles Pajeau and launched at the New York Toy Fair in 1915. By 1975 more than 100 million sets, packaged in distinctive cylindrical boxes, had been sold.

In Britain there was renewed interest in wooden toys in the 20th century. Such companies as Chad Valley (est. 1820; Chad Valley used as trademark from 1897) of Birmingham and the Lines family firm (est. 19th century; later Lines Bros Ltd) in London made a wide range of wooden toys, while new companies such as Forest Toys (1918–39) of Brockenhurst, Hampshire, produced a great variety of small, hand-carved and painted animals.

LARGE WOODEN TOYS

The rocking-horse first appeared in Britain in the early 17th century and reached its apogee in the mid-19th century with the highly popular "bow" rocking-horse (named after the shape of its rockers) which was hand-carved from laminated pine, then gessoed and painted. By 1870 metal cradles were attached to a secure wooden base to prevent the horse from overturning. Important makers include William Gabriel (active 19th century), Frederick Ayres (1864–1940), Lines, and Scott & Walker (1915–26).

Wooden versions of steam trains and motor cars became popular as the horse was superseded. Early pedal cars (c.1910) made by Lines are reasonably inexpensive to collect. More expensive, and more sought after, are the pedal cars made by Lines Bros Ltd in the 1930s with pneumatic tires, electric lights, klaxon horns, and wooden bodies. The best toboggans were made in the USA, Canada, and Scandinavia.

PAPER AND PAPER-ON-WOOD TOYS

In Britain, toy theaters were among the most popular wood and paper toys of the 19th century. Invented c.1811 by William West, they were available as "penny plain" or "tuppence colored." Some of the finest examples are those by Benjamin Pollock (1856–1937).

In the USA, among the best-known toymakers were Jesse A. Crandall and Charles M. Crandall, whose company (1840s–1905) was based in New York City. Early and unusual Crandall toys are very collectible; examples from the 1870s include "Crandall's District School" and the "Menagerie." Other notable manufacturers produced cheaper, wooden versions of tinplate toys; such companies included W.S. Reed Toy Co. (1876–97) and Milton Bradley & Co. (est. 1860), based respectively in Leominster and Springfield, Massachusetts, and R. Bliss.

▲ **Rocking-horse**
Made from carved and hand-painted laminated pine, this English horse can be dated to the mid-19th century by several features: sharply bowed rockers, dark dapple-gray paintwork, glass eyes, real horse-hair, finely modeled neck muscles and a long, narrow head turned to the right. An original brass-studded leather harness would be a bonus.
(mid-19th century; ht 2m/6ft 7in; value **H***)*

▼ *Ocean Wave* **by W.S. Reed Toy Co.**
This is a typically high-standard American paper-on-wood toy. Details are provided by chromolithography. The sails and sailors are made of cardboard, and the main structure, masts, and rudders of wood. Unusually, the maker's initials have been added – stamped on the cargo.
(1880s; l. 46cm/18in; value **G***)*

German-born publishers such as Ernst Nister (active late 19th–early 20th centuries) and Raphael Tuck (1821–1900) established companies in London producing movable books written in English (and therefore suitable for the USA) but printed in Germany. Raphael Tuck & Sons (est. 1882) began making jigsaw puzzles *c.*1890.

In the early 20th century new technology again brought changes in manufacturing techniques. Dissected puzzles became known as "jigsaw puzzles" after the type of saw used to make them, and, with the advent of cheap paper supplies, card replaced wood in less expensive puzzles. Few puzzles made after the 1920s have attracted collectors' interest, the notable exception being the highly sought after Chad Valley "Great Western Railway" promotional puzzles that were produced during the 1930s. One of the most valuable puzzles is the "Locomotive Erecting Shop at Swindon."

BOARD-GAMES AND JIGSAW PUZZLES

The earliest examples of board-games date from the mid-18th century. They were printed and then hand-painted and often had didactic or literary themes. After 1870 the development of chromolithography and cheap wood-pulp paper and board led to mass production, with the paper sections being laid down on folding board rather than on canvas or linen. After World War I themes became increasingly literary; for example, from 1917 Frederick Warne & Co. in London based games on Beatrix Potter's *Peter Rabbit* books. Games centered on such cartoon characters as Felix the Cat, Bonzo the Dog, and Pip, Squeak, and Wilfred were produced in the 1920s, and from the 1960s film and television themes (such as James Bond and *Thunderbirds*) became popular.

By the end of the 19th century thousands of games were produced each year in the USA. Milton Bradley (*b.*1830) was producing more than 400 games and puzzles, and in 1920 Milton Bradley & Co. bought McLoughlin Bros (est. 1858), one of its major rivals. Another giant manufacturer was Parker Brothers (est. 1883), in Salem, Massachusetts, which in 1935 produced *Monopoly,* and in 1949 *Clue* (*Cluedo* in Britain).

The jigsaw puzzle – or "dissected puzzle" – was the brainchild of John Spilsbury (*c.*1739–69), a London cartographer and engraver who used dissected maps to teach geography. Very early examples were made from engraved and hand-colored sheets of paper laid on wood and dissected by hand-cut wavy lines, with no interlocking pieces; from the mid-19th century, high-quality, hand-colored lithographs were used. Double-sided puzzles ("double dissections") were also produced. Most of these were made by board-game manufacturers.

After 1870, with the advent of chromolithography, the variety of subject-matter increased to include animals, nature, children's stories, and even propaganda.

▲ **Two board-games**
Wallis's Loco Game of Railroad Adventure (left) by Wallis (1775–1847) and *A Survey of London* (right) by William Darton (1755–1819) are typical of 19th-century board-games, being made of hand-colored, canvas-mounted sections of lithographed paper for storage in a slipcase, and having topical or educational themes.
(*Wallis's Loco Game of Railroad Adventure; 1840s; w. 38cm/15in; value* **C***; A Survey of London; c.1820; w. 61cm/24in; value* **C***)*

▲ **Teaching puzzle by J.W. Barfoot**
"The Child's Own Clock," a dissected British puzzle, exemplifies the educational nature of many 19th-century toys. The hand-painted lithograph illustrations are cut in wavy lines with no interlocking pieces, and are designed to teach children how to tell the time. The maker's characteristic "pink rose" signature is visible next to the number IIII.
(*c.1860; w. 38cm/15in; value* **A***)*

▲ **Board-game**
This British board-game was mass produced by an unknown manufacturer in the early 20th century. Its appeal lies both in the charm of its illustrations and in the theme of space travel (fueled by the invention of the airship) – of more interest to collectors than moralistic games.
(*c.1900; w. 38cm/15in; value* **C***)*

KEY FACTS

Wooden toys
- DATING early examples are more intricately carved, more highly decorated, and more valuable
- COLLECTING good condition, and the original paintwork and boxes, are essential for maximum value

Paper and wood-on-paper toys
- QUALITY examples produced between 1880 and 1914 (the golden age of chromolithography) are sought after because of the high-quality printed decoration
- DATING paper gives a clue to age: early examples use better quality "rag" paper, which acquires an attractive patina with age; later examples use wood-pulp paper, which yellows with age
- COLLECTING pieces with original, undamaged, unblemished, unfaded paper are most sought after

Board-games and jigsaw puzzles
- CONDITION board-games and puzzles must be in good condition and complete
- COLLECTING the original box and instructions are essential for maximum value; an unusual or cult theme enhances collectibility; 20th-century examples are generally inexpensive to collect

Early American toys

The American toy industry began in earnest in the 1830s, when the development of transportation by railway and canal made mass production and distribution viable. From the mid-19th century American toy manufacturers produced a wide range of tinplate toys notable for their ingenious design, hand-painted decoration, and charm. Steel was used by the turn of the century to produce friction toys and, later, pressed-steel cars and trucks. By the 1880s cast-iron toys and banks were being produced in large quantities and remained an almost exclusively American phenomenon.

▼ **"Charles" hose reel by George W. Brown & Co.**
This early American tinplate toy is exceptionally rare and valuable. It's design, pull-along mechanism and precise hand-painted decoration are typical of 19th century American tinplate toys.
(c.1867; l. 58cm/22¾in; value Q)

▲ **"Amos 'n' Andy" car by Louis Marx & Co.**
This American toy is based on the *Amos 'n' Andy* radio series, which took the USA by storm. The Marx company produced a vast range of well-made but inexpensive tinplate toys, many characterized by light-hearted and humorous designs.
(1930s; l. 20cm/8in; value E)

TINPLATE TOYS
Tin toys are made from thin sheet steel plated with tin. The first American tin toy manufacturer, Francis, Field & Francis (1838–1870s; also known as the Philadelphia Tin Toy Manufactory) in Philadelphia, Pennsylvania, produced a range of tinplate toys, especially pull-along trains. Tin was a difficult medium to work in, and these early tin toys were of simple design and painted in brilliant colors, to which hand-painted and, later, hand-stenciled decoration was added. George W. Brown & Co. (est. 1856) in Forestville, Connecticut, was probably the first maker to introduce a clockwork mechanism into an American toy, and went on to produce a range of charming tinplate mechanical toys. In 1868 Brown merged with J. & E. Stevens & Co. (est. 1843) in Cromwell, Connecticut, which resulted in the hugely popular Stevens & Brown velocipede.

From c.1914 to c.1942 Ferdinand Strauss produced lithographed tin toys such as "Ham & Sam the Minstrel Team" and "Jackee the Horn Pipe Dancer." Louis Marx (1896–1982) worked for Strauss for several years before setting up his own business in 1919. Marx became the largest toy manufacturer in the world and by the 1930s had set up a factory in Britain, at Dudley, near Birmingham. J. Chein & Co. (est. 1903) in Harrison, New Jersey, was a pioneer in the production of cheap lithographed sheet-metal toys, in which the tin sheet was printed with the design and

▼ **"Hill Climber" racer car by D.P. Clark & Co.**
Clark was one of the first companies to produce pressed steel cars with a flywheel mechanism. The term "hill climber" was used by many manufacturers to describe toy cars with a large iron flywheel that drove an extra set of wheels. However, Clark made the name its own by stamping it on the underside of its toys for a time. This example is in the colors of the American team in the 1903 Gordon Bennett Racing Trophy in Ireland.
(c.1903; l. 31cm/12in; value D)

color and then pressed into shape. The company made brightly-colored wind-up toys such as roller-coasters, Ferris wheels and merry-go-rounds, as well as many different versions of the popular *Popeye* comic strip characters, until 1979.

STEEL TOYS
With the advent of the motor car came an enthusiasm for toy automotive vehicles. Early manufacturers include D.P. Clark & Co. (est. 1898) in Dayton, Ohio, which was founded to manufacture the automotive friction toys patented by Israel Donald Boyer and his wife Edith on 2 November 1897. In these the flywheel and friction mechanism was combined with sheet-steel and wood bodies to produce a range of trains, novelty toys, and automotive toys. The last included Clark's "Hill Climber" range of cars, sturdily built and decorated with hand-painted stripes to resemble real cars. Even more sturdy were the cars and trucks produced by Fred Lundhal, who in 1921, in Moline, Illinois, first produced 20-gauge steel toy vehicles with a heavy baked-enamel finish. The company, known as "Buddy 'L'," became a large and prestigious toy manufacturer, known for the accuracy, size, and strength of its trucks, fire-trucks, and Model Ts. Kingsbury Manufacturing Co. (1919–42) in Keene, New Hampshire, produced a range of land-speed record cars in the 1920s and 1930s. Other Kingsbury car bodies were made from lightweight steel, which allowed for sharper, more authentic detail in the pressing process.

CAST-IRON TOYS
Although cast-iron toys were produced in the 1860s, they did not appear in great numbers until the 1880s, and by the 1920s and 1930s they were being superseded by lithographed tinplate toys. They were usually cast in several parts which were then pinned, bolted, or riveted together. "Bell toys" are an American phenomenon; first patented in 1874, they consist of designs incorporating two cast-iron wheels enclosing a bell that sounds when the toy is pushed or pulled along. Some of the finest

early cast-iron toys were produced by the Hubley Manufacturing Co. (est. 1894) in Lancaster, Pennsylvania, which after 1909 manufactured them as well as cast-iron hardware and novelties. Early toys included horse-drawn wagons, fire-engines, circus trains, and guns; an automotive line added later was particularly successful, especially the 5-ton trucks with the Keystone emblem on the side. The company rode out the Depression with "N.D.Q." ("nickel, dime, quarter") toys, but ceased toy production in 1942.

From 1920 to the 1930s the Dent Hardware Co. (est. 1895) in Fullerton, Pennsylvania, produced toys notable for their exceptionally fine casting, which makes them easy to identify even though they are unmarked. In 1921 the Arcade Manufacturing Co. (1868–1942) in Freeport, Illinois, produced its first "Yellow Cab," which was an instant success. The company slogan – "They Look Real" – reflected the quality of its cast-iron cars, probably one of the most successful toy car lines in the USA. Much of the company's success was due to the Mack truck series, which remained perennially popular; the Mack "Dump Truck" was one of the best- and longest-selling toys in the Arcade line.

CAST-IRON BANKS

The golden age of American cast-iron savings banks lasted from c.1869 to c.1910. There are two types of bank: still and mechanical. Still banks are primarily repositories and usually take the form of an animal or a human figure with a coin slot. Mechanical banks have moving parts and springs, and a sequence of movements can be triggered either by simply depositing a coin or, more commonly, by depositing a coin and pulling a lever.

John Hall of Watertown, Massachusetts, is generally credited with the first cast-iron mechanical bank – "Hall's Excelsior" – which was patented in 1869 and manufactured by J. & E. Stevens & Co. The charm and simple ingenuity of the design made the bank so

successful that it was produced for many years and is therefore one of the easiest banks to find (although rarely in good condition). One of the most ingenious designers was Charles A. Bailey, who patented his first mechanical bank in 1880. His output was so prodigious that he is believed to have been responsible for some 20 percent of all American cast-iron banks, many of which were produced by the most prolific cast-iron bank manufacturer, J. & E. Stevens & Co. Both Kyser & Rex (1879–98) in Philadelphia, Pennsylvania, and the Shephard Hardware Manufacturing Co. (1882–92) in Buffalo, New York, were hardware manufacturers which diversified into mechanical banks.

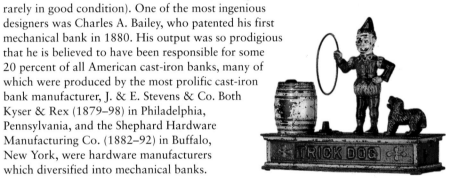

◄ **"Paddy and the Pig" bank by J. & E. Stevens & Co.**
The design of this cast-iron bank, which was patented by James H. Bowen on 8 August 1882, is typically humorous and a reflection of the ethnic stereotyping of the period. Paddy sits with a jug of whiskey poking out of his pocket; when a coin is placed on the pig's snout and a lever behind Paddy is pressed, the pig lifts its left leg to kick the coin toward him. Paddy then obligingly opens his mouth and sticks out his tongue to catch it, while rolling his eyes.
(c.1882; ht 25cm/9¾in; value G)

▼ **"Trick Dog" bank by the Hubley Manufacturing Co.**
Patented on 31 July 1888, this bank was produced for more than 50 years. Its popularity may be due to the simple yet entertaining movement: the coin is placed in the dog's mouth, and when the lever on the right-hand side of the base is pushed down the dog jumps through the hoop and the coin disappears into the barrel. On later versions the words "TRICK DOG" are inscribed on the base.
(c.1890; l. 21.5cm/8½in; value E)

▲ **"Two Frogs" bank by J. & E. Stevens & Co.**
This hand-painted bank was designed by James H. Bowen. The coin is deposited on the front legs of the small frog; when a lever behind the large frog is depressed, it opens its mouth and the small frog kicks the coin inside. The lush green foliage on the base is a typical feature of Bowen's excellent designs.
(c.1882; l. 21.5cm/8½in; value H)

KEY FACTS

Tinplate toys
- COLLECTING early American tinplate is rare and therefore valuable in any condition; later tinplate pull-along animals are more common; paintwork may be in good condition, but is liable to flake off because toys were often poorly primed

Cast-iron toys
- RESTORATION many toys have been repainted; poor restoration can result in "measle"-like patches where paint-remover has gone too deep
- REPRODUCTIONS reproduction cast-iron toys proliferate but are of little value; check for rough, ill-finished castings, poor detail, and any evidence of removal of a label or lettering

Cast-iron banks
- CONDITION good condition is vital because cast iron is difficult to repair
- RESTORATION original paintwork will have depth of color, a satiny patination, and perhaps fine crazing
- REPRODUCTIONS reproductions and fakes outnumber originals: check for rough surface with blurred details; ill-fitting pieces; a rusty, unpainted finish

Marks
Louis Marx & Co. (1919–82)

Tinplate

New technology arising from the Industrial Revolution made it possible to use tinplate rather than wood to make toy figures, horse-drawn carriages, and, later, boats, submarines, motor cars, and airships. Germany led the field with such famous factories as Märklin and Bing. In France the major toy-producer was Fernand Martin, which made high-quality and attractive novelty figures, while in Britain the firm of Frank Hornby was the market leader. In the USA the first tinplate factories opened in the 1830s, although tinplate toys were only produced for a short period there, since cast iron was the preferred material. Tinplate declined in popularity in the mid-20th century, when plastic toys from the Far East became widely available.

Germany

Early producers

The earliest producers of tinplate toys included Rock & Gräner (1815–1905), in Biberach an der Riss, and Lütz (1846–1905), in Ellwangen. Among their toys were horse-drawn carriages, railway locomotives, boats, soldiers, dolls' house furniture, and hand-painted dioramas. Toys made by Günthermann (est. 1877) in Brandenburg are distinguished by the vitality and humor of the designs: machine-pressed tinplate figures of dancing couples, boys flying kites, and the well-known range of Gordon Bennett racing cars. Another renowned company is Lehmann (est. 1881), also in Brandenburg, whose mass-produced novelty toys were inexpensive and popular. However, from the mid-19th century the production of tinplate toys was mainly centered on Nuremberg, where there was a pool of skilled labor.

NUREMBERG FACTORIES

Ernst Planck (1866–c.1935) made a range of novelty toys that included optical toys and magic lanterns as well as boats, and used steam and electric power. At the quality end of the market was Buchner (active 1880s), which specialized in coaches and horse-drawn carriages, and Staudt (est. 1867), which made horse-drawn carriages, omnibuses, and fire-engines, clockwork trains, boats, and carousels, and hand-painted novelty toys.

Another phenomenon of the mass production of lithographed tinplate was the penny toy. Production peaked c.1906 but continued into the 1930s. Boats,

▲ **Frog by Günthermann**

The eccentric humor of Günthermann's toys is exhibited in this painted frog, with its tailcoat, bow-tie, hat, and pince-nez. The elegant clothing is somewhat marred by flaking paintwork – a common problem with less expensive novelty toys, which were often poorly primed.
(c.1898; ht 18cm/7in; value **G**)

motor cars, aircraft, and novelty items were popular and usually had a simple push-along action or a flywheel; more unusual were items such as tiny telephones, birdcages, and sewing machines.

World War I stopped the worldwide export of German toys; after the war Germany resumed exporting, but to a changed market. Demand was now for less expensive and less exclusive toys, and makers catered to this with lighter, less complex models, simplified pressings, cheaper clockwork motors, and less detailed lithography. Schreyer & Co. (1912–78; trademark Schuco) produced novelty toys noted for their robust mechanisms and ingenious action – the range of clockwork figures included a Charlie Chaplin who twirled his cane as he walked. Schreyer was also known for its cars, often with complex mechanisms. Tipp & Co. (known as Tippco; 1912–71) made character toys, motorcycles, cars, trucks, and airplanes, and, after 1933, a fine range of military vehicles. In the 1920s and 1930s, Karl Bub (1851–1960s) produced a range of attractive limousines, coupés, and cabriolets, some still hand-painted. Another prolific manufacturer of toy cars in the 1920s and 1930s was Distler (c.1900–1962), which made such lithographed toys as 70cm (27½in) limousines. The clockwork cars were offered with or without electric light; larger cars are more stylish and collectible.

KEY FACTS

- **IMPORTANT FACTORIES** Nuremberg: Günthermann, Plank, Schreyer & Co., Tipp & Co., Distler & Co.; Other: Rock & Gräner, Lütz, Lehmann
- **CONDITION** good condition is very important as lithographed tinplate is almost impossible to restore properly; poor restoration detracts greatly from value
- **COLLECTING** tinplate toys made before 1895 are usually hand painted, with motor vehicles, aircraft, and fire appliances the most sought after, as well as toys with a short production run; later tinplate: this is flimsier with less detailing, but also less expensive than earlier work; large or fine boats are perhaps the most popular of later tinplate toys; with all examples, the original packaging adds greatly to value

Marks

Nuremberg: Buchner (active 1880s); marked with the initials "CB" inside the letter "M" and the word "Buchner"

Nuremberg: Ernst Plank (1866–c.1935)

Nuremberg: Günthermann (1887–1965)

Brandenburg: Ernst Paul Lehmann (est. 1881)

▼ *Wilhelm II* **paddle-steamer by Rock & Gräner**

This clockwork paddle-steamer was formerly attributed to Lütz. The detail, finish, and quality of construction justify its high value.
(1880; l. 71cm/28in; value **I**)

Märklin

The company was established in Göppingen in 1856 by Theodor Friedrich Wilhelm Märklin. In 1888 Theodor's sons Eugen and Carl assumed control, changing the name to Gebrüder Märklin. By 1895 the company catalog included the classic range of boats, trains, and horse-drawn vehicles that was to make it a world leader.

BEFORE 1914

From the mid-1890s Märklin made boats. The very earliest were somewhat crude in design, but they were characterized by solid construction, thickly applied paintwork, lavish hand-painted detail, and realistic fittings. The detail included deck fittings, lifeboats, masts, riggings, guns, and model sailors. The somewhat oversized proportion of these fittings gave the boats a freedom of design and charm that the more precisely modeled boats made after 1920 lost. Later models became increasingly sophisticated and were powered by clockwork, steam, or electricity. Popular lines remained in production over a long period. The high quality associated with Märklin is epitomized by the large ocean liners built mostly to order from 1909 to 1912. Surviving examples are rare and very expensive.

The number of cars produced was small, since the company concentrated on quality rather than quantity, making a limited range of expensive and often specially commissioned models. They were introduced in 1900, and pre-1914 examples are rarer than boats and trains made at the same time. Märklin cars are solid and well built in heavy-gauge tinplate. The severe style is offset by the superb finish produced by the thick paintwork and hand-painted detail; other luxuries included brass bonnet trims, pierced radiator grilles, and distinctive headlamps with concave lenses. Expensive and exclusive at the time of production, these cars were a great commercial success and are now highly collectible, but comparatively rare and correspondingly highly priced.

AFTER 1914

Märklin produced a limited special range of battleships during World War I, and pre-war boat designs were still made in the inter-war years. Many of the boats were steam-powered, but spirit-fired boilers were gradually replaced by clockwork motors, which were cheaper and safer. The cars became simpler, and the toy boats became closer to real boats in scale, with metal flags and stamped or stenciled portholes; both cars and boats were subsidiary to Märklin's trains. However, in the

▶ *Kronprinz Wilhelm*
ocean liner
Such toy vessels were the finest made in the world at the time of production. They were generally made to order, with a clockwork (as here), steam, or electrical mechanism, in rising order of cost. Boats are more prone to damage than other tin toys and should be checked carefully for missing details, repainting, and rust damage.
*(c.1911; l. 94cm/36½in; value **O**)*

▲ **Limousine**
This solidly built tinplate limousine is rare, but typical of the superb vehicles made during Märklin's golden era (1895–1914). It has a characteristically sturdy appearance, waisted wheel spokes, lamps with concave lenses, and realistic detail, including luggage straps, removable spare tires, and a pierced luggage rack, as well as a complex steering mechanism.
*(c.1910; l. 31cm/12in; value **L**)*

▶ **Racing car**
The mint condition of this clockwork racing car adds considerably to its value, as does the rare presence of the driver. It is an unusual example of a post-World War II factory-built model that has survived untouched with its original tissue wrapping and display plinth, as well as its box.
*(c.1950; l. 36cm/14in; value **G**)*

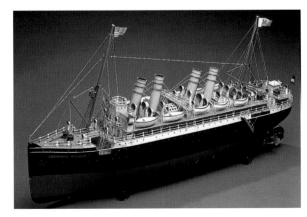

1930s the company produced a successful range of car construction kits. A standard chassis kit could be used with different component kits to construct six contemporary vehicles, the rarest and most collectible being the armored car, with painted camouflage, and the limousine, with spring suspension.

Märklin had been licensed to make Meccano before World War I. After the war it started to make its own very similar range, which was produced until the 1950s. From 1935 it also began to produce its own range of diecast toy vehicles: military vehicles, racing cars, limousines, and touring cars, all based on contemporary German models with the exception of a Buick produced in 1949. Production ceased in 1972.

KEY FACTS

- **STYLE** toys are constructed of heavy-gauge tinplate with a thick, almost creamy, paint finish; early vehicles and boats are filled with lifelike detail; solid, almost severe, design is combined with massive mechanisms and powerful springs
- **COLLECTING** most examples are rare and very valuable, especially the ocean liners built to order between 1909 and 1912; diecast cars produced in the 1940s and 1950s are more common but still have the quality casting and precise detail associated with Märklin; check for restoration on all toys, which may only be visible under UV light; a total repaint, which can be difficult to detect if of high quality, will affect value

Marks

The Märklin mark changed; this is one of the most common; boats usually marked on rudder

See also Trains: Märklin, p.464

Bing and Carette

After Märklin the two most important German factories producing tinplate toys during the late 19th and 20th centuries were those of the firms of Bing and Carette, both based in Nuremberg.

BING

Gebrüder Bing was founded by the brothers Ignatz and Adolf Bing in 1863. Originally a wholesale company, during the 1880s it had the sole buying and distribution rights for Lütz (est. 1846) in Ellwangen. Bing started its own production of toys in 1879.

From 1895 to 1905 Bing's toy boats were on a par with those of Märklin. Examples made before 1903 have hand-painted portholes and metal flags, after which flags were lithographed and portholes transfer-printed. Bing's boats were accurate representations of the real models, as were its cars, produced from 1902. Early car production aimed at a limited production of high-quality, expensive models with realistic detail. Although they were more mechanically accurate than Märklin cars, their more lightweight construction, rounded contors (especially the coal-scuttle bonnet), and fine hand-painted finish and lining achieved an overall lighter touch.

From c.1905 Bing inclined more toward quantity than quality, with its first lithographed small cars appearing c.1906; by 1914 most Bing cars were made from lithographed tinplate. Bing's originality sometimes gave rise to eccentricity; for example, the "American Platform" motor fire-truck used a ship's wheel to turn the platform-raising mechanism, while novel "Tuff Tuff" leather bellows recreated the sound of the engine. The toys reflected advances in real cars: the squared-off bonnet of a 1908 lithographed tinplate tourer was replaced c.1912 by the new convex shape.

During World War I, Bing adapted the lithograph decoration to transform its cars into wartime vehicles for the home market. It produced a popular range of Model T Fords c.1922, and in the late 1920s began to use electric power. Neither innovation prevented Bing's decline and its takeover by Karl Bub (est. 1851) in 1933.

▲ Car by Bing
Of characteristically high quality, this four-seat rear-entry tonneau has a light construction and fine, hand-painted finish with lining. The realistic details include a nickeled handbrake, a steering wheel, and headlamps. The clockwork mechanism is still working, as is the bellows horn.
(c.1906; l. 21cm/8¼in; value H)

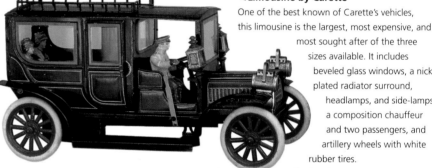

◄ Limousine by Carette
One of the best known of Carette's vehicles, this limousine is the largest, most expensive, and most sought after of the three sizes available. It includes beveled glass windows, a nickel-plated radiator surround, headlamps, and side-lamps, a composition chauffeur and two passengers, and artillery wheels with white rubber tires.
(c.1911; l. 40cm/15¾in; value I)

▼ Fire-engine by Bing
Fire-engines are generally very popular with collectors. This clockwork example has many realistic details: an air chamber, a reservoir, a bell, and two composition firemen. The hand-painted finish is chipped, and one of the headlamps and the hoses are missing, but there has been no attempt at repainting.
(c.1910; l. 26cm/10¼in; value H)

CARETTE

Georges Carette & Cie was founded in 1886 by the Frenchman Georges Carette, who lived and worked in Nuremberg, where he had been an apprentice in the Bing factory. From c.1900 the company began making toy cars, and went on to become one of the most prolific manufacturers of a range of elegant and well-made vehicles. Carette's cars are stylish, and often have fine-painted tinplate chauffeurs and passengers. Designs were often available in different versions, enabling customers to choose one of three sizes, a hand-enameled or a lithographed model, metal wheels or rubber tires, and a number of optional mechanisms and extra features including side-lamps and glass windows. Thus the price for one of the most famous and collectible Carette cars – a limousine with four side windows made c.1911 – could range from 1s 9d to 20s. Most sought after are the larger and more expensive cars, hand-painted and with luxury details. Although there was some limited production during World War I, Carette was forced to flee Germany in 1917, and the company ceased trading.

KEY FACTS

Bing (1879–1933)
- STYLE uses a lighter-gauge tinplate than Märklin; the more expensive cars are hand-painted, the less expensive are lithographed
- CONDITION good condition is essential because restoration of hand-painted and lithographed tinplate is difficult and can greatly reduce value
- DATING wheels help to date a model: early examples have plain wheels with thin spokes and rims; later, less expensive models have plain, thick spokes; by 1914 models have spoked wheels with stretched rubber tires
- PACKAGING original packaging is rare and adds value; it should be plain cardboard or a wooden box with a simple trademark or line engraving

Marks
Applied by transfer, embossed on tinplate, soldered plate with mark

Carette (1886–1917)
- STYLE similar to Bing, but the most expensive models are much larger and more elaborate; early models are of lightweight tinplate, sometimes with a lithographed gold lining; distinctive concave brackets connect the running-board to the subframe
- COLLECTING several versions of one model were often made

Marks
Applied by transfer, but not often used

See also Trains: Bing and Bassett-Lowke, p.465

Other European countries

In the late 19th and early 20th centuries German manufacturers dominated the production of tinplate toys in Europe and exported toys worldwide. However, good-quality tinplate toys were produced in other European countries.

BRITAIN

While Germany dominated production, demand for home-produced tinplate toys in Britain was small. However, British manufacturers were supremely successful in the production of tinplate novelty biscuit tins, commissioned by such companies as Huntley & Palmer and Crawford's. Popular forms included cars, omnibuses, vans, boats, airplanes, and racing cars.

One of the most successful of all British toymaking companies was established by Frank Hornby in Liverpool in 1901. The original name, Mechanics Made Easy, was changed to Meccano in 1907. The company produced construction sets, consisting of painted steel strips and accessories that could be assembled into a variety of models. From 1932 to 1940 the company introduced a range of Constructor Car and Airplane sets, and the even more sought-after factory-assembled "non-constructor" cars.

Triang was established in 1919 by William, Arthur, and Walter Lines, sons of the founders of Lines Bros Ltd, as an offshoot of the original firm. Most successful of its tinplate toy range was Minic – a range of pocket-sized clockwork cars produced from 1935 to 1963 and designed to compete with the highly successful mass-produced diecast cars. Mettoy Co. Ltd (1936–83) was founded in Northampton by Philip Ullman, former head of the German toy manufacturing company Tipp & Co. (Tippco) and made lithographed tinplate vehicles.

FRANCE, ITALY, AND SPAIN

Fernand Martin & Cie began production in its Paris factory in 1880. By 1900 the company was a major manufacturer and exporter of a range of ingenious novelty toys, which were mass-produced and powered by elastic bands or clockwork. They were based on such characters as dancers, duellists, barbers, street violinists, butchers, policemen, and gymnasts, and closely resemble the figures made by the German firm of Lehmann (est. 1881) in Brandenburg.

◄ **Cars and airplane by Meccano**
Meccano cars were made of good-quality tinplate, painted and sold in top-quality cardboard boxes. These No. 2 Constructor Cars were available with a diecast driver, a handbrake, and electric lighting. Fewer "non-constructor" cars were made, and they are more collectible.
(c.1934; Constructor Car: l. 28.5cm/11in; value C; non-constructor car: l. 23cm/9in; value E)

▲ **Minic Rolls-Royce by Triang**
This painted tinplate Rolls-Royce was top of the highly successful Minic series. The wheels, which are liable to perish, are in very good condition, which adds to the value of this piece.
(1939; l. 10cm/4in; value G)

▲ **Racing car by C.I.J.**
C.I.J.'s P2 Alfa Romeo always carried the racing number 2. Made of painted tinplate and run by a powerful clockwork mechanism, the car came in different colors, each one identifying a different major European racing team: red was for Italy. The fine details include leather bonnet straps, knock-off wheels, and hinged filler caps. It was produced in at least three series; earlier versions have large, smooth tires.
(mid-1930s; l. 52cm/20½in; value G)

During the inter-war years French manufacturers produced some of the finest tinplate toy cars in the world. C.I.J. (Compagnie Industriel de Jouets; 1902–64), in Paris, produced a range of well-made racing cars, the most famous of which was the P2 Alfa Romeo, modeled on the actual car, produced in the mid- and late 1920s in a range of colors, each associated with an international racing team. C.I.J. also made promotional models of Citroën cars, including the Traction Avant, for André Citroën (est. 1923). When Citroën was taken over in 1933 C.I.J. made promotional model cars for Renault until c.1960. Model versions of real cars were made by J.E.P. (Jouets de Paris), founded in 1899 as the Société Industrielle de Ferblanterie; in 1928 it was renamed Jouets de Paris, and in 1932 Jouets en Paris. In the 1920s and 1930s it produced a fine range of famous cars, which brought it to the forefront of toy car production.

Italian and Spanish manufacturers produced tinplate toys for their respective home markets. Ingap (Industria Nazionale Giocattoli Automatici Padua) started production in 1922, making mainly cars in thin tinplate and bright colors; a popular novelty toy of the 1930s was "Felix the Cat" with a three-wheeled cart. The Spanish company Paya was founded by the Paya brothers in Ibi, near Alicante, in the early 20th century, and is best known for its range of train sets and motor vehicles, including its famous Bugatti, produced between 1930 and 1948.

KEY FACTS

- BISCUIT TINS only valuable in perfect condition
- MECCANO well-used Meccano is not collectible; look for unused pre-war complete boxed sets; factory-built model cars; rare pieces (often small or with an unusual function) produced in the inter-war years; avoid repainted parts
- C.I.J. CARS Alfa Romeos: rare colors (white, orange, metallic blue, metallic red) can treble or quadruple value; check for front-end rebuilding, roll damage, and bent axles; Citroëns: the rarest and most collectible are the B2 taxis, the Traction Avant, and the Kergresse Half Track designed for crossing the Sahara Desert
- MARKETS Italian and Spanish tinplate toys are mainly collected in the home market

Marks

Lines Bros Ltd: this is the mark used for their Triang range of toys

Mettoy Co. Ltd: this mark was introduced in 1936 and used until c.1965

Trains

The first European model trains, produced *c.*1850, were of very simple design, of sturdy construction, and not very realistic. It was only at the end of the 19th and beginning of the 20th centuries that forms and mechanisms were developed, particularly by such famous German firms as Märklin, Bing, and Carette & Cie, which dominated the market completely before World War I, and later British firms including Hornby. In the USA outstanding trains were made by the Lionel Corporation and the Finch & Voltramp Electric Manufacturing Co. Trains are driven by steam, clockwork, or electricity and are made in a variety of gauges ranging from the early wide II, III, and IV through to the modern narrow 00 and H0 ones.

Germany and Britain

Märklin

Like those of other makers, early trains by Märklin (est. 1859) were simple but solidly constructed; they were not very realistic and had exaggerated domes, lamps, and fittings. In 1891, at the Leipzig Toy Fair, Märklin introduced a major development in the manufacture of toy trains: standardized gauges – 0 (35mm/1⅜in), I (48mm/1⅞in), II (54mm/2⅛in), and III (75mm/3in).

BEFORE 1945

The early 1900s were the first "golden age" of Märklin trains. The simple early designs were superseded by a range of realistic, detailed trains with a distinctive heavy style and a superb, thickly lacquered finish. A number of large, Gauge III locomotives were produced, but by 1910 there was an increasing demand for smaller, Gauge I and 0 Gauge models. Märklin also made an unrivaled range of rolling stock and accessories, from ornate station buildings to signals and lamps.

A large proportion of Märklin production at this time was geared to its highly successful export market. For the USA, a cow-catcher pilot was added to what was essentially a German locomotive, while an Alpine railway summer coach was aimed at the Swiss market. Especially sought after are the 0 Gauge circus wagons, which could be customized for different circuses.

After World War I, production picked up slowly. Both Gauge I and 0 Gauge models were produced for Britain, but the large locomotives were too big for the new-style, smaller-scale homes, and by 1938 Gauge I was obsolete. Märklin's heavy, thickly painted trains began to look old-fashioned; from 1930 the company invested in new tooling, and launched a range of detailed, specialized, international trains. This expensive, high-quality range included the Swiss *Crocodile*, the American *Commodore Vanderbilt*, and a number of British locomotives. The British series is especially popular; the fine, smooth lacquer is typical of the thinner, more even paint finish found from the 1930s. Most sought after are the green and the black versions of LNER's (London & North Eastern Railway's) *Cock o' the North* (1935–7).

AFTER 1945

In 1948 Märklin made several changes to its range. The 00 Gauge introduced in 1935 was not as realistic as that produced by British companies, so in 1948 the range was reworked, and the H0 Gauge was launched, with powerful, heavily built trains. Their diecast metal bodies had more accurate proportions: narrower, with a slightly matt finish, and a new type of coupling. By the late 1950s the solidity and quality of Märklin's trains had re-established the company's worldwide reputation. The 0 Gauge had disappeared by 1954; a major innovation two years later was the use of plastic, and by the late 1960s plastic was used for almost all trains.

▼ Gauge III train
Made for the British market, this unusually large tinplate train has a locomotive, a tender, and a coach. It is loosely based on London & North Western Railway stock and has several features typical of 1900–1914 production, such as solid construction and dense lacquer finish.
*(c.1904; l. 1.2m/3ft 11in; value **K**)*

▲ CCS 800 *Crocodile* locomotive
The Swiss-outline *Crocodile* (also made before the war in 0 Gauge) was one of the most popular of the H0 Gauge electric articulated locomotives launched in the late 1940s. It has the typical detailed, diecast, painted metal body with a slightly matt finish. This example is in good condition, with its original sturdy cardboard box.
*(c.1952; l. 23cm/9in; value **G**)*

KEY FACTS

1890–1914
- STYLE heavy, well-made trains, with little attempt at realism; early Gauge I, II, and III were gradually replaced by 0 Gauge
- POWER mainly powered by steam or clockwork; occasionally electric, from 1898; early steam mechanisms can be dangerous
- COLLECTING fine early pieces are very valuable; careful restoration of painting can be detected with UV light

1918–1940
- STYLE more realistic trains, with almost scale-length locomotives and coaches; detailed wagons with rare special loads, e.g. skis, armored cars, aircraft
- COLLECTING pieces from 1920s are generally less valuable, except for large Gauge I and 0 Gauge trains

Dating
- COUPLINGS couplings help to date pieces: pre-1904, simple tin loop coupling; *c.*1904–*c.*1913, hook coupling; from 1913, sliding drop link coupling
- CATALOGS from *c.*1910, catalog references were stenciled or lithographed on the sides of trains or stock

Marks
This mark was often applied to Märklin trains from *c.*1932, usually on the underside

See also Tinplate: Märklin, p.461

Bing and Bassett-Lowke

The history of the German firm of Bing and the British firm of Bassett-Lowke are inextricably linked. In 1900 the British entrepreneur Wenman Bassett-Lowke met Stefan Bing, the director of Gebrüder Bing, and the two men became business associates. The German firm supplied Bassett-Lowke with trains for sale through both its retail outlet in London and its mail order catalogs. This successful relationship remained until Bing was acquired 1933 by Karl Bub (est. 1851).

BING

Gebrüder Bing (1863–1933), in Nuremberg, manufactured a wide variety of trains, and by 1900 production was second only to that of Märklin. Bing trains ranged from mass-produced, lithographed tinplate "starter" kits to expensive, high-quality, large Gauge III and IV locomotives. Powered by clockwork and steam, Bing trains were lighter in style and more detailed than those of Märklin. In 1901 Bing began the "Black Prince" series for Bassett Lowke, while continuing to make trains under its own name for the middle and bottom ranges of the British and German markets.

After World War I, Bing simplified its train line. The range remained large, but the top-quality trains were less expensive. Production of mostly pre-war locomotives continued, but quality deteriorated in the 1920s. In 1921 Bing produced a new range of coaches for Bassett-Lowke of high-quality lithographed tinplate, known as the "1921 stock." In 1923 the British railway companies merged into a network of four large companies – GWR, LNER, LMS, and SR – and Bing had to adapt to the new liveries; pre-war locomotive designs were often combined with 1921 rolling stock painted over in the new liveries. A popular "own brand" series was the inexpensive 4-4-0 locomotives, loosely based on British trains, with the same body shell painted in the different liveries of the various companies. These remain popular, especially the Caledonian livery version. Despite its success, Bing was taken over in 1933. Stefan and Franz Bing then started a new company, Trix, and in 1935 launched a 00 Gauge tabletop electric train set. A British branch (1935–58) was set up with Winteringham, the manufacturing division of Bassett-Lowke.

W.J. BASSETT-LOWKE & CO.

W.J. Bassett-Lowke & Co. (1899–1969) was established in Northampton by Wenman Bassett-Lowke. He was an entrepreneur rather than a manufacturer, and sold

components for steam trains and locomotives through his mail order business. After meeting Bing in 1900 Bassett-Lowke realized the enormous market potential in Britain for Bing's high-quality trains, and, with the designer Henry Greenly, Bing made a fine range of 0 Gauge and Gauge I trains for the British market. In 1908 Bassett-Lowke & Co. set up its own manufacturing branch with George Winteringham. Bassett-Lowke also collaborated with Georges Carette & Cie (1886–1917) in Nuremberg, which manufactured a superb range of tinplate coaches and wagons (c.1912–14) for the firm.

The association with Bing continued after the war, although Bassett-Lowke increasingly used Winteringham, producing such successful ranges of locomotives as the live-steam "Mogul" range (from 1925), in the livery of all four national railway companies, and the *Flying Scotsman* (1933–1950s), a fine, realistic scale model. After World War II Winteringham produced lithographed tinplate trains and, until 1958, the Trix Twin range, as well as an expensive range of locomotives designed and hand-built by two freelance engineers, Victor Hunt and Victor Reader.

▼ **Gauge I 4-4-0 train by Bing for W.J. Bassett-Lowke & Co.**
This large-scale Gauge I train – one of the sturdy "112" series of tank locomotives – is made of painted tinplate and powered by clockwork. It is typical of the less expensive trains that Bing made for the mid-range of both the British and the German markets.
(c.1905; l. 25.5cm/10in; value D)

▲ *Flying Scotsman* **locomotive and tender by W.J. Bassett-Lowke & Co.**
First produced in 1933, Bassett-Lowke's LNER *Flying Scotsman* represents the high point of the company's production at this time. Designed by the managing director, Robert Bindon-Blood, the *Flying Scotsman* remained a popular model until the 1950s, and is highly sought after today. Made of lithographed tinplate in 0 Gauge, it has an electric mechanism and is a realistic and accurate model of the real locomotive. This particular example has the most valuable livery – an experimental blue that was briefly used by British Railways.
(c.1951–2; l. 51cm/20in; value G)

KEY FACTS

Bing
- STYLE trains are of lighter construction and better, more realistic modeling than Märklin trains; the most expensive models were hand-painted, the less expensive were lithographed
- RANGE a wider range than Märklin's was produced, and examples are therefore easier to find, especially less expensive models
- COLLECTING generally less expensive than Märklin trains; models after the 1920s are more affordable

W.J. Bassett-Lowke & Co.
- RANGE an eclectic range, mostly high quality, was produced by a select variety of makers to its own specifications
- COLLECTING Bing/Greenly models, mostly pre-World War I, are the most sought after; peak quality was reached in the 1950s, and hand-built locomotives of this era are very valuable
- DATING marks and couplings are good dating guides: pre-1914 trains are often unmarked; from c.1925, Winteringham's own products almost always marked with Bassett-Lowke trademark

Marks
W.J. Bassett-Lowke & Co.: applied by transfer, this mark mainly appears on locomotive tenders

See also Tinplate: Bing and Carette, p.462

Hornby

BEFORE 1938

After World War I, Britain was reluctant to import German toys; in June 1920, with his slogan "British Toys for British Boys," Frank Hornby launched the first 0 Gauge Hornby train sets. These early, clockwork sets were crude, sturdy, and toylike, and by 1923 were being replaced by more realistic designs. Colorful and durable, the later range was spray-painted, with some high-quality lithographed parts. The first electric train was produced in 1925; these early "Metropolitan" locomotives are highly popular with collectors.

From the early 1930s the Hornby Series range became increasingly realistic. Rare, and correspondingly valuable, models include locomotives such as the *County of Bedford*, the *Bramham Moor* Hunt Class LNER

locomotive, and the 1937 version of Southern Railway's Schools Class *Eton*. Hornby made a wide range of accessories: wagons, stations, and even sections of cardboard countryside with loofah hedges. Among the rarest of the Private Owner Vans series is the bright yellow Colman's Mustard one (1923–4). The finest, largest, and most accurate of all Hornby Series trains was the 4-6-2 LMS *Princess Elizabeth* (1937–40).

Post-World War II production suffered as a result of worn tooling and the lingering effects of war production. Redesigned in 1946, the new 0 Gauge trains were generally of poorer quality; lightweight tinplate and plainer, simpler trains contributed to the general decline, as did the success of the Hornby-Dublo range introduced in 1938. The last 0 Gauge material was sold in 1969.

AFTER 1938

In 1938 Hornby launched the Hornby-Dublo range to compete with the successful 00 Gauge systems of Märklin (est. 1859) and Trix (1935–58). Unlike the Hornby 0 Gauge, Hornby-Dublo was accurate and well modeled from the start. Cheaper clockwork versions were also available but were only produced until 1940, making them rare and sought after today.

▼ Hornby Series *Eton* locomotive and tender
The 4-4-0 0 Gauge Schools Class *Eton* locomotive is one of Hornby's most realistic models. Made of painted tinplate, in Southern Railway livery, the locomotive cab includes such features as the sloping sides found on the real train, which were necessary for negotiating the narrow tunnels at Hastings in Sussex. Although the tender does not share quite the same attention to detail, this particular model remains rare and highly collectible.
*(c.1938; l. 36cm/14in; value **G**)*

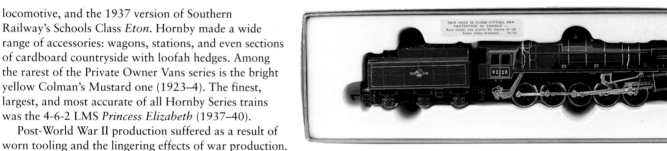

▼ Hornby-Dublo *Sir Nigel Gresley* passenger set
Sir Nigel Gresley was one of the first locomotives in the Hornby-Dublo range. The trains were beautifully designed, with finely detailed, diecast metal bodies and articulated tinplate coaches. This model is one of the rare clockwork versions, produced only from 1938 to 1940; it has the correct two-rail track and original box.
*(1939; l. 45cm/17½in; value **E**)*

When production resumed after World War II, the Hornby-Dublo range was simpler. In 1953 Hornby began to produce trains in the nationalized British Rail liveries, but subsequent production was dull – if good quality – until 1957, when the company decided to upgrade and replace its entire range. Some very fine models were produced, such as the *Dorchester* and *Ludlow Castle* locomotives. From 1960 to 1964 high-quality plastic was used for a range of freight stock with diecast chassis, and both plastic and tinplate for passenger stock.

The cost of the upgrading operation resulted in Hornby's being taken over by Triang in 1964; Dublo production passed to G. & R. Wrenn of Basildon. Triang had built up a successful range of inexpensive electric trains, and in 1959 it introduced its own "TT" miniature range of trains (in production until 1967). Triang-Hornby (the name from 1964) produced a number of collectible locomotives, including *Lord of the Isles* (GWR), *Sir Winston Churchill* (Battle of Britain Class), and *Evening Star*. After Triang's demise in 1971, the Triang-Hornby range continued with Hornby Railways, which has dominated the British market for 00 Gauge trains ever since. A fine example of its superb range of locomotives is the Schools Class *Stowe* locomotive and tender, which is highly popular with collectors, as is much of its 1970s and even its 1980s range.

▲ Triang-Hornby *Evening Star* locomotive and tender
The *Evening Star* was the last steam locomotive built by British Rail; this fine plastic model was also one of the last locomotives developed by Triang-Hornby, which went into receivership in 1971. The motor is inside the tender, enabling the locomotive to be more finely modeled.
*(1971; l. 28.5cm/11in; value **A**)*

KEY FACTS

- HORNBY-DUBLO pre-war Hornby-Dublo examples are rare but less popular because of metal-fatigue problems
- TRIANG nostalgia has extended the collectible range to include Triang; excellent condition and the original packaging are essential
- HORNBY RAILWAYS 1970s and 1980s Hornby Railways models are now collectible
- BEWARE early electrically powered locomotives are popular but may be dangerous
- GENERAL COLLECTING some 1920s pieces are very collectible, such as Colman's Mustard van and Control System accessories; 1930s pieces are most sought after: rarities include Private Owner Wagons and such accessories as the electrically lit station, signal gantry, water tower, and signal cabin; countryside sections; and "K" series miniature oilcan; good condition and original boxes are essential

Marks
Hornby: either in raised relief or, for Meccano, stamped into metal; transfer style and location will date the train

See also Tinplate: Other European countries, p.463

Other countries

EUROPE

Such French firms as Favre in Paris were known for charming, lightweight, tinplate, carpet toy trains with delicate detail. Later makers included J.E.P. (est. 1899 as the Société Industrielle de Ferblanterie) in Paris, known as Jouets en Paris from 1932. Its 0 Gauge electric trains approached models in their accuracy of design, as shown in the J.E.P. Nord 4-6-0 and the "Golden Arrow" Pullman cars produced *c.*1930. The French Hornby factory (Hornby AcHO) began production in 1921 and its toys were aimed specifically at the home market. Originally in Paris, the factory relocated to Bobigny in the early 1930s; it continued production until 1973. Other notable French manufacturers include Fournereau (active 1930s and 1940s), and the company of AS, which is still in production today. Particularly popular in the 1960s were plastic H0 Gauge railways made by the French firm of Jouef. Some models were produced under contract to Playcraft (est. 1955 in London), the sister company to Mettoy (1936–83).

Notable North Italian toy train manufacturers include Elettren (est. 1945), Rivarossi (est. late 1940s), and Biaggi (active 1950s), while such Swiss makers as Buco (1944–mid-1950s), Fulgurex (est. 1946), and HAG (est. 1949) are noted for their precisely modeled trains. Fulgurex and HAG were previously known for 0 Gauge production, but both now manufacture H0 Gauge. Also based in Switzerland, the firm of Wilag (active 1960s–1970s) produced replicas of Märklin Gauge I coaches for Fulgurex in the 1960s and 1970s; these were long (57cm/22½in) and finely modeled.

THE UNITED STATES AND JAPAN

In the USA the firm of Ives (1868–1928) in Bridgeport, Connecticut, produced a wide variety of toy trains, ranging from tinplate and cast-iron carpet toy trains to the first 0 Gauge electric system in the country, launched in 1910. Its later trains could not compete with the German imports they were based on, and in 1928 the company was taken over by the Lionel Corporation (1901–69) in New York. Lionel dominated the American market after World War I, producing trains in 0 Gauge (35mm/1⅜in). Lionel had also introduced its own non-standard size known as the American Standard Gauge (57mm/2¼in; this is slightly larger than the normal Gauge II) in 1906.

Lionel's main rival was the firm American Flyer (1907–*c.*1960) in Chicago, Illinois, which from 1934 produced a popular range of electric-powered 0 Gauge trains (rarely found in Europe). Other notable American toy train makers include Carlisle & Finch (1896–1915), the Voltamp Electric Manufacturing Co. (est. 1879) in Baltimore, Maryland, and Dorfan (1924–34) in Newark, New Jersey. Bachmann, in Philadelphia, Pennsylvania, is currently the largest company; production is carried out in Asia, and highly detailed ranges are designed for the home and European markets on 00 and H0 Gauge.

Before World War II a few unusual Japanese 0 Gauge electric locomotives and stock were imported into the USA and UK in semi-realistic outline. In the case of Japanese sets for the English market, this meant that an accurate steam shunting engine (copied from the English maker Leeds Model Co.) would come with a rake of coaches of American appearance, with open verandah ends. In the late 1950s and 1960s Tokyo companies such as Tenshodo, KTM, and Alco manufactured superb H0 Gauge models in brass, almost exclusively for the American market. They were often sold unpainted, with remarkable detail, and were very expensive when new.

▲ **"Mountain Etat" locomotive and tender by Biaggi**
This Italian locomotive and tender is in fact a model of a French design. Made of diecast metal and painted a somber gray-green, the 4-8-2 locomotive has a "Mountain" wheel arrangement.
(1952; l. 61cm/24in; value **G***)*

▼ **Electric 0 Gauge locomotive by the Lionel Corporation**
Made in the USA, this metal diecast 2-6-2 steam locomotive and tender is typical of Lionel's popular range. Its well-built trains are generally more popular with American than with European collectors.
(c.1935; l. 51cm/20in; value **B***)*

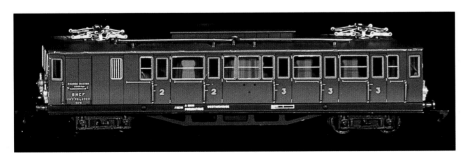

▼ **Electric train by AS**
This is one part of a modern, three-part French train, which is made in the traditional style. The section shows the Second and Third Class compartments. AS is one of the few firms still producing such older-style trains of interest to some collectors.
(1985; l. 31cm/12in; value **B***)*

KEY FACTS

- **SIZE** early models tend to be in larger gauges (e.g. Gauge I in Europe or Standard Gauge in the USA) and more elaborate; later models became increasingly smaller to meet the demands of smaller homes and to be of a more middle price range: 0 and 00 gauge shrank to the "subminiature" gauges of N (9mm) and Z (6.5mm).
- **IMPORTANT FACTORIES** France: Favre, J.E.P., Hornby AcHO, Fournereau, AS; Italy: Elettren, Biaggi, Rivarossi; Switzerland: Buco, Fulgurex, Wilag; USA: Ives, Lionel, American Flyer, Carlisle & Finch, Voltamp Electric, Dorfan, Bachmann; Japan: Tenshodo, KTM, Alco
- **COLLECTING** German, early French and early American trains are generally the most popular; many of these trains were expensive when made, and this is reflected in the current value; other very collectible lines are: Hornby AcHO, post-war mint and boxed Lionel sets, which are popular in the USA but not in Europe

Lead and plastic figures

The first mass-produced figures were made in Germany in the 18th century. These "flats" (*Zinnfiguren*) were produced by pouring a tin alloy through two separately engraved molds clamped together. "Semi-flats" (also known as "semi-solids") are more three-dimensional, while "solids" are fully rounded, three-dimensional figures made of solid lead alloy and cast from a mold. They might be cast in one piece, or in parts that are assembled later. A major breakthrough in the production of lead figures was the technique of hollow-casting, in which molten lead is sluiced around a composite mold, pioneered in 1893 by the British company Britains (est. 1845) in London.

There is a fundamental distinction between toy figures and model figures. Toy figures are generally mass-produced for the children's market, while model figures are miniature representations, perfect in every detail, and made to an exact scale.

FRANCE

One of the earliest makers of solid lead figures was Lucotte (1760–1825), in Paris, which specialized in contemporary French military pieces. These early solid figures were cast in separate parts in a lead, tin, and antimony alloy. Of extremely high quality, they were popular at the time and widely exported, and are much sought after today. In 1825 C.B.G. Mignot (est. 1825) in Paris took over Lucotte and extended the range to include figures from many periods of French history and the series "Ancient and Modern Armies of the World."

GERMANY

German toymakers were swift to adapt production to compete with the solid French figures. The best-known and most prolific German manufacturer was the firm of Georg Heyde (*c.*1845–1949) in Dresden, which used the same solid-cast technique as Mignot. A military line was produced in boxed parade and battle sets, but Heyde also introduced set pieces or display sets with non-military themes, which are among the most sought after of its production; for example, the Indian Durbar

▲ Arab oasis set piece by Georg Heyde
Heyde of Dresden extended the appeal of solid-cast figures by producing non-military set pieces such as this Arab oasis. Large sets like these show Heyde's production at its best.
*(1920s; figures ht 54mm/2¼in; value **D**)*

display included palm trees, elephants with howdahs, bullock carts, and mounted camels, as well as infantry. Heyde's figures were mostly made in the now-standard size of 54mm (2¼in).

Johann Haffner (1863–93), in Fürth, near Nuremberg, manufactured finely cast flats, semi-flats, and solids of mainly French and Prussian troops, which were exported to France and Britain. Georg Spenkuch (1870–1924), in Nuremberg, made flats, semi-solids, and solids in varying sizes and great quantity. Ernst Heinrichsen (est. 1839), also in Nuremberg, made flats and semi-flats in a huge variety of sets, covering a wide range of themes, from the Classical world and medieval tournaments to the Napoleonic Wars. The most prolific contemporary manufacturer of traditional German flats was Aloys Ochel (est. *c.*1925) in Kiel. Before 1939 Ochel acted as agent for Heinrichsen; the company's own range covers all periods and includes individual portrait models of famous generals, as well as such accessories as war elephants and siege weapons.

During the 1920s and 1930s two German makers produced figures in composition (a mixture of china clay, sawdust, and glue, supported by a wire armature). The firm of Otto and Max Hausser (est. 1910) in Ludwigsburg called its material "Elastolin." Production started with animal figures, followed by a range of military figures from 1912. Pre-war character figures included Frederick the Great and George Washington; from 1933 the emphasis was on German leaders such as Hitler, Hess, and Goering. In the late 1940s Hausser produced plastic models. Lineol (est. 1923) in Brandenburg also produced composition figures, but its range was more finely detailed than Hausser's and consisted largely of German troops produced as part of Hitler's political propaganda.

◄ "Grand Garde" by Lucotte
This solid lead figure of a soldier from the Napoleonic Grand Garde has many of the characteristics of the high-quality production associated with the Paris-based firm of Lucotte; these include superb hand-painted detail, the soldier's wide stride, the company mark of a bee (Napoleon's personal emblem), and the letters "L.C.." The body and head of Lucotte figures were cast separately, and the head was inserted into the neck using a plug; accessories such as weapons and knapsacks were soldered onto the figure at a later date.
*(c.1820; ht 6cm/2⅜in; value **B**)*

▼ "Charlie Chaplin" by Georg Heyde

This beautifully detailed lead figure of Charlie Chaplin, the celebrated stage and screen entertainer, portrays him in one of his most characteristic poses. It was produced in the 1920s by Heyde for the British firm of W.J. Bassett-Lowke & Co., of model railway fame. It is part of a very rare series of probably no more than five figures.
*(c.1920; ht 54mm/2¼in; value **D**)*

BRITAIN

British toy figures are almost synonymous with the company Britains (est. 1845) in London. In 1893 William Britain, the founder's son, developed the new method of "hollow-casting" that was to revolutionize production. Britains rapidly dominated the market, and holds an unrivaled popularity today.

The accuracy of Britains' military uniforms was part of its figures' appeal; soldiers were hand-painted by outworkers using contemporary lithographs. By 1900 Britains was producing more than 100 different sets. Alternatives to the military range were railway figures and footballers; more civilian lines were developed after World War I, including a "Home Farm" and a zoo series.

Vehicles and (highly collectible) airplanes were added to the military range, together with soldiers from many different countries. From 1936 Britains reflected the country's rearmament drive with a now rare range of troops in battledress with military equipment.

Production restarted after the war with a limited range and an emphasis on export. The Coronation provided a boost in 1953; on offer in that year only was one of Britains' largest-ever sets (228 figures). The higher cost of materials in the 1950s resulted in the production of "short" sets and individual "Picture Pack" figures. In 1953 Britains acquired Herald Miniatures, which produced plastic figures. By 1960 the government had banned the use of lead in toys, but Britains had already launched its plastic "Swoppet" series (1959). This consisted of well-sculpted plastic figures (including knights, cowboys, and infantry) with interchangeable parts: bodies, heads, and equipment could be swopped between figures. The Swoppet range was part of Britains' golden age of plastic (1959–67), which also included the best civilian and zoo figures it ever produced. From the mid-1960s, quality declined.

Britains continued to produce metal figures. In 1972 a range of "new" soldiers was launched, aimed primarily at the adult collector. From 1983 Britains produced these in a range of instantly successful, limited-edition boxed sets; these have already begun to appreciate in value.

Despite the dominance of Britains there were several other distinguished British makers. John Hill & Co. (Johillco; 1898–1960), in London and Cheshire, was one of the first to produce individual figures rather than boxed sets. Charbens & Co. Ltd (1920–55), in London, produced a mainly non-military line; its circus series of 1935 is popular. Taylor & Barrett (1920–39), also in London, was known for its non-military sets, including a zoo series. Pixyland Toy and Manufacturing Co. (c.1920–33), again in London, began production with military figures; from 1925 it produced farm and zoo figures, and the character figure range for which it is best known.

Post-war makers include Philip Segal (1938–50), in Christchurch, Hants, who made a rare set of footballers and other non-military models. Timpo (1943–79), in London and Lancashire, produced hollow-cast figures until 1956, after which plastic was used; its "Ivanhoe" series of 1955 is sought after. Cherilea Products (1946–61), in Blackpool, made hollow-cast and plastic figures, the plastic being largely an adaptation of the hollow-cast range. One of its most outstanding figures is the Black Prince.

THE UNITED STATES

In the USA the manufacture of lead figures developed separately from the European tradition. The two major makers in the 1920s and 1930s were Barclay and Manoil, both in New York City, producing scale soldiers and other figures. Gray Iron (1920–39) was the only American company to make figures of cast iron. From c.1950 Louis Marx (1919–82), in New York, made plastic models of American presidents, as well as boxed sets of figures from the Frontier Wars, and playsets of unpainted plastic figures with buildings and equipment.

▲ "Swoppet" knight by Britains

The Swoppet range of plastic figures retained the strong sculptural quality associated with Britains' hollow-cast figures. The Swoppet figures have movable heads and arms, and accessories can be swopped among others in the range. *(c.1960; 5cm/2in; value A)*

▼ Cartoon characters by Pixyland

These painted hollow-cast lead figures of Squeak (left), Pip (middle), and Wilfred (right) are based on contemporary cartoon characters in the British *Daily Mirror* newspaper. Cartoon and film characters became very popular in the 1920s. *(c.1925; ht 5cm/2in; value A)*

KEY FACTS

General
- CONDITION lead figures: check for oxidization (surface powdering), which can be a major problem
- COLLECTING military flats are popular only in Germany; figures made by Heyde, and by other early German manufacturers of solid and hollow-cast figures, are much sought after; Lucotte figures are very rare and highly collectible; Mignot production is less popular because it was produced over such a long timespan; British figures other than Britains' are becoming increasingly popular, in particular civilian ranges; American figures are not usually popular in Europe

Britains
- SETS sets must match; outworkers' painting styles differed, so check for consistent paint style
- COLLECTING complete sets in the original box, with figures and box in excellent condition, are most sought after; early military sets and early individual figures are rare and valuable; plastic models are becoming popular but only if in excellent condition; Britains' figures are very popular in the USA

Marks
Otto & Max Hausser: mark used on the Elastolin range of toys

Lineol: 1930s style mark used only on the base of boxes in the 1930s

Britains: mark appears on boxes from the 1890s to the 1960s

Diecasts

Miniature toy vehicles were produced from the early 20th century in lithographed tinplate or from crudely cast lead, but after World War I casting techniques improved and so did the quality of diecast models. The innovative Tootsie Toys dominated the American market for a time, but Frank Hornby's Dinky Toys swiftly became the world leader in diecast toys.

A problem with diecast mazac (a magnesium and zinc alloy) toys, first noted in the 1930s, is fatigue, visible as distortion or crumbling. Early, minor damage can be kept in remission by careful handling and avoidance of extremes of heat and light.

TOOTSIE TOYS

The name "Tootsie Toys" was first used in 1922 to describe the range of small, diecast metal toys made by the Dowst Manufacturing Co. (est. 1876) in Chicago. Dowst pioneered the use of mazac, which was lighter and harder than lead, and also developed the new technique of injection-molding. Attractive and affordable, Tootsie Toys included cars, trains, and aircraft, and the range became highly successful. From the mid-1920s such realistic detail as recessed lines around the engine compartment and doors was added. In the late 1920s the "Funnies" series was launched, based on American comic characters such as Andy Gump, Moon Mullins, and Smitty; this series is now rare and much sought after. By the early 1930s the Tootsie Toy car range had reached its peak; among the finest models were copies of real makes such as Graham and La Salle. Quality declined in the 1940s, with cruder modeling and less realistic detailing, leading to even simpler designs in plastic by the 1970s.

DINKY TOYS

The first Dinky Toys was made in April 1934. Produced by Frank Hornby, the founder of Meccano (est. 1901) in Liverpool, they were a development of the "Modeled Miniatures" series of figures launched in 1931 as accessories for Hornby railways. Pocket-sized vehicles were produced in 1933 and called "Dinky Toys" from the following year. Hornby used the injection-molding process pioneered by Tootsie Toys, replacing lead with mazac in 1934. Small and inexpensive, Dinky cars soon enjoyed the same huge success in Britain that Tootsie Toys had in the USA. The wide range of tiny vehicles included vans, racing cars, saloon cars, sports cars, and tractors; airplanes, boats, and military vehicles were

▼ Tootsie Toys "Fly-n-Giro" by the Dowst Manufacturing Co.
The finest Tootsie Toy models were produced in the early to mid-1930s, and included, in 1934, an early version of this unusual aircraft. Even more rare, and more valuable, is the version shown here, which was made from a different casting.
*(c.1937; l. 15cm/6in; value **B**)*

▼ Dinky Toys No. 24 Series motor cars by Hornby
Sets of Dinky Toys are highly sought after, and as this one is complete, in its original box, and extremely rare, its price will be correspondingly high. These painted diecast saloon cars have many of the characteristics of early Dinky cars: stylish contemporary designs, bright colors, smooth hubs, and white tires. There is a small amount of fatigue present, but careful handling and storage will prevent further deterioration.
*(c.1935; l. 36cm/14in; value **K**)*

▲ Dinky Toys "Thunderbird 2" by Hornby
This painted diecast model of Thunderbird 2 is based on Gerry Anderson's *Thunderbirds* television series for children. The first version, shown here, was pale green, and is more interesting and more valuable than the later version produced in metallic blue/green from 1973.
*(c.1967; l. 25cm/9¾in; value **B**)*

produced as World War II loomed. Vehicles were made in sets or series – complete examples are very rare and sought after. Collectible sets include the first 28 Series delivery vans, the 24 Series saloon cars, the 23 Series racing cars, and the 25 Series lorries. In 1940 production of Dinky Toys stopped as Meccano transferred to war production.

After the war, manufacture of toys restarted gradually as Meccano moved back to peacetime production. Very early post-war models were produced from adapted pre-war dies, and still had such features as smooth wheel-hubs and white tires. However, there are differences: post-war vehicles are drabber in color, have thicker axles, and are generally less rare and less collectible than pre-war models. In 1947 Dinky launched a new "Supertoy" range of larger vehicles, which included the 501 "Foden diesel 8-wheel wagon." The "Guy" lorries series that formed part of the range was expanded to include delivery vans with advertising transfers, including Weetabix (rare and very collectible). Many new ranges were introduced throughout the 1950s.

In 1956 the first Corgi diecast cars appeared, and Dinky was compelled to update and innovate. Older models were produced in new color combinations, including bright, two-tone variants of such models as the Jaguar XK 120. Boxed gift sets with specially designed folding lids appeared in 1963–4. This period (1958–64) is generally considered the golden age of Dinky Toys. However, the cost of the overhaul meant that the toys were too expensive for the market; the ensuing financial crisis led to a takeover by Triang in 1964. Triang tried to rationalize production: saloon models were simplified, and packaging changed to card and cellophane, then to plastic boxes. Successes included film and television tie-ins, such as the models of spacecraft from *Thunderbirds*. Airfix took over the Dinky Toys range in 1971. Quality deteriorated: colors became more garish, and detailing and packaging more crude; cars from this period are generally far less collectible. In 1979 the factory closed.

MATCHBOX, CORGI, AND SPOT-ON

One of the greatest rivals of Dinky was Lesney (est. 1947) in London, which in 1948 introduced a range of diecast toys and by 1950 was among the leading manufacturers. In 1952 the company produced a miniature (scale 1:75) Coronation Coach. The success of this model encouraged Lesney's co-founder Jack Odell to launch the "Matchbox" 1:75 series of contemporary vehicles in 1953. These simple and affordable pocket-sized toys, packaged in a box designed as a matchbox, were an immediate success, and their value has increased significantly over recent years, particularly for rare color varieties. In 1956 Lesney introduced the "Models of Yesteryear" series, which appealed to adult collectors. Both series were at their peak in the early 1960s, and models from those years are the most collectible. From the late 1960s quality declined, and in 1982 Lesney was taken over by Universal Holdings of Hong Kong.

The other major rival to Dinky was Corgi, part of the Mettoy Co. (1936–83) set up in Northampton by the German Philip Ullman. Inspired by the success of Dinky, in 1956 it launched the Corgi range of small diecast toys. The high standard reflected the skills of the German diemakers and resulted in immediate success. New features included plastic windows, spring suspension (from 1959), bonnets and doors that opened, and folding seats (from 1963). The company pioneered film and television tie-ins in the 1960s, one of the most famous results being the James Bond Aston Martin D.B.5., which sold nearly 3 million copies.

Although Corgi cars were at their peak in the 1960s, they maintained their quality until the early 1970s, and between 1970 and 1972 produced such sought-after models as the "Noddy" and "Magic Roundabout" cars. From the mid-1970s there was a rapid decline, and in 1983 Mettoy went into receivership. A management buyout was followed by a takeover by Mattel in 1992, when production was moved to China; a further management buyout took place in 1995, and Corgi Classics is still flourishing with a range of collectors' vehicles, mainly intended for adults.

Spot-On diecast models were made by Triang from 1959. Their reduction from real vehicle to model scale (1:42) was more successful than that of Dinky or Corgi, and they were made in a variety of rich colors, with extra features such as electric headlamps and "Flexomatic" suspension. One of the most famous models, introduced in 1963, is the London Transport "Routemaster" bus. Spot-On production ceased in 1967.

MAKERS IN GERMANY, FRANCE, ITALY, AND DENMARK

Manufacturers in most industrialized countries produced a range of diecast toys for both home and export markets. In Germany, Märklin (est. 1859) produced a high-quality range of diecast vehicles, notable for their precision casting from 1935 to 1977. Schuco (the tradename of Schreyer & Co.; 1912–77) made a range of diecast cars in the 1960s, and other German companies, such as NZG (est. 1968) and Gama (the post-World War II trademark of the Fürth-based company of Mangold), are still producing cars and commercial and industrial vehicles.

The French Dinky factory continued independent production after the Airfix takeover of the British Dinky line and made some first-rate diecast models between 1969 and 1972. Its range of GMC lorries and special sets, and especially its Citroën Presidentielle, are all sought after. Other French companies of note include Solido (est. 1932; from 1980 part of Majorette), now best known for a military range first produced in 1961, and C.I.J. (Compagnie Industriel de Jouets; 1902–64), in Paris.

The best Italian diecast toys were made in the 1960s: most collectible are the attractive, high-quality vehicles produced by Mercury. In Denmark, Tekno (1948–72) developed a fine range of diecast vehicles, reaching its peak of production in the 1960s. Its Mercedes-Benz 230 SL is much sought after, as are its commercial lorries and vans in unusual liveries, such as United Nations, *Disney Weekly*, Tuborg, and Carlsberg.

◀ Matchbox Commer pick-up truck by Lesney

This painted diecast Commer truck is a commercial version of the Hillman Minx, and is a typical example of a 1950s Matchbox vehicle, complete with metal wheels and original box. The 1962 two-color version has plastic wheels and a more elaborate box; as comparatively few were made, it is more valuable. Certain Matchbox toys have increased in value considerably over recent years.

(1958; l. 4cm/1½in; value C)

◀ Mercedes-Benz 230 SL by Tekno

Made by the Danish manufacturer Tekno from 1963, the Mercedes-Benz 230 SL is one of the finest toy cars the company produced. Made of painted diecast metal, it is supremely well modeled, with fingertip steering action. Its original box adds to its value as one of Tekno's most collectible high-quality cars.

(c.1968; l. 10.5cm/4in; value A)

▼ Citroën Presidentielle by Dinky Toys (France)

After the British company had been taken over by Airfix, the French Dinky factory at Bobigny continued to produce toys, going from strength to strength until the early 1970s, when this superb car was made. This model, complete with its presidential flag, was the finest diecast car that the French company produced. The example that is shown here is a special edition with electric headlamps.

(c.1972; l. 20cm/8in; value D)

KEY FACTS

- CONDITION models and boxes must be in excellent condition; pre-war Dinky Toys are a specialized field because of fatigue problems – look for cracking, crumbling, and distorted shapes, and check extent and severity carefully to plan viability of damage limitation
- BRANDS Tootsie Toys are popular with collectors in the USA; Dinky Toys are the most popular field in British diecast-toy collecting; Corgi is the next most popular make, followed by Matchbox; Tekno, Märklin, and French Dinky are all high quality and desirable, with Mercury and Solido in the next rank
- COLLECTING collectors usually seek to fill gaps in established collections; rare colors add enormously to value; sets are most sought after when complete and in good condition; rare color versions may transcend brand ranking

Marks

Dinky Toys mark introduced in April 1934; the mark shown here was used in the 1950s and 1960s

DINKY TOYS

Other post-war toys

After World War II there were significant changes in toy manufacturing. In 1939 German toymakers had dominated the world market, but by 1945 the German economy was in ruins and many German toymaking companies had collapsed. Japanese manufacturers swiftly replaced them, producing inexpensive but well-made tinplate, and later plastic, toys. In the USA the production of a wide variety of media-based toys reflected the increased consumerism and the effect of both television and film.

EUROPE

Although some of the well-known German toymakers were still in operation after the war, their ranges tended to be simpler and often included pre-war models. The well-established firms of Gama (est. 1882), Günthermann (1877–1965), Tipp & Co. (known as Tippco; 1912–71), and Technofix, all located in or near Nuremberg, produced tinplate cars based on American prototypes, while Märklin (est. 1859), in Göppingen, continued limited production of some of its 1930s constructor vehicles until 1954. Other Nuremberg firms included Johann Distler & Co. (c.1900–1962), Arnold (est. 1906), and Schuco (the tradename of Schreyer & Co.; 1912–77). Distler made a successful range of cars, one of the most collectible of which is the Electromatic 7500 Porsche first made in 1956. In the late 1940s Arnold produced its famous clockwork-driven "Mac" motorcycle, with a rider that mounted and dismounted as the bike moved in a circle. Schuco produced high-quality, finely lithographed, and excellently detailed tinplate vehicles, the most sought after of which are its constructor lorries and fire-engines.

In post-war Britain, Meccano (est. 1901) in Liverpool gradually restarted production of its perennially successful Constructor sets, which comprised strips of pierced steel that could be constructed into a range of different models. Traditional tinplate toys were still made by such established British companies as Mettoy (1936–83) in Swansea, which from the 1950s made very simple, inexpensive toys with basic mechanisms. At the firm of Triang (est. 1919) in London, production continued of its wide range of Minic toys (first introduced in 1935), including a fine clockwork fire-engine, until 1963. British tinplate toys declined in popularity during the 1950s and were eventually ousted by inexpensive mass-produced toys manufactured in Hong Kong and, during the 1960s and 1970s, China.

JAPAN

During the late 1940s and early 1950s, Japanese companies produced tinplate, celluloid, and plastic toys that reflected the American culture of the Allied Occupation army. Such large American firms as Cragstan (est. c.1955) and Rosko found it profitable to commission Japanese firms to make toys for them, in order to capitalize on the cheap and efficient Japanese labor force. Although many of these toys were only intended to have a short life, they remain very popular with collectors today. During the early 1950s production increased rapidly, and Japan enjoyed world supremacy until the 1960s, when China, Thailand, Malaysia, and Singapore entered the market.

► "Expert Motorcyclist" by Masudaya

The firm of Masudaya is one of the many Japanese companies that flourished after World War II, producing tinplate toys such as this motorcyclist. American distributors such as Cragstan imposed Western taste, which is reflected in the styling of the motorbike and the design of the original box. The battery-operated mechanism allows the rider to mount and dismount while the bike circles.
(c.1958; l. 22.5cm/8¾in; value **C**)

▼ "Merry Clown" by Technofix

An early example of post-war tinplate toys by this Nuremberg firm, this clockwork toy is of extremely good quality. Later in the 1950s Technofix gained a reputation for making brightly colored, inexpensively lithographed toys, which are very often affordably priced. This eye-catching clown is driven by clockwork and whizzes along nodding his head.
(c.1951; ht 10cm/4in; value **B**)

Among the most popular Japanese toys during the early post-war period were tinplate cars based on American models. Collectible examples include Ford convertibles, various types of police car, and Cadillacs, which are now particularly popular. Notable Japanese toy car manufacturers – all based in Tokyo – included Alps Shoji Ltd (est. 1948), which produced a fine friction-driven 1952 Cadillac convertible, and Ichiko Kyogo Ltd (1950s–1960s), known for its car range, which included the famous "Oldsmobile 88" (1959). Motorcycles were made by companies including Masudaya (est. 1924) and Marusan (1950s–1960s), both in Tokyo. Marusan's models were based on the real Sunbeam motorcycle and side-car combination – an accuracy of modeling characteristic of the company, which was noted for its small but high-quality and finely detailed range of cars. These are now considered among the finest of post-war Japanese toys.

With the development of space exploration during the 1950s there was an increase in the production of space-related toys, including spacecraft, astronauts, and robots. Many such toys are battery-operated, sometimes performing sophisticated functions. One of the most famous and collectible toys is a tinplate and plastic robot first produced in 1956 by Nomura (est. c.1920) in Tokyo. Called "Robbie the Robot," the robot was based on the character in the film *Forbidden Planet* (1956),

◄ "NASA Space Shuttles" by Masudaya

In the late 1970s Masudaya produced two versions of the NASA Space Shuttle. Both were made of lithographed tinplate and plastic, but they differed in the battery-operated mechanism: the white shuttle turned and its lights flashed, while the more expensive silver version could be steered using a remote-control device. These space shuttles are regarded as among the most collectible new tinplate toys made in Japan.
(c.1979; l. 27.5cm/10¾in; value **A**)

▼ "Goofy the Walking Gardener" by Marx

This clockwork, lithographed tinplate toy is one of the many Disney models made under license by the American firm of Marx. The paintwork of many of these toys, which are still fairly common, will be worn, and many may have lost their rubber ears and boxes. The excellent condition and original box of this example, however, make it valuable.
(c.1955; ht 22.5cm/8¾in; value D)

▼ "Dalek" by Marx

This American-made, molded-plastic "Dalek" is a toy version of the original Dalek from the BBC *Dr Who* television series. The battery-operated mechanism allowed it to imitate the movement of its sinister prototypes. Repeat showings of the original, plus several new series of *Dr Who*, have sparked a cult following, and production of the Dalek has restarted using original tooling. Good condition and an original box are essential when collecting such recent, mass-produced toys, since they are unlikely to be rare.
(1964; ht 17.5cm/7in; value A)

and, with its rounded limbs (its legs house the batteries), has a friendly rather than a sinister appearance. All robots enjoy an enthusiastic following with collectors, although few are found in good condition as they were easily damaged. Space toys include flying saucers, spaceships, rockets, and lunar modules, many clearly inspired by science fiction rather than by real spacecraft. Collectible toys include the "Space Giant" (1950s) and the "NASA Space Shuttle" (1979), both by Masudaya.

Among the most imaginative early post-war toys are Japanese novelty toys. Interesting battery-operated examples include the cigar-smoking "McGregor" by Nomura, "Fido the Xylophone Player," and the amusing "Wee-Wee Bonnie Doggie," both by Alps Shoji Ltd.

THE UNITED STATES

During the post-war years, merchandizing associated with films, television series, cartoons, and comics has played an increasingly important part in successful toy marketing. Particularly popular are character figures; for example, the manufacturer A.C. Gilbert (1908–66) in New Haven, Connecticut, produced a plastic "James Bond 007" action figure (*c.*1965), based on the hero of the *Thunderball* film of 1965.

Other characters from the *Thunderbirds* and *Stingray* children's television puppet series have a cult following among collectors today. Cartoon characters, including Yogi Bear and the Flintstones, also translated well into highly successful toys. *The Flintstones* television cartoon appeared in 1960, and in 1961 Louis Marx (1919–82), in New York City, issued a 50-piece playset to complement the series. The success of "G.I. Joe," a plastic, jointed soldier launched in 1964, spawned a number of action figures based on popular film and television series. The phenomenally successful *Star Wars* films from 1977 to 1983 gave rise to a huge variety of spin-off toys, including "Jabba the Hutt" playsets, which, owing to their number and recent production, are unlikely to be rare.

► "G.I. Joe" by Hasbro

The original, jointed plastic "G.I. Joe" action figure was first produced by the American firm of Hasbro in 1964; manufacture ceased in 1984 owing to lack of demand. The company reintroduced the figure and the British factory version, Action Man, again in 1993. The new version featured here is a female "G.I. Joe" and is smaller and less valuable than the original.
(1993; ht 25.5cm/10in; value A)

The film-maker Walt Disney was an astute business-man, and toy production associated with his films was syndicated from the 1920s. Ever popular characters include Mickey Mouse, Minnie Mouse, Donald Duck, and the Three Little Pigs. Post-war Disney toys are less rare and less collectible than pre-war examples, although Linemar, the Japanese division of Marx, produced a plastic and tinplate clockwork figure of "Pinocchio" in the late 1950s that is now rare, as relatively few examples were made. Marx made a friction-powered, lithographed tinplate toy called "Mickey Mouse Mouseketeers Moving Van" (*c.*1958). The huge and expanding range of Disney toys remains highly popular with collectors.

KEY FACTS

General points
- CONDITION good condition is vital for battery-operated tinplate toys; check for damage caused by leaking batteries and faulty or damaged wiring, which is difficult to repair
- BOXES these are often works of art in themselves and can add to a toy's value; must be in good condition
- COLLECTING rarities can be very valuable; late models are currently of relatively small value but may appreciate if in mint condition and boxed

Media-based toys
- COLLECTING trends are unpredictable; use quality and perfect condition as criteria; toys from successful film and television series are usually the most popular

Disney toys
- CONDITION good condition is essential, especially for less rare pieces
- FAKES beware fakes – usually made in Asia – of early pieces: these are generally crude and non-prototype
- DATING the early Mickey Mouse was a thin, toothy, more rat-like figure, with a tail and "pie-cut eyes"; by the 1950s he was plumper and often had no tail; the early Donald Duck has a longer bill than later versions
- VALUE an early date and rarity determine value; some early unlicensed pieces are very rare, but toys made under license are usually more valuable
- COLLECTING Disney toys are popular worldwide

Marks
Germany: Johann Distler & Co. (1900–1962) based in Nuremberg

Japan: Alps Shoji Ltd (est. 1948) based in Tokyo

Japan: Ichiko Kyogo Co. Ltd (1950s–1960s) based in Tokyo

See also Tinplate, pp.460–63; Diecasts, pp.470–71

In the 18th and early 19th centuries, "Oriental" was a catch-all term used in Europe and North America to describe the artifacts and styles of ornament emanating from China, Japan, Turkey, North Africa, the Middle East, and the Indian sub-continent. However, subsequently, the description has been more strictly applied to those works of art produced for both domestic consumption and export in the East Asian countries of China, Japan, and Korea. Today, numerous utilitarian, decorative, and ritual wares of the most outstanding craftsmanship are available to collectors of Oriental art, notably figures, vases, bowls, bottles, boxes, pictorial panels, and furniture. Also sought after are items worn with traditional Japanese dress; these range from beads (*ojime*) and toggles (*netsuke*), to seal cases (*inro*) and sword-guards (*tsuba*). Much of the lasting appeal of these artifacts resides in their exotic designs and motifs, and use of time-consuming decorative techniques such as lacquering and *cloisonné* and *champlevé* enameling, which were so popular that they have been widely copied in the West. The diverse range of materials from which these objects are crafted includes precious and base metals, and indigenous materials such as bamboo, ivory, and jade, the latter prized in the Orient above gold as a symbol of human virtue.

Detail of a screen (left) This Chinese cinnabar lacquer screen, made during the reign of Emperor Qianlong, is carved in high relief, and depicts a five-clawed dragon chasing a flaming pearl (*1736–95*).

Moon flask (above) Characteristic of transitional pieces of Chinese *cloisonné*, this flask stands on a cast-bronze base and displays complex designs embellished with decorative gilding (*17th century*).

Oriental Works of Art

Metalwork

Asia has produced some of the most elegantly crafted metalwork in the world. Techniques and themes were introduced in one area and were spread by craftsmen and trade to others. Shapes created in one medium, often ceramics, were copied in another, such as bronze, and the same motifs appear in objects made of metal, jade, and lacquer. The countries of East Asia display a most inventive use of metals and the most technically accomplished metalworking.

BRONZE

Bronze, an alloy of copper and tin, was used in China from the pre-Shang period to make weapons and ceremonial vessels. These vessels were cast first in clay molds and later using the lost-wax technique, in a range of shapes and with recurring decorative motifs, such as monster masks (*taotie*). Ancient pieces soon came to symbolize the virtues of the past, and from the Han period were already collectors' items. During the Ming and Qing periods many ancient forms were copied, including such vessels as those made for carrying liquids (such as *hu*) or for containing foods (such as *ding*). Where these had served originally as ritual containers, their imitations were used as flower vases and incense burners.

◄ Chinese *Buddha*
This small, portable gilt-bronze image of the Buddha would have been used for private contemplation, as much larger images placed in temples were for public devotion. In both large and small sculptures of the Buddha the bronze surface is generally gilded, although the tightly coiled hair, as seen in this figure, might be left untouched.
(18th century; ht 16.5cm/6½in; value G)

▼ Chinese moon flask
The gourd form and central mandala suggest that this flask was made for Buddhist use. This piece is typical of the 16th- and 17th-century transitional period between early and late Chinese *cloisonné*, when designs diversified into naturalistic motifs and the palette was widened to include semi-translucent shades and mixed colors.
(17th century; ht 27cm/10½in; value I)

◄ Chinese vase and cover
The *hu* vessel was originally for ritual use as a wine container, and was equipped with rings or handles and sometimes with a lid and chains. Decoration might be elaborate or, as in this cast-bronze example, consist of concentric bands and monster masks (*taotie*, barely discernible). The green encrustation will have been produced by humid, enclosed conditions such as those found in a grave.
(206 BC–AD 220; ht 41cm/16in; value G)

BEWARE

In China the respect for ancient bronzes has meant that for centuries wares have been copied, refashioned to incorporate ancient elements, "aged" to produce an artificial patina, and had false inscriptions added to them. This practice was a sign of esteem for an earlier period and was not always intended to deceive. Cast rather than incised reign marks are a better indication of authenticity. Bronzes bearing marks of Emperor Xuande (1426–35) are often in fact of later manufacture. Those with gold and silver inlay and colored patination generally date from the Qing reign period. With *cloisonné* wares, molded reign marks are more reliable than incised ones. False bases bearing marks for the mysterious Emperor Jiangtai (1450–57) may be fitted to later wares.

Naturalistic forms developed in parallel with the utilitarian and ritual ware, often expressed in representations of animals and birds. As Buddhism spread throughout East Asia, gilt-bronze statuettes of the Buddha and his disciples were produced for the faithful. Chinese bronze mirrors and bells were adapted by Korea and Japan to their own taste, and bronze spoons and eating bowls were produced in Korea, where good brassware is still made.

The Japanese tea ceremony favored antique Chinese models for flower vases for use during the ritual. In the 18th century, religious themes began to yield to naturalistic representations in bronze and to figures drawn from mythology and everyday life, a trend that accelerated as Buddhism declined in the late 19th century. The developing export market provided an opening for these new, naturalistic bronzes.

CLOISONNE

This French word describes a product often thought of as essentially Chinese, but the technique was introduced into China from Western Asia. Soft glass pastes, colored by the addition of minerals and metallic oxides, are applied within fields or *cloisons* formed by wire soldered or glued to a metal surface. Firing melts the enamel and fuses it to the metal, after which it is ground flush with the surface.

Cloisonné wares were first made in China in the 14th century. The earliest range of colors was simple: dark green, an intense cobalt blue, red, yellow, and white, on a background of turquoise blue. Early 15th-century pieces served mainly religious and ceremonial purposes and they often have

◀ **Pair of Japanese cranes**
These two silvered-bronze birds stand in typically contrasting poses, their plumage skilfully suggested by the juxtaposition of silvered and undecorated areas. Meticulous skill in metalworking, combined with the need to diversify, led to the production of such fine examples of metal sculpture.
(19th century; ht 23.5cm/9in; value H)

▼ **Chinese vase and cover**
This vase is an example of Chinese export silverware, intended for Western trade and tourists during the 19th century. It is worked in repoussé on a matt surface and is decorated with various auspicious emblems, some Buddhist (the lion finial), some imperial (the phoenix), and others traditional (peonies and prunus).
(19th century; ht 46cm/18in; value H)

be broadly divided into iron and alloy examples. Iron *tsuba* developed from the crafts of early armorers and swordsmiths. In the 16th century, as demand increased, specialist metalsmiths emerged, such as the Goto family (active until the 19th century), who worked exclusively in *shakudo* and gold. Prohibitions in the 1870s on the carrying of swords brought these crafts to an end, and metalsmiths turned to the production of other wares.

▼ **Two Japanese *tsuba***
Tsuba, often sold in sets of two to four, combine unvarying shape with enormous variety of decoration. The example on the left is a signed iron *tsuba* that is carved with a stylized butterfly; the one on the right is made of parcel-gilt iron and has been finely carved with a tree, banded hedge, spider, and two wasps.
(17th century and early 19th century; diam 8.5cm/3½in; 7.5cm/3in; values F and G)

technical imperfections. They tend to be heavy, as the enamel decoration is applied to a cast-bronze base. Nonetheless, their artistic refinement and deep colors are highly regarded by collectors.

Subsequent diversification of early designs and colors led to the production of many imposing pieces for the Qing rulers, distinguished by convoluted designs, a lustrous finish, and much use of gilding. Animal and bird figures became increasingly popular, and rose-pink was added to the range of colors in the 18th century. Chinese *cloisonné* appears to have first reached Europe during the 19th century, and it is still exported from China, often as small and inexpensive objects.

In Japan *cloisonné* enameling was introduced later than in China. From the 17th century the Donin family produced *cloisonné* medallions as decoration for sword fittings. During the 1830s, the first large pieces were produced. While Chinese Ming models were influential, Japanese colors were more sombre. From the mid-19th century, Japanese craftsmen aimed to reduce and ultimately eliminate the use of wires in *cloisonné* enameling. By 1889 they succeeded in inventing *musenjippo*, where the wires were removed before firing, and later made *plique à jour* enameled wares, the effect of which was akin to stained-glass windows.

OTHER METALS

Such precious metals as silver and gold have generally been used in East Asia for decorative inlay. Korean 19th-century iron brushpots and tobacco-boxes were inlaid with intricate silver designs.

From the 17th to the mid-20th centuries, China produced silverware specifically for export to the West. Some pieces copied classical Western models, but many were reproductions of Chinese designs. Japanese craftsmen worked in many metals: silver, iron, lead, copper, pewter, and other alloys, notably copper and gold (*shakudo*) and copper and silver (*shibuichi* or *rogin*), achieving rich patinas through pickling alloys in acidic solutions. Their most outstanding products were articulated iron animals, reptiles and birds, and *tsuba* (sword-guards). *Tsuba* can

KEY FACTS

Dates of principal Chinese and Japanese dynasties

CHINA	JAPAN
Shang (*c*.1600–*c*.1050 BC)	Asuka (*c*.550–710)
Zhou (*c*.1050–256 BC)	Nara (710–94)
Han (206 BC–AD 220)	Heian (794–1185)
Tang (618–907)	Kamakura (1185–1333)
Song (960–1279)	Muromachi (1333–1568)
Yuan (1279–1368)	Momoyama (1568–1600)
Ming (1368–1644)	Edo (1600–1868)
Qing (1644–1911)	Meiji (1868–1912)

Bronze
- DATING archaic forms (e.g. from the Han dynasty) are revered in China, but beware as the objects may be of Ming or Qing manufacture
- INSCRIPTIONS Chinese bronzes with Islamic inscriptions suggest a Ming date
- FIGURES gilt bronze was favored for Chinese Buddhist and Daoist images; Japanese bronze figures of the late 19th century are particularly lively

Cloisonné
- TECHNIQUE *cloisonné* (enclosures for enamel paste formed by fixing wire onto a metal surface) should not be confused with *champlevé* (enclosures cast in the metal or hollowed out from it)
- EARLY CHINESE CLOISONNE bronze wires attached by solder; can be slightly flawed due to imperfect firing
- LATER CHINESE CLOISONNE die-drawn copper wires, often fixed with vegetable adhesive; a smooth finish, the result of repeated firings and polishings
- JAPANESE CLOISONNE in later 19th-century wares there is an absence of wires; vivid colors

Other metals
- INLAY gold and silver often used in East Asian wares
- CHINESE EXPORT SILVER popular throughout Europe and the USA from *c*.1800

See also Silver: Teapots and tea services, pp.248–9

Carvings

NETSUKE AND OJIME

In the absence of pockets in traditional Japanese wear, small personal possessions such as *inro* (seal case) were suspended on cords tightened by an *ojime* (bead), and attached to a *netsuke* (toggle), through two drilled holes. The cord passed behind the sash holding a gown together and was kept from slipping by the *netsuke*. Another type of elongated *netsuke* gripped the sash at top and bottom. Japanese adoption of Western dress meant that by the early 20th century the need for such arrangements had disappeared.

▲ **Japanese** *netsuke*
A large *nio* (guardian deity) would watch over a Buddhist temple. This miniature wooden figure was said to offer similar protection to whoever wore it. The eyes are inlaid with horn.
(19th century; ht 6cm/2½in; value E)

Netsuke, probably known by the late 16th century, were originally formed from natural objects. They evolved into a flattened button shape, then took two further forms: a shallow bowl covered by a metal lid ("mirror-lid" *netsuke*) and a three-dimensional carving. At first often made by artisans active in other crafts, by the early 18th century *netsuke* were made by specialized craftsmen. Stylistic schools emerged, and individual carvers might sign their works. The range of subject matter was wide; the natural world provided inspiration and figures from mythology and popular religion were common, human figures less so, although foreigners and low-class people appealed in the hierarchical society of pre-Meiji Japan. Most striking are *netsuke* of ghosts and supernatural beings and mask *netsuke*. Although most examples are in carved wood and ivory, others are made from silver, hardstones, tortoiseshell, pottery, and stone; they could also be lacquered or inlaid. *Netsuke* functioned as personal seals, as containers, and as ashtrays in smoking sets. *Ojime* were always small, generally round or oval, but sometimes in a naturalistic form. Wood, pottery, and silver were common materials, and some were richly decorated.

SNUFF BOTTLES AND CARVED GLASS

The practice of taking snuff, introduced from the West probably in the late 17th century, spread from the court throughout China during the following century. Bottles, already in use for storing powdered medicines, were judged suitable containers for the new substance. A stopper, very often in a different material, was added, from which a small spoon hung down into the flask.

Through much of the 18th century glass was the chief material for snuff bottles. Hardstones were used, particularly nephrite jade, of which plentiful supplies became available toward the end of that century. Porcelain and organic substances such as ivory, amber, and lacquer provided other materials. Enameling and *cloisonné* were applied as decoration to appropriate surfaces. The technique of painting inside glass seems to have been perfected only toward the end of the 19th century. Snuff bottles are still produced in present-day China for sale as tourist items.

The practical requirement to carry snuff securely permitted little experimentation with the basic form of bottles, but there is considerable variety of outline. Some were adapted from natural objects, such as nuts. Bottles in jade, hardstones, ivory, and lacquer were frequently carved, generally in shallow but sometimes in deep relief, with appreciation of the decorative value of darker or lighter areas. Carved overlay glass decoration was known from the first decades of the 18th century, with up to five colors being applied. The skills of glass overlay and glass carving were extended to larger vessels as glass production flourished under early to mid-Qing rule (17th–18th centuries). Vases and bowls in clear, translucent, or opaque glass were fluted, faceted, cased in overlay, or carved with inscriptions and designs in low

▲ **Japanese** *netsuke*
Ivory was especially well suited to the carving of realistic, miniature representations in the round, as seen in this gamboling tiger. The eyes are inlaid in horn. The piece is signed by the artist Mishu. Tigers are seen as symbols of power in East Asia, and even this tiny figure would be credited with protective virtues. Although *netsuke* were no longer in use as part of everyday attire in the 20th century, their artistic appeal has remained strong.
(20th century; ht 4cm/1½in; value G)

◀ **Chinese snuff bottle**
This amber snuff bottle with lapis lazuli stopper is carved in shallow relief with a figure in a landscape. Snuff bottles were fashioned from a range of materials, but rarely from jadeite and coral, although these were often used to make stoppers (possibly because they were generally available only in small quantities). Some of the early 18th-century snuff bottles may have been adapted from medicine bottles. By the late 19th century, snuff bottles were produced as souvenirs for tourists. Some were adapted from or into decorative forms such as pendants, or served as small sculptures.
(1750–1850; ht 6.5cm/2½in; value G)

in China as an artistic medium. Bamboo stem was used for cylindrical objects such as brushpots, the root for figures and landscapes to be carved in the round. Bamboo could be treated in various ways. With *liuqing* (literally "retaining the green"), a section of the green outer skin was retained and the surrounding skin scraped off to reveal the flesh as ground. With ageing, the retained skin yellowed, while the flesh darkened. Veneer was formed by cooking and pressing a layer of yellow inner skin, then pasting it over wooden objects. The great centers of bamboo carving were in south-eastern China, where Nanjing and Jiading (both in Jiangsu Province) produced excellent schools of carvers such as the Zhu family. Carvers in one medium would also work in others. Such fine woods as box and red sandalwood (zitan) were used, as were bone, soapstone, and rhinoceros horn (strictly a mass of solid hair), as well as an array of different hardstones.

Both Japan and Korea have a long tradition of using carved wooden masks in certain types of drama (for example the *Bugaku* and *No*), as well as for religious rituals. The masks usually portray contorted faces exhibiting an exaggerated human emotion. Japanese woodcarvers have manufactured figures of vivid imagination and fine technical skill. By contrast, the Korean preference in wood-carving is for objects of great simplicity that are skilfully carved in such a way as to exploit the grain of the wood to achieve their best effect.

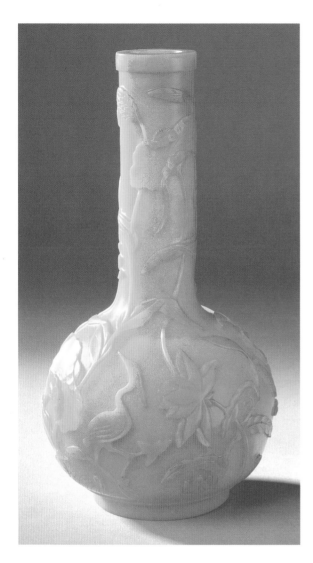

▲ Chinese bottle
This yellow glass bottle, carved with small birds among flowers, was probably intended to imitate amber. The taste in China for yellow carved glass objects was strong during the 18th and 19th centuries.
(19th century; ht 26cm/10¼; value **E***)*

relief, generally by jade craftsmen. Wheel-engraving, stippling, and etching were other techniques employed on glass. Much colored glass deliberately imitated jade and other hardstones, gold, amber, and coral.

BAMBOO AND OTHER CARVINGS
Bamboo is traditionally precious to the Chinese as a symbol of integrity and source of artistic inspiration. In use from the ancient dynasties, it was adopted by 16th-century scholar-officials during the Ming dynasty as a medium for carving figures, landscapes, and objects for their writing desks. Such pieces are characterized by high relief and openwork, simple designs, and good modeling. However, figure-carving gradually declined as artists increasingly sought to convey styles of painting and calligraphy on bamboo. From the early 19th century, shallow relief and linear styles predominated and bamboo veneer was commonly used. Bamboo persists

▼ Chinese brushpot
The creator of this brushpot, carved with figures, seal characters, and an inscription, was the statesman Li Hongzhang (1823–1901), who left both signature and carved seals on his work. The use of polished hardwood for the base and rim was frequent from the late 17th century. This style of brushpot is still common in China.
(1880; ht 12.5cm/5in; value **F***)*

▲ Japanese *inro* with *ojime*
This attractively carved, wooden, two-case *inro* features Hotei, the god of happiness, who is symbolized by his protruding belly, bulging sack, large feather fan, and young attendant.
(19th century; ht 8cm/3in; value **C***)*

KEY FACTS

Netsuke and ojime
- TYPES netsuke: button; shallow bowl with lid; three-dimensional figure; ojime: round or oval bead
- MATERIALS netsuke: wood and ivory most common, but other materials used; ojime: wood, pottery, or silver
- PERIOD OF PRODUCTION 17th to 20th centuries, with the best period during the first half of the 19th century
- INFLUENCES earlier subjects may show a Chinese influence; later figures may be more realistically carved
- BEWARE netsuke: artificially aged ivory or forged signatures; ojime: fakes are rarer

Marks
Some pieces signed on the underside or body with maker's name – this does not guarantee a higher price

Snuff bottles
- USAGE some bottles seem intended for display only, and a few, such as double bottles, as pieces of sculpture
- CHANGES may be adapted from porcelain medicine bottles or hardstone pendants (check for threading holes)
- COLLECTING the absence of a stopper and spoon from a snuff bottle does not detract from its interest

Marks
Reign and personal names may appear

Bamboo
- COLOR worked bamboo ranges from lemon yellow to almost black, with reddish-brown the preferred tone; generally, the older the object, the deeper the color
- SIGNATURES AND SEALS may indicate a style not period
- DATING this can be difficult; reign marks do not appear; dating follows cyclical pattern, giving more than one possible date
- CARE polishing eventually produces a patina; bamboo tends to crack so protect from climatic extremes
- BEWARE original signatures can be scraped off and new ones carved over in order to inflate the price

See also Lacquerware, pp.526–7

Lacquerware

The lacquer tree, *Rhus vernicifera*, tapped for its sap from which lacquer is prepared, is native to China, Korea, and Japan. Very thin layers of lacquer are applied to a base, usually of wood or cloth, each layer being allowed to dry before the next is applied. The resulting surface is hard enough to be carved, is resistant to water, heat, and insects, and can be used in food vessels. The uses of lacquer and its decorative possibilities appear to have been known from late Neolithic times in both China and Japan. Styles and techniques passed between the three East Asian countries, although principally from China eastward. All three countries continue to produce lacquerware today.

▼ Chinese tray
Mother-of-pearl inlay has been a form of decoration on lacquer in China since the Tang period, and it became most popular during the Ming period. After lacquer had been applied to a base and had dried, a design was carved on the body and the resulting space was filled with mother-of-pearl.
(1368–1644; l. 31cm/12in; value I)

CHINA

From being a protective coating, lacquer was developed for increasingly elaborate forms in China during the Han period (206 BC–AD 220). During the Tang period (618–907), the technique of dry lacquer (*jiazhu*) evolved, whereby layers of cloth, successively soaked in lacquer, were molded over a solid core. This technique was particularly used for the manufacture of Buddhist sculpture. Further innovation in the 13th and 14th centuries led to the taste for red lacquer, produced through the addition of cinnabar to pure lacquer, to lacquering in gold, and to various styles of shallow and deep carving, such as the *guri* scroll pattern. Carved scenes in polychrome lacquer and mother-of-pearl inlay were popular in the Ming period (1368–1644), and decorative themes include flowers, birds, dragons, and Buddhist emblems. The Qing court, especially Emperor Qianlong (1736–95), favored carved red lacquer, and the association of Chinese lacquer with this style probably dates from around that time. A tradition of plain, undecorated lacquer, especially for interior surfaces, has nonetheless always existed alongside the elaborate patterns.

Within China, lacquered wares were highly prized. From the Tang period, such goods were exported to Japan; and the Ryukyu Islands, between China and Japan, as well as Korea, may have served as stepping stones for the transmission of Chinese techniques and styles to Japan. From the 16th century, Chinese lacquer was among the luxury goods exported to the West. Export lacquer for the European market was known as "Coromandel" lacquer, as it was transported by ship along the Coromandel coast in India.

▼ Chinese stem cup
The "butter-lamp" form of cups such as this one, together with the characters in Tibetan script, lotus flowers, and other Buddhist motifs, carved in red on a black background, suggests that they were intended for a lamaist Buddhist temple. Polychrome carving through up to four alternating layers of colored lacquer (red, yellow, black, and green) had evolved by the Song period. Such heavily carved wares might be used as stands for porcelain teabowls.
(1736–95; ht 13cm/5in; value H)

▲ Chinese vase
Each side of this baluster-shaped vase is carved in relief with groups of scholars in landscape settings, surmounted by Immortals. The form is ancient and the feeling of classical antiquity is enhanced by the archaic-style gilt-bronze handles. This vase bears a seal mark of the Qianlong reign period.
(1736–95; ht 39cm/15¼in; value I)

KOREA

Lacquering processes were known in Korea during the first millennium BC. Korean craftsmen, moreover, took their skills to Japan during the Nara period (710–94) and the Momoyama period (1568–1600). Smooth-lacquered wares are common, but carved lacquer is not found. Instead, the finest Korean lacquerware is inlaid with mother-of-pearl, of which the country has plentiful native supplies. This is applied either in ground powder form or as whole pieces of shell, on a background of black, dark-brown, or red lacquer. Certain items of furniture, such as low tables, chests, and boxes, are treated in this way. Chests and boxes are generally finished with brass hinges and locks. A product unique to Korea is ox-horn decoration, consisting of translucent pieces of horn painted on the reverse, which are then glued to a wooden frame and polished to reveal the design underneath.

► Japanese box and cover
The rich ornamentation of this box includes areas in *takamaki-e*, *hiramaki-e*, *togidashi maki-e*, and *kiragane*. The interior and underside are in *nashiji*. The rims are in silver. Indigenous supplies of gold, silver, and copper allowed Japanese lacquer craftsmen to make extensive use of these metals in developing decorative techniques. Natural scenes and objects and literary themes are frequent subjects.
(19th century; l. 13cm/5in; value E)

▲ Japanese incense cabinet (*kodansu*)
This cabinet was used to store the implements that were needed in the Japanese game of mixing and identifying incenses. The techniques that are employed in its decoration are *hiramaki-e*, *kiragane*, and *nashiji*.
(19th century; w. 8cm/3in; value F)

▲ Japanese four-case *inro*
The cow and her calf on this brown lacquer *inro* are executed in gold and silver *hiramaki-e*. The cord-guides through which the cord was passed, beginning and ending at the top before both ends were threaded through the *ojime* and fastened to the *netsuke*, are visible on each side of the case. This example is signed "Jitokusai Tachibana Gyokuzan." *Inro* have long been popular with foreign collectors.
(19th century; ht 7cm/2¾in; value E)

JAPAN

During times of social and artistic exchange between Japan and China, as in the Nara (710–94) and Kamakura (1185–1333) periods, Chinese techniques and tastes influenced the evolution of Japanese lacquer, especially in such areas as dry lacquer (Japanese *kanshitsu*), used in Japan as in China for Buddhist sculpture, and carving. However, during periods of relative isolation in Japan's history, such as the Heian period (794–1185), Japanese craftsmen pushed other techniques, particularly in gold decoration, along their own characteristic paths.

For example, during the Heian era, the process of *maki-e* (literally "sprinkled illustration") was perfected. From the initial technique of sprinkling gold or colored filings onto a design in wet lacquer, more elaborate methods developed, giving highly sophisticated results. Techniques included *hiramaki-e*, where the gold design is level with the surrounding ground; *takamaki-e*, where the design is built up with lacquer or other substances above the surrounding surface before the gold powder is applied; *togidashi maki-e*, where the colored or metallic design is covered with lacquer, which is then polished down to reveal the pattern; and *kiragane*, where pieces of cut gold or silver are positioned so as to form a design in the lacquer. The *nashiji* (literally "speckled pear skin") technique of scattering gold filings in a bed of wet lacquer is frequently used on interior surfaces such as inside drawers or boxes.

For food purposes, such as bowls and other containers, plain red lacquer pieces are preferred. Negoro lacquers apply red over black; as the piece ages and becomes worn, the black underlay begins to show through. Regional styles from the Ryukyu Islands and Hidehara in northern Japan offer distinctive applications of basic techniques. Namban (literally "southern barbarian") lacquerwares, often combining Chinese, Japanese, and Indian motifs and with much use of mother-of-pearl inlay, were produced for export both to European traders and missionaries in the 16th and 17th centuries. The popularity of Japanese lacquers in Europe sparked a fashion in the late 17th century for "japanning" furniture, trays, and other objects; however, this was not done in lacquer, which was unobtainable in Europe, but in shellac, a resinous varnish, which was obtained from the lac insect.

Japanese lacquering skills are much in evidence in the production of *inro* (seal cases), small containers formerly carried, suspended from a sash, by Japanese men. *Inro* generally held personal seals, powdered medicine, and pills in up to five neatly interlocking compartments. They were nearly always lacquered on a wooden body, which might require laborious work by a specialist artisan to produce the correct fit, before being passed on to a lacquerer for finishing. *Inro* craftsmen worked separately from those producing *ojime* (beads) and *netsuke* (toggles). While rarely constituting a formal set, *inro*, *ojime*, and *netsuke* should nonetheless present a harmonious ensemble. From the Edo period (1600–1868) onward, families of lacquerers and individuals are known, and many pieces, including *inro*, carry signatures and seals.

A decline in the quality of Japanese lacquer in the early 19th century was reversed when foreign demand for lacquerware rose after the country was opened up to Western visitors in the late part of the century. Lacquer is still produced in Japan, using traditional skills.

KEY FACTS

- **WARES** furniture, writing cases, vases, bowls, trays, and boxes; Japanese masks, armor, and *inro*
- **FORMS** Chinese vases may copy ancient bronze and ceramic forms
- **DECORATION** polishing, carving, inlay with precious and semi-precious metals, and mother-of-pearl; Japanese *maki-e* (sprinkling with metallic filings)
- **QUALITY** on Japanese pieces lacquer should be rich and lustrous, and the line of the design clear and firm;
- **WEAR** Chinese and Japanese lacquer may show signs of repair or re-lacquering; Chinese Song-period pieces – may display hairline crackling; Yuan period – may have deeper crackles; recent Japanese Negoro wares – may bear simulated signs of age; intentional copying of style may be a sign of respect, with no intention to deceive

Marks
Chinese lacquer may carry a reign mark and an artist's signature on an inset plaque or incised on the base; Japanese lacquer may bear a signature, seal mark, or monogram, but these should not be assumed to give reliable information on the piece: successive generations of artists within a school may use the same pen name; the names of famous lacquerers may be appended to a previously unsigned piece or one of recent manufacture; and signatures may be forged

See also Carvings, pp.524–5

Jade

Jade is intimately associated with China, where for millennia it has been prized even above gold, as a symbol of human virtue. Its smooth finish and gentle gleam have been enhanced in the hands of the Chinese by dazzling craftsmanship and artistic refinement. The earliest pieces of worked jade excavated in China date from *c.*4500 BC. The round *bi* disc and the square *cong*, both pierced by a central hollow, were Neolithic forms; the *bi*, taken to symbolize heaven, has endured as a form to this day. The early ritual significance of jade gradually yielded to an appreciation of its aesthetic qualities. By the Han period (206 BC–AD 220), ancient jades were already being sought by collectors.

CHARACTERISTICS

The term "jade" (Chinese *yü*), which is sometimes applied loosely to a range of hardstones, strictly signifies only nephrite and jadeite, two separate minerals. Most Chinese jades are fashioned from nephrite, for which the mines in eastern Central Asia, particularly the Chinese region of Xinjiang, have been the principal source of supply; "spinach-green" nephrite from the area around Lake Baikal in Siberia was used by the Chinese from the 18th century. The largest source of jadeite is Myanmar (Burma), from where it has been imported into China.

Characteristic colors of nephrite are yellow, white, black, and green, and shades of these; the ranges of brown and green tones are particularly varied. A single, non-adulterated color is highly valued. With jadeite, by contrast, green, white, and red may be found in a single piece. A successful piece of worked jade displays the craftsman's ability to use juxtaposed areas of color and mottling to good effect. Because jade is an extremely hard material it cannot be carved, and it is therefore shaped using saws, discs, and drills in conjunction with abrasive powders that are harder than the jade itself. The techniques used to work jade have changed little since the earliest times.

▼ Chinese libation cup with three dragons

This jade cup is an example of the taste for *fanggu* ("imitating the ancient"). It was clearly inspired by the form of the *gui*, a round vessel with handles, originally intended for offering sacrificial food or wine. The writhing dragons add a dramatic touch. This example skilfully blends the creamy and gray shades of nephrite.
(17th century; diam. 13cm/5in; value G)

▲ Chinese pendant

Jadeite and nephrite are of differing composition, hardness, and density, with jadeite being the harder and denser of the two. The glassy brilliance of this apple-green jadeite pendant, carved with a peach, gourds, and a bat, is typical of the green shades of jadeite. Other colors are red and white, and the combination of all three in a single carving can produce a striking effect. Jadeite's brilliant appearance makes it a favorite medium for jewelry. Much is produced in Hong Kong.
(18th–19th century; ht 5cm/2in; value H)

▶ Chinese dish

The translucency and delicacy of this "spinach-green" nephrite dish, carved in the center with chrysanthemums, show how finely jade can be worked. This piece hints at the "Indian" style favored by the Emperor Qianlong (1736–95), who established a specialized workshop for the production of jades in this style. The technique often involved carving the material down to the point of transparency. Such pieces might then be decorated with gilt or inlaid with precious stones. Supplies of nephrite became abundant in the late 18th century, after Qianlong had brought under his control the jade-rich areas in eastern Central Asia now known as Xinjiang. The fractures clearly visible on this piece are common, as jade is such a hard but brittle material.
(18th–19th century; diam. 14.5cm/6in; value E)

STYLISTIC VARIATIONS

From the beginning, jade has generally been worked either in a formal style, incorporating archaic shapes, geometric patterning, and repeated motifs, or in a naturalistic way, expressed in representations of animals, birds, humans, and eventually plants. The ritual value attached to jade showed itself in an abstract style, while the stone's appeal to the senses encouraged at the same time a livelier style based on natural forms. Both of these approaches endure to this day.

During the Song period (960–1279), a strong "archaizing" style developed, known in Chinese as *fanggu* ("imitating the ancient"), as one aspect of a revival of interest in the values of the past. Cups, vases, ceremonial objects, and pendants were produced, clearly inspired by ancient models. This trend persisted through the Ming and Qing periods (1368–1911). In reaction, Ming scholar-officials favored a freer, naturalistic style for the jade objects that adorned their studies.

KEY FACTS

- **TYPES** jadeite and nephrite (true jade)
- **PROPERTIES** extremely hard (jadeite harder than nephrite), but also very brittle: it can shatter if dropped on a hard surface, and a piece may be chipped or broken; cold to the touch; weight: jadeite heavier than nephrite; jade cannot be scratched by an ordinary steel penknife, but jadeite can scratch nephrite
- **COLOR** green; gray-green; brown; yellow; black; white (nephrite: "mutton-fat" jade is the most highly prized in China); subdued colors usually nephrite; stronger colors (sometimes a mixture) usually jadeite; natural flaws or variegations not seen as imperfections; beware of jadeite that has been artificially aged by rubbing down
- **DECORATION** can be polished: jadeite is glossy and nephrite has an oily appearance
- **ITEMS** ritual and ceremonial wares; decorative items and jewelry (jadeite)
- **DATING** this is difficult; the heavier, more elaborate, and intricate a piece is, the more likely it is of recent date

Ivory

Ivory, the tusk of the elephant and other animals, has long been appreciated for its tactile surface and adaptability to carving, especially in miniature. All of the tusk can be used; the hollow root can be fashioned into a vase or brushpot, and the tip into miniature figures or toggles. Throughout South, South-East, and East Asia, ivory has had many decorative functions.

◄ Chinese Daoist deity
The high forehead and the rough staff of this elderly figure suggest that he is Shoulao, the Daoist god of longevity. The colored areas of ivory, which is the result of pigment, enhance the warm patina of this finely executed piece. The skills that had been acquired in carving Christian religious images for export were frequently applied in the Ming and Qing periods to the creation of representations of Daoist and Buddhist deities.
*(16th–17th century; ht 11cm/4¼in; value **E**)*

CHINA

Although ivory has never been held in as much esteem in China as jade and bamboo for carving, it has been worked since Neolithic times. As the mammoth that supplied ivory for the earliest pieces gradually died out, ivory objects from the early Ming period were fashioned from material imported mainly from South-East Asia and India, with some from East Africa.

Early uses of ivory were often as decorative inlay, and perhaps for that reason not much has survived from pre-Ming times. Figure-carving developed as a craft only in the 16th century, associated primarily with the south-eastern coastal province of Fujian. Through the area's trade with the Spanish colonies in the Philippines, Chinese ivory workers were commissioned to produce Christian religious images for use in Spanish colonial churches, copying European work. Adapting these foreign models to their own beliefs and tastes, they created Daoist and Buddhist figures for distribution within China, in addition to secular figures and erotic subjects, which were sometimes known as "medicine women." Ming-period scholars generally rejected ivory as a medium for accessories for their studies; but by the Qing period, ivory wrist-rests and brush holders were acceptable.

From the 18th century, Canton was the principal center for ivory production and the export to the West of intricately carved objects such as card-cases, architectural models, and concentric balls. Ivory proved exceptionally suitable for such elaborate work. Rising imports of unworked ivory into China during the 19th century were matched by swelling exports of carvings. Highly detailed pieces are still made, especially in Hong Kong.

JAPAN

Japanese ivory production has always relied on imported supplies. Although ivory was known before, it was only in the middle years of the Edo period (1600–1868) that craftsmen started to use it for the carving of *netsuke* (toggles), and then perhaps under the influence of Chinese figure-carving. The heyday of Japanese ivory figure-carving came in the late 19th century. The decline in the wearing of traditional costume, the carrying of arms, and the production of Buddhist images, which set in after the Meiji restoration of 1868, led to the weakening of crafts that had served these customs. Skills went into the creation of new objects, such as ornaments, encouraged by an expanding foreign demand. Carved ivory figures are among the finest products of this wave of activity. Professional associations ensured that standards of work were high. A favorite subject besides figures was fruit carved out of ivory and stained in realistic colors. Other forms of decoration were gilding and inlay with semi-precious substances, or ivory might be combined with carved wood in a single piece.

▼ Chinese card-case
This case, carved with outlined panels in relief of figures relaxing in gardens of pine and willow, is typical of the ivory wares that were exported to the West from Canton throughout the 19th century. In contrast to the simplicity of carved figures, objects were often worked in elaborate patterns of medallions, cartouches, and borders, or in deep relief.
*(19th century; ht 12cm/4¾in; value **D**)*

▼ Japanese Basket-seller and Boy
This lively group illustrates the suitability of ivory for detailed carving as well as the skill of this craftsman. It is signed "Jogyoku" on a red lacquer tablet. Figures depicting trades, young girls in traditional dress, and everyday scenes were very popular.
*(19th century; ht 26cm/10¼in; value **G**)*

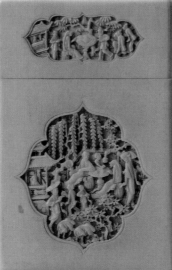

KEY FACTS

- PROPERTIES strong, but may break if dropped on a hard surface; does not burn easily, but deteriorates in hot, dry conditions
- COLOR the natural color of ivory varies according to its provenance; it absorbs oils and stains and can thus be artificially colored; polishing and handling will produce a golden- to dark-brown patina
- THE CITES CONVENTION both China and Japan are signatories to this convention, which regulates trade in such substances as ivory; camel bone is a modern substitute in China for ivory; Hong Kong remains an important center for ivory carving
- CONDITION cracks occur with age – these are not imperfections; check for artificial cracking and also ageing with tea

Marks
A signature may be marked on an attached lacquer tablet

See also Carvings, pp.524–5

The antiques and memorabilia included in this section – scientific instruments; sporting and rock and pop memorabilia; cameras and optical toys; metalwork; and boxes and bottles – are quite distinct in terms of their respective categories, and also, generally, in the types of collector to whom they appeal. However, despite such differences, many of these artifacts are coveted for fundamentally similar reasons. For example, items as diverse as candlesticks and tankards, snuff-boxes and perfume bottles, and sextants and microscopes are all appreciated for the aesthetic qualities of the materials – notably various alloys, hardwoods, and types of glass – from which they are made. The qualities of construction, design and, where applicable, decorative embellishment also figure large in the appeal of these artifacts. The items featured in this section range from the mundane to the esoteric, from vinaigrettes to optical toys and electric guitars. Nevertheless, a 17th-century celestial globe, an 18th-century brass warming-pan, a 19th-century tortoiseshell cardcase, and a late 20th-century female pop star's sequinned bustier can all be equally admired for the extraordinary inventiveness and craftsmanship that successfully integrate their form and their function.

Detail of a medicine chest (left) This British domestic medicine chest, made in mahogany, also has miniature scales, weights, and a pestle and mortar for preparing medicines at home *(c. 1870)*.
Weathervane (above) Made in the USA and now regarded as folk art, this traditional copper weathervane in the form of a cow has turned a very desirable shade of green over the years *(c. 1865)*.

Miscellaneous

Scientific and medical instruments

In the 16th century Copernicus suggested that the earth was not at the center of the cosmos, and Vesalius's dissections of humans transformed our understanding of anatomy. Building on these foundations, the 17th century was one of momentous scientific and medical advances: Galileo became the first astronomer to use a telescope, William Harvey discovered the circulation of the blood, and Isaac Newton formulated his basic laws of physics. This was also the age of European expansion and, as the New World was settled, the world was mapped. Among the tools that have helped to extend humankind's knowledge and physical wellbeing are globes, planetaria, surveying and navigational instruments, telescopes, microscopes, and medical instruments.

Globes and planetaria

The acquisition and study of globes, planetaria, and related instruments has long been popular. They display great diversity both in themselves and in the ways in which they developed according to discoveries and political change. To some collectors, globes are scientific instruments or three-dimensional maps; to others they are fascinating items of furniture. Planetaria are models that illustrate the motions of some or all of the stars and planets in the solar system. Early models depict the Ptolemaic (earth-centered) system; from the 17th century most show the Copernican (sun-centered) system.

GLOBES

Most globes consist of a papier-mâché shell covered with a layer of plaster and decorated with 12 hand-colored, printed-paper strips known as "gores." The globe was normally fitted with a brass meridian ring, and generally mounted in or on an oak stand with a horizon band showing a zodiac calendar scale. Globes are principally of two types: celestial (a map of the stars) and terrestrial (a map of the earth); until the late 19th century most globes were made in pairs.

Globes are thought to have been made in ancient times, but the first record of a European celestial globe dates back to the 10th century; the first European terrestrial globe was made c.1492 in Nuremberg by the German merchant Martin Behaim. In the 16th and 17th centuries new printing techniques and astronomical advances led to the production of many fine globes, particularly in Nuremberg. By the late 17th century it was the fashion to carry a miniature globe in the pocket to aid discussion of geography and the voyages of discovery: hence the nickname "gentleman's toy." From the late 19th century it became common for schools and libraries to own globes for educational purposes, and

most were between 20cm (8in) and 37cm (14½in) in diameter. Major makers in the 18th and 19th centuries include Charles François Delamarche (1740–1817) in Paris, Johann Georg Klinger (1764–1806) in Nuremberg, Newton & Sons (active 1782–1861) in London, and Jan Felkl (1817–87) in Prague.

PLANETARIA

The planetarium is a descendent of the armillary sphere – a skeletal celestial globe composed of rings ("armillae") showing the paths of the stars and planets. Although the term "planetarium" is widely used to refer to any replica of the solar system, there are three distinctive types of model: the planetarium, the orrery, and the tellurian. Planetaria show the relationships between the earth, moon, sun, and planets; some are surrounded by metal rings, which represent the polar circles, the tropics, and the equator. Large, complex planetaria are known as "orreries." More common are telluria, which are principally concerned with the relationship between the earth and the sun. Most models have hand-driven mechanisms, which move the outer balls around the fixed ball at the center; a few rare examples are powered by clockwork.

Makers include George Adams I (1709–72) and Newton & Sons, both in London.

◄ **Pocket terrestrial globe by Charles Smith & Son**
With hand-colored printed gores, this globe depicts the geography of 1834, and the tracks of Captain Cook's third voyage. Typically, a celestial chart lines the fishskin-covered case.
(mid-19th century; diam. 7.5cm/2¾in; value H)

▼ **Planetarium**
The lacquered, silvered-brass British model shown below has a gilded sun and ivory planets; its geared motion is encased in a polygonal drum after a design by John Bleuler (active 1790–1829).
(18th century; diam. 22cm/8½in; value N)

► **Celestial globe by Johann Doppelmayr (1677–1750)**
This typical German globe, measuring 20cm (8in) in diameter, has hand-colored printed gores depicting the stars and constellations, and an oak stand with a horizon ring showing the zodiac calendar, saints' days, and points of the compass
(early 18th century; ht 28.5cm/11in; value I)

KEY FACTS

Globes
- SIZE between 2.5cm/1in and 1.8m/6ft in diameter
- CASES British pocket globes are usually enclosed either in black fishskin-covered or turned wooden cases
- SIGNATURES most makers signed their work and, until the 19th century, dedicated the globe to a patron
- CONDITION avoid badly damaged examples
- COLLECTING look to see where the prime meridian is to help determine the country of origin: on French-made globes the prime meridian may run through Paris; table globes (diam.: 30.5cm/12in) and pocket globes (diam.: 7.5cm/3in) are most commonly found

Planetaria
- SIZE between 20cm/8in and 1.2m/4ft in diameter
- COLLECTING all models are very rare – most are in museums or private collections; avoid incomplete planetaria; signatures are usually on the upper plate

Surveying and navigational instruments

Many surveying instruments, used for mapping land and in construction, and navigational instruments, used to determine position at sea, still exist in fine condition. Until the 1930s most were commissions, so designs vary.

▼ Surveying compass by W. & L.E. Gurley
A telescope with a bubble level and a vertical circle has been added to this American compass, enabling it to be adapted as a theodolite.
(c.1860; ht 17.5cm/7in; value F)

SURVEYING INSTRUMENTS
The best-known surveying instruments are surveying compasses, levels, and theodolites. The surveying level, invented in the 18th century by the British instrument-maker Jonathan Sissons (1690–1747), is a telescope topped with a bubble level, which enables the user to line the telescope parallel to the horizon; the telescope moves on a horizontal plane and checks that two points are level.

The theodolite, although first invented in the mid-16th century, was only developed in the 18th century. It is similar to a surveying level but more sophisticated, as the telescope moves not only on a horizontal but also on a vertical plane, enabling it to measure a horizontal angle and an angle of elevation. The theodolite can be fitted with two bubble levels to enable the user to position the instrument flat; most theodolites have compasses.

The basic design of both instruments altered little throughout the 19th century. Most changes were intended to improve the instruments' accuracy; significant developments include the invention of the Vernier scale, where two scales, one of a very detailed calibration, were used in conjunction with one another to give a highly accurate reading, and the addition of magnifying glasses to the instruments so that the scale could be read more precisely.

NAVIGATIONAL INSTRUMENTS
Most navigational instruments work by enabling the user to determine the altitude of the sun or a star above a given point and from this work out the latitude, giving the position at sea. The first instrument of this type was probably the mariner's astrolabe, a flat disk developed by the Portuguese in the late 15th century with a rule known as an "alidade" fitted across the diameter; when the alidade was aligned with the sun, the user could work out the sun's altitude. In the early 17th century the nautical quadrant was developed: a quarter-circle with a bob or plummet, which hung vertically from the right-angle at the top of the instrument; the quadrant was fitted with viewing holes (or "sights"), one at the right angle and one below it. The instrument was aligned so that the sun was visible through the sights when the plummet hung perpendicular to the horizon. Measuring the angle where the plummet cut the graduated edge of the quadrant would determine the sun's altitude.

The octant was invented in 1730 by the British maker John Hadley and manufactured until *c*.1900, mostly in London. In the form of an eighth of a circle with a graduated scale, it used mirrors to measure angles of up to 90 degrees. Most octants were of mahogany or ebony, with brass, ivory, or boxwood scales, and between *c*.26cm (10¼in) and 46cm (18in) in radius. Some octants are signed but the signature is likely to be the name of the retailer rather than the maker. The sextant was developed *c*.1767; with an arc of 60 degrees, it was more accurate than the octant and measured angles of up to 120 degrees. Early examples were made in ebony, but most later ones were made of brass. Some fine instruments by such makers as Edward Troughton (*d*.1836) featured silver, gold, or even platinum scales. Other notable makers include Jesse Ramsden (*d*.1800).

▲ Theodolite by Marc Secretan (*d*.1867)
In lacquered brass with two bubble levels, this French theodolite has the twin vertical circles known as a "double-vertical" design. Superbly made, it shows the best of machine work allied to hand finishing by craftsmen. British instruments are typically less complex although still of high quality.
(c.1850–1900; ht 46cm/18in; value F)

▼ Octant by John Fuller
In ebony, ivory, and brass, this British octant features an accurate Vernier scale. It is signed by Fuller but, like most octants, was probably made in London.
(c.1780; ht 35cm/13¾in; value F)

KEY FACTS

- MATERIALS fine 16th-century instruments are often made of gilded copper or brass
- DECORATION since the 17th century most makers have concentrated on producing practical instruments; ornamentation is mainly confined to extremely valuable commissioned pieces
- CASES surveying instruments were almost always originally supplied in mahogany or oak cases; look for the maker's trade label in a case, as this enhances value
- SIGNATURES in general, signed instruments are more collectible than unsigned examples
- CARE do not polish instruments; seek expert advice from a specialist restorer before cleaning
- CONDITION surveying instruments were always highly priced, and most have been well looked after; an instrument should be in as original a condition as possible – try to avoid instruments stripped of their patination, as these are merely decorative; instruments should be complete and in working order, as restoration is expensive; octants and sextants: check that mirrors and shades (added for protection when looking at the sun) are present
- COLLECTING early instruments can achieve extremely high prices – many are museum pieces; more affordable 19th-century instruments exist in large numbers

Telescopes and microscopes

Telescopes and microscopes have long played a major role in the quest for scientific knowledge. The first prototypes of the tubular telescopes and microscopes, which are familiar today, were invented between 1590 and 1610 by the Dutch glasses-makers Hans and Zacharias Janssen in Middelburg. The Janssens discovered that an image can be magnified to great effect when several lenses are used in conjunction with one another. The degree of magnification was dependent mainly on the lens quality and the distance between the lenses.

▼ Reflecting telescope by George Adams I

The leather-covered tube, screw-rod focusing for the mirrors, and folding tripod table-stand on this finely decorated, lacquered-brass British example are classic late-18th-century elements.

(late 18th century; l. 38cm/15in; value **H**)

TELESCOPES

As lenses in the early 17th century were inaccurate, telescope-makers struggled to produce telescopes that gave sharp magnified images. The first telescopes were refracting telescopes, so-called because they used lenses to refract the light and focus it on the eye-piece. This type of telescope was first used for astronomy by Galileo in 1610. The basic design of the refracting telescope has changed little since the 17th century; most developments were concerned with minimalizing color and shape distortion, the most notable being the invention in 1758, by the optician John Dollond (1706–61), of a lens, which corrected both types of distortion.

The second type of telescope is the reflecting telescope, invented in the mid-17th century, which used a mirror rather than a lens to focus the light on the eye-piece. Reflecting telescopes were especially popular in the 18th century because they were not subject to chromatic and spherical aberration. They were usually smaller than refracting telescopes, and their

size also contributed to their popularity. By the 19th century lens design had improved so considerably that refracting telescopes regained their popularity. Many telescopes were produced in the 18th and 19th centuries for the large numbers of affluent, educated, amateur scientists who were fascinated by astronomy. Leading makers include George Adams I (1709–72), in London, who produced many fine instruments for his wealthy patrons, among them George III; notable 19th-century makers include Marc Secretan (*d.*1867), in Paris, and Joseph Fraunhofer (1787–1826), in Munich.

MICROSCOPES

There are two main types of microscope: the simple microscope, which is composed of a single lens with a handle and a slide platform or "stage" on which the sample sits, and the compound microscope, composed of two or more lenses (three is the typical number) fitted inside a brass or wood-and-pasteboard tube. Both the lens nearest the sample and the slide platform can usually be adjusted to allow for focusing. The microscope came into use in the early 17th century and initially suffered from the same problems of color and shape distortion as the telescope due to inaccurate lenses. However, as it developed in the mid-18th century with advances in optics, the microscope became an essential tool in medicine and science.

Microscopes vary greatly in design: some are exceedingly grand with intricate decoration, elaborate stands, and a range of complex accessories; others are more humble, such as students' microscopes, pocket microscopes, or botanical microscopes – usually a type of simple microscope, which could be taken out into the field. Quality also varies greatly: instruments by Powell & Lealand (active 1841–1911) and Andrew Ross (active 1830–59) are representative of the finest British production. Also highly prized are instruments by Nachet & Sons and Secretan, in France, and the camera-makers Carl Zeiss and Ernst Leitz, in Germany.

▲ Student's microscope, probably by Hartnack

The microscope featured here (probably French) is made of lacquered brass with a decorated iron base. An instrument of this type would have been sufficient for the basic experiments of a student, being simple to use, small, portable, and inexpensive, yet still of good quality.

(19th century; ht 30.5cm/12in; value **B**)

◄ Microscope by W. Watson & Sons

Produced in London, this monocular instrument has a binocular attachment (not shown) and a mahogany case complete with accessories. High-quality, oxidized- and lacquered-brass instruments such as this were popular with professional and amateur scientists.

(late 19th century; ht 43cm/16¾in; value **H**)

KEY FACTS

- LENSES telescopes: early 17th-century telescopes suffer from many defects due to poor-quality lenses; lack of sharpness of the image, colored light fringes, low light intensity, and very long focal length; from the mid-18th century lenses became more sophisticated and telescopes more accurate
- COLLECTING telescopes: avoid damaged or incomplete examples, as they are expensive to repair; many survive from the 18th and 19th centuries; microscopes: these are also available in huge numbers and a wide variety of designs; avoid damaged instruments: they should be optically complete; instruments should never be polished and should always come complete with the original case
- BEWARE the collecting field is vast, and would-be enthusiasts of microscopy are recommended to seek professional advice before purchasing an instrument

Medical instruments

Antique medical instruments, associated items such as cabinets, glassware, porcelain, furniture, books, illustrations, and other medical ephemera, have a wide and growing following among collectors worldwide.

MEDICINE-CHESTS

During the 18th and 19th centuries, most middle- and upper-class households possessed at least one domestic medicine-chest. These chests or cabinets contained labeled bottles of medicines, jars for ointments, powder canisters, a mixing slab, a pestle and mortar, and other useful items such as an apothecary's balance with weights. Often they came with a booklet advising the householder how to prepare remedies for various ailments and in what doses to administer them. Some households had homeopathic medicine-chests, equipped with rows of phials and instructions to enable the patient to mix their own natural remedies.

The exterior of the medicine-chest was usually intricately executed by a cabinet-maker, and very often, reflected contemporary furniture designs. Some examples were embellished with inlay, ivory, or mother-of-pearl decoration, chinoiserie designs, and fine gold or silver fittings. The interior of the chest was normally divided by shelves and drawers, with a secret shelf for bottles containing poisons often hidden at the rear. Most medicine-chests could be locked to keep the contents safe from prying hands.

▼ Medicine-chest

The 19th-century British mahogany medicine-chest below is of the kind that would have been found in a middle-class household. It is of average width and comes complete with bottles, scales, pestle and mortar, and labeled ointment jars and powder canisters.
(19th century; w. 30.5cm/12in; value H)

MEDICAL INSTRUMENTS

The development of anaesthetics and antiseptics in the 19th century enabled surgeons to extend the boundaries of medical knowledge and carry out increasingly complex operations. Their work demanded the design of sophisticated surgical instruments, which often exhibited fine, intricate workmanship. Especially notable are instruments by the Frenchman Joseph-Frédéric Charrière (1803–76), who produced designs for several major French surgeons.

Many devices were designed for blood-letting, a popular treatment for ailments of all kinds in the 19th century; these include lancets and scarificators – the latter pierced the skin in several places at once. Other somewhat macacolordevices include trepanning (skull-boring) instruments, lithotomy devices for removing gallstones, obstetric and gynecological instruments, catheters, and post-mortem sets. Surgical sets were usually in cases: either plush-lined fitted, and covered with gilt-embossed fishskin or leather, or mahogany decorated with brass or mother-of-pearl inlay.

Other areas of collecting include dental instruments and ear-trumpets. Surviving 19th-century dental instruments are either those used for cleaning, such as tooth scrapers, or those used for extraction, such as tooth keys and elevators. Ear-trumpets, which were made in large numbers and a wide variety of designs in the 19th century, range from the simple horn shape to complex dome-shaped devices. From the 19th century materials include horn, tortoiseshell, silver, gold, Bakelite, and plastic. Some instruments were finely decorated: silver-plated examples by F.C. Rein & Son (1851–1917), in Britain, were engraved with flowers, birds, and animals.

▲ Trepanning drill

Usually such instruments as the steel-and-bone trepanning drill shown here (probably French) were part of a set; matching devices include braces, and elevators to raise the head.
(c.1820; l. 23.5cm/9¼in; value G)

▲ Ear-trumpet

Ear-trumpets were mass-produced in Europe in the 19th century in a wide range of forms. The example above is a "one-draw," hoof-shaped, German ear-trumpet. The metal has been oxidized for decoration and protection. Other typical designs include horn-shaped, swan-neck, banjo-shaped, bell-mouth, and long, tube-shaped trumpets.
(19th century; l. 31cm/12in; value C)

KEY FACTS

Medicine-chests

- SIZE average width: 30.5cm/12in
- CASES most early chests were made of oak with iron fittings; later examples were of mahogany, some with brass banding; more exotic chests were made of ebony or rosewood and walnut, others of Chinese lacquer
- COLLECTING chests should be as complete as possible; bottles are often of mixed designs, many without their original stoppers
- BEWARE some chests still contain original medicines: always seek expert advice to find out how to dispose of them, as they may be poisonous

Medical instruments

- MATERIALS surgical instruments: early instruments are usually made of iron with bone or ivory fittings; some were richly decorated; ear-trumpets: early examples were made of cow horn; later examples are of various materials, including composition and metal
- CASED SETS most cases are mahogany, but embossed leather cases were popular in France and Germany
- CONDITION avoid polished instruments; ear-trumpets: forms are often simple, so damage should be obvious
- COLLECTING extreme care should always be taken when handling sharp instruments; cased sets should be as complete as possible; "married" sets will be less valuable than a set with all its original parts; trepanning and amputation sets are the most common

Sporting memorabilia

Sporting memorabilia encompass a wide range of diverse items, from equipment and clothing used in a match or game (such as bats, balls, bails, stumps, clubs, gloves, and boots) to autographs, presentation awards (including medals, trophies, belts, plates, and caps), decorative items (from commemorative ceramic wares to items of jewelry), and even literature. The broad selection of collectible objects, the strongly international flavor of the subject, and the diverse range of different sports covered make this a highly accessible area to a wide range of collectors. Five of the most popular sports among collectors are soccer, cricket, tennis, golf, and, particularly in the USA, baseball.

◄ *Wisden's Cricketers' Almanack*

This most celebrated of sporting annuals takes its name from John Wisden, the Sussex and All England fast bowler, who brought out the first edition in 1864. Very early editions can be distinguished by their pink wrappers, but the yellow wrapper that is used today has a long history, as shown here. *(1914–19; value J)*

ASSOCIATION SOCCER

The cornerstone of many soccer memorabilia collections is the match program. Program collecting became very fashionable in the 1960s, so examples from that period abound; of most interest to collectors are the rarer Football Association (F.A.) Cup Final and international programs dating from the last quarter of the 19th century. Caps are also popular among collectors. Those awarded by the English F.A. in the pre-World War II era international matches are of a velvety material and embroidered in metal thread with a rose. The color of the cap is indicative of the opposition: purple for matches against Scotland, maroon for matches against Wales, and white for those against Ireland. These caps also feature the year in which the match took place. Those awarded after the war are blue in color and embroidered both with details of the year in which the match took place and the opposing team. Most of the international caps are valuable.

The most desirable medals on the market are those awarded to F.A. Cup winners. Those awarded to present-day players are similar in design to late Victorian medals; the earliest English F.A. Cup winners' medals from the 1870s and 1880s are much smaller. Decorative objects with a soccer theme were rarely made, so late 19th- and early 20th-century examples can be valuable. Most popular are bronze or spelter figures of players in action, but Staffordshire mugs and vases printed with scenes of matches or portraits of players are also highly collectible.

◄ **Soccer cap**

English international caps awarded after World War II are always embroidered with the year and the opposition. This cap, from the Tour of Canada in 1950, is made of a blue velvety material, is embroidered in thread with three lions, and has a tassel and braiding. *(c.1950; value E)*

▼ **Soccer cards**

Bubble gum or cigarette cards representing famous soccer players were issued in large quantities in the 1950s and 1960s. These cards were usually offered in sets of 25 or 50; a full set is more collectable than a part one. Similar cards featuring baseball players were issued in the USA, and are very popular among collectors of all ages. *(c.1958; ht 8–10cm/3–4in; value for a full set A)*

CRICKET

Autographs, photographs, printed ephemera, trophies, regalia and wonderful works of art form the focus of interest for collectors, most of whom are English or Australian. Unless signed or associated with a particular match, bats and balls have to be very early in date – 18th or early 19th century – to have inherent value, because, unlike golf or tennis, the basic design of cricket equipment has changed very little over the past 150 years. With cricket, it is the personal association and historical record that collectors value. Books on or related to the game have been published since the early 18th century, and these are extremely popular with dedicated cricket fans. Most notable is the cricketer's bible, *Wisden's Cricketers' Almanack*, which has been published annually since 1864.

TENNIS

The game of lawn tennis was invented by Major Walter Wingfield in 1874. Even though the game is relatively young, early lawn-tennis rackets are very scarce today. The shape of the racket, unlike that of the cricket bat, changed significantly between the mid-1870s and the 1930s, so examples from the 1870s, distinguished by their asymmetrical heads, may be of considerable value, even without any specific association with a known player. Rackets that are associated with legendary players such as Fred Perry can be immensely valuable. When Perry's trophies were sold at Christie's, South Kensington, in 1997, the racket with which he beat Jack Crawford at Wimbledon in 1934 realized the breathtaking sum of £23,000 (US$34,500).

Also of appeal to collectors are novelty items, such as clocks, teapots, toast-racks, and even dinner gongs, that reflect the early popularity of the game; particularly unique to tennis is the wide range of jewelry that features racket-and-ball motifs. The tennis equivalent to *Wisden* is Ayres' *Law Tennis Almanack*, which was edited by Wallis Myers and published between 1908 and 1938, the year of Myers' death. In fine condition, a full set of the *Almanack* is highly rated. Wimbledon programs from the 1930s or earlier are now rare. The first championship that was held at the present site in Church Road was in 1922; before that the club was located at Worple Road, also in Wimbledon. Only 160 people attended the first Wimbledon championship held in 1877, and a program for that year would fetch a very high sum.

GOLF

Golf has its origins in Scotland, where it is recorded as having been played as early as the 15th century. The production of golfing equipment was centered around St Andrews on the east coast of Scotland, home to many courses. Early makers were often also leading golfers, and their golf balls and clubs are now very sought after. Other collectables include bags, tees, medals, trophies, decorative silver or ceramic wares, and cigarette cards.

The earliest-known golf balls, dating from the early 19th century, have stitched leather covers and feather stuffing. In 1848 the gutta golf ball or "gutty" was launched, made of gutta-percha, a moldable rubbery substance. Gutta balls were mass-produced at a fraction of the cost of feather balls; they were also much more robust, and by the late 1850s feather balls were no longer made. In 1898 the inventors Coburn Haskell and Bertram Work designed a ball with internal windings of rubber thread and an external shell of gutta-percha. The first "Haskell" golf balls were unpredictable, but later models were far superior to the "gutty." In the 1920s the liquid core and dimpled cover became standard, and until the advent of the one-piece rubber golf ball, in the 1960s, little changed in the manufacture of golf balls.

Most early clubs were hand-crafted and made solely of wood; until the late 1850s, iron-headed clubs were used only as a last resort to rescue golfers from a bad lie, as feather golf balls were too fragile to withstand the force of an iron. The earliest clubs were known as long-nosed clubs and had long, slender wooden heads. This design became less fashionable *c.*1850, after the invention of the "gutty," and by the 1880s the club head was shorter, the face deeper, and the neck thicker. By the 1890s golf-club manufacture began to show the effect of industrialization: clubs were made in greater numbers and more quickly and inexpensively than earlier models. Finishing was still carried out by hand, but the general construction of the club was done by machine.

◀ Advertising figure by Dunlop

This figure, made of plaster and papier-mâché, is one of a number of golf-ball advertising figures made by manufacturers in order to promote their sports equipment. This popular example was manufactured in Britain by the Dunlop Tyre and Rubber Co. Similar figures were made by other golf-ball makers, including Golf Ball Developments of Birmingham, which produced Penfold, and the Silvertown Company of London, which made the Silver King.

(c.1925; ht 40cm/15¾in; value D)

▶ Tennis rackets

Together with presentation trophies, rackets are probably the most collectable of all items of tennis memorabilia. One of the best methods of identifying and dating a racket is by looking at the design of the head, although collectors should be aware that the heads can sometimes become distorted if any of the strings are broken. The example featured on the left, with a slightly tilted head, dates from the early days of lawn tennis in the 1870s; it is distinguishable from a real-tennis racket, such as that from the 1870s shown in the center, by its much lighter frame. The example on the far right, which features a square head, is a lawn-tennis racket and dates from the 1880s.

(c.1870s–80s; l. 69cm/27in; left G; center G; far right C)

▶ Baseball

Items that have a specific association with the most celebrated sports stars are those that raise the highest prices among collectors. A baseball such as this, signed on the sweet spot by Babe Ruth (of the New York Yankees) and in good condition, is very desirable.

(c.1930; value I)

BASEBALL

Baseball collecting dates back to the end of the 19th century, when cards picturing the top players of the day appeared as premiums in cigarette packs. Throughout the 20th century these "freebies" have been sold in all shapes and sizes with sweets, savory snacks, and, most popular of all, bubble gum. A copy of the most sought-after baseball card, the "T206 Honus Wagner" ("T206" being the card's catalog number), recently sold for a record amount. Wagner, the top baseball player of the early 20th century, demanded that the card be pulled from distribution as he did not want his likeness to be used to promote smoking; as a result only about 50 examples are known to exist.

In recent years interest in other areas of baseball memorabilia has grown, and items as varied as match programs, press pins, presentation rings, and artifacts used in the World Series championships are now highly sought after by collectors. However, items of equipment as well as of sportswear used by players are the most collectable. Kit worn by the greats of the game can be exceptionally high in price; clothing worn by Lou Gehrig, on whom the Hollywood baseball film *Pride of the Yankees* was based, has been known to reach a premium. Any item associated with Babe Ruth is also certain to be extremely sought after by dedicated fans.

KEY FACTS

- ITEMS varied: include sports equipment, sportswear, caps, medals, press pins, figures, ceramics, cigarette cards, programs, photographs, and autographs
- CONDITION soccer: programs, especially examples from after World War II, should be in good condition; folds, creases, and tears will reduce the value; cricket: the binding of *Wisden* dramatically affects the value; try to obtain copies in their original binding rather than rebound copies; hardbacks published before 1940 in original cloth binding are most sought after
- COLLECTING proof confirming the origin of a piece is desirable; soccer: medals awarded for participation in F.A. Cup Finals and caps awarded for international games are most sought after; cricket: due to the proliferation of material, collectors often concentrate on a single player, county, or area of collecting; *Wisden*: a whole set will be very valuable, but a long run may also be of considerable value
- FAKES soccer: watch out for copies of programs, especially those from historically important games such as the first F.A. Cup Final at the Empire Stadium in 1923

Marks

Golf: most early iron clubs were made by blacksmiths and are not marked; later iron clubs typically feature the maker's name stamped on the back of the head

See also Textiles: Costume – Menswear, p.345

Cameras and optical toys

Although each is a distinct collecting area in its own right, cameras and optical toys often overlap. Both are connected with the presentation of a visual image either as a still portrait (two- or three-dimensional) or as a moving picture; both are linked to stereoscopy and the development of the photograph. Although the earliest optical toys date back to the mid-17th century, and camera production dates back to the early 19th century, collecting in an organized way only began in the early 1970s with auctions in London. By the end of the 1970s, groups for both subject areas were set up throughout the world. Camera collecting now seems to have reached a period of consolidation, but optical toys are becoming increasingly popular.

▲ **Field camera by Thornton-Pickard Co.**
Made in Britain from brass and mahogany, this design of field camera was the standard wood camera from the 1890s to the 1920s. The largest makers of this type of camera were the firms of Thornton-Pickard Co. and J. Lancaster.
*(c.1900; ht 21.5cm/8½in; value **B**)*

EARLY CAMERAS

The first cameras were simply boxes; the British pioneer of photography, William Henry Fox Talbot (1800–77), used a box with a lens at one end and sensitized paper inside. During the early years designs were made by such firms as Giroux and Lerebours in France, and Horne and Thornthwaite in London; in the USA designs in the style of a camera by W. & W.H. Lewis, in New York ("Lewis-pattern" cameras) were popular.

The sliding box camera, which enabled focusing, was introduced in the late 1840s. In the 1850s designers such as Thomas Ottewill, in Britain, made hinged models that folded flat; F.R. Window's design of 1861 developed the idea even further by using a rack and pinion, rather than the simple "push–pull" action, to control focusing. The box design lasted until the 1870s, by which time bellows were almost universal; however, the form was revived in the late 1880s for mass-produced amateur cameras.

FIELD CAMERAS

The design of portable cameras was facilitated by the introduction of a concertina bellows between the lens and the plate-holder. W. & W.H. Lewis patented the first bellows camera in 1851. Two other influential British cameras – one patented in 1856 by Captain Francis Fowke, the other designed in 1857 by C.G.H. Kinnear – inspired field cameras by firms such as P. Meagher (est. *c*.1859), and J. Lancaster (est. 1835), in Birmingham. The brass and mahogany field camera, epitomized by the designs of the Thornton-Pickard Co., in Altrincham, which were popular from the 1890s to the 1920s, enabled amateurs and professionals to carry their equipment easily, and played a major part in promoting serious photography.

BOXFORM CAMERAS

The invention of rollfilm in the 1880s not only allowed cameras to become much smaller but also meant that multiple pictures could be taken easily at one time. In 1888 the British-made Luzo camera and the first camera by the American firm of Kodak Co. (est. 1885) were produced in a design that remained popular until the 1960s – that of rollfilm inside a simple box. The Kodak Brownie, designed in 1900, was one of the most popular cameras of this type, and was widely copied in different materials (in metals and, later, Bakelite and plastic) and designs suited to contemporary fashions and styles.

FOLDING CAMERAS AND 35MM CAMERAS

The folding hand-camera with a lens panel coming forward on a baseboard further improved focusing. It was very compact and portable and could be used with interchangeable lenses. Notable designs were made by Kodak in the USA, the Houghton-Butcher Manufacturing Co. (1925–*c*.1963) in Britain, and Zeiss Ikon (est. 1926) in Germany, until *c*.1960 when 35mm cameras became more fashionable.

The first 35mm cameras were made in the early 1900s. The negative was very small, so many more pictures could be taken on a single load than on conventional rollfilm. The Leica I launched the format in a popular way in 1925, followed by the Zeiss Ikon Contax I in 1932. The 35mm single lens reflex (SLR) developed the format to its current compact style.

▲ **No. 2 Brownie camera and original box by Kodak**
The Brownie camera first came onto the market in 1900 and remained in continuous production until 1967. This type of boxform camera was tremendously popular, as it was not only simple and inexpensive to manufacture but also produced good-quality photographic results. Kodak made many variants of the Brownie, as did other makers in Britain, Europe, and the USA. The model shown here is the No. 2 Brownie. It made use of the larger 120-format rollfilm, which gave bigger, 5.5 x 8.5cm (2¼ x 3¼in) negatives.
*(c.1901; ht 10cm/4in; value **A**)*

▼ **IIIg camera by Leica**
The IIIg (1957–1960) was the last of the Leica cameras to be made with a screw-fitting lens and represented the pinnacle of development in a line of cameras introduced with the Leica I in 1925. From 1954 a method of mounting lenses with a bayonet-fitting was introduced – this method is still used today.
*(c.1958; w. 135mm/5¼in; value **F**)*

OPTICAL TOYS

The optical toy – closely associated with some areas of photography – is a loose term used to cover devices that aim to give an illusion of movement or present a change of scene to the viewer. At their simplest they may just be a sheet of paper with a view that changes when observed by reflected or transmitted light, but at their most complex they can rival the cinema in vividly presenting colored movement.

"Persistance-of-vision" devices – such as the phenakistiscope (1832), the zoetrope (1833), and the praxinoscope (1871) – are optical toys that present a series of similar pictures so that, when viewed in the appropriate way, they give an impression of movement. The best examples date from the early years of the 19th century to its third quarter. Children's toy versions were introduced c.1880s by makers such as Ernst Planck.

▶ Zoetrope

The zoetrope was one of the earliest devices to exploit "persistence of vision," whereby the brain combines a series of similar pictures to create an impression of movement. The zoetrope was introduced in 1833, but most 19th-century examples date from the 1860s and 1870s; 20th-century examples are smaller and less collectible.
(c.1880; ht 35cm/13¾in; value D)

The concertina peep-view presents a series of cut-out pictures joined together within a bellows, or inserted into a specially made box. A hole at one end allows the viewer to see a three-dimensional scene, such as the Thames Tunnel or Crystal Palace or other British tourist spots. They usually date from the early to mid-19th century. Peep-boxes allowed the viewer to look into a box containing a lit scene, and were often presented by itinerant showmen from the mid-1700s. The idea developed from the *vue d'optique*, a printed image or design, which, when viewed from the correct angle, gave a realistic representation of a scene.

The Great Exhibition of 1851 in London gave a boost to stereo-photography, in which two images taken from slightly different viewpoints were combined to give the impression of depth. Photographers used a single camera with two lenses, or one with one lens, and took two photographs from different angles. Between the 1850s and the 1900s they produced them as paper prints, albumen prints, gelatin-silver prints, and daguerreotypes. Subject-matter included topography, genre scenes, individuals, and still-life scenes. Such stereographs (stereo pairs made by different

photographic processes) were and are collectible. A stereoscope (viewing device) was used to view the photographs; these ranged from hand-held mahogany and walnut boxform viewers, in use from the 1860s, to the simple "Holmes-pattern" viewer – an unenclosed stereoscope with a base, sliding stage to hold the stereograph, and two lenses at the front set into a viewing hood – which was popular between 1890 and 1920. Table and floor-standing viewers were produced until the 1930s.

The magic lantern (slide projector) was recorded as early as 1641 but developed as an art form in the late 18th and the 19th centuries, before cinema relegated it largely to educational use. Mahogany and tin lanterns appeared as single models, as double (biunial) models, with two lanterns side by side, and as triple (triunial) versions. The larger the number of lanterns, the greater the scope for creating special effects; by projecting images on top of each other, these devices could be used to create three-dimensional images or give the impression of movement. Slides include long, hand-painted procession ones; wood-mounted slipping ones, with two pieces of painted glass, which gave the impression of movement; and hand-cranked ones, which created kaleidoscopic effects. Later transfer processes facilitated the mass-production of slides.

▼ Praxinoscope by E. Reynauld (1844–1918)

The praxinoscope works on the same principles as the zoetrope: a series of similar images merge together to create an impression of motion. With the praxinoscope the viewer looks into mirrors instead of directly at the picture strip. Here the mock theater frontage helps to add a sense of occasion.
(c.1870; w. 26cm/10¼in; value G)

▲ Magic lantern by Ernst Planck

This device has a lamphouse at the back, which holds a light source, and a lens, which focuses the image from a slide onto a screen. Lanterns by Planck were toys; other designers made elaborate versions for theater, scientific purposes, or lecturing.
(c.1890; ht 18cm/7in; value A)

KEY FACTS

Cameras

- **MATERIALS** nickel plating was typical from the late 1890s; chrome plating dates from the mid-1930s
- **TYPES** these are varied, ranging from the simplest early ones to sliding boxform, field, folding, and 35mm cameras
- **FILM** dry plates were first used in 1871; rollfilm was introduced from the mid-1880s; the first 35mm cameras from the early 1900s used standard movie film
- **FEATURES** red bellows were used until c.1910, and black bellows date from c.1900
- **MAJOR MANUFACTURERS** Kodak Co.; Houghton-Butcher Manufacturing Co.; Coronet Camera Co. (c.1928–63); Zeiss Ikon; Leica
- **CONDITION** in general, the older the camera, the less important the condition
- **COLLECTING** patent numbers aid with dating; Leica I (1925); Leica II (1932–48); Leica III (1933–9); early cameras, especially ones exemplifying groundbreaking design or technology developments, are especially sought after; an original box in good condition will add value

Optical toys

- **DESIGNS** optical toys include phenakistiscopes, zoetropes, praxinoscopes, concertina peep-views, stereographs, and magic lanterns; some lanterns are double (two lanterns side by side) or even triple
- **MAJOR STEREOGRAPH MAUFACTURERS** leading British makers include: Francis Bedford (active 1857–69), London Stereoscopic Co. (active 1854–1890s), and G.W. Wilson (active 1850s–1870s)
- **CONDITION** examples should be as clean as possible; any cleaning should be carried out by a professional conservator; the optical toy should come complete with its original images
- **COLLECTING** peep-boxes: the viewing boxes are far rarer than the prints; most collectible examples are finely detailed, hand-painted slides

Metalwork

Makers of metalwork have generally been concerned with producing everyday, utilitarian items, which were not intended for posterity. Demand has risen among collectors due to the scarcity of early metalwork. Designs for both pewter and brass loosely follow contemporary silver styles. Collectors today often buy metalwork because of its affinity with oak furniture, and enjoy the reflected light of brass and copper in period settings.

BRASS AND COPPER

The earliest European brass (an alloy of copper and zinc) originated in medieval times. The Low Countries and Germany were the main producers until the 18th century, owing to their reserves of calamine (an essential, zinc-based constituent of brass) and their access to rivers for both power and transport. "Brass" was used as a term to cover all yellow metal alloys, including what is now called "bronze" (an alloy of copper and tin), hence such varied items as bronze cooking-pots and bronze figures were often referred to as "brass." It was not until the 18th century, when advances in technology led to the separation of ores and the introduction of new casting methods, that the terms "brass" and "bronze" were first used correctly according to their constituent alloys; for this reason there is often some confusion in the description of pieces made from these early metals.

▲ **Brass pricket candlesticks**
Such candlesticks as these German examples were made for both ecclesiastical and secular use. Iron prickets and the high-dished drip trays are early features on candlesticks, since candles tended to be very messy. These candlesticks were cast in different sections and are held together by an iron rod through the middle.
(c.1680–1720; ht 48cm/19¼in; value G)

◄ **Brass candlestick**
This type of cast-brass candlestick, first made in the 17th century, is unique to England. Named a "trumpet-base" candlestick after the shape of the spreading foot, which resembles a trumpet, it is found with both a ribbed stem, as in this example, and a plain one. Both are sought after by collectors. One of the ways in which authentic examples can be identified is the evidence of lathe-turning marks under the foot.
(c.1670; ht 20cm/8in; value G)

Early metalwork production in the Low Countries and Germany included candlesticks, chandeliers, cooking-pots, pans, jugs, bowls, and alms dishes. A large amount of metalwork was exported from Antwerp and Amsterdam, mostly to Britain and Spain. In the 16th century the quantity of brass alms dishes and bowls produced in Nuremberg and exported around Europe, judging from how many still exist and are frequently found at auction, must have been phenomenal. It is known that a certain number were mass-produced, because the embossed decoration was punched out from the back using a series of iron or bronze stamps rather than carried out free-hand.

In Britain the industry only took off in the mid-17th century. Until then almost all metalwork had been imported, and, even though much brass continued to be brought in, the main impetus to domestic production was the Thirty Years War (1618–48), which restricted

trade and impelled Britain to develop its own industry. One of the most beautiful early items, in a design unique to England, was the trumpet-based candlestick. The simple design and the pleasing shape has led to this being one of the most popular candlesticks with collectors today.

During the 18th century a large number of European metalworkers, fleeing the religious persecutions in Europe, settled in Britain, bringing with them their skills and knowledge. Wares included large numbers of pairs of brass candlesticks, boxes, warming-pans, and kettles. Bristol and, increasingly, Birmingham became the main brass-making centers, the latter becoming famous for the production of small, inexpensive items such as buttons, buckles, toys, furniture mounts, and cutlery.

The Netherlands became a major producer during the 18th century, specializing particularly in engraved brass tobacco-boxes and embossed or repoussé work (decoration pushed out from the back). This can be seen on many items of sheet brass. Iserlohn in north-west Germany was another center of production of tobacco boxes, many of which commemorated victories in battle.

With the advances in mechanization and mass production in the 19th century, many of the small braziers, founders, and metalworkers were supplanted by factories capable of keeping up with demand for

▼ **Brass warming-pan**
This example is typical of British, late 18th-century warming-pans. The cover is made of pierced, embossed, rolled, sheet brass, the handle of an attractive fruitwood. These are much rarer than the ubiquitous copper warming-pans and thus more expensive. However, they are far less expensive than earlier brass warming-pans with wrought-iron handles and very elaborate piercing and engraving.
(c.1780–1820; ht 1.1m/3ft 7in; value D)

▲ Copper jelly mold
Jelly molds, used in middle- and upper-class households during the 19th century, were produced in large numbers and a great variety of designs. There should be evidence of tinning on the inside, and the best examples are struck with the retailer's or the maker's name or registration number. They should also be of a reasonable weight. The jelly mold featured above is a relatively rare design.
*(c.1860–80; ht 15cm/6in; value **B**)*

▲ Pewter baluster measure
This form is unique to pewter. These measures were made in graduated sets in huge numbers for taverns in Britain during the Victorian period; consequently many can still be found today and can be purchased very reasonably. Often they are collected as runs to decorate dressers.
*(c.1840; ht 16cm/6¼in; value **A**)*

► Gilded copper weathervane
Weathervanes were often gilded or painted, but if left plain copper or worn they turn a weathered green (verdigris), which is extremely desirable. They have become the epitome of American folk art and therefore command a large price, especially if sold with an impressive provenance.
*(c.1875; ht 47cm/18½in; value **H**)*

wares both in Britain and throughout the Empire. Much 19th-century brass is often neglected by collectors, who may feel that it does not capture the imagination of earlier, individually cast and crafted pieces. However, some of this commercial material, including runs of copper saucepans, jelly molds, measuring jugs, brass and copper *jardinières*, and brass candlesticks, is becoming increasingly popular with collectors. Such pieces tend to be inexpensive and generally easy to find.

PEWTER
Although pewter (an alloy of tin, lead, and often traces of copper and antimony) wares were made in substantial numbers from medieval times, very little early pewter has survived. It is known from inventories that most 17th-century households owned some pewter items, including chargers and plates, candlesticks, flagons, and tankards, but much of this has over the years been melted down and re-cast into more fashionable styles, or discarded completely. Much pewter is plain, but one of the most desirable types of decoration is "wrigglework", where the pewterer has drawn a design such as a flowering vase on a plate with a rolling punching tool. Such decoration greatly enhances the value of a piece.

Pewter declined in popularity during the 18th century, as competition from the increasingly inexpensive ceramics, glass, and silver industries grew. By the 19th century the staple fare that kept pewterers going was tavern mugs, which needed to be unbreakable. Industrialization led to the mass production, by larger metalwork companies, of both spun and electroplated pewter, known as "Britannia" metal, which today is virtually uncollectible.

In the USA pewter designs copied European styles, but much later. For example, porringers, which were popular in Britain around the late 17th and early 18th centuries, are often found, but were made some 60 to 80 years later than their European predecessors.

IRON AND TIN
Cast iron, used in the 16th and 17th centuries to make fire-backs and some fire-dogs, was first used on a large scale in the 19th century by commercial firms such as the Coalbrookdale Co. (est. 1708) in Shropshire. The best wrought-ironwork tends to come from Italy or Spain, probably because the climate of those countries encouraged the use of decorative iron balconies and window grilles. The skills used in making these also went into producing items such as tall iron candlesticks, locks, and fire-furniture. As iron is so hard, it is difficult to date, but generally the higher the quality, the earlier it is likely

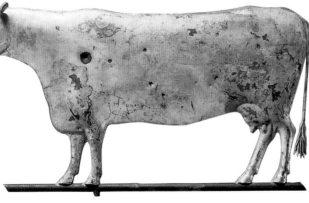

to be. In the 18th century many blacksmiths turned their hands to simple wrought-iron rushlights, which were made for the agricultural workers who could afford neither brass candlesticks nor the candles to burn in them.

In the 18th and 19th centuries tin-plated sheet-iron wares were typically covered with black asphaltum, heat-dried, and then painted with brightly colored flowers. In the USA these wares were known as "Toleware" or "Tolerware." Much tinplate was produced in Pennsylvania and fashioned into coffee-pots, trays, tea-caddies, sconces, skimmers, milk pans, and buckets. Other ways of decorating tin included piercing or punching.

Weathervanes were made and used all over Europe, most of them being cockerels on church spires, but in the USA the tradition was turned into an art form. Most examples were made during the second half of the 19th century, and are in a variety of imaginative forms, in either gilded or painted copper or cast iron.

KEY FACTS

General
- CONDITION chandeliers and candlesticks should show scratches in the drip-trays, where the candle wax has been scraped off over the years
- BEWARE avoid investing in any piece of metalwork with solder or repairs: a common place to find solder repairs is where the stem joins the foot of a candlestick – such a repair makes it impossible to assess whether the foot and the stem are "married"

Brass
- CANDLESTICKS Georgian (*c*.1700–*c*.1790) examples have a vertical seam that joins the two cast halves of the stem: the foot is cast separately and joined by a tang protruding through the foot and hammered over to keep it secure; reproduction candlesticks are core-cast and usually do not have any seams
- CHANDELIERS 18th-century chandeliers have seamed arms if British (if not seamed they are either European or later), and old hand-cut screw threads joining arms to nozzles; machine-cut, regular threads indicate a date after 1840; a chandelier with hollow arms will have been made for electricity from *c*.1900; if it is old and converted the wires will go up the outside of the branches and then through the drip-trays and nozzles
- PATINA originals have a mellow, coppery-brass color and a natural build-up of color
- REPRODUCTIONS some Flemish and German brass candlesticks were reproduced at the end of the 19th century and today from East Asia: most are in a yellow brass and often have a fake, greenish, applied patina
- CONDITION over-polishing can lead to small holes, which reduce value

Pewter
- PLATES AND CHARGERS genuine British examples were hammered in the booge (i.e. the sloping sides of the plate) to strengthen them after casting; the hammer marks should be visible
- GERMAN ALMS DISHES these have been copied and reproduced for the last 200 years: the later ones are lighter and thinner and have poorer repoussé work
- REPRODUCTIONS 20th-century reproductions are thin and brittle, and have a "soapy" feel

Iron and tin
- COLLECTING wrought iron should show signs of being hammered; Pennsylvania tinplate is becoming increasingly sought after in the USA

See also Arts and Crafts: Metalwork, pp.382–5; Oriental Works of Art: Metalwork, pp.522–3

Folk art

The term "folk art" encompasses a wide range of objects, including paintings, sculptures, and domestic wares, that epitomize the craft traditions and social values of mainly rural communities.

EUROPEAN ORIGINS

The German-speaking immigrants arriving in America throughout the 18th and early 19th centuries contributed to a boom period in American folk art. While 48 of the 50 states recorded significant Germanic settlements, Pennsylvania was most transformed by the arrival of Austrians, German Palatinates, Alsacians, and Prussians who assimilated into the dominant English colonial culture, while maintaining their own traditions.

As well as Germans, central European and Scandinavian communities came to the Lancaster, Lebanon, and Buckinghamshire counties of Pennsylvania from the 18th century onward, making furnishings and household items that evoked the forms and motifs of the old world. Folk art incorporated materials as diverse as ceramics, wood, tin, and paper, with animals such as turkeys, dogs, and horses frequently depicted.

Painting was one of the most revered skills and could turn an ordinary item into a stunning piece of art. Itinerant painters decorated anything from walls to boxes. Motifs such as the tulip – a symbol of a contented home life – crop up time and again, as does the peacock – associated with the resurrection of Christ – and the red rose, which signified God's love.

BOXES AND CHESTS

Small decorative boxes, known as "Schmückkästchen," held textile accessories, ribbons, trinkets, and personal keepsakes – and were traditional gifts within the Pennsylvannia German community. These boxes were usually constructed of thinly milled pine, cedar, or poplar with fine, dovetailed corner joinery, pinned bottom and top boards, and punch-decorated sheet-tin hinges and lock hasps. Their owners, many of whom lived in the Lancaster area, inscribed their names in ink. Red, blue, or blue-green ground colors were applied directly to the bare-wood surface rather than over a priming ground of paint. These colors were then overlaid with patterns of stylized flowers, vines, and pinwheels, which were laid out with a compass and painted free-hand. A protective layer of over-varnish was

then applied to the painted decorated surface. The punch-decorated, sheet-tin hardware of many boxes evoked the patterned punch-work of traditional tinsmiths in the local community.

The notion of using a compass to create a decorative pattern was replicated with chests. Such chests were made by many central European immigrants living on isolated farms. Many young girls preparing for marriage had a dower chest, into which they stowed household items, such as linen and needlework. The chests were painted with European motifs, including hearts, tulips, and birds, and later with symbols of the new democracy, such as eagles.

CARVED ANIMALS AND BIRDS

Pennsylvania was also home to German immigrant carver Wilhelm Schimmel (1817–90) who created brightly painted carved birds, animals, and other figures. Acquiring wood from the local sawmill and at barn raisings, Schimmel traded food, drink, or lodging for his work. The saloons and taverns he frequented displayed his work, while residents regularly bought his work for 10 to 25 cents. Larger figures such as eagles – which Schimmel referred to in German as "Vögels" – commanded higher sums. Several of his larger eagles with full wingspans were displayed atop flagpoles, and as ornaments on the crests of gables or in gardens. Schimmel would typically coat the finished carving with a thin layer of gessolike plaster, which served as a priming layer of his colorful painted surfaces and details. Pigments appear to have been common household oil paints, probably salvaged from discarded cans or leftovers found on his travels.

His eagles with spread wings demonstrated his technique of constructing forms and then delineating their surface details. The eagle would have a central body, head, leg and base section into which the separate wings were shallowly mortised and glued in place.

METALWARE

Another popular form of American folk art was the cast-iron or copper weathervane. Wooden patterns were the first step in the production of most hollow-bodied copper weathervanes in the second half of the 19th

◀ **Lidded treen canister**
A turned, poplar-lidded treen canister, with green and yellow leaf and dot decoration on a burnt orange ground. Canisters or Schmück-kästchen, like this, came in various styles, with lids of different types; popular forms had either domed or flat tops, or lids that slid open to reveal their contents, be it sewing accessories or trinkets. This piece, and the two illustrated below, all form part of the Dr. Donald A. Shelley Collection, and so command relatively high prices today.
(c.1800; h 16cm6¼in; value I)

▲ **Carved and painted eagle, by Wilhelm Schimmel**
A pine eaglet, painted with red, black, and yellow spots on an ivory background, the heart-shaped wings descending to tail feathers. Schimmel worked confidently using a folding pocket knife. Common to many of his pieces are the broad facets left on the surface of his carvings, made by the blade, and which he rarely sought to refine.
(late 19thC; h 17cm/6¾in; value O)

◀ **Compass box, Lancaster County, Pennsylvania**
A poplar and pine polychrome-decorated compass box, with punched sheet-iron latch and escutcheon, and a single drawer. Chests like this were often decorated with patterns set out by complicated overlapping lines and deeply scribed with a compass to create the design that was selectively filled in with paint. This example has a profuse, stylized, red-and-white decoration on a blue ground.
(c.1800–1840; w. 40.5cm/16in; value Q)

◄ Hackney horse weathervane

Made by Eugene Morahan, this weathervane is thought to have been made for industrialist William Henry Moore and modeled on his favorite mare. Although many workshops made copper weathervanes using cast-iron molds, a number of larger workshops used molten lead to make a second mold. The copper sheet was then placed between the iron mold and the lead and hammered into shape, thus creating a positive and negative impression. The finer details were further sharpened by hand before the two sheets of copper were soldered together to make the weathervane, and gilded.
(c.1912; h 240.5cm/94¾in; value **M***)*

massive strips from the upper jaws of right and bowhead whales. Those with the requisite tools and skills did the carving, lathe turning, and decorating. While scrimshaw is regarded as primarily an American art form, superb scrimshaw was produced aboard ships of other nations too, such as Britain and Australia.

FRAKTUR

The German immigrant population in Pennsylvania produced Fraktur – brightly colored, illuminated manuscripts – from the 18th century. A "Taufschein," for example, was a document recording the birth and baptism dates of children born to these early settlers. Using goose-quill pens with steel nibs, schoolmasters and itinerant artists would draw up these records for local families. Devotional motifs such as angels, crowns, and the symbolic tulip derived from the Lutheran religion, and these were combined with astrological and natural symbols such as hearts and stars, as well as pictures; images of the family in formal dress were common. Other types of Fraktur included "Vorschriften" – handwriting samplers, bookplates, and house blessings.

▲ Engraved whale's tooth

A fine example of scrimshaw, this whale's tooth is decorated with images symbolizing US nationalism: the spread eagle, the American shield, and the red, white, and blue flag.
(19thC; h 18cm/7in; value **J***)*

century. Cast-iron molds were made from the patterns, into which sheets of copper were hand-hammered.

To paint tinplate – known as tôleware – a similar method to the imitation lacquer technique known as japanning was used. The base coat is usually made of asphaltum, a tar-like substance that provides a glossy, opaque background. Oil paint was then stenciled or handpainted on top, in floral or abstract patterns. Tôleware was time-consuming to make and so was often reserved for special occasions and given as wedding gifts.

SCRIMSHAW

The New England whaling industry brought scrimshaw to American folk art. This involved the making of knickknacks, novelties, keepsakes, and tools from bone or ivory derived from whales and other marine mammals. Most scrimshoners were young men who sought to relieve the tedium of whaling voyages, which often lasted years with long stretches of relative idleness. Creative hobbies were known aboard whale ships more than any other maritime vessels. Veteran whalers who had honed their skills over several voyages probably made the most intricate scrimshaw. Ship carpenters and coopers made finely crafted pieces too. Scrimshawing involved extracting and preparing the raw material, such as bone and teeth from sperm whales, and baleen, a dark, resilient substance taken in

► Fraktur

A Manor Township, Pennsylvania watercolor and ink on paper haussegen (house blessing), dated, with central cartouche enclosing script flanked by tulip vines arising from pots and perched birds in shades of blue, yellow, red, orange and green. A common feature of all existing examples of fraktur is that they are all characterized by extensive use of brightly colored inks and careful script.
(1822; width. 39.5cm/15.5in; value **H***)*

◄ Red tôleware coffee pot

This coffee pot is typical of the domestic wares that were produced in this medium, which also commonly included candlesticks and trays. The tapering shape of the pot, the yellow and ivory floral decoration, and the goose-neck spout are typical features of the craft. The majority of tôleware was painted on a black ground, with red and yellow examples proving rare.
(c.1840; h 25.5cm/10in; value **L***)*

KEY FACTS

- **PAINTED BOXES, FURNITURE AND OTHER ITEMS** items with their original paint are highly sought after by collectors. Check that the paint is original – put onto the wood by its maker or first decorator – rather than "old" paint which may appear aged but hides an earlier, worn surface. Worn paint is only acceptable if it is old or original. Boxes with vibrant decoration, or that are inscribed with an original name, date and/or place always command a premium.

- **FRAKTUR** condition is very important; many pieces were rolled up and kept in chests or blanket boxes, and this will have helped to preserve them to some extent. Colors should be vibrant and any damage such as fading or foxing must be minimal, and should not affect the motifs.

- **WEATHERVANES** unusual subjects and pieces that are three-dimensional rather than two-dimensional are hotly contested by collectors. Weathering such as verdigris is acceptable on copper parts but rust on other metals is less so.

- **PROVENANCE** evidence of the original maker or owner will increase the value of an item. Pieces from landmark collections – such as that of Dr. Donald A. Shelley – will command higher prices

Boxes and bottles

Cases and boxes were manufactured for the purpose of holding or encasing an item or substance. Perhaps less obvious is the sheer range of receptacles made to contain often mundane but sometimes obscure or exotic articles. The materials from which boxes are made are equally wide-ranging. While gold, silver, and other metals may be used for the most elegant pieces, less expensive materials, including tortoiseshell, mother-of-pearl, and wood, were also used. Bottles were used to contain perfume, usually an expensive commodity. Perfume would be bought and decanted into one's personal perfume bottle, and as such the bottle would be as much a reflection of the owner's personality and taste as of his or her wealth or lack of it.

Cases and boxes

The collecting of boxes has always been fashionable or popular, if for no other reason than that the scope and variety of a collection are only limited by the imagination and pocket of the collector. The variety of cases and boxes offered in almost any material is almost limitless, ranging from snuff-boxes and cardcases to vesta (or match) boxes, cigarette cases, and small receptacles made of treen (turned wood). With a certain amount of luck a very reasonable collection can be accumulated for a fairly modest sum.

▲ **Snuff-box**
This French silver snuff-box is decorated with an enameled scene reminiscent of paintings by the French Rococo painter Antoine Watteau.
(19th century; diam. 9cm/3½in; value D)

SNUFF-BOXES

The widespread taking of snuff appears to date from around the beginning of the 18th century, although there were certainly aficionados of the practice prior to that time. Early snuff-boxes are similar to tobacco-boxes in form, except for the important distinction that the covers were hinged rather than of the lift-off variety – a design that allowed the user freedom of both hands and also helped to prevent accidental spillage of the fine powder.

A vast quantity of silver snuff-boxes were manufactured in the late 18th and early 19th centuries to provide for the popularity of snuff-taking. New mechanical techniques ensured a plentiful supply of relatively inexpensive sheet silver from which boxes could be cheaply made to satisfy the growing demand. Decoration of such boxes varied widely, from simple engine-turning or bright-cut engraving, which gave a sparkling effect when caught by the light, to far more extravagant boxes depicting hunting scenes or stories from Classical mythology. The larger boxes, typically measuring 9–12cm (3½–4¾in) in length and known as "table snuff-boxes," would probably have been used after dinner, when a host would offer his guests snuff from a communal box. During the early 19th century "castle-top" snuff-boxes were introduced; the principal makers included Nathaniel Mills, a Birmingham silversmith whose work is highly desirable – particularly his "castle-tops" depicting such famous buildings and landmarks as Windsor Castle and Westminster Abbey. By the mid-19th century the habit of snuff-taking had begun to decline, and the manufacture of snuff-boxes decreased as a result.

CARDCASES

The custom of "leaving one's card" dates back to the early 19th century and is grounded in a highly formal etiquette of introductions and visits. "Visiting" was largely a female occupation; visits were to be short, and Mrs Beeton, in her *Book of Household Management*, recommends a stay of no more than 15 to 20 minutes, in which serious discussions were to altogether avoided. The purpose of a visit could be indicated by turning up different corners of the card; for example, if one was calling at a house to enquire after an illness, the lower right-hand corner was turned up.

The earliest cardcases were made of silver, probably because of its status value, and were sharply rectangular in shape and lightly decorated with engine-turning or scrollwork and foliate patterns. In time this gave way to a more shaped rectangular form, complementing scrollwork decoration. As with snuff-boxes, the main center of production was Birmingham, and important manufacturers included such silversmiths as Joseph Willmore and Taylor & Perry. As with snuff-boxes, the most desirable examples are those decorated with topographical scenes, or castle-tops depicting Windsor Castle, Westminster Abbey, St Paul's Cathedral, and other famous landmarks. The earlier castle-tops had scenes on both sides, and the later ones a scene on one side only; the reverse often came with a plain cartouche where the owner's initials could be engraved. Gentleman's cardcases were generally smaller, and often curved so as to fit more readily into a waistcoat pocket. Cardcases made from tortoiseshell and mother-of-pearl are common, and lacquered, papier-mâché, and wooden cases can also be found fairly readily. Carved ivory cases, particularly those from China, are popular, and Japanese ivory cases decorated with *shibayama* work are highly sought after. Gold cardcases are extremely rare and priced accordingly.

▲ **Castle-top cardcase by Daniel Pettifer**
This British cardcase is stamped with a view of St John's College, Cambridge, and was made in Birmingham, where a great deal of inexpensive silver was manufactured during the 19th century. The silver on these cardcases is often very thin.
*(1858; ht 10cm/4in; value **H**)*

▲ **Cardcase**
This Chinese tortoiseshell and silver cardcase has been applied with figures stamped out of sheets of silver. It is difficult to identify imitation tortoiseshell, but the colors tend to be muddier than in the real material.
*(c.1880; ht 11cm/4¼in; value **A**)*

VESTA AND CIGARETTE CASES

The invention of the friction match was a boon to society, and alleviated a small part of the drudgery of daily life. However, due to the volatile nature of early matches, or "lucifers" as they were called, it quickly became apparent that a special container was required to store these matches for reasons of safety. Thus was born the "vesta" box, or "matchsafe" as it was known in the USA. The earliest examples were for use around the home and often took the form of cylinders of figures (such as animals). The invention of the safety match during the 1830s allowed matches to be carried on the person. The earliest form of vesta case was probably no more than a snuff-box converted to a vesta case by the addition of a striker. The production of vesta cases dates from *c.*1870; it reached its height at the turn of the century, and slowly petered out with the introduction of the cigarette lighter and the book of matches. By the time of World War II the vesta case had all but disappeared.

For such a mundane object, the designs and workmanship exhibited were of the highest quality. The most basic design is rectangular, sometimes plain, but often engraved with foliage or engine-turned decoration, with a hinged lid that snaps tightly shut for safety. The most collectible and expensive vesta cases are those with enameled decoration applied to the front, ranging from simple flats, flowers, and dogs' heads to very complex sporting scenes, and mild erotica. Unusual shapes, including railwaymen's lamps, rugby balls, animals, and fish, are also popular, as are cases with aphorisms such as "I'll find matches if you find baccy" or "A match for you at any time," and those incorporating whistles and photograph frames. Vesta cases were also made of inexpensive materials to allow those of more modest means to acquire them. Cases in silver plate, gun metal, brass, and tinplate were common, often in novelty shapes. North American silver and silver-plate vesta cases are often distinctively rectangular in shape and are profusely decorated with stamped-out scenes.

▲ **Vesta case**
Novelty vesta cases in the forms of fish, boots, pigs, cows, tubes of paint or, as in this British silver case, bears, are enormously popular with collectors. The small ring on the side was for attaching the case to a fob chain so that it could be kept in a waistcoat pocket.
*(c.1880; ht 2.5cm/1in; value **D**)*

▶ **Treen powder-box**
This plum-shaped treen box for storing cosmetic powder is made of carved boxwood. The shape is very plain, and the box has a screw-on lid. Boxwood was popular from the early 18th century onward, and was used in Victorian times for a wide variety of items, including bottle cases, tea-caddies, and powder-boxes.
*(c.1820; ht 11.5cm/4½in; value **G**)*

◀ **Cigarette case**
Although cigarette cases are generally not very popular with collectors, as modern cigarettes do not fit into the old size of box, and the habit of smoking is increasingly discouraged, examples with such images as this are very collectible. The nude woman on this enameled German cigarette case is typical of the rather risqué designs on some cigarette cases and matchboxes made during the Victorian and Edwardian periods. More explicit images were often hidden under the lids.
*(c.1910; ht 8.5cm/3¼in; value **F**)*

Cigarette cases were introduced in the late Victorian period, and are less widely collected – indeed, the standard plain rectangular case seems to have fallen from favor altogether, no doubt partly because modern cigarettes do not fit the old-size boxes. Nevertheless, cases with enameled fronts do have a following, with mildly erotic nude scenes being especially popular. Such scenes are often discreetly hidden underneath a double-hinged cover. Scenes of sporting interest and those featuring animals are also sought after.

OTHER BOXES

"Treen" is a generic term for small household items made from a single piece of turned or, more rarely, carved wood, produced throughout Europe and the USA. Although made from medieval times, the best-known objects date from the 17th century onward; the practice reached its apogee at the end of the 18th century. A bewildering range of wares was made: trenchers, bowls, spoons, spice-boxes, drinking-vessels, butter-markers, snuff-boxes, pestles and mortars (used by apothecaries), and nutmeg graters, which were often double-lidded, the first lid enclosing the grater and the second opening the repository for the whole spice. Woods used include fruitwoods (such as apple or pear), indigenous woods such as walnut, sycamore, yew, and maple, and exotic woods such as ebony, mahogany, and lignum vitae.

Patchboxes were made to hold tiny cut-out paper shapes that were originally worn by women to mask unsightly smallpox scars. However, the practice became fashionable throughout the 18th century when both men and women applied the patches as imitation beauty spots. Patchboxes are usually rectangular or oval, decorated with enameling or engraving; a mirror on the inside of the lid enabled the user to apply the patch accurately to the desired place.

KEY FACTS

- **SNUFF-BOXES** always with hinge to enable easy access; most desirable examples were made with unusual decoration including those with enameled scenes, or depicting hunting scenes or Classical mythology, and with castle-tops; beware of examples with overstretched lids that do not close properly, worn engraved decoration that lacks sharpness, chipped enamel, and modern plastic "enamel"
- **CARDCASES** the most desirable examples are castle-tops, especially those showing a famous or an unusual sight, or those made from such materials as carved ivory, tortoiseshell, or mother-of-pearl
- **VESTA AND CIGARETTE CASES** the pocket vesta case is very collectible; novelty shapes, such as fish and animals, are popular; decoration includes simple enameled design, and mild Victorian and Edwardian erotica, which are especially popular with collectors
- **TREEN** woods tend to be hard, tightly grained types; particularly popular are wares with good patination and such carved details as dates, initials, and mottoes

See also Silver: Miscellaneous, pp.258–9

Enamel boxes

By the mid-18th century the production of English pictorial enamels had emerged at a factory in the rural London suburb of Battersea. Looking to mirror French gold snuffboxes and elegant porcelain objects from the German factory in Meissen, Battersea enamels reflect the forms and decorative style of Continental pieces.

However, they were manufactured with inexpensive materials and ornamented with fused-in pictures that could be reproduced in multiple copies using the

▼ Birmingham Jacobite enamel snuff-box

The interior of this rare snuff-box, bears a portrait of Bonnie Prince Charlie. Such portraits of heroes were a popular decorative theme, as were patriotic images of national events, political slogans, and mottoes, particularly for items intended as souvenirs or sentimental gifts.

(c.1755; diam. 6cm/2⅜in; value **H**)

techniques of transfer printing and overpainting. Many boxes feature figural designs that looked for inspiration to Parisian fashions and the courtly manner of 18th-century taste. Others show subjects based on classical mythology and allegories – which allowed for a graceful way of depicting nude human figures in the guise of gods and goddesses, nymphs, and putti. Other figural motifs for Battersea enamel boxes were based on the popular oil paintings of the French artist Jean Antoine Watteau and his followers – light-hearted scenes of ephemeral pleasures. To a palette of clear, vivid colors ranging from deep pink, blue, light yellow, and reddish brown were later added other hues including pea green, turquoise, claret, lavender, plum, and olive.

After the closure of the Battersea factory in 1756, the production of enamel boxes was taken up at workshops in Bilston, Birmingham, and other towns in the Midlands region of England. Bilston boxes were often decorated with romantic and pastoral scenes, architectural motifs, and finely-painted arrangements of flowers surrounded by richly colored or gilded borders. Raised patterning produced by building up the enamel is also

associated with Bilston work, which was of a very high quality.

Among the leading manufacturers of small painted enamel boxes using Battersea techniques during the second half of the 18th century was the Liverpool ornamental tile manufacturer Sadler and Green, a leading maker of transfer-printed enamels. In Birmingham the factories of John Taylor – known for small portraits and French-style pictures – and Boulton and Fothergill were also well known. Painted work associated with Birmingham includes sunlit lakeside scenes featuring couples in fashionable dress strolling along the banks with swans drifting across the water, as well as detailed classical subjects. Small winged insects often crop up amid verdant foliage framed within brightly colored borders.

Other popular motifs for enamel boxes include hunting and sporting themes, Italian landscapes with classical ruins, harbor scenes with ships or countryside views featuring cows grazing, and commemorative portraits of actors, actresses, or royal personages. A few Birmingham makers exported enamels to the Continent and the United States. For American patrons these included commemorative boxes with stylized portraits of George Washington or the American eagle.

The towns of Wednesbury and Wolverhampton near Bilston were also important centers for painted enamels. The workshop of Samuel Yardley at Wednesbury became a major source for English enamels until it ceased manufacturing in 1840. The enamel boxes produced at his factory tend to be quite small and embellished with boldly outlined designs that typically featured scenes of topical interest or regional views and landscapes applied over a dense white background.

ÉTUIS

Other popular enamel boxes include dainty slender vessels called étuis, shaped either as flattened ovals, slightly tapering toward the base, or in round, baton-like forms. The oval examples often feature emblems or scenes bordered by scrolling patterns highlighted with gilt or gold-colored enamel, while baton-shaped étuis frequently boast all-over floral decoration including finely painted rosebuds or flower sprays. An étui may contain miniaturized sewing implements – needles, thimble, and narrow scissors – or delicate writing tools comprising a slim folding metal penholder, a tiny screw-top glass inkbottle, and a foil-thin ivory plaquette for writing notes. Étuis were also made to hold sticks of sealing wax, toothpicks, or needle-shaped bodkins for drawing ribbons through garments.

◄ Bilston enamel patch-box

This small box is inscribed "The Gift of a Friend," within a monochrome garland, on a pale blue base. Such a box would have been used for storing beauty patches, worn by the aristocracy to emphasize their looks.

(c.1800; l. 4cm/1¼in; value **D**)

▼ South Staffordshire enamel table snuff box

Like many enameled pieces, this snuff box features a scene from an oil painting by Jean Antoine Watteau – in this case La Cascade. Referred to as fête galantes or fêtes champetres such images portray typical aristocratic outdoor pursuits, often within a border of elaborate scrollwork – a characteristic decorative device of the Rococo period.

(c.1770; l. 8cm/3in; value **I**)

▲ Large South Staffordshire enamel étui

An étui is a small box containing various articles such as scissors, tweezers, a miniature spoon, pencil, and ivory memorandum slip. The finest étuis came complete with their contents, while others were sold empty, their use to be decided by the owner. This example depicts a portrait of lady Fenhoulet, the lid decorated with floral cartouches.

(c.1760; l. 11cm/4¼in; value **H**)

▲ Chinese export "famile rose" ogee lozenge-section tea caddy and cover

"Famille rose" describes the palette of colors used for decoration, which centered around pink. Large numbers of pieces were made for export to the West during the 18th, 19th, and early 20th centuries, with early pieces being of the finest quality. Collectors buy the best they can, as these are likely to remain desirable. It became common practice for wealthy families to commission Chinese painters to decorate pieces with their armorial bearing in the 18th century.

(c.18th century; ht 12.5cm/5in; value E)

Tea caddies

Tea first reached Europe during the first half of the 17th century – an exotic luxury imported from China. Despite its enormous expense, this fragrant leaf came to play an important role in fashionable circles during the 18th century, and led to the inauguration of new social rituals, particularly for women. The tea ceremony, with its emphasis on elegance of presentation, furnished the host with the opportunity to make not only an elaborate display of wealth, but also to demonstrate a command of etiquette, conversation, and refined behaviour while at the same time extending hospitality to guests.

Because tea was imported in large chests and sold loose, a tea canister was necessary for storage. With a pierced spoon a small quantity of tea would be taken from a canister and placed in the teapot, which would then be filled with freshly boiled water.

In early examples, made of Chinese or European porcelain, the lid of the canister was used as a measure. Bottle-shaped canisters based on Oriental jars in porcelain, glass, silver, and enamel gave way from the 1730s to box, bombé or vase forms embellished with Rococo flowers or chinoiserie decoration. In the 1770s and 1780s drum and oval shapes were popular, although by this time the tea caddy had found favor.

By the late 18th century tea had become more widely available, and caddies were now frequently much larger in size. Porcelain factories from Meissen to Worcester produced examples featuring delicate painted decoration of birds, cherubs, or chinoiserie scenes in soft and bold hues. The Chinese maintained a robust trade in porcelain until the early 20th century.

Emulating a small chest, the tea caddy was a small ornamental box in mahogany or walnut or decorated with exotic veneers such as shagreen, tortoiseshell, lacquer, leather, or mother-of-pearl. Most were quite small and frequently fitted with a lock to prevent

▲ Sheffield-plated oval tea caddy

From the end of the 18th century, tea caddies were mass-produced in thin-gauge sheet silver in a variety of classical shapes – square, oval, or oblong – and decorated with simple bands of beading, fluted or ribbed patterns, gadrooning, and flower garlands. This example is of simple oval form, with bead borders and a flower finial. It is engraved on the front with a crest and a foliate wreath.

(c.1785; h 13cm/5¹⁄in; value C)

servants from pilfering. Caddies contained lead-lined compartments to hold 'Green' and 'Bohea' tea as well as a small glass bowl for blending the tea or holding sugar. The term "caddy" derives from the Malaysian word *kati* – a unit of weight equal to about 3/5 of a kilogram – that was used from the 1770s when tea began to be imported via Malaya and Java.

▲ Birmingham enamel tea caddy

A Birmingham enamel tea caddy, with scenes depicting "Pyramus and Thisbe," "Persius and Andromeda" and scenes from "The Ladies Amusement." Such mythological scenes were common on enameled wares during the second half of the 18th century, reflecting the Rococo tastes of contemporary aristocracy.

(1760; ht 8.5cm/3¹⁄in; value I)

▶ Regency tortoiseshell tea caddy

By the early 19th century, tea caddies were made in larger sizes and from a range of exotic-looking materials. This example has the form of a pagoda, with a serpentine top, brass fittings, and ball feet. Regency tea caddies were also made in shapes based on architecture or in the form of a sarcophagus with lions'-paw feet and inlaid with robust decorative designs in contrasting wood marquetry, or brass inlay. Papier mâché and Tunbridge ware were also use, as was the mixed-metal technique – silver decorated with metals including copper, nickel, and brass – that found special favor in the USA.

(Early 19th century; w. 19cm/7¹⁄in; value E)

KEY FACTS

Enamel boxes
- DECORATION Battersea: elegant portraits and lighthearted French subjects; Bilston: Romantic and pastoral scenes, architectural motifs; Birmingham: lakeside views, insects, classical subjects and commemorative portraits

Tea caddies
- WARES Early examples small; bottle shapes based on Oriental jars
- DECORATION Rococo flowers and chinoiserie designs
- COLLECTING in good condition, tea caddies embellished with veneers are highly collectible

See also Boxes and bottles, pp.546–547

Perfume bottles

Until the 19th century the design of perfume bottles was very much governed by the nature of scent itself. Since scent is very volatile the bottles had to be airtight and impervious to light, and since scent was very costly, the bottles were made also to reflect this.

▲ Perfume bottle

This double-ended bottle in glass and silver was designed to contain perfume in the end (left) that has the flip top lined with cork; the other end (right) was intended to hold smelling salts and has a screw top.
(c.1870; w. 12cm/4¾in; value A)

EARLY PERFUME BOTTLES

Liquid perfume dates from around the mid-17th century. At this time, glass was considered unworthy to hold the very expensive perfumes, so precious metals and hardstones were used instead. Glass was not used until the end of the 18th century, reaching its heyday in the Victorian period. Of particular note are British double-ended scent bottles, a combination of scent bottle at one end and a smelling-salt bottle or vinaigrette at the other.

Vinaigrettes were tiny hinged boxes which opened to reveal a perfume-soaked sponge that was used to combat offensive odours. The earliest vinaigrettes were usually small rectangular boxes with hinged lids. Inside were pierced grilles, behind which lay the sponge. The interior of the box was gilt-lined, to prevent the liquid from eating into the metal, and a small ring added to one side, allowed the owner to wear it on a necklace or chatelaine. By the early 1800s vinaigrettes had grown in size (up to 4cm/1/2in) and bore more elaborate decoration: intricate scrollwork, flower and foliate designs, figural and animal designs within cast raised flower and shell borders, and lids featuring personal coats of arms or initials.

In the 18th century, perfume bottles were often made of colored faceted glass; the caps at each end were of silver, silver gilt, or even brass. While these bottles were mass-produced, all pockets were catered for, and some of the most expensive are set with coral or turquoise and have silver cagework overlay. Novelty shapes are unusual, but double-ended bottles shaped as horns are popular. Cameo glass scent bottles are also very popular today. These bottles consist of two layers of glass, the outer layer being cut away to reveal the differently colored glass underneath. The bottles took various forms, most notably animal heads, swans, eagles, owls, and even crocodiles, and the most noted exponents were Thomas Webb & Sons (est. 1837) in Stourbridge, England. Another unusual novelty form are the silver-topped bottles made to resemble speckled birds' eggs, the tops of which were sometimes formed as birds' heads. Scent phials known as "Oxford Lavenders" were produced in vast quantities in the 19th century and were very inexpensive. They tended to be discarded after use and have consequently been christened "throw-aways."

Other materials from which perfume bottles are made include procelain; the most desirable were produced at Meissen in Germany, where bottles were made from the early 18th century, and at the British factories of Chelsea, Coalport, Derby, Worcester, and Wedgwood. Examples in gold and silver were made in the 16th and 17th centuries before being largely supplanted by glass versions, only to enjoy a small renaissance in late Victorian Britain.

▲ Perfume bottle made by Meissen

This delicate perfume bottle is decorated in the Rococo Revival style (applied flowers in soft pastel colors and painted insects), which was hugely popular in Europe throughout the mid- to late 19th century. The petals on the flowers on porcelain bottles are vulnerable to chipping, and broken examples should be avoided as they are difficult to repair.
(mid- to late 19th century; ht 8cm/3in; value B)

◄ Perfume bottle

Made in Britain, this perfume bottle, which would probably have decorated an Edwardian dressing-table, is typical of the period in its use of elegant cut-glass decoration and its paneled design. Bottles such as this were not sold complete with perfume, which would have been bought separately and then decanted. The cut-glass stopper would have been used to dab on the perfume.
(1910; ht 23cm/9in; value A)

► Perfume bottle

This British scent bottle was made in Birmingham, where a large quantity of inexpensive 19th-century silver was manufactured. Silver scent bottles are much less common than glass and often have glass inner sleeves to protect the metal from being tarnished through contact with the perfume. The hallmark usually appears on the lid and the base.
(1891; ht 9cm/3½in; value C)

KEY FACTS

Glass
- IMPORTANT MAUFACTURERS Britain: Webb & Sons; France: the Saint-Louis Glassworks, Lalique, and Daum
- COLLECTING double-ended examples are the most common; cameo glass by Webb, early Bohemian *Milchglas* (milk glass), and silver ends should bear appropriate hallmarks

Porcelain
- IMPORTANT MANUFACTURERS Chelsea, Coalport, Derby, Worcester, Wedgwood, and Meissen
- COLLECTING beware of examples with chips or cracks, which can be difficult or expensive to repair

Silver
- IMPORTANT MANUFACTURERS Sampson Mordan & Co. of London; wares should bear their mark
- COLLECTING novelty scent bottles in the forms of various animals are rare and very desirable; all bottles should bear a full set of hallmarks

20th century
- COLLECTING unopened bottles, or those in original packaging, are generally more valuable; visual attractiveness dictates the value of unsigned bottles; Czech bottles: colors such as turquoise blue and brown are rarer than clear or pastel tones

◄ **Shoe-shaped perfume bottle, designed by Hoffman**
Hoffman's designs often feature details of an extremely intricate nature, as here, in this black crystal bottle with jade "knot" stopper. The decoration includes elaborate enameled and jeweled metalwork.
(c.1920s; l. 1.5cm/4½in; value L)

20TH-CENTURY PERFUME BOTTLES

Until the end of the 19th century, perfume was sold to be mixed and decanted into scent bottles. However, by the 1900s, large perfume and fashion houses had begun to sell bottles filled with their own scent, which made decanting unnecessary.

Collectors of 20th-century bottles tend to concentrate on examples by a particular parfumier, such as Coty, Guerlain, or Bourjois, or collect those by fashion houses including Chanel, Dior, or Schiaparelli. Bottles made by well-known glassmakers – Lalique or Baccarat – are also desirable, as are those from Czech glass factories. Bottles reflect the fashions of the time: Art Nouveau and Art Deco in the early years of the century, followed by the elegance and exuberance of fashion's post-war "New Look" and the "Pop" era of the 1960s.

In the 1920s and 1930s Czechoslovakian glass factories exported vast numbers of perfume bottles, usually Art Deco in style with cut decoration. The stoppers were elaborately decorated and could be three times taller than the bottle itself. Figural stoppers are highly desirable to collectors, and bottles by Czech designers such as Hoffman are highly collectible.

As the market for perfume grew so, too, did the number of companies hoping for a share in it. In 1921 Coco Chanel launched her first

► **Enameled and gilded perfume bottle**
An Art Deco glass perfume bottle with a gilded metal and cloisonné enamel stopper and suspended metal and glass ornaments. The dauber is marked "De Vilbiss," indicating the prolific manufacturer of perfume daubers and atomizers of the period. During this time, it was typical for the De Vilbiss name to feature on such products and not the name of the glassmaker, despite the fact that, frequently, makers included the Steuben, Cambridge, or Fenton glassworks.
(c.1920s; ht 12cm/4¾in; value H)

fragrance, "No. 5," as a means of allowing those who could not afford her clothes to enjoy something with the Chanel magic. Since then, perfume and cosmetics have become the mainstay of the fashion industry. Couturiers who followed in her footsteps include Elsa Schiaparelli (1890–1973).

In France, the Lalique company created flaçons for around 60 parfumiers, after René Lalique(1860–1945) developed a new technique of press-molding glass that enabled bottles to be mass-produced and hand-finished. For example, the bottle Lalique designed for François Coty's (1874–1934) fragrance "Muguet" (c.1913) is a simple shape with decoration restricted to a stained and molded stopper and gold label. Lalique also made stand-alone bottles that were sold from the company's catalog. Many designs are notable for their decorative stoppers – one famous range in the shape of fruits and flowers.

Perhaps Lalique's most recognizable commission was the bottle created by René's son Marc for Nina Ricci. The bottle for "L'Air du Temps," with its stopper in the form of two doves representing peace and love, dates from 1951. The perfume was created in 1948 to reflect the exuberance following the end of World War II.

Lalique's competitors included the French factory, Baccarat, which made bottles for parfumiers including Houbigant, Guerlain, Christian Dior, and Piver. Bottles were made in the Art Nouveau and Art Deco styles and then, in the 1930s, examples with a Surrealist influence were made for Schiaparelli and Elizabeth Arden. Before World War II Baccarat and other bottles were often sold in luxurious, fitted, velvet-lined boxes.

The increase in mass production after World War II saw many new perfumes produced, often to compliment the latest fashions. Christian Dior's "New Look" of 1947 had its own scent – Miss Dior – named after the couturier's sister. Other fragrances of the late 1940s and 1950s include "Quadrille" by Balenciaga and "Trésor" by Lancôme.

An innovation of the time was the novelty bottle: cats, dogs, and owls were among the creatures created in glass and used for perfume. Many of these bottles were aimed at the burgeoning teenage market and companies making them included Avon and Max Factor.

Bottles from the 1960s and 1970s, by the likes of Avon and Biba, are collected today, as are scents by celebrity names such as Elizabeth Taylor, Cher, and Dali.

Toward the end of the 20th century, parfumiers began to create special-edition fragrances which are starting to be collected to make the "set." For example, Jean Paul Gaultier's scent, sold in a bottle inspired by the singer Madonna in the female form and Gaultier himself in the male form has seen several new interpretations.

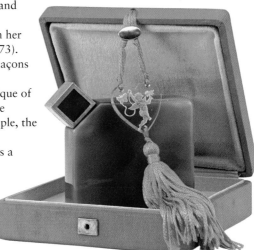

▲ **Ybry "Desir du Coeur" Baccarat perfume bottle.**
The bottle is made of pink crystal with a stopper and enameled metal cover. It is presented in a box that comes complete with a René Lalique glass pendant and tassel. At the start of Lalique's collaboration with parfumiers, he was commissioned by, among others, François Coty who invited René Lalique in 1908 to produce glass labels for his perfume bottles. Coty's aim was to make luxury affordable to more people.
(c.1926; ht 10cm/4in; value G)

◄ **Salvador Dali "Factice" perfume bottle.**
Celebrity-created perfumes became increasingly popular during the second half of the 20th century. Here, the artist Salvador Dali was invited to create a fragrance line by Cofci in 1981. The scent – a combination including rose and jasmine – was launched in 1985, in a dark-blue glass bottle featuring a Surrealist nose and lips. The design was inspired by Dali's painting, 'Apparition du Visage de l'Aphrodite de Cnide dans un Paysage' (1981).
(c.1983; ht 31.5cm/12½in; value E)

See also Silver: Miscellaneous, pp.258–9; Glass: Cut glass, pp.29969, Cameo glass, pp.300–1

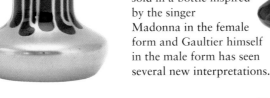

Rock and pop memorabilia

The international market for rock and pop memorabilia arguably began in 1981, when the first sale dedicated to such material was held at Sotheby's in London. The event created enormous interest among buyers and the media worldwide, and rock and pop auctions are now held on a regular basis internationally. Beatles memorabilia is a clear market leader, often achieving record-breaking prices, and this reflects the enormous impact that the Beatles had, and still have, on rock music. Although the focus of the market in general is on the 1960s – often regarded as rock's "golden age" – rock and pop is a market that caters for all tastes and pockets, and offers a wide variety of material to both the new and seasoned collector. Details of provenance (written or visual proof of an item's authenticity) are of the utmost importance, particularly when collecting clothing or instruments.

SIGNED EPHEMERA

Perhaps the most popular area of collecting is autographed material. Commonly seen items are autograph albums, signed photographs or records (and increasingly CDs), concert programs, and posters. The most collectible of all signed rock ephemera is that autographed by the Beatles, although collectors should be careful not to be fooled by forgeries. Among other hand-written material, the highest prices are commanded by Beatles lyrics by John Lennon and Paul McCartney, which sometimes provide an important record of how their songs evolved. In general, autographed or manuscript items of rock stars who are no longer alive with fetch premium prices owing to the finite supply of material.

PRESENTATION DISCS AND AWARDS

Awards, as a representation of an artist's success, can be highly collectible. Presentation (or gold) discs first appeared in the USA in 1958, awarded by the RIAA (Recording Industry Association of America) in recognition of record sales. Equivalent awards were not presented in Britain on a formal basis until the 1970s, with sales monitored and awards given by the BPI (British Phonographic Industry). In the USA, gold-colored discs are used for both gold and platinum awards, while in Britain there is also a silver disc category. American awards have altered in style over the years and this can help in authentication; British awards are basically unchanged. Grammys and Ivor Novello awards appear far less frequently on the market; these are felt by artists to be more important and personal than gold or silver discs, because they usually represent overall achievement rather than the number of records sold. This, allied with the fact that far fewer are awarded, means that they are highly prized among collectors.

▲ **Bob Dylan album cover for Good As I Have Been To You**
The desirability and value of this album cover are greatly increased by the notoriously rare presence of the artist's signature. An earlier signed piece, from the 1960s or 1970s, would be especially desirable.
(1992; value N)

▼ **Platinum Disc presented to Elton John**
Presented in recognition of sales of more than 1 million copies of the 1978 album *A Single Man in the USA*, this disc was auctioned by Elton John in 1988, together with stage costumes and other memorabilia. Platinum discs were first introduced by the RIAA in 1976 and are awarded for a single selling over 2 million copies and an album selling over 1 million copies.
(1978; ht 53cm/21in; value H)

▼ **Bustier by John Paul Gaultier worn by Madonna**
Madonna caused a sensation when she first appeared in her now famous bustiers, originally designed for her 1990 "Blond Ambition" world tour. This particular example was sold for charity in 1992.
(1990; value J)

CLOTHING

Ever since Elvis Presley donned his famous gold lamé suit in the 1950s, clothing has played a fundamental part in rock and pop. The Beatles were probably the first pop stars to be real trendsetters: their hairstyles and clothes, from Chelsea boots to psychedelic shirts, were copied by millions of fans. Since the 1960s, fashion and music have developed hand in hand; with the advent of glam rock and punk in the 1970s, musicians became as well known for their images as for the music they created.

Many artists, including Gary Glitter, Elton John, Prince, and Madonna, are famous for the theatricality of their costumes, and their distinctive, custom-made outfits are highly collectible. The value of ordinary items of clothing is increased if they are particularly associated with the star – for example, Buddy Holly's spectacles or Michael Jackson's fedora hats – or if they featured on an album cover, in a tour, or in a video. Worn clothes are more highly prized than pristine items.

Since the mid-1980s charity auctions have been a feature of the rock and pop world, with musicians often donating items of clothing and personal possessions, which sometimes fetch extraordinarily high prices. It is important to be sure of a piece's authenticity before buying. Artists have sometimes signed the soles of shoes or a piece of clothing; there may be a photograph of the artist wearing the garment in question, or it may be accompanied by a letter guaranteeing its provenance.

▲ Gibson ES335 electric guitar used by Roy Orbison

Although not primarily known as a guitarist, the singer Roy Orbison used this black Gibson ES335 during recording sessions when he was a member of the highly successful Traveling Wilburys. Other members of the group included Bob Dylan, George Harrison, Jeff Lynne and Tom Petty. Orbison's reputation as a musician will ensure that this piece maintains a high value, although the most startling prices are paid for guitars that were owned and played by guitar legends such as Jimi Hendrix or Eric Clapton.
(c.1980; value K)

► Beatles poster

This colorful poster, which was used to promote the Beatles' appearance at the New Brighton Tower in 1963, is an early piece of Beatles memorabilia and thus highly collectible. Posters in general were not designed for long-term use, and were usually disposed of after serving their purpose; they are therefore rare and will be highly sought after.
(1963; ht 76cm/30in; value G)

INSTRUMENTS

At the heart of rock and roll is the electric guitar, and examples owned and played by such guitar heroes as Jimi Hendrix, Eric Clapton, and Pete Townshend have sold for substantial figures. An instrument used for a major recording or live performance will hold the greatest attraction for collectors. A recent appearance on the market is the "signer" – a guitar never actually used by a star but signed by and associated with him or her owing to its make. "Signers" are more affordable alternatives to a guitar that was actually owned by an artist.

Size affects the collectibility of an instrument: guitars make ideal display pieces, while drums and pianos can be difficult to house. Complete drum kits are rare, and many collectors would be happy to own a single piece of a kit or perhaps just the drum skin. Drum kits associated with the most famous rock drummers – Ringo Starr, John Bonham (Led Zeppelin), Keith Moon (The Who), and Ginger Baker (Cream) – are of considerable collector value, as are pianos played by such stars as Elton John, Paul McCartney, and John Lennon.

MISCELLANEOUS

A diverse range of other material regularly appears at auctions and in collectors' fairs, including unsigned promotional items, concert posters, programs and handbills, unpublished photographs, and rare recordings. Most items were originally inexpensive to buy and are usually still very affordable. The magic surrounding some rock stars is such that even everyday personal possessions, including automobiles, documents, and furniture, can become highly desirable. Lennon's psychedelic Rolls-Royce Phantom V became the most expensive item of rock and roll memorabilia when it sold for a record-breaking price in New York in 1985.

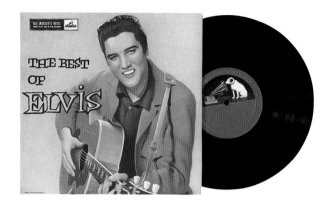

▲ *The Best of Elvis* album

Elvis was one of the most prolific recording rock artists. This album, issued on the HMV label, is in an unusual 10-inch format. It is in near-mint condition, and this will be reflected in the value.
(1957; ht 25.5cm/10in; value C)

KEY FACTS

Collecting
- NAMES the bigger the star, the higher the price: Elvis, Buddy Holly, the Beatles, Jimi Hendrix, and Jim Morrison are all highly collectible owing to their legendary status

Signed ephemera
- AUTOGRAPHS Beatles: owing to the demand in the 1960s, Beatles' signatures were often forged – by family members, employees, and even the Beatles themselves; genuine signatures most likely date from late 1962 to late 1964; examples after that date are less common
- PHOTOGRAPHS Beatles: signed publicity photographs were widely distributed; autographs are usually printed in blue or black, are very neat, and have an unnatural consistency of ink
- BEWARE owing to the rise in values for autographs, modern forgeries exist; attend auctions and collectors' fairs for tips on authenticity; buy from reputable sources who offer a money-back guarantee
- CONDITION this is crucial in determining value, unless a document is so rare that poor condition is less of a consideration; sympathetic restoration in a poster is acceptable; tears through signatures, or paper loss, can lead to a substantial depreciation in price

Presentation discs and awards
- COLLECTING discs presented to the artist are highly sought after, followed by discs given to those closely involved in the production of an album or single

Clothing
- ORIGINALITY the more distinctive and identifiable the clothing, the more desirable it will be; proof of provenance is important; an outfit featured on an album cover or worn extensively on tour will be more valuable than items used as everyday wear
- CONDITION signs of wear and tear, and even damage, can help establish authenticity; original labels are useful

Instruments
- CONDITION this is often irrelevant, as wear suggests use: Hendrix's smashed guitars raise premium prices
- COLLECTING guitars are most popular with collectors

Miscellaneous
- PRODUCTS items produced to cash in on Beatlemania, such as clothing and make-up aimed at female fans, are becoming increasingly valuable
- COLLECTING original packaging is vital; boxed items in mint condition command the best prices

See also Textiles: Costume, pp.342–45

Where to buy

Antiques can be purchased from a wide range of specialist and non-specialist outlets. The former category includes auction houses and antiques shops, fairs, and markets, while the latter embraces jumble sales, charity shops, car-boot and garage sales, junk shops, and the private advertisement sections in local newspapers.

AUCTION HOUSES

There is no doubt that auction houses provide one of the most exciting ways of buying antiques and collectibles. They offer the private buyer the opportunity to compete with the trade on equal terms, and the fact that most auction lots are bought by the trade, and that, because they have a business to run, members of trade hardly ever pay "over the odds" to secure a lot, private buyers can purchase at what might be called "wholesale prices." The most **prestigious auction houses** internationally are Sotheby's and Christie's, and most of the people attending their city sales are either dealers or serious collectors. Every country has many **independent auctioneers**, for example in Britain there is Lyon and Turnbull in Edinburgh, Dreweatt Neate in Newbury, Wallis and Wallis in Lewes, Cheffins in Cambridge, and Woolley and Wallis in Salisbury, all of whom hold excellent sales.

It is usually true that you will pay more for a lot in the leading city auction houses, and less in regional ones. A **"sleeper"** (a fine-quality piece not hitherto recognized either for what it actually is, or its true worth) can be found anywhere.

Information about the objects for sale comes in the form of a **catalog**, which is either available at the **preview** (a few days before the sale), or, depending on the importance of the sale, by post weeks, or even months, in advance. Catalogs list the objects for sale – **the lots** – with each lot having its own number. Catalogs for important sales include a description of each lot, the auction house's opinion on the date or period of the object, and advice on damage or alterations. Most catalogs carry an estimated price guide (**estimate**) for each lot, which is the price the auction house expects the object to achieve and, as such, is only a guide for prospective buyers. Before **bidding** for lots at a sale, you have the opportunity to examine them at a preview, usually one or two days in advance. If you require any additional information, you can ask someone in charge. Some of the major auction houses will also provide, on request, a **detailed report** on the condition of an object. If you subsequently discover any faults or damage not listed, you have grounds for recourse. However, you should always make up your own mind regarding damage, authenticity, and price. Indeed, the **"Conditions of Sale"** carried in many catalogs serves as a disclaimer against any incorrect description or attribution, although in recent years some auction houses have given a five-year guarantee against selling a forgery.

At many smaller auction houses you can turn up at the saleroom on the day of the sale, bid for what you want, and give your name and address when you secure a lot. However, at most major auction houses you must register in advance, or on arrival. You will then be given a **bidding number**, on a card or "paddle." If you can't attend the sale, you can leave an instruction with the auction house for someone to bid on your behalf. You should stipulate the maximum price you are prepared to pay (the bidder will invariably try to secure the lot for as little as possible), and they can expect a tip from you in the region of 5–10% of the **hammer price**.

Auctioneers usually start the **bidding** just below the estimate. If there are no bids at this point, he will ask for a lower sum, and perhaps lower it further, until he receives the first bid. He then conducts the bidding in increments of between 5 and 100%. You can enter the bidding at any stage, by attracting his attention with your paddle, a nod, or a raised hand. Once he has your attention, he will come back to you to see if you wish to continue bidding. A nod indicates your acceptance of the new increase; a shake of the head indicates your withdrawal. You can also offer a bid above the previous one, but less than the increase he asks for. He may accept this if he feels the bidding is reaching its conclusion. When the auctioneer appears to have only one bidder left, he will check to see if anyone else is interested, and then signal the end of the bidding by banging his hammer (gavel) on the rostrum. If you have been successful, he will take your name or bidding number, at which point you have entered into a **legal contract** between buyer and seller, and you are liable for the **hammer price**, the **buyer's premium** charged by the auction house (between 15–20% of the hammer price), plus VAT or any similar state tax on that premium. You will be given a set number of days to clear your purchase(s) from the premises, and you can expect to be charged **storage costs** exceeding that period.

When attending auctions, it is also worth noting that some lots are either left unsold, or "bought in" by the auction house itself, because they fail to reach a **"reserve"** price that has been agreed in advance between the seller and the auction house.

PROFESSIONAL ANTIQUES DEALERS

Despite the numerous auctions held every day of the week, the primary source of antiques for most buyers remains the antiques dealer, of which there are two basic types: generalists and specialists. Both can be encountered at a variety of locations, notably big-city showrooms, small high-street shops in towns and villages, covered and open-air antiques markets, and international, national, and local antiques fairs. As with auction houses, price levels tend to reflect the prestige of both the dealer and the location from which they are selling. For example, prices tend to be higher at an international antiques fair than in a local high-street shop. However, like auction sales, for the most part, they are simply a reflection of the quality of the pieces for sale. In other words, prestigious locations do not preclude competitive prices.

When buying from a dealer, you should always ask **"what's your best price,"** or **"what can you do,"** on any piece you are interested in. There are a number of significant advantages in buying from a dealer that can outweigh any short-term financial gain from buying at auction. Firstly, many reputable dealers allow you to purchase on a **sale-and-return** basis. Secondly, if you cultivate a good relationship with a reputable dealer, he or she will invariably go out of their way to find something you may be looking for, even if they don't have it in stock. Moreover, their prices tend to become more and more competitive the more you deal with them. Thirdly, dealers can be very generous with their knowledge of antiques, especially if you are enthusiastic.

A further advantage lies in buying from antiques dealers who are members of an **antiques trade association**. To become a member of a professional body applicants must have been registered and trading for a minimum of three years, and be proposed and seconded by existing members. An applicant is also subject to a **"vetting"** process, which includes an unannounced visit to his or her premises to check that all items displayed are properly labelled with accurate descriptions, etc. Membership is reviewed annually, and any departure from the **code of practice** will result in expulsion.

OTHER SOURCES

It can be worth looking for antiques and collectibles in **jumble sales** and **charity shops**. However, the onus is entirely on the purchaser, as no descriptions or guarantees are provided. Both **car-boot sales** and **garage sales** have proliferated and, like jumble sales and charity shops, they can be sources of good-quality antiques or, more likely, collectibles. Indeed, some **"amateur" antiques dealers** use boot sales as regular or occasional outlets for their wares, although in most cases be prepared to sift through piles of household junk to find any elusive treasures. It is normal to haggle over the asking price.

Some finds can be had at junk shops. Many **local newspapers** carry advertisements for antiques and collectibles in their "For Sale" sections. The majority are inserted by private individuals, most of whom are keen to get rid of something and raise some money in the process. Again, it's down to your own judgement. However, always ask for a **written receipt**, which should include a description of the object, the date of purchase, the price paid, and the name and address of the vendor. This is very unlikely to give you any legal redress if the seller has misrepresented the item, but, if the worse comes to the worse, and it turns out you have purchased **stolen goods**, the receipt will at least show that you bought in good faith. The primary disadvantage is that any purchase is a case of **caveat emptor** ("let the buyer beware"). In other words, the onus is once again entirely on the purchaser, and there is little or no legal redress against misrepresentation.

BUYING OVERSEAS

Finally, in recent years the antiques trade has become increasingly international, with more and more private buyers purchasing antiques and collectibles during holiday or business trips abroad. However, many countries now have strict laws regarding the **export of works of art** and antiques from their country of origin. Consequently, if you are thinking of buying overseas, always check the regulations with the appropriate embassy beforehand. Equally, on return, always declare the items, together with a **valid receipt**, at Customs. Although **duty** isn't usually payable on items over 100 years old, objects of more recent manufacture can be liable. So, again, check with the relevant **Customs** prior to departure.

BUYING ON THE INTERNET

Buying antiques and collectibles on the internet is remarkably simple. You can use online auctions (items are offered on a website for a fixed period for you to bid on); live auctions (bid at auction house sales in real time); or online absentee bidding (submit a bid to an auction house that a clerk will action at the auction itself). Many dealers have websites that allow you to view and buy direct.

If you are new to buying antiques online, it pays to consider a few tips. First, check the authenticity of the auction house or dealer – many will be registered with an official association – and make sure that they list all of the information that you would expect to find in a regular auction catalog. Antiques-related sites on the internet are now numerous, so narrow your search when looking for a piece: consider color, date, designer, manufacturer, and country of origin. Never be tempted to buy anything that you have not seen a visual reference for, and request additional photographs if you want to see more. If in doubt about a piece, double-check with other reliable sources – it is not uncommon for sellers to make mistakes. Finally, before buying a piece, make sure all payment and shipping costs have been explained to you, and check that the site is secure before sending personal and card details.

Contact the trade associations for more information on antiques shows. For antiques dealers (too numerous to name), please consult the many directories available.

BRITAIN

ASSOCIATIONS

British Antique Dealers' Association (BADA)
20 Rutland Gate, London SW7

Association of Art and Antique Dealers (LAPADA)
535 King's Road, London SW10

MAJOR AUCTION HOUSES

Bonhams Knightsbridge
Montpelier Street, London SW7

Bonhams
101 New Bond Street, London W1Y

Cheffins
The Cambridge Saleroom
2 Clifton Road
Cambridge CB1 4BW

Christie's
8 King Street
St James's, London SW1

Christie's South Kensington
85 Old Brompton Road
London SW7

Dreweatts
Donnington Priory Salerooms.
Donnington,
Newbury, Berkshire RG14 2JE

Gorringes
15 North Street
Lewes, East Sussex BN7 2PD

Lyon & Turnbull
33 Broughton Place
Edinburgh EH1 3RR

Sotheby's
34–35 New Bond Street, London W1

Wallis and Wallis
West Street Auction Galleries
Lewes, East Sussex BN7 2NJ

Woolley and Wallis
51–61 Castle Street
Salisbury, Wiltshire SP1 3SU

MAJOR ANTIQUES SHOWS

Alexandra Palace Antique and Collectors Fair
Alexandra Palace, London N20

Fine Art & Antiques Fair
Olympia
Kensington, London W14
BADA Antiques & Fine Art Fair
Duke of York's Headquarters
London SW3

The Chelsea Antiques Fair
Chelsea Old Town Hall
King's Road, London SW3

Grosvenor House Art & Antiques Fair
Grosvenor House Hotel, London W1

LAPADA Antiques Fair
Royal Academy of Arts,
6 Burlington Gardens
London W8

LAPADA Antiques Fair
National Exhibition Center
Birmingham

The National Glass Collectors Fair
The Heritage Motor Center
Gaydon, Warwickshire

ANTIQUES MARKETS AND CENTERS

Alfies Antiques Market
13–25 Church Street
London NW8

Antiquarius
King's Road
Chelsea, London SW3

Bartlett Street Antiques Center
5–10 Bartlett Street, Bath BA1

Bermondsey Market
Bermondsey Street, London SE1

Camden Passage
Islington, London N1

Grays Antique Market
Davies Street, London W1

The Ginnel
Harrogate Antique Center
The Ginnel
Off Parliament Street
Harrogate HG1

Preston Antique Center
The Mill
New Hall Lane
Preston, Lancashire PR1

Taunton Antiques Market
25–29 Silver Street
Taunton, Somerset TA1

THE UNITED STATES

ASSOCIATIONS

Antique Appraisers of America Inc,
386 Park Avenue South,
New York NY 10016

National Art & Antiques Dealers' Association (NAADA)
12 East 56th Street
New York NY 10022

Art and Antique Dealers League of America (AADLA)
353 East 78th Street
New York 10021

MAJOR AUCTION HOUSES

Christie's
502 Park Avenue
New York NY 10022

Sotheby's
1334 York Avenue
New York NY 10021

Sotheby's
215 West Ohio Street
Chicago IL 60610

Alderfer Sunford Auction Company
501 Fairgrounds Road
Hatfield PA 19440

Bonhams & Butterfield
220 San Bruno Avenue
San Francisco CA 94103

William Doyle Galleries
175 East 87th Street
New York NY 10128

Ken Farmer Auctions
and Estates
105a Harrison Street
Radford VA 24141

Freeman's
1808 Chestnut Street
Philadelphia PA 19103

Garth's Auctions
2690 Stratford Road
Box 369
Delaware OH 43015

James D Julia Inc
PO Box 830
Fairfield MA 04937

North East Auctions
93 Pleasant Street
Portsmouth NH 03801

David Rago Auctions Inc.
333 North Main Street
Lambertville, New Jersey 08530

Skinner Inc.
357 Main Street
Bolton MA 01740

Skinner, Boston
63 Park Plaza
Boston MA 02116

MAJOR ANTIQUES SHOWS

The American Antiques Show
The Metropolitan Pavilion
125 West 18th Street
New York NY

Heart of Country Antiques Show
Opryland Hotel
2800 Opryland Drive
Nashville TN 37214

New York Winter Antiques Show
Seventh Regiment Armory
67th Street and Park Avenue
New York NY 10021

Washington Antiques Show
Omni Shorham Hotel
2500 Calvert Street
Washington DC

Connecticut Spring Antiques Show
State Armory, Hartford CT

Philadelphia Antiques Show
103rd Engineers Armory
33rd and Market streets
Philadelphia PA 19104

Baltimore Museum Antiques Show
Baltimore Museum of Art
10 Art Museum Drive
Baltimore MD 21218

Mid-Week Manchester Antiques Show
Sheraton Tara
Wayfarer Inn, Bedford NH

New Hampshire Antique Dealers
Association Show
Center of New Hampshire
Holiday Inn
700 Elm Street, Manchester NH 03101

Riverside Antiques Show
New Hampshire
State Armory
Canal Street
Manchester NH 03101

Fall Show at the Armory
Seventh Regiment Armory
67th Street and Park Avenue
New York 10021

Ellis Memorial Hospital Show
The Cyclorama
539 Tremont Street, Boston MA

International Fine Art and Antique
Dealers Show
Seventh Regiment Armory
67th Street and Park Avenue
New York NY 10021

San Francisco Fall Antiques Show
Fort Mason Center
Festival Pavilion
San Francisco CA 94123

Ellis Memorial Hospital Show
The Cyclorama
539 Tremont Street,
Boston MA

International Fine Art and Antique
Dealers Show
Seventh Regiment Armory
67th Street and Park Avenue
New York NY 10021

San Francisco Fall Antiques Show
Fort Mason Center
Festival Pavilion
San Francisco CA 94123

Glossary

abalone shell ear-shaped shell lined with mother-of-pearl.

abrash variation of color shades created by the use of yarns from different batches.

Abstract Expressionism movement in painting and ceramics that emerged in the mid-1950s in the USA, characterized by gestural, random marks and compositions.

acanthus stylized, leaf-shaped ornament representing the plant *Acanthus spinosus*, popular in Classical architecture and often used as a carved or inlaid motif.

acid etching technique involving treatment of glass with hydrofluoric acid, giving a matt or frosted finish.

Adam style Neo-classical style, first introduced in Britain by the architects Robert Adam and James Adam during the second half of the 18th century and characterized by motifs such as husks, palmettes, and festoons.

Aesthetic Movement decorative arts movement with a strong Japanese influence, which flourished in Europe and the USA from c.1860s to the late 1880s.

agate ware type of pottery resembling agate due to the partial blending of different colored clays.

air twist decorative spiral pattern formed in the stem of a glass by twisting a trapped air bubble.

alabastron small bottle or flask, used in ancient Egypt.

albarello Italian term for a drug jar, generally of waisted, cylindrical form, originating in Persia in the 12th century but adopted by almost every major European country from the 15th century.

alla certosina type of decoration using inlays of bone and ivory.

alloy mixture of metals; in the context of silver, the base metals added to silver to strengthen it. Sterling silver is 92.5 percent pure and is usually mixed with copper.

Amen glass rare type of Jacobite glass that incorporates into the decoration verses of a hymn ending with the word Amen, thought to date from after the Battle of Culloden in 1746.

American Belleek late-19th-century American version of the thinly potted wares originally made at the Belleek factory in Ireland.

amphora Classical two-handled globular vessel used for storing wine or oil.

andirons iron supports for resting burning logs in a fireplace.

aniline dye synthetic, industrial dye used in textile and carpet manufacture from the 1850s. It produces strong, bright colors that are cruder than those of traditional vegetable dyes.

annealing process by which silver is heated and then rapidly cooled in order to soften it sufficiently to be workable. Also refers to slow cooling of hot glass, which reduces internal stresses that may cause cracking once the glass is cold.

anthemion stylized Classical ornament based on the honeysuckle flower.

apostle spoon silver spoon with a finial molded in the form of one of the 12 Apostles; particularly popular in the 16th and 17th centuries.

appliqué applied ornamentation that is made separately and then attached to an object. It also refers to the decorative application of a second fabric to the main fabric ground.

apron band or shaped "skirt" of wood that is attached to the top of a table or chest-of-drawers, or runs beneath the seat rail of a chair.

arabesque term for intricate decoration comprising stylized, intertwined leaves and scrolls.

arbor round, steel spindle or shaft on which a wheel pinion, lever, or anchor is mounted in a clock.

arcading series of decorative linked arches derived from architecture.

arcanist one who knows the formula (*arcanum*) for manufacturing hard-paste porcelain.

architrave molded framework; in Classical architecture, the lowest part of an entablature.

armadio Italian term for a linen-press or wardrobe.

armoire French term for a linen-press, wardrobe, or large cupboard.

armorial crest or coat of arms.

armorial wares ceramic, glass, or silver wares decorated with coats of arms or crests.

Art Deco style characterized by geometric forms and bright, bold colors, popular from c.1918 to 1940. The name is taken from the 1925 Exposition des Arts Décoratifs et Industriels Modernes in Paris.

artificial porcelain *see* soft-paste porcelain.

Art Nouveau movement and style of decoration characterized by sinuous curves and flowing lines, asymmetry, and flower and leaf motifs, prevalent from the 1890s to c.1910.

Arts and Crafts Movement 19th-century artistic movement, led by William Morris, which advocated a return to quality craftsmanship and simplicity of design in the face of mass production.

asmalyk five-sided woven trappings, used to decorate the bride's camel during a wedding procession.

assay testing of a metal alloy to establish its purity and consistency.

astragal small, semi-circular molding; term applied to the glazing bars on cabinets and bookcases.

automata term covering a variety of mechanical toys, usually clockwork.

automaton clock clock with a strike performed by mechanically operated figures.

autoperipatetikos clockwork figure, usually bisque-headed, that will glide along a smooth surface when rolled. Autoperipatetikos is the Greek word for "self-propelling," applied to Enoch Rice Morrison's walking doll (1862) and often used for other clockwork dolls.

Bacchic figures, jovial or drunken, relating to Bacchus, the Roman god of wine and festivities.

bachelor chest small, multi-purpose chest-of-drawers with a hinged top.

backboard the wood (often unpolished) used to in-fill the back of furniture made to stand against a wall.

backplate rear of the two plates supporting a clock or watch movement, on which details of the maker are often engraved.

baize woollen fabric resembling felt, usually green and used on games tables.

Bakelite early form of plastic invented by L.H. Baekeland in 1909 and used to make a variety of domestic objects.

balance spring spring acting on the balance wheel of a watch to counteract the force of the mainspring, the equivalent of the pendulum in a clock, developed shortly after c.1675.

ball-jointed term applied to a doll whose limbs are attached by a ball and socket, allowing the greatest possible movement.

baluster double curved form that swells at the base and rises in a concave curve to a narrow stem or neck.

banding veneer cut into narrow strips and applied to create a decorative effect; usually found around the edges of tables and drawer fronts.

barley twists spiraling columns popular on 17th-century furniture.

barometer instrument for measuring atmospheric pressure.

Baroque extravagant and heavily ornate style of architecture, furniture, and decoration that originated in 17th-century Italy. Characterized by an abundant use of cupids, cornucopia, and similar decorative motifs set in curvaceous designs.

baroque pearl irregularly shaped pearl.

basalte unglazed, very hard, fine-grained stoneware stained with cobalt and manganese oxides, developed by Wedgwood c.1768.

base metal non-precious metal such as iron, brass, bronze, or steel.

basketweave decorative relief pattern resembling woven willow or cane; applied to the borders of plates and dishes.

Bauhaus German school of architecture and applied arts founded in 1919 by Walter Gropius. The Bauhaus style is characterized by austere, geometric forms and modern materials such as tubular steel.

beading decorative border of tight beads, either cast and applied, or embossed.

beat scale graduated scale fixed to the case interior of many Vienna regulators, and used to measure the regularity of the pendulum swing.

bébé French term for a doll with a short chubby build, representing an infant rather than an adult.

bell-flower *see* husk.

Belle Epoque ("beautiful period") term describing the lavish, ornate styles in fashion from the late 19th century to World War I.

bent-limb term applied to a doll with five-piece body and curved arms and legs.

bentwood solid or laminated wood steamed and bent into a curvilinear shape. The process was developed by Michael Thonet in the early 19th century.

bergère French wing armchair or a chair in similar style with upholstered back and sides and deep seat.

Berlin ironwork black ironwork jewelry made during the Franco-Prussian war (1813–15) in exchange for gold jewelry surrendered for the war effort.

Berlin woolwork type of needlework based on published patterns; popular during the 19th century.

berrettino gray-blue tin-glazed ground used on 16th-century Italian maiolica; first introduced in Faenza c.1520.

bevel decorative angled edge of a mirror.

bezel ring, usually brass, securing the glass dial cover on a clock or watch. Also refers to the groove or inner rim of a cover, for example on coffee-pots.

bianco di Faenza type of maiolica, developed in mid-16th-century Italy, covered in a thick, milky-white glaze. It is usually cursorily decorated in a restricted palette of ocher, yellow, and blue with figures, flowers, or coats of arms.

Biedermeier bourgeois style characterized by simple, heavy, Classical forms; popular in Germany and Scandinavia c.1815–c.1848.

bird-cage support mechanism, located at the top of the pedestal, that enables some tripod tables to swivel.

biscuit (bisque) unglazed porcelain or earthenware fired once only. Popular for Neo-classical porcelain figures because it Classical marble sculptures. Also used for making dolls' heads.

blanc-de-Chine translucent white Chinese porcelain, unpainted and with a thick glaze. It was made at kilns in Dehua in the Fujian province from the Song Dynasty and copied in Europe.

blanks undecorated ceramic wares.

bleu lapis a deep cobalt blue ground of almost purplish tone, introduced at the Vincennes porcelain factory in 1753.

bleu persan ("Persian blue") rich, purplish, ultramarine ground associated with late 17th-century faience from Nevers in France.

blowing (also known as free blowing) technique of blowing a molten mass of glass through a long, hollow metal pipe into a desired shape.

blown-three-mold American term for mold-blown glass.

blowout *see* mold blowing.

blue and white white ceramics with painted or printed cobalt-blue decoration.

blue-dash charger tin-glazed earthenware charger on which the deep rounded rim is decorated with broad, sloping dashes of cobalt blue, applied with a sponge to suggest twisted rope.

bob disc-shaped weight at the bottom of the pendulum rod on a clock.

bobbin type of turning in the shape of a bobbin or reel found on the legs of 17th-century furniture.

bocage French term for trees or foliage in the form of an arbor surrounding or supporting a pottery or porcelain figure.

bombé bulbous, curving form, favored for wares made during the Rococo period.

bonbonnière small box or dish made for holding sweets.

bone-ash burnt, crushed animal bone that is added to soft-paste porcelain mixture to fuse the ingredients.

bone china classified as a soft-paste porcelain consisting of petuntse (china stone), kaolin (china clay), and dried bone.

bonheur de jour lady's small writing cabinet-on-stand, popular in the 18th- and 19th-centuries.

bonnet head doll wearing a hat or bonnet molded as an integral part of the head.

booge sloping sides of a plate or dish.

boot-button eyes black wooden eyes with metal loops on the back, used on early teddy bears.

boteh stylized cypress-leaf motif, used in Persian and Caucasian rugs and carpets.

bottle glass colored glass used for utensils such as bottles, as distinct from quality or clear glass.

Boulle marquetry decorative inlay named after André-Charles Boulle, usually using tortoiseshell and various other materials, such as brass, pewter, ivory, and mother-of-pearl. The technique was revived in Britain between c.1815 and 1840 and known as "Buhl" work.

bow front outward curved front found on case furniture.

bracket clock type of spring-driven clock, sometimes known as a mantel, table, or shelf clock, designed to stand on furniture, shelves, or wall brackets.

bracket foot squared foot used on furniture from c.1725 and 1780.

brandy saucepan small, bulbous or baluster-shaped saucepan, usually with a handle at right angles to the pouring spout.

break arch arch at the top of the dial of a clock.

breakfront term for a piece of furniture with a protruding central section.

bright-cut engraving type of engraving in which the metal surface is cut at an angle to create facets that reflect the light. Popular in the Neo-classical period.

Bristol glass colored glass, mostly blue, made in Britain from the late 18th to the mid-19th centuries.

Britannia metal metal substitute for silver, actually a form of electroplated pewter.

Britannia standard the highest standard of silver used in the making of wrought plate, being 95.8 percent pure and compulsory in Britain from 1697 to 1720.

brodérie perse French term for cut-out floral and bird motifs in printed cottons and chintzes sewn onto plain quilts.

broken pediment pediment, or triangular superstructure, in which the central apex is absent and often filled with a carved motif.

brownware salt-glazed brown stoneware, especially that made in England in Nottingham, Derby and elsewhere .

brushpot small Chinese or Japanese pot used for holding brushes used for calligraphy and painting.

buffet term for a two-part sideboard.

bun foot type of small, bulbous foot used on clocks and furniture from the 17th century.

bureau writing desk with a fall or cylinder front, enclosing a fitted interior, with drawers below.

burnishing method of polishing metals or gilded surfaces by applying friction with a hard tool made of agate to create a luster.

cabinet wares cups, saucers, and plates made for display rather than use.

cabochon gemstone (often heavily flawed) with an uncut but highly polished surface.

cabriole leg leg of elongated and gently curving S-shape, popular on European furniture from the late 17th century.

cachepot ornamental container for flower-pots. A smaller form of *jardinière*.

caddy container for tea.

caddy spoon spoon for measuring tea out of the caddy. Made in vast quantities from the late 18th century.

caillouté ("pebbled") irregular pattern of meshed ovals, usually gilded, resembling pebbles and used on Sèvres porcelain in the late 1760s.

calendar aperture window in a clock dial displaying the day of the month and sometimes the month or year.

cameo hardstone, coral, lava, or shell carved to show a relief design (usually a bust or head in profile) against a contrasting colored background.

cameo glass glass with two or more different-colored layers, with a carved design in relief. The relief design is often finely engraved to add definition.

canapé type of French settee with padded back and seat, open arms, and often elaborately decorated frame.

caneware pale, straw-colored unglazed stoneware made by the firm of Wedgwood from 1770.

cannetille type of gold or silver filigree in the form of tightly coiled wire scrolls or rosettes, used in jewelry.

canted/chamfered surface created by cutting off the angle of a piece of furniture at 45 degrees. The surface is often decorated with fluting or fretwork.

canterbury small stand or rack with partitions for storing sheet music.

canvaswork embroidery worked with counted stitches on an open-weave canvas.

capital head or top part of a column or pilaster.

capricci fantasy scenes, often appearing on marquetry furniture.

carat measurement of gold. One carat equals 200mg.

carcase basic structure of a piece of furniture; often forms foundation for veneering.

cardcase case for holding visiting cards.

carpet toy toy that can be played with only on the floor – for example, a train that does not fit any standard track or a toy airplane that cannot fly.

carriage clock small, portable, spring-driven clock, produced mainly by French makers during the 19th century.

cartel clock type of ornate, spring-driven wall-hung clock, produced mainly in France during the 18th century.

carton cardboard composition, used for some dolls' bodies in the 1920s and 1930s.

cartoon design for a carpet or tapestry, often copied onto squared paper to make it easier to follow.

cartouche decorative motif in the form of a scroll of paper with rolled ends, bearing a picture, motif, or monogram. Also used to describe a frame, usually oval, decorated with scrollwork.

carver 19th-century term for an elbow dining-chair.

caryatid draped female figure of Greek origin acting as a column support.

case furniture furniture such as chests, coffers, cupboards, and bureaux.

cash pattern Oriental ceramic pattern based on the design of beribboned coins with a square central hole.

cassapanca type of settle derived from the *cassone*, with a back and sometimes armrests.

cassone Renaissance Italian chest, often highly decorated with carving and inlay.

caster vessel for sprinkling salt, pepper, or sugar. Also refers to wheels, usually made of brass, wood, or ceramic, on furniture, which allows them to be moved around easily.

casting method of making objects by pouring molten metal or glass into a mold or cast made from sand, plaster, or metal, conforming to the shape of the finished object.

castle-top type of cardcase, snuff-box, or vinaigrette depicting a famous British building.

caudle cup silver cup with a cover designed to keep its contents warm. Originally held caudle, a spiced gruel laced with wine.

celadon semi-opaque, green-tinted glaze used first on wares made during the Chinese Song Dynasty.

cellaret lidded receptacle for cooling and storing wine.

celluloid original trade name for Pyroxylin, an early and highly flammable form of plastic.

centerpiece ornament designed to occupy the center of a dining-table.

chaise-longue upholstered chair with an elongated seat to support the legs in an horizontal position.

chamberstick type of utilitarian candlestick with a short stem and saucer-like base.

champlevé ("raised field") type of enameling set into grooves or recesses cut in a metal surface.

chapter ring part of a clock dial on which the hour and minute numbers are engraved, attached, or painted.

character doll doll with a realistic rather than idealized expression.

charger large, flat plate or dish.

chasing method of decorating metal (usually silver) using hammers and punches to push metal into a relief pattern. Unlike engraving, chasing does not involve removal of metal.

chesterfield deep-buttoned, upholstered settee.

chest-on-chest tall chest-of-drawers, mounted on another similar, slightly larger chest, also known as a tallboy.

chest-on-stand tall chest-of-drawers on a stand, also known as a highboy.

cheval mirror tall, free-standing mirror supported by a four-legged base.

chevron linked zigzag motif.

chiffonnier side cabinet with or without a drawer and with one or more shelves above.

china originally an alternative term for Chinese porcelain. Since the early 19th century the term has been used to refer to bone china.

china clay *see* kaolin.

china stone *see* petuntse.

Chinese export wares Chinese porcelain was made specifically for export to Europe from the 16th century to suit European tastes. Silver in similar styles was made from the 17th century.

chinoiserie decoration consisting of Oriental-style figures and motifs, such as pagodas, pavilions, birds, and lotus flowers, that permeated Europe from the Far East; prevalent from the late 17th century.

chocolate cup large cup with two handles, a cover, and a saucer.

chronometer extremely precise timekeeper, developed for use at sea to enable accurate determination of longitude.

chryselephantine combination of ivory and a metal, usually bronze; used for Art Deco figures.

cire perdue *see* lost-wax casting.

cistern chamber containing the mercury at the base of the tube of a barometer.

clair-de-lune translucent blue glaze introduced in Chinese porcelain from the Qing period.

claret jug ewer or jug, usually glass with silver or electroplate mounts, used for serving claret.

claw-and-ball foot foot modeled as a ball gripped by an animal's claw or bird's talon.

claw setting type of jewelry setting in which the gemstone is secured by projecting prongs.

cloisonné enamel fired into compartments (*cloisons*) formed by metal wires.

closed-back setting type of jewelry setting in which the back of the gemstone is covered with metal.

cloth doll term for a doll made from fabric, sometimes known as a rag doll.

coaster saucer or small tray, on which a bottle slid or was passed round the table.

cockbeading bead molding applied to the edges of drawers.

coffer traveling chest with handles and a domed lid but without feet, usually made of oak.

coiling method of forming ceramic objects by coiling long clay strips into the desired shape. The resulting ridges are smoothed out.

collar rim of a wine-cooler, often detachable.

collet setting type of jewelry setting in which the gemstones are set in a metal ring or band.

commedia dell'arte figures from Italian comedy theatre. The characters were modeled in porcelain at Meissen, Nymphenburg, and other Continental factories.

commode French term for a chest-of-drawers. Also refers to a type of furniture concealing a chamber-pot.

composition inexpensive substance made from, variously, cloth, size, wood, wood pulp, plaster of Paris, glue, and sawdust, used for making dolls' heads, bodies and limbs, and other toys.

cong Neolithic Chinese ritual vessel, originally of jade but later copied in ceramics.

console table intended to stand against a wall, between windows, also known as a pier table.

core forming (core winding) method of producing glass objects by building up a core of mud, straw, and clay around a metal rod, which is then dipped into molten glass.

cornice horizontal top part or cresting on a piece of furniture.

count wheel (locking) wheel with segments cut out of the edge or with pins fitted to one face, which controls the striking of a clock.

cow creamer silver or ceramic jug or boat for pouring cream, modeled as a cow.

crabstock type of handle or spout molded as a gnarled crab-apple branch.

crackled glaze (craquelure) deliberate cracked effect achieved by firing ceramics to a precise temperature.

crazing tiny, undesirable surface cracks caused by shrinking or other technical defects in a glaze.

creamware cream-colored earthenware with a transparent lead glaze, developed by Josiah Wedgwood c.1760.

credence table type of small table originally used for storing food before serving or tasting. Now refers to a semi-circular table with a hinged top.

credenza long side cabinet, with shelves at either end.

crewelwork embroidery using crewel, a fine, two-ply yarn. Often used to decorate curtains and bed-hangings in Britain and North America.

crinoline group pairs of complementary porcelain figures making romantic or chivalric gestures.

crizzling network of fine lines or cracks in glass.

crossbanding veneered edge to table tops and drawer fronts, at right angles to the main veneer.

cruet frame holding salt-cellars, casters, and other vessels containing condiments.

crystal glass *see* lead glass.

Cubism early 20th-century art movement characterized by distortion, angularity, geometric arrangements, and features of African sculpture.

cullet scraps of broken glass, used to help fuse new glass.

cup and cover bulbous turning common on furniture legs from the mid-16th century.

cushion drawer convex drawer found below a cornice that runs the full width of a piece of furniture.

cushion top rounded top found on many early English bracket clocks.

cut-card decoration flat shapes of applied silver, used as decoration and reinforcement, especially around the rims of tea- and coffee-pots. Common on 17th-century pieces by Huguenot silversmiths.

cut-down longcase clock that has been shortened.

date aperture see calendar aperture.

date letter letter identifying the year of assay of a silver object.

Davenport in Britain a small writing desk, usually with real and dummy drawers at side.

Delftware tin-glazed earthenware made in Delft in The Netherlands. Refers to British ware when it does not have a capital letter.

dep abbreviation of the French *depos* or the German *deponirt*, indicating a registered patent used on French and German dolls and often appearing as an incised mark on the bisque heads.

dessert service set of ceramic wares decorated en suite for serving dessert, including plates, compotiers, bowls, and tureens.

deutsche Blumen ("German flowers") naturalistic flowers or bouquets painted on European porcelain from the mid-18th century.

dial clock type of simple English wall clock with a round dial, glass cover held with a brass bezel, and a wooden case.

dial plate metal or wooden plate to which the chapter ring and spandrels are attached on a clock.

diamond-point engraving decorative designs on glass made by scratching the surface with a diamond-pointed stylus.

diaper decorative pattern of repeated diamonds or other geometrical shapes.

die-stamping method of production introduced at the end of the 18th century, whereby sheet silver is pressed between solid dies with complementary patterns to create or decorate an object.

disc joint joint made of discs of cardboard held in place by a metal pin; used to articulate soft toys and teddy bears.

dish ring silver ring used to keep hot dishes away from the table.

dished table top hollowed-out solid top, associated with tripod or tea tables with "pie-crust" edges.

Dog (Lion) of Fo mythical Chinese lion-spaniel, a guardian spirit of the temple of the Buddha (Fo).

dolls' hospital repair shop specializing in the restoration of dolls of all kinds; some cater for teddy bears as well.

doucai ("contrasting colors") type of ceramic decoration, introduced in 15th-century China, using overglaze enamels (red, yellow, purple, and green) within an underglaze-blue outline.

dovetailing series of interlocking joints, used to join sections of timber together.

"dragon's blood" red stain used on oak furniture.

drawer-lining side of a drawer.

drop handle pear-shaped handle popular during the late 17th and early 18th century on furniture and clocks.

drop-in seat upholstered seat frame that sits in the main framework of a chair.

dropleaf type of table with a pivoted leg to support the extended leaf but without understretchers.

dumb waiter type of furniture with a central shaft and circular trays, which often revolves; used by dining guests to help themselves to additional plates, cutlery, and food.

duration period for which a clock runs between winding.

Dutch term for German wooden dolls; probably a corruption of *Deutsch* meaning "German" (a word often found on the heads of German wooden dolls), rather than "Dutch."

duty dodging practice of transposing marks on silver objects to avoid paying duty.

earthenware term for a type of pottery, which is porous and requires a glaze.

ébeniste French term for a cabinet-maker.

ebonized wood stained and polished black to simulate ebony.

ecuelle covered shallow bowl usually with two flat handles at the rim, and a stand.

egg head rare type of miniature doll molded as a porcelain head only, with no torso.

eggshell porcelain type of slip-cast, razor-thin porcelain made in 19th-century Japan and Europe.

Eight Immortals legendary or historical individuals associated with Daoism and depicted on Chinese ceramics.

Eight Precious Things symbols of the Chinese scholar, namely the musical stone, jewels, a coin, a pair of books, an open-tied lozenge and a closed-tied lozenge, and an artemisia leaf, often represented on ceramics.

electroplating method of plating one metal with another (usually silver over an alloy) using an electric current. The process was patented in the 1830s and gradually superseded Sheffield plate.

electrotype creating a reproduction by taking a mold of an object and depositing onto it a thin layer of metal using an electric current.

embossing method of creating relief ornament on metal by hammering or punching from the reverse.

Empire style style inspired by the civilization of ancient Rome and celebrating the empire of Napoleon I, c.1804–15. It typically features such motifs as palmettes, winged lions, and sphinxes. The Second Empire style refers to the revival of Neo-classicism during the reign of Napoleon III (1852–70).

enamel form of decoration involving the application of metallic oxides to metal, ceramics, or glass in paste form or in a oil-based mixture, which is then usually fired for decorative effect.

end support central support at the sides of a writing or sofa table.

engine-turning decorative, textured patterns, created by turning metal on a machine-driven lathe.

engraving decorative patterns cut into a metal surface using a sharp tool.

entablature horizontal beam that surmounts architectural columns. Divided into the cornice (top), frieze (middle), and architrave (bottom).

entrée dish shallow silver dish with a flat bottom and domed cover.

entrelac interlaced tendril decoration of Celtic origin used on jewelry and revived by Arts and Crafts designers.

epergne silver or glass centerpiece consisting of a central bowl and several smaller bowls that can usually be detached; used from the mid-18th century to display and serve fruit and sweetmeats.

erasure removal of an existing coat of arms on silver, which is sometimes replaced by new arms.

escapement device regulating the transfer of power from the weights or spring to the movement in a clock.

escritoire cabinet with a fall front that lowers to form a writing surface.

escutcheon brass plate surrounding and protecting the edges of a keyhole, sometimes with a cap or cover on a pivot.

étagère two- or three-tiered table intended for displaying objects or serving food.

Etruscan style style characterized by the use of red, black, and white and motifs such as lions, griffins, and sphinxes; popular in the late 18th and 19th centuries following the rediscovery of ancient Etruscan sites and artifacts.

everted outward-turned or flaring, usually describing a rim.

ewer large jug with a lip that is often part of a set with a basin. Ewers originally held the water used by diners to wash their hands during meals, prior to the introduction of the fork.

excelsior soft mixture of long, thin wood shavings used for stuffing teddy bears.

faceted decorative surface cut into sharp-edged planes in a criss-cross pattern to reflect the light.

façon de Venise ("in the style of Venice") highly decorative and ornate glassware imitating 15th-century Venetian glass, often with elaborate lampwork on the stem.

faience French term for tin-glazed earthenware.

fall front flap of a bureau or secrétaire that pulls down to provide a writing surface.

famille rose palette used on 18th-century Chinese porcelain, which includes a dominant opaque pink. Much copied in Europe.

famille verte palette used from the 17th century on Chinese porcelain, distinguished by a dominant bright apple green.

fashion doll French doll, usually with a kid body and bisque head, dressed in elaborate and fashionable attire, produced between c.1860 and 1890 in Paris. Also known as "*Parisiennes.*"

fauteuil French term for an armchair.

"Favrile" type of iridescent glass developed by Louis Comfort Tiffany using metallic oxides.

feather banding two narrow bands of veneer laid in opposite diagonals, also called herringbone banding.

Federal style American version of the Neo-classical style, popular from c.1789 to c.1830.

fêtes galantes open-air scenes of aristocratic amusement that were a favorite theme of French Rococo painters.

field large area of a rug or carpet usually enclosed by borders.

figuring pattern made by the natural grain of wood.

filigree openwork silver or gold wire panels, sometimes decorated with beads.

finial decorative turned knob.

fire gilding *see* mercury gilding.

firing process of baking ceramics in a kiln. Temperatures range from 800° to 1100°C (1500–2000°F) for earthenware to 1400°C (2550°F) for the second firing of hard-paste porcelain.

flagon jug with a lid, usually tall and cylindrical in shape.

flambé glaze made from copper, usually deep crimson, flecked with blue or purple, and often faintly crackled.

flame veneer veneer cut at an angle to enhance the figuring.

flange collar or rim applied to an object to strengthen it or for attaching it to another object.

flashing technique in which a glass object is covered with another layer of differently colored glass; the two layers are fused by firing. Overlay refers to a similar process but with thicker layers of glass.

flat chasing chasing on a flat metal surface, leaving an impression of the punched pattern on the reverse.

flatware term embracing all flat objects, such as plates and salvers, but more specifically applied to cutlery.

flatweave type of rug or carpet made with only warps and wefts, using no knots and thus having no pile.

flirty eyes glass dolls' eyes that open and close and move from side to side.

fluting pattern of concave grooves repeated in vertical, parallel lines. The opposite of gadrooning.

foot-rim projecting circular base on the underside of a plate or vessel.

four-headed doll set produced by the German firm of Kestner comprising a doll with a socket body and detachable head (usually with a girl-doll face); sold with three interchangeable character heads.

free blowing *see* blowing.

French joint type of joint used on French dolls where the limbs are all attached to a ball fixed to one of the limbs.

fretwork pierced geometric decoration; may be used to decorate a frieze. Blind fretwork is when the decoration is not pierced through.

frieze long, ornamental band.

frigger decorative or novelty glass object, such as a bell, pipe, or walking stick.

fritware type of grainy, white-bodied Islamic ceramic ware, perhaps made to imitate imported Chinese porcelain.

fuddling-cup vessel of three or more cups linked at the base and with intertwined handles.

fusee spirally grooved metal cone taking up a wire or gut line wound round the spring barrel of a spring-driven clock. The fusee equalizes the force of the spring as it runs down, ensuring accurate timekeeping.

gadrooning decorative edging consisting of a series of convex, vertical, or spiraling curves.

Gainsborough chair deep armchair with an upholstered seat and back, padded open arms, and, usually, carved decoration.

gallery wood or metal border around the top edge of a table or a coaster.

galletto rosso decorative ceramic pattern of red-and-gold Chinese cockerels, devised at the Italian factory of Doccia.

garniture set of three or more vases of contrasting forms, intended for display on a mantelpiece.

gateleg hinged leg that pivots to support a drop leaf on a table.

gather *see* paraison.

gauge thickness of sheet metal or the diameter of a wire.

Geneva enameling painted enamels on a metal base, often used for decorative plaques in jewelry.

gesso plaster-like substance applied in thick layers to an inexpensive secondary timber before carving, gilding, and painting.

gilding method of applying a gold finish to a silver or electroplated item, ceramics, or glass.

gilt bronze *see* ormolu.

gimbals pivoted rings used in marine chronometer boxes to keep the chronometer level.

girandole A candle holder or sconce with a mirrored back, designed to hang on a wall.

glaze glassy coating that gives a smooth, shiny surface to ceramics and seals porous ceramic bodies.

gloss-gilding gilding of porcelain using gold in solution, introduced at Meissen in the 1820s.

Gobelins Name given to the Manufacture royale des meubles de la couronne, which was established under Louis XIV in 1663 for the production of royal furnishings.

going barrel cylindrical brass drum containing the mainspring and transmitting power directly to the wheels of the train in a spring-driven clock. It is used in clocks without a fusee.

gold-ruby glass deep-pink glass made with gold chloride, invented in 17th-century Germany.

googly eyes large, round eyes on dolls that look sideways.

Gothic decoration in the style of Gothic architecture, featuring such motifs as pinnacles, crockets, and trefoils. The style was revived from the 1820s in Europe and from the 1840s in North America.

Gothick 18th-century Gothic Revival decoration, more fanciful than the 19th-century revival.

graining painting an inexpensive wood such as pine or beech to simulate a more expensive timber such as mahogany.

grande sonnerie system of striking that repeats the last hour after each quarter has been chimed.

grand-feu ("high-temperature") French term for a palette used on tin-glazed earthernware limited to green, blue, purple, yellow, and orange. Petit-feu (low fired) enameling allows for a greater range of colors to be used.

Grand Tour term describing period of education and travel in Europe undertaken from the 18th-century by British aristocrats' on coming of age. On their travels they often collected works of art.

granulation method of creating relief designs on gold jewelry by soldering grains of gold onto a metal base.

Greek key design based on ancient Greek decoration.

griffin mythical animal with the head, wings, and claws of an eagle but a lion's body. It was a popular motif in the Regency and Empire periods.

grisaille painted decoration using a mainly black and gray palette and resembling a print.

grotesque type of Classical ornament composed of linked motifs, such as human figures and masks, and fantastical animals, such as sphinxes; widely used in the Renaissance period.

gloss-gilding secondary borders on either side of the main border of a rug or carpet.

guardstripe secondary borders on either side of the main border of a rug or carpet.

guéridon small table or candlestand on a pedestal foot, often with a specimen marble top.

guglet water-bottle with a bulbous body and tall neck.

guilloche Neo-classical pattern of twisting bands, spirals, double spirals, or linked chains.

guilloché translucent enameling, usually applied over an engraved or engine-turned metal base to create the shimmering effect of watered silk.

gul Persian term for "flower." Stylized geometric flower pattern that appears in many variations on Ottoman and Turkoman carpets.

gutta-percha fibrous, rubbery material used to make dolls' bodies and heads, and also golf balls, in the late 19th century.

hairy-paw foot paw foot carved to give a furred appearance, first seen in the 18th century.

half hunter watch with a hinged front cover with a small glazed aperture, revealing part of the dial.

hallmark mark on silver that indicates it has been passed at assay. The term derives from the Goldsmiths' Hall, London, where marks were struck.

hard-paste porcelain also known as true porcelain. It was first made in China using the combination of kaolin (china clay: 50%), petuntse (china stone: 25%), and quartz (25%).

hardstone generic term given to non-precious stones.

hardware locks, hinges, escutcheons, and other metal attachments on furniture.

harlequin term used to describe a set of chairs that are similar but do not match.

Hausmaler ("home painter") German term for an independent painter or workshop specializing in the decoration of porcelain and glass.

haute couture made-to-measure garments bearing the designer's label.

heaped and piled accidental concentrations of cobalt blue in 14th- and 15th-century Chinese blue-and-white porcelain. Copied by Qing potters.

herati diamond-shaped motif flanked by four serrated leaves, used in Persian carpets.

herringbone banding *see* feather banding.

highboy American term for a chest-on-stand.

highbrow early form of china doll.

Hispaño-Moresque ware wares made in Spain (particularly in the South), which were decorated in the style of Islamic art.

Hochschnitt see relief engraving

hollow-ware any hollow items such as bowls, teapots, jugs; distinct from flatware.

honey gilding method of applying gold leaf to glass or ceramics using honey as a fixative. Honey gilding has a warmer hue than mercury gilding.

hood part of a longcase clock that contains the dial and movement.

hu Chinese bronze vessel, originally made for ritual use.

Huguenots French Protestants, many of whom settled in England and The Netherlands after the Revocation of the Edict of Nantes denied them religious freedom in 1685. Many were skilled silversmiths, cabinet-makers, and weavers, who introduced French styles into the Dutch and English decorative arts.

hunter watch with an opening front cover that protects the glass cover of the dial.

husk Neo-classical decorative motif of formalized leaves.

Hyalith glass colored glass, either sealing-wax red or jet-black, produced in Bohemia from 1819.

hybrid paste formula that combines the ingredients of hard-paste and soft-paste porcelain in an attempt to produce a more malleable body.

hygrometer device for measuring humidity on barometers.

Imari Japanese porcelain with dense decoration, based on brocade patterns, in a palette that is dominated by underglaze blue, iron red, green, manganese, yellow, and gold.

inclusions natural flaws in gemstones.

indianische Blumen ("Indian flowers") European adaptation of the decoration on Japanese Kakiemon and Chinese *famille verte* porcelain.

infinite repeat device on rugs and carpets in which incomplete medallions are "cut" by the borders.

inlay setting of one material (e.g. marble, wood, metal, tortoiseshell, or mother-of-pearl) in another (usually wood).

inro Japanese seal cases.

intaglio incised design, as opposed to a design in relief.

intaglio carving type of carving whereby forms are sunken into, as opposed to molded onto, a surface.

intaglio engraving method of decorating glass by hollowing out a design below the surface. Also called *Tiefschnitt*.

intaglio painted eyes painted eyes with concave pupils and irises, hollowed out of a doll's head.

iridescent glass glass with a lustrous appearance, shot through with a range of colors.

ironstone see Mason's Patent Ironstone China.

istoriato narrative decoration on Renaissance Italian maiolica plates.

Iznik brilliantly decorated and much-imitated tin-glazed earthenware made in Anatolia (now Turkey). The palette comprises a brilliant turquoise, green, blue, and later red. Decorated with stylized flowers and arabesques.

Jackfield ware black glazed pottery, made in England in the late 18th century (especially at Jackfield, Shropshire).

Jacobethan 19th-century revival of motifs such as strapwork and grotesques found on 16th- and 17th-century decorative arts. The term is a combination of "Elizabethan" and "Jacobean."

Japanesque term used to describe European designs, c.1862 to 1900, inspired by Japanese art.

japanning painting and varnishing in imitation of Oriental lacquerwork. Popular in Europe from the 17th century.

jardinière plant container made from a variety of materials, including glass, silver, or pottery.

jasper ware hard, fine-grained colored stoneware developed by Wedgwood in the 1770s.

Jersey fabric that has no distinct rib, originally made of wool on the island of Jersey but now of various fibres. Used for making teddy bears.

jeweling technique of applying colored drops of glass onto a glass object to imitate gemstones. Also refers to a similar technique using drops of enamel on porcelain.

jufti knot in a rug or carpet that is tied over four as opposed to the usual two warp strands.

Jugendstil German and Austrian term for the Art Nouveau style. Named after the Munich-based publication *Jugend*.

juval type of woven Turkoman bag.

Kakiemon type of Japanese porcelain named after a family of potters, who may have introduced it in the Arita district of Japan during the 17th century. Designs are often asymmetrical in a palette of iron-red, cerulean-blue, turquoise-green, yellow, aubergine, and gold.

kaolin (china clay) fine, white granite clay used to make hard-paste porcelain.

kapok extremely lightweight fiber made from seed pods and used for stuffing teddy bears.

karakusa "octopus" scrollwork pattern common on late 17th-century Japanese porcelain.

kendi Persian term for a globular-bodied porcelain drinking vessel with a short spout made in 15th- and 16th-century China for export to the Middle East.

kneehole desk desk with a recessed central cupboard below the frieze drawer. One of the most well-known types was the *bureau Mazarin*.

knop decorative knobs on lids and covers or the projection or bulge in the stem of a glass or candlestick.

koro Japanese incense burner.

kraak Dutch term for Chinese blue-and-white wares, named after the Portuguese ships called carracks, which were used to export them.

krater large vase originally used for mixing wine and water in ancient Greece.

Kufic type of Arabic calligraphy, often used in stylized form on many Islamic artifacts, including carpets and pottery.

lacquerwork layers of varnish prepared from the sap of the *Rhus vernicifera* tree, used as a ground for Oriental decoration. European imitations are known as "japanning" and vernis Martin.

ladder-back vernacular chair with a series of horizontal back-rails.

lambrequin Baroque border pattern of lacework, scrolls, and scalloped drapery.

lamination method of gluing together sheets of wood with the grain in different directions to produce a material that is thinner and lighter than solid wood. Synonymous with the furniture manufacturer John Henry Belter.

lampwork method of producing decorative glassware by manipulating rods or tubes of glass over a flame. First used in 15th-century Venice.

lantern clock earliest English domestic clock, made almost entirely from brass. It is weight-driven and strikes the hours on a bell.

latten old English word for brass.

latticinio Venetian technique of working a clear glass vessel with opaque-white or colored glass canes.

lattimo see milk glass.

Laub- und Bandelwerk (leaf and strapwork) decoration of interwoven leaves and strapwork, often surrounding a cartouche. Most popular during the 18th century.

lead glass (crystal glass) type of glass, discovered c.1676, containing a high proportion of lead oxide, from which it obtains a particularly clear brilliance.

lead glaze clear glaze generally composed of silicaeous sand, salt, soda, and potash mixed with a lead component.

lenticle small, glazed section of the trunk door of a longcase clock, through which the pendulum can be seen.

linen-press term for cupboard with shelves (presses) for storing linen and clothes.

lingzhi fungus motif, found on Chinese porcelain and symbolizing longevity.

lion's-paw foot foot carved as a lion's paw, popular in the 18th century and during the Empire and Regency periods.

lithography method of polychrome printing in which a design is drawn in ink on a stone surface and transferred to paper. Lithographic prints were also used to decorate ceramics.

lithophane thin, low relief porcelain plaque that reveals a picture when held up to the light. Also called "Berlin transparency."

Lithyalin glass type of glass patented by Friedrich Egermann in Bohemia in 1829. Intended to imitate hardstones, it is opaque and usually marbled.

loading system for strengthening and stabilizing candlesticks and sometimes candelabra, whereby an iron or wooden rod is secured inside the body using pitch or plaster of Paris.

longcase clock weight-driven, floor-standing clock with a pendulum and weights.

loo table large Victorian card or games table, usually circular.

loper pull-out arm used to support the hinged fall of a bureau.

lost-wax casting method of casting bronze or another metal in which a wax model is enclosed within a plaster mold, the wax is then heated and replaced with molten metal to form the object.

loving cup two-handled cup, generally urn-shaped.

lowboy American term for a small dressing table.

lowbrow late-19th-century, china-headed doll with short, curly hair worn low on the forehead.

lusterware pottery with an iridescent surface produced using metallic pigments, usually silver or copper.

luting method of joining together separate pieces of clay with liquid slip.

maiolica tin-glazed earthenware produced in Italy from the 14th century.

majolica corruption of the term maiolica, which refers to type of 19th-century earthenware in elaborate forms with thick, brightly colored glazes.

maki-e ("sprinkled illustration") Japanese decorative technique of sprinkling gold or colored filings onto a design in wet lacquer.

Manierblumen ("mannered flowers") loose representation of scattered flowers, used on 18th-century European porcelain.

Mannerist style decorative style of the late 16th century, employing twisted, exaggerated, and bizarre forms often entrapped by strapwork and grotesques.

marchand-mercier dealer in luxury products in 18th-century Paris.

marotte doll's head mounted on a stick or baton which often plays music when twirled. Produced from the late 19th century.

marquetry use of veneer and often other inlays to make decorative patterns in wood.

married term referring to an item of furniture that has been made up from two or more associated pieces, usually from the same period.

martelé French term for silverware with a fine, hammered surface first produced in France and revived by the American Gorham & Co. during the Art Nouveau period.

marvering technique in which threads of softened glass are trailed over an object and rolled on flat surface to smooth them together.

Mason's Patent Ironstone China fine, porcellaneous stoneware first made in 1813 in Staffordshire, England, by Charles James Mason.

matchsafe American term for vesta box.

matrix hardstone, such as opal or turquoise, embedded in its parent rock. Much used in Arts and Crafts and Art Nouveau jewelry.

matting decorative surface on metal created either by applying acid or using small punches or hammers to create dense patterns of dots or indentations.

MDF medium density fibreboard, made from compressed particles of wood and used in the construction of furniture.

meiping Chinese term for a type of inverted pear-shaped vase.

menuisier French term for a joiner.

mercury gilding highly dangerous method of gilding, in which an amalgam of mercury and gold is brushed onto a surface then heated until mercury burns off as vapor.

metal term used to describe the fused materials from which glass is made.

meuble en deux corps cupboard made in two sections, enclosing drawers in both the top and bottom.

mihrab hollow or niche in the wall of a mosque that faces toward Mecca; often adopted as a structural element of the design in a rug or carpet.

milk glass term for glass made with tin oxide, which turns it an opaque white. Developed in late 15th-century Venice.

millefiori ("thousand flowers") glassmaking technique whereby canes of colored glass are arranged in bundles so that the cross-section creates a pattern. Commonly used in glass paperweights.

Mina'i enameled ceramics decorated with figures, made in 12th- and 13th-century Persia.

mitten hands or feet dolls' hands or feet stitched in one block, with no separation between fingers and toes.

mixed twist term for the stem of a glass that incorporates an opaque twist with an air twist.

Modernism style of the 1920s and 1930s inspired by a need to break with the past and to express the spirit of a new machine age. It rejected ornamentation in favor of geometric forms and smooth surfaces.

mohair plush fabric woven from the silky fleece of an angora goat and commonly used for making teddy bears.

monochrome decoration executed in a single color.

monteith large, shallow bowl with a detachable collar and scalloped rim from which wine glasses were suspended to cool in iced water.

moon dial/moonphase subsidiary dial usually fitted in the arch of a clock or in a watch to show the phases of the moon.

moons air bubbles in porcelain paste that expand during firing, leaving translucent spots.

Moreen an inexpensive imitation in wool or cotton of moiré silk.

mortise *see* pegged furniture.

mote spoon small metal spoon with a pierced bowl used to skim tea leaves, with a tapering, pointed stem to unblock the spout of a teapot.

mold blowing method of producing glass objects by blowing molten glass into a wooden or metal shaper or mold.

movement all the parts of a clock mechanism that lie behind the dial.

Mudéjar term for Islamic designs used on Spanish decorative arts.

muffle kiln chamber inside a kiln that prevents ceramic wares with enamel decoration from being damaged by the flames during firing.

mule chest chest with drawers in the base. Forerunner of the chest-of-drawers.

mystery action mechanism that causes a battery-operated toy to turn to the left or right at regular intervals and to pull away from an object after a collision.

mystery clock novelty clocks, usually 19th century, with no apparent connection between the movement and pendulum or hands.

Nasrids the last ruling Muslim dynasty in Spain (1232–1492).

Ne Plus Ultra body doll's body jointed at the knees and elbows and with the thighs forming part of the torso.

Neo-classicism mid- to late-18th-century style of architecture and decoration based on the forms of ancient Greece and Rome. Characteristic elements include Classical motifs such as garlands of flowers, palmettes, husks, vases, urns, key patterns, and mythical creatures.

nest of tables set of four occasional tables that slide one beneath the other when not in use. Also known as quartetto tables.

netsuke decorative toggles for securing personal possessions in traditional Japanese dress.

nickel any of various white alloys of copper, zinc, and nickel used in electroplating as a base for coating with silver.

niello compound of silver, lead, copper, and sulfur applied to metal and fired to create a lustrous black surface.

nigoshide extremely fine milky-white ceramic body used to make Japanese Kakiemon porcelain.

nozzle detachable top on a candlestick in which the candle is placed.

nutmeg grater silver or wooden box containing nutmeg and a grater, usually for sprinkling nutmeg on ale.

oeil de perdrix ("partridge eye") pattern of dotted circles in enamel or gilding; introduced at the Sèvres porcelain factory from the late 1760s.

ogee shallow, double S-shape curve.

OG (ogee) clock type of mass-produced American wall clock with an ogee-molded wooden case.

ojime small, round, or oval beads for tightening cords holding small personal possessions in traditional Japanese dress.

onion pattern popular decorative pattern in blue underglaze employed at Meissen and other Continental factories from the 18th century.

opaline glass translucent white (opalescent) glass made with oxides and bone ash. It reveals a red or yellow tint ("fire") when held up to the light.

opaque twist (cotton twist) twist or spiral created in the stem of a glass by introducing a strand of opaque-white or colored glass.

open-back setting jewelry setting in which the back of the gemstone is exposed.

open head open-crowned head covered with a pate (either cork or cardboard) with wig attached. Found on most bisque dolls.

open mouth parted lips of a doll which are really open (as opposed to an open-closed mouth).

openwork pierced decoration.

orders the most important elements of Classical architecture. An order comprises a base, shaft, column, entablature, and capital in one of the following styles: Doric, Ionic, Corinthian, Tuscan, or Composite. Used on all the decorative arts, particularly from the 18th century.

ormolu ("gilt bronze") gilded, brass-like alloy of copper, zinc, and tin, used for mounts on fine furniture.

overglaze term for any porcelain decoration painted in enamels or transfer-printed on top of a fired glaze.

ovolo molding making an outward curve across a right angle.

oyster veneer veneer formed by cutting smaller branches of trees, transversely across the end grain, producing small circles, which are then laid onto the furniture to resemble a pile of logs.

pad or club foot rounded foot that sits on a circular base, used in conjunction with cabriole legs on furniture.

pagoda top decorative top, used mainly on longcase clocks reflecting Oriental architecture.

pair case a double case on watches used from the 17th century: an inner one for the movement and an outer one that was usually decorated.

palette range of colors used in the decoration of ceramics.

Palladian style Classical style of architecture as interpreted by the Italian architect Andrea Palladio (1508–80) in his seminal work *Quattro Libri*. Palladianism was introduced into England in the 1730s by Lord Burlington and William Kent.

palmette decorative Classical motif based on the fan-shaped leaf of a palm tree.

pancheon deep, usually earthenware, bowl traditionally used for the mixing and rising of yeast dough.

paperweight eyes realistic glass dolls' eyes with white threads running through the irises, giving an impression of depth.

papier-mâché combination of molded paper pulp, whitening agent, and glue, used during the 19th century for the construction of dolls' heads and bodies, furniture, and domestic objects.

paraison bubble of molten glass on the end of a pontil rod or blowpipe that has been partially inflated.

parcel gilding gilding that only partially covers a metal or ceramic surface.

parian semi-matt porcelain made with feldspar and therefore not requiring a separate glaze. Also called "statuary porcelain," it became known as parian because of its similarity to the white marble from the Greek island of Paros.

Parisienne see fashion doll.

parquetry geometric marquetry made from veneers of various woods.

parure matching set of jewelry, comprising necklace, earrings, and pin. A "demi-parure" comprises matching earrings and pin.

paste mixture of ingredients from which porcelain is made. Also refers to cut and polished glass imitating gemstones.

patchbox rectangular or oval box for holding "beauty spots" or patches.

patchwork textile made by piecing together scraps of fabric, often used for making quilts.

pate crown piece found under the wig that covers the hole in some dolls' heads; made from cardboard, cork, or plaster.

pâte-de-verre ("glass paste") translucent glass created by melting and applying powdered glass in layers or by casting it in a mold.

patera circular or oval, fan-like decorative medallion popular in the Neo-classical period.

pâte-sur-pâte type of ceramic decoration involving low-relief designs carved in layers of slip and resembling cameos.

patina fine surface sheen on metal or wood that results from ageing, use, or chemical corrosion.

pavé setting in jewelry, gemstones set so close together that no backing material is visible.

peachbloom ceramic glaze derived from copper, ranging in hue from pinkish red to cloudy green, first seen in Chinese wares of the Qing Dynasty.

pearlware fine earthenware, similar to creamware but with a blueish glaze, introduced by the firm of Wedgwood c.1779.

pedestal desk flat desk, usually with a leather top, that stands on two banks of drawers.

pediment equivalent in Classical architecture of a gable: a triangular head or topping. A "broken" pediment has the apex of the triangle removed.

peg doll or peg wooden early wooden doll with simple, peg joints.

pegged furniture early joined furniture constructed by a system of mortises (slots) and tenons (tongues), held together by dowels (pegs).

Pembroke table small, two-flap table that stands on four legs.

pendulum metal or wood rod with a flat or bulbous bob fixed to the end, which swings at a fixed rate and controls the timekeeping of a clock.

penny wooden simple, inexpensive, wooden dolls made in the 19th century.

petit-feu low-fired enamel decoration on ceramics. The palette is much broader than the earlier *grand-feu* colors.

petite sonnerie clock that strikes the hours and the quarters only, but usually repeats *grande sonnerie*.

petuntse (china stone) bonding mineral essential for making hard-paste porcelain or bone china.

pewter alloy of tin or lead (and usually a variety of other metals), used for utilitarian domestic ware.

Piano Baby collectors term for all-bisque porcelain figures of crawling or seated children, made by the Heubach factory in Thuringia and intended for display on a piano.

pie-crust top carved decorative edge of a dished-top tripod or tea table.

piercing intricate cut decoration, originally done with a sharp chisel, later with a fretsaw, and finally with mechanical punches.

pier glass tall, narrow mirror intended to hang between the windows of a drawing-room.

pietre dure ("hardstones") used to decorate furniture and used in jewelry making. The most famous center of production was Florence in Italy.

pilaster flat, rectangular Classical column.

pile weavings rugs and carpets made with knots, clipped to create a pile.

pinchbeck alloy of copper and zinc, invented c.1720 as a substitute for gold and widely used in jewelry.

planishing technique of producing a smooth finish on metalwork by gently hammering or rolling the surface.

plastic synthetic material with a polymeric structure, which can be easily molded when soft and then set.

plate term originally applied to domestic wares made of silver and gold but now also used for articles made of base metal covered with silver, e.g. Sheffield plate and electroplate.

platform base three- or four-cornered flat table bases supporting a central pedestal and standing on scrolled or paw feet.

plinth the square base at the bottom of a column, for example on candlesticks or longcase clocks.

plique-à-jour technique in which a backed, many-celled metal mold is filled with translucent enamels. When the backing is removed, the finished piece resembles stained glass.

plush warp pile fabric with a long, loosely woven cut pile, used to imitate fur.

plywood form of laminated wood with the grain of the alternate layers set at right angles.

polescreen small, adjustable firescreen.
polychrome decoration executed in more than two colors.

pontil iron rod attached to the base of a glass object to support it while it is finally shaped.

pontil mark mark left on the base of a glass object by the pontil iron.

porringer straight-sided or bulbous silver or pewter vessel with two handles, made between c.1650 to c.1750 for soup or caudle (a warm, sweet, spicy drink).

portrait doll doll intended to represent a particular person sometimes similar only in name. The term is used to describe early Jumeau dolls.

Post-modernism reaction against Modernism, which began during the 1950s and promoted the reintroduction of bright colors and decorative, often with architectural-style components.

potash glass strong type of glass made from potash, lime, and silica. Also called *verre de fougère* or *Waldglas*.

pot board lowest shelf of a court cupboard or open dresser.

pounce box/pot cylinder or bottle with sprinkler for "pounce," a powder used to dry ink before blotting paper was invented.

poured wax term for dolls with hollow or shoulder heads, made by repeated dipping into molten wax until a substantial shell is achieved, which is then painted.

powder-blue mottled blue ground achieved by blowing dry pigment onto a ceramic body through gauze.

Prattware type of creamware decorated in high-fired colors including ocher, green, brown, and blue.

prayer-rug usually small rug on which Muslims kneel to pray. Many incorporate a mihrab or arch.

pressed wax (solid wax) term for dolls with solid carved-wax heads, made prior to the introduction of poured wax.

press-molding technique that involves pouring molten glass into a metal mold and pressing it to the sides using a metal plunger. Also refers to the molding of ceramic figures or applied ornament by pressing clay into an absorbent mold.

pricket metal spike on a candlestick for securing the candle.

provenance documented history of any antique item, passed on to each new owner. An unusual or notable provenance may enhance the value of a piece.

prunt blob of glass applied to a glass body for decoration. Prunts are sometimes impressed with a decorative stamp to form "raspberries."
puce purple red color formed from manganese oxide, which was used on ceramics.

pumpkin head type of wax-over-papier-mâché doll with molded hair, popular in Britain and Germany in the mid-19th century.

punch'ong type of grayish-green celadon stoneware, with stamped decoration filled with slip. Made in Korea from the 14th to the 16th century.

punch-bowl large bowl on a stepped or molded foot.

putti naked cherubs.

puzzle jug jug with a globular body, openwork neck, and between three and seven spouts.

quaich type of silver drinking bowl with flat handles, originating in Scotland.

quatrefoil shape or design incorporating four foils or lobes.

Queen Anne style style characterized by plain surfaces and octagonal/hexagonal geometric shapes and faceting, popular during the 1710s and 1720s. It was revived during the second half of the 19th century.

Queensware alternative name given by Wedgwood to its creamware in honor of Queen Charlotte, who commissioned a creamware tea service from Wedgwood in 1765.

rail horizontal splats of a chair back.

raising process of making hollow-wares by hammering sheet metal over a stake or anvil. The metal is annealed to make it easier to work.

rat-tail tapering rib strengthening the bowl and stem of a spoon.

redware stoneware, generally unglazed and often decorated with applied motifs in relief.

reeding decoration created by narrow, convex moldings in parallel strips and divided by grooves.

Reformation religious and political movement in 16th-century Europe that began as an attempt to reform the Roman Catholic Church and resulted in the establishment of the Protestant churches.

Régence the forerunner of the Rococo style in France, characterized by symmetrical, heavy forms typical of the Baroque but with elaborate scrollwork. It takes its name from the regency of Philippe, duc d'Orléans (1715–23).

Regency style of British origin, named after the period during which George, Prince of Wales (later George IV) was Prince Regent (1811–20) and characterized by heavy, broadly Classical forms and ornament such as winged lions, masks, and palmettes. Stylistically term covers the period c.1790 to 1830.

register plates scale of a barometer against which the mercury level is read.

regulator extremely accurate clock, used as a standard by which other clocks may be set.

reign marks four- or six-character marks on Chinese porcelain or bronzes denoting the name of the emperor and, on six-character, the dynasty. They do not necessarily indicate the period of manufacture as they were often copied.

relief engraving method of decorating glass by wheel-engraving to leave the design standing proud. Also called *Hochschnitt*.

Renaissance flowering of Classical scholarship, scientific, and geographical discovery at the end of the Middle Ages. In the decorative arts it was characterized by the use of elaborate grotesques, arabesques, flower swags, and scrollwork. This style was revived in the mid-19th century.

repeat work device that enables a clock to repeat the last hour or quarter-hour when a cord is pulled or a button depressed.

repoussé ("pushed out") term for embossing. More precisely the secondary process of chasing metal that has been embossed to refine the design.

reserve space within a ground, left blank for decoration.

Restoration re-establishment of the monarchy in 1660 in Britain; also the reign of Charles II (1660–85). Also the re-establishment of the monarchy in France under Louis XVIII (1814–24) and Charles X (1824–30).

reticulation intricate pierced decoration on thin-walled porcelain.

Revocation of the Edict of Nantes the Edict of Nantes, promulgated by Henry IV in 1598, granted freedom of religion to French Protestants. Its revocation by Louis XIV in 1685 led to many French Protestants (Huguenots) fleeing religious persecution and settling in England and The Netherlands.

ribbon plates plates with pierced borders through which to thread ribbons for hanging on a wall.

rinceaux type of scrolling foliage ornament.

ring method wooden animals for arks and farmyards, made in Germany in the 19th and early 20th centuries using the ring method. A large circle of wood was turned to produce the animal in cross-section. The animals were then cut from the ring in slices. The legs were separated and details, such as the ears and horns, were added.

robin's-egg glaze speckled dark blue and turquoise glaze developed in China during the 18th century.

rocaille ("rockwork") French term for an irregular form of decoration seen on Rococo wares. It incoporates shellwork and jagged rockwork.

Rococo decorative style that evolved in the early 18th century partly as a reaction to the Baroque. It featured asymmetrical ornament and flamboyant scrollwork.

rod bear early type of Steiff teddy bear with metal rod jointing.

rose Pompadour French term for the rich, deep-pink glaze introduced at the Sèvres porcelain factory as a ground color. Named after Louis XV's famous mistress, the Marquise de Pompadour.

rosso antico red-bodied ware developed by Wedgwood in the late 18th century.

roundel round, flat ornament.

rule join type of join on furniture contrived in such a way that, when open, no separation shows between the two joined parts.

rummer short-stemmed drinking glass, traditionally used for drinking rum and water.

runner name given to long, narrow rugs, generally c.2.6m (8ft 6in) long by 1–1.2m (3ft 3in–4ft) wide.

runners strips of wood on which drawers slide.

Sabot French term for the gilt-bronze "shoe" at the bottom of furniture legs.

saber leg outward-curving leg, shaped like the curved blade of a saber, that became fashionable on late-18th-century Empire and Regency chairs.

sacque 18th-century woman's dress with drapes falling in long pleats at the back.

Safavids dynasty that ruled Persia (now Iran) from 1501 to 1732.

salt collectors' term for a salt-cellar.

salt glaze thin, glassy glaze applied to some stoneware and produced by throwing salt into the kiln at the height of firing. The glaze may show a pitted surface, known as "orange peel."

salver flat, round dish, sometimes with feet, similar to a tray but smaller and without handles.

sancai ("three color") Tang period wares made as funerary goods and decorated with viscous lead glazes.

sangam Korean celadon wares inlaid with black-and-white clays.

sang-de-boeuf brilliant red ceramic glaze developed in early 18th-century China.

Savonnerie French rug or carpet with a dense pile, named after the French carpet manufactory established in Paris during the early 17th century. The term is sometimes also applied to similar carpets made elsewhere in Europe.

scagliola decorative material imitating marble or hardstones and made from hardened and polished plaster and chips of marble.

scale pattern ornament of overlapping scales. Also called imbrication.

Schnelle German term for a tall stoneware tankard with tapered sides made in the Rhineland, especially in Siegburg during the second half of the 16th century.

Schwarzlot German term for black lead enamel painting on porcelain and glass used from the second half of the 17th century.

sconce candle socket of any candle holder or a type of bracket candle holder attached to a wall.

scratchweight note made of the weight, in ounces and pennyweights troy, of a silver article at assay, usually hand-engraved lightly on the base or reverse.

scroll/flying scroll curved decoration, particularly used for handles. Flying scroll is an upward scrolling handle that is joined to the body at the base of the scroll only.

seams visible joins in metalwork that has been cast in several pieces.

seat rail framework that supports the seat of a chair and holds the legs together.

Secessionist movement formed in opposition to established artistic taste, which emerged in Munich, Berlin, and Vienna toward the end of the 19th century. It advocated a purer, more abstract style of design.

secrétaire writing cabinet with a fall front that lets down to provide a writing surface.

secrétaire à abattant type of writing cabinet with a fall front and resting on a chest-of-drawers or small cupboard.

serpentine undulating convex and concave form.

settle earliest form of seating for two more people.

sgraffito form of ceramic decoration incised through a colored slip, revealing the ground beneath.

shagreen untanned leather, originally the skin of the shagri, a Turkish wild ass, but now used to include sharkskin.

Shakers religious communities in North America, noted for their simple, pared-down furniture and artifacts.

shakudo alloy of copper and gold, used in Japanese metalwork.

Sheffield plate silver substitute used from c.1740, made by binding and fusing together sterling silver and copper.

shelf clock American term for a bracket or mantel clock.

shellac resinous varnish obtained from the lac insect and used in japanning.

shibuichi alloy of copper and silver used in Japanese metalwork.

shi-shi Buddhist lion motif used on Oriental porcelain.

shoe projecting piece rising from the back rail of a chair seat into which the base of the splat is fixed.

shoulder outward projection of a vase under the neck or mouth.

shoulder plate area of a doll's shoulder-head below the neck.

shu fu opaque white Chinese porcelain with a grayish-white glaze and incised with the characters *shu* and *fu*, meaning "Privy Council."

side chair chair without arms, designed to stand against a wall.

signer a guitar never used by a famous musician but signed by and associated with him or her due to its make.

silvered brass brass that is colored silver by the application of a silvering compound.

silver gilt silver covered in a thin layer of gold.

singerie French term for ornament featuring monkeys (*singes*), popular during the 18th century combined with chinoiserie decoration.

skeleton clock clock with pierced or fretted frame revealing the mechanism.

slab-building early method of forming ceramic objects by assembling slabs of clay and luting them together.

slat-back chair type of 17th-century chair with slats across the back.

sleeping eyes eyes that can move from open to closed, mainly found on French bisque dolls.

sleeve vase tall vase of long thin tubular shape.

slip smooth dilution of clay and water used in the making and decoration of pottery.

slip-casting manufacture of thin-bodied ceramic wares and figures by pouring slip into a mold.

slip-trailing application of slip onto a ceramic form as a wary of decorating the surface.

slip-in seat *see* drop-in seat.

slipware type of red-bodied earthenware decorated largely with slip in contrasting colors.

slit head type of wax-over-papier-mâché doll made in Britain in the early 19th century.

slop-bowl bowl for tea rinsings.

snuff-box hinged box, often highly decorated, used from the early 18th century for storing snuff.

snuffers scissor-like implements for trimming and collecting candle wicks.

socket head type of doll's head in which the base of the neck is rounded so that it fits into a cup shape at the top of the body.

socle block or slab that forms the lowest part of the pedestal of a sculpture or decorative vase.

soda glass (soda-lime glass) very light type of glass produced from soda, lime, and silica.

sofa table rectangular table with two hinged flaps at the ends designed to stand in front of a sofa.

soft-paste porcelain (artificial porcelain) porcelain formula made from a range of ingredients, which may include soapstone or bone-ash, but without the kaolin used in hard-paste porcelain.

solder lead applied to repair cracks and holes in silver.

solid wax *see* pressed wax.

soumakh a type of flatwoven textile made by the weft-wrapping technique, used especially in the Caucasus and north-western Persia.

spade foot tapering foot of square section.

spade hands crude hands with little detail, found on early German wooden dolls.

spandrel element of a design, closing off a corner: two spandrels make an arch shape.

sparrow-beak jug jug with a simple, triangular spout.

spelter zinc alloy, an inexpensive alternative to bronze. Used in the production of figures.

spindle term used to denote object in the shape of a spinner's spindle. Specifically the upright of a spindle-back chair.

splat central upright in a chair back, loosely applied to all members in a chair back.

sprig applied or relief ceramic ornament, not necessarily consisting of sprigs of foliage, made by press-molding.

squab cushion loose flat cushion on the seat of a chair.

stain method of coloring glass or ceramics.

stampino Italian term for blue-and-white stencil decorations, used on porcelain made at the Italian factory of Doccia factory.

standard required amount of pure silver in an alloy.

stereograph photograph made of two images taken from slightly different viewpoints to give the impression of depth.

sterling silver British term for silver that is at least 92.5 percent pure.

stiles back uprights on a chair and other pieces of furniture.

stipple engraving method of decorating glass by tapping a hard steel or diamond point against the surface to build up a pattern of small dots.

stippling technique of creating intricate painted designs on ceramics by applying dots of color with the point of a brush. Characteristic of the Capodimonte porcelain factory in Italy.

stirrup cup silver or silver-gilt cup used for drinking prior to making a journey or going hunting. Usually shaped as the head of an animal.

stoneware type of pottery fired at a higher temperature than earthenware, making it durable and non-porous. May be covered in a salt glaze.

strapwork decorative ornament resembling a series of thongs, rings, and buckles, used mainly in the 16th and 17th centuries and revived in the 19th century.

streamlining style with flowing curved lines and aerodynamic form, prevalent in American design of the Art Deco period.

stretcher rail joining and stabilizing the legs of a chair or table.

strike/silent lever or hand on the dial of a clock that enables the striking mechanism to be shut off.

stringing decorative inlay using thin strips of wood or metal.

studio pottery/glass pottery or glass that has been individually designed and crafted.

stumpwork raised needlework on a ground of cotton or cotton wool, formed as three-dimensional panels and often mounted as pictures. Popular during the 17th century.

subsidiary dial small dial contained within the main clock dial, typically showing seconds, date, or strike/silent indication.

sulphide small, opaque-white medallion made of china clay or glass paste enclosed in transparent glass.

sumptuary laws laws forbidding the import, ownership, or manufacture of luxury goods.

Sussex chair chair with an ash frame and rush seat, based on a traditional country design and popularized by William Morris in the 19th century.

swags decoration of hanging chains of flowers or husks.

swan-neck cresting type of broken pediment with two S-shaped curves, one of which is reversed.

swan-neck handle curved handle, popular in the 18th century.

swivel head type of doll's head made separately from the shoulders and fitted later, allowing the head to swivel.

table ambulante French term for a small, portable occasional table.

tallboy *see* chest-on-chest.

tallcase clock American term for a longcase clock.

taotie monster masks found on Chinese bronzes.

taperstick small candlestick for holding a taper (thin candle) for lighting pipes and melting sealing wax.

tapestry western European flatwoven textile.

tassie cameo portraits made from a glass paste cast in a mold, produced in Scotland from 1766.

tavern clock weight-driven wall clock, with a large dial and long trunk.

tazza large, shallow bowl on a stemmed foot made in glass, silver, and ceramics from the 16th century.

teapoy small piece of free-standing furniture designed for holding tea.

tear air-bubble in the stem of a drinking glass shaped like a tear-drop.

tenmoku Japanese term for a molasses-colored glaze, made from iron oxide.

tenons *see* pegged furniture.

terracotta lightly fired red earthenware, usually unglazed.

tester canopy or ceiling over a bed.

tête-à-tête tea or coffee service for two. Also term for a 19th-century "love seat."

theodolite sophisticated form of surveying instrument used to measure angles of elevation and horizontal angles.

throwing the technique of shaping ceramic vessels by hand on a rotating wheel.

thrown chair chair constructed from turned pieces of wood, made in Britain from the 16th century.

thumbpiece flange attached to a hinged lid, which, when pressed by the thumb, raises the lid.

timepiece clock without a striking mechanism.

tin glaze glassy glaze made opaque by the addition of tin oxide and commonly used on earthenware.

tinplate thin sheets of steel coated with a tin-based alloy.

Toby jug 18th- or 19th-century jug representing a seated Englishman with a three-cornered hat and a mug of ale.

Toleware/Tolerware tinplated sheet iron covered with black asphaltum and painted with brightly colored flowers. Produced in Pennsylvania in large quantities in the 18th and 19th centuries.

tooled gilding that has been worked with a tool into a decorative pattern.

topsy-turvy dolls rag doll that has two torsos, each with a different head, one hidden beneath the reversible skirt.

torchère candlestand.

tortoiseshell ware creamware decorated with mingled glazes to produce a variegated effect.
toys small, inexpensive items such as buckles and buttons mass-produced in silver and brass in the late 18th and 19th centuries. Also small porcelain novelties.

trailing method of decorating glass by laying molten glass onto the body in a line, spiral, or lattice pattern. The trails are sometimes combed to create festoons.

train interconnected series of wheels and pinions forming the movement of a clock.

transfer-printing transfer of an inked image from an engraved plate to paper or to a sheet ("bat") of tacky glue and from there to a ceramic object.

Transitional in French furniture-making, style created from the fusion of Neo-classical decoration with Rococo forms.

treen small household items made from turned or carved wood.

trefid spoon with a broad, flat stem ending in a trefoil shape.

trefoil decorative motif shaped like clover, with three pronounced lobes.

trelliswork geometric decoration in the form of a trellis.

trembleuse French term for a saucer with a raised ring to hold a cup to avoid spillages.

tripod table small table with a round top supported by a three-legged pillar, originally made for serving tea.

trompe l'oeil pictorial decoration intended to deceive the eye.

à la troubadour French version of the Gothic Revival style.

trunk middle section of a longcase clock, either solid or glazed and usually with a door at the front.

tsuba Japanese sword-guards.

tube-lining type of ceramic decoration in which thin trails of slip are applied as outlines to areas of colored glaze.

tumbler cup round-bottomed drinking vessel weighted at the base so that it will always return to an upright position if upturned.

tureen large bowl usually on a foot, often with handles and a cover. Used for serving soups and sauces.

turning process by which a solid piece of wood is modeled by turning on a lathe.

two-faced doll doll with a revolving head, showing different expressions or colors at the front and back. Three-faced dolls were also made.

tyg large mug with two, four, or more handles and sometimes several spouts.

underglaze color or design painted before the application of the glaze on a ceramic object. Blue is the most common underglaze color.

up/down dial subsidiary dial commonly found on marine chronometers, which indicates how much time remains before the clock must be wound.

veneer thin slice of expensive and often exotic timber applied to an inexpensive secondary timber (carcase) using glue.

Vernier scale sliding calibrated scale used in conjunction with a fixed scale to obtain a highly accurate reading on a barometer or surveying instrument.

vernis Martin type of japanning or imitation lacquerwork invented by the Martin family in Paris in the 18th century.

verre églomisé glass that has been decorated on the reverse with silver or gold leaf, which is covered with a varnish to protect it.

vesta case/box silver matchbox for early vesta matches, which were easily flammable and needed such protection.

vide poche French term for a small table or dish in which the contents of pockets may be emptied.

Vienna regulator extremely precise and finely made weight-driven clocks, either wall-hanging or floor-standing, produced in Austria during the first half of the 19th century.

vinaigrette small, hinged box to hold a sponge soaked in vinegar or perfume to combat offensive odors.

vinyl non-flammable, flexible yet tough form of plastic used from the 1940s.

vitrifiable colors colored enamels that become fixed and glassy when fired.

Vitruvian scroll pattern of repeating spiral scrolls (volutes) derived from Classical architecture.

wainscot chair early joined chair with a paneled back, open arms, and wood seat.

waiter small salver, less than 20cm (8in) in diameter.

Walzenkrug German term for a cylindrical tankard.

warp foundation material running the length of a carpet. Before weaving can begin, warps need to be correctly positioned on the loom. The warp is generally made from silk, cotton, or wool.

watch stand Victorian flatback piece with a hole in which to place a watch, used as a mantelpiece ornament.

wax over doll made of wax-over-composition, produced mostly in France and Germany in the 1870s.
weft horizontal threads in the foundation of a rug that are interwoven with the warps. In most flatweaves, the visible surface of the rug is composed of weft threads.

Wellington chest tall, narrow, relatively plain type of chest named after the Duke of Wellington.

whatnot mobile stand with open shelves, often made of mahogany.

wheel engraving method of decorating glass by cutting it using a small rotating wheel fed with an abrasive.

whitework embroidery in white thread on a white ground.

Willow pattern mock-Chinese decorative pattern, used on blue-and-white transfer-printed wares. The pattern shows two figures crossing a bridge, with a third in pursuit.

Windsor chair type of country chair with a spindle back and legs.

wine cooler container sometimes lined with lead for holding iced water to cool wine bottles, made in marble, wood or silver.

wine funnel silver funnel used to decant wine from the bottle at the dinner table.

wine taster shallow, circular silver vessel with a raised center used for assessing the color, clarity, and taste of wine.

wing chair fully upholstered chair with wings at the sides to protect the sitter from draughts.

wirework decorative use of interwoven wires.

wreathing spiraling indented rings inside thrown pottery, left by the potter's fingers, or caused by distortions during the firing process.

wrigglework decorative patterns on pewter made with punches. Popular on 17th-century pewter wares.

wucai ("five-colored") type of ceramic decoration developed in 16th-century China using the same palette as *doucai* but within overglaze black or red, instead of underglaze-blue outlines.

Zwischengoldglas ("sandwich gold glass") decorative gold leaf design between two layers of glass, developed by Bohemian glassmakers in the early 18th century.

Bibliography

GENERAL

Fleming, John and Honour, Hugh: *The Penguin Dictionary of Decorative Arts* (London, 1989)
Haslam, M.: *Marks and Monograms of the Modern Movement: 1875–1930* (Guildford, 1977)
Jervis, Simon, ed.: *The Penguin Dictionary of Design and Designers* (London, 1984)
Knowles, Eric: *Miller's 100 Years of the Decorative Arts* (London, 1998, first published 1993 as *Miller's Victoriana to Art Deco*)
Miller's Antiques Price Guide (annual)
Miller, Judith and Martin, eds: *Miller's Understanding Antiques* (London, 1997)
Murray, Peter and Linda: *Dictionary of Art and Artists* (London, 1997)
Savage, George, ed.: *Dictionary of Antiques* (London, 1978)
Turner, Jane, ed.: *Dictionary of Art* (London, 1996)

ART DECO

Arwas, Victor: *Art Deco* (London, 1980)
Arwas, Victor: *Art Deco Sculpture* (London, 1992)
Cheney, Sheldon and Martha: *Art and the Machine* (New York, 1992)
Dufrene, Maurice and Duncan, Alastair: *Authentic Art Deco Interiors from the 1925 Paris Exhibition* (Woodbridge, 1989)
Duncan, Alastair: *American Art Deco* (London and New York, 1986)
Duncan, Alastair: *Art Deco* (London, 1988)
Duncan, Alastair: *Art Deco Furniture: The French Designers* (London, 1984)
Fusco, Tony: *Art Deco: Identification and Price Guide* (New York, 1993)
Gabardi, Melissa: *Les Bijoux de l'Art Deco aux années 40* (Paris, 1986)
Green, Oliver: *Underground Art* (London, 1990)
Kardon, Janet, ed.: *Craft in the Machine Age: 1920–45* (New York, 1995)
Marcilhac, Félix: *Jean Dunand: His Life and Works* (London, 1991)
McCready, Karen: *Art Deco and Modernist Ceramics* (London, 1995)
Miller's Antiques Checklist: *Art Deco* (London, 1991)
Wilson, Richard with Pilgrim, Diane and Dickran, Tashjian: *The Machine Age in America: 1918–1941* (New York, 1986)
Raulet, Sylvie: *Art Deco Jewelry* (London, 1985)

ART NOUVEAU

Amaya, Mario: *Art Nouveau* (London and New York, 1966)
Aslin, Elizabeth: *The Aesthetic Movement: Prelude to Art Nouveau* (London, 1969)
Barilli, Renato: *Art Nouveau* (London, 1966)
Battersby, Martin: *Art Nouveau* (London, 1969)
Bayer, Patricia and Waller, Mark: *The Art of René Lalique* (London, 1988)
Becker, Vivienne: *Art Nouveau Jewelry* (London, 1985)
Cooke, Frederick: *Glass* (London, 1986)
Dawes, Nicholas M.: *Lalique Glass* (New York, 1986)
Duncan, Alastair: *Art Nouveau* (London, 1994)
Duncan, Alastair: *Fin de Siècle Masterpieces from the Silverman Collection* (New York, 1989)
Feinblatt, Ebria: *Toulouse-Lautrec and his Contemporaries: Posters of the Belle Epoque from the Wagner Collection* (Los Angeles, 1985)
Grover, Ray: *Art Glass Nouveau* (Rutland, 1967)
Hanks, D.A.: *The Decorative Designs of Frank Lloyd Wright* (New York, 1979)
Hutter, Heribert: *Art Nouveau* (London, 1967)
Johnson, Diane Chalmers: *American Art Nouveau* (New York, 1979)
Koch, Robert: *Louis C. Tiffany's Glass-Bronzes-Lamps* (New York, 1971)
Miller's Antiques Checklist: *Art Nouveau* (London, 1992)
Revi, Albert Christian: *American Art Nouveau Glass* (Camden, NJ, 1968)
Sembach, K.-J.: *Henri Van De Velde* (London, 1989)
Timmers, Margaret: *The Power of the Poster* (London, 1998)
Vergo, P.: *Art in Vienna, 1898–1918* (London, 1975)
Waissenberger, Robert, ed.: *Vienna 1890–1920* (New York, 1984)
Weill, Alain: *The Poster: A Worldwide Survey* (London, 1985)
Weisberg, Gabriel P.: *Art Nouveau Bing: Paris Style 1900* (New York, 1986)
Wilk, C.: *Thonet: 150 Years of Furniture* (New York, 1961)
Zapata, Janet: *The Jewelry and Enamels of Louis Comfort Tiffany* (London, 1993)

ARTS AND CRAFTS

Anscombe, I. and Gere, C.: *Arts and Crafts in Britain and America* (London, 1978)
Bowman, Leslie Green: *American Arts and Crafts* (Los Angeles, 1990)
Cathers, Beth and Volpe, Tod: *Treasures of the American Arts and Crafts Movement: 1890–1920* (New York, 1987)
Cathers, David M.: *Furniture of the American Arts and Crafts Movement* (Philmont, 1996)
Freeman, John Crosby: *The Forgotten Rebel* (Watkins Glen, 1966)
Gere, Charlotte and Munn, Geoffrey: *Artists' Jeweler: From the Pre-Raphaelites to the Arts and Crafts Movement* (Woodbridge, 1989)
Kaplan, W.: *Charles Rennie Mackintosh* (Glasgow, 1996)
Naylor, Gillian: *The Arts and Crafts Movement: A Study of its Sources, Ideals and Influence on Design Theory* (London, 1990)
Tracey, Berry B.: *19th-Century America: Furniture & Other Decorative Arts* (New York, 1970)

CERAMICS

Adams, Elizabeth: *Chelsea Porcelain* (London, 1987)
Atterbury, Paul and Batkin, Maureen: *Dictionary of Minton* (Woodbridge, 1990)
Bailey, Betty and Twitchett, John: *Royal Crown Derby* (London, 1976)
Barber, Edwin Atlee: *The Pottery and Porcelain of the United States* (New York, 1976)
Battie, David, ed.: *Sotheby's Concise Encyclopedia of Porcelain* (London, 1990)
Branyan, Lawrence, French, Neal, and Sandon, John: *Worcester Blue and White Porcelain* (London, 1989)
Carswell, John: *Chinese Blue and White and its Impact on the Western World* (Chicago, 1985)
Charleston, Robert, J., ed.: *World Ceramics* (London, 1982)
Coysh, A.W. and Henrywood, R.K.: *Dictionary of Blue and White Printed Earthenware* (Woodbridge, 1989–90)
Cushion, J.P.: *Handbook of Pottery and Porcelain Marks* (London, 1996)
Cushion, John and Margaret: *A Collector's History of British Porcelain* (Woodbridge, 1992)
Dawes, Nicholas M.: *Majolica* (New York, 1990)
Fay-Halle, Antoinette and Mundt, Barbara: *Nineteenth Century European Porcelain* (London, 1983)
Frelinghuysen, Alice Cooney: *American Porcelain* (New York, 1989)
Gabszewicz, Anton and Freeman, Geoffrey: *Bow Porcelain* (London, 1982)
Garner, Harry: *Oriental Blue and White* (London, 1970)
Gaston, Mary Frank: *American Belleek* (Paducah, 1984)
Godden, Geoffrey: *Caughley and Worcester Porcelain* (Woodbridge, 1981)
Godden, Geoffrey: *An Illustrated Encyclopaedia of British Pottery and Porcelain* (Leicester, 1992)
Godden, Geoffrey: *Lowestoft Porcelain* (Woodbridge, 1985)
Godden, Geoffrey: *Minton Pottery and Porcelain of the First Period, 1793–1850* (London, 1968)
Godden, Geoffrey: *Mason's China and Ironstone Wares* (Woodbridge, 1980)
Godden, Geoffrey: *Ridgway Porcelain* (Woodbridge, 1985)
Godden, Geoffrey: *Staffordshire Porcelain* (London, 1983)
Holgate, David: *New Hall* (London, 1987)
Howard, David: *Chinese Armorial Porcelain* (London, 1974)
Kovel, Ralph and Terry: *Kovel's New Dictionary of Marks: Pottery and Porcelain 1850 to the Present* (New York, 1986)
Langham, Marion: *Belleek* (London, 1993)
Lawrence, Louis: *Satsuma* (London, 1991)
Lockett, Terence and Godden, Geoffrey: *Davenport: China, Earthenware, and Glass* (London, 1989)
Macintosh, Duncan: *Chinese Blue and White Porcelain* (Woodbridge, 1994)
Medley, Margaret: *The Chinese Potter* (Oxford, 1976)
Menzhausen, Ingelore: *Early Meissen Porcelain in Dresden* (London, 1990)
Messenger, Michael: *Coalport* (Woodbridge, 1996)
Miller's Antique Checklist: *Porcelain* (London, 1996)
Miller's Collecting Pottery & Porcelain (London, 1997)
Pugh, P.D.: *Staffordshire Portrait Figures* (London, 1990)
Reilly, Robin: *Wedgwood* (London, 1989)
Ruckert, Rainer: *Meissener Porzellan 1710–1810* (Munich, 1966)
Sandon, Henry: *Royal Worcester Porcelain* (London, 1995)
Sandon, John: *Dictionary of Worcester Porcelain* (Woodbridge, 1993)
Sandon, John: *Starting to Collect Antique Porcelain* (Woodbridge, 1997)
Savage, George: *Seventeenth and Eighteenth Century French Porcelain* (London, 1960)
Savage, George and Newman, Harold: *An Illustrated Dictionary of Ceramics* (London, 1992)
Savill, Rosalind: *The Wallace Collection Catalog of Sèvres Porcelain* (London, 1988)
Schiffer, Nancy: *Japanese Porcelain, 1800–1950* (West Chester, 1986)
Twitchett, John: *Derby Porcelain* (London, 1980)
Van Lemmen, Hans: *Tiles: A Collector's Guide* (London, 1979)
Watney, Bernard: *English Blue and White Porcelain* (London, 1973)
Watney, Bernard: *Liverpool Porcelain of the Eighteenth Century* (Shepton Beauchamp, 1997)
Whiter, Leonard: *Spode* (London, 1978)
Wilson, Timothy: *Italian Maiolica* (Oxford, 1989)
Wojciechowski, Kathy: *Nippon Porcelain* (West Chester, 1992)

CLOCKS & WATCHES

Allix, Charles and Bonnert, Peter: *Carriage Clocks: Their History and Development* (London, 1974)
Britten, F.J.: *Britten's Watch and Clockmaker's Handbook, Dictionary and Guide* (London, 1982)
Britten, F.J.: *Old Clocks and Watches and their Makers* (London, 1975)
Cescinsky, Herbert and Webster, Malcolm R.: *English Domestic Clocks* (London, 1976)
Dawson, P.G., Drover, C.B., and Parkes, D.W.: *Early English Clocks* (Woodbridge, 1982)
Gould, Rupert T.: *The Marine Chronometer: Its History and Development* (Woodbridge, 1989)
Hawkins, J.B.: *Thomas Cole and Victorian Clockmaking* (Sydney, 1975)
Jagger, Cedric: *Clocks* (London, 1975)
Lee, R.A.: *The Knibb Family: Clockmakers* (Byfleet, 1964)

Loomes, Brian: *Early Clockmakers of Great Britain* (London, 1981)
Loomes, Brian: *Painted Dial Clocks* (Woodbridge, 1994)
Loomes, Brian: *Watchmakers and Clockmakers of the World: Volume Two* (London, 1989)
Mercer, Tony: *Chronometer Makers of the World* (Colchester, 1991)
Miller's Antique Checklist: *Clocks* (London, 1992)
Miller's Clocks and Barometers Buyer's Guide (London, 1997)
Roberts, Deryck: *British Skeleton Clocks* (Woodbridge, 1987)
Roberts, Deryck: *The Bracket Clock* (London, 1982)
Roberts, Deryck: *The English Longcase Clock* (London, 1989)
Robinson, Tom: *The Longcase Clock* (Woodbridge, 1981)
Rose, Ronald E.: *English Dial Clocks* (Woodbridge, 1978)
Sellink, Dr J.L.: *Dutch Antique Domestic Clocks* (Leiden, 1973)
Tardy: *The French Clocks* (Paris, 1982)
Tyler, E. John: *Black Forest Clocks* (London, 1977)
White, George: *English Lantern Clocks* (Woodbridge, 1989)

DOLLS & TEDDY BEARS
Bailly, Christian: *Automata: The Golden Age, 1848–1914* (London, 1987)
Bristol, Olivia and Geddes-Brown, Leslie: *Dolls' Houses: Domestic Life and Architectural Styles in Miniature from the 17th Century to the Present Day* (London,1997)
Cieslik, Jurgen and Marianne: *Button in the Ear* (Jülich, 1989)
Cockrill, Pauline: *The Teddy Bear Encyclopedia* (London, 1995)
Coleman, Elizabeth Anne, Dorothy and Evelyn Jane: *The Collector's Encyclopedia of Dolls: Volume 1* (New York, 1968)
Coleman, Elizabeth Anne, Dorothy and Evelyn Jane: *The Collector's Encyclopedia of Dolls: Volume 2* (New York, 1986)
Earnshaw, Nora: *Collecting Dolls' Houses and Miniatures* (London, 1989)
Hillier, Mary: *The History of Wax Dolls* (London, 1985)
Miller's Antiques Checklist: *Dolls & Teddy Bears* (London, 1992)
Miller's *Collecting Teddy Bears & Dolls: The Facts At Your Fingertips* (London, 1996)
Pearson, Sue: *Bears* (London, 1995)
Pistorius, Rolfs Christel: *Steiff Sensational Teddy Bears, Animals and Dolls* (Cumberland, 1991)

FURNITURE
Agius, Pauline: *British Furniture, 1880–1915* (Woodbridge, 1978)
Agius, Pauline and Jones, Stephen: *Ackermann's Regency Furniture and Interiors* (Ramsbury, 1984)
Alcouffe, D.: *Le Mobilier du Musée du Louvre* (Dijon, 1993)
Bahns, J.: *Zwischen Biedermeier und Jugendstil* (Munich, 1987)
Barquist, David I.: *American Tables and Looking Glasses* (New Haven, Connecticut, 1992)
Beckerdite, Luke, ed.: *American Furniture* (New England, 1997)
Boccador, J.: *Le Mobilier français du moyen âge à la renaissance* (Paris, 1988)
Chinnery, Victor: *Oak Furniture* (Woodbridge, 1986)
Claret Rubira, J.: *Meubles de estilo español desde el gótico hasta el imperio* (Barcelona, 1972)
Collard, Frances: *Regency Furniture* (Woodbridge, 1983)
Comstock, Helen: *American Furniture* (New York, 1962)
Cooper, Wendy: *The Classical Taste in America 1800 to 1840* (New York, 1994)
Dell, T.: *Furniture in the Frick Collection* (New York, 1992)
Edwards, Ralph: *The Shorter Dictionary of English Furniture: From the Middle Ages to the Late Georgian Period* (London, 1964)
Edwards, Ralph and Jourdain, Margaret: *Georgian Cabinet-Makers* (London, 1946)

Fastnedge, Ralph: *Sheraton Furniture* (London, 1962)
Feulner, A.: *Kunstgeschichte des Möbels* (Berlin, 1980)
Fitzgerald, Oscar: *Three Centuries of American Furniture* (New York, 1982)
Forman, Benno M. and Norton, W.W.: *American Seating Furniture, 1630–1840* (New York, 1988)
Garvan, Beatrice B.: *The Pennsylvania German Collection* (Philadelphia, 1982)
Gilbert, Christopher: *Furniture at Temple Newsam House and Lotherton Hall* (London, 1978)
Gillham, Leslie, ed.: *Miller's Furniture Buyer's Guide: Late Georgian to Edwardian* (London, 1998)
Goyne Evans, Nancy: *American Windsor Chairs* (Winterthur, 1996)
Granjean, S.: *Empire Furniture, 1800–1825* (London, 1996)
Groth, H. and von de Schulenburg, F.: *Neo-classicism in the North: Swedish Furniture and Interiors, 1770–1850* (London, 1990)
Hayward, Helena, ed.: *World Furniture* (London, 1990)
Hechsher, Morrison H.: *American Furniture at the Metropolitan Museum of Art: Late Colonial Period, Queen Anne and Chippendale* (New York, 1985)
Janneau, G.: *Le Mobilier français* (Paris, 1967–74)
Jervis, Simon: *Victorian Furniture* (London, 1968)
Joy, Edward Thomas: *English Furniture* (London, 1977)
Kane, Patricia: *Three Hundred Years of American Seating Furniture* (New York, 1976)
Kenny, Peter: *Honoré Lannuier: Cabinetmaker from Paris* (New York, 1998)
Kirk, John: *The Shaker World* (New York, 1997)
Kjellberg, Pierre: *Le Mobilier français du XVIIIe siècle* (Paris, 1989)
Miller's Antiques Checklist: *Furniture* (London, 1991)
Miller's Collecting Furniture: The Facts at Your Fingertips (London, 1995)
Miller's Late Georgian to Edwardian Furniture Buyer's Guide (London, 1998)
Musgrave, Clifford: *Regency Furniture: 1800 to 1830* (London, 1970)
Paz Aguiló, M.: *El mueble clásico español* (Madrid, 1987)
Pradère, A.: *Die Kunst des französischen Möbels: Ebenisten von Ludwig XIV. bis zur Revolution* (Munich, 1990)
Richards, Nancy E. and Goyne Evans, Nancy: *New England Furniture at Winterthur: Queen Anne and Chippendale Periods* (Winterthur, 1997)
Schwarz, Martin D., Stanck, Edward J., and True, Douglas K.: *The Furniture of John Henry Belter and the Rococo Revival* (New York, 1981)
Stevens, Christopher Claxton and Whittington, Stewart: *18th Century English Furniture: The Norman Adams Collection* (Woodbridge, 1983)
Symonds, R.W. and Whinneray, B.B.: *Victorian Furniture* (London, 1987)
Thornton, Peter: *Seventeenth Century Interior Decoration in England, France, and Holland* (London, 1978)
Walkling, Gillian: *Bamboo: Antique Bamboo Furniture* (London, 1979)
Ward-Jackson, Peter: *English Furniture Designs of the 18th Century* (London, 1984)
Watson, Francis: *The History of Furniture* (London, 1976)

GLASS
Battie, D. and Cottle, S., eds: *Sotheby's Concise Encyclopedia of Glass* (London, 1991)
Bickerton, L.M.: *Eighteenth Century English Drinking Glasses: An Illustrated Guide* (Woodbridge, 1986)
Boggess, Bill and Louise: *Identifying American Brilliant Cut Glass* (West Chester, 1991)
Bray, Charles: *Dictionary of Glass: Materials and Techniques* (London, 1995)
Broizova, Jarmila: *Bohemian Crystal* (Prague, 1984)
Charleston, R.J.: *English Glass and the Glass Used in England c.400–1940* (London, 1984)
Curtis, Jean-Louis: *Baccarat* (London, 1992)
Dodsworth, Roger: *Glass and Glass-making* (Buckinghamshire, 1982)

Frothingham, Alice Wilson: *Spanish Glass* (New York, 1964)
Hajdamach, Charles: *British Glass, 1800–1914* (Woodbridge, 1991)
Haynes, E. Barrington: *Glass Through the Ages* (Harmondsworth, 1970)
Husfloen, Kyle: *Collector's Guide to American Pressed Glass 1825–1915* (Radnor, 1992)
Klein, Dan and Lloyd, Ward: *The History of Glass* (London, 1984)
Lattimore, Colin R.: *English 19th-Century Press-Molded Glass* (London, 1979)
Melvin, Jean S.: *American Glass Paperweights and their Makers* (New York, 1970)
Miller's Antiques Checklist: *Glass* (London, 1994)
Norman, Barbara: *Glass Engraving* (Rutland, 1987)
Olivié, Jean-Luc and Petrova, Sylvia: *Bohemian Glass* (Paris, 1990)
Philippe, Joseph: *Le Val-Saint-Lambert: Ses cristalleries et l'art du verre en Belgique* (Liège, 1980)
Slack, Raymond: *English Pressed Glass, 1830–1900* (London, 1987)
Spillman, Jane Shadel: *American and European Pressed Glass in The Corning Museum of Glass* (Corning, 1982)
Spillman, Jane Shadel: *The American Cut-Glass Industry* (Woodbridge, 1996)
Spillman, Jane Shadel, and Frantz, Susanne K.: *Masterpieces of American Glass: The Corning Museum of Glass, The Toledo Museum of Art, Lillian Nassau Ltd.* (New York, 1990)
Swan, Martha Louise: *American Cut and Engraved Glass: The Brilliant Period in Historical Perspective* (Radnor, 1994)
Tait, Hugh, ed.: *Five Thousand Years of Glass* (London, 1991)
Welker, John: *Pressed Glass in America: Encyclopedia of the First Hundred Years, 1825–1925* (Ivyland, 1985)
Wilson, Kenneth M.: *American Glass, 1760–1930* (New York, 1994)

JEWELRY
Becker, Vivienne: *Antique and Twentieth Century Jewelry* (Colchester, 1980)
Becker, Vivienne: *Fabulous Costume Jewelry* (Exton, 1993)
Bennett, David and Mascetti, Daniela: *Understanding Jewelry* (Woodbridge, 1989)
Bury, Shirley: *Jewelry 1789–1910: The International Era* (Woodbridge, 1991)
Bury, Shirley: *Sentimental Jewelry* (London, 1985)
Cartlidge, Barbara: *Twentieth-Century Jewelry* (New York, 1985)
Clifford, Anne: *Cut Steel and Berlin Iron Jewelry* (Bath, 1971)
Flower, Margaret: *Victorian Jewelry* (London, 1967)
Gere, Charlotte: *European and American Jewelry, 1830–1914* (London, 1975)
Gere, Charlotte: *Victorian Jewelry Design* (London, 1982)
Hinks, Peter: *Nineteenth Century Jewelry* (London, 1975)
Hinks, Peter: *Twentieth Century Jewelry* (London, 1983)
Kelley, Lyngerda and Schiffer, Nancy: *Costume Jewelry: The Great Pretenders* (West Chester, PA, 1987)
Mary, Peter: *Collecting Victorian Jewelry* (London, 1970)
Miller's Antiques Checklist: *Jewelry* (London, 1997)
Munn, Geoffrey: *The Triumph of Love: Jewelry 1530–1930* (London, 1993)
Newman, Harold: *An Illustrated Dictionary of Jewelry* (London, 1981)
Phillips, Clare: *Jewelry: From Antiquity to the Present* (London, 1996)
Shields, Jody: *All that Glitters* (New York, 1987)

MISCELLANEOUS
Alsford, Denis B.: *Match Holders: One Hundred Years of Ingenuity* (Atglen, 1994)
Bennion, Elisabeth: *Antique Medical Instruments* (London, 1980)
Brett, Vanessa: *Guide to Pewter* (London, 1981)

Coe, Brian: *Cameras: From Daguerrotype to Instant Cameras* (London, 1978)
Crompton, Dennis: *Servants of Light: the Book of the Lantern* (Ripon, 1997)
Delieb, Eric: *Investing In Silver* (London, 1970)
Delieb, Eric: *Silver Boxes* (London, 1979)
FitzMaurice Mills, John: *Encyclopedia of Antique Scientific Instruments* (London, 1983)
Fresco-Corbu, Roger: *Vesta Boxes* (Cambridge, 1983)
Furjanic, Chuck: *Antique Golf Collectibles* (Iola, 1997)
Gentle, Rupert and Feild, Rachael: *Domestic Metalwork, 1640–1820* (London, 1994)
Helliwell, Stephen: *Collecting Small Silverware* (London, 1988)
Henderson Ian T. and Stark, David I.: *Golf in the Making* (London, 1979)
Herbert, Peter and Schiffer, Nancy: *Antique Iron* (Exton, 1979)
Hornsby, Peter R.G.: *Pewter of the Western World, 1600–1850* (Exton, 1983)
Laney, Dennis: *Leica Collectors Guide* (Hove, 1992)
Launert, Edmund: *Perfume and Pommanders* (London, 1985)
Maycock, Stephen: *Miller's Rock & Pop Memorabilia* (London, 1994)
Olman, John M. and Morton W.: *The Encyclopedia of Gold Collectibles* (Alabama, 1985)
Padwick, E.W.: *A Bibliography of Cricket* (London, 1984)
Peal, Christopher: *Pewter of Great Britain* (London, 1983)
Pritchard, Michael and St Denny, Douglas: *Spy Cameras: A Century of Detective and Subminiature Cameras* (London, 1993)
Ricketts, Howard: *Objects of Vertu* (London, 1971)
Sanders, Eugene and Christine: *Pocket Matchsafes* (Atglen, 1997)
Turner, Eric: *Brass* (London, 1982)
Turner, Gerard L'E.: *Antique Scientific Instruments* (Poole, 1980)
Turner, Gerard L'E.: *Collecting Microscopes* (London and New York, 1981)
Wing, Paul: *Stereoscopes: The First One Hundred Years* (Nashua, 1996)

ORIENTAL WORKS OF ART
Garner, H.: *Chinese and Japanese Cloisonné Enamels* (London, 1970)
Hutt, Julia: *Understanding Far Eastern Art* (New York, 1987)
Kerr, Rose: *Later Chinese Bronzes* (London, 1990)
McKillop, Beth: *Korean Art and Design: The Samsung Gallery of Korean Art* (London, 1992)
Peterson, Harold, ed.: *Chinese Jades: Archaic and Modern* (London, 1977)
Rawson, Jessica, ed.: *British Museum Book of Chinese Art* (London, 1992)
Smith, Lawrence and Harris, Victor: *Japanese Decorative Arts from the 17th to the 19th Centuries* (London, 1982)
Watson, William, ed.: *The Great Japan Exhibition: Art of the Edo Period, 1600–1868* (London, 1981)
Whitfield, Roderick, ed.: *Treasures from Korea: Art Through 5000 Years* (London, 1984)

POST-WAR DESIGN
Bryars, M. and Flinchum, R., eds: *50 American Designers* (Washington, 1994)
Dormer, Peter: *Design Since 1945* (London, 1995)
Duncan, Alastair: *Modernism: Modernist Design, 1880–1940* (Woodbridge, 1998)
Fiell, C. and P.: *Modern Furniture Classics Since 1945* (London, 1991)
Garner, Philippe: *Sixties Design* (London, 1996)
Heisinger, K.B. and Marcus, G.H.: *Landmarks of Twentieth Century Design: An Illustrated Handbook* (New York, 1993)
Jackson, L.:*"Contemporary": Architecture and Interiors of the 1950's* (London, 1994)
Jenkins, Steven: *Midwinter Pottery: A Revolution in British Tableware* (Shepton Beauchamp, 1997)
Julier, Guy: *Twentieth Century Design* (London, 1998)
Lyall, S.: *Hille: 75 Years of British Furniture* (London, 1981)

Miller's Collecting the 1950s (London, 1997)
Sparke, P.: *A Century of Design* (London, 1998)
Sparke, P.: *An Introduction to Design and Culture in the 20th Century* (London, 1986)

RUGS & CARPETS
Aschenbrenner, Erich: *Oriental Rugs: Volume 2 Persian* (Woodbridge, 1981)
Bateman Faraday, Cornelia: *European and American Carpets and Rugs* (Woodbridge, 1990)
Bennett, Ian: *Carpets of the World* (London, 1978)
Bennett, Ian: *Oriental Rugs: Volume 1 Caucasian* (Woodbridge, 1981)
Black, David: *Oriental Carpets* (London, 1982)
Edwards, A. Cecil: *The Persian Carpet* (London, 1953)
Jarry, M.: *The Carpets of Aubusson* (Leigh-on-Sea, 1966)
Jarry, M.: *The Carpets of the Manufacture de la Savonnerie* (Leigh-on-Sea, 1966)
Jourdan, Uwe: *Oriental Rugs: Volume 5 Turkoman* (Woodbridge, 1989)
Middleton, Andrew: *Rugs and Carpets* (London, 1996)
Thompson, Jon: *Carpet Magic* (London, 1983)
Thompson, Jon: *A Return to Tradition* (London, 1986)
Tzareva, Elana: *Rugs and Carpets from Central Asia* (Harmondsworth,1984)
Von Rosenstiel, H.: *American Rugs and Carpets* (London, 1978)
Willborg, J.P.: *Textile Treasures from Five Centuries* (Stockholm, 1995)

SILVER
Brett, Vanessa: *The Sotheby's Directory of Silver* (London, 1986)
Clayton, Michael: *The Collector's Dictionary of Silver and Gold of Great Britain and North America* (Woodbridge, 1985)
Davis, Frank: *French Silver, 1450–1825* (London, 1970)
Glanville, P.: *Silver in Tudor and Early Stuart England* (London, 1991)
Grimwade, Arthur: *London Goldsmiths 1697–1837: Their Marks and Lives* (London, 1976)
Grimwade, Arthur: *Rococo Silver, 1727–1765* (London, 1974)
Hartop, Christopher: *The Huguenot Legacy* (London, 1996)
Hayward, J.F.: *Huguenot Silver in England 1688–1727* (London, 1959)
Langford, Joel: *Silver: A Practical Guide to Collecting Silverware and Identifying Hallmarks* (London; 1991)
Marquardt, Klaus: *Eight Centuries of European Cutlery* (Stuttgart, 1997)
Miller's Antiques Checklist: *Silver & Plate* (London, 1994)
Miller's Silver & Sheffield Plate Marks (London, 1993)
Newman, Harold: *An Illustrated Dictionary of Silverware* (London, 1987)
Oman, Charles: *English Domestic Silver* (London, 1967)
Pickford, I., ed.: *Jackson's Silver and Gold Marks of England, Scotland and Ireland* (Woodbridge, 1989)
Rowe, Robert: *Adam Silver (1765–1795)* (London, 1965)
Truman, Charles, ed.: *Sotheby's Concise Encyclopedia of Silver* (London, 1993)

TEXTILES
Bath, Virginia Churchill: *Needlework in America: History, Designs, and Techniques* (London, 1979)
Beck, Thomasina: *The Embroiderer's Story: Needlework from the Renaissance to the Present Day* (Newton Abbot, 1995)
Blum, Dilys E.: *The Fine Art of Textiles* (Philadelphia, 1997)
Blum, Dilys E. and Haugland, H. Kristina: *Best Dressed: Fashion from the Birth of Couture to Today* (Philadelphia, 1998)
Brett, Gerard: *English Samplers* (London, 1951)
Bridgeman, H. and Drury, E.: *Needlework: An Illustrated History* (London, 1978)
Bryson, Agnes F.: *Ayrshire Needlework* (London, 1989)
Earnshaw, Pat: *Needlelace* (London and New York, 1991)

Edwards, Joan: *Sampler Making 1540–1940* (Dorking, 1983)
Farrell, Jeremy: *Umbrellas and Parasols* (London, 1985)
De la Haye, Amy, ed.: *The Cutting Edge: 50 Years of British Fashion, 1947–1997* (London, 1997)
Granick, Eve: *The Amish Quilt* (Intercourse, 1989)
Hughes, Robert: *Amish: The Art of the Quilt* (London, 1994)
Humphrey, Carol: *Samplers* (Cambridge, 1997)
Inder, P.M.: *Honiton Lace* (Exeter, 1971)
King, Donald: *Samplers* (London, 1960)
Kiracofe, Rod: *The American Quilts* (New York, 1993)
Laver, James: *Costume and Fashion: A Concise History* (London, 1995)
Leszner, Eva Maria: *Stickmustertücher* (Rosenheim, 1985)
Levey, Santina M.: *Lace: A History* (London, 1983)
Orlofsky, Myron and Patsy: *Quilts in America* (New York and London, 1974)
Reigate, Emily: *An Illustrated Guide to Lace* (Woodbridge, 1986)
Ring, Betty: *Girlhood Embroidery: American Samplers & Pictorial Needlework, 1650–1850* (New York, 1993)
Ring, Betty, ed.: *Needlework: An Historical Survey* (Pittstown, 1984)
Rothstein, Natalie, ed.: *Four Hundred Years of Fashion* (London, 1984)
Sichel, Marion: *History of Men's Costume* (London, 1984)
Sichel, Marion: *History of Women's Costume* (London, 1984)
Soltow, Willow Ann: *Quilting the World Over* (Radnor, 1991)
Tarrant, Naomi E.A.: *The Development of Costume* (London, 1994)

TOYS & GAMES
Ayres, William S.: *The Warner Collector's Guide to American Toys* (New York, 1981)
Barenholtz, Bernard and McClintock, Inez: *American Antique Toys* (New York and London, 1980)
Carlson, Pierce: *Toy Trains* (New York and London, 1986)
Foster, Michael: *Hornby-Dublo Trains* (London, 1980)
Franklin, M. J.: *British Biscuit Tins* (London, 1984)
Fuller, Roland: *The Bassett-Lowke Story* (London, 1984)
Gardiner, Gordon and Morris, Alastair: *Metal Toys* (London, 1984)
Gardiner, Gordon and O'Neill, Richard: *Toy Cars* (London, 1985)
Garratt, John, G.: *The World Encyclopedia of Model Soldiers* (London,1981)
Graebe, Chris and Julie: *The Hornby Gauge "0" System* (London, 1994)
Hammond, Pat: *Triang Railways* (London, 1993)
Hornby, Frank: *Life Story of Meccano* (London 1979)
Johnson, Peter: *Toy Armies* (London, 1982)
Joplin, Norman: *British Toy Figures 1900 to the Present* (London, 1987)
Joplin, Norman: *The Great Book of Hollow-cast Figures* (London, 1993)
Joplin, Norman: *Toy Soldiers* (London, 1994)
Joyce, J.: *Collectors' Guide to Model Railways* (Hemel Hempstead, 1977)
King, Constance: *Metal Toys and Automata* (London, 1989)
Kurtz, Henry I. and Erlich, Burtt: *The Art of the Toy Soldier* (London,1979)
Marchand, F.: *Motos-Jouets: L'Automobiliste* (Paris, 1985)
Miller's Antiques Checklist: *Toys & Games* (London, 1995)
Opie, James: *The Great Book of Britains* (London, 1993)
Pressland, David: *Pressland's Great Book of Tin Toys* (London, 1995)
Reder, Gustav: *Clockwork, Steam and Electric: A History of Model Railways up to 1939* (Middlesex, 1972)
Tempest, Jack: *Collecting Tin Toys* (London, 1987)

Index

Page numbers in *italic* refer to illustrations;
page numbers in **bold** refer to main entries

A

Aalto, Aino 456
Aalto, Alvar 415, 417, *417*, 419, 448, 450, *450*, 456
Abaquesne, Masséot 156
Abels, Gustav *293*
"Academic" period, Meissen **176**, 207
accessories, costume *346*, *346*
acid etching, glass 279, *279*, **295**, *295*, 398
Acier, Michel-Victor 176
Ackermann, Rudolf 117
Acoma pottery 171, *171*
"acorn" clocks 357
acorn knops, drinking glasses *281*
"Act of Parliament" clocks 352
Adam, James 166, 330
    Works in Architecture 60
Adam, Robert 166
    bookcases 96
    cabinets 85, 93, 95
    candlesticks and chandeliers 231, 307
    Neo-classical style 37, 89, 330
    painted furniture 25
    pier and console tables 58
    tureens 242
    Works in Architecture 60
Adam, William *240*
Adam fluted legs *20*
Adams, George 532, 534, *534*
"Admiral" carpet 331, *331*
"Admiral Fitzroy" barometers 364, *365*
advertising
    fans 346
    posters 410–11, *410*, 444–5
    sporting figures *537*
    trays *454*
Aesop 186, 201
Aesthetic Movement 84, 146, 147
    bureaux 101
    chairs 35
    furniture **372**, 373
    porcelain 215
    tiles 155
Affleck, Thomas 31, 62, 89
Afghanistan, rugs and carpets 325
African art 415, 418, 438
Afshar rugs 319
agate glass 284
agate ware **163**
Aimone, C.A. 84
air-twist stems, drinking glasses 279, 281, *303*, *303*
Airbourne International 451
Airfix 516, *517*
Aizdu Bamboo Co. 84
Akstafa *322*, 323
alabastron *284*
albarelli 152, *152*, 154
Albert, Prince Consort 264, 268, *308*, 484
Albrecht V, Duke of Bavaria 498
"album" quilts 341, *341*
Alcaraz 331, *331*
Alchimia 465, 466, 471
Alco 513
Alcock, Samuel & Co. 209, 211, 213
Alcora 150
Aldegrever, Heinrich *158*
Aldgate 162
Aldis 483

ale glasses *281*
Alessi 469, 472–3
Alexander Doll Co. 493
Alexander I, Tsar 219
Alexander II, Tsar 219
Alexandra, Princess 266
Alfonso III, King of Spain 416–17
alkalis, glass 276
alla certosina inlays 25
Allison, Michael *68*
almandine garnets 262
Alps 74, 77
Alps Shoji Ltd 518, *519*
alterations, furniture **26–7**, *26*
Althof Bergmann 494, *494*
amaranth **22**, *22*
Amberina glass 287, *287*
amboyna **22**, *22*
"Amen" wine glasses *278*, 294
America *see* United States of America
American Belleek 221, *221*
American China Manufactory 220, *220*
American China Works 221
American "Chippendale"
    chairs **31**, *31*
    tables 19
American Civil War 338
American Encaustic Tiling Co. 155
American Flyer 513
American War of Independence *58*, 257
amethysts *262*
Amish quilts 341, *341*
amphora 300
Amstel 186, 187
Amstelhoeck factory **395**
Amsterdam 36, 73, 86, 160, 540
Amsterdam School 395
Anatolia 316, 317, 320, 326
anchor escapement, clocks 350, 351, *351*
anchor pins *269*
andirons *384*
André, Emile 391
Andries, Jaspar 162
Androuet du Cerceau, Jacques, *Petites Grotesques* 72
aneroid barometers **365**, *365*
angle barometers **364**, *364*, 365
Anglo-Irish glass 296, 298, 307
Angoulême, Duke of 195, *195*
animals
    folk art 542
    jewelry 268
    porcelain 213, *213*, 217
    soft toys 495, *495*
Annagelb glass 285
Annagrün glass 285
Annapolis, Maryland 60
Anne, Queen of England 162, 498
    see also Queen Anne style
annular knops, drinking glasses *281*
Ansbach 99, 159
"Antique" style dining-chairs **38**
Antwerp 162
    escritoires 102
    glass 302
    metalware 540
    tiles 155
    tin-glazed earthenware 160
apostle spoons **244**, *244*, 245
Apple Inc. 473
applied decoration, ceramics **124**, *124*
appliqué
    pictures *338*
    quilts 340, *340*

aquamarines *262*
"Arabesque" service 194, *194*
Arabia 477
Arad, Ron 468
Arak 319
Arcade Manufacturing Co. 505
"Archaic" period, maiolica 152
"Archaic" wares, Chinese ceramics 139
Archelais, Jules *197*
Arequipa Pottery 380, *380*
Argand, Aimé 307
Argand lamps 307, *307*
Argy-Rousseau, Gabriel 399, *399*, **430**, *430*
Argyle Street Tea Room, Glasgow 373, *373*
Arita porcelain 142, *142*, 143, **146**, *146*, 147
armadio (linen-press) 73
armchairs 19, 29, *29*, **30–2**, *30–2*, **34–5**, *34–5*, *375*
Armenians 321
armillary spheres 532
armoires **73–5**, *74–5*
armorial wares, glass 288, *297*
Armstrong, William 218
Arneson, Robert 463, 477
Arnold 518
Arnold, John Roger *360*
Arrailos 331
arraiolos (embroidered carpets) 331
Arredolce 453
Art Deco **414–45**
    ceramics 414, **422–7**, *422–7*
    clocks 361
    costume 344
    furniture *415*, **416–21**, *416–21*
    glass 276, **428–35**, *428–35*
    jewelry **438–9**, *438–9*
    metalwork **436–7**, *436–7*
    perfume bottles 549, *549*
    posters 414, **444–5**, *444–5*
    sculpture 415, **440–3**, *440–3*
    silver 259
    watches 367
"Art Furniture" 467
Art Nouveau **386–411**
    ceramics **394–7**, *394–7*
    furniture **390–3**, *390–3*
    glass 276, 301, **398–403**, *398–403*
    jewelry **406–7**, *406–7*
    metalwork **404–5**, *404–5*
    perfume bottles 549
    posters **410–11**, *410–11*
    sculpture **408–9**, *408–9*
    silver *235*, *254*, 259, *259*
    wardrobes 77
art potteries 377, 378, **422**
Art Union of London 214
Art Workers' Guild 370, 372
Arte joven 388
arte povera 99, 101
Artek 417, *417*, 450
Arteluce 453, 471
Artemide 453, *471*
Artifort 451
Artigas, Josep Llorens 422
Artigues, Aimé-Gabriel d' 299
Arts Craft Shop, Buffalo, NY **385**
Arts and Crafts Exhibition Society 370, 372
Arts and Crafts Movement **377–85**
    ceramics 370, **376–81**, *376–81*
    costume 342

furniture 101, 111, *370*, **371–5**, *371–5*
    jewelry **406**, *406*
    metalwork **382–5**, *382–5*
Artworkers' Guild 376
aryballos 276
AS company 513, *513*
Aschaffenburg 178
Ashbee, Charles Robert 370
    Guild of Handicraft 372, 373, **382**
    jewelry **406**, *406*
    metalwork **382**, *382*
Askew, Richard 210
asmalyk (camel trappings) 325, *325*
Astbury, Thomas 165
astrolabes 533
Attwell, Mabel Lucie 427, 441
Au Bon Marché 414, 418
Aubusson
    carpets 314, 327, **329**, *329*
    tapestries 115
    upholstery 34
Audemars Piguet 367
Auffenwerth, Sabina 177
Auffenwerth family 177
Augarten Factory 189
Augsburg
    cabinets-on-stands 86
    escritoires 102
    Hausmaler 177
    occasional tables 66
Auguste, Henri 231
Augustus III, Elector of Saxony 235
Augustus the Strong, Elector of Saxony 173, 174, 175
Ault, William 377
Ault Pottery 376
aumbries 72
"Aurelian" wares 396
Austin, Walter 216
Austria
    Art Deco *414*, *424*, *424*, *432*, **436**
    Art Nouveau 388, **392–3**, 396–7, l *400*, *400*, 407
    Biedermeier style 32
    bonheurs du jour 104
    ceramics **396–7**, *424*, *424*
    chests 71
    clocks 353
    dining-chairs 38
    dolls 480
    furniture **392–3**
    glass *278*, *279*, *291*, *291*, *293*, **400**, *400*, **432**
    jewelry 407
    metalwork **436**
    mirrors 113
    porcelain **188–9**, *188–9*
    posters 444
    pot-cupboards 110
    secrétaires 103
    silver 238
    wardrobes 77
    Wiener Werkstätte **405**
Autio, Rudy 476, **477**, *477*
autographs, rock and pop memorabilia 550
automata 494, *494*
automaton clocks **362**, *362*, 363
Avril, Jane 410, *410*
awards, rock and pop memorabilia 550, *550*
Axminster carpets 330, *330*
Ayres, Frederick 502
Ayrshire whitework 338, *338*

B

Baccarat
  cameo glass 301, *301*
  cut glass 299, *299*
  jeweling 305
  lighting 306, 307
  opaline glass *286*
  paperweights 308, *308*, 309
  perfume bottles 549, *549*
  "tinted-rose" wares 287
Baccetti, Andrea 93
Bacchus, George & Sons 291, *291*, 309, *309*
Bach, Martin 402
Bach, Oscar 436, 437
Bachelier, Jean-Jacques 193, *193*
bachelors' chests **80**, 80
Bachmann 513
backgammon tables *68*
Badlam, Stephen 89
bags 346
Bailey, Charles A. 505
Bailey, William Willis 213
Baillie Scott, Mackay Hugh 370, 372, 373, *373*
Bain, Alexander 361
Bakelite 415
Baker, Ginger 551
Baker, Josephine 415, 444
Bakewell, Benjamin 297
Bakewell's 297, 301, 305
Bakker, Gijs 470
Bakst, Léon 415, 430
Baldwyn, Charles 216
Balenciaga, Christóbal 344, *344*
Balikesir 326
Balkans, kilims 326
Ball, William 200
ball knops, drinking glasses *281*
ball stoppers, glass *280*
Ballets Russes 415, 430–1
balloon-back chairs 21, *40*
balls
  baseball *537*
  golf 537
Balmain, Pierre 344
Balmoral Castle 342
Balsamo-Stella, Guido 432
Baltimore, Maryland 56, 60, 171, *341*
Baluchistan 326
baluster legs *20*
baluster stems, drinking glasses *281*
Balzac, Jean-François 230
Bamberger Metallwerkstätte *417*
bambocci 72
bamboo
  carvings 525, *525*
  imitation 84
bangles 267, *267*, 439, *470*
"banjo" barometers 364–5, *364*, *365*
"banjo" clocks 353
banks, cast-iron **505**, *505*
"bantamwork" screens 114
Baotou 327
"Barbie" dolls 493, *493*
Barbin, François 192
Barclay 515
Barfoot, J.W. *503*
Bargello stitch, canvaswork 337, *337*
barilla, glass 276
Barker, John *208*
Barker Brothers Furniture Co. 421
barley twist legs *20*
Barlow, Arthur 377

Barlow, Edward 351
Barlow, Florence 377, *377*
Barlow, Hannah 377
Barnard, Edward & Sons 251
Barnard, John *230*
Barnsley, Ernest 372
Barnsley, Sidney 372, 419, *419*
barometers **364–5**, *364–5*
Baroque style
  cabinets-on-stands 86
  dining-chairs 36
  display cabinets 92
  easy chairs 30
  figures 174
  furniture 20
  glass 278
  mirrors 112, *113*
  porcelain *191*
  pottery 156
  silver **230**, 237, 250
  tables 58, *59*
  wardrobes 77
Barovier, Angelo 276
Barovier, Anton 288
Barovier, Ercole 432, *432*, 457, *457*
Barovier & Toso 457, *474*
bar pins 265
Barr, Flight & Barr 208, *208*, 212
Barr, Martin 208
Barraclough & Sons *229*
barrel decanters *280*
Barrias, Ernest 408
Barrois, Madame 485
baseball **537**, *537*
baskets
  Belleek 218, *218*
  porcelain *181*
  pottery *165*
  silver 226, **239**, *239*
Bassano 154
Bassett-Lowke, W.J. & Co. **511**, *511*
"bat-printing," porcelain 211
Bateman family 251
Battersea enamels 546
Baudot, Guillaume *254*
Baudouine, Charles A. *76*
Bauhaus 415
  ceramics 424
  furniture 416, 420
  metalwork 436, *436*, 437
Bavaria 159
Baxter, Thomas 208, 209, *209*, 212
Baxter, Geoffrey 457
Bayreuth 159, *159*
"Beaconsfield" wardrobes 76
"Beaded" pattern, flatware 245
beakers
  glass 279, *284*, *285*, 288, *290*, *292*, *298*, *304*
  porcelain *173*, *193*
  silver *227*, **246**, *246*, 247
bears *see* teddy bears
The Beatles 550, *551*
Beatty, Frank 445
bébés 488–9, *488–9*
Bechstein 372
Beckford, William 59
bedroom suites 83
beds **116–17**, *116–17*, *391*
bedside tables **110–11**, *110*
Beebe, Robert 445
beehive feet, drinking glasses *281*
beeldenkast (cupboard) 72, 78
Beeton, Mrs 544

Behaim, Martin 532
Behrens, Peter 404, 405
Beijing 327 , 405
Beilby, Mary 289
Beilby, William 289
Beilby family 289, *289*
Bel Geddes, Norman 415, 437, *437*
Belfast Glassworks 296
Belfort, May 410
Belgium
  Art Deco ceramics 423, *423*
  Art Nouveau 388, **392**, 393
  furniture **392**, 393
  glass 282, **298–9**, *299*
  lace 347
  posters 410, *410*
  samplers 339
Bell, John 214
Bell, Vanessa 372
"Bell toys" 504–5
bell-shaped drinking glasses *281*
Belleek 218, *218*, 221
Belleville 198
Belloni *364*
bells, glass *310*
Belouch 324, 325, *325*
Belter, John Henry **35**, *35*, 45
Bemrose, William *210*
"Bemrose" garniture *210*
Benckgraff, Johann Kilian 180
"Benedict" wardrobes 76
Benesch, Markus *465*
Bennett, Mr 406
Bennington, Vermont 170, *170*, 171, 214, 216
Benson, William Arthur Smith **382–3**, *383*
Bentley, Percival A. 361
Bentley, Thomas 166
bentwood chairs **41**, *41*, 392
Bérain, Jean I 38, *156*, 192
Bergama *320*, 326
bergères 30, 31, *31*, 32
bergères en confessionnal 30, *30*
Berkemeyer glasses 289
Berkey & Gay 117
Berks County, Pennsylvania 71
Berlin
  bureaux 99
  faience 159
  glass 290
  porcelain **180**, *180*, **182–3**, *182–3*, 185
"Berlin ironwork" jewelry 271, *271*
Berlin porcelain factory 396, 485
"Berlin transparencies" 185
Berlin woolwork 34, *337*, 337, 339
Berliner Metallgewerbe 416–17
Bernard, Nicholas 62, *64*
Bernard, Oliver 419
Bernhardt, Sarah 389, 407, 410
Bernini, Gian Lorenzo 92
Bertoia, Harry 448, 451, *451*, 452
Bertrand-Parand, F.J. *232*
Beschefer, James 259
Beshir 324, 325
Bessarabia 326, *326*
Beswick, John 217
Bettignies, Amélie de 186
Beurdeley, Louis-Auguste-Alfred 94

"Biedermeier" dolls 482, 485
Biedermeier period
  commodes *82*
  easy chairs 32, *32*
  glass 288, 290, *290*, 298
  porcelain 181, 182, 189, 220
  pot-cupboards 110
  secrétaires 103
  tables *67*
  wardrobes 77
Biemann, Dominik 293, *298*
Bigaglia, Pietro 308
bijouteries 92
Billingsley, William 210, 212
Biloxi Pottery 380
Bilston enamel 546, *546*
Binder, Joseph *414*, 444
Bing, Adolf 508
Bing, Franz 511
Bing, Gebrüder 495, 496, **508**, *508*, 511
Bing, Ignatz 508
Bing, Samuel 392, 404
Bing, Siegfried 388, 389, 391
Bing, Stefan 511
Bing & Grondahl 397
Binns, Richard William 215
Binns, Charles Fergus 462
birch **22**, *22*
birds, folk art 542, *542*
bird's-eye maple **22**, *22*
Birge and Fuller *357*
Birmingham
  brass 540
  cardcases 544
  enamel 546, *547*
  silver 225, 231, 232, 233, *548*
biscuit porcelain 194, *199*
biscuit tins 509
bisque
  dolls **486–91**, *486–91*
  fairings **185**, *185*
black basalte 166, *166*
Black Forest 360, 396
Black Forest clocks **362**, *362*, 363
Blairsy, Léo Laporte 409
blanc-de-Chine 124, 137, 173, 192
blanket chests 71, *71*
blankets, Native American Indian 332–3, *332*
blazes, cut glass *280*
"bleeding bowls" 259
Bleuler, John *532*
Bliss, Rufus 499, *499*
Bliss (R.) Manufacturing Co. 502
Bloomfield, John Caldwell 218
Bloor, Robert *210*
blowing glass 276
"blown-three-mold" glass 282
"blowout" technique, glass 398
blue-and-white wares
  Chinese 134, *134*, 136, **138**, *138*
  Dutch 160
  Japanese 142, *142*
  porcelain **204–5**, *204–5*
  printed wares 167, *167*
  underglaze blue decoration **204**, *204*
  Worcester 203
"blue-dash" chargers 162, *162*
board-games **503**, *503*
boat-shaped teapots 249, *249*
boats, tinplate 506, 507, *507*, 508
bobbin knops, drinking glasses 281
bobbin lace 347, *347*
bobbin-turned chairs *21*

bobbin-turned legs *20*
Boch Frères 423
bodies, dolls **480**
Bohemian glass 276
　cameo glass **301**
　candelabra *306*
　colored glass **284**, *284*, **285**, *285*, 286
　cut glass **298**, *298*
　enameled glass **288–9**, *288–9*, 290, *290*
　engraved glass 278, **292**, 293, *293*
　gilding **304**, *304*
　sulphides 305
Bohemian porcelain 177, 184, 189
Boizot, Louis-Simon 194
"Bokhara" carpets 325
Bologna *78*
Bolsover, Thomas 256
bombé bureaux 99
bombé commodes **80**, *80*, 84
Bonaparte dynasty 268
bone china 122, 211, 213, 214, 216
bone inlays 25
Bonham, John 551
bonheurs de jour 66, 104, *104*
bonnet top pediments 89
"bonnet-head" dolls *484*
bonnets 343
Bonnin, Goussin 220, *220*
Bonnin & Morris 220, *220*, 221
Bontems, Blaise 494
bookcases **96–7**, *96–7*, *374*, 420
　secrétaire bookcases *103*
books, cricket 536, *536*
bookshelves 97, *97*
bookstands 97, *97*
Booth, Enoch 165
boots 343
Bordalo, Rafael *151*
Bordeaux 68, 74
Borderel & Robert 436
Boreman, Zachariah 210
Borgfeldt, George 490
Borromini, Francesco 92
Bos, Cornelis 160
Bosque Redondo 332
Boston
　chests-of-drawers *81*
　chests-on-chests 89
　glass 297
　high chests-of-drawers 87
　silver *248*
　tables *59*, *64*
Boston & Sandwich Glass Co. 283, 287, 301, 309, *309*, 311
Bottengruber, Ignaz 177
Böttger, Johann Friedrich 173, 188
bottle rings, silver *255*
bottle vases, porcelain 200, *221*
bottles
　glass *284*, **310–11**, *311*, *524*
　Oriental ceramics *133*, *134*, *136*, *138*, *139*, *141*, *143*, *144*
　pottery *162*
　snuff bottles **524**, *524*, 525
　see also perfume bottles
Bouchardon, Edmé 174
Boucher, François 84, 178, 188, 193, 196
Boucheron 404, 438, 439
Boulle, André-Charles 25, 38, 55, 65, 69, *94*
　bombé commodes 80
　bureaux Mazarins 107
　clock cases 355
　display cabinets 92
　marquetry 86
　writing tables *105*
　see also Buhl work
Boullework *see* Buhl work

Boulton, Matthew
　candlesticks 233
　cut-steel jewelry *265*
　Sheffield plate 256
　silver *234*, 243
Boulton and Fothergill 546
Bouraine, Marcel-André **440**, *440*
Bourbon Restoration 329
Bouval, Maurice 408, 409
Bovirke and France & Sons 450
Bow 144
　blue-and-white wares **204**, *204*, 205
　copies 199
　figures **129**, 202, *202*
　porcelain *122*, 200, **202**, *202*
Bowen, James H. *505*
bowl shapes, drinking glasses *281*
bowls
　glass *276*, *279*, *283*, *284*, *289*, *296*, *300*, *431*
　Oriental ceramics *132*, *138*, *139*, *140*
　porcelain *122*, *177*, *423*
　postmodernist *472*, *473*
　pottery *149*, *150*
　silver **250–1**, *437*
　studio ceramics *461*, *462*
Bowyer, William *352*
box-settles 42, *42*
boxes **544–7**, *544–7*
　enamel **546**, *546*
　etuis **546**, *546*
　folk art **542**, *542*
　lacquerware *527*
　Oriental ceramics *135*
　porcelain *215*
　tea caddies **547**, *547*
Boyer, Edith 504
Boyer, Israel Donald 504
Boyer, Victor *198*, 199
Boyle, Robert 364
Boyne, Battle of the (1690) 294
BPI (British Phonographic Industry) 550
bracelets **267**, *267*, *406*, *438*, *439*, *452*
"bracket-and-overmantel" style 39
bracket clocks **356–8**, *356–8*
bracket feet *20*
Braga *151*
Brameld family 213
Brandjes, Weduwe N.S.A. & Co. 395, *395*
Brandt, Edgar 429, 436, 437
Brandt, Marianne 415, 436
Branzi, Andrea 471
brass **540–1**, *540*
　beds 117
　clocks 352
　inlays *25*, *25*, 38
Braun 454, 455
break-front bookcases 96, 97
breakfast tables **54–5**, *54–5*
breeches 345
Breguet, Abraham-Louis 359
Breslau 177
Bretby Art Pottery 377
Breuer, Marcel 415, 416, *416*, 417, 419, *447*
Brianchon, Jules-Joseph-Henri 199
Briant, Thomas 200
Briati, Giuseppe 307
Bridge, John *254*
bridge fluting, cut glass *280*
Bridgewater 90
bright-cut engraving, silver **226**, *226*
Brighton Pavilion 84
"Brilliant" period, American glass 297, *297*, 298
brisé fans 346
Brislington *162*
Bristol
　clocks 355

delftware 162, *162*
glass 286, *286*, 304
porcelain 200, *200*, 203, 204, 205, **207**, *207*
Britain
　Art Deco
　　ceramics **426–7**, *426–7*
　　furniture **419**, *419*
　　glass 433
　Arts and Crafts Movement
　　ceramics **376–7**, *376–7*
　　furniture **370**, *370*
　beds 116, 117
　Berlin woolwork 337
　bonheurs du jour 104, *104*
　bookcases **96–7**, *96*, *97*
　brass **540**, *540*
　bureaux **98**, *98*, 100–1
　cabinet-makers' marks 76
　cabinets-on-stands 86
　canterburies 108, *108*
　ceramics
　　Art Deco **426–7**, *426–7*
　　Art Nouveau **396**, *396*, 397
　　Arts and Crafts **376–7**, *376–7*
　　porcelain **200–18**, *200–18*
　　pottery **162–9**, *162–9*
　　studio ceramics **460–1**, *460–1*
　chairs
　　construction 19
　　country chairs 33, *33*
　　dining-chairs 36, *36*, 38, *38*, 39, 40, *40*
　　early chairs 29, *29*
　　easy chairs 30, *31*, 34, *34*
　　hall chairs 32, *32*
　chaises-longues 43, 44
　chests 70, 71, *71*
　chests-of-drawers **78–81**, *78–81*, 83, *83*, *85*
　chests-on-chests **88**, *88*
　clocks **354**, *354*, **355**, *355*, **359**, *359*
　commodes 81, *85*
　costume 342, *343*, 344
　crewelwork **336**, *336*
　Davenports 106, *106*
　display cabinets **92–3**
　dolls 480, *482*, 483, *484*, *484*, *492*, 493
　dolls' houses **498–9**, *498*
　dressers **90–1**, *90–1*
　dumb waiters 109, *109*
　escritoires 102, *102*
　glass 276, 278
　　Art Deco 433
　　Art Nouveau **401**, *401*
　　cameo glass **300–1**, *300–1*
　　candlesticks *306*
　　colored glass **286**, *286*
　　cut glass **296**, *296*
　　enameled glass **289**, *289*, 290, **291**, *291*
　　engraved glass **294–5**, *294–5*
　　gilding **304**
　　lamps **307**, *307*
　　mid-century modern glass 457
　　paperweights *309*, *309*
　　pressed glass **283**, *283*
　　studio glass **475**
　　sulpides 305
　high chests-of-drawers 87, *87*
　imitation bamboo furniture 84
　jewelry 264, **406**, *406*, 452
　kneehole desks 107, *107*
　knife-boxes 118
　lace 347, *347*
　linen-presses 74, 75, *75*
　mid-century modern furniture **449**
　mirrors **112–13**, *112*, *113*

night tables **110**, 111, *111*
painted furniture 74
peat-buckets 119
pedestal desks 107, *107*
perfume bottles **548**, *548*
pot-cupboards 111, *111*
quilts 340, *340*
regulators 360, *360*
rock and pop memorabilia 550
rugs and carpets 330, *330*
salon suites 44
samplers 339, *339*
screens *114*, 115
secrétaires 103, *103*
settees 42, *42*
settles 42, *42*
shawls 343
side cabinets 94, *94*, 95
sideboards 61, *61*
silver **224**, *224*
　candelabra **234–5**, *234*, *235*
　candlesticks **230–3**, *230*, *231*, *233*
　dining silver **236–43**, *236–43*
　drinking vessels **246–7**, *246–7*
　flatware **244–5**, *244–5*
　hallmarks 225
　miscellaneous **258–9**, *258–9*
　serving beverages **248–53**, *248–52*
　serving wine and spirits **254–7**, *254–7*
sofas 45
stools 28, *28*
stumpwork 336
tables
　breakfast tables *54*
　center tables 55
　console, pier and side tables 58, *58*
　dining-tables **50–3**, *50–3*
　dressing tables **62–3**, *63*
　dropleaf tables 49
　drum tables *54*
　early tables 46, *46*, 47, *47*
　games and work tables **68–9**, *68*, *69*
　gateleg tables 48
　occasional tables 66, *66*, 67, *67*
　Pembroke tables 56, *56*
　serving tables 60, *60*
　sofa tables 57, *57*
　Sutherland tables 49
　tea tables 64
　tripod tables 64, *64*
　writing tables 105, *105*
teapoys 65, *65*
teddy bears 496, **497**, *497*
tiles 155, *155*
toys **509**, *509*, **516–17**, *516–17*
　lead and plastic figures **515**, *515*
　soft toys **495**, *495*
　trains **512**, *512*
　wood and paper toys 502, *502*, 503, *503*
trays 118, *118*
wardrobes 76, *76*, 77, *77*
washstands 111, *111*
whatnots 109, *109*
wine coolers and cellarets 119
Britains 499, 514, 515, *515*
"Britannia" metal 541
"Britannia" standard, silver **224**, *250*
British National Dolls *480*, 493, *493*
British Plate Glass Manufactory 112
Brittany 74
Brocard, Philippe-Joseph 291, 304
Brock, Robert *247*
Brock, Sir Thomas 214, 408
Brocket Hall 37
brodérie perse quilts 341
Broders, Roger 444, *444*
Brodie, Francis *58*

broken-arch pediments *87, 89*
broken pediments *89*
Brongniart, Alexander 194
bronze 540
　gilt bronze (ormolu) decoration 25
　Oriental **522**, *522, 523*
　sculpture 408, 440, *440, 441*
Brooklyn, New York City 220
Brooklyn Flint Glass Co. 297
Brower & Rusher 240
Brown, Ford Madox 371, *371*, 377
Brown, George W. & Co. 504, *504*
Brown-Westhead, Moore & Co. 215
Brownfield, W. & Sons 215
Bru, Léon Casimir 487
Bru Jeune & Cie 487, *487*, **488**, *488*, 489
Bruant, Aristide 410
Bruckmann, Peter 404–5
Bruckmann & Söhne 404
Bruges lace 347
Brühl, Count Heinrich von 175
Brummell, George "Beau" 270, 345
Brunetti, Gaetano, *60 Different Sorts of Ornament* 37
Brunetto, Tomas *151*
Brunswick 159
Brunswick tea tables 64
brushes, silver *259*
brushpots *525*
Brussa, Angelo 288
Brussa, Oswaldo 288, *288*
Brussels lace 347, *347*
Brustolon, Andreas 30, *30*, 59
Brychtova, Jaroslava 456–7
Bub, Karl 506, 508, 511
Bubb, J. 498
Buchanan Street Tea Room, Glasgow 373
Buchner 506
buckelplatte 160
bucket-shaped drinking glasses *281*
buckets **119**, *119*
buckles, silver **259**, *259*
Buco 513
Buddha 522, *522*
Buddhism 327, 522
Buen Retiro *123*, **190**, *190*
buffets 60, 61, 90
Bugatti, Carlo 389, 393, *393*, 405, *405*
Buhl work (Boullework)
　bureaux 100
　chairs 38
　clocks *356*
　tables 55, *55*
　wine coolers and cellarets 119
　writing tables *105*
bulb vases **310**, *310*
Bulle clocks 361, *361*
bullet-shaped teapots, silver 248, *248*, 249
Bullock, George *52*, 100, 107, 119
bun feet *20*
Buquoy, Count Georg Franz August Langueval von 285
bureau à cylindre 99, *99*, 100
bureau à rognon 100
bureau cabinets *26*
bureau de dame 99, *99*, 100, *100, 101*, 104
bureau Mazarin 107, *107*
bureau plat 105
bureaux **98–101**, *98–101*
bureaux cabinets 98, *98*, 101
bureaux-on-stands *104*
Burges, William 53, 254, 371
Burgundy 73, *73*
Burke, Edmund *305*
Burlington, Lord 58, 112
Burmantofts Faience 377
"Burmese" glassware 286, 287, *287*

burnishing, gilding **125**, *125*
Burns, Robert 309
burr-elm 22
burr-walnut 23, *23*
burr-yew 23, *23*
Burslem 166, 168, 211
Bush 455, *455*
Bushman of London *352*
Bustelli, Franz Anton 179, *179*, 190
busts
　parian **214**, *214*
　porcelain *195*
Bute, John Stuart, 1st Marquess of *237*
Buthaud, René 415, 422, *422*
butler's-trays 66, *118*
butter dishes, glass *296*
butter-pats, pottery *171*
Butterfield, William *111*
butterfly pins *265, 271, 406*
butterfly tables 49
butterfly veneering 24, *24*
buttoned upholstery 45
buttoned-back chairs 21, 34
Butz, Mary *339*

C

cabaret sets, porcelain *197*
cabinet cups 182, *183*
cabinet-makers' marks **76**
cabinet plates, porcelain 216
cabinets 373, *375, 390, 391, 421, 449*
　bureaux cabinets 26, **98**, *98, 101*
　cabinets-on-stands 86, *86, 371*
　display cabinets 86, **92–3**, *92–3*
　side cabinets **94–5**, *94–5*
　writing cabinets-on-stands **104**, *104*
　see also cupboards
cabochons, gemstones *262*
cabriole legs *20*
cachepots, stoneware *166*
caddies, silver 250, *250*, 251
caddy spoons, silver **245**
Caen lace 347
Caernarvon 91
Cafe family 230
Cailland of Paris *358*
Cairo 316, 317, 331
Caithness Glass 309
calamander 22, *22*
calcedonio glass 284
calcium carbonate, glass 276
calculators 455
Caldas da Rainha 151, *151*
Calder, Alexander 452
"California Decorative" furniture 375
Californian School **381**
Callot, Jacques 188, *188*, 191
Callowhill, James 215, *215*
Callowhill, Thomas Scott 215, *215*
Calvert, Isabella *340*
Cambrian Works, Swansea 212
Cambridge, Duke of *212*
cameo glass **279**, *279*, **300–1**, *300–1*, 398
cameo pins *265*
cameos
　jewelry **263**, *263, 265*, **265**
　tassies 305, *305*
cameras **538**, *538*
camisoles *343*
campaign beds 117
campaign chest-of-drawers 83
Campin, Robert 114
canapés (sofas) 34, **42–3**, *42, 45*
candelabra
　Art Nouveau *404*
　glass **306**, *306*
　silver **234–5**, *234–5*
candlestands 66
candlesticks

brass 540, *540*
　glass 306, *306*
　silver **230–5**, *230–5*
caned seats, dining-chairs 38
canes, glass paperweights 308
caneware 166
cannetille, gold 262, *262*
Canova, Antonio 300
Cantagalli, Ulysse 154
"Canton" wares 136, *137*
canvaswork 337, *337*
Capodimonte *123*, **190**, *190*
Cappellini 468
Cappleman 298
caps
　football 536, *536*
　"night" 345
car mascots *428*
carafes, glass *276, 282*
carats, gold 262
card-racks, pottery *167*
card tables 68–9, *68, 69*
cardcases **529**, **544**, *544*
Cardeilhac 404
Carder, Frederick 402, 434
Cardew, Michael 460
cards, sporting memorabilia *536*, 537
care, furniture **27**, *27*
Carette, Georges & Cie 508, *508*, 511
Carlin, Martin 61, 66
Carlisle, Earl of 234
Carlisle & Finch 513
Carlton House, London 105
Carlton House desks 105
Carlton Works 427, *427*
Carltonware 427
Carlu, Jean 444
Carmarthen 91
"Carnival" glass 283, *283*, **435**
Carolean chairs *21*
Caroline Matilda, Queen of Denmark 187
carpets *see* rugs and carpets
carriage clocks 359, *359*
Carrier-Belleuse, Albert-Ernest 197
cars, toy 504, *504*, 507, *507*, 508, *508, 509*, **516–17**, *516–17*, 518
cartel clocks **353**, *353*
Carter, Howard 415
Carter, Stabler & Adams 427
Carter, Truda *427*
Carter & Co. 427
Cartier 367, 438, *438*, 439
Cartier, Louis 439
Cartlidge, Charles 220
Cartlidge & Co. 220, *221*
carving
　furniture 24, *24*, 71
　jewelry 262, *262*
　Oriental **524–5**, *524–5*
carvings, folk art 542, *542*
Casati, Cesare 471, *471*
cases **544–5**, *544–5*
caskets, silver 226
Cassandre, Adolphe Mouron 444
cassapanca 44
Cassiers, Henri 411
Cassina 416, 418, 449, *468*
cassoni **70**, *70, 73*
cast iron 541
　beds 117
　toys 504–5, *505*
Casteldurante 153
Castellani family 262, 265, 266, 267
Castelli 154, *154*
casters
　dining-tables 52
　furniture styles *20*
casters (pepper), silver **258**, 259

Castiglioni, Achille 453
Castiglioni, Pier Giacomo 453
casting
　ceramics 123, *123*
　glass 276
Castle, Wendell *466*, 467
Catherine the Great, Empress of Russia 165, 187, 219
Catteau, Charles 423, *423*
Caucasus, rugs and carpets 320, **322–3**, *322–3*, 326
caudle cups, silver 259
Caughley 167, 205, *205*, 209
celadon **123**, *123*, **132**, *132*, 133, 141
celery vases, glass 282
cellarets **119**, *119*
celluloid dolls **493**, *493*
Celtic motifs 406
Centennial Exhibition, Philadelphia (1876) 220, 297, 378
center tables 55, *55*
centerpieces, silver 238, *238*
Century Guild 372
Ceramic Art Co. 221
ceramics **120–221**
　Art Deco **414**, **422–7**, *422–7*
　Art Nouveau **394–7**, *394–7*
　Arts and Crafts 370, **376–81**, *376–81*
　collecting and care **128–9**, *128–9*
　fakes and forgeries **126–7**, *126–7*
　materials and techniques **122–5**, *122–5*
　mid-century modern **458–63**, *458–63*
　Oriental pottery and porcelain **130–47**, *130–47*
　porcelain **172–221**, *172–221*
　pottery **148–71**, *148–71*
　studio ceramics 425, **460–3**, *460–3*, **476–7**, *476–7*
Cervantes, Miguel *214*
Chad Valley 492, 495, 497, *497*, 499, 502, 503
Chaffers, Richard 200, 204, 205, *205*
chains, jewelry **266**
chairs
　Art Deco **416–17**, *416, 417, 418, 420, 421*
　Art Nouveau *392*
　Arts and Crafts 371, *371–4*, 374
　backs *21*
　construction 19, *19*, **40–1**
　country chairs 33, *33*
　dining-chairs **36–41**, *36–41*
　early chairs 29, *29*
　easy chairs **30–2**, *30–2*, **34–5**, *34–5*
　hall chairs 32, *32*
　mid-century modern 448, *448*, **450–1**, *451*
　postmodernist *466*, 468, *468–9*, 469
　side chairs 19, 31, 36, *36, 37, 38, 39*
chaise caquetoire (gossiping chair) 29
chaises-longues 43, *43*, 44, *44*
chalcedony glass 284, *284*
Chamberlain, Humphrey 208
Chamberlain, Humphrey junior 208
Chamberlain, Robert 208
Chamberlain & Co. 208
Chambers, Sir William 58, 88, 231
chambersticks, silver **231**, 233
champagne glasses 295
champagne pitchers, glass *287*
Champion, Richard 207
champlevé enamel, watches 366
chandeliers, glass **307**, *307*
Chanel, Gabrielle "Coco" 272, 273, 344, 346, 549
Chantilly lace 347
Chantilly porcelain 144, **192**, *192*, 193
Charbens & Co. 515
chargers *128, 146, 154, 162, 162, 376,*

422, *461–3*, *476*
Charles I, Duke of Brunswick 180
Charles I, King of England *336*
Charles II, King of England 44, 162, 244, 294, *294*
Charles III, King of Spain 190
Charles X, King of France 329
Charles X furniture 22, 59, 82
Charleston, South Carolina 89
Charlotte, Princess of Prussia *182*
Charlotte, Queen of England 68, 69, 165
Charol, Dorothea 442
Charpentier 298
Charrière, Joseph-Frédéric 535
Chase, Martha 492
Chase Brass and Copper Co. 437
chasing silver **226**, *226*
Chatsworth House, Derbyshire 95, 115
Chauvet 408
checkered diamond cut glass *280*
cheese bells, pottery *169*
Chein, J. & Co. 504
Chelaberd *323*
Chelsea porcelain 144, 200, **201**, *201*, 203
  blue-and-white wares 186, 204
  Chelsea-Derby period 201, 206
  clocks *123*
  copies 199
  figures 168
  saucers *129*
Chenghua period ceramics 134, 135, 139
Chéret, Jules 410
Cheret, Louis-Jean-Baptiste *257*
Cherilea Products 515
Cheshire 91
Chester, silver hallmarks 225
Chesterfield sofas 44
chests **70–1**, *70–1*, 73, 78, *467*, 542
  medicine chests **535**, *535*
chests-of-drawers **78–85**, *78–85*
  bachelor's chests **80**, *80*
  bombé commodes **80**, *80*, 84
  campaign chest-of-drawers 83
  chests-on-chests **88–9**, *88–9*
  chests-on-stands 87
  commodes **80–2**, *80–2*
  high chests-of-drawers **87**, *87*
  Wellington chests 83, *84*
cheval mirrors 113, *113*
cheval screens **115**, *115*
Cheverton, Benjamin 214
Cheverton's Reducing Machine 214
Chevrot 488
Chi Chi *323*
Chiavari 449
Chicaneau, Pierre 192
chiffoniers 94, *94*, 95
Chihuly, Dale 457, 474, *475*
Chiltern Toys 495, 497
China
  cardcases 544
  carvings **524–5**, *524*, *525*
  furniture 37, 86, *86*, 112
  ivory **529**, *529*
  jade **528**, *528*
  lacquerware **526**, *526*
  metalwork 522, *522*, 523, *523*
  porcelain fakes and copies **126**, *126*
  pottery and porcelain 92, **131–40**, *131–40*, 460
  rugs and carpets **327**, *327*
  screens 114, *114*
  silver *252*
  stoneware 122, 123
  tea caddies **547**, *547*
  see also chinoiserie
china dolls **485**, *485*
Chinchilla 331

chinoiserie
  blue-and-white wares 204
  cabinets-on-stands 86
  chairs *21*
  chests-of-drawers 84
  display cabinets 92–3
  glass *304*
  handles *21*
  needlework pictures 338
  porcelain 203, 206, *206*
  settees 42
  sideboards 60
  silver **226**, *226*, 249
chintzes, quilts 340, *340*
Chiparus, Dimitri (Demêtre) 415, *415*, **440–1**, *440*
Chippendale, Thomas
  bookcases 96
  chests-on-chests 88, 89
  commodes 81
  dining-chairs 37, 40
  dining-tables 50
  display cabinets 92–3, *92*
  drawer construction 18
  easy chairs 31, 32
  The Gentleman and Cabinet-Maker's Director 31, 32, 37, 40, 42, 44, 60, 62, 65, 81, 87, 88, 92, 96, 105, 111, 115, 118
  high chests-of-drawers 87
  mirrors 112
  piecrust "supper" tables 65
  screens 115
  settees 42, *44*
  side chairs 37
  sideboards 60
  trays 118
  washstands 111
  writing tables 105
Chippendale style
  chairs *21*
  chests-of-drawers *81*
  dining-chairs 39, *40*
  handles *21*
  mirrors 113
  settees *44*
  tables 53, *53*, 65
  see also American "Chippendale"
chocolate-cups, porcelain *211*
chocolate-pots, silver 252, 253, *253*
Choisy-le-Roi 287, 328
chokers 266
Choson period ceramics **141**
christening gowns, whitework *338*
christening ware, silver 227, *229*, 247
Christian VII, King of Denmark 187
Christian, Philip 204, 205
Christofle 253, 436, 437
chronometers 360, *360*
chryselephantine *415*, 440, 442
Churro sheep 332
çiçims 314, **326**
cigar bowls *405*
cigarette cases *415*, **545**, *545*
C.I.J. (Compagnie Industriel de Jouets) 509, *509*, 517
Cincinnati 378
cire perdue see lost-wax casting
cisterns 119
Citroën, André 509
Cizhou wares 132
Clapton, Eric 551
Clare, Joseph *241*
claret-jugs, silver 254, 255
Clark, D.P. & Co. 504, *504*
Clark, Ossie 344
Classical Greek style, porcelain *197*
Classical style furniture *20*
  see also Neo-classical style

claw-and-ball feet 20
"claw" beakers 279
claw settings, jewelry **263**, *263*
claw tables 54, 64
Clay, Henry 118
cleaning ceramics **128**
Clement, Jean 250
Clichy Glassworks 308, *308*
Cliff, Clarice 127, **426**, *426*, 427
Clifton 495, *495*
clip pins, Art Deco **438**, *438*
clocks **348–67**, *348–67*
  Art Deco *437*
  bracket clocks **356–8**, *356–8*
  carriage clocks **359**, *359*
  ceramic 123, 184, 198, 201, 395
  electric clocks **361**, *361*
  longcase clocks **354–5**, *354–5*
  mechanics **350–1**, *350–1*
  mid-century modern *455*
  novelty clocks **362–3**, *362–3*
  precision clocks and chronometers **360**, *360*
  wall clocks **352–3**, *352–3*
  watches **366–7**, *366–7*
cloisonné enamel
  jewelry **263**, *263*
  Oriental **522–3**, *522*
cloisonné wares, porcelain 215
closed-back settings, jewelry **263**, *263*
clothing **342–6**, *342–6*
  accessories **346**, *346*
  menswear **345**, *345*
  rock and pop memorabilia 550, *550*
  womenswear **342–4**, *342–4*
club-shaped decanters *280*
clubs, golf 537
cluster rings **264**, *264*
"Clutha" glass 401, *401*, 402
coaching tables 66, *67*
Coalbrookdale Co. 541
"Coalbrookdale" porcelain 209
Coalport 209, *209*, 210, 220
  dessert dishes *129*
  export wares 216
  Japanesque style 215, *215*
  parian busts and statues 214
  Rococo Revival 213
coasters, silver **255**, *255*
Coates, Wells 419
coats 345
Cobb, John 65, 81
Coca-Cola 454, *454*
cockade fans 346
cocktail shakers 437
"cocktail" watches 367
Cocteau, Jean 461, *461*
Codd, Hiram 311
coffee-cups and cans, porcelain *189*, *190*, *203*, *210*, *211*
coffee-pots
  Art Deco *414*
  folk art 543
  porcelain *173*, *176*, *177*, *180*, *189*, *194*, *198*, *200*
  silver 224, **252**, *252*, 253
coffee services, silver *436*
coffers 27, **70–1**, *70*, 73, 78
Cogswell, John 89
coiling, ceramics **122**
cold enameling, glass 278
cold gilding, glass 279, 304
Coleman, William Stephen 377
Colenbrander, Theodoor C.A. 395
Colin, Paul 444
Colinet, Claire-Jeanne-Robert **441**, *441*, 442
Colinet Glassworks 302
collecting

ceramics **128–9**, *128–9*
  furniture 27
collet settings, jewelry **263**, *263*
Collinson & Lock 372
Collot, E.O. *199*
Cologne 158, 164
Colombo, Joe 453
Colonna, Edouard 391
Colotte, Aristide 431
colored twists, drinking glass stems **303**
coloring
  ceramics **124–5**, *124*, *125*
  glass 278, *278*, **284–7**, *284–7*
Columbian World Fair (1892–3) 297
Columbine 174
Colombo, Gino 455
commedia dell'arte figures *179*, 191, 192
commemorative ware
  glass 283
  mugs *125*
commode en tombeau 80, *80*
commodes 27, 78, **80–2**, *80–2*, 84, 85
  bombé commodes 80, *84*
  Maggiolini commodes **82**, *82*
  commodes (night tables) 110, *110*, *111*
Compagnie des Arts Français 418, 423
compasses *533*
Complin, George 210, *210*
composition dolls **493**
computers 473
Comtoise longcase clocks 355
Comyns, William 259
Condé, Louis-Henri of Bourbon, Prince of 192
confidantes 34, 44, *45*
Congreve, Sir William 363
conical feet, drinking glasses *281*
Connecticut 170, *170*, 353
console desserte 60, **61**
console tables 47, **58–9**, *58–9*
Consolidated Lamp & Glass Co. 434–5, *434*
construction, furniture **18–19**, *18–19*
  chairs 19, *19*
  chests and coffers **70**
  chests-of-drawers **79**, 83
  dolls **480–1**, *480–1*
  drawers 18
  pegged construction 18
  tables 18–19, *18*
  wardrobes **77**
Conta & Boehme 185
"conversation" chairs 31, 34
Cook, Captain *532*
Cook, William 209, *209*
Cookworthy, William 207, *207*
Cooper, Austin 445
Cooper, Susie **426**, *426*, 427
Copeland 169, 214, *214*
Copeland & Garrett 485
Copenhagen
  glass 290
  porcelain 187, *187*
Coper, Hans 460–1
Copier, Andreas 456
copper **540–1**, *541*
  Arts and Crafts 383
coral jewelry 262, *262*, 264
Corbusier *see* Le Corbusier
cord quilting 340
cordial glasses *281*
core forming, glass **274**
Corgi 516, *517*
Cork Glass Co. 296, *296*
corkscrew stems, drinking glasses *281*
Corning Glass Works 297
Cornwall, dressers 90
Coro **272–3**, *272*
"Coromandel" lacquer 526

screens 114, *114*
corsets 342, 344
cosmetic boxes, porcelain *199*
cosmetic pots, porcelain *190*
costume **342–5**, *342–5*
    accessories **346**, *346*
    menswear **345**, *345*
    rock and pop memorabilia 550, *550*
    womenswear **342–4**, *342–4*
costume jewelry **271–3**, *271–3*
Cotswold School 372, 373, 419
cotton
    quilts 340
    rugs and carpets 315
"cotton-stalk painter" 206
cotton-twist stems, drinking glasses 303
Coty 549
Coudray, Barbe 192
country chairs 21, *33*, *33*
Couper, James & Sons **401**, *401*, 402
court cupboards 60, 90
Courtenay, Hercules 62
cow creamers
    ceramic *163*
    silver **251**, *251*
Cowan, Reginald Guy 425
Cowan Pottery Studio 425, *425*
Cozzi **191**, *191*
Cozzi, Geminiano 191
Crace, John Gregory 371, 372
Crafts Revival Movement 465, 467
The Craftsman 374
"Craftsman" furniture 374, *374*
Cragstan 518
Crailsheim 159
"Cranberry" glass 287, 311, *311*
Cranbrook Academy of Art **421**, 425, 463, 467
Crandall, Charles M. 502
Crandall, Jesse A. 502
Crane, Walter 376, *376*
Crawford, Jack 536
Crawfords, biscuit tins 509
"Crazy Alice" dolls 484
crazy patchwork quilts 340, 341
cream-boats, silver 251
cream-jugs
    porcelain *198*, *207*
    silver *229*, **251**, *251*
creamware 123, 157, 161, **165**, *165*, 205
credence tables 47, *47*
credenzas 94, *94*, 95
Creil 157
Cremer, W.H. & Son 483
Crespin, Paul *224*, 238, 239, 241
Cressent, Charles 80, *84*, 112
Creswick, T.J. & N. *258*
Creussen 158
crewelwork **336**, *336*
cricket **536**, *536*
"Cries of Berlin" figures 180
"Cries of Zurich" figures 187
"Cris de Londres" figures 174
"Cris de Paris" figures *174*
Crisp, Nicholas 200
crisseling, glass 276
cristallo glass 276, 288, 292, *292*
crocheted lace *347*
crocks, stoneware *170*
crops, glass *310*
Cros, Henri 399
Crosby, Benjamin *97*
cross-cut diamond, cut glass *280*
cross stitch, canvaswork 337
crossbanding 24, *24*
Crouch, John *237*
Crown Derby 210
Crown Works 426
cruet frames, silver **258**, *258*, 259

crystal glass **276**
Crystal Palace Art Union 214
crystallo-ceramic process, sulphides 305
Cubism 414, 418, 424, 438
cuckoo clocks 362, *362*
Cuenca 331, *331*
cufflinks **270**, *270*
cullet, glass 276
Culloden, Battle of (1746) 294
Cumberland, Henry Frederick, Duke of 50
Cumberland-action tables 50
cupboards
    court cupboards 60, 90
    cupboards and linen-presses before 1840 **73–5**, *73–5*
    dressers **90–1**, *90–1*
    early cupboards and *meubles en deux corps* 72, *72*
    pot-cupboards **110–11**, *110*, *111*
    spice cupboards 91
    wardrobes **76–7**, *76–7*
    see also cabinets
"Cupid" pins *269*
cups
    porcelain *122*, *125*, *126*, *182*, *183*, *211*
    silver 227
    see also coffee-cups
"curricle" chairs 31
curtains, crewelwork *336*
cut glass *280*, **296–9**, *296–9*
    techniques **279**, *279*
    types *280*
cut-card decoration, silver **227**, *227*
cut-steel jewelry *265*, 271
cutlery, silver **244–5**, *244–5*
cutlery-urns **118**, *118*
cuvette à fleurs 193
cylinder knops, drinking glasses *281*
Cyprus, glass 305
Czechoslovakia
    Art Deco **432**
    glass **432**, 456–7, 475, 549

D

Dagestan 322–3, *323*
Dagly, Gerard 80, 86, 104
Dagoty factory **195**
Daguerre, Dominique 66
Dailey, Dan 474, *475*
Dali, Salvador 452, 468, *549*
Daly, Matthew *376*
Damascus 149
Damm pottery *159*, 178
Dammouse, Albert 399
Dancer, J.B. 534
Danel & Cie 489
Danhauser, Josef Ulrich 67
Daniel, H. & R. 211, *211*
Dansk International Design 454, *454*
Dantesque *see* Renaissance Revival
Daoguang period ceramics 140
Daoism 327, 529, *529*
Darly, Matthias 37
Darmstadt 404
Darte, Jean-François 195
Darte, Joseph 195
Darte, Louis-Joseph 195
Darte Frères **195**
Darton, William *503*
Darwin House, Buffalo 374
Dasson, Henri 94
Daum, Antonin 398
Daum, Auguste 398
Daum, Paul 429
Daum Frères 301, 390, 398, *398*, 399, 409, *429*, 429, 431
Davenport porcelain 211, 213
Davenports **106**, *106*
David, Emile *438*

David, Jacques-Louis 44
Davidson, George & Co. 283, *283*
Davis, Harry 216, *216*
Davis, William 200, 203
Dawenkou culture, ceramics 131
Day, Robin 448, 449
day-beds 43
De La Cour, William 37
De Lucchi, Michele 467, *467*, 471
De Morgan, William 149, 155, 370, 376, *376*, 377
De Pas, Gionatan *451*
deadbeat anchor escapement, clocks 351
Deakin, Charley 125
Deale, John Henry 330
Dean's Rag Book Co. 495, 497, *497*
Dearle, John Henry *377*
Decalcomania 75
Decamps, Ernest 494
Decamps, Gaston 494
decanter stands, silver 255
decanter wagons, silver 255
decanters
    glass *254*, 276, *279*, *280*, *285*, *286*, *289*, *293*, 296–8
    labels 255
    silver **254**, *254*, 255
Deck, Joseph-Théodore 394
Décoeur, Emile 422
Décorchement, François-Emile 399, *414*, 430
découpage 99
Degen, Pierre 470
Dehua porcelain **137**, 192
déjeuner sets, porcelain *189*
Delafosse, Jean Charles 75
Delaherche, Auguste 379, 394, *394*
Delamarche, Charles François 532
Delatte, André 431
"delft racks" 90
Delftware 92, 123, *128*, **160–1**, *160–1*, 204
Delftware, English *162*, *162*
Della Robbia Pottery 377, *377*
DeLosques, Daniel 444
Denmark
    Art Deco metalwork **436**
    Art Nouveau ceramics 396, **397**
    dining-tables 50
    easy chairs 31
    furniture 450, *450*, 451, *451*
    glass 456, *456*
    jewelry 452, *452*
    lighting 453, *453*
    metalwork **405**, **436**
    mirrors 112
    porcelain 187
    tables 64
    toys 517, *517*
Dent 359
Dent Hardware Co. 505
dental instruments 535
Denton, Samuel *356*
Depree of Exeter *360*
Depression (1930s) 216, 221
Depression glass 283, **435**
Derain, André 415, 422
Derby porcelain 203
    blue-and-white wares 205
    Chelsea-Derby period 201, 206
    domestic wares **210**, *210*
    early wares **206**, *206*
    figures 168, 206, *206*, **210**, *210*, 213
Derbyshire 91, 95
Derbyshire, John & Co. 283
Derrez, Paul 470, *470*
Deruta 152, *152*, 154
Descomps, Joé 441
Deskey, Donald 415, *415*, *420*,

420, 421, 437
desks
    Aesthetic Movement *372*
    Art Nouveau *390*
    Carlton House desks 105
    kneehole desks **107**, *107*
    pedestal desks **107**, *107*
    post-war design *419*, *421*
    roll-top desks 99, 101
Desprès, Jean 439
Desprez, Barthélemy 305
dessert dishes, ceramic *129*
dessert services, porcelain *211*, 213
deutsche Blumen 175, *176*
Deutscher Werkbund 404, 415
Devon, dressers 90
Devonshire, Duke of 95
Di Scavini, Enrico 492
Diaghilev, Sergei 440
dial clocks **352–3**, *352*
dials, clocks **350**, *351*, *354*
diamond-cut ball stoppers, glass *280*
diamond-point engraving, glass **278**, *278*, *292*, *292*
diamonds
    cuts *262*
    earrings 267, *267*
    pins 265
    rings 264, *264*
Dickens, Charles 217, 218
die-stamping
    gold 262
    silver **227**, *227*
diecast toys **516–17**, *516–17*
Diederich, Wilhelm Hunt 425, 436, 437
Dieppe *86*
Dietrich, Marlene 443
Dihl, Christophe 195
Dihl factory **195**, *195*
Ding wares 132
dining-chairs **36–41**, *36–41*
dining silver **236–43**, *236–43*
dining-tables **50–3**, *50–3*
Dinky Toys 499, **516**, *516*, 517, *517*
dinner services, porcelain **175**, *175*, 196, *212*
Dior, Christian 272, *273*, *273*, 344, 447, 452, 549
Directoire period
    commodes 81, *81*
    serving tables *60*
    sideboards 61
dished foliate chairs *21*
dishes
    jade *528*
    Oriental ceramics *133*, *134*, *137*, *142–6*
    porcelain *189*, *191*, *201*, *211*, *219*
    pottery *149*, *150*, *153*, *157*, *159*, *161*, *163*, *170*
Disney, Walt 495, 519
display cabinets 86, **92–3**, *92–3*
displaying ceramics **128**
Distel Factory 395, *395*
Distler, Johann & Co. 506, 518
Ditzinger, Gustaf Adolph *59*
Dixon, James & Sons *241*, 254
Dixon, Tom 468, *469*, 471, 475
Doat, Taxile 394
Doccia **191**, *191*
Dodd, Margaret 477
"dog-kennel" dressers 91
Doggett, John *112*
"dognose" spoons 244
Dol-Toi 499
Dollond, John 534
dolls **478–99**
    automata 494, *494*
    bisque **486–91**, *486–91*

china **485**, *485*
construction and features
   480–1, *480–1*
fabric and rag dolls **492**, *492*
later dolls **493**, *493*
papier-mâché **482**, *482*
parian **485**, *485*
poured-wax **483**, *483*
wax **484**, *484*
wood **482**, *482*
dolls' houses **498–9**, *498–9*
domed feet, drinking glasses *281*
domed pediments *89*
domestic wares
   mid-century modern **454–5**, *454–5*
   postmodernist **472–3**, *472–3*
Donath & Co. 184
Donin family 523
doorstops, glass 311
Doppelmayr, Johann *532*
Dorfan 513
"Dot" period, Meissen **176**
doucai style, ceramics 134, 135, *139*
Doucet, Jacques 344
Doughty, Dorothy 217
Doughty, Freda 217
Doulton, Henry 377
Doulton & Co. 217, *217*, 370, 376, 377,
   377, **426**, 427, *427*
dovetail joints 18, *19*
Downing, Andrew Jackson, *The
   Architecture of Country Houses* 76
Dowst Manufacturing Co. 470, *470*
dragon carpets 322, *322*
drainers, pottery *161*
draw-leaf tables 46
drawers
   construction 18, *19*
   see also chests-of-drawers
Drayton, Grace Debbie 491
"Dream Babies" 491, *491*
Dresden
   furniture 74, 99
   porcelain 174, **184**, *184*, 185, 189
Dresser, Christopher 215, 254, 370, 376,
   377, *377*, **383**, 401, *401*
dressers **90–1**, *90–1*
dresses 342–4, *342–4*
dressing mirrors 113
dressing-table silver 259, *259*
dressing tables **62–3**, *62–3*, *393*, *469*
dressoirs 90
Dreyfuss, Henry 437
drinking glasses *279*
   British 294
   enameled glass 288–9, *288*
   parts *281*
   styles *281*
   twisted stems 279, *281*, **303**, *303*
drinking vessels, silver **246–7**, *246–7*
drinks cabinets *375*
Drocco, Guido *468*
Droog 471
dropleaf tables 18, *18*, **49**, *49*
drug jars *152*, *160*
drum-shaped teapots **249**
drum tables 54, *54*, 105
Dryad Works 373
Du Barry, Madame *197*
Du Jardin, Edouard *410*
Du Paquier, Claudius 188
Dublin, glass 296, *296*
Dubois, Abraham *248*
Dubois, Robert 186
Dubreuil, André 468
Duesbury, William the elder 201, 206
Duesbury, William the younger 210, *210*
duet stands *109*
Duffner & Kimberly 403

Dufrène, Maurice 418
Dufy, Jean 423
Dufy, Raoul 422
"Duke of Cambridge" dinner service *212*
dumb waiters **109**, *109*
"dumps," glass 311
Dunand, Jean 415, *415*, 418,
   436, 437, 439
Dunlap, John 89
Dunlap, Samuel 89
Dunlap family 87
Dunlop *537*
Dunlop, Conyers *354*
Dunlop, Sybil 439
Dupas, Jean 422, 423, 445
Duplessis, Jean-Claude 193, *193*, 196
Dupont, Pierre 328
D'Urbino, Donato *451*
Dürer, Albrecht 153
Durham quilts 340, *340*
Dutch *see* Netherlands
Dutch Baroque silver 237
Dutch East India Company 64, 142,
   160, 338
Duvivier, Claude 234
Dux Porcelain Factory 424
Dwight, John 164, 200
Dylan, Bob *550*

E

Eames, Charles 421, 448, *448*
Eames, Ray 448, *448*
ear-trumpets 535, *535*
earrings 267, *267*, *268*, *271–3*
earthenware **122**, *122*
   American 170, 171
   Belleek 218, *218*
   Chinese 131, *131*
   creamware **165**, *165*
   Dutch 160
   English delftware 162, *162*
   faience 159, *159*
   glazes 123
   maiolica **152–4**, *152–4*
   majolica **169**, *169*
   Spanish 150
   tiles 155
East India Companies 64, 86, 114, 136,
   142, 160, 162, 175, 338
East Indies *82*
East Liverpool, Ohio 221
Easter eggs, porcelain *182*, 183
Eastern European furniture 71, 100, 103
Eastlake, Charles Locke 371
easy chairs **30–2**, *30–2*, **34–5**, *34–5*
Eberlein, Johann Friedrich 174
Ecole des Beaux Arts, Paris 408
ecuelles, porcelain *188*
Eden Toy Inc. 495, *495*
Edinburgh
   clocks 355
   silver hallmarks 225
Edison, Thomas 402
Edkins, Michael 289, 304
Edo period
   ivory 529
   lacquerware 527
Edward VII, King of England 345
Edwardian period
   bookcases 97
   bureaux *100*, 101
   chests-of-drawers *82*, *83*, 85
   clocks 355
   dining-chairs *41*
   dressing tables 63
   jewelry 264, 266, *267*, *268*
   pot-cupboards 110
   secrétaires *103*
   sofas 45

wardrobes 77, *77*
washstands 111
Edwards, John 483, *483*
Edwards & Roberts 85, 101, 107,
   109, *118*
Egermann, Friedrich 285, *285*
Egyptian glass 276, 284, 305
Egyptian style
   furniture 20, *35*, 59
   jewelry 270
Ehrenreich, Johann Ludwig Eberhard 187
Eichbaum, William Peter 297
eight cut, gemstones 262
Eisch, Erwin 474
Eisert, Peter 293
electric clocks 361, *361*
electrogilding, silver **227**, *227*
electroplating 235
electrotyping 235
Elers, David 164
Elers, John 164
Elettren 513
Elfe, Thomas 89
Elgin 499
Elimeyer *235*
Elizabeth I, Queen of England 294
Elizabeth II, Queen of England 492, 499
Elizabeth Christine of Brunswick-
   Wolfenbüttel *236*
Elizabethan Revival, dining-chairs 39
Elkington & Co. 235, 238, **240**, 254
Ellison Glassworks 283
elm 22, *22*
Elmes, Willard Frederick 445, *445*
Elmslie, George Grant 375
Elton, Sir Edmund 376
Elton Ware 376
embossing, silver **226**, *226*
embroidery **336–9**, *336–9*
emerald cut gemstones *262*
emeralds *262*
Empire style
   beds 116–17, *117*
   chairs 19, *21*, 31, 32
   chandeliers 307
   clocks 358
   commodes 82
   dressing tables 62, *62*
   mirrors 113
   porcelain 182, 194, *194*, 196, 220
   pot-cupboards 110
   rugs and carpets 329
   secrétaires 103
   tables 51, 59
"*en tremblant*" jewelry 265
enamel and enameling
   boxes 546, *546*
   ceramics 125, *125*, **138**
   cigarette cases 545
   cloisonné 263, *263*, **522–3**, *522*
   Geneva enameling 263, *263*
   glass 278, *278*, **288–91**, *288–91*
   guilloché **263**, *263*
   jewelry 263, *263*, 268
   perfume bottles 549
   plique-à-jour 404, 407, *407*, 523
   snuff-boxes 544
engagement rings 264, 268, *268*
engine-turning, silver **227**, *227*
England *see* Britain
"English Dresden" 209
English Toy Co. 499
Englund, Eva 474, 475
engraving
   glass **278–9**, *278–9*, **292–5**, *292–5*
   silver **226**, *226*, 237
Enriquez, Don Fadrique, 26th Admiral of
   Castille *331*
Ensell, Edward 297

entre-fenêtre panels *329*
entrée dishes, silver **240**, *240*, 241
epergnes
   glass 311, *311*
   silver 238
Ersari 324, 325, *325*
Erzgebirge 502
Escalier de Cristal 298, 299
escapement, clocks 350, 351, *351*
escritoires 72, 88, **102–3**, *102*, 104
étagères 97, **109**
etching, glass 279, *279*, 295, *295*
Etling, Edmond & Cie 428, *428*, 429
Etling Foundry 440
Etruria 166
Etruscan glass 276, *276*
Etruscan style
   furniture 37, 43
   jewelry 265, 267
etuis 546, *546*
Eugénie, Empress 40, 94, 342, *485*
Eureka Clock Co. 361, *361*
European rugs and carpets **328–31**,
   328–31
Evans, David 212
Evans, Paul 466, 467
Evans & Cartwright 499
evening bags 346
ewers
   Oriental ceramics *132*, *136*
   pottery *150*
Excise Acts (Britain) 296, 303
Exeter, carpets 330, *330*
Exhibition of Modern Art in Decoration
   and Furnishing, London (1928) 419
expanding bracelets 267
export wares
   Chinese ceramics **135–6**
   Japanese ceramics 142, *142*
Exposition des Arts Décoratifs et
   Industriels Modernes, Paris (1925) **414**,
   418, 422, 424
extending dining-tables 51, *51–3*, 52–3
eyes, dolls 481

F

Fabergé, Carl *263*
fabric dolls 492, *492*
fabrics *see* textiles
faceted stems
   candlesticks 306
   drinking glasses *281*
façon de Venise glass 276, 278, 279,
   292, *292*, **302**
Faenza 152, *152*, 153, *153*, 154,
   156, 160
Fahrenheit scale, thermometers 364
Fahrner, Theodor 406, 407, 439, *439*
faience 123
   French *128*, **156–7**, *156–7*
   German 159, *159*
   Portuguese 151
   Spanish 150, *150*
faience fine 157
fairings 185, *185*
fakes
   ceramics **126–7**, *126–7*
   furniture **26–7**, *27*
   silver 228, 229
   Staffordshire figures 168
Falcon Glassworks 289, 305
Falconet, Etienne 176
Falize, Lucien *263*, 404
Falkenberg, G. 240
famille rose 136, *136*, 137, 138, *138*,
   140, 161, *547*
famille verte 136, *136*, 138, 161,
   175, 192

fanghu vases *140*
fans 344, *346*, *346*
Far Eastern rugs and carpets **327**, *327*
Farnell, J.K. & Co. 495, 497, *497*
Farny, Henry 378
Farrell, Edward 234
fashion, and postmodernist design 473
fashion dolls **486–7**, *486–7*
Fausel, Charles 480
fauteuil à la reine 21
fauteuil en cabriolet 30
fauteuils (open armchairs) 30, *31*, *32*, 34
Fauves 415
faux cameo glass 301, *301*
Favre 513
Favre-Bulle, Monsieur 361
"Favrile" glass 402, *402*
fede rings 268
Federal style
    beds 116, *117*
    chairs *21*
    dining-tables 51
    handles *21*
    linen-presses 75
    mirrors 113
    Phyfe school 43
    sideboards 60
    silver *248*, *251*
    tables *68*
feet
    drinking glasses *281*
    furniture styles *20*
Feilner, Simon 178, 180, *180*
Felkl, Jan 532
female images, sculpture **408–9**, *408–9*,
    440, *440*, *441*
Fenton, Christopher Webber 171, 221
Fenton Art Glass Co. 283, 435
Ferdinand IV, King of Naples 190
Ferner, F.J. 177, *177*
Ferniani family 154
Festival of Britain (1951) 449
Feuillâtre, Eugène 389, 404, 407
Feuillet 199
Feure, Georges de 389, 391, *391*, 404
"Fiddle and thread" pattern, flatware
    245, *245*
Fiesta ware 425
figures, ceramic *128*, *129*, 217, *217*
    Art Deco **423**, *423*, *424*, 427
    Art Nouveau 397, *397*
    Belleek **218**
    Berlin 182, *183*
    Bow *129*, 202, *202*
    Buen Retiro 190
    Capodimonte 190, *190*
    Derby 168, 206, *206*, **210**, *210*, 213
    Dresden 184, *184*, 217
    fairings **185**, *185*
    fakes and forgeries 126, *127*
    Frankenthal 178, *178*
    Fürstenberg **180**, *180*
    Gardner *219*
    Ludwigsburg 179, *179*
    Meissen **174**, *174*, 176, *176*,
        181, *181*, 210
    Naples 190, *190*
    Nymphenburg 179, *179*
    Paris *199*
    Plymouth *207*
    pottery 159, *161*, 165
    Rockingham 213, *213*
    Royal Worcester 215
    Sèvres *194*, 408, *409*
    Staffordshire *168*, *168*, 210
    Tournai 186, *186*
    Vienna 188, *188*
    Zurich 186, *187*
    see also sculpture

figures, glass 302, *302*, 428
figures, lead and plastic **514–15**, *514–15*
filigree patterns, glass 279
Filmer, T.H. 95
Finland
    furniture *450*
    glass 456, *456*
Finmar Ltd 417, *417*, 419
fired gilding, glass 304
firescreens 115
firing feet, drinking glasses *281*
fish slices, silver **245**, *245*
Fisher, Alexander 383
Fisher Price 499
Fitzroy, Admiral Robert 364, *365*
"Five Towns" 211
flambé glazes 183
flame stitch, canvaswork 337, *337*
flanged feet, drinking glasses *281*
flashed glass 278, **285**, *285*
flasks
    glass 276, *278*, 288
    Oriental metalwork *522*
flat molded stoppers, glass *280*
"flatback" figures 168, *168*
flatware, silver **244–5**, *244–5*
flatweaves, rugs and carpets 314, *314*,
    326, *326*
Flaxman, John 166, 300
Flemish
    bobbin lace *347*
    mirrors *112*
    silver 246
    tables 46
Flight, John 203, 208
Flight, Thomas 203
Flight & Barr 208
Flight, Barr & Barr *208*
Flight family 208
Flockinger, Gerda 452
"Flora Danica" service 187, *187*
Florence
    ceramics 152, 154, 190
    chairs 30
    display cabinets 92
    jewelry 263, *265*
    pietre dure 67
Florentine stitch, canvaswork 337, *337*
"Florian" ware 396
Flos 453
flower-pots, porcelain *202*
flowers, language of 268–9
flute drinking glasses *281*, *292*
flux, glass 276
foam upholstery 451
fob seals *270*
foldover tables 48
Foley 427
folio stands **108**, *108*
folk art **542–3**, *542–3*
Follot, Paul 404, 415, 418, *418*
Fontaine, Pierre 28, 329
    Receuil de décorations intérieures
    28, 38, 59, 82
Fontainebleau 46, 72, 196, 198, 328
Fontainebleau School 156, 160
Fontenay, François Eugène de 299
foot shapes, drinking glasses *281*
footwear 343, 344
Ford, John 309
Forest Toys 502
forks, silver 244–5, *244–5*
Fornasetti, Piero 466, *467*, *469*
Forst, Eusebius Anton *182*
Fortuny, Mariano 344
Fostat 316, 331
Foster, Norman 468
Fostoria Glass 435
Fothergill, John 233

Fouquet, Georges 407
Fouquet, Jean 439
four-poster beds 116, 117
Four Seasons, glass figures 302, *302*
Fourdinois, Alexandre-Georges 94
Fourdinois, Henri-Auguse 94
Fournereau 513
Fournier, A.M.E. 28, *28*
fourreaux 342
Fowke, Captain Francis 538
Fox, George *232*
Fraktur **543**, *543*
frames, silver **259**, *259*
Frampton, George 408
France
    armoires 73, 74, *74*
    Art Deco 414
        ceramics **422–3**, *422*
        furniture **418**, *418*
        glass **428–31**, *428–31*
        jewelry 439
        metalwork **436**, *436*
        sculpture **440–1**, *440–1*
    Art Nouveau 388
        ceramics **394**, *394*
        furniture 390, *390*
        glass **398–9**, *398–9*
        jewelry 407
        metalwork 404, *404*, 405
        sculpture 408, *408*
    automata **494**, *494*
    bags 346
    barometers *365*
    beds 116–17, *117*
    bonheurs du jour 104
    bookcases 97
    bureaux 98, 99, *99*, 100
    cabinet-makers' marks 76
    canapés 42
    chairs *21*
        dining-chairs 36, 38, **40**, *40*, 41
        easy chairs 30, *30*, *34*, *35*
    chaises-longues 43, *43*, 44
    chests 70
    chests-of-drawers 79, 83
    chronometers 360
    clocks 351, 353, *353*, 355, 356,
        356–8, 358, **359**, *361–3*, 362, 363
    commodes 80, *80–2*, 81, 82, *84*
    costume 340, 342, *342*
    desks 107
    display cabinets 92, 93, *93*
    dolls 480, 482, 484, *484*, **485**, **486–9**,
        486–9, 493, *493*
    dressing tables 62, *63*
    dumb waiters 109
    étagères 109
    fans 346, *346*
    furniture 18, 451
    glass 276
        Art Deco **428–31**, *428–31*
        Art Nouveau 398–9, *398–9*
        cameo glass 301, *301*
        candlesticks 306
        colored glass 286, *286*, *287*, *287*
        cut glass 298, **299**, *299*
        enameled glass 290, **291**, *291*
        gilding 304
        mold-blown glass 282, *282*
        paperweights **308**, *308*
        sulphides 305
    jewelry *264*, *270*
    lace 347
    lead figures **514**, *514*
    meubles en deux corps 72, *72*, 88
    mirrors 112, 113
    night tables 110, *110*
    perfume bottles 549
    porcelain **192–9**, *192–9*

posters 410, *410*, 444
pot-cupboards 110
pottery **156–7**, *156–7*
quilts 340
regulators **360**
rugs and carpets 328–9, *328–9*
salon suites 44
samplers 339
screens 115
secrétaires 103, *103*
shawls 343
side cabinets 94, *94*, 95, *95*
sideboards 61
silver
    candelabra 234
    candlesticks 230, *231*, *232*
    decorative tableware 238
    entrée dishes 240
    hallmarks 225
    monteiths 257, *257*
    salt-cellars *258*
    sauceboats *241*
    scarcity **250**
    tea-urns *253*
    wine tasters *254*
snuff-boxes *544*
sofas 45
stools 28, *28*
tables
    breakfast tables *54*
    center tables 55, *55*
    console, pier and side tables
        58, *58*, 59
    dining-tables 50, *53*
    early tables 46
    games and work tables 68, *68*, *69*
    occasional tables 66, *66*
    serving tables *60*, 61
    tripod tables 64
    writing tables 105
toys **509**, *509*, 517
trains 513
wardrobes 77, *77*
watches *366*, 367
writing cabinets-on-stands 104
Franche-Comté 355, 359
Francis I, King of France 46, 72
Francis, Field & Francis 504
Francis Joseph, Emperor of Austria 189
Frankenthal 178 *178*, 179
Frankfurt 73, *73*, 74, 159
Frankish glass 279, 282
Frankl, Paul T. 415, **420**, *420*, 421
Franklin, Benjamin 168
Fraunhofer, Joseph 534
Fray, M. *241*
Frederick, Prince of Wales 238, 241
Frederick the Great, King of Prussia
    180, 182
Frederick William III, King of Prussia 182
Frederike, Princess of Prussia 182
free blowing, glass **276**
Free Renaissance style, dining-chairs 39
Freeman, Philip *239*
French jet 268
French polishing 23, 40
French Revolution (1789–99) 68, 194,
    250, 329, 345
fretted legs *20*
Friedeberg, Pedro 469, *469*
Friedlander-Wildenhaim, Marguerite
    424, *424*
friggers **310**, *310*
Fritsche, William 295
fritware 149, *149*
Frodsham, Charles 359, *359*
fruit stands, silver *227*
Fry, Roger 372
Frye, Thomas 202

Frytom, Frederik van 160
Fukugawa Porcelain Manufacturing Co. *147*
Fulda 159
Fulgurex 513
Fulham 164
Fuller, John *533*
Fuller, Loïe 389, 409
Fulper Pottery Co. 379, *379*
funeral jars *131*
"Funk" ceramics movement 463, 477
funnel-shaped drinking glasses *281*
funnels, silver **255**, *255*
furniture **16–119**
  Aesthetic Movement 372
  Art Deco 415, **416–21**, *416–21*
  Art Nouveau **390–3**, *390–3*
  Arts and Crafts 101, 111, *370,* **371–5**, *371–5*
  care **27**, *27*
  construction **18–19**, *18–19*
  decoration **24–5**, *24–5*
  dolls' house *499*
  marriages, alterations and fakes **26–7**, *26–7*
  mid-century modern **448–51**, *448–51*
  miscellaneous **108–19**, *108–19*
  Modernism 418, *419,* 420, 421
  postmodernist **466–9**, *466–9*
  seat furniture **28–45**, *28–45*
  storage furniture **70–97**
  styles **20–1**, *20–1*
  tables **46–69**, *46–69*
  woods and patination **22–3**, *22–3*
  writing furniture **98–107**, *98–107*
Furniture Shop, San Francisco 375
Fürstenberg **180**, *180*
fusee, clocks **350**
Futurism 414

G

Gabriel, William 502
Gaillard, Eugène 389, 391, 407
Gaillard, Lucien 404, 407
Gainsborough armchairs *34*
Galéries Lafayette 414, 418, 423
Galileo 534
Gallé, Emile 301, 389, 390, *391,* **398**, *398,* 399
"galleyware" 162
Gama 517, 518
games *see* toys and games
games tables **68–9**, *68–9*
Ganado 333
Gansu 327
Gardner, Francis 219, *219*
Garneray, L. *196*
garnets *262,* 266
garnitures, porcelain 203, 210
Garrard, Robert *236*
Garrards 238
Gate, Simon 293, *293,* 432
gateleg tables 18, **48**, *48,* 50
Gates, John Monteith 434
Gatti, Giovanni Battista 95
Gaudí, Antoní 393, *393*
Gaultier *480,* **487**, *487,* **489**, *489*
Gaultier, François 487, 489
Gaultier, Jean Paul 345, *549,* **550**
Gee, John 37
Gehrig, Lou 537
Gehry, Frank *466*
Gelly, A. *258*
gemstones **262**, *262*
  Art Deco jewelry 438
  necklaces 266, *266*
  rings 264, *264*
  settings 263, *263*
  symbolism 269

General Ceramics 425
Genet & Michon 428
Geneva enameling **263**, *263*
Gennerelli, Amedeo 441
Genoa
  furniture 30, 80, 99, 110
  lace 347
Gentile, Carmine 154
Gentile family 154
George I period
  chests-on-chests 88, *88*
  easy chairs *30*
  kneehole desks 107
  settees 42
  silver 241
  tables 64
George II period
  chests-on-chests 88
  commodes 81
  dining-tables 50
  easy chairs *34*
  kneehole desks 107, *107*
  knife-boxes 118
  pedestal desks 107
  settees 42
  tables 19, 58, 64
George III, King of England 68, 69, 208, 257, 534
George III period
  chairs 19, 21
  chests-of-drawers *81*
  chests-on-chests 88, 89
  clocks 354
  commodes 81, *85*
  dining-chairs 37
  kneehole desks 107
  pot-cupboards 110
  sideboards 60
  silver *242*
  wine coolers and cellarets *119*
George IV, King of England 43, 58, 69, 84, 105, *212,* 289
George IV period
  silver 234
  tables *57*
  see also Regency period
George Street Pottery 426
Georgene Averill Manufacturing Co. 492
Georgian period
  bureaux *98*
  chests-of-drawers **81**
  mirrors 112
  wine coolers and cellarets 119
Georgian Revival sideboards 61
Gerdago **443**, *443*
Gérin, Claude-Humbert 193
Germain, Thomas 242
"Germantown" yarns 332
Germany
  Art Deco **432**
    ceramics **424**, *424*
    furniture **416–17**, *416–17*
    metalwork **436**, *436*
    sculpture **442–3**, *442–3*
  Art Nouveau
    ceramics 396, 397
    jewelry 407
  automata 494
  Bauhaus 415, 416
  Berlin woolwork 337
  Biedermeier style 32
  bombé commodes 80
  bonheurs du jour 104
  brass 540, *540*
  bureaux 99
  cabinets-on-stands 86
  ceramics
    Art Deco **424**, *424*
    Art Nouveau 396, 397

mid-century modern ceramics 461
  porcelain **173–85**, *173–85*
  pottery **158–9**, *158–9*
  stoneware *123*
  tiles 155
chests 70, 71
clocks 353, 362, *362*
coffers *70*
commodes 82
cupboards 73, *73*
dining-chairs **39**, 41, *41*
dining-tables 50
dolls 480, 482, *482,* 484, *484,* **485**, *485,* **490–1**, *490–1,* **492**, *492,* 493
dolls' houses **498**, *498*
dumb waiters 109
escritoires 102
glass 276, **432**, **474**, 475
  colored glass 284
  enameled glass **288–9**, *288–9,* **290**, *290*
  engraved glass 278, **292**
globes 532, *532*
jewelry 452
Jugendstil **404–5**, 406
lead and plastic figures **514**, *514*
mirrors 112, 113
night tables 110, *110*
painted furniture 74
posters 444
pot-cupboards 110
purses *346*
samplers 339
secrétaires 103
sideboards 61
silver 225, *232,* 235, *236,* 238, *242,* 246, *248*
soft toys 495, *495*
tables 46, *47,* 58, 59, 64
teddy bears 481, **496**, *496*
toys **506–8**, *506–8,* 517, 518, *518*
trains **510–11**, *510–11*
wardrobes 77
wood and paper toys 502, *502*
Geslend Co. 487
Gesmar, Charles 444
Gessner, Salomon 187
gesso, gilt 25
Ghiordes, rugs 320, *320*
Ghiordes knot **315**, 320
giardinetto rings 264, *264*
Gien 157
Gilardi, Piero 468
Gilbert, A. 441
Gilbert, A.C. 519
Gilbody, Samuel 204, 205
gilding
  ceramics **125**, *125,* 181
  furniture **25**, *25*
  glass 279, *279,* **304**, *304*
  silver **227**, *227*
Giles, James 203, 289, 304
Gilet 199
Gilhooly, David *476,* 477
Gille 199
Gillow, Richard 51, *51,* 52
Gillow of Lancaster 371
  chests-of-drawers 85
  commodes (night tables) 110
  cutlery-urns *118*
  Davenports 106
  dining-chairs 37, 38, *38*
  dining-tables 51, 52
  dressing tables *63*
  linen-presses *75*
  night tables 110
  pot-cupboards 111
  sideboards 60
  sofas 43

tables *66*
  whatnots 109
  wine coolers and cellarets 119
gilt-bronze decoration, furniture **25**, *25*
gilt gesso 25
gimmel rings *268*
Gimson, Ernest 372, *372*
ginger jars *427*
Ginori, Carlo 191
Giovannoni, Stefano 472
girandole earrings 267, *267*
girandoles *112*
Girard 488
Giroux 538
Girshfeld, Natalya A. *219*
Giuliano, Carlo 266
Giuliano family 266, 267
Giulio Romano 46
Givenchy, Hubert de 344
Gladstone, W.E. 214
Glasgow School 375, **383**, *383*
Glasgow Style 388
glass **274–311**
  additions **302–5**, *302–5*
  Art Deco **428–35**, *428–35*
  Art Nouveau 301, **388**, **398–103**, *398–103*
  cameo glass **300–1**, *300–1*
  carved glass **524–5**, *525*
  colored glass **284–7**, *284–7*
  cut glass 280, **296–9**, *296–9*
  decanters 254
  decoration **278–9**, *278–9*
  enameled glass **288–91**, *288–91*
  engraved glass **292–5**, *292–5*
  forming techniques 276
  forms and styles *280–1*
  friggers **310**, *310*
  gilding **304**, *304*
  lampwork **302**, *302*
  lighting **306–7**, *306–7*
  materials **276**
  mid-century modern **456–7**, *456–7*
  miscellaneous **310–11**, *310–11*
  mold-blown glass **282**, *282*
  paperweights **308–9**, *308–9*
  perfume bottles 548, *548*
  postmodernist **474–5**, *474–5*
  pressed glass **283**, *283*
  twisted stems **303**, *303*
The Glasshouse 475
glazes, ceramics **123**, *123,* 460
Glitter, Gary 550
globes 532, *532*
globular decanters 280
gloss-gilding 181
gloves 343, 344
Goa 67
gobelet à la reine 193
Gobelins, furniture 86, *86*
goblets
  glass *292–5, 301, 302, 304, 305, 400*
  silver 247
Godard, A. 441
Goddard, John *102*
Goddard family *102*
Godwin, Edward William 370, 372, *372*
going barrel, clocks 350, *351*
gold **262**
  bracelets and bangles 267
  chains 266
  earrings 267, *267*
  hallmarking 225
  rings 264, *264,* 270
  watches 366
  see also gilding
"Gold Anchor" period, Chelsea **201**, *201*
gold-ruby glass 284, *284,* 292
Goldrubinglas 284

Goldscheider, Paris 440
Goldscheider, Vienna 408, 424, *424*, 443
Goldsmiths and Silversmiths Co. *243*
Gole, Pierre 86, 92
golf **537**, *537*
gondola chairs *21*
Gonzaga, Ludovico, Duke of Nevers 302
Gonzaga family 302
"Googly" dolls 490, **491**, *491*
Gorham Manufacturing Company *229*,
    238, *257*, **385**, *385*, 437, *437*
Gory, Affortunato 441
"Gosford Castle" service *212*
Goss 211, 214, 218
Goten, Jacobo van der 331
Gotha 178
Gothic Revival style
    bookcases 97
    bureaux 101
    chairs *21*
    chaises-longues 44
    clocks 357, *357*
    dining-chairs 39, *39*
    dining-tables 52, 53
    furniture 20, 371
    porcelain 196, 198
    silver *246*, 249
    tables 59
    wardrobes 76
Gothick style
    dressing tables 63
    settees 42
    sideboards 60
Goto family 523
Göttschalk, Moritz 498, *498*
Gotzkowsky, Johann Ernst 180
Gouda 160
Gould family 230
Goupy, Marcel **430**, *430*
Gouyn, Charles 200
Graham, George 351, 360
Grainger, Thomas 208, *208*
graining 75, 84
Grand Tour 58, 67, 346
grandfather clocks *see* longcase clocks
"granite ware" 171
La Granja de San Ildefonso 289, *289*, 298
Grant, Duncan 372
Grant of London *357*
granulation, gold **262**, *262*
Grassi, Anton 188
Graumans, Rody 471
Graves, Michael 469, *469*, 472, 473
Gray, A.E. & Co. 426
Gray, Eileen 418
Gray Iron 515
Great Exhibition, London (1851) 34, 40,
    41, 94, 95, 155, 169, *198*, *209*, 214,
    238, 286, 291, 294, *294*, 296, 305,
    307, 308, 337, 346, 363, 365, 539
Grecian style
    clocks 357
    furniture *21*, 38, 76
    jewelry 265, 267
The Greek A factory 161, *161*
Green, Guy 155
Greene, Charles Sumner 370, **374**,
    375, *375*
Greene, Henry Mather 370, **374**, 375, *375*
Greener, Henry & Co. 283
Greenly, Henry 511
Greenwood, Frans 292
Gregory, Albert 216
Gregory, Mary 311
Gregory, Waylande 425
Gresley, Cuthbert 216
Gretsch, Dr Hermann 424
Gribelin, Simon 237
Gribelin family 237

Gricci, Giuseppe 190
Grice, Edwin 300
gridiron pendulums, clocks 351
Griffen, Smith & Hill 171, *171*
Grima, Andrew 452
Grödnertal dolls **482**, *482*
Groenekan, Gerard van der 416, *416*
Grohe, Guillaume 94
Grohe, Jean-Michel 94
Gropius, Walter 415, 416, 420
Gros, Louis-Benjamin *105*
gros point de Venise 347, *347*
Grotell, Maija 425, 462, *463*
Groult, André 414
Grue, Francesco Antonio Xaverio 154, *154*
Grue family 154, *154*
Grueby 377
Grueby, William 370, *370*, 379
Grueby Pottery 155, *379*
Gruelle, John 492
Guan wares 132, 139
Guangzhou 136
Gubbio 153
Gudenberg, Wilhelm Wolff von 395
Güell, Count Eusebi 393
Guerbe 409
Guérhard, Antoine 195
guéridon (candlestand) tables 67, *67*
Guerriero, Alessandro 466
Gufram 468, *468*
Gugelot, Hans 455
guglets 162
Guilbert, Yvette 410
Guild of Handicraft 372, 373, **382**,
    382, 406
guilloché enameling, jewelry **263**, 263
Guimard, Hector 390, 391
guitars 551, *551*
gul motif, rugs and carpets 320, 324
Gund Manufacturing Co. 496
Günthermann 506, *506*, 518
Gurley, W. & L.E. *533*
Gurschner, Gustav 400, 409, *409*
Gustavian style *31*, 59
Gustavsberg 424, 461
guyuexuan wares 138
gypsy rings 264, *264*

H
Haarlem 160
Hacker, Christian 498, *498*
Hackwood, William *127*
Hadid, Zaha 469, 473
Hadley, James 215, *215*, 216, 217
Hadley, John 533
Haebler, Carl 442
Haffner, Johann 514
HAG 513
Hagler, Stanley **273**, *273*
The Hague 36, 73, 74, 86, 186
Hague School **385**
Haile, Thomas "Sam" 460
hair, dolls 481
hair embroidery 338
hair jewelry **269**
Hald, Edvard 293, *293*, 432, *456*
Haley, Kenneth 435
Haley, Reuben 434
half-hoop rings 264
half-pillar and splat shelf clocks 353
half-tester beds 116
Hall, John 374, 505
Hall, William 372
hall chairs **32**, *32*
Hall China Co. 425
Hallett, William 88
hallmarking **225**, *225*
    silver fakes 228, *228*
Hamada, Shoji *122*, 460, *460*

Hamilton, Sir William 300
Hamleys 483
Hammann, Adolph 184
Han period ceramics 131
Hanau 159
hand-piercing, silver **226**, *226*
Handcraft 374
Handel, Philip Julius 403
Handel Co. 403, *403*
handkerchief tables 49
handkerchiefs, lace *347*
handles, furniture styles *21*
hanging bookshelves *97*
Hanley 211
Hannam, Thomas *237*
Hannong, Paul Antoine 178
Hanover 159
"Hanoverian" pattern, flatware 244, *244*
"Hans Sloane" wares 201
Hansen, Fritz *447*, *450*
Hansen, Johannes 450
hard-paste porcelain **122**, *122*, 173
harewood **22**, *22*
Haring, Keith 473
Harlequin 174, *174*
"harlequin" Davenports *106*
Harlingen 160
Harrach Glassworks 285, *285*, 286, 298,
    301, 457
Harradine, Lesley 217, 427, *427*
Harrison, John 351, 360
Hartgring, W.P. 395
Hartnack 534
Hasbro *519*
Haskell, Coburn 537
Haskell, Miriam **273**, *273*
hats 343, 344, 345, *345*
Haupt, Georg 31, 58, *59*
Hausmaler **177**, *177*, 183, 188
Hausser, Otto and Max 514
haute couture 342, 344
Hautin & Co. 285
Haviland, Théodore & Cie 423
Haviland & Co. 199
Haweis, Mrs, *Beautiful Houses* 39
Hawkes, T.G. & Co. 297, *297*
Hawkes, Thomas G. 297
Haydn, Joseph 109, 188
Hayes, Rutherford 199
Hazel Atlas Glass Co. *435*
heads, dolls **480**
Heal, Ambrose 373
Heal & Son 63, *111*, 373, 419, *419*
heart rings 268, *268*
Heath, John 201, 206
Heaton, Maurice 435
Hébrard, A.A. 405, *405*
Heckert, Fritz 290
Heemskerk, Willem Jacobsz van 292
Heian period lacquerware 527
Heiligenstein, Auguste-Claude **430–1**
Heinrichsen, Ernst 514
Heintz Art Metal Shop 385, *385*
Hellenistic period glass 276
Hellot, Jean *193*
Hendrer, Madame 492
Hendrix, Jimi 551
Henningsen, Poul 453, *453*
Henrietta of Cleves 302
Henry II, King of France 88
Henry VIII, King of England 330
Henry, John Sollie 373
Henshall, William 218
Hepplewhite, George
    bookcases 96
    *The Cabinet-Maker and Upholsterer's
    Guide* 28, 32, 37, 56, 62, 69, 75, 85,

    89, 93, 96, 116, 118
    dining-chairs 37, *37*
    easy chairs 31
    knife-boxes 118
    sideboards 60
    tambor writing tables 98
    wardrobes 76
Hepplewhite Revival 85
Hepplewhite style
    chairs *21*
    settees *45*
Herald Miniatures 515
Herculaneum 25, 37, 38, 166, 188, 190
Hereke 316, 321
Heriz 318, *318*
Herman, Sam 475
Herman Miller Co. 421
Heron, Susanna 470
herringbone veneering **24**, *24*
Herter Brothers 35
Hess, Frank 273
Hesse, Ernst Ludwig, Grand Duke von 404
Hetsch, Gustav Friedrich 187
Heubach 185
Heubach, Christoph 491
Heubach, Ernst 491
Heubach, Gebrüder **491**
Heubach, Philipp 491
L'Heure Electrique *361*
hexagonal decanters *280*
Heyde, Georg 514, *514*
Heylyn, Edward 202
Hidehara 527
Hideyoshi, Toyotomi 141, 142
High-Tech design 471
High Wycombe 33
highboys 87
"highbrow" china dolls 485, *485*
Hill, John & Co. 515
Hill, Thomas "Jockey" 210
Hille Co. 449
Hindley & Wilkinson 101
Hipp, Matthäus 361
hippy clothes 345
Hirado porcelain **145**, *145*
Hiramatsu, Yasuki 470, *470*
Hispaño-Moresque
    ceramics 150, 152
    furniture *88*
Historismus glass 288, 290, *290*
Hoare, J. & Co. 297, *297*
Hoare, John 297
hob-nail cut glass *280*
Hobbs, Brockunier & Co. 287
Hochschnitt decoration, glass
    278, 290, 293
Höchst 159, *159*, **178**, *178*,
    179, 180, 199
Hoeker, W. 395
Hoffman 549, *549*
Hoffman, Wolfgang 421
Hoffmann, Josef 389, 432, 460
    ceramics 400
    furniture 392–3
    jewelry 407
    metalwork 405, *405*, 436
Hofkellereiglas 288
Hogarth, William 237
Hohenstein, Adolpho 410
Hohlwein, Ludwig 444
Holbein, Hans the Younger 266, 317, *317*
"Holbein" pattern, rugs and carpets 317,
    317, 320, 323, *323*, 330, 331
"Holbeinesque" pendants 266, *266*
Holdship, Josiah 205
Holdship, Richard 205
Holland *see* Netherlands
Holland, Henry 58, 81, *249*
Holland & Sons *76*, 101

Holly, Buddy 550
Holmegaard 456, *456*
Holmes, William *243*
Holophane Glass Co. 434
Holy Roman Empire 288
Holzschnittblumen 175
Homer Laughlin China Co. 425
honey gilding, glass 279
Hongwu, Emperor 133
Hongzhi period 134
Honiton lace 347, *347*
Honoré factory **195**
Hooke, Robert 364
Hoosemann, Franz 408
Hope, Thomas 38, 55
    Household Furniture and Interior
    Decoration 38, 54, 59, 110
Hope-Jones, Frank 361
Hopi pottery 171
Hopkins, W. & E. *270*
Hoppenhaupt, Johann Christian 112
Hornby **512**, *512*, 513, *516*
Hornby, Frank 509, 512, 516
Horne and Thornthwaite 538
Horner, Charles *406*
Höroldt, Johann Gregorius 173, *173*,
    175, 177, *177*
horse covers, soumakh *326*
horses, ceramic *131*
Horst, Philip *248*
Horta, Victor 388, 389, 391, *391*, 392
Houghton-Butcher Manufacturing Co.
    538
Houghton Hall, Norfolk 50
Howard & Sons 371
Howard Miller Clock Co. 453, *455*
Howell & James 377
Howorth *364*
Hubbard, Elbert 375, 384
Huber, Patriz 407
Hubley Manufacturing Co. 505, *505*
Hueck, Eduard *404*, 405
Hüet, Christophe 174
Huguenots
    furniture 36, 58, 86
    silver 227, 230, 237, 238, 241,
    250, 252, 256
Hukin & Heath 254
Hulanicki, Barbara 344
Humbert & Söhne *242*
Humpen glasses 288, *288*, 290
Hunebelle, André 428
Hunger, Christoph Conrad 187, 188, 191
Hunt, John S. *247*
Hunt, Victor 511
Hunt & Roskell 238, *247*
hunting-cased watches *366*
Huntley & Palmers 509
Hunzinger, George 84
Huret, Calixte 486, 487
Huret, Maison 485, *486*, *486*
hutch chests 70–1
Hutton, John 457
Huygens, Christiaan 351
Huysum, Jan van 161
hyacinth-bulb vases, glass **310**, *310*
Hyalith glass **285**, *304*
Hyatt, Isaiah Smith 493
Hyatt, James Wesley 493
"hybrid hard paste" 207
hydrofluoric acid, etching glass 279, 295
hygrometers 365

I

Ibn Batuta 316
ice pails
    porcelain *195*, *212*
    pottery *154*
Ichiko Kyogo Ltd 518

Ideal Novelty & Toy Co. 481,
    481, 496, *496*
littala 456, *456*
Imari porcelain **143**, *143*, 146, *146*, 161
    copies 173, 192, 208, 210
Imberton, I.J. 291, 304
Imperial factory, St Petersburg **219**, *219*
Imperial Glass Co. 283, 435
Ince, William 89
    The Universal System of Household
    Furniture 62, 64, 81, 92, 93, 105
Ince & Mayhew 37, *58*, 81, 92
incense-burners *144*
incense cabinets *527*
India
    Kashmir shawls 343
    quilts 340, *340*
    tables 67
    teapoys 65
Indiana Glass Co. 282, 283
indianische Blumen 175
Indians, North American *see* Native
    Americans
Industrial Revolution 182, 209, 294
Ingap 509
Ingermann, Christian Heinrich 235
inkstands, silver **258–9**, *258*
inkwells
    copper *384*
    Oriental ceramics *145*
inlays
    Buhl decoration 38, 55, *55*
    furniture **25**, *25*
inro 524, *525*, 527, *527*
insect motifs, jewelry 268
intaglio
    glass engraving **278**, *278*
    reverse intaglio technique *270*
intercalaire glass 398
international exhibitions **34**
    see also individual exhibitions
International Exhibition,
    Antwerp (1894) 299
International Exhibition,
    Barcelona (1929) 416–17
International Exhibition, Liège (1905) 392
International Exhibition, London (1862)
    53, 84, 108, 370, *371*
International Exhibition, Paris (1861) *198*
International Exhibition, Paris (1867)
    34, 85, 94, *198*
International Exhibition, Paris (1878)
    291, 300, 301
International Exhibition, Paris (1889)
    300, 394
International Exhibition, Paris (1900)
    93, 389, 394, 395, 407, 414
International Exhibition, Paris (1955) 299
International Exhibition of Modern
    Decorative Art, Turin (1902) 374,
    389, 393
inverted-pear-shaped teapots, silver
    248, 249
Iran *see* Persia
Ireland
    dressers 91
    glass 282, **296**, *296*, 307
    lace 347
    peat-buckets *119*
    porcelain **218**, *218*
    rugs and carpets **330**, *330*
    silver 225, 255, *255*, 257
    tables *55*
Irish trifid feet *20*
Irminger, Johann Jakob 173
Ironbridge 209
Ironside, Edward *231*
ironstone **167**, *167*
ironwork **541**

beds *116*, 117
    domestic wares *454*
    jewelry 271, *271*
    Oriental 523
    toys **504–5**, *505*
Iserlohn 540
Isfahan 316, *316*, 318, *318*
Islamic pottery **149**, *149*, 155
Islamic-style glass 288, 290, 291, *291*
Isokon 416, 419
Istanbul 316, 317, 321
istoriato maiolica 153, *153*, 154, *154*, 156
Italy
    Art Deco ceramics 423, *423*
    Art Deco glass **432**, *432*
    Art Nouveau furniture *388*, **393**
    beds *116*, 117
    bookcases 96
    bureaux 99, 100, 101, *101*
    canapés 42–3, *42*
    cassoni 70, *70*
    chairs 29
    chaises-longues 43
    chests-of-drawers *78*, *79*
    commodes **82**, *82*
    cupboards 72
    dining-chairs 36, 39
    display cabinets 92, 93
    dolls **492**, *492*
    easy chairs **30**, *30*
    escritoires 102
    fans 346
    furniture **449**, *449*, 451, 466
    glass **288**, *288*, 304, **432**, *432*, 457,
        457, **474–5**, *474*
    ironwork 541
    jewelry *262*, 265
    lace 347
    lighting 453, *453*
    linen-presses **73**
    marble 67, *67*
    metalwork **405**
    mirrors 112
    night tables 110
    painted furniture 74, 75
    porcelain **190–1**, *190–1*
    posters 410
    postmodernism 466–7
    pottery **152–4**, *152–4*
    settees 42
    settles *44*
    side cabinets 94, 95
    silver 225, *252*
    Stile Liberty 410
    tables 46, 55, 58, *59*, 65, 67, 105
    tiles 155
    toys **509**, 517
    wardrobes 77
Ive, Jonathan 473
Ives 513
ivory
    Art Deco sculpture **440**, *440*, *441*, 442
    cardcases 544
    inlays 25
    netsuke 524
    Oriental **529**, *529*
    porcelain copies 215
I.W.C. 367
Iznik-style glass 288
Iznik tiles *155*
Iznik wares **149**, *149*, 376

J

Jack, George 371
jackets *345*
Jackfield ware **163**
Jackson, Michael 550
Jackson & Graham 101
Jacob, François-Honoré-Georges 82

Jacob, Georges I 32, 37
Jacob-Desmalter & Cie 110
Jacobean period
    chairs *21*
    crewelwork 336, *336*
Jacobethan style
    beds 117
    dining-chairs 39
    mirrors 113
    sideboards 61
    tables 47
Jacobite glasses 294
Jacobs, Isaac 304
Jacobsen, Arne 450, *450*
jacquard carpets 330
Jacquet-Droz family 494
jade, Oriental **528**, *528*
jadeite 528, *528*
Jaeger le Coultre 367
James II, King of England 294
Jamieson, Mrs 338
Jansen, Jacob 162
Janssen, Hans 534
Janssen, Zacharias 534
Japan
    cabinets-on-stands 86
    carvings **524**, *524*, 525, *525*
    ceramics **142–7**, 460
    clocks 352
    ivory **529**, *529*
    lacquerware 526, **527**, *527*
    metalwork 522, 523, *523*
    mid-century modern 455
    screens 114
    soft toys 495
    toys **518–19**, *518*
    trains 513
Japanese influences
    Aesthetic Movement 372
    Art Nouveau 394, 395
    Arts and Crafts Movement 370, 376
    furniture 53
    glass *291*
    porcelain 197, *197*, *215*, *215*, 221
Japanese Palace, Dresden 174
japanning **25**, *25*, 84, 527
    clocks 354
    furniture *41*, 80, 86, 93
    screens 114–15
    toleware 543
    trays 118
    vernis Martin 66, 80, *84*, 95
Japonisme 394
Jardell, Alexis 297
jardinières 123, *124*, 156, 169, 209, *477*
jars
    glass 299
    Oriental ceramics *136*, *137*, 142
    pottery *153*, *171*
Jarves, Deming 283
Jarvie, Robert 370, **385**, *385*
jaspe glass *284*
jasper ware **127**, 164, 166, *166*
"*Jaspisporzellan*" 173
Jeanette Glass Co. 283
Jeanneret, Pierre 418
Jefferson Co. 403
jelly glasses *281*
jelly molds, copper *541*
Jennens & Bettridge 63, 95, 118, *118*
Jensen, Georg 405, *405*, 436, 452, *452*
J.E.P. (Jouets de Paris) 509, 513
Jerome, Chauncey 353, 357
jet 268, *268*
"jewel-and-eye" decoration, glass 305
jewelry **260–71**
    Art Deco **438–9**, *438–9*
    Art Nouveau *388*, **406–7**, *406–7*
    bracelets **267**, *267*

cameos **263**, *263*
carving 262, *262*
costume jewelry 271–3, *271–3*
earrings 267, *267*
enameling 263, *263*
gemstones 262, *262*
men's jewelry 270, *270*
metals 262
mid-century modern 452, *452*
mosaics 263, *263*
necklaces, pendants and lockets 266, *266*
pins 265, *265*
postmodernist 470
rings 264, *264*
sentimental jewelry 268–9, *268–9*
settings 263, *263*
jeweling, glass 305, *305*
Jiading 525
Jiajing period ceramics 134, 135
Jiangtai, Emperor 522
Jiaqing period ceramics 140
jigsaw puzzles **503**, *503*
Jingdezhen 133, 134, **136**, 137, 138, 140, 160
Joel, Betty 419
Johillco 515
John, Elton 550, *550*, 551
John Lewis Partnership 426
Johnson, Amy 442
Johnson, Edmund 96
Johnson, J.F. *419*
Johnson, Thomas 402
Johnson Furniture 421
Johnstone Jupe & Co. 51, *51*
joined construction, furniture 18, *19*
joined stools **28**, *28*
"jolly boats," silver 255
Jones, George & Sons 169, *169*, 215
Jones, Henry *356*
Jones, Owen 53
Joseff, Eugene **272**, *273*
Josephine, Empress 195, 342
Joubert, Gilles 81
Jouef 513
Jouve, Georges 461, *461*
"joyned" tables 46
Jüchtzer, Christian Gottlieb *181*
jufti knot *315*
jugendstil 388, 400, 404, 406
Jugiez, Martin 62, *64*
jugs
    glass *286*, *294*, *304*
    pewter *404*
    porcelain *194*, *198*, *201*, *205*, *207*
    pottery *122*, *151*, *164*, *165*, *426*
    silver **228**, 229, **251**, *251*, 254, *254*, 255
    stoneware *123*
    Toby jugs *163*
Juhl, Finn 450, *450*
Jumeau **486**, **488**, *488*, 489, 490, 493
Jumeau, Emile 486
Jumeau, Pierre François 486, 487
Jump, Joseph *352*
Jun wares 132, *132*, 139
Junger, Hermann 452
Jupe, Robert 51, 52
Jura 355
juval (bag) *324*
J.V.C. *455*

K

Kaga wares **146**, 147
Kagan, Vladimir 448, *449*
Kåge, Wilhelm 424, 461
Kakiemon porcelain **144**, *144*, 161
    copies 173, 192, 201
Kalo Shop **385**

Kamakura period lacquerware 527
Kämmer, Ernst 490
Kämmer & Reinhardt *480*, *481*, **490**, *490*, 491, *491*, 492, 493
Kandinsky, Wassily *416*
Kändler, Johann Joachim 174, *174*, 175, *175*, 176, 190
Kangxi period ceramics 126, 136, 137, 138, 146, 173, *202*
kaolin 207
Kapoudjian, Hagop 321
Karabagh rugs 320, 322, 323, *323*, 326
Karelian birch 22
Karl Theodore, Elector Palatinate 178
Karlsbad 290
Karpen, S. 421
Kartell 455
Kashan
    pottery 149
    rugs 316, *316*, 318, *319*, 322
Kashgai rugs 319, *319*, 326
Kashgar 327
Kashmir shawls 343, *343*
Kassler, Arthur 442
Kaston, Henryk 452, *452*
Kastrup *456*
Katz, Adolph 273
Kauffer, Edward McKnight 445
Kayser & Söhne 405
Kayseri 321
Kazak rugs 320, 323, *323*
Kéléty, Alexandre 441
Keller, Joseph 295
Kellinghusen 159
Kennedy, Jackie *493*
Kent, Rockwell 437
Kent, William (architect) 88, 92, 112
    bookcases 96
    settees 42
    tables 58, *58*, 60
Kent, William (potter) 126, *168*
Kenton & Co. 372
Keramis 423, *423*
Kestner & Co. **490**, *490*, 491, *491*, 493
Kestner, Adolphe 490
Kestner, Johannes Daniel 490
Keswick School of Industrial Arts **383**
Ketterer, Franz Anton 362
kettles, silver 253, *253*
Kewpie dolls 490, **491**, *491*
Khamseh rugs 319
Khotan 327
Kilian Bros 84
kilims **314**, *314*, **326**, *326*
Killarney 55
King, Jessie M. 406, *406*
King, Thomas, *The Modern Style of Cabinet Work Exemplified* 59
"King Umberto" carpet *316*
"King's" pattern, flatware 244, 245, *245*
Kingsbury Manufacturing Co. 504
Kingston, Duke of 234, 242
kingwood 22, *22*
Kinkozan IV 147
Kinnear, C.G.H. 538
Kirchner, Johann Gottlieb 174
Kirk, William Boyton 218
Kirman 149, 316, 318, 322
Kirschner, Maria 400
kit-cat glasses *281*
Kiz rugs *320*
Klein, Calvin 345
Klemm, Richard 184
Klimt, Gustav 388
Klinger, Johann Georg 532
Klinger, Johann Gottlieb 175
Klinkosch 238
Le Klint 453

"Klismos" chair 38, *39*
Kloster-Veilsdorf 178
Knatchbull, Sir Edward 50
kneehole desks **107**, *107*
Knickerbocker Toy Co. 496
knife-boxes **118**, *118*
knife rests, glass 311, *311*
Knight, Laura 426
knives, silver 244–5, *244–5*
Knoll, Florence 421, 451
Knoll Associates 417, 451, *451*
Knoll International 466
knops, drinking glasses *281*
knots, rugs and carpets *315*
Knowles, Taylor & Knowles Co. 221
Knox, Archibald 382, *382*, 406
Knox Bennett, Gary 471, *471*
Knütgen family 158
Kocks, Adrianus 160
Kodak Co. 538, *538*
Kok, J. Jurrian 395
Konya 320, *321*, 326, *326*
Koppel, Henning 452, *452*
Koppelsdorf porcelain factory 491
Köpping, Karl **400**
Korea
    carvings 525
    ceramics **141**, *141*
    lacquerware **526**
    metalwork 522, 523
Korhonen, Otto 417
koro 144
Koryo period ceramics **141**
Kosta 456
Kothgasser, Anton 288, 290
Kozan, Makuzu 147
kraak wares 135, *135*, 142, 151, 160
Kramer, Sam 452, *452*
Krog, Arnold 397
Krug, Arnold 187
Kruse, Käthe 492, *492*
KTM 513
Kuba 322–3, 326
"Kuba dragon" carpets 322
Kubachi 149
Kubrick, Stanley 451
Kuchler, Louis 442
Kugelbauchkrug 158, *158*
Kuhn, John 474
Kum Kapi *315*, 316, 321, *321*
Kunckel, Johann 284, *284*
"Kunckel red" glass 284
Künzli, Otto 470
Kuramata, Shiro 468–9
Kurdish rugs 320, 326
Kurfürstenhumpen glasses 288
Kütahya wares **149**
Kuttrolf flasks 290
Kyoto, ceramics **147**
Kyser & Rex 505

L

La Hubaudière, Antoine de *157*
La Mésangère, Pierre de, *Collection de Meubles et Objets de goût* 82
labels
    decanter 255
    wine **255**
Labino, Dominick 457, 474
lacca povera ("poor-man's lacquer") 75
lace **347**, *347*
lace-twist outline stems, drinking glasses *281*
Lachenal, Raoul 422
Lacloche Frères 439
lacquer 25, *25*
    cabinets-on-stands 86, *86*
    Oriental **526–7**, *526–7*
    screens 114

trays 118
lacy glass 283, *283*
ladder-back chairs 21, 33, *33*
Ladik 320, *320*
ladles, silver 245, *257*
Lafite, Gaston *407*
Lalique, René 414
    glass 389, **428**, *428*, 429, 434, 435, 549, *549*
    jewelry 407, *407*
    metalwork 404
Lalique, Suzanne 422–3
Lalive de Jully 60
Lambert, Leopold 494
Lambeth 162, *162*, 164
Lambeth School of Art 377
Lamerie, Paul de 229, 234, 239, 241, 250, 252
lamination, Belter's process 35, *35*
lamps *see* lighting
lampwork 302, *302*, 308
Lancashire, dressers 90, 91
Lancaster, J. 538
Lancaster County, Pennsylvania 71, 87, *91*
Landberg, Nils 456
Landelle, Charles *183*
Lane, Danny 468
Langlois, Pierre 81
lantern clocks 350, *350*
Lanz, Johann Wilhelm 178
lapis lazuli 262
Larche, Raoul 409
Laroque, Pierre 30
Latrobe, Benjamin 38
latticinio glass 287, *287*, 308
lattimo glass 284
Laub- und Bandelwerk ("leaf-and-strapwork")
    ceramics 188
    glass 289
Läuger, Max 389, 396
Laurel, Pierre 441
Lawson Time Inc. *437*
Le Corbusier 414, 415, 418, *418*, 420
Le Creusot Glass Factory 305
Le Faguays, Pierre 440, *440*
Le Masson, Louis *194*
Le Nove 154
Le Riche *194*
Leach, Bernard 126, 460, *460*
lead figures **514–15**, *514–15*
lead glass 276, 296
lead-glazed ceramics 123, **163**, *163*
Lebanon County, Pennsylvania *71*
Lechevallier-Chévignard, George 422
Lechevrel, Alphonse Eugène 300, 301
Ledru, Léon 299
Lee, Henry 445
Leeds 165, *165*
Leeds Model Co. 513
Leerdam Glassworks 456
Lefebvre, Piat *329*
Legrain, Pierre 418
Legras, Auguste JF 431, *431*
legs, furniture styles *20*
Lehman, Caspar 278, 293
Lehmann, tinplate toys 506, 509
Lehmann, Les Neveux de J. 440
Leica 538, *538*
Leithner, Joseph 188
Leitz, Ernst 534
Leleu *404*
Lelli, Angelo 453
Lemaire, George 408
Lenci 423, *423*, 492, *492*
Lennon, John 550, 551
Lenox Inc. 221
Lenz, Philip 442
Léonard, Agathon 398, *399*

Lerebours 538
Leroy, Desiré 125, 216, *216*
Lesney 517, *517*
Lessieux, Louis 411
Lethaby, William 372
Leuteritz, Ernst August 181, *181*
Levasseur, Etienne 81
Levens Hall, Westmorland 340
Lewis, W. & W.H. 538
L'Herminotte, Joannes Andreas Gerardus *230*
Li Hongzhang *525*
libation cups, jade *528*
Libbey Glass Co. 301
Libensky, Stanislav 456–7
Liberty, Arthur Lasenby *373*, 382, 406
Liberty & Co. 126
    costume 342
    furniture 63, 101, 373, *373*
    jewelry 406
    metalwork 382, *382*
    rugs and carpets 321
library *bergères* 31, *31*
library bookcases *96*
library steps 66
library tables 54, **105**
Licensing Act (1860) 255
Lichte 185
lighting
    Art Deco *429*
    Art Nouveau 388, 398, **402–3**, *402–3*, *404*, **409**, *409*
    Arts and Crafts 377
    candelabra 234–5, *234–5*, **306**, *306*, *404*
    candlestands 66
    candlesticks 230–5, *230–5*, **306**, *306*, *385*, 540, *540*
    glass *291*, **306–7**, *306–7*
    mid-century modern **453**, *453*
    postmodernist *471*
    table-lamps *384*, *402*
lily vases, glass *298*
Limbach 178
Limbert, Charles P. 375, *375*
lime glass 276, 293
Limehouse porcelain 200, *200*, 204, 205
Limoges
    dolls 489, *489*
    porcelain 193, 196, **199**, *199*, 423
Limosin, Léonard 198
Linck, Konrad 178
Lindberg, Stig 461
Lindfren, Johan *31*
Lindner, Doris 217
Lindstrand, Vicke 293, 433, 456
Linemar 519
linen, whitework 338
linen-presses **73–4**, **75**, *75*
Lineol 514
Lines, G. & J. 499
Lines Bros 493, 499, 502, 509
Linke, François *84*, 93, *93*, 94–5, *115*, *117*
Linning, Johann-Christian 80
Linossier, Claudius 436, *436*, 437
Linthorpe Pottery 376, *377*
lion-mask handles *21*
Lionel Corporation 513, *513*
Lipofsky, Marvin 474
Lisbon 151, *151*
lit à la duchesse 116
lit en bateau 117, *117*
lithography
    ceramics **125**, *125*
    paper toys 502
    posters 410
lithophanes 181, *185*, **185**
Lithyalin glass 285, *285*
Littler, William 202
Littleton, Harvey K. 457, 474

Liverpool
    blue-and-white wares 204–5, *205*
    clocks 355
    delftware 162
    porcelain 200
    tiles *155*
Lob, J.M. 395
Lobmeyr, J. & L. 291, *291*, 293, *293*, 298, 304, 305, *305*, 432
Lobmeyr, Josef 298, **400**
Lobmeyr, Ludwig 400
Lock, Matthias 60, 112, *112*
Lock, Nathaniel 225
Locke, Joseph 287, *287*, 295, *295*, *300*, 301
lockets 266, *266*, 269
Loetz 432, *432*
Loetz-Witwe, Johann **400**, *400*, 401
Loewy, Raymond 421, 454
Loffler, Bertold 397
Lombardy 73, *73*, *78*
Lomonosov porcelain factory 219
London
    barometers 364
    clocks 354, 355
    delftware 162
    porcelain 200
    silver hallmarks 225
    street fashion 344
"London Scenes" tea service *216*
London Underground *445*
longcase clocks **354–5**, *354–5*
Longines 367, *367*
Longqing period ceramics 134
Longquan celadons 132, *132*, 133
Longton Hall 202, *202*, 204, 205, 206, 211
Longwy factory 422, *422*
loo tables 53
Looking Glass and Picture Frame Factory *112*
looms, rugs and carpets 315
Lorenz, Oswald 184
Lorenzl, Joseph 424, **443**, *443*
lost-wax casting, silver 224
Lotto, Lorenzo 317
"Lotto" pattern, rugs and carpets 317, 330, 331
"Lotus blossom" carpets *327*
Loudon, John Claudius, *Encyclopaedia of Cottage, Farm and Villa Architecture and Furniture* 76
Louis XIII, King of France 30, 328
Louis XIII clocks 356
Louis XIV, King of France 156, 250, 328
Louis XIV period
    canapés 42
    chairs 19, *19*, 30, 31
    chaises-longues 43
    commodes 80
    dining-chairs 36, 40
    mirrors 112
    tables 58, *59*
Louis XV, King of France 178, 192, 193, *193*, 197, 342
Louis XV period
    armoires *74*
    bombé commodes 80, *80*
    chairs 30
    chaises-longues *43*
    chests-of-drawers 85
    clocks 356
    commodes 81
    dining-chairs 40
    display cabinets 93
    easy chairs *34*, 35
    night tables 110, *110*
    tables 58, *58*, 59, 66, *66*, 68
    tables à gibier 61

wardrobes 77
Louis XV Revival
    chairs 35
    vitrines 92
Louis XVI, King of France 64, *178*, 197, 297, 342
Louis XVI period
    armoires 75
    beds 117, *117*
    chairs *21*
    chests-of-drawers 85
    commodes 81, *81*
    dining-chairs 37, 40
    dining-tables 50
    display cabinets 93
    easy chairs *34*, 35
    mirrors 113
    night tables 110
    screens *115*
    tables 58, *66*
Louis XVI Revival
    canapés 45
    rugs and carpets *329*
    side cabinets 94–5
    sofas 45
Louis XVIII, King of France 299, 329
Louis Philippe, King of France 329
"Louis" style, wardrobes 77
Louise, Princess of Prussia 182
Louvre, Paris 328, *328*
love seats 34
"Lovis" 411
Low, Catherine *339*
Low Art Tile Co. 155
Low Countries
    brass 540
    furniture 42, 71, **72**, 79
    glass *276*, *292*, 302, 306
    porcelain **186**, *186*
    see also Belgium; Netherlands
lowboys 62, *62*, 87
"lowbrow" dolls 485
Löwenfink, Adam Friedrich von 178
Lowestoft, blue-and-white wares 205, *205*
lozenge stoppers, glass *280*
Lucchese, Francesco *475*
Luce, Jean 423, 431
Lucite 272
Lück, Carl Gottlieb 178
Lück, Johann Christoph Ludwig *188*
Lück, Johann Friedrich 178
Luck, K.G. *178*
Lucotte 514, *514*
Ludwigsburg *179*, *179*, *186*, 187, 199
Lund, Benjamin 200, *200*, 203, 205
Lundberg, Theodor *397*
Lundhal, Fred 504
Lundin, Ingeborg 456
Lunéville 156
luster glazes, ceramics 125, *125*, *150*
lusters, glass candlesticks 306, *306*
Lütken, Per 456
Lütz 506, 508
Lutz, Nicholas 309
Luzo cameras 538
Lyncker, Anton 186
Lyons 156, 343, 359
lyre-back chairs *21*, 38
lyre clocks 353, 358
Lyse, Anthony de 294
Lyttleton, Sarah, Lady 109

M
McBirney, David 218
McCabe 359
McCain, Mac 476
MacCarthy, D. 186
McCartney, Paul 550, 551
machine lace *347*

machine-piercing, silver 227, *227*
McIntire, Samuel 116
Macintyre & Co. 396, *396*
Mackennal, Bertrand *408*
Mackenzie, Bertrand *408*
Mackintosh, Charles Rennie 370, 372, 373, *373*, 375, 383, 389, 393, 405
Mackmurdo, Arthur Heygate 372
McLaren, Malcolm 344
McLoughlin Brothers 499, 503
Maddox of London 83
Madonna 550, *550*
Madoura *461*
Madrid 190
Madrid royal tapestry factory 331, *331*
Maggiolini, Giuseppe 58, 82
Maggiolini commodes **82**, *82*
magic lanterns 539, *539*
Magistretti, Vico 453, *471*
Magnus, G.E. 95, *95*
mahogany 22, *22*
    chests-on-chests **88–9**
Maigelein 276
Main, John 248
Mainz 74
Mainz, Elector of 178
maiolica 123, **152–4**, *152–4*
La Maison de l'Art Nouveau, Paris 388, 391, 392
La Maîtrise 414, 418, 423
majolica **169**, *169*
    American 171, *171*
Majorelle, Louis 389, 390, *390*, 429
Majorette 517
Makepeace, John 467
Makkum 160
Málaga 150
Mallard, Prudent 117
manganese oxide, glass 276
Mangold 517
Manierblumen 175
Manises 150
Manner, Frederick Schneider 445
Mannerism
    cassoni 70
    cupboards **72**, *72*, 73
    mirrors 113
    tables 46–7
Mannheim 178
Manoil 515
Manship, Paul 425
Mansion 82
Mantegna, Andrea 153
mantel clocks 356, **358**
Manwaring, Robert 37
"Manx" tripod tables 64
maple, bird's-eye 22, *22*
Maples 95
Mappin & Webb *245*
Mappin Bros *233*
Marasali 323
marble
    side cabinets 95
    tables 67, *67*
Marcolini, Count Camillo **176**, 181
Mare, André 415, 418
Margaret, Princess 492
Maria Luisa, Queen of Spain *190*
Marie Antoinette, Queen of France 40, *178*, 194, 342
Marieberg 187
Marinot, Maurice 429, *429*
Märklin, Carl 507
Märklin, Eugen 507
Märklin, Gebrüder **507**, *507*, **510**, *510*, 512, 517, 518
Märklin, Theodor Friedrich Wilhelm 507
marks
    cabinet-makers' **76**
    ceramic fakes and forgeries 127

Chinese porcelain **139**, *139*
    hallmarks **225**, *225*
    Sheffield plate and electroplate 233
Marot, Daniel 36, *39*, 59
    Livres d'Appartements 36
Marot style chairs *21*
marqueterie sur verre 398
marquetry **24**, *24*
    Buhl decoration 38, 55, *55*
    bureaux 100, 101
    cabinets-on-stands 86, *86*
    chests-of-drawers *83*, 84
    clocks 354, *354*
    dining-chairs **36**, *36*
    display cabinets 92
    Maggiolini commodes **82**, *82*
    tables 65, *65*
marquise rings 264, *264*
marriages **26**
Marseille, Armand **491**, *491*
Marseilles 156, *157*, 340
Marsh, Charles A. 483
Marsh & Tatham 38, 107
martelé glass 398
Martens, Dino 457
Martin, Fernand & Cie 509
Martin, Robert 376, *376*
Martin brothers 370, 376
Martin family 80, 84, *84*
Marusan 518
Marx, Louis 504, *504*, 515, 519, *519*
Mary II, Queen of England 162, *162*
    see also William and Mary period
"Mary Gregory" glass 311, *311*
Mashad 318
Mason, Charles James 167
Mason, John 476
Mason's Patent Ironstone 167, *167*
Massachusetts 49, 89, *89*
Massier, Clement 394, *394*
Masson, Nicolas-Richard *242*
Masudaya 518, *518*, 519
Matchbox **517**, *517*
matches, vesta cases **545**
Mather, Charles 445
Mathews, Arthur 375
Mathews, Lucia 375
Matisse, Henri *293*, 415, 422
Mattel 493, *493*, 499, 517
matting, silver **227**, *227*
Mattoni, Andreas 290
Mauboussin 439
Maurer, Ingo 471, *475*
Maw & Co. 376, *376*
May, Ada 442
Mayhew, John 89
    *The Universal System of Household
    Furniture* 62, 64, 81, 92, 93, 105
Mayodon, Jean 422
Mazarin, Cardinal Jules 30, 107
Meagher, P. 538
measures, pewter *541*
Meccano 499, 507, 509, *509*, 516, 518
meccha gilding, furniture 25, 42
Medaillonbecher 304
medallions, sulphides **305**, *305*, *308*, 309
medical instruments **535**, *535*
Medici, Francesco I de 190
medicine-chests **535**, *535*
Meech, Annette 475
Meech, Herbert John 483
Meeks, Joseph & Sons 35
Meier, Otto 461
Meier-Graefe, Julius 404
Meiji period ceramics 146
Meilo, Franco *468*
meiping wares *133*, *138*
Meissen 144, 178, 180, 183, 193, 396
    copies and imitations 184, 186, 190,

199, 201, 202, 203, 206, 209, 213
    cups and saucers *122*
    "Dot" ("Academic") period **176**
    early porcelain 173, *173*
    fakes and forgeries *127*
    figures **174**, *174*, 176, *176*,
        181, *181*, 210
    Hausmaler **177**, *177*
    Marcolini period **176**
    19th-century **181**, *181*
    perfume bottles 548, *548*
    sweetmeat dishes *125*
    tablewares and services **175**, *175*
    tea caddies 547
Meissonnier, Juste-Aurèle 37, 42, *58*, 74,
    234, 242
Meizan, Yabu 147
Mekeren, Jan van 36, 84, 86
Melchior, Johann Peter 178, 179
Memling, Hans 317
"Memling" pattern, rugs and carpets 317
memorial pictures, needlework 338
Memphis Group 465, *465*, 466, 467, *467*,
    469, *472*, *472*, 473
Mendini, Alessandro 472, 473, *473*
Mennecy 186, 187, **192**, *192*
Mennicken, Jan Emens 158
Mennicken family 158
Mennonite quilts 341
men's jewelry **270**, *270*
menswear **345**, *345*
Mercier 263
mercurial pendulums, clocks 351
mercury gilding 25, 279
Mercury toys 517
mercury twists, drinking glass stems 303
Merino sheep 332
Merovingian glass 282
Merrythought Ltd 495, 497, *497*
Merton Abbey Workshops 371, 376, 384
Meshed 149
Mesopotamia
    glass 276
    pottery 149, *149*
Messagé, Léon 93
metal furniture **451**, *451*
The Metal Pot 160
metallic oxides, colored glass 278, 284
metals, postmodernist furniture **468–9**
metalware **540–1**, *540–1*
    Art Deco **436–7**, *436–7*
    Art Nouveau **404–5**, *404–5*
    Arts and Crafts **382–5**, *382–5*
    folk art **542–3**, *543*
    Oriental **522–3**, *522–3*
metamorphic furniture
    commodes (night tables) 111
    tables 66
Methodist Church, United States *341*
Metlicovitz, Leopoldo 410
Metoy Co. 517
Metthey, André 422
Mettlach 158
Mettoy 509, 513, 518
meubles d'appui 94
meubles en deux corps 72, *72*, 88
Meydam, Floris 456
Meyer, Christian 81
Meyer, Franz Ferdinand 177, *177*
Meyer, Friedrich Elias 174, *175*
Meyer, Wilhelm Christoph 180
Meyrs Neffe 290, 432
Mezence, Mlle de *422*
Michaud, R. *444*
Michtom, Morris 496
micro-mosaic inlays 55
microscopes **534**, *534*
mid-century modern **447–63**
    ceramics **458–63**, *458–63*

domestic wares **454–5**, *454–5*
    furniture **448–51**, *448–51*
    glass **456–7**, *456–7*
    jewelry **452**, *452*
    lighting **453**, *453*
Middelburg 72
Middle Ages, tables 46
Mies van der Rohe, Ludwig 416–17, *417*
Migéon, Pierre 110
Mignot, C.B.G. 514
Mihalik, Julius 425
Mikado Co. 84
Milan 154, *154*, 347
Milan Triennale (1954) 454
Milchglas **288**, 289
Mildner, Johann Josef 304
military beds 117
military wristwatches 367, *367*
milk-jugs, porcelain *205*, 207
Millar, J.B. 295
millefiori, glass paperweights
    308, *308*, 309
Miller, Fritz von 404
Miller, Herman 448
Miller, James A. 384
Mills, Nathaniel 544
Milne, A.A. 497
Milne, Robert *355*
Milton, John 300
Milton, May 410
Milton Bradley & Co. 502, 503
Milton Ernest Hall, Bedfordshire *111*
Mina'i pottery 149
mineral-water bottles 311
Ming period
    ceramics 126, 128, 131, **133–5**, *133–5*,
        137
    ivory 529
    jade 528
    lacquerware 526
miniatures, jewelry **269**
Minton & Co. 209, 211, 213
    Art Nouveau ceramics 396, *396*
    Arts and Crafts ceramics 376, 377
    export wares 216
    Japanesque style **215**
    majolica 169, *169*
    parian ware 214, *214*
    saucers *125*
    studio pottery 370
    tiles 155
    vases *124*
Mintons Art Pottery Studios 377
mirrors 112–13, *112–13*, *391*
    dressing tables 62, 63
    silver frames **259**, *259*
    on wardrobes 77
"Mission oak" 374
Mistinguett 444
mixed twists, drinking glass stems
    303, *303*
"Mizpah" pins 269
"mochaware" 170
"mod" style, clothes 345
Modern Movement **415**
    furniture 418, **419**, 420, 421
    metalwork 437
    origins of 370
Modernismo 388
Mohn, Gottlob Samuel 288, 290
Mohn, Samuel 290, *290*
Moje, Klaus 474
Moje-Wohlgemuth, Isgard 474
Molaroni *154*
Molitor, Bernard 82
Mollino, Carlo 449
Molyneux, Edward 344
Monart glass 401, *401*
Moncrieff Glassworks 309, 401, *401*

Mondrian, Piet 420
Mongolian rugs and carpets 327
monk's tables 42
Monnoyer, Jean-Baptiste 161
monochromes, Chinese porcelain
    138–9, *139*
Montanari, Augusta 483, *483*
Montanari, Richard 483
monteiths, silver **257**, *257*
Montelupo 153, 154
Montereau 157
Montgomery dressers 91
Monti, Raphaelle 214
Montpellier 156
Mooleyser, Willem 292
Moon, Keith 551
moon flasks *522*
Moorcroft, William *124*, 396, *396*
Moore, P. & Co. *97*
Moore, Thomas 330
Moore, William *58*
Moore & Gumley 25
Moors 78, 331
Morahan, Eugene *543*
Morel, Jean-Valentin *253*
Morel-Ladeuil, Léonard 235
"Morgan" cup *300*
Morgenthaler, Sasha 493
Morimura, Iczaemon 147
Morland, George *118*
Mornaix, Charles Sallandrouze de la *329*
Morris, George Anthony 220, *220*
Morris, Henry 212
Morris, Marshall, Faulkner & Co. 53, 370,
    370, 371, *371*, 377
Morris, William *286*, 472
    carpets 330
    ceramics 377
    furniture 53, 370, **371**, *371*, 374
    metalwork 382
    needlework 336, *376–7*
Morris & Co. 370, 371, 372
"Morris" chairs 371, 374
mortise-and-tenon joints *19*
Mortlake 164, *164*
Morton, Alexander and Co. 330
mosaic glass 284
mosaic quilts 340, *340*
mosaics, jewelry 263, *263*
Moser, Koloman 400, 405, 407, 432
Moser, Ludwig 279, 290
Moser, Ludwig & Sons 290, *290*, 304
Mosley, R.F. & Co. 257
mosque lamps 307
mote spoons, silver 245
"moth painter" 206, *206*
Motzfeld, Benny 475
mold-blown glass 276, **282**, *282*
molds
    copper *541*
    pressed glass 276, **283**, *283*
Mount Washington Glass Co. 286,
    287, *287*, 301
Mourgue, Olivier 451, *451*
mourning jewelry 264, **268**, *268*,
    269, 270
mourning pictures, needlework 338, *338*
Moustiers 150, 156
mouths, dolls 481
Mozart, Wolfgang Amadeus 109
Mucha, Alphonse *386–7*, 407, 410, *410*
mugs
    ceramic *125*, 208
    silver **247**, *247*
Muir, Jean 344
mule chests 71, 78
Müller, Albin *404*, 405
Müller, Desiré 399

Müller, Friedrich 482
Müller, Henri 399
Müller, J.G. 219
Müller, Karl 220
Müller Frères 398, 399, *399*, 431
Munden 159
Munich 178, 404
Murano *113*, 432, 457, 474–5
Murch, John *244*
Murcia 331
Murphy, H.G. 439
Murray, Keith 426, *426*, 433
Murrle, Bennett & Co. 406, *406*
Mürrle, Ernst 406
"muses' modeler" 202
Museum of Fine Arts, Boston 200
Museum of Modern Art, New York 448, 449, 452
Musgrave, James *251*
mushroom knops, drinking glasses *281*
mushroom stoppers, glass *280*
music
   music stands 108, **109**, *109*
   musical instruments **551**, *551*
   rock and pop memorabilia
      550–1, *550–1*
Musselburgh 202
mustard-pots, silver *226*, **258**, *258*, 259
Myers, Joel Philip 474
Myott, Son & Co. 424
mystery clocks **363**, *363*

N
Nabeshima porcelain **145**, *145*
Nachet & Sons 534
Nailsea 279, 310, *310*
Nailsea Glasshouse 310
Nakashima, George 448
Namban lacquerware 527
name pins 269
Nancy, glass 301
Nancy School 389, **390–1**, 395, **398**, 399
Nanjing 525
Nantes, Edict of (1685), Revocation of 36, 58, 227
Nantgarw 209, **212**, *212*
Naples
   coral jewelry 262
   furniture 80
   maiolica 152
   porcelain **190**, *190*, 191
Napoleon I, Emperor *35*, 38, 59, 67, 82, 110, 113, 182, 194, 195, 218, *219*, 329
Napoleon III, Emperor 113, 196, 342
Napoleonic Wars 105, 181
Nara period lacquerware 527
Nasenschrank 73, *73*
Nasrid dynasty 150
Nast, Nepomucene-Jean-Hermann 195
Nast factory **195**, *195*
National Exhibition, Paris (1823) 299
National Training School 377
Native Americans
   pottery 170, **171**, *171*
   weaving 332–3, *332–3*
Natzler, Gertrud 462, *462*
Natzler, Otto 462, *462*
Navajo Indians
   pottery 171
   weaving 332–3, *332–3*
navigational instruments **533**, *533*
necklaces **266**, *266*, *272*, *273*, *388*, *470*
needlepoint lace **347**, *347*
needlework **336–41**, *336–41*
   Berlin woolwork **337**, *337*
   canvaswork **337**, *337*
   crewelwork **336**, *336*
   pictures **338**, *338*

quilts **340–1**, *340–1*
samplers **339**, *339*
stumpwork **336**, *336*
upholstery 34
whitework **338**, *338*
see also costume
Nees, Joseph *179*
Negretti & Zambra 365
Nelson, Admiral 38, *338*
Nelson, George 421, 448, *449*, 453, 454, *455*
Nemours, Duke of 196
Neo-classical style 20
   architecture 182
   armoires **75**
   barometers *364*
   beds 116
   bookcases 96
   bureaux 99, *99*
   carpets 330
   chairs *32*
   chests-of-drawers 84
   chests-on-chests 89
   clocks 353, 358, *358*
   commodes **81**
   costume 342, 343
   dining-chairs **37**, 40
   dining-tables 50, 53
   display cabinets 93
   dressing tables 62, 63
   easy chairs 31, *35*
   glass *286*, 291, 293, *293*
   jewelry 264, 268, *270*, 271
   knife-boxes 118
   mirrors 113
   night tables 110
   porcelain 176, *176*, 178, 179, 180, *180*, *181*, 186, 187, *187*, 188, 189, *189*, 193, **194**, *194*, 196, 206, *206*, 207, 208, *209*, 219
   pot-cupboards 110–11
   secrétaires 103, *103*
   serving tables 60, *60*
   side cabinets 95
   sideboards 61
   silver **230–1**, *230*, 232, 234, 237, *237*, 238, 242, 243, *243*, 247, 249, 250, 251, 252, *252*, 255, *257*, 258
   sofas *43*, 45
   stoneware **166**
   tables 56, 58, 65, *69*
   washstands 111
   wine coolers and cellarets 119
   writing tables 105
Neo-Gothic style
   furniture 371
   jewelry 271
Neo-Renaissance porcelain 183
Neolithic period ceramics 131, *131*
nephrite **528**, *528*
Nero, Emperor 153
nests of tables *66*, 67
Netherlands
   armoires 74, *75*
   Art Deco furniture **416**, *416*
   Art Nouveau ceramics **395**, *395*
   brass 540
   bureaux 99, 100, 101
   cabinets-on-stands 86
   chair construction 19
   chairs 29
   chests-of-drawers 78, 83, *83*, 84
   clocks 354, *354*, 356
   cupboards 72, *72*, 73
   dining-chairs 36, *36*, 40
   display cabinets 92, 93
   glass 278, 456
   kneehole desks 107
   painted furniture 74

peat-buckets 119
porcelain 186
pottery **160–1**, *160–1*
samplers 339
screens *114*
secrétaires 103
settees 42
settles 42
silver *239*
tables 46, 64
tiles 155, *155*
wardrobes 77
netsuke 524, *524*, 525, 527, 529
Neudeck 179
Neuss, Georg Christoph *232*
Nevers 156, *156*, 302
"Nevers" figures 302, *302*
"New Canton" 202
New Edwardian clothes 345
New England
   chairs 30, 31
   clocks 353
   high chests-of-drawers 87
   pottery 170–1
New England Glass Co. 283, *283*, 287, *287*, 301, *308*, 309
New England School 379
New Hall **207**, *207*, 209
New Hampshire 87, 89
"New Look," clothes 344
New York
   chairs *30*
   dining-tables *51*
   high chests-of-drawers 87
   Phyfe school 43
   porcelain 220, 221
   pottery 171
   silver 246
   tables 55, 68
   wardrobes 76
Newbould, Frank 445
Newcastle light baluster stems, drinking glasses *281*
Newcastle-upon-Tyne 292
Newcomb College Pottery 380, *380*
Newell, Steven 475
Newlyn School **383**, *383*
Newport, Rhode Island 87, *102*
Newport Pottery 426
Newson, Marc 468
Newton & Sons 532
Nicholas of Russia *182*
Nichols, Maria Longworth 378
"Nichols Chinese" carpets 327
Nicolson, Michel Angelo, *The Practical Cabinet-Maker, Upholsterer and Complete Decorator* 43
Niderviller 156
Niedermayer, Johann Joseph 188
Niedermayer, Matthias 189
niello 227
Nienhuis, Bert 395, *395*
Nigg, Joseph 188
"night" caps 345
night tables **110–11**, *110*
Nijinsky, Vaslav 441
Nîmes 156
Ningxia 327, *327*
Nippon wares **147**
"nipt-diamond-waies" glass 279
Nishapur 149
Nister, Ernest 503
Noah's Arks 502
Noguchi, Isamu 448
Noke, Charles 217
Nomura 518, 519
Non-Such Flint Glassworks 304
"nonsuch" chests 71
Noritake Co. 147, *147*

Normandy 74, 359
North America *see* United States of America
Northumberland County, Pennsylvania 71
Northwood, J. & J. 300
Northwood, John 295, 300, 301, 401
Northwood, Joseph 295, 300
Northwood Glass Co. 283, *283*
Norton, Alexander *119*
Norton family 170, *170*, 171
Norway, silver *247*
Norwich 162, 343
Nottingham *164*
Novak, Bretislav Junior 475
novelty clocks **362–3**, *362–3*
Nuremberg
   brass 540
   faience 159, *159*
   furniture 102
   glass 284, 289, 293, 302
   toys **506**
Nylund, Gunnar 461
Nymphenburg 179, *179*, 190, 199
NZG 517

O
O-Luce 453
oak 23, *23*
occasional tables **66–7**, *66–7*
Ochel, Aloys 514
Ochsenkopfhumpen glasses 288
octants 533, *533*
Odell, Jack 517
Odiot 238, 256
Oeben, Jean-François 81, 99
"OG" clocks 353
ogee bracket feet *20*
ogee-shaped drinking glasses *281*
Ohio 171, 282
Ohio Valley School **378**, 379
Ohr, George E. 370, 380, *380*
Ohrström, Edvin 456
oil bottles, Oriental ceramics *141*
oil gilding
   furniture 25
   glass 279
oil lamps, glass 307, *307*
ojime 524, 525, *525*, 527
Olbrich, Josef Maria 404, *404*, 405, 407
old cut, gemstones *262*
"Old English" pattern, flatware 245, *245*
"Old French" style, dining-chairs 40
"Old Kutani" style, ceramics 146, *146*
Olivetti 455, 472, *472*
Olsen, Michel *247*
Omega watches 367
Omega Workshops 372
One Off Ltd 468
one-piece quilts **340**
O'Neill, Rose 491
Onondaga Shops 374, *374*, 384, *384*
opaline glass 284, *286*, 287, 291, 304
opals 262
opaque twists, drinking glass stems **303**, *303*
open-back settings, jewelry **263**, *263*
Oporto 151
optical toys 538, *539*, *539*
Orbison, Roy *551*
Oriental art **492–501**
   carvings **524–5**, *524–5*
   ivory **529**, *529*
   jade **528**, *528*
   lacquerware **526–7**, *526–7*
   metalwork **522–3**, *522–3*
   pottery and porcelain **130–47**, *130–47*
   rugs and carpets **316–27**, *316–27*
Oriental influences, Art Deco 415, 418, 422

Oriental style
  carpets 330
  chests-of-drawers *83*, 84
  see also chinoiserie;
    Japanese influences
Orleans, Dukes of 112, 192, 196
Orme, Charles *364*
ormolu **25**, *25*
Orrefors 293, *293*, 432–3, *433*, 434, 456, *456*, 475
orreries 532
Orvieto 152
Osler (F. & C.) Glasshouse 296, 306, *307*
Osterley House, Middlesex 330
Osterspey, Jakob 178, *178*
Ott & Brewer 221, *221*
Ottewill, Thomas 538
Ottoman Empire, rugs and carpets **317**, *317*, **320–1**, *320–1*, 326
Oude Loosdrecht 186, 187
oval-shaped teapots **249**
overcoats 345
overlay glass 278, **285**
  cut glass 296, 298
  glass paperweights 308
Ovid 153
Owen, George 124, *147*, 215, *215*
ox-horn decoration, Korea 526
Oxford, clocks 355
oyster plates, porcelain *221*
oyster veneering **24**, *24*

P
P. & Cie *253*
pad feet *20*
painted furniture **25**, *25*, 84–5
  commodes *80*
  fakes 27
  provincial armoires 74–5, *74*
painting, folk art 542
Pairpoint Corporation 403, *403*
Paisley shawls 341, *341*
Pajeau, Charles 502
Pakistan, rugs and carpets 325
Palace of Westminster 39
Palatinate 178
Palazzo Reale, Turin 99
palisandre 22
Palissy, Bernard 151, 169
Palitoy 497
Palladian style
  architecture *75*
  furniture 88, 92, 96
  mirrors 112
"Pallas" flatweaves **326**
Pallme-König & Habel **400**, *400*
Palme, Franz Joseph 295
Palmqvist, Sven 456
Palmyra 75
pan-top drinking glasses *281*
Panasonic 455, *455*
Panton, Verner *447*, 451, *451*
paper toys **502–3**, *502–3*
paperweights, glass 305, **308–9**, *308–9*
papier-mâché
  chairs *21*
  dolls **482**, *482*
  dressing tables 63
  side cabinets 95
  tables 67
  trays 118, *118*
  wardrobes 76–7
Papworth, Edgar the younger *214*
Paquin, Mme Joseph 344
parasols **346**, *346*
"parcel gilding," silver 227
Parchment Convent, Youghal 347
Pardoe, Thomas 212
Pargeter, Philip 300

parian busts and statues **214**, *214*
parian dolls **485**, *485*
parian ware 216, 221
Paris
  Art Deco jewelry 439
  cabinet-makers' marks 76
  clocks 355, 358, 359
  mirrors 112, 113
  porcelain **195**, *195*, **198–9**, *198–9*
  posters 444
  shawls 343
  tables 66, 68
  watches 367
Paris-Lyon-Méditerranée (P.L.M.) railway 444, *444*
Paris School 389, **391**, 392, 393
"*Parisiennes*" 486
Parisot, Pierre 330
Parker, John *231*
Parker, George 80
  A Treatise of Japanning and Varnishing 86
Parker & Wakelin 234
Parker Brothers 503
parlor suites 44, 45
Paros 214
parquetry **25**, *25*, 65, *65*
partners' pedestal desks *107*
Passavant, Claude 330, *330*
paste jewelry **271**, *271*
patchboxes 545, *546*
patchwork quilts 340, *340*, **341**, *341*
pâte-de-cristal 430
pâte-de-verre 276, 398, **399**, *399*, *414*, 430, *430*
pâte-sur-pâte **124**, *124*, 196, *197*, 199, 396
Patek Philippe 367
patination, furniture *23*
Patou, Jean 344
Patrick, John *364*
Patti, Tom 474
Paul, Bruno 421
Paulin, Pierre 451
pavé settings, jewelry **263**, *263*
Paya 509
Pazyryk 316
Peachblow glass 287
pear-shaped teapots, silver **248**, *248*, 249
pearlware **165**, *165*, 167
Pearson, John 383
peat-buckets **119**, *119*
"pebble" pins 265, *265*
Pêche, Dagobert 400, 421, 432, 436
Peck, Lucy 483
pedestal desks 107, *107*
pedestal dining-tables 50–1, *50*, 52
pedestal stems, drinking glasses *281*
Pedigree 493
pediments, chests-on-chests *89*
peep-boxes 539
peg tankards, silver 246, *247*
pegged construction, furniture 18, *19*
Peiser, Mark 474
PEL 419
Pellatt, Apsley 295, 305, *305*
Pembroke tables 18, 49, 54, **56**, *56*, 69
pendant earrings 267, *267*
pendants 266, *266*, *399*, 406, *407*, *438*, *528*
pendule de voyage 359
pendule religieuse clocks 356
pendule sur socle clocks 355
pendulums, clocks **351**
Peninsular War (1809–14) 83, 331
Pennington, James 204
Pennington, John 204
Pennington, Seth 204
Pennington family 204, 205

Pennsylvania
  furniture 87
  glass 282
  pottery 171
  quilts *341*
  samplers *339*
Pennsylvania Dutch
  chairs 33
  chests 71, *71*
  dressers *91*
Pennsylvania German folk art 542, *542*, 543
Pennsylvania German quilts 341
"Pennsylvania slipware" 170
Penrose, George 296
Penrose, William 296
Penyamian, Zareh 321
"Peony and dragon" rugs 327
Percier, Charles 28, 329
  Receuil de décorations intérieures 28, 38, 59, 82
Perebedil 323
perfume bottles *see* scent bottles
peridot *262*
Perriand, Charlotte 418
Perrot, Pierre-Josse 328, *328*
Perry, Fred 536
Perry, Commodore Matthew 146
Persia
  pottery **149**, *149*
  rugs and carpets 316, *316*, **318–19**, *318–19*, 326
Persian knot *315*
Pesce, Gaetano *468*, 471
Peterinck, François-Joseph 186
Petit, Jacob **198**, *198*
Pettifer, Daniel *544*
pewter **541**, *541*
  Art Nouveau *404*
  Arts and Crafts 382, *382*
Pfohl, Karl *285*
Phalibois, Jean Marie 494, *494*
Philadelphia
  chairs 30, 31, *31*
  chests-on-chests 89
  clocks 355
  dining-tables *51*
  glass 297
  high chests-of-drawers 87, *87*
  porcelain 220
  Rococo-style furniture 62, *62*
  silver *248*, 251
  tables *64*
Philadelphia Chippendale style 62
Philadelphia Tin Toy Manufactory 504
Philip V, King of Spain 331
Philippe, Alfred 272, *272*
Philippe, Paul 442–3, *442*
Philipson 337
Phoenix Glassworks *435*
Phoenixville, Pennsylvania 171
photography 538, *538*
Phyfe, Duncan 38, **43**, *43*, 51, *57*, 68, 116
"Piano Babies" 185
piano rests, glass 311
"piano-top" Davenports *106*
Pianon, Alessandro 457, *457*
Picasso, Pablo 452, 461, *461*
Pickering, William 97
pickle stands, porcelain 206
picture frames, silver 259, *259*
pictures
  Berlin woolwork *337*
  canvaswork 337, *337*
  clocks *362*
  needlework **338**, *338*
  stumpwork 336, *336*
piecrust "supper" tables *65*

pier mirrors 113
pier tables **58–9**, *58–9*, 60
pierced decoration, ceramics **124**, *124*
Pierotti, Henry 483
Pierotti family 483, *483*
Pierre, François 309
pietre dure
  inlays 25, 67
  jewelry **263**, *263*, 265, *265*
  pins 265, *265*
Pietsch, Karl 293
Piffetti, Pietro 99
pile weavings, rugs and carpets **315**, *315*
Pilgrim Fathers 337
Pilkington Brothers 77
Pilkington's Tile & Pottery Co. 376
"pillar and scroll" clocks 357
pillar cut glass *280*
"pillar" rugs 327
Pillement, Jean 58
pillow lace **347**, *347*
Pinchbeck, Christopher 271
pinchbeck jewelry **267**, 271
pine **23**, *23*
Pineau, Nicolas 58, 112
Pins 265, *265*, 268, 269, 271–3, 406–7, *438*, 452
Pit-a-Pat 499
pitchers
  glass *287*
  porcelain *220*, 221
pittoresque movement *see* Rococo style
Pitts, Thomas 238
Pitts, William 238
Pittsburgh 171, 297
Pittsburgh Flint Glass Manufactory 297, 301, 305
Pixyland Toy and Manufacturing Co. 515, *515*
Planché, Andrew 206
Planck, Ernst 506, 539, *539*
planetaria **532**, *532*
plaques, ceramic *127*, 183, *183*, *394*
plastics
  bags 346
  dolls **493**, *493*
  figures **514–15**, *514–15*
  furniture 451, 468
  jewelry *439*, 452
  mid-century modern 455
plate-buckets **119**
plates
  Art Nouveau 396
  glass 293, 297, *311*
  porcelain *176*, *182*, *187*, *194*, 196, *202*, *208*, *212*, *213*, 216, *219*, *221*
  pottery *162*
  ribbon plates **185**
  silver 236, *236*
platform lever escapement, clocks 350, *351*
platinum jewelry 262
platters, pottery *157*, *167*
Plaue an der Havel 185
Plaue Factory 185
Playcraft 513
plique-à-jour enamel 404, 407, *407*, 523
Plummer, John 246
plus-fours 345
Plymouth 205, **207**, *207*
plywood furniture 450, *450*
Po-Hing 215
pocket watches **366**, *366*
Poertzel, Otto 442, *442*
Pohl, Wilhelm 295
point d'Alençon lace 347
point d'Argentan lace 347
point de France lace 347
point de gaze lace 347, *347*

Poiret, Paul 344
Poirier, Simon-Philippe 66, 80
Pokal drinking glasses *281*
Poland, *bonheurs du jour* 104
polescreens *114*, **115**
Pollard, William 212
Pollock, Benjamin 502
Polo, Marco 316
Polonaise rugs 316, *316*
polychrome wares **134**, **161**
Pomone 418, *418*
Pompadour, Madame de *193*, *197*
Pompeii 25, 37, 38, 75, 166, 188, 190, 194
Pompeiian Style, porcelain *197*
Pompone 414
Pont-aux-Choux 157
Ponteur 453
Ponti, Gio 423, *423*, 449, *449*, 466, *467*
pontil marks, glass 276
Ponzio, Emanuele 471, *471*
Poole Pottery 427, *427*
Poor, Henry Varnum 425, 462, *463*
Pop art 344, 453, 454, 471
pop memorabilia 550–1, *550–1*
porcelain *122*, **122**, **172–221**, *172–221*
    Austria **188–9**, *188–9*
    Britain **200–18**, *200–18*
    China **132–40**, *132–40*
    fakes 126
    France **192–9**, *192–9*
    Germany **173–85**, *173–85*
    Ireland **218**, *218*
    Italy **190–1**, *190–1*
    Japan **142–7**, *142–7*
    Korea 141
    Low Countries **186**, *186*
    porcelain-mounted furniture 61, *63*, 64, 66, *66*, 95, 103
    Russia **219**, *219*
    Scandinavia **187**, *187*
    Spain **190**, *191*
    Switzerland **186–7**, *186–7*
    United States **220–1**, *220–1*
Porceleynen Lampetkan 160
Porceleynen Schotel 160
porringers, silver *224*, **259**, *259*
"Port furniture" 74
Portici 190
Portland, Duchess of 300
Portland vase 300, 301, 401
portraits
    sulphides **305**, *305*, *308*, 309
    tassies *305*, *305*
Portugal
    furniture 29, 46, 77
    mirrors 112
    pottery 151, *151*
    rugs and carpets **331**, *331*
Pössneck 185
posters
    Art Deco *414*, **444–5**, *444–5*
    Art Nouveau **410–11**, *410–11*
    rock and pop memorabilia 551, *551*
postmodernism **465–77**
    domestic wares **472–3**, *472–3*
    furniture **466–9**, *466–9*
    glass **474–5**, *474–5*
    jewelry **470**
    lighting **471**
    studio ceramics **476–7**, *476–7*
posy bowls, glass *276*
posy rings *264*
pot-cupboards 60, **110–11**, *110*, *111*
pot-pourri jars, porcelain *184*, *192*, *213*
potash glass **276**, *276*, *284*
potassium carbonate, glass 276
potboards 90
Poterat family 192

Potschappel 184
Potsdam 182
Potsdam Glasshouse 284
Potter, Beatrix 495, *495*, 503
"Potteries" 211
pottery **148–71**, *148–71*
    Britain **162–9**, *162–9*
    France **156–7**, *156–7*
    Germany **158–9**, *158–9*
    Islamic **149**, *149*
    Italy **152–4**, *152–4*
    Netherlands **160–1**, *160–1*
    Portugal 151, *151*
    Spain **150**, *150*
    tiles **155**, *155*
    United States **170–1**, *170–1*
potting pans, porcelain *203*
pouffes 28, 34
Poulsen, Louis 447, 453, *453*
poured-wax dolls **483**, *483*
powder-boxes 545
Powell, William 216
Powell, Harry J. 401, *401*
Powell, James 433
Powell, James & Sons 279, *286*
Powell, Phillip Lloyd 467
Powell & Lealand 534
Powers, Hiram 214
Powolny, Michael 397, 400, 432
Prague, glass 285, 290, 293
Pratt, F. & R. & Co. 165
Pratt family 165
Prattware **165**
praxinoscopes 539, *539*
prayer-rugs 314, 318, *319*, 320, *320*, *321*, 323, *323*, 325, *325*
Pre-Raphaelite Brotherhood 342
precision clocks 360, *360*
Preis-Kassler Foundry (PK) 442
Preiss, Ferdinand **442**, *442*
Preissler, Daniel 177
Preissler, Ignaz 177, *177*, 289, *289*
Presley, Elvis 550, *551*
press-molding, ceramics **123**, *123*
pressed glass 276, **283**, *283*
presses, linen **73–4**, **75**, *75*
Pressnitz 177
Price, Kenneth **476**, *477*
pricket candlesticks *540*
prie-dieu (kneeling chair) 34
Primavera 414, 422, *422*
Prince 550
Printemps 414, 422
printing, ceramics **125**, *125*
prism cut glass *280*
Pritchard, Jack 416, 419
Privat-Livemont, T. 410, *410*
The Product Matters Company 471
programs
    soccer 536
    tennis 536
provincial chairs *21*, *33*, 33
prunts, glass 279
Prussia 182
"Prussian" service 182
Prutscher, Otto 400, *400*, 432
Przyrembel, Hans *436*
Pueblo Indians 332
Puente del Arzobispo 150
Pugin, Augustus Welby Northmore 39, 52, 59, 370, 371
    Gothic Furniture in the Style of the Fifteenth Century 39
Puiforcat, Jean Emile 436, *436*, 437
Pulpitel, Milos 457
"pumpkin-head" dolls **484**, *484*
punch-bowls
    ceramic *425*

    glass *283*, 297
    silver 256, **257**, *257*
punch ladles, silver 245
punk style, clothes 345
Purcell, Feick & Elmslie 375
Purcell, William Gray 375
purpleheart 22
purses 346, *346*

Q

Qianlong emperor 526, *528*
Qianlong period ceramics 136, 138, 139, *139*, 140, *140*
Qing period
    ceramics 131, 137, **138–40**, *138–40*
    ivory 529
    jade 528
    lacquerware 526
Qingbai wares 132, *132*
Qom 316
quaiches, silver **247**
"Quaint Furniture" 374
Quant, Mary 344
Quare, Daniel 364, *366*
quarter-veneering 24, *24*
quartetto tables 67
Queen Anne style
    Arts and Crafts furniture 371
    chairs 19, *19*, 30
    chests-on-chests 88
    lowboys 62
    mirrors 112
    settees 42
    silver 230, 232, *235*, 249, 252
    tables 49
Queen's Burmese glass 286
"Queen's" pattern, flatware 245, *245*
"Queen's ware" 165
Quezal Art Glass & Decorating Co. 402, *402*, 403, 435
quilts **340–1**, *340–1*
Quimper 157, *157*
Quistgaard, Jens Harald 454, *454*

R

Rabanne, Paco 344
Rabery & Delphieu 489
Race, Ernest 449
Rachette, Jean-Dominique 219
rackets, tennis 536, *537*
racks **108–9**, *108–9*
Radio City Music Hall, New York 420
radios 455, *455*
Raeren 158, 164
rag dolls 492, *492*
Raimondi, Marcantonio 153
"Raised Anchor" period, Chelsea **201**
Rambouillet 194
Rams, Dieter 455
Ramsden, J. *364*
Ramsden, Jesse 533
Ramsden, Omar *382*, 383
Ramshaw, Wendy 470
Randall, John 209, *209*
Randall, Thomas 126
Randolph, Benjamin 31
Ranftbecher **278**, 290
Raphael 153, 195
"raspberries", glass 279
ratafia drinking glasses *281*
Rathbone, Harold 377
Rato, Royal factory of *151*
Ravenscroft, George 276, 296, 306
Ravinet d'Enfert *436*
Reader, Victor 511
reading stands **108**
Récamier, Mme Juliette 44
recliners *392*
"Red Anchor" period, Chelsea **201**

Red House Glassworks 300
red lead, glass 276
redware **164**
Reed (W.S.) Toy Co. 502, *502*
reeded legs 20
refectory tables **46–7**, *46*
"regard" pins 269
Régence period
    canapés 42
    chairs 19, 30
    commodes 80
    mirrors 112
    silver *253*
    tables 58, 61
"Regency" glass 296
Regency period
    bookcases 97
    bureaux 100
    canterburies *108*
    carpets 330
    chairs *21*, 30, 37, 38, *38*, 40
    chaises-longues 43
    clocks 357, *357*
    Davenports 106, *106*
    dressers 90
    glass *298*, 307
    handles *21*
    linen-presses 75, *75*
    mirrors 113, *113*
    peat-buckets *119*
    pedestal desks 107
    pot-cupboards 110–11
    Sheffield plate 256
    side cabinets 94, *94*
    silver **232**, 234, 236, 237, *237*, 238, 239, 242, *243*, 247, 255, 256
    sofas 43, 45
    tables 46, 51, 57, 59, 65, *65*, 66, 105, *105*
    teapoys 65, *65*
    washstands *111*
    wine coolers and cellarets 119, *119*
registration marks, silver 233
Regnauld, Victor 196
regulateurs 355
regulators 360, *360*
Rehm, Wilhemine 425
Rehn, Jean Eric 31
Reichsadlerhumpen glasses 288
Reid, John 453
Reid, Sylvia 453
Reid, William 200
reign marks, Chinese porcelain 139, *139*
Reiling, Reinhold 452
Reilly & Storer 255
Rein, F.C. & Son 535
Reinhardt, Franz 490
Reinicke, Peter 174, *174*
Reissner, Stellmacher & Kessel 389
relief diamond cut glass *280*
relief engraving, glass **278**, *278*
Renaissance Revival
    beds 117
    bureaux 101
    chairs *35*, 39
    dining-tables 53
    display cabinets 93
    jewelry 265
    parlor suites 45
    pediment *89*
    porcelain 181, 196, 198
    side cabinets 94, 95
    wardrobes 77
Renaud *408*
rent tables 54
Repository of Arts 117
repoussé work *see* embossing
restoration
    ceramics **129**

furniture 26
silver 244
Restoration (Bourbon)
commodes 82, *82*
Sèvres porcelain **196**, *196*, 197
Restoration (English), dining-chairs 36
Revere, Paul 225, 257
Revere Copper and Brass Co. 437
Révérend, Claude 192
reverse intaglio technique *270*
Revolutionary dials, clocks 358
revolving bookcases 97
Reyhanli 326
Reynauld, E. *539*
Reynolds, James 62
Rhead, Frederick Hurten 378, 381, *381*, 425
Rhenish Glasshouse 290, *290*
Rhineland
glass 282, 305
Rhenish stoneware 158, **164**
Rhineland Rubber & Celluloid Co. 493
"Rhinoceros" vases 213
Rhodes, Zandra 344
RIAA (Recording Industry Association of America) 550
ribbon pins *265*
ribbon plates **185**
Richard-Ginori 191, 423, *423*
Richardson, W.H., B. & J. 286, 291, 295, 296, 300, 301, 401
"Richelieu" pattern, flatware *245*
Ridgway 211, *211*, 213
Rie, Lucie 460–1, *461*, 462
Riedel, Gottlieb Friedrich 179
Riedel, Josef 285
Riegel, Ernst 404
Riemerschmid, Richard 396
Riesener, Jean-Henri 81, 99
Riessner, Stellmacher & Kessel (R.S.K.) 397, *397*
Rietveld, Gerrit 415, 416, *416*, 417
Ringler, Joseph Jakob 178
rings *264*, **264**, 268, *268*, **270**, *407*, *439*
rinsers, glass *297*
Rio Grande 332
Riquer, Alexandra de 411, *411*
Risenburgh, Bernard van 110
Risler & Carré *234*
Rivarossi 513
Rivière, Maurice Guiraud 441
rivières 266, *266*
robe à l'anglaise 342
robe à la française 342
Robert *157*
robes 342, *342*
Robinson, Edkins & Aston *234*
Robinson, Sarah 480
Robinson & Leadbeater 214, *214*
Robj 423
Rock & Gräner 498, 506, *506*
rock and pop memorabilia **550–1**, *550–1*
rocking chairs 33
rocking-horses 502, *502*
Rockingham, Marquess of 213
Rockingham-glaze ware *170*, 171, 221
Rockingham porcelain **213**, *213*
Rococo Revival 20
bonheurs du jour 104
bureaux 101
chairs 35
clocks *358*
dining-chairs 40, 41
dining-tables 53
dressing tables *63*
mirrors 113
porcelain 181, *181*, 183, *183*, 184, *184*, 196, *198*, *199*, 209, *209*, 211, 213, *213*
side cabinets 95
silver 232, *233*, 242, *242*

sofas 45, *45*
tables 55, 59, 69
wardrobes 77
Rococo style 20
American "Chippendale" chairs 31, *31*
bombé commodes 80
bookcases 96
bureaux 99, *99*, 100, *100*
canapés 42, *42*
candelabra 234, *234*
ceramics 151
chairs 30, **37**, *37*
chests-on-chests 88–9
clocks 353, *353*, 356
commodes 81
costume 342
display cabinets 92
étagères 109
figures 174
glass chandeliers 307
handles *21*
linen-presses **74**
mirrors 112, *112*, 113
night tables 110
Philadelphia style **62**, *62*
porcelain 175, *175*, 178, 179, *179*, 180, *180*, 186, 187, *187*, 188, 191, 193, 194, *201*, 206, 208, *220*
pottery 156, *156*, *157*
rugs and carpets 328
settees 42
sideboards 60
silver 230, *230*, 236, 237, 238, 239, 241, 242, 248, 249, 250, 252, 253, 257
tables 59, 64, *64*
wine coolers and cellarets 119
writing cabinets-on-stands 104
Rodney decanters *280*
Roentgen, David 58, 81, 99
Rohde, Gilbert 421
Rohde, Johan 405
Rohlfs, Charles **374**, 375
Rohmer, Madame Marie Antoinette 485, *485*, **486**, *486*
Rolex 367, *367*
roll-top desks 99, 101
"rolling ball" clocks *363*
rolling pins, glass *310*
Rollos, Philip *236*
Roman Empire
glass 276, 278, 279, 282, *282*, 284, 300, *300*
jewelry 263, *263*
Romanesque style, wardrobes 76
Romantic Revival
porcelain 198
tables 59
Rome 30, 92
Römer glasses 289, 290, *290*
Rooke, Herbert K. 411
Rookwood Pottery 155, 370, 378, *378*, 381, 425, *425*
Roosevelt, Theodore 496
Rorstrand 461
"Rosalie" armchairs *35*
rose cut, gemstones *262*
Rose, John 209
Rose, Thomas 209
Rosebud 493
Rosen, Anton 405
Rosenthal 424, *424*
Rosenthal and Maeder (RuM) 442
Roseville Pottery 370, 378, *378*, 425, *425*
rosewood **23**, *23*
Belter's lamination process **35**, *35*
Rosko 518
Ross, Andrew 534
Rossetti, Dante Gabriel 371, 377

"*rosso antico*" 166
Rotaflex 453
"Rothschild Imperial Silk Hunting" carpet *316*
Rotterdam 160
Rouard, Georges 430
Rouen 151, 156, *156*, 157, 192
Roullet, Jean 494
Roullet & Decamps 494
Rousseau, Jean-Jacques *194*
Roux, Alexander 95
Roux, Edouard 150
Royal Bonn 221
Royal Copenhagen 397, *397*
Royal Crown Derby 210, 216, *216*
Royal Danish Porcelain Factory 187, *187*
Royal Doulton 217
Royal Porcelain Factory, Berlin 180, *180*, **182–3**, *182–3*, 185
Royal porcelain factory (Copenhagen) 397
Royal Society scale, thermometers 364
Royal Worcester 221
figures 215, 217, *217*
hand-painting 216, *216*
Japanesque and Eastern styles 215, *215*
maiolica 169
parian busts and statues 214
Roycroft Furniture Shop 370, **375**, *375*
Roycroft Metalwork Shop **384**, *384*
Rozenburg factory 395, *395*
Ru wares 132
Ruba Rhombic *434*, **435**
Rubenstein, Ida 441
rubies *262*
Rubinglas 284
Rudney II, Emperor 293
rugs and carpets **312–33**
Britain and Ireland **330**, *330*
Caucasus **322–3**, *322–3*
Europe **328–31**, *328–31*
Far East **327**, *327*
flatweaves **314**, *314*, 326, *326*
layout **314**, *314*
Ottoman Empire before 1700 **317**, *317*
Ottoman Empire after 1700 **320–1**, *320–1*
Persia before 1800 **316**, *316*
Persia after 1800 **318–19**, *318–19*
pile weavings **315**, *315*
Spain and Portugal **331**, *331*
United States **332–3**, *332–3*
Western Turkestan **324–5**, *324–5*
Ruhlmann, Jacques-Emile 414, 415, **418**, *418*, 423
rummers *281*
Rundell, Bridge & Rundell 234, *254*, 255, 256
runners 314
Ruskin, John 296, 370, 371
Ruskin Pottery 377
Russell, Gordon 372, 419, 449
Russia
ceramics 126
easy chairs 32, *32*
marble 67
night tables 110
porcelain **219**, *219*
secrétaires 103
sideboards 61
tables 50, 55
Russian Embassy, Washington 297
Ruth, Babe 537, *537*
Ruyckevelt, Ronald van 217
Ruyckevelt, Ruth van 217, *217*
rye whiskey decanters, silver *254*
Ryukyu islands 526, 527

S
Saarinen, Eero 421, 448, 451
Saarinen, Eliel 421, *421*
saber legs 20
Sabino, Marius-Ernest 428, *428*, 429
sablé work, purses 346
sacques, silk 342
saddle covers *327*
Sadler, John *155*
Sadler and Green 546
Safavids
pottery 149
rugs and carpets **316**, *316*, 318, 321, 322, 326
St Amand-les-Eaux *157*
Sainte Ange, Louis de la Hamayde de *329*
Sainte-Anne Glassworks 287, 299, 301, 305, 306, 307, 308
Saint-Cloud 144, 192, *192*
Saint Gobain Glasshouse 112
Saint-Laurent, Yves 344
Saint-Louis Glassworks 287, *287*, 299, 301, *301*, 305, 306, 308
Saint-Louis Müntzthal 287, 299, 301
Saint-Maurice 199
St Petersburg, porcelain 219
Sakier, George 435
Salem, Massachusetts 81, 89, 117, *117*
Salem secretary 96
salon suites **44–5**
Salor 324, *324*, 325
Salt, Ralph 168
salt-cellars, silver 258, *258*, 259
salt-glazed stoneware **123**, *123*, *170*
salvers, silver *226*, 237, *237*
Salvetat, Alphonse-Louis 196
Salviati *475*
Salviati, Antonio 302, 475
Samarkand 149
"Samarkand" carpets 327
Sambin, Hugues, *L'Oeuvre de la diversité des termes dont on use en architecture* 72
samplers **339**, *339*
Samson, Edmé & Cie **127**, *127*, 157, 192, 199
sand, glass 276
Sandoz, Edouard Marcel 423
Sandoz, Gerard 439
Sandwich, Massachusetts 283
sang-de-boeuf glazes 183
Santos Dumont, Alberto 367
Sanyo 455
sapphires *262*
Sardou, Victorien 410
Sarfatti, Gio 471
Sarouk 318
Sarpaneva, Timo 456, *456*
Saryk 324, *324*, 325
"Sasha" dolls 493
satin-birch 22
satinwood **23**, *23*
Satsuma wares *146*, **147**
Saturday Evening Girls' Club 379, *379*
sauce tureens 243, *243*
sauceboats
porcelain 187, 204, 220
silver **224**, 241, *241*
saucers
glass *304*
porcelain 122, 125, 126, 129, *173*, 203, 204, 210, 211
savings banks, cast-iron **505**, *505*
Savona 154, 156
Savonnerie carpets 30, 327, **328**, *328*, 329, 330
Saxbo 461
Saxe, Adrian 463

Saxony 158, 173
"Sayrafiyan" rugs 318
scagliola inlays 55, 67
Scandinavia
    Art Deco 417, 417, 432–3
    Biedermeier style 32
    ceramics 424, 461
    chests 71
    chests-of-drawers 82
    commodes 82
    domestic wares 454
    easy chairs 31, 31
    furniture construction 18
    glass 432–3, 456
    lighting 453
    mid-century modern furniture 450
    porcelain 187, 187
    secrétaires 103
    silver 246, 247
    studio glass 474
    tables 64
    wardrobes 77
    see also Denmark; Finland;
        Norway; Sweden
Scaramouche 174
Sceaux 156
scent bottles 548–9, 548–9
    glass 279, 285, 301, 311, 429
    porcelain 198
    silver 259
Schadow, Johann Gottfried 182
Schaper, Johann 289
Scheidt, Carl von 290
Scheier, Edwin 462, 462
Scheier, Mary 462, 462
Schellink, Sam 395
Schiaparelli, Elsa 272, 272, 344, 549
Schimmel, Wilhelm 542, 542
Schinkel, Karl Friedrich 59, 182
Schlesische porcelain factory 184
Schliepstein, Gerhard 424, 424
Schmelzglas 284
Schmidtcassel, Gustav 443
Schmitt et Fils 481, 489
Schmuz-Baudiss, Theodor Hermann 396
Schnackenberg, Walter 444
Schneegass, Gebrüder 498
Schneider, Charles 430, 431
Schneider, Frederick 445
Schnelle 158, 158
Schobinger, Bernhard 470, 470
Schoen, Eugene 421
Schoenhut, Albert 502
Schönheit, Johann Carl 176
Schouman, Aert 292
Schrank 73
Schreckengost, Victor 425
Schreyer & Co. 495, 506, 517
Schruder, James 239
Schubert, Franz 109
Schuco 495, 496, 496, 506, 517, 518
Schumann, Carl 424
Schuppe, John 251, 251
Schwaben Creek, Pennsylvania 71
Schwanhardt, Georg the Elder 293
Schwanhardt, Heinrich 292, 293
Schwarzlot (black monochrome)
    decoration
    glass 289, 289
    porcelain 177, 177, 188, 188
scientific instruments 532–5
    globes and planetaria 532, 532
    medical instruments 535, 535
    surveying and navigational instruments
        533, 533
    telescopes and microscopes 534, 534
Scotland
    Arts and Crafts Movement 373
    dressers 91

glass 309, 309
jewelry 265, 265
samplers 339
shawls 343
sideboards 26
silver 247, 248, 248, 255
whitework 338, 338
see also Britain
Scott, Sir Walter 39, 198
Scott & Walker 502
screens 114–15, 114–15, 420, 469
screws 19
scrimshaw 543, 543
scriptors 104
scrolled pediments 89
sculpture
    Art Deco 415, 440–3, 440–3
    Art Nouveau 408–9, 408–9
    parian busts and statues 214, 214
    postmodernist 472
    sculptural ceramics 476
    see also figures
seal-bottles, glass 310, 311
seal rings 270
Sears, Roebuck & Co. 454, 495
seat furniture
    chairs 29–41, 29–41
    settles and sofas 42–5, 42–5
    stools 28, 28
seaweed marquetry 24, 24
Second Empire
    rugs and carpets 329
    Sèvres porcelain 196–7
Second Republic, Sèvres porcelain 196
secrétaire à abattant 102, 103
secrétaire à capucin 104
secrétaires 72, 102, 102–3, 103
    secrétaire bookcases 96, 97
    secrétaire chests-on-chests 88
    secrétaire commodes 78
    secrétaire display cabinets 93
Secretan, Marc 533, 534
Seddon, George & Sons 37, 42
Sedgley, Walter 216
Seditionaries 344
Segal, Philip 515
Seger, Hermann 183
Seger-Porzellan 183
Seichur 322, 323
Seikozan studio 146, 147
Seljuks 317
semainiers 103
Senneh 318, 326
Senneh knot 315
sentimental jewelry 268–9, 268–9
serapes 332, 333
Serjeants-at-Law rings 270
serpent bangles 267, 267
serpent rings 264, 264
serpent-stemmed goblets 302
Serrurier-Bovy, Gustave 392, 392
"Service des Pêches" 196
serving tables 60–1, 60–1
Seto wares 146, 147
settees 42, 42, 44, 44, 45
settings, jewelry 263, 263
settles 42, 42, 44, 374
Seuter, Abraham 177, 177
Seuter, Bartholomäus 177
Seven Years War (1756–63) 176, 180,
    188, 193
Sèvres porcelain 176, 192, 193–4,
    193–4, 198
    Art Deco 422–3, 422
    Art Nouveau 394, 394, 399
    copies and imitations 186, 197,
        197, 203, 212, 216
    cups 125
    figures 194, 408, 409

late 19th century 197, 197
    porcelain plaques for furniture 61, 63,
        64, 66, 66, 95, 103
    redecorated wares 126, 126
    Restoration Period 196, 196, 197
    Second Republic and Second Empire
        196–7, 196–7
sextants 533
Seymour, Thomas 58, 60
Seymour family 58
sgabelli chairs 32
Shah Abbas 316
Shakers, chairs 33, 33
Shang period ceramics 131
Shaw, Richard Norman 371
shawls 343, 343
Sheffield
    flatware 245
    silver 225, 231, 232, 233
Sheffield plate 235, 256
    cleaning 229
    coffee-jugs 252
    inkstands 259
    monteiths 257
    sauce tureens 243
    tea caddies 547
    tea-urns 253
    tureens 242
    wine coolers 256, 256
"shelf" clocks 357, 357
shellac, japanning 25
Shelley Pottery 414, 427
Shenandoah Valley 87, 171
Shephard Hardware Manufacturing Co.
    505
Sheraton domed pediments 89
Sheraton style
    bureaux 100, 101
    chests-of-drawers 85
    dining-chairs 39, 41
    display cabinets 93
    mirrors 113
    sofas 45
    tables 69
Sheraton, Thomas
    bookcases 96
    The Cabinet Dictionary 31, 32, 50, 56,
        57, 67, 84, 97, 103, 108, 109, 116
    The Cabinet-Maker and Upholsterer's
        Drawing Book 31, 37, 56, 60, 61, 69,
        75, 85, 89, 96, 103, 109, 111
    canterburies 108
    dining-chairs 37
    dressing tables 62
    dumb waiters 109, 109
    secrétaires 103
    sideboards 60
    tambor writing tables 98
    work tables 69
Sherratt, Obadiah 168, 168
sherry glasses 305
shield-back chairs 21, 37, 37
ship's decanters 280
shipwreck cargoes 137, 137
Shire, Peter 472–3, 473
Shirvan 322–3, 322, 326
shoes 343, 344, 344
    ceramic 128
Shortt, William Hamilton 361
Shrewsbury, Earl of 211
Shropshire dressers 90, 91
shu fu wares 133
side cabinets 94–5, 94–5
side chairs 19, 31, 36, 36, 37, 38, 39
side tables 47, 47, 58–9, 59
sideboards 26, 60–1, 60–1, 373, 392, 448
Siegburg 158, 158
signet rings 264, 270, 270

Silber & Fleming 498
Silesia
    glass 184, 189, 278, 289, 292, 298
    regulators 360
silica, glass 276
silk, rugs and carpets 315
silk-boxes, porcelain 215
Silk Route 316, 327
Silla period ceramics 141
sillón de fraileros (monk's chair) 29, 29
silver 222–59
    Art Deco 437, 437
    Art Nouveau 395, 395
    Arts and Crafts 382, 382
    candlesticks 230–5, 230–5
    cardcases 544, 544
    care 229
    collecting 229
    decoration 226–7, 226–7
    dining silver 236–43, 236–43
    drinking vessels 246–7, 246–7
    electroplating 235
    electrotyping 235
    engraving 237
    fakes 228, 229
    flatware 244–5, 244–5
    forming methods 224
    hallmarking 225, 225
    influence on porcelain 201, 201
    jewelry 262, 265, 266, 267, 267
    miscellaneous 258–9, 258–9
    Oriental 523, 523
    perfume bottles 548, 548
    serving beverages 248–53, 248–53
    serving wine and spirits 254–7, 254–7
    Sheffield plate 256
    snuff-boxes 544, 544
    vesta cases 545
Simmen, Henri 422
Simmen, O'Kin 422
Simon & Halbig 490
Simpson, John III 163
Simpson, Ralph 163
Sinclair, Clive 455
"Sindy" dolls 493
Singer, Susi 425
"Sino-Portuguese" style, ceramics 151
Sissons, Jonathan 533
Sit, Ventura 289, 298
Sitzendorf 184
Sivas 321
Skeaping, John 427
skeleton clocks 363, 363
skimmers, silver 245
Sklarzska Poreba 298
"Skyscraper" furniture 420, 420
slab-building, ceramics 122
slat-back chairs 33
slate, simulated marble 95, 95
Slater, Eric 427
slide projectors 539, 539
slip-casting, ceramics 123, 123
slip-trailing, ceramics 124, 124
slipware 163, 163
    American 170, 170, 171
    studio ceramics 460
"slit-head" dolls 484, 484
slit-tapestry kilims 314
Sloane, Sir Hans 201
slop bowls, porcelain 192
slumping, glass 276
Smart, George 338
Smee, William & Sons 83, 106
Smethurst 307
Smith, Benjamin 237
Smith, Benjamin II 243
Smith, Charles & Son 532
Smith, E. & Co. 155
Smith, George 51, 61, 113

Cabinet-Maker and Upholsterer's Guide, Drawing Book and Repository 59
A Collection of Designs for Household Furniture and Interior Decoration 38, 39, 43, 57, 61, 97, 108, 117
Smith, Thomas Carll 220
Smith Pottery 170
snake chains 266
snuff bottles 524, *524*, 525
snuff-boxes *227*, **544**, *544*, *546*
snuffers, silver **231**, 232–3
soccer 536, *536*
Società Richard of Milan 191
Société des Artistes Français 440, 441
Société Française de Fabrication de Bébés et Jouets (S.F.B.J.) 488, **489**
Société Industrielle de Ferblanterie 509, 513
Société Nobel Française *493*
soda glass 276, *276*, 298
soda siphons *437*
sodium carbonate, glass 276
sofa tables **57**, *57*
sofas 43, *43*, 44–5, *45*, 449, *450*, 467
soft-paste porcelain **122**, *122*
soft toys **495**, *495*
Soho Plate Co 234
soldiers, lead 514, *514*, 515
Soldner, Paul 476
Solido 517
Solis, Virgil *158*
Solon, Léon 396
Solven, Pauline 475
Somerset, dressers 90
Song period
    ceramics *122*, 131, **132**, *132*, 139, 149, 460
    jade 528
Sonneberg dolls 482
Sonnenschein, Valentin *186*, 187
"Sons of Liberty" punch-bowl 257
Sony 455
Soper, Eva *217*
Sorgenthal, Conrad Sörgel von 188, 189
Sorrento *65*
Sotheby's 550
Sottsass, Ettore 455, 466–7, *467*, 471, *471*, 472, *472*, 473, *473*
Soulie, Alice 444
soumakhs **314**, *314*, **326**, *326*
soup tureens **242**, *242*, 243
Southern School 380
Southwark, London 162
Southwark, Philadelphia 220
souvenirs, porcelain 208, *208*
Sowerby, John 283
spade feet *20*
Spain
    Art Nouveau furniture **393**
    cabinets-on-stands 86
    chairs 29, *29*, 36
    chests-of-drawers 78, 79
    commodes 82
    glass 276, **289**, *289*, **298**
    ironwork 541
    painted furniture 74
    porcelain **190**, *191*
    posters 411
    pottery **150**, *150*
    rugs and carpets **331**, *331*
    samplers 339
    silver hallmarks 225
    tables 46, *46*, 47
    tiles *155*
    toys 509
    vargueños 78, 88, *88*, 98, 102
    wardrobes 77
"Spanish" feet *20*

Spanish Netherlands 72, 73
Sparks, George 209
"spatterware" **170**, 171
Spaun, Max Ritter von 400
Spenkuch, Georg 514
spice cupboards 91
spider-leg tables *48*, **49**
Spilsbury, John 503
spiral stems, drinking glasses *281*
spire stoppers, glass *280*
spittoons *125*, *166*
splat-backed chairs 19, *21*
splayed feet *20*
splits, cut glass *280*
Spode *125*, 167, 211, *211*
"spongeware" **170**, 171
spoons, silver **227**, **244–5**, *244–5*
sporting memorabilia 536–7, *536–7*
Spot-On **517**
sprigging, ceramics **124**, *124*
Sprimont, Nicholas **201**, *201*, 238, 241
springs 34, 44, 45
Stabler, Harold 439
Staffordshire
    art pottery 396
    blue-and-white printed wares 167
    creamware 165
    enamel *546*
    fakes and forgeries **126**, *127*
    figures **168**, *168*, 210
    ironstone 167
    lead-glazed wares 163
    majolica 169
    mugs *125*
    porcelain **211**, *211*
    stoneware 164, *164*
stained glass 278, **285**, *386–7*
Staite Murray, William 460, *460*
Stalker, John 80
    A Treatise of Japanning and Varnishing 86
Stamford 163
Standard-Möbel Lengyel & Co 416, *416*
stands **108–9**, *108–9*
Stangenglas 289
"star" carpets *317*, 330
Star Encaustic Tile Co. 155
Starck, Philippe 467, 468, *468*, 472
Starr, Ringo 551
Starr, Theodore *235*
State porcelain factory (Berlin) 424, *424*
State porcelain factory (Russia) 219, *219*
statues *see* figures; sculpture
Staudt 506
steel
    cut-steel jewelry **265**, 271
    toys **504**, *504*
Steel, Thomas 213
"steeple" clocks 357, *357*
Steiff, Margarete 481, 492, 495, *495*, **496**, *496*
Steiff, Richard 496
Steiner, Jules Nicholas **489**, *489*
stem cups, lacquer *526*
stems, drinking glasses *281*, **303**, *303*
stereoscopes 539
sterling standard, silver 224, 225, 262
Steuben Glassworks 402, *402*, 403, **434**, *434*
Stevens, J. & E. & Co. 499, 504, 505, *505*
Stevens & Williams 286, 295, 301, 401, 402, 433
stick barometers **364**, *364*, 365
Stickley, Albert 374
Stickley, Gustav 370, 374, *374*, 375, **384**, *384*
Stickley, John George 374
Stickley, L. & J.G. 374, *374*
Stickley, Leopold 374

Stickley Brothers Co. 374
Stickley family **374**, 375
De Stijl 416
Stile floreale 388
Stile Liberty 388, 393, 410
Stinton, Harry 216, *216*
Stinton, James 216
Stinton, John 216, *216*
stipple engraving, glass **278**, *278*, **292**
stirrup cups, silver **247**, *247*
Stöer, Lorenz 86
Stoke-on-Trent 167, 169, 209, 211, 214
Stölzel, Samuel 188
stomacher pins 265
stone china 167
stoneware **122**, *122*
    American **170–1**, *170*
    Chinese 131, 132, 137
    English **164**, *164*
    German **158**, *158*
    glazes 123
    Korean 141
    Meissen 173
    salt glazes 123, *123*
    Wedgwood **166**, *166*
stools 28, *28*, *465*, *467*, *468*
stoppers, glass *280*
storage furniture **70–97**
    bookcases and bookshelves **96–7**, *96–7*
    cabinets-on-stands **86**, *86*
    chests and coffers **70–1**, *70–1*
    chests-of-drawers **78–85**, *78–85*
    chests-on-chests **88–9**, *88–9*
    cupboards and linen-presses before 1840 **73–5**, *73–5*
    display cabinets **92–3**, *92–3*
    dressers **90–1**, *90–1*
    early cupboards and meubles en deux corps **72**, *72*
    high chests-of-drawers **87**, *87*
    side cabinets **94–5**, *94–5*
    wardrobes **76–7**, *76–7*
Storr, Paul 234, *239*, 249, *249*, 256
Stourbridge glass 287, 295, *295*, 300, *310*, **401**
Stowe, Solomon *353*
strainer cups, porcelain *192*
Strasbourg 156, *156*, 178
Strass, Georges-Frédéric 271
Strauss, Ferdinand 504
strawberry diamond, cut glass *280*
"streamlining" 415, 437
striking mechanism, clocks 351
stringing **24**, *24*
strip quilts 340, *340*
Stuart, Charles Edward ("Bonnie Prince Charlie," the "Young Pretender") 294
Stuart, James "Athenian" 75, 89
Stuart, James Edward (the "Old Pretender") 294
Stubbs, George 166
Studio Alchimia 466
studio ceramics **425**, **460–3**, *460–3*, **476–7**, *476–7*
Studio Glass Movement, 474
stumpwork **336**, *336*
Stuttgart 179
Subes, Raymond 436, 437
Süe, Louis 415, 418, 436
sugar-baskets, silver **250**, 251, *251*
sugar-bowls
    porcelain *191*, *193*
    silver **250–1**
sugar casters *250*
sugar sifters *127*, *156*
suites *see* parlor suites; salon suites
suits, menswear 345
sulphides, glass **305**, *305*, *308*, 309
Sultanabad 319

"Sultan's Head" prayer-rugs *321*
Summers, Gerald 419
"supper" tables **65**
Suprematism 219
surface engraving, glass **279**, *279*
surveying instruments **533**, *533*
Susse Frères 408
"Sussex" chairs 371, *371*
Sutherland, Duchess of 49
Sutherland tables **49**, *49*
"Swan" service, Meissen 175, *175*
Swansea
    dressers 90, 91
    porcelain 209, **212**, *212*
Swatch 473, *473*
Swatow wares **137**
Sweden
    armoires 74
    bombé commodes 80
    ceramics 461
    clocks 353
    commodes 82, 85
    dining-tables 50
    easy chairs 31, *31*
    furniture construction 18
    glass **292**, 293, *293*, 456, *456*
    mirrors 112, 113
    night tables 110
    painted furniture 74, *74*
    porcelain 187
    sideboards 61
    tables 58, 59, 64
sweetmeat dishes *125*
Swid Powell 473, *473*
Switzerland
    chests 70, 71
    clocks 361, 362
    painted furniture 74
    porcelain **186–7**, *186–7*
    trains 513
    watches *366*, 367, *367*
swivel seals 270
sword-guards **523**, *523*
Symbolist movement 408
symbols
    Chinese rugs 327
    sentimental jewelry **268**
Syon House, Middlesex 330
Syria, glass 276

T

table à gibier 61
table à transformation 66
table ambulante 66
table-cabinets 86
table clocks 356
table de cabaret 66
table de chevet 110, *110*
table en bureau 80
table en chiffonière 66, *66*
table-lamps *384*, *402*
table rafraîchissoir 66
table vitrine 92
tables **46–69**
    Art Deco *415*, *417*, *418*
    Art Nouveau *393*
    console, side and pier tables **58–9**, *58–9*
    construction **18–19**, *18*
    dining tables **50–3**, *50–3*
    dressing tables **62–3**, *62–3*
    drum, breakfast and center tables **54–5**, *54–5*
    games and work tables **68–9**, *68–9*
    gateleg and dropleaf tables 18, *18*, **48–9**, *48–9*
    "joyned" and draw-leaf tables 46
    library tables 105
    occasional tables **66–7**, *66–7*

Pembroke and sofa tables 18, 56–7, 56–7
postmodernist 466
refectory tables 46–7, 46
sideboards and serving tables
    60–1, 60–1
spider-leg tables 49, 49
Sutherland tables 49, 49
tea tables and tripod tables 19,
    64–5, 64–5
tilt-top 18–19, 18
writing tables 105, 105
tablet-back chairs 21
Tabriz 317, 318, 318, 322
Tagliolini, Filippo 190
Tagliapietra, Lino 474, 474
Tahmasp, Shah 316
Takaezu, Toshiko 463, 463
Talavera de la Reina 150
Talbert, Bruce J. 53
Talbot, Suzanne 418
Talbot, William Henry Fox 538
tallcase clocks see longcase clocks
tambour writing tables 98, 100
Tang period
    ceramics 126, 131, 131, 460
    lacquerware 526
tankards
    glass 279, 288
    Oriental ceramics 142
    pottery 158
    silver 226, 228, 246–7, 246–7
tapering decanters 280
tapersticks, silver 231, 231
tapestries 314, 314
tapis-ras 329
target stoppers, glass 280
Tassie, James 305
Tassie, William 305
tassies, glass 305, 305
tatting 347
tavern clocks 352–3
taxation, glass 286, 296, 303
Taylor, Fred 445
Taylor, John 546
Taylor, Samuel 250
Taylor, W. Howson 377
Taylor, William 163
Taylor, William Watts 378
Taylor & Barrett 515
Taylor & Perry 544
tazze, glass 286, 297, 401
tea caddies 547, 547
    porcelain 178, 186, 205
    silver 227, 250, 250, 251
tea-kettles, silver 253, 253
tea services
    metalwork 436
    porcelain 147, 182, 213, 216,
        218, 218, 424
    silver 249, 252
tea tables 64, 64
tea-urns, silver 253, 253
teabowls, porcelain 203
Teague, Walter Dorwin 415, 421, 434,
    434, 437
teapots 473
    metalwork 436
    porcelain 175, 187, 195, 205, 218
    pottery 122, 127, 156, 164, 426
    silver 248–9, 248–9
teapoys 65, 65
Tearle, Thomas 225, 252
Technofix 518, 518
teddy bears 481, 481, 496–7, 496–7
Teddy Boys, clothes 345
Teec Nos Poc 333
Tehran 316
Tekke 324, 324, 325
Tekno 517, 517

telescopes 534, 534
telescopic dining-tables 51, 51
televisions 455
tellaria 532
temperature-compensating pendulums,
    clocks 351
Temple Newsam House, Leeds 307
Templier, Raymond 439
ten Broek, Willem Frederik 444
Teniers, David 188
Tenshodo 513
tent stitch, canvaswork 337, 337
terracotta, Native American 171
Terry, Eli 353, 357
tester beds 116, 116
tête-à-tête (love seat) 34
Teutonic glass 282
textiles 334–47
    accessories 346, 346
    costume 342–5, 342–5
    lace 347, 347
    needlework 336–9, 336–9
    quilts 340–1, 340–1
    rugs and carpets 312–33, 312–33
theatres
    posters 410, 410
    toy theatres 502
theodolites 533, 533
thermometers 364
Théroude, Alexandre Nicolas 494
Thieme, Carl 184, 184
Third Republic, Sèvres 197
Thirty Years War (1618–48) 71, 540
Thompson, Robert ("Mouseman") 419
Thonet, Gebrüder 392, 392, 416, 418
Thonet, Michael 41, 41, 392
Thornton-Pickard Co. 538, 538
Thorvaldsen, Berthel 187
Thrace 326
threading, lampwork 302
"three deck" clocks 357
thrones 30
throwing, ceramics 122
"thrown" chairs 29
Thuillier, A. 489
Thuringia
    dolls 485, 490, 491
    porcelain 178, 184, 185, 189
Tibet, rugs and carpets 327, 327
Tiefenfurt 184
Tiefschnitt engraving, glass 278, 292, 293
tiepins 270, 270
Tiffany, Charles Lewis 385, 402
Tiffany, Louis Comfort 385, 400, 402,
    403, 407
Tiffany & Co.
    flatware 245
    glass 300, 388, 401, 402–3, 402
    jewelry 407, 407, 439
    lighting 409
    metalwork 385
    silver 229, 437
    Tiffany Studios 385, 401, 402–3, 402
"Tiffany" style 388, 388
tiles, pottery 155, 155
tilt-top tables 18–19, 18
Timms & Webb 373
Timpo 515
tin 541
    toleware 541, 543
    toys 504, 504, 505, 506–9, 506–9
tin-glazed earthenware 123, 123
    Dutch pottery 160
    English delftware 162, 162
    faience 156–7, 156–7, 159, 159
    maiolica 152
    tiles 155
Tinworth, George 377

Tiny Toy 499
Tipp & Co. (Tippco) 506, 509, 518
toasting glasses 281
tobacco jars, ceramic 376
Toby jugs 163
Toft, Thomas 163
Tofts, Albert 408
toilet mirrors 113, 113
toilet tables 62
tôle peinte trays 118
toleware 541, 543
Tompion, Thomas 354
Tonwerke Kandern 396
Tooth, Henry 376, 377
Tootsie Toys 516, 516
top hats 345, 345
topaz 262
torchères (candlestands) 66
Torricelli, Evangelista 364
tortoiseshell
    cardcases 544
    tea caddies 547
tortoiseshell ware 163
Toulouse, John 203, 207
Toulouse-Lautrec, Henri de 410, 410
toupie feet 20
Tournai
    carpets 329, 329
    porcelain 186, 186, 187
Toussounian family 321
Town & Emmanuel 66, 101
town weaving, rugs and carpets 315, 315,
    318, 320
Townshend, Pete 551
Townsend family 102
toys and games 500–19
    diecasts 516–17, 516–17
    dolls' houses 498–9, 498–9
    early American toys 504–5, 504–5
    lead and plastic figures
        514–15, 514–15
    soft toys 495, 495
    teddy bears 496–7, 496–7
    tinplate toys 506–9, 506–9
    trains 510–11, 510–11
    wood and paper toys 502–3, 502–3
    see also dolls
"Trafalgar" chairs 38
trailing, glass 279
trains 510–11, 510–11
transfer-printing 125, 125
    blue-and-white wares 205
    tiles 155
Transitional period
    bureaux 99
    Chinese ceramics 136, 136, 137,
        142, 160
    commodes 81, 85
"Transylvanian" rugs 317, 320, 323
travel posters 411, 411, 444–5, 444, 445
trays 118, 118, 283, 526
treen 545, 545
"trefid" spoons 244, 244, 245
"Trench" watches 367
Trent Tile Co. 155
Trenton, New Jersey 171, 221
trepanning drills 535
trestle tables 46
Triang 498, 499, 509, 509, 512, 512,
    516, 517, 518
"Triangle" period, Chelsea 201
tribal weaving, rugs and carpets 315, 315,
    319, 319
tric-trac tables 68
Trifari 272, 272
trifid feet 20
tripod tables 19, 54, 64–5, 64–5, 68
Trix 511, 512
trolleys 417

Troughton, Edward 533
trousers 345
truckle beds 116
trumpet-shaped drinking glasses 281
trumpeter clocks 362
Tschirnhausen, Ehrenfried Walther von
    173
tsuba (sword-guards) 523, 523
tube-lining, ceramics 124, 124, 396, 397
Tuck, Raphael 503
Tucker, Thomas 220
Tucker, William Ellis 220, 220
Tudor Toys 499
"Tudorbethan" dining-tables 52
"Tudric" pewter 382, 382
tulipwood 23, 23
tumbler cups, silver 246, 247
tumblers, glass 289
Tunbridge Wells 338
Tunbridgeware 65, 65
Tunstall 211
tureens
    glass 299
    porcelain 177, 178, 200
    pottery 151, 157, 167, 218
    silver 242–3, 242–3
Turenne, Vicomte de 242
Turin 154
Turkestan, rugs and carpets 324–5,
    324–5, 327
Turkey
    rugs and carpets 320–1, 320–1
    tiles 155
"Turkey" carpets 321, 330
Turkish knot 315, 319, 320
Turkoman carpets 320–1, 324
Turner, Thomas 205
turning, chairs 29, 29
turquoises 262
Tuscany 29, 72, 73, 86, 152
Tutankhamun, Pharaoh 415, 438,
    439, 441
twisted stems, drinking glasses 303, 303
Two Gray Hills 333
Tynietoy 499
typewriters 455
Tyrol 159

U
Ullman, Philip 509, 517
Ullmann, Franz 293, 293
underglaze colors, ceramics 124, 124
    underglaze blue 173, 204, 204
underwear 343
Unger Bros 407
unguentarium 282
Union Porcelain Co. 220–1, 221
United States of America
    American "Chippendale" chairs
        31, 31
    Art Deco 415
        ceramics 425, 425
        furniture 420–1, 420–1
        glass 434–5, 434–5
        metalwork 436–7, 437
    Art Nouveau
        glass 402–3, 402–3
        jewelry 407, 407
    Arts and Crafts 370, 370
        ceramics 378–81, 378–81
        furniture 374–5, 374–5
        metalwork 384–5, 384–5
    automata 494
    bags 346
    beds 116, 117, 117
    bureaux 99
    canvaswork 337, 337
    ceramics
        Art Deco 425, 425

Arts and Crafts **378–81**, *378–81*
    mid-century modern ceramics
      462–3, *462–3*
    porcelain **220–1**, *220–1*
    pottery **170–1**, *170–1*
    studio ceramics **476–7**, *476–7*
    tiles 155
chair construction 19, *19*
chests-of-drawers *81*
chests-on-chests **89**, *89*
clocks 351, **353**, *353*, **355**, *355*,
    357, *357*
costume 342
country chairs 33, *33*
crewelwork 336, *336*
dolls 480, **492**, *492*, 493
dolls' houses 498, **499**, *499*
domestic wares 454
dressers 91
easy chairs 30, **31**, 35, *35*
escritoires *102*
folk art **542–3**, *542–3*
glass 276
    cameo glass **301**
    candlesticks 306
    colored glass 286, **287**, *287*
    "Cranberry" glass 311, *311*
    cut glass **297**, *297*
    lamps 307
    mid-century modern glass 457
    mold-blown glass 282, *282*
    paperweights **308**, *309*, *309*
    pressed glass **283**, *283*
    studio glass **474**
    sulphides 305
handles *21*
high chests-of-drawers **87**, *87*
imitation bamboo furniture 84
jewelry 268, *270*
lead and plastic figures **515**
lighting *453*
linen-presses 74, 75
lowboys 62, *62*
metalwork **384–5**, *384–5*
mid-century modern furniture **448**, *448*
mirrors 112, *112*, 113
needlework pictures 338, *338*
painted furniture 74
parlor suites 45
Pennsylvania Dutch chests **71**, *71*
pewter 541
Philadelphia style **62**, *62*
Phyfe school **43**, *43*
posters **445**
postmodernist furniture **467**
quilts **340–1**, *340–1*
regulators 360
rock and pop memorabilia 550
rugs and carpets **332–3**, *332–3*
samplers 339, *339*
side cabinets 95
sideboards 60, *60*
silver 225, **235**, *238*, 240, 245,
    246, 248, 250, 251, 252, 254,
    257, 257, 259
soft toys 495, *495*
tables 56, 57, 58, *59*
    breakfast tables 55
    butterfly tables 49
    dining-tables 51, *51*
    dropleaf tables *49*
    games and work tables *68*
    tea tables *64*
    tripod tables 64
teddy bears **496**, *496*
tinware 541
toys **504–5**, *504–5*, 516, *516*,
    518, **519**, *519*
trains **513**, *513*

wardrobes *76*
washstands 111
wood and paper toys 502, *502*, 503
United States Pottery 171, 214, 221
United Vienna and Gmund Ceramics
    Factory 397
Universal Exhibition, Paris (1937) 414
Universal Holdings of Hong Kong 517
Universal watches *367*
upholstery
    easy chairs 34
    foam 451
    sofas 45
uranium glass 282, 285, *285*
Urbino 153, *153*, 154, 156
urn splat chairs *21*
urns, tea 253
Ushak 317, *317*, 321, *321*, 329, 330
Utility furniture 449
Utrecht 30, 160
"Uxbridge" chairs *31*

V
Vacheron & Constantin 367
Val-Saint-Lambert Glasshouse 299, 304,
    310, *311*, **431**, *431*
Valenciennes lace 347, *347*
Valentien, Albert Robert 378, 381
Valentien, Anne Marie 381
Valentien Pottery 380, *381*
Vallin, Eugène 391
Van Briggle, Artus 378
Van Briggle, Henry *380*, 381, *387*
Van Cleef & Arpels 272, 439
Van de Velde, Henri 388, 392, *392*, 396,
    396, 404, 431
Van der Hoef, Christiaan J. 395
Van Eenhoorn family 161
Van Erp, Dirk 370, **384–5**, *384*
Vandenberge, Peter 477
Vandercruse, Roger 81
vargueño (writing desk) 78, 88, *88*, 98,
    102, 104
varnish, furniture 23
"vase" carpets 316
"Vaseline" glass 286, *286*, 311
vases
    Art Deco ceramics *414*, *422*,
      423, *425–9*
    Art Nouveau ceramics *394–7*
    art pottery *376–80*
    glass *279*, *287*, *290*, *291*, *295*,
      298, *300*, *398–402*, *428*, *430–5*,
      456, *457*, *474–5*
    lacquer *526*
    metalwork *405*, *436*
    Oriental ceramics *132*, *135*, *138–41*,
      143, *146*, *147*
    Oriental metalwork *522*, *523*
    porcelain *180–2*, *182*, *196*, *197*, *199*,
      200, *203*, *206–9*, *215*, *216*, *221*
    postmodernist ceramics *473*
    pottery *151*, *152*, *154*, *169*, *170*
    stoneware *122*, *166*
    studio ceramics *460–2*
Vassou, Jean-Baptiste *92*
Vauxhall 200, *200*, 204, 205
Vauxhall glass jewelry *271*
vegetable dishes, silver *240*
veneering 24, *24*
Venetian Revival glass 286
Venice
    bureaux 99
    ceramics *153*
    chairs 30
    glass 276, 279, **284**, *284*, 288, *288*,
      292, 294, 302, *302*, 304, 307, 308, 457
    mirrors 112, 113, *113*
    painted furniture *80*

porcelain 191
Venini, Paolo 432, *432*, 457
Venini Glassworks 432, *432*, 457, *457*
Venturi, Robert 466, *466*, 473
Verbilki 219
verge escapement, clocks 350, *351*
verge watches 366, *366*
Verlys 428, **434**, *434*
Vermeulen *354*
Vernier scale, barometers 364
vernis Martin 66, 80, *84*, 95
verre de fougère 276
Verrerie d'Andelys 434
verreries parlantes 398
Versailles 112, 250, 328
Verzelini, Jacopo 294
vesta cases **545**, *545*
Vever, Henri 407
Vever, Maison 407
Vever, Paul 407
Vezzi **191**, *191*
Vezzi, Francesco 191
Vichy brothers 494, *494*
Victoria, Queen of England 49
    commemorative ceramics 213
    commemorative glass 283
    costume 342
    Diamond Jubilee souvenirs 265
    dolls 483
    dolls' houses 498
    engagement ring 264
    glassware 286
    mourning jewelry 268
    sentimental jewelry 269
    sulphides 308
Victoria and Albert Museum, London
    200, 213
Victorian domed pediments *89*
"Victorian Ladies" series *217*
Victorian period
    Berlin woolwork 337
    bookcases 97
    bureaux *100*, 101
    canterburies *108*
    chairs 21, 34, 35, 39
    chaises-longues 44
    chests-of-drawers 83, *83*, 85
    clocks 355, **357**
    commodes (chests-of-drawers) 81
    commodes (night tables) 111
    costume 342
    Davenports 106
    dressing tables 62–3
    dumb waiters 109
    figures 168
    folio stands *108*
    glass 311
    jewelry 264, 265, 266, 267, *267*,
      268, *269*, 270, *270*, *271*
    majolica 169
    parian ware 214
    pedestal desks 107, *107*
    pot-cupboards 110, *111*
    screens *115*
    silver **232–3**, *234*, 235, 238, 239,
      249, *249*
    sofas 45
    tables 47, 49, *49*, 52–3, 55, 69
    wardrobes 76, *77*
    washstands 111
    whatnots 109
    wine coolers and cellarets 119
Vidie, Lucien 365
Vienna
    furniture 38, 66, *86*, 99
    glass 288, 290
    porcelain **188–9**, *188–9*, 190
Vienna ceramics factory 397
Vienna regulators **360**, *360*

Vienna Secession 101, 375, 388, 392, 396
Viero, G.B. 154
Viertel, Augustus *290*
Vignelli, Lella **454**, 455
Vignelli, Massimo **454**, 455
Vile, William 65
Vile & Cobb 37
village weaving, rugs and carpets **315**,
    315, **319**, **320**, *320*
Villeroy, Duke of 192
Villeroy, George 346
vinaigrettes 548
Vincennes 178, 192, **193**, *193*, 201
Vincent, René 411
Vineland Flint Glassworks **435**, *435*
Vinogradov, Dmitri 219
vinyl dolls 493
Vionnet, Madeleine 344
Visscher, Anna Roemers 292
Vistosi *453*, 457, *457*
Vitra 469
vitrified colors, glass 291
vitrines 92, *370*
Vivant Denon, Baron, *Aventures dans la
    basse et la haute Egypte* 38, 59, 61,
    82, 110
Vizagapatnam 65, 67
Vizner, Frantisek 475
Vlaminck, Maurice 415
Vodder, Niels 450
Voigt brothers 184
Volkstedt 184
Volland & Co. 492
Vollmer, Philip 420
Voltamp Electric Manufacturing Co. 513
Von Nessen, Walter 437
Vonêche Glassworks 298, 299, *299*
Voulkos, Peter 463, **476**, *476*, 477
Voysey, Charles Francis Annesley 330,
    372, *372*, 373
Vries, Hans Vredeman de 29, 46–7,
    73, 160
Vuillard, Edouard 422

W
Waals, Peter 372, 419
Wade Ceramics 217
Wagenfeld, Wilhelm 432
wainscot chairs 29
waistcoats 345, *345*
"waiters" 237
"wake" tables *48*
Wakelin, Edward *231*
Waldglas 276
Wales
    dressers 90, *90*, 91
    porcelain **212**, *212*
    see also Britain
Walker, Izannah 492
Wall, Dr John 200, 203
wall clocks **352–3**, *352–3*
wall masks 424, *424*
Wall Street Crash (1929) 221
Wallendorf 178, 185
wallets, canvaswork 337
walnut **23**, *23*
    chests-on-chests **88**, *88*
    dining-chairs **36**, *36*
    kneehole desks **107**, *107*
Walpole, Sir Robert 50
Walter, Alméric 399, *399*, 430, *431*
Walter, Ludwig 442
Walter Kidde Sales Co. *437*
Walters, Carl 425
Walton, George *370*, 373
Walton, John 168
Walzenkrug 159, *159*
Wanli period ceramics 134, 135, 160
wardrobes **76–7**, *76–7*

warming-pans 540
Warne, Frederick & Co. 503
Warth 158
"Wartime" series, figures 217
Warwick cruet frames 258
Washington, George 168, 220, 338, 338
washstands 111, 111
watches 366–7, 366–7, 473, 473
    pocket 366, 366
    wristwatches 367, 367
water droppers 131
water gilding, furniture 25
Waterford Glass House 296
Waterloo Glass House 296
Watkins, David 470
Watson, W. & Sons 534
Watteau, Antoine 84, 84, 95, 175, 178,
    180, 184, 184, 188, 196, 546
Waugh, Sidney 434
wax dolls 483–4, 483–4
"wax-over" dolls 484, 484
waxjacks 231
Wear Flint Glass Works 297
weathervanes 541, 541
    folk art 542, 543
weaving see rugs and carpets; tapestries
Webb, Philip 370, 371, 371
Webb, Thomas & Sons 286, 295,
    296, 296, 300, 300, 301, 301,
    401, 548
Webb & Hammond 276
Weber, Karl Emmanuel Martin ("Kem")
    421, 421, 437, 437
wedding dresses 342
wedding rings 264
Wedgwood
    agate ware 163
    Art Deco 426–7, 426
    art pottery 377
    creamware 157, 165, 205
    fakes and forgeries 127
    furniture plaques 85
    imitations 195
    majolica 169, 169
    parian ware 214
    pearlware 165
    stoneware 164, 166, 166
    vases 124
Weesp 186, 186, 187
Wegely, Wilhelm Kaspar 180
Wegner, Hans 448, 450
Weigel, H. 183
Weiss, Reinhold 454
Weisweiler, Adam 22, 81
Weller, Sam 378
Wellings, Norah 492
Wellington, Duke of 83, 182
Wellington chests 83, 84
Wentworth estate 213
West, William 502
West Bend Aluminum 437
West Indies 74, 82
West Midlands 91
West Pans 202
West Virginia, glass 282
Western Turkestan, rugs and carpets
    324–5, 324–5
Westerwald 158, 158, 164
Westmorland 90
Westwood, Vivienne 344, 344
whale-oil lamps 307
Whallis, Ernst 409
whatnots 97, 109, 109

wheel barometers 364–5, 364
wheel engraving, glass 278–9, 278–9,
    293, 293, 294, 294
Whieldon, Thomas 126, 127, 163,
    166, 169
Whipham, Thomas 242
whiskey decanters, silver 254
Whistler, Laurence 295, 457
Whitaker, Henry, Practical Cabinet
    Maker and Upholsterer's Treasury of
    Designs 53
Whitby jet 268, 268
White, J.P. 373
White House, Washington 38, 297
White Star factory 160
Whitefriars Glassworks 279, 401, 401,
    433, 433, 457
whiteware 164
Whitework 338, 338
Whittock, Nathaniel, The Decorative
    Painters' and Glaziers' Guide 84
Whitty, Thomas 330
Wickes, George 234
Widdicomb, John 421
Wiener Werkstätte 388, 389, 432
    ceramics 425
    furniture 392–3
    glass 400
    jewelry 407
    metalwork 405, 405, 436, 437
Wieseltheir, Vally 425
Wilag 513
Wilcox & Co. 377
Wilde, Oscar 215
Wileman & Co. 427
Wilkens, M.H. & Sohne 405
Wilkins, Liz 377
Wilkinson, A.J. Ltd 426
Wilkinson, Henry & Co. 233
Wilks's Warehouse 337
Willard, Aaron 353
Willard, Simon 353
Willems, Joseph 201
Willets Manufacturing Co. 221
William III, King of England 162, 162,
    292, 294
William IV, King of England 208, 213, 213
William IV period
    dining-chairs 38
    dining-tables 51
William and Mary period
    cabinets-on-stands 86
    chairs 21
    chests-on-chests 88
Williamite glasses 294
Williams, Richard & Co. 296
Williamson, W. & Sons 95
Willkommhumpen glasses 288
Willmore, Joseph 544
"Willow" pattern 165, 167, 167
Willow Street Tea Room, Glasgow 373
Willson, T. 76
Wilmann, Phillip 442
Wilson, Henry 406
Wilson, John 305
Wilson, Joseph 200
Wilson, William 433
Wilton carpets 330, 330
Wincanton 162
Winchester 163
Window, F.R. 538
Windsor, Duke of 345
Windsor chairs 21, 33, 33

wine-bottle collars, silver 255
wine cisterns 256
wine coasters, silver 255, 255
wine coolers 119
    silver 256, 256, 257
wine funnels, silver 255, 255
wine glasses see drinking glasses
wine jugs, silver 254, 254, 255
wine labels, silver 255
wine tasters, silver 254
wing armchairs 19, 30–1
Wingfield, Major Walter 536
Winter, Friedrich 278, 292, 293
Winteringham, George 511
Wirkkala, Tapio 456
"witch" balls, glass 310
Witzel, Josef R. 411
WMF see Württemberg Metalwork
    Factory
Wohnbedarf 416
Wolff, David 278, 292
"Wolff" glass 292
Wolfsohn, Helena 184
womenswear 342–4, 342–4
wood 22–3, 22–3
    dolls 482, 482
    folk art 542
    marquetry 24, 24
    Oriental carvings 524, 524, 525
    parquetry 25, 25
    postmodernist furniture 469
    toys 502–3, 502–3
    treen 545, 545
    veneering 24, 24
    see also furniture
Wood, Beatrice 462, 462
Wood, Ralph 163, 169
Wood & Sons 426
Woodall, George 279, 300, 300, 401
Woodall, Thomas 300, 301, 401
Woodman, Betty 463, 477
woodworm 27
wool
    Berlin woolwork 337
    canvaswork 337
    crewelwork 336
    needlework pictures 338
    rugs and carpets 315
Worcester, Battle of (1651) 292
Worcester porcelain 200, 203, 203, 207,
    208, 208, 210
    blue-and-white wares 186, 204,
    204, 205
    Chamberlain's 208
    copies 199
    Flight's 208
    flower- and bird-painting 216
    Grainger's 208
    redecorated wares 126
    tea caddies 547
Work, Bertram 537
work tables 69, 69
World War I, watches 367
World War II, watches 367
World's Fair, New York (1939) 414
World's Fair, St Louis (1904) 496
Worth, Charles Frederick 342
Wrenn, G. & R. 512
Wright, Charles 242
Wright, Frank Lloyd 420
    ceramics 147, 147
    furniture 370, 374, 375, 420, 421
    metalwork 384

Wright, John 235
Wright, Russel 421, 437
Wright & Mansfield 65, 85, 95, 101
wristwatches 367, 367
writing furniture 98–107, 98–107
    bureaux 98–101, 98–101
    davenports 106, 106
    escritoires and secrétaires 102–3, 102–3
    library and writing tables 105, 105
    pedestal and kneehole desks 107, 107
    writing cabinet-on-stands 104, 104
    writing tables 54, 105, 105
Wrotham 163
wucai style ceramics 134, 134,
    135, 138, 140
Württemberg, Duke of 179
Württemberg Metalwork Factory (WMF)
    389, 389, 405, 432, 433
Würzburg 99
Wyatt, James 37, 231
Wyatt, William 372
Wylie & Lochhead 373

X
X-frame chairs 29
X-frame stools 28
Xinjiang 316, 327
Xuande period
    bronzes 522
    ceramics 126, 133, 134, 138

Y
Yager, Jan 470
Yangshao culture, ceramics 131
Yaozhou 132
Yardley, Samuel 546
Yarkand 327
"Yei" rugs 333, 333
"Yeibichai" rugs 333
"yellow-ware" 170, 171
yew 23, 23
Yixing wares 137, 164
Yomut 324, 325, 325
Yongle period ceramics 133, 138
Yongzheng period ceramics 136, 138,
    139, 139
Yorkshire 91
Young, William Weston 212
Youngman 408
Ysart, Paul 309, 309, 401
Ysart, Salvador 401
Yuan period ceramics 131, 133, 133
Yue period ceramics 131, 131, 141
Yuruk rugs 320

Z
Zach, Bruno 424, 443, 443
Zanesville 378
Zanotta 451
zebrawood 22
Zeeland 72, 78
Zeiss, Carl 534
Zeiss Ikon 538
Zen, Carlo 393
Zhengde period ceramics 134, 135
Zhou period ceramics 131
Zhu family 525
Ziegler & Co. 319, 319
Zijl, Lambertus 395
zoetropes 539, 539
Zoritchak, Yan 475, 475
Zuccheri, Toni 474, 474
Zurich 186–7, 186, 187

Acknowledgments

The publishers would like to thank the following people and organizations for supplying pictures for use in this book or for allowing their pieces to be photographed.
A&C: The Arts & Crafts Furniture Company, East Sheen, SW14; **AD:** J. Alastair Duncan, Ltd. New York, NY; **ADAGP:** Associeté des Auteurs dans les Artes Graphiques et Plastiques; J **AE:** Antiquorum and Etude Tajan, "The Magical Art of Cartier" Auction 19.11.96; **AG:** Andrew and Jojo Grima, Vieux Gstadd, Switzerland; **AH:** America Hurrah Archive, New York, NY; **AHO:** gift of Arthur A. Houghton Jr.; **AJ:** Andy Johnson; **AL:** courtesy of Adrian Little; **AM:** Arthur Middleton, 12 New Row, Covent Garden, London WC2; **AMA:** Annie Marchant; **ASG:** AS Antique Galleries, 26 Broad St, Salford, Manchester M6; **B:** Beamish, The North of England Open Air Museum, County Durham; **BC:** courtesy of Bunny Campione; **BDG:** collection of Barbara & David Goldberg; **BIR:** Birmingham Museum & Art Gallery; **BK:** Bukowskis, Stockholm, Sweden; **BLA:** H. Blairman & Sons, London W1; **BLH:** Brian & Lynn Holmes, Grays Antique Market, London W1; **BM:** British Museum; **BO:** Bonhams, London; **BOG:** Joan Bogart, Rockville Centre, New York, NY; **BR:** Bruun Rasmussen, Copenhagen, Denmark; **BRI:** Bridgeman Art Library; **BSCH:** courtesy Bernhard Schobinger represented through PRO LITTERIS Switzerland; **BW:** Barometer World Ltd, Okehampton, Devon; **BWH:** The Big White House, UK; **CA:** Christie's Amstersdam; **CAG:** Cheltenham Art Gallery & Museums, Gloucestershire; **CAM:** collection of Cranbrook Art Museum, Bloomfield Hills, Michigan, USA; **CB:** collection Cobra and Bellamy, 149 Sloane St, London SW1; **CCG:** courtesy of Charles Cowles Gallery, New York, NY; **CCM:** Cambridge & County Folk Museum; **CG:** Christie's Glasgow; **CGE:** Christie's Geneva; **CGI:** Cora Ginsberg, Inc., New York, NY; **CH:** Chris Halton; **CI:** Christie's Images; **CL:** courtesy of Christopher Littledale, The Sussex Toy and Model Museum; **CMG:** Corning Museum of Glass, New York, NY; **CNY:** Christie's New York; **CRB:** Carswell Rush Berlin, Inc. New York, NY; **CS:** Christopher Sheppard Ltd, 11 St George St, London W1; **CSK:** Christie's South Kensington; **CW:** Charlie Woodage, The Mall Antiques Arcade, The Lower Mall, 359 Upper St, London N1; **DACS:** Design and Artists Copyright Society; **DG:** collection of D. Gallion & D. Morris; **DI:** Deco Inspired, 67 Monmouth St, London WC2; **DMc:** Daniel McGrath; **DN:** Dreweatt's, Donnington, Newbury, Berkshire; **DOR:** Dorotheum, Vienna, Austria; **DR:** David Rago Auctions, Lambertville, NJ; **DRO:** Derek Roberts, 25 Shipbourne Road, Tonbridge, Kent; **DS:** David Schorsch, Hitchcock House Antiques, Inc. Woodbury, Connecticut; **DT:** courtsey of Donna Thynne; **DTC:** Design20c, Surrey; **EOH:** The End of History, New York, NY; **EPC:** Elizabeth Prime Collection, New York, NY; **EVD:** Etienne & van den Doel, The Hague, The Netherlands; **FAC:** Farnham Antiques Centre; 27 South St, Farnham, Surrey; **FDE:** Flying Duck Enterprises; 320–322, Creek Rd, Greenwich, London SE10; **FRE:** Freeman's, Philadelphia, Pennsylvania; **GA:** Mary Wise and Grosvenor Antiques Ltd, 27 Grosvenor St, London W8; **GC:** Gerry Clist; **GDG:** Geoffrey Diner Gallery, Washington, DC; **GJ:** Georg Jensen, 15 New Bond St, London; **GM:** Galerie Maurer, Munich, Germany; **GORB:** Gorringes, Bexhill, East Sussex; **GRA:** courtesy Galerie Ra, Amsterdam, The Netherlands; **GRN:** Gail Reynolds Natzler/courtesy of Couturier Gallery, Los Angeles, CA; **GU:** Güell Family Collection, Spain; **HA:** Hirschl & Adler Galleries Inc., New York, NY; **HAK:** F.J. Hakimian, Inc., New York, NY; **HAL:** The Hali Archive, London; **HAW:** Gerard Hawthorn, 104 Mount St, London W1; **HD:** Halcyon Days, London W1; **HE:** Hermitage, St Petersburg; **HJ:** Hugh Johnson; **HL:** gift of Mr and Mrs Harold Ludeman; **HOL:** Holsten Galleries, Stockbridge, MA; **HPM:** Het Princesshof Museum; **HS:** gift (funds) Harriet Smith; **IB:** Ian Booth; **IP:** Ian Pout, Teddy Bears of Witney, 99 High St, Witney, Oxfordshire OX8; **IS:** Israel Sack, Inc. New York, NY; **JA:** coll G. N. Bradfield; **JBT:** John Bigelow Taylor, NYC; **JCH:** John and Carole Hibel, H. & D. Press Inc.; **JE:** John Eskenazi, Ltd, Clifford St, London; **JG:** James and Nancy Glazer Antiques, Pennsylvania; **JH:** Jeanette Hayhurst, 32a, Kensington Church St, London W8; **JHA:** Jonathan Horne Antiques Ltd, at Sampson & Horne Antiques, Mount Street, London, W1; **JJE:** John Jesse, 160 Kensington Church St, London W8; **JJO:** John Joseph, Grays Antique Market, London W1; **JN:** John Nicholsons, Haslemere, Surrey; **JP:** coll. J. P. Axelrod; **JS:** courtesy of John Sandon; **JWH:** John White; **JWI:** Justin Windle Photography; **L:** Leyland's, New York, NY; **L&T:** Lyon & Turnbull, Edinburgh, Scotland; **LB:** Linda Brine, Assembly Antiques Centre, 5–8 Saville Row, Bath, BA1 2QP; **LCG:** Lesley Craze Gallery, London EC1; **LFA:** Law Fine Art, Berkshire; **LK:** Leigh Keno, New York, NY; **LKM:** Leo Kaplan Modern, New York, NY; **LM:** Leeds Museums and Art Galleries/Temple Newsam House, Leeds; **LN:** Lillian Nassau Ltd, New York, NY; **LTM:** London Transport Museum; **LOS:** Lost City Arts, New York, NY; **LP:** Larry L. Peltz; **LU:** Luna, Nottingham, UK; **M:** Mayorcas Ltd, 8 Duke St, London SW1; **MA:** gift of Mr Maynard T Allen; **MAB:** Museum of Fine Arts Boston/Centennial Fund, Gift of John Goelet, and unrestricted textile purchase funds.; **MAC:** Macklowe Gallery, New York, NY; **MAL:** Mallett & Son (Antiques) Ltd, New Bond Street, London; **MAP:** Memphis and Post, Milan, Italy; **MAR:** S. Marchant and Son, 120 Kensington Church St, London W8; **MAZ:** Ivor Mazure, 9 Roupell St, London SE1; **MBU:** Museum of Applied Arts, Budapest; **MG:** Macklowe Gallery, New York, NY; **MGA:** Marilyn Garrow, 6 The Broadway, White Hart Lane, London SW13; **MGE:** Maison Gerard, New York, NY; **MJ:** Margot Johnson, Inc., New York, NY; **ML:** collection of Marion Langham; **MLA:** Mark Laino, Philadelphia, PA; **MM:** Martin Morris; **MMA:** The Metropolitan Museum of Art/Rogers Fund, 1952 (52.118). Photograph copyright 1989 The Metropolitan Museum of Art; **MN:** Martin Norris; **MP:** courtesy Max Protetch Gallery, New York, NY; **MPO:** Madeleine Popper, Grays Antique Market, London W1; **MR:** Melvin M Rose/Howard Agriesti/Cleveland Museum of Art; **MT:** M. Tehran, Hamburg, Germany; **MW:** Mark J. West, www.markwest-glass.com; **MWP:** Museum of Worcester Porcelain; **NAC:** Neal Auction Company, New Orleans, LA; **NB:** Neil Bingham; **ND:** Nicholas M Dawes, New York, NY; **NF:** Nick Forder; **NH:** Nicholas Harris Gallery, 564 Kings Rd, London SW6; **NN:** Nick Nicholson, Hawkley Studios; **NTW:** The National Trust, Waddesdon Manor/Eost & Macdonald; **NW:** Nigel Williamson; **OB:** collection of Olivia Bristol; **OH:** Olde Hope Antiques, Inc., New Hope, PA; **OPG:** Octopus Publishing Group Ltd; **P:** Phillips, London; **PBA:** Pierre Bergé & Associés, Paris, France; **PC:** Private Collection; **PCA:** Patric Capon, London N1; **PM:** Pine Mine, London SW6; **PMA:** Philadelphia Museum of Art/The Joseph Lees Williams Memorial Collection; **PO:** Pieter Oosthuizen, The Georgian Village, Camden Passage, London N1; **POOK:** Pook & Pook, Downingtown, PA; **PP:** Pro-Photo; **PW:** Peter Willborg, Sibyllegatan 41, Stockholm, Sweden; **PWA:** Pam Walker; **QU:** Quittenbaum, Munich, Germany; **R:** Rennies Seaside Modern, 47 The Old High Street, Folkestone, Kent; **RC:** Royal Copenhagen; **RCA:** Rupert Cavendish Antiques, London SW6; **RD:** Royal Doulton Ltd; **RDA:** R. Davies; **RH:** R. Holt & Co. Ltd. 98 Hatton Garden, London EC1; **RJ:** Roderick Jellicoe Fine Porcelain, 114 Kensington Church St, London W8; **ROC:** The Robert Opie Collection, The Museum of Advertising and Packaging, Gloucester, GL1; **RP:** Richard Purdon, 158 High St, Burford, Oxfordshire; **RR:** Robert Rust, Roycroft Shops Inc., East Aurora, NY; **RRPL:** Collection Cowan Pottery Museum at the Rocky River Public Library, Rocky River, Ohio; **RS:** Robin Saker; **RSB:** Rita Smythe, Britannia Antiques, Grays Antique Market, London W1; **RYA:** Robert Young Antiques, Battersea Bridge Rd, London SW11; **S:** Sotheby's; **SA:** Sotheby's Amsterdam; **SC:** Simon Cherry; **SCH:** Stuart Chorley; **SCP:** SCP Ltd, London EC2; **SCR:** Sandra Cronan Ltd, 18 Burlington Arcade, London W1; **SDR:** Sollo:Rago Modern Auctions, Lambertville, NJ; **SF:** The Silver Fund, London SW1; **SG:** Samarkand Gallery, 8 Brewery Yard, Sheep St, Stow-on-the-Wold, Gloucestershire; **SHK:** Sotheby's Hong Kong; **SJ:** Sheila & Norman Joplin; **SK:** Skinner, Auctioneers and Appraisers of Antiques and Fine Art, Boston and Bolton, MA; **SL:** Sotheby's London; **SNY:** Sotheby's New York; **SP:** Sue Pearson, Antique Dolls and Teddy Bears, 18 Brighton Square, Brighton; **SPA:** Spectrum Antiques, Grays Antique Market, London W1; **SPL:** Sotheby's Picture Library; **SS:** Sotheby's Sussex; **ST:** Steve Tanner; **STG:** gift of Steuben Glass; **STO:** Steinbeck & Tolkein, 193 Kings Rd, London SW3; **STR:** The Stradlings, New York, NY; **SWE:** Sweetbriar Gallery, Helsby, Cheshire; **TBM:** The Brooklyn Museum/Dick S. Ramsay Fund; **TC:** Textile Company, PO Box 2800, London N1; **TD:** Tom Dixon/Space Ltd, 12 Dolland St, London SE11; **TDG:** The Design Gallery, Westerham, Kent; **TEN:** Tennants Auctioneers, Leyburn, North Yorkshire; **TF:** Fusco & Four Associates, Brighton, MA; **TG:** Tadema Gallery, Camden Passage, London N1; **TGW:** T.G. Wilkinson Antiques, Petworth, West Sussex; **TK:** Tim Knox; **TO:** Titus Omega, London N1; **TR:** Tim Ridley; **20thC:** 20th Century Design; 274 Upper St, London N1; **VA:** Victoria & Albert Museum, London; **VH:** Valerie Howard, 2 Campden St, off Kensington Church St, London W8; **VDB:** Van den Bosch, London N1; **VZ:** Von Zezschwitz, Munich, Germany; **W:** Wartski, 14 Grafton St, London W1; **WA:** Witney Antiques, Witney, Oxfordshire; **WB:** William Bedford PLC, London; **WCGL:** Worshipful Company of Goldsmiths' Library and Assay Office Collections; **WD:** William Doyle Galleries, New York, NY; **WG:** Weinstein Galleries, New York, NY; **WIM:** Wimpole Antiques, Grays Antique Market, London W1; **WKA:** Wiener Kunst Auktionen - Palais Kinsky, Vienna, Austria; **WM:** courtesy of The Wedgwood Museum, Barlaston, Staffs; **YAG:** Yale University Art Gallery/The Mabel Brady Garvan Collection; **WW:** Woolley & Wallis, Salisbury, Wiltshire; **YC:** Yesterday's Child, Angel Arcade, 118 Islington High St London N1

Acknowledgments in page order
Back jacket top row L-R: SDR, L&T, PAR; **Back jacket bottom row L-R:** L&T, POOK, DRA, FRE; **Spine:** RGA; **Front top row L-R:** VZ, L&T, DRA, DRA, AA; **Front bottom row L-R:** FRE, FRE.
1 SL, **2/3l-r** SL, AH, OPG/BO/PP, OPG/MT/TR, SL, OPG/SL/PP, SL, OPG/CSK, OPG/CSK, **4** OPG/AM/PP, **6l** OH, **6tr** SL, **6c** CI, **6br** SL, **7l** OPG/SL/TR, **7tc** DRA, **7bc** CI, **7br** BO, **10** SL, **11l** CI, **11br** CSK, **12tc** CI, **12tr** CI, **12cl** CI, **12bl** CI, **12br** SPL, **13l** OPG/CSK, **13tcl** SL, **13tc** SL, **13tr** SL, **13cr** SL, **13bcl** OPG/P, **13bc** SL, **13br** CI, **14tl** SS, **14tc** SL, **14tr** CI, **14bl** CI, **14bc** SL, **14br** BRI/CAG, **15tl** SL, **15tc** CI, **15tr** OPG/SL/PP, **15bl** OPG/ASG/JWI, **15bc** SNY, **15br** BO, **16** OPG/SL/PP, **17tr** OH, **22tl** OPG/PP, **22tc** OPG/BO/TR, **22tcr** OPG/SL/PP, **22tr** CI, **22cl** OPG/SL/PP, **22c** OPG/SL/PP, **22bl** OPG/BO/TR, **22bc** OPG/RYA/PP, **22bcr** OPG/PP, **22br** OPG/BO/TR, **23cac** OPG/PP, **23tl** CI, **23tc** OPG/BO/PP, **23tr** OPG/PP, **23cl** OPG/PM/IB, **23cbc** OPG/PP, **23bl** OPG/BO/PP, **23bc** OPG/SL/PP, **24tl** OPG/BO/TR, **24tc** OPG/BO/TR, **24tr** OPG/PP, **24c** OPG/PP, **24cr** OPG/SL/PP, **24bl** OPG/SL/PP, **24bc** CI, **24br** OPG/SL/PP, **25r** SPL, **25tl** OPG/BO/PP, **25cl** OPG/BO/TR, **25c** OPG/SL/PP, **25bl** CI, **25bc** CI, **25br** OPG/BO/TR, **26tl** SL, **26bl** SPL, **27tr** OPG/BO/TR, **27bl** CI, **28t** OPG/SL/PP, **28cr** CI, **28bl** CSK, **29l** SS, **29tr** SPL, **29b** P, **30tl** CI, **30tr** CI, **30b** LK, **31l** OPG/SL/PP, **31tr** IS, **31br** CI, **32r** OPG/BO/PP, **32t** CI, **32b** CI, **33l** SS, **33r** DS, **33b** OPG/BO/PP, **34l** CSK, **34t** CSK , **34br** CSK, **35l** BOG, **35r** SPL, **35b** MJ, **36l** SPL, **36tr** OPG/SL/PP, **36br** SPL, **37tl** CI, **37tr** CI, **37b** CI, **38l** OPG/BO/TR, **38tr** IS, **38b** CI, **39l** HA, **39tr** CSK, **39br** CSK, **40l** OPG/BO/PP, **40tr** CSK, **40br** CSK, **41l** CSK, **41r** OPG/IB, **41b** CSK, **42l** CI, **42t** SPL, **42b** CI, **43t** CI, **43bl** HA, **44l** SPL, **44tr** CI, **44br** SPL, **45l** CI, **45t** BO, **45b** SPL, **46tr** B, **46b** CI, **47r** P, **47t** SPL, **47bc** CI, **48tr** CI, **48bl** CSK, **48br** CI, **49tr** IS, **49c** OPG/CW/IB, **50t** SPL, **50b** CI, **51r** SNY, **51b** P, **52tr** SPL, **52cl** CSK, **52b** CSK, **53t** SPL, **53b** CSK, **54l** CI, **54tr** SPL, **54b** CI, **55r** CI, **55t** CI, **55bl** HA, **56l** SPL, **56r** SPL, **56b** IS, **57tr** IS, **57b** SPL, **58l** CI, **58t** P, **58b** CI, **59l** CI, **59tr** CI, **59bc** CRB, **60l** P, **60tr** P, **60b** IS, **61t** CI, **61b** OPG/TGW, **62t** P, **62bl** LK, **63l** CI, **63r** OPG/BO/PP, **63bl** SPL, **64r** LK, **64t** IS, **64bl** OPG/SL/PP, **65r** OPG/BO/TR, **65tl** OPG/BO/PP, **65b** SPL, **66t** OPG/BO/TR, **66bl** CI **66br** CI, **67r** CI, **67t** CI, **67bl** OPG/SL/PP, **68l** OPG/BO/TR, **68tr** CI, **68b** IS, **69l** CSK, **69tr** CSK, **69b** P, **70l** CI, **70tr** P, **70b** CI, **71tr** SS, **71bl** OH, **72t** CI, **72b** CSK, **73l** CI, **73r** CI, **73b** CI, **74tl** SA, **74tr** CSK, **74b** CI, **75l** CI, **75tr** SPL, **76tr** NAC, **76bl** CSK, **76br** SPL, **77tr** CSK, **77bl** SPL, **78t** CI, **78bl** CI, **78br** P, **79tl** RYA, **79tr** CI, **79b** OPG/SL/PP, **80r** CI, **80t** P, **80bl** SPL, **81tl** LK, **81tr** CI, **81b** CI, **82l** P, **82t** SPL, **82b** OPG/RCA, **83l** OPG/BO/PP, **83tr** CSK, **83br** CI, **84l** SPL, **84tr** CI, **84br** SNY, **85r** CI, **85t** CI, **85bl** OPG/SL/PP, **86t** CI, **86cr** CI, **86bl** P, **87r** CNY, **87t** LK, **87bl** CI, **88l** P, **88r** CI, **88b** CI, **89** CNY, **90l** P, **90t** CI, **90b** BO, **91l** CI, **91br** JG, **92l** CI, **92tr** CI, **92br** SPL, **93tr** CSK, **93b** SPL, **94l** OPG/WB, **94tr** SPL, **94b** P, **95l** P, **95tr** CSK, **96l** SPL, **96r** IS, **97l** CI, **97r** CI, **97b** OPG/CW/IB, **98l** SPL, **98r** SL, **99tl** CI, **99tr** CI, **99bl** LK, **100l** SPL, **100tr** CI, **100b** CSK, **101tr** P, **101b** CSK, **102t** CI, **102bl** CI, **102br** IS, **103l** SPL, **103r** CSK, **103b** P, **104r** BO, **104t** P, **104b** CI, **105t** SPL, **105bl** CI, **105br** CI, **106l** SPL, **106r** SL, **106b** CSK, **107l** P, **107r** CSK, **107b** CI, **108tr** OPG/BO/TR, **108bl** CI, **108br** OPG/SL/PP, **109r** CSK, **109t** CI, **109b** SPL, **110tr** OPG/SL/PP, **110bl** CI, **110br** CI, **111r** CI, **111t** OPG/CW/IB, **111b** SPL, **112l** SPL, **112r** SPL, **112b** CNY, **113r** SPL, **113t** OPG/BO/PP, **113b** CI, **114l** OPG/BO/TR, **114tr** CI, **114br** CI, **115tr** SPL, **115b** P, **116t** CI, **116b** CI, **117r** IS, **117tl** CI, **117bl** BO, **118l** OPG/SL/PP, **118t** CI, **118cr** OPG/IB, **118br** CI, **119l** CI, **119r** OPG/SL/PP, **119b** CI, **120** SL, **121t** CI, **122l** SL, **122tcl** OPG/P, **122tc** OPG/P, **122tr** BO, **122bl** CI, **122bcl** OPG/P, **122bcr** OPG/P, **122br** SL, **123tl** SL, **123tc** SL, **123tr** SL, **123cr** SL, **123bl** OPG/P, **123bc** SL, **123br** CI, **124tl** OPG/JH, **124tc** SL, **124tr** P, **124bl** SPL, **124bc** BO, **124br** OPG/P, **125tl** SL, **125tc** OPG/P, **125tr** OPG/P, **125bl** OPG/P, **125bc** CI, **125br** OPG/P, **126tr** SL, **126b** OPG/P, **126br** SL, **127r** P, **127tl** OPG/JS/CH, **127tc** SL, **127cl** OPG/DT/CH, **127bl** SNY, **127bcl** WM, **128tcr** OPG/CSK, **128tr** OPG/CSK, **128bl** OPG/CSK, **128bc** OPG/CSK, **128br** SL, **129l** OPG/P, **129tc** OPG/P, **129tr** OPG/CSK, **129br** OPG/CSK, **131tl** SL, **131tr** SNY, **131b** SL, **132l** SL, **132r** SL, **132b** SL, **133l** SL, **133r** SL, **133b** SL, **134l** SL, **134t** SL, **134br** SL, **135tl** SL, **135b** SL, **136l** SL, **136r** SL, **136b** SL, **137tl** MAR, **137tr** CI, **137b** SL, **138l** SL, **138t** SL, **138b** CI, **139l** CI, **139r** CI, **139b** CI, **140r** SPL, **140t** SL, **140bl** CI, **141l** CI, **141r** SL, **141b** SL, **142l** SL, **142r** SL, **142b** CI, **143r** OPG/P, **143t** SL, **143bl** SL, **144l** SL, **144tr** OPG/CSK, **144bl** SL, **145l** SL, **145t** SL, **145b** OPG/CSK, **146tr** OPG/CSK, **146bl** SL, **146br** SPL, **147l** OPG/CSK, **147r** CI, **147b** SL, **149r** SL, **149tl** SL, **149b** SL, **150l** SL, **150r** OPG/P, **150b** SL, **151tc** SL, **151cr** OPG/P, **151b** BM, **152l** SL, **152t** SL, **152br** SL, **153tl** SL, **153cl** SL, **153bc** SL, **154r** OPG/P, **154t** SL, **154b** CI, **155tl** SL, **155tc** OPG/CSK, **155tr** JHA, **155cr** CI, **155bl** SL, **155bc** OPG/DR,

156t SL, **156c** OPG/CSK, **156bl** SL, **156br** CI, **157l** CI, **157tr** VH, **157b** CI, **158r** OPG/CSK, **158t** SL, **158b** SL, **159l** SL, **159r** OPG/P, **159b** SL, **160t** OPG/SL/IB, **160bl** OPG/P, **161r** OPG/CSK, **161tl** OPG/P, **161bl** OPG/S, **162r** OPG/P, **162tl** SL, **162b** SL, **163l** JHA, **163r** CI, **163b** SL, **164r** SL, **164t** SL, **164b** CI, **165r** P, **165bl** OPG/CSK, SL, **166t** OPG/CSK, **166b** SL, **167l** OPG/P, **167r** OPG/JS/CH, **167t** P, **168l** JHA, **168r** OPG, **168b** OPG/JS/CH, **169r** OPG/RSB/PP, **169t** SL, **169bl** OPG/RSB/PP, **170l** CI, **170t** STR, **170br** ND, **171tr** CI, **171b** ND, **173t** SPL, **173b** BR, **174tr** CI, **174bl** CI, **174br** CI, SPL, **175tr** CI, **175bc** CI, **176l** SPL, **176tc** CI, **176b** CI, **177l** SPL, **177r** CI, **177t** SPL, **177bc** CI, **178l** CI, **178t** SPL, **178b** CI, **179cl** CI, **179b** SPL, **180l** CI, **180r** SPL, **180b** CI, **181tr** SPL, **181c** SPL, **181b** SPL, **182l** SPL, **182r** SPL, **182t** SPL, **183r** P, **183bl** SPL, **184l** SPL, **184tr** SPL, **184b** CI, **185tl** OPG/P, **185tr** OPG/P, **185bl** OPG/P, **186l** SPL, **186t** CI, **186br** SPL, **187tr** CI, **187c** SPL, **187b** SPL, **188tr** CI, **188bl** SPL, **188br** SL, **189l** SPL, **189tr** SPL, **189b** CI, **190l** CI, **190r** CI, **190b** VA/RDA, **191tc** SL, **191c** OPG/P, **191br** SL, **192l** SL, **192tr** OPG/P, **192b** SPL, **193tr** CI, **193c** CI, **193b** SPL, **194tr** SPL, **194c** SPL, **194b** SPL, **195r** SPL, **195t** SPL, **195b** CI, **196l** CI, **196tr** SPL, **196b** SPL, **197tl** SPL, **197tr** SPL, **197b** SPL, **198l** SPL, **198t** OPG/CSK, **198b** OPG/CSK, **199l** CI, **199r** OPG/P, **199b** SPL, **200r** P, **200t** SPL, **200b** SPL, **201r** OPG/JS/CH, **201c** CI, **201bl** P, **202l** CI, **202r** P, **202b** OPG/P, **203r** CI, **203c** CI, **203b** CI, **204tl** OPG/P, **204c** OPG/P, **204b** OPG/JS/CH, **205l** P, **205bl** OPG/P, **205br** OPG/P, **206r** CI, **206t** OPG/P, **206bl** CI, **207l** P, **207r** RJ, **207b** CI, **208r** OPG/P, **208t** P, **208b** P, **209l** P, **209r** P, **209b** GA, **210r** OPG/P, **210t** P, **210bl** SL, **211l** CI, **211r** OPG/P, **211b** OPG/P, **212l** SPL, **212r** SPL, **212b** OPG/P, **213r** OPG/P, **213tr** P, **213b** TEN, **214l** OPG/P, **214tr** OPG/P, **214b** OPG/P, **215l** P, **215r** CI, **215b** P, **216l** OPG/P, **216tr** SPL, **216br** P, **217l** RD, **217r** MWP, **217b** OPG/P, **218tr** OPG/CSK, **218c** OPG/CSK, **218bl** OPG/ML/PP, **219r** MAZ, **219tl** SPL, **219c** SPL, **220tl** TBM, **220br** STR, **221r** DRA/BDG, **221tl** STR, **221b** STR, **222** OPG/CSK, **223tr** SPL, **224l** CI, **224tr** CI, **224br** OPG/CSK, **226tl** CI, **226tc** SNY, **226tr** OPG/CSK, **226cl** CI, **226bl** OPG/S, **226bc** SPL, **226br** OPG/CSK, **227tl** OPG/CSK, **227tc** OPG/CSK, **227tr** CI, **227cl** CI, **227bl** OPG/CSK, **227bc** CI, **227br** OPG/CSK, **228tc** WCGL, **228bl** WCGL, **228bc** WCGL, **228br** WCGL, **229tr** OPG/NH/SCH, **229bl** OPG/HJ, **229br** OPG/HJ, **230l** CI, **230t** SNY, **230br** SPL, **231tl** CI, **231tr** CI, **231b** CI, **232l** CI, **232tr** CI, **232c** CI, **233r** OPG/CSK, **233tl** CI, **233bl** SPL, **234l** SPL, **234tr** CGE, **234b** SPL, **235r** OPG/CSK, **235t** OPG/NH/SCH, **235bl** CI, **236l** CI, **236r** CI, **236t** CI, **237tr** CI, **237bl** CI, **238t** OPG/CSK, **238b** OPG/NH/SCH, **239r** OPG/CSK, **239tl** OPG/CSK, **239b** CI, **240t** SPL, **240cr** CI, **240b** CI, **241l** OPG/SS/IB, **241tr** CGE, **241b** SPL, **242l** CI, **242t** CGE, **242bl** SPL, **243r** OPG/CSK, **243tl** BRI, **243b** CI, **244l** SPL, **244tr** SPL, **244bl** SPL, **244br** OPG/CSK, **245r** OPG/CSK, **245tl** CI, **245b** CI, **246l** CI, **246c** CGE, **246br** OPG/CSK, **247tl** CI, **247tr** CI, **247b** CI, **248l** SPL, **248tr** OPG/CSK, **248br** YAG/MB, **249tl** CI, **249tr** OPG/CSK, **249b** CI, **250tl** OPG/CSK, **250tr** CI, **250bc** OPG/CSK, **250br** CGE, **251tl** SPL, **251tr** CI, **251cr** CI, **251b** OPG/SS/IB, **252tl** CI, **252tr** SNY, **252b** OPG/SS/IB, **252br** SPL, **253tl** CGE, **253tr** CI, **253b** SPL, **254l** CGE, **254r** OPG/NH/SCH, **254b** CI, **255l** OPG/SS/IB, **255r** OPG/CSK, **255b** OPG/CSK, **256r** OPG/CSK, **256b** CI, **257r** CI, **257tl** SPL, **257b** CI, **258l** OPG/SS/IB, **258r** OPG/SS/IB, **258tc** CGE, **258b** CI, **259tl** OPG/CSK, **259tc** CI, **259tr** OPG/CSK, **259bl** OPG/NH/SCH, **259bc** OPG/SS/IB, **260** SCR/GC, **261tr** OPG/MPO/PP, **262l** OPG/RH/PP, **262tc** SPL, **262tr** CI, **262cr** SPL, **262br** SPL, **263tl** CI, **263tc** CI, **263tcr** OPG/CSK, **263tr** OPG/CSK, **263cl** CI, **263c** SPL, **263ccr** OPG/CSK, **263bl** CI, **263bc** SCR, **263bcr** SPL, **263br** OPG/CSK, **264t** OPG/BLH/PP, **264tl** CI, **264tr** OPG/BLH/PP, **264cl** OPG/WIM/PP, **264bl** OPG/BLH/PP, **264bc** OPG/JJO/PP, **265l** OPG/MPO/PP, **265t** W, **265tr** OPG/BLH/PP, **265b** CI, **265br** CI, **266tl** OPG/JJO/PP, **266tr** OPG/BLH/PP, **266bl** CI, **266br** OPG/MPO/PP, **267tl** CI, **267tc** OPG/BLH/PP, **267tr** OPG/BLH/PP, **267bl** CI, **267bc** CI, **267br** OPG/WIM/PP, **268l** OPG/PC/PP, **268r** OPG/WIM/PP, **268t** OPG/JJO/PP, **268br** SCR, **269l** SPL, **269tr** OPG/SPA/PP, **269c** OPG/BLH/PP, **269b** SCR/GC, **270l** SCR, **270t** OPG/BLH/MPO/JJO/PP, **270tc** SCR, **270tr** SCR, **270b** SCR, **270bc** CI, **270br** CI, **271l** OPG/MPO/PP, **271tc** SCR, **271tr** OPG/MPO/PP, **271b** SCR, **272** PC,**273** PC, **274** SL, **275tr** SL, **275bl** DRA, **276r** OPG/JH/PP, **276t** SL, **276b** SL, **277tr** OPG/JH/PP, **277cl** SL, **277bl** SL, **277br** OPG/JH/PP, **278tl** SL, **278tc** CI, **278tr** OPG/JH/PP, **278bl** SL, **278bc** SL, **278br** VA/DMc, **279tl** OPG/JH/PP, OPG/JH/PP, **279tr** MW, **279bl** OPG/JH/PP, **279bc** SL, **279br** OPG/JH/PP, **281l** OPG/JH/PP, **282r** OPG/MW/IB, **282b** OPG/JH/PP, **283tr** CMG/HL, **283c** OPG/JH/PP, **283bl** CMG, **284r** SL, **284tl** SL, **284b** SL, **285l** SL, **285r** OPG/MW/IB, **285b** SL, **286l** OPG/MW/IB, **286r** OPG/MW/IB, **286b** OPG/MW/IB, **287l** OPG/MW/IB, **287r** CMG, **287b** CMG/HS, **288l** CI, **288r** OPG/MW/IB, **288t** SL, **289l** CI, **289r** OPG/MW/IB, **289b** CI, **290l** SL, **290t** OPG/MW/IB, **290br** OPG/MW/IB, **291l** OPG/MW/IB, **291r** OPG/JH/PP, **291b** SPL, **292l** CI, **292tr** CI, **292br** SL, **293r** CI, **293t** CI, **293bl** CI, **294l** SPL, **294tr** OPG/MW/IB, **294b** OPG/MW/IB, **295l** OPG/MW/IB, **295tr** SL, **295b** OPG/MW/IB, **296l** CI, **296tr** CI, **296br** OPG/JH/PP, **297tl** SL, **297c** OPG/MW/IB, **297br** CMG/MA, **298l** SPL, **298t** OPG/MW/IB, **298br** OPG/MW/IB, **299l** OPG/MW/IB, **299r** OPG/MW/IB, **299b** OPG/MW/IB, **300l** CMG/AHO, **300t** MAL, **300br** SPL, **301r** OPG/MW/IB, **301tl** CI, **301b** OPG/MW/IB, **302tr** CS, **302bl** SL, **303l** OPG/JH/PP, **303tr** MW, **303cr** OPG/JH/PP, **303b** OPG/JH/PP, **304l** SL, **304t** OPG/MW/IB, **304b** SL, **305t** SPL, **305c** OPG/MW/IB, **305bl** OPG/MW/IB, **306l** SL, **306tr** OPG/MW/IB, **306br** CI, **307l** CI, **307r** MAL, **307b** OPG/MW/IB, **308l** SNY, **308tr** SNY, **308br** SNY, **309l** SNY, **309tr** SWE, **309b** SPL, **310tr** OPG/JH/PP, **310cl** OPG/MW/IB, **310bl** CI, **310br** OPG/MW/IB, **311l** OPG/JH/PP, **311r** OPG/MW/IB, **311c** OPG/MW/IB, **311b** l OPG/MW/IB, **312** OPG/MT/TR, **313r** RP, **314tr** OPG/SL/TR, **314bl** OPG/SL/TR, **314br** OPG/PC/TR, **315tr** OPG/SL/TR, **315c** OPG/SL/TR, **315bl** OPG/SL/TR, **315br** OPG/SL/TR, **316r** CI, **316b** MAB, **317tr** CI, **317b** MBU, **317br** MBU, **318l** OPG/SL/TR, **318tr** OPG/SL/TR, **318br** RP, **319l** HAL, **319r** CI, **319b** CI, **320l** HAL, **320r** HAL, **320t** CI, **321r** OPG/SL/TR, **321tl** HAL, **321b** OPG/SL/TR, **322l** HAL, **322r** OPG/SL/TR, **322t** HAL, **323l** CI, **323tr** HAL, **323b** OPG/SL/TR, **324r** OPG/PC/TR, **324tl** HAL, **324b** RP, **325l** OPG/SG/TR, **325tr** SG, **325b** RP, **326r** RP, **326t** OPG/SL/TR, **326b** OPG/SL/TR, **327t** JE, **327c** PW, **327b** l RP, **328t** NTW, **328b** MMA, **329tl** SL, **329tr** OPG/SL/TR, **329c** OPG/SL/TR, **329b** OPG/SL/TR, **330l** LM, **330r** OPG/SL/TR, **330b** HAK, **331r** HAK/JBT, **331tl** PMA, **331b** PMA, **332l** CI, **332r** CI, **332t** CI, **333l** CI, **333t** CI, **333bl** CI, **334** AH, **335tr** OPG/SL/TR, **336tr** OPG/M/PP, **336bl** CGI, **336bc** CGI, **337r** OPG/MGA/PP, **337tl** P, **337b** CGI, **338r** OPG/MGA/PP, **338t** OPG/SL/TR, **338bl** SNY, **339r** SNY, **339tl** CGI, **339bl** WA, **340tr** SL, **340cr** TC, **340bl** B, **341l** AH, **341t** AH, **341b** AH, **342l** SL, **342r** CI, **343l** OPG/TC/TR, **343tr** OPG/SL/TR, **343cl** OPG/SL/TR, **343b** OPG/SL/TR, **344r** OPG/PC/IB, **344t** CB/SL/TR, **344b** OPG/STO/TR, **345l** CI, **345r** OPG/SL/TR, **345b** OPG/SL/TR, **346t** OPG/SL/TR, **346c** OPG/SL/TR, **346b** CI, **347tl** OPG/SL/TR, **347tr** OPG/SL/PP, **347cl** OPG/SL/PP, **347c** OPG/SL/PP, **347cr** OPG/SL/PP, **347b** OPG/MGA/PP, **347bl** OPG/MGA/PP, **347bc** OPG/MGA/PP, **347br** OPG/MGA/PP, **348** SL, **349tr** CSK, **350tr** CSK, **352bl** CSK, **352br** CSK, **353tr** SL, **353bl** SPL, **354tr** CSK, **354bl** DRO, **355l** SL, **355r** CSK, **355c** DRO, **356l** CSK, **356tr** CSK, **356c** CSK, **357tr** SL, **357b** CSK, **358tl** CSK, **358cr** CSK, **358bl** CSK, **359r** CSK, **359bl** PCA, **359br** CSK, **360l** CSK, **360r** CSK, **360c** CSK, **361l** CSK, **361r** SL, **361bc** SL,**362l** SL, **362tr** CSK, **362b** SL, **363tr** SL, **363c** CSK, **363bl** CSK, **364l** CSK, **364tr** CSK, **364br** CSK, **365l** CSK, **365r** BW, **365bc** BW, **366l** SPL, **366tr** CSK, **366bc** CSK, **367l** CSK, **367r** CSK, **367tc** SPL, **367bc** CSK, **368** L&T, **369** DRA, **370l** BRI/VA, **370t** CI, **370b** DRA, **371tr** BRI/CAG, **371bl** VA, **372l** CI, **372tr** CI, **372br** CI, **373tl** BLA, **373c** SPL, **373br** CI, **374r** DRA, **374tl** WD, **374b** CI, **375b** DR, **375tl** ND, **375tr** DRA, **376l** CI, **376t** SS, **376b** SPL, **377r** CI, **377tl** P, **377b** OPG, **378** DRA, **379** DRA, **380** DRA, **381** DRA, **382b** DN **382cl** TO **382cr** VDB **382tc** WW **383b** GDG **383c** TDG **383t** L&T **383bl** DR **384br** DR **384tl** DR **384tr** DR **385b** FRE **385cl** MAC **385cr** DR **385tr** DR **388bl** L&T **388tr** DR **389bl** TO **389br** L&T **389tl** DR **391bl** DOR **391cr** DR **391tl** MAC **392l** CA, **392tr** CI, **392b** CI, **393l** BRI/GU, **393tr** CI, **394l** CI, **394t** VA, **394b** BRI/HE, **395l** SPL, **395r** HPM, **395b** PO, **396l** OPG/SL/IB, **396t** BO, **396b** SPL, **397l** P, **397c** CI, **397br** RC, **398tl** CI, **398br** CI, **399tc** CI, **399c** SNY, **399b** CI, **400t** CI, **400tr** SPL, **400b** OPG, **401tl** CI, **401tr** CI, **401b** BM, **402bl** FRE **402br** FRE **402tc** DR **402tr** SK **403b** DR **403tc** POOK **404t** SPL, **404bl** CI, **404br** CI, **405r** CI, **405c** OPG/NH/SCH, **405bl** SPL, **406l** CB, **406tr** TG, **406cr** OPG/PP, **406b** TG, **407l** TG, **407tr** CB, **407b** TG, **408tr** OPG/ASG/JWI, **408bl** OPG/ASG/JWI/©DACS 1998, **408br** BO, **409tl** OPG/ASG/JWI, **409tr** OPG/ASG/JWI, **409b** SPL, **410l** CSK, **410tr** CI/©ADAGP, Paris and DACS, London 1998, **410br** CI, **411l** CSK, **411tc** CI, **411br** CI, **412** MR, **413tr** CI, **414t** CI, **414bl** CI, **414br** BO, **415l** CI/©ADAGP, Paris and DACS, London 1998, **415t** CI/©ADAGP, Paris and DACS, London 1998, **415br** AD/GNB, **416t** CI/©DACS 1998, **416br** SPL, **417tl** CI, **417tr** SPL, **417bl** SPL, **418tl** CI, **418tr** CI, **418b** CI, **419t** L&T, **419bl** LFA, **420l** CI, **420tr** SNY, **420br** CI, **421tr** CAM, **421b** AD/DG, **422l** CI, **422tr** CI, **422b** SPL, **423tr** SPL, **423c** SPL, **423bl** CI, **424l** SPL, **424tr** SPL, **424b** BRI/BO, **425l** RRPL/LP, **425r** AD/JP, **425b** AD/JP, **426l** CI, **426tr** BO, **426b** WM, **427tl** RD, **427bl** CI, **427br** CI, **428l** ND, **428t** BO, **428br** BO, **429t** SPL, **429b** SPL, **430l** CI, **430t** SPL, **430b** SPL, **431b** DN **431tl** LN **431tr** MAL **432br** DR **432l** VZ **432tc** PC **433bl** BK/©ADAGP Paris and DACS London 2008 **433cr** JH **433tl** VZ **435bl** GORB **436r** SPL, **436b** P, **437l** SPL, **437t** OPG/MGE/SC, **437br** OPG/NH/SCH, **438l** TG, **438r** CI, **438b** AE, **439l** JJE, **439r** TG, **439t** OPG/JJE/PP, **440r** CI/©ADAGP, Paris and DACS,London 1998, **440t** CI, **440bl** OPG/ASG/RS, **441t** SPL, **441b** SPL, **442l** OPG/ASG/JWI/©DACS 1998, **442r** P, **442b** SPL, **443tl** OPG/ASG/RS, **443tr** SPL, **443b** OPG/ASG/RS, **444tr** CI/©ADAGP, Paris and DACS, London 1998, **444bl** CSK, **445l** CI, **445r** CI, **445b** CI/LTM, **446** BK **447** LOS **448l** OPG/20thC/TR, **448tr** OPG/CSK/IB, **448b** BO, **449bl** SDR **449cr** L&T **449tl** SDR **450b** SDR **450cl** SK **450tr** sk **451bl** BO **451br** JN **451tc** FRE/©ADAGP Paris and DACS London 2008 **451tl** BO **452b** SK **452l** SK **452r** SF **453bc** SK **453br** SDR **453tl** SDR **453tr** WKA **454l** OPG/DI/TR, **454r** OPG/BO/PP, **454t** OPG/BO/PP, **454b** OPG/BO/PP, **455b** L **455cl** L&T **455cr** DTC **455tc** QU **456b** WW **456tl** BK **456tr** EOH **457b** QU **457cl** QU **457cr** SDR **457tr** QU **458l** OPG/DI/TR, **458r** OPG/R/IB/©Estate of Eric Ravilious 1998, **458t** OPG/FDE/TR, **458b** OPG/NB/TR, **459r** OPG/BO/PP, **459t** OPG/BO/PP, **459bl** OPG/BO/PP/©DACS 1998, **461bl** PBA **461cr** SDR **461tc** JN **461trc** SDR/©ADAGP Paris and DACS London 2008 **461tr** SDR/©ADAGP Paris and DACS London 2008/Succession Picasso,Paris 2008 **462b** SDR **462l** SDR **462tc** SDR **463b** SDR **463r** SDR **463tl** SDR **464** GM **465** GM **466** SDR **467bl** SDR **467br** SDR **467t** QU **468br** BK **468tl** QU **468tr** SDR **469bc** SDR **469bl** SCP **469tl** L&T **469tr** MAP **470bl** BSCH **470cr** LCG **470tr** GRA **471bc** DTC **471cl** DOR **471cr** SDR **471tr** FRE **472br** BWH **472cl** DTC **472tr** SDR **473bc** BWH **473bl** ML **473tl** GM **473tr** GM **474bc** BK/©ADAGP Paris and DACS London 2008 **474br** HOL **474tr** QU **475bl** EVD **475c** LKM **475tl** EVD/ADAGP Paris and DACS London 2008 **475tr** SDR **476bc** SDR **476tl** SDR **476tr** SDR **477bc** SDR **477cr** SDR **477tl** SDR **478** OPG/CSK, **479t** SP, **480l** CSK, **480t** CSK, **480br** OPG/FAC/TR, **481l** NN, **481r** SP, **481b** OPG/SS/RS, **482l** CI, **482t** SP, **482b** SL, **483r** SL, **483t** OPG/YC/IB, **483bl** CI, **484r** OPG/SS/RS, **484t** SP, **484bl** SL, **485l** SL, **485r** SPL, **485b** OPG/SS/RS, **486r** SL, **486bl** SL, **487r** SL, **487tl** CI, **487b** CSK, **488l** SL, **488tc** SL, **488tr** SL, **488br** CI, **489l** SPL, **489r** OPG/PWA, **489b** SL, **490l** SPL, **490r** SL, **490t** SPL, **491r** SPL, **491tl** CSK, **491b** SPL, **492l** OPG/BC/PP, **492tr** OPG/SS/RS, **492b** SPL, **493tl** OPG/FAC/TR, **493tr** OPG/FAC/TR, **493bl** SP, **494l** SL, **494t** SPL, **494br** SL, **495l** CSK, **495tr** CSK, **495cr** OPG/FAC/TR, **495b** CSK, **496tr** CI, **496bl** SP, **496br** SP, **497tl** SP, **497tr** SP, **497bl** OPG/IP/RS, **497br** SP, **498l** OPG/OB/ST, **498tr** OPG/CCM/TR, **498b** OPG/NF/TR, **499l** OPG/EPC/TK, **499tr** OPG/OB/ST, **499br** OPG/OB/ST, **500** CSK, **501tr** OPG/CSK/IB, **502l** OPG/PC/MN, **502r** CSK, **502br** CSK, **503r** CSK, **503t** CSK, **503bc** OPG/PC/MN, **504l** CNY, **504r** CI, **504b** CSK, **505t** CSK, **505cr** CSK, **505bl** CI, **506t** CSK, **506bl** CSK, **507tr** CSK, **507c** CI, **507b** CI, **508t** SPL, **508cr** SPL, **508bl** SPL, **509tl** CSK, **509c** CSK, **509br** SPL, **510r** CSK, **510bl** CI, **511tr** OPG/CSK/IB, **511bl** OPG/CL/IB, **512l** OPG/CL/MN, **512cr** OPG/CL/IB, **512bl** OPG/CSK/IB, **513t** CSK, **513c** OPG/CL/MN, **514l** OPG/NW/AJ, **514t** OPG/CSK/IB, **514br** CSK, **515t** OPG/AL/AJ, **515b** OPG/SJ/AJ, **515tr** CSK, **516c** OPG/CSK/IB, **516bl** CSK, **517t** OPG/CSK/IB, **517cr** CSK, **517b** CSK, **518t** OPG/CSK/IB, **518c** CSK, **518b** OPG/PC/MN, **519l** OPG/CSK/IB, **519tr** CI, **519b** CSK, **520** PC, **521tr** OPG/CSK, **522l** OPG/CSK, **522t** SHK, **522br** OPG/CSK, **523r** SPL, **523tl** OPG/CSK, **523b** OPG/CSK, **524l** OPG/CSK, **524r** OPG/CSK, **524b** CI, **525l** OPG/CSK, **525tr** OPG/CSK, **525b** SHK, **526l** HAW, **526r** CI, **526b** P, **527l** OPG/CSK, **527tr** HAW, **527bl** OPG/CSK, **528r** OPG/CSK, **528t** SPL, **528bl** OPG/CSK , **529r** OPG/CSK, **529tl** HAW, **529b** OPG/CSK, **530** OPG/AM/PP, **531tr** CI, **532tr** CSK, **532cr** CSK, **532b** CSK, **533l** CSK, **533r** CSK, **533b** CSK, **534l** CSK, **534tr** CSK, **534b** CSK, **535tr** CSK, **535cr** CSK, **535bl** CSK, **536l** CG, **536t** BO, **536b** BO, **537l** BO, **537tr** L, **537b** CSK, **538l** CSK, **538tr** CSK, **538br** CSK, **539l** ROC, **539tr** CSK, **539b** CSK, **540l** SS, **540r** SS, **540t** SS, **541tl** OPG/MM/AMA, **541cl** SS, **541bc** CI, **542bl** POOK **542cr** POOK **542tr** POOK **543bc** POOK **543tl** SK **543tr** SK **544l** OPG/BO/PP, **544tr** BO, **544br** OPG/BO/PP, **545tc** CSK, **545cr** BIR, **545bl** CSK, **546bc** HD **546br** HD **546cl** HD **546cr** HD **547bl** HD **547br** FRE **547tl** DN **547tr** WW **548l** CSK, **548tr** OPG/CSK, **548bl** LB, **548br** CSK, **549bl** DRA **549br** DRA **549tl** DRA **549tr** DRA **550r** SL, **550tc** OPG/CSK/IB, **550b** SL, **551l** OPG/CSK/IB, **551r** SL, **551b** OPG/SL/IB

General Editor's Acknowledgments

I would very much like to thank the editorial, design, and production team at Mitchell Beazley for all the long hours, dedication, and skill they have committed to the production of the *Miller's Antiques Encyclopedia*. To Liz Stubbs (Senior Editor) for her efficiency in successfully running this large and complex project and for her tremendous patience and encouragement in her day-to-day dealings with me and all the contributors. To Clare Peel (Assistant Editor) for the intelligence of her editing and, for her cheerful, helpful disposition. To Paul Drayson (Senior Art Editor) and Adrian Morris (Designer) for their wonderful and original designs, and for tackling the vast array of source material so effectively. To Maria Gibbs and Donna Thynne (Picture Researchers) for liaising with auction houses, dealers and museums to obtain the photographs essential to the quality of the book. And finally, to Alison Starling (Executive Editor) and Vivienne Brar (Executive Art Editor) for knowledgeably overseeing this enormous project from beginning to end.

I also owe a tremendous debt to the excellent contributors, all experts in their field, for their fascinating and illuminating text.